London Boroughs & Postcode areas

1. Kensington & Chelsea
2. City of London

D0875063

London Gazetteer

Russ Willey

London Gazetteer

Russ Willey

Chambers

Chambers
An imprint of Chambers Harrap Publishers Ltd
7 Hopetoun Crescent, Edinburgh, EH7 4AY

This edition published by Chambers Harrap Publishers Ltd 2007
Hardback edition published 2006

© Chambers Harrap Publishers Ltd 2007

A CIP catalogue record for this book is available from the British Library.

ISBN 978 0550 10326 0

Map of Greater London showing postcode areas © PC Graphics
London Connections map © Association of Train Operating Companies,
reproduced by permission

Photographic acknowledgements: Chris Christodoulou: St Luke's; Hare and
Humphreys: Bloomsbury, Brompton, Covent Garden, Strand (King's College
chapel); Royal Borough of Kensington & Chelsea: Fulham Road, Holland Park,
North Kensington, Sloane Square; London Borough of Haringey: Wood Green;
London Borough of Harrow Communications Unit (photographer: Dermot
Carlin): Harrow, Headstone Manor, Stanmore; London Borough of Merton:
Wimbledon Park; London Borough of Sutton Heritage Service: Carshalton
Beeches; Visit London: Columbia Road, Southwark, Strand (Royal Courts of
Justice), Tower. Other photographs by the author.

Editor: Hilary Marsden
Publishing Manager: Patrick White
Prepress: David Reid, Nicolas Echallier

Designed and typeset by Chambers Harrap Publishers Ltd, Edinburgh
Printed by Tien Wah Press (PTE.) Ltd., Singapore

Introduction

The purpose of the *London Gazetteer* is to provide concise information about every part of Greater London, whether large or small. For understandable reasons, most books about London persistently revisit the same areas, but this book aims to redress the balance by telling the story of even the remotest corners.

It is a cliché that there is nowhere in the world like London. The Danish town planner Steen Eiler Rasmussen gave the subtitle *The Unique City* to the English edition of his 1934 treatise on London's architecture. But the city's uniqueness resides in more than just its buildings. No other metropolis has welcomed so many settlers over so many centuries. Nowhere else has been home to so many famous and infamous residents or inspired so many works of art, music and literature. And, for better or worse, it is doubtful whether any other world-class city has grown in such an unregulated fashion.

All this character and heritage is spread far beyond the bounds of the Circle Line or the congestion charging zone. Inevitably, only a small proportion of London's seven million inhabitants live in the city centre. The most populous boroughs are Barnet and Croydon, in the far north and south. And although there are common features, no two places look quite alike or share the same history. It is rare for even the most apparently colourless of places to be without some distinctive aspect, even if it consisted of nothing more than empty fields until developers laid out streets of semis between the wars.

London's architectural highlights are not restricted to Westminster and the City. There are stately homes at Osterley Park, Syon Park and Kenwood. William Morris's delightful Red House can be found in an obscure part of Bexleyheath named Upton. The remains of a Roman villa stand beside Orpington station. East Finchley has one of London's oldest working cinemas. Great industrial structures like Bankside power station have been converted to cultural uses in central London, but others continue to serve their original purpose further downriver or beside railways and canals.

The delights of the central London parks cannot compare with the sights and smells of Kew Gardens, the undulations of Hampstead Heath or the vast expanse of Richmond Park. Here and there, outer London still has chunks of ancient woodland that have barely changed in a thousand years.

Not all the city's most illustrious residents and visitors have lived in Hampstead, Chelsea or Soho. Charles Darwin retired to what is now the outer south-eastern corner of London; Karl Marx flitted here and there (especially when the rent collector was due) before settling in west Kentish Town; W B Yeats wrote some of his finest poetry in Bedford Park; Voltaire exiled himself to Wandsworth. Émile Zola and Camille Pissarro photographed and painted the evolving suburb of Norwood.

Half a dozen great London names reappear in accounts of different localities. Henry VIII hunted deer in almost every available wood, common and park. The highwayman Dick Turpin seems to have frequented half the taverns in what is now the metropolitan area. Charles II and Nell Gwynne allegedly trysted in a score of love nests. More verifiably, Charles Dickens drank in pubs far and wide. Several writers seem to have moved to a new locality almost annually, including Richard Sheridan, Leigh Hunt and J M Barrie. Space does not permit these events to be mentioned in the entries for every place in which they may have occurred.

The absorption of foreign settlers has been crucial to the city's success. The thousands of Huguenots who fled from persecution in the 17th and 18th centuries long ago dissolved in the London melting pot. The city had a thriving German community in the 19th century, many of whom anglicized their names – especially after the outbreak of World War I – and so have disappeared from view. Other minorities retain their identity but have moved on from the places they first made home. Jewish East Enders have migrated to the borough of Redbridge or the north-western suburbs. The Irish have deserted Kilburn for greener pastures. The Cypriots of Green Lanes are moving to quieter corners of Haringey. Chinatown was once in Limehouse; now it is in south Soho, but a second outpost has been mooted for the Thames Gateway. Many who have come to London during the last half-century still have their favoured spots. The Polish community is concentrated in Ealing and west Hammersmith, while Koreans have colonized New Malden. South Africans have made Wimbledon theirs, while Acton has Australians, New Zealanders and Japanese. Brick Lane is Banglatown. Southall is Little India – but so is Wembley. Brixton and Peckham are the best-known centres for the city's scattered black community, the former primarily Caribbean, the latter mainly west African.

Each place on the map of Greater London has played a part in making the city what it is today. A gazetteer must be an alphabetically ordered work of reference, but perhaps the most misleading way to look at London is to compartmentalize it in this way. The city has grown organically, spreading outwards from the centre and from market towns now swallowed in the metropolis, as well as from transport nodes – especially river crossings and Victorian stations – and even from amusement parks and cemeteries. With the exception of some isolated hamlets, all the parts of London are interlinked, and often merge at indistinct borders. Their pasts and futures are bound up together.

Russ Willey
London, 2006

Notes on the Layout

Each entry generally includes: an indication of where the place is and what it is like; some explanation of how it got its name, especially if this is interesting; a potted history of its development; and, if applicable, a few remarks on notable buildings, natural features, events and former residents, and selected artistic works that feature the place or were produced there. If the place has given its name to something else, this is often mentioned – Vauxhall, for example, has become a Russian word for 'station'.

Almost every town, village, district and locality shown in any recent street atlas is listed, together with all underground and mainline stations, even if their names are not commonly applied to the vicinity – except for some with locational affixes, such as Penge East or Finchley Central. Major thoroughfares are frequently included, as are some minor ones if they define a specific locality, for example Hatton Garden. Place names that are solely used by estate agents are mentioned only when they carry a special resonance. Public parks and housing estates are listed if they are particularly large or otherwise significant. Obscure electoral wards and obsolete place names are usually excluded unless they conveniently bestow an identity on an otherwise anonymous spot.

The book is arranged in alphabetical order, ignoring spaces between words. Information is occasionally recapped when a single place has a double identity, such as Malden Manor and Old Malden. For each entry, the place name is followed by that of the parent borough (or boroughs), even where the child may be better known than the parent, for example, **Wimbledon**, *Merton* – or where the two share the same name: **Greenwich**, *Greenwich*. London has 32 boroughs, plus the City of London, where things still operate a little differently.

Pronunciation guidance is given whenever there may be doubt, using standard English characters except that a rotated 'e' indicates the 'indeterminate vowel sound' known as a schwa – as in 'hommətən' for Homerton. A letter in parentheses denotes a sound that is barely or optionally articulated, as in 'bron(d)sb(ə)ry' for Brondesbury.

Landscape, structures, people and events are considered under the most specific possible heading, although if they are of exceptional importance they may be mentioned elsewhere as well. The construction (and sometimes demolition) of buildings can often take years, but for the sake of brevity only the completion date of works is usually given.

Narratives for larger districts are intended to pull together the highlights of the more comprehensive entries for their constituent parts, so they should be read in conjunction with each other. Cross-references are indicated in SMALL CAPITALS. The inclusion of all stations, no matter how localized their name, means that one small street may be examined in some depth while a similar street elsewhere may not be mentioned – which is just the luck of the draw. Goodge Street and Warren Street, for example, are accorded little histories, while nearby Howland Street has to be ignored.

The relevant postal district or postcode area is appended to each entry. Where there are two or more, they are listed in approximate order of predominance. However, few districts in London have clearly defined borders, so this information should not be taken as gospel. For the same reason, a precise description of an area's extent is rarely attempted.

Population figures from the 2001 census are cited where one or more 'output areas' roughly match the extent of a listed place. However, electoral boundaries are frequently drawn so as to include a similar number of voters in each local government ward within a borough, so the data may not always give a true representation of a place's magnitude. Demographic highlights are often provided, where these are available and illuminating. In the absence of ward data, distinctive characteristics of local school rolls are sometimes summarized. Preference is given to information about primary schools, since these have smaller catchment areas and therefore better reflect the community in their immediate vicinity. However, caution should be exercised in drawing conclusions from this information, because state school rolls are often skewed away from upper income groups and (obviously) towards younger families. The fact that a high proportion of pupils at a school speak Twi-Fanti does not necessarily mean that the neighbourhood is dominated by people of Ghanaian origin.

Notes on the Layout

To avoid excessive repetition, the nearest station, tram stop or riverboat pier is usually given only when it has (or used to have) the same name as the place in question. Underground lines and mainline service providers are shown for each station, together with its fare zone(s).

Suggestions for further reading are given wherever possible. These range from slim pamphlets to multi-volume works such as Neil Rhind's study of Blackheath or David Pam's history of Enfield. Preference is given to works still in print. For London-wide books, see the select bibliography on page x.

The addresses of relevant websites are provided, especially if they are run as community resources rather than advertising vehicles. However, many of the finest neighbourhood sites have disappeared already, after being created with benevolent intentions or optimistic entrepreneurialism during the first internet boom. Some sites have closed through fear of being held liable for damages in legal actions. In the absence of a worthwhile community resource, websites (including those of churches and schools) that provide information on aspects of local history or a district's key attraction are often listed. All these sites were live at the time of publication, but the rapidly changing nature of the medium may mean that some have since disappeared or fallen into disuse.

Surprisingly often, there is still disagreement over spellings, the most common being place names ending in 'hill', which are sometimes rendered as one word, sometimes as two: Rosehill and Rose Hill, for example. This occasionally represents a distinction between, say, a road or topographical feature and the settlement built there, but more often it is just different ways of writing the same thing. In such cases preference is given to the more prevalent usage. The same rule is applied to the presence or absence of apostrophes, for example in King's Cross or Earls Court. Practice has often changed over the centuries, but the modern form is generally used throughout an entry for the sake of consistency, as is the case with spellings generally. References to the Artisans', Labourers' and General Dwellings Company, for example, do not use the 'Artizans' spelling that the company preferred at the time.

Key to icons used in the text:

⊠ Postal district

↳ Population

🚍 Railway or underground station; tram stop

🚢 Riverboat pier

📖 Further reading

@ Website(s)

Acknowledgments

Chris Barrett, John Black, Gavin Curry, Jackie Danicki, Lindsey Denford, Sarnjit Dhanda, Eliza Easton, Lucy Gaster and family, Fabian and Rosy Hamilton, Juliet Haydock, Sue Hennessy, Julia Hilton, Paul Humphreys, Sarah Joyce, Sofina Khan, Kate Lewis, Frances Leviston, Jan Newbigin, Nic Oatridge, Alison Pickering, John A Prichard, Vera Romanovskya, Reem Saif, Marian Sheil, Don Tait, Roger Trew, Barnard Turner, Brian Willey, June Willey, Karen Woo; my agent Andrew Lownie and editor Hilary Marsden; Patrick White at Chambers; and the staff of London's local history libraries and the Guildhall library.

Select Bibliography

Civic historians are for the most part out-and-out copyists, and the tribe that inflicts itself on London is no exception.
Cyril Philips Bryan, *Roundabout Harley Street* (1932)

The author has drawn on a vast array of sources in compiling this gazetteer. Many of these works are now out of print and held in just one or two local libraries. Several have only ever existed as typed – or even handwritten – manuscripts. No attempt has been made to catalogue all these sources, but a few general and specialist works merit individual mention.

For in-depth information on the city's man-made environment, the London volumes of the *Buildings of England* series are unsurpassable. Quotations from 'Pevsner' in the text of this gazetteer usually refer to the latest editions of these marvellous works. The many volumes of the *Survey of London* are meticulous architectural and topographical examinations of narrowly defined areas – mostly single parishes in inner London. But with several years separating the publication of each study, only a few are still in print and relatively up to date. The latest in the series is a three-part study of Clerkenwell. The more recent volumes of the *Victoria County Histories*, especially of Middlesex, have proved invaluable to the author. These histories are also becoming available online. There are cul-de-sacs in the City of London with more of a story to tell than certain remote suburban sub-districts; Hibbert and Weinreb's *The London Encyclopaedia* is the ideal reference book to consult about these, and much more. English Heritage's *London Suburbs* is a beautifully illustrated study of the domestic architecture overlooked in most guides to the capital.

The many guidebooks aimed at visitors understandably focus on central London and the more picturesque outlying 'villages', like Hampstead, Highgate, Dulwich, Greenwich and Richmond. Among the most popular are the annual *Time Out* guide, *Lonely Planet London* and the *Rough Guide to London*. There are numerous handbooks devoted to specific aspects of metropolitan life, from eating and drinking, museums and galleries, shopping, cycling and job-hunting to London for children, vegetarians, Christians, and gays and lesbians. If you are house-hunting, especially in inner London and the more popular outer suburbs, Carrie Segrave's annual *London Property Guide* is highly recommended.

New histories of London come out almost annually. In recent years the most popular of these have been Peter Ackroyd's quirky but erudite *London: the Biography* and A N Wilson's *London: A Short History*. *The Times History of London* makes good use of maps and pictures. John Richardson's *Annals of London* is highly recommended as a descriptive chronology of key events. *The Oxford Dictionary of London Place Names* by A D Mills provides much more detail on the subject than brief etymologies attempted here.

For greater detail about lesser locations there are innumerable volumes by local historians, and reference to these is often made under the relevant entry. 'Further reading' listings should not be treated as exhaustive or, unless otherwise stated, as recommendations. Preference is given to readily available works, but some are out of print or hard to find. Many are of the 'East Cheam in Old Pictures' variety or are simply pamphlets, but some have academic credentials, such as Gillian Tindall's examination of Kentish Town, Alan Warwick's chronicle of Norwood and Harold Dyos's seminal treatise on Camberwell (sadly out of print). More recent works worthy of special mention include the very personal accounts by Melanie McGrath, John Gross and Edward Platt dealing with Silvertown, Mile End and the Western Avenue respectively. David Kynaston's four-volume history of the City of London is both authoritative and enlightening. Historical Publications' district histories are usually very well researched and written.

Each of London's four major street atlases possesses its own strengths. Philip's *Ordnance Survey Atlas* is especially helpful for identifying communal dwellings like blocks of flats; Collins' colour coding makes land use very clear; the AA's *Street by Street Atlas* has the best labelling of amenities; while the Geographers' *A–Z London Atlas* remains the great all-rounder. For a different aerial perspective, GetMapping's *London Photographic Atlas* makes stunning use of satellite images.

The internet provides an ever-changing torrent of information about London. For present-day facts and listings, the most comprehensive citywide resources are www.londontown.com and the official tourist site www.visitlondon.com. The best news resources are www.bbc.co.uk/london, www.thisislondon.com and www.thisislocallondon.com. Useful neighbourhood pages are mentioned under the relevant entries. The websites of the London boroughs continue to exhibit staggering variations in quality. Among the best are those of Sutton, Croydon, Kensington and Chelsea, Kingston, Brent and Barking and Dagenham. Reports from the government's Office for Standards in Education – available at www.ofsted.gov.uk – often provide revealing data not just about schools and other educational establishments, but about the demographics of their catchment areas and the languages spoken by a locality's ethnic minorities. Two other sites deserve special praise: www.london-footprints.co.uk has suggestions for self-guided walks, with excellent historical background material, while www.ideal-homes.org.uk is a splendid pictorial resource for those with an interest in the suburbs of south-east London.

A selection of material from the *London Gazetteer*, primarily relating to lesser-known localities, is reproduced at www.hidden-london.com.

Glossary

acre
A measure of land area in the imperial system, equal to 4,840 square yards (4,047 square metres). Although most authorities now use the metric unit of measurement for area, the hectare, the more familiar acre is used throughout this book. There are approximately 2.5 acres in one hectare. There are 640 acres in one square mile.

Black Death
A virulent pneumonic and bubonic plague that spread across Europe from Asia between 1347 and 1353, killing approximately 25 million people.

chapel of ease
Until the late 19th century, parishes outside towns often covered a very large area, and many villages and hamlets were a considerable walking distance from the nearest church. For the convenience of remote parishioners, a local chapel was often built as a subsidiary to the parish church. As districts became suburbanized, these chapels of ease usually evolved into fully-fledged churches with their own parishes, and sometimes spawned chapels of ease of their own.

dates of reigns
Dates of events and periods are generally stated in the text (eg in the 1820s), rather than as references to the monarch on the throne at the time. However, the main periods of residential building in the two centuries before World War I are sometimes identified by the name of the reigning monarch: Georgian, 1714–1830 (including the Regency period, 1811–20); Victorian, 1837–1901; and Edwardian, 1901–10.

dissolution of the monasteries
The closing of England's monastic institutions in the late 1530s, when their assets and treasures were confiscated by the king. The move was part of the Reformation in England, instigated by Henry VIII after the Pope refused him a divorce from his first wife, Catherine of Aragon. Some of the buildings formerly occupied by these institutions were taken over by the newly established Church of England; others were sold to private individuals or donated to charitable organizations. The remainder fell into ruin and were later demolished.

Domesday Book
A survey of all lands in England, ordered by William I, the Conqueror, in 1086, detailing their value, ownership etc, for tax purposes; it is so called because it was considered to be as authoritative as Judgement Day or 'doomsday'. The survey constitutes the most comprehensive report on the economic condition of settlements and landholdings before the modern era, and provides the first record of the existence of many of the villages that now make up Greater London.

enclosure
The process by which common land was closed off to public use and ownership passed to individual landowners. Much of the land in the area of modern London (as elsewhere in the country) remained available for common use as recently as the early 19th century. Common land was used for grazing livestock, digging peat, gathering firewood and drying washing. But the existence of so many commons acted as a brake on economic growth, so Parliament progressively divided up common land among those who had the capital to invest in its improvement, whether through more efficient farming methods or by building on it. Enclosure was the single most influential factor in the development of outer London before the coming of the railways.

glebe
Church-owned land providing an income in rent etc. for the resident Anglican priest or minister.

Grand Junction/Union Canal
The Grand Junction Canal in west London (and its Paddington and Slough branches) and the Regent's Canal in east and central London became the Grand Union Canal in 1929 after the merger of the Grand Junction, Regent's and Warwick Canal companies. The Grand Junction Canal opened in stages between 1796 and 1805, the Paddington branch opened in 1801, and the Regent's Canal in two stages in 1816 and 1820. The Grand Union Canal was nationalized in 1948, and is now managed by British Waterways.

Greater London Council (GLC)

The Greater London Council was established with the creation of the much larger county of Greater London in 1965, and took over the responsibilities of the London County Council. The Conservative government abolished the GLC in 1986, dividing its powers between borough councils and unelected 'residuary bodies'. After a 13-year interregnum, the Greater London Authority was established as an elected regional assembly and government for London, headed by the Mayor of London.

Great Fire of London

A major fire in the City of London from 2–5 September 1666. The surveyors appointed after the fire reported that 436 acres were destroyed inside and outside the city walls; this included about five-sixths of the city within the walls. Their report listed losses as '400 streets, 13,200 dwelling-houses, 89 churches [besides chapels]; 4 of the city gates, Guildhall, many public structures, hospitals, schools, libraries, and a vast number of stately edifices'. As well as the Guildhall, the 'public structures' included St Paul's Cathedral, the Royal Exchange, the Custom House, Bridewell and other prisons, and four bridges across the Thames. Although 100,000 people were left homeless, only 9–16 deaths were reported.

Great Plague

An outbreak of disease, believed to have been bubonic plague, in London in 1665–6, and one of the last widespread outbreaks in Europe. Although the outbreak may have begun in the winter of 1664–5, the plague spread rapidly in the unusually warm spring and summer of 1665 and is believed to have killed up to a fifth of London's population. The death toll began to decline in autumn 1665 but continued at a low level until September 1666, when the Great Fire destroyed the City's rats and their plague-carrying fleas.

green belt

Open land surrounding a town or city, where building or development is strictly controlled; the aim is to prevent urban sprawl and protect the countryside from further encroachment. A narrow 'green girdle' around London was proposed to the Greater London Regional Planning Committee in 1933 and became the basis of the Green Belt (London and Home Counties) Act 1938. The Town and Country Planning Act 1947 permitted local authorities to prevent development in green-belt areas, and a national green-belt policy was codified in 1955. London's green belt is not only the oldest in England but also, at 486,000 hectares, the largest. It is under threat in Hertfordshire and Sussex, and particularly in areas of south Essex that fall within the Thames Gateway development area.

hide/hyde

A measure of land area, usually the amount considered adequate to support one family and its dependents. The area varied in size according to the quality and fertility of the land, but was usually 60–120 old acres, or 15–30 modern acres (60,000–120,000 square metres).

hundred

The division of a county for administrative, military and judicial purposes, from Saxon times until the 19th century. Each hundred had enough land to support 100 households (*see* **hide/hyde**) and was headed by a hundred-man, who was responsible for its administration, justice, and supplying and leading its military forces.

jerry-building

The construction of flimsy buildings cheaply, quickly and incompetently.

Knights Hospitallers/Knights of St John

The Knights Hospitallers of St John of Jerusalem was a military religious order named after the hospital at Jerusalem that cared for pilgrims to the Holy Land. Initially the Order cared for sick pilgrims but subsequently it also took on a military role, defending the pilgrimage routes. After the Holy Land fell to the Muslims in 1291, the Order established its headquarters first in Rhodes and then in Malta. The English branch of the Order was dissolved at the Reformation, although its work with the sick continued elsewhere in Europe. A British branch, the British Order of St John, was re-established in the 19th century and founded St John Ambulance in 1877, training lay people to administer emergency medical care.

Knights Templar

The Order of Poor Knights of Christ and of the Temple of Solomon was a military religious order founded in Jerusalem in 1119–20 to protect pilgrims travelling to the Holy Land, and played an important role in the Crusades. The Order's independence, power and wealth led to it becoming Europe's banker in the 13th century, but also inspired the hostility which brought about its suppression in 1307–14 for alleged heresy.

Lammas land

The church festival of Lammas on 1 August each year celebrated the harvesting of the grain crops. Lammas land was land opened up to use by commoners, primarily to graze their livestock, after the harvest had been gathered in.

listed building

A building, or other man-made structure, judged to be of architectural or historical importance and therefore legally protected from demolition or alteration. The buildings are categorized as Grade I, II* or II and placed on a register. Most listed buildings are rated as Grade II; Grade II* buildings (about 4 per cent) are deemed especially significant; and Grade I buildings (about 2 per cent) are defined as being of 'exceptional interest'. Not all listed buildings are beautiful or ancient; some are chosen because they represent a good example of a disappearing style of architecture, even though the style may be disappearing for a valid reason, as is the case with some recently listed 1960s tower blocks.

London County Council (LCC)

The London County Council succeeded the Metropolitan Board of Works (MBW) in 1889 and assumed an enlarged portfolio of responsibilities. The MBW was created in 1856, the first single organization to take a co-ordinated approach to creating, maintaining and improving public amenities and services across the county of London; vestries, boards of health and other local authorities retained responsibility for matters that did not cross parish or borough boundaries. One of the MBW's first achievements was the construction of the sewage disposal network on which much of London still depends today. The most visible legacy of the MBW and LCC's early activities is a constellation of public parks, created when it became apparent that speculative builders would otherwise cover every inch of former farmland. Later, the LCC began to build housing estates and clear slums. The LCC was replaced by the Greater London Council with the creation of the much larger county of Greater London in 1965.

Ofsted

The Office for Standards in Education (Ofsted) was established in 1992, replacing HM Inspectorate of Schools. It conducts regular inspections of all state schools and colleges, as well as other childcare and educational facilities. Inspectors' reports include information on the characteristics of each institution, which can provide an insight into the demographics of its catchment area.

out-county

A term used of an area outside the then boundaries of the county of London but in which a London council had an interest, eg through the construction of a housing estate.

parish

An administrative subdivision: ecclesiastically, a subdivision of a diocese representing an area with its own church and priest; and in civil administration a subdivision of a county and the smallest unit of local government in England. Parishes have probably existed since pre-Conquest times, and the ecclesiastical and lay responsibilities devolved to parish level were administered by vestry boards from about the eleventh century until the late 19th century. The ecclesiastical and civil functions were separated in the late 19th century.

Pevsner

A reference to the London volumes of *The Buildings of England*. The architectural historian Sir Nikolaus Pevsner worked on this magnificent series of books until his death in 1983, creating an architectural record unmatched anywhere in the world. Later editions have been revised by several authors, but this book does not attempt to assign individual responsibility for specific remarks.

Poor Law
The system for providing social welfare in England (and subsequently the UK) from the 16th century until the 20th century. The maintenance of the poor – the unemployed, ill, elderly, orphaned etc. – was the responsibility of the parish in which they were resident, and was financed by a rate (property tax) levied in each parish. Amendments were introduced in the 19th century which encouraged the development of poor law unions and workhouses (*see* **union** and **workhouse**). Social services began to be provided by the state in the early 20th century, starting with the old age pension and national insurance introduced before World War I, and the remnants of the Poor Law were abolished in 1948 with the creation of the welfare state.

ragged school
Voluntary schools for destitute children, set up by charities and often providing food, clothes and accommodation as well as free education.

ribbon development
The extensive building of residential property along the side of a main road leading out of a town or village.

rookery
A crowded, dilapidated and crime-ridden slum area.

stucco
White plaster or cement used to cover exterior brickwork to give the appearance of stone. The effect is usually augmented by using widely spaced straight grooves to break up large surface areas. Stuccoing was considered indispensable in London's more upmarket residential developments during the 18th and 19th centuries. Most stucco is nowadays painted a creamy white.

toll road/turnpike
A road with a gate or barrier preventing access until a toll was paid, common from the 16th to the 19th centuries. From the early 18th century, turnpike trusts were formed by local business people, who levied tolls on stretches of road running through the district and used the money received to maintain the road. The first turnpike road was authorized in 1663 for part of the Great North Road in Hertfordshire, and the first trusts were established on the 13 main roads to London between 1706 and 1750. Road maintenance became the responsibility of local authorities after 1888.

union
Following legislation in 1834, Poor Law Unions were formed by groups of parishes which were responsible for the funding and administration of the Poor Law in the area covered by the union. The unions were run by boards of guardians, whose responsibilities were expanded later in the 19th century to include some aspects of education and hospital provision. They were abolished and their responsibilities transferred to county councils in 1930.

vestry
A room in a church where meetings were commonly held to deal with the administration of the local parish, and by extension the administrative body. The vestry board was usually responsible for both ecclesiastical and lay matters administered at parish level, such as the Poor Law. The boards were replaced in the late 19th century by parochial church councils, which administer the affairs of the ecclesiastical parish, and parish councils, which deal with local government matters affecting the civil parish.

workhouse
Originally the poor were provided with Poor Law relief in their own homes, or accommodated in their parish's poorhouse. Workhouses, combining the provision of accommodation with the provision of work, developed gradually until legislation in 1834 made poor relief available only in the workhouse. Conditions were harsh and abuses were common. Workhouses were abolished by the Local Government Act 1929.

Abbey Mills • *Merton see* MERTON ABBEY MILLS

Abbey Mills • *Newham*

A commercial and industrial district by the River Lea, situated south of STRATFORD High Street and taking its name from watermills belonging to Stratford Langthorne Abbey, a Cistercian monastery founded in 1134 by William de Monfichet. The abbey stood in the marshes, on the present-day Channelsea River, and was endowed with estates in WEST HAM. It remained a wealthy and influential landowner until the dissolution of the monasteries in the 1530s. The first record of a mill here was in the early 14th century. The district is more properly known as MILL MEADS (and, on its eastern side, West Ham Mills) but developers are calling it Abbey Mills because the pumping station of that name is a much-admired masterpiece of Victorian public works engineering, nicknamed 'the cathedral of sewage'. Designed by Sir Joseph Bazalgette, the pumps draw sewage from the drains of north London and send it down to the filter-beds at BECKTON. Because it is still in use, the magnificent interior, with its ornate cast iron, is not open to the public. Landscaping work is planned to enhance views of the pumping station from nearby footpaths. In recent years, there has been extensive regeneration in the neighbourhood, with the replacement of disused factories by shed-type warehouses. On the eastern bank of the Channelsea River is the Abbey Mills Riverine Centre, established by an Islamic trust in the mid 1990s for the development of a mosque. It was formerly the site of a chemical works.

✉ E15

Abbey Road • *Westminster/Camden*

A musically famous street with contrasting social characteristics in its northern (KILBURN) and southern (ST JOHN'S WOOD) halves. Abbey Road was created in 1829 from an existing farm track called Abbey Lane as part of the development of St John's Wood. Its name derived from the nearby presence of Kilburn Priory. In the 1840s, developers put up tasteful villas in a variety of Gothic-influenced styles, many of which survive today. After 1851, slightly less exclusive properties were built on the west side of the locality and the entire area was virtually gapless within a couple of decades. St Mary's Church and St John's Wood Synagogue were built on Abbey Road to serve the area's two main religious communities. The southern part of the road and its neighbourhood generally maintained its high social status but towards Kilburn properties were subdivided and some suffered from neglect. Wartime bomb damage exacerbated the decline and the local and county councils cleared a large area in the north-west and built the high-rise Abbey Road estate in the early 1960s. Later in the decade the Greater London Council built the Ainsworth estate to the east of the road. Following a schism within British Jewry, the New London Synagogue was founded in 1964, at first holding services in Lauderdale Road, MAIDA VALE. All four members of the Beatles attended a memorial service here for their manager Brian Epstein in 1967. The synagogue relocated to Abbey Road in 1970. The Abbey Road ward, which covers the southern part of the street and its hinterland, has a relatively high number of residents aged over 75. Many homes are privately rented and the number of single-parent households is very low. Fifty-five per cent of 16- to 74-year-olds are qualified to degree level or above. Forty-five per cent of residents are Christian and 16.4 per cent are Jewish.

Abbey Road is best known for the EMI recording studios and the Beatles' album that took its name from the address; the famous cover photograph shows the band members on a zebra crossing in Abbey Road. Occasional public events are held at the studios, which are nowadays especially involved with film scores. The street is also responsible for another famous name: the Abbey National (now Abbey) banking group, which was born from a merger of the National Building

Society and the Abbey Road and St John's Wood Permanent Building Society.

⊠ NW8; NW6

♁ 9,554 (Westminster's Abbey Road ward)

📖 Brian Southall et al, *Abbey Road*, Omnibus, 2002 (history of the recording studio)

Abbey Wood • *Greenwich/Bexley*

An affordable dormitory district situated south of THAMESMEAD, which it prefigured. It is named after the ancient woodlands that surround the remains of LESNES ABBEY, founded in 1178. The abbey's site was close to a marsh that was prone to flooding as the Thames frequently overflowed its banks. The monks had to maintain the river wall to prevent the floods, which allowed the development of a small settlement here. The hamlet had only a hundred inhabitants when the North Kent Railway arrived and a small station opened in 1850, and its setting remained rural for the rest of the 19th century. To the south, the Royal Arsenal Co-operative Society began building the BOSTALL estate from about 1900. Further expansion came with the construction of a tram depot, which was subsequently converted into a bus garage. In the 1950s, sales of land by the contracting WOOLWICH ARSENAL allowed the council to build the Abbey Wood estate on land west of Harrow Manor Way. For a while the estate was a boom town, attracting industry and more housing. Local amenities followed, but only after pressure from community activists. Half the housing is now owner-occupied and Abbey Wood constitutes a useful first step on the property ladder for cash-strapped homebuyers, especially those with children.

⊠ SE2

♁ 13,372

🚆 South Eastern Trains (zone 4)

📖 Darrell Spurgeon, *Discover Woolwich and Its Environs*, Greenwich Guidebooks, 1996

Acton • *Ealing*

A large suburb situated between EALING and CHISWICK, now mainly residential but formerly of major industrial significance. First recorded in 1181, Acton's name translates roughly as 'oak farm'. Acton is one of the few places in London with evidence of Stone Age worship. A Bronze Age cemetery has also been located and relics have been found indicating two phases of Roman activity. The area surrounding the village of Acton remained arable farmland until the latter half of the 19th century, but suburban development was well advanced by the outbreak of World War I. The district was at one time famous for its laundries and SOUTH ACTON gained the nickname 'Soapsuds Island'. Between the wars, Acton became a 'suburb of production'; in the 1930s it was Britain's largest industrial area south of Coventry. The evolution of Acton's land use has resulted in a variety of housing styles, from Victorian villas, through cottage estates to council tower blocks. Some parts have recently been 'rediscovered' by home buyers, notably the estate agents' favourite, Poets' Corner. The roads nearest Chiswick are also considered highly desirable. WEST ACTON is especially popular with the Japanese community because of the Japanese school there. Many of the larger properties have been subdivided into flats, often rented by young professionals and/or transient Antipodeans. Just by Acton Central station are the Goldsmiths' almshouses, now let on a commercial basis, although members of the Worshipful Company of Goldsmiths are given preference. Acton has more Tube and rail stations to its name than anywhere else in London: one for each point of the compass, plus Acton Central, ACTON TOWN and Acton Main Line.

In 1959, Acton County Grammar School pupils Roger Daltrey, John Entwistle and Pete Townshend formed the Detours band, later to become The Who. Adam Faith, the pop superstar turned actor, grew up on a council estate in Acton Vale.

⊠ W3

♁ 41,208 (Acton Central, East Acton and South Acton wards)

🚆 First Great Western Link (Acton Main Line, zone 3); Silverlink Metro (Acton Central, zone 2)

📖 Averil and Thomas Harper Smith wrote and published a series of books covering even the most recondite aspects of Acton's history

@ www.users.globalnet.co.uk/~ajk/acton (Acton History Group site)

Acton Green • *Ealing*

The southernmost part of ACTON, bounded by Acton Lane and the tracks of the District Line and the North London line. The Battle of TURNHAM GREEN ranged across and beyond Acton Green Common in 1642. By 1790

Acton Green had ten acres of orchards and market gardens, occupying around a quarter of the common's total area. A small hamlet grew up on the south side of the green, with more cottages following at the southern end of Acton Lane. Some grander villas appeared here and there, notably Fairlawn House and, later, Fairlawn Villa. All of Acton's commons were enclosed in 1859, at first boosting the concentration of orchards here, but soon resulting in strips of land being sold off for housebuilding. Streets were laid out on farmland and paddocks belonging to the Rothschilds of GUNNERSBURY. The locality also gained its share of laundries as Acton became London's 'Soapsuds Island' from the 1860s. Acton Green station (now CHISWICK PARK) opened in 1879, prompting the rapid completion of the suburbanization process. The Church of St Alban the Martyr was consecrated in 1888 and the Fairlawn Park estate took the place of Fairlawn House in the following year. By the start of the 20th century, Acton Green was also becoming home to workshops and factories, notably the electrical and defence equipment manufacturer Evershed and Vignoles. In the early 1960s the company employed 1,500 workers here. Its factory was redeveloped as luxury flats and a small trading estate in the 1990s, a period when most of Acton Green's shops and industrial premises made way for residential new builds or conversions. Estate agents prefer to use the name Chiswick Park for the whole neighbourhood, despite the efforts of Acton Green residents' association. The green itself lies at the south-eastern corner of the residential locality and covers 15 acres.

✉ W4

🚆 District Line (Chiswick Park, zone 3)

@ www.actongreen.org.uk (residents' association site)

Acton Town • *Ealing*
Although not widely used, except by London Underground, this term is worth employing to differentiate ACTON town centre from its sprawling surroundings. This locality was Windmill Hill in the early 19th century, later shortened to Mill Hill. From 1877 William Willett laid out the Mill Hill Park estate in the extensive grounds of a house that had stood in present-day Avenue Crescent. This was Acton's earliest higher-class suburban project, and one of the few that later escaped wholesale redevelopment by the council. The station

that opened just to the south west was named Mill Hill Park in 1879 and renamed Acton Town in 1910. The station was rebuilt in 1932 by Charles Holden for the arrival of the Piccadilly Line. Later in the 1930s the Edwardian municipal buildings were extended to provide an assembly and concert hall. Elsewhere on the High Street, continuing rebuilding and refacing of shops and other businesses has created a wholly unappealing impression. Acton cannot compete with EALING as a shopping destination and the state of the local economy is reflected in the 99p stores that seek to outdo the pound stores but are in turn undercut by the 98p stores. The Acton Central ward has relatively high numbers of tenants who rent privately or from a housing association. At 41 per cent, the proportion of residents qualified to degree level or above is more than twice the national average and indicates the area's popularity with young professionals who cannot yet afford Ealing or CHISWICK.

✉ W3

🚶 13,442 (Acton Central ward)

🚆 District Line; Piccadilly Line (zone 3)

Addington • *Croydon*
A North Downs village lying two and a half miles east of SOUTH CROYDON. The name relates to a Saxon landowner and the manor was mentioned in Domesday Book, when it was held by Tezelin, the king's cook. Addington was the site of one of Henry VIII's hunting lodges. Addington Palace, a rather plain mansion built in 1780 with grounds landscaped by Capability Brown, was a home of the archbishops of Canterbury in the 19th century. During the 20th century it was successively a diamond merchant's home, a Red Cross hospital, a hotel and a music college, and it is now a country club. Five archbishops of Canterbury are buried at the Church of St Mary the Blessed Virgin and are remembered in many memorials, decorations and windows around the church, which dates from 1080 but is now mainly Victorian, following extensive renovations. Addington has a cricket club founded in 1743 and several golf courses in the surrounding parkland. Addington Hills are to the west, near UPPER SHIRLEY. The village has kept itself at arm's length from the much larger settlement of NEW ADDINGTON to the south-east, but has suffered a decline with the loss of its school and village shop. The arrival of the Croydon Tramlink has helped its accessibility, but the stop is not conveniently situated

because the line needs to bear southwards for New Addington.

> ✉ Croydon CR0

> 🚊 Croydon Tramlink, Route 3 (Addington Village)

> 📖 Frank Warren, *Addington: A History,* Phillimore, 1984

Addiscombe • *Croydon*

A Victorian and interwar extension of CROY-DON, which lies to the west. Although there is no mention of Addiscombe before the 13th century, it may take its name from the same landowner who earlier gave his name to AD-DINGTON. Addiscombe Place was a grand mansion built in 1703 by William Draper, son-in-law of the diarist John Evelyn. It later became home to Lord Hawkesbury, whose gardener James McPhail shaped the destiny of British sandwiches and salads with his *Treatise on the Culture of the Cucumber*, describing an 'advantageous method of cultivating that plant'. Lord Liverpool lived at Addiscombe Place for many years before he became prime minister and often entertained George III there. In 1809, the East India Company Military Seminary was established at the mansion. Among the college's distinguished staff was the chemist Edward Frankland, 'the father of valency'. The college closed in 1861 and the training of Indian Army officers transferred to Sandhurst. Within a few years, six new roads lined with villas had replaced Addiscombe Place and most of its outbuildings. Ashleigh and India, a pair of houses built in 1848 as homes for professors, remain today on Addiscombe Road. The parts of Addiscombe that had not been built up with Victorian terraced houses were filled by detached and semi-detached houses during the 1930s. Addiscombe tramstop stands on the site of the former Bingham Road station, while the old Addiscombe station has been demolished and replaced by housing. Croydon council has recently created the four-acre Addiscombe linear park between Morland Road and Dalmally Road on the site of the former railway line. New trees and shrubs have been planted and the park has a footway and cycle track along its length.

The novelist and poet D H Lawrence lodged at 12 Colworth Road from 1908 to 1912, while teaching at Davidson High School.

> ✉ Croydon CR0

> 👥 15,402

> 🚊 Croydon Tramlink, Routes 1 and 2

> 📖 Steve Collins et al, *The Book of Addiscombe,* vol 1, Halsgrove, 2000; vol 2, Halsgrove, 2002

Adelphi • *Westminster*

The name has dropped out of use, but this was once a fashionable quarter situated south of the STRAND and east of CHARING CROSS. The name, which comes from the Greek word for 'brothers', strictly referred to Adelphi Terrace, but by extension covered the buildings of the neighbouring streets, all developed by Robert, James and John Adam between 1768 and 1774. There was a year's pause halfway through construction when the trio ran out of money, and the development never made them any profit. The grandiose architecture was largely the work of Robert Adam, who also created KENWOOD House, half of Fitzroy Square and the interior of Syon House, the centrepiece of SYON PARK. A subterranean network of passages and arched vaults, described as 'a very town' by one writer, led down to the Thames. The Adelphi was popular with leading figures from artistic and literary circles, and residents have included the actor-manager David Garrick, the poet Thomas Hood and the writers John Galsworthy and J M Barrie. Adelphi Terrace was demolished in 1936 but most of the other streets remain intact, notably the premises of the Royal Society of Arts in John Adam Street.

The present Adelphi Theatre was built in 1930 in Maiden Lane on the north side of the Strand, on a site occupied by three earlier theatres since 1806. It has been reported that the ghost of actor William Terriss often walks the building. An 'Adelphi melodrama' was a kind of populist play put on at the theatre during the late 19th century.

> ✉ WC2

> 📖 David G C Allen, *The Adelphi Past and Present: A History and Guide,* Calder Walker, 2001

Agar Town • *Camden* (pronounced 'aygar')

Former name for the canalside locality situated east of CAMDEN TOWN, remembered now only in Agar Grove. From 1789 this was the private estate of William Agar of Elm Lodge. In the 1810s, Agar fought a desperate battle to prevent the cutting of the Regent's Canal through his property, although his underlying motive may simply have been to maximize the compensation he received. Agar died in 1838 and his widow soon began to grant building leases on part of the estate, while retaining Elm Lodge. The jerry-built settlement that took root here was later described as a 'suburban Connemara' for its alleged predominantly Irish population, and nicknamed 'Ague Town' for its poverty and ill health. Depictions of Agar Town as the worst kind of filthy slum may have been exaggerated but the residents were undeniably poor and conditions were insalubrious. St Thomas' Church was built on Wrotham Road in 1864, at the very time that the old town was disappearing beneath the tracks and goods yards that accompanied the opening of the Midland Railway's St Pancras station. The displaced inhabitants mostly moved to neighbouring districts like KENTISH TOWN. St Thomas's was damaged by wartime bombing and demolished in the early 1950s, when its parish was united with that of St Michael's Church, CAMDEN ROAD. After the goods yards became redundant, part of the site was opened as Camley Street Natural Park in 1984, while Fairview Estates developed Elm Village, an award-winning mix of social and private housing. Much of the remainder of the district falls within the KING'S CROSS railway lands, an area now undergoing massive development and regeneration.

✉ NW1

📖 Steven Denford, *Agar Town: Life and Death of a Victorian 'Slum',* Camden History Society, 1995

@ www.victorianlondon.org/districts/agartown.htm (1851 account of local conditions)

Albany Park • *Bexley*

A lacklustre housing estate lying on high ground overlooking the Cray Valley, midway between SIDCUP and BEXLEY. This was formerly the site of Tanyard and Hurst farms, part of the estate of the Vansittart family of FOOTS CRAY. New Ideal Homesteads laid out the estate and made up its name in the mid 1930s, publishing a sales brochure with the implausible pledge that 'the charming countryside shall permanently retain the rural character of its vistas and shall not suffer disfigurement in any way'. Although the Dartford Loop railway line had been built in 1866, it was the developers who opened a station here in July 1935. NIH built at almost twice the housing density recommended by Bexley council and priced its properties as low as £395, making them affordable for working-

class families wanting to escape inner London. The settlement was extended southeastwards with the building of the Royal Park estate, begun in the early 1940s and completed after World War II. In 1965 the green-roofed parish church of St Andrew's was built on Maylands Drive. Pevsner called it 'ingenious, fashionable and slightly absurd'. The granting of parochial status was a special concession as Albany Park fell well short of the 10,000 population normally required. Albany Park has been cited as one of Sidcup's prime areas of residential growth, but it shows no outward sign of vitality. The shops of Norman Parade are almost entirely closed down and derelict, and the property company that owns them had no plans for their redevelopment at the time of writing. Hurst Place is a much-altered 18th-century mansion, now in use as a community centre.

In 2003, Riverside Road resident Ian Robb made the local news when he withheld part of his council tax in protest at Bexley council's alleged neglect of Albany Park. 'I have lived here 22 years and watched it gradually go downhill,' Mr Robb was quoted as saying. 'The place is dying … Because we are off the beaten track, the council doesn't want to know.'

✉ Bexley DA5; Sidcup DA14

🚉 South Eastern Trains (zone 5)

Aldborough Hatch • *Redbridge*

A semi-rural residential locality situated north of the Eastern Avenue (A12), just beyond NEWBURY PARK. The name probably derives from the family who built a hall here, while the hatch (a wicket gate) would have led into HAINAULT Forest. Writing in his *Environs of London* in 1792, Daniel Lysons described the hall as 'a capital mansion situated in the forest'. The woods provided a living for the local charcoal burners and foresters, and game for the frequent royal hunts. Before the extensive deforestation of the 1850s, according to local historian George Tasker, 'the hamlet consisted almost entirely of four or five mansions within a stone's throw of each other, and a farm or two'. By way of compensation for the destruction of the woodland the government contributed towards the cost of building St Peter's Church, using stones from the old Westminster Bridge. The Eastern Avenue brought the builders with it in the late 1920s and early 1930s, including Suburban Developments (London) Ltd, which laid out the Aldborough Grange estate on land east of Aldborough Road North. Designation as green-belt land has restricted further expansion into the farmland on the north side of the road. The Aldborough ward has a culturally diverse population. Slightly more than 50 per cent of residents are Christians and the main religious minorities are Jews and Hindus.

Aldborough Hall is now an equestrian centre, while Aldborough Hall Farm runs a pick-your-own operation and a farm shop.

✉ Ilford IG2

♦ 11,611 (Aldborough ward)

Aldersbrook · Redbridge/Newham

A well-preserved Edwardian estate surrounded by open land on the south side of WAN-STEAD. The present name dates from the 16th century and refers to alders growing beside a tributary of the River Roding. Before this, it was called Nakedhall – an allusion to the exposed position of the manor. The dynasty that owned Wanstead House steadily acquired and altered the farmland of Aldersbrook from 1786 onwards, knocking down its manor house, selling land to the Corporation of London for use as a cemetery and auctioning building plots from 1899. The plots' conditions of sale included clauses stipulating that the properties be relatively expensive, especially on the edges of the estate, where the £500 detached houses had views over WANSTEAD PARK and WANSTEAD FLATS. These sold to the professional classes, while the £300 semi-detached and terraced houses on the main streets attracted lower middle-class occupiers, usually to rent rather than to buy. More than a thousand homes were built by 1910 and the variety of developers, combined with the rapidly changing architectural fashions of the time, resulted in a miscellany of styles. Some properties that were bombed in World War II were rebuilt in styles almost indistinguishable from their predecessors. In the 1960s, council housing replaced the children's home and isolation hospital that had stood on Aldersbrook's western and eastern sides respectively. South of Aldersbrook Road, Heatherwood Close juts into Wanstead Flats where Aldersbrook Farm used to stand. Redbridge council belatedly designated Aldersbrook a conservation area in 2002.

✉ E12; E11

📖 Kathryn Morrison and Ann Robey, *One Hundred Years of Suburbia: The Aldersbrook Estate in Wanstead 1899–1999*, Royal Commission on the Historical Monuments of England, 1999

Aldersgate · City

One of only two primarily residential wards in the CITY OF LONDON (because it includes much of the BARBICAN) and also a former name of Barbican Tube station. An aperture in the Roman defences that surrounded the City was added here sometime after the construction of the wall itself, perhaps in the early 4th century. The Aldersgate name, relating to a man named Ealdrēd, probably dates from the late Saxon period. When James VI and I came from Scotland to London in 1603, he entered the city by this gate and statues of him were erected here, seated on horseback outside the gate and on his throne on the inner side. By the 1650s the wide road was lined with impressive houses and was described by a contemporary writer as 'resembling an Italian street more than any other in London'. In 1667, John Milton wrote much of *Paradise Lost* in a house nearby. Aldersgate Street holds a special significance for Methodists, for it was at a religious meeting here on 24 May 1738 that John Wesley felt his heart 'strangely warmed' as he listened to a reading of Martin Luther's preface to the *Epistle to the Romans*. Wesley went on to found a network of evangelical societies, at first within the Church of England, which later formed the nucleus of the Methodist Church. Aldersgate was demolished in 1761; Thomas More House in the Barbican stands near its site. Aldersgate Street now constitutes the very southernmost end of the A1 and extends just south of the Museum of London rotunda to meet St Martin's le Grand. There has been a public house on the site of the Lord Raglan, at 61 Aldersgate Street, since Shakespeare's day – indeed, the Bard is said to have been among its regulars. It was rebuilt in the mid 19th century, and renamed then after the Crimean War commander. Across the road, Postmans Park has a permanent display of commemorative tiles dedicated to ordinary people who heroically gave their lives in order to save others. North of the rotunda, the jutting edges of the Barbican residential complex filled most of the east side of Aldersgate Street in the early 1960s. Commercial offices (and one apartment block) formed an unbroken wall of stone and glass south of the junction with Long Lane at the beginning of the 21st century.

The Museum of London adjoins the Barbican complex. Its exhibits include the Great Fire Experience, reconstructed Victorian shops, the gilded Lord Mayor's coach, a Roman horse skeleton, and grim 18th-century prison cells, complete with prisoner graffiti.

Outside the entrance to the museum a bronze memorial in the shape of a flame marks the site of Wesley's conversion.

✉ EC1; EC2

🏃 1,600

🚇 Circle Line; Hammersmith & City Line; Metropolitan Line (Barbican, zone 1)

📖 Alfred Lubran, *A Snippet of Information about Aldersgate, a London District*, Narbulla Agency Press, 1972

@ www.museumoflondon.org.uk

Aldgate • *City*

Often regarded as the point where the EAST END meets the CITY OF LONDON, Aldgate is now a street running east of Leadenhall Street, which becomes Aldgate High Street at the junction with the Minories. One of the four original entrances to the City, Aldgate was the easternmost gate in the Roman wall, rebuilt in 1606 and then removed in the 1760s to ease traffic congestion. Though it is usually believed to mean 'old gate', the name might be a corruption of 'ale gate', as refreshments were provided here for thirsty travellers. St Botolph's Church, which is probably of Saxon foundation, has been periodically enlarged and rebuilt. Its parish, which comprises the City ward of Portsoken, stands on land reputedly granted by King Edgar to 13 knights who had performed brave deeds to prove their worth. In 1107 the Prior of Aldgate founded the monastery of Holy Trinity just outside the gate. It acquired great wealth and significance but was given by Henry VIII to Sir Thomas Audley at the dissolution of the monasteries and was soon dismantled. In 1710, Sir John Cass founded a school here for 90 poor children. Aldgate has one of the most historic parish pumps in London, first erected above St Michael's well at the end of the 16th century. The well was filled in for health reasons in 1876 and mains water was piped to the pump. Like neighbouring SPITALFIELDS, Aldgate benefited from the economic vitality brought by successive waves of immigrants, notably Huguenots, Irish and Jews, but following destruction by World War II bombs and 1960s planners, it now consists principally of uninspiring commercial premises encircled by a traffic-clogged one-way system.

The medieval English poet Geoffrey Chaucer lived at Aldgate from 1374 to 1386, during which time he wrote several works, including *Troilus and Criseyde*. The poet Edmund Spenser was born locally in 1552 and the philosopher Jeremy Bentham was baptized at St Botolph's Church in 1748. Novels set in Aldgate include Gerard Williams' *Dr Mortimer and the Aldgate Mystery* and several works by Ralph Finn.

✉ EC3

🚇 Circle Line; Metropolitan Line (zone 1)

📖 Malcolm Johnson, *Outside the Gate: St Botolph's and Aldgate, 950–1994*, Stepney Books, 1994; Lazarus Sheridan, *Aldgate & Roundabout*, Azalpress, 2002 (reissue of a 1939 work with a new introduction by the author)

Aldgate East • *Tower Hamlets*

A London Underground station located on WHITECHAPEL High Street at the corner of Commercial Street. Aldgate East lay at the boundary of Holy Trinity Priory from its foundation in 1107 until the dissolution of the monasteries in the 16th century. Whitechapel High Street was originally 'Algatestrete' and was probably bordered by open waste until at least the 13th century, when the first dwellings appeared. Over successive centuries the street gained early forms of industry, tall houses and hostelries, with a maze of alleys behind. The Metropolitan Railway Co. and Metropolitan District Railway Co. jointly opened the first Aldgate East station in 1884, four years before Jack the Ripper set to work close by, speeding the clearance of the alleys. In the early part of the 20th century the EAST END's new Jewish community, refugees from Russia's pogroms, created a tailoring district here. In 1936 a replacement Aldgate East station was built, 300 yards east of its predecessor, with new tunnelling and longer platforms, relieving a bottleneck in the underground system and allowing the closure of nearby St Mary's station. After World War II, bomb sites and slums were cleared and replaced by the blur of businesses, educational institutions and rag trade wholesalers that characterize the eastern edge of the City, which continues to eat away at Whitechapel at this point. The street scene by the station is presently dominated by the blank white panels of the Forum, a conference centre with a fitness club. The Aldgate Union project promises 'total transformation' but some uncertainty hangs over the final form that this will take. The Women's Library, on Old Castle Street, was converted from a Victorian washhouse in 2001.

Elizabeth Garrett Anderson, the first British

woman to qualify as a doctor, was born at 1 Commercial Road in 1836.

> ✉ E1

> 🚇 District Line; Hammersmith & City Line (zone 1)

> @ www.aldgateunion.com

Aldwych • *Westminster*

A grand crescent breaking away from the STRAND and rejoining it a few hundred yards further on, created by the cutting of KINGS-WAY in 1905 and named Aldwych by the London County Council. Although the street is relatively new, it commemorates a site of exceptional importance during the Dark Ages. When the Saxons colonized the London area in the 5th century, after the Romans had departed, they established a riverside market town beyond the city walls, calling it Lundenwic. The Thames was much wider then, and the Strand marks its shoreline. In 886, Alfred the Great captured London from the marauding Danes, refortified the city and moved the trading activities of Lundenwic within it. A century or more later, a Danish community resettled the vicinity of the old market (which is what 'Aldwych' means). The Church of St Clement Danes is said to be the burial place of the half-Danish Harold I, Harefoot, who ruled England from 1035 to 1040, first as regent for his half-brother and then as king. Centuries later, Samuel Johnson worshipped at the church, and its bells say 'Oranges and lemons' in the famous nursery rhyme. It was gutted by fire caused by bombing during World War II but has since been restored. Modern Aldwych contains Australia House, India House and Bush House, home of the BBC World Service. The World Service is to relocate to Broadcasting House (see GREAT PORTLAND STREET) around 2011.

The Aldwych farces are a series of plays written by Ben Travers and first performed at the Aldwych Theatre between 1925 and 1933. The composer Ivor Novello lived in Aldwych for most of his adult life.

> ✉ WC2

> 🚇 formerly on the Piccadilly Line, although Aldwych station (once known as Strand) closed in 1994; it is occasionally used as a location for television and film productions

Alexandra Palace • *Haringey*

North London's answer to the CRYSTAL PALACE crowns the 313-foot summit of MUSWELL HILL, west of WOOD GREEN. At the end of the 1850s the Great Northern Railway Co. opened Wood Green (now Alexandra Palace) station and the Great Northern Palace Co. acquired Tottenham Wood Farm. The latter company opened a pleasure garden and then reused materials from the international exhibition held at South Kensington in 1862 to build the first Alexandra Palace. A railway branch line connected the palace with HIGHGATE station on Archway Road. Nicknamed 'Ally Pally', the exhibition hall burned down within days of its inauguration in 1873. A new palace opened two years later, with more emphasis on cultural and educational facilities than some of the showier exhibition halls built elsewhere at that time. Perhaps because of this, the venue was almost continuously beset by financial difficulties and a consortium of local authorities had to step in and rescue it in 1901. Alexandra Palace served as a prisoner of war camp in World War I and the BBC transmitted the world's first public television broadcasts from a studio here in 1936. The palace's dedicated railway line closed in 1954. The Greater London Council managed the site from 1966 and passed control to the London Borough of Haringey in 1980, whereupon half the palace was again ruined by fire. Part of it was restored in 1990 but the rest is still awaiting renovation. Haringey council cannot afford to carry out the work and has obtained government permission to offer the building for commercial development on a 125-year lease. Meanwhile the palace serves as a minor exhibition and events centre. It also has an ice rink, a theatre and a pub, appropriately named the Phoenix.

The sightline towards St Paul's Cathedral from the palace's dilapidated viewing terrace is designated a 'landmark viewing corridor', which new building must not obstruct. Even trees must be cut back if they grow too tall.

> ✉ N22

> 🚇 WAGN Railway (zone 3)

> 📖 Ken Gay, *Palace on the Hill*, Hornsey Historical Society, 1992; Fred Clarke, *Tales of the Alexandra Palace and its People*, Rocket, 1995

> @ www.alexandrapalace.com

Alexandra Park • *Haringey*

A hillside public park in the grounds of ALEXANDRA PALACE and the late Victorian and Edwardian residential locality to its north. This was part of TOTTENHAM Wood until most of the trees were cleared in the late 18th century and the land was turned over to farming. After the death of Thomas Rhodes in 1856, his

Tottenham Wood Farm was sold to become the site for Alexandra Palace and its 180 acres of parkland. Over the course of its existence the park has had a swimming pool, athletics ground, horse-racing track and dancing and banqueting facilities at Blandford Hall. In the early 1880s the London Financial Association acquired much of the northern part of the park for residential development. Unlike the effect of CRYSTAL PALACE on SYDENHAM, the nearby presence of a great exhibition hall failed to inspire potential homebuyers and it was not until the end of the century that plots began to sell with any rapidity. The Rhodes family's former home at Tottenham Wood House survived at the junction of Alexandra Park Road and Albert Road into the 1890s. After 1901 the consortium of local authorities that had acquired Alexandra Palace sold more land and the area filled with streets of well-built, red-brick terraces over the next decade. Although out of fashion for a period after World War II, when some of the properties were allowed to deteriorate, Alexandra Park has now become a desirable place to live, being a little more affordable than neighbouring MUSWELL HILL. Many homes have been restored to a high standard, with the retention of period features. By Haringey's standards, the Alexandra ward's ethnic profile is exceptionally white, and levels of employment, academic qualifications and owner occupation are high. At Rhodes Avenue Primary School fewer than 20 per cent of pupils are from ethnic minorities, which is a low figure for the Wood Green area.

The surviving part of the park is recognized as the borough's most ecologically valuable site, with meadow, scrub, formal parkland and a lake. There is a conservation area in the south-east corner, next to the reservoir, with mainly ash woodland and some mature oaks that were part of Tottenham Wood. Blandford Hall burned down in 1971 and birch trees now dominate its site.

✉ N22

🚶 10,475 (Alexandra ward)

All Saints • *Tower Hamlets*
Poplar's parish church and the Docklands Light Railway station named after it, both situated on the south side of East India Dock Road. The first religious institution in the district was Poplar Chapel, built by the East India Co. as a chapelry of Stepney. In 1817 Poplar became a parish, with All Saints consecrated as its parish church in 1823. It was one of very few works by the architect Charles Hollis, who won the vestry committee's design competition under the pseudonym 'Felix'. The concealment of his identity did not prevent accusations of favouritism as he had previously been a clerk to a prominent parishioner, and the West India Dock Co. complained, in vain, to the bishop. Built in Greek style from Portland stone, the church stands on Bazely Street, originally Bow Lane. Hollis was also responsible for the rectory. All Saints' churchyard was closed for burials in 1862 and then was progressively opened up to the public as a recreation ground and gardens. Immediately after the construction of the church, quality housing began to appear around it, prompted by the growth of London's docks and the creation of the East India Dock Road. Although a few 19th-century houses survive, many others were damaged by bombing during World War II and demolished afterwards. The council tower blocks that replaced them in the 1950s and 1960s dominate much of the area. All Saints station occupies the site of the North London Railway's Poplar station, which operated from 1866 to 1945.

✉ E14

🚈 Docklands Light Railway, Stratford branch (zone 2)

📖 Stephen Porter (editor), *Survey of London, vols 43 and 44: Poplar, Blackwall and the Isle of Dogs, the Parish of All Saints*, Athlone Press, 1994

Alperton • *Brent*
Once the smelliest place in Middlesex, Alperton is regarded as the southernmost part of WEMBLEY. First recorded in 1199, the name may relate to a Saxon landowner or may have meant 'apple farm'. By 1433 the village had a wooden bridge across the River Brent. Stag-hunting was a popular pursuit hereabouts in Tudor and Stuart times. Alperton in the 17th and 18th centuries was a typical country village with a handful of farms and labourers' cottages, a smithy and a couple of inns. Its transformation began with the arrival of the Grand Junction (now Grand Union) Canal in 1801. Pleasure boats brought day-trippers and anglers. Brickworks were established, shipping their products by barge, a means of transport also adopted by farmers sending hay for London's horses. In the latter part of the 19th century Henry Haynes became Alperton's grandee. The son of a local hay dealer, he owned 70 of the village's 100 buildings and

employed most of the workforce at his brick-works. Haynes built cottages, shops, a church and the Alperton Park Hotel. By this time Alperton had become the most industrialized village in the Wembley area, reeking of horse manure, sewage and pig dung and polluted by dusty brickfields. Tile and brick-making ceased around 1890 and the newly created Wembley urban district council helped to clean up the noxious industries from 1894. Alperton's station opened in 1903, originally as PERIVALE–Alperton. Early 20th-century businesses included mushroom cultivation and the manufacture of rubber products, fireproofing and Wooler's 'Flying Banana' motorcycles. The construction of the North Circular Road (A406) brought more industry in the 1920s and 1930s. The district was almost fully built up by 1933 but underwent a decline after World War II, with a fall in population. From the 1970s, East African Asians, many of Gujarati origin, began to move to Alperton. The new community brought a revival to the shopping parade on Ealing Road, selling a variety of specialist products – especially jewellery, sometimes crafted at home. The locality has been called an 'Asian HATTON GARDEN'. Fourteen per cent of Alperton's employed population works in manufacturing, the highest proportion in London.

Built on the newly opened North Circular Road in 1938, the Ace Café is located near the PARK ROYAL junction, on the Alperton/STONE-BRIDGE border. It achieved legendary status as a bikers' hangout in the 1950s and 1960s, visited by rock 'n' roll luminaries like Gene Vincent and Billy Fury. The café closed in 1969 but reopened in 2001 after a total refit.

✉ Wembley HA0

� 12,323

🚇 Piccadilly Line (zone 4)

📖 M C Barrès-Baker, *Alperton*, Grange Museum of Community History and Brent Archive, 2001

@ www.ace-cafe-london.com

Alton Estate • *Wandsworth*

An extensive and historically significant municipal estate situated on ROEHAMPTON's border with RICHMOND PARK. Much of the land hereabouts constituted the grounds of Parkstead, a Palladian villa built in the 1760s for Lord Bessborough and later renamed Manresa House. Parts of its grounds were developed from around 1850 as a high-class suburban estate known as Coombe Park or Roehampton Park. Alton Lodge was an early 19th-century villa on the Kingston Road, occupied by Dr Thomas Hake from around 1854 until 1872. In 1951 the architect's department at the London County Council selected this area as the site for one of the largest and most radical housing developments ever undertaken in London. The best villas and some of the land-scaping were preserved but 130 acres were otherwise totally cleared to make way for the project. The Scandinavian-inspired Alton East was completed in 1955 and it was followed four years later by the much larger Alton West, which was influenced by the high-rise creations of the French architect Le Corbusier. Both stages include a mix of tower blocks, maisonettes and terraced houses, permitting a combination of high population density and extensive open spaces. The slabs on stilts of Downshire Field were the estate's most important innovation but novel construction, heating and ventilation systems were also employed. In 2002 Wandsworth council took back control of the estate from the residents' management organization, following its declaration of insolvency. This brought to an end the largest such venture in the UK, which had been overwhelmingly supported in a ballot of tenants three years earlier. The Alton estate has an ethnically diverse population, speaking Croatian, French, Portuguese and several African languages. The estate is now a conservation area and most of the buildings also have listed status.

Dr Thomas Hake of Alton Lodge was a cousin of General Gordon of Khartoum and a friend of Dante Gabriel Rossetti. The poet and painter stayed at Alton Lodge in 1872 while recovering from a mental collapse.

✉ SW15

Anerley • *Bromley*

Now an unfashionable collection of cul-de-sacs located on the south-western side of PENGE. The northern dialect word 'anerly' means 'alone' or 'only', and Anerley House (later called Anerley Lodge) was the first dwelling on this part of what was then Penge Common. The house belonged to William Sanderson, a Scottish silk manufacturer who had bought a large building plot after the common was enclosed in 1827. When the newly created London and Croydon Railway Co. sought to lay its tracks across his land, it is said that Sanderson demanded a halt for his own use in travelling up to London. The station opened in 1839, in turn giving its name to the settlement that eventually grew up nearby. For a while, a section of the old Croydon canal remained here, attracting anglers and visitors to the tea gardens that adjoined the station. Anerley's subsequent growth was stimulated by the building of the CRYSTAL PALACE, and the Anerley Lodge estate was sold off in two phases after Sanderson's death in 1871. But as housing density increased, Anerley progressively declined in desirability and this is now one of the most built-up parts of the borough. The former Anerley Town Hall is a library and a recreational and community centre.

Edward Lear's limerick makes it clear how Anerley's name is pronounced: 'There was an Old Person of Anerley, / Whose conduct was strange and unmannerly; / He rushed down the Strand / With a Pig in each hand, / But returned in the evening to Anerley.' The poet Walter de la Mare lived at three houses in the area from 1899 to 1925, including Thornsett Road, where he found himself a next-door neighbour of the plumber Thomas Crapper.

> ✉ SE20

> 🚂 Southern (zone 4)

> 📖 Peter Abbott and the Anerley Writers Circle, *The Book of Penge, Anerley and Crystal Palace*, Halsgrove, 2002

> @ www.virtualanerley.com (community site)

Angel, Edmonton • *Enfield*

A shopping area situated at the point where the North Circular Road (A406) now passes beneath Fore Street (A1010). Its full title is Angel Corner, UPPER EDMONTON. Like the better-known ANGEL, ISLINGTON it takes its name from an inn that stood here from at least the 17th century. Another popular inn, the Bell, lay to the south on Fore Street. There was much demolishing and rebuilding of these taverns over the centuries, and some interchanging of names, and no trace of the originals remains. They were a focus of EDMONTON social life, hosting everything from riotous fairs to petty sessions and manorial courts. A sorry-looking borough plaque at the site of the Angel announces that the STAMFORD HILL and GREEN LANES Turnpike Trust met here from 1713 until 1826. Fore Street was built up as early as the mid 18th century and four pairs of adjoining brown-brick houses survive north-west of the crossroads, at Angel Place. South of the junction the area filled with cheap tenements from the early 19th century, almost all of which have now been cleared

away and replaced. From the 1860s the Angel became a destination for horse-drawn omnibus services and in the early 20th century for some of London's first motor buses. Shopping parades lined each side of Fore Street south of the Angel. The North Circular Road was diverted beneath Fore Street via an underpass from 1997, greatly easing the junction's traffic congestion and improving the environment. The shops that presently stand at the Angel, Edmonton are very much a local amenity, with little to attract visitors from further afield.

William Cowper's comic poem *The Diverting History of John Gilpin* (1785) tells the story of a Londoner whose runaway horse carried him ten miles past the Bell, where he was supposed to be having his wedding anniversary dinner. Wetherspoon's Gilpin's Bell pub on Fore Street commemorates the verse but occupies a former motorcycle shop.

> ✉ N18

Angel, Islington • *Islington*

A commercial quarter and busy road junction at the southern end of Islington High Street, best known to non-Londoners for its place on the Monopoly board. Goswell Road follows a Saxon route out of the City, and the Romans are also believed to have built a road through here. A tavern may have been established as early as the 13th century, with a sign showing the Angel of the Annunciation with the Virgin Mary. However, the first public house that definitely stood here was the Sheepcote in 1614 and the first confirmed use of the Angel name came when this house was rebuilt in 1638. The new structure was a coaching inn with a galleried yard, offering entertainment by groups of travelling actors and players. It was popular with overnight guests who were travelling to the City but did not want to risk highway robbery on the hazardous last stretch of their journey. Following the creation of what became CITY ROAD in 1761, a turnpike was set up at the Angel; it was moved eastward in 1800. The galleried inn was demolished in 1819 and rebuilt in Flemish style at the end of the 19th century. A horse-drawn tram service reached here in the 1870s and Angel Tube station opened in 1901. By this time the surrounding area had become very run-down but since World War II a long programme of slum clearance and rebuilding has progressively erased the substandard properties. In recent years the Angel locality has been transformed again, with the erection of commercial and apartment complexes. A branch of the Co-operative Bank has taken the place of the pub, and the reconstructed Tube station is now part of the Angel Square complex.

Inspired by the French Revolution, the republican Thomas Paine probably wrote the first part of *The Rights of Man* while staying at the Angel in 1790, although some have suggested that he was at the Old Red Lion. Waddington's brought fame to the Angel by including it in the British version of the Monopoly board game, which the company first produced in 1935. The classic version of the board remains unchanged, although in a 'Here and Now' limited edition produced in 2005 to mark the British version's 70th anniversary, the Angel was replaced by the Hammersmith Apollo.

✉ N1

🚇 Northern Line (zone 1)

Angell Town • *Lambeth*

Now a large housing complex on the BRIXTON/STOCKWELL border, Angell Town takes its name from the eccentric landowner John Angell, who died in 1784. His grandfather Justinian had acquired the land by marriage. Angell Town was built up in the early 19th century as a desirable estate for the new middle classes. Most of the old town was replaced in the 1970s by a council estate that combined 1960s-style tower blocks with the newer concept of overhead walkways and linking bridges, some of which were later removed in an attempt to prevent robbers and vandals from making easy getaways. A bridge was supposed to cross Brixton Road to the social facilities on the Stockwell Park estate, but it was never built. Angell Town soon gained a reputation for neglect and decline and became stigmatized as a 'sink' estate. In a scheme notable for the high level of residents' participation in the consultative process, the estate was radically redeveloped from the mid 1990s. The deck-access system was converted to a street format based on terraced houses with individual entrances, and unused garages were replaced with shops and community facilities. A central green space, created with children in mind, is called Little Angells.

In 1999 the Metropolitan Housing Trust commissioned an angel sculpture for the estate from the artist Jason Gibilaro.

✉ SW9

@ www.londontimebank.org.uk/angelltown

Angel Road • *Enfield*

The main east–west route through EDMONTON, with its continuation of SILVER STREET. The road was called Watery Lane in 1557 and Marsh Lane in the late 16th century, taking its present name in the 1870s from the inn standing at the corner of Fore Street. A station opened on the London and Northern Railway line to Broxbourne in 1840, originally called Water Lane. This was too early to bring suburbanization to the vicinity since Londoners were not at that time prepared to countenance living so far from their place of work, partly because fares were high and services slow. Angel Road itself was also liable to flooding by Pymmes Brook. However, the railway did encourage industrial growth on the highly affordable marshland between the station and the River Lea, a process that accelerated at the beginning of the 20th century. By this time terraced housing was spreading outwards from the western part of Angel Road, helped by improvements in bus services and later by the introduction of trams. In 1927 Angel Road became part of the North Circular Road (A406), bringing still more factories. Edmonton council began to put up housing in the area in the 1930s and chose Angel Road as a prime zone for the building of tower blocks in the early 1960s. Inevitably, factories have closed or moved away in recent decades and several former industrial sites have been converted to other uses, notably at Glover Drive, where Tesco and Ikea superstores have opened.

Introductory offers caused a small riot to break out when Ikea began trading here in 2005. The store opened its doors at midnight but had to close again after just 30 minutes when it was overwhelmed by customers, fights broke out and a man was stabbed. Tottenham MP David Lammy complained that Ikea should have known that offering cheap prices in a deprived area would cause a rush.

✉ N18

🚇 'one' Railway (zone 4)

Aperfield • *Bromley* (pronounced 'apperfield')

BIGGIN HILL was once known as Aperfield and some maps still refer to the eastern side of the town by this name, although most residents are unfamiliar with it. Originally Appuldre (apple tree), the name grew to Apuldrefeld (apple tree field) and then contracted to its present form. Like many other parts of present-day London, the estate was given by

William I, the Conqueror, to his brother, Bishop Odo of Bayeux. Two centuries later lord of the manor Henry de Apuldrefeld obtained the right to hold a fair and market here. In the 17th century Aperfield was in the possession of the Earl of Sussex, who leased it to a widow named Ann Brasier. The manor's last owner was Frederick Henry Dougal of Wandsworth, who bought it at auction in 1895. Dougal divided his new property into small plots, which he sold cheaply, setting in train the disjointed creation of Biggin Hill. The house at the centre of the manor, a second-rate mansion called Aperfield Court, was pulled down around 1905, the year of Dougal's death. Aperfield now displays the unco-ordinated architectural style that is characteristic of its adoptive parent.

In 1998 a Lebanon cedar in Aperfield Road became one of the '21 great trees of London' chosen to receive commemorative green plaques in a scheme to recognize and protect significant trees.

✉ Westerham TN16

Archway • *Islington*

Archway Road skirts the eastern side of Highgate Hill and the Archway locality is at its southern end. In the early 19th century work had begun on a tunnel under Hornsey Lane but the roof collapsed, bringing the lane down with it. This forced a change of plan and in 1813 a cutting was dug and a Roman-style viaduct built to carry Hornsey Lane across it. JUNCTION ROAD was constructed at the same time as a feeder for the new road. However, the viaduct proved too narrow for the volume of traffic and the present Archway Bridge opened in 1900. Much of the locality's original development was as cheap housing for working people who were displaced from ST PANCRAS and SOMERS TOWN by the railway building of the mid 19th century. The Archway Tavern was built in 1888, the third public house on the site in three centuries. Archway station was the northern terminus from 1907 to 1939 of what is now the High Barnet branch of the Northern Line, during which time the station was called HIGHGATE. After this, the Archway name took hold in the area, which had formerly been considered part of UPPER HOLLOWAY. Locals are keen to see Archway tower and mall redeveloped but the necessary investment has been hard to find. Archway Bridge is known locally as 'suicide bridge'.

Archway was the scene of the third and final 'brides in the bath' murder, committed by George Joseph Smith at 14 Bismarck Road, now Waterlow Road. Smith drowned Margaret Lofty in the bath just two days after he had married her in December 1914.

Saint Etienne's *Archway People*, New Model Army's *Archway Towers* and The Boo Radleys' *Blue Room in Archway* all take a jaundiced view of life in the neighbourhood. Sarah Cracknell sings, 'There are some nice parts of London / You can see them from here.'

✉ N19

🚇 Northern Line (zones 2 and 3)

📖 Simon Morris and Towyn Mason, *Gateway to the City: The Archway Story*, Hornsey Historical Society, 2000

Ardleigh Green • *Havering*

A comfortably-off locality, usually regarded as the northernmost part of HORNCHURCH, although some link it with GIDEA PARK or even UPMINSTER. It was first recorded as Hadley in the 14th century, evolving through Hadley Green and Hardley Green before attaining its present form around a century ago. Like Barnet's Hadley, the original name probably indicated a heathland clearing. However, an alternative theory suggests a link with the de Badele family, who lived in the area around 1325. A hamlet was in existence by the early 17th century and the Spencer's Arms inn later became popular with agricultural labourers. A few villas were built in the late 19th century, including Hardley Court, but the surroundings remained very rural until the opening of SQUIRREL'S HEATH (now Gidea Park) station in 1910. From 1927 the builders E A Coryn and Sons developed the Haynes Park estate. Haynes Park Road was later renamed Ardleigh Green Road but Haynes Road remains. Ardleigh Green junior and infants' schools opened in 1933. Essex County Council bought Hardley Court and 15 acres of land for £9,000 in 1946. The house was used as a teacher-training college for several years before the first part of what is now Havering College was built in the grounds in the late 1950s. Most of the college's present buildings date from two phases of construction in 1962 and 1971. Hardley Court was renamed Ardleigh House and leased to the local community association. Owing to its poor state of repair, the building was demolished and replaced in the late 1960s, since when it has continued to serve as a meeting place and adult education centre. In a reflection of the absence of change in the area, there are no pupils at Ardleigh Green Junior School for whom English is not their first language, and population mobility is very low. Ardleigh Green's shops also serve EMERSON PARK.

> ✉ Hornchurch RM11

> @ www.ardleighhouse.org.uk

Arkley • *Barnet*

An extended village situated on the far western edge of BARNET. Arkley was first recorded in the 14th century and the name is of uncertain origin. It may refer to a meadow where closed baskets (then called arks) were made from wickers or reeds. Arkley windmill was built in 1806 and survives today in the back garden of a private house. In the second half of the 19th century the village had a post office, store and tearooms, and the high and secluded setting made it a desirable place to build substantial country houses – a practice that continued into the early 20th century, although with diminishing grandeur. Ribbon development began to reach here from Barnet in the 1930s but was halted by the outbreak of World War II. Green-belt legislation prevented excessive incursions into the neighbouring fields when development resumed along Barnet Road after the war. Building in the latter part of the 20th century was limited to the creation of a few cul-de-sacs of executive homes and blocks of private flats on the sites of larger old houses. In a few cases, the original garden wall encloses the new properties. The Poor Clare Monastery moved to the far north of Arkley from WESTBOURNE PARK in 1970. Such is Arkley's reputation that some developers and estate agents attach its name to new properties on the west side of CHIPPING BARNET, at DUCKS ISLAND and even in the south-east corner of Borehamwood, over the county boundary in Hertfordshire. At the far end of Barnet Road lies Arkley Park, an estate of upmarket trailer homes for retired people.

Several houses in Arkley were requisitioned for military purposes in World War II, notably the now-demolished Arkley View, which housed the Radio Security Service monitoring operation from 1940. Suspicious-sounding broadcasts were transcribed and a despatch rider took them to Bletchley Park in Buckinghamshire for decoding. The RSS was made up of part-time amateurs, such as the historian Hugh Trevor-Roper (later Lord Dacre), and did such good work here – sometimes decoding messages before they had reached Bletchley Park – that the service was subsequently integrated within the military intelligence communications division MI8.

> ✉ Barnet EN5

Arnos Grove • *Enfield*

A classic station and its immediate vicinity, keeping NEW SOUTHGATE at arm's length from SOUTHGATE. In the 14th century this area was Armholt Wood, and later Arnolds. When the City banker James Colebrook bought the estate in 1719 he built a mansion called Arnolds in Cannon Hill, Southgate. Locals called the estate Arno's and the subsequent owner Sir William Mayne, later Lord Newhaven, adopted this convention by renaming the house and estate Arnos Grove, which is now pronounced as though it never had an apostrophe – unlike, for example, Arno's Vale in Bristol. From 1777 until 1918 the estate belonged to the Walker brewing family, which increased its landholding to over 300 acres by buying neighbouring Minchenden. In 1928 Lord Inverforth, who had bought the estate from the last of the Walker brothers, sold the southernmost 44 acres to Southgate council, the mansion to the North Metropolitan Electricity Supply Co. for use as offices, and the rest to builders. North Metropolitan enlarged the mansion and encased it in red brick; it is now an upmarket residential care home called Southgate Beaumont. Arnos Grove station opened on the far south side of the estate in 1932. One of London's finest pieces of railway architecture, designed by Charles Holden, the station was for its first year the northern terminus of the Piccadilly Line. There was some debate over its name: Arnos Park was considered and might have been more appropriate, since this was the name the council had given to the neighbouring open space, which has meadowland, a railway viaduct, a stretch of Pymmes Brook and traces of a former loop of the New River. The area north of the park was built up by 1939 as the classy Minchenden estate, with Arnos Grove as its central avenue. More recently, privately built flats have been added near the park in Walker Close.

> ✉ N11; N14

> 🚇 Piccadilly Line (zone 4)

> 📖 R Garnier, *Arnos Grove*, Georgian Group Journal, no. 8, 1998

Arsenal • *Islington*

A Tube station and former football stadium in north HIGHBURY, south of FINSBURY PARK. In 1913, St John's College of Divinity leased its sports ground at Highbury to WOOLWICH AR-SENAL Football Club, which had been founded in 1886 as the works team of the Royal Arsenal at Woolwich. Tottenham Hotspur and Orient football clubs (the latter then playing at Clapton) objected to the relocation but were overruled. The club's achievements were modest until Yorkshireman Herbert Chapman took over as manager in 1925. A strict disciplinarian and canny businessman, Chapman guided Arsenal to FA Cup victory in 1930 and then to three league championships. To honour the club's successes, Gillespie Road station was renamed Arsenal in 1932. Highbury stadium was erected during the following few years, to the design of Archibald Leitch, who was responsible for most of the great British stadia built before and after World War I. St John's College was demolished after a fire in 1946 and the institution subsequently relocated to NORTHWOOD before settling in Bramcote, Nottinghamshire in 1969. Among Arsenal's successes in recent years have been three Premiership titles and four FA Cup wins, including a 2005 victory over Manchester United that was the first final to be decided on penalties. The club moved to the newly built Emirates stadium at Ashburton Grove in nearby DRAYTON PARK for the 2006–7 season. Highbury's art deco east and west stands are now being converted into apartments, while the north and south stands will be replaced by business units, apartments and a restaurant, and the pitch will become a commemorative area and community garden. The project is due to be completed around 2010.

Football scenes for the movie *The Arsenal Stadium Mystery* were filmed at Highbury stadium in 1939, with several leading players taking part. Nick Hornby's 1992 memoir *Fever Pitch* evokes the pains and joys of being a fanatical Arsenal supporter.

✉ N5

🚇 Piccadilly Line (zone 2)

📖 Phil Soar and Martin Tyler, *The Official Illustrated History of Arsenal*, Hamlyn, 2003

@ www.arsenal.com (Arsenal Football Club site)

Ashburnham Triangle • *Greenwich*

A conservation area in south-west GREENWICH, consisting of nine streets and some later cul-de-sacs, bounded by Greenwich South Street, Blackheath Road and Greenwich High Road. John Ashburnham, who came from a Sussex family of 'stupendous antiquity', acquired the land here as part of a sub-

stantial inheritance in 1755. His new possession included the Chocolate House, which stood nearer BLACKHEATH and had gained its name from tastings of drinking chocolate held there when the beverage first came into fashion. The mansion was renamed Ashburnham House in 1820. From around this time the family laid out streets and housing to the west of South Street, with the scheme gaining full momentum around the middle of the century. Most of the little estate consisted of tasteful stuccoed terraced houses, together with several public houses, including the Guildford Arms and the Ashburnham Arms. In the 1880s the Ashburnhams began to sell off the estate in stages and Ashburnham House was demolished to make way for further development. Blackheath High School opened on Catherine Grove in 1904. The school was converted to apartments about a century later and three new houses were built in the former playground. Most of Ashburnham Triangle's original housing has survived unspoilt, although the triangle was one of the last of the current conservation areas to be designated in Greenwich. Through traffic is kept out of Ashburnham Retreat so that it can serve as a children's play street.

The thriller writer Edgar Wallace was born in 1875 at 7 Ashburnham Grove, which now displays an unofficial plaque. A biography harshly calls the area a 'London slum'. Wallace's unmarried, show-business parents offered him up for adoption when he was nine days old.

✉ SE10

📖 Diana Celia Rimel, Tony Lord & Pat Ward, *Ashburnham Triangle*, Ashburnham Triangle Association, 1994

Ashburton Grove   *see* DRAYTON PARK

Avery Hill • *Greenwich*

A Victorian mansion, park and mid-20th-century housing estate, situated east of EL-THAM. It is possible that the name refers to an aviary that may have existed here in the early 19th century. A map of 1805 calls the area Pollcat End. John Thomas North was nicknamed 'the nitrate king' for the wealth he accumulated dealing in sodium nitrate from Chile and he devoted a large part of his fortune to building Avery Hill House in 1891. He dismissed the architect for going 50 per cent over budget in creating what was virtually a small palace. North died only five years after the house was built and the London County Council then acquired the building and its 86 acres of grounds, which in 1903 were opened to the public as Avery Hill Park. In 1906 Avery Hill House became the nucleus of Avery Hill College of Education, which was enlarged soon afterwards with the purchase of two nearby properties. The Crown sold 68 acres of neighbouring farmland for development in 1936. Several builders collaborated in laying out a set of streets, which were named after the fields and woods that they replaced. After the war the LCC took over and completed the estate, building a school and blocks of flats, to the annoyance of some early residents. The GLC added a final phase, which included a nursery and retirement flats, before handing the estate over to the London Borough of Greenwich in 1980. Avery Hill College merged with Thames Polytechnic in 1985 and is now part of the University of Greenwich. The cam-

pus is situated on either side of Avery Hill Park. The library, once the great hall of North's mansion, is a listed building, as is the adjacent glass-domed winter garden. The university is hoping for a lottery grant to enable much-needed restoration work to be carried out in the conservatory. Student social facilities are centred on the recently opened second phase of the student village – a courtyard development of flats for 1,300 occupants. The village includes the Dome, a purpose-built venue with capacity for 1,000.

✉ SE9

📖 Keith Wells, *The History of Avery Hill Housing Estate*, self-published, 1995; David Shorney, *A History of Avery Hill College*, Thames Polytechnic, 1989

Bakers Arms • *Waltham Forest*

A crossroads on the Lea Bridge Road where High Road LEYTON meets WALTHAMSTOW's Hoe Street. Formerly known as Leyton Corner, the locality now shares the identity of its unprepossessing public house, which was named in honour of the neighbouring almshouses built in 1857 by the London Master Bakers' Benevolent Institute. The Greater London Council subsequently converted the almshouses into one-bedroom flats, after a change of heart over their proposed demolition to allow road-widening. The Bakers Arms area has expanded to absorb the former hamlet of Knotts Green, just to the east, home for many years of the Barclay banking family. Leyton leisure lagoon is the principal local amenity. The rail users' group for the Barking to Gospel Oak line is campaigning for a new station to be opened at Bakers Arms.

✉ E10; E17

Baker Street • *Westminster*

One of London's most famous thoroughfares, with deerstalker imagery along its length, running northwards from Portman Square to the south-western edge of REGENT'S PARK. Building began here in 1755 and the street was named after the developer, Sir Edward Baker. Baker Street gained one of the first underground stations in London when the short stretch from Paddington to Farringdon opened in 1863. The actress Sarah Siddons and the politician and prime minister William Pitt, the Younger, lived in Baker Street, but its most famous resident is the fictional detective Sherlock Holmes, who was supposed to have lodged at 221B, an address that did not actually exist at that time. Most Sherlockian scholars advocate number 31 as the likely real address (assuming Conan Doyle ever had a specific location in mind) while a minority prefer 111. In Holmes's day, Baker Street proper was only a quarter of a mile in length, with 80 buildings, but it later incorporated York Place and Upper Baker Street. Imposing mansion blocks were built towards the nor-

thern end of Baker Street in the 1920s, while commercial premises lined the rest of the street. The headquarters of the ABBEY ROAD Building Society (later the Abbey National, and now Abbey) occupied the site of 221B Baker Street from 1932 until 2002, during which time the company answered thousands of letters addressed to the great detective. The Sherlock Holmes Museum now deals with the correspondence – and claims the precious address, although it is really at 239 Baker Street.

Madame Tussaud opened her first permanent waxworks museum on Baker Street in 1835. The museum relocated to its present site on Marylebone Road in 1884 and is now the capital's most popular paying attraction after the London Eye. Britain's first planetarium opened next door in 1958 and closed in 2006.

Gerry Rafferty's ballad *Baker Street* was first a hit in 1978. It has since been covered by bands as disparate as Foo Fighters and Undercover.

✉ W1; NW1

🚇 Bakerloo Line; Circle Line; Hammersmith & City Line; Jubilee Line; Metropolitan Line (zone 1)

📖 Sir Arthur Conan Doyle, with notes by Leslie S Klinger, *The New Annotated Sherlock Holmes*, Norton, 2005

@ 221bakerstreet.org (privately operated Sherlock Holmes site); www.madame-tussauds.co.uk

Balham • *Wandsworth*

An increasingly fashionable south London suburb situated between TOOTING and CLAPHAM. Baelgenham, which probably means 'smooth or rounded enclosure', was established around the 8th century, when woodland still covered much of the area. It remained an insignificant hamlet until the mid 1770s, when the first large houses began to appear on Balham Hill. Continued growth led to the establishment of shops, with more than 20 businesses in place by the 1820s. More villas followed, often with fine gardens, but these began to be overrun by suburban house-building following the arrival of the railway in 1856. A year earlier, Balham had become a parish in its own right, gaining independence from STREATHAM. The station relocated to its present site in 1863. Towards the end of the 19th century, the Hyde Farm and Heaver estates completed the build-up. What is now the Northern Line arrived in Balham in 1926. In the 20th century, construction mainly replaced existing properties, often with blocks of flats. The most monumental block was Du Cane Court on Balham High Road. Completed in 1936, its 647 apartments were claimed to be the largest set of flats under one roof in Europe. Flats also replaced the Balham Hippodrome cinema (originally the Duchess Palace Theatre) in the early 1950s. Over the past few decades Balham has become popular as a more affordable residential alternative to Clapham. Fifty-seven per cent of 16- to 74-year-olds in Balham are qualified to degree level or higher.

The founding of the Balham group in the early 1930s marked the beginning of the British Trotskyist movement. The group's members were soon expelled from the British Communist Party, which they had accused of slavishly following a Stalinist orthodoxy.

Balham was dubbed 'Gateway to the South' in Peter Sellers' rendition of a sketch by Frank Muir and Denis Norden, and 'the ugliest and most abominable of London's unpleasing suburbs' by *Swallows and Amazons* author Arthur Ransome, who stayed here briefly. Probably because it typifies the sprawling anonymity of south London, Balham's name has cropped up in numerous musical and literary works, from Chilli Willi and the Red Hot Peppers' album *Bongos over Balham* to Chris England's cricket travelogue *Balham to Bollywood*. The Balham Alligators are a Cajun rock band whose output includes the 1996 album *Gateway to the South*.

✉ SW12

👤 12,840

🚇 Southern (zone 3); Northern Line (zone 3)

📖 Graham Gower, *Balham: A Brief History,* Wandsworth Borough Council, 1990; Patrick Loobey, *Balham and Tooting,* Tempus, 2001

@ www.balham.com (community site)

Ballards Lane • *Barnet*

A busy road linking FINCHLEY CENTRAL with NORTH FINCHLEY. This was an important medieval thoroughfare, named after a family who were living here in 1263. It was originally called Overstreet, contrasting it with Nether Street, which ran in parallel to the west. The estate of Ballards Reding, later Wimbush Farm, stretched across to FALLOW CORNER. By the 15th century large houses set in spacious grounds were appearing along the lane. Many of these properties were rebuilt in the 17th century. With the construction of Regent's Park Road the lane became a turnpike in 1826 and was extended north to a new junction with the Great North Road (now High Road), bringing an increase in development. By 1851 the lane had 56 houses and a further seven under construction, which was positively heaving for such a rural outpost of London at this time, and made it the most populous part of Finchley. Most of Ballards Lane was rebuilt again from the early years of the 20th century onwards, much of it with parades of shops and flats, and it has lost character as a result. The surrounding area has become popular with London's Japanese community and Ballards Lane has several suppliers of goods and services targeted at this market.

✉ N3; N12

Bandon Hill • *Sutton*

Also spelt as a single word, Bandon Hill is a railside residential locality lying east of WALLINGTON. The discovery of Roman funeral urns in the 1970s indicates the presence of a burial ground on the site of the present Bandon Hill Cemetery as early as the 2nd century AD. The manor of Bandon was first recorded in 1203. There is a slight possibility that early resident Roger de Bandon brought the name with him from elsewhere but it is much more likely to derive from 'bean down' – the hill where beans are grown. In the Middle Ages, Bandon was a more important settlement than nearby BEDDINGTON but its precise location is now forgotten. Loosely gathered around a manor house, the village probably lay between Beddington and WADDON. The tautological name Bandon Hill was a later invention, applied to the rising ground south-east of Beddington, the settlement that began to take shape here in the late 19th century and the cemetery that opened in 1899. Bandon Hill was an unplanned development, built a few houses at a time by small-scale speculators. The short-lived Bandon railway halt brought some early commuters. The first streets to be filled were Upper Road, the west side of Plough Lane and Beddington Grove Road (now Sandy Lane North), which had an inn. Bandon Hill Primary School stands on the original site of St Michael and All Angels Church, which moved further west to SOUTH BEDDINGTON in 1907. A Methodist church opened in 1912. The settlement expanded progressively throughout the 20th century until all available gaps were plugged with the exception of the cemetery, two sports grounds and Mellows Park, which has tennis courts, a children's playground, bowling green, pavilion and fruiting community garden.

The African–British composer Samuel Coleridge-Taylor, best-known for *Hiawatha's Wedding Feast*, was buried at Bandon Hill Cemetery in 1912.

> ✉ Wallington SM6

> 📖 Hedley Marne Gowans et al, *Courts of the Manors of Bandon and Beddington, 1498–1552*, Sutton Libraries and Arts Services, 1983

Banglatown *see* BRICK LANE

Bank • *City*
The central bank of the United Kingdom, located at the heart of the 'square mile' that constitutes London's prime financial district. The Bank of England began in 1694 as a commercial operation providing funds for a war against France. At first the bank operated out of Mercers' Hall and then Grocers' Hall before acquiring its governor's mansion on Threadneedle Street as the site for its own premises in 1724. By the end of the 18th century the bank had become such a venerable institution that the dramatist Sheridan dubbed it 'the Old Lady of Threadneedle Street'. Gradually it became the dominant issuer of notes and the chosen bank of most departments of state but it was not until the 19th century that the Bank of England fully acquired its present national role. To the untrained eye, the bank's present headquarters appear to be an architecturally harmonious achievement but the building is actually the product of several controversial stages of construction, extension and reconstruction. George Sampson set the Palladian tone, Sir Robert Taylor oversaw enlargement to the east and west boundaries at Bartholomew Lane and Prince's Street, and Sir John Soane expanded the bank northwards to Lothbury and created magnificent banking halls. Between the two world wars the bank was further enlarged in the only direction left: upwards. This project necessitated the recon-struction of most of Soane's interiors, although attempts were made to retain the character of the original halls. Nowadays, the bank's primary responsibilities are setting interest rates to keep inflation low, issuing banknotes and striving to maintain a stable financial system. The Bank of England Museum traces the institution's history and displays a collection of ingots, coins and banknotes.

The present Bank station is an amalgamation of City station, which operated the 'drain' service to Waterloo from 1898, and Bank, which was opened by the City and South London Railway Co. in 1900 and became the eastern terminus of the Central London Railway later that year. The station has been nicknamed 'the worm' for its twisting network of pedestrian tunnels interconnecting its platforms and those at MONUMENT.

> ✉ EC2

> 🚇 Central Line; Northern Line; Waterloo & City Line; Docklands Light Railway terminus (zone 1); escalator link with Monument

> 📖 Maberley Phillips, *The Bank of England: Its Origin and Development*, Ian Henry, 1997

> @ www.bankofengland.co.uk

Bankside • *Southwark*
A revived riverside cultural destination, situated on the south side of the Thames between BLACKFRIARS and SOUTHWARK Bridges. Bankside has had a remarkably consistent history as a place of often bawdy entertainment. As it fell outside the City's jurisdiction, it was free to allow practices outlawed elsewhere. The ladies who worked at Bankside's houses of ill repute were known as 'Winchester geese' because of the tolerance extended by the bishops of Winchester, who owned the properties and benefited from the tax revenues. Bankside's oldest theatre was the Rose, built around 1587; it had disappeared before the outbreak of the Civil War. The Globe, where William Shakespeare was a shareholder and premiered many of his plays, was put up in 1599 and destroyed in a fire started by a cannon during a performance of *Henry VIII* in 1613. It was rebuilt but the new theatre also had a short life, making way for tenements in 1644 after being closed by the Puritan administration two years earlier. Later in the century Sir Christopher Wren watched the building of ST PAUL'S Cathedral from a house on Bankside's waterfront. Beer was another of Bankside's attractions. The Anchor brewery

on Park Street was founded in 1616 and by the mid 19th century was reputedly the largest in the world. Its owner, Barclay Perkins, merged with Courage, another Southwark brewer, in 1955. The Anchor closed in 1981 and the buildings were demolished. The brewery represented part of the industrialization of Bankside, creating a growing working-class population as Southwark expanded southwards. Peabody Square off Blackfriars Road was one of the biggest late-Victorian experiments in providing purpose-built model homes for the working poor. Bankside suffered like other riverside areas from German bombing in World War II and post-war industrial decline but recent years have seen an upturn in its fortunes, bringing it round full circle to its original role. The remains of the Rose theatre were discovered in 1989, reviving public interest in the area's dramatic past which was already being encouraged by American actor-director Sam Wanamaker. His plans to rebuild the Globe took many years to bear fruit but in 1996 a recreation of the 17th-century theatre (based on scholarly guesswork) was opened on a site by the Thames not far from the original's home. As a tourist attraction it was topped by the conversion of Sir Giles Gilbert Scott's Bankside power station into the Tate Modern art gallery by the Swiss architects Herzog and De Meuron. Vinopolis, at Bank End, is a museum devoted to wine and its history, with tutored wine tastings and artefacts dating back to 2000BC.

✉ SE1

🚢 Bankside pier

📖 Leonard Reilly and Geoff Marshall, *The Story of Bankside*, London Borough of Southwark, 2001

@ www.london-se1.co.uk (community site); www.southbanklondon.com (arts events site)

Barbican • *City*

Originally a defensive structure atop the City walls (pulled down in 1267), then a street and now a housing estate in the north-west corner of the CITY OF LONDON. The term 'Barbican Centre' is often used for the entire development, but strictly refers only to its arts complex. In the 19th century the Barbican was a warren of factories, warehouses, markets and shops, but much of it was razed by fire in 1902 and the remainder was devastated in the Blitz. In 1956, housing minister Duncan Sandys recommended the creation of a model post-war neighbourhood with schools, shops and amenities as well as homes. The architects Chamberlin, Powell & Bon were appointed to design the complex, including the tallest residential blocks in Britain; with 43 storeys, these were only recently eclipsed by Manchester's Beetham Tower. The first of 2,000 flats were completed in the early 1960s. The arts centre was built between 1971 and 1982 at a cost of £153 million. Its buildings are on ten floors, the lowest being some distance underground. The Barbican's rain-stained, hammered concrete slabs detract from its aesthetic appeal but it has achieved Grade II-listed building status by virtue of its distinctive character.

The Museum of London has several paintings of the Barbican and its surroundings, notably Harold Hussey's depiction of the scene before building began but after the clearance of the former bombsite, revealing the colossal scale of the project.

✉ EC2

🚇 Circle Line; Hammersmith & City Line; Metropolitan Line (zone 1)

📖 D Heathcote, *Penthouse over the City: The Barbican and Modern Urban Living*, Wiley-Academy, 2004

@ www.barbican.org.uk (Barbican Centre site); www.barbicanliving.co.uk (Barbican estate site)

Barking • *Barking & Dagenham*

A major east London centre, situated south of ILFORD and east of the River Roding. Evidence of Roman occupation has been discovered here and Barking was one of the earliest Saxon settlements east of London, established on a habitable site near navigable water. St Erkenwald founded Barking Abbey in 666 and William I, the Conqueror, used it as a temporary headquarters while the Tower of London was being constructed. From the 14th to the 19th centuries, the main industry was fishing, with a fleet operating out of Barking Creek. In addition, many of Henry VIII's ships were repaired and maintained in the area, barges transported locally grown potatoes and onions to the City, and timber from Epping Forest was sent for navy shipbuilding at WOOLWICH. The abbey escaped the first wave of religious suppression in 1536 but was dissolved in 1539. The Crown retained control of the estate until 1628, when it was bought by Sir Thomas Fanshawe. St Margaret's Church, where Captain Cook was married in 1762, and the Abbey ruins are now a designated preservation area. Fishing became especially important in the first half of the 19th century and the town's population more than doubled without its area significantly increasing, which created localized slum conditions. Barking New Town was laid out east of the new STRATFORD to Tilbury railway line but its two-storey, bay-windowed houses were intended for City office workers, not trawlermen. The fishing industry was hit by economic difficulties from the late 1850s and collapsed when the major trawler operator moved his fleet to Norfolk in 1865. Riverside and creekside factories began to provide alternative employment and Barking resumed its growth, with terraced housing of varying quality spreading outwards over the rest of the century. Barking Park opened on Longbridge Road in 1898 and has been described as probably the finest municipal park in east London. From the earliest years of the 20th century Barking council progressively cleared rundown streets and put up new houses and, later, blocks of flats. Between the wars commercial builders extended the town eastwards to UPNEY and the London County Council laid out the vast BECONTREE estate to the northeast. The largest post-war development was the THAMES VIEW estate, on the marshes to the south. The council is presently overseeing the regeneration of the town centre in a scheme that will enliven the shopping area, while providing up to 4,000 new homes with a mix of tenures. Even bigger developments are underway at BARKING REACH (also known as Barking Riverside), where four phases of construction will provide homes for 26,000 people over the next quarter of a century, together with new schools, parks and other amenities.

Barking was the childhood home of the footballers Bobby Moore, Trevor Brooking and John Terry, England rugby stalwart Jason Leonard and the singer Billy Bragg.

✉ Barking IG11

♟ 38,556 (Abbey, Eastbury, Gascoigne and Longbridge wards)

🚍 c2c; Silverlink Metro; District Line; Hammersmith & City Line (zone 4)

📖 Richard Tames, *Barking Past*, Historical Publications, 2002

Barking Reach · *Barking & Dagenham*
A major 21st-century urban community named after the stretch of the Thames downstream of GALLIONS REACH. While the new town of THAMESMEAD grew up on the south shore from the mid 1960s, industrial and utility usage continued to dominate the marshland on the northern bank. However, the landscape is now changing with its designation as a 'key housing site' within the THAMES GATEWAY master plan. Redevelopment began in the late 1990s with Bellway Homes' Great Fleete estate at the western end of Choats Road, near the pre-existing THAMES VIEW estate. Although people will live anywhere in London if the price is right, the appeal of Barking Reach is presently limited by its poor access to public transport. An extension of the Docklands Light Railway constitutes the cornerstone of plans to address this issue, possibly with an interchange on c2c's Fenchurch Street to Tilbury line, between the present BARKING and DAGENHAM DOCK stations. The completed township will have a mix of housing types and tenures and its own civic amenities, with new employment opportunities created nearby. The intentions are honourable but *Guardian* architecture critic Jonathan Glancey has called Barking Reach 'low-grade subtopian housing: isolated, boring, and a nesting ground for future disaffected teenagers'.

✉ Barking IG11

Barkingside · *Redbridge*
Despite accusations of 'chav' characteristics, Barkingside is an unobjectionable interwar suburb situated at the south-western corner of FAIRLOP plain. The name was first recorded in 1538 and derives from its location on the Barking side of HAINAULT Forest, at the boundary of the old parish. By 1840, Barkingside and its neighbouring hamlets and mansions had grown sufficiently populous to warrant the building of Holy Trinity Church at MOSSFORD GREEN, but in 1876 James Thorne found that the settlement was 'merely a gathering of a few small houses along a crossroad, and a few others by a scrubby green; the inhabitants are chiefly engaged in agriculture'. Soon after Thorne made his observations Dr Thomas Barnardo established his village home for girls at Mossford Green, with its own church and hospital. It is said that Barkingside station, opened on the Great Eastern Railway in 1903, owes its ornate style to the frequent royal visits to the home, which is now designated a conservation area. The construction of the Eastern Avenue (A12) in 1925 encouraged southward expansion towards GANTS HILL and the absorption of Mossford

Green and FULLWELL, where new facilities were added after World War II. Green-belt legislation prevented post-war expansion east of the railway, which became part of the Central Line in 1948. New Anglican and Roman Catholic churches were built in the mid 1950s. Jews held services in Barnardo's church until the conversion of a former primary school to a synagogue at NEWBURY PARK in 1981. Barkingside's focal High Street distinguishes the suburb from the neighbouring sprawl of 'greater' Ilford but the predominance of independent retailers and fast-food outlets reflects its declining importance as a shopping area. Redbridge council has spoken of 'regenerating' Barkingside town centre, but at the time of writing, plans do not amount to more than building a few affordable homes and tidying up the look of the High Street. The Barkingside ward is the largest in the borough, both in terms of area and population, and includes most of Gants Hill. It boasts wide religious diversity, with significant numbers of Christians, Jews, Hindus, Muslims and Sikhs.

> ✉ Ilford IG6

> ♟ 11,303

> 🚃 Central Line (zone 5)

Barnehurst • *Bexley*

A comfortable commuter-belt territory lying north-east of BEXLEYHEATH. The May Place estate had been in existence since the 15th century and in the hands of the Barne family from 1750. In the latter part of the 19th century the house was occupied by Colonel Frederick Barne, who was also chairman of the Bexleyheath Railway Co. 'Hurst' used to mean a 'woody bank', but the Barnehurst name was simply an invention for a station in the middle of nowhere. Only 15 people lived within half a mile of the station when it opened in 1895 and not a single first-class season ticket was sold for over ten years. The lane that served the station was called Hills and Holes until the 1920s, when it was renamed Barnehurst Road and 600 homes were put up on land acquired from Michael Barne, a descendant of the owners of May Place. Shops were built on Midfield Parade in 1928. Wates was among the various later developers, laying out the Barnehurst Park estate in 1933 on land to the south of Mayplace Road. With prices as low as £535 for a four-bedroom house, this was one of the most affordable new estates in London, although the fourth bedroom measured less than eight feet by seven. Crayford urban dis-

trict council acquired May Place in 1938, and what remains of it now forms part of the clubhouse for Barnehurst golf course. More than a thousand homes were damaged during the Blitz, resulting in extensive rebuilding after the war. Modern Barnehurst is an ethnically uniform locality with 95 per cent of residents classified as white. Eighty-four per cent of homes are owner-occupied.

May Place used to be the seat of the lord of the manor and was the home of Admiral of the Fleet Sir Clowdesley Shovell, commander-in-chief of the Royal Navy until he was shipwrecked off the Scilly Isles in 1707 and strangled by a fisherwoman for the emerald ring he was wearing.

> ✉ Bexleyheath DA7

> ♟ 10,277

> 🚃 South Eastern Trains (zone 6)

> 📖 Edward O Thomas, *The Story of Barnehurst*, Bexley Education and Leisure Directorate, 1998

> @ www.barnehurst.com (community site)

Barn Elms • *Richmond*

Now the collective name for the eastern part of the BARNES peninsula, Barn Elms was originally the manor house of Barnes and the home of a succession of notable figures from the 16th to the 19th centuries. From 1894 until 1939, the Ranelagh Club was situated here, providing sporting facilities comparable with those at HURLINGHAM. The clubhouse was damaged by fire in 1954 and subsequently demolished. Barn Elms' Victorian reservoirs, which became redundant after the inauguration of the Thames Water Ring Main in the mid 1990s, have been spectacularly transformed into the 64-acre London Wetland Centre, funded by the building of luxury housing nearby. The £16-million project was the brainchild of the naturalist and artist Sir Peter Scott, who wanted to bring the sight of rare ducks, geese and swans to city dwellers. The western side of the reserve is devoted to reconstructions of 14 wetland habitats, including Siberian tundra, tropical swamps and an Australian billabong. Walkways and hides help visitors get close to the waterfowl without disturbing them and there is a lakeside observatory with displays of the different migration routes of the birds that visit the reserve.

In the early 18th century, Jacob Tonson, founder of an elite political society called the Kit-Cat Club, lived at Barn Elms and provided a room in his home as one of its meeting places. The home farm where William Cobbett practised experimental agriculture in the late 1820s disappeared under Barn Elms reservoirs in the 1890s. Cobbett is believed to have written much of his campaigning treatise *Rural Rides* while based here.

✉ SW13

@ www.wwt.org.uk/visit/wetlandcentre

Barnes • *Richmond*

A classy riverside settlement situated to the north-west of PUTNEY. Domesday Book had the first authenticated appearance of the name, which means what it says: this was the place of the barns that stored grain for the manor of MORTLAKE. When Barnes became a manor in its own right, under the ownership of the dean and chapter of ST PAUL'S Cathedral, the manor house was built at BARN ELMS and was later enlarged into an aristocratic mansion. Further inland, Barnes remained a remote farming community for several centuries. The most noteworthy event was a dispute in 1589 that resulted in the men of Barnes refusing to let their Putney neighbours continue to share Barnes Common with them. Perhaps surprisingly, given its proximity to the Thames, the village developed around the green, which had three ponds. Milbourne House has faced the green since the 15th century, albeit in several incarnations. The parish had around 200 residents by 1600 and at least two inns by 1637. Barnes Street, now Barnes High Street, was in existence by 1700. Several villas and mansions were built in the 18th and early 19th centuries, notably along the riverside on the Terrace. The population had grown to 860 by the time of the first census in 1801. The Barnes peninsula was especially isolated until the opening of HAMMERSMITH Bridge in 1827, affording its market gardeners improved access to their primary market and bringing residential potential to the locality later called CASTELNAU. The arrival of the railway in 1846 opened up the wider district to development. The original station building survives, making this one of the oldest such structures in Greater London. Barnes Bridge was built in 1849 to carry the loop line of the London and South Western Railway across the Thames to Chiswick, bringing a second station to the village. An embankment was constructed to raise the line as it approached the bridge, blocking the riverside path. At this time, much of the waterfront area was still covered by market gardens. These were sold in 1865 to the British Land Co., which laid out a tight network of terraced cottages. Over the next hundred years middle-class suburban developments filled the area more densely, together with some later pockets of council housing. St Mary's Church was devastated by a fire in 1978 and has been completely rebuilt, but with great sympathy for its medieval origins. Much of the village is now designated the Barnes Green conservation area. This is a popular place of residence for established figures in the arts and media, and Barnes High Street and its offshoots have individually-owned boutiques specializing in foodstuffs, clothing and interior design. Only the Grand Pond survives from the original trio at the heart of the village, and is now called Barnes Pond. Barnes Fair is held annually on the green on the second Saturday of July.

The novelist and dramatist Henry Fielding lived briefly at Milbourne House in the mid 18th century before leaving for southern Europe in a vain attempt to improve his failing health. The rock star Marc Bolan was killed in a car crash on Queens Ride in 1977. The sycamore tree that his car hit is now the site of a shrine to his memory.

✉ SW13

👥 9,823

🚋 South West Trains (Barnes; Barnes Bridge, zone 3)

📖 Maisie Brown, *Barnes and Mortlake Past*, Historical Publications, 1997

@ www.barnes-online.co.uk (local online newspaper site); www.barnesvillage.org.uk (Barnes Community Association site)

Barnes Cray • *Bexley*

An industrial and working-class residential outpost of CRAYFORD, located to the north-west of Dartford, Kent. This was said to have been the site of Ellam, a medieval manor house. Like nearby BARNEHURST it takes its present name from the Barne family, who owned land on the edge of the Crayford Marshes from the mid 18th century. Maiden Lane has farm buildings and cottages that may be over 300 years old. Iron Mill Lane is named after a mill that made plate for armour. In a 'swords to ploughshares' conversion, the mill later switched to producing Vitbe flour. Barnes Cray and the neighbouring hamlet of Perry Street became increasingly industrialized in the latter part of the 19th century, with brickworks inland, mills and wharves by the river and factories alongside the railway line. After the outbreak of World War I, Vickers laid out a garden village here for employees at its Crayford munitions works. Six hundred cottages were built in a variety of styles with the aid of a grant from the War Office. Vickers already had experience of this kind of development, having built Vickerstown at Barrow-in-Furness in the early years of the 20th century. Each of the homes here had at least three bedrooms and more than half were constructed using roughcast concrete blocks. The iron church of All Saints was established in 1917. After the war Crayford council built more housing to the north. The iron church was never upgraded and when it closed in 1960 it was not replaced. Barnes Cray Primary School is on Iron Mill Lane. The national educational standards agency Ofsted describes the school's catchment area as 'very mixed … [with] high social deprivation' and says that 'many pupils come from homes suffering severe economic stress'. East of Thames Road (A206), Barnes Cray remains entirely industrial, with extensive waste treatment and transfer facilities around Crayford Creek.

Geoffrey Whitworth was a leading campaigner for the popularization of theatre and in 1918 he attended a play-reading by Vickers workers that inspired him to form the British Drama League. The drab but culturally vital building that bears his name was opened in 1959 by Dame Sybil Thorndyke as the home of the British Theatre Group. Located on Beech Walk, the theatre hosts around a dozen week-long productions every year.

✉ Dartford DA1

📖 Katherine Harding and Denise Baldwin, *Along the River Cray: A Pictorial History of the Cray Valley*, Bexley Libraries, 2003

@ www.thegwt.org.uk (Geoffrey Whitworth Theatre)

Barnet • *Barnet*

An elongated and elevated suburb five miles west of ENFIELD and eleven miles from the centre of London. The name was first recorded around 1070 and derives either from a corruption of 'burnt', indicating the clearance of former woodland, or from 'bergnet', an Old English word describing an area with a little hill. The variant form 'Barnetley' was in use for several centuries, the affix signifying a clearing. EAST BARNET may have been the earliest part of the district to be permanently inhabited and a church stood here by 1140.

However, a more significant settlement soon evolved on the higher ground to the north-west following the establishment of a market by the abbey of St Albans. From the 14th century the new centre was known as CHIPPING BARNET (Barnet market), although the alternative name West Barnet was employed for a while. To the east of the Great North Road (as it later became) the settlement of HADLEY took root on the edge of ENFIELD CHASE. The Battle of Barnet took place on Hadley Green on a foggy Easter Sunday in 1471. This was a key battle in the Wars of the Roses, in which Edward IV and the Yorkists slew the Earl of Warwick, the Kingmaker, and vanquished Henry VI. Horse-trading has always played an important role at Barnet fair, which was first held in 1588. During the 17th and 18th centuries Barnet thrived as a coaching stop, gaining a notorious number of inns. Purer waters were drunk at the physic well, on what is now Wellhouse Lane. The Great Northern Railway reached NEW BARNET in 1850. This was too early for hordes of potential commuters to consider living so far out of London but it sowed the seeds of high-class suburban development in the area formerly known as LYONS-DOWN. HIGH BARNET station opened in 1872, cementing the popularity of yet another alternative name for the market town. Speculative builders began to lay out the first streets of terraced and semi-detached houses from the end of the 19th century, and between the wars the whole district expanded rapidly, stretching out to ARKLEY in the west and to the newly opened underground station at COCKFOSTERS in the east. To the south, hitherto sporadic growth in OAKLEIGH PARK reached a climax, completing a built-up continuum with the separate parish of FRIERN BARNET. After World War II, the inception of the green belt prevented further expansion to the north and west, where open farmland remains. In 1965 this southern tip of Hertfordshire joined neighbouring parts of Middlesex to form the London Borough of Barnet. With the district fully built up and unable to spread outwards, recent housebuilding has mainly consisted of the replacement of older, space-consuming properties with compact apartment blocks, but the best of Barnet's Georgian and Victorian heritage is protected within conservation areas.

Since the mid 19th century 'barnet' (via Barnet fair) has been cockney (originally thieves') rhyming slang for one's hair.

✉ Barnet EN5

50,640 (East Barnet, High Barnet, Oakleigh and Underhill wards)

Northern Line (zone 5); north-eastern branch terminates at High Barnet station

Pamela Taylor, *Barnet and Hadley Past*, Historical Publications, 2002

@ www.barnet4u.co.uk (community site)

Barnet Gate • *Barnet*
A western satellite of BARNET, located beyond ARKLEY at the junction of Barnet Road and Hendon Wood Lane, and surrounded by woodland, sports grounds and other green-belt land. The gate prevented cattle from straying onto Barnet Common. It was first called Grendel's Gate, after the monster slain by Beowulf, and it has been suggested that the use of such a portentous name may indicate a place of some significance in Saxon times. It was certainly more important than it is now, for manor courts were held here in the Middle Ages and Hendon Wood Lane was a busy thoroughfare that may have been a Roman road. The settlement lay on the edge of Southaw, a large wood belonging to the abbey of St Albans, much of which was obliterated by the creation of CHIPPING BARNET. From the 13th century there were brickworks here, and these were still in existence in 1896. Barnet Gate Farm was established around the end of the 18th century. The extensively altered Gate public house is of Victorian origin, and was originally called the Bell. Dating from the same period, Bell's Cottages have also been renovated. Barnet Gate Wood is a remnant of ancient woodland but has become overgrown with rhododendron, which is impeding the renewal of native trees and shading out most of the woodland flowers.

The British Library's collection includes the *Barnet Court Book*, a record of a manor court held at Barnet Gate in 1354.

Barnet EN5; NW7

Barnet Vale • *Barnet*
The north-western quadrant of NEW BARNET, filled mainly with owner-occupied late Victorian and Edwardian housing. The terrain slopes markedly from the heights of CHIPPING BARNET and HADLEY down to the Pymmes Brook as it flows through EAST BARNET, but Barnet Vale's name is the invention of developers, with no recorded history before the modern streets appeared. Construction radiated slowly outwards from New Barnet station after it opened in 1850, at first along the newly

built Station Road (later the location of a town hall and courthouse) and Leicester Road, leaving the older Potters Lane untouched. A second phase of development travelled northwards across the meadows towards Monken Hadley Common. Remaining gaps were filled at intervals throughout the 20th century, mainly with 'courts' and cul-de-sacs, and there was commercial development in the 1960s on Station Road. St Mark's Church, in Potters Road, was consecrated in 1899. It was one of two unfinished places of worship by the architect John Pearson, who died in 1897; the other is St John's Cathedral in Brisbane, Australia. Use of the building is shared with local Orthodox Christians, the congregation of the Greek Orthodox Church of St Catherine within St Mark's Church. Clifford Road has some well-run allotments, with grassed paths and small ponds that promote a rural appearance. The allotments are flanked by a sports ground and golf course to the north and Cromer Road Primary School to the south. Cromer Road once housed Maw's Pharmaceuticals, famous for its cotton wool. The factory stood here from 1921 until 1982, when it was replaced by the Boleyn Way estate.

Barnet EN5

Barnsbury • *Islington*
London's pioneering gentrified locality, consisting of a mix of older terraces and squares and modern council blocks in north-west ISLINGTON. The 13th-century Berners family gave its name to a large manor, of which present-day Barnsbury covers just a small part. Legal obstacles prevented building on the land until the 1820s, significantly later than nearby districts such as CANONBURY. During the 1830s an eccentric Frenchman named Baume set up the short-lived Barnsbury Park Community, a co-operative community with a farm and a college, settled by radical tailors and shoemakers. Elsewhere, the rows of narrow-fronted terraces were destined to house a lower class of occupant than its developers intended, especially when the building of the railways prompted the more prosperous to migrate to more distant suburbs. Many larger houses were subdivided for multiple occupancy, or even turned into factories. During the 1970s some of the most run-down parts were demolished and the council and Barnsbury Housing Association built new homes. The latter also restored some older properties. Around this time the pendulum began to swing back in favour of city

dwelling and Barnsbury's protracted decline was reversed. Young professionals flocked in and the district became known for its 'liberal intelligentsia', including numerous writers and journalists, as well as Tony Blair before he became prime minister in 1997. The locality's long spell out of fashion has, ironically, preserved many features, since speculators did not deem the area worthy of redevelopment. There is evidence that prices here have subsequently escalated to the detriment of the sense of community fostered by the first wave of gentrifiers, with household incomes now typically in six figures.

| ✉ | N1; N7 |

| 👥 | 10,274 |

| 🚌 | Silverlink Metro (Caledonian Road and Barnsbury, zone 2) |

| 📖 | Mary Cash, *An Historical Walk through Barnsbury*, Islington Archaeology and History Society, 1981 |

Barons Court • *Hammersmith & Fulham*

A made-up name for the compact residential locality situated between HAMMERSMITH and WEST KENSINGTON. Hammersmith (or Margravine) Cemetery was consecrated in 1869 and soon afterwards Major Sir William Palliser built the first suburban houses to its east. Palliser was the inventor of armour-piercing projectiles known as Palliser shot, while his wife was famous as the model for Sir John Millais's portrait *Charlie is my Darling*. The Barons Court name was Palliser's playful allusion to nearby Earls Court; there is no evidence of any specific baron having lived here. Established in 1886, the Queen's Club claims to have been the first multi-purpose sports complex anywhere in the world. It is now best known for the pre-WIMBLEDON Stella Artois tennis championships held every June and is the national headquarters for real tennis and rackets. After recovering from the bankruptcy of their West Kensington Estate Co., William Gibbs and John Flew ventured into Barons Court, graduating from stucco to red brick as they moved west of Vereker Road and building a bridge over the railway line to improve access. Barons Court station did not open until 1905, 30 years after the construction of the line. Art deco terraced houses went up on Barons Court Road in the 1930s and flats replaced some bomb-damaged houses after World War II. Talgarth Road was the home of the Royal Ballet School (originally the Sadler's Wells Ballet School) from 1947. The lower school moved

to the White Lodge, RICHMOND PARK in 1955 and the upper school to Floral Street, COVENT GARDEN in 2003. The Barons Court building has become home to the London Academy of Music and Dramatic Art. The 60-seat Barons Court Theatre is located in the cellar of the Curtains Up pub on Comeragh Road. Barons Court has a high level of mobility, as the welter of 'for sale' boards suggests.

Mahatma Gandhi lived on Barons Court Road while studying law and visited the Congregationalist church on Castletown Road that has since become the Bhavan institute for Indian art and culture.

| ✉ | W14 |

| 🚇 | District Line; Piccadilly Line (zone 2) |

| 📖 | Robert T Holt and John E Turner, *Political Parties in Action: The Battle of Barons Court*, The Free Press, New York, 1968 (a study of political campaigning here in 1964) |

| @ | www.queensclub.co.uk |

Barwell • *Kingston*

A hamlet in south-west CHESSINGTON, situated just north of Chessington World of Adventures. The Barwell name is of 13th-century origin, and may have meant 'the place near a spring (or pool) where barley is grown'. Evidence suggests that Barwell has been occupied since Roman times and has been a farm since medieval times, when it also had a dovecote. The farm probably took in fields to the south, including Winey Hill. The Barwell estate, later known as Barwell Court, was first owned by Merton Priory and was annexed to the 'honour' of Hampton Court after the dissolution of the monasteries, together with part of nearby HOOK. In 1587 Elizabeth I granted Barwell to Thomas Vincent, after which it passed through a succession of private hands. Little is known of the original manor house, but hearth tax returns of 1664 showed that it had six fireplaces. In the 18th century the farm covered 250 acres. By 1872 the original manor house had been replaced by the present mansion, which had six bedrooms, a walled kitchen garden and three wells supplying spring water. It has since been divided into three luxury homes, while a separate house has recently replaced a nearby industrial building. Former farm buildings are now used as livery stables. In 1937 Surbiton council bought 24 acres at Winey Hill from Lady Barker for £5,000 and this is now a public open space. The Sir Francis Barker recreation ground and Barwell business park are on, respectively, the west and east sides of Leatherhead Road.

Barwell Court served as a rehearsal studio in the late 1970s and 1980s, owned by the Sony and Virgin record companies. The Boomtown Rats stayed in the house for several months and Marillion wrote their album *Misplaced Childhood* there.

✉ Chessington KT9

Battersea • *Wandsworth*

An increasingly upmarket district that nevertheless retains many council-built flats, situated on the south bank of the Thames, northeast of WANDSWORTH. It is one of the oldest recorded place names in the London area. A late seventh-century charter makes reference to 'Badrices ege', the island of a man called Badric. In 957 King Eadwig gave Battersea to one of his ministers, together with pasture at Penge. The parish church of St Mary was in existence by 1157, although nothing of the original structure has survived. The Abbey of Westminster held the manor at the time of the dissolution of the monasteries, when it passed to the Crown, and then in 1627 to the St John family, whose manor house stood east of the church. In 1700 Sir Walter St John founded Battersea's first school. Industries were established on reclaimed marshland beside the Thames, including a shot foundry, a whiting (whitewash) works and a brewhouse at NINE ELMS. From the 1740s to 1756, decorative enamel boxes were made at York House, and several other manufacturing businesses were equally short-lived. St Mary's Church was rebuilt in the mid 1770s. Most of the manor house was demolished in 1793, and later became the site of flour mills. Away from the river, most of Battersea was used for market gardening, with a few clusters of dwellings around the church and in Falcon Road and Bolingbroke Grove. The coming of the railway to Nine Elms and CLAPHAM JUNCTION and in 1858 the simultaneous opening of Chelsea Bridge and BATTERSEA PARK prompted developers to lay out estates of reasonably priced housing for the middle classes all along the route to CLAPHAM COMMON, while Sir Walter St John's school was rebuilt. Shortly afterwards, however, Battersea was divided up by an increasing number of railway lines and as a result property prices dropped, with some of the larger houses being subdivided to allow occupation by 'persons of humbler circumstances'. New stations were opened at Battersea Park and QUEENSTOWN ROAD and grids of terraced cottages were laid out, including in

the 1870s the Shaftesbury Park estate, the work of the same philanthropic company that later built QUEEN'S PARK. By 1871 the population of Battersea had increased almost tenfold in 40 years and it tripled again before the end of the 19th century, when most of the residents were skilled artisans employed in local service industries. The Latchmere estate of 1903 was the first to be built by a London County Council borough. Battersea council was a famously progressive body, in 1906 gaining the first British-born black councillor, John Richard Archer. In 1913 Archer was elected mayor, another first. Blocks of municipal flats replaced much of Battersea's Victorian housing before and for several decades after World War II. The most unspoilt part is the old village, south of the church. In recent years, much of the riverside has filled with luxury apartment complexes, of which the most impressive is the Montevetro building. Price's candle factory, which took the place of York House, has been converted into flats.

Battersea was the birthplace of the television personality Michael Aspel. Other former residents include the author G K Chesterton and the artist-craftsman Eric Gill.

✉ SW11

♦ 62,811 (Latchmere, Northcote, Queenstown, St Mary's Park and Shaftesbury wards)

📖 Patrick Loobey, *Battersea Past*, Historical Publications, 2002

Battersea Park • *Wandsworth*

A feature-filled public park occupying 200 acres of the Thames riverside between BATTERSEA and NINE ELMS. This was formerly Battersea Fields, an isolated spot that became popular as a duelling ground in the early 19th century; in 1829 the Duke of Wellington, then the prime minister, and the Earl of Winchelsea confronted each other here but no blood was spilt. The fields later became a venue for less noble forms of contest, and the fighting and brawling was stimulated by the presence of several disorderly taverns. The Royal Commission on Metropolitan Improvements was established in 1843 and its recommendations resulted in the acquisition of the fields, as well as the creation of the Chelsea Embankment and Chelsea Bridge. Sir James Pennethorne created the initial plan for Battersea Park, which was laid out from 1846 and officially opened by Queen Victoria in 1858. Work on the park continued with the excavation of the ornamental lake in 1861 and the planting of

27

the sub-tropical garden in 1864. In the following year the opening of Battersea Park station brought tens of thousands of visitors on a daily basis. Battersea Dogs' Home, sandwiched between two railway lines just off Battersea Park Road, moved here from HOLLOWAY in 1875. The land surrounding the park was sold by the Crown for development between 1880 and 1900. Pleasure gardens covering 37 acres of Battersea Park were laid out in 1951 for the Festival of Britain. The park's funfair closed in 1974. Buddhist monks and nuns built a peace pagoda beside the riverside promenade in 1985 to commemorate the 40th anniversary of the bombing of Hiroshima. The Duke of Edinburgh reopened the park in 2004 following an £11 million programme of improvements. Victorian and post-war features have been restored, new fountains added and the promenade widened. The park's many other attractions include a children's zoo, boating lake and art gallery.

Creative works mentioning the park include Petula Clark's 1954 single *Meet Me in Battersea Park* and the 2001 books *After Battersea Park*, by Jonathan Bennett, and *The Battersea Park Road to Enlightenment*, by Isabel Losada.

✉ SW11; SW8

🚆 Southern (zone 2)

📖 *Battersea Park*, Friends of Battersea Park, 1993

@ www.batterseapark.org

Bayswater • *Westminster*

A self-enclosed enclave of hotels and high-class housing lying north of KENSINGTON GARDENS. Bayswater began as a hamlet located close to present-day LANCASTER GATE but the name now covers a wide area stretching west to NOTTING HILL, north as far as WESTBOURNE GREEN and east to PADDINGTON – or even beyond, to MARBLE ARCH. In 1380 this was Bayard's Watering Place. The water was provided by the stream later known as the Westbourne, while a bayard was a bay (chestnut) horse, though some suggest the name may have come from a resident called Baynard. The hamlet was intermediately known as Bayswatering, while Bayswater was first recorded in 1659, when just a handful of houses stood here. Apart from some tea gardens, a lying-in hospital and the inevitable inn or two, Bayswater remained entirely undeveloped at the start of the 18th century. Speculative builders began to grab the land here in 1809, led by BOND STREET printmaker Edward

Orme. Single and paired villas with gardens were the favoured types of dwellings built initially but tree-lined, terraced avenues, squares and crescents rapidly extended the district in the 1840s and 1850s. A 'splendid new town' had come into existence by the time Bayswater station opened in 1868. Artists and writers came here when the district was still semi-rural but were soon succeeded by more conventional members of the upper classes. Bayswater was nicknamed 'Asia Minor' in 1885 and Indian fruits and vegetables were on sale in the local shops, but the customers were military and administrative professionals with south Asian experience rather than immigrants from the subcontinent. Greeks and Jews also settled here, establishing their own places of worship on Moscow Road and St Petersburgh Place respectively. Late in the 19th century some of the earliest houses were rebuilt, while others were replaced with flats. Hotels and mansion blocks made up the lion's share of replacement building between the wars. From the early 1960s some new hotels were added, while older ones were converted into flats. Bayswater was designated a conservation area in 1967, constraining subsequent redevelopment. Since the 1980s Bayswater has been the focus of a wave of settlement by Middle Eastern expatriates, who patronize the shops and services on QUEENSWAY and EDGWARE ROAD.

The engineer Rookes Crompton electrically illuminated his house in Porchester Gardens in 1879. A 'dry land sailor' used to be known as a Bayswater Captain.

✉ W2

👥 8,145

🚆 Circle Line; District Line (zone 1)

📖 James Dowsing, *A Guide to Bayswater*, Sunrise Press, 2001

Beckenham • *Bromley*

BROMLEY'S little sister lies two miles to its west. The name is generally held to derive from Beohha, a Saxon farmer. The river that flows through the town is called the Beck, but this is a 'back formation', ie the name Beckenham came first and the river was named after it. The discovery of pottery dated to the period 900–1150 is evidence of previously unknown Saxon–Norman occupation. The site, on what is now Fairfield Road, was abandoned early in the Middle Ages and was not reoccupied until houses began to line the High Street in the late 17th century. Because Beckenham was off the main route carrying traffic from Kent into London that ran through nearby Bromley, it became popular as a country retreat at this time, retaining its appeal for more than a century. One of the grandest mansions was Beckenham Place, built in the late 1770s for wealthy local landowner John Cator. Much of its surrounding parkland was later sold off for building, including a station in 1857. What remains of Beckenham Place Park contains one of the few surviving areas of ancient woodland in Greater London. Rapid development ensued over the next three decades, with detached properties for the middle classes and terraced cottages for the workers who provided their services, while shopping parades marched in all directions. After World War I, compact, densely packed terraces of houses covered the remaining fields in the southern half of the district and the council compulsorily purchased and widened the High Street. Bomb damage during World War II led to clearance for council flats and town houses, and for new commercial property, though as a shopping centre Beckenham has been totally eclipsed by nearby Bromley.

The comedian Bob Monkhouse was born in Beckenham in 1928. In 1969 David Bowie founded the Beckenham Arts Lab at a pub on the High Street, while living in Foxgrove Road.

✉ Beckenham BR3

🚊 South Eastern Trains; Southern; Croydon Tramlink interchange (Beckenham Junction, zone 4)

📖 Eric R Inman and Nancy Tonkin, *Beckenham*, Phillimore, 2002

@ www.beckenham.net (commercial local information site)

Beckenham Hill • *Lewisham*
A station and road located between BECKENHAM Place Park and BELLINGHAM. This was Stumps Hill when John Cator acquired and rebuilt Beckenham Place in 1773. The CATFORD loop line was built in 1892 by the Shortlands and Nunhead Railway Co., an offshoot of the London, Chatham and Dover Railway. The company opened a station at Beckenham Hill, even though the area was almost entirely unpopulated, and for many years this was said to be 'the quietest suburban station of all'. Unusually for the line, the main station building was constructed on the same level as the platforms, which were sheltered by a pair of gener-

ous canopies. Large forecourts were provided on each side of the road to provide turning space for horsedrawn vehicles. Only a handful of buildings had appeared on Beckenham Hill Road by the early 20th century, including the neo-Georgian Red House. The locality remained peacefully rural until the LCC's Bellingham estate spread in this direction in the 1920s. Even in 1959 the station's platforms were still lit by gas lamps. At the last local government boundary change, the whole of Beckenham Place Park became part of the London Borough of Lewisham. The mansion serves as a clubhouse for Beckenham Place Park golf course. A strip of Stumpshill Wood survives at the southern end of Beckenham Hill Road, opposite the council's Beckenham Hill estate.

The original members of the rock band Status Quo, as they were later to become, got together in 1962 at Sedgehill School, which is located to the north-west of the Beckenham Hill estate.

✉ SE6

🚊 South Eastern Trains (zone 4)

Beckton • *Newham*
The former home of the world's biggest gasworks and now a docklands development area, situated west of Barking Creek and north of the Royal Albert Dock. The first intrusion into the hitherto empty East Ham Levels was the construction of the Northern Outfall Sewer in 1864, pouring raw waste into the Thames until the building of a treatment works 25 years later. The sewage works subsequently became the largest in the country and today serves a population of three million, treating over 200 million gallons a day. In 1870 the Gas, Light and Coke Co. established its London base here. Housing was built for the workers and the whole 400-acre site was named Beckton after the governor of the company, Simon Adams Beck. At its peak, Beckton supplied gas to over four million Londoners, as well as manufacturing by-products such as creosote, fertilizers, inks and dyes. It was not until the switch to natural gas in the 1960s that the works were scaled down. The neighbouring marshland was formerly occupied by hundreds of garden allotments and was also the site of a prisoner of war camp during World War II. Docklands regeneration in Beckton has created a cluster of industrial and commercial 'parks' and thousands of new homes. Beckton is ethnically diverse, and has large numbers of single people, lone parents and students.

During its dereliction, the old gasworks site was often used as a film and television location, most notably for the Vietnam scenes in Stanley Kubrick's *Full Metal Jacket* and for James Bond's disposal of Blofeld down a chimney in *For Your Eyes Only*.

✉ E6

👥 13,112

🚈 Docklands Light Railway (Beckton; Beckton Park; zone 3)

Becontree • *Barking & Dagenham* (pronounced 'beckәntree')

A gargantuan council estate covering four square miles of former fields, heath and parkland north of DAGENHAM. It has been claimed that its name was shortened to the present form because Beacontree, an old local name, was one letter too long to fit on bus destination blinds. However, there is little evidence for this since both spellings have been in use for centuries. Some modern maps still prefer the alternative spelling. Much of the area was part of Parsloes, once the largest manor in Dagenham and the property of the Passelewe family in 1257. The most recent incarnation of the manor house was demolished in 1925 owing to its dilapidated condition. VALENCE House, the district's only other piece of heritage, was preserved as a showpiece for the new estate. Begun in 1921, Becontree was the flagship of the London County Council's 'cottage estate' housebuilding programme and was intended to accommodate 100,000 people. Most of the houses were constructed in red brick with tiled roofs. A railway line brought materials from the Thames docks and 50 miles of roads were laid out for what was called the world's greatest public housing project. Parsloes Park was opened to the public as part of the ceremony marking the inauguration of the estate. Many of the first residents came from LIMEHOUSE, where a slum clearance programme was under way at the time. By the 1930s, Becontree had grown larger than many provincial cities. But the LCC's ambitions could not be fully realized on an estate so lacking in education, healthcare and social facilities; and the housing, though adequate, was plain and monotonous. Had it not been for the creation of the Ford motor works, unemployment would have been an added burden. Some of the estate's early drawbacks have been overcome but the township is still not well-endowed with amenities. With the trends towards smaller families and more people living alone, Becontree's population is now much smaller than originally envisaged. Most residents are white, but there is also a sizeable black British community, of Caribbean and African descent. Bengali, Urdu, Punjabi and Albanian are among the minority languages spoken.

✉ Dagenham RM8, RM9 and RM10

👥 29,874 (Becontree, Valence and Heath wards)

🚈 District Line (zone 5)

📖 Robert Home, 'A Township Complete in Itself', Barking & Dagenham Libraries and UEL School of Surveying, 1997; Andrzej Olechnowicz, *Working-Class Housing in England between the Wars: The Becontree Estate*, Clarendon Press, 1997

Becontree Heath • *Barking & Dagenham*

A historic administrative centre situated in the north-eastern corner of BECONTREE. In medieval times this was probably the meeting place of the court of the Becontree hundred, which then extended as far as Havering. But by the late 18th century Becontree Heath presented a more lawless aspect. The cottagers who made their living from the common land did not take well to judicial interference and were frequently at odds with the parish constable. In 1819 the vicar acquired a pair of stocks at his own expense for the chastisement of miscreants. He may also have been displeased by the growing number of Methodists here. By the mid 19th century Becontree Heath was the only remaining unenclosed common in the district and it became a prime spot for hay and straw dealers. Everything changed in the 1920s with the construction of the London County Council estate at Becontree, when a civic centre, cinema, shops and houses were built. The council acquired and preserved what remained of the heath in 1931. Most of the borough's central offices are still located at Becontree Heath, at the junction of Wood Lane and Rainham Road, behind which lies Central Park. The Heath ward is 92 per cent white, and households are divided almost equally between owner-occupancy and council tenancy. The number of residents with a higher educational qualification is less than a third of the national average.

✉ Dagenham RM8 and RM10

👥 9,649 (Heath ward)

Beddington • *Sutton*

A very varied district situated between CAR-

SHALTON and the WADDON area of CROYDON, treated by many as though it is part of WALLINGTON. The name is associated with a Saxon landowner. Around 900, Edward the Elder, king of Wessex, gave Beddington to the minster at Winchester, his capital. Bishop (later Saint) Ethelwold of Winchester died here in 984. By the time of Domesday Book, the bishops had lost Beddington and it was split into two manors. During the 14th century Sir Nicholas Carew acquired a large estate and built a moated and fortified mansion. Sir Francis Carew laid out magnificent gardens where the first English oranges were grown in the 17th century. The wall of the orangery, with its heating ducts, is still standing. Another Sir Nicholas rebuilt Beddington Place in the early 18th century, though older parts survive – notably the great hall, which is probably late 15th century. The Carews' ownership came to an end in 1859 when Charles Hallowell Carew sold the estate to clear his gambling debts. The mansion became an orphanage and underwent further alterations. It is now a school for children with moderate learning difficulties. From 1864 to 1891 Alexander Bridges was the rich rector of St Mary's Church, parts of which date back to the 11th century. Bridges acquired and re-landscaped much of the adjoining park, saving it from property developers, and funded the restoration and extension of the church in the late 1860s. He and his wealthy neighbours resisted the opening of a station in Beddington and they had no financial need to sell land for housing, so Wallington grew at Beddington's expense in the late 19th century. It was not until after World War I that rapid suburbanization began. Among the industries and utilities to the north on Beddington Lane is a sewage treatment works, constructed in the mid 19th century on part of the Carews' deer park after the members of Croydon Board of Health had been threatened with imprisonment for discharging the borough's untreated sewage into the River Wandle. The sewage works is a sanctuary for several rare species of birds.

✉ Wallington SM6; Croydon CR0

♦ 20,364 (Beddington North and Beddington South wards)

🚋 Croydon Tramlink, Route 1 (Beddington Lane)

📖 Ronald Michell, *The Carews of Beddington*, Sutton Libraries and Arts Services, 1981

Beddington Corner • *Sutton/Merton*
An assortment of industry, terraced housing and wilderness lying on the east side of the River Wandle south of MITCHAM COMMON. Although the name is used to denote the junction of Goat Road, Carshalton Road and London Road, its origin lies in its former location at the north-west corner of BEDDINGTON parish. HACKBRIDGE and Beddington Corner now have their own parish church, built on London Road in 1931. Mill Green business park has engineering, manufacturing and a journalism training centre. Once there were lavender and leather works here, the latter giving their name to the Skinners Arms and Goat public houses. Beddington Corner is earmarked for further housebuilding and Sutton council has designated it an 'area of special local character' to regulate its development.

Tom Francis and Eric Montague's book *Old Mitcham* tells of a band of Galician Gypsies that once lived in a field near Willow Cottage at Beddington Corner, before departing for America. When the Gypsy leader's daughter died, she was buried in MITCHAM churchyard with an elaborate funeral, her body bedecked with gold and silver coins.

✉ Mitcham CR4

📖 Tom Francis and Eric Montague, *Old Mitcham*, Phillimore, 1993

Bedfont *see* EAST BEDFONT

Bedford Hill • *Wandsworth*
A curving, one-mile road connecting BALHAM with STREATHAM, via TOOTING BEC Common. Originally a private drive leading to the long-gone Bedfordhill House, it takes its name from the dukes of Bedford, who owned an estate here in the 18th century. The Priory is a Gothic villa built in 1822 on the edge of Tooting Bec Common, and a rare survivor of its kind. The house was the scene of the mysterious death of Charles Bravo in 1876. Bravo was probably poisoned by his wife but there were other suspects with their own potential motives. No one was ever convicted of the crime, which has since been the subject of print and television investigations. Most of the hill was built up in the last quarter of the 19th century, notably by Alfred and George Heaver, whose Bedford Hill estate consisted of six roads of generously proportioned red-brick houses. Apart from some shabby shops at the Balham end of the road, this is a pleasant locality but it lacks architectural consistency as there have been additions in almost every decade. The Priory was converted to flats in 1982, and houses have been built in its grounds. In the 1980s,

Bedford Hill

31

Bedford Hill was south London's best-known red-light district but heavy policing subsequently reduced streetwalking to a comparatively low level. Plans to turn a minor offenders' hostel into a rehabilitation unit for dangerous offenders, including rapists and paedophiles, prompted demonstrations and blockades in 2001; the Home Office subsequently put the proposal on ice. The Bedford, at 77 Bedford Hill, is a former *Evening Standard* pub of the year that once had a seedy reputation. Nearly 60 per cent of the residents of the Bedford ward are single and more than half are qualified to degree level or higher, although 15 per cent of homes do not have central heating.

✉ SW12; SW17; SW16

♦ 13,017 (Bedford ward)

@ www.thebedford.co.uk (pub site)

Bedford Park • *Ealing*

An influential 'new model suburb' created after 1875 in the south-east corner of ACTON by the speculator Jonathan Carr. Prompted by the arrival of the Metropolitan Railway at TURNHAM GREEN, Carr bought 24 acres of land with the intention of building a settlement that would be affordable yet stylish. He named the project after the dukes of Bedford, who owned property here in the 17th century, and commissioned E W Godwin to design the first houses. However, the architectural press criticized the interiors, though Godwin had previously worked on the CHELSEA homes of Wilde and Whistler. Anxious to avoid damage to the development's reputation, Carr sacked Godwin and brought in R Norman Shaw, the leading architect of his day. Shaw's Queen Anne architecture has been nicknamed 'Wrenaissance' – long rows of houses, some with balconies, differentiated by detailing in the gables, windows and tall chimneys. There was hot-water plumbing, and the airy rooms looked out onto tree-lined avenues. These well-received homes formed the heart of Bedford Park but Shaw resigned in 1880, frustrated with Carr's exacting demands and slow payment of his bills. The building of the next five years was the work of E J May, a pupil of Shaw, and the differences in the designs represent an evolution rather than a change of direction. Carr commissioned progressively larger houses with more generous gardens, but his company failed in 1886. The remaining plots were sold to an assortment of developers and construction continued until the outbreak of World War I. Unlike many of the more austere Victorian 'model' communities, Bedford Park had an inn, a club and an art school as well as the customary church. The area suffered a decline during the post-war years, and delays in granting statutory protection allowed several houses to be demolished and replaced by blocks of flats in the early 1960s. Preservation groups have since prevented any further destruction and Bedford Park is once again highly popular with the middle classes.

W B Yeats lived in Bedford Park for most of the 1880s and 1890s, and wrote the *Lake Isle of Innisfree* at 3 Blenheim Road. Camille Pissarro's painting of *Bath Road in Bedford Park* (1897) is in the Ashmolean Museum, Oxford.

✉ W4

📖 Tom Greeves, *Bedford Park: The first garden suburb*, Bedford Park Society, reprinted 2000

@ www.bedfordpark.org (Bedford Park Society site)

BedZED • *Sutton*

A 'carbon neutral' community dubbed 'the UK's largest eco-village' built on the three and a half acre site of an old sewage works lying between London Road and Beddington Lane in HACKBRIDGE. Archaeological excavations at the site have uncovered prehistoric flint and Roman ceramic building material. The BEDDINGTON Zero Energy Development, completed in 2001, is a Peabody Trust project in association with the BioRegional Development Group, actively supported by Sutton council. Its cutting-edge architecture addresses environmental, social and economic needs and employs various methods of reducing energy, water and car use. These include integrated photovoltaic panels and a combined heat and power plant fuelled by wood waste (generated by tree surgery) from the boroughs of Sutton and Croydon. The most distinctive features are the colourful rotating wind cowls that use wind power to ventilate the units naturally. BedZED incorporates 82 homes and around 20 businesses, including the offices of the architects responsible for the project. Despite the relatively high density of BedZED, all the houses have roof terraces or gardens. The site's community facilities include a sports pitch and clubhouse, and the neighbouring landfill site has been transformed into parkland. BedZED won two awards for housing design in 2000. Like most utopian schemes, BedZED has its flaws and some residents express mixed feelings about having moved here, but its creators' intentions are admirable and further schemes of this nature would greatly enhance London's social housing stock.

✉ Wallington SM6

@ www.bedzed.org.uk

Belgravia • *Westminster*

Probably London's most desirable address, Belgravia is a Georgian estate of terraces, crescents and squares situated between KNIGHTS-BRIDGE and VICTORIA. In 1677, at the age of 21, Sir Thomas Grosvenor of Eaton in Cheshire married the twelve-year-old Mary Davies. In doing so he gained possession of Ebury manor, which covered north MAYFAIR, PIMLICO and Belgravia. Their son Richard laid out GROSVENOR SQUARE in Mayfair, but it was more than a century before his grandson developed the land south-west of HYDE PARK CORNER, prompted by the rebuilding of Buckingham House (now Buckingham Palace). The Grosvenors, who still own the estate, also held the title Viscount Belgrave; hence the name of the new district's central square and by extension the name Belgravia. The construction of Belgravia was entrusted to the Norfolk builder Thomas Cubitt and his brother Lewis. Additional work was contracted to a syndicate that included the architect George Basevi, who was responsible for much of Eaton Square. Cubitt excavated the marshy clay and made bricks from it, building on the exposed underlying gravel. Some material was also brought from the excavation of ST KATHERINE'S Docks. The architecture of Belgravia is remarkable for its grandeur and sense of unity – and because so much has survived intact. As well as providing residences of the very highest quality, Belgravia is home to several embassies; the earliest to locate here was the Austrian Embassy, in the 19th century.

Chopin gave his first London recital at 99 Eaton Place in 1848. The district has been the subject of several novels, mostly mysteries and romances. Among the more recent is Robert Barnard's *A Scandal in Belgravia*.

The Grenadier pub, on Wilton Row, was the officers' mess for the Grenadier Guards in the 1830s. It is said to be haunted by the ghost of an army officer who died after he was flogged for cheating at cards.

✉ SW1

👥 8,949 (Knightsbridge and Belgravia ward)

📖 James Dowsing, *Belgravia: Home of London's Rich and Famous*, Sunrise Press, 1999

Bellenden • *Southwark*

A renewal area covering much of south-west PECKHAM, taking its name from Bellenden Road, formerly Basing Road. The area was built up with terraced housing in the mid 19th century. By the late 20th century many of the properties were in a run-down condition, but had nevertheless managed to escape the widespread demolition that had obliterated most of Victorian Peckham. Bellenden had already attracted a small artistic community when it was designated a renewal area in 1997. The ten-year project is improving both the housing and the surrounding environment, in close consultation with the local community. The scheme has had a transformative effect, and Bellenden Road is now crowded with bars, organic cafés, ethnic food shops and other niche retailers. However, some observers have expressed concern that gentrification is prompting the departure of the original residents whom the project was designed to benefit.

The artist Tom Phillips and sculptor Antony Gormley created street furniture for the renewal area at their adjoining Bellenden Road studios.

✉ SE15

Bell Green • *Lewisham*

A socially and geographically depressed locality, set in a hollow amidst the rolling hills of SYDENHAM. Formerly called Sydenham Green, its present name may derive from a public house. Until the early 19th century this was common land occupied by a handful of elegant properties, but enclosure in 1810 changed its character forever. Bell Green was divided into smallholdings, most of which were accompanied by rude cottages, and it became a village of humble farmers divided by a maze of paths. In 1851 the Sydenham (later CRYSTAL PALACE) Gas Company erected its gasworks here, enabling this to be one of the first parts of London to be 'lit up'. Dwellings were built for the gasworks' employees and Bell Green soon became the most overcrowded part of Sydenham. Charles Booth, the great observer of London's social conditions, wrote at the end of the 19th century that 'Bell Green is the one really poor district in this quarter of London'. Much of the slum housing survived until the late 1960s, when it was replaced with council flats. Gas production ceased in 1968 and the site became a gas distribution centre for the surrounding area. Subsequent rationalization of the gas mains and storage facilities released the majority of the site for redevelopment in the early 1990s. The dominant feature of the first phase was the construction of a Savacentre hypermarket and its car park. The second phase will include a DIY store and associated garden centre, retail warehousing and a restaurant. The Livesey Memorial Hall will be retained as a social club. About 156 residential units are proposed for the final phase.

The Rolling Stones' Bill Wyman grew up at 38 Miall Walk, and went to school in nearby PENGE.

✉ SE26; SE6

Bellingham • Lewisham

An interwar municipal estate situated south of CATFORD. The name is of 10th-century origin and probably denoted 'the water meadow of Beora's people' – Beora may have been a nickname meaning 'the bear'. The Abbot of Ghent sold the sub-manor of Bellingham in the mid 13th century but the first significant building did not take place until the opening of the station in 1892, which revived the almost forgotten Bellingham identity. After World War I, Lewisham council planned to build housing here, mainly to ease inner city overcrowding, especially in DEPTFORD and BERMONDSEY. The council's subsequent failure to deliver on its commitment prompted the London County Council to step in and construct an estate between 1920 and 1923. A much larger development was afterwards built to the south-west and called DOWNHAM. The 17th-century weatherboarded and timber-framed farmhouse of Bellingham Farm was demolished in 1932; the site is now in the middle of Waterbank Road. The 'cottage estates' like Bellingham Green consisted of relatively well-proportioned semi-detached and terraced houses, but blocks of flats were erected south of Southend Road in the late 1930s. In recent years several disused shops have been replaced by community project offices, while an impressive 'leisure and lifestyle' centre opened in 2004. Most of Bellingham's residents are white, but there are significant minorities of black Caribbean and black African origin. Nearly half the homes are now owner-occupied.

The boxer Henry Cooper lived in Farmstead Road from 1940 to 1960. In 1963 Cooper trained for his fight with Cassius Clay (later known as Muhammad Ali) in the Fellowship Inn's ballroom, which was temporarily converted into a gymnasium. 'It was quite an event in Bellingham,' Cooper later recalled.

✉ SE6

♦ 13,642

🚉 South Eastern Trains (zone 3)

@ www.ideal-homes.org.uk/lewisham/bellingham.htm (London surburban history site)

Belmarsh see THAMESMEAD SOUTH WEST

Belmont • Harrow

The family-friendly locality of Belmont fills the gap between KENTON and STANMORE. James Brydges, the phenomenally wealthy owner of CANONS PARK, was dissatisfied with the view along the western avenue from his mansion, so he created a mound called Belmont and had a summer-house built at its summit, probably in the 1720s. Throughout the 19th century the area remained wholly unspoilt, with just a few scattered gentlemen's residences. William Loudon established a model farm on Kenton Lane around 1810 and its main buildings survive today. A row of cottages called Belmont Terrace was built to the east in 1827, on Honeypot Lane. Towards the end of the century the railway came through on its way from HARROW to Stanmore but it was not until 1932 that a station opened at Belmont, in response to the first stirrings of suburban growth and with the financial assistance of the developers. Over the rest of the decade the area was very rapidly built up with middle-class housing, accompanied by shops and the Essoldo cinema at Belmont Circle. Belmont Primary School opened in 1938 and construction of St Anselm's Church began the same year, using materials and furnishings from a demolished church of the same name that had stood in Davies Street, MAYFAIR. The section of the railway from Belmont to Stanmore closed in 1952, leaving Belmont as the terminus of the branch line, which closed completely in 1964. The cinema was demolished in 1970 and replaced by a supermarket. Belmont is dominated by owner-occupied homes, and nearly a quarter of the population is of Indian descent. There is also a significant Jewish minority. At Belmont First and Middle Schools on Hibbert Road, fewer than half the pupils speak English at home.

John Mantle's novel *The Bloody War, Mate*, published in the USA in 2003, is based on the author's recollections of growing up in Tenby Avenue during World War II.

✉ Harrow HA3; Stanmore HA7

♦ 9,506

Belmont · *Sutton*

The southernmost part of Sutton, situated on the edge of the North Downs, and allegedly the original home of the racecourse now located at Epsom. Until the 19th century this was an exposed spot called Little Hell, although 'hell' may simply have been a dialect version of 'hill'. Sometime in the late 1840s an Epsom lime-kiln worker is said to have dug up a bucket half-filled with precious coins and used his new wealth to fund a trip to California to join the gold rush. On his return this unnamed entrepreneur established the California Hotel here. When a station opened in 1865, it too was named California. However, goods intended for delivery here were sometimes shipped to America by mistake, so the stationmaster's wife came up with the name 'Belmont' in 1875. Building to the west of the railway line began in the following decade, replacing lavender, peppermint and strawberry fields. The Victorians took advantage of Belmont's healthy, accessible and affordable setting to build hospitals and other institutions. The South Metropolitan (later Sutton) Schools were a children's home for vagrants and orphans from south London, afterwards serving as a workhouse, a prisoner of war camp and a training centre. A mental hospital was founded in 1877, subsequently gaining national renown as a centre for nervous disorders. Belmont's main phase of suburban growth came in the years after World War I and the locality was fully built up by 1930. The California Hotel took a direct hit by a bomb during the Blitz and was rebuilt after the war as the Belmont. The council's Shanklin Village estate added 424 deck-access flats and maisonettes in the 1960s. The mental hospital became an extension of the Royal Marsden Hospital in 1963. The Sutton Schools were demolished in 1982 and replaced by housing. Belmont's population is 88 per cent white but there are small minorities, classified as 'Asian or Asian British' and 'Chinese or other ethnic group'.

✉ Sutton SM2

♦ 9,790

🚃 Southern (zone 5)

📖 Patricia Berry, *Cheam and Belmont in Old Photographs*, Sutton, 1993

Belsize Park · *Camden*

A (relatively) poor man's HAMPSTEAD, situated to its south-east. The sub-manor of Belsize was first recorded in the early 14th century and Belsize House in 1496. The name derives from Bel-assis, meaning 'beautifully situated'. Well-to-do Londoners built country houses in Belsize in the 17th century, each with its own spacious grounds. Among these was a rebuilt Belsize House, where a sub-lessee nicknamed 'the Welsh ambassador' opened pleasure gardens in 1720. These briefly attracted high-class visitors, including the Prince and Princess of Wales, but like all London pleasure gardens they soon descended into bawdiness and vulgarity, offering entertainments such as mudwrestling and illegal gaming. The gardens were closed in 1740. Belsize was divided into nine leasehold estates in 1808, each based on a single house and its parkland. Early exploitation of the leases was limited to the construction of a handful of lodges and villas, while a new and exceptionally grand Belsize House appeared. Terraces of houses were built north of England's Lane in the mid 1820s but the main phase of suburbanization came after 1850. One by one the country houses were demolished and their grounds covered with detached or semi-detached houses. Each development was given the name of the house it replaced, such as the Rosslyn Grove estate and the Hillfield estate, but the largest was the Belsize Park estate on the site of Belsize House, which ultimately gave its name to the entire suburb. Sussex builder Daniel Tidey was responsible for the first stage of Belsize Park's development, putting up five-storeyed stuccoed houses, but he over-extended himself and went bankrupt in 1870. William Willett and his son, also William, led the next phase, preferring a variety of red-brick designs. Separate 'village centres' evolved on England's Lane and HAVERSTOCK HILL and at BELSIZE VILLAGE. Flats came very early to Belsize Park, built privately from the 1880s and by Hampstead council after 1905. In the 1930s, refugees from central Europe established a synagogue and a Viennese theatre club and opened continental-style cafés. Flat-building reached a peak around this time, when many Victorian properties were replaced. The most impressive of the blocks was the recently restored Isokon development on Lawn Road by the modernist architect Wells Coates. Throughout its existence Belsize Park has acted as a more affordable alternative to Hampstead. The principal change has been that most residents now rent or own flats in subdivided houses rather than occupying the whole property, although gentrification since the 1970s has resulted in the reunification of a number of homes.

Belsize Park has always attracted artists, writers and entertainers. The artist Robert Bevan lived locally and painted several views of the neighbourhood, including *A Street Scene in Belsize Park* (1917), which shows the influence of his acquaintance Paul Gauguin. Other residents have included the composer Frederick Delius, authors Jerome K Jerome, Nicholas Monsarrat and Agatha Christie, actors Sadie Frost, Jude Law, Hugh Laurie, Kate Winslet and Helena Bonham Carter, film director Tim Burton and comedians David Baddiel and Frank Skinner.

✉ NW3

👥 11,653 (Belsize ward)

🚌 Northern Line (zone 2)

📖 Leonie Cohn and Adrian Shire (eds), *Belsize 2000: A Living Suburb*, Belsize Conservation Area Advisory Committee, 2000; Christopher Wade (ed.), *The Streets of Belsize*, Camden History Society, 1991

Belsize Village • *Camden*

An agreeable group of shops and eateries centred around the junction of Belsize Lane with the pedestrianized Belsize Terrace, built on the site of Belsize Farm. The village was part of the BELSIZE PARK estate, first developed by Daniel Tidey from the 1850s and then by William Willett senior, one of the progenitors of the garden suburb concept. Willett built the first shops, originally called Belsize Park Terraces, in a style that has been described as 'standard speculator's Italianate'. He gave up some of his land in 1876 to widen Upper Belsize Terrace (now Belsize Terrace) and create a village green. Belsize Village later evolved into a service zone for the grander homes in neighbouring streets, with a set of mews for servants and horses. Today, the presence of a few empty retail premises betrays the stronger pulling power of nearby HAVERSTOCK HILL, but this is a charming spot, much loved by local residents. The diminutive village square is a popular hang-out on a warm day, although there have been problems with loitering youths and some anti-social activity.

✉ NW3

Belvedere • *Bexley*

A diverse industrial and residential district on land rising from the Thames north-west of ERITH. From the mid 17th century three substantial villas were successively erected beside a crossroads at Blinks Hill on LESSNESS HEATH.

The last of these was named Belvedere House, from the Italian meaning 'beautiful view'. Built in the 1770s, the house became home to a series of peers and knights, culminating with the philanthropist and reformer Sir Culling Eardley. In the mid 19th century, several factors combined to render the area ripe for profitable growth: the establishment of industries beside the Thames, the arrival of the North Kent Railway, and Eardley's willingness to develop his estate with housing for the middle classes. The village gradually expanded from a focal point near the present library. Meanwhile, the riverside hamlet of Picardy became LOWER BELVEDERE, a settlement of terraced cottages for workers at the nearby factories and wharves. Eardley sold up in 1864 and his house became a seamen's mission. Apart from some development towards the south in the 1930s and some bomb damage during World War II, UPPER BELVEDERE remained unspoilt until the demolition of Belvedere House in 1959. Thereafter, many of the larger Victorian properties were subdivided into flats or knocked down and replaced with maisonette blocks or other compact dwellings. Despite the changes, the name of Upper Belvedere retains a cachet locally. In common with much of outer south-east London, the population is predominantly white; a small minority of residents are of Indian origin, mostly Sikhs. Belvedere's industrial half is earmarked for further growth, as part of schemes to boost employment in the Thames Gateway region.

Long-running plans to build a huge waste incinerator on a 40-acre riverside site here are the subject of a public inquiry at the time of writing.

✉ Belvedere, DA17

👥 10,839

🚌 South Eastern Trains (zone 5)

📖 John A Prichard, *Belvedere and Bostall: A Brief History*, Bexley Libraries, 1974

@ www.ideal-homes.org.uk/bexley/belvedere.html (London surburban history site)

Benhilton • *Sutton*

A little-used name for the north-east quadrant of SUTTON, except in the context of All Saints Church and All Saints School. The name Benhilton was originally a medieval version of 'bean hill', with 'ton' added later, so this was an area where (broad) beans were cultivated, probably in a strip-farming system by tenants of Chertsey Abbey, which owned the manor of Sutton. There was woodland too, and Benhill Wood survived until the mid 19th century, when it was cleared to make way for housing after Thomas Alcock became lord of the manor. Alcock laid out Benhill Road, Benhill Street (now Benhill Avenue) and Benhill Wood Road and divided the land along them into building plots. The north end of the area was the Benhill estate, which was for large upper-middle-class houses; to the south lay the poorer Newtown. In the 1860s Alcock endowed All Saints Church for the newly formed parish of Benhilton, and an accompanying school was created at the same time. However, these were still early days for suburbanization of such a distant locale and take-up of the land was sluggish. Many plots remained unfilled until after World War I. Sutton council built a new Benhill estate in the early 1970s, with 429 flats and maisonettes. The estate has recently undergone a much-needed regeneration programme, but the high costs borne by leaseholders have caused controversy. Nowadays, the section of the High Street between St Nicholas Way and Throwley Way (pedestrianized in the 1980s) is Sutton's main shopping thoroughfare, although once that was the area around the Green to the north.

✉ Sutton SM1

Berkeley Square • *Westminster*
An aristocratic quadrangle in central MAYFAIR, which once rivalled GROSVENOR SQUARE as the most fashionable spot in the WEST END. Berkeley House was built on the north side of PICCADILLY in the 1660s for the first Lord Berkeley, with grounds stretching far into Mayfair. The house was sold in 1696 with the stipulation that its grounds be preserved, thus setting aside the space that became the square. After the demolition of Berkeley House in 1733, exceptionally grand properties were built on three sides of the very oblong 'square'. The northern half of the former Berkeley House garden was railed in, while the southern half became the front garden of what is now Lansdowne House, completed by Robert Adam in 1762 for John, Earl of Bute. Its garden and the front rooms of the house were lost in a road scheme in the 1930s, when the drawing room was reinstalled at the Philadelphia Museum of Art and the dining room went to New York's Metropolitan Museum of Art. The house became the exclusive Lansdowne Club, which boasted that it was the only London club to admit women on equal standing with men. Later in the 1930s, 20 of the original houses on the east side of the square were knocked down and replaced by an office building. The last private house in the square went on the market in 1953 at an asking price of £27,000, and the square is now entirely occupied by high-status offices, clubs and other amenities for the very wealthy. Jack Barclay's Rolls-Royce and Bentley showroom is perhaps the world's most prestigious outlet for these vehicles. The BP pension fund acquired over 100 properties in and around the square in 1967 for £12 million and sold them to a private Middle Eastern investor for over £300 million in 2001.

The square was home to the writer Horace Walpole, the statesmen George Canning and Winston Churchill and the general Lord Clive. John Balderston's twice-filmed 1929 play *Berkeley Square* is an early time-travel romance. Berkeley Square's fame comes above all from the wartime song *A Nightingale Sang in Berkeley Square*, recorded by Vera Lynn, Glenn Miller, Frank Sinatra and countless others. BBC TV's Edwardian mini-series *Berkeley Square*, first aired in 1998, told the story of three nannies struggling to improve themselves in the face of a rampant class system. Tim Hindle's book *The Sultan of Berkeley Square* examines the rise and fall of the Polly Peck business empire, whose headquarters were located here.

✉ W1

📖 B H Johnson, *Berkeley Square to Bond Street: Early History of the Neighbourhood*, London Topographical Society, 1952

Bermondsey • *Southwark*
A densely developed – and developing – district, occupying a broad swathe of inner south-east London between TOWER Bridge and the OLD KENT ROAD (A2). Bermondsey's Old English name meant 'Beornmund's island' and points to its genesis on habitable ground amid the marshes. Evidence has been found of Roman and Saxon occupation. The dominant institution until the Reformation was St Saviour's Monastery – Bermondsey Abbey – which was founded for the Cluniac order by merchant Aylwin Child in 1089 on a site to the south of Tower Bridge. Nearby St Mary Magdalene's was built as a parochial church in the 14th century and rebuilt in 1680. Bermondsey's plentiful supply of water and strong links with the City of London favoured the growth of its leather industry, with

tannery pits dotting the area. Thomas Keyse's discovery of a spa in 1770 created a fashionable resort but its popularity was short-lived, the spa closing in 1804. Another side to the area was starkly embodied by Jacob's Island, a riverside slum depicted by Charles Dickens in *Oliver Twist*. The island lay east of St Saviours Dock and south of Bermondsey Wall, where the now-hidden River Neckinger enters the Thames. Bermondsey's growth was encouraged by the opening of the capital's first passenger railway, from Spa Road to DEPTFORD, in 1836; it was soon extended from LONDON BRIDGE to GREENWICH. The borough's population grew rapidly from 27,465 in 1851 to 136,660 in 1891. Southwark Park Road developed into its main shopping street and Southwark Park its only significant open space. The continuing importance of the leather trade was illustrated by the building of the Leather Market on Weston Street in 1833 and the ornate Leather, Hide and Wool Exchange on the corner of Leathermarket Street in the late 1870s, when St Crispin's Church was dedicated to the patron saint of leather and shoes. The Bermondsey wharves brought food processing as an industrial spin-off, and Hartley's Jams established a factory on Rothsay Street. The living conditions of the urban poor inspired the work of the philanthropist and MP Alfred Salter, whose wife Ada became mayor of Bermondsey in 1922. She and her fellow councillors were active in replacing slums with 'modern' tenements, planting trees and turning open spaces into playgrounds. The area suffered greatly in World War II and post-war rebuilding did not treat it kindly. Industries such as leather died away but the Leather Market and the neighbouring Exchange were saved from demolition in 1993 and converted into workspaces. The regeneration of the warehouses to the east of Tower Bridge at SHAD THAMES has brought the Design Museum and other attractions. The fashion designer and Bermondsey resident Zandra Rhodes established the Fashion and Textile Museum at 83 Bermondsey Street. Hundreds of bric-à-brac stalls operate at the Friday morning antiques market in Bermondsey Square. There are also warehouse-based antiques dealers in Bermondsey Street and Tower Bridge Road. Bermondsey Square is presently the focus of a regeneration project, due for completion in 2007, but the market will continue to operate throughout and after the construction work. An even larger regeneration project in the Bermondsey Spa area is due for completion in 2011.

Fête in Bermondsey by the 16th-century Flemish artist Joris Hoefnagel is now in the Marquess of Salisbury's collection at Hatfield House. The singer and actor Tommy Steele was born in Bermondsey in 1936.

> ✉ SE16; SE1
>
> ♦ 34,505 (Grange, Riverside and South Bermondsey wards)
>
> 🚇 Jubilee Line (zone 2)
>
> 📖 Mary Boast, *The Story of Bermondsey*, London Borough of Southwark, 1997
>
> @ www.visitsouthwark.com/bermondsey-antiques-market; www.ftmlondon.org (Fashion and Textile Museum site)

Berrylands • *Kingston*

The eastern part of SURBITON, mostly built up between the wars. 'Berry' was a variant of the Old English 'beorg', or barrow. The manor of la Bergh was recorded in 1241 and a licence granted the enclosure of land at Berowe in 1439. For almost half a millennium the area was to remain in agricultural use, dominated latterly by two large farms – Berry Lodge, on the Tolworth border, and Berrylands to the north. Surbiton council opened a sewage works north of the railway line at Berrylands in 1913. Houses had begun to spread across the fields before World War I but the watershed event was the opening of the Kingston by-pass (A3) in 1927. Berrylands was soon being aggressively marketed as a new suburban haven, marking the end of the dairy herd at Berry Lodge Farm and its supply of milk to Surbiton. Seven local developers clubbed together to find over 90 per cent of the cost of building Berrylands station, which opened in 1933. The following year saw the creation of a small park with a swimming pool called Surbiton Lagoon. The much-loved pool closed for repairs in 1979, never to reopen, and the site is now occupied by the houses of Meldone Close. Kingston University's plans to build a 1,000-bed 'student village' on a disused part of the sewage works were rejected in 2003, when the site's status as metropolitan open land was reaffirmed. Nearly 90 per cent of Berrylands' residents are white. The proportion of one-person households is very high for a suburban district. The Surbiton Racket and Fitness Club is based in Berrylands and is home to the 26.2 Road Running Club.

> ✉ Surbiton KT5; Kingston upon Thames KT1
>
> ♦ 9,278

🚌 South West Trains (zone 5)

Berry's Green • *Bromley*

A straggling North Downs farming hamlet situated in the southern part of the borough. Although shown on most maps, Berry's Hill is not widely recognized locally. Instead it is treated either as an extension of CUDHAM or of BIGGIN HILL, which lie to the east and west respectively. The manor of Berterye was recorded in a charter dated 1145, affirming that tithes were to be given by one Hamo Maminot to the Bishop of Rochester. A map of 1819 locates Bury's Farm here. Bungalows and mobile homes are now set incongruously amidst the woods and farms of this most rural part of Greater London. Cudham's former jail is now a public house. Cudham Church of England Primary School lies a little further along Jail Lane. On Berry's Hill, Cudham tithe barn has been converted to office use and currently houses a publisher and event organizer specializing in classic cars. To the south-west of Berry's Green is Cherry Lodge, a private golf club laid out in 1968 on 130 acres of former farmland. To the south-east is Blackbush Shaw, a 25-acre Woodland Trust property open to the public.

✉ Westerham TN16

Bethnal Green • *Tower Hamlets*

One of the most archetypal EAST END neighbourhoods, situated immediately north of WHITECHAPEL and STEPNEY. It was recorded as Blithehale in the 13th century, when a hamlet began to grow around the site of the present Tube station. By the 16th century merchants and noblemen were building large houses in the fields and Bethnal Green remained a pleasant country retreat on the outskirts of London until about 1700. Thereafter, houses began to line Dog Row (now CAMBRIDGE HEATH Road) and Bethnal Green soon developed into one of the first manufacturing districts in the East End, becoming a separate parish in 1743. It gained fame for its chairmaking and silk-weaving, though market gardens clung on in the eastern part. During the following century Bethnal Green became London's poorest quarter, described by Karl Marx as a 'notorious district' because of its child labour. From the 1860s philanthropists like Angela Burdett-Coutts and George Peabody built solid, if disheartening, tenement housing for the poor. Baroness Burdett-Coutts also sponsored the construction of a spectacular market hall in COLUMBIA ROAD, which was never a success, although the street market has evolved into London's most popular flower market. The original buildings of what became the Victoria and Albert Museum in SOUTH KENSINGTON were re-erected on Cambridge Heath Road between 1868 and 1872 and they now house the Museum of Childhood, which draws nearly a quarter of a million visitors annually. The work of eradicating the slums was taken up in 1900 by the newly created metropolitan borough of Bethnal Green, which also built libraries and washhouses. Bethnal Green Tube station was the scene of the worst civilian disaster of World War II when 173 people, 62 of them children, were killed in a stampede to shelter here during an air raid in March 1943. The clearance of slums and bomb sites in the 1950s broke up long-established communities and, in a creative but doomed response to the problem, the council turned to building clusters of highrise blocks where old neighbourhoods could be re-established vertically. Bethnal Green is now a chequerboard of council and housing association projects dating from every decade since the late 19th century. Some of the few surviving Victorian terraces have undergone gentrification in recent years, with an artistic community forming on the SHOREDITCH border. Like SPITALFIELDS to the west, Bethnal Green has long been a first home for new waves of immigrants, from Huguenot weavers in the 16th and 17th centuries to the South Asian community of today. Over a third of Bethnal Green's residents are now Bangladeshis.

In an early reference to the locality, the medieval ballad of the *Blind Beggar of Bednall Green* tells of a poor man whose daughter marries a knight for a dowry of £3,000 in gold. The song may have been written in the reign of Elizabeth I, though it was subsequently much revised. A sundial in Vallance Road recreation gardens marks the spot where William Booth began his outdoor preaching, before going on to found the Salvation Army in 1878. London's most notorious post-war criminals the Kray twins lived on the same road in a house nicknamed Fort Vallance.

✉ E2

🚶 25,440 (Bethnal Green North and Bethnal Green South wards)

🚌 'one' Railway; Central Line (zone 2)

📖 Gary Haines, *Bethnal Green*, Tempus, 2002; Tim Baker (ed.), *History of the County of*

Middlesex: Early Stepney with Bethnal Green, Victoria History of the Counties of England, 1999

Between the Commons • *Wandsworth*

An estate agents' term for the pricey area between Wandsworth and Clapham Commons, with Broomwood Road as the central axis. Rapid growth in the value of houses has eroded former diversity in favour of upper middle-class homogeneity; some have even spoken of a 'huntin', shootin' 'n' fishin' set'. Tim Butler, in his study of London gentrification (see below), found evidence of a 'staging post' mentality in Between the Commons. It is an area for people moving up in the world, who hope to do well enough to soon move out of London altogether.

✉ SW11

📖 Tim Butler, 'Thinking Global but Acting Local: The Middle Classes in the City', Sociological Research Online, vol. 7, no. 3, 2002 (www.socresonline.org.uk/7/3/butler.html)

Beulah Hill • *Croydon*

This leafy road, linking KNIGHT'S HILL with South Norwood Hill, has been lined with houses since the mid 19th century, though more sparsely then than now. The name is a romanticized version of the original Bewly Hill. The British Museum holds the Beulah Hill treasure trove, 138 gold and silver coins dating from the reign of Edward III, which were discovered in 1953. In 1831 the springs that form the source of the River Effra were opened as Beulah Spa, with a maze and gardens laid out by Decimus Burton. Michael Faraday analysed the water and endorsed its quality. Johann Strauss, the Elder, and his orchestra performed here twice in 1838. For a while the spa drew coachloads of visitors, but the appeal faded in less than two decades. In Charles Dickens' *Sketches by Boz* it is remarked that 'the Gordian knot was all very well in its way … so is the maze at Beulah Spa'. Burton's Tivoli Lodge (originally Rustic Lodge) is the sole surviving structure, at the entrance to a recreation ground on Spa Hill, which is fringed by a small arc of woodland. Beulah Hill remained a distinct settlement until the early years of the 20th century, but has now been absorbed into Upper Norwood. It retains several imposing Victorian houses, most notably St Valery, built in 1880 by Sextus Dyball for a wealthy bookmaker and now divided into flats. At the top of the hill is Beaulieu Heights, with its ITV transmitter. This wooded park is also known as a gay cruising area, and was the scene of a homophobic murder in 2002.

Beulah Hill was the home of the great Victorian preacher C H Spurgeon and of the organist and composer Thomas Attwood, whose friend Felix Mendelssohn twice stayed at his villa. The hill also had Little Menlo, the home of the English agent for Thomas Edison, where the phonograph was first demonstrated in this country. Admiral Robert Fitzroy, captain of HMS *Beagle* when Charles Darwin undertook his famous voyage and subsequently founder of the Meteorological Office, is buried in the churchyard of All Saints, Beulah Hill.

✉ SE19

Bexley • *Bexley*

The district of Bexley lies on the eastern side of the borough, mostly south of the East Rochester Way (A2). BEXLEYHEATH is located to the north-west and SIDCUP to the south-west. Bexley grew up around its mills beside the River Cray, which is bridged by the High Street. Its Old English name, Byxlea, is theorized to have denoted a settlement in a box wood clearing – but some experts disagree, arguing that box trees would have been unlikely to flourish on this terrain. In 814 Kenulph, King of the Mercians, granted lands here to the Archbishop of Canterbury. St Mary's Church is of 13th-century origin and records of 1241 show a manor house on the site of Hall Place. Around 1540 Sir John Champneis (or Champneys), Lord Mayor of London in 1534, started the present Hall Place, probably using material salvaged from demolished monasteries. His son Justinian extended the house in 1556, and Robert Austen more than doubled its size in the mid 17th century. In 1623 William Camden granted the manor of Bexley to Oxford University, which used the revenue to fund a professorship of history. Styleman's almshouses were built in 1755, at a time when the High Street was filling with merchants' homes. In the 1770s a weatherboarded watermill was built on the riverside, together with Cray House, which was probably the home of the mill's owner. The Bexley National Schools were established on Bourne Road in 1834. After Bexley station opened in 1866, the town and outlying villages like COLDBLOW and BRIDGEN began to expand. Built on the grounds of Parkhurst House and Marl House, the Parkhurst estate offered large villas with long gardens for wealthier commuters. Semi-detached properties followed in the decade from 1876. St John's Church was built on Parkhill Road in 1882. Extensive suburbanization took place in the 1920s and 1930s, a process accelerated by the electrification of the railway. After World War II, green-belt legislation preserved the open land to the south and east. This, combined with the village centre's designation as a conservation area in 1972, has restricted opportunities for commercial or residential growth, while enhancing the appeal of OLD BEXLEY. Hall Place has been home to a notorious rake, a music hall star and a school, and is now a civic amenity with delightful gardens. In 2005 Bexley Heritage Trust applied for lottery funding to enhance its facilities and undertake further restoration.

The former Conservative prime minister Edward Heath served as Member of Parliament for Bexley (ultimately Old Bexley and Sidcup) from 1950 to 2001.

✉ Bexley DA5

👥 10,043 (St Mary's ward)

🚆 South Eastern Trains (zone 6)

📖 Malcolm Barr-Hamilton and Leonard Reilly, *From Country to Suburb*, Bexley Libraries, 1995

@ www.hallplace.com;
www.bexleycivicsociety.org.uk

Bexleyheath • *Bexley*

The commercial centre of the borough and a densely built-up suburb, situated to the north-west of BEXLEY. The hamlet of UPTON is of medieval origin and the Crook Log public house is said to date from 1605, but the present-day town centre had nothing but a lone tree and an old windmill until the early 19th century. Farms on the edge of Bexley Heath (as it was) grazed some cattle and sheep on the scrub, but the presence of highwaymen made the heath notoriously dangerous for Kentish travellers to cross. The Crayford and Bexley enclosure acts were passed in 1812 and 1814, partly to get rid of squatters who had begun to move here, and the first legitimate community began to establish itself soon afterwards. Oak House was one of the earliest and largest homes to be built, around 1817. By 1831 the settlement had a church and a market, although the population did not rise much above 2,000 for several decades. Upton was still rural when William Morris and Philip Webb built the Red House in 1860. Trinity Baptist Chapel and Christchurch were built towards the western end of the Broadway, and each is handsome in its own way. Until Bexleyheath station opened in 1895, the settlement was known as Bexley New Town. The station was sited well to the north-west of the town centre because railway director Robert Kersey owned the Brampton Place estate and wanted to profit from its development. Oak House was used as council offices from 1903 and a clock tower was erected in the market square in 1912. Following the railway's electrification in 1926 there was a surge in housebuilding and neo-Georgian shops lined the Broadway. New Ideal Homesteads bought and erased Pelham Farm in 1932, allocating a site for Pelham Primary School. By 1938 all available land for a mile around had been built on. From the 1960s, the centre of Bexleyheath was wholly rebuilt. As local historian Malcolm Barr-Hamilton put it, 'Only the clock tower has survived the remorseless onslaught of Bexleyheath's miserable piecemeal redevelopment'. Oak House was demolished and new civic offices opened in 1980. The Broadway shopping centre was built on the site of Hides department store, the Lord Bexley Arms and Victorian shops that had survived interwar reconstruction. An Asda supermarket replaced the Bexleyheath Bowl and Regal cinema in 1987 and a larger bowling complex was built on a former playing field and war memorial gardens. In 1989 the Woolwich Building Society moved from Equitable House, WOOLWICH to its new corporate headquarters in Bexleyheath. Developments in the 1990s included the part-pedestrianization of the Broadway and the construction of the 126-room Swallow (now Marriott) hotel and the Cineworld multiplex cinema. Broadway Square was completed in 2001. Bexleyheath is classified as a 'metropolitan centre' by the Thames Gateway London Partnership and is a target for further commercial development.

The singer/songwriter Kate Bush was born at Bexleyheath Maternity Hospital in 1958 and grew up in EAST WICKHAM. The formula 1 motor racing tycoon Bernie Ecclestone and the cookery writer Delia Smith were educated in Bexleyheath and both left school at the age of 16.

✉ Bexleyheath DA6 and DA7

👥 20,777 (Brampton and Christchurch wards)

🚆 South Eastern Trains (zone 5)

📖 John Mercer, *Bexley and Bexleyheath: A Pictorial History*, Phillimore, 1995; J C M Shaw,

The Bexley Heath Phenomenon, Bexley Libraries, 1983

Bexley Village *see* OLD BEXLEY

Bickley • *Bromley*

A highly desirable and architecturally lush part of BROMLEY, bordering CHISLEHURST. The name was first recorded in 1279 and may have referred to a woodland clearing belonging to a man called Bicca, or to a clearing on or near a pointed ridge. The area was virtually uninhabited until the 18th century, apart from a hamlet called Cross in Hand, which lay near the present Chislehurst Road. A hunting lodge surrounded by fox-frequented heathland was in the hands of the Wells family from 1759 and the lodge was progressively enlarged to become Bickley Hall. Deptford shipbuilder John Wells bought the 1,200-acre estate from his brother in 1812 but began to sell it off when he lost money in a Maidstone bank crash in 1841. The first roads had been laid out with villas for the upper middle classes by the time that SOUTHBOROUGH (later Bickley) station opened in 1858. Amidst alleged chicanery the Bickley Park estate was acquired by George Wythes, who employed some of the finest architects of the era to build even more superior homes for merchants and bankers, with gardens of two to five acres. When Chislehurst station opened in 1865 it was briefly called Chislehurst and Bickley Park. Wythes built St George's Church on Bickley Park Road in 1865 and gave the site for Bickley Park Cricket Club, which was founded in 1868. The church has a monument to the Wythes family. A water tower was erected at the top of Summer Hill as a landmark for the estate. Wythes' first architect was R Norman Shaw but Bickley's principal creator was Shaw's protégé Ernest Newton, who built 8 Page Heath Lane for himself in 1884. Over the following two decades Newton designed a series of distinctive properties in a style that became increasingly neo-Georgian. From 1905, Newton's successor C H B Quennell laid out a more homogeneous little suburb around the church. The Wythes left Bickley around 1908 and Bickley Hall was leased to a private school. The hall was demolished in 1963 (as was the water tower around the same time) and its remaining parkland was developed with expensive houses, although these occupied smaller plots than the Victorian and Edwardian homes. Over the course of the 20th century the impracticable grandeur of many of the early villas resulted in their demolition or conversion into flats, but there are also numerous survivors and even the replacements are exclusive. Bickley is so popular that estate agents lend its name to neighbouring localities like WIDMORE and Southborough, which provide the area's limited shopping amenities. Like most of the borough, Bickley's population is over 90 per cent white and there is almost no council housing.

The children's writer Enid Blyton taught at Bickley Park School immediately after World War I. This independent day school for boys now operates a preparatory and pre-preparatory school at two sites on Page Heath Lane.

✉ Bromley BR1

♦ 13,904

🚆 South Eastern Trains (zone 5)

📖 Muriel V Searle, *Bickley, Widmore and Plaistow*, European Library, 1990

@ www.bickleypark.co.uk (Bickley Park Cricket Club site)

Biggin Hill • *Bromley*

Once a famous airfield, now a crowded residential district, situated two miles south-east of NEW ADDINGTON. Biggin Hill probably takes its name from a hilltop 'bigging' or habitation. It has been said that it 'started almost in the middle of nowhere, and then grew'. This process began when the Wandsworth speculator Frederick Dougal bought APERFIELD manor at an auction in 1895, subsequently selling off parcels of the land. Growth proceeded at a slower pace after Dougal's death in 1905, but by the outbreak of World War II the township was well developed and there was little further construction for nearly two decades. During the 1950s, All Saints Church, Peckham, was brought here brick by brick and re-erected as St Mark's. When the Macmillan government of the 1960s decreed that every borough should undertake a programme of council house building, the reluctant Bromley council seized upon this remote corner of its fiefdom as a suitable place to fulfil its obligations. Private builders, too, put up houses and flats wherever land could be acquired, prompting from Pevsner the comment that it is 'a place to make even the most ardent free-enterpriser admit the virtues of planning'. Many houses are sited on the hillsides, resulting in split-level layouts with steep gardens. The absence of a rail link has made Biggin Hill a very affordable place to live and new properties continue to be built wherever planning permission can be obtained, with growth between 1971 and 2001 estimated at around 40 per cent. Given the lack of public transport, it is not surprising that Biggin Hill's households have more cars than any other ward in the Greater London area.

Biggin Hill occupies an important place in British history as a military airfield, familiarly known as 'Biggin-on-the-Bump' or simply 'Biggin'. In World War II it became a Spitfire station and was attacked a dozen times during the Battle of Britain. Offensive missions flew from here after the pressure for defensive action was relieved. The airfield was downgraded to non-operational status in 1958 and the Royal Air Force finally left in 1992. The North Camp plays host to a Battle of Britain open day every September, as part of the Biggin Hill International Air Fair. When Croydon airport closed, most of the operators who had not already made the move came to Biggin Hill, which is now the most popular light aviation centre south of London, with a collection of thriving light aircraft clubs. A new passenger terminal handles executive charter flights and occasional scheduled diversions.

✉ Westerham TN16

♟ 10,131

📖 Josephine Cole, *Biggin Hill: Then and Now*, Tempus, 1999

@ www.bigginhillairport.com

Billingsgate · *City/Tower Hamlets*
A wholesale fish market formerly located in the CITY OF LONDON ward of the same name and now based in DOCKLANDS. Billingsgate probably began as a Roman watergate on the Thames and it was used by the Saxons as a small port for general cargo. Most of London's fish was landed upstream at Queenhithe until the late 15th century, after which it began to decline as a result of its inaccessibility to larger vessels. Billingsgate's status was officially recognized by an Act of Parliament of 1699, which established 'a free and open market for all sorts of fish whatsoever'. Sales were made in wooden sheds until the construction in 1850 of the first trading hall, which was replaced by a larger structure in 1877. This building survives today on Lower Thames Street. With the widening of that road in the late 1960s, trading at Billingsgate became increasingly impractical and the market transferred to a renovated warehouse at the West India Docks in 1982. Each year since the move the Lord Mayor of London has presented the nominal rent to the Mayor of Tower Hamlets

in the form of a gift of fish, which is then distributed to old people's homes in the borough.

The old market caught the attention of many artists, attracted by the opportunity to present life in the raw. William Hogarth's exuberant *Shrimp Girl* (c.1750) hangs in the National Gallery. The swearing of workers in the market made Billingsgate – and its fishwives – synonymous with coarse language.

✉ EC3 (old Billingsgate); E14 (new Billingsgate)

📖 Colin Manton and John Edwards, *Bygone Billingsgate*, Phillimore, 1989

@ www.billingsgate-market.org.uk

Birkbeck · *Bromley*
Situated between ANERLEY and ELMERS END, this is no longer a distinct place, just the identity of a station and tramstop. The Birkbeck Freehold Land Society built several estates in the London area during the second half of the 19th century. Its name honoured Dr George Birkbeck, the physician, philanthropist and co-founder of the London Mechanics' Institution, which later became London University's Birkbeck College. The society began laying out housing here in the 1870s and the parish church of St Michael was consecrated in 1908. The creation of Allen Road just before World War I marked the completion of the Birkbeck estate. Although the estate straddled the railway, it was not until 1930 that a station was added. Behind the station is Beckenham Cemetery, opened in 1876 by what has become Britain's oldest surviving commercial cemetery company, now called Birkbeck Securities Ltd. Among the graves are those of the plumber Thomas Crapper, the cricketer W G Grace and the car manufacturer Frederick Wolseley.

Walter de la Mare, best known for his children's poetry, lived in Mackenzie Road from 1899 to 1908.

✉ SE20; Beckenham, BR3

🚌 Southern (zone 4); Croydon Tramlink, Route 2 (zone 4)

The Bishops Avenue · *Barnet*
An ultra-exclusive street running from the northern tip of HAMPSTEAD HEATH to EAST FINCHLEY. Neighbouring Winnington Road is almost as well-heeled. HIGHGATE golf course lies to the east and HAMPSTEAD GARDEN SUBURB to the west. The name derives from the bishops of London, who owned a large hunting park in the area during the late Middle Ages. This is probably the most 'desirable'

address outside central London, if you like ostentatious displays of wealth. One house, The Towers, sold for around £10 million in 1992 – a phenomenal price at that time. Its features include an island with palm trees in the middle of its indoor swimming pool. Another, the twelve-bedroom, eleven-bathroom Summer Palace, built in 1991, has a brass and crystal glass lift, a comprehensive leisure complex and a central atrium. A Middle Eastern businessman bought it in 1995 for £6.75 million. Prices on the avenue have continued to spiral and when Toprak Mansion went on the market in 2005, offers in the region of £50 million were sought. Barnet council has taken exception to some of the more vulgar monstrosities built in the last decade or two, but realistically the avenue is beyond redemption and might as well be allowed to continue as an object of amazement and amusement. However, since London's millionaires prefer to live in BELGRAVIA or KENSINGTON, some properties have lain vacant in recent years and the latest trend is for their replacement by upscale, low-rise apartment blocks.

The entertainer Gracie Fields used to live on the Bishops Avenue. 'Why not talk about Bishops Avenue / I've got a lovely house on Bishops Avenue,' sang Elton John in his 1988 parody of *Give Peace a Chance*.

✉ N2

Bishopsgate • *City*

A former Roman road and now the City of London's highest rising street, with office towers clustered around its southern half. Bishopsgate (A10) runs north from Gracechurch Street to NORTON FOLGATE. The gate in the city wall was called *Porta Episcopi* in Domesday Book, and this was anglicized as Bishopsgate by the 12th century. It is said that the name refers to Saint Erkenwald, who was Bishop of London for eleven years in the late 7th century. Houses began to appear on both sides of the gate in the 13th century and by the 16th century the whole road was lined with buildings, including the merchants' residences of Crosby Place and Gresham House and the churches of St Botolph, St Helen and St Ethelburga. Like many of the gates in the City wall, Bishopsgate was demolished in 1761. Continuous rebuilding has left nothing of the medieval street except for the core fabric of the surviving churches. The most pleasing remnants of the Victorian era are Dirty Dick's pub and the Bishopsgate Institute, both near PETTICOAT LANE. Crosby Place's great hall survived until 1908, when, threatened by the prospect of demolition, it was taken down and rebuilt on CHEYNE WALK in Chelsea. From the 1960s a succession of office blocks and towers has made Bishopsgate one of the City's most unashamedly commercial thoroughfares. At its northern end the BROADGATE complex borders the street's west side. The NatWest Tower was completed on the site of the former Gresham House in 1981, when it became Britain's tallest building. A bird's eye view reveals the tower to be designed in the shape of the National Westminster Bank's symbol: three intersecting chevrons forming a chopped-cornered triangle. The bank moved out in the early 1990s and the building has since been renamed Tower 42. In 1993 a massive IRA truck bomb killed a freelance photographer and caused £350 million worth of damage when it exploded outside 99 Bishopsgate. This marked the culmination of a terrorist campaign against City targets, prompting the Corporation of London to create the so-called 'ring of steel' that reduced access to the central part of the City and placed police checkpoints on the remaining routes. East of Bishopsgate the Swiss Re building at 30 St Mary Axe has become one of London's favourite landmarks since its completion in 2004 on the site of the Baltic Exchange, which was the victim of another IRA bomb. This bulbous tower is commonly known as 'the Gherkin'. Another spectacular tower is planned for Bishopsgate but its construction is dependent on planning permission and market conditions.

A tax record for 1596 notes that William Shakespeare was lodging in the parish of St Helen's, Bishopsgate, but there is no confirmation that this was *the* William Shakespeare. The dramatist was familiar with Crosby Place and used it as the setting for Gloucester's plotting in *Richard III*.

✉ EC2; E1

👤 106

@ www.bishopsgate.org.uk (Bishopsgate Institute); www.tower42.com; www.30stmaryaxe.com

Blackfen • *Bexley*

A district on the northern fringe of SIDCUP populated predominantly by white owner-occupiers. Its name is self-explanatory: this was an area of dark-coloured marshy ground. Blackfen was first recorded in 1241 as part of the manor of BEXLEY. Days Lane Farm and

Black Fenn Farm were mentioned in 17th-century documents. In 1770 one of Blackfen's cottages was converted to a sham chapel with a little spire, to enhance the southward view from Danson House. Blackfen itself had no grand house with attendant servants' lodgings, unlike neighbouring BLENDON and LA-MORBEY, and the land remained entirely in agricultural use until the 1920s. With the break-up of the DANSON estate and improvements in nearby railways and roads, New Ideal Homesteads and other speculative builders seized on Blackfen as a development prospect. Between 1930 and the outbreak of World War II almost all the fields were covered with houses, while shopping parades appeared on Blackfen Road and at the Oval. C R Leech built the Queenswood and Westwood estates on either side of Blackfen Road, offering semi-detached, three-bedroomed houses for £675. Unusually, self-built properties were a feature of other streets. Blackfen Central School opened for juniors in 1933 and Blackfen Girls' School in 1938. The latter is now the borough's most popular school. Growth continues in Blackfen, with new homes shoehorned in wherever opportunities arise.

One of the rare uses of a machine gun in a British bank robbery occurred in Blackfen in August 1993.

✉ Sidcup DA15

🚶 10,419 (Blackfen and Lamorbey ward)

📖 Susan J Ilott, *Blackfen: From Country to Suburb*, Bexley Libraries, 1977

@ www.ideal-homes.org.uk/bexley/ blackfen.html (London surburban history site)

Blackfriars • *City*

A historic religious and theatrical site located at the eastern end of Victoria EMBANKMENT, now dominated by a railway terminal and gyratory traffic system. The Black Friars (or Dominicans) were so called because they wore long black mantles over their white robes. In 1224 the friars established a priory on the east side of Shoe Lane and moved to what is now the east side of New Bridge Street in 1278. The Dominican Order established more than 50 priories in England but this was probably the most important and it was the site of early parliamentary conclaves. The order in England was dissolved by Henry VIII in 1538. Unlike some other religious buildings, the priory did not survive to serve a different purpose. It was reduced to a pile of rubble

when the actor James Burbage acquired much of the site to build the Blackfriars Theatre in 1596. William Shakespeare was involved in the enterprise and bought a house in nearby Ireland Yard. The theatre closed in the Civil War and was demolished in 1655. Playhouse Yard marks its site. Blackfriars Bridge was built in 1769, using funds generated from rents on the houses and shops of London Bridge. Structural problems caused by water scouring necessitated its replacement exactly a century later. Blackfriars Railway Bridge has also been built twice; the piers of the original still protrude from the water. In 1864 the London, Chatham and Dover Railway Co. opened Blackfriars station on Ludgate Hill. The station moved to its present site by the river in 1886. Subsequent extensions and alterations have only served to compound its status as the ugliest main-line terminal in London. A radical remodelling by the architects Alsop and Störmer, planned in the late 1990s, has yet to start. The nearby Black Friar is regarded as the finest Arts and Crafts pub in London. East of Blackfriars station a bombed-out warehouse was converted into the Mermaid Theatre in the late 1950s, but has primarily been used as a conference facility and nightclub in recent years.

Early on 18 June 1982 the body of Italian financier Roberto Calvi was found hanged under Blackfriars Bridge, his pockets stuffed with bricks and stones. Calvi, dubbed 'God's banker' because of his ties to the Vatican's bank, IOR, had been seeking help for his failing Banco Ambrosiano after escaping house arrest in Italy.

✉ EC4

🚆 South Eastern Trains; Thameslink; Circle Line; District Line (zone 1)

⛴ Blackfriars Millennium pier

Blackheath • *Lewisham/Greenwich*

A pretty village and common, separated from GREENWICH PARK by Shooters Hill Road and originally centred around the junction of the roads to GREENWICH, WOOLWICH and LEE. Most of the heath, which got its name either from the colour of the soil or from its bleakness, was in the hands of the earls (originally barons) of Dartmouth from 1673. In addition to its use as pasture, Blackheath was extensively quarried for gravel, particularly in the 18th century. This left a terrain of craters and ravines, a few of which survived to be filled with bomb rubble after World War II; subsidence here in April 2002 caused serious disruption for months afterwards. The first street to be completed was the prosperous Dartmouth Row in the 1690s, but with that exception the Dartmouths were slow to grant leases on their freehold and the heath in 1780 had just a few roadside cottages on its southern edge. It was over the next 25 years that a settlement developed, expanding after the Napoleonic Wars and acquiring the name Blackheath Village. Its present charm and popularity owe much to the survival of properties dating from this period. North-east of the village's central triangle, impressive residences went up on land belonging to the speculator John Cator after he began to sell leases in 1793. South Row (which did not survive the Blitz) and Montpelier Row were constructed as three-storey terraces, while The Paragon is a unique crescent of seven pairs of houses linked by colonnades, designed by Michael Searles. The North Kent Railway Co. opened Blackheath station in 1849 after local objections prevented the cutting of a line through Greenwich Park. The railway stimulated a housing boom in the 1860s and 1870s, and several of the original cottages were cleared to make way for more salubrious properties. At this time, the heath itself passed into the hands of the Metropolitan Board of Works after the Earl of Dartmouth agreed to waive his manorial rights. Its 270 acres are now given over to kite-flying, jogging and other leisure activities. Salem House in Dickens' novel *David Copperfield* was modelled on a Blackheath school. The late-Victorian Blackheath Halls and the neighbouring Conservatoire of Music and the Arts are on Lee Road.

Blackheath has a proud sporting history. It was the site of the first golf club in England, laid out by James I, and Blackheath was one of the founder members of the Rugby Football Union. The Blackheath Harriers Athletics Club moved south to HAYES in 1927.

✉ SE3

☃ 25,116 (Lewisham's Blackheath ward and Greenwich's Blackheath Westcombe ward)

🚌 South Eastern Trains (zone 3)

⎙ Neil Rhind, *Blackheath Village and Environs, 1790–1970*, vol 1, Bookshop Blackheath, 1976

@ www.blackheath.org (Blackheath Society site)

Blackheath Park · *Greenwich*

A late Georgian and early Victorian private estate, south-east of BLACKHEATH village, bordering KIDBROOKE. Not all maps show the name, but estate agents are very fond of it. Despite modern intrusions, this remains one of the most distinctive residential districts in London. It is also known as the Blackheath Cator estate, after Bromley businessman John Cator. He bought the land cheaply and demolished Wricklemarsh House, a classical mansion built for Sir Gregory Page by John James, who had worked with Hawksmoor and Wren. After Cator died in 1806, his heirs began to sell off plots of land and Blackheath Park took shape during the 1820s and 1830s. Another flurry of building followed in the late 1850s and again in the 1930s, when the expiry of leases removed constraints on infilling. The Cators installed lodges at the main entrances to the estate and granted land for St Michael and All Angels Church, and later for the Blackheath Conservatoire of Music and the Arts and Blackheath Concert Hall. After World War II, the local authority and the London County Council compulsorily purchased several plots and put up blocks of flats, but resistance by preservation groups reduced the intended scale of development. The estate retained its private status, with the municipal authorities contributing to the freeholder's maintenance fund. Private housing schemes, principally by Span Developments Ltd, also resulted in the demolition of original properties, mainly between 1957 and 1965. Although the Span development encountered opposition at the time, it has been widely acknowledged since as representing the best in contemporary design.

The philosopher John Stuart Mill lived at 113 Blackheath Park for 20 years and wrote *On Liberty* and *Utilitarianism* there. Blackheath Park's other distinguished residents have included Richard Bourne, who founded P&O, the wine merchant Robert Barrow, and the shipbuilder Sir Alfred Yarrow.

✉ SE3

Blackheath Vale · *Lewisham*

An artificial depression and the settlement that lies within it, lying north of BLACKHEATH village. Encroachment by the Earl of Dartmouth brought him possession of this part of the heath around 1700; the vale itself was created by the extraction of sand in the mid 18th century. The first structures were two windmills, erected on the perimeter in 1770, which stood for nearly 70 years. After the excavators abandoned the pit, the Dartmouth estate granted leases for livery stables and cottages, and between 1789 and 1810 a small village grew up in this dry and sheltered basin. Blackheath Brewery produced ales, stouts and porter from about 1823 until 1875, around which time most of the original cottages in the vale were pulled down. Their successors included more substantial, semi-detached properties as well as All Saints' Primary School. After World War II, the bomb-damaged Talbot Houses had to be demolished and were replaced by Goffer's House. Terraced cottages that blend passably with their Victorian neighbours have filled other gaps more recently.

✉ SE3

Blackhorse Road • *Waltham Forest*

A station and commercial thoroughfare in west WALTHAMSTOW. Originally called Werdestrete, the road came into existence in Saxon times as a route from the common lands of HIGHAM HILL to the nearest mills, at what is now LEA BRIDGE. 'Blackhorse' is a corruption of Black House, a mansion that stood at the southern end of the road in the 18th century. The Warner family acquired the crumbling Black House in 1813 and replaced it with a Regency villa called the Clock House. Perhaps to make a deliberate contrast with the earlier property, the Warners built their new home using white Suffolk bricks. Commercial and industrial properties began to line Black Horse Lane later in the century and its southern section was renamed Black Horse Road in 1888. Around this time Sir Courtenay Warner began to lay out streets of terraced housing on the family's extensive estates in Walthamstow and LEYTON and he instigated the construction of the Tottenham and Forest Gate Railway to boost the popularity of the project. The line opened in 1894, as did Black Horse Road station, sited on the eastern side of the road. The Victoria Line arrived here in 1968, adopting a one-word spelling of 'Blackhorse' and creating the only intermediate interchange on the Gospel Oak to Barking line. The old mainline station was demolished in 1981 and its platforms were moved west to allow the creation of a common entrance for the two services. The Clock House still stands at the western end of Mission Grove. The much-altered villa was restored in the early years of the 21st century.

✉ E17

🚇 Silverlink Metro (zone 3); Victoria Line (zone 3)

Blackwall • *Tower Hamlets*

A historic riverside district situated east of POPLAR. The name probably derives from the embankment built to prevent tidal inundation, although there is a legend that Alfred the Great had a weir constructed nearby to strand invading Danish ships that had sailed up the River Lea. The first wharves appeared at Blackwall in the late 15th century. This was later than the developments between ST KATHERINE'S and LIMEHOUSE but 200 years before the drainage of STEPNEY Marshes (on what became known as the Isle of Dogs) allowed waterfront construction on the peninsula, so Blackwall long remained an isolated satellite of the port of London. Shipbuilding and repairs were carried on, and the *Mary Rose* was refitted here in 1514. Blackwall had a proud maritime tradition and both Walter Raleigh and Admiral Lord Nelson are said to have had homes in the area. The first colonists of Virginia sailed from Blackwall in 1606, and later the East India Docks attracted a thriving international trade. Today, Blackwall is best known for its tunnels under the Thames, opened in 1897 and 1967. Until recently, Blackwall had a declining residential population and a high level of social deprivation, but luxury riverside apartments began to be built from the late 1980s onwards. The latest and largest of these is New Providence Wharf, which has 550 apartments, a hotel, and an office, shopping and leisure complex. It has no perceptible link with the neighbouring community or Blackwall's heritage; its promotional literature referred, without apparent irony, to 'this brave new world'.

Most London-based television dramas have fictional settings, like Walford in *EastEnders* and Sun Hill in *The Bill*, but Blackwall was the home of Blue Watch, the firefighters of Carlton's series *London's Burning*, which ran from 1988 to 2002.

✉ E14

👥 11,939 (Blackwall and Cubitt Town ward)

🚇 Docklands Light Railway, Beckton branch (zone 2)

📖 Stephen Porter (ed.), *Survey of London, vols 43 and 44: Poplar, Blackwall and the Isle of Dogs, the Parish of All Saints*, Athlone Press, 1994

Blendon • *Bexley*

A pleasant suburban locality situated midway between BEXLEYHEATH and SIDCUP. The first known resident was Jordan de Bladindon, who built a house here in the 14th century. In the 1650s the house's Royalist owners had to mortgage the estate to pay a fine imposed on them after the Civil War, but they regained possession following the Restoration. The house later came into the hands of Jacob Sawbridge, an MP and director of the South Sea Company, whose collapse in 1720 owing to speculation mania caused a national financial crisis. A new Blendon Hall was erected in 1763, accompanied by significant improvements to the 90-acre grounds. Like most of the surrounding area, the construction of the Rochester Way (A2) was the catalyst for Blendon's suburbanization. The house and grounds were put up for sale in 1929 and bought for £29,000 by D C Bowyer, a prominent local builder. Bowyer's homes attracted middle-class buyers, but the new residents were not rich enough to fulfil his hopes of converting Blendon Hall into a private school, so the 20-bedroom mansion was demolished and replaced by more housing. The Blendon and Penhill ward has a high proportion of married, Christian owner-occupiers, who are overwhelmingly of white British origin.

✉ Bexley DA5

👥 10,418 (Blendon and Penhill ward)

📖 Roger Mayo, *Blendon: From the Earliest Times*, Bexley Local Studies and Archive Centre, 2002

Bloomsbury • *Camden*

London's principal academic and cultural quarter, noted for its fine squares; COVENT GARDEN lies to the south and EUSTON to the north. From the 13th century this was the manor of Blemund'sbury, probably named after one William Blemund, whose family originated from Blémont in France. The Earl of Southampton laid out London's first formal square in 1661 as a kind of forecourt to his mansion, Southampton House, and the Duke of Montagu built Montagu House on Great Russell Street in 1679. The latter mansion soon burned down but was quickly rebuilt. A succession of high-class developments progressed westwards and northwards over the course of the 18th century to form the present grid of handsome streets and squares, of which the finest is Bedford Square and the largest is RUSSELL SQUARE. Following the death of Sir Hans Sloane, the government acquired his collection of antiquities for the nation and bought Montagu House, which opened to the public as the British Museum in 1759. The museum extended the collection with a wealth of books, artefacts, relics and classical sculptures, via donations, government purchases and trophies from imperial expansion and military victories, including the Rosetta Stone and the Parthenon sculptures known as the Elgin Marbles. By 1820 the museum had entirely outgrown its accommodation and Sir Robert Smirke was appointed to design new buildings. Construction began in 1823 and a series of new wings enlarged, and then replaced, Montagu House over a period of three decades. A reading room followed, and new galleries and wings have continued to expand the British Museum ever since. University College London (as it is now called) was founded in 1828 and eight years later became part of an overarching body called the University of London, which also incorporated King's College. The college's first home was the Wilkins Building, erected on land that had been intended for yet another Bloomsbury square. Like the British Museum, the university has grown inexorably and now fills a swathe of Bloomsbury east of GOWER STREET. Nearly 30 per cent of Bloomsbury's residents are students. Only 19 per cent of the population is married and there are very few children. With around five million visitors a year the British Museum is rivalled only by the National Gallery and Tate Modern as London's most popular attraction.

The Bloomsbury Group, active in the early part of the 20th century, was a school of socially aware men and women of letters, of whom the best known was Virginia Woolf. The group first came together in 1904, meeting at the Gordon Square home of Clive and Vanessa Bell. Other prominent members included the biographer Lytton Strachey and the economist John Maynard Keynes.

✉ WC1

👥 9,224

📖 Jean Moorcroft Wilson, *Virginia Woolf's London: A Guide to Bloomsbury and Beyond*, Tauris Parke, 2000; Brian Girling, *Holborn, Bloomsbury and Clerkenwell*, Tempus, 2000

@ www.thebritishmuseum.ac.uk; www.lon.ac.uk (University of London)

Blythe Hill • *Lewisham*

A roughly conical hill rising to almost 200 feet, located on the west side of CATFORD.

Although marked as such in some street atlases, Blythe Hill is not generally recognized as the identity of the wider locality. A Roman road supposedly ran across the hill from the direction of NUNHEAD. Designed by Samuel Teulon in 1842, Blythe Hill House was one of the last mansions to be built in the parish of Lewisham. The enclave of housing around Blythe Hill Lane was begun in the 1860s, when the Blythe Hill Tavern was built on Stanstead Road (A205). Most of the area's present-day properties are Edwardian. Blythe Hill House was demolished around 1895 and its grounds became part of BROCKLEY Farm. The London County Council acquired 18 acres of the farm in 1935, which were opened to the public as Blythe Hill Fields. Trees were planted to mark the coronation of George VI in 1937 and part of the park was converted to allotments during World War II. Lewisham council took over Blythe Hill Fields from the GLC in 1971. The Blythe Hill Tavern is now an Irish pub, which stages regular traditional music sessions.

Blythe Hill is the title of a song by local musician Gordon Giltrap and of a jazz track and album by John Rangecroft, Marcio Mattos and Stu Butterfield.

✉ SE6

Bond Street • *Westminster*

London's most expensive street for retailers, according to recent research on land values, running north from PICCADILLY to OXFORD STREET through the eastern part of MAYFAIR. Bond Street was begun in 1686 and its name honours Sir Thomas Bond, who helped restore Charles II to the throne. New Bond Street, added in two stages, reached Oxford Street in the 1720s. Almost from its creation Bond Street has been a fashionable address. Among the 18th-century lodgers and residents who helped popularize it were the writers Jonathan Swift, Edward Gibbon, Laurence Sterne and James Boswell, the statesman Lord Chatham (William Pitt, the Elder), the poet James Thomson and Admiral Lord Nelson. By the end of that century the street was lined with tailors, jewellers, chemists, perfumers, and purveyors of every kind of superior foodstuff. Georgian Bond Street was not just the best place to shop, it was the best place to be *seen* shopping; 'Bond Street Loungers' were men who took equal pleasure in adorning themselves and in surveying the titled ladies who promenaded in the afternoons. In Regency times, Beau Brummell reigned supreme among all the dandies, making the reputation

of his tailor, Weston, in Old Bond Street. Every variety of merchant in search of a smart address wanted to set up shop here. Samuel Chappell, the music publisher, arrived in 1811. Asprey's, the jewellers, moved to New Bond Street from MITCHAM in the 1830s. In 1873 Richard Benson and William Hedges began making cigarettes at 13 Old Bond Street. In 1891 the Northumbrian ladies' outfitter Fenwick's opened its London branch in New Bond Street. Art galleries and auctioneers fitted in splendidly amidst the goldsmiths and china shops, culminating in the arrival of Sotheby's at its present location in 1917. Two years later came the photographic dealer Wallace Heaton. Mid-20th-century incomers included tour operators, airline offices and employment agencies. Bond Street continues to attract the most prestigious names, especially in contemporary couture. During the 1990s, DKNY and Gianni Versace opened showrooms in Old Bond Street, while Louis Vuitton and Tommy Hilfiger came to New Bond Street. Nearby South Molton Street is a pedestrianized echo of the Bond Street retail experience.

Around the corner at 25 Brook Street is the Handel House Museum, which was home to the great composer from 1723 until his death in 1759. Rock guitarist Jimi Hendrix lived next door in 1969. The poet, painter and engraver William Blake lived at 17 South Molton Street.

✉ W1

🚇 Central Line; Jubilee Line (zone 1)

📖 Jean Desebrock, *The Book of Bond Street Old and New*, Tallis Press, 1978

Borough • *Southwark*

SOUTHWARK's historic commercial centre, noted especially for its inns. The name recalls the presence of a defensive 'burgh' protecting LONDON BRIDGE. The Church of St George the Martyr was built in the 12th century and Marshalsea gaol was in existence by 1381, when it was attacked during the Peasants' Revolt. In the *Pickwick Papers*, Charles Dickens described Borough as home to 'several ancient inns; great rambling queer old places with galleries and passages'. The most illustrious of these was the Tabard, from which the pilgrims of the *Canterbury Tales* began their journey. Pilgrimage Street, Manciple Street and Pardoner Street all commemorate Chaucer's tale tellers. The White Hart Inn was the headquarters of Jack Cade during his revolt of 1450 against Henry VI. A 17th-century print shows a Civil War fort on Borough High Street guarding the southern approaches to London from Royalist attack but most of the Borough was burned down in 1676, in the so-called Little Fire of London. The Tabard was rebuilt as the Talbot after the fire – the change of name apparently being the result of a misunderstanding by the signwriter. The timbered and galleried George Inn was also rebuilt and is the only survivor from the days when the inns thrived on their position serving the stagecoach route from London to the south coast, and when St Margaret's Hill, now part of Borough High Street, formed a wealthy enclave amidst the surrounding poverty of Southwark. St George's Church was stoutly rebuilt in the mid 1730s. The Talbot was pulled down in 1875 despite protests and Marshalsea gaol met the same fate, to less dismay, in 1887. Borough station opened three years later. Borough market is of medieval origin and has traded at its present site for 250 years. In response to declining business, the wholesale market has recently expanded into retail, focusing itself on the 'foodie' consumer, with an emphasis on organic and speciality farmers' produce.

Charles Dickens' father was imprisoned in the Marshalsea and the author made it the birthplace of Little Dorrit. Borough market pops up in several British films, including *Lock, Stock and Two Smoking Barrels*, *Wilde* and *Bridget Jones's Diary*. The Borough is the setting for the opening part of Sarah Waters' 'lesbian Victoriana' *Fingersmith* (2002).

✉ SE1

🚇 Northern Line (zone 1)

📖 Mary Boast, *The Story of the Borough*, London Borough of Southwark, 1997; Ptolemy Dean et al, *The Borough Market Book: From Roots to Renaissance*, Civic Books, 2004

@ www.boroughmarket.org.uk

Bostall Heath • Greenwich/Bexley

An expansive area of former common land situated north of EAST WICKHAM and BEXLEYHEATH. The developed part is often known simply as Bostall, a name that probably derives from Old English words meaning 'a secure place', since it provided refuge from the regular flooding of the lower-lying land nearer the Thames. The commoners resisted attempts by Queen's College, Oxford to enclose and develop the heath in the 1880s. The college had appointed a local solicitor and builder, whose

homes were trashed during riotous scenes, and the authorities drafted in 200 extra police and called out the fire brigade to hose down the mob. The battle was resolved in court, when Queen's College lost the case and then lost interest in the land, and the Metropolitan Board of Works acquired and preserved 155 acres. East of Knee Hill the large gardens of some Victorian properties have become part of the woodland again, including an ornamental pond. The Royal Arsenal Co-operative Society built housing to the north-west from the end of the 19th century, digging a chalk mine to provide material for road foundations and plasterwork in the houses. The land to the south-east of the preserved heath and woodland was developed in the 1930s. The council restrained the more impatient aspirations of speculative builders but construction nevertheless exceeded 500 homes a year for most of the decade, mostly large three-bedroom semi-detached houses. Cabbage fields between Abbott's Walk and King Harolds Way were covered with the distinctive bungalows of the St Hilary estate. To the south, the orchards of Dixons Farm were built over, although some fruit trees survived in back gardens. Shops, schools and in some cases roads did not come until after the first residents had moved in. Bostall suffered some serious bomb damage during World War II owing to its proximity to targets in ERITH. A single parachute mine damaged more than a thousand properties in 1941. After hostilities ended the remaining empty corners of the district were temporarily used for prefabricated accommodation before their replacement by more semi-detacheds. St Andrew's Church began as a wooden structure in 1935 and was replaced by a permanent building on the same site in 1957. Methodist and Roman Catholic churches were also built in the 1950s. In 1984 St Andrew's became the mother church of the newly created parish of Bostall Heath. A large Victorian house on Bostall Hill called Shornells, which the Co-operative Society had used as a training centre, was replaced by the Greenwich and Bexley Cottage Hospice in 1994. A second phase of the hospice's development was completed in 2003. Co-operative Woods has one of London's best camping and caravanning sites, located off Federation Road and open all year round.

✉ SE2; Bexleyheath DA7

📖 John A Prichard, *Belvedere and Bostall: A Brief History*, Bexley Libraries, 1994

Boston Manor • *Hounslow/Ealing*

A Tube station and Jacobean mansion and their immediate vicinity, located on the HANWELL/BRENTFORD border. This was Bordeston in 1377, so the name has nothing to do with any other Boston and is probably related to a Saxon farmer named Bord. Boston Manor was built in 1623 for Lady Mary Reade in preparation for her marriage to Sir Edward Spencer of Althorp. A merchant banker, James Clitherow, bought the house in 1670 and immediately set about enlarging it and adding some ornamentation. Another James Clitherow and his wife Jane entertained William IV and Queen Adelaide to dinner here in 1834. From the mid 19th century, houses began to line Boston Road as Hanwell stretched out its tentacles following the arrival of the Great Western Railway. The Metropolitan District Railway skirted the northern edge of the mansion's grounds in 1880 and Boston Road station was built, opening up the southern part of Hanwell to suburban development. The station was renamed Boston Manor in 1911. The Clitherow family remained at Boston Manor until 1923, when most of the grounds were sold for housebuilding and Hounslow council bought the house. Although its exterior is dour, some of the rooms and furnishings are splendid, especially the elaborate state drawing room on the first floor. The walls are hung with paintings from the borough's art collection. Opening times are limited but admission is free. Former farmland to the south and west of the house is now a public park, bisected by the M4 motorway.

✉ W7; Brentford TW8

🚇 Piccadilly Line (zone 4)

@ www.hounslow.info/bostonmanor

Botany Bay • *Enfield*

A remote hamlet situated on the Ridgeway (A1005), which links west ENFIELD with the M25 at Potters Bar. It takes its name from the former Australian penal colony, implying an isolated settlement in the same way that 'WORLD'S END' was used two miles to the south. The hamlet came into being after the enclosure of ENFIELD CHASE in 1777 and it had gained its cheeky name by 1819, when C G Greenwood identified it on his map of Middlesex. Botany Bay has been home to a series of simple chapels during its short life

and still has one today. The first was in existence by 1851 and had links with a now-obscure evangelical sect called the Countess of Huntingdon's Connexion, but it did not see out the century. Terraced cottages and some of the larger properties are of Victorian origin, while 20th-century amenities include the Robin Hood public house and a farm shop. Botany Bay Cricket Club is located on East Lodge Lane and since 2000 the Right Start Montessori School has operated from a unit in its grounds. In 2001 Enfield council contemplated relocating Enfield golf course to Rectory Farm but the incoming Conservative administration abandoned the proposal a year later. The council firmly opposes attempts to develop Botany Bay in almost any way, stating that 'the character and prominent ridge-top location of the village means that no sites exist where further building development will not harm the green-belt setting or the landscape of the Enfield Chase heritage area. The council will therefore resist development on backland sites, in spacious gardens and grounds, and in substantial gaps along road frontages.'

East Lodge Gardens hosts an 'antiques village' and a balloon flight operator. A permissive path crosses Bay Farm, which keeps geese, sheep and shire horses.

✉ Enfield EN2

Botwell • *Hillingdon*

Much of the heart of modern HAYES was once called Botwell and the old identity is still visible in the names of roads, community facilities and the local ward. First recorded in 831, this was the site of a spring with supposedly curative properties; 'bōt' was an Old English word for 'remedy'. Botwell was still a quiet farming village when the Grand Junction (now Grand Union) Canal crossed the southwest corner of the district in the mid 1790s. A few substantial houses were erected on Botwell Lane in the early 19th century but economic activity had only progressed as far as brick-making when the Great Western Railway was constructed through the area in 1838. A station opened in 1864 and the decision to omit Botwell from its name soon consigned the old village name to history. Factories were built and houses and shops for their workers followed until what was by then called HAYES TOWN was fully built up by the outbreak of World War II. The oldest part of Botwell is now designated a conservation area. Botwell Green is a six-acre open space and the site of a proposed community leisure centre. More than two-thirds of the residents of the Botwell ward are white but a significant minority are of Indian origin.

✉ Hayes UB3

🏃 12,432

🚆 First Great Western Link (Hayes and Harlington, zone 5)

Bounds Green • *Haringey/Enfield*

A recently troubled area located just under a mile to the north-west of WOOD GREEN. The name was first recorded as Le Boundes and may derive from a family that lived here in the 13th century. Bounds Green remained a small farming hamlet until the late 19th century, with a few cottages, a tavern and a brickworks. Suburban houses began to appear with the outward spread of Wood Green, and Bounds Green infants' and junior schools were built in 1895. The junior school now occupies all of the Victorian buildings, while the infants' school has new premises of its own. Electric tram services began in 1906 and many Edwardian properties survive from the consequent phase of housebuilding. The suburban build-up was completed following the opening of Bounds Green station on the London Electric Railway (now the Piccadilly Line) in 1932. Like others on this stretch of line, the station was designed by Charles Holden but its appearance is more angular than most. Factories were established in the decades before and after World War II, at first individually and later on an industrial estate. In the late 1970s an old warehouse was converted for use by Middlesex Polytechnic (now University). The building has since been converted again, into residential apartments. Elsewhere in the locality former industrial premises have been replaced by housing. Since the early 1980s Bounds Green has attracted an expanding number of Greek, Turkish and Asian residents, relocating from longer established communities a mile or two to the south-east. Almost half the pupils at Bounds Green junior and infants' schools have English as a second language. Among the schools' many ethnic minorities the most distinctive is a Congolese contingent. In June 2003 the *Mail on Sunday* led with the decision of Lauren Booth, half-sister of the prime minister's wife, to leave 'crime and drug-infested' Bounds Green for a life in rural France. Ms Booth acknowledged that other parts of London suffered worse problems but was especially disturbed by what she saw as the unresponsive attitude of the local police in the face of rising disorder and anti-social behaviour.

Jerome K Jerome, the author of *Three Men in a Boat*, probably had his first experience of boating on a waterlogged brickfield in Bounds Green.

✉ N11

🏃 10,905

🚆 Piccadilly Line (zones 3 and 4)

Bow • *Tower Hamlets* (pronounced to rhyme with 'go')

A socially and geographically unfocused residential district situated between MILE END and the River Lea. Around 1100, Henry I's wife Matilda commissioned the construction of a bridge across the river, allegedly after she had fallen in during an attempted crossing. The bridge's innovative arched shape was the source of the early name for the hamlet that grew up here: Stratford Bow. Along with STRATFORD Langthorne on the opposite bank and Bromley to the south (now usually called BROMLEY-BY-BOW), this became an early centre for trade and industry, notably milling, baking and cloth-dyeing. By the 17th century Bow was the most important settlement between Stepney and the Lea, and wealthy gentlemen kept country homes here until they were driven away by industrial and suburban expansion. In the mid 18th century Bow gained fame for its porcelain, examples of which are in the British Museum. In 1764 the Whitsuntide festivities that had given MAY-FAIR its name were transferred to the banks of the Lea after they became too rowdy for the sensitivities of the London gentry. Behaviour here was even worse and the fair was described as 'two weeks of saturnalia when all habitual restraints and standards were cast aside'. By the 1820s the district was being built up with compact terraced houses for the lower middle classes and the new residents' objections sealed the fate of the event. The fairground is recalled in the name of Fairfield Road, which in 1860 became the site of Bryant and May's match factory. A famous strike in 1888 has left the factory with a reputation for Dickensian exploitation, when in fact working conditions were relatively healthy and the owners were of a benevolent inclination. A huge new factory was added in 1911, capable of producing ten billion matches a year. The interwar and post-war periods saw a repetition of the typical east London pattern: blocks of council flats replacing run-down terraced houses, historic buildings and disused factories; new immigrant communities (black and Asian) replacing old ones (mainly Irish); and, more recently, the arrival of young professionals in search of affordable property. The trendsetting gentrification project was the conversion in the late 1980s and early 1990s of the former match factory into the Bow Quarter. Since then, further complexes of apartment blocks have been springing up in every available space and prices have rocketed – admittedly from a relatively low base. Bow's main point of difference is that upmarket shops and restaurants have not followed the residential influx to a matching degree, perhaps because neither BOW ROAD nor ROMAN ROAD offers the right environment.

Chaucer, in the prologue to *The Canterbury Tales*, says of the Prioress, 'Frenssh she spak ful faire and fetisly [elegantly] / After the scole of Stratford atte Bowe, / For Frenssh of Parys was to hir unknowe'; the sardonic suggestion is that the Prioress spoke French with the anglicized accent she had learned in her convent, the Benedictine nunnery of St Leonard, Bromley. William Hargreaves composed the music hall favourite *Burlington Bertie from Bow* in 1915.

✉ E3

👤 19,218 (Bow East and Bow West wards)

Bow Church • *Tower Hamlets*
A Docklands Light Railway station named after St Mary's Church, which stands at the eastern end of BOW ROAD. St Mary's is one of only two medieval churches in the borough and was established in 1311 as a chapel of ease to STEPNEY. Parts of the present building date from its founding and from the late 15th century. St Mary's became a parish church in 1719, when rebuilding was proposed. However, lack of funds prevented this, and subsequent 19th-century proposals, from being implemented. Despite the nearby presence of a mid-19th-century pub called the Bow Bells, this St Mary's should not be confused with the Church of St Mary-le-Bow, which is located in CHEAPSIDE and possesses the true Bow bells, nor with Bow Road Methodist Church, which stands on the corner of Merchant Street. BOW station opened in 1850 on the North London Railway, with services to POPLAR. The Great Eastern Railway later added through services to FENCHURCH STREET and Southend in Essex. The station stood on the north side of the road and was rebuilt in much-enlarged form in 1870. The new struc-

ture had a concert hall above the booking office, which was used for cultural and educational purposes and later became the Bow Palais. Passenger services ceased in 1944, although the line continued to carry freight until its closure in 1981, after which the station buildings were demolished. The site is now occupied by a car hire firm. A new station called Bow Church opened on the opposite side of the road in 1987 as one of the original stops on the DLR network. The station is situated midway between the church and Bow Road Tube station.

In 1882 Theodore Bryant of the Bow matchmaking company Bryant and May paid for a statue of prime minister William Gladstone to be erected in St Mary's churchyard. According to the early feminist Annie Besant, some of the 'match girls' who worked for Bryant and May 'cut their arms and let their blood trickle on the marble paid for, in very truth, by their blood'. Even in recent years the statue has been periodically splashed with red paint in recollection of this story.

✉ E3

🚉 Docklands Light Railway, Stratford branch (zone 2)

Bow Common • *Tower Hamlets*
Historically a poor quarter, situated southeast of MILE END. The area was industrialized in the mid 19th century as factories moved towards the River Lea from districts such as WHITECHAPEL, and the Great Central Gas Co. built gasworks to supply the CITY OF LONDON. A proposal to create VICTORIA PARK here in the 1840s was vetoed in favour of a more northerly site. In 1883 the Congregationalist clergyman and anti-poverty campaigner Andrew Mearns observed, 'Out of 2,290 persons living in consecutive houses at Bow Common, only 88 adults and 47 children ever attend' a place of worship, a situation that he blamed on the conditions in which they lived. 'Block of streets between Gale Street and Furze Street are the worst in the district, worse than almost any district in London. Three policemen wounded there last week,' wrote Charles Booth, the social reformer and statistician, a few years later in notes for *Life and Labour of the People of London*, his classic study of London poverty. The streets were offensively nicknamed the 'Fenian Barracks' on account of their Irish inhabitants. There has been much slum clearance since, and the replacement of buildings damaged in the Blitz. More recently, much of the council's housing stock has been

refurbished or replaced by housing association properties. St Paul's Church, originally built in 1858, was bombed in World War II and a new church was subsequently built on the site that was consecrated in 1960. Designed by two radical architects in their twenties, with a Marxist vicar for a client, this Modernist building made ground-breaking use of space and is now a Grade II*-listed building. The Church of the Holy Name and Our Lady of the Sacred Heart opened in 1894. It is now London's Vietnamese Roman Catholic church. The Fern Street Settlement is a community charity founded in 1907 by Clara Grant, headmistress of Devons School. She introduced a ceremony that became known as 'Farthing Bundles', whereby any child who could pass under a small wooden arch without bending their knees would receive a parcel of toys for a farthing. The heavily wooded Tower Hamlets Cemetery is a 33-acre public park and nature reserve.

An attempted wages snatch in 1961 from an armoured truck in Bow Common has been cited as a turning point in British criminal conduct. Police opened fire on robbers armed with sledgehammers and pick-axe handles. From then on, it is said, raiders began to carry firearms.

✉ E3

📖 R Beer and C A Pickard, *Eighty Years on Bow Common*, Fern Street Settlement, 1987

Bowes Park • *Haringey/Enfield* (pronounced 'boze')

A mixture of Victorian and interwar terraced housing, situated between WOOD GREEN and PALMERS GREEN. Bowes was a Norman manor and the name may derive from John de Arcubus, meaning 'of the bows', who owned land here in 1274. In 1412 Henry IV granted the manor to the dean and chapter of ST PAUL'S Cathedral. Bowes manor house lay to the northeast, near the present Sidney Avenue, and became noted for its landscaped gardens. The avenue's name recalls Thomas Sidney, one of several aristocratic residents. The 370-acre Bowes Farm estate, much of which was woodland, survived until the end of the 18th century. Thereafter, the Ecclesiastical Commissioners, who had succeeded St Paul's as the landowners, began to lease plots of land on which some large houses were built. However, the commissioners retained the freehold interest in most of the manor until much later. The Great Northern Railway Company built a branch line from Wood Green to Enfield in

1871 and opened Bowes Park station nine years later in response to the area's growth. Another phase of housebuilding filled the remaining gaps in the 1930s and 1940s, mainly with bay-fronted semi-detached and terraced houses. Most of Bowes Park's public amenities were added during this period. Bowes Primary School's pupils reflect the area's diverse social and ethnic profile: some are from well-off families, others from overcrowded homes, and 62 per cent of children come from homes where English is the second language. Gujarati and Turkish are the most commonly spoken languages after English. Some children are from Somali and Kosovan refugee families. In Enfield's Bowes ward, 12 per cent of residents are Muslims and 8 per cent are Hindus. Bowes Park has suffered difficulties with antisocial behaviour but a combined council and community initiative, begun in 1996, succeeded in reducing some of the problems and improving the look of the area.

✉ N11; N13; N22

👤 11,678 (Enfield's Bowes ward)

🚃 WAGN Railway (zones 3 and 4)

Bow Road • *Tower Hamlets*

A section of the A11 running from MILE END east towards STRATFORD. Bow Road formed a section of the route to Colchester in the Middle Ages, when it was flanked by wide bands of manorial waste (common land). The eastern end of the road was the focus of the medieval village of Bow, but only St Mary's Church remains from this period. An irregular collection of 19th- and 20th-century buildings line the road today, many of them dismal. The most interesting exceptions are relics of bygone civic investment in Bow, and most no longer serve their original purposes, including the former electricity showrooms, POPLAR Town Hall and Bromley Public Hall. An Italianate courthouse of 1860 has been replaced by the intimidating bulk of Thames magistrates' court. The first Bow Road station opened on the Great Eastern Railway's BLACKWALL branch line in 1876. The station was rebuilt on the north side of the road in 1892. The separate Bow Road Tube station opened in 1902 on the Metropolitan District Railway, in a scheme co-funded by the London, Tilbury and Southend Railway, to relieve overcrowding on its service into FENCHURCH STREET. The attractive Wellington Buildings, located just around the corner on Wellington Way, were built to house residents who were displaced by the construction of the line and the station. Bow Road was also served by the Hammersmith & City Railway from 1936. Bow Road main-line station closed in 1949. The original station buildings survive, as does the bridge that carried the railway over the road.

> ✉ E3

> 🚇 District Line; Hammersmith & City Line (zone 2)

Brackenbury Village • *Hammersmith & Fulham*

An estate agents' and property developers' label for the area between RAVENSCOURT PARK and Hammersmith Grove, which saw numerous conversions and restorations in the late 20th century, with an accompanying influx of specialist shops and eateries. From the 1860s, terraced cottages and some substantial houses were built on former market gardens and brick-fields and the present streetscape was almost complete in 1890. By the mid 20th century many of the properties were in such a run-down condition that the council considered demolishing some streets and replacing them with municipal housing. Instead, the homes were progressively improved and from the early 1980s gentrification took hold. With Tube stations at three corners and its varied and pretty architecture, Brackenbury Village (or simply Brackenbury) is now one of the most desirable neighbourhoods in inner west London. The cluster of shops at the junction of Brackenbury Road and Aldensley Road adds to the sense of community. The impact of a strip club's arrival in an area popular with young families was the subject of a television documentary in 1999.

There is another Brackenbury Village in north ICKENHAM (London Borough of Hillingdon) but the name is not widely used. Aylsham Drive is its main thoroughfare.

> ✉ W6

Brent Cross • *Barnet*

A road junction and the shopping centre named after it, situated beside the River Brent in south HENDON. Brent station opened when the underground extension to EDGWARE was completed at the end of 1923. At around the same time, Hendon Way (A41) and the North Circular Road (A406) sliced through the locality, creating the Brent Cross intersection. The present flyover was constructed in 1965. Much of the Brent Cross site was occupied by a sewage farm from 1886 to 1935. The shopping centre, with its John Lewis and Fenwick department stores, opened in 1976 with a fully enclosed and air-conditioned format and a late-opening policy that were novel in Britain at that time. Brent station was then renamed Brent Cross, but the dreary trek from the station to the shopping centre only serves to emphasize its dedication to the motorized shopper. For those without a car, arrival by bus is the better option. Brent Cross was extended and refurbished in 1997 and now contains 110 retail outlets. Owners Hammerson and Standard Life have hopes for further expansion in the direction of CRICKLEWOOD, as the government has rejected plans to enlarge the centre any further on its existing site. Their proposals include thousands of new homes and a cluster of office towers, as well as more shops and a pedestrianized Victorian-style high street.

Brent Cross should not be confused with the commercial zone of Brent Park, which includes the Ikea and Tesco superstores. This is located two miles along the North Circular to the south-west of Brent Cross.

> ✉ NW4; NW11

> 🚇 Northern Line (zone 3)

> @ www.brentcross-london.com

Brentford • *Hounslow*

A centre of industry and commerce since the Middle Ages, situated two miles west of CHISWICK. The River Brent was named by the Celts, but it is not clear whether the original ford was a crossing of that river or the Thames. There is no direct evidence to support the legends that Julius Caesar crossed the Thames or fought a battle here in 54BC. With its good river and road connections, Brentford developed early as a trading place and was granted the right to hold markets and fairs in 1306. The construction of a new bridge across the Brent in 1446 contributed to the emergence of a settlement on the west bank known as BRENTFORD END. On the instructions of Henry VIII, part of the common land north of the High Street was commandeered for archery practice and by 1596 this area was known as the Butts. Brentford grew in importance as a coaching stop and market town during the 17th century, with shops, inns, warehouses and dwellings, surrounded by orchards and market gardens. Middlesex county court sessions were held here and, later, parliamentary elections – leading to erroneous claims that it was the county town. In the late 1680s the landlord of the Red Lion inn began to build houses at the Butts and these properties survive today as an unexpectedly glorious enclave. During the 19th century, industry expanded along the OLD BRENTFORD waterfront and the residential character of the town became increasingly working-class. Brentford Football Club was founded in 1889 by members of the town's rowing club who wanted to pursue a winter sport (a vote of eight to five decided it would be association rather than rugby football). The club moved to its present ground at Griffin Park in 1904. By the early 20th century the High Street (A315) had become a bottleneck that was choking the free movement of traffic into London. Plans for a Brentford bypass were delayed by World War I and then merged into a grander scheme to create a series of new approach roads to London. The Great West Road (A4) opened in 1925, precipitating a new wave of industrial development. Brentford's 'golden mile' of art deco factories, built by the likes of Smith's crisps and Maclean's toothpaste, caused J B Priestley to liken a drive along the Great West Road to a vista of California. Before and after World War II, private builders spread streets of terraced houses across the remaining open land, while the borough council cleared slums and built flats and houses. On the Great West Road, the Firestone building was demolished in 1980 but the Beecham building survived a similar threat. The road has been undergoing a renaissance in recent years and several major companies have plans in hand for new or redeveloped office complexes, including much-needed landscaping improvements. Although Brentford's manufacturing heyday is long past, it is home to the Brompton folding bicycle, winner of the Queen's Award for Export in 1995. The redevelopment of disused sites has continued into the 21st century with privately built apartment complexes at Brentford Lock, while the council plans a major regeneration programme, beginning in 2006. The area's visitor attractions include Waterman's Arts Centre, the Musical Museum and the KEW BRIDGE Steam Museum. 'Is Brentford the first base in an alien assault on the planet Earth?' This is one of the questions posed in the *Brentford Trilogy*, a comic sci-fi series now on its eighth volume, by Robert Rankin.

✉ Brentford TW8

👫 10,745

🚌 South West Trains (zone 4)

📖 Gillian Clegg, *Brentford Past*, Historical Publications, 2002; Carolyn and Peter Hammond, *Brentford*, Tempus, 2004

@ www.brentfordtw8.com (community site); www.brentford-online.com (local online newspaper site)

Brentford End • *Hounslow*

This is the rarely heard name for the part of BRENTFORD west of the River Brent. It was at the 'Brentford end' of ISLEWORTH parish. One of the first notable landowners here was Humphrey Noye, son of Charles I's attorney general and a Royalist commander in the Civil War. Noye's property was appropriated by the Parliamentarians in 1643 and leased to a poor craftsman who took the opportunity, along with others, to plunder it. The distinguished engraver and calligrapher George Bickham taught writing and engraving at Brentford End in the first half of the 18th century, though he mainly lived at BUNHILL Fields. Brentford End's suburban development began early in the 20th century, houses replacing nurseries and market gardens best known for their strawberries. Some very plain council terraces came later. Syon Mission Church is on Beech Avenue. There is commerce and industry north of the railway line and beside the Brent.

In 1994 a *Sunday Times* article carried claims that female gangs such as the 'Cherry Crescent posse' and "Busch Corner girls', named after streets in Brentford End, were among the toughest teenage criminals in west London, preying on young businesswomen travelling home at night on public transport.

✉ Brentford, TW8

Brentham • *Ealing* (pronounced 'brentəm')

One of London's hidden gems, Brentham garden estate was laid out in NORTH EALING during the early years of the 20th century. The estate backs onto Pitshanger Park, beside the River Brent from which it takes its name. The earliest roads, those with the Woodfield name, were a co-operative creation but their architecture differed little from speculatively built terraces built elsewhere around this time. The tenants' association bought more land in 1905 and 1907 and its leader, Henry Vivian, pushed through more innovative principles of street layout and house design. The architects Parker and Unwin were brought in to create Britain's first 'co-partnership garden suburb', intended to provide cottage homes for working people who invested their savings in the scheme and received dividends for keeping their property in good repair. The Arts and Crafts architecture exhibits a delightful variety of stylistic detail while retaining a thematic harmony. The community's focal point is the Brentham Club on Meadvale Road, which organizes a wide range of activities. Unlike many such centres – at least those of such quality – the club building is not a conversion of some pre-existing gentleman's home but was built for the purpose in 1911. From that year until 1947 the estate had its own railway halt on the main line between WESTBOURNE PARK and GREENFORD. Brentham's identity is no longer widely recognized beyond the immediate neighbourhood; it is often considered part of what estate agents call PITSHANGER VILLAGE. On the fringes of the estate some properties have been disfigured with pebbledashing or even stonecladding but the heart of Brentham is a wonderfully preserved conservation area.

✉ W5

📖 Aileen Reid, *Brentham: A History of the Pioneer Garden Suburb 1901–2001*, Brentham Heritage Society, 2001

@ www.brentham.com (Brentham Heritage Society site)

Brick Lane • *Tower Hamlets*

A market street in SPITALFIELDS, running south from SHOREDITCH station towards ALDGATE EAST and noted for its Bangladeshi community and south Asian cuisine. Joseph Truman established a brewery here in the late 17th century and built some houses to its south that also survive. A market began to operate in the 18th century and Brick Lane became a 'high street' for London's Russian and Polish Jews from the late 19th century. In the early 1970s, immigrants from Bangladesh began to settle here and the first 'Indian' restaurant opened in 1974. Brick Lane now has the densest concentration of curry houses on one street in the country. Pavement touts try to hustle you into one of 50 restaurants, which adds to the atmosphere for some visitors but deters others. An international curry festival is held every September and other culinary events take place throughout the year. Branding the area 'Banglatown' was an attempt by restaurateurs to imitate the success of CHINATOWN and has been endorsed by Tower Hamlets council. Brick Lane also has a cultural community centred on the old Truman brewery, which has been converted into studios for artists, musicians and fashion designers. The annual Brick Lane Festival began in 1997 and now attracts tens of thousands of visitors. Held in mid-September under the auspices of the Ethnic Minority Enterprise Project, the event presents a global mix of food, history and culture.

Monica Ali's 2003 novel *Brick Lane* tells the story of a teenaged girl who moves from a Bangladeshi village to an East End tower block following her arranged marriage.

✉ E1

📖 Sean Carey, *Curry Capital*, Institute of Community Studies, 2004; Tarquin Hall, *Salaam Brick Lane: A Year in the New East End*, John Murray, 2005

@ www.visitbricklane.com (community site); www.bricklanefestival.com

Bridgen • *Bexley*

A little-used name for a compact locality situated on the western edge of BEXLEY. This was a long-established farming hamlet, mostly consisting of cottages strung along Bridgen Road. The Anchor and Cable inn stood here in 1681, later becoming the Blue Anchor. In the late 18th century, William Cope built Bridgen Place, subsequently the home of the Reverend Edward Cokayne Frith. At the start of the 20th century Bridgen had just 80 inhabitants but it soon fell victim to the expansion of Bexley and BEXLEYHEATH. *Kelly's Directory* for 1924 lists a boot repairer, painter and confectioner among the tradesmen of Bridgen, as well as the gardener at Bridgen Place and the publican of the Blue Anchor. Despite its prettiness, the pub was demolished and replaced in 1928, partly owing to its dilapidated condition but also because the brewery wanted to build larger premises to cope with the growing population of its catchment area. Neighbouring cottages were also pulled down around the same time. Bridgen Place was razed around 1930 and replaced with the semi-detached houses of Arbuthnot Lane, named after a latter-day owner of the residence. Bexley Park Wood was part of the deer park enclosed for the use of the lords of Bexley manor. There is a footpath through the park, which now includes the former Murchison Road allotments.

The notorious criminal Kenneth Noye, jailed in 2000 for a 'road rage' murder committed in 1996, owned a house in Bridgen Road for 15 years, under the alias Anthony Francis, and his Land Rover was registered at this address, although he lived in Sevenoaks.

✉ Bexley DA5

Brimsdown • Enfield

The borough's principal commercial zone, now called a 'business area'. Brimsdown lies east of ENFIELD and west of King George's Reservoir, and constitutes a large section of the Lee Valley industrial corridor. It was originally called Grimsdown, and no one is sure how the 'G' became a 'B'. The railway station opened in 1884, followed by Brimsdown power station in 1903. The proximity of water, rail and power brought manufacturing to Brimsdown, including Enfield Rolling Mills, which used to receive copper by barge via the River Lee Navigation. Following several factory closures, Brimsdown won regeneration funding in the mid 1990s. Modern industry includes Johnson Matthey's refinery on Jeffreys Road, where silver salts for the photographic and pharmaceutical industries are manufactured using recycled metal. In addition, there are several wholesale and retail warehouses. The Mossops Creek permissive path gives access to the River Lea towpath from Brimsdown. A new footbridge links the walk with Mossops Creek Park on the opposite bank. The creek, which joins the River Lee Navigation near the bridge, is thought to have been formed when Mossop and Co. extracted gravel here in the second half of the 19th century.

There is a residential side to Brimsdown, a patch of mixed housing west of the railway line. At Brimsdown Primary School on Green Street, 60 per cent of the children are from minority ethnic groups and 29 languages are spoken, according to a 2002 report by the educational standards agency Ofsted.

The England football captain David Beckham played for Brimsdown Rovers as a youth.

✉ Enfield EN3

🚉 'one' Railway (zone 5)

Britannia Village • Newham see WEST SILVERTOWN

Brixton • Lambeth

The beacon of south London's black community, Brixton lies east of CLAPHAM and north of STREATHAM and each of its main thoroughfares has a distinct character. Acre Lane, BRIXTON HILL (A23) and Coldharbour Lane all existed as medieval routes. Brixton was 'Brixiges stan' when it was first recorded in 1062, and later Brixistan, which means 'the stone of Brixi'. The stone probably stood on Brixton Hill and marked a meeting place for the hundred court, which administered the medieval district of which Brixton was the capital; Brixi was a short form of Beorhtsige, a popular Saxon name meaning 'bright victory'. As the woodland was cleared, farms were established, which later turned to market gardening and rearing game to supply the London markets. Despite its ancient origins, Brixton did not evolve into a significant settlement until the early 19th century, when the enclosure of the manor of LAMBETH and the construction of new bridges across the Thames began to draw the first City gentlemen in search of sites for their country retreats. Detached villas and up-market terraced houses were sufficiently numerous on Brixton Road and Brixton Hill by the early 1820s to warrant the building of St Matthew's Church. With the coming of the railways in the late 1860s, first at Loughborough Park, speculative builders began a rapid development of the district with two- and three-storey terraced housing for the lower middle classes. Brixton Road became a shopping centre, with a street market on Atlantic Road. The purpose-built Bon Marché department store and the artificial lighting that gave its name to Electric Avenue were pioneering developments in British retailing. Brixton's monotonous residential streetscape was the subject of jibes; it was referred to as a 'nightmare of the mediocre' by *The Speaker* magazine in 1903. As a result of bomb damage, slum clearance and the end of 99-year leases, much of Brixton was rebuilt from the middle of the 20th century, a period that also saw the early arrival here of migrants from the Caribbean, partly because Lambeth council was more welcoming than others. However, the poor economic and housing conditions experienced by many of Brixton's black residents, combined with what were perceived as racist policing tactics, caused tensions that boiled over into unrest in 1981. Hundreds of buildings and cars were damaged in what was London's largest civil disturbance of the century, usually referred to as the 'Brixton riots', although some black Londoners object to that term, seeing the events as a righteous uprising. Less serious riots followed in 1985 and 1995, again sparked by policing incidents. In recent years, Brixton has become known for the relatively free availability of drugs on its streets, especially cannabis, and has been the subject of experiments in 'tolerant' law enforcement. Meanwhile, legitimate trades in exotic fruits, vegetables and fish, specialist record shops and entertainment palaces such as the Ritzy cinema, Fridge nightclub and Academy live music venue have made Brixton south London's liveliest shopping and leisure centre.

With its almost iconic cultural status, Brixton makes frequent appearances in works of music and literature, including The Clash's *Guns of Brixton*, local author Alex Wheatle's books, such as *Brixton Rock* and *East of Acre Lane*, and Nicholas Wright's play *Vincent in Brixton*, which takes artist Vincent van Gogh's 1873 stay in Hackford Road as the inspiration for a fictional love story. The Black Cultural Archives and Museum at 378 Coldharbour Lane records the history of London's black community.

✉ SW9; SW2

👤 52,852 (Brixton Hill, Coldharbour, Ferndale and Tulse Hill wards)

🚌 South Eastern Trains; Victoria Line (zone 2)

📖 Alan Piper, *A History of Brixton*, Brixton Society, 1996; J Dudman, *London: Brixton and Norwood*, Sutton, 1995

@ www.brixtonsociety.org.uk (local amenity society site)

Brixton Hill • *Lambeth*

Brixton Hill is a slope rising towards STREATHAM, rather than a summit in itself. It was on this hill that Brixi may have placed the boundary stone that gave its name to BRIXTON. Long before it gained its present identity, this stretch of Roman road was Brixton or Bristow Causeway. The thin strip of Rush Common that lines part of the eastern side of the road results from conditions accompanying the enclosure of Brixton's wastes. In 1802 Christopher Hall, a SOUTHWARK merchant, acquired 62 acres that lay south of the present Blenheim Gardens, where a windmill was erected in 1816 and still stands today. Hall's main use for his land was earth excavation for brick-making but in 1819 part of the land became the site for the Surrey house of correction, now Brixton Prison. Hall also sold land for the construction of Brixton Hill Reservoir in 1834. Residentially, the road and its hinterland developed according to Lambeth's typical three-stage process that began with Georgian villas, then saw these hemmed in or replaced by Victorian and Edwardian semi-detached and terraced houses, and concluded with widespread post-war demolition to make way for council houses and flats. In the Brixton Hill area few properties remain from the earliest stage – Raleigh House and New Park Court are among the more notable exceptions

– but there are plenty from the second stage, and Rush Common and Brixton Hill comprise a conservation area. The Blenheim Gardens estate, built in the early 1970s, is one of Lambeth council's more successful architectural projects. A quarter of the residents of the Brixton Hill ward describe themselves as black or black British, and nearly two-thirds as white. The ward scores poorly on several indices of deprivation, but not as badly as some other parts of the borough.

✉ SW2

👤 12,458

@ www.brixtonsociety.org.uk/trailone.htm

Broadgate • *City*

An 'office city', rivalling the BARBICAN as the Square Mile's biggest building project since the Great Fire of London. Some maps apply the Broadgate name to the whole north-eastern projection of the City. The scheme was first mooted by British Rail in the mid 1970s as a means of funding the rebuilding of Liverpool Street station. It eventually got underway a decade later in the wake of the boom that followed stock market deregulation. British Rail sold the site of Broad Street station and the hinterland of LIVERPOOL STREET to a joint venture by developers Rosehaugh and Stanhope Properties. Broad Street station closed in 1986, with its services transferring to Liverpool Street, and the first two new buildings opened in the same year. Arup Associates – later joined by Skidmore, Owings & Merrill – were responsible for the brutalist architecture, which was disliked by some for its overbearing style. By 1991 the 29-acre site had 13 buildings, mainly clad in pink granite. On the far side of the station is the black and grey monolith of Exchange House, one of the last phases to be completed. It is as much a bridge as a building but the scale of the engineering achievement cannot excuse its ugliness. The social focus of the complex is Broadgate Arena, which is encircled by tiers of shops, bars and restaurants. The arena hosts cultural events in summer and is converted into an ice rink from October to April, hosting the Broomball League. Broadgate underwent a £35 million refurbishment in 2004, when sweeping staircases were installed in the foyers to promote workers' fitness by discouraging use of the lifts.

Scenes for Paul McCartney's 1984 film *Give My Regards to Broad Street* were filmed at the old station.

✉ EC2

📖 Les Hutton et al, *Broadgate*, Davenport, 1991

@ www.broadgateestates.co.uk

Broad Green • *Croydon*

A gateway to CROYDON, Broad Green straddles the London Road south of THORNTON HEATH. The name, which is self-explanatory, dates back to at least the 16th century. Broad Green was a small settlement on the edge of Croydon Common until the 19th century, when it began to attract some impressive houses. Broad Green House was built in 1807 and was later joined by several other properties named after the locality and by Croydon Lodge. In the early 1850s the Archbishop of Canterbury, John Sumner, paid for the construction of Christ Church on the road that now bears his name. Towards the end of the century speculative developers began to buy up the mansions and replace them with streets of terraced houses for the lower middle classes. Various amenities were provided and an old beer shop was rebuilt as the Star Hotel. Kidderminster Road and Nova Road were laid out on the site of Broad Green Place, with the imposing shops of Royal Parade fronting London Road. Chatfield Road and Montague Road filled the grounds of Broad Green House, although the house survived as a school. Croydon Lodge survived until the 1920s, when it was replaced by Elmwood Road. Over the course of the 20th century Broad Green declined and parts of the area were rebuilt by the council, including the Kingsley Road estate to the west of Mitcham Road. London Merchant Securities built City House on London Road in the late 1960s and leased it to the Philips electronics company as its UK headquarters. Broad Green has been the recipient of significant regeneration funding in the past decade and a smart new library was built on Canterbury Road in 1998. Fairview New Homes acquired the freehold of City House in 2006 for conversion to residential apartments. The population of the Broad Green ward is 53 per cent white, 23 per cent Asian or Asian British and 19 per cent black or black British. A high proportion of the working population is in semi-skilled and unskilled manual jobs. Broad Green is rated the third most deprived ward in the borough, after NEW ADDINGTON and Fieldway.

✉ Croydon CR0

🚹 14,866

📖 Raymond Wheeler, *Images of Norbury, Thornton Heath and Broad Green*, Tempus, 2000

Broadwater Farm • *Haringey*

An ill-famed but much improved housing estate in west TOTTENHAM. The original Broadwater Farm covered 119 acres of the huge Downhills estate, which had been in existence since the mid 15th century and included Broadwater Farm by 1728. By the outbreak of World War I, private and municipal housebuilding had filled most of this side of Tottenham but a large part of Broadwater Farm survived. Tottenham council acquired the land and opened it as Lordship recreation ground in 1932. Soon after its formation in 1965, Haringey council took the south-eastern corner of the recreation ground for a flagship housing project. Completed in 1973, the Broadwater Farm estate consists of 12 concrete-panelled blocks of flats, most of which have four to six storeys, originally with a deck access system of pedestrianized walkways. By 1976 the design faults, lack of amenities and fear of crime on the estate resulted in more than half of those on the council's housing waiting list refusing accommodation there, and there was a long list of transfer requests from existing tenants. In October 1985 the death of a black woman, Cynthia Jarrett, in a police raid on her house led to the Broadwater Farm riot in which PC Keith Blakelock was hacked to death. During the ten years from 1993, comprehensive improvements were carried out to make the estate a more humane place to live. Disused shops have been replaced by smart new homes and overhead walkways have been dismantled. The estate-based management programme designed to address the social problems in Broadwater Farm has been relatively successful, partly through the use of 'super-caretakers' and also because the neighbourhood is so well-defined; elsewhere, projects have attempted to encompass 'communities' with which residents do not identify. The estate's football club, Broadwater Farm United, offers an inclusive training and playing programme for young residents. 'The Farm', as the estate is known, now has some successful light industrial units and just over a thousand homes, few of which are empty.

Junior Delgado and Little T's 1985 reggae track *Broadwater Farm* came out before the riots of that year, but was re-released afterwards and widely banned.

✉ N17

☐ Lord Gifford QC, *The Broadwater Farm Inquiry*, Karia Press, 1986

Brockley • *Lewisham*

A pleasing Victorian suburb situated south of NEW CROSS and west of LEWISHAM. The name was first recorded in the early 1180s and probably meant 'woodland clearing belonging to a man named Broca'. Alternatively, the 'brock' element could have indicated the presence of badgers or a brook. A house called Forest Place was in existence by the late 16th century, and a village evolved in the vicinity of the Brockley Jack public house during the 18th century. Following enclosure in 1810, Brockley Green Farm, Manor Farm and Brockley Farm became the dominant landholdings. The latter used Forest Place as its farmhouse. Brockley Green Farm belonged to the governors of Christ's Hospital and was bought by the London and Croydon Railway Co. in 1836. From the late 1840s the Tyrwhitt-Drake family began to build large terraced houses for the upper middle classes in place of their market gardens in Upper Brockley, around the present-day hub of Brockley Cross. Forest Place was demolished around 1870 when the Earl of St Germans sold the adjoining land to build more housing for the professional classes. Brockley station opened in 1871, Brockley Lane station (now closed) in 1872 and CROFTON PARK station in 1892. Hilly Fields was acquired by the London County Council and opened to the public in 1896, following a campaign led by housing reformer and National Trust founder Octavia Hill. It is said that few households in the streets around Hilly Fields were without a 'maid of all work' at that time and this side of Brockley is now a conservation area. Houses for the less wealthy were built west of Brockley Road, where subsequent redevelopment has left a variety of 20th-century styles, especially where the area merges with Nunhead. Parts of Brockley Road still have the air of a village high street although many of the shops have the low-rent appearance typical of much of inner south London. Brockley has a high concentration of young singles, many living in subdivided houses. There are twice as many 20–29-year-olds and unmarried people as the national averages, and half as many pensioners.

Brockley has been home to music hall performer Marie Lloyd, humorist Spike Milligan (who joined the Young Communist League of Brockley), and G K Chesterton's fictional detective Mr J G Reader. In 2003 the BBC1 documentary *Worlds Apart* showed two Brockley families – one in a council flat and the other in a seven-bedroom house – living contrasting existences while sharing the same streets.

✉ SE4

🚶 13,697

🚊 Southern (zone 2)

☐ Harry Monk, *The Muffin Man and the Herring Barrow*, Deptford Forum, 1995

Brockley Hill • *Harrow/Barnet*

Situated north-east of STANMORE, Brockley Hill constitutes the northernmost section of the A5 in Greater London and is the site of a Roman settlement. There have been suggestions of prehistoric occupation at Brockley Hill, but little evidence has been found. Stories that Julius Caesar fought a battle nearby or that the Romans built a 'city' here are almost certainly fanciful. However, most scholars now believe that Brockley Hill was the site of Sulloniacae, a posting station on Watling Street located halfway between London and St Albans. The station was recorded in the Antonine itinerary, a third-century list of routes and stopping places in the Roman Empire. There was certainly a pottery operating here from around AD 75 to AD 160, which specialized in lidded bowls and jars, flagons and mortaria (mixing bowls). Surrounding woodland seems to have been cleared to grow crops, although this may have been at a later phase of Roman occupation. But despite extensive excavations since 1937, proof of a larger settlement has not been found. Archaeologists continue to search for more substantial Roman remains, both at Brockley Hill and at mooted alternative locations such as BURNT OAK. The site is a scheduled ancient monument. From the 17th to the 19th centuries, development along Brockley Hill was mostly limited to a handful of substantial houses and the creation of Brockley Hill Farm. In 1882 Mary Wardell converted Sulloniacae, her house on Wood Lane, into a children's convalescent home. After military use in World War I, the Royal National Orthopaedic Hospital acquired the home as a country branch. Many more buildings have since been added and the process continues today, partly funded by the sale of 'excess' land for residential development. Land at the bottom of Brockley Hill, on the corner of London Road, was bought by the Ministry of Works in 1946 and used for assorted government offices, including those of the Ministry of Defence. The site was vacated in the 1990s and much of it has now been redeveloped with high-class housing, with the nine-hole Brockley Hill golf park to the north.

✉ Stanmore HA7; Edgware HA8

Bromley • *Bromley*

A major commercial centre and focal point of outer south-east London, located nine miles from CHARING CROSS in the upper valley of the River Ravensbourne. It was 'Bromleag' in 862, from Old English words meaning 'the heath where broom grows'. Broom is not so common nowadays, but the yellow-flowered shrub formerly covered many woodland clearings in the London area and gave its name to BROMPTON, BROOM HILL and Broomfield House in PALMERS GREEN, as well as to the sweeping devices that were made from its twigs. An Anglo-Saxon settlement developed around the site now occupied by the market square, and Gilbert Glanville, Bishop of Rochester, built a palace nearby in 1185. The bishop's successors encouraged pilgrims to visit St Blaise's well, which was fed by a spring whose waters tasted of iron. In 1205 King John granted a charter to the town's market, which specialized in the wool trade. Despite its important institutions, Bromley had only 129 households in the 1660s, when the almshouses of Bromley College were built. A separate hamlet had by this time evolved to the south, at BROMLEY COMMON. Bromley flourished as a spa town after the rediscovery of the St Blaise's well in 1754. A new episcopal palace was constructed in 1775, surrounded by a moat. The last Bishop of Rochester to be based at Bromley Palace moved away in 1845. Bromley station (now Bromley South) opened in 1858 and the first substantial villas appeared soon afterwards. A second station (now Bromley North) opened in 1878 and whole estates of middle-class housing began to spread out from the centre, including 'New Bromley' to the north-east, together with clusters of cottages for artisans. The railway also brought suburban growth to peripheral hamlets like BICKLEY and SUNDRIDGE. Central Bromley was fully built up by the outbreak of World War I and subsequent change has been limited to the replacement of large houses and some factories with compact houses or blocks of flats. Bromley Palace was converted into a teacher training college in the 1930s and now forms the core of Bromley Civic Centre. The Church of St Peter and St Paul was rebuilt in the 1950s following wartime devastation. Major developments in recent decades have included the pedestrianization of the High Street, the construction of a library and theatre block in 1975 and of the Glades shopping centre in 1991. In the following year Lord Archer opened the neighbouring Pavilion Leisure Centre. Bromley's rivalry with CROYDON and KINGSTON as south London's leading shopping destination has been undermined in recent years by competition from the Bluewater centre in Kent. Some prestigious stores have closed and their places have been taken by relatively downmarket outlets. An area action plan, under discussion in 2006, aims to redress the decline by creating new shops, housing, leisure, cultural and community facilities and public spaces.

The writer H G Wells was born in 1866 over a shop at 47 High Street – now the site of a branch of Primark. The author Hanif Kureishi grew up here in the 1960s and later mocked Bromley in *The Buddha of Suburbia*. Bromley's (non-existent) Green Midget Café was the setting for Monty Python's 'spam' sketch, which has led to the word 'spam' being used to describe repetitive nonsense, including junk mail, sent over the internet. In the 1970s the Bromley Contingent was a faction of punk fashionistas and early followers of the Sex Pistols. The original line-up of Siouxsie and the Banshees emerged from the contingent.

✉ Bromley BR1 and BR2

♦ 14,499 (Bromley Town ward)

🚆 South Eastern Trains (Bromley North, zone 4; Bromley South, zone 5)

📖 Patricia Knowlden, *Bromley: A Pictorial History*, Phillimore, 1990

@ www.the-glades-bromley.co.uk (shopping centre); www.theambassadors.com/Churchill (Churchill Theatre); www.bromleymytime.org.uk (borough leisure resources)

Bromley-by-Bow • *Tower Hamlets*

A historic East End district situated between BOW and POPLAR. 'Bromley' is a corruption of Old English words meaning 'woodland clearing with brambles', and the extended name avoids confusion with its south London namesake. It was earlier known as Bromley St Leonard, after the Benedictine priory of St Leonard, once the oldest religious house in east London. After the dissolution of the monasteries, the manor was granted to Sir Ralph Sadleir, principal secretary of state to Henry VIII. The British Museum holds his account of the estate's properties, drawn up in

1540. By this time, Bow had gained ascendancy over Bromley, but Bromley became a popular place to build rural retreats from the early 17th century. A hunting lodge that stood on what is now St Leonard's Street was said to have been built by James I. Later known as the Old Palace, the building was split into two residences in 1750. From the 1820s, Bromley began to fill with noxious industries and workers' housing, some built by charities, some by profiteering jerry builders. Much of Bromley was a slum by the late 19th century and it became an early target for civic improvement. Bromley Public Hall was built on Bow Road in 1880 as the vestry hall for St Leonard's parish. The replacement of the palace by a school in 1894 caused an outcry and played a pivotal role in promoting future (often unsuccessful) attempts to preserve east London's heritage. The interior of the state room was salvaged and can be seen at the Victoria and Albert Museum. From the 1930s the London County Council began a massive slum clearance programme, erasing the old village green with its houses and inns. Ruinous bomb damage in World War II brought further clearance after 1945 and municipal and social housing now fills almost the entire area. Seventy-two per cent of homes here are rented from the council or a housing association, an extraordinarily high figure. The largest ethnic minority is of Bangladeshi descent, followed by white Britons. The Bromley-by-Bow Centre on Bruce Road is a community regeneration organization that aims to harness the energies and abilities of local people through a variety of integrated projects, linking health with education and enterprise, for example, or environment with training and family support.

The political economist David Ricardo, the son of a Dutch Jewish stockbroker, grew up in Bromley St Leonard in the late 18th century. Kingsley Hall is said to have been the first purpose-built community centre designed for the needs of local people. It has also given house room to a variety of groups and movements, including the suffragettes and the Jarrow marchers. Later it was a base for the psychoanalyst R D Laing. A blue plaque records Mahatma Gandhi's stay at the hall, which is now home to the Gandhi Peace Foundation.

✉ E3

🏃 11,581

🚇 District Line; Hammersmith & City Line (zones 2 and 3)

@ www.kingsleyhall.freeuk.com (site includes local history); www.bbbc.org.uk (Bromley-by-Bow Centre)

Bromley Common • *Bromley*

An elongated settlement stretching between BROMLEY and FARNBOROUGH. A hamlet was in existence at Bromley Common by the 16th century. The diarist John Evelyn was robbed on the common in 1652, when his assailants jumped out from behind a large oak tree. Enclosure of the common's 300 acres began in 1764 and the Pye House, later the Crown public house, opened in the following year. The Rookery and Oakley House were the most substantial mansions built on the edge of the common in the 18th century. The latter became the home of Admiral Cornwallis, who fought at the Battle of Trafalgar. Following the second stage of the common's enclosure in 1821 villas were built on Hastings Road (A21), with a row of cottages on present-day Oakley Road (A233). The village had expanded significantly by the late 1830s and two of the cottages were converted into an infants' school, while Holy Trinity Church was built in an economical style known as Commissioners' Gothic. A purpose-built school opened beside the church in 1847. To the north, the area around Chatterton Road was nicknamed 'the building field' in the 1870s, when it rapidly filled with terraced cottages, accompanied by shops and a large public house, now the Chatterton Arms. The 1880s saw the opening of a hospital for infectious diseases, the improvement of Holy Trinity and the building of St Luke's Church, although its tower was not completed until 1910. A bus garage opened in 1924 and another phase of expansion later in the decade necessitated more school building. To the west, the Norman family preserved the grounds of The Rookery until the army took over the house during World War II. The Rookery burned down in 1946 while still under military occupation, after which green-belt legislation prevented development and ensured that much of this area remains open space still. Bromley Technical College was built on The Rookery's site in 1965 and this has since become the main campus of Bromley College. The isolation hospital, later a geriatric care facility, was demolished and replaced by housing in the mid 1980s. Oakley House has become a Masonic hall that also serves as a conference, banqueting and wedding venue. Three-quarters of the homes in the Bromley Common and Keston ward are owner-occupied, but there is also a relatively high proportion of social housing.

Richmal Crompton, author of the *Just William* books, lived with her mother at 9 Cherry Orchard Road from 1917 to 1928. She wrote the first nine books in the series here and later moved to The Glebe, Oakley Road.

✉ Bromley BR2

👪 14,171 (Bromley Common and Keston ward)

📖 Amanda Peckham and Gill Humby, *From the Workhouse to the Pye House: A History of Bromley Common*, Local History Publications, 2000; Mary Cadogan, *Richmal Crompton and her Bromley Connections: The Woman Behind William*, Lilburne Press, 2001

@ www.bromley.ac.uk (Bromley College site)

Bromley Park • *Bromley*

A pair of late Victorian estates in north-west BROMLEY, wedged between Beckenham Lane (A222) and London Road (A21). Bromley Park was a small country estate straddling London Road and belonging to the Blyth family from 1769. The family began developing the estate with large houses for the middle classes from the late 19th century, and left the area after selling off the last part of the estate in 1913. Most of the area now marked on maps as Bromley Park was actually part of a neighbouring estate that ran south from Bromley Hill (A21) to Beckenham Lane, where an entrance lodge stood near the present Highland Road. That estate was in existence by the 17th century and Bromley Hill House was built in the late 1760s on the site of a farmhouse. Around 1801 the estate was acquired by Charles Long, with the encouragement of his friend William Pitt, the Younger, who lived not far away at HOLWOOD. Long, who later became first Baron Farnborough of Bromley Hill, beautified the grounds and progressively enlarged the house into an Italianate mansion in a series of stages that lasted almost until his death in 1838. Bromley Hill remained in the possession of the Long family until 1881 when it was acquired for development by Samuel Cawston. The resulting Bromley Hill estate quickly filled most of the house's grounds. Cawston built Christ Church on Highland Road in 1887, using the architect who had designed most of the estate's well-proportioned residential properties. Bromley Hill House served as a convalescent hospital for Canadian soldiers from April 1915 to the end of August 1918. The house survives, in mangled form, as the Bromley Court Hotel.

✉ Bromley BR1 and BR2

Brompton • *Kensington & Chelsea*

A prosperous quarter centred on Brompton Road, which runs south-westward from KNIGHTSBRIDGE Tube station. The street is much mentioned in chic circles, but the locality's name has yielded to the greater cachets of CHELSEA, Knightsbridge and SOUTH KENSINGTON. There was a heathland village here in medieval times and 'Broom Farm' was first recorded in 1294. The marshy ground was drained in the 16th century and converted into fruit gardens. Brompton Park nursery was established in 1681, on land where the Victoria & Albert Museum now stands; it has given its name to a flower, the Brompton stock, a large, usually red, biennial variety. During Victoria's reign, Brompton became a fashionable district in which to live and an estate was laid out with the inelegant, and thankfully short-lived, moniker of Bromptonville. A reputation for healthy air attracted a number of private hospices, including Brompton Hospital, now converted into one of the most expensive addresses in London. In 1868 the Metropolitan Railway opened Brompton (GLOUCESTER ROAD) station, but after the Piccadilly Line reached the area in 1906, Brompton's name was dropped. There was also a Brompton Road station on the Piccadilly Line, between Knightsbridge and South Kensington, from 1906 to 1934. Brompton Cross, where Brompton Road meets Draycott Avenue, has been known since the mid 1980s for its fashion boutiques and has been nicknamed the 'Tiara Triangle'. Brompton Oratory is one of London's trendiest places of Roman Catholic worship. Properly called the Oratory of St Philip Neri, this thoroughly Italianate group of buildings dates mainly from the late 19th century.

Ruth Ellis, the last woman to be hanged in Britain, lived in a bedsit at 44 Egerton Gardens and managed a members-only drinking club in Brompton Road.

✉ SW1; SW3

👪 9,313

🚇 Circle Line; District Line; Piccadilly Line (Gloucester Road, zone 1)

📖 Richard Tames, *Earls Court and Brompton Past*, Historical Publications, 2000; Hermione Hobhouse (ed.), *Survey of London, vol 41: Southern Kensington: Brompton*, Athlone Press, 1983

Brondesbury • *Brent* (pronounced 'bron-(d)sb(ə)ry')

A classy residential district in north KILBURN, set on a ridge that runs from HAMPSTEAD to HARLESDEN, dividing the surroundings into two drainage areas. It may take its name from the same man who gave his name to BROWNS-WOOD PARK. By 1538 Brondesbury possessed a moated manor house in the area now known as BRONDESBURY PARK. During the 1860s, Brondesbury Heights developed rapidly because of the arrival of the Hampstead Junction Railway and the sale for housing of land owned by the Ecclesiastical Commissioners. The manor had lain within Willesden parish but the growth led to an early separation when the parish of Christ Church was created in 1866. By the 1890s the district had been almost entirely built up with high-class housing and had gained a significant Jewish community, for whom a synagogue was built. During the first half of the 20th century many of the impracticably large properties were replaced by more affordable houses or subdivided into flats but the area retained its superior status. The manor house was demolished in 1934 after serving as a girls' boarding school. More than 200 council houses were built in the 1960s and 1970s, while private developers found a few gaps to fill. A trend towards insensitive alterations to surviving Victorian properties was curbed by the designation of a conservation area in 1990. Also in that year Christ Church was innovatively and tastefully subdivided to create residential apartments, combined with a smaller church, which council tax bills refer to as 'Flat 22'. The Shree Swaminarayan Temple on Willesden Lane is one of London's few purpose-built Hindu temples.

The Brondesbury Tapes is an album of homemade recordings by Giles, Giles and Fripp, a forerunner of the progressive rock band King Crimson. The tracks were laid down in 1968 but only released in 2001.

✉ NW6

🚉 Silverlink Metro (zone 2)

Brondesbury Park • *Brent*

A leafy locality lying on the western side of KILBURN. It is built on and named after the grounds of BRONDESBURY manor house, which in 1789 were landscaped by Humphry Repton. In 1856 Lady Elizabeth Salusbury sold the leasehold interest in the house to the Ecclesiastical Commissioners, who released successive plots for building throughout the rest of the century. Brondesbury Park and its exten-sion Salusbury Road were created as an access spine. The new road cut the manor house off from its entrance on Willesden Lane and was extended to WILLESDEN GREEN (in the NW2 postal district) in 1901. In response to the growth of the area, St Anne's Church was built on Salusbury Road in 1905, Brondesbury Park station opened in 1908 and the ward of Brondesbury Park was created in 1909. Manor House Drive was laid out following the demolition of the manor house in 1934. The drive's double-fronted houses have up to eight bedrooms. Elsewhere, many Victorian houses have been converted into spacious flats. The Russian Orthodox Church in Exile opened the Convent of the Annunciation in Brondesbury Park in 1960. Recent residential developments include the gated estate of Honeyman Close, which has upmarket communal leisure facilities. St Anne's Church was impressively rebuilt in 1998 and the building is shared with St Andrew's United Reformed Church and the London Interfaith Centre. The Brondesbury Park ward has many young single people living in privately rented accommodation, but also a high proportion of pensioners. Around two-thirds of residents are white.

✉ NW6

🚶 11,643

🚉 Silverlink Metro (zone 2)

Brook Green • *Hammersmith & Fulham*

HAMMERSMITH's sought-after north-eastern corner, taking its name from a narrow, wedge-shaped green that was traversed by a brook running south from SHEPHERD'S BUSH. This section of the brook was called the Black Bull ditch, after an inn that it passed. Almshouses were built on the south side of the green in 1629. With the aim of saving girls 'from the deluge of vice', Mrs Francis Carpue established a school in 1760 that later evolved to become St Mary's Roman Catholic College. Brook Green was formerly marshy and contaminated by waste that ran off nearby brickfields but orchards were planted following improvements in drainage. An annual fair was held from 1800, but it became too rowdy and was banned after 1823. Cheap terraced houses were built to the east of the green and were principally occupied by Irish labourers. The *Kensington Gazette* called the area a 'rookery' and cholera broke out in 1859. The houses that filled the area over the rest of the century were of better quality and although their architecture is varied, the overall effect is harmonious.

Meanwhile, Brook Green maintained its popularity with benevolent institutions; William and Catherine Booth began the work of the Salvation Army in a small house on the green, ST PAUL'S School relocated here and its trustees, the Mercers' Company, later added a girls' school. Caterers J Lyons expanded their Cadby Hall factory to take over the buildings of St Mary's College in 1925, paying enough to enable the college to buy magnificent premises at STRAWBERRY HILL. St Paul's School (boys) moved to CASTELNAU in 1968 but the girls' school has remained here. The Lyons site was redeveloped in the early 1980s, with offices on Hammersmith Road and expensive houses and flats behind. The former Osram lamp factory has been converted into a Tesco supermarket, with Peabody Trust housing. Several large companies have offices in or around Brook Green, notably EMI Music. Residents of the ward are likely to be young, unmarried, living alone and qualified to degree level or higher.

The most illustrious member of staff at St Paul's Girls' School has been Gustav Holst, who was director of music from 1905 until his death in 1934. Holst wrote the *Brook Green Suite* for the school's junior orchestra. It is a suite for strings, consisting of a prelude, air, and dance. Brook Green was also home to the Victorian actor Sir Henry Irving.

✉ W6

♦ 11,522 (Avonmore and Brook Green ward)

Broom Hill • *Bromley*

Originally a hamlet on high ground just to the west of ORPINGTON's High Street, also known as Broomhill. It takes its name from the shrub that grew here, which was used locally for broom-making. Bonnet-making was another cottage industry on the hill. The hamlet is mentioned in Orpington's 18th-century parish records. A document from 1791 states that 'Elizabeth Leet of Broomhill was … said to be married to John Walker though not believed'; she died aged 30, probably from smallpox. From 1819 the Zion Chapel occupied what is now Devonshire Road. The chapel was converted into two dwellings in the 1840s, subsequently 4 and 6 Broomhill Cottages, which survived until 1935. On the southern side of the hill, the Knoll estate was the first part of Orpington to undergo suburbanization, because of its proximity to Orpington station. 'Picturesque' detached houses were erected and a golf course laid out in the early years of the 20th century. These were followed by the Knoll Park and Mayfield estates in the 1920s. The golf links were built over and the clubhouse became St Nicholas' School, which in turn was replaced by more houses, those of Bancroft Gardens, in 1969.

Sir Malcolm Campbell, who set successive land and water speed records in his car and boat both named *Bluebird*, practised flying from fields on Broom Hill in the 1910s.

✉ Orpington BR6

Brownswood Park • *Hackney*

A little-used name for the section of FINSBURY PARK that lies between Blackstock Road and GREEN LANES, in the borough's extreme north-western corner. Brownswood was the local manor from the 13th century. An early version of the name indicates that the lord of the manor may have been called Brand. In 1852 the New River Co. constructed filter-beds on the west side of Green Lanes and 150 acres of surrounding land began to be built up soon afterwards. Within two decades there were over a thousand homes on the Brownswood Park estate, mostly occupied by the professional classes, including those deriving their income from rents and dividends. Wesleyan Methodists built an impressive church at the western end of Wilberforce Road in 1875, replacing a corrugated iron building; the church was demolished in the 1960s. Brownswood was the largest part of South Hornsey until its transfer to Stoke Newington's care in 1900. Pressure on space prompted the popular Brownswood Bowling Club to move north to Green Lanes in 1911, where it added facilities for croquet, tennis and other games, later succumbing to compulsory purchase as part of the WOODBERRY DOWN site. Brownswood's section of Seven Sisters Road remained primarily residential until the 1920s, when shops began to replace houses along its eastern side. Blackstock Road also evolved as part of the Finsbury Park shopping district. During the 1990s the filter-beds were filled in and more housing built. The erection of barriers to convert streets into cul-de-sacs results from efforts to prevent the area's use as a red-light district. The north-eastern end of Seven Sisters Road has the only 'hotel zone' in the borough. The Brownswood ward has a high proportion of young, single, university-educated residents.

✉ N4

♦ 11,331 (Brownswood ward)

Bruce Grove • *Haringey*

A station and street in central TOTTENHAM, with nearby Bruce Castle as the principal place of interest. The Bruce family built Tottenham manor house here in the mid 13th century but Edward I sequestered their property after Robert the Bruce rebelled and became king of Scotland in 1306. The house was rebuilt in 1514 on a scale that would befit visits from Henry VIII and Elizabeth I. The house was known as 'The Lordship' until the late 17th century, when it was remodelled and named Bruce Castle. With the break-up of the manorial estate in 1789 a new road called Bruce Grove was laid out, and semi-detached villas were erected on part of its south-western side. Almshouses were built at the northern end of the road in the early 19th century. In 1827 the Hill family acquired Bruce Castle and converted it into a school. For its first six years the school's headmaster was Rowland Hill, who later devised the basis of the modern postal service. The area remained popular with wealthy merchants, especially Quakers, until the arrival of the railway in 1872. Cheap housing for working-class commuters filled the area over the remainder of the century, with shops and places of entertainment around the station. After the school's closure in 1891, the local board (forerunner of the urban district council established in 1894) bought Bruce Castle and opened the grounds as a public park in the following year. The house is now a museum of local history, with a special collection devoted to the postal service. The Tottenham Carnival is held in Bruce Castle Park in late June. Slightly less than half the residents of the Bruce Grove ward are white and over a third are black or black British. At Bruce Grove Primary School on Sperling Road almost two-thirds of children speak English as an additional language.

✉ N17

🏃 11,997

🚃 'one' Railway (zone 3)

@ www.haringey.gov.uk/leisure/ brucecastlemuseum.htm

Brunswick • *Camden*

A concrete megastructure and its immediate environs, built in the late 1960s on the borders of ST PANCRAS and BLOOMSBURY, north-east of RUSSELL SQUARE. This was the site of a series of Georgian and Victorian terraces, deemed substandard and overcrowded by the council but almost certainly capable of rehabilitation. The architect Patrick Hodgkinson created a pair of layered terraces consisting of flats with glazed 'winter gardens', shops at ground level and car parking below. Many aspects of the original plan never came to fruition: a third set of flats was proposed for Handel Street in place of the Territorial Army centre; the shopping area was to have been glazed over; the concrete was to have been painted cream to match the neighbouring Georgian stucco; and the centre was originally intended as a private development by Marchmont Properties, but Camden council stepped in to take responsibility for the housing. The Brunswick Centre was conceived as a nucleus for the future redevelopment of the entire neighbourhood, which also failed to materialize. Despite the many mutations, the centre is reckoned an architectural success and was given Grade II-listed status in 2000. The Brunswick (as it is now styled) has recently been redeveloped by Allied London Properties, with its shopping centre branded as 'Bloomsbury's high street'. A newly-built Waitrose supermarket closes off one end of the radically transformed retail and restaurant area. Facing Brunswick Square is the Renoir cinema, one of London's leading independent arthouse cinemas. At the 1991 census, 64 per cent of homes in Brunswick ward were one-person households, the highest proportion in London. Brunswick is no longer a ward.

When Thomas Coram's Foundling Hospital was pulled down in the 1920s, its archive was relocated to 40 Brunswick Square. The Foundling Museum's collection includes works of art by Hogarth, Gainsborough and Reynolds as well as social history objects relating to London's first children's home.

✉ WC1

@ www.thebrunswick-london.com (Allied London Properties site about the Brunswick redevelopment); www.coram.org.uk/ heritage.htm (Coram Family site)

Brunswick Park • *Barnet*

A very mixed industrial and residential district situated north of NEW SOUTHGATE and east of FRIERN BARNET, separated from OSIDGE by Pymmes Brook. The Great Northern Railway Co. opened a cemetery beside its railway line in 1861, with its own siding so that coffins could be brought by train from KING'S CROSS. It is now called New Southgate Cemetery. To its north, former sewage works have been converted into a lushly vegetated public open space called Brunswick Park, through which the Pymmes Brook trail runs. Brunswick Park Primary School sits at the park's north-western corner. Brunswick (now New Southgate) recreation ground opened on Oakleigh Road South in 1892, when the first suburban houses were beginning to appear. From the 1920s Brunswick Park saw significant industrial development on land released by the cemetery company north of Waterfall Road, where Standard Telephone and Cable established a factory that employed 14,000 people at its peak. This was a target for enemy attacks in World War II and V1 rockets fell here in 1944. Northern Telecom (Nortel) manufactured telecommunications equipment here from 1989 but left in 2000. The site has since been rebranded the North London Business Park and is the focus of efforts to fill it with a variety of commercial users, although this is proving a challenge. A second industrial area on Oakleigh Road South is being redeveloped for mixed use, including private and social housing. The Brunswick Park ward has a varied socio-economic profile, with some pockets of hardship, but the typical resident is married with children, lives in a mortgaged semi-detached or terraced house and works as a lower level manager for a small business. Twelve per cent of Brunswick Park residents are retired.

Brunswick Park is also the name of a street, ward and recreation ground in north-east CAMBERWELL (London Borough of Southwark).

✉ N11

⫯ 14,668

Bulls Cross • *Enfield*

A rural settlement, situated south-west of the junction of the M25 and the Great Cambridge Road (A10). The name may originate from a family living in the area from the 13th century. Capel Manor, on Bullsmoor Lane, is London's only specialist college of horticulture and countryside studies. It occupies the site of an ancient manor established in the late 13th century, and takes its present name from the Capel family (later lords of Essex), who lived here in the 15th and 16th centuries. The existing manor house was built in the 1750s. The college was established in 1968 in an attempt to bring life back into the derelict buildings and restore the gardens, which now have 30 richly planted acres and 50 themed gardens open to the public, with the accent on the educational and the informative. The 19th-century Myd-

dleton House, used by the Lee Valley regional park authority, has a garden that was made famous by the plantsman E A Bowles. It fell into decay and is being restored as an example of a 20th-century plantsman's garden. Bowles was born here in 1865, and died here in 1954. He published books on this garden and on growing crocus, narcissus and colchicum.

The northern part of Bulls Cross lies to the north of the M25, and across the Hertfordshire border.

✉ Enfield EN1 and EN2; Waltham Cross EN7

📖 Valerie Carter, *Forty Hill and Bulls Cross* (3rd edn), Enfield Preservation Society, 1995

Bullsmoor • *Enfield*

The northernmost part of the built-up spread of ENFIELD, occupying roughly the quadrant between TURKEY STREET and the M25, which separates it from Hertfordshire. Bullsmoor sounds like a close relation of nearby BULLS CROSS but it gained its name from a local family called Bell – the modern spelling is a corruption influenced by its neighbour. Bullsmoor (or Belsmoor) Lane was first recorded in 1572. Bullsmoor Place was the home of Colonel Thomas Boddam in 1800. The Great Eastern Railway built its line to Cheshunt across the moor in 1891. By 1914, housing was spreading into Bullsmoor from Hertford Road, and the subsequent construction of the Great Cambridge Road (A10) created a pincer movement of development. After World War II, Enfield council built houses on former market gardens between Turkey Street and Bullsmoor Lane, with a library and community centre. Land east of the railway was preserved as Aylands open space – a name preferred to its former identity of Dung Field. Bullsmoor Comprehensive School opened in 1977. Now renamed Lea Valley High School and Sports College, the school has a growing roll and was almost totally rebuilt in 2005. Almost 40 per cent of students qualify for free school meals and a similar proportion have English as an additional language. Nearly 200 students are from refugee families, mostly of Turkish origin. Across the rail tracks, on the Elsinge estate Honilands Primary School serves a narrower catchment area than Lea Valley and has a higher percentage of white British students, but a similar proportion come from deprived households.

✉ Enfield EN1 and EN3

Bunhill • *Islington*

Bunhill is an electoral ward taking its name

from a graveyard located at the southern end of CITY ROAD. Bunhill Fields, which is a corruption of Bone Hill Fields, had been associated with interments since Saxon times and became a Quaker burial ground in 1665, the year of the Great Plague. It was popular with Dissenters of various denominations because the ground was unconsecrated. John Bunyan, William Blake and Daniel Defoe are buried here, but their memorials do not mark the precise sites of the graves as there has been so much disarrangement. By the 1800s the graveyard had become so overcrowded as to constitute a health hazard, although it was not closed until 1863. STOKE NEWINGTON'S Abney Park had by then become London's first choice for Nonconformist burials. The Corporation of London then took over Bunhill's maintenance and part of it was laid out as a garden in 1960. Fewer than a fifth of the homes in Bunhill ward are owner-occupied, with the majority of residents renting from Islington council or a housing association. Two-thirds of households have no access to a car.

John Milton lived in Artillery Row, now Bunhill Row, from 1663 to 1674. Here he completed *Paradise Lost* and wrote its sequel *Paradise Regained* and the poetic drama *Samson Agonistes*.

> ✉ EC1
>
> ♟ 10,055
>
> 📖 Susan Black, *Bunhill Fields: The Great Dissenters' Burial Ground*, Brigham Young University Religious Studies Center, 1990
>
> @ www.quakerinfo.com/bunhill.shtml (privately operated Quaker information site)

Burnt Oak • *Barnet*

A deprived community located on the southern side of EDGWARE, dominated by the London County Council's WATLING estate. Evidence has been found of a Roman rubbish pit dating from around AD 300. Most of the cultivated land here had been enclosed by the latter part of the 16th century. A common field called Sheveshill lay near the site of the Tube station and disappeared sometime around the 1830s, when a workhouse for 350 inmates was built at Redhill. A school for 150 children was added to this in 1859, and houses went up in North, South, and East Roads soon afterwards, presumably to serve the workhouse. The workhouse infirmary has since evolved to become Edgware Community Hospital. A farmhouse was built to the south – and it still had a cow-keeper in 1922. Burnt Oak remained predominantly rural until 1924 when the underground station opened and the London County Council bought land to build 4,000 homes. The Watling estate was complete by 1930 and included good provision of green spaces but a variety of other amenities were not made available until later. Private companies then built on the estate's perimeter, notably the Sheffield-based firm Henry Boot and Son, which developed the site of Burnt Oak Farm after 1930. Many residents found employment at the de Havilland aircraft works in Stag Lane. Since World War II, houses and flats have replaced some commercial premises and the old Redhill Hospital buildings. Barnet council has targeted Burnt Oak for various regeneration efforts, such as the demolition of 45 vandalized garages and their replacement by affordable homes in 2002. On almost every index of deprivation, Burnt Oak ranks the highest in the borough and it is the most densely populated. The ward also has the borough's highest proportion of disabled people and relatively large numbers of white Irish and black residents. At 33.7 years, the average age of Burnt Oak residents is relatively low, mainly because of the large number of households with children, including many single-parent households.

The first Tesco supermarket opened in 1929 in Burnt Oak, although founder Jack Cohen had already been selling groceries in the markets of east London for a decade. Boosey and Hawkes moved their musical instrument factory from Burnt Oak to Croxley Green, near Watford, in 2002 after 77 years in this area.

> ✉ Edgware HA8
>
> ♟ 15,243
>
> 🚇 Northern Line (zone 4)

Bury Street • *Enfield*

A former hamlet in LOWER EDMONTON centred on the thoroughfare of that name, which was split in two by the creation of the Great Cambridge Road (A10) in the 1920s. From the mid 17th century Bury Street was one of the four constituent wards of Edmonton. The ward took in an extensive area; its main settlement was WINCHMORE HILL. Bury Hall was a grand Jacobean house, enlarged in 1750, and owned by only three families in its 300-year existence. Its last private owner was William Bowater, the paper-maker. When the hall was auctioned by Harrods in 1914 the particulars of sale stated that its cellar 'covers a larger area than the house, and is believed to have been connected with a subterranean passage that linked up the old houses in Bury Street, and connected with the Church'. Despite this boast the property did not meet its £5,500 reserve price, and subsequently it was demolished to make way for the Great Cambridge Road. Housing began to line Bury Street from the end of the 19th century, but much of the vicinity remained covered by nurseries until its interwar development. The street now crosses the railway via a bridge, which replaced a level crossing and its keeper's cottage. Bury Street West and Little Bury Street, which crosses Salmon's Brook, retained some delightful 18th-century cottages until they were knocked down in the 1930s. One of the few grander survivors is Salisbury House, on Bury Street West. Sensitively restored by Enfield council in 1992, it now serves as an arts centre and a meeting place for various societies. The house adjoins Bury Lodge Park, which has an ornamental garden and a play area for children. The much larger Jubilee Park, on Galliard Road, has extensive recreational facilities.

✉ N9

@ www.lower-edmonton.co.uk/buryst.html (regularly updated private site)

Bushey Mead • *Merton*

A compact set of terraces for the upwardly mobile situated between RAYNES PARK and WIMBLEDON CHASE stations. From the 1890s, suburban houses began to appear on Kingston Road and Bushey Road and after 1900 streets started to sprout southwards off Kingston Road, starting with Chestnut Road and Bronson Road and steadily proceeding westwards. As construction progressed, styles became grander and the more ambitious properties were given bay windows and decorative flourishes. Although all terraced, the houses have been described as 'really aiming to be miniature Victorian villas'. They had small front gardens with railings and privet hedges, while the avenues came to be mostly tree-lined. The twelve parallel streets were all in existence by 1907, although their completion took a little longer as they were gradually extended south to reach Bushey Road. The last piece of the jigsaw was the addition of Approach Road in 1913, linking Kingston Road to Grand Drive and thence to Bushey Road. Several builders had a hand in the estate's development, but the largest partnership was that of local auctioneer and surveyor P J Dixon and his bro-

ther, who maintained a management office on Approach Road. Part of the estate was built on land that had belonged to the parish vestry and was known as Poors Wood. But this name clearly lacked social cachet so Bushey Mead was conceived, after Bushey Meadows, the fields that lay to the south. The streets were popularly referred to as the 'Twelve Apostles', a nickname said to have been invented by the local district nurses. Across Bushey Road lie the Prince George's playing field and a David Lloyd sports centre.

✉ SW20

Bush Hill • *Enfield*

A name occasionally used to distinguish the vicinity of the road of that name (much of which runs along the western edge of Bush Hill Park golf course) from the larger settlement of BUSH HILL PARK in southern ENFIELD. Only one modern street atlas still makes this distinction although Bush Hill and Bush Hill Park were separate estates for several centuries. The former was the older of the two, but the latter was the first to be sold for development and became the site of a station bearing its name. As a result, most residents now consider the whole area to be Bush Hill Park. Sir Hugh Myddleton acquired the Bush Hill estate while he was overseeing the creation of the New River and rebuilt Bush Hill House around 1609. His heirs seem to have sold the estate by 1650. By 1664 Bush Hill House was the largest residence in the parish, assessed for 31 hearths. The house was recased in brick in the 1850s and leased to the shipping magnate Samuel Cunard until 1878. At the end of the century the southern part of the estate was sold for development, while the house (by then called Halliwick) and its grounds became a girls' boarding school. From 1911 the school catered specifically for disabled girls. Housebuilding resumed in the Bush Hill area after World War I with the laying out of the New River estate. The first houses in Sittingbourne Avenue and Faversham Avenue were occupied by 1926 and the modern appearance of the locality was largely fixed by the mid 1930s. The council put up some housing in Halliwick's grounds in the 1960s and the charity I CAN took over the college in 1985 but closed it in 1993. By this time the house had been rebuilt to such an extent that almost nothing of the original mansion remained and it was demolished to make way for Laing Homes' Cunard Crescent.

✉ N21

Bush Hill Park • *Enfield*

A socially advantaged settlement situated on the southern side of ENFIELD. The small estate of Bush Hill Park originated in 1671 and a 'commodious brick mansion' of that name was in existence by 1724. This was also known as the Clock House, from a clock tower that was removed in 1875. The Bush Hill Park Co. began to build suburban houses on the estate in 1877. Prompted by the growth of the area (and stimulating more) the Great Eastern Railway opened a station on the previously existing branch line to ENFIELD TOWN in 1880. Bush Hill Park Golf Club was founded in 1896 and originally occupied the site now covered by the lovely Queen Anne's Gardens. When that land was sold for housing in 1911 the club moved to its present home on Enfield's Old Park estate. Development in Bush Hill Park took different forms on either side of the railway line. To the west were wide, tree-lined roads with well-proportioned houses and large gardens. Much of this side is now designated a conservation area, shaped remarkably like a map of Great Britain and Northern Ireland. Across the tracks the Cardigan estate was laid out from 1889 with terraced houses intended for the working classes. This portion of Bush Hill Park was entirely built up by the outbreak of World War I. The western part continued to fill up after the war and Bush Hill Park House remained as a private residence, though with much smaller grounds, until it was pulled down in 1929. After World War II many of the best houses from the first phase of Bush Hill Park's development were demolished and replaced by privately built blocks of flats. In 1974, Enfield council compulsorily purchased properties north of Main Avenue and demolished Fifth, Sixth and Seventh Avenues to put up a housing estate. Extensive Roman remains were discovered in the process and the new cul-de-sacs were given Roman-related names. The Bush Hill Park ward has the highest proportion of owner-occupied housing and of married couples with children in the borough. Employment levels are high and crime is low.

In 1975 two IRA gunmen shot dead the writer and broadcaster Ross McWhirter on the doorstep of his home in Village Road. McWhirter had publicly campaigned against the IRA and had offered a reward for information leading to the arrest of anyone involved in its London terror campaign.

✉ Enfield EN1

🏃 13,346

🚌 'one' Railway (zone 5)

📖 Denis Hoy, *From Fields to Flats: A History of Bush Hill Park and St Stephen's Church*, Edmonton Hundred Historical Society, 1998

Bushy Park • *Richmond*

The second-largest but least-known of the eight royal parks of London, situated between TEDDINGTON and the Thames at HAMPTON COURT. A Bronze Age barrow and burial mound has been excavated near Sandy Lane and its contents are in the British Museum. There is evidence of medieval settlement and traces of the largest and most complex field system in Middlesex. The park was created in the early 16th century to provide a hunting ground for Hampton Court and the Longford River was cut across the park in the late 1630s to provide the palace with fresh water. Sir Christopher Wren created Chestnut Avenue as a formal approach to Hampton Court Palace, with the Arethusa, or Diana, fountain as its centrepiece. The earls of Halifax beautified the park in the early 18th century but also enclosed it with a wall. A footpath named Cobblers Walk recalls Timothy Bennet's successful campaign in the early 1750s to regain access for the public; the HAMPTON WICK shoemaker was so pleased with his achievement that he wrote a play on the subject. Teddington Hockey Club began playing in Bushy Park in 1871 and is the world's oldest hockey club with a continuous history. In 1900 Queen Victoria gave Bushy House to the Commission of Works for the establishment of the National Physical Laboratory. The laboratory remains on the same site, where it has vastly expanded the scale of its operations. Among its many roles, the NPL is responsible for regulating GREENWICH Mean Time. George V gave permission for Upper Lodge to become a home for Canadian convalescents during World War I, and in World War II the park became the site of Camp Griffiss, which General Dwight Eisenhower made the centre for planning the 1944 D-Day invasion. Eisenhower moved to a quiet cottage here to escape the distractions of central London, bringing only a naval aide, an orderly and 'two negro soldiers', who all stayed with him until the end of the war. The park has few facilities but an abundance of pastoral scenery, including woodland gardens. The Bushy Park History Centre at Upper Lodge is open to visitors by appointment.

✉ Teddington TW11; East Molesey KT8; Hampton TW12; Kingston upon Thames KT1

📖 Kathy White and Peter Foster, *Bushy Park: Royals, Rangers and Rogues*, Foundry Press, 1997

@ www.royalparks.gov.uk/parks/bushy.park; www.bushy.org.uk (Friends of Bushy and Home Parks site)

Butlers Wharf *see* SHAD THAMES

Butts Farm • *Hounslow*

A former model farm in north HANWORTH, now densely built up, except beside the River Crane. Prehistoric pottery has been uncovered here. With the success of his retail business in WESTBOURNE GROVE, William Whiteley bought Glebe Farm and Butts Farm in 1891 and added neighbouring Rookeries Farm three years later to create a 200-acre agricultural estate that provided fresh produce for his store. Whiteley built villas for the farm's managers, cottages for labourers and a chapel. The farm bred cows, pigs, poultry and rabbits and there were orchards and fruit gardens. Despite his enormous wealth Whiteley spent much of his time living in a bungalow on the farm. Some of the cottages and the former chapel survive but much of the farm was developed with housing by New Ideal Homesteads in the mid 1930s. After World War II the council built an estate of terraced houses and four-storey blocks of flats, set around two greens. Remaining farm buildings were replaced in 1976 by light industrial units. Richmond Housing Partnership took over management of the Butts Farm estate in 2000, after tenants narrowly voted in favour of the arrangement. The association has been making efforts to improve the poor state of the environment, but can do little about the problems of social deprivation, which are some of the worst in the borough. In January 2004 police on the estate made one of the first ever uses of new laws empowering them to prevent small gatherings.

✉ Feltham TW13

Cable Street *see* ST GEORGE IN THE EAST

Caledonian Road • *Islington*
A characterful north-south route running through the western edge of ISLINGTON. In 1826 a company was formed to build a road from KING'S CROSS to HOLLOWAY ROAD. Originally named Chalk Road, it ran through the open COPENHAGEN Fields for most of its length. In 1861 it was renamed Caledonian Road, after the Royal Caledonian Asylum, founded in 1815, which had moved to Copenhagen Fields in 1827. The asylum cared for 'the children of soldiers, sailors and mariners, natives of Scotland, who have died or been disabled in the service of their country; and the children of indigent Scotch parents residing in London, not entitled to parochial relief'. Like REEDHAM Asylum near Purley, the building has gone but its purpose survives in the form of a charitable trust. Terraced houses were built for the middle classes in 1850s, but soon slid downmarket into occupation by the working classes, often with more than one family to a house. PENTONVILLE Prison was built on land to the south of the asylum in 1842. The Great Northern Hospital stood on Caledonian Road until 1884. In 1892 the first public baths in Islington, with first- and second-class facilities, were built on the hospital site. The baths were demolished and rebuilt in 1980 and are universally known as the Cally Pool. Most decades of the 20th century saw further development of some kind, including the construction of post-war council flats, and more housing in the 1980s, mainly at the northern end of the road. Caledonian Road is a comparative rarity in today's London: a proud and close-knit working-class community. However, its relative affordability is attracting increasing numbers of young graduates. The Bemerton estate, which has had problems with anti-social behaviour, has recently undergone a £10 million improvement programme. The area north-east of Caledonian Road station is earmarked for the construction of a huge waste transfer station, with associated developments, decanted here as part of Arsenal Football Club's relocation. Caledonian Road is home to numerous alternative charities and community organizations, related to issues as diverse as gay rights and counselling, pacifism, Tibetan Buddhism, and support for prisoners' families. There is also a number of home improvement outlets, specializing in ironwork, glass, paint and second-hand furniture.

The London Canal Museum, on New Wharf Road, was built as a cold store in 1863, to preserve ice imported from Norway to make ice cream.

✉	N1; N7
👤	11,566 (Caledonian ward)
🚉	Silverlink Metro (Caledonian Road and Barnsbury, zone 2); Piccadilly Line (zone 2)
@	www.canalmuseum.org.uk

Camberwell • *Southwark*
A socially mixed Victorian suburb situated west of PECKHAM. Camberwell was first recorded in Domesday Book but its name is of uncertain origin. The village was of some medieval significance and St Giles' was the mother church of a parish that took in DULWICH and Peckham. King John enjoyed hunting here and, much later, so did Charles I and Charles II. In 1615 the vicar of St Giles' established Wilson's School, which has since decamped to SOUTH BEDDINGTON. During the 18th century market gardening became very important to the village and the construction of new roads and bridges brought the first commuters as early as the 1780s. High-class terraced houses were built in the 1820s and 1830s, but by the mid 19th century terraces of much smaller dwellings were covering much of the district. The annual fair on Camberwell Green was abandoned in 1855 as Camberwell became a 'walking suburb', with clerks tramping north to the City each morning. Those who could afford it took the new horse-drawn omnibuses and for a while the rich lived cheek

by jowl with the poor. The arrival of horse-drawn trams in the 1870s made Camberwell even more accessible but less desirable, and the old Georgian properties were sub-divided for multiple occupancy by the working classes, growing numbers of whom began to work in small-scale local industries and the building trade. Housebuilding for the middle classes continued in the south of Camberwell into the 1880s. The Free Library and Art Gallery moved from Battersea to Camberwell in 1887 and over the following decade the philanthropist John Passmore Edwards funded new buildings that became the South London Gallery and the Camberwell School of Art (now Camberwell College of Arts). In 1910 the Peabody estate at Camberwell Green brought the first of many flats, culminating in system-built blocks in the 1960s and 1970s. Along the main roads the ground floors of terraced houses have been converted for retail or service use. Many older properties have been restored in recent decades as Camberwell has been rediscovered by the middle classes. Part of southeast Camberwell is now a conservation area.

The Camberwell Beauty (*Nymphalis antiopa*) is a velvety chocolate-brown butterfly, rarely seen because it migrates each year from Scandinavia. The name comes from its first recorded sighting, on Coldharbour Lane in 1748. *Camberwell Beauty* is also the title of a V S Pritchett story and of the humorist Jenny Eclair's debut novel. George Gissing proposed the title *Miss Lord of Camberwell* for his story of romance in London's new suburbs, but his publisher persuaded him to change it to *In the Year of Jubilee*. Former Camberwell residents include the 19th-century poet Robert Browning and the actor Michael Caine. A large marijuana cigarette is dubbed a 'Camberwell carrot' in the cult film *Withnail and I*.

✉ SE5

♦ 35,229 (Brunswick Park, Camberwell Green and South Camberwell wards)

📖 Mary Boast, *The Story of Camberwell*, London Borough of Southwark, 2000; H J Dyos, *Victorian Suburb*, Leicester University Press, 1961 (definitive but rare)

@ www.southlondongallery.org; www.camberwell.arts.ac.uk; www.camberwellonline.co.uk (blogger's local information site)

Cambridge Heath • *Tower Hamlets*
The neglected north-eastern corner of BETHNAL GREEN. There is no connection with the

university town; the Saxon who gave his name to the heath was probably called Centbeorht, which might as easily have been corrupted to Canterbury as Cambridge. The heath lay on a gravel plateau surrounded by marshland and was part of the 'waste' of STEPNEY manor in the Middle Ages. Apart from a house that was described as 'ancient' in 1275 there was very little building among the vegetable patches and hayfields until cottages began to appear in the mid 18th century. Later that century a more intense period of development began which produced terraced houses, factories and chapels. During the first half of the 19th century the locality was almost fully built up, although a windmill survived in 1836. Among the active builders here was the London Society for Promoting Christianity among the Jews, which built Palestine Place. Cambridge Heath station opened on the Great Eastern Railway's new branch line to Enfield in 1872. Most of the residents were poor, especially in the streets around the railway line and the Regent's Canal and on Russia Lane. London's greatest philanthropic developer, the Peabody Trust, built its first Bethnal Green blocks here in 1910 and municipal flats began to replace slum housing after World War I. Bethnal Green borough council, at that time under communist–socialist control, built the Lenin estate in 1927, and the incoming liberal–progressive administration changed the estate's name to Cambridge Heath the following year. Municipal building continued up to and after World War II and Cambridge Heath remains dominated by blocks of flats, including some recent private builds and conversions mostly targeted at young singles. Local commercial premises generally operate at the lower end of the market, with the notable exception of a private art gallery.

✉ E2

🚌 'one' Railway (zone 2)

Cambridge Park • *Richmond*
The story of this part of east TWICKENHAM, south of Richmond Bridge, follows, with a few variations, a typical pattern: some distance from the City a wealthy personage creates a substantial estate with a grand house at its heart, but as communications improve the grounds are gradually sold off for suburban housing and in time the original edifice succumbs to the developer's bulldozer. A Jacobean mansion, built around 1610 and enlarged in the 1650s, stood for a century and a

half before acquiring the name Cambridge House from Richard Owen Cambridge, an author, poet and friend of Dr Johnson and of Horace Walpole, who lived at STRAWBERRY HILL. In 1795 the Cambridge family watched over Maria Fitzherbert, the clandestine 'wife' of George, Prince of Wales (subsequently the Prince Regent, and then George IV), while she stayed nearby at MARBLE HILL. In the 1850s the future Edward VII used to sneak out from Kew Palace to cavort with his friends at the riverside here. Factories, as well as houses, covered much of the 74 acres of parkland in the early years of the 20th century. Richmond ice rink opened in 1928, but closed four years later because of financial difficulties, reopening in 1934. Finally overwhelmed by its encroaching neighbours, Cambridge House was demolished in 1937. The ice rink closed for good in 1992, to be replaced by executive-style homes.

> ✉ Twickenham TW1

> 📖 M Bunch, *Cambridge Park, East Twickenham*, Borough of Twickenham Local History Society, 1992

Camden Road • *Camden/Islington*

A former turnpike road connecting CAMDEN TOWN with Holloway's NAG'S HEAD locality, skirting KENTISH TOWN and TUFNELL PARK en route. Together with SEVEN SISTERS Road, Camden Road formed a major through route from Camden to TOTTENHAM, reaching HOLLOWAY in 1826. Housebuilding lagged behind the road's progress. The Camden end was lined fairly quickly with compact terraced houses but development did not reach Holloway until the 1850s, when more substantial terraces and large semi-detached villas were built. Camden Town station (now Camden Road) opened on the corner of Royal College Street in 1870 on a line that had originally been intended to carry freight from the Regent's Canal to the London docks. A literary and scientific institution called the Athenaeum was established in 1871 at the junction of Camden Road and Parkhurst Road, later serving as a banqueting hall and rehearsal studio before its replacement by a petrol station. At the southern end of the road, St Michael's Church was consecrated in 1894. Its imposing bulk is marred by the failure to build a planned tower. The Aerated Bread Co. operated a factory on the other side of the road from 1915 to 1938. Its site is now occupied by a high-tech Sainsbury's, with associated housing and workshops. Camden Road was spared

wholesale redevelopment in the 1960s and 1970s but several council estates were built in its hinterland and run-down properties were replaced untidily. The presence of a media community in the neighbourhood is reflected in the changing nature of the road's bars and other amenities, while the retail scene near the southern end is dominated by overspill from Camden Town.

The French poets Arthur Rimbaud and Paul Verlaine stayed on Royal College Street in 1873.

> ✉ NW1; N7

> 🚇 Silverlink Metro (zone 2)

Camden Town • *Camden*

A swarming 'market town', located a mile north of EUSTON. Camden takes its name from Charles Pratt, 1st Baron Camden from 1765 and 1st Earl Camden from 1786, whose family owned the KENTISH TOWN estate in the 18th and 19th centuries. Pratt was a man of many titles, including Viscount Bayham, but the Camden tag related to his CHISLEHURST property, Camden Place. An Act of Parliament of 1788 authorized him to develop the land to the east of what is now Camden High Street and George Dance junior devised a plan for a neoclassical estate, but the parsimonious Pratt chose a less ambitious option. Land to the west of the modern High Street belonged to Lord Southampton, who began to exploit it in the early 19th century. The arrival of the Grand Union Canal from Birmingham in 1814 provided an early spur to growth in the north. Commercial activity was forbidden south of Camden's flight of locks so factories and warehouses clustered here, with attendant workers' housing. In 1822 Camden Town became the first London home of Charles Dickens, when he was ten years old and the district was still surrounded by fields. The now-demolished house, at 16 Bayham Street, was probably the model for Bob Cratchit's home in *A Christmas Carol*. In the mid 1830s the Euston–Birmingham railway brought the noise and dirt of sidings and goods yards and Camden Town's still new gentlemen's residences were subdivided into lodgings for Irish and Italian immigrants. Camden at that time has been described as the 'tradesmen's entrance to the capital'. Shops and places of entertainment later flanked the High Street, including the Camden Theatre, now the Camden Palace. Camden Town Tube station opened on what is now the Northern Line in 1907, but this failed to draw wealthier commuters and the pattern of social decline continued in the first half of the 20th century. Municipal housing replaced some bomb sites and run-down streets after World War II, when a Greek-Cypriot community took root. In the 1960s, Camden Town began to regain popularity with the middle classes, who refurbished dilapidated properties. Small-scale infilling is of a particularly high quality in Camden because much of it was done by architects building their own homes. Camden market began in 1974 in the former Dingwall's packing case factory at Camden Lock and gained a Sunday licence two years later. The market has since spread to fill every available open space nearby and offers an increasing range of covered sites. The emphasis is on youth-oriented clothing but there are also hundreds of stalls devoted to handicrafts, artwork, music and food. There are predictions that visitor numbers could reach an astonishing 40 million a year. Government statisticians report that Blackpool pleasure beach is Britain's number one leisure destination – but that is only because they do not measure Camden market's hordes.

In 1911 Walter Sickert founded the Camden Town Group of post-Impressionist artists, which included Augustus John, Lucien Pissarro and Wyndham Lewis. A fine example of the school is C W R Nevinson's grim yet romantic view of *The Towpath, Camden Town, by Night* (c.1912), in the Ashmolean Museum, Oxford. An unofficial plaque at 8 Royal College Street marks the house where the French poets Paul Verlaine and Arthur Rimbaud lived briefly in 1873, having fled France and the scandal created by their relationship. In the mid 1990s Camden Town gained a different cultural reputation, as London's prime centre for alternative nightlife and the cradle of Britpop, nurturing bands like Blur, Echobelly and Sleeper, while Oasis made it their London base.

✉ NW1

♦ 22,064 (Cantelowes and Camden Town with Primrose Hill wards)

🚇 Northern line (zone 2)

📖 Jack Whitehead, *The Growth of Camden Town*, Jack Whitehead, 1999

@ www.camdentown.co.uk (community site); www.camdennewjournal.co.uk (online version of local newspaper); www.camden.tv (downloadable local videos); www.camdenlock.net (largest of several sites devoted to the market)

Canada Water • *Southwark*

A former dock and now a regeneration zone in ROTHERHITHE. Canada Dock was constructed in 1876 on the site of two former timber ponds and was the first major scheme of the Surrey Commercial Docks Co., an amalgamation of former rivals. The dock took its name from its specialization in Anglo-Canadian trade. The proximity of the East London Railway posed difficulties for the builders, who used enormous amounts of concrete to ensure that the line would never be flooded. Huge new warehouses were built alongside the new dock, each capable of holding 35,000 tons of grain. In 1926 two neighbouring timber ponds were replaced by Quebec Dock, which was connected to Canada Dock. In the early 1980s, following the progressive closure of the Surrey Docks and their reinvention as SURREY QUAYS, all of Quebec Dock and most of Canada Dock were filled in. Surrey Quays shopping centre covered the bulk of the Canada Dock site and the Mast leisure park replaced the dock's southern goods yard with a nine-screen cinema, a bingo hall, a ten-pin bowling alley and several 'formula' restaurants with an emphasis on American cuisine. The remaining northern portion of the dock was reduced in depth and reeds were planted to encourage waterfowl. The Daily Mail Group's Harmsworth Quays printing works was built on the site of Quebec Dock. Canada Water station opened in 1999, providing an interchange between the East London line and the newly built Jubilee line extension. Canada Water is set for major redevelopment in the next few years, as the result of a joint initiative by Southwark council and British Land Canada Quays Ltd. Proposals include a library, leisure facilities, a department store and a new public space with the Canada Water dock at its heart. The plans include around 2,000 new homes in mixed styles and tenures, and around 100,000 square feet of new office, business start-up and live-work space.

Harmsworth Quays doubles as Carver's printing works in the James Bond film *Tomorrow Never Dies*.

✉ SE16

🚇 Jubilee Line; East London Line (zone 2)

@ www.canadawater-southwark.com (council redevelopment and community site)

Canary Wharf • *Tower Hamlets*

An 86-acre office estate occupying much of the former West India Docks in the north-west corner of the ISLE OF DOGS. The *Guinness Book of Records* has rated it the world's largest commercial development and this is probably the only part of London that is indistinguishable from the downtown district of a modern American city. The original Canary Wharf was constructed in 1937 for unloading and storing fruit from the Canary Islands. Following the closure of the docks in the late 1960s, Limehouse Studios took over the quayside warehouses and began to make television programmes. Following its establishment in 1981, the London Docklands Development Corporation began to promote the wharf to real-estate investors. The initial adviser-cum-developer was the American entrepreneur G Ware Travelstead but he was unable to secure the necessary funding for his scheme, so the Canadian developers Olympia and York stepped in, signing an agreement with the LDDC in 1987. Olympia and York created a masterplan for the site based on its previous successful projects in Toronto and at Battery Park City in Manhattan, which included the World Financial Center. However, unlike the New York project, which echoed the existing streetscape, Canary Wharf represented an entirely new departure for London. Nearby residents reacted sceptically to the plan but the television studios were demolished within months. Canary Wharf was laid out as four neighbourhoods, each grouped around a public space and Cesar Pelli's art deco-influenced tower at One Canada Square was completed in 1990. At just over 800 feet, this remains the tallest building in London. The rest of the first phase was completed two years later, at a time of plunging commercial property values. The developer went into administration, leaving more than half the office space unlet and aggravating the doubts of potential tenants. As the market recovered a refinancing deal created a new consortium that included Olympia and York's owner, Paul Reichmann. The consortium bought Canary Wharf back from the administrators and completed the second phase in 1997. The Jubilee Line extension, which had been delayed by the absence of promised funding from the developers, was completed in 1999. As a result of its eventual success, Canary Wharf has gone on to consume the neighbouring HERON QUAYS, which had initially been planned on a much more modest scale, and new phases continue to unfold on adjoining sites. The project caused consternation to the Corporation of London, the governing body of the CITY OF LONDON, which suffered an exodus of finan-

cial corporations and reacted by relaxing planning restrictions. The opening of Jubilee Place boosted Canary Wharf's role as a shopping centre in 2004. In March of that year the Songbird consortium acquired two-thirds of the share capital in the Canary Wharf Group plc for about £1.1 billion. Around 70,000 people presently work at Canary Wharf, with 95 per cent of existing space leased. When all available sites have been fully developed, the estate may have more than twice the floor space and working population than in 2006.

Canary Wharf provided the backdrop for scenes in *Batman Begins* and *Basic Instinct 2*.

✉ E14

🚇 Jubilee Line; Docklands Light Railway, Lewisham branch (zone 2)

⛴ Canary Wharf pier

📖 S K A Naib, *London Canary Wharf and Docklands: Social, Economic and Environmental*, University of East London, 2002

@ www.canarywharf.com (developer's site); www.mycanarywharf.com (commercial local information site)

Cann Hall • *Waltham Forest/Newham*
An electoral ward located in south-east LEYTONSTONE. This was a small manor, also known as Canons Hall, with a history dating from Norman times when it belonged to Holy Trinity monastery in ALDGATE. Cann Hall later became the country estate of the Colegraves and many of the streets here are named after branches of the family. The hall and the buildings of Cann Hall Farm were pulled down when the estate was built up between 1880 to 1895. The housing is mostly in compact terraces and there is an imposing primary school. There has been some recent infilling and the construction of a new Methodist church. At the western end of Cann Hall Road is the Thatched House, well-known as a local landmark. An inn of this name stood in the vicinity from the 18th century, but the present terraced establishment dates from 1875. WEST HAM Cemetery lies in the south of the locality, just within the Newham borough boundary. Almost half of Cann Hall's residents are from ethnic minorities, the largest single group being of black Caribbean origin. Around half the pupils at Cann Hall Primary School have English as an additional language and 33 other languages are spoken. Children enter the school with levels of attainment that are

well below average, according to a 2000 report by the educational standards agency Ofsted.

✉ E7; E11

♦ 11,388

Canning Town • *Newham*

A solidly working-class district, though with less industry than before, situated north of the ROYAL VICTORIA Dock and east of the River Lea. The settlement was originally called Hallsville and probably took its modern name from George Canning, briefly prime minister in 1827, or his son Charles Canning, first viceroy of India from 1858 until his death in 1862. Others suggest that the name came from a mid-19th-century factory, possibly a cannery, but historians have failed to trace its identity. The opening of a railway station (initially called Barking Road) in 1847 stimulated early jerry-built development, mostly without proper drainage, leaving the population prone to outbreaks of disease. The fastest phase of growth came after the 1880s, in the heyday of the ROYAL DOCKS. The area's greatest employer was the Thames Iron Works, Victorian shipbuilders to the world and the original home of WEST HAM Football Club. Thirty-eight spectators died at the ironworks when the slipway collapsed at the launch of the warship HMS *Albion* in 1898. The docks brought about significant immigration and Canning Town had the largest black population in London by 1920. Ironically, this was the year that comedy writer Johnny Speight was born here. He went on to create the bigoted television character Alf Garnett. The area was heavily damaged in the Blitz, leading to the construction of numerous council tower blocks after the war. The partial collapse of the Ronan Point tower block, in the CUSTOM HOUSE area, in 1968 marked the start of a withdrawal from high-rise solutions to accommodation needs throughout the UK, and beyond. More recent development has taken the now typical form of smaller units in a never-ending series of cul-de-sacs, built by housing associations. Poverty and unemployment are high and at Hallsville Primary School over three-quarters of the pupils are eligible for free school meals.

East London's association with criminal gangs has survived longest in Canning Town, still notorious at the end of the 20th century as the last bastion of old-fashioned East End criminality. Nevertheless, the grim surroundings seem frequently to have inspired humour in the residents; the comic actors Reg Varney, Marty Feldman and Windsor Davies all grew up in Canning Town.

✉ E16

♦ 23,339 (Canning Town North and Canning Town South wards)

🚇 Jubilee Line; Docklands Light Railway, Beckton branch (zone 3)

📖 Howard Bloch and Nick Harris, *Canning Town*, Nonsuch, 2005

Cannon Hill • *Merton*

A green and pleasant south-eastern corner of RAYNES PARK, some of which lies above the 70 foot contour, and so about 30 feet higher than most of its environs. For centuries this was part of the 'waste' land of Merton manor, wild and uncultivated. When the canons of Merton Priory acquired the manor in 1121, they set about improving the land and eventually sold it for farming. In 1763 William Taylor built Cannon Hill House, an impressive stuccoed mansion with surrounding parkland adjoining Cannon Hill Farm. A City businessman, Richard Thornton, bought the estate in 1832 and lived in the house until his death in 1865. Edward Rayne, meanwhile, acquired most of the neighbouring farmland as part of his WEST BARNES estate. Thornton left over £3 million in his will, the largest fortune of his times, which was progressively diminished by dispersal throughout an ever-extending family. The Cannon Hill estate remained in the hands of the executors until World War I. The grounds continued to be used by the Thornton family for game shooting, while the house became dilapidated and had to be demolished. In the 1920s the council built the pleasing Whatley and Cannon Hill estates, while builder George Blay laid out a series of roads, including Grand Drive and the streets branching off it, and followed this with developments around Cannon Hill Lane during the 1930s. Blay's properties were mostly affordable but well-proportioned terraced houses supported by council subsidies, some for sale and others to let. With the co-operation of Blay and the council, and the generosity of benefactors – notably Joseph Hood MP – much of Cannon Hill was saved from development and remains open space. Cannon Hill Common, opened as a park in 1927, has a central area designated as a wildlife reserve. According to the 2001 census, the typical Cannon Hill resident is likely to be a white, married owner-occupier who is a little older than the average Londoner.

✉ SW20; Morden, SM4

👤 9,286

📖 Evelyn M Jowett, *Raynes Park with West Barnes and Cannon Hill: A Social History,* Merton Historical Society, 1987

Cannon Street • *City*

One of the CITY OF LONDON's longest streets and the site of its most symbolically important relic. Linking the MONUMENT to St Paul's Churchyard, Cannon Street traces the route of the ancient riverside track that ran alongside the Thames towards the STRAND. It was first recorded in 1183 as Candelewrithstret, the street of the candlewrights. The City ward of Candlewick derives its name from the same source. Cannon Street used to stretch only as far west as Walbrook. It took its present form in the mid 1850s, when a path was cleared through a network of small lanes south-east of ST PAUL'S and the whole route was widened. Cannon Street station and its accompanying bridge over the Thames opened in 1866. The station served as the new terminus of the South-Eastern Railway, which had originally run into London Bridge station, and remains the terminus for services from the Kent coast. British Rail reconstructed the bridge in 1981 and an office block was built over the station later in the same decade.

Sometime in the Middle Ages a limestone monolith was placed in the middle of Cannon Street, where it may have acted as a focus for judicial proceedings. Over the years, it became the subject of various legends, including that a Trojan king had brought it there, that it marked the site of Druidic sacrifices, and that London's prosperity depended on its safekeeping. Edward III made it the axis of the City's trade when he granted Londoners the right to hold markets within a seven-mile radius of London Stone, as it had come to be known. In 1742 a chunk of the original block was set into the wall of St Swithin's Church. When wartime bombing destroyed the church, the Corporation of London moved the stone to GUILDHALL. It now sits in a niche in the façade of the Chinese bank that stands on the site of St Swithin's.

✉ EC4

🚆 South Eastern Trains (zone 1); Circle Line; District Line (zone 1)

Canonbury • *Islington*

A Georgian and early Victorian suburb in east ISLINGTON, fringed by post-war council estates. Canonbury, the 'manor of the canons' of St Bartholomew's Priory in SMITHFIELD, was first recorded in 1373. Canonbury House was in existence by this date and stood isolated here for almost four centuries. The house underwent a succession of alterations and partial demolitions, of which the lasting results are a 16th-century tower (now a Masonic research centre) and an east range that survives as part of Canonbury Place. In the early 17th century the scientist and philosopher Sir Francis Bacon spent the last ten years of his life at Canonbury House and the writers Oliver Goldsmith and Washington Irving later lodged in the tower. By 1730 the Canonbury tavern had been built to the north-east of the house, drawing crowds to its tea gardens. In the late 18th century the stockbroker John Dawes began to erect villas around what remained of the house, including a new Canonbury House in 1795. In 1803 the Earl of Northampton leased more land for building and developers added short rows of houses but progress was sporadic and many gaps remained in the second quarter of the century, when St Paul's Church and St Stephen's Church were built on Hopping Lane and Canonbury Road respectively. Terraces and pairs of villas spread across Canonbury from the 1850s and Canonbury station opened on Newington Green Road in 1858. The present station on Wallace Road replaced it twelve years later. Hopping Lane was renamed St Paul's Road in 1862. The Georgian heart of Canonbury did not suffer the same degree of social decline that affected most of Islington from the end of the 19th century. It dipped in the 1930s but was quick to recover after World War II. The borough and county councils built estates on the overcrowded outskirts, mostly on a small scale and near the main roads. By far the largest project, the Marquess estate was completed in 1976 to widespread acclaim but has since required costly rehabilitation. The Estorick Collection of Modern Italian Art opened at Northampton Lodge in 1998. The gallery focuses on early-20th-century Futurist art and is open from Wednesday to Sunday. The Hen and Chickens pub on St Paul's Road has a popular upstairs theatre.

The writer Evelyn Waugh lived in Canonbury Square in the late 1920s, as did George Orwell in 1945, the year that saw the publication of *Animal Farm* – and the birth of film director Alan Parker in Canonbury. The poet Louis MacNeice lived on Canonbury Park South between 1947 and 1952.

✉ N1

👥 9,899

🚍 Silverlink Metro (zone 2)

📖 Mary Cosh, *History of St Stephen's Church, Canonbury: The Building and the People from its Consecration in June 1839 to June 1989*, St Stephen's Church, Canonbury, 1989

@ www.estorickcollection.com; www.henandchickens.com

Canons Park • *Harrow*

A METROLAND dormitory suburb situated between STANMORE and EDGWARE, especially popular with north London's Jewish community. The name comes from the former landowner, the canons of the Priory of St Bartholomew the Great, West SMITHFIELD, which was granted six acres of land here in 1331. James Brydges, afterwards the first Duke of Chandos, created the palatial mansion of Canons around 1718. To complete the ostentatious set-up, Brydges had an orchestra accompany his meals and hired Handel as resident composer. 'Having such a composer was an instance of real magnificence … such as no prince or potentate on earth could at that time pretend to,' wrote John Mainwaring in his *Life of Handel* (1760). The mansion survived for less than 30 years before a much smaller substitute took its place, built mainly with materials reclaimed from the demolition of its predecessor. Other parts of the original mansion were sold as architectural salvage and the original colonnade now stands in front of the National Gallery in TRAFALGAR SQUARE. Around 1898, Arthur du Cros, founder of the Dunlop Rubber Co., acquired the house and surrounding grounds and commissioned Charles E Mallows to redesign the gardens, which were considered to be amongst the finest of the Edwardian era. The house was bought by the North London Collegiate School in 1929, while the Canons Park Estate Company built up the neighbouring land with a startling variety of properties, from modest semi-detached houses to extravagant so-called mansions. The arrival of the Metropolitan Railway in 1932 contributed to the success of the development, which is known as the Du Cros or DC estate. Harrow council is presently restoring some of the historic features of Canons Park open space with support from the Heritage Lottery Fund. The Canons ward has an exceptionally large number of pensioners, raising the average age of residents to 43.2 – much older than in most other parts of London. At least half of the white residents of Canons Park are Jewish. There is also a significant Indian minority, most of whom are Hindus.

The television personality Esther Rantzen and actress Rachel Weisz went to the North London Collegiate School. The actress Maureen Lipman is a former Canons Park resident.

✉ Edgware HA8

👥 10,091 (Canons ward)

🚍 Jubilee Line (zone 5)

Carnaby Street • *Westminster*

A pedestrianized thoroughfare running parallel with the middle part of Regent Street, to its west. The street was laid out in the 1680s and the first property known to have stood here was Karnaby House, built by bricklayer Richard Tyler. The house may have been named after the village of Carnaby in Yorkshire. By the mid 19th century most of the street was given over to trades of various kinds and a number of the premises were subsequently converted to sweatshops working for the gentlemen's outfitters in nearby Savile Row. In the 1950s some of these tailors began to produce more distinctive garments for direct sale, including suits for the smartly dressed Mods of the early 1960s. Off-the-peg fashion retailers soon joined the party and within a few years Carnaby Street and its immediate neighbours had become world famous for their trendy unisex boutiques. At the height of 'swinging London' only the King's Road offered serious competition. Slow decline set in at the end of the 1960s, with periodic attempts to reverse it. The street was garishly refurbished by the council in 1973, and during the 1990s local traders attempted to 'reposition' the area as West Soho, with very limited success. The latest idea, promoted by landowners Shaftesbury plc, is simply to brand it 'Carnaby'. The street has taken a turn for the better lately, and offers an increasingly eclectic selection of clothes and accessories amid a dwindling proportion of gimmicky tat. Several cult brands have recently opened flagship outlets here and the danger now is that bigger names will flock to the street and homogenize it.

'Everywhere the Carnabetian army marches on,' declared Ray Davies in the Kinks' 1966 hit *Dedicated Follower of Fashion*, but by 1977 Carnaby Street was 'not what it used to be' according to The Jam's B-side of that name.

✉ W1

📖 Paolo Hewitt and Sean Body (eds), *The Sharper Word: A Mod Anthology*, Helter Skelter, 2002; Peter Roy Myatt, *Carnaby Street Study*, Greater London Council, 1975

@ www.carnaby.co.uk (Shaftesbury plc's local information site)

Carshalton • *Sutton* (pronounced 'carshawl-tən')

A popular suburb situated east of SUTTON, Carshalton began life as a 'farmstead by a river source, where watercress grows', or so its name suggests. Few parts of Greater London can be said to have reached their peak in the late 13th century but this was the time when Carshalton's weekly market was at its height, and before prolonged wet weather made the clay soil harder to farm. After a decline in the late Middle Ages, Carshalton revived during the 17th and early 18th centuries when watermills and accompanying industry sprang up along the River Wandle and the mill owners sold off the hinterland for merchants' houses. In Carshalton Park a grotto and ornamental canal were created as part of a landscape garden that was never completed. Around 1707 Sir John Fellows, subsequently the sub-governor of the ill-fated South Sea Co., employed Charles Bridgeman to landscape the grounds of Carshalton House. A water tower with a Delft-tiled plunge bath and a folly called The Hermitage survive. By the mid 19th century Carshalton was the largest settlement for miles around, with a diversity of buildings that extended from grand houses to squalid tenements. Then came a second phase of decline after railway stations opened in Sutton and WALLINGTON but not in Carshalton, owing to objections from the owner of the Carshalton Park estate. The construction of the Sutton to Mitcham line in 1868 eventually brought a passenger station, but the absence of a goods yard was economically disadvantageous. By the end of the 19th century Sutton had become the area's commercial centre, a shift that preserved some of Carshalton's village character. The sale of the Carshalton Park estate led to housebuilding on the land between the village and the railway from the early 1890s. Suburban development swamped the rest of Carshalton in the 1920s and 1930s, and most of the large houses were demolished as their grounds were sold. Honeywood is the borough's heritage centre. It stands in Honeywood Walk at the west end of Carshalton Ponds.

✉ Carshalton, SM5

🚶 19,580 (Carshalton Central and Carshalton South and Clockhouse wards)

🚆 Southern; Thameslink (zone 5)

📖 Wilks and Rookledge, *The Book of Carshalton*, Halsgrove, 2002

Carshalton Beeches • *Sutton*

A southern extension of CARSHALTON popular with upmarket commuters. Much of Carshalton Beeches was formerly part of Barrow Hedges Farm, named after three ancient burial mounds located on the north side of the Oaks Park. For centuries it was strip-farmed common land. Because the SUTTON to CROYDON railway line was forced to swerve south of the village centre, Carshalton's nearest station was originally at WALLINGTON but a halt was provided at the Beeches, named after an avenue of beech trees that the line crossed at this point. This was in sparsely populated territory known as Carshalton Fields, leased by Croydon council from the lord of the manor. The halt was little used in its early years because the steam-hauled shuttle service was infrequent and slow. After World War I, the railway company electrified the line and built a proper station, called Carshalton Beeches, at the halt, making it a regular stop for the London service. The effect was transformative. Within a few years almost all of Carshalton Fields had been covered with housing, much of it of good quality and with generous gardens. With the additional benefit of its elevated setting, the Beeches soon became a more prestigious address than the village itself. Later expansion further south reached new heights of comfort and even ostentation.

Little Holland House stands at 40 Beeches Avenue. This was the self-built home of artist and craftsman Frank Dickinson, who died in 1961. His design for the Grade II*-listed Arts and Crafts interior was inspired by the ideals of William Morris and John Ruskin. The house now belongs to Sutton council and is open to the public on the first Sunday of each month and on bank holidays.

✉ Carshalton SM5

🚆 Southern (zone 5)

📖 Arthur Edward Jones, *From Medieval Manor to London Suburb: An Obituary of Carshalton*, self-published, 1965

@ www.sutton.gov.uk/leisure/heritage/lhh.htm (Little Holland House page on borough council site)

Carshalton on the Hill • *Sutton*

A Victorian suburb that now fills the south-eastern corner of CARSHALTON but originally stood alone in the foothills of the North Downs. In the late 1860s, William Alfred Gale laid out a handful of streets on Sandpiece and Vicars Cross Shotts, two field strips that had belonged to the WOODCOTE estate, and built some substantial villas and the Stanley Hotel. Carshalton on the Hill gained a reputation for its attractive setting and unpolluted south-westerly breezes, drawing visitors from as far afield as continental Europe for holidays or convalescence. The Stanley Hotel prospered for a while but the inception of nearby building work was a blight from which it never fully recovered. The work in question was part of a plan to develop the settlement much more intensively but the absence of mains water and gas proved a deterrent to potential buyers. This lack of amenities resulted in the subdivision of several properties and even their occupation by squatters. Towards the end of the 19th century a clearance programme resulted in the demolition of many of the larger houses and their replacement by more affordable homes. The Stanley Hotel closed in 1897 and the premises were given over to charitable use. The Children's Infirmary opened in 1909, again taking advantage of the clean country air. When Queen Mary became patron of the hospital five years later it was renamed in her honour. In the 1950s the Foundation Hospital for mentally handicapped children transferred to the site and amalgamated with Queen Mary's to create the country's first comprehensive paediatric hospital. With the decline in demand for long-term care facilities, Queen Mary's Hospital closed in 1993 and its functions transferred to ST HELIER. Most of the site has since been redeveloped with private sector housing.

✉ Carshalton SM5

Castelnau • *Richmond* (pronounced as in 'neither castle nor city')

An urban village centred on a 'boulevard' that leads from BARNES to HAMMERSMITH Bridge. The Castelnau area is increasingly considered to include BARN ELMS Common and playing fields. When Major Charles Lestock Boileau built his home here he called it Castelnau House after his family's former estate of Castelnau de la Garde, near Nîmes in France; Boileau's family were Huguenots who had fled to England to escape religious persecution and

settled in Mortlake. In 1843 Boileau began to build Castelnau Villas and several rows of cottages. Holy Trinity Church was consecrated in 1868, by which time the settlement had around 800 residents and 140 houses, many of which were substantial detached properties with large gardens. The population had more than doubled by the time Holy Trinity became a parish in 1888. After Boileau's death in the following year, Upper Bridge Road was renamed Castelnau. With the sale of the Boileau estate, more streets were laid out and lined with housing over the next two decades. In 1928 the London County Council built 640 houses on the western side of Castelnau, with streets named after deans of St Paul's, the former lords of the manor of Barnes. This increased the housing stock to 2,000 and the population to over 5,000. Castelnau House was demolished in the early 1960s and replaced by a public library. The north-western rim of the peninsula has the Harrodian, Swedish and St Paul's schools. To the east, the former Harrods Depository and a pair of Victorian factories were redeveloped in the late 1990s as Harrods Village. A cluster of chic restaurants and bars has coalesced at the Hammersmith Bridge end of Castelnau.

The travel writer Eric Newby and humorist Arthur Marshall were both born in Castelnau. Folk singer Sandy Denny died in a fall at a friend's Castelnau home in 1978.

✉ SW13

📖 Rev S Linton, *The History of Castelnau*, self-published, 1968

Castle Bar Park • *Ealing*

A station and public park with plentiful sports facilities situated in north-west EALING. 'Castle Bar' may refer to a castellated mansion that once stood in a 'bær', Old English for 'swine pasture'. The Italianate mansion Castle Hill Lodge was built for Henry Beaufoy and was bought in 1795 by Maria Fitzherbert, the clandestine 'wife' of George, the Prince of Wales (subsequently the Prince Regent, and then George IV). Edward, Duke of Kent, father of Queen Victoria, bought the house in 1800 and lived there for several years. The lodge was demolished in 1827 and replaced by Kent House, now the St David's Home for Disabled Ex-servicemen, primarily those from the Royal Navy and merchant navy. The Ecclesiastical Commissioners sold five acres of glebe land on Castle Hill in 1852 and around 20 houses were built here over the following decade. From the 1860s a variety of minor schemes speckled the locality with prestigious villas for the gentry of Ealing, but a much more ambitious scheme to lay out the entire area was not realized. Many of the properties have since been replaced by small blocks of private flats, but several survive as part of the Castlebar conservation area. Less imposing homes started to fill the locality more densely from the late 1870s but some plots were not built upon for several decades. St Benedict's Roman Catholic Church, begun in 1895, is now Ealing Abbey. The London County Council began the Cuckoo estate to the west of the railway tracks in the mid 1930s, and Castle Bar Park station was opened to serve it. Cuckoo Hill was once known as Blood Croft, and was said to be an ancient battleground. By the outbreak of World War II, the Cuckoo estate had 1,600 houses and 18 shops, laid out on 'garden city' principles. It is now a conservation area but the designation came too late to prevent detrimental modifications to many properties. Wates built the much-admired Lakeside estate in 1966 on the site of a house called The Grange, preserving much of its landscaped grounds. The Castlebar area has a number of schools, including several small private establishments. Castlebar School caters for young children with learning difficulties.

Charlie Chaplin was educated at the Central London District School, which stood on the site of the Cuckoo estate until 1932.

✉ W13; W7

🚆 First Great Western Link (zone 4)

Castle Green • *Barking & Dagenham*

A residential counterpart to the adjoining RIP-PLESIDE commercial locality, located north of Ripple Road (A13) on the border between BARKING and DAGENHAM. It takes its name from the former Ripple Castle, a minor mansion with a castellated front half, which stood here from c.1800 to 1930. The area is also known as Goresbrook Village, after a small stream that makes its first appearance in Goresbrook Park and flows south to Dagenham Dock. A gore was a wedge-shaped strip of land but also Essex dialect for a 'muddy obstruction in a watercourse'. After the demolition of Ripple Castle the area was built up as Barking and Dagenham expanded to meet each other between the wars. This is an area with social difficulties and it has been the focus of a variety of projects designed to improve the quality of life of its residents. In 2001, following a six-month community involvement project, the prestigious Random

Dance Company put on six performances of *CastleScape*, a work featuring 50 local residents, inside a geodesic dome on Castle Green recreation ground. The Castle Green Centre, which opened on Gale Street in 2005, unifies an extraordinarily wide variety of community resources. These include a crèche and nursery, the Jo Richardson Community School, a library, an adult college, a theatre, entertainment and conference spaces, and sports and catering facilities. At the Jo Richardson School the vast majority of pupils are of white British descent and have below average levels of ability at the time of joining.

✉ Dagenham RM9; Barking IG11

@ www.barking-dagenham.gov.uk/castlegreen (community centre site)

Catford • *Lewisham*

A much-redeveloped town centre surrounded by late Victorian and Edwardian housing, situated on the River Ravensbourne south of LE-WISHAM. Perhaps surprisingly, the name is not some arcane corruption, but probably does mean that wild cats used to frequent the ford that is now the site of Catford Bridge, although an alternative explanation is that 'the cat' was a local landowner's nickname. The name was first recorded in 1254, around the time that the Abbey of Ghent, which had owned the land hereabouts since at least the early tenth century, sold it off as a sub-manor. Two moated houses are recorded as having been built thereafter, one near Catford Bridge and the other at RUSHEY GREEN. Each of these houses had become the nucleus of a small hamlet by the mid 18th century. The green was enclosed in 1810, and soon built upon. The opening of Catford Bridge station on the Mid Kent Railway in 1857 encouraged the construction of houses for the more affluent middle classes. In 1875 the Lewisham board of works built offices here, which later became the town hall, and in the 1880s parades of shops lined Catford Broadway and the parish church of St Laurence was consecrated. With the opening of Catford station in 1892 and the arrival of tram services, suburban development began in earnest. Landowners sold their farms and major developers built extensive estates for clerical commuters, with some light industry to the south. Between the wars, numerous places of entertainment were built, including a theatre, concert hall and greyhound stadium, together with new shops on the Broadway. Lewisham Town Hall was demolished and rebuilt in 1958 and the council radically redeveloped the town centre from the early 1960s, with blocks of flats and a shopping centre. The brutalist office tower Eros House replaced the Lewisham Hippodrome and the Gaumont cinema. St Laurence's Church was demolished and replaced by the council's Laurence House, and a new church was built on Bromley Road (A21). Catford Stadium closed without warning in 2003 and is being replaced by mixed-tenure housing. The council's area action plan, under discussion in 2006, seeks to improve the town centre and build its role as an 'attractive, safe and animated' shopping, cultural and leisure destination.

After his father's discharge from the army, Spike Milligan's family came from India to live in Catford. His poem 'Catford 1933' is reproduced in Kenneth Baker's anthology *London Lines*. In March 1966 the 'Battle of Mr Smith's Club' brought about the downfall of south London's most powerful criminal gang, the Richardsons, and led to the revenge killing of George Cornell by the Kray twins.

✉ SE6

👥 27,246 (Catford South and Rushey Green wards)

🚆 South Eastern Trains (Catford and Catford Bridge, zone 3)

📖 Darrell Spurgeon, *Discover Sydenham and Catford: A Comprehensive Guide to Sydenham, Crystal Palace, Forest Hill, Catford, Hither Green and Grove Park*, Greenwich Guidebooks, 1999

@ www.catford.towntalk.co.uk (commercial local information site)

Chadwell Heath • *Barking & Dagenham/ Redbridge*

Although it is postally a part of ROMFORD and administratively mainly in the borough of BARKING & DAGENHAM, Chadwell Heath really marks the easternmost extent of the IL-FORD district. Records of Chadwell go back to the 14th century, although the heath was called Blackheath until a little after 1600. Chadwell is almost certainly a corruption of 'cald wielle', Old English for a cold spring, so the associations with St Chad are wishful thinking. The water from the well was said never to have dried up and to have been good for eye complaints. Whalebone Lane is so called because of the arch made out of a pair of giant ribs that stood for two centuries at a tollgate on the High Road to Romford, the

whale in question having been stranded in the Thames in 1658. The heath was enclosed by the Crown in 1860 and part of it survives as St Chad's Park, the oldest park in the borough. The district now covers a much larger area than did the original heath, since it has absorbed the neighbouring hamlet of Chadwell Street (which is the part within the borough of Redbridge). Suburban development began at the end of the 19th century and most of the present housing stock dates from between the world wars. The two halves of Chadwell Heath exhibit different socioeconomic characteristics. Home ownership (usually with a mortgage) is highest on the Redbridge side. The part that lies within Barking & Dagenham has a higher proportion of white, working-class council tenants. The district's principal employer is the Dairy Crest milk processing plant on Selinas Lane, which doubled its capacity in 2001. WEST HAM United's training ground is a modest facility located off Saville Road.

Chadwell Heath has briefly been home to the 18th-century feminist Mary Wollstonecraft and the boxer Frank Bruno.

✉ Romford RM6 and RM8

👥 20,329 (Barking & Dagenham's Chadwell Heath ward and Redbridge's Chadwell ward; there has been a Chadwell ward since 1552)

🚆 'one' Railway (zone 5)

📖 D Hewson, *Chadwell Heath and the Road to Romford Market*, Sutton, 1995

Chalk Farm • *Camden*

The calmed-down side of CAMDEN TOWN, situated to the north-west of the market area. Its name comes not from the nature of the soil but from Lower Chalcots Farm, which extended across much of what is now PRIMROSE HILL. 'Chalcots' derived in turn from the Old English 'caldicote', meaning cold cottages. In the 17th century Lower Chalcots farmhouse became a public house, with gardens and an assembly room offering entertainment to walkers. When the railway line to EUSTON was built through in 1837, Lord Southampton sold land for the construction of sidings and locomotive sheds. Houses and pubs for the railway workers were built on the 'island' between the tracks and the Regent's Canal. The underground station opened in 1907. Chalk Farm's landmark is the Roundhouse, a former railway engine shed turned arts venue. Among its varied past repertoire, the Roundhouse has hosted a 'dialectics of liberation' conference organized by psychiatrist R D Laing in 1968 and influential gigs by the Doors (available on DVD) and the Ramones. The building subsequently fell into disuse but has recently been impressively remodelled as a creative centre and performance space. The Pirate Castle was built in 1977 at Gilbeys Wharf, which is named after a former gin warehouse. The castle is home to a boating club and youth activities centre founded by Viscount St Davids, who lived nearby. In 1994 former goods yards on Chalk Farm Road were replaced by a superstore and a housing association estate of 200 homes. The commercial premises of Chalk Farm Road include antique and bric à brac shops and Marine Ices, possibly London's best-loved ice cream parlour.

'Chalk Farm' is cockney rhyming slang for the arm. Its best-known musical association is with 'nutty boys' Madness, but Chalk FarM (sic) is also the name of a Los Angeles rock band.

✉ NW1; NW3; NW5

🚇 Northern Line (zone 2)

📖 Bob Carpenter, *A Heritage Trail around Chalk Farm and Primrose Hill*, Camden Leisure Services, 1993

@ www.roundhouse.org.uk

Chalkhill • *Brent*

A 'remade' housing estate situated on the east side of WEMBLEY PARK, and separated from NEASDEN by the River Brent. Although not shown on maps, the name is widely used locally. Now considered a part of WEMBLEY, Chalkhill was a manor within the ancient parish of KINGSBURY at the time of Domesday Book. The land here once belonged to Edward the Confessor, and later to Westminster Abbey. Chalkhill was built up as a 123-acre METROLAND estate in the mid 1920s, when the Empire Exhibition was held at Wembley Park. Chalkhill House, which had evolved from a dwelling of medieval origin, was used as a school after World War II and was demolished in 1963. In the 1970s most of the suburban housing was replaced by an estate of high-density flats. These in turn were demolished 30 years later in a project entitled 'Remaking Chalkhill'. The last remaining symbol of the old estate came down in 2002 when council leader Ann John blew up the chimney of the boiler house that used to provide heating for more than 1,300 residents. Councillor John said, 'We are saying goodbye to the bad things such as vandalism and disrepair and have listened to what our residents want and need from their homes'. The final 160 homes of 're-made' Chalkhill were completed in 2003. The new housing is undoubtedly an improvement on what went before but still smacks of tight cost control and a lack of room to breathe. Chalkhill's residents are primarily of black African, Pakistani and black Caribbean descent, and numerous refugee families have been placed here.

✉ Wembley HA9

Chancery Lane • *City/Camden/Westminster*

A focal thoroughfare for the London legal profession, running between FLEET STREET and High Holborn. Soon after the middle of the 12th century the Knights Templar created New Street as a route between their old headquarters in HOLBORN and their 'New TEMPLE'. In 1232, Henry III founded the Domus Conversorum on New Street, which occupies a bleak place in the history of Jewish persecution. It was England's principal house of indoctrination, where Jews who had been coerced into renouncing their faith were interned away from their community and instructed in the Christian religion. Henry also closed the schools of law in the City, an act which led to the foundation of the Inns of Chancery (a contraction of Chancellery), where legal students served apprenticeships. In 1377, Edward III gifted the former Domus Conversorum to the Keeper (later Master) of the Rolls of the Court of Chancery and by the early 15th century the road was becoming known as Chancery Lane. The Inns of Chancery ceased to serve an educational role after the Civil War and thereafter functioned as professional clubs. By the 1770s the lane had taken on a decidedly urban character and it retains many Georgian buildings, which form part of the Chancery Lane conservation area. With the steady rise of the legal profession, solicitors took premises here, as did suppliers such as wig makers, strongbox makers, law stationers and booksellers. The Inns of Chancery closed one by one and some of their buildings were replaced by public institutions with legal connections. The Public Record Office was built in stages during the second half of the 19th century and the building has recently been skilfully adapted to house King's College's Maughan Library. The Patent Office was established in 1852 and based in Southampton Buildings, where it shared accommodation with the Secretaries of Bankrupts and Lunatics. The office expanded to fill several neighbouring buildings and remained on Chancery Lane until the late 1990s. The Law Society of England and Wales is headquartered at 113 Chancery Lane. Chancery Lane is also home to the Official Solicitor to the Supreme Court. The Historical Manuscripts Commission was based just off Chancery Lane, in Quality Court, until its amalgamation with the Public Record Office in 2003. The London Silver Vaults are an underground storehouse for antique and modern silverware. They are open to the public and silversmiths sell their wares there.

'Long Chanc'ry-lane retentive rolls the sound / And courts to courts return it round and round;' wrote Alexander Pope in *The Dunciad*. Izaak Walton, the 'father of angling', worked as a linen draper in Chancery Lane from 1627 to 1644.

✉ WC2; EC4

🚇 Central Line (zone 1)

📖 Aidan Lawes, *Chancery Lane 1377–1977*, National Archives, 1996; A K Bruce, *Chancery Lane and its Memories*, Butterworth, 1949

@ www.thesilvervaults.com

Chapel End • *Brent*

A little-used name for the (now) central part of WILLESDEN, distinguishing it from CHURCH END to the west. The name derived from the WILLESDEN GREEN Independent (Congregational) Chapel, built in 1820 at the junction of the High Road (A407) and DUDDEN HILL Lane. The locality has also been called Queenstown, to mark a visit by Queen Victoria in 1837. In the mid 19th century this was a settlement of agricultural labourers but it evolved into a middle-class suburb from the 1870s, after the coming of the railway and the sale of farmland to developers. A larger chapel was built just to the west to serve the growing population and the original building was used as a Sunday school until its demolition in 1908.

✉ NW10

Chapel End • *Waltham Forest*

A densely populated part of north WALTHAMSTOW with a wide variety of ethnic minorities, including Asian, Turkish and Greek communities. Established in 1303 as the manor of Walthamstow Sarum, its present name came into use after the late 1430s, when Sir William Tyrwhitt founded a chapel here, which adjoined his manor house of Salisbury Hall and was dedicated to Edward the Confessor. The chapel was in ruins by 1650 and attempts to re-

build it foundered. As the hamlet of Chapel End grew, a new chapel of ease was built by Lewis Vulliamy in 1830 and dedicated to St John. This was replaced by the present church, which was built in 1926 in response to the suburban development of the area, much of which was the work of the Warner family, Walthamstow's pre-eminent builders. With the arrival of the North Circular Road (A406) in the late 1920s, factories were built in the north of the district, and this industrial zone continued to grow until the 1960s. Sports grounds occupy much of the east side of Chingford Road, together with Sir George Monoux College, formerly a grammar school and now a sixth form college. LLOYD PARK is situated to the southwest. Most homes in Chapel End are owner-occupied and a high proportion of these contain dependent children. At Chapel End Junior School, 56 per cent of children come from ethnic minorities and a quarter do not speak English as their first language.

The author James Hilton partly modelled the protagonist of his novel *Goodbye Mr Chips* on his father, who was head teacher of Chapel End School. The character was also influenced by one of Hilton's teachers at Sir George Monoux School. Old boys of Monoux include the jazz musician Sir Johnny Dankworth and the footballer Teddy Sheringham.

✉ E17

👥 11,098

@ www.george-monoux.ac.uk

Chapel Market • *Islington*

A thriving but threatened street market, located off the southern end of Liverpool Road, near the ANGEL, ISLINGTON. Townhouses with rear gardens were built along what was then Chapel Street late in the 18th century. A fire-engine house was erected in 1792 and heightened in 1822; it survives today but in poor condition. To the annoyance of the well-heeled residents, costermongers began to sell their wares along the street and by the 1860s a fully fledged and relatively reputable market was in operation. Official designation as a street market came in 1879. In 1882 John James Sainsbury opened his first Islington shop at 48 Chapel Street, managed for a while by his eldest son, John Benjamin. The venture was so successful that the Sainsburys opened three more shops in the street, including their first branch specializing in poultry and game. By the 1890s Chapel Street had one of the two largest markets in the Clerkenwell and Islington areas, divided about equally between food and non-food stalls. Furniture, earthenware, second-hand clothing and drapery were among the most popular merchandise. The council renamed the street Chapel Market in 1936. A few mainstream retailers and fast-food outlets now occupy premises towards the eastern end of the street but for the most part it remains a traditional and unpretentious market, still selling mainly household goods and food. It is open every day except Monday. There are many high-street stores nearby, while the large N1 complex on Liverpool Road has a multiplex cinema and extensive facilities for eating (especially oriental) as well as shopping (chiefly fashion). Despite its continuing popularity, Chapel Market is vulnerable to a future change of use owing to the high value of land in Islington.

The essayist Charles Lamb lived at two addresses in Chapel Street at different times in the late 1790s. Madame Vasso, a medium formerly consulted by Sarah, Duchess of York, gave tarot readings at a sanctum in Chapel Market in the mid 1980s.

✉ N1

Charing Cross • *Westminster*
The geographical centre of London, located immediately east of TRAFALGAR SQUARE at the western end of the STRAND, which formerly marked the boundary between the City of London and the City of Westminster. The medieval village of Charing probably took its name from the Saxon 'char', a turn, referring either to the bend in the Thames or in the westward road from the City. Edward I placed a wooden cross here in 1290 to mark the final resting point of his wife's funeral procession on its way to Westminster. This was replaced by a monument sculpted from Caen stone and raised on marble steps. Eleanor's cross was demolished in 1647 and its stone was used to pave WHITEHALL. An equestrian statue of Charles I was erected in its place in 1675 and now marks the exact point from which all distances from London are measured. As the point of entry into Whitehall, Charing Cross was for centuries the scene of rebellious confrontations and subsequently of hangings and beheadings. The royal mews and great offices of state stood on the Westminster side of Charing Cross, while slums lay to the north and east. Charing Cross Hospital was founded in 1818 as the West London Infirmary and Dispensary and gained its present name in 1827. Charing Cross station and hotel occupy

the site of Hungerford Market, which had been rebuilt in 1833 as a two-storey emporium. The station was designed by the engineer John Hawkshaw in 1863, and its Renaissance-style hotel facing the Strand is the work of Edward Middleton Barry. Barry also designed a replica of Eleanor's cross, sculpted by Thomas Earp, which was placed in the station's forecourt. In 1905 the roof of Charing Cross station collapsed, killing six people and destroying the Avenue Theatre. Charing Cross Hospital moved five miles away to Hammersmith in 1959. In addition to an unexciting cross-section of offices, shops, pubs and eateries, the Charing Cross locality is noted for its dealers in stamps and coins.

No. 36 Craven Street was the home of the American scientist and statesman Benjamin Franklin between 1757 and 1775. The house has recently become a museum and educational facility. In a lecture at Charing Cross Hospital in 1906 Ivan Pavlov described experiments in which he had conditioned dogs to salivate at the sound of a bell. With proper cockney pronunciation, Charing Cross is rhyming slang for 'horse'.

✉ WC2

🚆 Main-line: South Eastern Trains; Southern (southern counties and Kent coast) London Underground: Bakerloo Line; Northern Line (zone 1)

@ www.benjaminfranklinhouse.org

Charing Cross Road • *Westminster*
A street famed for its bookshops, running north from TRAFALGAR SQUARE to ST GILES Circus. Crown Street and Castle Street formerly followed this route and their improvement was primarily a slum clearance and road-widening project, replacing St Martin's Lane as the area's principal northbound thoroughfare. Despite suggestions that the new street should be named Alexandra Avenue or Nelson Avenue, it was opened in 1887 as Charing Cross Road, a choice apparently preferred by the local inhabitants. The Duke of Cambridge performed the opening ceremony and the midpoint junction with SHAFTESBURY AVENUE was named Cambridge Circus in his honour. Leicester Square station was built in 1906. Its Cranbourn Street entrance replaced three houses belonging to Lord Salisbury, which had to be compulsorily purchased from the reluctant peer. Also in 1906, William and Gilbert Foyle relocated the bookshop they had founded three years earlier to its present

site in Charing Cross Road. Even before the road's creation booksellers had operated in the southern part of the area and the arrival of Foyles encouraged the trade to spread along its full length. Recent rent rises have forced away some specialists but many remain, while big-name book superstores also deem it essential to have a presence here. Retailers in Cecil Court, a side street near Trafalgar Square, specialize in antiquarian books.

The book *84, Charing Cross Road* is the story of the American writer Helene Hanff's 20-year correspondence with Frank Doel, of the antiquarian booksellers Marks and Co., at that address, which is now the site of a bar. The book has been adapted for the stage and screen.

✉ WC2

🚇 Northern Line; Piccadilly Line (Leicester Square, zone 1)

Charlton • *Greenwich*

A residential and industrial district situated between GREENWICH and WOOLWICH. First recorded in Domesday Book, the name means 'homestead belonging to the churls'. Churls constituted the lowest rank of freemen in medieval English society. From 50BC to AD250, a large Romano-British settlement occupied the ridge to the north of what is now CHARLTON VILLAGE. A Saxon village later grew up to the south-west, and St Luke's Church was in existence by the 11th century. Following the construction of the palatial Charlton House in the early 17th century, the village grew slowly until the arrival of the railway half a mile to the north in 1847. The Bowater estate was laid out on the border with Greenwich from the 1850s, while industry began to fill the riverside at what became known as NEW CHARLTON. On the west and east sides of the district respectively, the Eastcombe and Little Heath areas were built up towards the end of the 19th century, while the village expanded. The Maryon Wilson family gave Charlton sandpits in Hanging Wood to the London County Council in 1891 and one pit became the nucleus of Maryon Park. Charlton Athletic Football Club was founded in 1905 and moved to the Valley, the site of another of the sandpits, in 1920. Maryon Wilson Park was created across Thorntree Road from Maryon Park in 1926. Much of the area was built up by the Metropolitan Borough of Greenwich between the wars, beginning with the attractive cottages of the Charlton estate. From 1930 the council and private developers jointly built the Horn-

fair and Thornhill estates in the former grounds of Charlton House. After World War II the council built the larger estates on both sides of Charlton Road. Charlton Athletic returned to the Valley in 1992, after a seven-year absence during which fans had waged a vigorous campaign for the stadium to be rebuilt. Two-thirds of the residents of the Charlton ward are white British. The largest minority is of black African origin. The ward has an even spread of socio-economic classes and almost equal numbers own their home or rent it from the council or a housing association.

Maryon Park achieved cult significance in 1966 as the key location for Michelangelo Antonioni's film *Blow-Up*, starring David Hemmings. In 1999 Channel 4 chose Elliscombe Road as the location of its '1900 House', for the television series of that name. The idea was to take a Victorian house, remove all elements of the 20th century, and film a family coping for three months without access to modern amenities. No. 50 Elliscombe Road was a real find for the producers because under plasterboard and wallpaper lay all the features they needed to make the series a reality, including pipes for gas lighting that were in working order.

✉ SE7

🚶 12,608

🚇 South Eastern Trains (zone 3)

📖 John G Smith, *History of Charlton*, Charlton Society, 1996

@ www.charlton-athletic.co.uk

Charlton Village • *Greenwich*

The old centre of CHARLTON, as opposed to the much larger and newer suburb that has since engulfed it. St Luke's Church was first mentioned in 1077, when it lay at the centre of an extensive parish. Charlton House was built for Sir Adam Newton, tutor to Prince Henry, the elder son of James I. The house was completed in 1612, the year the prince died. Newton died in 1629, leaving money that was used to rebuild St Luke's. From 1767 the manor and the house belonged to the Maryon Wilsons, the family that later tried to develop HAMPSTEAD HEATH. In 1879 they enclosed the green in front of Charlton House and added it to their grounds. From around this time the section of street called the Village filled with shops. The White Swan inn was built in 1889, while the Bugle Horn was formed from three late-17th-century cottages. A drinking fountain and war memorial were erected at the junction of the Village and Charlton Church Lane in 1902 and 1920 respectively. In 1925 the Metropolitan Borough of Greenwich bought Charlton House and opened the grounds as a public park. The house is now a community centre and events venue. Despite the modernization of some premises, the village retains much of its charm.

Spencer Perceval, the only British prime minister to have been assassinated, is buried in St Luke's churchyard. The poet Walter de la Mare was born in the village in 1873.

✉ SE7

The Chase *see* DAGENHAM EAST

Chase Cross • *Havering*
An estate predominantly of 1930s bungalows on the north-eastern edge of COLLIER ROW. The name probably dates from the 18th century, when the crossroads here stood close to the 'chase', or hunting ground, of HAINAULT Forest. The forest was cleared in the 1850s and converted to agricultural use. When the ROMFORD building company Preedy Brothers acquired the farmland, it laid out roads and built several types of bungalow, mostly with large gardens. The properties went on sale in 1933, priced from £300 to £400, and the firm based its sales office at 2A Chase Cross Road. Advertisements spoke of the 'dry and invigorating air' and productive, loamy soil of this 'charming, picturesque district'. Even the smaller properties had 'three nice rooms and scullery, larder, deep sink, coal shed and lavatory' and were built with British labour and materials. Two-storey houses later filled out the area. Chase Cross School opened in 1949 and was renamed Bower Park on its 40th anniversary. According to the educational standards agency Ofsted, most pupils come from the local community, 'which has higher than average levels of unemployment and social disadvantage'.

✉ Romford RM5 and RM1

Chase Side • *Enfield*
A charming residential locality situated north-west of ENFIELD TOWN, clustered along the road of the same name. This Chase Side should not be confused with a section of the A111 in SOUTHGATE, although both are so called because of their former location beside ENFIELD CHASE. The road was in existence by 1572, when it was called Woodside, and a loose collection of dwellings grew up here during the 17th century. By 1686 the locality was known as Chase Side but the road was not given that name until after 1803. By this time the enclosure of Enfield Chase had encouraged the building of houses and shops, which were later joined by a brewery (which switched to cotton dyeing for a while), a short-lived paper-making factory and some small chapels and schools. Builders laid out new streets on either side of the road later in the century. The Church of St Michael, GORDON HILL and Chase Side was consecrated in 1874 and Congregationalists began the construction of Christ Church in the same year. In the following year a five-bed cottage hospital opened, which later expanded to become Enfield War Memorial Hospital. Chase Side Board School opened on Trinity Street in 1901. A village pond used to flank Parsonage Lane but it was filled in to allow for road widening in 1906. The parish had been granted 200 acres of land west of Chase Side after the enclosure and used the rental income to supplement the poor rates. Enfield council progressively sold the land for building during the course of the 20th century. Enfield War Memorial Hospital closed in 1984 and the site was sold for redevelopment. The southern half of Chase Side is part of the Enfield Town conservation area.

In September 1827 the essayist and poet Charles Lamb and his sister Mary came to live at the Poplars, Chase Side. The following month they moved to the house next door, lodging with the Westwood family for six years, after which they moved to EDMONTON.

✉ Enfield EN2

Cheam • *Sutton*
A favoured interwar suburb with some impressive older houses and cottages, situated west of SUTTON. The name may be a corruption of two words meaning 'village by the tree stumps'. Cheam was granted to the cathedral priory of Christchurch, Canterbury in 1018 and a church built soon afterwards was dedicated to a former archbishop, St Dunstan. The village had around 150 inhabitants at the time of Domesday Book, when the archbishop owned five slaves. By the 14th century Cheam had been split into east and west manors, each of which had its own village. East Cheam (later known as LOWER CHEAM) was the larger of the pair. From the 14th to the 16th century Cheam was known for its potteries, which specialized in making jugs. Whitehall was built on Malden Road around 1500 and is

Greater London's finest early example of a medieval hall house (a house in which the main living area was not open to the roof). The house was later extended and weatherboarded and is now open to the public. Henry VIII acquired the manors of Cheam after commissioning the construction of Nonsuch Palace in the neighbouring parish of CUDDINGTON in 1538. Cheam School was founded sometime before 1646, and may have used either Whitehall or West Cheam manor house as its original home. The manor house was demolished in 1796. At the 1801 census, the 616 inhabitants were concentrated in three clusters: around Whitehall, around the church and on the High Street. On the north side of the parish, CHEAM COMMON was enclosed by 1810. When Cheam station opened in 1847, it had at first little effect on the character of the village. St Dunstan's was rebuilt in 1864 but the chancel of the medieval church was preserved as the Lumley chapel, the borough's oldest building. By the outbreak of World War I, housing was spreading here from Sutton and in the 1920s the old village was overwhelmed by houses and shops, many built in mock-Tudor style. The High Street was blighted by road widening but a medieval cottage was saved by moving it to its present site on the Broadway in 1922. The new district of NORTH CHEAM grew up to the east of WORCESTER PARK in the 1930s. St Alban's Church was built on Gander Green Lane in 1930 with materials salvaged from Cheam Court Farm. The suburb had largely assumed its present-day appearance by 1939, with terraced and semi-detached homes filling the north of the district and larger detached properties in the south. Among the indicators of affluence in Cheam are very high proportions of owner-occupied homes and households with access to two or more cars. At an average 6.4 rooms per household, residents have more space than almost any other Londoners. Cheam also has a disproportionately large number of people aged over 60.

The poet Abraham Cowley died here in 1867. The entertainer Harry Secombe lived in Cheam Road for 32 years and the second volume of his autobiography is entitled *Strawberries and Cheam*. The Exits' late-1970s mod-revivalist song *Cheam* features on several compilation albums, including *This is Mod, Volume 2*.

✉ Sutton SM3, SM2 and SM1

♟ 9,695

🚃 Southern (zone 5)

📖 Martin Andrew, *Francis Frith's Around Cheam*, Francis Frith Collection, 2005; Sara Goodwins, *Cheam Past and Present*, Sutton, 2003

@ www.sutton.gov.uk/leisure/heritage/whitehall

Cheam Common • *Sutton*

A little-used name for the north-western part of CHEAM bordering WORCESTER PARK. Formerly a 320-acre common filling the northern part of Cheam parish, by 1810 the common had been enclosed and divided with hedges into compact fields. As neighbouring suburbs began to grow in the mid 19th century, brickworks were established at Lower Farm and on other parts of the common, while the first suburban streets came early to the corner that offered easy access to Worcester Park station. The British Land Co. laid out Longfellow Road and Washington Road in the late 1860s, and Cheam Common Elementary School opened. The red-brick church of St Philip, Cheam Common was consecrated in 1876. When the brickfields were exhausted, the abandoned sites were developed into terraces of cottages and an isolation hospital set up by Epsom rural health authority in the 1890s. The final stage of the suburbanization of Cheam Common was driven by an unusually entrepreneurial farmer, William J Lavender. Recognizing the potential of his territorial assets, Lavender first started a haulage business, bringing building materials to other contractors in the area and using his farmhouse as the base for his business. He then teamed up with F J Farrell, already an established builder, to develop the farm with roads and housing. Lavender and Farrell went on to collaborate on projects in nearby localities, like the Manor Drive estate at Malden Green. The well-regarded Cheam Common Infants' and Junior schools opened in 1932 and 1935. In the 1950s most of Cheam Common's remaining cottages were pulled down and replaced by semi-detached properties. MacMillan House, a large office block, now occupies the site of Lower Farm's farmhouse. St Philip's Church was demolished because of subsidence in 1978. More housing was built following the closure of Cheam Hospital in the 1990s.

John Major, prime minister from 1990 to 1997, lived in Longfellow Road as a child.

✉ Worcester Park KT4

Cheapside · *City*

The CITY OF LONDON'S main shopping street for the past millennium, running eastwards from ST PAUL'S towards BANK. It takes its name from 'chepe', a Saxon word for a market. The street connected the southern end of the Roman Watling Street with the main City settlement to its east and its alignment was dictated by a convenient bridging point across the (now subterranean) River Walbrook. The Church of St Mary-le-Bow stood here by 1091, when it was seriously damaged in a storm. Market buildings were constructed from the late 12th century, with low roofs that later formed viewing platforms for tournaments. At that time the layout of Cheapside was more like a marketplace than a street: up to 62 feet wide but with very narrow exits at each end. Side streets acquired names that indicated their early specializations: fishmongers traded on Friday Street, while Honey Lane and Wood Street are self-explanatory. Cheapside itself became the centre of the jewellery trade, where most London goldsmiths sold their wares, but it was destroyed in the Great Fire of 1666. It was laid out afterwards with the bottlenecks removed, forming a continuous link with Poultry, the connecting street to its east. Sir Christopher Wren rebuilt St Mary-le-Bow in 1680, with a tower that used the Roman gravel roadway as its foundations. By tradition, a true cockney must be born within the sound of the church's bells. It took some time for Cheapside to recover from the economic effects of the fire but in 1775 a visitor observed that with its 'many thousands of candles … the street looks as if it were illuminated for some festivity', although this was just for everyday trade. Most of the street was rebuilt with offices from the late 19th century, and especially before and after World War II. When Sir John Bennet's clock shop closed in 1933, motor manufacturer Henry Ford bought the 'Cheapside clock' that had hung outside. In that same year a commentator wrote that 'dingy-looking brown buildings have been replaced by tall and handsome buildings which give Cheapside the appearance of a new street'. History has not looked so kindly on most of these blocks but Bow Lane retains quaint shopfronts from the late 18th and 19th centuries. Conventional retailers on Cheapside are nowadays outnumbered by services providers for City workers, such as opticians, building societies and mobile phone stores.

Thomas More, statesman and author of *Utopia*, was born in Milk Street in 1478. Just across Cheapside, Bread Street was the birthplace of two poets, John Donne and John Milton.

✉ EC2

📖 Walter Thornbury, *Old London: Cheapside and St Paul's*, Village Press, 1986; Hermione Hobhouse, *The Ward of Cheap in the City of London*, Ward of Cheap Club, 1963

Chelsea · *Kensington & Chelsea*

A fashionable quarter for nearly half a millennium, Chelsea lies on the north bank of the Thames between PIMLICO and FULHAM. Speculation on the origin of its name has settled on something between a chalk wharf and a gravel bank. It was farmland from the time of Domesday Book until the early 1520s, when Sir Thomas More built Beaufort House. Henry VIII developed a liking for Chelsea during his visits to More (whom he later had executed), and bought a manor house here, but found it too small and built a new one in what is now Cheyne Walk. This started a trend, and a succession of grand retreats appeared over the following 200 years, with a supporting village of working people growing up on the river bank. The separate hamlet of Little Chelsea sprouted closer to KENSINGTON, an area of heathland and nurseries. Several eminent literary and scientific figures lived in Chelsea in the 17th century, but their fine houses have all disappeared. Perhaps the greatest was Shaftesbury House, which stood from 1635 to 1856, spending its latter years as the parish workhouse. In 1682, Charles II founded the Royal Hospital, which was completed by Christopher Wren in 1690. This was, and remains, a home for old or disabled soldiers, who became known as Chelsea pensioners. Ranelagh Gardens, now part of the hospital's grounds, were originally the estate of Richard Jones, first Earl of Ranelagh, and were laid out as pleasure gardens after his death. Unlike many such places of amusement, the gardens managed to keep out hoi polloi and remained a playground of the rich and titled until the Napoleonic Wars. They are now the setting for the immensely popular Chelsea Flower Show, held every May. A little further west is the Chelsea Physic Garden, one of the world's oldest botanical and medicinal gardens, founded in 1673 by the Worshipful Society of Apothecaries of London. During the 18th century, Chelsea's proximity to WESTMINSTER was the downfall of its palaces and gardens. Lodges and townhouses replaced them and the modern street plan was laid out. The poorer inhabitants were pushed westward to the WORLD'S

END district, which was the subject of slum clearance and municipal building of flats in the mid 20th century.

Chelsea's contributions to a variety of crafts are reflected in some of the names it has spawned. Chelsea buns and Chelsea porcelain were popular in the 18th century. In the 1960s, ankle-length, elastic-sided footwear sold in the KING'S ROAD acquired the name Chelsea boots. Wags have recently nicknamed sports utility vehicles 'Chelsea tractors'. Chelsea has been particularly popular with the world of arts and letters, and famous residents have included the writers Charles Kingsley, Oscar Wilde and Bram Stoker, the composer and actor Noël Coward and the artist David Hockney.

✉ SW3; SW10

⚲ 25,111 (Cremorne, Royal Hospital and Stanley wards)

🚢 Cadogan pier

📖 Patricia E C Croot (editor), *A History of the County of Middlesex: Chelsea*, Victoria County History of the Counties of England, 2004; John Richardson, *The Chelsea Book: Past and Present*, Historical Publications, 2003

@ www.mychelsea.net (commercial local information site)

Chelsea Harbour • *Hammersmith & Fulham*

An upmarket but slightly dated residential and commercial development occupying a triangular site between CHELSEA Creek and the West London railway line in south-east FULHAM (not Chelsea). It was formerly part of the industrial district of SANDS END and most of the 17-acre site was occupied by a coalyard. In the late 1980s the property division of shipping conglomerate P&O created what it called 'a unique world of homes, flats, offices, restaurants and shops' focused around a 50-berth yacht marina and the 21-storey Belvedere Tower. An underground car park provided spaces for a remarkable 1,350 vehicles. Perhaps surprisingly, in view of its rateable value, Hammersmith & Fulham council tried to offload Chelsea Harbour to Kensington & Chelsea but the royal borough declined the offer, despite the enthusiasm of many residents. The shopping mall failed to appeal to tenants or customers and has been converted into a trade centre for the interior design industry. The Conrad Hotel has 160 suites, a conference centre and health club. In 2000, P&O sold Chelsea Harbour to a consortium led by the Berkeley Group for £59 million. In the following year P&O sold off nine acres of undeveloped neighbouring land, including the disused Lots Road power station, to a consortium led by Taylor Woodrow. This site became the subject of lengthy planning wrangles, especially over the proposed height of its tower blocks of apartments.

✉ SW10

🚢 Chelsea Harbour pier

@ www.chelsea-harbour.co.uk (commercial and property information site)

Chelsfield • *Bromley*

Because of the location of the station, this has become the name for the south-eastern part of ORPINGTON, and is a completely separate locality from CHELSFIELD VILLAGE; it has sometimes been called New Chelsfield. In 1868 the South Eastern Railway's 'new main line' opened between CHISLEHURST and Tonbridge. Chelsfield station was built in open country, almost a mile from the village that it was intended to serve. Little development took place in the immediate vicinity of the station until 1925, when Homesteads Ltd purchased much of the Chelsfield Park estate. The company divided the site into generously proportioned plots and built houses and bungalows for sale or rent; the rental properties were later sold. In 1951 the newly-formed Chelsfield Park Residents' Association acquired the estate's recreation ground from Homesteads Ltd for £100. The ground has cricket and tennis facilities and is enclosed by Homestead Road, Oxenden Wood Road and Worlds End Lane. During the 1950s and 1960s, Chelsfield and GREEN STREET GREEN expanded across the cornfields to meet each other, with new estates at Glentrammon Road, Highfield Avenue and Windsor Drive, which gained its own shopping facilities, and in 1961 Homesteads extended Chelsfield Park south-eastwards towards JULIAN BRIMSTONE. In 1984 Homesteads transferred the covenants of the Chelsfield Park estate to the residents' association, which has continued to enforce the various restrictions, notably those that prevent the construction of more than one building per plot. Since the plots can be up to an acre in size and 750 feet in length, this has maintained an exclusive character in the area south of the station. A handful of recent properties have been built in Chelsfield using the traditional Kentish knapped-flint technique, although these are overwhelmed by their less vernacular neighbours. Chelsfield Hall Farm survives in the far south-west, on the edge of Green Street Green. Chelsfield has become popular as a place of residence for south Londoners who have 'done well', especially in fields such as sport and self-employed trades.

As a girl, *Railway Children* author Edith Nesbit's nearest station was Chelsfield, a three-mile walk from Halstead Hall, in Kent.

> ✉ Orpington BR6
>
> ♦ 14,068 (Chelsfield and Pratts Bottom ward)
>
> 🚌 South Eastern Trains (zone 6)
>
> @ www.chelsfieldpark.co.uk (commercial local information site); www.chelsfield-park-residents-association.co.uk

Chelsfield Village • *Bromley*

The original heart of CHELSFIELD, situated a mile to the east of the 'new' Chelsfield that has grown up around the railway station. The name was recorded in Domesday Book as 'Cillesfelle', but transcription errors were common in that survey, and in the following year another document rendered it as 'Chilesfeld'. The name may have indicated a 'chilly field', given the exposed nature of the high ground, but was more likely to have derived from ownership by a man called Cēol. The Church of St Martin of Tours is of early Norman origin, and was altered and enlarged in the 13th century. In 1290, Otto de Grandison granted Chelsfield a charter declaring that 'there may be one market at my manor of Chelsfield each week on Monday, and one fair each year, at the same, lasting 3 days'. Several lanes converge on the village and drovers would stop here to obtain water for their livestock and ale for themselves. The Five Bells public house takes its name from the unusual number of bells that the church used to have. The present Court Lodge and its farm have stood near the church since at least the 18th century; in Kent, manor houses were often called 'court lodge' because manorial courts were held there. Fire destroyed many of the farm buildings in 1857, probably as a result of arson. Lord of the manor William Waring then built a new farmhouse nearby, renting the lodge and its garden to a succession of London businessmen. In 1928 the ORPINGTON bypass (A224) divided the village from the church and Court Lodge, and some houses were built by the roadside. Had it not been for the interruption of World War II and the subsequent introduction of green-belt legislation, the village would probably have been joined to Orpington by further development. The church was restored in 1950 after wartime damage and has been well-maintained since. In the village itself, Victorian farm labourers' cottages have been altered and gentrified but many properties retain their rustic charm. Chelsfield Park Hospital on Bucks Cross Road has 50 beds, three theatres and an assisted conception unit.

The novelist Miss Read (born Dora Shafe) moved from Hither Green to Chelsfield in 1921, at the age of seven. Her *Fairacre* books, although set in the Cotswolds, were based on her childhood experiences in the village, the village school and surrounding countryside. Miss Read's autobiographical *Time Remembered* (1986) portrays Chelsfield and its inhabitants in the 1920s.

> ✉ Orpington BR6
>
> 📖 Geoffrey Copus, *Chelsfield Chronicles: Annals of a Kentish Parish*, CAT Designs, 2004; Edward Hasted, *Hasted's History of Chelsfield*, ed. John W Brown, Local History Reprints, 2001
>
> @ www.chelsfieldevents.co.uk

Chequers • *Barking & Dagenham*

The vicinity of the Chequers public house on the A1306 in DAGENHAM. Chequer Fields were so called because of their multi-coloured, chequerboard appearance and in the 18th century they gave their name to the Chequers Inn, which has since been rebuilt. The London County Council put up housing at Chequers Corner in the 1920s, while large-scale industry colonized the land to the south, notably in the form of the Ford motor works. Following the cessation of car production here in 2001 the Chequers Lane area has become the focus of major regeneration activity. The London Development Agency is leading a mixed-use project at Chequers Corner, for which land has been compulsorily purchased. All this activity has forced the relocation of the Sunday morning market on Chequers Lane, and will probably result in its ultimate closure. Meanwhile, Barking & Dagenham council has been investing to improve the existing built-up area as a place to live, work and shop.

> ✉ Dagenham RM9

Chessington • *Kingston*

A heavily developed mid-20th-century suburb occupying most of the tongue of the borough that protrudes south beyond HOOK. Cisendone

– 'the hill of a man named Cissa' – was mentioned in Domesday Book, and St Mary's Church appears in Merton Priory records of 1174. Chessington Hall was built in the early 16th century and from the 1750s it was home to the playwright Samuel Crisp. The novelist Fanny Burney was a frequent guest at the hall and wrote part of her second novel, *Cecilia*, in the summerhouse during the early 1780s. Chessington Hall was rebuilt in 1832 and St Mary's Church was restored in 1854. Chessington Court lay to the north, across a mile of open farmland. Stimulated by the arrival of the Kingston bypass (A3/A309), private and municipal housing began to fill the fields from the late 1920s and soon replaced Chessington Court. In 1931 Chessington Zoo opened in the 65-acre grounds of Burnt Stub, a 19th-century house built on the site of a predecessor that had been burnt down to a stub by Parliamentarians during the Civil War. The arrival of the railway at Chessington South was important to the success of the zoo and a baby elephant attended the station's opening ceremony in 1939. Later in the same year, George VI opened RAF Chessington as a barrage balloon centre for the defence of London. The base was used throughout World War II and was subsequently converted to military medical use. After the war the council built more estates in the area, including 400 homes in the grounds of Chessington Hall in the 1950s. The hall itself survived a little longer but was demolished in 1965. Having spent its latter days as a US air force base, RAF Chessington was sold by the Ministry of Defence and housing was built on the site in the mid 1990s. On Garrison Lane, Chessington Community College has evolved out of Fleetwood School. The college is likely to be almost wholly rebuilt over the next few years. The zoo has become Chessington World of Adventures – Greater London's only full-scale theme park – and Burnt Stub is now Hocus Pocus Hall. The park is divided into themed areas, with rides, fairground attractions and wild animals, and is outer London's most popular paid-for visitor attraction, drawing 1.5 million fun-seekers a year.

The singer Petula Clark lived in Salmons Road as child, attended Lovelace Primary School and performed at street parties in Bolton Close and Hook's Vallis Way to celebrate the end of World War II.

✉ Chessington KT9

18,209 (Chessington South, and Chessington North and Hook wards)

South West Trains (Chessington North; Chessington South, zone 6)

Mark Davison, *Chessington Remembered*, Mark Davison, 1999; C H Keeling, *Chessington Story: The Story of the Chessington Zoological Garden*, Clam, 1996

@ www.chessington.co.uk (Chessington World of Adventures site)

Cheyne Walk • *Kensington & Chelsea* (pronounced 'chainy')

A celebrated creative hotbed located on CHELSEA'S Thames embankment south of the mid-section of the KING'S ROAD. A Buckinghamshire gentleman, Charles Cheyne, who had got rich by marrying into the Cavendish family and later became Viscount Newhaven, bought the manor of Chelsea on an instalment plan between 1657 and 1661. The riverside walk that later took his name was already well-endowed with inns, coffee houses and some grand houses by that time and more building leases were granted by Cheyne's son after he inherited the manor in 1698. The resulting street is of great architectural merit – most of the properties are listed buildings, right down to their garden walls and railings and the phone box by Albert Bridge – but it is most famous for the dazzling array of talented individuals that has lived and worked here. The list includes Thomas More, Hilaire Belloc, George Eliot, Elizabeth Gaskell, Dante Gabriel Rossetti, Philip Wilson Steer, the Brunels, Sylvia Pankhurst, Mick Jagger and Keith Richards. The artist J M W Turner died in Cheyne Walk. Henry Fielding, Tobias Smollett, William Holman Hunt and James Whistler lived around the corner in Lawrence Street. The Cheyne Row house and garden of the 'Sage of Chelsea', the Victorian writer and historian Thomas Carlyle, is now owned by the National Trust. The great hall of the 15th-century mansion Crosby Place was brought here stone by stone from BISHOPSGATE and re-assembled in 1910. It is now a private residence. The council drew up a plan to demolish almost half of Cheyne Walk after World War II but was dissuaded and restricted its activities to tastefully rebuilding a pair of houses as flats. Turner's house had been damaged in the war and the London County Council rebuilt it to look as it had before. In 1982 Kensington & Chelsea council opened to the public Cremorne Gardens, on a corner of the site of the former Cremorne pleasure gardens. Understandably, Cheyne Walk has some of London's highest property values. In the 1980s, house prices breached the £1 million barrier. In the early 21st century they approached £10 million.

Tate Britain has Sir Max Beerbohm's evocative cartoon *The Small Hours in the Sixties at 16 Cheyne Walk* (1916).

✉ SW3; SW10

📖 Reginald Blunt, *In Cheyne Walk and Thereabout*, Mills and Boon, 1914

Child's Hill • *Barnet*

A socially diverse community straddling the FINCHLEY ROAD south of GOLDERS GREEN, with Jewish, Arabic and Somali groups among its minorities. The name probably refers to a former resident – possibly Richard Child, who was living around here in 1321. Historically, the ownership of Child's Hill was disputed by the manors of HENDON and HAMPSTEAD, with the former eventually winning. It was one of the Hendon area's first industrial districts, with brick and tile making in the early 19th century and hand-laundering that served the gentry of Hampstead. One laundry was used as a chapel until the building of St Mary's Church in 1856. The arrival of the Finchley Road spurred further growth from the late 1820s, when a tollgate was set up near the Castle Inn. An indication of the early significance of Child's Hill is that this was the name given to what is now CRICKLEWOOD station when it opened in 1870. Child's Hill became one of the poorest parts of Hendon urban district, its housing described by one councillor in 1903 as a 'disgrace to civilization'. A tram link with Cricklewood opened in 1909 and in 1914 the council chose Child's Hill for its first housing estate, consisting of 50 dwellings. Semi-detached houses were added around Child's Hill Park in the 1930s. During the early 1960s, the council used its powers to move industry out of Granville Road and into new accommodation beside the North Circular Road (A406). The priciest homes tend to lie in the south of the locality, off Hendon Way, notably on the exclusive Hocroft estate.

Founded in 1967, Child's Hill Gymnastics Club has a successful competition record, both nationally and internationally. The club was originally based at Child's Hill School but now uses Metropolitan Police facilities in COLINDALE.

✉ NW2; NW11

👥 17,261 (London's most populous ward)

📖 Stewart Gillies and Pamela Taylor, *Hendon,*

Child's Hill, Golders Green and Mill Hill, A Pictorial History, Phillimore, 1993

@ www.childs-hill.com (Child's Hill Gymnastics Club site)

Chinatown • *Westminster*

Once a term applied to LIMEHOUSE, Chinatown now identifies the compact neighbourhood around Gerrard Street and Lisle Street, north of LEICESTER SQUARE. The Chinese call Gerrard Street *Tong Yan Kai*, 'Chinese street' in Cantonese. A handful of Chinese restaurants were established in SOHO during World War II, when they became popular with soldiers who had acquired a taste for the food abroad. Later, Chinese entrepreneurs began to buy up and convert the rundown properties south of SHAFTESBURY AVENUE. This coincided with an influx of agricultural workers from Hong Kong, who had been forced out of their traditional occupations by changes in the world rice markets. Many found work in the catering trade, often living nearby in tied accommodation, and a variety of other businesses sprang up to serve the new population. Increasing prosperity allowed most members of the community to reside further afield but Chinatown's role as a trading zone is stronger than ever, catering to the Chinese population from all over south-east England. There are oriental arches at each end of Gerrard Street, the street signs are bilingual (as are the notices in the bookmakers) and the telephone kiosks are miniature pagodas. Westminster council has pedestrianized Gerrard Street and parts of Macclesfield Street and Newport Place. Since 1973, the Chinese New Year has been celebrated here on the Sunday closest to the New Year with lion dances and other festivities; the date of the New Year varies because it depends on the phases of the moon, but usually falls between mid January and mid February. The activities of triad societies such as 14K, Shui Fong and Wo Shing Wo cause some problems in Chinatown, though these rarely affect anyone outside the Chinese community. Work began in 2006 on a three-year facelift for the area, which will include the installation of a 'real' Chinese gate on Wardour Street.

The poet John Dryden once lived at 43 Gerrard Street. His blue plaque is one of the oldest in London.

✉ W1

📖 Steve Lau, *Chinatown Britain*, Chinatown Online, 2003

@ www.chinatown-online.co.uk (education

and information site about the UK's Chinese community); www.minquan.co.uk (Chinese anti-racism charity site)

Chingford • *Waltham Forest*

A collection of marshland and forest hamlets, unified by railway-era suburbanization, situated north of WALTHAMSTOW. The name may be derived from words meaning 'ford of the stump-dwellers', a reference to houses built on poles to keep them clear of the marshy ground, but others have suggested that 'ching' is a corruption of 'shingle'. Either way, the early riverside settlement was probably located in modern SOUTH CHINGFORD. The first church was erected on CHINGFORD MOUNT in the twelfth century, when patches of Epping Forest were beginning to be cleared, afterwards becoming the sites of Chingford's disconnected hamlets. Three hundred years later Henry VIII commissioned the building of a lodge in Fairmead Park, two miles to the north-east of the Mount, to provide a grandstand view of the hunt in Epping Forest. This is now a museum of the forest's history and is known as Queen Elizabeth's Hunting Lodge. Chingford remained a quiet parish, isolated by the River Lea and the forest and lacking public transport until the railway was extended here from Walthamstow in 1873. Even then, expansion proceeded slowly. The Chingford Rise estate was the first to be laid out, in the mid 1880s, but the project was unsuccessful and the land went back on the market in 1897. In the early 20th century, building proceeded slowly at a handful of locations until after World War I, when two decades of rapid growth saw most of the district covered by suburban housing, along with some industry in the south-west. During this period, the railway was also hugely popular with day-trippers to Epping Forest, who arrived in their tens of thousands on public holidays. Because suburban development came relatively late, Chingford was not built up with the same dense layout that characterized many late Victorian street plans, like that of Walthamstow. The builders nevertheless exploited their sites aggressively, demolishing the few older houses that the district possessed at that time. The arrival of the North Circular Road (A406) in 1928 boosted Chingford's appeal to the newly car-owning middle classes. After World War II, the London County Council acquired the FRIDAY HILL estate for municipal housing, and private builders filled the few remaining gaps elsewhere. Today the only undeveloped areas are Chingford Plain, which has a public

golf course, and Pole Hill, once owned by Lawrence of Arabia. To the west lie the King George's and William Girling reservoirs. The former was opened in 1913 by George V and the latter in 1951, also by its namesake, who was chairman of the Metropolitan Water Board.

✉ E4

♦ 50,784 (Chingford Green, Endlebury, Hatch Lane, Larkswood and Valley wards)

🚇 'one' Railway (zone 5)

📖 Barbara Ray, *Chingford Past*, Historical Publications, 2003; Stephen Pewsey, *Chingford: The Second Selection*, Tempus, 2002

@ www.chingfordhistory.org.uk (Chingford Historical Society site); www.colind.homechoice.co.uk (a resident's view of Chingford)

Chingford Green • *Waltham Forest*

The modern heart of CHINGFORD, located south-west of the station. It began life as a forest hamlet in the late 17th century and a weatherboarded cottage survives from this period on the Green Walk. Like much of Chingford, poor road connections with London deterred the gentry from establishing country retreats here until the late 18th century, when a handful of substantial houses appeared, for example west of the green at Mount Echo. One of the country's largest sets of staghound kennels operated from Kilgreana, also known as Chingford Lodge, from 1798 to 1806. The kennels are long gone but the house survives, divided into two properties, as part of a conservation area. In the early 1840s a local grandee, Robert Boothby Heathcote, commissioned Lewis Vulliamy to design the Church of St Peter and St Paul, which replaced CHINGFORD MOUNT'S All Saints as the parish church. Secular ascendancy was assured by the opening of the station and the arrival of piped water in the 1870s. Shortly afterwards the Bull and Crown public house was built to serve day-trippers to Epping Forest. Designed in French Second Empire style, the building is now Grade II-listed. Suburban housing filled much of the neighbourhood in the late 19th and early 20th centuries and the church was enlarged in 1903. Chingford Town Hall was built on the Ridgeway in 1929 and this now houses the borough's engineering and planning departments. Recent developments include the flats and houses of Echo Heights, in Mount Echo Drive. The Chingford Green ward has a relatively elderly population, and 93 per cent of residents are white.

✉ E4

👥 9,497

Chingford Hatch • *Waltham Forest*

The south-eastern part of CHINGFORD, situated north of HIGHAMS PARK. The name was first mentioned in 1487, although Simon and William de la Hache were recorded as living here in the early 13th century. A hatch was a gate, probably used here to prevent cattle from straying from their pasture on the edge of Epping Forest, and the locality is sometimes referred to simply as 'the Hatch'. Walthamstow worthy Sir George Monoux owned a house and 13 acres of land here at the time of his death in 1544. Although a small village had evolved by the late 18th century, it was not until the early 20th century that radial expansion from CHINGFORD GREEN reached this far. Much of the area is often now called FRIDAY HILL, following the London County Council's construction of the estate of that name in the 1950s. Widespread change followed all across the district, as weatherboarded cottages and a Wesleyan chapel gave way to new houses, car-body repairers replaced wheelwrights, and unsightly shops were built on a service road beside Hatch Lane. The Manor Hotel (later the Horseless Carriage and then the Wheelwrights pub) stood at the corner of Hatch Lane and Friday Hill. It was controversially demolished in 2003 and replaced by the fortress-like Ashton Court, a stylish apartment development by Fairview New Homes, which paid £2.5 million for the site.

✉ E4

👥 9,879 (Hatch Lane ward)

Chingford Mount • *Waltham Forest*

The commanding height of CHINGFORD, located on its western side. The parish church of All Saints was founded here in the twelfth century and some of the early stonework survives in the present structure, together with additions from the following three centuries. All Saints was later rededicated to St Peter and St Paul but this name moved to the new church on CHINGFORD GREEN when that was built in 1844. STOKE NEWINGTON'S Abney Park Cemetery Co. established Chingford Mount Cemetery in 1884, on the site of Caroline Mount House in Old Church Road. The cemetery's original chapel and lodges have not survived.

The old church fell into ruin but Louisa Heathcote of FRIDAY HILL paid for its restoration in 1930, when Chingford's phenomenal interwar growth created a need for more places of worship. One of the busiest builders in the area at this time was Reader Bros, which had begun in Hackney in the 1890s. Members of the Reader family lived in one of the company's newly built houses on Wellington Avenue. Parades of shops serve the local community but Chingford Mount is no longer a focus for the wider district.

Members of the Kray family are buried at Chingford Mount Cemetery, including the notorious gangster twins Ronnie and Reggie.

✉ E4

📖 Josephine Boyle, *Builders of Repute: The Story of Reader Bros*, Suitable Press, 2002

Chipping Barnet • *Barnet*

The western part of the BARNET district, also known as HIGH BARNET. The 'chipping' element derives from the Saxon 'chepe', a market. King John granted the abbey of St Albans a formal market charter in 1199 although unofficial trading had already been carried on here for the previous hundred years. The town developed around this weekly trade and by providing services to travellers at the junction of the Great North Road and the St Albans Road. The eastern side of what is now the High Street was part of Hadley. The Church of St John the Baptist was built on Wood Street some time in the first half of the 15th century, replacing a chapel of ease to EAST BARNET. Queen Elizabeth's School was founded on Wood Street in 1573 and a fair operated at Chipping Barnet from 1588. Permanent houses and shops began to line the High Street and a few timber-framed structures are still in existence, although much altered. To the west, Wellhouse Lane, off Wood Street, marks the site of the former physic well, a chalybeate spring popular in the 17th century. Samuel Pepys was among its pilgrims, returning for second helpings despite being feverish after drinking five glasses on his initial visit. Some Georgian and early Victorian properties survive on Wood Street (now a conservation area), one of which is now Barnet Museum. An enclosure act of 1815 permitted the erasure of a public racecourse and of much of Barnet Common, which was mostly given over to haymaking. The market was relocated around 1860 and began to decline, restricted to selling cattle in its latter years. The arrival of the railway prompted the construction of a few suburban villas at the end of the 19th century but most of Chipping Barnet was built up in the 1920s and 1930s, merging with Underhill to the south and connecting with Arkley to the west. Further expansion was restricted by green-belt legislation after World War II. The Spires shopping centre opened on the west side of the High Street in 1969. The ward of High Barnet has a predominantly white population, which is relatively old, well-educated and affluent.

✉ Barnet EN5

♦ 96,187 (parliamentary constituency)

Chislehurst • Bromley

A pretty suburb situated south-west of SIDCUP with an old village centre and common, and plenty of greenery and 19th-century cottages. First recorded in 974 as a patch of stony woodland, a settlement had developed around the Scadbury estate by the mid-13th century. Camden Place, now a golf clubhouse, is named after William Camden, the Elizabethan antiquary who lived in Chislehurst from 1609 until his death in 1623. Lord Chief Justice Charles Pratt lived here and took the title of Camden when he was made a baron in 1765, subsequently bestowing the name on north London's CAMDEN TOWN. When Napoleon III and his family were expelled from France in 1871 after the country's defeat in the Franco-Prussian War, the imperial family moved to Camden Place. Napoleon died in 1873 and was buried at the Roman Catholic church in Chislehurst until the Empress Eugenie removed his body to Farnborough, Hampshire. Around this time, the 'new' end of Chislehurst began to develop near the railway station, which opened in 1865. The town became suburbanized between the wars and merged with Sidcup in 1934 to form a larger urban district. Part of the old parish of Chislehurst was 'lost' to BEXLEY when the London boroughs were reorganized in 1965.

Chislehurst Caves, off Old Hill, are a disused chalk mine with several miles of passageways split into three sections, colourfully named Saxon, Druid and Roman, although evidence of such early usage is flimsy. The caves were last worked in the 1850s. When the railway reached Chislehurst the caves became a tourist attraction. They were used for military purposes in wartime, for mushroom farming between the wars and have represented a thaesium mine on the planet Solos for an episode of *Dr Who*. During the 1960s, Status Quo, Jimi Hendrix and Pink Floyd all per-

formed here. In 1974 Led Zeppelin launched their Swan Song label with a party in the caves. Guided tours operate most days.

Sir Malcolm Campbell, who set land and water speed records, was born in Chislehurst on 11 March 1885, and was buried next to his parents at St Nicholas' Church in 1949.

✉ Chislehurst BR7

♦ 14,739 (the Mottingham and Chislehurst North ward adds another 10,114)

🚃 South Eastern Trains (zone 5)

📖 Muriel Searle, *Chislehurst in Old Picture Postcards*, European Library, 1998; T A Bushell, *Imperial Chislehurst: The Story of a Kentish Village*, Barracuda, 1974

@ www.chislehurst-society.org.uk; www.rands.holman.org/Chislehurst.html (Chislehurst Guide site)

Chislehurst West • Bromley

Now the commercial heart of CHISLEHURST, situated on the north-west side of the wider residential district. Until the mid 19th century this was the hamlet of Prick End and it is not hard to understand why the Victorians renamed it, although Prickend Pond remains. The separate hamlet of Red Hill, which had two brickworks, was absorbed later as Chislehurst expanded towards MOTTINGHAM. From the 1880s the main thoroughfare, then called Chislehurst West, was built up with generously proportioned two- and three-storey terraced houses, many of which had shops at street level. Surviving older cottages were converted for commercial use and the road was soon renamed the High Street. A Sainsbury's supermarket was built in the mid 1970s at the expense of some of the Victorian properties. Chislehurst West is now noted as an eating and drinking destination.

✉ Chislehurst BR7

Chiswick • Hounslow (pronounced 'chizzik')

A west London suburb filling the peninsula between HAMMERSMITH and BRENTFORD. The name means 'cheese farm' and was in use by 1000. Chiswick came into being as a Thames-side fishing village, clustered around the church of St Nicholas by 1181. The present church dates from the 15th century, but was mostly rebuilt in 1884. The 16th-century Walpole House is the grandest of Chiswick Mall's villas, though much altered, and illustrates the stature of the village's residents at that time. By the late Middle Ages, Chiswick encompassed the neighbouring villages of Little Sutton, TURNHAM GREEN and STRAND ON THE GREEN, across the peninsula. Chiswick House was built in Palladian style by the Earl of Burlington in 1729. Of modest proportions by aristocratic standards, its splendid decor and ornate ceilings have been faithfully restored by English Heritage. Both the house and its estate were enlarged by Burlington's heirs, the dukes of Devonshire. To the north-east of Chiswick House lived the artist William Hogarth from 1749 until his death in 1764. His house is now a museum. From the second quarter of the 19th century, the orchards and market gardens of the Chiswick peninsula began to fill with housing. Chiswick New Town was an early project for the working classes, now replaced by council flats. The Glebe estate to its north was more upmarket. On Chiswick's northern edge BEDFORD PARK set a new standard for suburban housing after 1875. By this time Turnham Green had become the commercial heart of Chiswick. Before the end of the 19th century developers had begun to demolish large villas and replace them with mansion blocks or smaller, more densely packed houses. The Turnham Green area is now synonymous with Chiswick for many Londoners, and is popular for its restaurants, cafés and specialist shops. Chiswick's river front and Strand on the Green are the least changed parts of this mini-conurbation, the former still grand, the latter hanging on to quaintness.

Erin Pizzey founded the world's first refuge for battered women in Chiswick in 1971. Linoleum and Cherry Blossom shoe polish were created in Chiswick. Chiswick's appeal to the literary community is reflected in its role in several novels, including William Thackeray's *Vanity Fair* and John Fowles' *A Maggot*. Like Deptford, Chiswick was home to an eponymous independent record label during the punk rock era; Chiswick Records' most notable signing was The Damned. Chiswick was also the birthplace of rock musician Phil Collins.

✉ W4

♦ 21,225 (Chiswick Homefields and Riverside wards)

🚃 South West Trains (zone 3)

📖 Gillian Clegg, *The Chiswick Book: Past and Present*, Historical Publications, 2004 (a little encyclopaedia of Chiswick); William Percy Roe, *Glimpses of Chiswick's Development*, W P Roe, 1999

@ www.chiswickw4.com (community website)

Chiswick Eyot · *Hounslow* (pronounced 'chizzik ait')

A narrow, uninhabited island lying off Chiswick Mall in a stretch of the Thames known as Corney Reach. This is the most easterly of London's eyots and the only such obstacle in the course of the University Boat Race. Flint tools and Neolithic and Roman pottery have been discovered here, indicating the possibility of a small settlement. By 1800, osier beds around the island were producing reeds that were used to make baskets for the market gardens of CHISWICK. Commercial cultivation continued until the mid 1930s, when the borough of Brentford and Chiswick bought the island from the Ecclesiastical Commissioners. Chiswick Eyot used to be more than an acre larger than it is now, but all of the part that used to lie within the Hammersmith borough boundary has fallen into the Thames. This erosion problem prompted a proposal in the 1970s to flatten the entire island but the plan was shelved in the face of public resistance. Instead, the banks were shored up during the following decade. In 1993 Chiswick Eyot was declared a local nature reserve, and put under the care of English Nature. The island is accessible at low tide but the Chiswick lifeboat has sometimes been called out to rescue explorers marooned by rising waters.

✉ W4

@ www.urban75.org/vista/eyot.html (island panorama via webcam)

Chiswick Park · *Hounslow/Ealing*

A station, business park and (arguably) the neighbouring residential area on the CHISWICK/ACTON border. The use of the name for this north-western corner of Chiswick is a relatively modern and misleading coinage. The original Chiswick Park was part of the Duke of Devonshire's Chiswick House estate and lay well to the south. This area was the farmland where Thomas Kemp Welch, inspired by the success of BEDFORD PARK, tried in vain to create a garden suburb called Chiswick Park in the 1880s. Staveley Road now covers the site of Chiswick Park Farm. For reasons best known to itself, the Metropolitan District Railway Company renamed ACTON GREEN station Acton Green & Chiswick Park in 1887 and it became plain Chiswick Park in 1910. The most likely explanation is that the Chiswick name carried a greater cachet than Acton's, as it still does. Good quality terraced houses for the working classes began clustering around the station from its inception, in the area still more properly known as Acton Green. The London General Omnibus Company built its maintenance and engineering works opposite GUNNERSBURY station in 1921 and the facility employed 3,500 staff at its peak. Maintenance work transferred to Elstree in 1956 and London Transport closed its engineering operation here in 1988, leaving the 30-acre site available for redevelopment as a different kind of Chiswick Park. The Anglo-Norwegian Kvaerner Group has constructed eleven office buildings accommodating around 7,500 people in what is said to be the largest such project in London since CANARY WHARF, although PADDINGTON WATERSIDE can also lay claim to this distinction. The tenant profile is mixed but is aimed primarily at the high-tech and new media sectors. The landscaping provides an 'inner garden', said to make reference to both Monet's paintings and to Chinese influences of the 19th century, while the 'outer landscape' is a simpler and more functional design that includes peripheral car parking and arterial corridors between the buildings.

✉ W4

🚇 District Line (zone 3)

@ www.chiswick-park.com (business park site)

Church End · Barnet

The old heart of FINCHLEY, representing the south-west quadrant of the parish, usually now called 'Finchley Central'. An excavation at St Mary's School in 1990 revealed evidence of early medieval occupation, probably peaking between 1150 and 1250. The parish church of St Mary was first documented in 1274. From the mid 14th century, when much of the area was part of Bibbesworth manor, the Great North Road (as it later became) ran to the east of Church End, attracting commerce away to what is now EAST FINCHLEY, and the old village became a woodland backwater, though the church was rebuilt in the 15th century. In 1826, Regent's Park Road was constructed as part of a new through route from west London to the north and Church End slowly regained some vitality. Some Bibbesworth land was sold for building and Christ's College was founded on Hendon Lane in 1858. The college's first buildings have not survived but the main block of 1861 has, with a distinctive 'pepper-pot' stair-turret. Following the arrival of the railway in 1867, Lichfield Grove was laid

out on former Bibbesworth land and other developers targeted Hendon Lane and Grass Farm to its west, but progress was slow at first. Avenue House was built north of East End Road, and extravagantly rebuilt in the 1880s by H C Stephens of the ink-making family. Stephens left the house and grounds to the borough on his death and it is now the base for several local groups and charities, including the Finchley Society. NORTH FINCHLEY gained commercial superiority over Church End but residential development took off after the introduction of tram services in 1905 and the area was almost entirely built up by 1920. Flats and office blocks replaced many of the larger old properties after World War II but the Church End conservation area preserves the vicinity of Christ's College and St Mary's Church. Like much of the Finchley district, Church End has a large Jewish population and a smaller minority of Indian origin, including both Hindus and Muslims.

✉ N3

👤 13,810

Church End · Brent

A deprived locality in west WILLESDEN, on the borders of HARLESDEN and STONEBRIDGE. The church in question is St Mary's, which was situated near the local manor house and farmstead in a dead-end lane at the west or 'church' end of the village. The church is said to have been founded in 938, but the present Kentish ragstone structure dates from the mid 13th century, with Victorian additions. It is the oldest parish church in north-west London. St Mary's was once famous for its spring, which was credited with healing powers, and for its shrine to Our Lady of Willesden, which drew pilgrims to see a sacred black image. The neighbouring cemetery, Willesden Old Burial Ground, is reputedly the site of a 17th-century plague pit, and haunted by a hooded monk, dressed in white. The village was well-developed by the 18th century, with several inns. The parish register of St Mary's Church has entries in the 1720s for the baptism of 'Sarah, daughter of Tobias Eco [or Ecco], a black' and later of sons Tobias and John; these are among the first records of black residents in the London area. Church End remained primarily agricultural until the 1870s, when cheap housing began to be laid out for the working classes and the locality was almost entirely built over within 20 years. During the 1960s and 1970s, maisonettes and system-built council towers replaced much of the older housing in Church End. The charitable trust Fortunegate took over the Church End estate from Brent council in 1998 and began a major rehabilitation programme. Parts of the estate have since been transformed by this scheme but it remains beset by crime and violence associated with the crack cocaine and heroin trade. In 2002 a Somali refugee, Kayser Osman, was stabbed to death outside the Acorn Club on Taylors Lane. A jury found the then 14-year-old killer guilty of manslaughter but acquitted his 12-year-old cousin, one of the youngest people ever to stand trial for murder.

In 1997 the Archbishop of Canterbury led a group of religious leaders representing eight faiths from the Baha'i faith to Jainism in blessing the spring at St Mary's Church.

✉ NW10

📖 M C Barrès-Baker, *Church End and the Parish of Willesden*, Grange Museum of Community History and Brent Archive, 2001

@ www.brent-heritage.co.uk/church.end.htm (local history site)

Church End · *Redbridge see* WOODFORD

Church End · *Waltham Forest see* WALTHAMSTOW VILLAGE

Church Street · *Westminster*

A socially disadvantaged ward and diverse market street, situated on the west side of LISSON GROVE. Church Street was created in the 1790s as part of the development of LISSON GREEN, and ran west towards the parish church at PADDINGTON GREEN. A hay market opened on a three-acre site on the north side of Church Street in 1830, adding vegetables and general goods a year later. A grand collection of buildings was named Portman Market after Sir William Portman, who had owned much of the manor in the latter half of the 16th century. Better-off folk came to the market from further afield, including Mary Ann Evans, otherwise known as the writer George Eliot, who shopped every week at the post office and grocers. However, hopes that the market would rival COVENT GARDEN were never realized, despite a reconstruction scheme in 1900. The site was sold in 1906 and became a vehicle maintenance depot. Traders soon set up their stalls on the street instead. The neighbourhood was badly damaged during the Blitz and the old market site was redeveloped as part of the Church Street estate after the war. More council flats filled the street's hinterland

in the following decades, some controversially replacing properties that could have been restored. From the 1960s, trade in antiques and bric-à-brac flourished on Church Street. Alfie's Antique Market opened in 1976 on the site of Jordan's department store and is now home to over 100 dealers. There are more traders in nearby Bell Street, especially second-hand booksellers. The Church Street ward is ethnically diverse, with a large Muslim minority, many of whom are of Bangladeshi origin. The majority of homes are rented from the council or a social landlord, and 68 per cent of households – a very high proportion – have no car.

After his supposed death at the Reichenbach Falls, Sherlock Holmes first reappears to Dr Watson disguised as a Church Street bookseller in *The Adventure of the Empty House*.

✉ NW8; W2

🚶 6,490

📖 E McDonald and D J Smith, *Pineapples and Pantomimes: A History of Church Street and Lisson Green*, Westminster Libraries, 1992

@ www.alfiesantiques.com

City of London · *City*

The City with a capital 'C' always refers to the City of London, either in the literal geographical sense, or as a figurative term for London's financial centre. The City extends from CHANCERY LANE in the west to Mansell Street and Middlesex Street (PETTICOAT LANE) in the east. It is bounded by the Thames to the south and at its northernmost extremity it stops just short of OLD STREET. The Romans appear to have decided to make Londinium their capital soon after invading Britain in AD43 and built a defensive wall that encompassed 330 acres on its completion in the third century. With the departure of the Romans early in the fifth century, the Saxons established their main trading settlement in the vicinity of the ALDWYCH and the City fell into decline. The construction of the first ST PAUL'S Cathedral in 604 was the first sign of renewed growth and by the ninth century prosperity had returned, with CHEAPSIDE becoming London's high street. Although the Normans made WESTMINSTER their seat of government, William the Conqueror built a castle that later became the TOWER of London at the south-east corner of the City. Richard I allowed Londoners to choose their own mayor and the Guildhall was constructed in the early 15th century as a form of parliament for representatives from the City's merchant guilds. The establishment of the Royal Exchange in 1570 consolidated London's role as a leading international trading centre, but like most of the City's buildings it burned down in the Great Fire of London in 1666. The medieval street plan was retained in the City's reconstruction, but brick and stone were used for the replacement buildings, rather than wood. Sir Christopher Wren was commissioned to rebuild the City's churches, including St Paul's Cathedral. The BANK of England was founded in 1694 and evolved into the official custodian of the nation's currency over the course of the following century. Other great financial institutions also assumed their modern form during this period, including the insurance brokers Lloyd's of London and the main clearing banks. The MANSION HOUSE, the official residence of the Lord Mayor of London, was completed in 1752. Britain was relatively unaffected by the wars that blighted Europe for more than two decades from 1792, allowing London to assume an unrivalled position as the mercantile centre of a growing empire. However, with more than 100,000 inhabitants crammed into the square mile, the vast majority of Londoners reaped scant reward from the City's wealth and the reality of daily life was dark, dirty and noisome in the warrens of tenements in the poorer quarters. A great change came with the building of the railways in the mid 19th century. Together with other improvements in transport and increasingly affordable fares, the railways stimulated a suburban building boom that allowed an exodus of residents. The destruction wreaked in World War II resulted in the clearance of most of the surviving dwellings and workshops, although the subsequent construction of the BARBICAN brought the return of a residential and cultural aspect. From the late 1980s the regeneration of DOCKLANDS posed the most serious threat to the City's vitality since the Romans left. The Corporation of London reacted by relaxing some of its strict planning controls, improving streetscapes and embarking on a worldwide promotional drive. Despite the loss of some major corporations, construction of new floorspace recovered – most visibly in the form of 30 St Mary Axe, better known as the Gherkin – and the City's daytime population remains massive; more than a quarter of a million people commute into the City every day. Boundary changes in 1994 increased the City's area to 779 acres and added more than 30 per cent to its population – mainly from the Golden Lane and Mansell Street housing estates. The City experienced a surge in the building of residential units in the late 1990s, rising from almost none in 1994 to nearly 500 in 1999, split almost equally between new buildings and office-to-flat conversions. In the early years of the 21st century the craze faded, especially for conversions. The City's demographic profile is radically different from that of any other local authority in London. Sixty per cent of residents are qualified to degree level or higher and a similar proportion of households have only one occupant. The proportion of residents aged under 19 is less than half the national average.

✉ EC1; EC2; EC3; EC4

👤 7,185

📖 David Kynaston, *The City of London*, Pimlico, 2006 (abridged edition of 4-vol. history); Nikolaus Pevsner et al, *London: City of London*, Yale University Press, 2002; Warren Grynberg, *Images of the City of London: The Square Mile Revealed*, Breedon Books, 2005

@ www.cityoflondon.gov.uk

City of Westminster *see* WESTMINSTER

City Road • *Islington/Hackney*
Timber merchant and sawmill pioneer Charles Dingley devised his scheme for a new route linking the CITY OF LONDON with the ANGEL, ISLINGTON in the mid 1750s. The road developed as a series of individual sections, which were eventually unified as the City Road in the 1860s, when a tollgate that stood near the present OLD STREET station was removed. Some of the road's architectural and historical highlights are listed here in south–north order. Finsbury Barracks, built in 1857 as the headquarters of the Royal London Militia, now houses the Honourable Artillery Company, the second most senior regiment in the Territorial Army. In 1777, John Wesley founded the chapel known as 'the cathedral of world Methodism'. He lived, preached, died and was buried within the confines of the little complex of buildings that now serves as an active memorial to his work. Wesley's house and a museum of Methodism are the chapel's neighbours. The associated Leysian Mission was a philanthropic project founded in 1886 by the old boys of the Leys School, Cambridge. The mission operated from two smaller sites before the construction of the present grand edifice in 1904, which has recently been converted to apartments. Moorfields Eye Hospital came to its present site in 1899, since

when it has been much enlarged. The Shepherd and Shepherdess ale house and tea garden operated at the corner of what is now Shepherdess Walk until around 1745, when it was replaced by the Eagle tavern, of *Pop Goes the Weasel* fame. A new Eagle tavern, combined with a 'Grecian theatre', was built in the 1820s. Music hall star Marie Lloyd started work here as a waitress, at the age of 15. City Road station opened on the City and South London Railway line in 1901. Stations on what is now the Bank branch of the Northern Line closed in 1922 for tunnel-widening work but unlike the others City Road never reopened, although remnants of it are still visible. City Road Basin is an arm of the Regent's Canal where timber was once unloaded for finishing in the locality. This area began to be regenerated in the late 1980s. The clock tower at the junction with Goswell Road was erected in 1905.

In 2002 celebrity chef Jamie Oliver launched his restaurant Fifteen in Westland Place. The opening marked the fruition of a training programme for unemployed would-be caterers, which was the subject of the television series *Jamie's Kitchen*.

✉ EC1; N1

Clapham • *Wandsworth/Lambeth* (pronounced 'clappəm', despite the jokey, mock-posh 'claahm' affected by some residents)

A stylish, socially and ethnically mixed neighbourhood situated south-east of BATTERSEA. The name derives from the Old English words 'cloppa' (rocks or hills) and 'ham' (a homestead or enclosed pasture), and was first recorded around 880 in the Anglo-Saxon Chronicle. By the 12th century St Paul's Church was the focus of a small village and in the latter part of the 17th century numerous Londoners settled here after plagues and fire ravaged the City. The diarist Samuel Pepys retired to Clapham and died in a house overlooking the common in 1703. Grand houses and terraces filled the Old Town and encircled the common during the 18th century and a new church, Holy Trinity, was built on CLAPHAM COMMON in 1776. Thomas Cubitt laid out the high-class CLAPHAM PARK estate after 1825 and within a decade the village had grown into an exclusive suburb on the edge of the metropolis. In the latter part of the 19th century trains and horse-drawn trams made Clapham accessible to clerks and artisans and its status declined as the population grew. Developers demolished and replaced most of the largest houses. The extension of the City and South London Railway to Clapham Road (now Clapham North station) and Clapham Common in 1900 cemented the change in character. Clapham South station opened in 1926. Following extensive damage during World War II, large parts of Clapham were redeveloped in the 1950s and 1960s, mostly with council housing, but many properties survive from the 18th and early 19th centuries. In recent times Clapham has become highly fashionable among families who might aspire to live in CHELSEA but cannot yet afford it, and property prices have risen accordingly. The district is also popular with young singles, often sharing rented accommodation. This revival in Clapham's desirability is reflected in the shops, bars and restaurants of Clapham High Street and Clapham Common South Side.

Clapham's name has had a variety of associations. To have 'been at Hadham and come home by Clapham' was 18th-century slang for having contracted gonorrhoea. William Wilberforce's anti-slavery movement was known as the Clapham Sect and its members were Claphamites. The phrase 'the man on the Clapham omnibus', meaning the average person, was coined in 1903 by Lord Bowen.

✉ SW4

👥 13,332 (Lambeth's Clapham Town ward)

🚌 Southern (Clapham High Street, zone 2); Northern Line (Clapham North, Clapham Common, zone 2; Clapham South, zones 2 and 3)

📖 Julie Myerson, *Home: The Story of Everyone Who Ever Lived in our House*, Flamingo, 2004; Peter Jefferson Smith and Alyson Wilson (eds), *Clapham in the Twentieth Century*, Clapham Society, 2002; Gillian Clegg, *Clapham Past*, Historical Publications, 1998

@ www.claphamhighstreet.co.uk (privately operated local information site)

Clapham Common • *Wandsworth/Lambeth*

One of south London's most important open spaces, the common juts into south BATTERSEA from the western side of CLAPHAM. From the time of Domesday Book this has been uncultivated land, split between the manors of Battersea and Clapham. The poor quality of the soil protected it from exploitation at a time when neighbouring fields came under the plough. A windmill was erected in 1631 and horse racing took place here from 1674. Certain problems arose cyclically, mostly revolving around issues of ownership and responsibility for the common's upkeep. The condition of the terrain was often allowed to deteriorate to an overgrown and boggy state before improvements were made. Owners of houses bordering the common periodically attempted to extend their properties onto the common land until legal measures forced them to retreat. In 1716 tensions over grazing rights erupted into a turf war when Battersea parishioners dug a boundary ditch bisecting the common. Clapham parishioners promptly filled it in. By the mid 18th century the common's edges had become a popular place to build one's country retreat, especially on the north side. The Pavement divided the common from Clapham's Old Town, and the Plough and Windmill public houses were well-established. Mount Pond had been formed by the extraction of gravel. Until the mid 18th century the common remained an important amenity for ordinary people, providing firewood and water as well as pasture for livestock, and even a place to string out a washing line between two trees, but these practices began to die out with the construction of more villas and institutions, especially private girls' schools. Sports clubs established themselves here, including Clapham Golf Club and Clapham Rovers Football Club. In 1877 the Metropolitan Board of Works acquired Clapham Common from the lords of the manors, relocating a bandstand here from SOUTH KENSINGTON in 1890. The common became a popular place for day trips, with a classier reputation than KENNINGTON. A group of houses replaced a grove of chestnut trees behind the Windmill Inn in the 1890s but the common's integrity has otherwise been preserved. Clapham Common now has dozens of pitches for almost every kind of outdoor sport and is a regular venue for fairs, rallies and concerts. The long-derelict bandstand was restored in 2006 at a cost of nearly £1m. The Clapham Common ward has an exceptionally high proportion of university-educated residents, many in their twenties. The common's role as an after-dark rendezvous for gay men attracted widespread coverage in 1998 when the Secretary of State for Wales, Ron Davies, resigned following an incident here.

In 1768 the American scientist and statesman Benjamin Franklin conducted experiments in pouring oil on troubled water on Mount Pond.

✉ SW4

♦ 12,270 (Lambeth's Clapham Common ward)

🚇 Northern Line (zone 2)

📖 Fiona Henderson et al, *The Story of Clapham Common*, Clapham Society, 1995

@ www.claphamcommon.org (Friends of the common site)

Clapham Junction • *Wandsworth*

A station, complex railway intersection and shopping area situated in south-west BATTERSEA. When a railway halt opened here in 1846, it was named after the best-known of the few buildings on the Old Portsmouth Road, the Falcon Inn. With the multiplication in the number of lines traversing south Battersea, the station was rebuilt in 1863 as Clapham Junction; the choice of name probably resulting from the greater cachet of Clapham as a smart suburb. From the outset Clapham Junction provided links to VICTORIA and WATERLOO stations in London and to most towns in southern England. The station was extended in the 1870s. The vicinity developed rapidly in the latter part of the 19th century but only a minority of the new residents used the trains in the early decades of the station's existence. Less wealthy commuters reached the city centre on foot, and later by tram or horse-drawn bus. From the 1880s, cheaper fares made rail travel affordable to labourers and artisans, helping to change the social profile of the neighbourhood. The Falcon was rebuilt as a hotel and the Arding and Hobbs department store opened on the opposite corner of the crossroads. The store's present appearance dates from 1910. Although the façades of the many outlets on St John's Hill, St John's Road and LAVENDER HILL have changed radically, there was little renewal of the built environment during the 20th century. In 1988, 35 people died in a rush-hour collision between trains to the south-west of the station. The subsequent inquiry into the crash recommended the installation of automatic train protection for the whole rail network, but the £750 million price tag precluded its implementation. After a very brief period in 2005 when it claimed to be Europe's busiest railway station, Clapham Junction has now reverted to the surer boast that it is Britain's busiest. The station has 16 active platforms and its own retail precinct. Arding and Hobbs is now part of the Debenhams group.

The film *Up the Junction*, based on the book by Nell Dunn, premièred at the nearby

Granada cinema in 1968. The Squeeze single track of the same name reached number two in the UK pop charts in 1979.

✉ SW11

🚌 Silverlink Metro (limited); South Eastern Trains; Southern; South West Trains; Virgin Trains (zone 2)

📖 V Mitchell and K Smith, *Clapham Junction: 50 Years of Change*, Middleton Press, 1997

Clapham Park • *Lambeth*

Located in the south-east corner of CLAPHAM, Clapham Park is a council estate combined with an agreeable community of terraced streets, which some prefer to consider 'the Abbeville Road area', rather than part of Clapham Park. In 1825 Thomas Cubitt bought 229 acres of Bleak Hall Farm and began to lay out the BRIXTON side of the district as the Clapham Park estate with his trademark Italianate villas, building a home for himself on Clarence Avenue. Development progressed slowly and it was not until the 1850s that most of the estate had been built up. By this time Clapham Park had become one of the most fashionable London addresses south of the river. From the 1880s the previously undeveloped area near CLAPHAM COMMON was laid out with streets of more compact housing, with Abbeville Road as the spine. Cubitt's house was demolished in 1905 and the spacious semi-detached houses of Rodenhurst Road filled its grounds. From 1929 to 1936 the London County Council laid out an estate of its standard neo-Georgian flats. The LCC resumed its programme after 1950, demolishing many of Cubitt's houses and building low-rise shops and flats in a Swedish-influenced style. Lambeth council completed the scheme after 1965 in yet another style. Problems of neglect caused social difficulties in the 1990s but the estate is currently the subject of a major regeneration effort. Meanwhile, on Abbeville Road, the upmarket florists and trendy cafés tell the story of the enormous rise in popularity of what estate agents have started to call Abbeville Village or Abbevillage. A third of Clapham Park's population consists of black and minority ethnic groups. There is also a relatively high proportion of retired people and, on the Clapham Park estate, single-parent families.

Clapham Park was home to the piano manufacturer Whelpdale Maxwell and Codd until it moved out in 2000 to cut costs.

✉ SW4

📖 Joanna Bogle, *One Corner of London: A History of St Bede's, Clapham Park*, Gracewing, 2003

@ www.claphampark.org.uk (regeneration project site)

Clapton • *Hackney*

The north-eastern quadrant of the borough, consisting of UPPER CLAPTON, LOWER CLAPTON, CLAPTON PARK and the MILLFIELDS and SPRINGFIELD PARK areas. The name was first recorded in 1339 as Clopton, which meant 'farmstead on a hill'. In common with other districts at a similar distance from the CITY OF LONDON, Clapton first developed as a rural retreat, then became built up into a 19th-century commuter suburb (aided by the arrival of rail and tram services in the 1870s) but went downmarket during the 20th century as the middle classes moved further out to the edge of the countryside. More recently, its population has regained a young professional contingent because of its relative affordability for would-be homeowners. Clapton's grandest mansion was Brooke House, formerly King's Place. Said to have been a residence of Henry VIII and later home to earls and barons, the house became a lunatic asylum in 1760. It was demolished after World War II, having suffered irreparable bomb damage. Many of Clapton's Georgian and Victorian buildings have been supplanted by public housing, either as part of slum clearance programmes or because they were allegedly too large for 20th-century living. Some smaller estates are replacements for housing destroyed in the Blitz. Clapton stadium was the home of Clapton (now Leyton) Orient. Later a dog track, the stadium had given way to housing by 1980. Clapton's focal point is the newly formatted roundabout at the junction of Lea Bridge Road with Upper Clapton Road and Lower Clapton Road. Once this junction was the site of Brooke House and of retail emporia, banks, drinking fountains and public conveniences; now there is a mosque and a college. The borough's 'North-East Neighbourhood' corresponds roughly with 'greater Clapton'. Forty-two per cent of the neighbourhood's residents are white British and the other main ethnic groups are non-British white, black African, black Caribbean and Indian. Christianity, Islam and Judaism are the principal religious faiths.

✉ E5

🚶 52,996 (Hackney's 'North-East

Neighbourhood', comprising Cazenove, Hackney Downs, Leabridge, New River and Springfield wards)

🚇 'one' Railway (zones 2 and 3)

Clapton Park • *Hackney*

A clash of Victorian terraced houses and council flats, located on the eastern side of LOWER CLAPTON and separated from HACKNEY MARSH by the River Lea Navigation. The London and Suburban Land Co. invented the Clapton Park name for an estate that it laid out in two phases in the late 1860s and early 1870s. Most of the land had previously been market gardens. Chatsworth Road provided the main shopping amenities. The short-lived Clapton Park Theatre opened on Glenarm Road in 1875. The area south of Redwald Road was the last to be developed, at the end of the 19th century. In 1928 Hackney council built some of its first homes here: 69 maisonettes around Daubeney Road. The London County Council laid out the low-rise Kingsmead estate in 1937 on 20 acres of Hackney Marsh. Hackney council added the system-built Clapton Park estate in the 1960s. Three decades later, all but one of its towers were demolished and replaced by more traditional houses and street patterns. The remaining block, Sudbury Court, was sold to a private developer, renamed Landmark Heights and given a (somewhat superficial) makeover. In 1994 *The Guardian* chillingly described the Kingsmead estate as 'a blighted labyrinth of five-storey concrete blocks that hits the headlines with depressing regularity. Remember the paedophile ring that led to the abuse and murder of teenage runaway, Jason Swift? The council gardener who held satanic masses and murdered his girlfriend's five-year-old son? The desperate legal measures adopted by the council in the face of a crime wave police seemed unable or unwilling to curb? That was Kingsmead.' Thirteen per cent of homes in the King's Park ward are single-parent households – twice the national average. The ward also has a high student population.

Julian Perry's 1990 painting *The Enchanted Castle*, in the Museum of London, depicts one of the Clapton Park towers surrounded by unfeasibly tall trees. The artist and sculptor Rachel Whiteread produced several photographic works based on the demolition of tower blocks on the estate.

✉ E5; E9

🚶 10,964 (King's Park ward)

Claybury • *Redbridge*

A little-used name for the northern part of CLAYHALL. Except for London Buses, most authorities nowadays describe the entire residential area as Clayhall. Like Clayhall, the name probably derives from the De la Clay family. In the 19th century, Claybury Farm stood where Claybury Broadway now runs parallel with part of Woodford Avenue. To the north was Claybury Hall and its surrounding parkland, laid out in 1789 by Humphry Repton for the owner, James Hatch. On the edge of the park the Victorians built the palatial Claybury Hospital in 1893, as a self-supporting community with capacity for 2,500 residents. In the 1960s, staff here pioneered a 'therapeutic community' approach to psychiatry and Claybury continued in use a hospital until 1997. Property developer Crest Nicholson has now converted it to housing with the aid of an enabling grant. Like other conversions of Victorian hospitals, the 'Repton Park' development is a mix of refurbished apartments and new homes, in this case mews and town houses, with a health club in the restored Victorian chapel and Great Hall. The grounds still cover 235 acres and are managed by the London Wildlife Trust. There are wildflower-rich meadows, rare acid grassland and the ancient woodland of Claybury Woods, with distinctive flora such as the wild service tree, wood anemone, Forester's woodrush, and broad-leaved helleborine orchid.

✉ Ilford IG5; Repton Park is in Woodford Green IG8

📖 Eric H Pryor, *Pictorial Review of Claybury Hospital*, Forest Healthcare Trust, 1996

Clayhall • *Redbridge*

A multi-faith residential district consisting of bungalows, semi-detached houses and housing association flats, situated north of GANTS HILL and south-east of WOODFORD BRIDGE. It probably takes its name from the De la Clay family, who were living here in 1203. Clayhall was first recorded in 1410. Although some manors remained in the possession of a single family for centuries, Clayhall changed hands with great frequency. From around 1608 to 1619, it was the home of Sir Christopher Hatton, cousin of a namesake who gave his name to HATTON GARDEN. From the wealth and nobility of its various owners, the 17th-century manor house would seem to have been substantial, but it was demolished in the mid 18th century and replaced by a farmhouse. A chapel built by Sir Christopher Hatton had become a barn by 1901. The farm was run by a succession of tenants until the estate was broken up for development in the mid 1930s and the farmhouse, barn and other outbuildings were demolished. The majority of Clayhall's properties are generously proportioned, bay-fronted semi-detached houses, now mostly pebble-dashed. The only council housing is the Tiptree estate, off Clayhall Avenue. Clayhall is one of the most diverse wards in London in terms of religious beliefs; Christians, Jews, Hindus, Muslims and Sikhs are all well-represented.

The Lifeline system of pocket alarms for elderly people living alone, which has been adopted nationwide, was pioneered in Clayhall. The borough's original Lifeline control centre was based at Clayhall's Stoneleigh Court, a sheltered housing unit, but a larger centre was soon required.

✉ Ilford IG5

♦ 11,855

Clay Hill • Enfield

A conservation area in north ENFIELD, on the edge of open country west of FORTY HILL. Although seemingly self-explanatory, the name may not be derived from the sedimentary deposit but from the surname of a medieval resident. The wider area is indeed formed of London clay but the distinctive characteristics at Clay Hill are patches of pebble gravel. In 1572 the road and the settlement were known as Bridge Street, but both had become Clay Hill by 1754. The Rose and Crown inn lay at the heart of the hamlet from its earliest days; it is said that the inn was once owned by Dick Turpin's grandfather and that the ghost of the highwayman and his horse have been seen here. Beggar's Bush fairs were held at the top of Clay Hill in the 1770s but later returned to SOUTHGATE, where they had first begun. The Church of St John the Baptist was built in 1858 but was soon closed for a while by the Bishop of London after James Whatman Bosanquet of Claysmore complained about 'mysterious mutterings' of a popish nature. Clay Hill House, now an old people's home, was built around 1860 for Joseph Toms of the Derry and Toms department store in Kensington. The improvement of railway services to ENFIELD TOWN in the early 1870s brought housebuilding to the south side of the hill later in that decade. The opening of a station at GORDON HILL in 1910 made the locality even more appealing to developers. In anticipation of the station's opening, Enfield council had

bought all 62 acres of Park Farm in 1909, and opened the land as Hilly Fields Park in 1911. Claysmore burned down in 1930 but the 18th-century Claysmore Lodge remains. Clay Hill is traversed by the Turkey Brook and local volunteers have laid a boardwalk through a particularly muddy part of the woods. Clay Hill has equestrian facilities at Kingswood and Brayside Farm, Enfield Cricket Club's ground is on Strayfield Road and Beggars Hollow is the access point for WHITEWEBBS golf course.

Novelist Captain Frederick Marryat and mathematician Charles Babbage both went to school in Clay Hill. The Bosanquets of Clay Hill were a distinguished Huguenot family. Bernard Bosanquet played cricket for England in the early 20th century and is credited with having invented the googly (also known as the 'bosie'). His son Reginald became a well-known television newsreader in the 1970s.

✉ Enfield EN2

@ www.hillyfields.info (Friends of Hilly Fields site)

Clementswood • Redbridge

One of the four most southerly Redbridge wards, constituting the south-eastern part of ILFORD. The name derives from the Clement family, who were smallholders around the 15th century. During the following century the farmland here was consolidated into a single property. In 1803 John Thompson bought Clements Farm and began to develop the estate with the assistance of his son. The Thompsons gave the name 'Clements' to their brick-built mansion, which was situated 200 feet north of the farmhouse. They also earned the opprobrium of the local populace by diverting Green Lane from its route across their land. A small riot broke out in 1826 when the family's brickfield workers were enlisted to resist a mass attempt to reopen the old lane. Following the death of William Thompson, who had been in financial difficulties, the estate was broken up and the mansion was demolished in 1880. Most of the farmland was covered with housing during the last two decades of the 19th century, while the north-western corner of the estate became part of Ilford's growing town centre. After World War II, many middle-class residents moved out to Essex and some properties were subdivided. St Clement's Church was demolished and replaced by flats; services were thereafter held on the second floor of the church hall. The majority of residents in the Clementswood ward are now Asian or Asian British, with both Indian and Pakistani origins well-represented. The Pakistani community is said to be London's largest. A very high proportion of households contain dependent children.

The Clementswood crystal set, a basic AM radio receiver that can be made at home, was created by an Ilford amateur radio enthusiast; he adopted the name after seeing and liking the name of Clementswood Bowling Club as he walked through South Park.

✉ Ilford IG1

👥 11,286

Clerkenwell • *Islington/Camden*

A former monastic settlement now turning increasingly hedonistic, located between KING'S CROSS and the CITY OF LONDON. Around 1140 Jordan de Briset and his wife donated land for a priory of the Order of the Hospital of St John of Jerusalem and the nunnery of St Mary. The sisters of the convent drew their water from a well that became known as the clerks' well because City students performed an annual miracle play close by. In 1370, Sir Walter de Manny established the Carthusian priory of Charterhouse (an anglicization of 'Chartreuse'), which was rebuilt after the dissolution of the monasteries as a rambling mansion, becoming Charterhouse Hospital and School in 1611 and now constituting London's most picturesque retirement home. The nunnery's buildings were also demolished after the dissolution but the clerks' well can still be seen through the window of an office block on FARRINGDON Lane. Parts of St John's Priory have survived and a revived 'venerable order' (of which the health care organization St John Ambulance is an offshoot) later returned to St John's Gate, where it maintains its headquarters and a museum. Richard Sadler opened a music hall and spa in north Clerkenwell in 1683; Sadler's Wells has since evolved via a series of rebuildings into one of London's leading venues for the performing arts, especially ballet and opera. From medieval times Clerkenwell attracted edge-of-City trades like jewellery, lock-making, printing, bookbinding, and the making and repair of clocks and watches – and there are still practitioners of several of these crafts here today. When many larger firms closed or moved out to suburban industrial estates, they left behind factories and warehouses that have now been converted for 'loft style living'. Clerkenwell also had a murky side too, and the House of Detention, formerly an underground prison, and the Old Sessions House, once the busiest

court in England, survive from its period as a den of thieves and receivers, pickpockets and coiners. In the 19th century the district was said to have the highest murder rate in London. Lenin produced 17 issues of the Russian revolutionary newsletter *Iskra* in 1902–3 at what is now the Marx Memorial Library on Clerkenwell Green. Most of Clerkenwell's housing still consists of Georgian terraces and municipal and philanthropic tenement blocks from the first half of the 20th century, but apartment complexes like Brewhouse Yard are filling the few available spaces. Numerous 'chilled' bars and minimalist restaurants cater to the new community of media-oriented young professionals.

George Gissing depicted the underbelly of Clerkenwell in his 1889 novel *The Nether World*. Arnold Bennett set his 1923 tale *Riceyman Steps* in Clerkenwell, although he did not know the area well and had to draw on William Pinks' study of the district (republished in 2001). Peter Ackroyd's 2003 story of medieval murder and religious intrigue is entitled *The Clerkenwell Tales*.

✉ EC1; WC1

👥 9,773

📖 William Pinks, *History of Clerkenwell*, Francis Boutle, reissued 2001; Richard Tames, *Clerkenwell and Finsbury Past*, Historical Publications, 1999

@ www.sja.org.uk/museum (St John's Gate museum pages of St John Ambulance site); www.sadlerswells.com; www.marxlibrary.net; www.cga.org.uk (Clerkenwell Green Association site, promoting local craftspeople and designers)

Clissold Park • *Hackney*

A much-loved 55-acre park located in northwest STOKE NEWINGTON. In 1790 the Quaker banker Jonathan Hoare commissioned his nephew Joseph Woods to build a mansion here, demolishing four houses on the north side of Stoke Newington Church Street in the process. Brick earth was excavated in the grounds, leaving two depressions that were later made into ornamental lakes. Hoare had previously lived across the road in Paradise Row and called his new home Paradise House. Within ten years financial difficulties forced him to move out and in 1811 the estate was sold to the Crawshay iron-making family. Eliza Crawshay inherited the property on her father's death in 1835, when she married the Reverend Augustus Clissold. From the mid

19th century, streets began to be laid out on former glebe land to the south. One of the first was Park Road, now Clissold Road. After the death of Augustus Clissold in 1882, the Ecclesiastical Commissioners bought the estate with the intention of profiting from a property development scheme. However, this was a time of popular and municipal enthusiasm for public open spaces and the Metropolitan Board of Works bought the house and grounds in 1887 for the creation of Clissold Park. Joseph Beck and John Runtz were leading proponents of the purchase and the twin lakes were named Beckmere and Runtzmere in their honour. The park was endowed with a lodge soon after it opened but this was replaced in 1936 by the flats of Clissold Court. Opposite the surviving Georgian houses of Paradise Row, a dip running along the edge of the park marks where the New River ran until this stretch was filled in during the 1950s. The council's Clissold Leisure Centre replaced inadequate swimming baths in 2001. Owing to serious defects with the building, the centre closed after 20 months, due to reopen in 2006.

Ernest Raymond's *We, The Accused* (1935) was described by John Betjeman as 'the greatest London novel … murder and autumnal mists in Clissold Park', though George Orwell thought it clumsy and long-winded.

✉ N16

👥 10,438 (Clissold ward)

📖 David Solman, *Clissold Park*, Abney Park Cemetery Trust, 1992

Clock House • *Bromley*

A station in west BECKENHAM and occasionally the name used for its vicinity, often spelt as a single word. Clock House Road runs from the station to ELMERS END, with the railway line on one side and the culverted Chaffinch Brook on the other. The original Clock House was a substantial red brick mansion built in the early 18th century near the Penge to Beckenham road. The house was occupied until his death in 1781 by Rear-Admiral Sir Piercy Brett, after whom Captain Cook named Cape Brett and Piercy Island in New Zealand in 1769. The clock on the stables gave Clock House its name, and the house gave its name to the station when it opened in 1890. The accompanying suburban expansion sealed the mansion's fate and it was pulled down six years later and the gardens, which had had a lake and fountain, became a nursery. The locality

was almost entirely built up by 1900, except for a site east of the station that was filled in 1906 by a parade of shops with flats above. Clock House stables survived until 1926, when the clock was removed and taken to Beckenham Place, where it survives today. The Clock House locality is mostly residential apart from a few offices along Beckenham Road. The impressive Beckenham Spa swimming pool and leisure centre opened in 1999 opposite the station. Like much of the borough, the demographic profile of the Clock House ward is much closer to the national average than most other parts of London.

The children's writer Enid Blyton lived as a child and young woman at homes in Chaffinch Road, Clock House Road and Elm Road between 1897 and 1915.

✉ Beckenham BR3

👥 15,757

🚉 South Eastern Trains (zone 4)

@ www.wbecra.com (West Beckenham Residents' Association site)

Clockhouse • *Sutton*

An anomalous enclave occupying a peninsula of the London Borough of Sutton, isolated from the rest of the borough by fields and golf courses but joined up with COULSDON, further to the south-east. Locals often refer to the area as 'the Mount', after its central road. This was formerly the open land of Clockhouse (or Clock House) Farm, which was associated with the village of WOODMANSTERNE and had eight cottages in the 19th century. Developers put up semi-detached houses here following the opening of Woodmansterne station in 1932 and Carshalton council built the Clockhouse estate after World War II, with local shops at Hillcrest Parade on the Mount. Privately built detached houses and council flats and maisonettes later extended the diversity. The clock-topped farmhouse that gave the estate its name lay across the Surrey border in Banstead and was demolished in the 1970s to make way for more houses. Among the most recent additions are housing association properties next to the Methodist Church on Whitethorn Avenue. Since a boundary change in 1993 the council has operated the sport and recreation facilities at Corrigan Avenue. The only direct way to reach Sutton town centre is to walk along bridlepaths, and most young residents are educated within the borough of Croydon, but residents have overwhelmingly rejected the opportunity to secede from

Sutton. Clockhouse formerly had the lowest population of any ward in all the London boroughs but has now been amalgamated with parts of CARSHALTON. A 2004 attempt to use census data to measure happiness found that the ward of Carshalton South and Clockhouse was the second 'happiest place to live' in London.

Clockhouse's most exciting event in recent years was the discovery of a suspected unexploded bomb in Longlands Avenue in 1998. An emergency planning team primed hundreds of residents for evacuation as Royal Engineers excavated the site but they found only a rusty bucket, a paint roller, a mower's handle and a scooter with one wheel missing.

✉ Coulsdon CR5

♁ 9,747 (Carshalton South and Clockhouse ward)

Cockfosters • *Enfield/Barnet*

'A metropolitan blend of open spaces, excellent facilities and easy commuting,' according to a recent property developer's blurb, but known to most as the station with the funny name at the northern end of the Piccadilly Line. In the 16th century this was the 'cock forester's estate', 'cock' meaning head or chief. Cockfosters developed as a hamlet long before most other parts of ENFIELD CHASE. It lay on the edge of woodland, halfway along the road from SOUTHGATE to Potters Bar. A LINCOLN'S INN barrister owned a house called Cockfosters in 1613 and a small group of cottages and houses had formed by 1754. The estate of Trent Park, now a Middlesex University campus, was created when Enfield Chase was enclosed and Cockfosters found itself standing near the main gate. Consequently, its growth from the end of the 18th century (when the Cock Inn was established) was in many ways as a service village for the Trent Park estate. Christ Church and the nearby Trent Church of England School, for girls and infants, were built at the expense of Robert Cooper Lee Bevan of Trent Park in the late 1830s. Little then changed in the village for almost a hundred years except that a subscription-funded boys' school opened in 1859 and two houses, Ludgrove Hall and Heddon Court, later became boys' preparatory schools. After the Piccadilly Line arrived in 1933, Heddon Court and Westpole Farm were sold for building and new streets were laid out. A shopping parade was built near the station. By 1939 Cockfosters was fully built up south of the station and had spread west

to meet NEW BARNET. The appearance of Cockfosters has been influenced by World War II, not by bombing but because the conflict brought housebuilding to a standstill. When the process resumed afterwards it was constrained by the new green-belt regulations, so suburban expansion came to an abrupt halt north of the station. To the west, Barnet council built an estate of 419 homes and commercial builders filled most of the remaining gaps during the 1950s. More recently some balconied apartments have been squeezed in. Cockfosters has several religious minorities, notably Jews, Muslims and Hindus, and a relatively high proportion of older people.

Osbert Sitwell, the poet and short-story writer, was educated at Ludgrove School, which he loathed. John Betjeman, poet laureate from 1972 until his death in 1984, taught at Heddon Court School from April 1929 to July 1930. He later recalled this period in his poem *Cricket Master*. German DJ Michael Burkat released his techno EP *Cockfosters* in 2000.

✉ Barnet EN4

♁ 12,536 (Enfield's Cockfosters ward)

🚇 Piccadilly Line terminus (zone 5)

Coldblow • *Bexley*

A semi-rural neighbourhood linking BEXLEY with the settlement of JOYDENS WOOD via Baldwyn's Park and Tile Kiln Lane. The latter name refers to the making of clay roof tiles here from the 16th century. The kiln was owned by Lesnes Abbey prior to its dissolution in 1525, but the production of tiles continued until around 1700. In the early 1880s, Bexley's growth as a prosperous suburb prompted the construction of a dozen or so substantial houses on Dartford Road and Wansunt Road. This enclave was much rebuilt and extended in the years before and after World War II and only two of the original properties survive. Some of the 20th-century houses are well-appointed, but only one is of architectural significance: a modernist 1930s house at 7 Hill Crescent. Coldblow is shielded from the A2 to the north by Churchfield Wood, a detached portion of Joydens Wood. A small area of the wood is dominated by field maple, a characteristic indicator of ancient woodland. The wood is privately owned but a public footpath runs along its length. There are deneholes south of Dartford Road. These medieval shafts, unique to north Kent and south Essex, were probably dug to extract good quality chalk to use as fertilizer, although some have argued that they were hiding places.

Just across the present borough border, the inventor and engineer Hiram Maxim worked on the construction of biplanes in Baldwyn's Park in the late 1880s and the 1890s. In an 1894 test flight he lifted that century's largest flying machine off the ground, albeit briefly. Maxim lived at Baldwyn's, a mansion situated in what became the grounds of Bexley Hospital.

✉ Bexley DA5

Coldharbour • *Greenwich*

A post-war council estate situated between MOTTINGHAM and NEW ELTHAM, sharing an electoral ward with the latter. Coldharbour Farm was identified on a map of 1759 and had formerly been part of ELTHAM'S Great Park. The farmhouse and its outbuildings stood near the southern end of what is now Speke Hill. In London's last sale of a large working farm for housing, Woolwich council bought 155 acres from the Crown Commissioners in 1946. Building began the following year and Aneurin Bevan, the Minister for Health, opened the first house in July 1947. In all, 1,700 homes were built and ten acres of open space and trees were retained. Two public houses were provided, despite advice from the London Brewers' Council that five were needed. The estate was completed in 1957, when Queen Elizabeth the Queen Mother visited and unveiled a commemorative plaque. The estate's main thoroughfare is William Barefoot Drive, which commemorates a former mayor of Woolwich. Other street names are drawn mostly from Kentish sources. Coldharbour has been poorly served by public transport; it was not until 1972 that the first bus route traversed the estate. Most local children attend Greenacres Primary School, on Witherston Way, which has an attached language impairment unit that takes pupils from across the borough. The educational standards agency Ofsted described the school as 'swiftly improving' in 2002. By London standards, a relatively small proportion of pupils are learning English as an additional language but 40 per cent are entitled to free meals. Coldharbour Leisure Centre, on Chapel Farm Road, hosts a variety of sports and 'wellness' activities.

✉ SE9

👥 5,700 (Coldharbour and New Eltham ward)

Coldharbour • *Havering*

A remote Thames-side industrial zone situated at the end of Coldharbour Lane in south RAINHAM. The promontory here is called Coldharbour Point and lies across the river from ERITH. The name is probably a reference to the bleakness of the location; a harbour was originally a place of shelter for wayfarers, not necessarily a haven for ships. Its earliest appearance on a map was around 1560 as 'Coleherbert', which was probably a confused spelling. Later maps show Great and Little Coldharbour. The distribution company Freightmaster is based here and operates a terminal with more than 150,000 square feet of warehousing, five acres of open storage and a long riverside frontage. Neighbouring landfill facilities operated by Cleanaway were due to expire in 2002 but planning permission has been granted for an extension to the site, allowing up to 18 years of further use. There are proposals for increased recycling of waste, including a plant generating electricity from gas. Coldharbour forms part of the Havering Riverside project, which could see much of Rainham marshes transformed into a series of major commercial and residential developments. Derelict concrete barges lying offshore formed part of World War II defences.

The London Loop is a 150-mile walking route that almost entirely encircles Greater London. The loop became fully walkable in 2001, beginning at Erith and ending on the opposite bank of the river at Coldharbour Point. Plans to extend the path through a nature reserve to Purfleet should make Coldharbour more accessible to the public.

✉ Rainham RM13

@ www.wheresthepath.com (privately operated information site about the London Loop and other walks)

Cole Park • *Richmond*

A privately built housing estate in north TWICKENHAM, tucked into a loop of the River Crane (which separates it from ST MARGARETS) where it nears the end of its circuitous journey to the Thames. Thomas Cole founded a brewery on London Road early in the 17th century and his descendants provided refreshment to local people for nearly 300 years. In the mid 1890s, George Cole sold the brewery, using part of the proceeds to clear the family's debts. He planned to invest the balance in laying out an estate of 140 detached houses with all the latest conveniences, including electricity, which had just arrived in Twickenham.

Cole and his agent drafted a scale of prices that rose to £1,000, or £70 annual rent, for a property with six bedrooms. There were to be landscaped communal areas, with facilities for croquet and tennis, and fishing in the River Crane. The first house on the Cole Park estate was completed in 1898 and 20 were occupied by the turn of the century. George Cole continued to direct the project until his death in 1910, when his brother took up the reins. The family trustees, now based in Cornwall, still own some property here. By the early 1970s, all the remaining gaps in Cole Park had been plugged by further housebuilding, including the low-roofed terraces of Lancaster Place. Despite the agreeable appearance of the homes, some have pocket gardens that betray the builders' desire to wring the maximum return from undersized plots.

✉ Twickenham TW1

📖 G E Mercer, *The Cole Papers*, Twickenham Local History Society, 1985

Colham Green • *Hillingdon*

A semi-rural locality situated between HIL-LINGDON and STOCKLEY PARK, dominated by Hillingdon Hospital. The manor of Colham Garden, alias Drayton, once covered a large area to the south of UXBRIDGE and Hillingdon. The name may be a corrupted reference to its location near the River Colne or to a landowner called Cola. The manor was first mentioned in an Anglo-Saxon charter of 831, and at the time of Domesday Book it was of greater significance than Hillingdon, while Uxbridge was merely its subsidiary. The long-vanished manor house stood to the north of the green, near what is now Hillingdon and Uxbridge Cemetery. The hamlet of Colham Green was in existence by the late 16th century and a house called Moorcroft may have been a centre for illegal Roman Catholic activity. This was the home in the 1590s of Henry Garnett, superior of the Jesuits in England, who was executed in 1606 as an accomplice of the Gunpowder plotters. In the mid 1740s Hillingdon vestry chose Colham Green as the site for the parish workhouse, which later became Uxbridge union workhouse. A schoolroom, chapel, infirmary and other buildings were added afterwards. The surrounding area remained virtually uninhabited in the 19th century, when the land was occupied by farms, gravel pits and brickfields. Moorcroft farmhouse was built early in the century and survives today, on Moorcroft Lane. Evelyns School was established at Colham Green in 1872 and

maintained close connections with Eton until it was closed in 1931. Much of Colham Green was built up with private estates before World War II and with the Violet Farm and Evelyns council estates afterwards. In 1930 control of the workhouse passed to Middlesex County Council which began to develop it as Hillingdon Hospital. The hospital was largely rebuilt in 1963 and is presently undergoing radical redevelopment, with an entirely new set of buildings under construction. A long-running but ultimately successful strike of domestic staff at the hospital became a socialist cause célèbre in the late 1990s. Older hospital facilities on the north side of Pield Heath Road have been replaced with housing, under the names Chantry Park and Kings Place. The surviving part of Colham Green is now a recreation ground. At Colham Manor Infants' School, slightly less than one-fifth of pupils come from minority ethnic backgrounds, and almost a third are eligible for free school meals.

✉ Uxbridge UB8

@ www.thh.nhs.uk (Hillingdon Hospital)

Colindale • *Barnet*

A commercial zone strung out along the A5 south of EDGWARE, with a hinterland of nationally important institutions. The name probably derives from 16th-century residents, the Colinn family. The settlement took root at the end of the 19th century, near the older but now-lost hamlet of Colindeep. Colindale has had a long association with aeronautics. In the years leading up to 1914, aircraft manufacturing and pilot training dominated the locality, and this expanded greatly after the outbreak of World War I, with associated industries attracted by government intervention. After the establishment of the Royal Air Force in 1918 it flew from HENDON aerodrome, which the government acquired in 1925. During World War II, the aerodrome became a transport, communications and training base, but its unsuitability for post-war jet aircraft meant that the last flying units left in 1957, although RAF Hendon officially closed only in 1988. The RAF Museum opened on the base in 1972, in two of the aerodrome's original hangers, which have been supplemented since by other exhibition halls. The GRAHAME PARK estate was built on the rest of the site from the late 1960s. On Aerodrome Road, to the south, the Peel Centre is the home of the Metropolitan Police Training Establishment. The Oriental City shopping and dining centre on

Edgware Road has two floors of specialist restaurants and import retailers, but faces an uncertain future. The British Library Newspaper Library, on Colindale Avenue, collects journals from all over the world and stores copies of all newspapers published in the UK. On the same road is the Health Protection Agency's Centre for Infections, formerly the Central Public Health Laboratory, the national base for infectious disease surveillance and specialist microbiology and epidemiology. The residential population of Colindale is relatively deprived, by the standards of a prosperous borough, with significant and diverse ethnic and religious minorities. More than a quarter of homes are rented from the council and a further 10 per cent from social landlords. With its social difficulties and recent closures of local employers, Colindale is at present the focus of a regeneration project which will include the construction of new rail bridges across Aerodrome Road to remove a traffic bottleneck and allow access to buses. Meanwhile, thousands of new homes are being built at Beaufort Park, a 25-acre section of the former aerodrome site.

Prompted by his acquaintance with the station as an airman at Hendon, T E Lawrence ('Lawrence of Arabia') adopted the pseudonym 'Colin Dale' when writing reviews for *The Spectator*, and a London-based techno DJ uses the same name today.

✉ NW9

👤 13,860

🚇 Northern Line (zone 4)

@ www.rafmuseum.com;
www.beaufortpark.co.uk

College Park • Hammersmith & Fulham

A late Victorian urban village in the far north of the borough, tucked between the railway line and the western end of HARROW ROAD. Some definitions of College Park's extent also take in the industrial estates west of Scrubs Lane. There was never a college here; the name derives from All Souls College, Oxford, which used to own the land. Its development during the last quarter of the 19th century was stimulated by activity on both sides. To the east, Kensal Green had been built up following the establishment of its cemetery. To the west, WILLESDEN JUNCTION station had opened in 1866. College Park has a high population turnover and a wide variety of ethnic minorities. It also has characteristics that make it ripe for gentrification, so it now presents contrasting aspects: some bay-fronted properties have recently been renovated while others remain run-down; there are smart new live/work units on Waldo Road and tatty shops along Harrow Road. The relatively unspoilt College Park Hotel is a local landmark, though there have been proposals to convert it into flats. The council's creation of a College Park 'home zone' is intended to make the roads safer by giving pedestrians priority over vehicles. Children from Kenmont Primary School played a part in the initiative's formulation. College Park Community Centre, on Letchford Gardens, hosts adult education courses, a youth project and meetings of the College Park residents' association.

✉ NW10

👤 7,643 (College Park and Old Oak ward)

Collier Row • Havering

The northernmost extent of Romford's miniconurbation, with green-belt parks and farmland on most sides. Some locals regard Collier Row as encompassing the whole of NORTH ROMFORD. Colliers were active here in the 15th and 16th centuries. These were charcoal burners, not miners, making their living from the forest that covered most of the manor of Gobions, also known as Uphavering. A manor house called Great Gobions lay on the south side of Collier Row Common, while another house called Gobions stood on the common's east side. The hamlet of Collier Row had 56 houses in 1670 and five inns were recorded a century later. The common land was enclosed in 1814 and a new road replaced an old track leading to NOAK HILL. During the agrarian boom of the mid 19th century, many farmhouses were built or rebuilt and the opening of ROMFORD station attracted some wealthy Londoners. A mission church was built for the village in the 1880s. Until the opening of Eastern Avenue (A12) in 1925, Collier Row remained a rural village, surrounded by fields of clover and hay. The improved access to London, combined with the outward growth of Romford, was the impetus for a major programme of speculative construction that lasted until after the outbreak of World War II. A shopping centre was provided at the top of Collier Row Road, with a cinema that did not survive the advent of television. In response to the area's explosive growth, two more Anglican churches were built before and after World War II and Corpus Christi RC Church opened in 1965. Very few residents of Collier Row come from ethnic minorities and the educational standards agency Ofsted has commented of one local school that its pupils 'are not well enough prepared for life in contemporary multicultural British society'.

✉ Romford RM5

📖 Brian Evans, *Romford, Collier Row and Gidea Park*, Phillimore, 1994

Colliers Wood • *Merton*

A former industrial village hemmed in by MERTON and TOOTING GRAVENEY. The name was first recorded in 1632 and refers to charcoal-burning, not mining. From 1755 a tollgate stood on the Merton Road (now High Street Colliers Wood) on the site of the present station, which gave rise to the alternative village name of Singlegate. Colliers Wood House, which had been home to Elizabethan and later notables, was rebuilt around 1780. By the early 19th century, mills beside the River Wandle were switching from grinding corn to printing textiles, an industry that soon employed the bulk of the local labour force. In 1851 only five per cent of the population worked in agriculture, a remarkably low proportion for such an out-of-the-way place. In the 1870s the 40-acre grounds of Colliers Wood House began to succumb to speculative building, at first in the direction of Tooting, then towards Merton. The tollgate was taken down and the first shops, a school and Christ Church were built. Colliers Wood House was demolished in 1904; its site is now occupied by the lower numbers of Clive Road and Warren Road. A tram service began in 1907 and streets of terraced houses were laid out on land belong to Emmanuel College, Cambridge. Builders squeezed in a last few pebble-dashed and mock-Tudor properties after the London Underground system was extended here in 1926. Later additions have included council flats, a 19-storey office block and a Savacentre, once said to be the largest hypermarket in Europe. Colliers Wood has seen a flurry of house-building in recent years owing to the spin-off effect of Tooting's growing popularity on neighbouring (and more affordable) localities. The ward has an ethnically diverse population, of whom two-thirds are white, without a bias towards any specific minority. A relatively high proportion of residents are in their twenties and living in privately rented accommodation.

✉ SW19

👥 9,293

🚇 Northern Line (zone 3)

Colney Hatch • *Barnet* (pronounced 'coney')

A recently transformed residential locality situated south of FRIERN BARNET, formerly famous for its enormous mental hospital. Colney Hatch was a hamlet in 1409 and the hatch may have been a gate providing access to Hollick Wood. In 1831, Colney Hatch had 33 inhabited houses but the hamlet was soon to be overwhelmed when it was chosen as the site for the new Middlesex County Lunatic Asylum. Built in 1851 in the style of an Italian monastery, Colney Hatch asylum had its own gasworks, shoemakers, brewery, bakery and farm and became the best-known institution of its kind in the London area – so much so that throughout Middlesex and beyond its name became synonymous with mental illness. It was the largest mental hospital in Europe and at one time housed 3,000 patients. The planned construction of the neighbouring Great Northern Railway line was one reason for the choice of the site and Colney Hatch station was opened specifically to serve the asylum. The old village expanded as a provider of goods and services for the asylum's staff but the larger settlement that grew up to the east was named NEW SOUTHGATE out of a desire to avoid the negative connotations of Colney Hatch. The station's name was later changed for the same reason and the asylum itself was renamed Friern Hospital in 1937. It closed in 1993 and a flock of developers descended on the site, now renamed Princess Park Manor. The main building has been converted into hundreds of luxury flats and many more big detached houses have been built in the grounds. The Colney Hatch name is still little used to define the neighbourhood and estate agents and some residents have been pushing the designation 'Friern Village' instead. Admittedly, this invention helps distinguish the development from the rather tired-looking terraced houses and shops of the adjacent thoroughfares.

'Colney Hatch' was cockney rhyming slang for a match.

✉ N11

@ www.princessparkmanor.net (property developer's site)

Columbia Road • *Tower Hamlets*

A horticultural market area in BETHNAL GREEN. There has been a market in Columbia Road almost since Bethnal Green came into existence and in 1869 the philanthropist Baroness Burdett-Coutts initiated the construction of a grand edifice, not unlike ST PANCRAS station in appearance, to house the purveyors of affordable fresh food to the people of the EAST END. It was intended that the market should have its own railway line and station but these never materialized and the market was not a success. The traders returned to their less-regulated street pitches, which the local residents preferred. The building was subsequently put to a variety of uses, including as cabinet-making workshops for Jewish immigrants. The magnificent Gothic fantasy was demolished in 1958 to make way for some of the most bland blocks of flats in the East End. The presence of a large Jewish community enabled the market to obtain a Sunday licence, as was the case for PETTICOAT LANE, and as Sunday trading became established the weekday market died out. From as early as 1927 various influences pushed Columbia Road towards a specialization in flowers and plants. The market now operates from 8am to 2pm every Sunday, with more than 50 stalls and almost as many shops and cafés. Ferociously busy in spring but crowded all year round, this is one of London's most distinctive street markets and its success has spawned a rash of 'homestyle' boutiques in neighbouring streets. The tight parking restrictions are rigorously enforced on Sunday, so visitors need plenty of change for parking fees, and to be prepared to cruise around for some time to find a parking spot. The local population is mainly Bangladeshi, with smaller numbers of black African, black Caribbean and Pakistani descent.

✉ E2

📖 Linda Wilkinson, *Watercress But No Sandwiches: 300 Years of the Columbia Road Area*, Jhera, 2001 (winner of the Raymond Williams Award for Community Publishing)

@ www.eastlondonmarkets.com

Commercial Road • *Tower Hamlets*
An EAST END thoroughfare connecting WHITECHAPEL with LIMEHOUSE and comprising the westernmost section of the A13. It is often thought of as a locality in its own right, neither a part of STEPNEY to the north nor WAPPING to the south. During the 19th century this important road had the distinction of bearing the heaviest volume of traffic of any thoroughfare in the world. It was made in 1803 to provide a direct link between the City and the new docks at Blackwall. Then came the East

India Dock Road and, a few years later, the Barking Road. The completion of an iron bridge over the River Lea also turned Commercial Road into the main highway between London and Tilbury. In 1870 the road was extended westward to its present endpoint at ALDGATE EAST. The junction formed by the extension later became known as Gardiner's Corner, after the Gardiner and Co. clothing store that stood there for a century from the 1870s. The transformation of the road into a densely populated neighbourhood began with the establishment of sugar refineries in ST GEORGE IN THE EAST, which led to the erection of small houses for local workers, many of whom were of German origin. Towards Stepney, speculative builders attempted to create a more exclusive residential district, with some early success. But the area went into a decline later in the century from which it is only now beginning to recover.

✉ E1; E14

📖 Ray Newton, Steve Kentfield and Tom Newton, *South of Commercial Road*, History of Wapping Trust, 2002

Coney Hall • *Bromley*
One of the constituent parts of WEST WICKHAM, with its own small shopping parade. Some authorities have placed the Roman settlement of Noviomagus near the present Layhams Road, although most prefer CRAYFORD. Coney Hall was first mentioned in the 17th century, when the farm's lease stated that the tenant had the sole right to catch coneys (rabbits) on nearby Jackson's Heath. The house was sufficiently grand to have its own rectory and assembly rooms. Following the death of lord of the manor Sir Henry Lennard in 1928, much of his Wickham Court estate was sold to Morrell's, which was also building on the western side of PETTS WOOD. Construction work on the estate's 1,000 homes began in 1933 and the shops of Kingsway Parade were built on the south side of Croydon Road. Many of the houses were in a standard style, with polygonal bay windows and half-timbered gables, and were priced more affordably than elsewhere in West Wickham, although this distinction has since diminished. As a result of Sir Henry's former opposition to the construction of roads across his land, the estate was initially difficult to reach and London Transport refused to provide a bus service on the hilly and narrow lanes. Morrell's responded by laying on a free coach connection with the nearest station at HAYES but the service

was withdrawn when the estate was completed. In 1937 Elsy and Jim Borders, the owners of 81 Kingsway, withheld their mortgage payments in protest at the alleged jerry-built condition of their new home. Hundreds more mortgage payers struck in sympathy around the country and the ensuing court case influenced the framing of the Building Societies Act in 1939, which strengthened the rights of mortgagors. During World War II, Canadian soldiers of the 3rd Field Regiment were billeted at Coney Hall. From 1956, Glebe Way linked Coney Hall with West Wickham's High Street, at last overcoming the problems of access. A Greenwich meridian stone in Coney Hall recreation ground marks the point of 0 longitude.

✉ West Wickham BR4

👥 14,923 (Hayes and Coney Hall ward)

📖 Joyce Moore, *Blow the Candle Out Honey*, self-published, c.1995 (wartime reminiscences of Coney Hall)

Coombe • *Croydon*
A broad swathe of south-east CROYDON without a place name on most maps, and it would be appropriate to revive the identity of the former hamlet of Coombe were it not for possible confusion with the one in Kingston. The name derives from Old English 'cumb', which is analogous to the Welsh 'cwm', a valley. The area was known in the 15th century as the 'borough of Coombe' and in Elizabethan times as Broad Coombe. The settlement consisted mainly of small cottages neighbouring the expansive Coombe estate, until grander properties began to appear early in the 19th century, several of which incorporated the Coombe name. Coombe Lane station opened on the WOODSIDE and SOUTH CROYDON Railway in 1885. Rebuilt and renamed Coombe Road in 1935, it closed in 1983. The Croydon Tramlink now approaches here via the old trackbed north of Coombe Road, and then swerves east to Lloyd Park. Recently built bungalows in Larcombe Close occupy the site of the former station. To the south-east, Coombe Wood was originally created as a site for conduits that supplied water to the Coombe estate. Open to the public since 1948, the wood has beech and pine woodland, ornamental gardens and a café.

✉ Croydon CR0; South Croydon CR2

Coombe • *Kingston*
A verdant residential locality situated north of

NEW MALDEN, with golf courses in most directions and RICHMOND PARK and WIMBLEDON COMMON just beyond. There is evidence of a Bronze Age camp at Coombe Warren. The Romans also settled here and Coombe is mentioned in Domesday Book. Coombe provided a well for HAMPTON COURT in the 16th century; the connecting pipeline still exists and the conduit room on Coombe Lane West is open from time to time. In the mid 19th century Coombe became popular with fashionable London society as a semi-rural retreat, and numerous substantial houses were built. John Galsworthy's father was responsible for developing much of Coombe Hill and the novelist turned to his birthplace as a setting for his Forsyte novels. Cedar Court, on Coombe Hill Road, was built originally in 1485 on the banks of the River Colne at Colchester, Essex. It was transplanted here in 1912 when William Thornton-Smith, a wealthy antiquarian, fulfilled his dream of placing a genuine Tudor property on a recently acquired plot next to Coombe Hill golf course. Unexpectedly, Coombe has one of London's most remarkable 20th-century houses: E Maxwell Fry's international modernist flourish, Miramonte, in Warren Rise. Built in 1937 and deservedly Grade II-listed, it is an L-shaped composition of glass and whitewashed concrete in horizontal bands, with a sun terrace on the flat roof. A cuboid outbuilding provides a garage with a flat above for the chauffeur. The house has recently been restored and extended, despite conservationists' objections to the alteration of the original plan. Woodlands Avenue has a group of Sunspan houses by the Canadian architect Wells Coates. Coombe has lately been one of the fastest growing parts of the borough, with developers willing to pay highly for any plot of land with planning permission. Galsworthy's Coombe Leigh has been demolished and its grounds are occupied by more recently built large houses. Another Galsworthy building, Coombe Ridge, is now a preparatory school.
The Australian soprano Dame Nellie Melba lived for a while at Coombe House, on Beverley Lane.

✉ Kingston upon Thames, KT2; New Malden KT3

👥 19,589 (Coombe Hill and Coombe Vale wards)

📖 Sue Lown et al, *A Fair and High Locality: Chronicle of Coombe Ridge House and 'The Manor of Coombe'*, PWP Press, 1996

Copenhagen • *Islington*

A designation sometimes applied (but no longer formally) to the area encompassing Islington's BARNSBURY and THORNHILL wards, which lie north and east of KING'S CROSS. Its name originates from Copenhagen House, the 17th-century residence of the Danish ambassador to Britain. In the late 18th century, Copenhagen Fields became a popular venue for radical demonstrations. In 1795, two such protests were attended by crowds of over 100,000, and one was followed by rioting in central London. Copenhagen House was demolished in 1852, when the market for live animals transferred here from SMITHFIELD. The relocation was not a success and this market was replaced for the first half of the 20th century by the Caledonian market, at which second-hand goods were sold. Much of the site is now occupied by council-built housing, and Barnard Park on Copenhagen Street and Caledonian Park on Market Road are the area's only remaining open spaces. Because of its high level of deprivation, the Copenhagen neighbourhood was Islington's chosen setting for its Sure Start initiative in 2001, tackling child poverty and social exclusion. At Copenhagen Primary School, two-thirds of the pupils speak English as an additional language and an even higher proportion is entitled to free school meals.

'Copenhagen Fields' is the name of a magnificent layout, at a scale of 2 mm to the foot, by the Model Railway Club. The model is set in the 1920–30 period, showing the area near the club's headquarters in Calshot Street, and includes Copenhagen Fields and the approaches to King's Cross, as well as the cattle market and CALEDONIAN ROAD and its station, with working London Underground line.

For the classic Ealing Studios film *The Lady-killers*, Mrs Wilberforce's house was specially built at what was then the end of Frederica Street, overlooking Copenhagen railway junction, at the southern end of Copenhagen Tunnel.

✉ N1

@ www.themodelrailwayclub.org

Copers Cope • *Bromley*

An electoral ward and former farm in north-west BECKENHAM. The name may be a corruption of 'cooper's copse'. Copers Cope House began life as a farmhouse, probably in the early 18th century. The house still stands on Southend Road (A2015) and is the most significant building of its age in Beckenham, but its appearance was altered when it was enlarged in the 19th century. Copers Cope Farm covered 250 acres and was acquired by Beckenham's leading landowners, the Cator family, in 1783. The Cators first sought to build houses on the land in 1813 but it was not until the 1860s that Copers Cope Farm began to be developed as NEW BECKENHAM. Lawn Road, Park Road and Brackley Road were all named after former fields. In 2005, Beckenham MP Jacqui Lait raised the issue of local overdevelopment in a parliamentary debate, 'with regard to more and more single family homes being torn down and replaced with apartment buildings', and specifically mentioned the Copers Cope area. As a result of the continuing conversions and replacements, the Copers Cope ward has a high proportion of single-person households and relatively few homes with dependent children. Like most of the borough, nine-tenths of residents are white.

✉ Beckenham BR3

♦ 14,229

Coppermills • *Waltham Forest*

A watery quarter lying beside WALTHAMSTOW Marshes on the southern banks of the River Lea reservoirs. A mill has existed here for many centuries. The present Coppermill building was erected two centuries ago and copper coins were minted here during the Napoleonic Wars. It was converted to a pumping station by the East London Waterworks Co. in the 1860s, when the tower was added. Nowadays, most of Coppermills is occupied by Thames Water's filter-beds and pumping stations, which replaced the LEA BRIDGE waterworks in 1972. Water from the New River arrives here after its journey south through Hertfordshire and Coppermills is a major supplier to the Thames Water Ring Main. The neighbouring residential area lies on the western edge of Walthamstow. At Coppermill Primary School on Edward Road nearly 60 per cent of the children come from minority ethnic backgrounds, mainly black Caribbean and Pakistani. Over a third of pupils have English as an additional language.

✉ E17

Copse Hill • *Merton*

A conservation area located south of WIMBLEDON COMMON. The hill itself lies towards the eastern end of the lane called Copse Hill. The first and grandest mansion to appear on Copse Hill was Prospect Place, built in the mid 18th century by a London goldsmith, with grounds that were later improved by

Humphry Repton. The estate was sold to developers in stages from 1851 and a handful of villas was erected on what was named the COTTENHAM PARK estate. Among these was The Firs, which was commissioned by two barristers, the Christian socialists Thomas Hughes and John Ludlow. Hughes wrote *Tom Brown's Schooldays* in the house in 1856. Christ Church was built at the expense of the hill's wealthy residents in 1860 and later enlarged. Prospect Place was pulled down in the 1860s to make way for the Atkinson Morley convalescent home, subsequently a hospital, which was funded by the bequest of a wealthy hotelier who had trained as a doctor. Terraced cottages with small front gardens lined Thurstan Road later in the 19th century. Copse Hill was widened in 1925 and much of its present housing dates from around this time. The Wolfson neurosurgery unit opened within the hospital during World War II. The Firs was demolished in 1957 and replaced by nurses' accommodation that retained the same name. In 2003 the facilities of the Atkinson Morley Hospital relocated to St George's Hospital in Tooting, but the Wolfson Rehabilitation Centre survives. Most of the 20-acre site is now earmarked for housing development and The Firs buildings are likely to be demolished, but much of the grounds will survive as metropolitan open space. Barham Road gives access to Fishpond Wood and Beverley Meads nature reserve, which has coppiced hazel and oak woodland, a pond system and acid grassland with a wide variety of species. Wimbledon Rugby Football Club plays at Beverley Meads.

✉ SW20

@ www.amhlung.org.uk (site of action group opposed to development of hospital site); www.wimbledonrfc.co.uk

Corbets Tey • *Havering*

A commuter village located south of UPMINSTER, to which it is now connected by suburban development. Since 'Corbinstye' was first recorded in 1461 there is certainly no truth in the story that Elizabeth I said to her servant 'Corbet, stay and ask the name of this place', and when told that it had no name decreed that it be called after her first words. Somewhat more likely is that Corbin was the landowner and Tey comes from the Old English 'tye' or enclosure. The medieval manor of Gaynes occupied most of the southern Upminster area and some of its land has been under cultivation for over 2,000 years. The

rubble-walled tower of the parish church of St Laurence dates from the early 13th century. There was a tannery at Corbets Tey from 1573 to 1635 and gravel extraction took place in the vicinity from the 18th century. The most notable survival at the centre of the old village is High House, a tall farmhouse built around 1700 and still possessing a virtually complete original interior. During the 1770s Sir James Esdaile commissioned a very grand manor house at Gaynes, with a 100-acre park created from the surrounding farmland. But within about 50 years most of the mansion had to be demolished to make the property affordable to a new buyer. Esdaile also built Harwood Hall in 1782, and its distinctive castellations were added a century later. It is now a Montessori school. The remaining east wing of the manor house at Gaynes stood until 1929, when it was pulled down to make way for what Pevsner calls 'singularly unexciting straight streets of dull houses', but a small part of the grounds survives as parkland. Corbets Tey has some early weatherboarded and half-timbered cottages but these have been overwhelmed by the contemporary development that has surrounded them.

The Corbets Tey gravel formation is a sedimentary layer that may have represented the north bank of the lower Thames during an interglacial phase of the Pleistocene epoch.

✉ Upminster RM14

📖 Edward George Ballard, *Our Old Romford and District: Including Hornchurch, Upminster, Cranham, Corbets Tey, North Ockendon*, Swan Libraries, 1981

Cottenham Park • *Merton*

A 'high-class' neighbourhood, as its creators called it, situated north of RAYNES PARK in WEST WIMBLEDON. When developers bought part of the Prospect Place estate in 1851 (see COPSE HILL), they named it Cottenham Park after former owner Charles Pepys, the Earl of Cottenham, who had recently completed his second term as Lord Chancellor. New roads were laid out and given aristocratic names that had associations with the estate. But only a few large houses were constructed, with their frontages at least 30 feet from the road. It was not until the interwar period that most of the area was built up, and the orchards and piggeries of Cottenham Park Farm survived until around this time. St Matthew's Church was completed in 1927, although services had been conducted in the east part of the structure from 1909. The church was destroyed by a flying bomb in 1944 and rebuilt in 1958. Some public spaces remain in Cottenham Park, in the form of allotments, a recreation ground and Holland Gardens, which were opened in 1929 in memory of Sir Arthur Holland, a former local resident and Wimbledon benefactor. Cottenham House is a Grade II-listed building with a steeply pitched slate roof and extensive landscaped grounds, parts of which are attributed to Humphry Repton.

✉ SW20

Coulsdon • *Croydon* (pronounced 'coolsdən', although some locals prefer 'coalsdən')

A comfortable 20th-century suburb located south-west of PURLEY. In the 19th century the village of Coulsdon consisted of a small group of houses clustered around the village green of what is now OLD COULSDON. Primarily because of the growth in popularity of Brighton, the country track that passed through SMITHAM Bottom was upgraded to a turnpike road in 1808 and by the 1820s 40 coaches were passing through every day. The coaching trade declined when the first railway line was built through the district in 1841 but no trains stopped here until 1889, when Coulsdon South station opened, originally as Coulsdon and Cane Hill. Most of the station's early users were visiting or working at the New Surrey Lunatic Asylum at Cane Hill. In around 1900, suburban roads were laid out south of the station, although the Corporation of London's acquisition of Farthing Downs prevented development from extending too widely in this area. The downs contain a Saxon cemetery and a Romano-British field system. Village residents continued to refer to the newly developing area as Smitham Bottom until the opening of Coulsdon post office here and the creation of the parish of St Andrew's, Coulsdon, in 1906. The parish did not gain a permanent church until 1915. By this time, stations had also opened at Smitham and further north at REEDHAM and 'new' Coulsdon began to grow in earnest after World War I. The urban district council of PURLEY and Coulsdon laid out Stoats Nest Village for ex-servicemen in 1919 and private development spread north-west of the Brighton Road (A23) to the edge of UPPER WOODCOTE, while the Dutch village was built in the far south. By the outbreak of World War II, extensive shopping facilities lined the Brighton Road, together with two cinemas, a library and the council's offices. By the 1960s continuous rows of housing stretched all the way from Croydon to Coulsdon South station, although the green belt afforded protection away from the main road. Later in the century, the road became a ribbon of offices, supermarkets and takeaways, notorious for its heavy traffic. However, the recently completed Coulsdon inner relief road aims to help 'make Coulsdon town centre a focal point of the local community once more'. Among the companies based in Coulsdon, the best known is Jane's Information Group, publishers of world famous titles about the defence industry. The South London Harriers athletics club and the Coulsdon Chess Fellowship are each among the most significant in London in their respective fields. Cane Hill Mental Hospital closed in 1991, although a medium-secure unit operated on the site until 2006, when the government agency English Partnerships began to review development options that included the creation of a business park here. According to the last census, typical Coulsdon residents are white, middle-aged, married, living in their own home and unlikely to be university educated.

✉ Coulsdon CR5

👤 25,445 (Coulsdon East and Coulsdon West wards)

🚆 Southern (Coulsdon South, zone 6)

@ www.southlondonharriers.org; www.ccfworld.com/Chess

Covent Garden • *Westminster/Camden*

A booming commercial zone situated east of SOHO and south of BLOOMSBURY. It is generally asserted that the name is a corruption of 'convent garden' but it is quite possible that 'covent garden' was the original version (since 'convent' derives from the Anglo-Norman 'covent') and that the name has always been rendered this way, at least in spoken form. The Romans did no more than pass through here but Saxons lived in the area after they established the settlement of Lundenwic, which flourished from AD 600. After 900, Viking attacks prompted the Saxons to move back within the walls of the CITY OF LONDON and there was little habitation here until the foundation early in the 13th century of the Benedictine convent of St Peter, WESTMINSTER. Following the dissolution of the monasteries, the Bedford family acquired the land, which remained in agricultural use until the fourth Earl of Bedford obtained a licence from the Crown in 1630 to lay out an estate here. This represented quite a coup, since requests for such licences were generally being refused at this time. Inigo Jones laid out a disciplined grid of streets around St Paul's Church and a central piazza. At first the highest class of citizens made their homes in Covent Garden but the area's universal popularity proved its undoing. Coffee houses, taverns, theatres and traders of all kinds attracted throngs of Londoners and the aristocrats beat a retreat, leaving ever more dubious characters in their wake. But even the vice trade was no match for the trade in flowers, fruit and vegetables that dominated Covent Garden from the 18th century. The market buildings of the present-day piazza were erected in 1830 and roofed over in 1870. Neighbouring slums were progressively cleared and replaced by 'model' housing for the working classes. To escape the traffic congestion of post-war London, the wholesale market relocated to NINE ELMS in 1973. The Greater London Council planned to demolish the market buildings but an exemplary community campaign brought a change of heart that resulted in their refurbishment in 1980 as a retail shopping complex. The redevelopment succeeded beyond the wildest dreams of its proponents and Covent Garden is now one of London's busiest destinations for shopping trips, dining out and general entertainment. The residential population has recovered as run-down old homes have been modernized, although the area retains a broad social mix, with many people still renting from the council or housing associations. Small businesses have been drawn in, especially those operating in new media sectors. The Royal Opera House re-opened in 1999 after a three-year reconstruction and refurbishment project that cost £178 million. It is the third theatre on the site, with operas and ballets having been performed here for more than 150 years.

The poet Andrew Marvell lived on Maiden Lane, where the artist J M W Turner was born above his father's barber's shop in 1775. Jane Austen stayed with her brother on Henrietta Street. James Boswell wrote *The Life of Johnson* while living on Great Queen Street, which was also home to the dramatist Richard Brinsley Sheridan and the poet William Blake. Among the many films that have used Covent Garden as a backdrop, the best known is 1964's *My Fair Lady*.

📧 WC2

🚶 10,645 (Camden's Holborn and Covent Garden ward)

🚆 Piccadilly Line (zone 1)

📖 John Richardson, *Covent Garden Past*, Historical Publications, 1995; Mary Cathcart Borer, *The Story of Covent Garden*, Robert Hale, 1984

@ www.coventgarden.uk.com (commercial local information site and online magazine); www.coventgarden.org.uk (Covent Garden Community Association site); www.coventgardenlife.com (commercial local information site; good for visitors); www.royalopera.org (Royal Opera House)

Cowley • *Hillingdon*

A ribbon development along the road from UXBRIDGE to YIEWSLEY, parallel with the Grand Union Canal to its west. It was first recorded in the tenth century as Cofenlea, 'the woodland clearing of a man called Cofa'. The twelfth-century St Laurence's Church was the smallest parish church in Middlesex and remains unenlarged today. Its parish covered a very irregular 300 acres, 'mixed up with HILLINGDON in such a way as defies description'. For this reason, the medieval history of Cowley is so closely bound up with that of Hillingdon as to have made the two indistinguishable at times. Houses and cottages lined the High Street in the 17th and early 18th centuries, including Vine Cottage, the Crown inn, Maygood's Farm, Poplar Cottage and Cowley House. A surprising number of these early properties have survived to the present day, although often much altered. In the 18th century the northern part of Cowley consisted almost entirely of over 300 acres of open space called Cowley Field. The ownership of the field was split between the manors of Cowley, Cowley Hall and Colham (see COLHAM GREEN). Cowley Field was enclosed in 1795, when the Grand Junction (later Grand Union) Canal was being built on its western side. The arrival of the railway at WEST DRAYTON in 1838 brought limited growth to the village, not in the form of suburban housing but by stimulating the development of the horticultural industry, which could rapidly deliver fresh flowers to COVENT GARDEN and SPITALFIELDS. Cottages were built for labourers who worked in the greenhouses and also at the extensive brickfields nearby. It was not until the 1890s that developers began to build estates of affordable housing, especially after the opening of a branch line and station in 1904, and the village merged with the hitherto separate settlement at COWLEY PEACHEY. The private builders were joined in their endeavours by the council after World War I. Despite these projects, many acres stretching towards PIELD HEATH remained under cultivation until after World War II. In the 20 years from 1945 the council built hundreds more homes at Cowley, many occupied by workers at the factories of Cowley Bridge, where a business park still operates. Cowley station closed in 1962, as did the line. Much of the High Street was rebuilt later in the 20th century, including with unprepossessing office blocks.

'One of the true British poets of the last half-century lived in Cowley,' says Iain Sinclair of Bill Griffiths, who has since exiled himself to north-east England.

✉ Uxbridge UB8

📖 C Cotton, *Uxbridge, Hillingdon and Cowley,* Sutton, 1995

Cowley Peachey · *Hillingdon*

The southern side of COWLEY – part commercial, part council-built – and the site of a junction on the Grand Union Canal. Westminster Abbey owned an estate here at the time of Domesday Book and this was granted to Bartholomew Peachey in 1252. When a settlement grew up in the later Middle Ages it took the name of the manor. Two timber-framed houses survive, perhaps from the 16th century. The Grand Junction Canal (as it was first called) came through Cowley Peachey in the mid 1790s. A packet boat service ran to PADDINGTON for a while, giving its name to an inn and the lane that crossed the canal. The Slough branch of the canal was one of the last to be built in Britain. Opened in 1883, it provides five miles of lock-free waterway along an almost straight line into the centre of Slough. In the early years of the 20th century Cowley Peachey was used as a dumping ground for silt dredgings taken from the canal, while a few factories appeared along the bank. By 1910 ribbon development connected the village with UXBRIDGE, via Cowley. Uxbridge borough council built an estate of grey terraced houses here in the mid 1950s. During the 1970s, soil, sand and gravel extraction eroded the land beside the canal, which rapidly became an eyesore as opportunists exploited it for fly-tipping. Cowley Peachey was formally designated a contaminated site in the 1980s. British Waterways has now cleaned it up and created a 120-berth marina with associated amenities for boat users, a visitors' centre and an urban park. The £3.5 million project was completed in 2002. The site incorporates the pre-existing Turning Point pub and restaurant.

✉ Uxbridge UB8

Cranbrook · *Redbridge*

A late Victorian and Edwardian estate in north ILFORD, also known as Cranbrook Park. The Cran Brook itself feeds the pond and lake in VALENTINES PARK. The first official mention of the manor of Cranbrook was in BARKING Abbey's records of 1347. At the northern end of the district a tannery operated from the mid 15th century until 1840. From the end of the 19th century, local MP Peter Griggs developed two estates of 'substantially built housing' called Central Park and Cranbrook Park. To the west, land on the edge of the WANSTEAD PARK estate was also sold for building. The 500-year history of Cranbrook Hall, which included holding prisoners from the Spanish Armada, ended with its demolition in 1900 to make way for the new housing. Cranbrook Castle, a folly erected in 1765 on what became the Port of London Authority's sports ground, survived until 1923. It had been intended as a mausoleum but was never used for the purpose. Shops were added on Cranbrook Road between 1924 and 1930. Like much of Ilford, the Cranbrook ward has a large Asian population, including Muslims, Hindus and Sikhs. There is also a significant Jewish minority. At the well-regarded Highlands Primary School, 84 per cent of the pupils have English as an additional language and 34 different languages are spoken. The school is accepting an increasing number of refugees and children from temporary accommodation. Cranbrook College, on Mansfield Road, is an independent school.

In 1995, PC Phillip Walters was shot and fatally wounded after being called to a disturbance at a house in Empress Avenue, where a police memorial has since been erected. PC Walters' convicted killer subsequently claimed £70 compensation from the Metropolitan Police for a gold tooth cap lost during the struggle between the two men, sparking death threats to his solicitors.

✉ Ilford IG1

👥 11,858

Cranford · *Hounslow/Hillingdon*

A HEATHROW satellite community, lying between HOUNSLOW and HAYES. Its name derives from the birds that once frequented the ford. An early Saxon settlement on the heathland, the manor of Cranforde is mentioned in Domesday Book and was later described as the prettiest village in Middlesex. By 1274 there was a bridge carrying the Bath Road over the River Crane, but the village remained a quiet backwater until the early 20th century, even experiencing a slight decline in the late 19th century as the railway took away coaching traffic. Cranford Park, once the grounds of Cranford House, lies beside the River Crane, immediately south of the M4. Cranford House was the home of the Countess of Berkeley, who so feared accusations of perjury regarding the claimed date of her marriage that she had constructed an escape tunnel that still runs under the park. The stable block is the most complete part of the remaining buildings of the house. Also in the park, St Dunstan's Church has a 15th-century tower and an 18th-century nave. In the churchyard is a memorial dedicated to the great post-war comedian Tony Hancock. Across the motorway, in a small extension of the park, are the remains of a moat marking the site of the manor house of Cranford-le-Mote, which was demolished in 1780. The High Street still has some 17th- and 18th-century buildings and the Round House, in which criminals were locked up overnight. Half of Cranford's residents are of Asian origin and the dominant faiths are Sikhism, Islam and Hinduism. There is also a small Somali community. Heathrow Airport has brought significant commercial development to the area.

Residential building in Cranford has spread west of the River Crane into the borough of Hillingdon. Its planners call the new locality Cranford Cross.

> ✉ Hounslow TW4 and TW5; Hayes UB3
>
> ♦ 10,936

Cranham · *Havering*

A suburbanized village occupying much of the territory between UPMINSTER and the M25. When it was first recorded in Domesday Book, Cranham manor may already have been in existence for several centuries. The early spelling 'Crawenho' indicates that this was 'a spur of land frequented by crows'. The parish was originally known as Bishop's Ockendon (or its Latin equivalent) but later took the name of its largest constituent manor. Cranham Hall was first mentioned in 1344, shortly before it was purchased by Sir Ralph St Leger, of Kent. Several changes of hands later, Sir William (later Lord) Petre bought the manor and rebuilt Cranham Hall around 1600. The hall was rebuilt again two centuries later and this version survives today as a retirement home. Cranham remained a very quiet agri-

cultural village throughout the 19th century. Apart from the hall, the first brick structure seems to have been a workhouse in 1828, since replaced by a pub. All Saints' Church was rebuilt in 1873 using some materials from its medieval predecessor. After the opening of nearby brickworks in 1900, Cranham began to grow, but only slowly. A widely advertised 1925 plan to lay out a garden suburb north of the railway line did not come to fruition. The council built a few houses in 1931 but rapid expansion did not occur until the sale of the Cranham manor estates in 1937. Most of the council's terraced houses and pebble-dashed semi-detached houses were erected in the 1950s, when Cranham's population trebled. The main shopping precinct is on Front (formerly Cranham) Lane, behind which is the District Line railway depot. South of the new centre is bungalow country, and beyond this lies the old village with a handful of Victorian cottages and the hall. A few executive-style homes have been added more recently. Cranham's demographics are out of the ordinary in many respects, even by Havering's standards. Ninety-five per cent of residents are white British and 82 per cent are Christians – the highest proportions in London. Pensioners occupy 35 per cent of all households. More than nine-tenths of homes are owner-occupied, and around half are owned outright – again the highest proportion in London.

The previous incarnation of Cranham Hall was as the home of General James Oglethorpe, founder of the American colony of Georgia. He died at the hall in 1785 at the age of 89. Oglethorpe has given his name to the local primary school – and to a university in Atlanta, USA. Streets laid out for council housing in Cranham have names with Georgian connections.

> ✉ Upminster RM14
>
> ♦ 12,242
>
> 📖 A W Fox, *A History of Cranham*
>
> @ www.users.globalnet.co.uk/-kelsey/ cranham.htm

Cranley Gardens · *Haringey*

A hillside residential locality in southern MUSWELL HILL, centred on the dog-legged avenue of the same name and overlooked by Queen's Wood. In 1928 a pot containing over 650 Roman coins was discovered in the vicinity. The Imperial Property Investment Co. bought farmland here from the Ecclesiastical Commissioners and built the first houses in

Cranley Gardens and Onslow Gardens in the 1890s. Lack of interest from potential home-buyers prompted the company to sell plots to other builders, who soon began work on Woodland Rise and Woodland Gardens. In around 1900 the Ecclesiastical Commissioners gave land at the corner of Park Road as the site for St George's Church but this was instead built on Priory Road. The locality was mostly built up before World War I and completely filled by the outbreak of World War II. Many of the early properties are well-proportioned but the quality of building seems inversely proportional to its altitude. During the first half of the 20th century Cranley Gardens had a station on the ALEXANDRA PALACE branch of the Great Northern Railway. After the Priory Road Church was destroyed by wartime bombing, a new St George's was built on the originally proposed site at the eastern end of Cranley Gardens. Following the demolition of HORNSEY'S structurally un-sound St Mary's Church in 1969, its parish was joined with St George's.

Rod Stewart joined the Faces and wrote his solo hit *Maggie May* while living in Ellington Road between 1969 and 1971. Dennis Nilsen, London's most notorious serial killer of modern times, lived and killed at 23 Cranley Gardens. Nilsen was caught in 1983 after body parts he had flushed down the lavatory blocked the drains, prompting the neighbours to call in Dyno-Rod.

> ✉ N10

> 📖 Brian Masters, *Killing for Company: The Case of Dennis Nilsen*, Arrow, 1995

Crayford • *Bexley*

The principal industrial zone in the borough, straddling the River Cray and the former Roman road of Watling Street, between BEXLEYHEATH and Dartford, Kent. Crayford Marshes have been the site of important archaeological finds, including rhinoceros bones, and evidence of an Iron Age settlement has been uncovered. Crayford was probably the site of the Roman settlement of Noviomagus, although other authorities place it at WEST WICKHAM. The Battle of Crayford, which took place in AD 456 or 457, played a decisive role in the formation of the kingdom of England, when Hengest's Anglo-Saxons drove Prince Vortimer's Britons out of Kent. The Anglo-Saxon Chronicle says that 4,000 men were slain. Domesday Book recorded the presence of a church, which was replaced by the present Church of St Paulinus around

1100, since when it has been much altered. The first Crayford manor house was built to the north-west of the church in the 14th century, when the town was granted a charter to hold an annual fair. The presence of the freely flowing river brought thirsty industries such as tanning, while barges were built at Crayford Creek. Huguenot refugees established the first calico bleaching works in the late 17th century, and later printed silk here. Crayford station opened in 1866. Machine guns and other armaments were manufactured north of Crayford Road, first by Hiram Maxim and from the end of the 19th century by Vickers, which also built some early flying machines. The company employed more than 14,000 workers during World War I. New Ideal Homesteads and other local builders laid out housing estates in the 1930s, but the location did not prove especially attractive to potential buyers. Vickers left Crayford in 1969 and its place was taken by distributors and small-scale manufacturers, the best known of which is Caterham Cars. A former British Telecom site has been redeveloped as Optima Park. Crayford greyhound stadium was relocated westward in 1985 to make room for a leisure centre and Sainsbury's and Homebase stores. Developments like the Tower retail park have drawn shoppers away from the High Street and Waterside but Bexley council has ambitious long-term plans to refocus the centre on Crayford Bridge, adding 'features of interest' and creating a new public park or open space. Crayford's population is almost exclusively white, and levels of educational attainment are generally low.

The occult novelist Algernon Blackwood was born at the manor house (now an adult education centre) in 1869. The house has an observatory in its grounds.

> ✉ Dartford DA1

> 🚶 10,290

> 🚆 South Eastern Trains (zone 6)

> 📖 Frances Sweeny, *Memories of Erith and Crayford*, Bexley Education and Leisure Services Directorate, 2002

> @ www.ideal-homes.org.uk/bexley/ crayford.html (London suburban history site)

Creekmouth • *Barking & Dagenham*

An industrial area lying to the east of BARKING Creek, which is the estuary of the River Roding. Creekmouth began life as a fishing hamlet and in 1739 Barking fishermen defied the Royal Navy press gang here in a significant act of civil disobedience. It took reinforcements from the dragoon guards to quell the insurrection, sometimes known as the Battle of Creekmouth. In the 1820s and 1830s the social reformer Elizabeth Fry had a home nearby, at which the family holidayed. During the latter part of the 19th century and the early 20th century a small settlement thrived here, served by a school, a mission church and the Crooked Billet pub, but Creekmouth has since succumbed entirely to trade and industry. The Crooked Billet has been rebuilt on the opposite side of River Road from its original site. The aircraft designer Sir Frederick Handley Page set up the first British aircraft factory at Creekmouth in 1909, making aircraft parts; the company moved to CRICKLEWOOD three years later. A power station was built in 1925, and was enlarged twice subsequently to become one of the largest steam-generating stations in Europe. The 200-foot-high Barking Creek Flood Barrier opened in 1982. It has a drop gate that is held out of the water when not in use, allowing the creek's use by commercial shipping, including turning oil tankers. Plans for future development envisage Creekmouth's continued role as a commercial zone but with scope for 'improvement and intensification'. The marshes here are a popular site for marine birds, and thus for birdwatchers.

⊠ Barking IG11

Crews Hill • *Enfield*

A horticultural heaven, situated two miles north-west of ENFIELD. Its name derives from a family that lived here in the mid 18th century. Crews Hill was part of the woodland hunting ground of ENFIELD CHASE and very little human activity took place here until after the enclosure and division of the chase in the late 1770s. By the early 19th century Trinity College, Cambridge owned most of the land here. The station opened in 1910 when the Great Northern Railway Co. extended the line as far as Cuffley in Hertfordshire. Crews Hill golf course was established on land bought from Trinity College in 1915. Theobalds Park Farm, which covered 140 acres, produced vegetables for the London markets and new nurseries were still being established in Crews Hill at a time when the wider trend elsewhere was for their closure and replacement by housing. A small estate of 102 bungalows was built in the early 1930s but soon afterwards Crews

Hill was included in a 'green girdle' plan to restrict development in north Middlesex, which evolved into green-belt protection after World War II. The nurseries progressively switched from production for London's wholesale fruit and vegetable markets to retail horticulture. Crews Hill is now utterly overgrown with garden centres and these are not loosely scattered but crammed together along a 'golden mile' east of the station. There are specialists in hardy plants, bonsai trees, landscaping and garden fencing and furniture. As well as all the nurseries, Crews Hill has an architectural reclaim merchant, on a site covering three-and-a-half acres, and an equestrian zone to the north with stables, paddocks and a stud farm. The Plough is a well-regarded example of the traditional English country pub and has a landscaped beer garden.

Bred by Lord Matthews of SOUTHGATE, the racehorse Crews Hill was a winner of eleven events, including the Stewards' Cup in 1981.

⊠ Enfield EN2

🚇 WAGN Railway (zone 6)

@ www.crewshill.com (local retail information site)

Cricklewood • *Brent/Barnet*

A changing and ethnically diverse district situated to the north-west of BRONDESBURY. Its name derives from Middle English words meaning an irregularly shaped wood. Though first identified separately from its parent manor of HENDON in the 13th century, Cricklewood did not develop beyond a small agricultural hamlet until the end of the 18th century. When the railway station opened in 1868 it was originally called CHILD'S HILL. With the arrival of the railway came sidings, yards and railway workers' cottages. Cricklewood Broadway (A5) became established as a shopping centre around the end of the 19th century, houses spread across the fields and industry began to flourish. The aircraft manufacturer Handley Page began production in Cricklewood in 1912 and inaugurated London to Paris flights from Cricklewood aerodrome in 1919. The following year saw the first-ever fatalities on a scheduled passenger flight, when an aircraft crashed into a house by the aerodrome. In the same year Frank Smith produced the first batch of his potato crisps in two garages behind the Crown public house. Bentley cars were built in Cricklewood from 1919 to 1931. During World War II, Handley Page manufactured Halifax bombers at Cricklewood. The Dubreq company produced the seminal Stylophone electronic organ here in the 1960s and 1970s. Cricklewood's residential population evolved over the second half of the 20th century with successive waves of settlement by Irish, Caribbean and Asian communities. In 1974 a police raid on the Carib club led to charges of affray, possession of offensive weapons and assault on police; none of the so-called 'Cricklewood Twelve' was convicted. The year 1977 brought the 'Battle of Grunwick', a historic industrial dispute centred on the right of a photo processing company's predominantly Asian, female workforce to join a trade union. In 1984 a huge fire destroyed most of Cricklewood trading estate. Cricklewood is presently undergoing massive regeneration, as brownfield sites fill with thousands of mixed-tenure homes, offices and leisure facilities.

The blues rock band Ten Years After named their 1970 album *Cricklewood Green*. *Cricklewood* was also the title of a 1997 album by Canadian experimental electronic musician David Kristian. Joe Strummer and the Mescaleros' *Willesden to Cricklewood* is a standout track from the album *Rock Art and the X-Ray Style*.

✉ NW2

🚆 Thameslink (zone 3)

📖 M C Barrès-Baker, *Cricklewood and Dollis Hill*, Grange Museum of Community History and Brent Archive, 2001

Cripplegate • *City*

The CITY OF LONDON'S most populous ward, taking in the eastern and central parts of the BARBICAN. Cripplegate was the northern entrance to the Roman fort, erected around AD 120, and stood at what is now the corner of Wood Street and St Alphage Gardens. The name probably derives from the Old English 'crypel-geat'; a cripple was 'one who can only creep' – which was the necessary way to duck under the original low arch. An alternative possibility is that it was a corruption of 'crepel', a burrow. St Giles's Church was built in 1090, probably on the site of a Saxon predecessor, and rebuilt in 1545 after a fire. The Cripplegate entrance was reconstructed at least twice and demolished in 1761. By this time, the formerly wealthy ward of Cripplegate had gone downhill and religious dissidents and journalists had come to live here. The most renowned thoroughfare was Grub Street, which had a community of hack writers and became a byword for 'persons who wrote for hire' and hence for literary efforts of low value. In a leap from the ridiculous to the sublime, Grub Street was renamed Milton Street in 1829. The street was subsequently denuded of dwellings following an influx of businesses to the area and an exodus of residents, a process that was bolstered by the extension of the underground railway line from Farringdon to Moorgate in 1865. Cripplegate was damaged beyond recognition by World War II bombing and the church needed comprehensive restoration. Most of the area was rebuilt with the massive concrete blocks of the Barbican, where the first homes were completed in the early 1960s. The remainder of the ward has been filled with office towers. The ward's residential population exhibits a high degree of affluence, although the level of car ownership is very low.

There is evidence that William Shakespeare was a parish resident in the late 1590s. Oliver Cromwell was married in St Giles's Church and the poet John Milton is buried here. The writer Daniel Defoe was born in Cripplegate ward in 1660. Giles Emerson's 2002 book *Sin City* describes the activities of the early-18th-century Farting Club of Cripplegate.

✉ EC2

👥 3,007

📖 Caroline Gordon and Wilfrid Dewhirst, *The Ward of Cripplegate in the City of London*, Cripplegate Ward Club, 1985

@ www.cripplegatewardclub.org

Crofton • *Bromley*

The western side of ORPINGTON, with a predominantly white, home-owning character. A Roman farming estate of about 500 acres existed here from AD 140 to around AD 400, with woodland and an arable and pasture field system. A 20-room villa housed the landowner's family and servants. Although modest in design and furnishings, it had underfloor heating and tiled floors in several rooms and there were barns and outbuildings. The surviving floors of ten rooms of the main house are protected inside a viewing building, which is open to the public from April to October. Crofton's name is of Old English origin and means 'farm on a rounded hill'. It has been rendered as Cropton, Crocton and Crawton at various times over the past millennium. Part of the revenue from the Crofton estate was given by Henry VIII to endow St Thomas's Hospital in Southwark. In his *History of Kent*, written at the end of the 18th century, Edward Hasted describes Crofton as lying in the middle of woods, and notes that it was 'said to have been once a parish of itself, and to have been destroyed by fire'. The arrival of the railway in 1868 brought some tentative suburban development and St Paul's Church was built on Crofton Road in 1887. Crofton was chosen as the site for Orpington's council offices in 1925 and it was during construction that the remains of the villa were uncovered. Most of Crofton was built up between the wars with bungalows and semi-detached houses, with some larger homes to the north. Shops were provided at Kelvin Parade. During the 1950s terraced housing and more compact semi-detacheds were built nearer the town centre. A new St Paul's Church opened in 1958 and the old church became the parish hall. The 200 acres of Crofton Woods, formerly known as Crofton Heath and now including Sparrow Wood, Roundabout Wood and Gumping Common, lie to the north-west. The ancient woodland shelters some uncommon plants and is also important for its insects, especially micro-moths. Among the larger trees are oak, ash, birch and aspen, while smaller varieties include hazel and hawthorn as well as rarer shrubs.

✉ Orpington BR5 and BR6

👥 14,180 (Farnborough and Crofton ward)

@ cka.moon-demon.co.uk/villa.htm (Crofton Roman villa site)

Crofton Park • *Lewisham*

The southern part of BROCKLEY, bordering HONOR OAK PARK. This was the location of the village of Brockley in the 18th century, centred on the Castle public house, later renamed the Brockley Jack. The part of Brockley that lay within the parish of Deptford consisted solely of farmland at that time. When the Catford loop line was built in 1892 a station was opened here, and a new name was required, since Brockley station was already in existence. Crofton Park's name appears to have been entirely an invention, with no basis in local history. The Brockley Jack was rebuilt in 1898 and shops surrounded the station. New roads were laid out to the south of the railway, including Crofton Park Road, which roughly followed the route of an old lane. The parish church of St Hilda, Crofton Park, was completed in 1908 in a variation on the Arts and Crafts style that has been called 'strange' and 'irresponsible'. The Crofton Park picture palace opened in 1913 and the building was extended in 1924. It later became the Rivoli ballroom. Brockley Hall Road is built on the site of the former home of the Noakes family of Bermondsey brewers. Brockley Hall stood for a century and a half but was demolished in 1932 following the death of its last owner, the eccentric Maude Noakes. The Crofton Park ward – which also takes in Honor Oak Park – is demographically typical of Lewisham, except for a higher level of owner occupation. Two-thirds of residents are white, while a quarter are black or black British.

The Rivoli ballroom is now used for banquets, political rallies and specialist dance nights. Among its many film and television appearances, the Rivoli was the location for Tina Turner's *Private Dancer* video and featured as a 1970s German dance hall in the 2001 thriller *Spy Game*, starring Robert Redford and Brad Pitt. The Brockley Jack has a popular upstairs theatre.

✉ SE4

👥 13,904

🚆 South Eastern Trains (zone 3)

@ www.croftonpark.com (community site); www.brockleyjack.co.uk

Croham • *Croydon* (pronounced 'cro'əm')

An electoral ward covering most of SOUTH CROYDON. The name was first recorded in 1225 as Craweham, 'a homestead or enclosure frequented by crows'. Croham Hurst is a 477-foot hill with evidence of intensive prehistoric use, including a burial mound that dates from around 2,000 BC. The absence of subsequent relics indicates that the infertile hilltop was abandoned when settlers moved to the valley to cultivate crops. The manor of Croham was one of four in the parish of SANDERSTEAD and was acquired in the late 16th century by Archbishop Whitgift. It later became the property of the schools that the archbishop founded in Croydon. In 1898 the governors of the Whitgift Foundation planned to sell the lower slopes for development, while offering the hilltop to the council. Following public protests the foundation sold the whole of Croham Hurst to Croydon corporation, while playing fields for Old Whitgiftians were laid out on Croham Farm. Croham Hurst School was founded in 1899 for day girls and boarders, and transferred to its present site in Croham Road in 1907. Croham Hurst Golf Club was established in the 1920s and suburban housing was built beyond the protected slopes, notably in the form of Richard Costain and Sons' Croham Heights estate in 1927. The Croham ward has a higher proportion of well-educated, young, single people than most parts of the borough.

✉ South Croydon CR2

👥 14,443

📖 Brian J Salter (ed.), *Selsdon and Croham*, Living History, 1983; Monica Sharpe, *Croham Hurst School*, Phillimore, 1998

@ www.croham.surrey.sch.uk (Croham Hurst School)

Crooked Billet • *Merton*
The south-easternmost tip of WIMBLEDON COMMON has a distinct, if little known, identity, taking its name from a popular pub that faces onto a small triangular green. Despite claims of a Cromwellian connection, the house probably dates from the early 18th century and became the Crooked Billet in the 1750s. However, the building has been so greatly altered that it is not deemed worthy of statutory listing. Around 1770 Cinque Cottages were built on the green, possibly as an illegal encroachment. The cottages were later divided into eight dwellings. Piecemeal redevelopment of the locality over more than two centuries has periodically altered the arrangement of the buildings, but several other properties survive from the 18th and early 19th centuries. The Hand in Hand public house had become the Crooked Billet's neighbour by 1890. Southside House, on nearby Woodhayes Road, was built by Robert Pennington, a friend of Charles II, as a safe haven for his family after his son died in the Great Plague; Pennington's descendants live here to this day. Their neighbour is King's College School, which took over a Georgian house in 1897 and has progressively expanded its premises since then.

Both pubs on the green are said to be haunted. The Crooked Billet's ghost is an Irishwoman who confines her wanderings to the cellars.

✉ SW19

Crossharbour • *Tower Hamlets*
A Docklands Light Railway station on the ISLE OF DOGS, just to the east of MILLWALL Docks, which was the station's original name in 1872. The Crossharbour name refers to the Glengall Bridge, which carried Glengall Road (later Glengall Grove) across Millwall Inner Dock. The bridge's construction was a concession by the developers to obtain planning approval for the dock when it was built in 1868. A century later the shipping line Fred Olsen Ltd put up two massive warehouses on the quayside to store fruit and tomatoes from the Canary Islands. The northern warehouse, known as J Shed, was refurbished and extended in 1984 at a cost of £7 million but the value of the site was increasing so rapidly that within four years the building had been demolished and replaced by the nine-block Harbour Exchange complex. Around the same time, K Shed (or Olsen Shed 2) was converted into the London Arena, a business and entertainment venue hosting concerts, ice shows and sporting events that closed in 2004. To the south of the bridge, the Glengall Bridge development, completed in 1991, provided more than half a million square feet of residential, commercial and retail space on either side of the Inner Dock. Across East Ferry Road is an Asda superstore, one of the earliest indicators of the renaissance of the Isle of Dogs when it opened in 1983.

✉ E14

🚉 Docklands Light Railway, Lewisham branch (zone 2)

Crossness • *Bexley*
Located at the northern tip of the ERITH marshes, Crossness is now an outpost of THAMESMEAD but this was an isolated spot when Victorian engineers chose it as the site for one of their characteristically grand public engineering projects. Sewage pollution had become a serious health hazard in London by the early 19th century and the 'great stink' of 1858 finally persuaded Parliament to act. Joseph Bazalgette and his colleagues devised and built a network of sewers that carried the city's waste water to two huge pumping and filtration stations on either side of the Thames, east of the metropolitan conurbation. At Crossness, four massive engines pumped effluent into a reservoir that held 25 million gallons. Opened in 1865 by the Prince of Wales (later Edward VII), who turned on the Prince Consort engine named after his father, the building was designed in ornate Romanesque style in gault brick, ornamented inside with painted ironwork. The old engines were decommissioned at the end of the 1950s and Thames Water now uses modern technology elsewhere on the site to process the effluent. As with all waste water plants, bad odours are a problem and hundreds of sprays have been mounted around the works to squirt perfume into the air on

hot days. Since 1985, the Crossness Engine Trust has rescued the Victorian machinery from rust and vandalism. The team of volunteers has progressively restored the old machinery and began to show the results to the public in 2001, with an accompanying exhibition on the history of sanitation, housed in the only Grade I-listed industrial building in south-east London. The surrounding marshland is a 50-acre wetland nature reserve and Thames Water has made use of redundant concrete pilings to create an artificial cliff with nesting ledges for birds and a bat cave. A tidal river used to flow from ELTHAM and enter the Thames just west of Crossness Point but this dried up as PLUMSTEAD marshes were enclosed and drained.

✉ Erith DA18

Crouch End • *Haringey*

A fashionable Victorian suburb centred around a confluence of routes a mile southwest of HORNSEY. The name is of Middle English origin, an 'end' being an outlying place, while a 'crouch' was a cross, which may have been placed here as a boundary post between two manors. During the late 18th century the village took shape as a congregation of labourers' cottages, though there were grander houses in the vicinity – two of which were later acquired by the Booths, the gin distilling family. The Hornsey enclosure award of 1813 prompted a gradual programme of housebuilding that accelerated rapidly after the opening of CROUCH HILL and Crouch End stations in the late 1860s. The latter is now closed and its disused line has become the Parkland Walk that traverses the district. During the 1870s and 1880s, Crouch End was entirely built over, with pressure from local worthies ensuring a high standard of construction. Civic pride shows in Crouch End's landmark, a clock tower erected by public subscription in 1895. A few post-war office blocks have marred its homogeneity, but Crouch End remains one of London's lovelier suburbs, with an eclectic selection of shops and restaurants in the streets converging on the Broadway – also the location of Hornsey Town Hall, an award winner when it was built in 1935. Hornsey College of Art, attended by the Kinks' frontman Ray Davies, later became the TUC College. A remarkable number of 1960s pop stars went on to buy homes in Crouch End and the area has acquired quasi-cult status among mid-ranking media personalities. The most prominent of recent developments has been the replacement of the old telephone exchange by an apartment complex with a fitness centre and a Marks and Spencer food store at street level.

Despite its outward gentility, Crouch End – according to Stephen King's short story of that name – conceals a gateway to a nightmarish parallel dimension behind its 'elderly brick houses like sleepy dowagers'.

✉ N8

♦ 10,762

📖 Ken Gay, *Hornsey and Crouch End*, Tempus, 1998

Crouch Hill • *Islington/Haringey*

The hill is part of the Northern Heights that extend eastward from HAMPSTEAD and HIGHGATE, while the road of that name links STROUD GREEN with CROUCH END. The farmland here was sprinkled with superior villas in the first half of the 19th century, of which a couple survive in altered form. Following the opening of the station in 1867, suburban housing was built along Crouch Hill and in new streets branching off it. To the east, John Farrer was responsible for Cecile Park in the 1880s and 1890s. To the west and along the upper section of Crouch Hill are houses by local builder W J Collins, influenced by the work of R Norman Shaw. No. 113 Crouch Hill is especially elaborate and may have been a show house for the estate. The ornate Friern Manor Dairy at No. 1 Crouch Hill dates from the same period. During the interwar years Crouch Hill saw extensive rebuilding along its southern half, and Islington council subsequently added some council housing, notably the Holly Park estate's 17-storey Ilex House, completed in 1972. Many of the area's larger houses have been subdivided into flats. The old dairy was converted into a bar and restaurant in 1997.

In Ken Macleod's 'future history' *The Star Fraction* (1995), teenage computer expert Jordan Brown flees his home at the top of Crouch Hill, which has become part of a fundamentalist Christian enclave called Beulah City.

✉ N4; N8; N19

🚆 Silverlink Metro (zone 3)

Crowlands • *Havering*

A messy area situated north-west of RUSH GREEN, with railside utilities and works, some skimpy greenery, and housing that looks uncomfortable about being here. It takes its name from a former landowner, John Crowland, whose family was living here in 1480. The land was known as Crowland by 1514 and as Crowlands by the 19th century. A map of 1805 shows 'Lowlands' north of London Road (A118) in the area of Crown Farm (formerly Pigtail Farm) but this was presumably a cartographer's error. The hamlet was originally focused on the junction of Crow Lane and Jutsums Lane, now the site of commercial premises and a recreation ground. The Eastern Counties Railway cut across the heathland in 1839. Work was once begun on a station at Crowlands, but it was never completed. When London Road School was built for 280 infants in 1908 its surroundings were still predominantly rural. Crow Lane at that time was a narrow winding road, bordered by ditches and large areas of gravel. The lane was loosely built up with compact houses from the early 1930s, when the school was enlarged, but seniors transferred to the Warren School in DAGENHAM in 1937. London Road School became Crowlands School in 1956 and a purpose-built nursery unit was added in 2001. There are pockets of social and economic disadvantage among the neighbourhood's mainly white, working-class population. Crowlands Heath Golf Club, situated to the south-west, on Wood Lane, has a links-style nine-hole course with naturally formed ponds and wetlands, and a driving range where golfers hit their balls into a lake. If the Crossrail project goes ahead to provide a new east–west railway route across London, Crowlands may be subject to considerable disruption, including the relaying of a gas pipeline.

✉ Romford RM7

Croydon • *Croydon*

The dominant commercial centre of outer London, situated 12 miles due south of St Paul's Cathedral. Croydon may have been settled by the Romans as a staging post on the road from the south coast to London – its position at the head of the River Wandle just north of a gap in the North Downs makes it a natural choice – but it was the Saxons who named it 'saffron valley'. The earliest mention of the parish church of St John the Baptist, at the heart of Croydon's old town, was in Domesday Book. Croydon was part of the archbishop of Canterbury's estates from Saxon times and six archbishops were buried in the church between 1583 and 1757. The archbishops' 1,000-year-old residence survives on Old Palace Road, as do Archbishop Whitgift's 16th-century almshouses on George Street.

From medieval times charcoal was burnt in the nearby woods and Croydon was the trading centre, making its streets some of the dirtiest in England. The market town grew as a coaching halt as Londoners started to flock to the south coast resorts from the late 18th century. The Wandle valley became heavily industrialized, with dozens of factories producing goods such as textiles and metals by 1800. The horse-drawn Surrey Iron Railway linked Croydon to WANDSWORTH from 1803 and the Croydon Canal opened in 1809. Neither survived beyond 1850, by which time steam trains were running to Croydon from LONDON BRIDGE. The boom in industry and transport created health problems for Croydon's growing population and its board of health, set up in 1849, took action by building a comprehensive sewerage system. St John's Church was rebuilt by Sir George Gilbert Scott after a fire in 1867. Croydon became a borough in 1883 and a county borough in 1889; a new town hall, designed by local architect Charles Henman, was opened on Katharine Street in 1896. Its predecessor was demolished as part of a programme of town centre improvements that included the widening of the High Street. WADDON'S wartime aerodrome became London's main civil airport in 1920. Croydon was hit by bombs during both world wars; V1 attacks in 1944 caused hundreds of deaths and destroyed at least a thousand homes. The Croydon Corporation Act of 1956 marked the start of a new era, with its drive to draw businesses from central London creating around six million square feet of office space. The FAIRFIELD Halls arts complex opened in 1962, a plan to redevelop the airport site for housing and light industry was approved in 1963 and the Whitgift shopping centre opened in 1969. What had seemed pioneering in the 1960s was already looking tired and ugly by the 1980s and Croydon's character became the subject of metropolitan disdain. The borough council has since been co-ordinating the wholesale redevelopment of the business, retail and leisure district and innovations in recent years have included the Clocktower arts centre, the Tramlink network and the Centrale shopping centre. More is to come, including Park Place – a shopping and dining complex with over a million square feet of floor space – which is expected to start trading in 2010, while the Croydon Gateway scheme will transform the vicinity of EAST CROYDON station.

In 1577 the comic play *Grim, the Collyer of Croydone* was performed before Elizabeth I; Grim was probably a mythical figure, identified with the devil because of his blackened clothes and features. Croydon band The Damned released the pioneering punk single *New Rose* in 1976.

✉ Croydon CR0

♦ 114,878 (Croydon Central parliamentary constituency)

🚆 Southern (West Croydon; East Croydon, zone 5); South Eastern Trains; Thameslink (East Croydon, zone 5)

🚊 Croydon Tramlink, Routes 1, 2 and 3 (George Street, Church Street, Centrale, West Croydon, Wellesley Road, East Croydon)

📖 John Gent, *Croydon Past*, Phillimore, 2002

@ www.croydononline.org (community site); www.croydonsociety.org.uk

Crystal Palace • Bromley

Three years after the triumphant Great Exhibition of 1851 in HYDE PARK, Queen Victoria opened the rebuilt and enlarged Crystal Palace in a quiet corner of SYDENHAM formerly belonging to Penge Place. The massive iron and glass structure, which had been nicknamed the 'Crystal Palace' by *Punch* magazine, was over 1,600 feet long and covered nearly 14 acres. Its creator, Joseph Paxton MP, was knighted for the achievement and his statue now stands at the entrance to the park. The new 200-acre park contained a magnificent series of fountains; the two largest basins have since been transformed to accommodate the athletics stadium and the sports centre. Water flowed through the fountains into a grand lake, which is now devoted to boating and fishing. Benjamin Waterhouse Hawkins, the draughtsman Darwin had employed on the voyage of the *Beagle*, constructed 29 life-size replicas of extinct animals, under the guidance of Professor Richard Owen, the man who invented the word 'dinosaur'. The park quickly became a sporting venue. It has been home to the Crystal Palace Athletics Club since 1868. Later, the cricketer W G Grace founded both the London County Cricket Club and the Crystal Palace Bowling Club – the bowlers used one of the carpeted long galleries of the palace – while palace workers formed Crystal Palace Football Club, originally nicknamed the Glaziers, in 1905. The Crystal Palace held every kind of national exhibition, including the world's first air show. In 1911 the palace hosted the Festival of Empire, held in honour of George V's coronation. After World War I, during which it served as a

naval barracks, it became the original home of the Imperial War Museum. Crystal Palace Football Club moved to nearby SELHURST PARK in 1924. Between 1933 and 1936, John Logie Baird pioneered the development of television in a complex beneath the palace's main concourse, and two decades later the BBC began full television transmissions here. The Crystal Palace was destroyed by fire on 30 November 1936 – an event so momentous that special trains were laid on for sightseers and more than a million people are said to have watched the blaze. After this, the popularity of the area began to wane. The Crystal Palace transmitter, which dates from the early 1950s, remains unique in being the only self-supporting lattice tower of this scale in the country (nearly all the rest are guyed masts). It is the tallest structure in London, with a height approaching 900 feet. Plans for radical redevelopment of the sporting facilities at Crystal Palace are undergoing a very long gestation.

The palace was a frequent source of artistic inspiration, especially for the Impressionists. Camille Pissarro's painting *The Crystal Palace* (1871) is in the Art Institute of Chicago.

✉ SE19

♦ 11,233 (the ward takes in much of Anerley and Penge)

🚆 Southern (zone 4); also, from 2010, the East London Line

📖 Jan R Piggott, *Palace of the People: The Crystal Palace at Sydenham 1854–1936*, C Hurst, 2004

@ www.crystalpalacefoundation.org.uk

Cubitt Town • Tower Hamlets (pronounced 'kewbit')

The south-eastern quadrant of the ISLE OF DOGS. During the 1840s most of the land here was acquired in four stages by William Cubitt, brother of the great London builder Thomas Cubitt and subsequently Lord Mayor of London. The ground was liable to flooding and the river wall was in need of repair, so the leases were relatively cheap. Cubitt commissioned a number of builders to erect wharves, mills and other dock-related industries along the river bank and terraces of three-storey houses inland. The streets followed the lines of former drainage ditches. As was the practice of the time, the development included a church and plenty of public houses, which were provided for the construction workers as much as for subsequent residents. The largest of the contractors built 181 houses and shops and three pubs, but many others were responsible for just a handful of properties each. This accounts for some of the variations in the finished effects, though the designs of successive houses were modelled on the earliest examples. By the early 1850s the whole area had taken the name Cubitt Town, even those parts not developed by the man himself. Almost all the work was completed by 1867. The township was well regarded for the neatness of the houses, the width of the roads and the absence of squalor and overcrowding. Nearly all of the original properties have since been replaced with council housing. Cubitt Town has a slightly larger proportion of white residents than most of the borough. Among the most common minority languages is Sylheti, which is spoken in the Sylhet region of eastern Bangladesh.

✉ E14

⑂ 11,939 (Blackwall and Cubitt Town ward)

Cuckoo Hill • *Harrow*

An undulating and upmarket locality situated between EASTCOTE VILLAGE and PINNER GREEN. The hill itself is at the midpoint of the road of the same name. Until the Ruislip Enclosure Act of 1804, Cuckoo Hill marked the eastern edge of RUISLIP COMMON, which was then an uninhabited wilderness. Cuckoo Hill Farm was at that time the property of the wealthy Eastcote heiress Elizabeth Rogers, who also owned several other farms in the parish. The farmhouse is still standing, although in altered form and hemmed in by suburban development, some of it distinctly grand, since the late 1920s. The UK branch of the Sathya Sai Education in Human Values Trust is based at The Glen in Cuckoo Hill. It is part of a world-wide, multi-faith programme intended to develop positive values in children and young people, although some have questioned its allegedly 'cultish' aspects.

The humorous Victorian writer and critic Barry Pain lived at The Circuits, Cuckoo Hill. The house, which was demolished in 1957, had been drolly named by a previous owner, Judge Alderson.

✉ Pinner HA5

Cuddington • *Sutton*

An exclusive enclave situated to the west of BELMONT and bordering the Surrey boroughs of Epsom & Ewell and Reigate & Banstead. The name, which refers to a Saxon landowner, may have originated as early as the eighth century. Cuddington is one of the 'finger parishes' of Sutton, so-called for their elongated north–south shapes. By 1538 the parish had acquired the stone church of St Mary, a manor house and a handful of productive farms. But this was the year in which Cuddington changed forever, for Henry VIII acquired the entire manor, obliterated all the existing buildings and commissioned the construction of Nonsuch Palace. The lord of the manor received the priory of Isleworth in compensation for his loss. Although primarily intended as a hunting lodge, Nonsuch was built and decorated to impressive standards of grandeur that were designed to rival Chambord, the Loire Valley palace of the French king Francis I. Work was close to completion when Henry died in 1547. Nonsuch remained in the possession of the Crown until Charles II gave it to his mistress Barbara Villiers, who demolished the palace in 1684 and sold off the materials. Cuddington was now a parish without a church and without many parishioners either. Nearly two centuries passed before civilization returned with the creation of WORCESTER PARK at the parish's northern end, where a new St Mary's Church was built in 1867 and rebuilt in 1895. The modern locality of Cuddington, however, lies well to the south-east, where the borough of Sutton juts into Surrey. Wrapped around Cuddington golf course, laid out in 1929, this is one of south London's most select neighbourhoods. Progressively developed in the course of the 20th century with increasingly grand homes (but no community facilities), even a bungalow here can fetch over half a million pounds.

Nonsuch Park, which contains the site of the palace and some relics of its heyday, lies west of CHEAM and beyond the Greater London boundary.

✉ Sutton SM2; Banstead SM7

📖 Charles Abdy, *A Brief History of Cuddington*, Nonsuch Antiquarian Society, 1995

Cudham • *Bromley*

A quiet village with several flint and red-brick buildings, lying two miles east of BIGGIN HILL. The church of St Peter and St Paul is of 12th-century origin, though much restored since. There is evidence that there has been a place of worship on this site since 900 BC and two yew trees in the churchyard may be 17 centuries old. Cudham's landowners have often been of noble birth but none have ever chosen to live here. In 1865 Richard Relph acquired the

Blacksmith's Arms, a property that dates from 1628, when it was a real smithy. The landlord's wife bore him 15 children, one of whom – born at the inn when Relph was at a remarkably advanced age – went on to become the celebrated music hall star 'Little Tich'. The houses and cottages of Cudham date mainly from the 19th century. Cudham Hall, built around 1850, served until recently as a trade union-run college of electrical and mechanical engineering. The hall is presently being converted to flats, with new outbuildings providing additional accommodation. Cudham's very grand vicarage later served as a sailors' convalescent home and a care home for the mentally ill. The surrounding farms were once known for growing dyer's weed (*Reseda luteola*), which produces a yellow pigment. Its cultivation ceased when the development of synthetic dyes rendered it uneconomic. Run by the Woodcraft Folk, Cudham environmental activities centre is set within a three-acre woodland site on New Barn Lane. It has a residential field studies unit, a camping area and a mini-farm.

In 1877, Louis Staunton confined his wealthy wife Harriet to a remote Cudham farmhouse and she died in an emaciated condition. Staunton and three co-conspirators received death sentences but these were later commuted because of doubts about their intent.

✉ Sevenoaks TN14

Custom House · *Newham*

A redeveloping dockland locality squeezed between CANNING TOWN and BECKTON. It takes its name from the Port of London's custom house, which was formally called the Dock Directors' Access Centre and stood beside the station and the ROYAL VICTORIA Dock. Following the establishment of the ROYAL DOCKS, the need for accompanying housing encouraged the brisk growth of this part of Canning Town in the 1880s. From the late 1920s Custom House was the home of WEST HAM Stadium, a speedway and greyhound track with a capacity of over 100,000. After World War II bomb-damaged terraced housing was replaced by council flats, notably the nine tower blocks of the Freemasons estate. One of its towers was Ronan Point, which partially collapsed after a gas explosion in 1968, killing five people. The disaster has been called 'modern architecture's Titanic' and it had a pivotal influence on subsequent designs for tall buildings. It has even been suggested that the effects of the terrorist attack on the

World Trade Center's twin towers might have been less catastrophic had lessons from Ronan Point been incorporated into their construction. West Ham Stadium was demolished in the 1970s and replaced by a maze of curling cul-de-sacs, many of the streets named after former speedway champions. The Admiral's Reach development, completed in 1993 by Barratt, occupies the site of the Freemasons estate. North of Newham Way (A13), the Terence McMillan Stadium has facilities for squash, football and athletics. The Custom House ward has a significant black African community, mainly speaking Yoruba, Twi and Swahili. Fifteen per cent of homes in the ward are single-parent households.

The custom house was refurbished in 1995 but, in an astonishing about-turn, it was then demolished to make way for the ExCeL exhibition and conference centre. Opened in 2000, the centre has 90,000 square metres of event space on a 100-acre site north of the Royal Victoria Dock. The £250-million construction project was the largest in east London since Canary Wharf. Three Docklands Light Railway stations serve the site: Royal Victoria and PRINCE REGENT for the western and eastern entrances respectively, and Custom House for the centre. ExCeL will host boxing, wrestling, judo, weightlifting and taekwondo in the 2012 Olympic Games.

✉ E16

♦ 11,875

🚇 Docklands Light Railway, Beckton branch (zone 3)

@ www.excel-london.co.uk

Cutty Sark · *Greenwich*

A riverside attraction in north-west GREENWICH, and the location of a Docklands Light Railway station since 1999. Built in Dumbarton in 1869, the *Cutty Sark* has a 152-foot main mast and boasted a top speed of 17 knots. This famous tea clipper made record-breaking voyages bringing tea from China and wool from Australia back to Britain. The ship's name, and the inspiration for its figurehead, comes from a Scottish legend, retold by Robert Burns, of Tam O'Shanter's admiration for a graceful young witch who wore a 'cutty sark', the dialect term for a short chemise. The ship was placed in a dry dock here in 1957 after featuring as a showpiece at the Festival of Britain in 1951. The Cutty Sark was ravaged by fire in May 2007 but much of the clipper's fabric had been removed for repairs at the time and it is hoped that restoration will be completed by 2010. The original plan for the DLR extension to LEWISHAM did not include a station here, but its potential convenience for tourists prompted key local institutions to help fund the construction costs. The station is ideal for visiting the maritime sights of Greenwich.

✉ SE10

🚊 Docklands Light Railway, Lewisham branch (zones 2 and 3)

@ www.cuttysark.org.uk

Cyprus • *Newham*

A rebuilt urban hamlet located north-east of the ROYAL ALBERT Dock, off Woolwich Manor Way (A117). The name dates from 1878, when it was named after the Mediterranean island that Britain had just leased from Turkey – the naming of new buildings etc after recent colonial acquisitions being a common practice in the 19th century. Also known as New Beckton, this tiny settlement with its shops and services was a 'self-supporting community', entirely owned by the Port of London Authority, providing homes for workers at BECKTON gasworks and the ROYAL DOCKS. Unlike the earlier workers' housing in 'old' Beckton, construction standards were not high and the absence of mains drainage contributed to the poor health of the residents. Council houses were built on Savage Gardens shortly before World War I. Much of the Victorian township was destroyed in World War II bombing and the council erected prefabricated houses in the neighbourhood after hostilities ended. Following the relocation of some existing noxious industrial plants in the 1970s, Cyprus became the site of the London Docklands Development Corporation's first sponsored housing project, with homes built by Barratt, Wimpey, Broseley and Comben. The rapid sale of the properties prompted the LDDC to release further land for residential building and drew more developers to DOCKLANDS. The Ferndale public house on Cyprus Place is the only remaining Victorian structure. South of the Docklands Light Railway station, the former quayside of the Royal Albert Dock has been transformed into the University of East London's Docklands campus. Opened in 2000, this is the capital's first totally new university campus in 50 years, and its most distinctive feature is a waterside row of drum-shaped halls of residence. A second phase of construction is due for completion in 2007.

✉ E16

🚊 Docklands Light Railway, Beckton branch (zone 4)

@ www.uel.ac.uk/campusdevelopments/ docklands

Dagenham • _Barking & Dagenham_

A working-class stronghold situated beside the Thames marshes east of BARKING. The name was first recorded around 687 and refers to the homestead of a man called Dæcca. The 'Dagenham Idol', a wooden figure dug out of the marshes in 1922, is possibly from the Bronze Age. It is believed that it was buried as a talisman to help crops grow. In 1205 Dagenham was large enough to have a chaplain and the parish church of St Peter and St Paul was probably built at a similar time. From the Middle Ages until the 20th century the appearance of Dagenham village did not change significantly. The main street, called Crown Street, ran east from the church and crossed the valley of the Wantz Stream. William Ford's School was founded in 1825 and continues to thrive despite the social difficulties of its catchment area. Dagenham Common survived longer than much of the heathland in the London area, but was enclosed after 1862. After 1921 the village was rapidly hemmed in to the south by industrial development on Dagenham Marshes – notably in the form of the Ford Motor Co.'s factory – and then to the north by the huge BECONTREE estate. Dagenham's population increased more than threefold between the wars. After World War II the council began to pull down decaying buildings and by the early 1970s almost every vestige of the old village had been replaced by municipal housing, while cottages on Church Street were demolished to provide a new village green. The parish church, vicarage and Cross Keys public house are now the only ancient structures. With the exodus of industry from the vicinity of DAGENHAM DOCK and CHEQUERS Lane, SOUTH DAGENHAM is set to become a major new township over the next two decades, as part of THAMES GATEWAY developments. At DAGENHAM EAST, a former quarry has been reclaimed as a 120-acre nature reserve. To the south-west the CASTLE GREEN Centre on Dagenham's border with Barking provides a wide range of amenities for both districts.

The England football manager Alf Ramsey, comedian and actor Dudley Moore and singer Sandie Shaw were all born in Dagenham, while footballer Jimmy Greaves and fashion designer Hardy Amies grew up here. The famous Dagenham Girl Pipers, the first all-female bagpipe band, was formed in 1930.

> ✉ Dagenham RM9

> ♟ 39,613 (Alibon, Goresbrook, River and Village wards)

> 🚇 District Line (Dagenham Heathway, zone 5)

> ▢ S Curtis, _Dagenham and Rainham Past_, Phillimore, 2000

Dagenham Dock • _Barking & Dagenham_

An industrial and bulk storage district built on DAGENHAM Marshes, south of the A13. The old docks were constructed in 1887 around Dagenham Breach, now a constricted industrial lagoon but originally a local beauty spot, created in the early 18th century by the Thames' irrepressible habit of breaking through flood defences. The docks' founder was William Varco, who lived at Mardyke Farm in what became SOUTH HORNCHURCH. HMS _Thunderer_, the last warship built on the Thames, was completed at the docks in 1911 and took part in the Battle of Jutland five years later. In the late 1920s the Ford Motor Co. built its massive car factory here. For British drivers, Dagenham's name became synonymous with Ford cars but the plant closed in 2001, although the site continues to be used for engine production and as a distribution depot. The remainder of the area is a motley collection of oil, coal and molasses depots, glass reclaimers, car breakers and container compounds. On CHEQUERS Lane, Barking Power Ltd has built a privately funded electricity generating station, which began to supply power to the national grid from 1995. The recently built Dagenham Dock viaduct carries the six-lane A13 dual carriageway across the area. Dagenham Dock is presently undergoing extensive regeneration as part of the Thames Gateway master plan. This is bringing new employment opportunities and, to the west, housing at BARKING REACH. Planners hope to shift the industrial emphasis in a greenward direction from its formerly dirty character.

✉ Dagenham RM9

🚇 c2c (zone 5)

Dagenham East • Barking & Dagenham
An industrial and recreational zone bordering the borough of Havering. Eastbrookend country park is a reclaimed tract of countryside that includes the Chase, a 120-acre nature reserve. From the 1920s until the early 1970s this was a gravel quarry, providing construction materials for the expansion of east London. Many of the exhausted pits were filled with rubble but others were simply abandoned, allowing wetlands and grasslands to form. The re-vegetation process was aided by the use of the land for horse grazing and by the designation of the Dagenham corridor as green belt. Much of the terrain is stony and prone to winter flooding, but the Chase harbours numerous animals and plants unusual in an urban setting. Over 140 bird species have been recorded, including kingfishers, woodpeckers, owls and lapwings. The small areas of woodland scrub have hawthorn, willow and the rare black poplar tree. In 1986 Barking & Dagenham council asked the London Wildlife Trust to take over management of the Chase and to develop it as a recreational and educational resource for the community. Rhône-Poulenc Rorer, whose factory is adjacent to the reserve, is a major sponsor of the project.

On the opposite side of Rainham Road (A1112) is the home of Dagenham and Redbridge Football Club. The club's Victoria Road ground originally belonged to Dagenham F C, which merged with Redbridge Forest in 1992.

✉ Dagenham RM10; Romford RM7

🚇 District Line (zone 5)

Dalston • Hackney (pronounced 'dawlstən')
KINGSLAND and Dalston are twin localities situated on the western side of HACKNEY, but the latter name is commonly applied to the whole district. First recorded in 1294, the settlement began life as Deorlof's farm. By the mid 18th century it consisted primarily of a handful of large houses and a cluster of cottages on the north side of Dalston Lane. In the early 19th century, a second cluster began to form at the western end of Dalston Lane, with terraced houses for the upper middle classes. Dalston Green, as it was known, had fused with the earlier hamlet by 1831 and building then began to spread southwards. The opening of Dalston Junction station in 1865 spurred further growth that soon created a continuum with Hackney. The last of the nurseries for which Dalston was known had disappeared by 1891. The suburb was deemed more respectable than most of its neighbours and apparently some professional families who tried moving further afield discovered too many working-class newcomers in the remoter suburbs and returned to Dalston. In 1905 the Four Per Cent Industrial Dwellings Co. built Navarino Mansions for Jews from the EAST END. After World War II, the county and borough councils cleared large areas – some bomb-damaged, some not – for a series of housing estates that now accommodate the majority of Dalston's inhabitants. Dalston Junction station closed in 1986 when services to Broad Street station ceased. It is scheduled to reopen as part of the East London Line extension. Holy Trinity Church, on Beechwood Road, is the 'clown's church', where the great Joey Grimaldi is honoured with a painting, a stained-glass window and a special prayer at the annual clowns' service on the first Sunday in February each year. Ridley Road market has nearly 200 pitches, and an emphasis on world foods. Dalston Culture House is a new arts venue, and home to the Vortex jazz club. Its creation marks the first stage of the development of Gillett Square as one of the 100 new squares for London promoted by the Mayor of London. Dalston's population includes representatives of all London's main ethnic communities. It is a deprived area, but no more so than the rest of the borough.

Dalston was the setting for J M O'Neill's 1987 novel *Duffy is Dead*. Razorlight's *Don't Go Back to Dalston* is an infectiously jaunty track from their album *Up All Night*.

✉ E8

🧍 10,358

🚇 Silverlink Metro (Dalston Kingsland, zone 2)

Danson Park • Bexley
A historic parkland site and surrounding suburban development, situated west of BEXLEYHEATH and south of WELLING. It was first recorded as 'Dansington' in 1294. The 18th-century mansion at its heart was designed by Robert Taylor, architect of the Bank of England, and the park was landscaped in the style

of Capability Brown. In 1881 Alfred Bean, then owner of the Danson estate, began to develop the neighbouring suburb of Welling. Bean died in 1890 but his widow survived him for 31 years, and it was only after her death that the Danson estate was divided into lots and sold. Bexley council bought the mansion and 224 acres of parkland for £15,000 in 1924 and spent another £3,500 converting the park for public use. The remainder of the estate was sporadically developed for housing over a period of nearly 15 years with a variety of styles and sizes, from semi-detached bungalows to mock-Tudor mansions, plus a handful of modernist villas. Danson Junior School opened on Dansington Road in 1933. Post-war change in the Danson locality has mostly been limited to the improvement and enlargement of existing properties. Like most of the borough, the population of the Danson Park ward is more than 90 per cent white. Eighty-four per cent of homes are owner-occupied. Levels of educational attainment are relatively low.

The Grade I-listed mansion in Danson Park has recently been restored by its leaseholder, English Heritage, while the stable block has been converted into a bar and restaurant. The park is probably the borough's finest open space and boasts extensive sporting facilities. The lake is used for boating and windsurfing.

✉ Welling DA16; Bexleyheath DA6

👪 10,315

@ www.ideal-homes.org.uk/bexley/danson-estate.html (London surburban history site); www.dansonhouse.com

Dartmouth Park • *Camden/Islington*

A group of well-built Victorian estates in south HIGHGATE. Dartmouth Park Hill was originally part of the oldest road in Highgate, a mucky track through thick forest that later became part of the manor and parish boundaries. The earls of Dartmouth acquired much of the land here in the 18th century. To the south-west of their estate, luxurious four-bedroom homes lined Grove Terrace in 1780. Other impressive houses were built on the peripheral roads in the first half of the 19th century. Opposite the southern tip of Highgate Cemetery is Holly Village, built in 1865 for the retired servants of the Burdett-Coutts family, who lived on the other side of Swains Lane. Whittington Hospital evolved from a workhouse infirmary established in 1869 by the Poor Law guardians of St Pancras parish. In the 1870s the Dartmouths began to develop their estate and few gaps remained by the end of the century. Dartmouth Park Road was endowed with some very spacious properties but those nearer Dartmouth Park Hill were priced more affordably. The terraced houses of Highgate New Town extended across the borough border into Islington during the 1880s, while the Conservative Land Society laid out Spencer Rise, Churchill Road and Ingestre Road near TUFNELL PARK. Around the same time the New River Co. built a pumping station and two covered reservoirs on the east side of Dartmouth Park Hill. Dartmouth Park Lodge became a gatehouse for Waterlow Park when it opened in 1891. Twentieth-century evolution consisted of gap-filling and the subdivision of larger houses. Camden council redeveloped Highgate New Town in the 1970s in a scheme that has been called 'architecturally sculptural, but socially disastrous'. Local resident and Camden councillor John Thane courted controversy in 2005 when he argued that Dartmouth Park was 'a nice hotchpotch but why should that make it a conservation area?'.

The operatic impresario Richard D'Oyly Carte lived at 2 Dartmouth Park Road in the early 1860s, with his parents and many siblings.

✉ NW5; NW6 (Holly Village); N19

Dawley • *Hillingdon*

A little-used name for an industrial and commercial zone in HAYES, situated south of the Grand Union Canal. The manor was listed in Domesday Book as Dallega. The statesman and writer Henry St John, Viscount Bolingbroke acquired the 17th-century Dawley House in 1725 and substantially rebuilt it; Dryden, Pope, Swift and Voltaire were among his visitors here. In 1755, Henry, Earl of UXBRIDGE added the manor to his extensive landholdings in the district and built a mile-long wall around Dawley House to keep out smallpox. Dawley House was demolished in 1776 and its once-beautiful gardens became brickfields. The de Salis family acquired the estate and sold it off little by little over the following 160 years. The Gramophone Co. (later EMI) moved its headquarters to Blyth Road in 1911 and opened a factory and recording studio here. It is said that the company bought all the chickens in the neighbourhood to prevent their cackling being picked up by the recording apparatus. Between the wars other manufacturers colonized the whole area between the canal and the railway line. By the early 1960s, EMI owned 150 acres of land and employed 14,000 staff. The company progressively withdrew from Dawley, relocating its offices, closing the factory, spinning off its central research laboratories and selling the site to a Far Eastern fund in 1999. A slow-moving regeneration programme is under way, but has been constrained by the designation of much of Dawley as a conservation area.

✉ Hayes UB3

📖 B T White, *The History of Dawley (Middlesex)*, Hayes and Harlington Local History Society, 2001

De Beauvoir Town • *Hackney* (pronounced 'de beaver' by purists, but *à la française* by most locals)

A contrasting community of council tower blocks and early Victorian villas in west DAL-STON, separated from HOXTON by the Regent's Canal. Richard Benyon de Beauvoir laid out the estate in the 1840s and its civilized proportions made it popular with wealthy commuters to the nearby City. The 20th century brought multi-occupation of many of the properties, accompanied by a general urban decay, and in the 1960s Hackney council demolished nearly a third of the original estate to build low- and high-rise flats. Since then, designation as a conservation area and a vigorous local campaign have made the most of what remains. De Beauvoir Square is well-preserved except on the east side, with the result that the flats of the Lockner estate have the best view. The main streets that border De Beauvoir exhibit the typical Hackney mix of low-rent shops and service industries. At De Beauvoir Primary School, 37 per cent of pupils have English as an additional language, with most at an early stage of English acquisition, according to a 2001 report by the educational standards agency Ofsted. A number of children come from families of refugees and asylum-seekers housed at nearby hostels. Population mobility is very high, with more than a third of pupils joining the school at other than the usual time of entry.

✉ N1

👤 9,928 (De Beauvoir ward, which includes Kingsland and part of Hoxton)

📖 Brian MacArthur (ed.), *De Beauvoir Town Millennium Scrapbook*, De Beauvoir Scrapbook Association, 1999 (a first-class community survey)

Denmark Hill • *Lambeth/Southwark*

A street and locality in south CAMBERWELL, connecting with HERNE HILL at its southern end. Originally Camberwell's High Street, the street was renamed in honour of Queen Anne's husband, Prince George of Denmark (1653–1708), who had a residence here. Limited suburban development began in the 1780s on land belonging to the de Crespigny family, French Huguenots who had settled here a century earlier. Their seat, Champion Lodge, was demolished in 1841 to make way for more housing. In the following year the writer John Ruskin moved into a detached house on the hill and stayed here for almost three decades. Even after the arrival of the railway in 1866, the emphasis remained on building substantial villas, rather than the high-density terraced houses that had consumed other parts of Camberwell. At the southern end, this restraint was the policy of the governors of the Dulwich College estate. Denmark Hill (now Lyndhurst) School opened on Grove Lane in 1905 and Ruskin Park was created two years later. In 1913, King's College Hospital relocated to new premises in Denmark Hill and established a separate school of medicine here. The school acquired a house on Champion Hill as a students' hall of residence. The Maudsley Hospital opened in 1923 as a London County Council hospital for the early treatment of acute mental illness; it is now part of the King's College campus. King's College added a dental hospital and teaching school in the late 1960s. William Booth College, on Champion Park, was built in 1932 by Sir Giles Gilbert Scott. Its monumental style is reminiscent of Scott's BANKSIDE power station, now the Tate Modern gallery. Council housing now occupies much of the hinterland but many older properties survive on the main road, including some detached houses from the early 19th century. The locality's main ethnic groups are of British, Caribbean and African descent. A government-sponsored survey conducted in 2003 rated Denmark Hill one of the noisiest roads in south London.

It has been claimed that the sport of roller hockey, now especially popular in the USA and southern Europe, was invented at Denmark Hill's Lava rink in 1885.

✉ SE5

🚃 South Eastern Trains; Southern (limited service) (zone 2)

Deptford • *Lewisham/Greenwich* (pronounced 'de(p)tfəd')

A historic Thames-side settlement, situated west of GREENWICH. Its name was first recorded in 1293 and is a corruption of 'deep ford'.

In *The Spirit of London's River*, L M Bates says of Deptford waterfront, 'This was the ground from which, more than any other, grew the British Empire'. Henry VIII founded a naval dockyard here in 1513 and within a century Deptford had become one of the country's leading ports and a major industrial suburb. Many of the greatest figures of 16th- and 17th-century English history had associations with Deptford. In 1577 Francis Drake sailed from Deptford via Plymouth on his three-year circumnavigation of the globe, claiming a portion of present-day California for Elizabeth I; on his return, Drake was knighted by the Queen after she had dined aboard the *Golden Hind* at Deptford. In 1593 the dramatist Christopher Marlowe was killed here, reputedly in a tavern brawl. Anthony Burgess's *A Dead Man in Deptford* is one of the works to suggest a conspiratorial aspect to his death. The diarist John Evelyn came to Deptford in 1652 to live at Sayes Court, a house belonging to his wife's family, which he rented to Peter the Great of Russia in 1698 during the Tsar's visit to learn the art of shipbuilding. Evelyn discovered woodcarver and sculptor Grinling Gibbons toiling in a lowly Deptford workshop and introduced him to Christopher Wren; Gibbons went on to become a master carver under five British sovereigns. Another illustrious diarist, Samuel Pepys, worked in Deptford as an admiralty official. The government and private dockyards of Deptford flourished during the Napoleonic Wars and Deptford New Town was laid out in the locality now known as ST JOHNS. The early arrival of the railway in 1836 brought new residents to Deptford but did not prevent dock-related industries moving to more convenient purpose-built sites elsewhere on the river. From the closure of the dockyard in 1869 and of the cattle market that replaced it in 1913, through World War II bombing and post-war industrial decline, Deptford has suffered a long and damaging period of deterioration but it is now the focus of extensive regenerative building, both commercial and residential, from Deptford Bridge in the south to the Pepys estate by the river. Deptford Creek is the planned site for further riverside developments. Deptford High Street still has terraced buildings from the late 17th century and the 18th century and, although these are sometimes hard to spot amidst the newer intrusions, they represent an undervalued part of London's architectural heritage. Deptford has a large black community, mostly of African origin. With few pensioners and many children, the average resident of Evelyn ward is aged only 30.7 years, compared with 38.6 years for England and Wales as a whole. Less than one-fifth of homes are owner-occupied and 15 per cent are single-parent households. Deptford has London's largest Buddhist community, comprising 4.4 per cent of the total population. According to a 2005 press story, a new mathematical formula has determined that the High Street is London's best place to shop.

The Deptford pink (*Dianthus armeria*) is a protected species of wildflower with diamond-shaped deep pink petals, but its name is apparently a case of mistaken identity. The National Maritime Museum has L S Lowry's nondescript *View of Deptford Power Station from Greenwich* (1959). The band Dire Straits was founded in Deptford in 1977, and Squeeze debuted on the ironically titled label Deptford Fun City. The seminal punk fanzine *Sniffin' Glue* flourished in Deptford around the same time. New indie stars Athlete have been called 'Deptford's answer to Steely Dan'.

✉ SE8

🚶 14,512 (Lewisham's Evelyn ward)

🚆 South Eastern Trains (Deptford, zone 2); Docklands Light Railway, Lewisham branch (Deptford Bridge, zones 2 and 3)

📖 Jess Steele, *Turning the Tide: The History of Everyday Deptford*, Deptford Forum, 1993; Neil Gordon-Orr, *Deptford Fun City: A Ramble through the History and Music of New Cross and Deptford*, Past Tense, 2004

@ www.deptford.towntalk.co.uk (commercial local information site)

Derry Downs · *Bromley*

One of the few Victorian developments in the Cray valley, located on the edge of the green belt south-east of ST MARY CRAY. There seems to be no record of the name before the second half of the 19th century, nor an explanation of its derivation. However, the words 'derry down' were often used meaninglessly in old ballads. From 1866 until around the end of the century houses were built on and near the road called Derry Downs, including some substantial villas. This was a piecemeal project, with plots sold separately and each house designed individually. In 1897 William Cook, the breeder of the ORPINGTON Buff chicken, lent his eldest son the money to buy Elm Cottage (now Elmdene, 51 Derry Downs). Cook's son appears to have started up a competitive poultry farm here, and the two fell out.

Rebuilding and expansion since World War II has altered the character of Derry Downs but several Victorian properties survive. The Cockmannings estate, jutting into pig-rearing country further to the south-east, takes its name from a house once owned by the Manning family, lords of the manor of KEVINGTON, and from the cockpit in its grounds. The neighbouring farmland, part of the North Downs, is criss-crossed with public footpaths and is popular with cross-country runners.

✉ Orpington BR5

Devons Road • *Tower Hamlets*

A lacklustre street and Docklands Light Railway station located between BOW COMMON and BROMLEY-BY-BOW. Devons Road was built up in the mid 19th century with terraced housing for the industrial workers of Bow and Bromley. In the early 1870s funds from the sale of the City Church of All Hallows, Staining, which stood near FENCHURCH STREET, were used to build All Hallows' Church here. Spratt's pet biscuit factory was built in Violet Road in 1899 and has now been converted into imposing flats and offices. Until World War II, Devons Road was a busy shopping street with market stalls but the area was earmarked for large-scale redevelopment almost as soon as hostilities ended and the Devons estate of 442 flats was completed in 1949, with more estates following later. The bomb-damaged All Hallows was rebuilt in 1955 and is now the parish church of Bromley-by-Bow. Two semi-derelict Victorian shops in Devons Road were the first properties to be managed by Acme Studios, marking the beginnings of an organization that became one of the greatest providers of working and living space for artists in the United Kingdom. Devons Road was formerly the site of British Railways' first all-diesel maintenance depot, situated beside the tracks of the Blackwall railway line but there was no station here until the Docklands Light Railway system opened in 1987. Devons Road's depressing post-war streetscape has been relieved recently by the construction of some pleasant social housing but the area remains down-at-heel, although it retains a hint of old EAST END character.

The Widow's Son pub, at 75 Devons Road, is also known as 'the Bun House'. Both names derive from the story of a widow who set aside a hot cross bun for her son, who was on a sea voyage. He never returned, so she hung the bun from the ceiling in mourning and repeated this act every Easter afterwards. When a pub was built on the site around 1848, the publican retained the custom and the annual 'hanging of the bun' was made a clause in the lease of the building. Sailors to this day perform the ceremony on Good Friday.

✉ E3

🚆 Docklands Light Railway, Stratford branch (zone 2)

Docklands • *Tower Hamlets/Newham/Southwark*

The area covered by the former ports of London, originally 'Dockland', a term invented by journalists at the beginning of the 20th century. Docklands extends from TOWER Bridge to BECKTON on the north side of the Thames, and from LONDON BRIDGE to ROTHERHITHE on the south. Nowadays, however, the term is often used in specific reference to the vicinity of CANARY WHARF. Waterfront development began at WAPPING and ST KATHERINE'S in the Middle Ages and progressively extended eastwards and across the river as Britain's role as a trading nation increased. From the beginning of the 19th century inland docks were constructed to improve handling capacity and provide greater security from theft. Shipbuilding was concentrated on the ISLE OF DOGS. Speculative builders crammed cheap housing for dockworkers into networks of narrow streets in districts like CANNING TOWN and POPLAR and – to a higher standard – in CUBITT TOWN. The London docks were ravaged by bombing in World War II and never fully recovered afterwards. The use of containers and the increased size of ocean-going vessels progressively rendered the facilities redundant from the 1960s and 18,000 jobs had been lost by the time the last docks closed in 1981. In that year, the London Docklands Development Corporation was established to find new uses for the derelict sites. On the south side of the Thames, the Surrey Docks (now SURREY QUAYS) were mostly filled in and covered by housing. In the north, most of Wapping Dock was also filled in but other large docks were preserved for their aesthetic value or for new purposes. St Katherine Docks became a marina, while the ROYAL DOCKS were used for watersports. North of the ROYAL ALBERT Dock a new town was built at Beckton. Commercial development was more tentative at first, partly owing to the precarious state of the economy at that time. The LDDC invested in infrastructural improvements, notably in the form of the Docklands Light Railway, and LONDON CITY AIRPORT opened in 1987. With the eventual success of the Manhattan-style project at Canary Wharf, financial companies have relocated to Docklands in droves, causing consternation in the CITY OF LONDON. Up-market apartment complexes have lined the riverside, and continue to push eastwards. Critics have expressed concerns about the architectural quality of some of the schemes and the fragmentation of long-established communities, but the economic success of Docklands regeneration is undeniable and will ensure that the last remaining disued sites are intensively exploited over the coming decade.

Stephen Poliakoff's 1991 film *Close My Eyes* captured the evolving new world of Docklands.

> ✉ E14; E16; SE16; E1

> 📖 Andrew Church, *Discovering Cities: London Docklands*, Geographical Association, 2003; Chris Ellmers and Alex Warner, *Dockland Life: A Pictorial History of London's Docks 1860–2000*, Mainstream, 2000; Janet Foster, *Docklands*, UCL Press, 1998

Dollis Hill • *Brent*

A multi-ethnic residential district situated between NEASDEN and CRICKLEWOOD, at one time known as Dollar's Hill. The name may be of 16th-century origin, and connected with a family called Dalley. Surprisingly, the etymology of nearby Dollis Brook may not be the same, although the spellings have converged owing to their proximity. Oxgate Farm, located at the southern end of Coles Green Road, was formerly one of WILLESDEN'S manor houses and is among the oldest buildings in Brent. The 96-acre Gladstone Park, created in 1901, dominates the district. The park was once the grounds of Dollis Hill House, built in the early 19th century and visited frequently by William Gladstone (prime minister four times between 1868 and 1894) when it was owned by Lord Aberdeen (prime minister 1852–5). The American author Mark Twain spent the summer here in 1900, writing that, 'From the house you can see little but spacious stretches of hay-fields and green turf … Yet the massed, brick blocks of London are reachable in three minutes on a horse.' Most of Dollis Hill's undulating meadows were obliterated by suburban housebuilding before and after World War I. Dollis Hill was an early place of migration for Jewish Londoners moving out of the EAST END. The progressively designed concrete synagogue opened in 1938. It is now in use as a school. Today, the main religious

minorities are Muslims and Hindus. Perhaps unexpectedly, Dollis Hill also has London's highest percentage of Irish residents (whether measured by place of birth or declared ethnicity), many of whom have 'graduated' here from districts like KILBURN and HARLESDEN. Dollis Hill House was badly damaged by fire in 1996 and plans for its restoration are still under consideration at the time of writing. The neighbouring walled garden, however, is kept in immaculate condition with flower displays changed three times a year, while the stable block hosts art exhibitions.

In 1934 the Post Office engineering research station opened in Brook Road. Two War Cabinet meetings were held in the bomb-proofed basement of an outbuilding there, and the wartime prime minister Winston Churchill briefly retained a flat at nearby Neville's Court. The research station was the British base of the 'innocent' in Ian McEwan's 1990 novel of that name. In the mid 1990s the property was sold to a developer who converted the main building into luxury flats and built a new housing estate on the rest of the site.

> ✉ NW2; NW10

> 👥 12,102

> 🚇 Jubilee Line (zone 3)

> 📖 M C Barrès-Baker, *Cricklewood and Dollis Hill*, Grange Museum of Community History and Brent Archive, 2001

Dormers Wells • *Ealing*

Primarily a group of council estates in northeast SOUTHALL, bordering GREENFORD. The well was first recorded in the 13th century, and was reputed to have medicinal properties. An 'old moated castle' called Dorman's Well may have been built for Edward Cheeseman, cofferer (treasurer) to Henry VII, and was certainly in the possession of Robert Cheeseman on his death in 1547, when a chapel also stood here. The Dorman's Well estate subsequently belonged to the lords of the manor of Norwood and the house is said to have gradually fallen into ruin. Only traces of the moat now survive. Dorman's Well had become a manor in its own right by the 18th century, consisting of a 108-acre farm. The present form of the name evolved in the 19th century, when Dormers Wells Farm was owned by the Earl of Jersey, as an outlying part of his OSTERLEY possessions. Dormers Wells remained little more than a single farm until after World War I, when developers began to build houses for the lower middle classes. Between 1926 and

1928 more than 700 houses were built in the neighbouring hamlet of Mount Pleasant, which lay just to the west and has since been absorbed within Dormers Wells. Boys' and girls' secondary schools opened in 1934. The council built up the area intensively from the 1960s, in the form of the Havelock, Windmill and Golf Links estates, which included a number of tower blocks. Problems of deprivation, crime, racism and drug use were widespread by the 1980s. As a result of a neighbourhood renewal initiative, there has been significant new building lately, generally of smaller blocks. Other measures, such as improved security and the installation of closed circuit television networks have made the area safer. Many of the streets of Dormers Wells are named after British inventors and discoverers, with no connection to the largely Asian population, most of whom are of Indian origin. There is also a small Somali community. Dormers Wells High School has faced obstacles in the past, partly because few of its pupils come from homes where English is the first language, but its performance has improved markedly in recent years.

✉ Southall UB1

🚶 13,073

Downe · *Bromley*

A country village and potential world heritage site located three miles south-west of ORPINGTON. The name was first recorded in 1283 and derives from the Old English dūn, a hill. It is claimed that the Post Office encouraged its spelling with an 'e' to avoid confusion with County Down in Ulster. This is a very scattered village, with weatherboarded cottages and brick and flint houses dotted around in all directions but especially to the south. A chapel was built in 1291 and may have stood on the site of the present St Mary's Church. The fabric of the present church dates primarily from the 16th century. Downe Court was built in 1690 on the site of an earlier manor house, which was probably surrounded by a moat. English Heritage has placed Downe Court on its register of buildings at risk because it is 'starting to show the effects of long term neglect'. On LUXTED Road, Petleys was built in the early 18th century and became a home of the Wedgwood pottery family. In 1842 Josiah Wedgwood's daughter Emma came to live at Down House, a former parsonage at the southern end of the village, with her husband Charles Darwin. The great scientist took a daily stroll around a circuit of the

grounds known as the 'sand walk', set up a laboratory in a brick hut and cultivated orchids in the greenhouse. Darwin lived at Down House until his death in 1882 and he wrote all his most important works here, including *On the Origin of Species by Means of Natural Selection*. Downe remained a farming village into the 20th century, producing fruit and vegetables for the London markets. With its isolated location, the village attracted walkers and cyclists to its tearooms and pubs. Numerous shops served the resident farm labourers. Down House became a Darwin museum in 1929 and was acquired by English Heritage in 1996. Darwin's study, where he did most of his writing and microscope work, has been recreated from photographs. Crammed with books, files and specimens, its amenities included a spittoon and a discreetly curtained privy. Modern educational displays fill the rooms of the first floor. To the south-east of the house is Downe Bank – or Orchis Bank, as Darwin knew it. Now a Kent Wildlife Trust property, the wood is rich in orchids and provides one of Britain's best displays of bluebells in spring. In 2006 the British government nominated Down House and the surrounding area in which Darwin walked and thought as a world heritage site. As the Department for Culture, Media and Sport has pointed out: 'Few properties and their environs can claim to have been as central to the life and work of one person as Down House'; Unesco's world heritage committee will decide whether to approve the nomination in summer 2007.

✉ Orpington BR6

📖 Janet Browne, *Charles Darwin: The Power of Place*, Jonathan Cape, 2002

@ www.english-heritage.org.uk; www.bromley.org/ciswebpl/Darwin (World Heritage Site nomination); cudhamanddowne.org (St Mary the Virgin Church, Downe site)

Downham · *Lewisham/Bromley*

A cottage estate, also referred to as a 'garden city', situated midway between CATFORD and BROMLEY. It is named after William Hayes Fisher, first Baron Downham, chairman of the London County Council until his death in 1920. From 1924 to 1930 the LCC erected a huge estate of 6,000 homes on former farmland, part of which had been a popular walking spot known as Seven Fields. Road names were taken from old field names and, for no recorded reason, from Devon resorts and

Arthurian legend. A further 1,000 homes were added in north Downham in 1937. Most of the tenants were relocated from decaying inner city areas on the south side of the Thames, such as BERMONDSEY, DEPTFORD and ROTHERHITHE. A population of more than 30,000 materialized where there had been a handful just a few years before. By the standards of the time, this was cheap, basic housing but it was eminently preferable to many post-war council estates. Many of the early residents, however, found the twelve shillings a week rent for a one-bedroom house too high and had to move. Right-to-buy legislation has now brought many homes into private ownership, but has perhaps also detracted from the sense of community, and Downham is more popular for its affordability than as the showpiece estate its creators intended. The old Downham baths and library are being replaced by the Downham lifestyle centre, which will include extensive leisure facilities and a health centre, community hall and library when it opens in 2007. Located in a 20-acre parkland setting, the lifestyle centre is the cornerstone of a government-backed initiative to 'restore focus and pride to the entire Downham area'. Some funds for the £16-million project will come from the sale of two surplus council-owned depots to Wates Homes for the construction of a residential estate with a proportion of affordable housing.

The Downham Tavern used to have a place in the *Guinness Book of Records* as Britain's largest pub. Built by the LCC in 1930, it could accommodate 1,000 customers.

✉ Bromley BR1

👤 14,311 (Lewisham's Downham ward)

📖 Alistair Black, *The Downham Estate, 1924–1939*, manuscript essay deposited with local libraries, 1985

@ www.downhamonline.org.uk (community site)

Downtown • *Southwark*

A riverside locality in east ROTHERHITHE, covering the area north of GREENLAND DOCK and south of Downtown Road. The Downtown estate was a large interwar scheme of mainly three-storey deck-access flats and maisonettes built in the classic municipal style and providing homes for workers at the Surrey docks. Downtown was very badly affected by bombing in World War II and the subsequent decline of the docks sealed the fate of the estate. Many of the properties had become van-

dalized squats by the time they came within the purview of the London Docklands Development Corporation in the early 1980s. Under the terms of the 'Downtown package' Southwark council and the LDDC worked with several housing associations and developers to build new town houses and apartments and refurbish viable older buildings. The new housing was initially well-signposted but this caused problems when some visitors to London found themselves in Downtown when they had expected to arrive in the WEST END. The final phase of the Downtown project is not yet complete because of protracted disagreements between the developers and local residents, many of whom have expressed a preference for things to remain 'low and green' and have formed the Downtown Defence Campaign to promote their position.

✉ SE16

@ www.downtowndefence.co.uk (community site)

Drayton Green • *Ealing*

A jumbled locality situated on the HANWELL/ EALING border. The green itself is an unexciting recreation ground. The name Drayton was first recorded in the 14th century and may have referred to a farm where loads were hauled up the slope from the River Brent. The words 'drag', 'draw' and 'dray' all derive from the same Norse word, 'draga'. The hamlet became known as Drayton Green to distinguish it from WEST DRAYTON, and it was also called Drayton in Ealing. In the early 19th century this was the only settlement north of the Uxbridge Road in Ealing parish, apart from Haven Green, which is now part of the town centre. At this time its few buildings occupied much the same positions as they had done almost two centuries earlier. The estate of Park House covered all the land west of Argyle Road, northwards over Cuckoo Hill to the Ruislip Road and was owned by Sir Archibald MacDonald, an MP who was Attorney-General in 1788–93 and subsequently a judge. Benjamin Sharpe bought the house in 1848 and it passed to his son, Sir Montague Sharpe, in 1883, but it was derelict not long afterwards and subsequently demolished. By this time, housing was converging on Drayton Green from the south and east, and Greenford Avenue, a new road from the Park Hotel, was made in 1886. Other new roads soon followed and Hanwell slowly encroached upon Park House. Drayton Bridge Road was constructed in 1897 and built upon around 1905, when

Drayton Green station opened. Ealing borough council acquired the four-acre green soon afterwards and preserved it as an open space. Middlesex County Council bought the Park House site for Drayton Manor School in 1926. Each side of the green now presents a different aspect: interwar suburban to the north, Victorian to the east, light industrial to the south, and modern municipal to the west. Drayton Green has a richly diverse ethnic mix, including residents of white, black African (especially Somali), black Caribbean and Indian backgrounds.

✉ W7; W13

🚆 First Great Western Link (zone 4)

Drayton Park • *Islington*

A residential and light industrial area centred on the street of that name in west HIGHBURY. The first roads were laid out around 1840 and development progressed gradually until the opening of the Great Northern Railway's CANONBURY spur line in 1874. New sidings and depots brought industry to the area, including a gasworks and paper-staining works. The council built its first depot here in 1937. Drayton Park suffered badly from wartime bombing and the London County Council compulsorily purchased and cleared land here in the 1950s. This is now a multi-ethnic community, with significant Turkish and Bengali minorities, and nearly 30 different languages are spoken at Drayton Park Primary School. Even so, half the households have a car, the highest proportion in the borough. The housing stock includes owner-occupied and privately rented homes, as well as some social accommodation. The Emirates Stadium in Ashburton Grove is the new home of ARSENAL Football Club, and opened in 2006; the much-delayed project has created a 60,000-seat stadium and associated community buildings, with the cost of relocating pre-existing industry and a waste recycling centre absorbing almost half the total budget. The stadium's construction has been more than just a football issue, as the project is the largest development in Islington for many years and has regeneration implications for the whole area.

John Lydon, formerly Johnny Rotten of the Sex Pistols, was born in Benwell Road in 1956, although he considers the street to be part of FINSBURY PARK. Prime Minister Tony Blair lived in Stavordale Road from 1976 until 1982, when he moved to Barnsbury.

✉ N5; N7

🚆 WAGN (zone 2); station open weekdays only, though football specials may be introduced

Drury Lane • *Westminster/Camden*

A historic COVENT GARDEN thoroughfare, representing the eastern edge of London's 'THEATRELAND'. Until the construction of Kingsway in 1905, this was the principal route from High Holborn to the STRAND, which it used to join at a point near St Clement Dane's Church. The road was described as 'old' when it was first recorded in 1199 and went under several names, including the Via de Aldewych and Fortescu Lane. Its present name derives from Drury House, built in the mid 16th century for Sir William Drury. By 1650, gentlemen's houses lined both sides of the lane and the first Theatre Royal was established in 1663. Nell Gwynne began selling oranges in Drury Lane around this time and soon made her first appearance on the theatre's stage. The Theatre Royal burned down in the early 1670s and was rebuilt with almost three times its original capacity. By this time the neighbourhood was acquiring a reputation for crime, disorder and prostitution. The actor David Garrick and writer Richard Brinsley Sheridan managed the theatre in the second half of the 18th century and it was rebuilt again in 1794 and finally in 1812. Drury Lane's impoverished conditions persisted until the late 19th century, when its squalid courts were cleared and replaced by model dwellings and commercial properties.

Drury Lane was the name of an amateur sleuth created by Ellery Queen in the 1930s. Lane was a Shakespearean actor, retired through deafness, who turned his keen intellect to solving 'tragedies' that had baffled the police.

✉ WC2

📖 Brian Dobbs, *Drury Lane: Three Centuries of the Theatre Royal, 1663–1971*, Cassell, 1972

Duck's Hill • *Hillingdon*

A rural community in west NORTHWOOD, formerly the site of the RUISLIP parish workhouse, when surrounding farmland was allocated to 'industrious, poor labouring men'. The name derives from a 16th-century landowner, not the local wildfowl. In the 1850s, Daniel Norton, an UXBRIDGE timber merchant, acquired Maze Farm and established the Northwood Park estate. Norton bought and demolished neighbouring properties to create a park of almost 200 acres, and rebuilt the farmhouse as Northwood Hall. The estate was sold in 1902 and Mount Vernon Hospital was built on the northern part, in French-chateau style. It has become a specialist cancer centre but there are plans to move the in-patient facilities to a new hospital at Hatfield, Hertfordshire, at the end of 2011. At Duck's Hill plantation, Joseph Conn built himself a large house that was used by American special forces during World War II for planning clandestine operations. It was renamed Battle of Britain House after the war, and served as a college before burning down in 1984. The site is now being allowed to return to woodland. Northwood Hall became a boys' school for a while, and then stood empty until it was bought in 1925 by Alfred Denville MP and converted into a rest home for retired actors. Now called Denville Hall, the house has recently been remodelled, with a crescent-shaped extension added within newly landscaped grounds. The Copse Wood estate comprised the northern extremity of the RUISLIP MANOR development.

> ✉ Northwood HA6

Ducks Island • *Barnet*

A compact, little-known locality situated in south-west BARNET, separated from TOTTERIDGE by Dollis Brook. Mays Lane runs across its northern edge. Ducks Island formerly lay isolated on the edge of Barnet Common, but was never cut off by water – and the brook rarely runs deep enough now to support waterfowl. The name may have been a humorous reference to the boggy clay terrain, which was fit only for ducks, or it may have referred to duck shoots that took place in the fields. During the latter part of the 19th century a cluster of dwellings formed around the junction of Mays Lane and Chesterfield Road and a mission hall was established. Streets of drab semi-detached houses were laid out on part of Whitings Hill Farm shortly before World War II and Barnet council added a small estate of 15 houses on Connaught Road in 1953. Ducks Island recreation ground has gardens and a children's play area.

> ✉ Barnet EN5

Dudden Hill • *Brent*

A little-used name for the residential locality created in the early 20th century on the north side of WILLESDEN. Dudden or Duddinghill field was first recorded in 1363. The name may be linked to the northern word 'dod', which can mean 'a distinct shoulder or boss of a hill'. A windmill stood in Dudden Hill field from around 1616 until the late 18th cen-

tury. By the mid 19th century much of the area belonged to Dudden Hill Farm. Passenger trains began to call at the Midland Railway's Dudding Hill station in 1875, but the service was abandoned at the turn of the century – just as development was taking off. The Dudding Park Estate Co. led this early phase of development. In 1909 the Metropolitan Railway Co. opened a station here, which they called DOLLIS HILL; the naming of the station has been the principal reason for the loss of Dudden Hill's identity. Dudden Hill Lane was widened in the early 1920s to allow improved access to the Empire Exhibition at Wembley. Medium-sized semi-detached houses filled the area north of the railway line in the decade before World War II. The sequence of streets was supposed to begin with consecutive letters of the alphabet, but last-minute planning changes caused a couple of omissions. There was some industry too, notably a manufacturer of telephone equipment. Willesden College of Technology opened on Denzil Road in 1934 and took over the buildings of the former Dudden Hill Lane School in 1964. It is now the Willesden centre of the College of North West London, one of the largest further education colleges in the UK. The Dudden Hill ward has a similar demographic profile to that of Brent as a whole, but with a slightly larger white population and fewer residents of Indian origin, though they are still the largest minority.

In Mark Haddon's best-selling novel *The Curious Incident of the Dog in the Night-Time*, Christopher goes to stay with his mother in Chapter Road, off Dudden Hill Lane (which he calls Hill Lane, probably because he misread his A–Z).

> ✉ NW2; NW10

> ♦ 13,350

> 📖 M C Barrès-Baker, *Neasden and Dudden Hill*, Grange Museum of Community History and Brent Archive, 2001

Dulwich • *Southwark* (pronounced 'dullitch' or 'dullidge')

A collegiate village situated five miles south of the CITY OF LONDON, hemmed in by more prosaic neighbours that have traded on its prestige. First recorded as Dilwihs in a charter signed by King Edgar in 967, the name derives from the Old English words 'dile wisc', meaning 'dill meadow'. Despite its close historical links with CAMBERWELL, to the north-west, Dulwich has remained distinct and has long been more exclusive. This is almost entirely due to the role of Dulwich College, founded in 1619 by the actor Edward Alleyn as the College of God's Gift, which consisted of almshouses and a school for under-privileged boys. To the north of the school, fine houses for City gentlemen filled DULWICH VILLAGE in the 18th century, and many survive to the present day. Villas and lodges also fringed the north side of the common, which was enclosed in 1805. There were humbler cottages too, but these have mostly gone. Sir John Soane built the school's picture gallery and the founder's mausoleum in 1814. A work of art in itself, the gallery has paintings by Rubens, Rembrandt, Van Dyck and Gainsborough. Most of the college buildings were erected in the late 1860s, financed by the sale of land to the South Eastern and Chatham Railway Co. Alleyn's School and James Allen's Girls' School are spin-offs from the college, and are located on opposite sides of East Dulwich Grove. Speculative builders created the new suburb of EAST DULWICH following the opening in 1868 of the station, which was originally called Champion Hill. NORTH DULWICH took shape at the beginning of the 20th century, after the sale of Dulwich House, while the main phase of development in WEST DULWICH came in the years before World War I. The governors of Dulwich College have preserved the surrounding fields either as parkland or playing fields to prevent the intrusion of suburbia, though the fringes were colonized by small blocks of London County Council flats after World War II. More recently, planning permission has occasionally been granted for luxury estates bordering the sports grounds in the south of the district. Many of the large Victorian and Edwardian houses in Dulwich have been subdivided into flats and occupied by young professionals but the village remains an exclusive enclave.

Literary figures educated in Dulwich have included Raymond Chandler and P G Wodehouse at Dulwich College; C S Forester and V S Pritchett at Alleyn's School; and Anita Brookner at James Allen's Girls; School. Jimmy Perry's suburban television comedy *The Gnomes of Dulwich* paired Hugh Lloyd and Terry Scott in the late 1960s. Both Mr Pickwick and Lady Thatcher bought retirement homes in Dulwich, although the latter hasn't occupied hers.

✉ SE21; SE22

♦ 20,778 (College and Village wards)

🚆 Southern (East Dulwich, zone 2; North Dulwich, zones 2 and 3); South Eastern Trains

(West Dulwich, zone 3

📖 Richard Tames, *Dulwich and Camberwell Past*, Historical Publications, 1997; Mary Boast, *The Story of Dulwich*, London Borough of Southwark, 1990

@ www.dulwich.co.uk (community site and portal)

Dulwich Village • *Southwark*

A charming road and a storybook hamlet, situated north of DULWICH College. Until the early 17th century, when Edward Alleyn acquired the lordship of the manor and established the college, this was an area of cornfields, with a few scattered windmills, farmhouses and cottages. From the early 18th century, and especially after the mid 1760s, college allowed wealthy Londoners – often the parents of pupils – to build substantial houses that would maintain their value, and that of the estate. A number of these remain, and only a few have been converted to flats or for other purposes. On Gallery Road, Belair is a well-proportioned villa built in 1765 for a Whitechapel corn merchant, and now housing a restaurant. Its grounds are open to the public. The college subsequently permitted more homes to be built, of a progressively more affordable character, but nevertheless kept the numbers down and the standards up. In 1860 the village pond was filled in, and covered by the shops of Commerce Place, now 25–49 Dulwich Village. Dulwich Park was formed in 1890 from the fields of Dulwich Court Farm and its neighbours. Soon afterwards, the Crown and Greyhound took the place of two 18th-century inns as the focal point of the village. Around this time, new streets of redbrick terraced houses linked Dulwich Village with Turney Road. Some of the village's cottage shops have been converted into homes. In the 20th century, building mostly took the form of pastiche replacements of Georgian properties. There are two primary schools, Dulwich Village and Dulwich Hamlet, both of which were rated as outstanding by the national education standards agency Ofsted in 2005. The Village ward, which includes HERNE HILL, is a highly atypical part of the borough: two-thirds of homes are owner-occupied, with an average of six rooms per household; 86 per cent of residents are white; and 56 per cent of 16- to 74-year-olds are qualified to degree level or higher.

✉ SE21

♦ 10,484 (Village ward)

Ealing • *Ealing*

The 'queen of the suburbs', situated west of ACTON and eight miles from central London. Ealing has been occupied since the Iron Age but the name is derived from the Old English Gillingas, which meant 'the settlement of Gilla's people' and was recorded as early as the 7th century. The parish church of St Mary's was built in the early 12th century and has since been much altered and enlarged. The early village of Ealing grew up around the church, while another hamlet evolved to the north, at Haven Green. Until the late 18th century these nuclei were surrounded by open countryside, bisected by a road running east to west that subsequently became Uxbridge Road (A4020) and the Broadway. Sir John Soane acquired Pitshanger Manor in 1800 and rebuilt most of it, while retaining an earlier west wing by George Dance. A later extension is now a repertory gallery of contemporary art, while the main house has a permanent collection of ceramics and is hired out for weddings and other functions. Ealing council has rebranded this double act the P M Gallery and House. With the arrival in 1838 of the Great Western Railway, speculative builders began to put up semi-detached houses for the new middle classes. Growth was slow until the 1870s but surged with the improvement of rail services in that decade. The formerly separate hamlet of Ealing Dean metamorphosed into WEST EALING as terraced and semi-detached houses formed a continuum with HANWELL, while another old hamlet, LITTLE EALING, experienced a wave of building after SOUTH EALING station opened in 1883. From just 4,000 a century earlier, Ealing's population had increased to 105,000 by 1901, the year that it became the first Middlesex borough to receive a charter and elect a mayor. Charles Jones, the borough surveyor for 50 years, was responsible for much of the new public building, including the Town Hall. EALING BROADWAY grew as a shopping centre, and open spaces such as Walpole Park contributed to Ealing's reputation as the greenest of London's boroughs. The coming of electric tram services to Uxbridge Road in 1901 and the electrification of the District Railway in 1908 brought more growth to fringe localities such as NORTHFIELDS. BRENTHAM garden suburb was built between 1901 and 1915 as an Arts and Crafts-inspired pioneering project in co-operative housing. Ealing boomed as London's industry increasingly moved west after World War I, benefiting from the construction of Western Avenue (A40) and the North Circular Road (A406) in the 1920s. Interwar developments in NORTH EALING included the mock-Tudor estate on HANGER HILL. After World War II, the borough continued to grow and change, with immigration creating several minority groups; of these, the most distinctive is Ealing's large Polish community, which has increased markedly in recent years as a result of Poland's accession to the European Union. Other eastern European nationals have also been drawn to the area. The subdivision of Victorian villas into flats has attracted young graduates, while the London campus of Thames Valley University is located on St Mary's Road.

Established in 1902, Ealing Studios was acquired in the early 1930s by Basil Dean, the owner of Associated Talking Pictures, with Michael Balcon joining as head of production in 1938. In the 1940s and 1950s the film studios became famous for the Ealing comedies. Among several productions with a strong London flavour were *The Ladykillers*, *The Lavender Hill Mob* and *Passport to Pimlico*. The BBC used the studios for several decades after film-making ceased, making classics of its own, like *Steptoe and Son*. Ealing was the birthplace of the writers T H Huxley, Nevil Shute and Frank Richards, the creator of Billy Bunter.

✉ W5; W13

♦ 52,305 (Cleveland, Ealing Broadway, Ealing Common and Walpole wards)

📖 Peter Hounsell, *The Ealing Book*, Historical

Publications, 2005; John Rogers and Reg Eden, *Ealing*, Tempus, 2004

@ www.ealing-web.com (commercial local information site); www.lammas.com (commercial local information site); www.ealingcivicsociety.org

Ealing Broadway • *Ealing*

The central shopping and leisure area of EAL-ING, occupying a curve of Uxbridge Road (A4020). Ealing (now Ealing Broadway) station opened at the corner of Haven Green in 1838 and over the second half of the 19th century the area to its immediate south became the focus for the new suburb's amenities. Sir George Gilbert Scott's Church of Christ the Saviour was consecrated in 1852 and was joined in the late 1860s by Ealing Broadway Methodist Church (now the Polish Church). Shops came first to the newly named High Street in the early 1870s, because of its greater proximity to the old village centre around St Mary's Church, but soon spread into the Broadway and then further east to the Mall. Municipal offices (now the National Westminster Bank) were built on the north side of the Mall in 1874 and these were replaced by the present town hall on the New Broadway in 1888. Electric tram services came to Uxbridge Road in 1901 and over the following few years a series of shopping parades replaced earlier houses (and almshouses), while Bond Street was created to provide another link to Ealing Green. South of Uxbridge Road, the Questors Theatre was founded on Mattock Lane in 1929 and now claims to be the largest amateur theatre in Europe, with 3,000 members, of whom 600 are actively involved in productions. A cinema and more blocks of shops were built in the 1930s. The hitherto separate Underground and main-line stations were combined as a single Ealing Broadway station in 1962. From around this time the council began to plan the redevelopment of the main shopping area and finally completed the Ealing Broadway Centre in 1985, with a library, multi-storey car park and dozens of retail units. The council designated Ealing town centre a conservation area in 1994. The Broadway has acquired an increasingly metropolitan flavour in recent years and chic boutiques and bistros have come to Ealing Green. To the north of Ealing Broadway station, Haven Green is a larger open space but marred by circling traffic, especially buses. The explosion of bars on and off the Broadway in recent years prompted Ealing North MP

Stephen Pound to describe central Ealing as a 'Las Vegas of drinking' in 2004. Four-fifths of residents of the Ealing Broadway ward are white and most adults are university-educated. A third of homes are privately rented and relatively few households have children.

W5

12,634

First Great Western Link; Heathrow Connect terminus; Central Line terminus; District Line terminus (zone 3)

@ www.questors.org.uk

Ealing Common • *Ealing*

A 40-acre open space in east EALING, and the electoral ward that surrounds it. In the Middle Ages the common covered some 70 acres but its extent was reduced as a result of progressive encroachment. Medieval tracks have been upgraded to become the roads that now frame and traverse it. From 1809 until his assassination in 1812, prime minister Spencer Perceval lived at Elm Grove, a house at the south-west corner of the common. In 1870 his son's widow sold the Elm Grove estate to the East India Company. Ealing Common station opened in 1879, when housing began to spread from the town in this direction. St Matthew's Church and several substantial detached houses were soon built on North Common Road, but the open fields of Fordhook Farm survived to the east until the end of the century. Building reached a peak in 1903, when some relatively new houses were demolished and replaced by blocks of flats. Spencer Perceval's youngest daughter bequeathed money for All Saints' Church to be built in his memory and Leopold de Rothschild gave the site, where Elm Grove had formerly stood. The church was completed in 1905. Ealing Common station was rebuilt for the arrival of the Piccadilly Line in 1932. The common continued to be used for grazing and donkey rides until well into the 20th century but dog-walking is now the prime animal activity. Funfairs are periodically held on the common, usually on bank holiday weekends. The Ealing Common ward has a well-educated population and its proportion of twenty-somethings is nearly twice the national average.

The Who's Pete Townshend was an Ealing Common resident at the height of the band's fame in the 1960s.

W5

12,804

District Line; Piccadilly Line (zone 3)

Earls Court • *Kensington & Chelsea*

A busy residential district and a location of exhibition halls in south-west KENSINGTON. From the time of Domesday Book this was the site of the manor house of the earls of Oxford, who were lords of the manor of Kensington. From the early 17th century they were superseded in this role by the earls of Warwick and Holland. The manor house lay to the east of what is now Earls Court Road, where a hamlet subsequently evolved. This side of Earls Court retains a faintly villagey air and is now a conservation area. Earls Court Farm occupied 190 acres on the west side of Earls Court Road and was the property of William Edwardes, created first Baron Kensington in 1776. The Edwardes family ran into financial difficulties and began to develop their land with housing after 1811, with streets bearing names relating to their home county of Pembrokeshire, in Wales. However, much of the farm survived until later in the century and in 1830 William Cobbett could write in *Rural Rides*, 'I came up by Earls Court, where there is, amongst the market gardens, a field of wheat'. The arrival of the railway made development a more viable prospect. Earls Court station opened in 1871 and was rebuilt seven years later on the site of the old farmhouse. Remaining open ground to the west of the station was used for fairs and exhibitions from 1887 and impressive buildings were constructed in the 1890s by Imre Kiralfy, who went on to create the WHITE CITY. Kiralfy's fairground included a big wheel that was two-thirds the height of the present London Eye but had a greater passenger capacity. It was later removed to Blackpool, Lancashire. The last major phase of residential development saw substantial mansion blocks erected in the 1890s and in 1902 the Kensington family sold off 82 acres of land and nearly 1,500 buildings at auction for £565,000 – the highest price then recorded for a London estate. The present Earls Court exhibition hall, home of the Ideal Home Show and a venue for rock concerts, opened in 1937. A second hall was added in 1991. In the mid 20th century many of the large terraced houses were subdivided into flats as the professional middle classes began to move away. In the late 1970s, Earls Court became known as a social gathering place for gay men, a role now largely supplanted by SOHO. The district has a highly transient population, especially of Antipodeans, and relatively few children or old people. Three-quarters of residents are white. The largest ethnic minority is classified as 'Chinese or other ethnic group' – which comprises primarily the area's Arabic community. More than half the adult residents are college educated and most households have only one occupant.

The London Academy of Music and Dramatic Art was based in Earls Court from 1945 until 2003, when it moved west to BARONS COURT. The academy's MacOwan Theatre remains in Logan Place. Rock star Freddie Mercury lived at Garden Lodge in Logan Place and died there in 1991.

SW5; W8

9,659

District Line; Piccadilly Line (zones 1 and 2)

Richard Tames, *Earls Court and Brompton Past*, Phillimore, 2000

@ www.eco.co.uk (Earls Court and Olympia exhibition halls site)

Earlsfield • *Wandsworth*

A late Victorian and Edwardian residential locality in south-east WANDSWORTH, on the eastern slope of the Wandle Valley. From the late Middle Ages, Garratt was the principal village in the manor of Allfarthing. By 1747 it had become famous for mock elections in which a mayor of Garratt was chosen by revellers on the basis of his physical deformity and witty speech. The elections became increasingly radicalized and died out early in the 19th century. In 1868, Robert Davis bought Elm Lodge on Allfarthing Lane and added a new house, which he called Earlsfield because Earl was his wife's maiden name. Davis bought another 59 acres of land in 1876 and began to lay out Earlsfield Road. Wandsworth Cemetery opened in 1878 on neighbouring land that belonged to Magdalen College, Oxford. Davis's original plan was to construct 300 spacious villas with quarter-acre gardens, designed by the architect Thomas James Lynes, who lived nearby in what is now Marcilly Road. A few were built at the upper end of Earlsfield Road, but Davis soon switched to compact terraces of houses that sold more quickly and brought him a higher return. Earlsfield station opened in 1884, and the following year the British Land Co. bought the lower part of Davis's estate and rapidly developed it. In 1890 St Andrew's Church replaced a mission church that had become inadequate for the growing congregation. Magdalen College's land east of the railway line was built up from 1900, proceeding in a generally easterly direction. Earlsfield House was rebuilt as a school in 1908, later serving as a children's home and then a boys' remand hostel. It closed in 1981 and was converted into flats. Earlsfield is popular with young adults, often sharing rented accommodation. Its ethnic composition closely matches that of the borough as a whole, which is 78 per cent white with a broad mix of minorities making up the rest.

The writer Louis de Bernières, an Earlsfield resident, portrayed the locality in *Sunday Morning at the Centre of the Earth*, his 1999 radio play in the style of Dylan Thomas's *Under Milk Wood*.

- ✉ SW18
- 👤 12,903
- 🚆 South West Trains (zone 3)
- 📖 W J Drinkwater, *Wandsworth, Earlsfield and Southfields*, SB Publications, 1993

East Acton • Ealing/Hammersmith & Fulham

With WORMWOOD SCRUBS to the north-east and WHITE CITY to the east, this is now one of the less prestigious corners of Acton but it was a distinct farming village as early as 1294. Some rural retreats started to appear from the late 16th century, slowly eroding the village green. In 1654 a goldsmith named John Perryn settled here, subsequently bequeathing his estate to the Worshipful Company of Goldsmiths. Over the following centuries the Goldsmiths' Company acquired additional land, put up 20 almshouses, promoted the building of a station (now Acton Central) and – after several failed attempts – instigated East Acton's suburbanization in the 1920s, following the construction of the Western Avenue (A40). Several streets were named after eminent goldsmiths such as Thomas Vyner and Martyn Bowes. The homes were relatively highly priced and were popular with civil servants and other middle-class professionals. At the same time the council built the East Acton estate on land that had been Acton Wells farm (and latterly a golf course). Several of the village's fields were preserved as sports grounds, most of which now belong to the Park Club, a 27-acre private facility off East Acton Lane. The King Fahad Academy opened in 1985, taking over the former St Anne's convent school, at which singer Dusty Springfield was a pupil.

Like NEASDEN and CHEAM, something about East Acton's character has made it a butt of anti-suburban humour. In George and Wee-don Grossmith's *The Diary of a Nobody*, Mr Pooter regrets visiting such an out-of-the-way place to attend the East Acton Volunteer Ball. A 1955 *Goon Show* lamented the dearth of earthquakes in East Acton. And in the BBC comedy programme *Sykes*, Eric Sykes and Hattie Jacques played a bumbling brother and long-suffering sister who lived at the fictional 24 Sebastopol Terrace, East Acton.

- ✉ W3; W12
- 👤 14,448 (Ealing's East Acton ward)
- 🚆 Silverlink Metro (Acton Central, zone 2); Central Line (East Acton, zone 2)
- 📖 Averil and Thomas Harper Smith, *East Acton Village*, Harper Smith, 1993

East Barnet • Barnet

A medieval village grew up around what is now the junction of East Barnet Road, Cat Hill and Church Hill Road but East Barnet's name is now used as an umbrella term encompassing NEW BARNET and OAKLEIGH PARK. St Mary's Church is of 12th-century origin, at the latest, and although much altered it is still recognizably Norman. St Mary's was the mother church of BARNET and the entire modern district can be said to have evolved out of East Barnet. A mill was recorded in 1291, when the village may have had around 30 dwellings. A mansion later known as the Clockhouse was documented in 1506 but this was one of few significant developments before the late 17th century, when City gentlemen began to establish rural retreats here. By then, CHIPPING BARNET had firmly established itself as the district's commercial centre. In the mid 18th century East Barnet gained a cottage school and the King's Head public house, while country seats were successively rebuilt in an increasingly uniform style. Leisurely growth over the following century was not much quickened by the opening of New Barnet and Oakleigh Park stations but there were suburban villas on a handful of new streets by 1900. The Clockhouse was replaced by a parade of shops in 1925, when suburbanization was getting properly underway – a process accelerated by the extension of the Piccadilly Line to Cockfosters in 1933. Soil excavated during the construction of the line was used to raise the flood plain in Oak Hill Park, which opened to the public in the same year. By the outbreak of World War II, long rows of semi-detached and terraced housing had replaced almost every pre-20th-century property. Completion of some projects had to wait until after the war but the later houses look the same as their 1930s forebears. The residents of East Barnet are mostly white, Christian, married and owner-occupiers – typical for the country as a whole, but less so for London.

Church Hill Road has been called 'the ghosts' promenade'; sightings have included knights on horseback, headless hounds and wandering noblemen. The root cause of these manifestations is said to be the denial of a Christian burial to the unpopular local landowner Geoffrey de Mandeville in 1144. The 18th-century prophetess Joanna Southcott, also known as 'Satan's mistress', apparently used to sit under an oak tree in what is now Oak Hill Park, which burst into flames on a clear day in the early 1930s. Nowadays the park hosts the East Barnet Festival in early summer each year. This free community music and dance event attracts around 25,000 visitors.

✉ Barnet EN4

👤 15,332

📖 Gillian Gear and Diana Goodwin, *East Barnet Village*, St Mary's Church, East Barnet, 1980

@ www.eastbarnetfestival.org

East Beckton • *Newham*

The massive scale of development in BECKTON during the 1980s prompted its subdivision by points of the compass. This part has become particularly visible because it is a bus destination. There has been a redefinition of the place name as commercial enterprises have pressed further and further eastwards across the former gasworks site since the 1990s. The former East Beckton district centre, with its Asda supermarket, has become simply Beckton district centre, as it now finds itself at the geographical heart of the new town. Retail parks and leisure venues dominate the 'new' east, with attractions that include a 75,000 square foot Savacentre and a multiplex cinema.

✉ E6

East Bedfont • *Hounslow*

A business and residential district situated south of HEATHROW airport; West Bedfont lies just outside the London boundary. Finds of Roman coins indicate the possible presence of a Roman villa, and the Saxons built a church here. The manor of East Bedfont was first recorded in the eleventh century and parts of St Mary's Church date from around 1150. In front of the church's south porch are two ancient yew trees, which were trimmed into the shape of a pair of peacocks in 1704. During the coaching era, East Bedfont lay at the midpoint on the second stage out of London, between HOUNSLOW and Staines. In 1826 its inns, of which the Black Dog was the most notable, were described as 'respectable and yielding good accommodation'. Until relatively recently, East Bedfont remained a charming backwater, with cottages and tall trees surrounding the green and pond, and some outlying timber-framed buildings that may be 500 years old. However, expansion towards FELTHAM altered its character in the second half of the 20th century, and the Bedfont Lakes Country Park project introduced an entirely new side to the district in the early 1990s. Former market gardens that had been worked for gravel and then used as landfill sites were intensively landscaped, using 70 million cubic feet of soil to form hills that became the highest point in the borough. This new amenity opened in 1995, with an accompanying business 'technopark' on its northern edge, which attracted computing corporations such as IBM and SAP. There is also an industrial park to the west. East Bedfont's residential population includes a significant Indian minority, though this is smaller than in other parts of the borough. In most other respects, the demographic profile is remarkably close to the national average.

Peter Harvey, the landlord of the Black Dog inn, invented a delicious fish sauce but resisted all offers to buy its recipe. However, when his sister married a London grocer in 1776, Harvey gave them the recipe as a wedding present and the couple set up a company to market the sauce. Crosse and Blackwell acquired the company in 1920. The recipe for Harvey's Sauce is no longer a secret and Mrs Beeton's directions can be found on several websites.

✉ Feltham TW14

👤 10,104

📖 Andrea Cameron, *Feltham, Hanworth and Bedfont: A Pictorial History*, Phillimore, 2002

@ www.communigate.co.uk/london/bedfontforum (community site); www.hounslow.info/bedfontlakes

East Cheam *see* LOWER CHEAM

Eastcote • *Hillingdon* (pronounced 'eastcət')

A METROLAND suburb born from a medieval village located east of RUISLIP, having formerly been part of its parish and manor. The name, which dates from the 13th century or earlier, means 'eastern cottages'; Ruislip at one time had a Southcote and a Westcote as well. During the Middle Ages the forest was cleared for arable farming and cattle grazing. Enclosures in 1804 brought the subdivision and hedging of Eastcote's farmland, most of which was given over to growing hay. In 1906 the Metropolitan Railway opened a halt in the locality formerly known as Field End and mains utility services were laid on soon afterwards. A station was built in 1910, when District Railway services began. While the area remained rural, the station drew London day-trippers and several tea gardens flourished in the vicinity. During the 1920s and 1930s, detached and semi-detached houses spread, first north of the railway, and then south to cover the former sports fields and pig farms. St Lawrence's Church was built on Bridle Road in 1933. At the outbreak of World War II, the government requisitioned a meadow at the northern end of Lime Grove and built a small military hospital. This proved surplus to requirements so the buildings were used as a barracks. After the war, the site became the original base for the communication interception operations of Government Communications Headquarters. The two remaining Colossus decoding machines that had helped break Germany's ciphers in the war were brought here from Bletchley Park, Buckinghamshire, and remained until GCHQ moved to its present home in Cheltenham. The site later became a government computer centre. The post-war housing shortage led the local authority to construct nearly a thousand new homes, together with schools and shops. Most of these properties are now privately owned. The vast majority of Eastcote's residents are white, and enjoy relatively high standards of living.

✉ Pinner HA5; Ruislip HA4

♟ 22,719 (Cavendish, and Eastcote and East Ruislip wards)

🚇 Metropolitan Line; Piccadilly Line (zone 5)

📖 Colleen A Cox, *A Quiet and Secluded Spot: Ruislip, Northwood and Eastcote, 1851–1881*, Ruislip, Northwood and Eastcote Local History Society, 1991 Ron Edwards, *Eastcote from Village to Suburb: A Short Social History, 1900–1945*, Hillingdon Borough Libraries, 1987

@ www.st-lawrence-eastcote.org.uk

Eastcote Village • *Hillingdon*

The original heart of EASTCOTE, located north-west of Bridle Road, is now called Eastcote Village to distinguish it from later development that spread outwards from the station. Bridle Road was so named following the Ruislip Enclosure Act, when it became a 20-foot-wide bridleway. Eastcote House was the home of the Hawtrey family and their descendants from about 1532 to 1880. Oliver Cromwell supposedly stayed at the house and billeted his troops here during the Civil War. Alice, Countess of Derby built the grander Haydon Hall around 1630, conceivably as a place to keep her possessions out of the reach of her corrupt son-in-law. Subsequently rebuilt and then extended, it was acquired in 1805 by Dr Adam Clarke, an eminent Methodist theologian. Eastcote remained an isolated community of about a hundred scattered farms and cottages, mostly near the River Pinn, until the late 19th century. The principal visitors by this time were cyclists taking rides into the countryside. From the 1920s, METROLAND engulfed the village, but several 16th- to 18th-century buildings remain. Eastcote House was demolished in 1964, although its dovecote and coach house survive. Haydon Hall met the same fate later in the decade, and its site is now Eastcote Cricket Club's ground.

✉ Pinner HA5

East Croydon • *Croydon*

The name of a station rather than a district of CROYDON, and the planned site for major new commercial developments. The station originally opened on the London and Brighton Railway in 1841; the company became the London, Brighton and South Coast Railway five years later. A new set of platforms for local trains was given its own name – New Croydon – in 1862, but the whole station was rebuilt as a united entity in 1894. From the early 1960s the vicinity of the station was almost wholly rebuilt with office blocks of varying heights. For a few years, the resulting skyline was as distinctive as that of CANARY WHARF – there was nothing else quite like it in the country. But the effect soon began to pall owing to the absence of any intrinsic architectural merit. The area is now the focus of the borough's plans for the regeneration of central Croydon. Former sidings and a goods yard adjoining the station are to be the location of the massive Croydon Gateway scheme, whose final form has been the subject of protracted debate.

151

The project is likely to entail the replacement of the Warehouse Theatre, an important arts venue housed in a former cement warehouse.

While waiting for a train at East Croydon, the writer D H Lawrence caught a chill that is said to have contributed to his eventual death from tuberculosis.

✉ Croydon CR0

🚌 Southern; South Eastern Trains; Thameslink (zone 5)

🚌 Croydon Tramlink, Routes 1, 2 and 3

@ www.warehousetheatre.co.uk

East Dulwich • *Southwark*

An up-and-coming Victorian suburb situated south of PECKHAM, and quite separate from the rest of DULWICH. The hamlet of East Dulwich was recorded in 1340 as having gardens, arable lands, heath and enclosures, and thus it remained for 500 years. With the introduction of a coach service to the City, a few large villas were erected between the 1830s and the 1850s, but these were overwhelmed by the speculative building that followed the arrival of the railway in 1868. The station was called Champion Hill for its first 20 years, and it was during this period that almost all the fields of East Dulwich were built over. Covenants prohibited 'offensive trades', ensuring that development was almost entirely residential. The northern part of the district, around the former hamlet of Goose Green, was swarmed upon by a host of small-scale entrepreneurial developers, who often constructed only a few short terraces of houses. Some houses were intended for two working-class families to share. East of Barry Road, the British Land Co. laid out the more spacious Friern Manor estate. At first a shortage of stopping trains and the absence of shops and services made it hard for landlords to let many of the completed houses, but at the beginning of the 20th century the introduction of a tram service and the opening of commercial and municipal facilities overcame these obstacles. On the fringes of East Dulwich a handful of large council estates were built from the 1930s onwards but the district did not experience the scale of post-war redevelopment that transfigured Peckham. East Dulwich is shedding its reputation as a dreary suburb, although claims that it has become 'the CROUCH END of south London' are premature.

The children's writer Enid Blyton was born in a flat above a shop in East Dulwich in 1897, but her family soon moved to CLOCK HOUSE.

✉ SE22

👤 10,840

🚌 Southern (zone 2)

📖 John D Beasley, *East Dulwich Remembered*, Tempus, 2002

East End • *Tower Hamlets*

A 19th-century term for the district lying east of the CITY OF LONDON. There is no agreed definition of its extent, but it corresponds roughly with the modern borough of Tower Hamlets. From the late Middle Ages housing and industry spread here from two directions: outwards from the City and northwards from the riverside at ST KATHERINE'S and WAPPING. By the early 17th century, despite Privy Council bans, some of the inner suburbs were already densely built-up. Noxious trades like soap boiling and tanning were concentrated here, because the prevailing wind blew the odours away from the City. But the wind was blowing from the east during the Great Fire of London, so the narrow streets and tumbledown tenements escaped destruction and grew ever more crowded. Huguenot weavers began to settle in SPITALFIELDS, the first of a succession of immigrant communities that helped make the East End the most economically vital part of the capital. By 1700, building had spread to MILE END and the population of east London was estimated at 91,000, a more than fourfold increase in a hundred years. During the 18th century large-scale industries like distilling, brewing and sugar-refining took on thousands of workers, many of whom were lucky if they had a single room to call home. Jewish immigrants began arriving in large numbers, often working in the garment trade. The creation of inland docks in the 19th century brought a flood of casual labourers in search of employment and London's first CHINATOWN evolved in LIMEHOUSE. In 1850 STEPNEY alone had a quarter of a million inhabitants. Child labour was especially rife in BETHNAL GREEN, and WHITECHAPEL gained the most notorious reputation of all through the crimes of Jack the Ripper in 1888. By this time, philanthropic individuals and societies were helping to clear the slums and put up 'model' housing, with healthy ventilation and drainage. They were soon joined in their efforts by the Metropolitan Board of Works and its successor, the London County Council, and much of the old East End was swept away in the first half of the 20th century. During World War II the area suffered worse bombing than any other part of London. When Buckingham Palace was hit by bombs in 1940, Queen Elizabeth (later the Queen Mother) famously remarked, 'Now we can look the East End in the face'. After the war, massive municipal schemes decanted East Enders into ranks of tower blocks, breaking up the traditional patterns of life. Many residents left for the new suburbs of outer London, while industries also moved away or closed down. Commonwealth immigrants, especially from what is now Bangladesh, added another dimension to the ethnic mix, most noticeably on BRICK LANE. DOCKLANDS regeneration has transformed the riverside since the early 1990s but elsewhere many parts of the East End retain some of the highest levels of deprivation in the country.

BBC1's long-running soap opera *EastEnders*, set in the fictional borough of WALFORD, provides the best-known media portrayal of the district but despite its racy storylines the show depicts a much blander East End than the real thing.

📖 Kate Gavron, Geoff Dench and Michael Young, *The New East End*, Profile Books, 2006; J Green, *A Social History of the Jewish East End in London, 1914–1939*, Edwin Mellen Press, 1991; Jerry White, *Rothschild Buildings: Life in an East End Tenement Block 1887–1920*, Pimlico, 2003 (reissue of prize-winning 1980 title); Alan Palmer, *The East End*, John Murray, 2000; Gilda O'Neill, *My East End*, Penguin, 1999

@ www.eastlondonhistory.com; www.eastendtalking.org.uk (children's site)

East Finchley · *Barnet*
A distinctly different community from its parent district, which lies across the North Circular Road (A406) to the north-west. As early as the 14th century a chain of little hamlets took root beside HORNSEY park on the newly created Great North Road (as it later became), and were collectively known as East End. The extended settlement slowly acquired more cottages, a couple of inns and a succession of large houses on the higher slopes but at the end of the 17th century it remained surrounded by open fields, now mostly denuded of trees. Pigs were reared on the common and traded at the Hogmarket. From around 1800 the Bishop of London began to sell building leases and villas lined the Great North Road and FORTIS GREEN Road. At the heart of the village, humbler dwellings multiplied and by the 1850s East End was the most populous part

of FINCHLEY, crammed with tenements and terraced houses. Expansion accelerated following the arrival of the railway in 1867 and the sale of more building leases from 1878. The centre of population shifted eastward as hundreds of inferior cottages were built, while larger houses were subdivided into lodgings when the wealthier classes fled. Conditions were often insanitary and East Finchley (as it had now become) gained a reputation for drunkenness, godlessness and a lack of moral restraint. Extensive bomb damage during World War II prompted the council to radically remodel the district afterwards. The first blocks of eleven-storey flats went up in the mid 1950s and municipal building continued for the next two decades. East Finchley is home to the UK headquarters of McDonald's, although Barnet council denied the company permission to open a restaurant here following local resistance. The ward remains relatively godless: at the last census 19 per cent of adults said they had no religion, the highest proportion in the borough. East Finchley also has Barnet's highest number of people living in flats.

Dating from 1910, when it began life as the Picturedrome, the Phoenix is one of the oldest working cinemas in the country. The cinema featured in Tom Cruise's *Interview with the Vampire*. East Finchley residents have included comedian and actor Peter Sellers, musicians Vivian Stanshall and Feargal Sharkey, and US chat show host Jerry Springer, who was born in Chandos Road.

✉ N2

🚶 14,534

🚇 Northern Line (zone 3)

📖 Carola Zentner, *Insider's Guide to Muswell Hill, Crouch End, Highgate and East Finchley*, Searchlight, 1995

East Greenwich · *Greenwich*
The industrial side of GREENWICH, including (by most definitions) the former marshland of the GREENWICH PENINSULA. One of the first structures here was the government powder magazine. Throughout the 17th century it tested, stored and distributed gunpowder, to the increasing apprehension of the growing residential population. The building was demolished in 1802 and the site later acquired by the Enderby family, Bermondsey tanners who had married into the whaling trade. One of the exploratory voyages that they funded resulted in the discovery of Antarctica's Enderby Land, as

it was named. Around the same time, local landowner George Russell built New East Greenwich, which consisted of a large tidal mill for grinding corn, together with workers' housing, some of which still stands, in River Way. The great mill became a chemical works in the 1840s before being replaced by a power station. In the 1850s the new technology of cable-making began life at East Greenwich, and the first Atlantic cable was made here. The site is still in use by Alcatel. In the 1880s the South Metropolitan Gas Co. built its East Greenwich works. The two gasholders were the biggest in Europe; only one holder in America ever surpassed them. The smaller of the pair still stands, described by Richard Boston in the *Guardian* as 'a very fine gasometer indeed with a visually intriguing criss-cross of girders that rather upstages the Dome'. The site of the former Annandale School, which has been relocated to MILLENNIUM VILLAGE, is under development by Durkan Homes as the 'SElect10n', a name derived from the postal district. East Greenwich Pleasaunce is a formal, tree-lined garden that serves as a burial ground for around 3,000 sailors who died at the Royal Hospital for Seamen at Greenwich.

✉ SE10

📖 Mary Mills, *Greenwich Marsh: The 300 Years before the Dome*, Greater London Industrial Archaeology Society, 1999

East Ham • *Newham*

A densely built-up former borough and a parish that was said to be haunted, situated a mile west of Barking. The Old English word 'hamm' indicated an area of dry land bounded by marshes or rivers. The manor of Hammarsh and the riverside marshes belonged to Westminster Abbey from at least the time of the Norman Conquest. St Mary Magdalene Church was built around 1130, and it is believed that the site was earlier used for burials. The church's original apse, chancel and nave have all survived, making this one of London's least modified medieval churches. By the late 12th century, documents were distinguishing Ham's eastern and western parts. WEST HAM grew slowly but East Ham remained an agricultural backwater until the late 19th century, with a weekly cattle market, potato farms and market gardens noted for their onions, especially pickling onions. Much of the district was developed by successive generations of the Ynes Burges family, who began to build on their century-old estate from the 1880s. Between 1891 and 1911 the population of the bor-

ough (as it became in 1904) quadrupled to around 133,000. This was not the consequence of industrialization in East Ham itself; most of the new residents commuted to work in the ROYAL DOCKS, BECKTON gasworks or the factories of neighbouring West Ham. A town hall was built in 1903 and the early 18th-century mansion Rancliffe House was demolished in 1908; its grounds now form Central Park. East Ham Jewish Cemetery was laid out in 1919 on Sandford Road and now has 40,000 serried graves. Having been so comprehensively built-up before World War I, there was little scope for further construction in the 1920s and 1930s but the council redeveloped much of the area after World War II, partly in response to heavy bomb damage. The ten-acre churchyard of St Mary Magdalene was designated a nature reserve in 1976. East Ham's population is primarily Asian, mostly of Indian origin but with large Pakistani and Bangladeshi communities as well. White and black residents make up a larger proportion towards the south of the district, where there are more council homes and fewer dependent children. BBC London made East Ham the focus of its 'Voices' project in 2002 because of its ethnic diversity.

East Ham was the birthplace of the wartime songbird Vera Lynn and the footballer Jimmy Greaves. The Granada cinema played host to the Beatles in 1963 and to a solo performance in 1964 by Phil Everly just after his brother Don had attempted suicide with a drugs overdose.

✉ E6

🚶 36,008 (East Ham Central, East Ham North and East Ham South wards)

🚇 District Line; Hammersmith & City Line (zones 3 and 4)

📖 Stephen Pewsey, *East Ham*, Sutton, 1996

@ www.bbc.co.uk/london/yourlondon/voices

East India • *Tower Hamlets*

A Docklands Light Railway station built on part of the site of the East India Docks in eastern Blackwall. In 1803 the success of the newly opened West India Docks prompted a group of merchants involved in trade with the East Indies to propose a similar scheme at BLACKWALL. Construction took three years and filled a 60-acre site. Brunswick Dock, which had opened in 1790, became the export dock, with an entrance basin to its east and a larger import dock to its north. At the same time

East India Dock Road was built as an extension of Commercial Road, providing a link with the City of London. The nearby Brunswick Hotel was renowned for its whitebait dinners but in the 1860s it became a hostel for emigrants to Australia and was demolished in 1930. The docks had already begun to decline when they suffered tremendous damage during the Blitz. The export dock never reopened and was replaced by Brunswick power station in 1956. The import dock was repaired but containerization and other changing circumstances rendered it increasingly obsolete and it was gradually filled in from the late 1960s. Only the entrance basin and sections of the dock wall now remain. In 1989 part of the site of the import dock became the *Financial Times* print works, which has since been converted into offices and a BT switching centre. Brunswick power station has been replaced by a luxury apartment complex. Other areas have been laid out with granite-faced office blocks in the characteristic DOCKLANDS style, with newly created water features and streets named after eastern herbs and spices. Tower Hamlets Town Hall stands on Clove Crescent.

> ✉ E14

> ♁ 11,496 (East India and Lansbury ward)

> ☒ Docklands Light Railway, Beckton branch (zones 2 and 3)

East Putney • *Wandsworth*

A residential conservation area on the WANDSWORTH/PUTNEY border, with a strong commercial presence on Upper Richmond Road. Wandsworth suffered a very high death toll during the Great Plague of 1665–6 and the bodies are reported to have been buried near the site of the station, which has been designated an archaeological priority area. Apart from a scattering of 18th-century mansions, the area did not begin to develop until the 1860s, when Wandsworth and Putney grew towards each other along WEST HILL, and detached and semi-detached villas appeared on Upper Richmond Road and Keswick Road. In 1880 East Putney station opened on the London and South Western Railway's line from Wimbledon to Waterloo. The District Railway service began in 1889 and the company bought the Clockhouse estate on West Hill, laying out Lytton Grove and the southern extension of Keswick Road on either side of the tracks. Oakhill Road was mostly built up between 1890 and 1900. Architectural styles adopted during this period included French Renaissance, Queen Anne and Italianate. From the 1930s, blocks of flats were inserted into the grounds of older villas and Portinscale Road was redeveloped. The main-line rail service to WATERLOO ceased to operate in 1941. Most residents of the ward live in what the council's conservation area statement calls 'large-scale intrusions' dating from the second half of the 20th century. East Putney's population is biased towards well-educated young adults, living in their own homes or renting privately. Eighty-six per cent of residents are white, and employment levels are very high.

East Putney is home to one of Britain's largest conglomerates, although many Londoners have never heard of it. Tomkins plc encompasses an international group of businesses making products for the industrial, automotive and building markets, with sales of approximately £3 billion a year. The company is based at East Putney House on Upper Richmond Road.

> ✉ SW15

> ♁ 13,196

> ☒ District Line (zones 2 and 3)

East Sheen • *Richmond*

A socially advantaged locality situated south of MORTLAKE and east of RICHMOND, which was originally called Sheen (or Shene). First recorded in 1247, East Sheen became a separate manor from Mortlake around 1500. The village was centred around Milestone Green, which lay where Upper Richmond Road now crosses Sheen Lane, with a few more dwellings where the lane meets Christ Church Road. East Sheen had 26 houses in 1617, by which time the two nuclei had probably joined. The 17th-century Temple Grove was the manor house of East Sheen and Westhall and took its name from the Temple family, later the viscounts Palmerston, who owned it until 1805. Around 1837, a younger son of the third earl of Dartmouth built Stanwell House at the north-west corner of East Sheen common, with decorative garden features reassembled from parts of old London Bridge, which had been demolished a few years earlier. The arrival of the railway at BARNES and Mortlake brought some early suburban development but the main spur to growth did not come until 1896, when 50 acres of the Palewell estate were sold, and other old estates soon followed. Temple Grove, which had latterly served as a boys' preparatory school, was demolished around 1900. By the early 1920s most of the area had been built up and the creation of a string of shops along Upper Richmond Road had given East Sheen retail ascendancy over the old district centre at Mortlake High Street. A final phase of housebuilding filled the remaining gaps south of Upper Richmond Road in the 1930s and Stanwell House was demolished and replaced by the flats of Courtlands. A London Bridge alcove survives in the residents' gardens. East Sheen has an overwhelmingly white, well-educated population including many families with young children. The 53-acre East Sheen Common is owned by the National Trust.

East Sheen was home to the Whig prime minister Earl Grey. Sir Tim Berners-Lee, inventor of the world-wide web, was born in East Sheen in 1955. The last home of 1970s rock star Marc Bolan was 142 Upper Richmond Road West, a large Victorian house with a corner location, surrounded by a high brick wall and foliage. It was only a short distance from here that Bolan met his death on Barnes Common in 1977.

> ✉ SW14; Richmond TW10

> ⑂ 9,744

> 📖 Raymond Gill, *The Growth of East Sheen in the Victorian Era*, Picton, 1996

East Wickham • *Bexley*

A former medieval manor that became part of suburban north Welling between the wars. 'Wikam' was first mentioned in 1240 and the reference almost certainly indicated a homestead associated with an earlier 'vicus', a Romano-British settlement that probably stood on Watling Street. 'Estwycham' was recorded in 1284, the prefix distinguishing the hamlet from West Wickham, which lies nine miles to the south-west. St Michael's Church is of 13th-century origin, although its west end was rebuilt in the 19th century. William Foster bequeathed funds for a school that was established on Upper Wickham Lane in 1727. Both the school and its buildings survive but in different places: the school has moved to Westbrooke Road, while its main building and the schoolmaster's house have been converted for residential use. The farmhouse at East Wickham Farm has a façade dating from 1843 but, like the church, its timbers are much older. In 1916 the Woolwich Arsenal erected the East Wickham hutments, an estate of prefabricated homes for wartime munitions workers, with amenities that included a theatre but excluded decent sanitation. Bexley council built 426 houses on the fields of East Wickham Farm in 1922, while private developers laid out neighbouring estates. Over a ten-year period from 1928, three schools opened and a new St Michael's Church was built. The medieval church is now used by a Greek Orthodox congregation and its brasses and other removable fittings have been transferred to the modern church. During the 1950s the surviving fields of East Wickham Farm were used as a landfill site, primarily for rubble from wartime bomb sites. An 84-acre area has since been levelled and planted with grass, with part being left to grow wild. The amenity is sometimes known as 'Fanny on the Hill park', after a nearby public house, but is properly called East Wickham Open Space. The East Wickham ward has an overwhelmingly white population, with a high level of home ownership but low educational attainment. The large number of pensioners accounts for the relatively high average age of 40 years.

The musician Kate Bush grew up at East Wickham Farm and continued living there with her family after her early success. East Wickham was the scene of rioting in 1993 when police battled to prevent marchers from reaching the British National Party headquarters in nearby Welling.

> ✉ SE18; Welling DA16

> ⑂ 10,383

> 📖 Peter Tester, *East Wickham and Welling*, Bexley Local Studies and Archive Centre, 1991

Ebury • *Westminster*

A half-recalled Saxon manor that once stretched from present-day OXFORD STREET southward to the Thames. In the 16th century Ebury Farm covered 430 acres and its farmhouse stood on the site of the modern VICTORIA coach station. The estate was regularly leased by the Crown to court favourites until James I sold the freehold in 1623. A Temple barrister, Hugh Audley, purchased the marshy manor; it descended in 1666 to his one-year-old grand-niece Mary Davies. Eleven years later Mary married Sir Thomas Grosvenor of Eaton in Cheshire. Their union was not a happy one: she went mad and he died young. But the Grosvenor family profitably developed the land and, as BELGRAVIA came into existence and grew, the Ebury name dropped out of widespread usage. It is remembered today primarily in the context of street names. Westminster council applies the name Ebury Village to a group of roads lying west of Victoria and has designated it an area of archaeological importance.

Mozart composed his first symphony when staying in Ebury Street in 1764. Ebury Street residents have included Ian Fleming, Noel Coward, Thomas Wolfe, Vita Sackville-West and George Moore, who wrote *Conversations in Ebury Street* in 1924.

✉ SW1

📖 Simon Jenkins, *The Selling of Mary Davies and Other Writings*, John Murray, 1993

Eden Park • *Bromley*

A compact and comfortable locality in south BECKENHAM, situated east of ELMERS END. This was part of the Langley estate, the eastern half of which has become PARK LANGLEY, and was formerly known as Bure Gates. William Eden leased land here from the Beckenham grandee Peter Burrell around 1782. Following Eden's arrival a confusion of similarly named farms evolved: Eden Farm in the north, Eden Park Farm in the centre and Park Farm to the south. A mansion built on Eden Farm in 1820 was called Eden Park from 1832. To the east of the Eden farms, the Harvington estate was developed from the 1870s with some very substantial houses, including Harvington, Homewood and Chalfont. In 1882 Eden Park station opened on the Mid-Kent line from Elmers End to HAYES. Most of the neighbouring land was not released for building until after World War I, when the area was developed as Beckenham Heights. This was propitious timing because the electrification of the railway in the mid 1920s encouraged commuters to move here. Wellhouse Road takes its name from a well house that was demolished during the building of Beckenham Heights; the dilapidated Eden Park mansion was pulled down at the same time. Crease Park was opened to the public by Alderman James Crease in 1936 and Beckenham council also acquired the surviving 117 acres of woods and open space of the Harvington estate for use as a sports ground. In 1994 a derelict former council depot on the Harvington estate was cleared by over 100 local young people to create what was claimed to be the largest skate park in south-east England. Following complaints about noise, Bromley council bulldozed the skate park in 2004.

William Eden's brother was the great-great-grandfather of Sir Anthony Eden, first Earl of Avon, who has been labelled the least effective British prime minister of the 20th century, primarily as a result of his handling of the 1956 Suez crisis.

✉ Beckenham BR3

♟ 14,751 (Kelsey and Eden Park ward)

🚆 South Eastern Trains (zone 5)

📖 Ian Muir and Pat Manning, *The Book of Monks Orchard and Eden Park*, Halsgrove, 2004

Edgware • *Barnet/Harrow*

An interwar middle-class suburb with a strongly Jewish character, situated three miles north-west of Hendon and split between two boroughs along the course of the former Watling Street (A5). The name meant 'Ecgi's weir' and was first recorded in an Anglo-Saxon charter of around 975 but was omitted from Domesday Book. Ecgi probably constructed his weir on what is now the Edgware Brook either to trap fish or to irrigate his field. It is said that medieval pilgrims travelling from London to St Albans would stop at Edgware to rest and to pray at St Margaret's Church, which was in existence by 1375. The church was rebuilt in 1764, when Edgware was becoming an important coaching halt, and a starting point for some services to London. Several inns were established and Edgware held fairs in the 18th and 19th centuries. The Great Northern Railway Co. opened its branch line to Edgware via MILL HILL in 1867 and was soon making a profit, but the indirect route discouraged potential commuters. As the coaching trade declined, wheelwrights and blacksmiths departed and the village became primarily agricultural. Only a few streets of terraced houses had been built by the outbreak of World War I. Services on what is now the Northern Line began in 1924, when the builders were already hard at work laying out new streets for the middle classes either side of Dean's Brook. They next turned their attention southwards to BURNT OAK, while the London County Council created the sprawling WATLING estate to the south-east. The completion of the Edgware Way bypass in 1927 brought a sea of detached houses to its hinterland but progressive northward expansion was halted by the outbreak of World War II, and subsequently restricted by green-belt regulation. Station Road is the main shopping street and has been declining in recent years, but the creation of the Mall Broadwalk has restored some vitality. Some ancient buildings survive on the west side of High Street Edgware, including the 17th-century White Hart Hotel, but many more have been lost through road widening. As well as its very large Jewish population, Edgware has significant Hindu and Muslim minorities, mainly of Indian origin. Relatively high house prices have discouraged younger, single home-seekers and Edgware was rated the hardest place in London to get a date in a 2002 survey.

Agatha Christie created the character Lord Edgware in a 1933 Hercule Poirot story. Jay Rayner's novel *Day of Atonement* is set among 'the thirteenth tribe of Israel: the wandering Jews of Edgware and WEALDSTONE'. The book was shortlisted for the Jewish Quarterly's novel of the year award in 1999.

> ⊠ Edgware HA8
>
> ♦ 49,983 (Harrow's Canons and Edgware wards and Barnet's Burnt Oak and Edgware wards)
>
> 🚇 Northern Line, Edgware branch terminus (zone 5)
>
> @ www.themall.co.uk/broadwalk (shopping centre site)

Edgwarebury • *Barnet*

Farming country straddling the M1 motorway and the Hertfordshire border north of EDG-WARE, also spelt as two separate words. To the east lies the oak woodland of Scratchwood, which dates from the last Ice Age, while vestiges of Celtic fields have been discerned to the north. 'Bury' was Old English for a manor or manor house and Edgwarebury seems to have been the focus of the manor of Edgware through the Middle Ages and beyond. The manor was owned by All Souls College, Oxford from 1443. A clause in Earlsbury Farm's lease in 1602 stipulated that the lords of the manor or their representatives should be given accommodation at the farmhouse when visiting the manor on official business. This farmhouse was replaced in the early 17th century by the timber-framed Bury Farm, which was extended in the 18th century. According to H S Geikie's *Notes on the Church and Parish of Edgware*, Dick Turpin is said to have poured boiling water over the householder, stolen his silver and raped his daughter. Edgwarebury Lane used to connect with Fortune Lane in Elstree until the fields were enclosed in 1854 and Edgwarebury Lane was diverted northward. Builders A W Curton created the upmarket Edgwarebury Lane estate in 1935, offering supersized properties such as a six-bedroom house for £1,785. Edgwarebury Park and cemetery lie on the edge of built-up Edgware.

Outside London since the last boundary change, the mock-Tudor Edgwarebury Hotel is popular among actors working at Elstree Studios. It has satisfied the studios' location requirements on many occasions – usually doubling as the home of some rich eccentric – including in three episodes of the *Avengers* television series.

> ⊠ Edgware HA8

Edgware Road • *Westminster*

A faintly Parisian-style boulevard with a strongly Middle Eastern flavour, running north-westwards from MARBLE ARCH to MAIDA VALE. Although there is another section of the A5 with the same name further north, it is the street separating PADDINGTON from MARYLEBONE that is usually meant by 'the Edgware Road'. This was part of the Roman road of Watling Street but despite its long existence there were few buildings here until modern times. Writing around 1596, Ben Jonson mentioned in *A Tale of a Tub* a Red Lion inn that probably stood on the Edgware Road. Other taverns came and went but the surrounding land remained in cultivation, latterly as market gardens. Development began in the 1790s, and over the following three decades the southernmost part was flanked by four-storey terraced houses for the upper middle classes, on the border of the fashionable new suburb of Tyburnia. Housing also spread southwards from Maida Vale. Between these residential ribbons, the road took on a more commercial aspect from its earliest days, with shops and workshops. In 1863 Edgware Road gained one of London's original underground stations on the inaugural line that ran between Paddington and FARRINGDON. From around this time some houses were converted to shops, offices or consulting rooms. A second, separate station opened on the Bakerloo Line in 1907. After the mid 1920s the houses began to be replaced by hotels or by shops with flats above. This process reached a peak in the 1930s, when the present streetscape came into existence. In the past 25 years, Edgware Road has become a focus for London's Arabic population, as has QUEENSWAY, its counterpart on the other side of Bayswater. The process may have begun with the tendency for wealthy Middle Eastern visitors to stay in hotels here and on nearby Park Lane, which led to the establishment of shops and restaurants dedicated to serving them. This in turn encouraged Arabic migrants, especially Lebanese, to settle in the area. The opening of Britain's first independent Islamic bank here in 2004 underlined Edgware Road's place at the heart of this community. Edgware Road has two landmark buildings by the Marylebone flyover: the blank-windowed Burne House telecommunications centre and the Hilton London Metropole, which is the capital's largest hotel, with 1,058 bedrooms and a 28-storey tower.

John Linnell's oil painting, *The East Side of the Edgware Road, Looking towards Kensington Gardens*, c.1812, belongs to HOLLAND PARK's Leighton House but has recently been exhibited at Tate Britain's gallery.

✉ W2

🚇 Bakerloo Line; Circle Line; District Line; Hammersmith & City Line (zone 1)

Edmonton • *Enfield*

An overly built-up former borough, situated north of TOTTENHAM. It was first recorded in Domesday Book, as 'Adelmetone', which was a farmstead belonging to a man named Éadhelm. At this time it was the smallest of the hundreds (administrative areas) of Middlesex, but nevertheless encompassed ENFIELD, Tottenham and South Mimms. Woodland covered much of the district and pig-keeping was the main form of agriculture. Market gardens were established after deforestation, while the road to Ware and Hertford, which became known as Fore Street for most of its length here, became the focus of ribbon development. Twin nuclei formed at EDMONTON GREEN, at the junction with Church Street in LOWER EDMONTON, and around the crossroads with SILVER STREET and Watery Lane (now ANGEL ROAD), which was the site of the ANGEL public house. Away from Fore Street, Edmonton became a desirable residential neighbourhood in the late 18th century but this did not last. By 1800 the gentry were moving out to SOUTHGATE and the place was inhabited by 'retired embroidered weavers, their crummy wives and tightly laced daughters', according to the scurrilous contemporary writer John Thomas Smith. It fell further as exploitative builders covered the central area with cheap housing in the latter decades of the 19th century. Nearer the River Lea, improvements in drainage permitted the establishment of industry on former marshland. The Great Cambridge Road (A10) brought more housing to the west of the district when it became the principal north–south route in 1924. That year also saw the start of municipal housebuilding in Edmonton, on the Hyde estate, south of Church Street. An RAF plane crashed onto the estate in 1938 and more than a dozen people died. The council built a number of tower blocks in the 1960s and 1970s and many of these properties are now being refurbished or replaced. The area beside the River Lea continues to provide some of the prime opportunities for initiatives of various kinds, although parts have green-belt protection. The leisure centre at PICKETT'S LOCK is being replaced by a regional athletics centre. Warehouses, business centres and superstores are filling disused industrial sites and some new housing has been built in the locality formerly known as MARSH SIDE. The regeneration of Edmonton Green is by far the largest project currently underway in the district.

The play *The Merry Devil of Edmonton* was published in 1608 and performed at the Globe. Supposedly based on a true story, it tells of a prankster who on one occasion fools the Devil himself. Edmonton was the 17th-century home of Elizabeth Sawyer, who was accused of having witched her neighbour's children to death and was hanged after the devil's mark was found above the base of her spine, a story that inspired two plays. Edmonton gave its name to the Hudson's Bay Co.'s Edmonton House in Alberta, Canada in 1785 and thence to the settlement that grew up around it, which is now far larger than its progenitor.

✉ N9; N18

👥 55,326 (Edmonton Green, Haselbury, Jubilee and Upper Edmonton wards)

🚉 'one' Railway (Edmonton Green, zone 4)

📖 Graham Dalling, *Southgate and Edmonton Past*, Historical Publications, 1996

Edmonton Green • *Enfield*

The focal point of LOWER EDMONTON, situated at the junction of Church Street, Hertford Road and Fore Street (earlier called Duck Lane here). Houses appeared around the green from the late 17th century and wholly encircled it in the following century. Fairs were held on Edmonton Green and menageries were exhibited here. A station opened in 1849 and the surrounding area was built up in the 1880s and 1890s. By the 1930s Edmonton Green had become a major shopping destination, drawing visitors from a wide catchment area. In the mid 1960s the newly formed Enfield council took over a project planned by its Edmonton predecessor, sweeping away 'substandard' Victorian housing and building a shopping centre, tower blocks and various amenities. The plan originally included a new civic centre but this element was subsequently abandoned. Edmonton Green was the largest municipally owned shopping centre in

London but by the end of the 20th century found itself losing out to competition at WOOD GREEN, WALTHAMSTOW and further afield, while ENFIELD TOWN and SOUTHGATE became more appealing to commercial investors within the borough. The close proximity of high-rise flats to multi-storey car parks proved an encouragement to crime. In one of the largest mixed-use schemes of its kind, Enfield council is now working with a property developer and a housing association to wholly redevelop the main facilities at Edmonton Green and the neighbouring housing. The £120 million project involves the replacement of the existing leisure centre, and the construction of a new shopping mall, Asda supermarket, primary care centre and bus station. The Green Horizons housing association will provide 750 new and 650 refurbished homes. Begun in 2000 and implemented in several phases, the project is due for completion in 2007. Edmonton Green is the most deprived ward in Enfield by most measures. It has the highest proportion of council housing of any ward, an ethnically diverse population and high levels of unemployment and crime.

A footbridge that led to nowhere in the old shopping centre was made famous by Michael Crawford as a roller-skating Frank Spencer in an episode of the 1970s television sitcom *Some Mothers do 'Ave 'Em*.

✉ N9

♀ 15,103

🚊 'one' Railway (zone 4)

Eel Pie Island • *Richmond*

Originally called Twickenham Ait, this is the largest island in London's stretch of the Thames, lying between TWICKENHAM and the HAM Riverside Lands. It is rumoured to have been the site of a monastery and much later was used as a 'courting ground' by Henry VIII. In the 18th century it attracted day-trippers, who came to picnic or fish here, and to enjoy the renowned pies that were made with locally caught eels. Although this is the most obvious explanation of the name, another story suggests that a royal mistress who had a house on the island called it Île de Paix, 'island of peace'. Many of the wood-frame properties date from the early 1900s, when they were used as summer houses by wealthy Edwardian Londoners. The structures survive well and fetch high prices. In the 1950s and 1960s, Eel Pie Island became famous for its noisy jazz club, where the Rolling Stones first emerged,

and The Who, Pink Floyd and Genesis also played gigs early in their careers. The island has even been called 'the place where the Sixties began'. Subsequently the Eel Pie Hotel became something of a hippie commune, to the disapproval of straight-laced locals. In 1996 a boatyard and 60 neighbouring artists' studios burnt down. An appeal brought donations from the local community in Twickenham as well as from famous rock stars, but only limited rebuilding has taken place so far.

The inventor Trevor Bayliss, best known for the clockwork radio, lived on the island, working from Haven Studio, a house-cum-shed with a heated swimming pool.

✉ Twickenham TW1

Elephant and Castle • *Southwark*

A busy road junction and its improving vicinity, situated in (and better known than) NEWINGTON, and often simply called 'the Elephant'. In 1641 John Flaxman set up a blacksmith's forge on an island site here to take advantage of the passing horse-drawn traffic. Around 1760 the smithy was converted to a tavern that displayed a sign of an elephant and castle. There is almost certainly no truth in the widely held belief that the name is a corruption of *Infanta de Castilla* ('princess of Castile'). The more likely connection is with the old heraldic symbol of an elephant with a castellated tower on its back, which was especially associated with the Cutlers' Company because of the use of ivory in knife handles. The tavern became a coaching halt and thus gave its name to the junction. This was already a densely built-up area by the time Charles Spurgeon established the Metropolitan Tabernacle in 1861. The tabernacle has been twice rebuilt since then but its original portico survives. The City and South London Railway arrived here in 1890 and the Baker Street and Waterloo Railway added a connection in 1906. Before the junction was overwhelmed by motor traffic, this was a locality where people came to socialize, shop and be entertained. In 1913 Désiré Pasquet observed in *Londres et les Ouvriers de Londres* that 'South London's central edifice is a public house – the Elephant and Castle'. Following its devastation during World War II, the area was clumsily redeveloped from the late 1950s with offices, academic buildings, housing estates and the Elephant and Castle shopping centre – a pioneer in its time but notoriously dismal now and not improved by its garish crimson cladding. With priority given to road traffic, pedestrians were forced into a network of subways. A £1.5 billion regeneration programme has recently begun, which will wholly remodel the area over a ten-year period, bringing new homes, shops and cultural and leisure facilities. One of the earliest projects will see the conversion of the southern roundabout into a landscaped T-junction with wide pedestrian crossings. WALWORTH'S Heygate housing estate will be demolished in a phased programme due for completion in 2009. Demolition of the shopping centre is planned to begin in the following year.

Shakespeare's *Twelfth Night* is set in Illyria but some have taken this to be an idealized England, citing as evidence Antonio and Sebastian's decision to lodge 'in the south suburbs, at the Elephant'. A shiny generating station in the centre of the Elephant and Castle roundabout doubles as a monument to local-boy-made-good Michael Faraday and his pioneering work on electricity.

✉ SE1; SE17

🚊 Southern; Thameslink; Bakerloo Line terminus; Northern Line (zones 1 and 2)

📖 Michael Collins, *The Likes of Us: A Biography of the White Working Class*, Granta Books, 2005

@ www.elephantandcastle.org.uk (regeneration programme site); www.into.org.uk (community and cultural site); www.metropolitantabernacle.org

Elmers End • *Bromley*

A mixed residential and commercial locality in south-west BECKENHAM. This was the end of the parish owned by the Elmer or Aylmer family, who were living here in the 13th century. Elmer Lodge was built around 1710 and surrounded by concentric moats. Cottages were built for 'industrious shepherds and labourers' in the late 18th century. Elmer Lodge was sold in 1820 when the vast Burrell estate was split up at auction. Croydon board of health purchased the building in the 1860s, filled in the moats and later created a sewage farm. Elmers End station opened in 1864 and, although most of the area remained rural, substantial houses began to line Croydon Road. The largest and most distinctive of these was Lymore (later Elmer Grange), built for a retired Welsh tailor about 1880. St James's Church was completed in 1888. Croydon Road recreation ground opened in 1890 and is more impressive than its prosaic name suggests. The park was endowed with a drinking fountain

and shelter designed in 'oriental' styles. More houses and shops appeared in the early 1900s and after World War I the council laid out an estate on Goddard Road, Shirley Crescent and Adams Road. The grounds of Elmer Grange were filled by Priory Close in the 1930s, although the house itself survived for another half-century. An Odeon cinema opened in 1939 and industry flourished south of the station. Throughout the second half of the 20th century Elmers End evolved in a progressively residential direction, mostly with the construction of blocks of flats. The Odeon proved to be very short-lived and closed in 1957. The old shepherds' cottages were replaced by council flats in 1962. The sewage farm closed in the 1960s, as did many of the factories from the 1970s onwards. The latter were mostly replaced by warehouses and in 1995 by a Tesco superstore.

In D H Lawrence's novel *Sons and Lovers*, published in 1913, the protagonist's elder brother William Morel dies of pneumonia in a boarding house in the 'dreary London village' of Elmers End. Lawrence had lived in nearby ADDISCOMBE.

✉ Beckenham BR3

🚊 South Eastern Trains (zone 4); Croydon Tramlink interchange

@ www.becrec.net (Croydon Road recreation ground site)

Elm Park • *Havering*

A 'wonder-town of homes', according to its developers, situated on the south-west side of HORNCHURCH. With financial support from the Halifax Building Society, the Liverpool-based company Richard Costain and Sons began building here in 1934, partly on the site of Elm Park farm. It is claimed that the layout was influenced by the garden city movement, but this is hard to detect. Costain ran free coach trips from EAST HAM for potential buyers, and part-funded the building of Elm Park's District Line station in 1935, after 500 homes had already been completed. It was the last station to open on the line. A 1937 advertisement promised 'space to breathe the clear air of open Essex. Compare these wide, clean avenues with the narrow, dust-laden streets in which many families unnecessarily remain when they could so easily live healthier, fuller lives at Elm Park.' Shortly afterwards, Tesco opened one of its earliest suburban stores here. By the outbreak of World War II the estate was three-quarters complete. When hostilities ceased, the council took on the remaining phase of development, though a planned cinema was never built. More shops were added in the 1950s, and later still came further housebuilding to the south, on part of the former Hornchurch airfield. Now one of the smallest of Havering's seven town centres, the shopping parade has a declining number of retail outlets, many of which have been replaced by fast-food takeaways. A community hall and annex was originally the Costain site canteen. Future development in Elm Park may include higher density housing, but the residents' association has expressed reservations about such proposals, preferring the neighbourhood to retain its suburban character. There are some problems with neglect and anti-social behaviour, particularly after dark. 'Between daytime and the evenings, Elm Park is like Dr Jekyll and Mr Hyde,' one resident has commented.

Elm Park is a predominantly white area, with only a few residents from ethnic minorities. At Dunningford and Benhurst primary schools, only one per cent of pupils speaks a language other than English at home. Nevertheless, recent ward elections have seen a consistently strong showing by candidates from Third Way, an obscure neo-fascist party with an emphasis on racial separation.

✉ Hornchurch RM12

♁ 12,048

🚇 District Line (zone 6)

Elmstead • *Bromley*

A diminutive and leafy locality situated between SUNDRIDGE and CHISLEHURST. The name was first recorded in 1320 as Elmsted, 'the place where elm trees grow', and the wood was Elmystediswood in 1392. This was part of the Bishop of Rochester's estate and used to provide timber for shipbuilding. A map of the early 1760s shows a house called Emsted Place and a gazetteer of 1797 added yet another variation on the name, by calling the hamlet Hemsted. The gazetteer reported that the hamlet had only one gentleman's house (presumably Emsted Place) and that this belonged to a PALL MALL bookseller. The rest of the locality was said to consist of 'good farms and labourers' cottages'. The railway line from ST JOHNS to Chislehurst was constructed in 1865 and Elmstead was the last station to open – in 1904. The 'Woods' addition to the name of the station came four years later, presumably to attract day-trippers. Most of the vicinity was built up in the early 20th century as part of the expansion of Chislehurst. Ravensbourne College of Design and Communication was created in the early 1970s and occupies an 18-acre site north of Walden Road. The surviving part of Elmstead Wood has paths that are part of the green chain walk that stretches across south-east London and the trees are mainly oak, sweet chestnut and hornbeam. Just beside the station is Elmstead Pit, formerly called Rock Pit, a small site with a nationally important exposure of the geological strata known as Blackheath Beds – marine deposits that were built up approximately 50 million years ago. They are rich in fossils and have yielded fish scales and shark fins. The pit is on land belonging to SUNDRIDGE PARK Golf Club and there is no public access.

A Sex Pistols gig at Ravensbourne College in 1975 influenced some of the audience to form the Bromley Contingent of punk disciples. The contingent included Billy Idol, a student at the college.

✉ Chislehurst, BR7

🚇 South Eastern Trains (Elmstead Woods, zone 4)

@ www.rave.ac.uk (Ravensbourne College of Design and Communication)

Eltham • *Greenwich* (pronounced 'eltəm')

A sprawling south-east London suburb, occupying most of the area between BLACKHEATH and SIDCUP. Eltham was first recorded in Domesday Book and its name could relate to a man called Elta, or to the Old English word 'el-fitu', a swan. Plantagenet kings chose Eltham as a place of rest en route to and from France and converted the manor house into a moated palace in the 14th century. In the 1470s Edward IV added a great hall for royal banquets. For reasons not known, Eltham was particularly popular as a place for the royal families to spend Christmas. The Tudor monarchs preferred Greenwich, and Eltham Palace declined in the 16th century and was ransacked in the Civil War. The trees of the palace's three parks, Great Park, Middle Park, and HORN PARK, were cut down and used for shipbuilding. After the Restoration the vintner and influential financier Sir John Shaw leased the Great Park and built Eltham Lodge in 1664. He did not attempt to rescue the palace and the great hall became a barn. The park is now Royal Blackheath Golf Course and the lodge is its clubhouse. The parish of Eltham had 30 other houses in the early 18th century but little trace of these remains. The High Street gained some characterful premises later in the century, of which a few survive, notably the Greyhound and Rising Sun inns. The arrival of the railway at what is now NEW ELTHAM brought early suburban development to the south-east in the 1880s but the land north of the palace remained in agricultural use until 1900, when Cameron Corbett began to lay out the ELTHAM PARK estate. To its west, the Ministry of Works built housing for Woolwich Arsenal munitions workers at WELL HALL during World War I. Woolwich council subsequently built the Page, Middle Park, Horn Park and COLDHARBOUR estates, while private developers capitalized on the construction of Rochester Way, providing homes for the new car-owning classes. During the 1930s Sir Stephen Courtauld leased the site of Eltham Palace, repaired the great hall and built a new house for himself and his wife Virginia, with lavish art deco interiors. The buildings were magnificently restored by English Heritage in the 1990s and opened to the public. A tragic event elsewhere in Eltham sullied the town's reputation in 1993, when black schoolboy Stephen Lawrence was murdered in a racist attack for which no one was ever convicted. Parts of Eltham continue to be regarded as crime hotspots. In 2002 bus drivers refused to enter the Middle Park estate following repeated attacks, robberies and racial abuse. In response to the damaging effects on Eltham's image, the South Greenwich Regeneration Agency devised 'rebranding' proposals in 2005, featuring the slogan 'Eltham: more than a town'.

The Flemish artist Sir Anthony Van Dyck spent one or more summers at Eltham Palace in the 1630s and painted several of his greatest works here.

✉ SE9

👤 50,202 (Eltham North, Eltham South, Eltham West, and Middle Park and Sutcliffe wards)

🚌 South Eastern Trains (zone 4)

📖 David Sleep, *Eltham*, Tempus, 2004; Colin Nutt, *The Eltham Palace Story*, English Heritage, 2004

@ www.thisiseltham.co.uk (community site); www.elthampalace.org.uk

Eltham Park • *Greenwich*

A primarily Edwardian estate situated in the north-east of ELTHAM. Although evidence of Roman occupation has been discovered in present-day Glenesk Road, the area remained virtually undeveloped until a mansion was erected in the 18th century. The final purchaser of the mansion and its adjoining farmland was Thomas Jackson, a civil engineer involved in the building of the Bexleyheath Railway, who died shortly before the line opened. His widow died in 1899 and the estate was soon bought by Cameron Corbett, the kingpin of London's suburban housebuilding programme at that time. Corbett developed the Eltham Park estate between 1900 and 1914 and built churches for four denominations. A station opened in 1908, originally as SHOOTERS HILL and Eltham Park. The most expensive houses were built close to the station but out of earshot of the trains, and had servants' quarters. Cheaper properties were built close to the line or on the estate's fringes. Corbett was a teetotaller so no public houses were provided; to this day a covenant prohibits the use of any premises for the sale of alcoholic beverages. When an off-licence eventually opened, it was situated on the bridge over the railway, not on Corbett's land. Many of the early residents worked at WOOLWICH ARSENAL or at other military establishments in the area and rented their homes at reasonable prices. From 1910 a tram service provided a direct link with WOOLWICH. The original Rochester Way came through the north of the district in 1932, but in the 1980s the estate and the neighbouring public park were split in two by the relief road (A2) that was cut alongside the railway line. Eltham Park station closed in 1985, when Eltham's new station opened.

The comedian Bob Hope was born in Craigton Road in 1903, and was christened Leslie Towns. The family migrated to America when he was four years old, settling in Cleveland, Ohio.

✉ SE9

Elthorne Heights • *Ealing*

A hotch-potch of interwar semi-detached houses and council tower blocks and terraced houses constituting the north-western corner of HANWELL, on its border with GREENFORD. Elthorne was a hundred, a medieval administrative division that took in Hanwell, Greenford, HARMONDSWORTH and WEST DRAYTON. Elthorne Heights was earlier considered a more prestigious name than that of Hanwell, but is now little used. This was the last part of Hanwell to be built up, and was saved from overdevelopment by the opening of the Brent Valley Golf Club around 1910. Soon afterwards developers laid out Studland Road and the streets to its north and almost all the available building land was filled by 1935. The borough council took over the golf club in 1938 and it became a public course. Elsewhere, the river's border has been preserved as part of Brent Valley Park. Mayfield Primary School on High Lane is a popular school with a culturally diverse intake. Some properties in Elthorne Heights are in a poor state of repair and the locality has had a problem with cardumping.

✉ W7

Elverson Road • Lewisham

A road and station in north LEWISHAM, on the borough's border with Greenwich. The diminutive street was laid out in the late 19th century. Elverson Road station, which opened ahead of schedule in November 1999, is only 500 yards from the branch terminus at Lewisham. Most stations along this route are seeing significant commercial, cultural or residential developments in their vicinity, partly prompted by the arrival of the Docklands Light Railway, but there has been little activity here beyond the creation of Elverson Mews, which consists of a handful of two-storey terraced houses. Brookmill Park was re-landscaped when the railway line was brought through and the River Ravensbourne has been rerouted along the park's eastern edge.

✉ SE8

🚇 Docklands Light Railway, Lewisham branch (zones 2 and 3)

Embankment • Westminster/City

Usually a shorthand term for Victoria Embankment, which runs from WESTMINSTER to BLACKFRIARS, but sometimes also encompassing Albert Embankment, on the south bank of the Thames, and Chelsea Embankment, all created as part of the same project. Parliament first approved a land reclamation scheme on the Thames mudflats in 1846. Although it would have benefits in improving the flow of the Thames and releasing land for building, a vital objective was to permit the creation of an efficient network of sewers beneath the new streets that would skirt the Thames. Progress was painfully slow at first and an exasperated Thomas Cubitt built a section of wall himself so that he could complete the development of PIMLICO. Two factors eventually drove the project forward: the establishment of the Metropolitan Board of Works in 1855 and the 'great

stink' of 1858, when sheets soaked with chloride of lime had to be hung in the windows of the Houses of Parliament. Joseph Bazalgette, the hero of Victorian sanitation, was appointed to oversee the project. Victoria Embankment opened in 1870, as did Embankment station on a section of line that was half buried in the newly reclaimed riverbank. Subsoil excavated during the construction of the line was reused to fill in behind the river wall, while topsoil for Victoria Embankment Gardens was dredged from Barking Creek. A granite monolith dubbed Cleopatra's Needle was shipped from Egypt and erected opposite the gardens in 1878. This had been hewn around 1475 BC and carved with the names of gods and pharaohs, with Cleopatra's name added later. At $68\frac{1}{2}$ feet in height, it is Britain's tallest obelisk cut from a single block of stone. George Vulliamy bracketed the needle with bronze sphinxes in 1880. It is said that they were supposed to face inwards but the workmen mounted them the wrong way round.

The author Rudyard Kipling's former home in Embankment Place is marked by a blue plaque.

✉ SW1; WC2; EC4 (Victoria Embankment)

🚇 Bakerloo Line; Circle Line; District Line; Northern Line (zone 1); short walk to Charing Cross

🚢 Embankment pier

📖 Robert J Harley, *London's Victoria Embankment*, Capital History, 2005; Stephen Halliday, *The Great Stink of London: Sir Joseph Bazalgette and the Cleansing of the Victorian Metropolis*, Sutton, 2001

Emerson Park • Havering

A pricey residential district situated northeast of HORNCHURCH. In 1895 William Carter of Parkstone in Dorset bought 20 acres of Nelmes Manor and Lee Garden Manor to build 'country villas for city gentlemen'. Carter put up a wide variety of dwellings, from bungalows to family houses with accommodation for servants, and named the estate after his eldest son, Emerson. Other developers added their own estates, such as Haynes Park and Great and Little Nelmes, but the original name has come to apply to the whole neighbourhood. It is now completely built over, with cul-de-sacs jutting into what were once the gardens of larger properties. Over 91 per cent of homes in Emerson Park are owner-occupied and a similar proportion of residents are white, although the district also has one of the borough's larger communities of Indian origin. At an average 6.2 rooms per household, residents have much more space than most other Londoners, and almost half the households have two or more cars. The well-regarded Emerson Park School is on the eastern edge of the district, beside the River Ingrebourne.

✉ Hornchurch RM11

♦ 11,396

🚉 'one' Railway, Romford to Upminster branch line (zone 6)

Enfield • *Enfield*

An extensive and diverse district centred on ENFIELD TOWN and encompassing a broad belt of localities such as SOUTHBURY, WORLD'S END, GRANGE PARK, GORDON HILL and BULLSMOOR. A settlement grew up around Enfield Green and St Andrew's Church in the Middle Ages. The wooded expanse of ENFIELD CHASE lay to the west, where haymaking and dairy farming became the predominant forms of agriculture after its enclosure and deforestation. Most of the land to the east, down to the River Lea, was occupied by arable fields, many of which were later converted to market gardens. The protected status of the chase and the inhospitable nature of the marshland by the Lea discouraged the early growth of outlying hamlets but the town itself flourished. Enfield Grammar School dates from 1557, and the New River was cut through the parish in 1613; its course has since been altered. By the mid 17th century the vicinity of the green was known as Enfield Town and villages were evolving at CLAY HILL and along the Hertford Road, notably at PONDERS END. Numerous fine houses were built or rebuilt during the 18th century in the town and the surrounding country. Gentleman's Row and Forty Hall are among the best survivors. The manufacture of muskets at ENFIELD LOCK from 1804 was an indicator of the district's early industrial potential and marked the birth of Enfield's important place in the history of gunmaking. In 1831 Enfield was the second most extensive parish in Middlesex, covering some 20 square miles. As the railway companies thrust four fingers of lines into the district from the mid 19th century, the discrete villages began to grow together, coalescing in the early 20th century. Factories were concentrated in the east, along the banks of the Lea, with accompanying housing for their workers. West of the

Great Cambridge Road (A10), constructed in 1924, developers built mostly for the middle classes. The industrial side of Enfield inevitably suffered most from bombing in World War II, and became the focus of the larger municipal housing projects in the 1960s and 1970s. 'Sunset' industries have closed down or moved away from the Lea Valley corridor in places such as BRIMSDOWN, sometimes to be replaced by wholesale or retail warehouses but in other cases leaving empty brownfield sites in need of regeneration. To the north and west of the town centre the green-belt status of open land has preserved the pre-war street plan and enhanced property values. In recent years Enfield has begun to present a more cosmopolitan aspect than many other districts on the fringes of Greater London, and is attracting unmarried young professionals as well as families, although the absence of a London Underground line is a deterrent for some. The most important modern projects have been the redevelopment of the Royal Small Arms Factory site as ENFIELD ISLAND VILLAGE and recent changes in the town centre.

Former Enfield residents include civil engineer Sir Joseph Bazalgette and Isaac D'Israeli, father of prime minister and novelist Benjamin Disraeli and a literary talent in his own right.

✉ Enfield EN1, EN2 and EN3

♦ 65,776 (Chase, Enfield Lock, Enfield Highway, Southbury and Town wards)

📖 David Pam, *A History of Enfield*, 3 vols, Enfield Preservation Society, 1990–4; Graham Dalling, *Enfield Past*, Historical Publications, 1999

@ www.enfield-online.co.uk (local information site)

Enfield Chase • *Enfield*

The original Enfield Chase was a great swathe of woodland that extended from BARNET to present-day ENFIELD. It was a favourite royal hunting ground (and supposedly a hideaway for Dick Turpin) until it was deforested in the 18th century. The country park of Trent Park is now all that remains, and the name Enfield Chase has become associated with the locality around the station, half a mile west of Enfield's centre. The Great Northern Railway Co. built a branch line from Wood Green as far as Windmill Hill in 1871, when much of the surrounding area was part of the Chase Park estate. Following the death of the landowner Francis Adams, his heirs sold the land for development in 1879. Shirley Road and Station Road were divided into building plots and soon lined with terraced houses. However, much of the area still remained unexploited at the end of the century. The railway line was extended in 1910, the old terminus was converted into a goods depot and Enfield Chase station was built to the east, at the foot of Windmill Hill. A succession of 20th-century additions to the housing stock has produced a mixed but satisfactory result, and the locality benefits from a diverse selection of shops around the station. The Chase ward takes in all the villages in the north-west of the borough, including BOTANY BAY, CREWS HILL, CLAY HILL and BULLS CROSS, but it does not extend as far south as Enfield Chase station. A fifth of homes in the ward are rented from the council.

The astronomer John Hadley was born in 1682 at Enfield Chase. He became a Fellow of the Royal Society in 1716 and built the first Gregorian reflector telescope in 1721.

> ✉ Enfield EN2

> ♦ 12,531 (Chase ward)

> 🚂 WAGN Railway (zone 5)

> 📖 David Pam, *The Story of Enfield Chase*, Enfield Preservation Society, 1984

Enfield Highway • *Enfield*

A relatively poor part of north-east ENFIELD, with Enfield College to its south. Known from 1572 as Cocksmiths End, the present name dates from the mid 18th century and derives from the hamlet's situation in the parish of Enfield on the main road from London to Hertford. St James' Church was built in 1832, at that time serving a largely rural congregation, many of whom were market gardeners. A church school opened the following year. In 1840 the extension of the Metropolitan Police area led to the establishment of a police station at Enfield Highway, from which policing was supervised as far afield as Cheshunt and Waltham Abbey. Workers from the nearby Royal Small Arms Factory set up what became the Enfield Highway Co-operative Society in 1872. The society opened branches across Hertfordshire and later built local housing for workers. By the beginning of the 20th century the area was filling rapidly with artisans' houses. The 34-acre Durants Park provided the main recreational space from 1903. In 1914 there were still farms, orchards and market gardens between Enfield Highway and PONDERS END but after World War I, industrial expansion at ENFIELD LOCK prompted a further surge in building and by the outbreak of the next war the area was fully built up, much of it with council housing. The shops that line Hertford Road today are not especially alluring but they attract steady custom. Two-thirds of homes are now owner-occupied while a fifth are rented from the council. Thirty-seven per cent of 16- to 74-year-olds have no educational qualifications.

> ✉ Enfield EN3

> ♦ 14,137

Enfield Island Village • *Enfield*

A 'flagship' development of 'regional significance', according to the government, built from 1997 to 2003 by Fairview New Homes on a 100-acre flood plain lying between the River Lea and the Cattlegate Flood Relief Channel. The site was formerly occupied by the Royal Small Arms Factory. Some original buildings have been retained and the design incorporates a network of waterways, creating a habitat for waterfowl. There are distinct neighbourhoods within the village, each with its own architectural variations. The council originally imposed a limit on the number of homes that could be built before shops and community services were provided, but this was later withdrawn. The developers also increased housing density from their original proposals, with a higher proportion of social accommodation, including some that went to asylum-seekers. Enfield Island Village featured prominently in a 2000 investigation by the BBC television programme *Panorama* into housing developments on contaminated land. This reported that a survey had found traces of toxic chemicals and metals such as lead, cadmium, arsenic and copper. The land has been 'remediated' by capping with a layer of clay to prevent contaminants leaching to the surface but there have been stories of children suffering dermatological problems after playing in their back gardens, and residents have been warned not to dig down more than three feet. There was further disquiet when Enfield's chief planning officer left to join the Fairview company. The borough subsequently convened a special panel that rejected allegations of official wrongdoing but recommended 'robust and permanent monitoring' of the site in the future. The panel's report was narrowly adopted by the council.

> ✉ Enfield, EN3

📖 Paul de Zylva et al, *Unsafe as Houses: Urban Renaissance or Toxic Time Bomb?*, Friends of the Earth and Enfield Lock Action Group, 2000

@ www.eivral.com (residents' association site)

Enfield Lock • *Enfield*

A redeveloped former industrial zone located on the banks of the River Lea and the River Lea Navigation channel in the far north-east of ENFIELD. A lock and a watermill operated here from medieval times and the mill may have been used for making gunpowder in the mid 17th century. The present lock and a surveyor's house were constructed on the Enfield cut of the Lee Navigation in the early 1790s. In about 1804 an arms factory was established and soon afterwards began to assemble muskets. The factory produced the first Enfield rifle in 1853. The Board of Ordnance took over production the following year and built the much larger Royal Small Arms factory. Enfield Lock station (originally called Ordnance Factory) opened on the Great Eastern Railway in 1855. The growing scale of production at the arms factory brought workers' housing to the surrounding area, especially in 1890s and the early 20th century. Arms manufacture reached a peak in World War II and so did the area that the factory occupied. With its testing ranges, the site covered around a hundred acres. Production declined after the war, although the enterprise still employed over a thousand workers in the 1970s. The factory closed in 1988 and most of the site is now occupied by ENFIELD ISLAND VILLAGE. The Enfield Lock conservation area covers the lock itself and the older neighbouring structures, including arms workers' cottages in Government Row that date from 1816. Houses and workshops have recently been built on part of the site of the former British Waterways maintenance depot south of the lock. The former Swan and Pike bathing pool is now a picnic area. The Enfield Lock ward covers the borough's north-eastern corner, including FREEZYWATER and Enfield Island Village. The ward is more than four-fifths white, but has a variety of ethnic minorities.

✉ Enfield EN3

👤 12,714

🚉 'one' Railway (zone 6)

📖 David Pam, *The Royal Small Arms Factory Enfield and its Workers*, Broadfield Publishing, 1998

Enfield Town • *Enfield*

A market town turned suburban centre, situated towards the western side of the wider ENFIELD district, nine miles due north of the CITY OF LONDON. The green to the south of St Andrew's Church was an early focus for parish activities, holding markets and fairs from 1303. Houses soon began to encircle the green, joined by inns from the 16th century. The establishment of a marketplace in 1632 created the nucleus for the development of the modern street plan, with houses soon spreading along Church Street, Silver Street and London Road. During the 18th century, fine houses dotted the surrounding fields and the path facing the Chase to the west became known as Gentleman's Row. The Reverend John Ryland opened a school on what is now Southbury Road, which at one point included the poet John Keats amongst its pupils. In 1849 the schoolhouse became Enfield Town station, at the end of the Great Eastern Railway's new branch line. However, the 45-minute journey to London was a deterrent to potential commuters and significant expansion did not begin until the introduction of workmen's fares and a shorter route to the city in the 1870s, when the station was rebuilt. Most of the town's older buildings were demolished at the end of the 19th century and the centre began to take on its present streetscape. Of the properties that survive, the finest group is the collection of Georgian and early Victorian houses in Gentleman's Row. Pearsons department store, founded in 1903, moved into its present premises on the site of Enfield manor house in 1928. The most visible change in the modern era has been the construction of the 12-storey Tower Point in the late 1960s. The block was radically revamped in 2005 and converted from office to residential use. A new shopping mall called PalaceXchange is due to open in late 2006, when Pearsons will be enlarged to connect with it. The Town ward is the most upmarket part of the Enfield district, where adults with degrees outnumber those with no qualifications and households with two cars outnumber those with none.

The comic actor Reg Varney unveiled the world's first ATM cash dispenser at Barclays Church Street branch on 27 June 1967.

✉ Enfield EN1 and EN2

👤 13,928 (Town ward)

🚉 'one' Railway (zone 5)

📖 Graham Dalling and Valerie Carter, *Enfield Town*, Enfield Preservation Society, 1988

Enfield Wash • *Enfield*

A grim part of north-east ENFIELD, commonly known as Horsepoolstones until the 18th century, although the present name was first recorded in 1675. A 'wash' was a place that regularly flooded, in this case because of the overflow from Maiden's Brook, which was called the Wash Brook in 1826. Ermine Street, the Roman road that ran through here, probably crossed the brook via a ford. In 1753 a young girl called Elizabeth Canning claimed to have been kidnapped near the corner of Hertford Road and what is now Ordnance Road and her alleged abductors were tried and convicted, but her story was subsequently discredited and she was sentenced to transportation. Dozens of pamphlets were written about the story, such was its notoriety. The construction of the railway line to Cambridge in 1840 brought some early growth to Enfield Wash and the British Land Co. developed the Putney Lodge estate from 1867. The 45-acre Albany Park consisted of farmland and allotments until their purchase by the council and Trinity College, Cambridge in 1902. The park was probably named after Leopold, Duke of Albany, the younger son of Queen Victoria. Neighbouring College Farm was used by drovers for overnight stops when taking their cattle to the London markets, and is now a council property. The opening of Great Cambridge Road (A10) in 1924 stimulated extensive private development during the following decade. Romford builders Newman Eyre laid out the Aylands estate in the north-west corner of Enfield Wash from 1933. Council rebuilding and private infilling have been the main aspects of post-war change and the skyline is now dominated by tower blocks. Enfield Wash has a diverse ethnic mix. At Albany School half the pupils are from white British backgrounds and the main minority groups are of 'other white', black African and black Caribbean origins. Around 100 pupils come from refugee and asylum-seeking families. Enfield Wash shares shopping amenities with neighbouring FREEZYWATER.

The old folk tune *Enfield Wash* is still popular at country dances.

✉ Enfield EN3

Erith • *Bexley* (pronounced 'earith')

A fast-growing and affordable THAMES GATEWAY district situated east of BELVEDERE. Evidence has recently emerged that a forest established itself here after the last ice age, stretching across what became the Thames to HORNCHURCH. The name Earhyth, which means 'muddy landing place', was first recorded in the seventh century when lands here were granted to the bishop of the East Saxons. Henry VIII established a naval storehouse at the end of West Street in 1512. The town briefly flourished as a summer resort in the mid 19th century after the opening of a steamboat pier, a hotel and the station. Riverside gardens were laid out, with a maze and arboretum. At the same time, the docks brought industrial growth, which accelerated over the second half of the century, when Erith's population increased tenfold. The town filled with terraced housing for workers, while lords of the manor the Wheatley family progressively developed a high-class suburb in the Lesney Park area. The Wheatleys built a new manor house in NORTHUMBERLAND HEATH and created Avenue Road as a direct route to the town. To the north-west, British Oil and Cake Mills built innovative concrete silos on Church Manor Way in 1916. In the first half of the 20th century the manufacture of armaments and cables were the dominant industries. Callender's laid a pipeline across the bed of the English Channel, which was used to supply fuel for the D-Day landings. As a consequence of its military significance, Erith was the target of heavy bombing during World War II and was radically redeveloped afterwards. A concrete pier was built in 1957 and the Pier Hotel was demolished to make way for warehouses. More historic buildings were lost in the 1960s but a few remain, notably the White Hart, St John's Church and Erith Library, which has a local museum. In 1999 a Morrisons supermarket was built on the site of the old deep wharf, retaining the pier and reviving a disused industrial part of the riverside. In 2004 funding was secured for a regeneration scheme that includes a public art project. Mainly because of its remoteness, Erith has some of the cheapest property prices in the London area, both for houses and flats. The decline of industry has freed up large areas for residential development and flats, town houses and maisonettes have sprung up all over the town in recent years. However, its low-lying situation beyond the Thames Flood Barrier may make Erith increasingly prone to flooding if global warming causes the expected rise in sea levels.

Alexander Selkirk, the real-life inspiration for Daniel Defoe's *Robinson Crusoe*, arrived back at Erith in 1711 after being rescued from his desert island. He is remembered in the names of Friday Road and Crusoe Road. The poet Wendy Cope was born in Erith in 1945. Former Conservative prime minister Margaret Thatcher met her husband Denis while campaigning in Erith in 1950. He was chairman of the family paint and chemical business, the Atlas Preservative Company.

✉ Erith DA18

👤 9,811

🚊 South Eastern Trains (zone 6)

📖 Frances Sweeny, *Memories of Erith and Crayford*, Bexley Education and Leisure Services Directorate, 2002

@ www.erithmuseum.org.uk

Essex Road • *Islington*

An evolving street running north-east from ISLINGTON GREEN in the direction of STOKE NEWINGTON. The route may be of Roman origin and was certainly well-established by the Middle Ages. The road has gone by a variety of names for part or all of its length, including Seveney Street, Lower Street and Lower Road. There were some substantial properties here by about 1600 but at the end of the 17th century several of these homes had been let as inns. Rows of cottages were built from the 1760s and over successive decades the pattern of construction became increasingly dense, urban and poor, spreading into a network of side streets in the early 19th century. Overcrowding became a serious problem. Philanthropic housing associations planned the first slum clearance programmes from the late 1870s and had almost totally rebuilt the area by the end of the century. The Great Northern and City Railway opened in 1904 with a station at Essex Road, at the corner of CANONBURY Road. After World War II much of the area was rebuilt again by the borough and county councils, notably in the form of the Marquess estate of the 1960s and early 1970s. Following Islington's gentrification, private developers have been building town houses and flats since the 1980s. Essex Road now possesses a diverse set of commercial premises, from dirt-cheap discount stores to exclusive little French bistros and quirky antique emporiums. Many shops occupy single-storey extensions built over the former front gardens of terraced houses. The more interesting establishments tend to lie near Islington Green but these are spreading north-eastward with Islington's ever-growing desirability.

In 1807 the poet Thomas Hood moved to 50 Lower Street with his parents, remaining there for 20 years. The composer Benjamin Britten had a studio in Halliford Street from 1970 to 1976. His opera *Death in Venice* was partly composed here.

✉ N1

🚊 WAGN Railway (zone 2)

Euston • *Camden* (pronounced 'yoostən')

A main-line railway terminus and its immediate vicinity, located north of BLOOMSBURY. Opened by the London and Birmingham Railway Co. in July 1837 and taking its name from neighbouring EUSTON SQUARE, this was London's second railway terminus after LONDON BRIDGE. The relatively steep slope down into the station presented problems and it was originally intended to terminate the line at CHALK FARM, which later became the site of the station's goods yards. The engineer in charge of the project was Robert Stephenson, son of the railway pioneer George Stephenson. Philip Hardwick designed the station buildings and a grand entrance focused on a propylaeum, or Doric gateway, which became known as the Euston Arch. Hardwick's son added a great hall in 1849 as the boardroom of the railway company, which had by then become the London and North Western. In the mid 1960s the station was completely rebuilt in conjunction with the electrification of the west coast main line. At the same time, the entrance structures and adjacent buildings were demolished to make way for a commercial development. Completed in 1978, the complex has half a million square feet of office space, including the headquarters of what is now Network Rail. Urban conservationists will never forgive British Rail for the destruction of the Euston Arch but large chunks of it were found in Surrey and Kent in 2005, giving hope that it might be reconstructed as part of a future redevelopment programme. Most of the Euston complex now belongs to Sydney and London Properties, which intends to work with local businesses and community groups to rebuild the area with a mix of offices, shops and homes.

Capital Radio operated for more than 20 years at Euston Tower, on the corner of Hampstead Road and Euston Road. The station went on the air in 1973, splitting into separate AM and FM services in 1989. Capital is now based in LEICESTER SQUARE.

✉ NW1

🚉 Main-line: Silverlink Metro (Midlands and suburban services); Virgin Trains (West Midlands, north-east England and Scotland); London Underground: Northern Line; Victoria Line (zone 1)

📖 A J Kellaway, *Great British Railway Station: Euston,* Irwell Press, 1994

Euston Square • *Camden*

A former residential rectangle now fused with the extended forecourt of EUSTON main-line station. Euston Square's name is little used except in the context of the Tube station, which lies to the west on the corner of GOWER STREET. Present-day Euston Road began life in the 1750s as part of the New Road, which served as the original 'north circular', taking traffic away from built-up London. Until the end of the 18th century the road marked the outer edge of the metropolis in the same way that the M25 does today. In the 1810s the northward expansion of BLOOMSBURY breached this barrier with the creation of Euston Square, named after the country seat of the second Duke of Grafton at Euston Hall in north Suffolk. The scheme was more of a road-widening project than the creation of a true square: a strip of garden was laid out on the north side of the New Road, with houses around it and on the south side of the main road. Euston Square soon gave its name to the neighbouring section of the New Road and to the new railway terminus. Gower Street station opened on the world's first underground railway in 1863 and was renamed Euston Square in 1909. The houses disappeared from the square long ago and the vicinity is now filled with a mixture of 20th- and 21st-century commercial and institutional premises, notably the buildings of the Wellcome Trust. A garden of sorts remains at Euston Square, with benches, lawns and beds of shrubs, but it is split in half by a bus lane that passes between stone lodges from the Victorian entrance to Euston station. As Camden council points out, tongue in cheek, this little park probably has more visitors than any other in the borough, but commuters rarely linger here on their way to the station.

The Wellcome Trust building at 183 Euston Road is presently being refurbished and is due to reopen in 2007, with events and exhibition spaces, a library of the history of medicine and other facilities.

✉ NW1

🚉 Circle Line; Hammersmith & City Line; Metropolitan Line (zone 1)

@ www.wellcome.ac.uk (Wellcome Trust site)

Fairfield • *Croydon*

The borough's most populous ward, taking in CROYDON town centre. The area was radically redeveloped from the late 1950s, and dispiritingly overwhelmed by high-rise office towers, an underpass and flyover, and several multistorey car parks. Opened in 1962, the Fairfield Halls consist of an 1,800-seat concert hall, the 750-seat Ashcroft Theatre and the 500-seat, multi-purpose Arnham Gallery. Fairfield is south London's leading cultural and entertainment venue, hosting popular and classical music concerts, wrestling, comedy, pantomime and ballet. The council's Vision 2020 scheme for the regeneration of central Croydon envisages the refurbishment and partial redevelopment of the Fairfield Halls as part of the creation of a new arts and cultural quarter. A low-level piazza will link the theatre with the nearby Queen's Gardens, while existing open space will be remodelled to provide a pedestrian boulevard connecting Queen's Gardens, Croydon College and EAST CROYDON station. Apartments will front the boulevard, and restaurants and cafés will surround the piazza, linking with a new entrance and foyer to the Fairfield Halls. Work is expected to begin in 2007. The Fairfield ward has a high proportion of young, single, well-educated residents. Almost half the homes are one-person households, many of which are privately rented.

The rock bands Nice, Soft Machine, Paul Kossoff and Caravan have all released live albums recorded at the Fairfield Halls, as did the pop group Bucks Fizz. Scenes in the film version of *The Da Vinci Code* were shot in the vicinity of the Halls.

✉ Croydon CR0

♦ 14,085

@ www.fairfield.co.uk

Fairlop • *Redbridge*

A semi-rural hamlet situated south-west of HAINAULT, primarily given over to recreation grounds and playing fields. The railway station opened in 1903 and ran a steam service until 1947, when the Fairlop loop became part of the London Underground network. Neighbouring Fairlop Plain, once a part of Hainault Forest, used to be the venue for an annual fair that took place beneath the Fairlop oak on the first Friday of July. This magnificent tree was blown down in 1820 after being killed by the many fires that had been lighted around it, although the fair continued until 1853. A 'new Fairlop oak' was planted at the centre of the FULWELL CROSS roundabout in 1951. Fairlop Plain was used as an aircraft base during World War II, but plans to create a civil airport were abandoned in 1953. Ilford council then bought the site from the CITY OF LONDON, and profited from the extraction of over a million cubic yards of gravel. The resultant hole was subsequently filled with refuse and has been landscaped to create Fairlop Waters golf course and country park. There is a nature reserve, an activity centre, and water sports and angling on Fairlop Lake. Plans to create Greater London's only horse racing course on greenbelt land at Fairlop Waters were rejected in 2002. The very large Fairlop Primary School caters for pupils from a wide catchment area. In 2001 the national standards agency Ofsted reported that more than 120 children came from families with origins outside the United Kingdom.

The *Fairlop Fair Song* is a traditional ballad that records the custom of riding through the fair while seated in boats.

✉ Ilford IG6

♦ 10,420 (this includes several surrounding localities)

🚇 Central Line (zone 5)

📖 P Kylin, *Fairlop Oak and Fairlop Fair*, self-published, 1982

Falconwood • *Greenwich/Bexley*

A privately developed, low-cost estate separated from ELTHAM PARK by Oxleas Wood and Shepherdleas Wood, and best-known to outsiders as a traffic-camera location monitoring a busy stretch of the A2. Falcon Wood was part of Eltham Palace's parkland from medieval times, and was said to derive its name from the Plantagenet kings flying their falcons here. After the Civil War the trees were felled for use in shipbuilding. In the 18th century a house named Falconwood stood on the east slope of SHOOTERS HILL. Until the late 19th century most of the present settlement of Falconwood was covered by West Wood, owned by Oxford University, lord of the manor of BEXLEY. This woodland was cleared in 1895 and replaced by Westwood Farm. In the early 1930s the farm was acquired by New Ideal Homesteads, south-east London's pre-eminent suburban housebuilders, for the creation of Falconwood Park, a south-westward extension of WELLING; NIH rarely built an estate without appending the word 'park' to its name, but here the suffix has not stuck. The developers erected over 2,000 properties at a total construction cost of £1.5 million, offering detached houses with two reception rooms, three bedrooms and a separate lavatory from an economical £559. The mock-Tudor shops and amenities of the Green covered the site of Westwood farmhouse. NIH contributed substantially to the cost of the 'functional and fashionable' station, which opened long after the rest of the Bexleyheath line, on New Year's Day in 1936. Later that year Falconwood Field was acquired as a public open space. The houses of Falconwood are almost exclusively owner-occupied and the residents are predominantly white.

> ✉ SE9; Welling DA16

> ♟ 10,535 (Bexley's Falconwood and Welling ward)

> 🚃 South Eastern Trains (zone 4)

Fallow Corner • *Barnet*
A very late Victorian neighbourhood situated at the southern tip of NORTH FINCHLEY. Although now focused on the corner of Granville Road and Finchley High Road, this was originally uncultivated land at the corner of FINCHLEY Common. Fallow Corner was first recorded in 1429 and Fallow Farm (originally Cobley's) was in existence from the late 17th century. A small workhouse stood near Fallow Corner from around 1768 and had become very overcrowded 20 years later. After the enclosure of the common in 1814, new roads were constructed, including Bow Lane, which was named after its shape, while Fallow Farm was much enlarged. The farmhouse stood just

west of the present Heatherdene Close and its estate remained in the possession of the Cobleys and their descendants the Clulow and Child families until the late 19th century. In its latter days the 80-acre estate was renamed Etchingham Park, after the Clulow family home in Sussex. The sale of the farm and the mooted arrival here of electric trams prompted a spate of activity at Fallow Corner in the very early years of the 20th century. Neighbouring Wimbush Farm was sold and its farmhouse demolished. The 13-acre grounds of another large house, Fallow Lodge, were divided into 101 plots and built on. Fallow Court Avenue was laid out around it. A mattress factory was built, with accommodation above, offering a same-day restuffing service. In 1903 a county school opened and in 1908 a cottage hospital, which was extended in 1922 and renamed Finchley Memorial Hospital. The few remaining gaps were built on around this time, including the site of Fallow Farm's farmhouse. Fallow Cottage was sold in 1939 to Wood and Wallers, who built flats on its site. Across the High Road, the Glebe Land has been preserved as sports and recreation grounds.

A blue plaque identifies the site of Joseph Grimaldi's former home at Fallow Cottage. The great clown lived here from 1806 until around 1815, returning each evening after his performances on the stage in London. Grimaldi's two-volume memoirs were edited by Charles Dickens and published in 1838. Five years later Dickens retreated to Fallow Farm in order to complete *Martin Chuzzlewit*.

> ✉ N12

Farnborough • *Bromley*
A suburban village situated on the edge of larch woods and open country, at the south-western extremity of ORPINGTON'S sprawl. An Anglo-Saxon charter identified the boundary of Farnborough in 862. The name referred to a small hill, overgrown with ferns. The manor of Farnborough belonged to the Duchy of Lancaster 'from the first erection of it', as Edward Hasted put it in his *History of Kent*. The powerful Simon de Montfort leased Farnborough Hall to Simon de Chelsfield in the mid 13th century. In 1639 a great storm destroyed the Church of St Giles the Abbot, which had to be rebuilt from scratch. Vestry records depict an active community in the 18th century, with plenty of takers for rewards that were offered for badgers' heads and the carcasses of foxes, polecats and hedgehogs. In 1845, Brom-

ley board of guardians built at LOCKSBOTTOM a union workhouse that subsequently evolved into Farnborough Hospital. Like DOWNE and GREEN STREET GREEN, Farnborough was popular with walkers and cyclists in the early 20th century and refreshment rooms abounded. The pretty village began to succumb to suburban development after World War I, causing the fragmentation of the area's long-established Gypsy community. When Urania Boswell, the queen of Kent's Gypsies, died in 1933 a crowd of 15,000 turned out to watch her funeral procession. Also known as Gypsy Lee, she was buried in St Giles' churchyard. After World War II the area north of the High Street filled with housing, but green-belt legislation prevented building further south. The developments included Darrick Wood, which is now Keniston Housing Association's largest estate, with around 360 houses and flats, and sheltered accommodation for the elderly. The Farnborough and CROFTON ward has an above-average proportion of older people, making for a high average age of 42.6 years. More than 95 per cent of residents are white. At Farnborough Primary School, pupils come from a broad range of socio-economic backgrounds, but relatively few are eligible for free school meals and attainment on entry is broadly above average, although spread across a wide range. None of the pupils is at an early stage of acquiring the English language.

The former England cricketer and current cricket commentator Chris Cowdrey, son of the great Colin, was born at Farnborough in 1957.

> ✉ Orpington BR6

> ♦ 14,180 (Farnborough and Crofton ward)

> ☐ Muriel V Searle, *Farnborough and Downe in Old Picture Postcards*, European Library, 1990

Farringdon • *City/Islington*

A historic underground station and its immediate environs, situated in south CLERKENWELL. Farringdon's name defines only a compact quarter because there are other well-known localities close by, such as SMITHFIELD and HATTON GARDEN. The city ward of the same name covers a much wider area. Documents of the late 13th century record William de Farindon (whose name is spelt several ways, sometimes within the space of a single paragraph), who was a goldsmith and a City of London alderman. This area lay well

away from the heart of medieval London and remained isolated until the River Fleet was covered in 1737 and Farringdon Street was constructed over it. Shoddy housing went up on Saffron Hill and the neighbourhood became seriously overcrowded. Work to extend Farringdon Street began in the early 1840s. Originally called Victoria Street, and later Farringdon Road, the new thoroughfare pushed very slowly north towards KING'S CROSS over the following two decades, cutting through the Saffron Hill slums; 1,600 homes were demolished and *The Times* estimated that 16,000 residents were displaced. The arrival of London's first underground railway brought further disruption in 1863, when Farringdon Street station opened. The station was relocated to its present position two years later when the line was extended to Moorgate and its spacious interior survives from that time. Warehouses, type foundries and other commercial and industrial premises were built along Farringdon Road in the 1860s and 1870s and a miscellaneous market began to operate, which later specialized in second-hand books. Some of the road's earliest buildings survive, mixed in with a largely unattractive set of office blocks from the latter part of the 20th century. *The Guardian* newspaper moved its headquarters to Farringdon Road in 1976. A newsroom, visitor centre and archive opened in 2002 in a converted Victorian warehouse. In recent years the Farringdon area has gained new residential accommodation, mainly well-appointed apartments for City businesspeople, and a variety of bars and nightclubs.

The Labour Party was founded in 1900 at a meeting of trade unionists and socialists held in a church hall at Caroone House, at the southern end of Farringdon Street. This was the former site of the notorious Fleet Prison, which was burned down in the Peasants' Revolt, rebuilt and finally demolished in 1846. Caroone House itself was demolished in 2004.

> ✉ EC1; EC4

> ♦ 868 (City wards of Farringdon Within and Farringdon Without)

> 🚇 Thameslink; Circle Line; Hammersmith & City Line; Metropolitan Line (zone 1)

Farthing Street • *Bromley*

A hamlet since Norman times, Farthing Street is a quiet echo of DOWNE, which lies three-quarters of a mile to the south. The name was first recorded in 1332, although 'street' was added later. 'Farthing' probably referred to land that made up a quarter of a larger estate, while 'street' would indicate that this was a row of dwellings, rather than just an empty cart-track. Nineteenth-century flint-faced houses with red-brick dressings are hidden away on a single-track lane with tall hedgerows, but overhead power lines strung across the village detract from its appeal. Farthing Street Farm was once noted for its strawberries, picked at dawn and delivered to the shops of BROMLEY by 9am.

> ✉ Orpington BR6

Feltham • *Hounslow* (pronounced 'feltǝm')

A sprawling suburban development located just inside the Greater London border, to the west of HANWORTH, with which it has a close historical association. A Saxon hamlet by the 8th century, its name means 'a settlement in a field'. Feltham had become a small village of around 100 people when the manor and surrounding houses and barns were destroyed by fire in 1634. The medieval church of St Dunstan survived the fire but was rebuilt in 1802. Heathland enclosure led to the development of market gardening, and a handful of mills were built beside the River LONGFORD. Agriculture remained the main occupation until the 1920s, after which unconstrained urbanization began. By the late 20th century, Feltham had become a run-down district, despite its convenience for Heathrow Airport. The Feltham First Regeneration Programme is injecting up to £160 million of private and public sector money into a large number of regeneration projects. Among the achievements to date are a new leisure complex, the refurbishment of a derelict office building as a hotel, and the construction of Feltham Gateway, a rail/bus terminus linked directly with Heathrow Airport and central London. Further projects are under consideration, including a complete redevelopment of the town centre. Perhaps surprisingly, Feltham has a loyal residential population; a recent survey found that more than half the locals questioned had lived here for ten years or more.

Freddie Mercury, legendary frontman of the rock group Queen, spent his teenage years in Feltham after his family moved there from Zanzibar in 1964. The band's guitarist, Brian May, grew up nearby, although the two did not meet at that time. After Mercury's death, his parents suggested converting the house into a museum, but the council was not prepared to assist in the project.

> ✉ Feltham TW13 and TW14
>
> ♂ 21,100 (Feltham North and Feltham West wards)
>
> 🚃 South West Trains (zone 6)
>
> 📖 Kenneth Baldwin, *Bygone Feltham*, Hounslow and District Historical Society, 1988

Fenchurch Street • *City*

An office-filled street curving south-westwards from ALDGATE, with a shipping-related past and one of London's most commuter-oriented railway stations. The Romans built several municipal structures at the western end of the street in the first and second centuries AD, including a military storehouse. The present name was first recorded in 1283 as Fancherchestrate and probably referred to a street by a church in a marsh. Alternatively, the first part could have come from 'faenum', or hay, indicating the presence of a haymarket. The church was presumably All Hallows, Staining, which stood in Mark Lane. In the late 18th century the East India Company built bonded warehouses on Fenchurch Street. The station opened in 1841 as the City terminus of the London and BLACKWALL Railway. In *London River* (1921), H M Tomlinson describes 'a cobbled forecourt, tame pigeons, cabs, a brick front topped by a clock-face: Fenchurch Street Station. Beyond its dingy platforms, the metal track which contracts into the murk is the road to China … It is the beginning of Dockland.' The names of some of the street's buildings indicate its mercantile connections: Black Sea and Baltic House, the Marine Engineers' Memorial Building and the offices of Lloyd's Register of Shipping. On its completion in 1957, the 14-storey Fountain House became Britain's first office tower block. Fenchurch Street station is heavily devoted to commuter traffic. Over 83 per cent of passenger arrivals at Fenchurch Street station take place during the morning peak period. Season tickets account for three-quarters of its passenger revenue.

The author Joseph Conrad frequented Fenchurch Street's bars and Ford Madox Ford recalled that 'Conrad could tell you where every husky earringed fellow with a blue, white-spotted handkerchief under his arm was going to … It most impressed the writer that in the station barber's shop was a placard that read: Teeth scaled two shillings, extractions sixpence … To come home from the great waters to that!' Fenchurch Street was the subject of a Baroness Orczy mystery in

1902 and the station appears – and disappears – in *The Hitchhiker's Guide to the Galaxy*.

✉ EC3

🚉 c2c; terminus of London, Tilbury and Southend line (zone 1)

📖 J E Connor, *Fenchurch Street to Barking (Eastern Main Lines series)*, Middleton Press, 1998

Ferrier • *Greenwich*

A large, multicultural housing estate in south KIDBROOKE, and 'one of the most deprived neighbourhoods in England' according to the council that is now overseeing its eradication. In 1970 the London Borough of Greenwich was handed the land occupied by the former RAF depot near Kidbrooke station and immediately began construction of the houses, maisonettes and tower blocks of the Ferrier estate. At the same time the dilapidated old station was rebuilt to cope with the surge in traffic. The subsequent deterioration of the estate, both structurally and socially, became a casebook example of urban decay. At the end of the 20th century the Ferrier estate was the focus of high-profile initiatives to make it a better place to live and politicians queued up for photo opportunities here. But in a subsequent admission of defeat, Greenwich council earmarked the estate for demolition, despite objections that too much of the substitute housing would be for private sale and that displaced residents would suffer as result of the break-up of close-knit ethnic groups. The council made efforts to address these concerns, consulting residents on each aspect of the regeneration proposals, with dedicated meetings for the estate's Chinese, Vietnamese and Somali communities. The estate will be progressively rebuilt on entirely different lines and will not be called Ferrier. The development will see 4,400 new homes, of which 1,910 will be 'affordable', with a school within an educational campus, improved transport links and community spaces. Ferrier tenants have been relocated across the borough, including to THAMESMEAD, PLUMSTEAD and WOOLWICH ARSENAL and some new housing has already been completed locally. The total cost of the project, which has been part-funded by the sale of council-owned land, will approach £1 billion, making this one of the largest such schemes ever undertaken in London. Work will probably be completed around 2011.

The popular journalist Garry Bushell sprang from what he described in 1979 as 'the towering concrete jumble I call home and the council so lovingly christened the Ferrier'.

✉ SE9; SE3

📖 Séamas Coileáin, *Voices of Ferrier*, Greenwich Community College Press, 1995

Figge's Marsh • *Merton*

A triangular open space and its neighbouring housing, located at the fork of London Road (A217) and STREATHAM Road (A216) in north MITCHAM. Figge's Marsh is nine miles from London, according to its 18th-century milestone, and is named after William Figge, who held the land from 1357. The marsh was formerly part of a continuous swathe of pasture land that stretched from CROYDON to Mitcham. By the 18th century, Swain's Farm and Pound Farm were cultivating flowers and herbs for the perfume and culinary markets. During the first half of the 19th century James Arthur of Pound Farm and neighbouring landowner Major James Moore grew opium poppies to produce morphine for medical use. Moore also grew hemp and the hallucinogenic wormwood, which was used in place of hops in some Mitcham ales. Housing closed in around the surviving 25 acres over the course of the 20th century, especially between the world wars, and the open space is now used as a gathering place for activities like parades and fun runs, as well as for flying model aircraft. Figge's Marsh was formerly home to TOOTING GRAVENEY Football Club (now merged into Tooting and Mitcham FC) and Mitcham Rugby Club. The Figge's Marsh ward has relatively high proportions of households with children and renting from the council, and significant black and Asian minorities. It is one of Merton's priority wards for action on areas of social concern, such as the welfare of single-parent families.

Daniel Defoe is said to have lived in a house on London Road near Figge's Marsh around 1688, when he was serving as a Nonconformist minister in Tooting, but the whole story is open to question. Other tall tales of Figge's Marsh revolve around sightings of the legendary Spring Heeled Jack on Streatham Lane (now Road) in the 1870s, sometime after his heyday. A local posse was got up in a vain attempt to catch the creature with the preternatural jumping ability.

✉ Mitcham CR4

👥 9,896

Finchley • _Barnet_

A famously conservative residential district, situated north of HAMPSTEAD GARDEN SUBURB. The evolutionary patterns of most outer London suburbs have been determined primarily by when and where their stations were built, but the shape of growth here was mainly driven by road construction. The hamlet of Finchley took root at Gravel Hill in the 12th century and St Mary's Church had been built by 1274. The settlement lay on the road from HENDON to WHETSTONE, far enough from Dollis Brook to avoid the risk of flooding but with its own supply of well-water. Around 1350 the Bishop of London allowed travellers to pass through Hornsey Park, creating a new northerly route that took traffic to the east of the village. The Great North Road (as it became) emerged from the park at Finchley's East End (now EAST FINCHLEY) and a string of cottages soon appeared here. The two halves of Finchley were linked by what is now East End Road. East End's concentration of inns, smithies and other providers of services to travellers made it Finchley's principal settlement by the 16th century. Gentlemen's residences were scattered loosely around the district, but none were of sufficient grandeur to form the nucleus of an additional hamlet. As the woodland was cleared, dairy farming and haymaking became the main forms of agriculture. In 1826 a northbound route from west London (called the FINCHLEY ROAD further south and Regent's Park Road here) met Hendon Lane at CHURCH END and connected with the Great North Road (now the A1000) via an extension of BALLARDS LANE. This helped to rejuvenate Church End but the greatest change was to the formerly barren common land at the new junction in the north, which, as NORTH FINCHLEY, became the main commercial centre. The arrival of the railways in the late 1860s and early 1870s had an effect but equally important was the introduction of electric trams to the main roads in the early years of the 20th century. Only at this point did developers begin to lay out residential streets on almost every remaining Finchley field, including the formerly uncultivated land at FALLOW CORNER. After the mid 1920s the North Circular Road (A406) swung across the south-west of the district, bringing housebuilding to its hinterland and separating East Finchley from its parent. One of the last corners to be built up was WEST FINCHLEY, which did not appear – as either a station or a place – until the early 1930s. Even here the station opened in response to housing development, rather than prompting it. The most significant change since World War II was the municipal redevelopment of East Finchley, which partially obliterated its original street pattern.

In the latter part of the 20th century Finchley was best known nationally as the constituency of Margaret Thatcher, prime minister from 1979 to 1990. She represented the seat from her parliamentary debut in 1959 until her retirement from the House of Commons at the 1992 general election. Finchley provided less controversial heroes in the four Pevensie children, saviours of Narnia in C S Lewis's stories and the 2005 film adaptation of _The Lion, the Witch and the Wardrobe_.

✉ N3; N2 (East Finchley); N12 (North Finchley)

ꝑ 58,141 (East Finchley, Finchley Church End, West Finchley and Woodhouse wards)

🚇 Northern Line (Finchley Central, zone 4; other stations listed under specific localities)

📖 Lynn Bresler (ed.), _Finchley Remembered_, Finchley Society, 2002

@ www.finchleysociety.org.uk

Finchley Central _see_ CHURCH END (BARNET)

Finchley Road • _Camden_

A long, curving highway running from ST JOHN'S WOOD to FINCHLEY, and specifically that part of it in the vicinity of Finchley Road Tube station, in south-west HAMPSTEAD. Excavation of the London Underground line here provided evidence that this was the furthest point reached by the glacial sheet that covered most of Britain during the last ice age. Finchley Road sliced through the demesne of FROGNAL in the late 1820s but a number of legalities prevented its commercial exploitation for several decades. Finchley Road station (now Finchley Road and Frognal) opened on the Hampstead Junction Railway in 1860. The Metropolitan Railway built a separate station in 1879 when the line was extended to WILLESDEN GREEN. By then the first signs of development were in evidence, with cottages on the former Finchley Road brickfield and, on the east side of the road, Holy Trinity Church and its vicarage. An ice skating rink opened in 1880 and the first shops appeared shortly afterwards. Within another decade the road had a string of houses, some of which were soon converted to shops at street level. Today the stretch of road between the

◄ **Addington** – The former palace of the archbishops of Canterbury is now a golf clubhouse

▲ The west side of **Aldersgate Street** has been lined with new office blocks in recent years

▼ **Aldborough Hatch** – Aldborough Hall Farm has a child-friendly barnyard and a farm shop

▲ Many properties in **Aldersbrook** retain their original porches and other Edwardian features

► Built in the mid-1860s, **Alexandra Palace** was north London's answer to the Crystal Palace, but has also been beset by fires

▲ **Alperton**'s Ace Café has been restored to its former glory and is once again popular with London's bikers

▲ **Archway** Bridge has spiked railings that attempt to deter suicide bids

◄ The tower blocks of the **Alton Estate,** seen from Richmond Park

▲ The Grade II-listed **Arnos Grove** station is regarded as one of the finest achievements of the architect Charles Holden

▲ A statue of Galatea reclining on a dolphin's back in the winter garden at **Avery Hill**

▲ John Doubleday's statue of Sherlock Holmes was erected outside **Baker Street** station in 1999

▲ **Bakers Arms** – The London Master Bakers' Benevolent Institute began building these almshouses in 1857

▶ The **Bank** of England moved to its present site in 1724 and the heart of the much-altered building is the work of Sir John Soane

◀ The Globe Theatre opened on **Bankside** in 1997, 200 yards from the site of its Shakespearean predecessor

▲ Sir Giles Gilbert Scott's **Bankside** power station became home to Tate Modern in 2000

▲ In 2002 the T-Rex Action Group erected this memorial at the 'Bolan tree' on Queen's Ride in **Barnes**

▲ **Barnes** developed around a village green and a trio of ponds, of which only the largest now remains

▲ The Catch is a sculpture at Fanshawe roundabout celebrating **Barking**'s fishing tradition

▲ Lauderdale Tower is one of three 400-foot residential skyscrapers on the **Barbican** estate

▲ The Tudor Hall began as a grammar school under a charter granted by Elizabeth I and is now part of **Barnet** College

▲ Hemingford Road in **Barnsbury**, an area that moved from irredeemable to irresistible in the space of a decade

▲ **Beckton** owes its existence to its gasworks and is named after the gas company's governor

▲ The **Battersea** Park peace pagoda was built by Japanese Buddhist monks and nuns in 1985

▶ **Bayswater** Road becomes London's largest open-air art gallery every Sunday

◄ **Bedford Park**'s houses are distinguished by individual architectural styling

▲ **Belsize Village** was a service zone for the grand homes of the neighbouring streets

▲ Eaton Square is the largest square in **Belgravia** and was laid out by Thomas Cubitt from 1827

▼ **BedZED**'s colourful roof cowls use outgoing stale air to warm incoming fresh air

▲ The **Belvedere** Social Club on Nuxley Road is one of several members-only establishments in the area

▲ **Blackfriars** – The back room of the Black Friar pub is unchanged from its Arts and Crafts remodelling of 1905

▶ Hall Place was built in 1537 and is now managed by the **Bexley** Heritage Trust

▲ The **Bishops Avenue** – Toprak Mansion was built for a Turkish entrepreneur and has recently been valued at £50 million

▲ **Bermondsey** antiques market is open on Friday mornings from 6am until 12 noon

▲ **Blackheath** – The Paragon is a unique crescent of seven pairs of houses linked by colonnades, by Michael Searles

▲ **Bloomsbury** – Restoration of the British Museum's Great Court and its central reading room was completed in 2000

▲ **Bow** Locks are situated where the multiple channels of the Bow Back Rivers merge to become Bow Creek

◄ **Borough** market has been undergoing major improvements to capitalize on the surge in popularity of its farmers' produce

▲ Many of **Brentham**'s houses were styled in the Arts and Crafts tradition in the early years of the 20th century

▲ **Brick Lane**'s curry houses and other south Asian restaurants are the best-known feature of London's 'Banglatown'

◄ The architectural highlight of **Brentford**, the Butts were developed from the late 17th century by a local pub landlord

▶ **Boston Manor** was built in 1623 for Lady Mary Reade in preparation for her marriage to Sir Edward Spencer of Althorp

▶ **Brixton**'s Ritzy cinema opened in 1911 as the Electric Pavilion and was restored and extended in the 1990s

▼ **Bruce Grove** – the former home of the family of Robert the Bruce is now a museum of local history

▲ Now Tower Hamlets register office, **Bromley-by-Bow**'s public hall was built in 1880 as the vestry hall for St Leonard's parish

◀ A Tridentine mass is held on Sundays at the Little Oratory, adjoining the London Oratory on **Brompton Road**

▲ **Bushy Park** is the second-largest but least known of London's eight royal parks

▲ The enormously successful markets in **Camden Town** are popular for their many food stalls, as well as fashion, crafts and music

▲ **Bunhill** Fields is the final resting place of the Christian writer John Bunyan

▶ **Canada Water** is a surviving part of the former Surrey Docks and is scheduled for a £1-billion redevelopment programme

◄ **Canary Wharf** is the focal project of the regeneration schemes that have transformed the Isle of Dogs since the late 1980s

▲ **Cannon Street**'s London Stone is a remnant of a monolith that assumed semi-mythical status in the Middle Ages

▲ **Canonbury** House was built at the end of the 18th century on the site of the west range of its much larger predecessor

◄ **Carshalton Beeches** – Little Holland House was the self-built home of the artist and craftsman Frank Dickinson

▲ This sign at **Catford** shopping centre features a domestic version of the feral felines that probably gave the district its name

▲ Substantial family homes lined **Castelnau** from the mid-19th century, creating a desirable boulevard between Barnes and Hammersmith Bridge

◄ **Chapel Market** has provided fresh produce to the people of Islington since the 1860s

▲ Built in 1612 and later the focus of **Charlton Village,** the palatial Charlton House is now a community centre and its grounds are a public park

▲ Enfield's **Chase Side** has a variety of brick, stuccoed and weatherboarded cottages and villas, most built in the early 19th century

▲ Lumley Chapel is the surviving portion of **Cheam**'s original church and is the borough's oldest building

▲ By tradition, a true cockney must have been born within earshot of the church bells of St Mary-le-Bow, **Cheapside**

▲ Cross Hall is one of a cluster of older buildings at the heart of **Chelsfield Village**

▲ **Chiswick** House is a Palladian villa built for the third Earl of Burlington in the late 1720s

▲ The monument to **Chislehurst** resident Eugène Napoleon, the Prince Imperial, who was killed on a British expedition to Zululand in 1879

▲ Looking like an oversized privy, this is the clerks' well from which **Clerkenwell** draws its name

▲ Designed by the Richard Rogers Partnership, the Lloyds Building was the most distinctive addition to the **City of London** in the 1980s

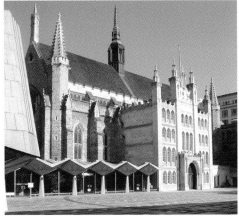

▲ Guildhall has been the administrative headquarters for the **City of London** since the Middle Ages

▲ **Clapham Common**'s Eagle Pond is a well-stocked coarse fishing lake of approximately one acre, which was de-silted in 2002

▲ Lenin used an office in this former charity school building on **Clerkenwell** Green, which is now the home of the Marx Memorial Library

▲ Warren Rise forms a border of Kingston's **Coombe** House conservation area, which has distinctive structures from the last four centuries

▲ **Columbia Road** in Bethnal Green hosts London's finest flower market every Sunday morning

▲ The former **Colney Hatch** asylum has been transformed into an upmarket residential estate and rebranded Princess Park Manor

▲ This clock tower is the surviving centrepiece of the market that was established on **Copenhagen Fields** in the mid-19th century

▶ **Coney Hall** – 81 Kingsway was the house where an influential mortgage strike began in 1937

◄ **Coppermills** – Reservoir No. 5 has an island that is of national significance as a roosting place for rarer birds than this Canada goose

▲ For lovers of opera and ballet, **Covent Garden** is synonymous with the Royal Opera House, which was radically reconstructed in the late 1990s

▲ **Cottenham Park** – The 3.5-acre Holland Gardens were opened to the public in 1929

▲ 23 **Cranley Gardens**, the former home of serial killer Dennis Nilsen

▲ Local miscreants were formerly locked up for the night in **Cranford**'s claustrophobic Round House

▲ **Crossness** pumping station was built as part of Joseph Bazalgette's masterplan for the improvement of sewage disposal in Victorian London

▲ **Crouch End** – The design for Hornsey Town Hall was influenced by a much grander Dutch counterpart in Hilversum

▲ **Cubitt Town** – Completed in 1905, the Carnegie library is a relatively old survivor in this heavily redeveloped Docklands locality

▲ **Croydon**'s Old Palace School was a property of the archbishops of Canterbury until 1780

▶ The ExCeL exhibition and conference centre at **Custom House** will host several events in the 2012 Olympics

▲ The **Cutty Sark** as it looked before it was ravaged by fire in 2007, and as it is hoped it will look again after restoration

▲ Created in the mid-1980s, the Hackney peace carnival mural on **Dalston** Lane seems likely to survive redevelopment plans

▲ Drum-shaped halls of residence for the University of East London were built at **Cyprus** in 1999

▲ Based in a quayside warehouse, the Museum in **Docklands** unites traditional museum displays, life-size reconstructions and multimedia technology

◄ **Downe** – Now a museum belonging to English Heritage, Down House was the home of Charles Darwin for the last 40 years of his life

▲ **East Finchley** – Projectionist Peter Bayley was awarded the MBE in 2002 for 42 years of service to the Phoenix cinema

▲ **Dulwich** – The original buildings of Edward Alleyn's College of God's Gift have been much altered in successive phases of restoration

▲ A wooden platform shelter at **East Acton** station, built by the Great Western Railway Co. in 1920

▲ **East India** Docks have been redeveloped with a complex of classy office blocks

▲ **East Sheen** – A pedestrian shelter from the medieval London Bridge survives in the gardens of the Courtlands estate

▲ The appalling shopping centre at **Elephant and Castle** is due to be replaced as part of the area's comprehensive regeneration

▲ St Paul's Cathedral forms a part of the Battle of Britain Monument on Victoria **Embankment,** which was unveiled by the Prince of Wales in 2005

▲ Edward IV was responsible for most of the surviving medieval parts of **Eltham Palace,** probably including the stone bridge that crosses its moat

▲ A customer smokes a hookah in an Arabic café on **Edgware Road**

▲ **Enfield Island Village** has been laid out around preserved buildings and artefacts from the former Royal Small Arms Factory

▲ A group of terraced cottages line the New River at **Enfield Town**'s River View

▲ Unprepossessing clothes stalls line Seven Sisters Road beneath the railway bridge in **Finsbury Park**

▲ The former Daily Express building at numbers 120–129 **Fleet Street** made pioneering use of curtain-walling techniques

▲ Augustus John is credited with coining the name '**Fitzrovia**' in honour of his favourite hostelry, the Fitzroy Tavern

▲ **Fleet Street** – The writers Dr Johnson, Voltaire, Thackeray and Dickens all drank at Ye Olde Cheshire Cheese

◀ Five Arches Bridge linked the estates of **Foots Cray** and North Cray Places in 1782

▲ **Forty Hill** – Sir Ncholas Raynton, a haberdasher and lord mayor of London, built Forty Hall between 1629 and 1636

▲ 20 Maresfield Gardens, in the **Frognal** area of Hampstead, was the home of the Freud family from 1938 to 1982

◀ **Fulham** Road's Michelin Building began life as a tyre-fitting garage in 1911 and was refurbished as a Conran restaurant in 1986

▲ 'Moscow Hall' was built at **Gants Hill** Central Line station in 1947 and restored to its original condition in 1994

▲ The Ecopark at **Gallions Reach Urban Village** is an affordable housing project with an emphasis on sustainability and low energy use

▲ Platform for Art is a London Underground project sponsoring billboard displays at **Gloucester Road** station

▲ **Grove Park** (Lewisham) – Chinbrook Meadows were improved in 2003, with new paths, trees and sports facilities and the 'naturalization' of the Quaggy River

▲ The **Gorringe Park** pub sign makes a visual pun on the area's unusual name

▲ Much of **Grays Inn** was rebuilt following wartime bomb damage but the styles blend well with surviving buildings from the 17th and 18th centuries

▲ The austerity of **Gower Street**'s Georgian architecture has been criticized in the past but its regularity now seems striking

▲ Most of the shops and restaurants on **Green Lanes** are run by members of London's Turkish community

▲ **Greenwich** – Inigo Jones' Queen's House and its later outbuildings and colonnades were converted into the National Maritime Museum in 1937

▲ The Battle of Barnet probably began on **Hadley Green**, which is encircled by listed buildings, including several stuccoed Georgian houses

▲ Artisans' cottages dominated the first phase of **Hampstead Garden Suburb** but these soon gave way to generously proportioned individual properties.

▲ **Hampstead** – The Admiral's House was built in 1700, with 'naval' roof features added later. It was depicted by Constable and featured in the film Mary Poppins.

▲ This tool store for a **Hampstead Heath** volunteer group has been used in the past as an ice house, a keeper's shed and a police hut

▲ The actor-manager David Garrick lived at **Hampton** from 1754 and commissioned the Shakespeare Temple to house a statue of the playwright

▲ The garden village at **Hanger Hill** has small blocks of flats disguised as Tudor houses

▲ Centred on Sloane Street, **Hans Town** was created from the 1770s onwards and extensively rebuilt in the 19th century to further enhance its prestige

◀ **Harley Street** was completed in 1770 and attracted the rich and famous before being colonized by doctors' practices from the mid-19th century

▲ Manor Farm Barn at **Harmondsworth** dates from the early 15th century and is the largest such structure in the London area

▲ **Harrow** School was founded in the late 16th century but the present appearance of the Old Schools dates from the enlargement scheme of 1819–21

◀ **Hatton Garden** is London's prime jewellery quarter and takes its name from Elizabeth I's 'dancing chancellor' Sir Christopher Hatton

▲ The well-preserved village green at **Havering-atte-Bower** has this group of weatherboarded cottages on its north side

▲ Constitution Arch at **Hyde Park Corner** is no longer surmounted by the statue of the Iron Duke that led it to become known as Wellington Arch

▲ **Hawley's Corner** – This thatched cottage provides accommodation for the manager of the Spinning Wheel pub and restaurant

▲ Parts of **Haydons Road** have a distinctly ramshackle appearance but the wider area is moving upmarket

▲ **Herons Quays** roundabout has Pierre Vivant's Traffic Light Tree, created from 75 working signal heads

▼ The 14th-century **Headstone Manor** House has recently been restored after a long period of neglect

▲ **Herne Hill** velodrome has been dedicated to track cycling and associated recreational uses since 1891

▲ Tin-roofed conveniences built for hop pickers at Lower **Hockenden** Farm

▶ The Old Forge is one of a pair of two-storey, 18th-century cottages in **Highwood Hill**

▲ In the mid-1770s **Highbury** Place became the first part of the district to be built up, on the east side of Highbury Fields

◀ Highgate – Designed by Berthold Lubetkin in the mid-1930s, Highpoint is regarded as among the most important modernist buildings in London

◀ The delightful gardens of **Holland Park** comprise the former grounds of Holland House, which was reduced to a shell by a wartime bomb

▶ The trusses of the glazed roof cast shadows in the atrium of **Hounslow**'s Treaty Centre, which replaced Edwardian civic buildings in the mid-1980s

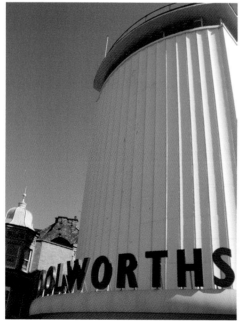

▲ The fluted corner tower of Woolworths in **Ilford** town centre, built in the 1950s for C&A

▲ **Holloway Road** – London Metropolitan University's graduate school was designed by Daniel Libeskind and opened in 2004

▲ **Kensington Gardens** – Designed by Sir George Gilbert Scott, the Albert Memorial was opened in 1872 and thoroughly restored in the 1990s

▲ In a flourish of civic pride, the London County Council endowed **Kennington**'s Brandon estate with Henry Moore's sculpture Reclining Figure No.3

▲ **Kensal Town** – Ernö Goldfinger's 30-storey Trellick Tower was completed in 1972 and is now Grade II* listed

▲ **Islington Green** – Built in 1911 as the Picture Theatre, this popular repertory cinema was relaunched as the Screen on the Green in 1981

▲ The top of the cylinder of the Grand Junction 90-inch engine on display at **Kew Bridge** Steam Museum

▲ **Kevington** lies just inside the south-eastern border of Greater London but has more in common with rural Kent

◄ **Kensington Olympia** opened in 1886 and was extended in the 1920s

◄ **King's Cross** railway lands are set for redevelopment, in one of the largest schemes currently planned in Europe

two stations is a lively strip of shops, bars and places of entertainment, dominated by the 02 Centre. Together with Kilburn High Road and Camden Town, Finchley Road is one of the borough's three designated zones for 24-hour-party licences.

'But here we are in the Finchley Road / With a drizzling rain and a skidding bus / And the twilight settling down on us.' So wrote Ford Madox Ford in one of his *Songs from London*, published in 1910.

✉ NW3

🚇 Silverlink Metro (Finchley Road and Frognal, zone 2); Bakerloo Line; Jubilee Line (Finchley Road, zone 2)

Finsbury • *Islington*

A very indistinct area situated north and north-west of the CITY OF LONDON. First recorded in the 13th century, the manor covered a swathe of the boggy moor that lay beyond the City wall. By the 15th century a manor house stood at what is now the corner of Finsbury Pavement and Chiswell Street. Houses and places of entertainment were built as the marshes were drained. James Burbage's Curtain Theatre in SHOREDITCH was described as being 'in Finsbury Fields'. Finsbury Square and Finsbury Circus were laid out in the late 18th and early 19th centuries as the nuclei of a high-class suburb that never achieved its full potential and subsequently converted to commercial use. Finsbury was a parliamentary constituency in the 19th century and the metropolitan borough of Finsbury was formed in 1901 from the CLERKENWELL parishes of St James and St John. Many of the borough's civic and public buildings lay in the vicinity of Rosebery Avenue and Finsbury's name thus came to be primarily associated with this neighbourhood. The borough took over Clerkenwell's stately Flemish Renaissance vestry hall as its headquarters. The council developed a 'Finsbury plan' to improve living conditions in this overcrowded area and its most notable success was the Finsbury health centre of 1938. In its present state, this is by no means a beautiful building but it has been Grade I listed for its significance to the modernist architectural movement. The borough was merged into Islington in 1965 and has begun to fade from memory. Some Clerkenwell estate agents still refer to properties in the Rosebery Avenue area as being 'in the heart of Finsbury' but most people now associate the name with the park that was created for the constituency's residents three miles to the north. After a long period of dereliction Finsbury Town Hall has recently been restored as a dance centre for the Urdang Academy.

The Finsbury constituency, once one of the largest in Britain, was traditionally a focus for political progressiveness. Charles Babbage, who invented the forerunner of the computer, addressed the political implications of mechanization in his Finsbury election campaign of 1832, while Thomas Wakley led demands for the extension of the franchise, the repeal of the Corn Laws and the abolition of slavery. In 1892, Dadabhai Naoroji became Britain's first Asian MP as the Liberal member for Finsbury. Naoroji has been called the 'grand old man of India' because of his later work as president of the Indian National Congress in its formative years.

✉ EC1

📖 Richard Tames, *Clerkenwell and Finsbury Past*, Historical Publications, 1999

Finsbury Park • *Islington/Hackney/Haringey*

A 115-acre public park and its multi-ethnic neighbourhood, situated north of HIGHBURY. The park was created from a surviving corner of HORNSEY Wood in the 1860s for the welfare of the residents of the parliamentary constituency of FINSBURY, an overcrowded inner city area that had no sizeable green spaces of its own. The constituency and the park lay at opposite ends of Islington parish and its trustees were instrumental in persuading the Metropolitan Board of Works to finance the project. The opening of the park came at a time when the neighbouring area was filling with two- and three-storey terraced housing for the middle classes. Many houses failed to find buyers of the intended means and were soon subdivided into single-floor flats. In some cases, each bedroom was occupied by a different family. New transport links improved Finsbury Park's appeal to commuters in the early 20th century. The Great Northern and City Railway (now WAGN Railway) arrived from MOORGATE in 1904, and two years later Finsbury Park became the northern terminus of the Great Northern, Piccadilly and Brompton Railway (now the Piccadilly Line). Edward A Stone's art deco Astoria cinema opened in 1930, with an ornate interior that creates the impression of a Moorish settlement at night. The Astoria subsequently became a noted live music venue and hosted the Beatles' Christmas shows in 1963. It is now home to the Universal Church of the Kingdom of God. The district's most overcrowded housing has been cleared and replaced by council flats. Elsewhere, multiple occupation remains widespread, although partial gentrification has taken place. Fonthill Road developed a rag-trade speciality in the 1960s and now has a Saturday market and daily shops specializing in cut-price designer clothing. It has been suggested that Finsbury Park's location 'in the armpit of three boroughs' has been at the root of some municipal neglect. However, a 1999–2006 regeneration programme delivered some benefits, including enhancements to the very busy bus and rail interchange. The park itself is now the responsibility of Haringey council, which restored it to something approaching its Victorian glory in a lottery-funded scheme, also completed in 2006. It has a small lake, plenty of trees and extensive sports facilities, and is often used for major events and concerts. Finsbury Park's community is culturally diverse, with no single ethnic group forming a majority. Blackstock Road has been dubbed 'Little Algiers' for the number of Algerian refugees who live in the vicinity.

The North London Central Mosque (commonly known as Finsbury Park Mosque) was at the centre of controversy in the early 21st century as an alleged base for Muslim extremists, attracted by the preaching of one of its imams, Sheikh Abu Hamza. The mosque was closed for over a year but reopened in 2005 under a more mainstream regime.

✉ N4

12,448 (Islington's Finsbury Park ward)

WAGN Railway; Piccadilly Line; Victoria Line (zone 2)

Jerry White, *Campbell Bunk: The Worst Street in North London Between the Wars*, Pimlico, 2003 ; Ken Gay, *Finsbury Park*, Hornsey Historical Society, 1996

Fish Island • *Tower Hamlets*

The borough's largest industrial area, situated in eastern OLD FORD, south of HACKNEY WICK. Fish Island is bounded by the River Lea, the Hertford Union Canal and the East Cross Route (A12), and is so-called because of its street names. Old Ford Road used to continue through the marshes and across the river and one large house, latterly known as King John's Palace, stood here until 1863. In 1865 the Imperial Gas Light and Coke Co. bought 30 acres of land as the site for a new works, but instead decided to build these on the east bank of the Lea in BROMLEY-BY-BOW. The company sold the site and the present network of streets was laid out, and filled with small houses and multi-storey factories. Until recently the island's largest employer was Percy Dalton's Famous Peanut Co., at the Old Ford Works in Dace Road. Fish Island is now dominated by waste disposal and recycling facilities and wholesale and distribution warehouses, together with some offices. In 2003 a 'gateway feature' created an improved urban space at the island's main access point (and terminus of the No. 339 bus route). Several vacant commercial properties have fallen into disrepair and the council has permitted their conversion to live–work loft apartments and artists' studios. The main site for the 2012 Olympic Games lies on the opposite bank of the River Lea and some or all of the area known as Fish Island South may be taken for related developments.

Channel 4's *Big Breakfast* was broadcast from the lock-keeper's cottage at Fish Island from 1992 to 2002. There were rumours that executive producer Bob Geldof would blow up the cottage on the show's final day but computer tricks were instead used to fake a disappearance and the cottage was subsequently sold as a family home.

✉ E3

Fitzjohn's Avenue • *Camden*

'One of the noblest streets in the world', according to the American magazine *Harpers* in 1883, connecting HAMPSTEAD with SWISS COTTAGE. This was formerly a track running northwards from ST JOHN'S WOOD to Hampstead, via Shepherd's Well, a spring that was the main source of the Tyburn River. Several prominent figures attempted in vain to prevent development here in the early 1870s, notably the philanthropist Octavia Hill, whose fund-raising campaign reportedly came within 1,000 pounds of achieving its target. But in 1875 the Maryon Wilson family, lords of the manor of Hampstead, sold 50 acres for development and named the old footpath Fitzjohn's Avenue after their estate at Great Canfield, Essex. 'Stately dwellings' were built in Queen Anne style with spacious grounds, and the avenue was lined with chestnut trees, later replaced with plane trees. Neighbouring streets were built up in the late 1870s and the 1880s. The development was an immediate success, proving especially popular with artists. Many of the properties have subsequently been subdivided, some into bed and breakfast accommodation, but the locality retains a prestigious reputation. The world-famous Portman Clinic, at 8 Fitzjohn's Avenue, is the only institution of its kind to offer psychotherapeutic help to adults, adolescents and children who suffer from sexual deviation or engage in delinquent behaviour. In the FROGNAL and Fitzjohns ward, 40 per cent of homes are privately rented, a very high proportion. Fitzjohn's Primary School has a number of refugee children, mainly of Kosovan origin. 'I went up to town on an invitation from some artistic people in Fitzjohn's Avenue: one of the girls was a Newnham chum. They took me to the National Gallery.' So says Vivie Warren in George Bernard Shaw's play *Mrs Warren's Profession*. Stella Gibbons wrote *Cold Comfort Farm* at 76 Fitzjohn's Avenue in 1932.

✉ NW3

♦ 11,632 (Frognal and Fitzjohns ward)

Fitzrovia • *Westminster/Camden*
From the 1930s, the area between GREAT PORTLAND STREET and GOWER STREET became known to its denizens as Fitzrovia. The district was first developed by Charles Fitzroy, lord of the manor of Tottenhall from 1757. The east and south sides of Fitzroy Square were designed by Robert Adam in 1794 and survive in their original form, in Portland stone. Fitzroy built for the upper classes, but they soon migrated south-westwards to Belgravia and Mayfair, forcing subdivision of the aristocratic houses into workshops, studios and rooms to let. Immigrants from France and other European countries replaced them and helped establish the district as a centre for the furniture trade by the end of the 18th century. Chippendale was among the craftsmen who set up shop here. The artist John Constable maintained a local residence, although he spent most of his time in HAMPSTEAD. Greeks and Italians brought new vitality to the area after World War II, followed later by Nepalese and Bengalis, but the area's originally jocular name began to fade from use, except by estate agents. Residents later revived it and their pressure resulted in the inclusion of Fitzrovia on Ordnance Survey maps from 1994. Today, around 6,500 people live in the area, while 50,000 work here. Fitzrovia's best-known thoroughfare is Charlotte Street, with its concentration of media companies and restaurants.

The writer George Bernard Shaw lived in Fitzroy Square from 1887 until his marriage in 1898. Early in the 20th century, the artist Walter Sickert and friends formed the Fitzroy Street Group, based in Whistler's former home at 8 Fitzroy Street. In the years before World War II, Augustus John and Dylan Thomas helped earn Fitzrovia a Bohemian reputation. John is credited with coining the name 'Fitzrovia' in honour of his favourite hostelry, the Fitzroy Tavern.

✉ W1; WC1 (between Tottenham Court Road and Gower Street)

🚇 Northern Line (Goodge Street, zone 1)

📖 Mike Pentelow and Marsha Rowe, *Characters of Fitzrovia*, Pimlico, 2002; Michael Bakewell, *Fitzrovia: London's Bohemia*, National Portrait Gallery, 1999

Fleet Street • *City*
The former home of London's newspaper industry; its name is still used as a generic term for the national press. The street originally emerged from the western edge of the CITY OF LONDON, crossed the River Fleet via a small island at present-day Ludgate Circus and led to WESTMINSTER via the STRAND. The river was later covered over after it became an open sewer. Fleet Street's association with printing began in 1500 with pioneer Wynkyn de Worde, who produced nearly 800 books at his workshop near Shoe Lane. The printing industry flourished here over the next 200 years but it was not until the beginning of 18th century that the first daily newspapers were published. Fleet Street at this time was a frantically busy part of the connecting route between the twin centres of London. It has been called 'a double street' because there was as much going on in its alleys and passageways as on Fleet Street itself. Protruding signboards were mounted above every doorway; one of these fell down in 1718 and killed four people, including the king's jeweller. By the early 19th century Fleet Street's newspapers had achieved massive circulations among both the working and middle classes. Publications ranged from scandal sheets like *John Bull*, through William Cobbett's polemical *Political Register* to *The Times*, which increased its size to eight pages in 1827. The *Daily Telegraph* arrived late on the scene in 1855 but soon outsold *The Times*. The *Evening Standard* evolved out of its daily counterpart in 1860. The press drove out most of Fleet Street's other businesses, especially after regional newspapers like the *Yorkshire Post* and *Manchester Guardian* began to open London offices here. In the first half of the 20th century the number of national newspapers halved from its peak of around two

dozen, while several of the survivors built imposing printing works, of which the finest is the art deco *Daily Express* building of 1932, clad in black glass, with a cinema-style foyer. All the major newspapers relocated their offices and printing works during the 1980s. News agency Reuters remained until 2003. Now the street mixes management consultants and investment specialists with shops and takeaways at street level to serve office workers.

Dr Samuel Johnson lived in Gough Square from 1748 until 1759, and it was here that he compiled the first comprehensive English dictionary. Now restored to its original condition, the house has panelled rooms, a pine staircase, and a collection of period furniture, prints and portraits. Johnson and Boswell whiled away many an hour in the Cheshire Cheese, a Fleet Street inn that has changed little to this day. George Dibdin Pitt's 'domestic drama' *Sweeney Todd, The Demon Barber of Fleet Street* (1842) has been called the first true crime play; much later it became a Stephen Sondheim musical. The story seems to have no basis in fact.

✉ EC4

📖 Roger Hudson, *Fleet Street, Holborn and the Inns of Court*, Haggerston Press, 1995; Ray Boston, *The Essential Fleet Street: Its History and its Influence*, Blandford, 1990

Foots Cray • *Bexley*

A commercial and residential area in southeast SIDCUP, also spelt Footscray. Archaeologists have recently found evidence of the deliberate burning of the woodland during the mesolithic period to promote the growth of hazel, and of increased agricultural activity in Roman times. Domesday Book recorded the landowner as Godwin Fot, who possessed a farm, four cottages and a mill and gave his name to the manor. Conveniently located where the Maidstone road crossed the River Cray, the village grew steadily over the following centuries. Around 1754, Bouchier Cleeve commissioned the building of Foots Cray Place, a Palladian mansion where he built up a noteworthy collection of art. In 1822 the house was acquired by the Chancellor of the Exchequer, Sir Nicholas Vansittart, later Lord Bexley. The Vansittart family retained a substantial landholding in the area for the next century. The arrival of the Sidcup bypass brought businesses here from the 1930s, and the centre of Foots Cray is now dominated by the industrial and commercial premises of

two business parks and the Coca-Cola and Schweppes bottling plant. There is scope for further industrial development on Powerscroft Road. Rectory Lane has All Saints Church and a terrace of Georgian houses, but the majority of residents live in more recent housing on or off Sidcup Hill and Cray Road. Foots Cray Meadows lie to the north of the built-up area and contain the remains of Foots Cray Place, which burned down in 1949. Kingfishers and ring-necked parakeets are among the park's plentiful wildlife. The Cray Meadows ward has relatively few young adults and a high proportion of retired people. Nearly three-quarters of homes are owner-occupied, but a significant minority are rented from housing associations. Ninety-four per cent of residents are white.

British settlers in Australia in the mid 19th century gave the name Footscray to what is now the Melbourne suburb of Maribyrnong.

✉ Sidcup DA14

👥 10,295 (Cray Meadows ward)

📖 Gertrude Nunns, *Foots Cray*, London Borough of Bexley Libraries and Museums Department, 1982

@ www.ideal-homes.org.uk/bexley/foots-cray.html (London surburban history site)

Forestdale • *Croydon*

A privately developed housing estate situated on the eastern edge of SELSDON, and sometimes considered to be part of ADDINGTON. Forestdale is separated from NEW ADDINGTON by Addington Court golf course, which was the first privately run golf course to be opened to the general public when it was established in 1932. The flats and houses of Forestdale were mostly built in the late 1960s, on former farmland. Wates added a development in the mid 1970s that won an industry award for the solar heating system installed in three of the houses. Since the opening of Croydon Tramlink in 2000, a 'gradient of desirability' has arisen, with property values showing a relationship with their proximity to tram stops, primarily the one at Gravel Hill. On Pixton Way, the Forestdale Forum hosts the meetings of several local clubs and societies. Croydon council became a joint trustee of the forum in 2004, in a bid to prevent the forfeiture of its lease. The Forestdale Centre is a shopping precinct located near the junction of Featherbed Lane and Selsdon Park Road. In addition to the Forestdale Arms pub, the centre is graced by McDermott's, which in 2005 was voted the best fish and chip shop in the London and south-east England region and came third in the national awards of a competition run by the Sea Fish Industry Authority.

✉ Croydon CR0

🚌 Croydon Tramlink, Route 3 (Gravel Hill)

Forest Gate • *Newham*

A truly multicultural district, with no single ethnic group constituting a majority, situated east of STRATFORD and its MARYLAND locality. Here was an entrance to Epping Forest, of which the nearby WANSTEAD FLATS are still considered a part. Dr John Fothergill established the extensive Ham House estate (as it was later called) from the early 1760s, filling the house and its gardens with 3,400 species of tropical plants. The Quaker philanthropist Samuel Gurney acquired the estate in 1812. Forest Gate station opened on the Eastern Counties Railway in 1841, an exceptionally early date for such a backwater, and an absence of passengers brought about its closure for two years from 1844. The Ham House estate was broken up and sold to developers in 1852. The land was filled by the WEST HAM and Jewish cemeteries, the Forest Gate Industrial School, the Gurney estate of substantial, middle-class housing and some lesser streets of artisans' dwellings. South of Romford Road (A118), compact terraced houses were built for clerks and skilled workers. Shops opened on Woodgrange Road, Upton Lane and Romford Road. During the remainder of the century an expanding network of rail and tram services drew day-trippers to Wanstead Flats and the Eagle and Child tea gardens became a popular resort. Forest Gate School must have seemed cursed in the last quarter of the century when more than 40 pupils died in three separate incidents. The school later became a hospital and its site is now occupied by housing and a small park. In the early 20th century, churches and associated schools were built, including several Roman Catholic institutions. Most of Forest Gate's Victorian housing has survived intact, although developers have recently been taking every opportunity to squeeze in new units. East Thames Housing Group built a pair of innovative 'eco-houses' in Eider Close in 2002. There is a small hotel zone opposite Forest Gate police station. North of the railway line the largest minority is white, followed by black or black British and then Asian or Asian British, of which the main sub-group is of Bangladeshi descent. To the south, the Asian community is larger and the main sub-group is of Indian descent. Christianity and Islam are the principal religions and places of worship have been built, or converted, for the minority religions.

On Boxing Day in 1966 Jimi Hendrix wrote and then performed *Purple Haze* at the Ace of Spades Club on Woodgrange Road; during demolition of the building for construction of the Channel Tunnel rail link a purple ceiling was uncovered behind a more modern one. Bodybuilder Arnold Schwarzenegger came to Forest Gate in the same year as Hendrix, and stayed here for over two years, sleeping on the couch at Wag and Dianne Bennett's house in Romford Road and training at the gym that they ran.

✉ E7

👥 26,563 (Forest Gate North and Forest Gate South wards)

🚌 'one' Railway (Forest Gate, zone 3); Silverlink Metro (Wanstead Park, zone 3)

📖 Dorcas Saunders, *Forest Gate*, Tempus, 1994

Forest Hill • *Lewisham*

Highly fashionable in the Victorian era, SYDENHAM's northern neighbour is today a less than lovely locale, but has recently begun to show signs of gentrification. Until the late 18th century it was simply called 'the Forest', and was almost entirely uninhabited. The original 'Forest Hill', now Honor Oak Road, was a grand avenue of well-proportioned merchants' houses built in the 1780s and its name was the developer's invention. Enclosure in 1810 initiated the suburbanization of the area, with height above sea level being a general guide to the grandeur of the villas. The smaller plots on lower-lying land were quickly built up with modest cottages, many wooden, especially along the major southbound routes of Dartmouth Road and PERRY VALE. Off these branched cul-de-sacs, as the many individual builders went their unco-ordinated ways. When the station opened in 1839, originally as Dartmouth Arms, it prompted the construction of homes for city businessmen, especially along London Road. In the 1850s the erection nearby of the Crystal Palace put a seal on the popularity of Forest Hill and most of the neighbouring localities. Among the many notable figures who moved here were the tea merchants Frederick Horniman and the Tetley family. Horniman established the museum and gardens in London Road that bear his name and later gave them to the public. The museum's speciality is the display of artefacts from other cultures and there is a particular emphasis on music. It is one of London's most visited attractions, largely because it draws so many school parties. Nowadays, Forest Hill is a jumble of Victorian terraces and post-war council blocks and has an air of stabilized decay. Estate agents eulogize the Arts and Crafts delights of houses by the master builder Edward Christmas, built between 1888 and the 1930s. Like most of the borough, Forest Hill has a sizeable black minority, of both Caribbean and African descent, but few residents of Asian heritage.

The notorious art forger Tom Keating was born into 'a large and poverty-stricken household in Forest Hill'. He gained fame during the 1970s and early 1980s for allegedly producing up to 2,500 forgeries. Francis Rossi, frontman of rock band Status Quo, was born here in 1949, into the Rossi ice cream family.

> ⊠ SE23

> ⋔ 14,039

> 🚍 Southern (zone 3)

> 📖 John Coulter and John Seaman, *Forest Hill and Sydenham in Old Photographs*, Sutton, 2003

> @ www.foresthill.org.uk (community site)

Fortis Green • *Haringey*

A leafy and lovely locality situated between MUSWELL HILL and EAST FINCHLEY, although many consider it simply the south-western corner of Muswell Hill. What became Fortis Green Road was just a track across Hornsey Common until the early 19th century. Enclosure allowed individual fields to be sold off to speculators and the hamlet began to expand outwards from the village green and the Clissold Arms. Two East Finchley brothers bought one of the fields in 1835 and built a pair of Italianate villas, Springcroft and Colethall (later Uplands). In 1853 an adjacent field was laid out with roads and divided into plots for sale to local builders. The resulting Harwell estate took several decades to complete, leading to an inconsistent but not unpleasing appearance. Fortis Green now consists of a mixture of late Victorian and early 20th-century semi-detached houses, with a few grand villas in the shady corners. The avenues are tree-lined almost to the point of being wooded. St Luke's Woodside Hospital and Thames Water's Fortis Green pumping station (with covered reservoir) are on Woodside Avenue, just north of Highgate Wood. More than half of the 16- to 74-year-olds in Fortis Green are qualified to degree level or higher, and employment levels are very high.

Two disparate bands emerged from Fortis Green in the 1960s. The Davies family, which spawned the Kinks, lived in Denmark Terrace. Brothers Ray and Dave attended what is now Fortismere School and first performed in public at the Clissold Arms. *Fortis Green* is the title of a Dave Davies song. 'Fairport', the house that gave its name to the folk band Fairport Convention, stands at the corner of Fortismere Avenue and Fortis Green Road.

> ⊠ N2; N10

> ⋔ 11,235

Fortune Green • *Camden*

A multicultural locality in WEST HAMPSTEAD, situated south-east of CRICKLEWOOD. In the 18th and 19th centuries the farmland and scattered cottages here belonged to a family named Flitcroft. A little building took place during the first half of the 19th century, but the first major development was the creation of HAMPSTEAD Cemetery in 1876. Among those buried here are the music hall star Marie Lloyd, surgeon Joseph Lister and artist Kate Greenaway. The remainder of the 50-acre Flitcroft estate was sold to speculative builders in the 1880s, while Hampstead vestry acquired and preserved the green itself. Together with the cemetery and neighbouring sports grounds, the green now forms the largest open space in West Hampstead. The annual Jester Festival takes place on the green around the second week of July each year. Fortune Green play centre opened in the 1980s and is much used by local children's groups. More than a third of homes in the Fortune Green ward are privately rented and there is a disproportionate number of university-educated residents in their twenties. Confusingly, there is another Fortune Green in the borough, at the end of Eversholt Street, near Euston station.

The novelist Evelyn Waugh was born at 11 Hillfield Road, off Fortune Green Road. The comic actor Tony Hancock once lived in the locality; ADDISCOMBE'S Bingham Road station (now replaced by a tramstop) posed as Fortune Green South in Hancock's 1961 film *The Rebel*.

> ⊠ NW6

> ⋔ 10,465

Forty Hill • *Enfield*

A comfortable residential locality on the north side of ENFIELD, taking its name from an Old English word meaning a patch of higher ground in a marsh. John Tiptoft, Earl of Worcester, is said to have built Elsing (or El-synge) Hall here in the 1460s. Sir Thomas Lovell, Speaker of the House of Commons and Chancellor of the Exchequer from 1485, lived here from 1492 and hosted frequent royal visits. It is said that Sir Walter Raleigh laid his cloak across a puddle at Elsing so that Eliza-beth I might cross without getting her feet wet, but other localities also lay claim to this legend. The house was demolished around 1660 and its site was lost until excavations 300 years later. Forty Hall was built to the south-west of Elsing for Sir Nicholas Raynton in 1636 and heavily modified around 1708. Raynton was a haberdasher and Lord Mayor of London in 1632. Other wealthy gentlemen built villas nearby in the 18th and early 19th centuries and several have survived, as have a few older cottages. The Bridgen Hall estate, which lay between Carterhatch Lane and Goat Lane, was sold for building in 1868. Streets were laid out but parts were later used for gravel digging and it was many decades be-fore the estate was completed. The introduc-tion of better bus services after World War I and the construction of the Great Cambridge Road (A10) in 1924 stimulated housebuilding on the eastern side of the locality. The built-up part of Forty Hill had mostly assumed its present form by 1939 and further development was prohibited by green-belt legislation after the war was over. Enfield council acquired the Forty Hall estate in 1951. The hall is Grade I listed and has served as the borough's arts and heritage museum since 1955 but this will move to ENFIELD TOWN in 2007.

Tate Britain gallery has John Hill's *Interior of the Carpenter's Shop at Forty Hill, Enfield*. Executed around 1813, the painting may de-pict Hill's own father at work.

> ✉ Enfield EN2 and EN1

> 📖 Valerie Carter, *Forty Hill and Bulls Cross*, Enfield Preservation Society, 1988

Foxbury • *Bromley*

The eastern side of CHISLEHURST consists mainly of woodland and open ground, situ-ated within the green belt and the Chislehurst conservation area. Foxbury Manor is a Grade II-listed Jacobean-style building located off Kemnal Road. It was built in 1876 as the home of the banker Henry J Tiarks, and subse-quently served as a women's training college for the Church Missionary Society and more recently as a conference centre. Set in eight

acres of gardens, there is planning permission to divide the manor into two residential wings and to build another large house in the grounds. Just to the north, a former Cold War nuclear bunker has been imaginatively and unrecognisably transformed into the Glass-house, a luxurious private home with state-of-the-art technological aids. The sports facil-ities at Foxbury, most of which belong to colleges or private clubs, include athletics grounds, tennis courts and shooting ranges. The Old Elthamians Association's land was purchased in memory of former pupils of MOTTINGHAM'S Eltham College who gave their lives in World War II. The Foxbury area also has Beaverwood, a girls' secondary school with a technology specialization, and Darul Uloom London, an Islamic school.

> ✉ Chislehurst BR7

> @ www.beaverwood.bromley.sch.uk; www.darululoomlondon.co.uk

Freezywater • *Enfield*

Also spelt as two words, Freezywater is a lack-lustre residential locality stuck out on a limb in the north-east corner of ENFIELD, south of the M25. A farm was first recorded here in 1768, taking its name from a local pond that was lost when sewage works were built on Rammey (or Ramney) Marsh. Freezywater was one of the last parts of Enfield to attract the interest of builders or housebuyers. To the west of Hertford Road (A1010), the United Counties Land, Building and Investment So-ciety acquired an estate near Freezywater Farm in 1881 and laid out Holly Road, Oak-hurst Road, and Holmwood Road. A few hou-ses had appeared by 1897 but other plots remained empty for decades. The parish church of St George and the neighbouring St George's School were built in the early 1900s. The electric tramway route along Hertford Road reached Freezywater in 1907. Despite these amenities, growth remained slow and the establishment after World War I of a new nursery (for raising fruit and vegetables, not children) indicated the continuing absence of demand. Freezywater eventually filled out with terraced and semi-detached houses in the decades after World War II. The vast ma-jority of residents are white although a grow-ing minority come from black Caribbean and black African backgrounds. The Freezywater business area on the eastern side of the local-ity is defined as a 'strategic employment loca-tion' but the council's proposals to improve its accessibility via a new (indirect) link to the

M25 from Mollison Avenue were rejected at a public inquiry in 2002. Rammey Marsh sewage works have been replaced by Innova Business Park, intended to be primarily a business park for science companies. But after a stuttering start the plan has been revised to include proposals for an academy school and 369 social housing units, mostly for rent.

> ✉ Enfield EN3

Friday Hill • *Waltham Forest*

A housing estate built by the London County Council north of CHINGFORD HATCH. This had previously been Jackatt Hill and its present name derives from John Friday, who was living here in 1467. In 1608, City merchant Thomas Boothby acquired the manor of Chingford Comtis, also known as Chingford Earls, and built a manor house here. A story that Friday Hill was inhabited by snakes and toads that spat fire was probably put about to keep intruders away from the grounds. The manor house was pulled down in 1838 and replaced by the present Friday Hill House, which was designed in Tudor style by Lewis Vulliamy for the Reverend Robert Boothby Heathcote. Some of the original panelling, fireplaces and other features were reused in the new house, and survive today. Boothby Heathcote also commissioned Vulliamy to build the new parish church of St Peter and St Paul at CHINGFORD GREEN in 1844. The grounds of Friday Hill House remained the last undeveloped tranche of CHINGFORD until the death of Louisa Heathcote in 1940 at the age of 86. After World War II the London County Council acquired the property and laid out a pleasant estate, with the house becoming a community centre. Most of the homes are now owner-occupied, while Friday Hill House continues to serve as an adult education centre and a meeting place for local societies, but its future role is uncertain. A plane tree on Friday Hill was awarded a green plaque in a 1998 scheme to recognize the '21 great trees of London'. Pimp Hall Park, to the north-west, has nurseries and a 17th-century timber-framed dovecote.

Boy band Friday Hill (made up of former members of Blazin' Squad) takes its name from this place.

> ✉ E4

> 📖 Arthur Lansdell Martin, *Chingford and the Boothbys of Friday Hill*, Chingford Antiquarian and Historical Society, 1964

Friern Barnet • *Barnet* (usually pronounced as in 'friar' by locals, but some prefer 'free-ən')

A medieval parish enveloped by a series of late-Victorian suburban estates, situated between NEW SOUTHGATE and NORTH FINCHLEY. From around 1274 this was 'Frerenbarnet', because this corner of Barnet was owned by the Order of the Hospital of St John of Jerusalem. The early village grew along Friern Barnet Lane in the vicinity of the medieval St James's Church and the parish extended north and south to include WHETSTONE and COLNEY HATCH. In the 16th century it was still mainly woodland and what few dwellings it had were loosely scattered. At the beginning of the 19th century this was still an entirely rural area; the parish had only 144 inhabited houses, of which 55 stood in the village of Friern Barnet itself. The population doubled over the next 40 years but total transformation came with the construction of the Middlesex County Lunatic Asylum at Colney Hatch in 1851. In the 1870s, James Thorne described Friern Barnet as a 'quiet, retired, and very pretty place, hardly to be called a village', with wealthy citizens' homes standing in spacious grounds, 'embowered among old elms and limes'. But Thorne reported that the speculative builders were already making inroads nearby and they closed in on the old village during the latter decades of the 19th century and the early years of the 20th, creating estates like Holly Park, Southgate Park, the British Land Co.'s White House estate and the Bethune Park Garden estate, which was promised to be the 'prettiest garden suburb to London'. But the heart of the village remained agricultural until after World War I. The council was a major builder before World War II and virtually the only builder for the two decades afterwards, constructing housing primarily in the north of the district and schools in all corners. Some early terraced houses were considered to be slums by the late 1950s, and accordingly cleared. Recent private projects have mostly involved replacing old houses with small blocks of flats, except for the conversion of Colney Hatch asylum into Princess Park Manor. To the south-east, Friern Bridge retail park has warehouse-style showrooms. Friern Barnet exhibits a similar demographic profile to that of the borough as a whole, except that it has more middle-aged residents and fewer retired people.

> ✉ N11; N12

> 👥 14,504 (Coppetts ward)

📖 Stewart Gillies and Pamela Taylor, *Finchley and Friern Barnet*, Phillimore, 1992

Friern Village *see* COLNEY HATCH

Frognal • *Camden*

An idyllic locality and leafy street meandering between HAMPSTEAD and WEST HAMPSTEAD. Perhaps unexpectedly, the name does signify that this was once a nook frequented by frogs. Frognal was recorded in the early 15th century as a 'customary tenement', an estate held on condition that the customs of the manor (of Hampstead) were adhered to, which involved performing certain tasks and making various payments. During the 17th and 18th centuries Frognal gained a reputation for the 'salubrity of its air and soil' and grew from a single house and farm to a collection of cottages and mansions, many of which adopted the Frognal name. These included Frognal Hall, Frognal Grove, Frognal Priory and, in 1806, Frognal Park – possibly the grandest of them all. The creation of the FINCHLEY ROAD rendered southern Frognal ripe for development, but a number of legalities prevented its exploitation until the 1870s, when the road called Frognal was extended southwards. Frognal House, at 99 Frognal, occupies the site of the original Frognal house. During the latter part of World War II, General de Gaulle lived at Frognal House, directing the efforts of the Free French forces. In the Frognal and Fitzjohns ward, 17 per cent of residents are Jewish and 59 per cent of 16- to 74-year-olds are qualified to degree level or above.

No. 20 Maresfield Gardens was the last residence of psychoanalyst Sigmund Freud after he fled Nazi Austria in 1938. He died here the following year, but his daughter Anna, the founder of child psychoanalysis in the UK, continued to live and work in the house until her death in 1982. The house is now a museum and visitors can see the library and study, which contain the great man's personal collection of antiquities and books as well as his psychoanalytic couch. The illustrator Kate Greenaway lived at 39 Frognal from 1886 until her death in 1901.

✉ NW3

👥 11,632 (Frognal and Fitzjohns ward)

🚆 Silverlink Metro (Finchley Road and Frognal, zone 2)

📖 Marina Warner, *20 Maresfield Gardens: The Freud Museum*, Serpent's Tail, 1998

Fryent • *Brent*

A large park and the neighbouring electoral ward, filling much of north KINGSBURY. Like FRIERN BARNET, the name derives from its early ownership by the friars of the Order of St John of Jerusalem. An original part of the ancient parish of Kingsbury, the Fryent estate was taken over by ST PAUL'S Cathedral in 1543 and remained in agricultural use until the 20th century. Between 1928 and 1931 the Ecclesiastical Commissioners divided up Fryent Farm and sold the parts to several private developers and to WEMBLEY council, which built a large housing estate here after World War II. Fryent Country Park was formed in 1967 by merging Barn Hill and Kenton Lane open spaces with the land of Bush and Hillhouse farms. The park's 260 acres have an undulating character, reaching a height of 206 feet towards the north-east. Most of London's parks were once farmland but usually all trace of their former life has been obliterated. Fryent is different: it has an ancient hedgerow system, farm ponds and hay meadow grasslands, as well as extensive woodland. Like the rest of Brent, the Fryent ward has a multicultural population, and most leading faiths are well represented, except Sikhism. Apart from English, the main languages spoken in the area are Gujarati, Urdu, Somali and Arabic.

✉ NW9; Wembley HA9

👥 11,888 (Fryent ward)

Fulham • *Hammersmith & Fulham*

A late-Victorian district occupying a wide Thames peninsula opposite Wandsworth. The Bishop of London acquired the manor of Fulham in 704 and Danish invaders landed here in 879. A fishing village grew up in the vicinity of the present PUTNEY BRIDGE station and Fulham High Street was in existence by 1391, when it was called Burystrete. The west tower of All Saints' Church was built around 1440. The earliest of the surviving buildings of Fulham Palace date from around 1480, when it became one of the bishop's country retreats. Medieval villages grew up at three distinct locations in Fulham in addition to the thriving old town: PARSONS GREEN, WALHAM GREEN and NORTH END. Fulham Palace became the bishop's main residence in the 18th century. Among the gentlemen's retreats built in the Georgian era were HURLINGHAM House, later home to the prestigious sports club, and Lord Craven's *cottage orné* north of the palace, built in 1780. The earlier Peterborough House was rebuilt around the same time. Over the course of the 19th century industry filled the former marshland of SANDS END and elsewhere terraces of suburban housing rolled out across the former market gardens and gentlemen's estates from the 1870s. North End was rebranded WEST KENSINGTON and FULHAM BROADWAY, at Walham Green, became Fulham's administrative and shopping centre. Peterborough House was demolished to make way for a pleasing estate that bears its name. Fulham Football Club built a permanent home on the site of Craven Cottage in 1896, 17 years after the club's foundation. In April 1904 Fulham Theatre held the first public experiment in 'talking pictures' with the aid of a phonographic soundtrack. Much of Fulham's new housing was built for the lower middle classes but by the 1920s large parts of the district had become wholly working class in character. Before and after World War II the borough council added several housing estates, most visibly on the eastern side of West Kensington. Fulham Palace ceased to be the bishop's official residence in 1973 and most of its grounds were opened to the public. Gentrification since this time has been so widespread throughout the district that it is hard to believe that Fulham had a poor reputation 50 years ago. The deserted industrial wasteland by the Thames at Sands End has provided the principal zone of opportunity for large-scale developers, beginning with CHELSEA HARBOUR in the 1980s and reaching a crescendo at IMPERIAL WHARF, which will not be completed for several years.

Fulham has been the scene of two high-profile murders in recent decades. In July 1986 estate agent Suzy Lamplugh went missing after leaving her Stevenage Road office; neither her body nor her presumed killer was ever found. In April 1999 television presenter Jill Dando was shot dead on her doorstep in Gowan Avenue. Local man Barry George was convicted of her murder in 2001 and sentenced to life imprisonment.

✉ SW6

👥 57,308 (Fulham Broadway, Munster, Palace Riverside, Parsons Green and Walham, Sands End and Town wards)

📖 Patrick Loobey, *Fulham*, Tempus, 2004; Barbara Denny, *Fulham Past*, Historical Publications, 1997

@ www.myfulham.co.uk (commercial local information site)

Fulham Broadway • *Hammersmith & Fulham*

A short stretch of FULHAM ROAD east of its junction with NORTH END Road, constituting the commercial heart of modern FULHAM. The locality was known as WALHAM GREEN until the late 19th century, when a flurry of commercial and residential development erased the old green and the former village's character. Walham Green station was renamed Fulham Broadway in 1952. The Broadway's evolution over the course of the 20th century produced an aesthetically unpleasing result, although much of the neighbouring housing stock has improved during Fulham's gentrification since the 1970s. A £70 million project has recently transformed the town centre, providing a new station building, shopping mall, restaurants, multiplex cinema, health club, offices and a new Methodist church; the development also includes roosting and breeding boxes for bats. Unlike nearby wards, Fulham Broadway has a relatively low proportion of owner-occupied homes, with roughly equal numbers of residents renting from the council, from social landlords and privately.

🚇 District Line (zone 2)

👥 10,189

Fulham Road • *Hammersmith & Fulham/Kensington & Chelsea*

A fashionable street extending two-and-a-half miles south-westwards from BROMPTON Cross to the grounds of FULHAM Palace. The 'way from Fulham to London' was first mentioned in 1372 and became a functional highway in 1410, when the Bishop of London caused STAMFORD BRIDGE to be built across Counters Creek, connecting CHELSEA and Fulham. By this time, hamlets existed at Brompton and WALHAM GREEN. In the early 17th century the first significant settlement midway along the road grew up at Little Chelsea, which was located to the north-east of Stamford Bridge. Elsewhere, open fields bordered the road on both sides until the mid 18th century, when speculative builders began to put up clumps of smart houses between the farms. Sections of the road had street lighting from 1806 and paving by 1845. From the 1840s the Royal Brompton Hospital took shape at the road's north-eastern end and a cancer hospital, now the Royal Marsden Hospital, moved to its present site in 1862. Houses of varying sizes and quality lined much of the rest of the road, together with private schools and asylums and St George's workhouse, which gained an infirmary in 1878. The far south-western end of the road was developed in the early 1880s, when builders were descending on Fulham en masse. From the late 19th century larger shops and places of entertainment appeared. Chelsea Football Club came into existence at Stamford Bridge in 1905. Michelin opened a delightfully ornate tyre-fitting garage at 81 Fulham Road in 1911, with offices above. The first blocks of upmarket flats were built nearby before World War I. Following an unexciting period before and after World War II, Fulham Road became fashionable in the 1960s, particularly at the Brompton end. Terence Conran opened the first Habitat store at 77 Fulham Road in 1964. Art galleries, antique dealers, jewellers and fashion houses later moved here from increasingly unaffordable MAYFAIR. In 1986 Conran founded a new venture, the Bluebird restaurant, housed in the immaculately refurbished Michelin building. In former Little Chelsea the progressive evolution of the old workhouse infirmary culminated in the opening of the £200-million Chelsea and Westminster Hospital in 1993. Its vicinity has a pleasing mix of pubs and eateries, independent shops and galleries, and a six-screen cinema. The supposedly Mediterranean feel of this stretch of the road has given rise to the nickname 'the beach'. The commercial section across the borough boundary is called Fulham Broadway. An integrated shopping and leisure complex has recently been built here.

'The Avenue' constituted a group of 15 artists' and sculptors' studios at 76 Fulham Road from the late 19th century. Alfred Gilbert created 'Eros' for PICCADILLY CIRCUS at No. 8 in 1893, and John Singer Sargent worked here for 20 years, lending his studio to James Whistler for a while in 1896.

✉ SW6; SW10; SW3

Fullwell Cross • *Redbridge*

A minor locality in north BARKINGSIDE, and a roundabout from which roads radiate in six directions. This may have been the site of one of Barking Abbey's medieval fields, Hanchemstede, later Hampstede Croft. Its modern name derives from Adam Fulwell, who leased a farm from the abbey at what became Fullwell Hatch. To the east stood the FAIRLOP oak, which boasted a trunk with a circumference of 36 feet. A Wapping man named Daniel Day started by the oak a fair held on the first Friday of July each year that came to be attended by thousands. Day was buried in 1767 in a coffin

made with wood from the tree. A 'new Fairlop oak' was planted at the centre of the roundabout as part of the Festival of Britain celebrations in 1951, around the time that most of the housing here was built. Fullwell Cross library and swimming baths, which have some architectural merit, were opened in 1968. The Fulwell ward, which takes in part of CLAYHALL, has few young single people, and educational attainment is relatively low. Judaism is the second religion after Christianity.

✉ Ilford IG6

♦ 11,269 (Fullwell ward)

Fulwell • *Richmond*

Something of an amenity centre for the neighbouring districts of HAMPTON, TWICKENHAM and TEDDINGTON, Fulwell lies just north of HAMPTON HILL. The name was first recorded in the 15th century and is probably a corruption of 'foul well'. Fulwell Lodge, later Fulwell Park, was built beside the River Crane sometime before 1623. By the middle of the 17th century a mill also stood beside the river, and its site is now marked by Mill Road. Fulwell station opened in 1864 and terraced and semi-detached houses were built to its south later in the century. Fulwell golf course filled much of the western half of the area in 1904. The district grew further in the early 20th century after the arrival of tram services, and in response to the increase in population the Church of St Michael and St George was built on Wilcox Road in 1913. In the same year the exiled king of Portugal, Manoel II, settled his new wife Auguste at Fulwell Park, from where he continued to strive for reconciliation with the republican government. Manoel died at Fulwell in 1932 without an heir and received a state funeral in Lisbon. Afterwards, Auguste returned to her native Germany, where she created a new Fulwell Park near Freiburg. The couple's house was demolished and the grounds were built over. The housing has since been supplemented by a great deal of infilling. Fulwell grew in significance as a transport hub over the course of the 20th century. Its tram shed was shared by trolleybuses from the 1930s and became one of the last depots to convert fully to motor buses in 1962. Residents of the Fulwell and Hampton Hill ward are 92.5 per cent white and employment levels are high. Three-quarters of homes are owner-occupied.

✉ Twickenham TW2; Teddington TW11

♦ 9,448 (Fulwell and Hampton Hill ward)

🚌 South West Trains (zone 6)

📖 Bryan Woodriff, *Fulwell: Home to Trams, Trolleys and Buses*, Middleton Press, 2003

@ www.fulwellpark.de (German-language site about the Fulwell Park in Germany)

Furzedown • *Wandsworth*

'A place where people of all ages can feel part of a safe, caring and creative community', according to the Furzedown Community Network. Furzedown is situated between Tooting and Streatham, in the southernmost extremity of the borough. The name is of relatively recent origin, dating perhaps from the 17th century, and refers to the gorse that grew here. Furzedown House was built in 1794 and was enlarged and endowed with a conservatory and a single-storey entrance lodge in the early 1860s. Soon after 1900 local builders began to lay out residential streets in the grounds of the house, beginning with Moyser Road, Pendle Road and Pretoria Road. Parkland that had been used as public open space and a golf course was lost to this development but Furzedown House was saved from demolition by the London County Council, which converted it into a teacher training college in 1915. Private development continued into the 1920s and St Paul's Church opened in 1925.

Wandsworth council provided a recreation ground and in the late 1920s built several hundred houses, comprising its largest interwar estate, in the south of the borough. Local doctor Norman Levinson founded the Furzedown Project in 1975 to provide a meeting place for older people. Furzedown Secondary School was formed in 1977 and merged with Ensham School in 1986 to become Graveney School. The school's buildings include Furzedown House. By the borough's standards (but not the country's), Furzedown has relatively few young adults and many retired people. Children at Furzedown Primary School come from 'a very mixed range of backgrounds', according to the national educational standards agency Ofsted, and 22 per cent are at the earliest stages of speaking English.

✉ SW17; SW16

👫 13,539

📖 Graham Gower, *Historic Furzedown*, Local History Publications, 1990

@ www.furzedown.net (Furzedown Community Network site); www.furzedownproject.org.uk; www.furzedown.org.uk (Furzedown School reunion site)

Gallions Reach • *Newham*

A Docklands Light Railway station named after the stretch of the Thames between Woolwich and Barking Creek. Gallions Point, at the entrance to the KING GEORGE V Dock, is nine nautical miles below London Bridge. The Galyons were a 14th-century family who owned property on the shoreline. The modern station is located to the north-west of its predecessor, 'Gallions', a ship-to-rail transfer point that opened in 1880 on the Port of London Authority's railway. A stylish hotel was built soon afterwards to accommodate travellers who were halting overnight. The station closed with the branch line in 1940, after the first air raid of the Blitz. The track was later repaired but the passenger service was not reinstated. With the closure of the ROYAL DOCKS and the gas production facilities at BECKTON, the area was earmarked for regeneration but it remained a wasteland until the late 20th century, when the most significant tenant was a go-karting track. In recent years several ambitious projects have transformed this brownfield site. These include the Gallions Reach retail park, which has more than 30 stores and 2,000 parking spaces, and the grey and forbidding UK headquarters of IVAX, a generic pharmaceuticals giant. The Royal Quay residential scheme will have around 450 apartments when it is completed sometime before 2010 and its centrepiece will be a refurbished Gallions Hotel, with a gymnasium, café/restaurant and bar. Further inland the social housing of EAST BECKTON provides for a less affluent community. At Gallions Primary School a majority of the children come from ethnic minorities and 18 languages are spoken. Over 70 per cent qualify for free school meals and there is a very high level of pupil turnover as a consequence of transience in the local population.

In 1878, Gallions Reach was the scene of one of Britain's worst-ever disasters when the *Princess Alice* pleasure steamer sank with the loss of more than 600 lives. *Gallions Reach* is the title of both a 'fantasia' by the light orchestral composer Peter Yorke and a bitter romantic novel by H M Tomlinson, published in 1927.

> ✉ E6

> 🚊 Docklands Light Railway, Beckton branch (zone 4)

> @ www.gallions-reach.co.uk (retail park site)

Gallions Reach Urban Village • *Greenwich*

A moderately priced housing estate within the new town of THAMESMEAD, just north-east of WOOLWICH. Archaeologists have found evidence of prehistoric human activity on the surface of the sandy clay here. The 'village' will ultimately consist of several thousand homes. According to figures from the London Planning Advisory Service, which co-ordinates strategic planning in the capital, the location was the sixth-largest undeveloped site in London. The village has a landscaped amenity called Gallions Hill and a shopping, leisure and residential zone called The Reach. Future plans include a riverside walk, a canal with ecologically managed environs and a wildlife 'corridor', and a district park of approximately 80 acres. There will also be a new primary school and live-work units. The tenure mix will mirror the whole of London rather than the proportions in the rest of Thamesmead. A small part of the village has been built as an 'eco-park', an affordable housing project with an emphasis on sustainability and low energy use. In a dissertation on urban utopias, Clare Freeman uses Gallions Reach as a case study in her argument that the 'urban village' concept is to some extent a marketing ploy (aimed at those providing funding as well as potential residents), rather than a truly radical approach to modern housing needs, and she suggests that a key aim has been to disassociate the development from its poorly regarded Thamesmead parent. However, she concedes that the deception may have been necessary to pull off even the limited achievement that this new community represents.

✉ SE28

@ www.gallionsha.co.uk (Gallions Housing Association site)

Gallows Corner • *Havering*

A major road junction and its immediate surroundings, situated to the north-east of GIDEA PARK. Here the Eastern Avenue splits into the Colchester Road (A12) and the Southend Arterial Road (A127). For several centuries this was an isolated country crossroads on the edge of Romford (or Harold's Wood) Common, frequented by highwaymen who committed numerous robberies. Criminals sentenced to death at the court of quarter sessions for the Liberty of Havering were executed here in the 16th and 17th centuries, as were some prisoners convicted at Chelmsford. The gallows, which stood close to the site of the present-day cricket pavilion, ceased to be used sometime in the 18th century and was taken down after 1815. The locality's character changed after the construction of the Southend Arterial Road in 1925. Houses and commercial amenities were built along the main thoroughfares in the late 1920s and Gallows Lane was widened and renamed Straight Road. Maresfield Crescent was created in 1937. Gallows Corner is now dominated by light industry, car dealerships and shed-style retail outlets, including a Tesco Extra superstore. Gidea Park and ROMFORD Cricket Club was formed in 1970 with the merger of two clubs which shared the facilities at Gallows Corner sports ground, formerly a secondary ground for Essex's county matches and also home to Romford Hockey Club.

Farnes Drive honours Ken Farnes, selected by *Wisden Cricketers' Almanack* as its 1939 cricketer of the year, who went to school in Romford and played for Essex and England.

✉ Romford RM2 and RM3

Gants Hill • *Redbridge*

A compact commercial and residential district centred on a transport hub two miles north of ILFORD. Its name relates to medieval landowners the Le Gant family, who originated from the Belgian city of Ghent. This was a purely agricultural district until after World War I, when the Corporation of London took advantage of government subsidies to begin laying out an estate of 2,000 cottages on farmland that stretched from just west of Cranbrook Road eastward to Horns Road. In 1921 the government had second thoughts about the whole scheme and withdrew its subsidies,

prompting the Corporation to call a halt to the project when only 220 homes had been built. The land reverted to the farmer, even though foundations had already been laid for many more properties. The Eastern Avenue (A12) cut through Gants Hill soon afterwards and Bradford developer Charles Henry Lord bought the abandoned site, profitably converting cottages that faced the new road into shops. The rest of the area was rapidly built up with affordable housing that abandoned the substantial proportions of earlier properties nearer Ilford. The art deco Savoy cinema (later an Odeon) became a local landmark in 1934. Gants Hill station opened on the FAIRLOP loop of the Central Line in 1947, with a lower level concourse that has been nicknamed Moscow Hall because of its resemblance to the station designs of the Moscow metro, though on a more modest scale. Bolstered by the new Tube connection, Gants Hill gained blocks of offices over the following two decades. The shopping centre has suffered a severe decline in recent times, with many premises lying empty and boarded up, while the Odeon was demolished in 2003 and replaced by flats. The cinema is remembered in a pavement mosaic placed outside a pizza restaurant the following year. In response to the pervading air of decline, Redbridge council convened a task force with representatives of the residential and business communities. The result was a 'town centre area action plan', most of which has yet to be implemented. Gants Hill has a substantial Jewish population, with synagogues and Jewish community centres and schools across the area.

Gants Hill was the childhood home of Louise Wener, who fronted the Britpop band Sleeper in the 1990s and is now an author. She has been quoted as saying, 'There's something about growing up in the dregs, the badlands, away from it all', where 'the main cultural attraction is its roundabout'.

✉ Ilford IG2

🚇 Central Line (zone 4)

Gascoigne • *Barking*

An electoral ward and housing estate in south BARKING. Dr John Bamber acquired the manor of Bifrons early in the 18th century and on his death in 1753 ownership passed to Sir Crisp Gascoyne (or Gascoigne), through his marriage to Bamber's daughter, Margaret. Gascoyne was a landowner in his own right and the first Lord Mayor of London to have lived at the MANSION HOUSE. Much of Bifrons manor was sold by Sir Crisp's wayward grandson Bamber Gascoyne to pay off gambling debts, and Bifrons manor house was demolished in about 1815. What remained of the estate descended through marriage to the marquises of Salisbury and was sold for building development after 1889. The modern Gascoigne estate, which lies between central Barking and the A13, is widely regarded as one of the borough's least desirable addresses. It consists primarily of 17 high-rise blocks, which have recently undergone refurbishment. The Gascoigne ward is one of the most racially mixed in the borough, and employment levels are very low. More than 15 per cent of homes are single-parent households. Gascoigne Primary School has a high, and rising, level of mobility – an indication of the changes taking place in the wider community. The 2001 report on the school by the educational standards agency Ofsted found that half the pupils spoke English as an additional language and nearly a quarter were from refugee families. Among the languages spoken were Albanian, Turkish and Lingala, a central African lingua franca.

✉ Barking IG11

♦ 9,371

Gidea Park • *Havering*
An expanded garden suburb situated just to the north-east of ROMFORD. At its inception in 1910 this was one of the most imaginative examples of enlightened town planning devised for Londoners who wanted to escape to the country. The name may derive from the Old English 'ged' and 'ea', meaning 'pike water', but it could simply mean giddy, or foolish. This would have been a reference to the outlandish architecture of the first Gidea Hall, which stood from the 13th century until 1718. Lady Jane Grey is said to have received tuition there. Its wooded park extended over 150 acres and its gardens grew vines, melons and oranges. The Georgian mansion that was built immediately after the demolition of the original hall survived until 1930, spending its latter years as the clubhouse for what is now Romford golf course. After the opening of the station in 1910, an idealistic Arts and Crafts project named Romford Garden Suburb began here, with designs that won an architects' competition. The homes were well-built, light and airy, and constructed in a variety of individual styles on the land attached to Gidea Hall. The retention of several features from the original estate – the orangery, lime

walk, ponds and a bathing temple – added a cachet to the marketing prospectus. Another competition, on a smaller scale, was held in 1934 and more housing followed, some of it equally innovative. Growth subsequently proceeded in the direction of the station, absorbing the hamlet of HARE STREET. Like much of easternmost Greater London, Gidea Park has a predominantly white population and a reasonably high standard of living.

The suburb's role as a refuge for East Enders was illustrated by Charles Kray, who once commented that if he had moved his family here, his twin sons might never have gone to the bad. Gidea Park was the boyhood home of radio and television presenter Noel Edmonds. The pop group Gidea Park had two minor hits in the early 1970s.

✉ Romford RM2

🚊 'one' Railway (zone 6)

📖 Brian Evans, *Romford, Collier Row and Gidea Park*, Phillimore, 1994

Gilwell Park • *Epping Forest, Essex*
With SEWARDSTONE and SEWARDSTONEBURY, between which it lies, this is the only corner of the extended metropolis that is not part of a London borough but falls within a London postal district. Henry VIII built a hunting lodge here for his son Edward, which he later granted to Sir Edward Denny of Waltham Abbey. It has remained privately owned ever since. The lodge was rebuilt in the late 18th century as the White House, with landscaped gardens adorned by a stone balustrade from old LONDON BRIDGE. The extravagance helped to bankrupt its owner and the Crown seized the property in 1812 and sold it at auction. The house had fallen into dereliction when W F de Bois Maclaren bought it in 1919 for £10,000 and presented it to the Scout Association. Gilwell Park now consists entirely of Scout facilities, both administrative offices and adventure sites. Among the park's features are the 'bomb-hole', which was created by a World War II air raid and enlarged to form a canoeing lake, and the Buffalo Lawn, which has a bronze buffalo given by the Boy Scouts of America. In 2003 a new lodge was opened in a woodland area to provide additional accommodation for the increasing number of Scouts visiting Gilwell Park from around the world for youth work, adult training and recreational purposes. Around 40,000 people now attend the centre each year and more lodges are expected to be built in the future.

The founder of the Scout Association, Robert Baden-Powell, was created Lord Baden-Powell of Gilwell in 1929.

✉ E4

📖 *Gilwell Park*, Scout Association, 1973

@ www.scouts.org.uk/nationalcentres/
gilwellactivity.html (Gilwell Park page of
Scout Association site)

Gipsy Hill • *Lambeth/Southwark*

A collection of Victorian villas and terraced houses situated north-west of CRYSTAL PAL-ACE, and noted for its fine views across London. A field at the foot of Gipsy Hill was said to have been used for the burial of plague victims. During the 17th and 18th centuries, the so-called NORWOOD Gipsies lived in the area and gave it its present name. Samuel Pepys recorded his wife's visit to their camp in August 1668 to have her fortune told. The most famous of all the mystics was Margaret Finch, who lived in a tepee-like structure made from branches, at the foot of an ancient tree. Allegedly, she was 109 when she died in 1740 and had to be buried in a deep, square box because she had sat cross-legged for so long that her limbs could not be straightened. Finch's successors lived on at the timber-built Gipsy House until the early 19th century. The area changed rapidly after Gipsy Hill station opened on the West End of London and Crystal Palace Railway in 1856. Christ Church was consecrated in 1867 and gained its statuesque tower in 1889. Blocks of flats were built between the world wars, and more have since replaced some of the largest houses. However, most of the Victorian and Edwardian properties have survived, although often in subdivided form. A quarter of the residents of Lambeth's Gipsy Hill ward are black or black British, and another 5.5 per cent are of mixed race. One-third of homes are rented from the council.

A pantomime called *The Norwood Gipsies* was staged at Covent Garden in 1777. The remarkable Annie Besant, theosophist, socialist, orator and Indian nationalist lived at 39 Colby Road from 1874 to 1893.

✉ SE19

🚶 13,601 (Lambeth's Gipsy Hill ward)

🚇 Southern (zone 3)

@ www.gipsyhill.org.uk (Christ Church parish
site)

Globe Town • *Tower Hamlets*

A collection of council-built properties located near the western end of ROMAN ROAD, east of BETHNAL GREEN. A track running north from STEPNEY was called Theven Lane in the Middle Ages, from the Old English plural of 'thief'. By the early 18th century it had been renamed Globe Lane, and later Globe Road, probably after a local inn. In the 1790s, land on the Eastfields estate was developed by a consortium of builders and the scheme had become known as Globe Town by 1808. More houses were added in the 1820s, which although small were well-built and aimed at a middle-class market. Globe Road and Devonshire Street station opened on the Great Eastern Railway in 1884 and closed in 1916. Inevitably for this part of east London, Globe Town had by this time become very run-down and it suffered the loss of many houses, factories and a church in World War II. In the late 1940s the borough council built the Rogers estate, named after a local war hero. This was followed by a succession of municipal projects that changed the face of Globe Town over the following three decades. In 1992 the crime-ridden Rogers estate was London's first to benefit from a government initiative called the 'design improvement controlled experiment' but the improvements were not sustained and the flats soon resumed their deterioration. Since then, housing associations have taken over the management of many of Globe Town's flats, while others have been sold privately. Globe Town has a large Bangladeshi community, as well as Turkish-, Arabic- and Cantonese-speaking minorities.

As a result of Tower Hamlets' short-lived division of the borough into seven 'neighbourhoods' in the 1980s, Globe Town must be the best branded locality in London, with stylish steel spheres mounted on brick columns or arches at every point of access.

✉ E2

🚶 11,801 (Mile End and Globe Town ward)

📖 Anne Cunningham, *Glimpses of Globe Town*,
Globe Town Neighbourhood Libraries
Service, 1988; Gerry Stoker and Vivien
Lowndes, *Tower Hamlets and
Decentralisation: The Experience of Globe
Town Neighbourhood*, Local Government
Management Board, 1991

Gloucester Road • *Kensington & Chelsea*

A commercial street and hotel zone running northward from SOUTH KENSINGTON towards

KENSINGTON GARDENS. From the early 17th century this was Hogs Moor or Hogsmire Lane and it was the site of an unsuccessful pleasure garden in the late 18th century. George III's sister-in law Maria, Duchess of Gloucester built herself a house on the lane in 1805, later known as Gloucester Lodge. The politician George Canning, briefly prime minister in 1827, lived here for a while. Much of the surrounding area was built up in the second quarter of the 19th century, including the modest Lee estate of 1825, Kensington New Town between 1837 and 1843, and Kensington Gate from 1850. The cosy, ornate St Stephen's Church was consecrated in 1867, and in the following year the Metropolitan Railway opened a branch line from EDGWARE ROAD to BROMPTON (Gloucester Road), as the station was originally called. Over the course of the 20th century numerous terraced houses on Gloucester Road were converted to hotels. In a more recent trend, big-name hoteliers have bought up whole groups of these establishments and united them under a single fascia. The locality also has many short-stay apartments and studio flats, while a plentiful supply of bars and restaurants caters to both tourists and residents. Around the corner on Cromwell Road, Holiday Inn's London Kensington Forum is London's second largest hotel. Opened in 1973, it has 910 rooms and its tower rises 27 storeys. In 1989 a large shopping and office complex was built behind Gloucester Road station, spanning the tracks. The Circle and District Line level of the station has become London Underground's prime setting for art exhibitions. An unused fourth platform is regularly filled with works by artists of international stature, sometimes publicizing temporary shows at London galleries.

The author J M Barrie lived at 133 Gloucester Road between 1895 and 1902, the period in which he conceived the story of *Peter Pan*. In his *Literary Guide to London*, Ed Glinert calls T S Eliot 'the Pope of Gloucester Road' in allusion to the poet's 25 years as church warden of St Stephen's Church. Eliot resided in nearby Grenville Place from 1933 to 1940.

✉ SW7

🚇 Circle Line; District Line; Piccadilly Line (zone 1)

Goddington • *Bromley*

The south-eastern part of ORPINGTON, built up during the late 1920s and 1930s. Goddington was once a small manor in the parish of Chelsfield, first recorded in the 13th century as the property of Simon de Godyn), His family came from a hamlet near Ashford in Kent, now spelt Godinton, where he also held the manor of Great Chart. In 1461 Edward Poynings inherited the manor, at the age of eleven. Henry VII later knighted him and made him Lieutenant of Ireland. The manor of Goddington grew to include parts of the parishes of Orpington and ST MARY CRAY, remaining an area of corn and hop fields until after World War I. The Park Avenue estate was laid out from 1926, when Gravel Pit Cottages were demolished to make way for Spur Road and the tree-lined drive that had led to Goddington House became Park Avenue. That house is now a retirement home belonging to the Methodist Ministers' Housing Society. Part of Goddington Park is protected chalk grassland, and mesolithic tools have been found here. Orpington Sports Club has been based in Goddington since the 1930s. When St Olave's Grammar School took over its Goddington Lane site in 1968, the sports club moved to the 23-acre Goddington Dene, south of the park. Westcombe Park Rugby Football Club moved here in 1990 and became the controlling force within the sports club.

✉ Orpington BR6

Golders Green • *Barnet*

Created by American property developers at the beginning of the 20th century, Golders Green is known particularly as a home of London's middle-class Jewish community. It is situated to the north-west of HAMPSTEAD HEATH. The name probably derives from a 14th-century resident called Godyere. A number of 'ornamental villas' were built from the late 18th century onwards, and the crossroads that forms the hub of Golders Green was created by the arrival of the FINCHLEY ROAD in the late 1820s. The London County Council's acquisition of Golders Hill House and its gardens in 1898 brought the first public park to the urban district of HENDON. This was followed by the rapid suburban development of the neighbourhood, and Golders Green's first shopping parade was established in 1908. The Golders Green Hippodrome opened in 1913. It has served as a music hall, cinema, theatre and BBC recording studio; the BBC put it up for sale in 2005. After World War I a large number of Jewish families began moving into the area's new housing from the crowded East End, and synagogues were built to serve the community. Immigrant Jews fleeing Nazi persecution augmented the settlement during the 1930s. At the same time, the builders Laing laid out the racetrack-shaped Golders Green estate in the south-west corner of the district. CRICKLEWOOD aerodrome had occupied the site from 1916 to 1930. The 1930s also saw the erection of mansion blocks in central Golders Green. The visible signs of Golders Green's Jewish character are diminishing as new ethnic minorities, especially Korean and Japanese, move in.

The London Cremation Society opened London's first crematorium on Hoop Lane in 1902. Those cremated here have included the psychoanalyst Sigmund Freud, former prime minister Neville Chamberlain, writer Bram Stoker, birth control campaigner Marie Stopes and ballerina Anna Pavlova. Badfinger, one of the most successful bands signed to The Beatles' Apple label, recorded at their studio in Golders Green. After the suicide of singer/ songwriter Pete Ham, albums of his demo tapes were released, entitled 7 *Park Avenue* and *Golders Green*.

> ✉ NW11

> 🚶 16,249

> 🚇 Northern Line (zone 3)

> 📖 Clive R Smith, *Golders Green As It Was*, self-published, 1998; Hilary J Grainger and Peter C Jupp (ed.), *Golders Green Crematorium, 1902–2002: A London Centenary in Context*, London Cremation Co., 2002

Goldhawk Road • *Hammersmith & Fulham*

Running west from SHEPHERD'S BUSH Green to STAMFORD BROOK, and becoming increasingly upmarket as it progresses westwards, this highway was created by the Romans as part of the Great West Road and takes its name from a family that lived here in the 15th century. It was little used in medieval times but gained a new lease of life when the stretch from Askew Road to KING STREET was relaid in the 1830s. This part was at first called Oxford Street Road or New Road, and smart houses began to spring up along its length. Goldhawk Road was described in the 1870s as 'the prettiest road out of London ... with its charming little villas coyly hidden behind low walls'. The roadside had trees and shrubs, grassy verges and a pond. With the coming of the tram at the end of the century the road took on a more urban character, but a marked contrast remained between the villas of the western section and the stuccoed terraces in the east. Goldhawk Road station opened in 1914, to co-incide with the eastward relocation of Shepherd's Bush station. The houses in the eastern terraces have mostly been subdivided as the area has declined in prosperity, with low-rent commercial premises at street level. There is a market by the Tube station, which specializes in fabrics. The Goldhawk industrial estate, off Brackenbury Road, has a very metropolitan mix of tenants that includes security services, laboratory instruments, health drinks and media services companies.

Business tycoon Richard Branson founded the Town House studios at 150 Goldhawk Road in 1979. Bob Dylan, Queen, Robbie Williams and all the major Britpop bands have used its facilities, and Elton John recorded his *Candle in the Wind* tribute to Diana, Princess of Wales here. Simon Bent's play *Goldhawk Road*, described by the *Evening Standard* as 'scathingly funny' and 'wickedly misanthropic', premiered at the nearby Bush Theatre in 1997.

> ✉ W12; W6

> 🚇 Hammersmith & City Line (zone 2)

Goodge Street • *Camden*

Like nearby WARREN STREET, Goodge Street's name is associated more with the Tube station than the thoroughfare, which runs westwards off TOTTENHAM COURT ROAD and soon becomes Mortimer Street. John Goodge obtained Crab Tree Field by marriage in 1718 and his sons developed the land in the 1740s. When the Northern Line station opened in 1907, it was at first named Tottenham Court Road, while the stop to its south was called OXFORD STREET. Within a year the company changed its mind and gave the two stations their present names. During World War II the government built a deep shelter linked to Goodge Street station, part of which was made available to General Eisenhower as his operational headquarters for D-Day. After the war the army used the shelter as a transit centre until it was damaged by fire in 1956. In the mid 1960s some of Goodge Street's cafés gained a reputation as hang-outs where illicit substances might be obtained. The surrounding area is now known for its electronics retailers, nearby academic institutions and the art galleries of Windmill Street. Scala Street boasts the delightful Pollock's Toy Museum.

Donovan's *Sunny Goodge Street* was one of the first pop songs to include an explicit reference to drug-taking. Judy Collins, Marianne Faithfull and Paul McCartney later recorded cover versions, and Tom Northcott's rendition topped the Canadian charts in 1967. For a while, Goodge Street's name became emblematic of the 'stoned' hippie lifestyle, even rating a mention on the American television cop show *Hawaii Five-O*.

- ✉ W1
- 🚇 Northern Line (zone 1)
- @ www.pollockstoymuseum.com

Goodman's Fields *see* LEMAN STREET

Goodmayes • *Redbridge*

A multiracial satellite of eastern ILFORD, separated from the BECONTREE estate by Goodmayes Park. Tradition has it that the name derives from John Godemay, a 14th-century landowner, but local historian Peter Foley argues that Godemay took his name from the place, not the other way around. Citing another local name, Mayfield, Foley suggests a link to the herbaceous plant madder, cultivated for dyeing in pre-industrial times. Like neighbouring SEVEN KINGS, this area was farmland until the end of the 19th century when local developer Cameron Corbett (later Baron Rowallan) erected the Mayfield estate south of the railway line and east of Goodmayes Lane. Corbett's Scottish origin shows in the names of many of the streets. To ensure the success of his project, he pressed for a railway station to serve the area and this opened in 1901. Shopping parades followed, on the High Road and Goodmayes Road. In 1909 the philanthropist Andrew Carnegie presented a public library and lecture hall. Today, the main local landmark is a Tesco superstore, opened in 1987 on land formerly occupied by railway sidings. In a relatively recent transformation, less than half of Goodmayes' population is now white and the second largest ethnic group is of Indian origin. The Muslim, Hindu and Sikh faiths are all well represented. Three-quarters of homes are owner-occupied. Goodmayes is looking the worse for wear nowadays, as east London's decline washes outwards across it.

Goodmayes was the home from 1924 to 1927 of the long-serving Labour politician Emanuel Shinwell. Actor Ian Holm was born in 1931 at Goodmayes Hospital, where his father, a psychiatrist, was superintendent.

- ✉ Ilford IG3
- 👥 10,994
- 🚇 'one' Railway (zone 4)
- 📖 Peter Foley, *Seven Kings and Goodmayes:*

Origins and Early Development, Heptarchy, 1993

Gordon Hill • *Enfield*

A street and station situated in a pleasant corner of north-west Enfield. This was part of the virgin territory of ENFIELD CHASE until its enclosure and division in the late 1770s, when much of the land was acquired by Trinity College, Cambridge. Only one house of note stood here at that time, which was the home of Lord George Gordon and later of Sir Thomas Hallifax, banker and Lord Mayor of London in 1776. In the late 1850s the North London Society bought Gordon House, demolished it and laid out streets, but a decade later only a few houses had been built on Halifax Road and Gordon Road. Services began at the unfinished Church of St Michael and All Angels, Gordon Hill and CHASE SIDE in 1874. It was almost 90 years before the west wall and narthex (entrance lobby) were completed. Separate schools for infants, boys and girls were built and later amalgamated on the boys' school site at the foot of Brigadier Hill. The North London Society began to extend its estate in the 1880s and built houses on the site of Gordon House in 1894. Gordon Hill station opened in 1910 when the Great Northern Railway line was extended to Cuffley in Hertfordshire but the area maintained a semi-rural aspect until the 1930s. Several compact apartment blocks have been built in new cul-de-sacs in recent years to capitalize on the locality's 'highly sought after' status. St George's RC Primary School, on Gordon Road, is regarded as one of the best state schools in London and most of its pupils come from very favourable social and economic backgrounds.

Lord George Gordon became notorious as the instigator of an anti-Catholic uprising in London in 1780. He led tens of thousands of Protestant demonstrators in a march on Parliament that turned into five days of destructive riots eventually put down by the army. Hundreds of rioters were killed and Gordon was charged with treason, but acquitted. He later converted to Judaism.

- ✉ Enfield EN2
- 🚇 WAGN Railway (zone 5)

Goresbrook Village *see* CASTLE GREEN

Gorringe Park • *Merton*

A rarely used name for the far northern part of Mitcham, south-east of Tooting station. Gorringe Park House was a three-storey villa that stood close to the site of present-day Gorringe Park Primary School, which is at the junction of Sandy Lane and Streatham Road. Around the beginning of the 20th century its grounds began to be carved up for suburban building, while James Pascall set up his confectionery factory on neighbouring farmland. Gorringe Park House became an orphanage, served as a convalescent home during World War I and was afterwards the base for a Christian Jewish mission. St Barnabas' Church, on Gorringe Park Avenue, was completed in 1914 by architect Henry Philip Burke-Downing. His imposing Gothic structure is now Grade II listed. Young's Gorringe Park pub is located on London Road, just by Tooting station.

✉ Mitcham CR4

@ www.gorringepark.merton.sch.uk

Gospel Oak • *Camden*

A socially polarized locality known to some as 'Hampstead Bottom', occupying the void between KENTISH TOWN and HAMPSTEAD. Gospel Oak's name derives from a tree under which a host of legendary figures are said to have preached, including St Augustine, Edward the Confessor, John Wesley and even St Paul. The tree marked the boundary between the parishes of Hampstead and ST PANCRAS. It vanished sometime in the mid 19th century; the uncertainty as to when exactly this occurred corresponds with the mythological nature of its history. Gospel Oak was just starting to be developed as a somewhat underprivileged suburb when railways seared through in all directions. From the 1850s compact terraced houses for the lower middle classes were built on land belonging to the Church Commissioners in the west and to Lord Mansfield and Lord Southampton to the east. The dense pattern of building left no room for greenery, except at Lismore Circus; a writer complained that 'in Oak Village there is not a sapling of that sturdy representative of English hearts to be found'. Two remarkable churches were erected in 1865 and 1901: St Martin's on Vicars Road, which Pevsner calls 'the craziest of London's Victorian churches', and All Hallows on Savernake Road, which he reckons a 'masterpiece'. By 1924 Gospel Oak had descended to 'shabby gentility on the very brink of squalor', according to John Buchan in *The Three Hostages*, although others recognized a community at ease with itself. Much of the district was rebuilt with low-rise council flats in the 1960s and 1970s. Studies have revealed many forms of deprivation and the area

has been the focus of regeneration spending on rebuilding and community projects. The area is poorly served by amenities and is notable for the sharp contrast between its rented flats and owner-occupied houses.

Ian Matthews, of Fairport Convention and Matthews Southern Comfort, released the solo album *Journeys from Gospel Oak* in 1974. Sinéad O'Connor's six-song EP *Gospel Oak* (1997) featured a cover photograph of the railway station. Comedian and television presenter Michael Palin moved into a terraced railway cottage in Gospel Oak in the 1960s and has since bought two neighbouring properties and knocked them all into one. Palin suggested in 2005 that he had grown too old to front world travel blockbusters and that his next project might be 'a history of Gospel Oak'. He has planted a new gospel oak at Lismore Circus 'pocket park'.

✉ NW5; NW3

♦ 10,465

🚉 Silverlink Metro (zone 2)

Goulds Green • *Hillingdon*

A half-developed locality situated just beyond the northern edge of STOCKLEY PARK. The family of John Golde was mentioned in local documents in 1373 and Goulds Grene was first recorded in 1592. The green was a southward extension of Hillingdon Heath, covering about 20 acres. By 1806 the hamlet was sufficiently significant to form one of the four divisions of HILLINGDON parish, along with Hillingdon East, Hillingdon Town and YIEWSLEY. A police station was in existence here by 1864. In the 1920s and early 1930s suburban development had stretched here from HAYES and there has been more since, but the Stables Farm survives. The farmhouse is home to a fireworks company, while the outbuildings and fields comprise Goulds Green Riding School.

The Goulds, a town in Newfoundland, Canada, may have been named by settlers who came from Goulds Green.

✉ Uxbridge UB8

Gower Street • *Camden* (pronounced to rhyme with 'power')

An elegantly sombre BLOOMSBURY street connecting Bedford Square and Euston Road, with a northern extension continuing to Hampstead Road. The street was built from the 1780s and retains one of London's longest sets of unbroken Georgian terraces. Critics decried its ugliness and the landowners, the Bedford estate, later added some stuccoed entrances to relieve the brown-bricked gloom. During Gower Street's development, a square was proposed near the northern end but the land was taken instead for what became University College London (UCL). The university was founded to provide an alternative to the Anglican-dominated colleges of Oxford and Cambridge and was nicknamed 'the godless institution of Gower Street'. The Wilkins Building opened in 1828 and the university has since progressively expanded to consume most of the east side of the street and the land behind it. University College Hospital opened on the west side in 1833, bringing surgeons and doctors to the residences nearby. The hospital was rebuilt in flamboyantly baroque style by Sir Alfred Waterhouse and his son Paul over the ten years to 1906. Now known as the Cruciform, this building became part of UCL's teaching facilities in 1996. The hospital moved into a spectacular pair of new buildings on Euston Road in 2005. Gower Street's edifying museums make it a miniature South Kensington. UCL's Petrie Museum and Grant Museum house, respectively, Egyptian archaeology and natural history collections, the latter featuring plenty of skeletons and mounted animals, including the marsupial wolf and the dodo.

After drawing up a list of the pros and cons of marriage, Charles Darwin proposed to his first cousin Emma Wedgwood, and married her in 1839. The newlyweds moved into a house on Gower Street, but three years later Charles's increasingly poor health prompted them to move to the country village of DOWNE. The Pre-Raphaelite artist Simeon Solomon trained at his brother's Gower Street studio, and had his first picture exhibited at the Royal Academy when he was only 18 years old. His later arrest for indecent exposure prompted a decline into alcoholism and poverty. Other Gower Street residents have included the engineer Richard Trevithick and the Italian patriot Giuseppe Mazzini.

✉ WC1

🚇 Circle Line; Hammersmith & City Line; Metropolitan Line (Euston Square, called Gower Street 1863–1909, zone 1)

@ www.uclh.nhs.uk (University College Hospital)

Grahame Park · *Barnet*

For most of the 20th century this locality in north-east COLINDALE was entirely given over to the activities of the Royal Air Force. The pioneering British aviator Claude Grahame-White founded the London aerodrome here in 1910. During World War I the airfield served as a base for the Royal Naval Air Service and the Royal Flying Corps, becoming RAF HENDON in 1927. Aircraft were manufactured and flown from Hendon for another ten years, after which its enclosure by suburban housing made aviation impractical, although it operated briefly as a fighter station during the Battle of Britain. From 1940 RAF Hendon became a transport, communications and training base, but its unsuitability for post-war jet aircraft meant that the last flying units left in 1957, although RAF Hendon officially closed only in 1988. The Greater London Council began construction of the Grahame Park estate on part of the former airfield in 1969. It was planned as a miniature new town, with council flats and houses at its core and private-sector and Ministry of Defence housing on the perimeter. Community facilities included a library, day centre and health centre, all with angular designs. Plans continued to evolve throughout the project's implementation, generally in the direction of downscaling. Barnet council made some worthwhile efforts to prettify the estate in the early 1990s but problems of crime and deprivation have persisted and a radical rebuilding programme is now planned. Over 3,000 new homes will be built, with improved transport links and new retail and community areas in a programme targeted for completion around 2020.

On Grahame Park Way, former aircraft hangars now house Britain's national aviation collection, the Royal Air Force Museum. Over 70 aeroplanes are on show and there is a special emphasis on the Battle of Britain, recalling the site's role as an operational centre in World War II.

✉ NW9

Grand Union Village · *Ealing/Hillingdon*

A mixed-use 'urban village' situated on Ruislip Road and Broadmead Road in north SOUTHALL, by the side of the Grand Union Canal. Originally a brickfield, the site was formerly the headquarters of Taylor Woodrow Construction and the company will continue to be based here once the 'village' is completed. Work began on the £130-million project in 2002 and should be completed by 2008. There will be more than 700 residential properties, from one-bedroom apartments to six-bedroom houses. Ten per cent of the homes will provide key worker accommodation, including 30 exclusively for teachers. Restaurants, shops and walkways will line the canal, with a commercial centre set around a new canal basin. Leisure facilities will include a sports complex and publicly accessible playing fields. Developer Bryant Homes (a division of Taylor Woodrow) made effusive claims about the ground-breaking nature of the village in its planning proposals, but local pressure groups have objected to aspects of the plans, which they say do not conform to principles of sustainability.

> ✉ Northolt UB5; Hayes UB4

> @ www.grandunionvillage.co.uk (Bryant Homes marketing site)

Grange Mills • *Lambeth*

One current street atlas shows Grange Mills as a locality in east BALHAM, but this is a cartographic error. It is merely a 24-unit commercial estate on Weir Road, of no more significance than hundreds of other such estates across London. Formerly Grove Road, the street was renamed to commemorate Benjamin Weir, who in 1902 bequeathed his house for the construction of a hospital. Around this time the grand villas on the south side of the road were replaced by well-proportioned terraced houses, interspersed with some light industrial premises. These included a Pickfords depot and the Clapham Park Bottling Co. Grange Mills was from the outset, and continues to be, a stationery works specializing in envelopes. Originally Chapman and Co., it is now Mekvale Envelopes plc. The ancillary buildings of Grange Mills today serve as distribution warehouses or as inexpensive offices for small companies and not-for-profit organizations, while others lie empty. Access to the Grange Mills enclave is via a narrow gap between two houses, beneath a quaint decorative arch.

> ✉ SW12

Grange Park • *Enfield*

A 'self-contained orchard city', as the local newspaper extravagantly described it in 1908, beside Salmon's Brook in north WINCHMORE HILL. The Old Park estate, north of Green Dragon Lane, occupied the area for centuries, possibly since the time of Domesday Book. The present Old Park House dates from 1735 and was home to the Clayton family and later the Ford family until 1909. In 1911 BUSH HILL PARK Golf Club took over the land surrounding the mansion, which is now its clubhouse.

The remaining parkland was built on and marketed as the Old Park Grange estate, with Grange Park station opening in 1910. ENFIELD Golf Club, founded in 1893, occupies the former fields of Old Park Farm. In 2001 Enfield council considered relocating the golf course and developing the site for social housing and a public park, but the plan was abandoned a year later after local elections led to a change of political control of the council. Adjacent to the golf course is Grange Park Primary School, which is very large, highly rated and oversubscribed. A fifth of its pupils come from other European countries, although most speak English fluently. The population of Grange ward, which includes BUSH HILL (but not BUSH HILL PARK), is 90 per cent white, and 85 per cent of property is owner-occupied.

> ✉ N21

> ♦ 11,605 (Grange ward)

> 🚆 WAGN Railway (zone 5)

> 📖 Douglas Haigh, *Old Park in the Manor of Enfield*, Enfield, 1977

Gray's Inn Road • *Camden*

A historic street running north-north-west from CHANCERY LANE station to KING'S CROSS. Gray's Inn itself is at the southern end of the road, on the west side. The 12th-century manor house here belonged to Sir Reginald de Grey, Chief Justice of Chester and Constable and Sheriff of Nottingham, who died in 1308. Some time in the 50 to 60 years following his death, a learned society of lawyers based itself at the manor house and by the 15th century Gray's Inn had become one of London's leading Inns of Court. The present central hall dates from 1558. Around 1600 Sir Francis Bacon laid out the inn's gardens with a network of pathways called 'walks', which were a novelty at the time. During the 1680s Robert Rossington pulled down most of the properties in what was then Gray's Inn Lane and replaced them with plain, four-storey terraced houses. The one surviving example of Rossington's development is at 55 Gray's Inn Road. The Calthorpe estate, built around 1820, was the first housing project of Thomas Cubitt, who went on to become London's greatest speculative builder; among his achievements are much of the housing in Belgravia, St Pancras and Clapham. Charles Dickens lived nearby at 48 Doughty Street, now the home of the Dickens House Museum. Gray's Inn Road has the ITN building, created in 1991 by Sir Norman Foster. The UCL Centre for Auditory Research was opened in 2005 next to the Royal National Throat Nose and Ear Hospital, funded by the Wellcome Trust.

The Water Rats public house has long been a venue for live music. Previously called the Pindar of Wakefield, after a traditional English ballad, it hosted Bob Dylan's London debut in 1962. Oasis attracted early interest when they played here in 1994.

> ✉ WC1

> @ www.graysinn.org.uk (Honourable Society of Gray's Inn website)

Great Ilford *see* ILFORD

Great Portland Street • *Westminster*

Not as grand-looking as it sounds, this commercial thoroughfare runs between OXFORD STREET and the eastern end of Marylebone Road, where Great Portland Street station is located. Like many streets in the vicinity, its name was a product of the marriage of estate owner Margaret Cavendish Harley to the second Duke of Portland. The car showrooms for which the street was once renowned have been driven away by fashion wholesalers and office furnishers, although it remains home to the Retail Motor Industry Federation. And there is still a Ryman stationers in the street where, in 1893, Henry J Ryman opened his very first store. To the west, Portland Place runs parallel with Great Portland Street, joining REGENT STREET via a dog-leg bend at Langham Place, the site of the BBC's Broadcasting House. The elliptical building was constructed in 1932 of ferro-concrete faced, aptly, with Portland stone. Eric Gill produced carvings for the interior and a free-standing relief of Prospero and Ariel above the front entrance.

On his visits to London in the 1820s and 1830s, the composer Felix Mendelssohn stayed in Great Portland Street at the home of a German iron merchant. Among the writers who lived here were James Boswell and Leigh Hunt. H G Wells was well-acquainted with the area; it is the setting for events in both *The Invisible Man* and his lesser-known story *The Crystal Egg*. The Invisible Man boarded in 'a large unfurnished room in a big ill-managed lodging-house in a slum near Great Portland Street'.

> ✉ W1

> 🚇 Circle Line; Hammersmith & City Line; Metropolitan Line (zone 1)

Great Stanmore *see* STANMORE

Greenford • *Ealing*

A moderately priced residential area with an industrial zone to its north, situated to the north-west of EALING. First recorded in 845, Greenford's name derives from a crossing of the River Brent. The little farming hamlet had both a windmill and a watermill by the 17th century, and the Coston and Ravenor families owned all the land. It is said that a survey carried out during the plague years found that Greenford was one of the three healthiest places in the country, with its inhabitants surviving much longer than the national average. At the end of the 19th century the village was beginning to grow but the population was still below a thousand. GREENFORD PARK Cemetery opened in 1901, and the extension of the Great Western Railway in 1904 gave impetus to the suburbanization process. The creation of the Western Avenue (A40) in the 1920s brought industrial development to the north of the area. One of the earliest arrivals was the tea and coffee producer J Lyons and Co. The Ravenors sold their farm to Ealing council in 1928 and Ravenor Park opened later that year. The 1930s saw the peak period of housebuilding in Greenford, mostly small and medium-sized semi-detached houses. Nearly all the early development was speculative, although the council built a couple of small estates. In World War II, Greenford was a major base for artillery storage and distribution, with over 2,000 workers employed at the site. Post-war developments consist mainly of flats and small houses. The Westway Cross retail park occupies the site of former factories near the Grand Union Canal. Holy Cross Church, on Oldfield Lane, is a small, flint-clad parish church with windows of medieval stained glass from King's College, Cambridge.

Opened in 1999, the London Motorcycle Museum has over 60 exhibits, with an emphasis on British machines. Situated on Oldfield Road South, where it utilizes some of the buildings of Ravenor Farm, it is open every weekend and on bank holidays.

> ✉ Greenford UB6

> 👥 38,852 (Greenford Broadway, Greenford Green and North Greenford wards)

> 🚇 First Great Western branch terminus (zone 4); Central Line (zone 4)

> 📖 Richard Essen, *Ealing, Hanwell and Greenford*, Sutton, 2000

Greenford Green • *Ealing*

The industrial part of GREENFORD lying north

of the station, now undergoing regeneration. In the 19th century, day-trippers would take a pleasure boat along the canal from PADDINGTON to this 'pretty place'. The chemist William Perkin, who pioneered the development of synthetic dyes for fabrics, opened the world's first commercial dye plant at Greenford Green in 1857, initially producing mauve and later magenta and alizarin red. This may sound like an obscure claim to fame, but it has been credited as 'the beginning of the commercialization of scientific invention'. The Science Museum has a bottle of Perkin's original mauve dye. Perkin retired from industry, aged 36, to return to pure science and later created one of the earliest synthetic perfumes. In 1906 he was awarded the inaugural Perkin Medal, now the highest honour in American industrial chemistry, to commemorate the 50th anniversary of the discovery of mauve. Greenford Green was the ideal site for industrial development in the early part of the 20th century. Its distance from central London made land relatively cheap and transport links were first class. The Grand Union Canal, the Great Western Railway and the Western Avenue (A40) all facilitated the movement of goods. J Lyons and Co. opened its factory at Greenford Green in 1921. Tea and coffee were processed and packed here, followed later by a range of grocery and confectionery lines. Tea and other bulk commodities were brought by barge from London docks, unloaded at a dedicated canal basin and moved around the site by an in-house railway. Ice cream was manufactured at the neighbouring Bridge Park factory from 1954. Lyons' parent company, Allied Domecq, closed the operation at Greenford Green in 2002. The residential part of Greenford Green has a large Asian community, mainly of Indian origin. Hinduism and Islam are the principal minority faiths. Over three-quarters of homes are owner-occupied.

✉ Greenford UB6

👭 12,466

📖 Simon Garfield, *Mauve*, Faber & Faber, 2000

@ www.kzwp.com/lyons/greenford.htm (Lyons' company history site)

Greenford Park • *Ealing*

The south-western part of GREENFORD, and one of the earliest suburban developments in the area, although it is not shown on most maps. The area was formerly 250 acres of common land known as Upper and Lower Town Fields. These were the two largest fields in Greenford, belonging to the wealthy Marnham family. From 1710 parts of the fields were bequeathed for charitable purposes, and these were later sold to liquidate the assets. In 1901 Greenford Park Cemetery opened on Windmill Lane (which recalls the presence of a 16th-century windmill). The Greenford Park estate was begun in 1908. The White Hart pub followed, at the junction of Windmill Lane and King's Avenue, together with a small parade of shops. To the north-west, the council acquired Marnham Fields as open space in 1932. The fields now form part of NORTHOLT and Greenford Countryside Park, and community woodlands have recently been planted here.

✉ Southall UB1; Greenford UB6

Greenhill • *Harrow*

The north-central part of HARROW, and an important shopping area. The name was first recorded in 1334 and the area may earlier have been known as Norbury. By the mid 18th century, Greenhill was a small hamlet of modest farms regularly spaced around the six-acre village green, which had halved in size by 1817. Harrow (later Harrow and WEALDSTONE) station opened in 1837 and within four years there were 28 houses in Greenhill, with 151 inhabitants. The Church of St John the Baptist was built in 1866, by which time the population had risen to around 400. Harrow-on-the-Hill station opened in 1880 and with its convenient location between two stations, Greenhill grew rapidly over the following three decades, prompting the rebuilding of St John's Church in 1904. Harrow Technical School was built on part of the Lowlands estate after its proprietor Isabella Rotch died in 1909 at the age of 100. The school later became Greenhill College and is now a campus of Harrow College. Shops began to line Greenhill Lane, which was renamed Station Road. Sopers (now Debenhams) became the borough's first department store in 1914, by which time Greenhill was part of a continuous ribbon of development stretching north to HEADSTONE and HARROW WEALD. The last gaps were filled in the 1920s, mainly by private developers, although 169 council houses were built in the vicinity of Elmgrove Road. The expansion of the shopping centre reached a peak during the 1930s and the Granada cinema was built in 1938 on the site of Greenhill manor house. Harrow civic centre was built in 1972 at the northern end of Station Road. By the borough's standards the Greenhill ward has a high proportion of single people in their twenties and relatively few households with children. Twenty-seven per cent of homes are privately rented. Slightly over one-quarter of residents are of Asian – mainly Indian – origin.

The punk fashion designer Vivienne Westwood was married in 1962 at St John's Church.

> ✉ Harrow HA1

> ♦ 9,324

> @ www.stjohn-greenhill.fsnet.co.uk (St John's Church site)

Greenland Dock • *Southwark*

The largest remaining dock in south London, situated east of SURREY QUAYS station. It was excavated in 1696 and originally named Howland Great Wet Dock after the family that owned the land. By the mid 18th century it had become a base for Arctic whalers and was renamed Greenland Dock. During the 19th century Greenland Dock handled trade in Scandinavian and Baltic timber and Canadian grain, cheese and bacon. The dock was enlarged in 1904 and closed in 1969, along with the rest of the Surrey Docks. The London Docklands Development Corporation commissioned a plan for mixed developments of squares and streets integrated into the existing environment and community. Between 1984 and 1990, 1,250 homes were built at Greenland Dock, notably townhouses and apartment blocks by the Danish company Islef. The scheme was a success and demand for the new housing exceeded expectations. In 1990 the Surrey Docks Watersports Centre and a waterside pub opened. The smaller South Dock now serves as a marina.

> ✉ SE16

> ⚓ Greenland pier

Green Lanes • *Hackney/Haringey/Enfield*

One of London's longest stretches of road with a single name, and the 'spinal chord' of Cypriot London, according to the magazine *New Society* in 1981. Green Lanes (A105) runs from Newington Green to BUSH HILL. This was part of an ancient route that led from London's SHOREDITCH through ENFIELD to Hertford, and may have been in use from the second century AD. The road connected a series of greens, most of which have since been lost, even in name. Among these were Beans Green at present-day MANOR HOUSE, Ducketts Green, and Elses Green, which lay at what is now the junction of WOOD GREEN'S High

Road and Lordship Lane. Drovers bringing animals to London for slaughter liked the road because it was less busy than other highways. It was formerly called Green Lanes for an even greater length than its present extent, but in the mid 19th century the southernmost part was renamed Southgate Road, and the section that passes through Wood Green became the High Street, which was changed to High Road around 1895. This was a time when developers were laying out a series of middle-class streets in Green Lanes' HARRINGAY hinterland and the main road was lined with long, imposing shopping parades. Over the first half of the 20th century the area declined in social status and many houses were subdivided, making property affordable to Turkish immigrants who arrived from Cyprus from the late 1950s onwards. A snowball effect strengthened the community here and the eastern Mediterranean ambience of the shops and cafés later drew Greek Cypriots too. Despite the intercommunal tensions and occasional violence of their native island, the two communities lived here in harmony. Many Greek Cypriots have since moved further north, although some continue to operate or work in businesses here. The Turkish Cypriots have increasingly been joined by compatriots from Turkey, and more recently by Kurds and Bulgarians. These ethnic groups also have a history of rivalry with the Turks but co-existence was peaceful on Green Lanes until conflict arose between Turkish and Kurdish gangs over drugs territory. In a mass street fight in 2002, four men were shot and another was stabbed to death. The stresses caused by this incident have mostly been resolved since as the communities strive to prove that the majority of their number are hardworking and respectable. Other south-eastern European minorities represented on Green Lanes include Kosovans and Albanians.

The area's harmonious fusion of Greek and Turkish Cypriots has been the subject of frequent media attention, including a 2001 BBC radio documentary entitled *Green Lines, Green Lanes*.

> ✉ N16; N4; N22; N13; N21

> 🚊 Silverlink Metro (Harringay Green Lanes, zone 3)

Green Park • *Westminster*

The smallest of the central London royal parks, situated east of HYDE PARK CORNER, in the apex of PICCADILLY and Constitution Hill, so-called because Charles II took his constitutional walks here. The park's existence was first recorded in 1554 when Sir Thomas Wyatt led a rebellion against the marriage of Mary I to Philip II of Spain. Duels were later fought here. Charles II enclosed the park with a brick wall in 1667, stocked it with deer and provided a ranger's house. The park was known at that time as Upper St James's Park but was commonly called Green Park by the mid 18th century. Green Park has always been plainer than its more illustrious ST JAMES'S neighbour, although little 'temples' were built to mark the end of the Austrian War of Succession and the first 100 years of the Hanoverian dynasty. Both were quickly destroyed in firework displays. The grass was kept verdant by the Tyburn River, which ran below the surface and later fed the Queen's Basin, a reservoir named in honour of Caroline, queen consort of George II. Caroline also endowed the park with a library and a new boulevard, Queen's Walk, which briefly attracted fashionable society away from St James's Park. When George III acquired Buckingham House the part of the park south of Constitution Hill was taken as the royal garden. The park was further reduced in size by the construction of three mansions on the east side of Queen's Walk. Green Park was officially opened to the public in 1826 and the (often mud-filled) reservoir was filled in. The Ranger's Lodge and Queen's Library were demolished by 1855. Twentieth-century modifications included the planting of hedgerows and some further attrition of the park's borders through road widening. Green Park station opened as Dover Street in 1906 and gained its present name in 1933. The Victoria and Jubilee lines came here in 1969 and 1979 respectively.

Claude Monet's 1871 painting of Green Park hangs in the Philadelphia Museum of Art.

> ✉ SW1
>
> 🚇 Jubilee Line; Piccadilly Line; Victoria Line (zone 1)
>
> @ www.royalparks.gov.uk

Green Street • Newham

A major shopping street and cultural centre for the community of UPTON PARK, occupying the borderland between EAST HAM and WEST HAM. Green Street House was built in the mid 16th century and later became known as Boleyn Castle. There is no evidence for the tradition that Anne Boleyn lived at the house but Richard Breame, the estate's owner and a servant of Henry VIII, may have boasted that the king courted his future bride here. Green Street House was used as a Roman Catholic school from 1869, when the owners demolished its gateway and began to develop the land facing the street. In the early 20th century the house became a maternity home and was then leased by West Ham United Football Club, which built a stadium in the grounds. Green Street House was allowed to deteriorate and was demolished in 1955. Queens market moved to its present location on Green Street in the 1960s and its traders now specialize in textiles, clothes and a range of exotic and everyday foods. The market operates on Tuesdays, Thursdays, Fridays and Saturdays. Newham council had proposed to sacrifice many of Queens market's shops in a major redevelopment scheme but to its credit it has kept all interested parties well-informed, listened to objections and revised its plans to allow all existing traders to remain. The regeneration of the market is planned for completion in 2010. The wards of Green Street East and Green Street West lie on either side of the road, north of the railway line. Slightly less than a third of the population is of Indian origin, while Pakistani, Bangladeshi, white and black minorities each account for about a sixth of the total. Islam is the principal religion. The percentage of adults in employment is relatively small, mainly because of the high numbers of students and homemakers. The average age is low and the number of people aged over 75 is almost a third of the national average.

The unsuccessful 2005 film *Green Street* starred Elijah Wood as an American who joins a 'firm' of aggressive West Ham fans known as the Green Street Elite. The film was made at the nearby THREE MILLS studios, with location shooting in the area.

> ✉ E7; E13; E6
>
> 👥 26,072 (Green Street East and Green Street West wards)
>
> @ www.newham.gov.uk/queensmarket

Green Street Green • Bromley

A former village now located at the tip of suburban London, south of ORPINGTON. The village was part of the manor of CHELSFIELD and was first recorded in the 1290s as Grenestrete. The name may carry more meaning than its simple appearance suggests: 'street' often indicated an Anglo-Saxon hamlet that stood on a former Roman road and the greenness of the street could indicate that it had fallen into disuse and become overgrown. The village green that gave Green Street its present name was not recorded until the 18th century. By this time the road had become busy again, with coaches travelling from London to the Sussex coast at Rye. In 1745 a gang of smugglers attacked customs officers on the road here. By the late 18th century the village possessed two inns: the Queen's Head and the Rose and Crown. Green Street Green was transformed after 1836, when John Fox established the Oak brewery, often called Fox's brewery. This grew into a much larger concern than the local brewhouses that characterized many other villages of the period. Houses clustered around it and a school opened in 1867. By the late 19th century Green Street Green had become a grimy industrial community, with the Fox family as its paternalistic grandees. To the shock of the villagers, the brewery ran into financial difficulties and closed in 1909, causing widespread unemployment. The village soon reinvented itself as a haven for Edwardian cyclists, with tearooms encircling the large green. Cottages with large gardens were advertised as 'suitable for fruit growing or poultry farming'. A row of shops was built in 1912, originally as the Broadway, later the High Street. After World War I both the council and commercial developers built houses and in 1938 St Mary's Church acquired a permanent building. In the mid 1940s plans were drafted for a very large 'model village' that would have swept away the old settlement and created a whole new town. Unexpectedly severe post-war economic conditions stymied this vision and instead Green Street Green spread more haphazardly towards Chelsfield, while green-belt restrictions prevented expansion to the south and west. A former coach house became the Greenwood Community Centre in 1952. The brewery site, latterly the home of a packaging company, was sold in 1992 for the creation of the Oaks estate. Although it seems an unusual name, there is another Green Street Green not far away, in the borough of Dartford, Kent.

Green Street Green was a minor hit single for the New Vaudeville Band in 1967. The band was fond of songs about places and had earlier achieved greater success with *Winchester Cathedral* and *Finchley Central*.

✉ Orpington BR6

📖 Marjorie Ford and Geoffrey Rickard, *The Story of Green Street Green*, Bromley Leisure and Community Services, 2004

Greenwich • *Greenwich*

A world heritage site located on the south shore of the Thames, opposite the ISLE OF DOGS. The name means 'green trading place or harbour' and it was first recorded in 964. It is likely that the Romans established some kind of settlement but little of the town's history is recorded until 1012, when the Danish fleet moored here and Archbishop Alphege was brutally murdered. Henry V's brother Humphrey, Duke of Gloucester, inherited land at Greenwich in 1427 and built himself a riverside house named Bella Court. After the duke's death Margaret of Anjou, wife of Henry VI, enlarged the house and renamed it Placentia, or 'pleasant place'. Henry VII made the new palace even grander and it became a favourite royal resort. Henry VIII was born here in 1491 and made further elaborate improvements to Placentia. Both his daughters, Mary I and Elizabeth I, were born at the palace and Elizabeth I spent much time there. James I presented the palace and its park to his wife, Queen Anne, who commissioned Inigo Jones to design a neighbouring house. Anne died before the Queen's House was completed and, on its eventual completion in 1635, Charles I gave it to his queen, Henrietta Maria. The Royal Hospital for Seamen was originally intended as a new palace for Charles II, to replace Placentia, which had suffered from being used as a biscuit factory and prisoner-of-war camp during the Commonwealth. However, by the time the building was nearing readiness, William and Mary were on the throne and they chose to live at HAMPTON COURT instead. The first pensioners arrived at the hospital in 1705. The hospital closed in 1869 and the Royal Naval College moved here from Portsmouth four years later. The college is now the centrepiece of the University of Greenwich. The Queen's House became the core of the National Maritime Museum in 1937. In addition to its historic public buildings, Greenwich has attractive residential parts, including MAZE HILL and the ASHBURNHAM TRIANGLE, and agreeable places to eat, drink and shop. Greenwich market, with 160 stalls, claims to be London's best source for handcrafted items but its future is uncertain. Greenwich Theatre and the Fan Museum are situated on Crooms Hill, where the poet Cecil Day-Lewis lived in the 1950s. EAST GREENWICH has an important industrial history and NORTH GREENWICH is the site of the former Millennium Dome, Britain's most visited – and vilified – paying attraction in 2000. Greenwich is the permanent resting place for the world's last tea clipper, the CUTTY SARK.

The rock band Squeeze emerged from Greenwich in the late 1970s. Of the band's many London-related songs, *King George Street* is the most local. It was released as a single in 1986.

✉ SE10

♦ 21,383 (Greenwich West and Peninsula wards)

🚆 South Eastern Trains; Docklands Light Railway, Lewisham branch (zones 2 and 3)

⛴ Greenwich pier

📖 Charles Jennings, *Greenwich*, Abacus, 2001; Clive Aslet, *The Story of Greenwich*, Harvard University Press, 2001

@ www.greenwichwhs.org.uk (Maritime Greenwich World Heritage Site)

Greenwich Millennium Village *see* MILLENNIUM VILLAGE

Greenwich Park • *Greenwich*

A royal park covering 183 undulating acres of south-east GREENWICH. Henry VI enclosed the park in 1433 and deer were introduced by Henry VIII, who was born at Greenwich. In the early 17th century James I had a wall built around the park and its gardens were laid out in the French style. Some of the trees planted at that time remain today and the formal layout remained virtually unchanged for 200 years. Flamsteed House was built in 1676 on the highest ground in the park as the home of the Royal Observatory. The observatory's greatest achievement was to devise the conventions of the prime meridian and Greenwich Mean Time. The Ranger's House, as it is now known, was built at the BLACKHEATH end of the park at the end of the 17th century and enlarged by the fourth Earl of Chesterfield, who acquired it as a retreat in 1748. The house has a gallery of Tudor portraits from the collection of the earls of Suffolk. Greenwich Park was fully opened to the public in 1830 but a biannual fair was abolished in 1857 because of rowdiness. The Royal Observatory is presently undergoing a £15 million redevelopment programme. The first phase was completed in 2006, with the opening of four new galleries devoted to timekeeping. The park will host equestrian events and the modern pentathlon during the 2012 Olympic Games.

✉ SE10

📖 Pat Pierce et al, *Greenwich Park*, Royal Parks, 1993; Angus Duncan Webster, *Greenwich Park: Its History and Associations*, Conway Maritime Press, reprinted 1971

@ www.royalparks.gov.uk/parks/greenwich_park; www.friendsofgreenwichpark.org.uk

Greenwich Peninsula • *Greenwich*

A tongue-shaped 285-acre regeneration site jutting into the Thames north-east of maritime GREENWICH. The area was formerly known as Greenwich Marshes or Bugsby's Marsh. Bugsby may have been the commander of a prison hulk that was once moored here, but it has also been suggested that the word is a corruption of 'boggarty', which meant 'haunted by sprites or spirits'. The methane gases of the marshes could have conjured up such manifestations. The stretch of the Thames between Blackwall Reach and Woolwich Reach, below Blackwall Point, is called Bugsby's Reach. Because they regularly flooded at high tide the marshes remained desolate until they were embanked and drained at the beginning of the 19th century. The newly reclaimed land was used first for grazing and then by industry, especially of the noxious kind. From the 1880s, the EAST GREENWICH gasworks filled the lion's share of the peninsula, with workers' housing and associated amenities, including the Church of St Andrew in the Marsh and the Dreadnought School. The opening of the Blackwall Tunnel in 1897 reduced the peninsula's isolation. Industry declined after World War II and a series of closures led to the demolition of almost all the houses, shops and public houses, and the church and school. Much of the peninsula lay derelict until the late 1990s, when the Millennium Dome, NORTH GREENWICH station and the MILLENNIUM VILLAGE brought a revival. The regeneration of the peninsula is planned for completion around 2015, by which time there will be more than 12,000 new homes, as well as office complexes, hotels and wide-ranging leisure facilities. Most residents of the Peninsula ward live in rented accommodation and the number of households with two or more cars is almost a third of the national average. The ethnicity of the peninsula's inhabitants is roughly in line with that of the borough as a whole, except that fewer residents are of black African origin, while the Bangladeshi community is relatively large.

✉ SE10

👤 10,155 (Peninsula ward)

Grosvenor Square • *Westminster* (pronounced gro-vnə)

One of London's grandest squares, located in north-west MAYFAIR, formerly home to the cream of English society and now better known for its American associations. In July 1725 the *Daily Journal* reported that 'Sir Richard Grosvenor ... is now building a Square called Grosvenor Square, which for its largeness and beauty will by far exceed any yet made in and about London'. Its stately terraces and then-private central garden made the development an immediate success. John Adams established the first American mission to the Court of ST JAMES here in 1765. Rebuilding in the late 18th and early 19th centuries served only to enhance the reputation of Grosvenor Square. Writing in 1935, Arthur Dasent called it the 'favoured home of the titled and untitled aristocracy of England over two centuries'. Reconstruction since that time has been less elegant but equally prestigious and has introduced hotels and offices in place of private residences. During World War II, American military officials operated from several buildings in the area, notably 20 Grosvenor Square, which is still used by the US Navy. The US Embassy filled the western side of the square in 1960 and statues of presidents F D Roosevelt and Dwight Eisenhower are among several memorials erected to honour American leaders and war heroes.

✉ W1

📖 Geoffrey Williamson, *Star-Spangled Square: The Saga of 'Little America' in London*, Geoffrey Bles, 1956

@ www.usembassy.org.uk

Grove Park • *Hounslow*

The south-western part of the CHISWICK peninsula, consisting of a popular residential zone and extensive sports grounds. The first Grove House stood here from as early as 1412. The Duke of Devonshire bought the estate in 1833 and remodelled the house. After the opening of Chiswick station in 1849 the duke began to plan a settlement at Grove Park but this was slow to get under way. Grove Park Hotel was built in 1867, followed by the first few houses and then St Paul's Church in 1872. The popularity of BEDFORD PARK prompted two attempts at building a garden suburb here; Thomas Kemp Welch advertised a development called CHISWICK PARK, and Jonathan

Carr, Bedford Park's creator, planned a new town called Burlingwick, which would have covered 330 acres and housed 40,000 people. Nothing so grand ever materialized and Grove Park continued to grow through a series of smaller projects, such as the Riverview estate of 1904. Soap-makers Dan and Charles Mason began to produce Cherry Blossom boot polish at their factory in Burlington Lane in 1906. The company acquired land on Duke's Meadows in the 1920s for a packaging plant and an employees' sports ground. The rest of the meadows were preserved by the council after schemes for a gasworks and a power station were dropped. The Kinnaird Park estate replaced Grove House following its demolition in 1928. There seems to be some truth in stories that the house's building materials were exported to the USA but they were not all reassembled in one place. In Staveley Gardens, the Chiswick Polish Co. built semi-detached houses for its workers in 1930 and maisonettes for retired employees in 1960. Cherry trees were planted to line the walks. Chiswick Quay is an estate of mid 1970s townhouses built around a marina that was once Grove House's ornamental lake and later a yacht and houseboat basin. Many of the large homes of the original Grove Park estate have been demolished and replaced by flats or smaller houses, but a few early villas survive, notably on Grove Park Road. The built-up stretch of the riverside has seen several new developments in recent years, mostly of modest proportions, including the conversion into flats of the RAF Association's former offices.

Duke's Meadows, to the south of Grove Park, is awash with sports facilities – for tennis, athletics, cricket and more – as well as with bases for rowing and sailing on the Thames. The University of Westminster's sports ground (formerly the Polytechnic stadium) has an impressive grandstand, in need of restoration at the time of writing.

Bernard Montgomery, later Field Marshal Viscount Montgomery of Alamein, lived on Bolton Road as a teenager. The actor John Thaw lived on Grove Park Road for 20 years from 1978.

✉ W4

🚃 South West Trains (Chiswick, zone 3)

Grove Park • *Lewisham*

A mixed settlement of council and private housing, separated by the railway line from the DOWNHAM estate to the south-west. This was dense woodland in the extreme south of the parish of LEE until the early 18th century. At that time, as local historian John King puts it, Grove Park 'just did not exist, in name or reality'. Thereafter, the trees were cut down and mostly used to make charcoal, hence the name of Burnt Ash Farm, which covered most of the area. A smaller farm, near present-day Somertrees Avenue, was called Grove Farm. A short-lived brickworks operated in the mid 19th century and some of its bricks were used locally to build a number of large houses. In the early 1870s a station was built and a road was constructed to provide a link to MOT-TINGHAM, and both were named Grove Park, after the farm. Throughout the rest of the century a handful of villas went up annually. In 1902, the Greenwich workhouse was built here. It served as a barracks during World War I and became a tuberculosis isolation hospital in 1926. In the same year the railway line was electrified and Lewisham council began building its 44-acre Grove Park estate. The council bought Chinbrook Meadows for use as a recreation ground. Sports grounds and private housing consumed Grove Park's remaining dairy pasture and plant nurseries in the 1930s, although a pig and poultry farm was subsequently established for wartime purposes. This survived until the construction of the Marbrook estate in the 1960s, which followed a number of smaller infill projects designed to address the post-war housing shortage. Private housebuilding has continued to the present day, including the redevelopment of the former Grove Park hospital site. More than four-fifths of the population is white, a high proportion by the borough's standards.

Edith Nesbit, author of *The Railway Children* and a founder member of the Fabian Society, lived in Grove Park from 1894 to 1899.

✉ SE12

♁ 14,010

🚆 South Eastern Trains (zone 4)

📖 John King, *Grove Park: The History of a Community*, Grove Park Community Group, 1982

Gunnersbury • Hounslow

A Tube station, park and a pair of mansions situated in the far north-western corner of CHISWICK. Gunnersbury is one of the few places in London to have been named after a woman, Gunnhildr, whose manor this was. There is no evidence for the suggestion that she was a niece of King Canute but she may have had Danish blood. Gunnersbury House was a Palladian mansion built in the mid 17th century for Sir John Maynard, the king's principal serjeant-at-law. Princess Amelia, daughter of George II, made the villa her summer residence from 1762 to 1786. The estate was sold in 1800 and the house was demolished and replaced by Gunnersbury Park and Gunnersbury House, later called the Large Mansion and the Small Mansion. In 1835 Gunnersbury Park was acquired and then enlarged by the banker Nathan Mayer Rothschild. His nephew Leopold de Rothschild bought Gunnersbury House in 1889 and put it to use as a guest house for visitors to Gunnersbury Park, who included Edward VII. After Leopold's death in 1917 the estate was split up. Part was sold for building, while the local boroughs bought the mansions and 186 acres of parkland. The Large Mansion is home to Gunnersbury Park Museum, which displays Ealing and Hounslow's local history collections. The Small Mansion is an arts centre. Gunnersbury station (originally Brentford Road) was rebuilt in 1966 with an 18-storey office block above, now occupied by the British Standards Institution. The Russian Orthodox Cathedral stands on Harvard Road, just south of the station. It was built in 1998 in the traditional 'Pskov' style, with an onion-shaped dome painted in blue with gold stars. Gunnersbury Triangle is a six-acre nature reserve on Bollo Lane, situated between railway lines. It has birch and willow woodland with an attractive pond, marsh and meadow, but not much in the way of rare species.

Gunnersbury Park hosts one of London's most popular summer festivals, the London Mela – a one-day celebration of Asian culture with attendances that approach 100,000. The comic actor Sid James lived on Gunnersbury Avenue in the 1950s. Gunnersbury is the name of one of the principal characters in Patrick Neate's 2003 novel *The London Pigeon Wars*.

✉ W3; W4

🚆 Silverlink (zone 3); District Line (zone 3)

📖 Ann Collett-White and James Collett-White, *Gunnersbury Park and the Rothschilds*, Heritage Publications and Hounslow Leisure Services, 1993

@ www.hounslow.info/gunnersburypark.htm (borough council site)

Hackbridge • *Sutton*

An area of declining industry and increasing housing, situated beside the River Wandle in north BEDDINGTON. The name was first recorded around 1235 and probably derives from the Old English words 'haca brycg', meaning 'the bridge at the hook-shaped piece of land'. As was the case along most of the Wandle, mills flourished from the Middle Ages, latterly specializing in tanning and the manufacture of parchment. The river divides at Hack Bridge and the two channels rejoin 500 yards to the north, creating an island that was used to lay out cloth for whitening in the sun. The Red Lion inn was built in 1721 and is by far the oldest surviving structure in the area. Hackbridge House was in existence by 1820, when it was the home of the Goad family, the area's leading landowners. In the mid 19th century the hamlet consisted of cottages grouped around the green, where most of the inhabitants worked for the Goads, with other homes for mill workers on Hackbridge Road. The Quaker banker and philanthropist Samuel Gurney built (or rebuilt) a house called Culvers and bred black swans on the river until his death in 1856. The crash of his bank ten years later led to the piecemeal sale of the estate, which stretched up towards BEDDINGTON CORNER. Hackbridge station opened in 1868 but failed to bring even patchy development to the area until the 1890s. Hackbridge House was sold in 1908, becoming a hotel and subsequently a base for army cadets, while an assortment of speculative builders covered much of the grounds with housing. Industry began to appear around 1910, first in the form a cardboard factory and then an engineering business that became the Hackbridge Cable Co. The Mullard radio works was established in the late 1920s. Another large house, Elmwood, was replaced by workers' homes in the early 1930s and All Saints' Church was built in response to the growth of the settlement. Hackbridge House was demolished and replaced by a housing estate in 1970. BEDZED eco-village was completed in 2001 on part of the site of Beddington sewage works. Less innovative new housing has been filling other brownfield sites in the area. Hackbridge Primary School opened in 2002 and 75 per cent of its pupils live in an area of disadvantage, determined by postcodes. A similar situation pertains at Culvers House Primary School. In the south of the locality, Wilderness Island is a 7-acre nature reserve, with a mosaic of ponds, sedge beds and damp hollows.

⊠ Wallington SM6; Carshalton SM5

🚍 Thameslink (zone 4)

Hackney • *Hackney*

Formerly 'that Arcadia beyond MOORFIELDS' and now a multicultural, multiracial, multilingual and multi-social district, situated three miles north-east of ST PAUL'S. Hackney probably takes its name from Haca, a Danish nobleman, and 'ey', an island, for the River Lea and its tributaries once dissected the area. The village had a church by 1275, when wealthy Londoners were already beginning to build country retreats here. In the 16th and 17th centuries the large, rambling houses of Hackney's aristocrats became a distinctive feature of the landscape. Samuel Pepys paid several visits to Hackney, 'which I every day grow more and more in love with'. By the 18th century Hackney's wealth, which remained remarkable, no longer derived from the presence of noblemen but from merchants, including Huguenots and Jews. Church Street (now the northern part of Mare Street) was lined with shops and houses by the 1720s, which spread outwards over the next century, while the formerly separate hamlet of Mare Street expanded to meet it. Hackney merged with its near neighbours at Homerton and Lower Clapton in the first quarter of the 19th century, when entrepreneurs began to actively exploit their leases in the area. Streets of substantial houses for the middle classes were laid out but the quality of building declined after the arrival of the railway in the 1850s, when larger old properties were demolished to make way for compact terraced housing. Private blocks of flats were built as early as the 1870s. By the end of the 19th century Hackney was looking increasingly like part of the EAST END, although only LONDON FIELDS, HOMERTON and outlying HACKNEY WICK suffered from widespread, entrenched poverty. Commerce thrived on Mare Street, where many of the shops were rebuilt on a grander scale and the Hackney Empire Music Hall opened in 1901. Soon after this, the London County Council built flats in London Fields and on Mare Street, initiating a process that would change the face of Hackney over the following decades. Industrial growth reached a new level of intensity between the wars, as did municipal building, with the borough and county councils each providing thousands of new dwellings. The flat-building programme was repeated after World War II, especially on bomb sites. Tower blocks grew higher with each passing decade until the late 1970s, while industry declined. Thereafter, different conditions prevailed and the main trends were towards refurbishment of existing properties, the rebuilding of large estates on a less impersonal scale and a growing role for housing associations. More recently, private building has increased and pockets of Hackney have become gentrified where Victorian streets have survived. Afro-Caribbeans began to replace Jews as the predominant minority from the 1960s and were later joined by immigrants from Africa, south Asia and the eastern Mediterranean.

In London's longest armed siege of modern times, gunman Eli Hall held out for 20 days in his bedsit on the corner of Marvin Street and Graham Road. Hall shot himself after being wounded in an exchange of fire with police in January 2003.

✉ E8; E9

� 64,589 (Chatham, Hackney Central, Hackney Downs, Queensbridge, Victoria and Wick wards)

🚉 Silverlink Metro (Hackney Central, zone 2)

📖 Alan Wilson, *Hackney Memories*, Sutton, 2004

@ www.hackneysociety.org; brickfields.org.uk (excellent local history site)

Hackney Downs • *Hackney*
Formerly common land, now a park and playing fields with neighbouring social housing in north HACKNEY, bordering SHACKLEWELL and

LOWER CLAPTON. The Great Eastern Railway Co. gained permission to build a branch line on the west side of the downs in 1867 and put up 150 houses for its construction workers on the site of a brickfield. Originally nicknamed 'navvies' island', this later became simply 'the island' and was described by the social reformer and statistician Charles Booth as a 'curious patch' of poverty. Hackney Downs station opened in 1872 and the vicinity immediately experienced a boom in building activity as established villas with large grounds were sold for the erection of rows of middle-class homes. Fearing that the common itself would soon succumb, the Commons Preservation Society took advantage of a new law to preserve it as a public open space. Downs Road and Downs Park Road were laid out along the common's northern and southern borders. The Grocers' Company founded Hackney Downs School in 1876. The school was taken over by London County Council in 1907. From the 1930s, municipal and philanthropic schemes erased many of the early streets. Local landowner Lord Amhurst wanted to upgrade the cottages of 'navvies' island' in the late 1950s but the council demurred, preferring to knock them down and build the Landfield estate. The largest project was the Greater London Council's Nightingale estate, completed in 1972, with tower blocks of up to 21 storeys. Most of that estate has been rebuilt on a more human scale since the late 1990s. Like many poorer parts of inner London, the ward of Hackney Downs has a growing number of young graduates, so the proportions of single people and one-person households are relatively high. Slightly more than half the residents are white and nearly 30 per cent are black or black British.

The playwrights Harold Pinter and Stephen Berkoff both went to Hackney Downs School, though neither of them much enjoyed the experience. Rebuilt as a comprehensive in 1968, the school subsequently became a symbol of the battle between the left and right wing in British education politics. Denounced by the government, its education association and the tabloid press as the worst school in Britain, Hackney Downs School closed at the end of 1995. Its supporters claimed that the school suffered from a difficult intake and neglected buildings.

✉ E5; E8

♦ 10,276

🚉 'one' Railway (zone 2)

📖 M O'Connor, E Hales, J Davies, S Tomlinson, *Hackney Downs: The School That Dared to Fight*, Cassell, 1999

Hackney Marsh • *Hackney*

The largest recreation ground in London and the second largest common after HAMPSTEAD HEATH, situated on the banks of the River Lea, east of CLAPTON. Hackney Marsh (frequently called Hackney Marshes) covers 336 fairly featureless acres. In 1185 the area was recognized as having two parts: the humbra or marshy meadow, and the quabba or bog. Hackney Marsh was also known as Hackney Mead in the 16th century, when it had a reputation as a haunt of highwaymen and robbers. From the Middle Ages this was Lammas land, where commoners had grazing rights after 1 August each year, by which time the hay crop should have been gathered in. In the 1880s suspicions arose that the landowners might try to build on the marsh and tensions were exacerbated when boys from the Eton Mission at HACKNEY WICK were banned from playing football here. The London County Council stepped in and acquired the land for £75,000, opening it to the public in 1893. The LCC carried out flood prevention works and later used building rubble to raise the level of the terrain. The National Projectile factory was built on part of the marsh in 1915 and its former site is now Mabley Green recreation ground in east Homerton. Thirty-seven acres were taken to build CLAPTON PARK'S Kingsmead estate in 1937. Hackney council is now responsible for the marsh, which has cricket, hockey and rugby pitches and a wildlife and conservation area. Kite-flying is popular but the marsh is best known for its football pitches, and especially for the scores of Sunday league games played here. Dubbed 'the spiritual home of parks football', Hackney Marsh is said to have the largest concentration of football pitches in Europe, although their number has been reduced in recent years. Mabley Green and parts of the marsh may be used as a car park for the duration of the 2012 Olympic games.

In a 1997 television commercial for Nike, since voted one of the 20 best-ever adverts by viewers, Sunday league footballers on Hackney Marsh were joined by Eric Cantona, Ian Wright, Robbie Fowler and David Seaman.

✉ E5, E9; E10

Hackney Wick • *Hackney/Tower Hamlets*

A run-down Leaside industrial area, now divided from the rest of HACKNEY by the East Cross Route (A12). A 'wick' usually signified an outlying dairy farm and the 'ferm of Wyk' was recorded in the 13th century. By the late 18th century the small hamlet had gained a silk factory and the Wick went on to play a distinguished role in east London's industrial history. Remarkably, the use of the word 'petrol' was pioneered in Hackney Wick, by Carless, Capel and Leonard, who carried on their oil wholesaling business here for over 100 years from 1860. Matchbox toys were later made at Lesney's factories. However, the growth of industry contributed to social decline in Hackney Wick, which was described in 1879 as a district of 6,000 people who had sunk to the lowest depths, and it became notorious for its jerry-built housing. The parish church of St Mary of Eton with St Augustine was founded in 1880 by Eton College, which wanted to perform charitable work in a poor part of London. From the 1930s the municipal authorities set about improving conditions in Hackney Wick, opening public baths and a library and clearing slums to put up blocks of flats, notably in the 1960s. Hackney Wick did not gain its station (originally intended to be called Wallis Road) until 1980, when the North London line was reopened to passenger services, although it had earlier been served by a station at VICTORIA PARK. After a period of dereliction, some disused industrial sites are now undergoing regeneration and a tentative gentrification has begun recently with artists buying long leases on old warehouses. Completed in 2003, ST MARY'S VILLAGE has replaced the tower blocks of the Trowbridge estate with a mixed tenure development of houses and flats. A third of homes in Hackney Wick are rented from a social landlord and another quarter from the council. Five per cent of households have neither central heating nor sole use of a bath or toilet, the highest proportion in London.

As plans stand at the time of writing, indoor sports facilities will be constructed at Hackney Wick for the 2012 Olympic Games, on the site of the Arena Field recreation ground and the former Hackney greyhound stadium. Tennis courts will replace Bow industrial park, south of the railway line. Kingsway International Christian Centre on Waterden Road, which is said to be the largest house of worship in Britain, with a capacity of 4,000, will have to move as a result of the Olympic redevelopment.

✉ E9; E15

> **♦** 11,049 (Hackney's Wick ward)

> **🚆** Silverlink Metro (zone 2)

> **📖** Vicki Cattell and Mel Evans, *Neighbourhood Images in East London: Social Capital and Social Networks on Two East London Estates*, York Publishing Services–Joseph Rowntree Foundation, 1999

Hacton • *Havering*

An unprepossessing hamlet situated between HORNCHURCH and CORBETS TEY. In *Place Names of Greater London*, John Field suggests that the name means 'farm on a hook-shaped piece of land', pointing out that Hacton is 'on the tongue of land formed by the junction of the Ingrebourne and a tributary'. The immediate surroundings are flat farmland, but the chimneys and pylons of industrial east London loom on the horizon. Nineteenth-century rural depopulation led to the loss of the cottages that once lined Hacton Lane. The recently extended White Hart was converted from two labourers' cottages around 1855. To the north, Hacton House has fallen within the encroachment of UPMINSTER. Built around 1770 by a London merchant, the house has been converted into flats. The Hacton Farm estate has 548 homes built by Hornchurch council before its absorption within Havering. The neighbourhood has an overwhelmingly white population, although a handful of residents speak Cantonese or Urdu.

Hacton Parkway is a part of the Green Chain walk beside the River Ingrebourne.

> **✉** Upminster RM14

> **♦** 12,494 (the ward includes the south-eastern part of Hornchurch)

Hadley • *Barnet*

A loosely scattered picturesque village also known as MONKEN HADLEY, situated to the north-east of CHIPPING BARNET. The name was first recorded as Hadlegh in 1248 and was formerly thought to mean 'a high place' but is probably derived from the Old English forms of 'heath' and 'lea'. A 24-acre common called Hadley Green lay on the edge of ENFIELD CHASE and the first residents were recorded here in the 14th century. St Mary's Church was built in 1494, according to the date inscribed on its west tower. A sizeable village grew up around the church and spread in every direction except onto the royal preserve of Enfield Chase. By the mid 17th century, houses ran in an unbroken line down to the High Street at Chipping Barnet. In 1741, Sir Jeremy Sambrook erected an obelisk to the north of the green, supposedly at the site where the Earl of Warwick had fallen in the Battle of BARNET, and cottages and inns formed a group here that became known as Hadley Highstone. The monument was relocated a century later, but there is no evidence of the authenticity of either its original or present position. In 1799, land to the east of the church was granted as compensation to parishioners for the loss of their rights on Enfield Chase after its enclosure. The 190 acres were sometimes called Hadley Wood but usually Hadley Common. Nineteenth-century additions to the housing stock around the green were generally of a high standard and a wide swathe is now a conservation area. To the south-east of the green, the British Land Co. bought Woodcock Farm in 1868 and laid out an estate as an extension of NEW BARNET. Some older houses were demolished in the early 20th century but Hadley's declining population rose again when new streets were laid out north-east of Chipping Barnet High Street. More suburban houses were built near COCKFOSTERS after its station opened in 1933. Hadley had a brewery for two centuries until 1938 and the site continued to function as a distribution centre until 1969. This was replaced by three luxury detached houses in 1996.

The missionary and African explorer Dr David Livingstone stayed at what is now Livingstone Cottage in 1857–8. Comedian Spike Milligan lived for many years at Monkenhurst, which was built in 1881 on The Crescent and which he saved from demolition. Father and son authors Kingsley and Martin Amis lived at Lemmons, formerly Gladsmuir House, and poet laureate Cecil Day Lewis died there during a visit in 1972.

> **✉** Barnet EN5

Hadley Wood • *Enfield*

The houses that Jack built, separated by MONKEN HADLEY Common from Hadley itself, which lies to the south-west. When ENFIELD CHASE was enclosed in 1777, surveyor Francis Russell built himself a mansion at Beech Hill Park, where he lived until his death in 1795. Shortly after Russell's death, Archibald Paris acquired the mansion, along with neighbouring farms totalling over 1,500 acres. Paris farmed the land until his retirement in 1850, when the estate was broken up for sale. Most of it was bought by Charles Jack, who kept the farm going for another two decades before declining grain prices prompted him to consider an alternative source of income. In 1885 Jack subsidized the construction of a station on the Great Northern Railway and began to build substantial houses around it, although only a few had been completed by the time of his death eleven years later. The new estate was to have been called Beech Hill Park, but when the station was opened as Hadley Wood the shorter name stuck. Jack's heirs and executors had planned to sell the whole of Beech Hill Park for building but were unable to get the price they wanted. A group of entrepreneurs bought the park after World War I and opened Hadley Wood Golf Club, with the mansion as its clubhouse. By this time Hadley Wood had around a hundred houses, a figure that was to treble by the outbreak of the World War II. Green-belt restrictions subsequently prevented unbridled expansion, but some new building was permitted, notably some American-style luxury properties on Camlet Way and smaller houses northwards to Wagon Road, while several of the earliest and largest villas were demolished and replaced by closes of smaller houses. Hadley Wood Primary School opened on Courtleigh Avenue in 1965. Hadley Wood now has nearly a thousand homes, many of which are highly valued, especially the grander properties on the south side, which are popular with minor celebrities and footballers.

Marguerite Radclyffe-Hall, author of the taboo-breaking lesbian novel *The Well of Loneliness*, moved to 67 Camlet Way in 1918 with her lover Una, Lady Trowbridge. The couple quit the 'modern, pretentious and very ugly house' after two years, tired of the suburban monotony and the distance from London.

✉ Barnet EN4

🚉 WAGN Railway (zone 6)

📖 Nancy Clark, *Hadley Wood: Its Background and Development*, Ward Lock, 1968 (difficult-to-find limited edition, but highly recommended)

Haggerston • *Hackney*

A poor but partially gentrifying locality situated between DALSTON and SHOREDITCH, to the east of Kingsland Road (A10). Haggerston was first recorded in Domesday Book as Hergotestane; the name probably derives from a Saxon farmer called Hærgod, who either had a 'ton' (farmstead) here or a stone that marked the boundary of his land. In 1685 Sir Robert Geffrye, a former Lord Mayor of London, left land on Kingsland Road for pensioners' almshouses and these were built in 1715. Haggerston was densely built up during the 19th century and became increasingly overcrowded, especially after the opening of its station on the East London Railway in 1869. In an attempt to improve public health, Haggerston baths were built on Whiston Road in 1904. The baths presently lie disused, but are Grade II-listed so emergency work has been undertaken to arrest their decay. In 1914, Sir Robert Geffrye's almshouses became a museum, which now has collections of furniture, textiles, paintings and decorative arts, displayed in a series of period rooms. A slum clearance programme led to the two-stage construction of 447 homes on the Haggerston estate. Haggerston West was built in the 1930s but Haggerston East had to be postponed until after World War II. Haggerston station closed in 1940 but is planned to be reopened in 2010 as part of the northern extension of the East London Line. The station may help to revive awareness of Haggerston's name, which has dropped out of common usage, possibly because of its ugly sound. The new Bridge Academy, for example, simply describes itself as being in 'south HACKNEY'. The academy has been built on the site of the former Laburnum Primary School and is due to reach capacity in 2013. Calculations by the Low Pay Unit have shown a high level of deprivation in Haggerston, although this is changing as more young graduates move in and private apartments are built. Forty-one per cent of residents are white British and the largest ethnic minorities are of black African, black Caribbean and Turkish origin. Haggerston has very few old people, especially aged over 75.

Haggerston was the birthplace in 1656 of Edmond Halley, the son of a wealthy soap boiler. Halley became the second Astronomer Royal and accurately predicted the return of the comet that now bears his name.

✉ E2; E8

👥 10,366

@ www.geffrye-museum.org.uk; www.bridgeacademyhackney.org

Hainault • *Redbridge*

A 20th-century urban creation situated in the north-east corner of the borough, three miles east of WOODFORD. The name comes from the Old English 'higne holt', meaning a wood belonging to a monastic community, in this case the Abbey of Barking. Hainault Forest once covered a swathe of the countryside hereabouts but was savagely cleared in 1851, with 2,000 acres of oaks felled in six weeks. In anticipation of housing development a station opened in 1903, only to be closed five years later as it was being used by fewer than 20 passengers a day. Hainault served as an airfield during World War I but reverted to farmland thereafter. In the 1930s the London County Council laid out extensive municipal housing to the north of the existing settlement, ensuring the success of the reopened station, which came within the London Underground system in 1948. This estate was part of Chigwell until local government reorganization in 1965 brought it within Redbridge. Hainault residents tend to be white and relatively old, with low levels of educational attainment. Twothirds of homes are now owner-occupied, with most of the rest rented from the council.

To the east are Hainault industrial estate and what remains of Hainault Forest. The latter is a country park with woodland, meadows, plains and a public golf course. It is designated a site of special scientific interest.

> ✉ Ilford IG6; Chigwell IG7

> ♦ 11,367

> 🚌 Central Line (zone 5)

> 📖 Georgina Green, *The Story of Hainault Forest*, Redbridge Libraries, 2002

The Hale • *Barnet*

A well-built interwar suburb situated on the border of EDGWARE and MILL HILL. The settlement lay in the north-west corner (halh; Old English 'corner, angle') of HENDON parish and was first mentioned in 1294. Twin hamlets had evolved by the mid 18th century: Upper Hale, focused around the junction of Deans Lane, Hale Lane, and Selvage Lane, and the smaller Lower Hale, centred on a village green that lay a short distance to the north-west. The Green Man inn stood at Upper Hale by 1751 and later became a meeting place for boxers and other sportsmen. Construction of the convent of St Mary at the Cross began in 1874 near Lower Hale and was completed in 1893, when a few villas were appearing along Hale Lane. From 1906 the Hale had a railway station, on an extension of the line that now terminates at MILL HILL EAST and very close to the present MILL HILL BROADWAY station, but this did not survive beyond the outbreak of World War II. The Hale remained a separate farming village until the mid 1920s, when the 110-acre Stoneyfields estate and Upper and Lower Hale farms

were all sold for building. Progress was not as rapid as the developers had hoped but the schemes were successful enough to attract other investors. The first shops were planned later in the decade, as was the Elmgate Gardens estate. Between Stoneyfields Lane and Edgware Way John Groom's Crippleage (later disabled persons' home) provided accommodation for 120 disabled women from 1932. The strikingly angular John Keble Church was built on Deans Lane in 1937, while hospital buildings were added at the convent. In the early 1990s private houses and a home for the elderly were built in the convent's grounds. John Groom's Home was replaced by housing later in the decade. The Hale's ward boundaries have been drawn for the convenience of bureaucrats rather than the community, so little can be gleaned from demographic data. Like much of the wider area, the Hale has a large Jewish minority.

> ✉ NW7; Edgware HA8

> ♦ 15,663

Hale End • *Waltham Forest*

A socially diverse locality situated south of HIGHAMS PARK, with which it shares a station. It is separated from WOODFORD by a thin stretch of Epping Forest. There was a Walter de la Hale living here in 1285 and a Thomas Hale in 1634. However, either could have taken their name from the place, since a 'hale' meant a nook. An 'end' was an outlying place, and this was one of several in WALTHAMSTOW. There had been a clearing in the forest here since Domesday Book and it was known as North End or Wood End until the present name established itself in the second half of the 17th century. Hale End was built up after the opening in 1873 of the railway station, which was originally called Hale End. Tottenham and Forest Gate Railway trains also began to serve the station in 1894, when it was renamed Highams Park to publicize developments in the grounds of Highams, and this has resulted in a blurring of the identities of the two places. With its improved communications, Hale End gained an industrial base, with an emphasis on what were then 'hightech' products. British Xylonite bought the 50-acre Jack's Farm in 1897 and began to make plastics here, later pioneering the manufacture of celluloid in this country. The company's Halex-branded goods came to dominate markets as diverse as toothbrushes and table tennis balls. Other firms specialized in electronic and scientific products. After

World War I, Walthamstow council built the Hale estate, while industry was boosted by the arrival of the North Circular Road (A406) in the late 1920s and continued to flourish into the early 1960s. The area has a mainly white population, with relatively few young adults. A new Hale End station has been proposed for a site between Wood Street and Highams Park stations but is unlikely to be built.

In 1909 two Latvian anarchists who had stolen wages from a factory in TOTTENHAM were cornered in Hale End after a chase involving murders and tram and van hijackings. Both men shot themselves rather than surrender, one by the railway embankment beside Winchester Road and the other in a cottage on Oak Hill.

✉ E4; Woodford Green IG8

👤 10,075 (Hale End and Highams Park ward)

🚃 'one' Railway (Highams Park, zone 4)

Ham · *Richmond*

An extended village situated to the west of RICHMOND PARK, across the Thames from TWICKENHAM. The name was first recorded around 1150 and derives from the Old English 'hamm', which here meant 'land in a river bend'. Henry V acquired the manor of Hamme Upkyngeston in 1415, bringing the village into a closer relationship with the royal estate at RICHMOND UPON THAMES. Ham House was built in 1610 for Sir Thomas Vavasour, knight marshal to James VI and I. Said to present more aspects of 17th-century life than any other house in the country, it was the meeting place of the original 'Cabal', Charles II's leading advisers between 1667 and 1673. Sports grounds and playing fields now surround the house, which belongs to the National Trust. Other large houses appeared in the 18th century, and many of these survive today, but in 1800 Ham was still primarily rural and most of the villagers were employed in agriculture. All of Ham's three large farms were owned by Lord Dysart of Ham House. Cottages spread along Ham Street and by 1851 the village had 236 dwellings. From the 1870s the farms began to convert to market gardening, cultivating fruit, beans and cabbages. Nearer the end of the 19th century, the Dysarts began to sell their land for development and villas were built for the upper middle classes. The council built some 'homes for heroes' after World War I, and gravel extraction created large pits that have since been filled and covered with houses. The character of the village changed radically from the late 1950s as a result of both municipal and private projects. Some of the smaller schemes were imaginative, especially those designed by Eric Lyons. The large Wates estate east of Riverside Drive included the Water Gipsies public house, the star-shaped St Richard's Church and a neighbouring primary school. There has been no further development of the water meadows known as Ham Riverside Lands since the Locksmeade estate was controversially approved in 1979. Elsewhere, infilling and redevelopment continue to be closely monitored by the local amenities group and residents' association. Some of Ham's public housing has significant levels of deprivation and a high number of single-parent families. Large parts of the riverbank became overgrown with scrub willow, horse chestnut and sycamore, which obscured the vistas created for the pleasure of the nobility, but recent work has helped restore the sight-lines.

The landscape painter John Constable stayed at Ham House as a guest of the Dysarts.

✉ Richmond TW10

👤 9,678 (Ham, Petersham and Richmond Riverside ward)

📖 Leonard Chave (ed.), *Ham and Petersham at 2000*, Ham Amenities Group, 2000

@ www.nationaltrust.org.uk (for Ham House)

Hammersmith · *Hammersmith & Fulham*

A strategically significant commercial and cultural centre located on the north bank of the Thames one-and-a-half miles west of KENSINGTON. Prehistoric pottery, flints and a leaf-shaped arrowhead have been found on the riverbank and there is also evidence of Roman habitation. Hammersmith developed as a Saxon fishing village and its name (which probably refers to the presence of a hammer smithy or forge) was first recorded in 1294. A foreshore of gravel, rather than the more common marsh, made Hammersmith a healthy retreat for jaded Londoners from the Middle Ages onwards and a chapel of ease, later St Paul's Church, was built in 1631. Further west, boat builders, lead mills and malthouses clustered around the outlet of Stamford Creek into the Thames. Catherine of Braganza, queen consort of Charles II, came to live on Upper Mall in 1687 after she was widowed, and several fine villas were later built by the river here. A ribbon of houses flanked the road to London by the early 19th century and

Hammersmith Bridge opened in 1827, stimulating development on both sides of the river. Hammersmith gained parochial independence from FULHAM in 1834. Away from the riverside, an attractive settlement evolved at BROOK GREEN. The Hammersmith and City Railway arrived in 1864. In the late 19th century KING STREET became the district's main shopping centre and the Metropolitan Board of Works opened RAVENSCOURT PARK to the public. Much of Hammersmith's architectural heritage was lost in the middle decades of the 20th century as the district became increasingly urbanized, but some important examples have survived. Subsequent gentrification has rehabilitated Victorian streets such as those in BRACKENBURY VILLAGE. Hammersmith flyover – dubbed 'the gateway to west London' – was built in 1961 and is now overlooked by the Ark, a love-it-or-hate-it copper-and-glass concoction that is one of several office blocks in the vicinity of Hammersmith Broadway. This is one of London's busiest traffic junctions, with a bus and Tube interchange and a shopping mall at its centre. Hammersmith has four noteworthy entertainment venues: the Apollo, a former cinema that now hosts major rock gigs; the Palais, a historic dance hall; the Riverside Studios, which comprises studio theatres, a cinema and an art gallery; and the Lyric, a 19th-century auditorium and a studio theatre encased in concrete. A pub crawl along the riverbank west of Hammersmith Bridge is a rewarding experience, both aesthetically and alcoholically. The Rutland and Blue Anchor pubs are on Lower Mall, which Pevsner calls 'Hammersmith's best street'. The Dove, on Upper Mall, is reputed to have Britain's smallest bar, with less than 33 square feet of floor space.

James Thomson wrote the words to *Rule Britannia* in an upstairs room at The Dove. The artist J M W Turner lived on Upper Mall from 1808 to 1814. On the same street, Francis Ronalds invented the electric telegraph in 1816, in the garden of a house in which designer-craftsman William Morris lived from the age of 45 until his death in 1896. Morris called the house Kelmscott after his Oxfordshire home and gave the same name to a publishing firm that he founded. Gustav Holst conducted the Hammersmith socialist choir at Kelmscott and composed an orchestral prelude and scherzo entitled *Hammersmith*. To have 'gone to Hammersmith' was 19th-century boxing slang for being soundly beaten.

✉ W6

   11,560 (Hammersmith Broadway ward)

   District Line; Hammersmith & City Line terminus; Piccadilly Line (zone 2)

   Jane Kimber and Francis Serjeant, *The Changing Face of Hammersmith and Fulham*, Breedon, 2002; Philip Whitting (ed.), *A History of Hammersmith*, Fulham and Hammersmith Historical Society, 1965

@   www.myhammersmith.co.uk (commercial local information site); www.lyric.co.uk; www.riversidestudios.co.uk

Hampstead • *Camden*

A stratospherically expensive hillside and heathside settlement, situated three miles due north of Paddington. The name 'Hemstede' was first recorded in 959 and simply means 'homestead'. The letter 'p' did not intrude until the mid 13th century. Hampstead manor house stood on what is now FROGNAL Lane. Hampstead began to develop as a fashionable spa in the 1790s, drawing both visitors and wealthy residents to the south-west edge of HAMPSTEAD HEATH. Fenton House, on Windmill Hill, is the oldest surviving example of a merchant's house from this period and is now the property of the National Trust. The much-extended Burgh House on New End Square now serves as an arts venue and local history museum. The spa became a place of debauchery, lewdness and drunken revelry and was closed. The same thing happened again when an attempt was made to revive it. However, these events did not prevent Hampstead's rapid growth 'from a little country village to a city', as Daniel Defoe put it in 1724. The poet John Keats lodged in the eastern half of what is now the Keats House Museum in 1818–19 and wrote *Ode to a Nightingale* under the plum tree in its garden. Stuccoed cottages and terraced houses spread down the hill towards London in the early 19th century but a vigorous conservation campaign restricted development on the heath, which attracted crowds from all over London as transport links improved. From the 1860s Hampstead underwent its most rapid phase of growth as luxurious detached houses were built on newly created streets. The *Hampstead and Highgate Express* was founded at this time and is probably London's most vigorous local newspaper, universally known as the '*Ham & High*'. Hampstead Drill Hall and Assembly Rooms opened in the late 1880s, later becoming a theatre and then the Everyman cinema. The underground station opened in 1907 but residents' protectionism thwarted another proposed station at NORTH END. The same vigilant attitude prevented significant disturbance to the built environment for most of the 20th century. In the middle decades of the century Hampstead became known for its free-thinking elite but with house prices now *starting* at £1 million, corporate executives have almost entirely supplanted liberal intellectuals. The shops and amenities of Heath Street and its neighbours reflect the community's wealth, with classy cafés and boutiques predominating. Locals waged a 12-year campaign against the opening of a McDonald's before losing the battle in 1991. Census statistics for Hampstead Town bear out its reputation; almost two-thirds of 16- to 74-year-olds are educated to degree level or higher and only 7 per cent have no qualifications. A quarter of Hampstead's adults are atheists.

The Admiral's House on Admirals Walk is said to have inspired the abode in *Mary Poppins* and was the home of George Gilbert Scott, architect of St Pancras station. Tate Britain gallery has Constable's painting of the house and Camden council has a collection of 19th-century memorabilia that belonged to Elizabeth Sharpe, who lived there from 1865 to 1905. The novelist John Galsworthy lived next door.

> ✉ NW3 (nicknamed 'NW twee')
>
> 👤 10,617 (Hampstead Town ward)
>
> 🚇 Northern Line (zones 2 and 3)
>
> 📖 Ian Norrie, *Hampstead: London Hill Town*, Wildwood House, 1981
>
> @ www.hamhigh.co.uk (*Ham & High* site); www.myhampstead.co.uk (commercial local information site)

Hampstead Garden Suburb • *Barnet*

The most architecturally successful of London's planned suburbs, situated to the northwest of HAMPSTEAD HEATH. Dame Henrietta Barnett, who lived at Hampstead's NORTH END, had witnessed the effect of the arrival of the railway in other parts of London and did not like the result – monotonous streets of middle-class housing laid out with little attempt to preserve any of the existing landscape, produce distinctive individual designs or provide homes for a variety of social classes, as a pre-existing village might have done. A handful of pioneering settlements had shown that things could be done better, like Rowntree's village for its workers at New Earswick

near York and London's co-operatively created BEDFORD PARK, although each of these was socially uniform in its own way. Faced with the impending arrival of the underground railway at GOLDERS GREEN, Dame Henrietta set up the Hampstead Garden Suburb Trust in 1906 and with the support of her influential contacts and the London County Council acquired the freehold on 243 acres of Eton College's land at Wylde's Farm. Parliament passed a special act to waive HENDON'S building regulations so that some of the roads might be quaintly narrow and houses of varying heights could sometimes be grouped together without the need for party walls to project above the roofline. The suburb was planned and built in several phases, beginning with an 'artisans' quarter' extending to the east side of the Finchley Road at TEMPLE FORTUNE. A central square was laid out at the suburb's highest point, with churches and communal buildings. More popular attractions like a pub or cinema or even shops were not permitted – and are still not – which has impaired the square's potential to act as a community hub. Nearer the extension to Hampstead Heath (which Dame Henrietta had earlier successfully campaigned to create) grander houses were built to help generate revenue for the whole scheme. The trust acquired additional parcels of land before World War I and these were mostly developed after the war by co-partners, who built commercially but had to follow strict guidelines. Raymond Unwin became the suburb's principal architect after the dismissal of the Italianate-inclined Edwin Lutyens, but many other practices played a part and all worked to the same harmonious ends. A vernacular Arts and Crafts style permeated the earlier phases, giving way to neo-Georgian when profit became the primary motivation. Hampstead Garden Suburb was intended as a utopian haven for Londoners of all classes but the typical resident is now likely to be white, married, middle-aged and university educated. The Henrietta Barnett School is rated one of the top ten state schools in the country.

The artist William Ratcliffe, a fringe member of the Camden Town Group, lived here and his painting of the suburb hangs at Tate Britain gallery. The actress Elizabeth Taylor grew up at 8 Wildwood Road.

> ✉ NW11; N2
>
> 👤 14,727 (Garden Suburb ward)
>
> 📖 Mervyn Miller and A Stuart Gray, *Hampstead*

Garden Suburb, Phillimore, 1992; Kathleen M Slack, *Henrietta's Dream: A Chronicle of the Hampstead Garden Suburb*, Hampstead Garden Suburb Trust, 1997

@ www.hgs.org.uk

Hampstead Heath • *Camden/Barnet*

North London's finest open space, situated on high ground north-east of the settlement of HAMPSTEAD. It was first recorded as 'a certain heath' in 1312 and as Hampstead Heath in 1543. The moorland landscape and varied habitat of the heath were created by a sandy ridge overlying a belt of clay, which formed springs and consequent muddy hollows, especially where sand and gravel had been extracted. A policy of 'judicious neglect' of most of these diggings has helped create the picturesque terrain of the modern era. From the 18th century the heath became a popular place for Londoners to take a walk in the fresh country air. Constable painted here in the 1810s. Later in the 19th century the railway brought day-trippers and revellers by the thousands – sometimes tens of thousands on bank holidays. The core of the heath was common land of the manor of Hampstead, on which lord of the manor Sir Thomas Maryon Wilson tried to build from the 1830s despite every kind of legal attempt being made to prevent him. When he started to build the first house near Whitestone Pond, members of the public tore down the walls as soon as the bricks had been laid. After Sir Thomas's death his more reasonable brother agreed to sell the heath's 200 acres to the Metropolitan Board of Works for £45,000. By an Act of 1871 the heath was preserved forever and sand and gravel extraction was prohibited. Subsequent additions of farmland and parkland have quadrupled the heath's size, with part of the grounds of KENWOOD forming the most recent extension in the 1920s. Hampstead Heath's larger ponds were originally created as reservoirs, although the water was never of very good quality and was primarily used for industrial purposes. Following the abolition of the Greater London Council, the Corporation of London became the custodian of Hampstead Heath in 1989. It has since committed itself to a broad strategy of minimum change following consultation that showed most users wanted it to stay just as it was. The main cause of friction has been the corporation's desire to charge bathers for their use of Highgate Ponds. Usage of the heath is estimated at around five million visits a year.

The heath's joys as a place of perambulation for the working classes were captured in Albert Chevalier's music hall song ''Appy 'Ampstead' in the 1890s. Hampstead Heath is cockney rhyming slang for 'teeth'; a Hampstead Heath sailor was a landlubber.

✉ NW3; N6; NW11

🚇 Silverlink Metro (zone 3)

📖 David McDowall, *Hampstead Heath: The Walker's Guide*, self-published, 1998; Alan Farmer, *Hampstead Heath*, Historical Publications, 1984

Hampton • *Richmond*

A settlement by a bend in the river (which is what its name means) in the south-west corner of the borough. The name is used both for the Thames-side locality west of BUSHY PARK and for the entire district that extends from MARLING PARK and NURSERYLANDS in the west to HAMPTON WICK, three miles to their east. The early village, surrounded by arable land, would have been centred on Thames Street and Church Street and the southern end of the High Street. There are records of a church on Thames Street, on the present site of St Mary the Virgin, in 1342. By 1500 the population of Hampton and Hampton Wick was over 300, a figure that had doubled by 1600 and doubled again by 1700. By 1840 there were five horse-drawn buses a day to London. The 1852 Metropolitan Water Act prohibited the London water companies from taking water from below the tidal reach of the river and the consequent building of a waterworks here was to change Hampton radically. Pumping stations, reservoirs, filter beds and associated buildings were constructed along the river, altering the appearance of the area and employing a large number of people in addition to the labour needed to build the works. Hampton station opened in 1864 and this stretch of the river, and its islands, became popular for houseboats, regattas and picnicking. The area around the station was mostly developed in the 25 years after 1880; the River Hill Estate (between Plevna Road and Belgrade Road) was laid out in 1878; and the area around Carlisle Park started to be developed, slowly, from 1897. In the same year Ashley Road was built after new buildings for the station were constructed on the north side of line. The levels of Garrick's Ait and PLATT'S EYOT were raised by the depositing on them of soil excavated during the construction of further filter beds in the last years of the 19th century. An open-air pool opened on the High Street in 1922 but closed in 1981 when it was no longer considered financially viable by the council. Local enthusiasts managed to keep it from being dismantled and it reopened in 1985 as a heated swimming pool, run as a not-for-profit venture and open all year round. The pump houses of the riverside waterworks are no longer in use but are listed buildings. Some of the filter beds are no longer needed but the land has a green-belt designation, which Thames Water wants to have lifted so that it can develop the area; so far, the company has been unsuccessful.

In 1754 the actor David Garrick came to Hampton House, now Garrick Villa, and built a 'temple' in the part of the garden separated from the house by the road and nearer the Thames.

> ✉ Hampton TW12

> � 18,506 (Hampton and Hampton North wards)

> 🚆 South West Trains (zone 6)

> 📖 John Sheaf and Ken Howe, *Hampton and Teddington Past*, Historical Publications, 1995

> @ www.hampton-online.co.uk (community site)

Hampton Court • *Richmond*

A royal palace, park and gardens, set in a loop of the Thames, south of BUSHY PARK and TEDDINGTON. By 1066 HAMPTON manor existed as an important agricultural estate with royal connections. The Knights Hospitallers acquired it in 1236 and in 1338 the manor buildings consisted of a chamber block, hall, garden and church. It was leased to Sir Giles Daubeney in 1494. He built a kitchen next to the hall, which survives as the Great Kitchen, and a courtyard and gatehouse. Cardinal Wolsey took the lease from 1514 and extended the existing buildings with a second courtyard of lodgings, Base Court and the Great Gatehouse. He also added a gallery for viewing the garden, constructed a grand chapel and introduced lavish suites for the king and queen. Henry VIII regularly used Hampton Court and by 1528 had made it his own. He extended the kitchens; built the Houses of Offices (the bakehouse and stores) and council chamber; rebuilt the chapel and great hall; constructed a system to bring drinking water from COOMBE Hill in Kingston; and improved sanitation. The Great House of Easement, a lavatory block, could seat 28. Henry built new apartments for himself (Bayne Tower) and his queen, and provided for his entertainment with bowling alleys, tennis courts, a hunting park and gardens. During the reign of James I, Hampton Court was the setting for a religious conference which led to the decision to publish the authorized version of the Bible commonly known as the 'King James' Bible. The buildings changed little until the reign of William III and Mary II (from 1689), who commissioned Sir Christopher Wren to remodel the palace. New apartments were built, overlooking a new privy garden, and the maze was planted. The full court was at Hampton Palace for the last time in 1737. The palace was opened to the public in 1838 and went through a period of restoration. In 1986 a fire destroyed some of the king's apartments; repairing the damage took six years. Hampton Court gardens attract over one million visitors a year and a flower show is held every July. Hampton Court station and the surrounding residential area of that name are located on the other side of the Thames in the Surrey borough of Elmbridge.

The French Impressionist Alfred Sisley was probably the greatest artist to have worked prolifically in the Hampton Court area, although he did not focus his attention on the palace itself. In a series of works painted in 1874, Sisley depicted the riverside, a regatta, the bridge across the Thames (from the side and below) and *The Road from Hampton Court*.

> ✉ East Molesey KT8

> 🚆 South West Trains (zone 6)

> ⛴ Hampton Court pier

> 📖 Simon Thurley, *Hampton Court: A Social and Architectural History*, Yale University Press, 2004; Lucy Worsley and David Souden, *Hampton Court Palace: The Official Illustrated History*, Merrell, 2005

> @ www.hrp.org.uk/webcode/hampton.home.asp (Hampton Court Palace site)

Hampton Hill • *Richmond*

The popular north-eastern corner of HAMPTON, bordering TEDDINGTON and FULWELL, with terraces of thriving specialist shops and restaurants. There is no detectable hill here; merely slightly higher ground that may once have lain above the Thames flood plain. Before the Act of Enclosure of 1811 the area that is now Hampton Hill was common land used for grazing cattle, the only buildings being Upper Lodge in BUSHY PARK and the windmill, which had been constructed in the 1780s to grind corn and grain. A map of 1839 shows the High Street, Burton's Road and Windmill Road, with a few buildings along the High Street and at the High Street end of Windmill Road, all surrounded by fields. By 1850 Hampton Hill had 24 traders, and the population grew as labourers constructing the waterworks along the river at Hampton came to live here, usually in very poor conditions. In 1863 St James's Church was built and its first vicar, a clergyman of private means named Fitzroy John Fitzwygram, set about building cottages and houses for the labourers and improving the facilities in the area. By the late 1870s the windmill had been demolished and the population had risen significantly. In 1890 the area, which had been known as the Common and New Hampton, was renamed Hampton Hill. At this time market gardens flourished in the Hampton area. A tram service began in 1903 and Hampton Hill was on the route from Stanley Road to HAMPTON COURT. The High Street saw some changes when the tramway converted from single to double tracks a little later, and some buildings had to be demolished to allow the road to be widened. During World War I a camp was set up for Canadian soldiers in Bushy Park, with Upper Lodge used as a hospital. Many of the soldiers who died there are buried in St James's churchyard. Most of the market gardens disappeared after World War II as more building took place. The site of the last, St Clare's, was taken in 1990 for a Sainsbury's supermarket. Very recent changes have been made to the stretch of the High Street between Windmill Road and Park Road, with some flats among the new building. Hampton Hill playhouse is a 200-seat theatre, with a 50-seat studio theatre, built in 1998.

Hampton Hill was the birthplace in 1947 of Queen guitarist Brian May. He was educated at Hampton School.

✉ Hampton TW12

♠ 9,448 (Fulwell and Hampton Hill ward)

📖 Borough of Twickenham Local History Society, *Old Hampton, Hampton Hill and Hampton Wick*, Hendon Publishing, 1982

@ www.localink.co.uk/hamptonhill (community site)

Hampton Nurserylands • *Richmond*

A modern housing estate in north-west HAMPTON, consisting of compact detached and semi-detached houses, arranged in narrow, curling cul-de-sacs. During the 1870s and 1880s, nurseries and market gardens covered the previously open farmland. There were 48 such concerns in 1912, but only eight remained by 1973, when the land was bought for housing development. Many of the estate's properties are owned by housing associations. Estate agents call Nurserylands a 'popular development' but there are problems with crime and anti-social behaviour and the council has been accused of allowing the neighbourhood to decline. 'When I got to Hampton Nurserylands, what an appalling sight met my eyes. Vandalized bus shelter, graffiti covered the phone kiosk and White House [community centre] walls, rubbish was lying around the recycling bins, weeds spilling out onto the pavement with plastic bags caught up. The area looked like an urban slum.' (Reader's letter to the *Richmond and Twickenham Times* in June 2000). In response to the situation, the borough's Youth Offending Team has made special efforts here. The council's 2001 crime audit stated that the team 'has been central to the Community Safety Strategy of reducing crime and anti-social behaviour in a crime hotspot, Hampton Nurserylands, and has been part of a joint motor project and a local football team for this area.'

✉ Hampton TW12

Hampton Wick • *Richmond*

The south-eastern annexe of TEDDINGTON, separated from the rest of HAMPTON by BUSHY PARK. A 'wick' was a harbour or trading place, and this landing point beside the Thames is likely to have been used to supply provisions for the original manor house of Hampton, which evolved into HAMPTON COURT. The construction of the wooden KINGSTON Bridge in 1219 added to the significance of the location, yet it remained an undistinguished hamlet for several centuries. In 1527 Cardinal Wolsey conducted negotiations at Hampton Court for an alliance with France, and the French ambassadors lodged in 'the village at the end of the park', which was probably Hampton Wick. Thomas Burdett bequeathed the sum of £50 to the poor of Hampton Wick in 1695, the profits to be spent on coals or wood and distributed yearly on St Thomas's Day in perpetuity. A few cottages survive at Hampton Wick from the early 18th century, but these do not seem to include The Hovel, which the Irish writer Richard Steele either rented or built for himself in 1707. Modern growth did not begin until the early 1830s, when the Church of St John the Baptist was built. The civil parish of Hampton Wick was created in 1831, covering 1,235 acres of land and 69 acres of water. Hampton Wick station opened in 1863. A Roman Catholic chapel was built in 1882, and a convent was added three years later. Most of the village was built up around the turn of the century. The former Hampton Court gasworks site on Sandy Lane is currently the focus of a major building project, which is planned to include a care home, crèche, shops, offices and around 200 apartments. The demographic profile of Hampton Wick closely mirrors that of the borough as a whole.

In the late 1970s television comedy *George and Mildred* the eponymous couple moved to the fictional Peacock Crescent on an executive housing estate in Hampton Wick after their EARLS COURT home was compulsorily purchased. 'Hampton' or 'Hampton Wick' is cockney rhyming slang for the male member.

✉	Kingston upon Thames KT1
👫	9,081
🚇	South West Trains (zone 6)
@	www.greenissues.com/Teddington (Sandy Lane developer's site)

Hanger Hill • *Ealing*

A delightful pair of interwar estates in NORTH EALING, especially popular with Japanese families. 'Hanger' meant a wood on the side of a hill or bank. Hanger Hill House, built in 1790, was the home of local landowners the Wood family until 1874. In the early years of the 20th century, the mansion became a golf clubhouse, while the adjoining fields were taken by ACTON aerodrome and the manufacturing facilities of the Alliance Aeroplane Co. With the construction of the Western Avenue (A40), the land was acquired for development and the Hanger Hill garden estate was laid out between 1928 and 1936. Consisting of short terraces of houses and three-storey blocks of flats, all in mock-Tudor style, the development is characterized by lovely gardens and vistas. The neighbouring Haymills estate is remarkable amongst London suburbs of the 1930s for the large number of buildings designed by a single practice, as a series of concentric crescents. Ealing council created a Hanger Hill electoral ward in 1999 in a move described as 'uniting the whole Hanger Hill community in one ward for the first time'. Ethnically, the ward is two-thirds white and the main minorities are of Indian and Japanese origin. After Christianity, the principal religions are Islam, Hinduism and Buddhism. Just over half the 16- to 74-year-olds are university educated. More than a quarter of the properties are privately rented.

West Acton Fox Wood is a nature reserve managed by the London Wildlife Trust. It has dense mixed oak woodland and two small wildflower meadows adjoining Hanger Hill Park, with a well-marked trail.

✉	W5; W3
👫	14,010
📖	Norman Pointing, *History of Hanger Hill, Ealing and the Church of the Ascension*, Diamond, 1990

Hanger Lane • *Ealing*

A highway connecting ALPERTON'S Ealing Road with GUNNERSBURY Avenue in EALING. Hanger Lane was a medieval route but its northward continuance over the River Brent was fragile, with the wooden bridge needing frequent repairs. In 1818 the lords of the manor of Ealing and Harrow disagreed over who should pay for the repairs and finally agreed to split the cost between them. The Western Avenue (A40) crossed Hanger Lane in 1930 and the Central Line station opened at the junction in 1947. The 'gyratory' roundabout here was regarded as an innovative traffic management system on its introduction but it remains one of London's most notorious blackspots – almost a byword for queues and delays. Like an old coaching stop, the junction has attracted restaurants and hotels, targeted more at business people than tourists. South of the gyratory to its finish at EALING COMMON, Hanger Lane is part of the A406 trunk road, better known as the North Circular.

✉	W5
🚇	Central Line (zone 3)
📖	Edward Platt, *Leadville: A Journey from White City to the Hanger Lane Gyratory*, Picador, 2001

Hans Town • *Kensington & Chelsea*

Now no more than the name of an electoral ward, Hans Town was a grand 18th-century suburb, centred on Sloane Street. Sir Hans Sloane was perhaps Chelsea's greatest benefactor. A president of the Royal Society, he moved to CHELSEA in 1742 and subsequently endowed the Chelsea Physic Garden. He was instrumental in founding the American colony of Georgia, and his scientific and literary collection became the nucleus of the British Museum after his death in 1753. In the 1770s the outward spread of London led FULHAM architect Henry Holland to spot an opportunity south of KNIGHTSBRIDGE. He acquired building rights from the Earl of Cadogan, who had come into possession of the land through his marriage to one of Hans Sloane's daughters. Spacious three-storey terraced houses were erected along the west side of Sloane Street and in Hans Place, then around Sloane Square, and finally in Cadogan Place in 1790. Holland built himself a mansion called Sloane Place in the south-western part of his 'town', with grounds landscaped by Capability Brown. Cadogan Square replaced this when R Norman Shaw and other architects redeveloped Hans Town a century later, after criticism of the district's bland and uniform architecture prompted the Cadogan estate to commission new designs. Each house was given its own distinctive detailing, further enhancing the prestige of the locality. The Hans Town ward has a very high proportion of privately rented properties, and 56 per cent of households have only one occupant.

Jane Austen stayed with her brother in Hans Place in 1814–15. The writer Arnold Bennett lived in Cadogan Square from 1921 to 1930.

> ✉ SW1

> 👥 9,335

Hanwell • *Ealing*

A likeable west London suburb, connected with EALING to its east via Uxbridge Road (A4020). The name probably refers to a stream (weille) frequented by cocks (hana). Fifth- and sixth-century Saxon graves have been discovered at the site of Oaklands School. By the time of Domesday Book, Hanwell belonged to Westminster Abbey. St Mary's Church was in existence by the twelfth century but has since been rebuilt three times. Buried in the crypt of the church is the merchant and travel writer Jonas Hanway, who introduced the umbrella to England in the 1750s. The last of the open land in Hanwell was enclosed in 1816 and several terraces of houses appeared during the following decade. Hanwell Lunatic Asylum (later St Bernard's Hospital) opened on the SOUTHALL border in 1831 and, after early difficulties, subsequently gained a reputation for the humane treatment of its patients. In 1836 Isambard Kingdom Brunel built the Wharncliffe viaduct for the Great Western Railway and Hanwell station opened

two years later. An oft-repeated story has it that Queen Victoria used to halt the royal train on the viaduct so that she could admire the view towards St Mary's. Only a few more homes were built following the creation of this early link to London and the main increase in Hanwell's population derived from the construction in 1856 of the Central London District School, near present-day CASTLE BAR PARK station. Hanwell's two cemeteries, flanking Uxbridge Road, were established in the 1850s, for the burial of Londoners from Kensington and Westminster. In the 1870s the viaduct was widened, the station was rebuilt and a full commuter service was laid on for the first time in response to growing demand. Hanwell became an urban district in 1895 and began to expand rapidly with the arrival of electric trams in 1901 but the district was absorbed by Ealing in 1926. In the 1930s the London County Council built the Cuckoo estate on the site of the Central London District School, but its imposing main building survives as Hanwell community centre. Terraced and semi-detached houses and other council flats filled most of the remaining land – and replaced earlier houses – in the years between the wars, although generous open spaces have been preserved in the Brent Valley. Contemporary Hanwell has a growing population of youngish professionals, especially in the southern part, and a variety of bars and restaurants to serve them. The population is mainly white, with a broad cross-section of ethnic minorities. Streets north-east of the station are named after English poets, so estate agents have tritely called it 'Poets' Corner' despite potential confusion with another Poets' Corner in ACTON.

In 1969 Hanwell community centre provided rehearsal rooms for rock bands Uriah Heep and Deep Purple. Much of the album *Deep Purple in Rock* was composed here.

> ✉ W7

> 👥 25,396 (Elthorne and Hobbayne wards)

> 🚆 First Great Western Link; Heathrow Connect (zone 4)

> 📖 Jonathan Oates, *Southall and Hanwell*, Tempus, 2002; Peter Hounsell, *Ealing and Hanwell Past*, Historical Publications, 1991

> @ www.hanwell.biz (privately operated community site)

Hanworth • *Hounslow*

An amorphous area of untidy housing, mixed

up with gravel pits and a few factories, lying just inside the Greater London border, to the east of FELTHAM. Hanworth was first recorded in Domesday Book. A 'worth' was an enclosed settlement, while the 'Han' element probably derives from a personal name. St George's Church was in existence by 1293. The manor of Hanworth came into the hands of the Crown through an exchange of lands in 1512. Hanworth House (also sometimes called Hanworth Castle or Palace) was the hunting lodge of Hanworth Park, which Henry VIII granted to Anne Boleyn for life. As Anne's life turned out to be shorter than expected, Henry later settled the property on his last wife, Katherine Parr. Princess Elizabeth (later Elizabeth I) came to live at Hanworth at the age of 15. In the second quarter of the 17th century the Hanworth Park estate was owned by Baron Cottington of Hanworth, and Queen Henrietta Maria stayed here in 1635 while the plague raged in London. Hanworth House was destroyed by fire in 1797 and a new house was built, but demolished three-quarters of a century later. The medieval church was rebuilt in two phases during the 19th century. In the late 1820s the 100-room Hanworth Park House was built to the north and this survives today, although its future ownership and use are uncertain. From 1917 until the opening of HEATHROW Airport, aircraft were built and tested in Hanworth Park, which is now public open space. The vast majority of Hanworth's residential and industrial premises were built between 1919 and 1939, including the development of BUTTS FARM, supplemented by post-war council estates. What had survived of the old village of Hanworth was mostly sacrificed to the construction of the M3 feeder road (the A316T) in 1973. Around a third of residents rent their homes from Hounslow council and there are problems associated with social disadvantage, more so in the Hanworth ward than Hanworth Park.

✉ Feltham TW13

♦ 21,391 (Hanworth and Hanworth Park wards)

📖 Andrea Cameron, *Feltham, Hanworth and Bedfont: A Pictorial History*, Phillimore, 2002

Harefield • *Hillingdon*

A large, self-contained village situated in the far north-western corner of Greater London. The name was first recorded in Domesday Book and was usually rendered as 'Herefeld' in the Middle Ages – possibly a reference to a field used by Danish invaders, 'here' being an Old English word for an army. Neolithic remains have been found in the parish, as well as fossils in the chalk. St Mary's Church is of 13th-century origin and is noted for its wealth of monuments. During the Middle Ages and 16th century, much of the parish consisted of moors and common land, with the cultivated lands of Harefield manor around the village. The 18th and 19th centuries saw the growth of several estates on which country houses were built, including Belhammonds, also known as Harefield Park, which later formed the core of Harefield Chest Hospital. The construction of the Grand Junction (now Grand Union) Canal on the western side of the parish at the end of the 18th century changed the character of this part of Harefield. By 1813 lime-kilns and copper mills lay along the northern part of the canal, and there were coal wharves north of Moorhall. The industrial area continued to expand throughout the century, but away from the canal Harefield remained one of the few places in Middlesex where the ancient pattern of an agricultural village survived into the second half of the 19th century, mainly because of the absence of a main road or railway. By the outbreak of World War I, houses were being built by the mills, around HILL END, along the main roads and round the village green. Large sand and gravel workings operated on the outskirts of Harefield between the wars but most of these are now disused or have become landfill sites, while much of the canalside industry has been replaced by offices and other business premises. UXBRIDGE council built nearly 500 houses between 1919 and 1951 around the common and in Northwood Road, and in SOUTH HAREFIELD and MOUNT PLEASANT. Subsequent development, both public and private, has been tightly constrained by the inclusion of almost all the surviving farmland within the green belt. During World War II, wounded Australian and New Zealand troops were brought to Harefield Hospital for treatment and many of those who died there are buried in St Mary's churchyard. Since its first heart transplant in 1980 the hospital has had a distinguished history of ground-breaking surgery. Plans to incorporate the hospital's facilities on the site of a new 'super-hospital' at PADDINGTON WATERSIDE fell apart in 2005, to the joy of Harefield's many supporters. Harefield village retains a genuinely rural character, though a fifth of its housing is owned by Hillingdon council. The population is 94 per cent white and educational attainment is relatively low. Car ownership is high, as it needs to be out in the sticks.

✉ Uxbridge UB9

♦ 7,090 (Harefield ward; by far the borough's smallest ward)

📖 Eileen M Bowlt, *Ickenham and Harefield Past*, Phillimore, 1996; Mary P Shepherd, *History of Harefield: The Story of the Hospital*, Quiller Press, 1990

@ www.rbht.nhs.uk (Royal Brompton and Harefield NHS Trust site)

Harefield Grove • *Hillingdon*

Only one London street atlas identifies this as a discrete locality, situated north of HARE-FIELD proper on Rickmansworth Road and consisting of little more than a farm and a mansion. There has been a farm here since at least 1684, when it was called Guttersdean Farm. In the late 19th century exotic fruits and vegetables were grown for the London market in over 100 greenhouses with 50 miles of hot water piping. Harefield Grove is a Grade II-listed house, probably of 18th-century origin but significantly altered on at least two subsequent occasions. It is most notable for its grounds, with lakes and a waterfall, which are among the few surviving landscaped gardens in London not to have been opened to the public. The house was restored and converted to offices in 1985.

A small studio was constructed at Harefield Grove Farm to create CI5's headquarters in the first series of *The Professionals*, a 1970s crime-action television drama. Some exterior scenes were shot at locations nearby.

✉ Uxbridge UB9

Harefield West *see* MOUNT PLEASANT

Hare Street • *Havering*

A former hamlet situated north of GIDEA PARK station, still shown on some relatively recent maps. Hare Street was the name for what is now the more prosaic Main Road and, as with HAREFIELD, the name probably relates to the Old English 'here', meaning an army. Its inns had a long history of serving travellers on the Great Road between London and East Anglia. Hare Street has been absorbed by Gidea Park, an inevitable consequence of its location between the park and the station of that name.

Humphry Repton lived in a cottage on Hare Street in 1786, shortly before he began his illustrious career as a landscape gardener; a plaque on the Lloyds Bank building marks the site. During World War I, Hare Hall became home to the Artists' Rifles, who constructed a model army camp in the grounds. The poets Edward Thomas and Wilfred Owen both trained at the camp.

✉ Romford RM2

Harlesden • *Brent* (pronounced 'harlzdən')

Variously called 'the West Bronx of London' and 'Jamaica Town', Harlesden is situated south of WILLESDEN and has the capital's highest proportion of residents of Caribbean descent. The name was first recorded in the eleventh century and is corrupted from Here-wulf's tun, or farmstead. Harlesden grew very slowly throughout and after the Middle Ages. By the mid 18th century the hamlet had a few dozen houses and two inns: the Crown and the Green Man. Even after enclosure in 1823, there was little building on the green that bordered the Harrow road. By the early 1840s Harlesden had a station (named Willesden) on the London to Birmingham line, which brought a few houses, a chapel and another inn. However, it was the replacement of this station by WILLESDEN JUNCTION in 1866 that wrought a transformation. Terraced houses and villas began to spread along the High Street and other existing roads. The distinctive All Souls' Church was completed in 1876 and after this date new streets were laid out in place of former orchards. In the ten years from 1881 the population of All Souls' parish increased from 2,390 to 9,929. A minority of the developments took the form of pricey villas but most consisted of terraced housing for the lower middle classes. The High Street gained its Jubilee Clock in 1887 to celebrate the 50th anniversary of Queen Victoria's accession, and in the following year Harlesden Green became the destination for the first horse-drawn tramway in north-west London. The High Street was lined with its present shopping parades in the 1890s and the Green Man was rebuilt in 1908 as part of a scheme that added more shops. By this time, Harlesden's prime landowner, All Souls College, Oxford, had started to lay out an estate that had almost 400 houses by 1914. The outbreak of World War I brought housebuilding to a halt but stimulated industrial growth in the south. By the 1930s the last of the open spaces and larger houses had been replaced by terraced houses and the middle classes had mostly departed as overcrowding increased. The council built blocks of flats after World War II, but not as many as it had intended because demand for housing was so urgent that there was no time to knock down and replace existing properties. From the late 1950s, immigration from the West Indies began to alter the district's character and as early as 1968 the Curzon Crescent estate had a Caribbean majority. The suddenness of this change, and a degree of civic neglect, caused social problems at first but in time led to the creation of one of London's most culturally effervescent communities. From the 1970s Harlesden became increasingly renowned for its live music, records shops, pirate radio stations and Caribbean food shops and restaurants. Since the 1990s regeneration projects have improved the High Street and the council-built estates, while gentrification has begun in the terraced houses. Even greater change is taking place on the nearby STONEBRIDGE estate, which had acquired a dire reputation. Forty-three per cent of Harlesden's residents are black or black British, of whom the majority are of Caribbean descent. Most householders rent their homes, primarily from housing associations.

The reggae artist Delroy Washington worked in a Harlesden record shop and members of reggae group Aswad grew up in the vicinity. BBC2's 2001 documentary series *Heart of Harlesden* showcased the area's cultural vitality.

> ✉ NW10

> ♟ 12,227

> 🚅 Silverlink Metro; Bakerloo Line (zone 3)

> 📖 M C Barrès-Baker, *Harlesden*, Grange Museum of Community History and Brent Archive, 2001

> @ www.brent-heritage.co.uk/harlesden.htm

Harley Street • *Westminster*

London's premier address for private doctors, Harley Street runs north from Cavendish Square to REGENT'S PARK along what was once the valley of the Tyburn River. From around 1719 Edward Harley, later the second Earl of Oxford, began to develop the Cavendish family estate, but Harley Street itself was not completed until 1770. Its architecture was widely scorned for its dullness but the sumptuous interiors, some by the Adam brothers, attracted the upper echelons of society, including Lady Nelson, the artist J M W Turner and statesman William Gladstone. The Duke of Wellington (as he later became) rented a house in Harley Street for his wife and children while he was away on his military campaigns. Foreign ambassadors chose the street for its quietness and the quality of its accommodation, and families from the country rented houses here during the London season. Around the mid 19th century, Cavendish Square became a prestigious location for physicians' consulting rooms and doctors began to colonize the southern end of Harley Street in order to be near the square. In 1829 John St John Long – 'the king of quacks' – set up shop here, offering his cures by rubbing and inhalation, and causing traffic jams as patients thronged to attend. Florence Nightingale moved to Harley Street in 1853 to become superintendent of a gentlewomen's nursing home. It was not until later in the century that the street acquired a cachet of its own, whereupon spacious rooms were subdivided into consulting suites, and large brass plaques were mounted on front doors because professional restrictions prevented other forms of advertising. By the 1920s the street had almost completely filled up with doctors and Brunswick Place was renamed Upper Harley Street to provide additional capacity. Harley Street lost some of its practices after the creation of the National Health Service, but it remains synonymous with expensive consultancy, including newer forms of treatment such as cosmetic surgery.

In Elizabeth Gaskell's *North and South*, heroine Margaret Hale lives in 'comfort and luxury' with her cousin Edith Shaw at 96 Harley Street. Charles Dickens made the street home to the obscenely wealthy Mr Merdle in *Little Dorrit*. Both novels were published in the 1850s.

> ✉ W1

> 📖 Percy Flemming, *Harley Street: From Earliest Times to the Present Day*, Lewis, 1939

Harlington • *Hillingdon*

A medieval manor and village transformed by later transport improvements, situated south of HAYES. This was Hygeredington in 831 and Hardington for several centuries after that. The Church of St Peter and St Paul was in existence by 1086, when the manor house stood nearby. The church's Norman south door is said to be the best in outer London. The centre of the village had shifted southwards by the 17th century and a small settlement had grown up at the WEST END of Harlington by the 1750s. To the north of the parish the Grand Junction (now Grand Union) Canal was constructed in the 1790s and the Great Western Railway was built through the district in the 1830s, although Hayes and Harlington station did not open until 1864. Cottages were built for brick-workers and new public houses joined the White Hart and the Red Lion. The intensity of brickmaking and gravel-working in the north was so great that much of the land was lowered by several feet. The presence of the railway and the canal brought factories to the DAWLEY area, and these in turn brought housing, especially semi-detached properties north of Pinkwell Lane in the 1930s, and some later council flats. This evolution consumed the former village of Pinkwell and merged with Hayes to the north – indeed, many consider this section to be part of Hayes rather than Harlington. The part of the parish that lay south of the Bath Road (A4) was taken by the air ministry in 1945 for the creation of what became HEATHROW Airport. The construction of the M4 motorway in the 1960s divided the area into two quite distinct parts. The area north of the motorway is now entirely filled with housing, while the old centre to the south has been protected from overdevelopment, although much of the village had already lost its original character as a consequence of the proximity of Heathrow. Harlington village was made a conservation area in 2005. At Harlington Community School, on Pinkwell Lane, the roll is ethnically very diverse and has a very high proportion of pupils with English as an additional language, but only a small proportion is at the early stages of language acquisition. The school's sports facilities are open to the wider community in the evenings and at weekends. Queen's Park Rangers Football Club trains at Imperial College's Harlington sports ground on Sipson Lane.

✉ Hayes UB3

🚆 First Great Western Link; Heathrow Connect (Hayes and Harlington, zone 5)

📖 Philip Sherwood, *Harlington and Harmondsworth*, Tempus, 2002

Harmondsworth • *Hillingdon*

A HEATHROW satellite village located south of WEST DRAYTON. Evidence has been found here of Iron Age huts and sixth-century Saxon dwellings. In 1069 William the Conqueror gave the parish church and the manor to the Benedictine Abbey of Holy Trinity (later known as St Catherine's) in Rouen, France. The abbey rebuilt the church and the oldest parts of the present structure date from the mid twelfth century. Around 1211 the abbey established a priory here that became increasingly unpopular for the taxes it imposed on the manorial tenants, who in 1281 burned down some of its buildings. The manor of Harmondsworth was appropriated in 1391 to Winchester College, which commissioned the construction of an aisled, timber-framed barn for the manor farm. Completed in 1427, it was the last in a series of vast medieval barns built on this site and survives today as the second longest in England. The Grange and Harmondsworth Hall were among the grandest of the homes built in the 17th century and both remain in existence, the former as offices and the latter as a hotel, with an 18th-century brick front. Once part of HOUNSLOW HEATH, the land around Harmondsworth was steadily enclosed from the 1750s and brought under cultivation. Orchards and market gardens were established in the latter part of the 19th century. The village grew slowly but did not change significantly from its medieval form until the opening of the Colnbrook bypass in 1929. This brought some suburban housing, and to the south of the village, commercial premises, notably in the form of Penguin Books in 1937. When the walls and roof of the Penguin warehouse were first erected, there were still cabbages growing amidst the stacks of books and the company's founder, Sir Allen Lane, insisted they should be sold to recoup part of the outlay. The development of Heathrow Airport since 1945 has erased all former traces of the parish south of the Bath Road (A4) but the village centre remains an authentic delight, and is now both a conservation area and an archaeological priority area. Horrifyingly, plans for a third runway at the airport threaten much of Harmondsworth's heritage, including the tithe barn. Harmondsworth has not acquired the diverse ethnic mix of other Heathrow 'suburbs', although a small minority speaks a language other than English, most commonly Punjabi, Bengali, Somali or Gujarati.

✉ West Drayton UB7

📖 Philip Sherwood, *Harlington and Harmondsworth*, Tempus, 2002

Harold Hill • *Havering*

A post-war 'new style suburb' in the northeast corner of Greater London, just inside the M25. From the Middle Ages the Havering submanors of Dagnams (originally Dagenhams), Cockerells and Gooshays covered roughly the area of the present estate. Dagnams was particularly grand and was visited by Samuel Pepys. From the early 19th century the area was progressively acquired by the Neave family, who made Dagnam Park their home. The Neaves created the 137-acre Harold Hill Farm in 1829 after they acquired the manor of Gooshays. Most of the farmland was sold to the tenants in 1919, but the family stayed on at Dagnam Park. In 1944 Professor Patrick Abercrombie earmarked the land for development as part of his Greater London Plan. The site's gross area was 1,387 acres, 549 acres of which were to be devoted to housing. The original intention was to name the estate Dagnam Park, but Harold Hill was chosen to avoid any confusion with DAGENHAM. Sir Arundel Neave voluntarily sold up and moved to his estate in Anglesey but several farms had to be compulsorily purchased by the London County Council in 1947. The following year saw the completion of 500 prefabricated homes in Magnolia Close. Construction of permanent dwellings began soon afterwards and continued for almost a decade. Most of the properties were two-storey houses in short terraces, with a few semi-detached houses. Blocks of flats were placed on higher ground, to provide tenants with good views and create a varied skyline. Two neighbourhood units with a total of 8,200 dwellings were built, with an industrial zone in the south-west corner. In the north-east corner, on the edge of the green belt, higher value homes were built as part of a plan to house a wider variety of tenants than was usual with council estates. By 1965 the estate had five churches, seven pubs and a dozen schools. Slightly over half of the houses are now owner-occupied, while nearly all the rest are still rented from the council. More than 96 per cent of residents are white, and educational attainment is low; over 40 per cent of 16- to 74-year olds have no qualifications at all. Harold Hill has problems with anti-social behaviour and has been the target of special police operations designed to counter what the local paper calls 'mob rule'.

Duck Wood serves as a community nature reserve. Its ancient hornbeam woodland is noted for carpets of bluebells and wood anemones.

✉ Romford RM3

👤 25,769 (Gooshays and Heaton wards)

Harold Park • *Havering*

The north-eastern part of HAROLD WOOD, occupying an isthmus of land between Colchester Road (A12) and the River Ingrebourne. In 1868 a wealthy Brentwood solicitor built himself a mansion, called Harold Court, to the south of the river and railway line. After the owner's bankruptcy the house served as a children's home, then a lunatic asylum and then a sanatorium. In 1959 it became a teacher training college and has now been converted into private flats. Horse Block Farm lay to the north-east of Harold Court Road. After World War I the Essex building company Iles and Co. laid out a bungalow estate here that it called Sunnytown; the company also created Sunnymede at Billericay. When Harold Court Primary School opened in 1929 the area still retained a rural character, but this was slowly eroded as further development filled the remaining land, including some industry beside the Ingrebourne.

✉ Romford RM3

Harold Wood • *Havering*

A Victorian railway township, now much enlarged and rebuilt, situated just over two miles north and a little to the east of HORNCHURCH. Harold's Wood was a large forest stretching some way to the north-west of the present district. Although King Harold once owned the estate there is no evidence that he ever visited it. After the trees were cut down in the 15th and 16th centuries the land became known as Harold's Wood (or ROMFORD) Common. Harold Wood Farm was probably established in the mid 18th century and was later acquired by local grandees the Neave family. The district of Harold Wood grew up some distance away, on 300 acres of Gubbins Farm, following the opening of the station in the late 1860s. The station was built with the sponsorship of the Harold Wood Estate Co., formed by a group of builders to exploit the potential for residential development here, in the first suburban scheme in the parish of Hornchurch. New roads were laid out and some expensive villas were built, together with the King Harold public house, but neither prosperous nor clerical commuters wanted to live so far out of London and the project foundered. In an indication of the slowness of the suburb's evolution, an iron church was provided in 1871 and it was almost 70 years before this was replaced by a permanent structure, St Peter's Church. Meanwhile, industrialization took the form of a brick company and later a provender mill on Gubbins Lane. In 1908 a Victorian house called The Grange became a children's convalescent home, which was to form the nucleus of Harold Wood Hospital, initially run by the borough of WEST HAM. Harold Wood's rural character finally vanished after World War I as the district filled with new housing, and Victorian properties were demolished to make way for more affordable dwellings. The brick company's site was built over in the late 1940s. Unilever acquired the mill in 1965 and its buildings were demolished around 1970. Three-quarters of homes here are owner-occupied, and 95 per cent of residents are white.

> ✉ Romford RM3

> 🚹 12,004

> 🚆 'one' Railway (zone 6)

> 📖 Chris Saltmarsh and Norma Jennings, *Havering Village to Harold Wood*, Phillimore, 1995

Harringay • *Haringey*

The grids off GREEN LANES, situated north of FINSBURY PARK. Harringay's name comes from the same root as its parent borough, as does that of its neighbour, HORNSEY. All are corruptions of 'Haringes hege', which meant an enclosure belonging to a Saxon named Haring, or perhaps Hær. Although Hornsey can lay claim to being the site of the original enclosure, Harringay House was built in this locality in the 1790s, probably on the site of a Tudor mansion. The massive property was built for Edward Grey, a London linen draper, who accumulated an estate of 192 acres by the 1820s. Grey died in 1838 and the estate was broken up and sold. The largest part was later acquired by the British Land Co., which rapidly laid out streets and building plots from the early 1880s. The company divided the extensive development into two halves: the Harringay Park estate in the south and the Hornsey Station estate in the north, each of which eventually contained over 1,000 houses. The rigidly gridded arrangement of the streets west of Green Lanes has given rise to the nickname 'the Ladder'. The grid is bisected by Haringey Passage, a well-maintained alley almost a mile in length. South Harringay (now Harringay Green Lanes) station opened in 1880 and Harringay West (now Harringay) opened on the more useful Great Northern Railway in 1885, the year in which Harringay House was demolished. To the east of Grand Parade, J C Hill laid out the Harringay Gardens estate on the former St John's Lodge Farm from the late 1890s. In 1927 the Greyhound Racing Association built Harringay Park, a stadium that later hosted speedway events as well as dog races. The Harringay Boxing and Ice Skating Arena opened on a neighbouring site in 1936,

and was famously used for prayer meetings by the Christian evangelist Billy Graham until its closure in 1958. The greyhound stadium closed in 1987 and the two sites are now occupied by a retail park. Harringay has been the focus of London's Cypriot community for several decades and its specialist shops line the Grand Parade section of Green Lanes. The Ladder makes up most of the ward of Harringay, which has a high proportion of well-educated young adults. Seventy per cent of residents are white, with the remainder drawn from a broad cross-section of ethnic minorities. More than a third of homes here are privately rented.

The actress Gillian Anderson grew up in and around Harringay and her parents kept on their flat here after the family moved to America, returning during school holidays.

> ✉ N4; N8

> 🚹 10,525

> 🚆 WAGN Railway (Harringay, zone 3); Silverlink Metro (Harringay Green Lanes, zone 3)

> 📖 Mike Ticher, *The Story of Harringay Stadium and Arena*, Hornsey Historical Society, 2002

Harrow • *Harrow*

An extensive suburban district that grew outwards from HARROW ON THE HILL after the coming of the railways. Harrow lies 11 miles north-west of central London. First recorded in the eighth century, the name derives from the Old English 'hearg', a pagan shrine. HEADSTONE manor house was the Middlesex residence of the archbishops of Canterbury from 1307 until 1546. The house is presently undergoing restoration, while its great barn has become the borough's heritage museum. In 1572 John Lyon founded Harrow School and the institution achieved a zenith of fashionability in the 19th century, expanding to fill most of the old village and consequently preserving its charm. The first Harrow station (now Harrow and WEALDSTONE) opened in 1837, bringing early growth to GREENHILL and Wealdstone. Later in the century housing began to fan out from Pinner Road (A404) into the newly invented localities of WEST HARROW and NORTH HARROW. Harrow was never a significant industrial district and the only factory of importance was that of Kodak Ltd, which opened in Wealdstone in 1890. New stations opened all around Harrow in the early 20th century and the town pushed further out in all directions except eastwards. Development reached a crescendo between the world wars, filling all the available space from NORTHOLT PARK in the south to Uxbridge Road (A410) in HARROW WEALD, and westwards to the edge of RUISLIP. Harrow Garden Village was created on the border with EASTCOTE, but the name was largely a marketing device and this was not the kind of pioneering scheme seen in BEDFORD PARK or HAMPSTEAD GARDEN SUBURB. Other affordable homes were built near RAYNERS LANE station and in SOUTH HARROW, which swallowed the old hamlet of ROXETH. Council estates changed the character of some areas in the third quarter of the 20th century, notably on the western side of Harrow Weald. Subsequent private development has mostly taken the form of compact blocks of flats, maximizing revenues from the very limited sites available. High-rise offices came to central Harrow in the 1960s and the shopping area was redeveloped from the late 1970s. Diana, Princess of Wales opened the St Ann's shopping mall in 1987 and St Ann's Road was later pedestrianized. The smaller St George's shopping and leisure centre was completed in 1996, and incorporates a nine-screen cinema. Changes to the built environment in recent decades have been relatively minor compared with the shift in the ethnic mix of the population; around a quarter of all residents can trace their origins to the Indian subcontinent.

✉ Harrow HA1

👥 88,189 (Greenhill, Harrow on the Hill, Headstone North, Headstone South, Marlborough, Roxbourne, Roxeth, Wealdstone and West Harrow wards)

📖 Don Walter, *Harrow A to Z*, Sutton, 2005

@ www.lifeinharrow.co.uk (local information site); www.harrowtimes.co.uk (online version of local newspaper)

Harrow on the Hill • *Harrow*
The southern part of central HARROW and one of London's most authentic-looking villages. Alternatively spelt in hyphenated form, and later known as Harrow Town, Harrow on the Hill was the site of the original hamlet in the early seventh century. The hill rises to 408 feet above sea level and was crowned by St Mary's Church from the 11th century. In the Middle Ages the church was one of the most important in Middlesex and was a peculiar of the Archbishop of Canterbury, who had a residence at SUDBURY and subsequently at HEADSTONE. A market was established in 1226. John Lyon, a yeoman of PRESTON, founded Harrow School in 1572, under a charter gran-

ted by Elizabeth I. On the completion of the schoolhouse in 1615 just one pupil was on the roll. Properties in the village were taken over as boarding houses for the pupils from the late 17th century but Harrow remained just one of many local grammar schools until it achieved a leap in its popularity early in the 19th century, and most of the working people in the village were soon serving the school in some way. The school buildings were doubled in size in 1821, a chapel was added in 1839 and numerous other buildings and purpose-built boarding houses followed. To the north of the school complex, the station opened in 1880 and the Roxborough and Northwick estates were laid out soon afterwards. By the end of the century, Harrow on the Hill had merged with GREENHILL to its north. The junction of Grove Hill and Lowlands Road (A404) is said to have been the scene of Britain's first fatal car accident, in 1899. With its little shops, tea-rooms and pubs, the village has changed little since that time, which has led to accusations of faux-nostalgia but the effect is delightful nonetheless. Lower down the slopes of the hill, modern commercial premises have inevitably intruded but the school's extensive grounds have preserved the open space to the east. In the Harrow on the Hill ward, half the residents are white and the next largest ethnic group is of Indian origin.

Old Harrovians include the statesmen Viscount Palmerston, Winston Churchill, Pandit Nehru and King Hussein of Jordan, the poet Lord Byron, and the writers R B Sheridan, Anthony Trollope and Richard Curtis. *Harrow-on-the-Hill* is the title of a poem by John Betjeman, in which he sees the hill as 'a rocky island … [with a] churchyard full of sailors' graves'.

✉ Harrow HA1

👥 10,632

🚆 Chiltern Railways; Metropolitan Line (Harrow-on-the-Hill, zone 5)

📖 Christopher Tyerman, *A History of Harrow School 1324–1991*, Oxford University Press, 2000

@ www.harrowschool.org.uk

Harrow Road • *Westminster/Brent*
London has several Harrow Roads, but the best-known is the stretch of the A404 running from MARYLEBONE to HARLESDEN. In *The Growth of St Marylebone and Paddington*, Jack Whitehead calls it a typical English road,

'which wandered from village green to village green, skirting the corners of large estates, avoiding ponds which have now been filled in for centuries, turning and looping for no apparent reason'. From PADDINGTON as far as KENSAL GREEN, Harrow Road runs close to the Grand Union Canal, which was constructed at the beginning of the 19th century. Most of the suburban development in the area from that time onwards evolved out of hamlets that had first taken root beside Harrow Road. The London Lock Hospital, with buildings designed by Lewis Vulliamy, moved to a site near the canal bridge in 1842. The hospital was the capital's only specialist medical centre for sufferers from venereal diseases and was funded partly by gifts and, from the 1860s, by a government subsidy in return for treating military patients. Paddington Infirmary was established nearby in 1867, eventually becoming the Harrow Road branch of St Mary's Hospital; today it is the luxury apartment development Carlton Gate. Harrow Road was entirely built up in the latter decades of the 19th century, but there has been much piecemeal replacement since then. In addition to residential properties there were many shops and public houses serving the inhabitants of the new suburbs in its hinterland, most of which were more affluent than the road itself. The successor to the Lock Hospital closed in 1952 and Vulliamy's main buildings were demolished. Westminster's Harrow Road ward has a relatively deprived population, with low home and car ownership. The main ethnic minorities are of black Caribbean and black African descent. There are relatively few older people, especially aged over 75.

Mick Jones, lead guitarist with The Clash, lived from 1973 to 1980 in the 21-storey Wilmcote House on the Warwick Estate. *Harrow Road* is a track by his later band Big Audio Dynamite, from the album *Planet BAD*.

✉ W2; W9; W10; NW10

♁ 8,621

Harrow Weald • *Harrow*

An elongated residential area situated west of STANMORE, with different characteristics in its northern, south-western and south-eastern parts. This was simply the Weald for most of its history, and the name derives from the Saxon word for a wood. The dense tree cover here was unfavourable to habitation in the Middle Ages but progressive northward deforestation eventually created an expansive common; the first settlement was in an area called the Lower End of the Weald. The London merchant Sir Edward Waldo acquired the manor of Marlpits in the 1680s and created Waldo's Farm from the part of the manor that lay in Harrow Weald. From 1759 the common was steadily enclosed and had been reduced to 685 acres in 1817. Only the northern tip of this acreage survives today, with the neighbouring Grimsdyke Open Space, named after a linear earthwork that may be of late Iron Age origin. During the 19th century several grand houses were built on the enclosed land, among them the home of Thomas Blackwell, who formed a food company with Edmund Crosse of nearby Clamp Hill. Harrow Weald Park was a mansion occupied by the gaming club owner Henry Crockford until his death in 1844 and was rebuilt in 1870 in sumptuous Victorian Gothic style, looking something like an Oxford college. When Harrow council later destroyed the mansion, retirement homes were built on part of the site, although most of its woodland survives. A rambling house called Grim's Dyke was the work of the architect R Norman Shaw in the early 1870s, and its 'Old English' style influenced the appearance of several other properties in the area. The librettist W S Gilbert spent the last years of his life at Grim's Dyke, which is now a hotel. Properties north of Uxbridge Road (A410) occupied extensive grounds but further south houses were built more densely, although still to a superior standard. A surge of development after World War I pushed the population up to 10,928 in 1931 and two 16th-century farmhouses, Wealdstone House and Harrow Weald House, were demolished around this time. After World War II the London County Council acquired 153 acres south of Uxbridge Road and built an estate for 5,000 people from London, making the High Road and High Street a dividing line in the area's character. On Brookshill, Weald College became the Harrow Weald campus of Harrow College in 1999. Almost three-quarters of Harrow Weald's residents are white, a high proportion by the borough's standards.

The notorious miser Daniel Dancer lived at Waldo's Farm in the late 18th century, but he refused to go the expense of cultivating the land. In wintertime Dancer defrosted food by sitting on it rather than light a fire, and knocked out his dog's teeth to avoid compensating neighbours if it attacked their livestock. Money was found hidden all around the farm after his death in 1794, including £2,500 in a dung heap.

✉ Harrow HA3

🚶 10,345

@ www.harrow.ac.uk (Harrow College site);
www.grimsdyke.com (Grim's Dyke Hotel site)

Hatcham • Lewisham

The name used for the area east of PECKHAM and north of NUNHEAD until well into the 20th century. Hatcham was first recorded in Domesday Book and the medieval manor house was rebuilt in 1775. The house was demolished by the Worshipful Company of Haberdashers, which laid out an estate of three-storey terraced houses from the 1860s to around 1900. Shop fronts were later added in the front gardens of houses on NEW CROSS Road. In 1923 NEW CROSS GATE station was given its present name, which was subsequently used to denote the vicinity. There have been efforts to revive Hatcham's identity, for example in the name of the conservation area that covers the Haberdashers' Company's estate.

✉ SE14

📖 Raymond Thatcher, *Hatcham and Telegraph Hill: An Historical Sketch*, Lewisham Historical Society, 1982

Hatch End • Harrow

The urbane but not urban northern tip of PINNER. Hatch End's name was first recorded in 1448, although the mention around 1300 of the surname de la Hacche indicates that the settlement may have been in existence even earlier. The hatch (gate) would have given access to Pinner Park, which belonged to the archbishops of Canterbury. Hatch End lay on the boundary between Pinner and HARROW WEALD and was divided between those parishes for the assessment of tithes. Dove House Farm was in existence by 1547 and by 1759 its farmhouse occupied a moated site. This was the home in the early 19th century of a horse dealer named Tilbury, who invented the two-wheeled carriage that bore his name. Napoleon III of France visited Dove House and copied its stables for those that he built for his palace at Chantilly. The Dove House estate was divided by the London and North Western Railway line in the late 1830s, and Pinner (later Hatch End) station opened in 1842. A high-class estate was being laid out at WOODRIDINGS by 1855, and in the same year the Royal Commercial Travellers' Schools relocated to Hatch End from WANSTEAD. The school buildings were subsequently enlarged several

times. The rest of Hatch End remained rural until Metropolitan Railway services began in 1886, when settlement spread westwards from Woodridings and northwards across Uxbridge Road (A410). St Anselm's Church was built in 1895, on Westfield Park. Hatch End station was tastefully rebuilt in 1911. Comben and Wakeling laid out the mock-Tudor Hatch End Park estate in the 1930s. As is common in such safe and desirable areas, a number of maisonette blocks were built in the second half of the 20th century, often with retired people in mind. One such block replaced Dove House farmhouse in the mid 1960s. The Royal Pinner School (as the Commercial Travellers' Schools had become) closed in 1967 and Harrow Arts Centre moved into the school's impressive Elliot Hall in 1988. In addition to its eclectic range of shops, Hatch End is regarded as the restaurant capital of the borough. At an average age of 41 years, Hatch End has a relatively mature – and affluent – population, with above average levels of car ownership, employment and owner occupation. The national educational standards agency Ofsted describes Hatch End High School (originally Blackwell County) as 'a 12–16 co-educational multi-ethnic comprehensive school with a wide social mix', and praises its high standards.

The novelist Ivy Compton-Burnett was born in Hatch End in 1884. Her father, a homeopathic doctor, moved the family to the Sussex coast in 1891 to give his children the benefit of sea air.

✉ Pinner HA5

🚶 10,098

🚌 Silverlink Metro (zone 6)

📖 Don Walter, *Pinner and Hatch End Past and Present*, Sutton, 2002

@ www.harrowarts.com (Harrow Arts Centre site)

Hatton • Hounslow/Hillingdon

Primarily a large service area for HEATHROW Airport, situated to the west of HOUNSLOW. The name is a corruption of 'heath ton' and was first recorded in Domesday Book. Edward III seems to have built a (long-lost) house here, which was known as Hatton Grange and was later granted to the priory of Hounslow. The hamlet lay on the edge of HOUNSLOW HEATH at the junction of several byways with the road to Staines and Bath. The Green Man inn, which dates from the late 18th century, is said to have been a favourite haunt of highwaymen. A timber-framed building at the north-eastern end of Hatton Road was converted to a mission church but no longer serves this purpose. Over the second half of the 20th century the old hamlet was almost entirely erased by the construction of warehouses and other service buildings for Heathrow Airport, one of which covered a prehistoric earthwork. Hatton Cross station opened in 1975 on the Piccadilly Line extension to Heathrow, and provides a bus interchange for the main-line rail service via Feltham. Hatton Green has a cluster of housing and the small and under-filled Hatton Cemetery lies further south, behind Hounslow Urban Farm on the edge of NORTH FELTHAM.

✉ Hounslow TW6 and TW14

🚇 Piccadilly Line (Hatton Cross, zones 5 and 6)

Hatton Garden • *Camden*
London's prime jewellery quarter, located just north of HOLBORN Circus. Hatton Garden takes its name from Sir Christopher Hatton, who acquired the property from the diocese of Ely. Hatton was both knighted and made chancellor by Elizabeth I, who had originally been attracted to him by his graceful dancing at a ball. Accordingly nicknamed the 'dancing chancellor', he was a major sponsor of Sir Francis Drake's round-the-world voyage. Drake renamed his flagship in honour of his patron, whose family crest featured a golden hind. From an early role as a cutting centre for Indian diamonds, Hatton Garden developed a trade in gold and platinum during the 19th century. The exploitation of South Africa's Kimberley diamond field brought a further increase in trade from the 1870s. 'The Garden' now boasts around 300 jewellery businesses, including 50 retailers. In July 1993 thieves stole jewels valued at £7 million from a Hatton Garden workshop belonging to the KNIGHTSBRIDGE jewellers Graff's: it was London's biggest gem robbery of modern times. Hatton Garden formed the backdrop for Guy Ritchie's heist movie *Snatch*.

Giuseppe Mazzini, the Italian writer and political leader, founded an Italian language school in Hatton Garden in 1841. In a small factory in Hatton Garden in the early 1880s the engineer Sir Hiram Maxim invented and perfected the Maxim gun, a single-barrelled machine gun that could fire 666 rounds a minute, which was adopted by the British army in 1891. In Ely Court, a narrow alley at the southern end of Hatton Garden, is the 18th-century Ye Olde Mitre public house. The present building replaced the original tavern built in 1546 by Bishop Goodrich of Ely.

✉ EC1

📖 H Marryat and Una Broadbent, *The Romance of Hatton Garden*, James Cornish and Sons, 1930

Havering-atte-Bower • *Havering*
An extended village standing on high ground three miles north of ROMFORD. 'Havering' is pronounced the same way as the verb, despite the fable of its origin. It is said that in the mid 11th century Edward the Confessor built a hunting lodge, often referred to as a small palace or 'bower'. The story goes that Edward was once approached here by a beggar asking for alms, to which he replied, 'I have no money, but I *have a ring*', which he handed over, and that is how Havering got its name. Furthermore, the same beggar is later supposed to have met some pilgrims and passed the ring to them, saying, 'Give this to your king, and tell him that within six months he shall die.' And this apparently came to pass. This is so far-fetched that it scarcely bears repeating, yet the ring in question retains a central position on the borough's coat of arms to this day as a result of the tale. The tower on the coat of arms represents the old palace, although it is topped with the horns of HORNCHURCH. There was certainly a royal house at Havering by the early 12th century, but the name probably derives from a landowner called Hæfer. A succession of royal associations came to an end during the Commonwealth when the house fell into decay and it was demolished early in the 18th century. Bower House was built nearby in 1729, perhaps using some of the old stones. This house was later enlarged and is now owned by the Ford Motor Co., which holds management training sessions and dealer presentations here. On Broxhill Road, an oval, three-storeyed, stuccoed villa called the Round House dates from 1794. The Church of St John the Evangelist was built in 1878 by the respected Arts and Crafts architect Basil Champneys. The church's thatched predecessor had reputedly stood on the site of a royal chapel. The present village is by no means unspoilt but retains sufficient older elements to give it some character, including weatherboarded cottages facing the green, which still contains stocks and a whipping post, and there are glorious views over Essex meadowland. Post-war expansion has been principally northward, but some residents of

the Hillrise estate to the south consider their community to be part of Havering.

✉ Romford RM4

📖 Marjorie K McIntosh, *A Community Transformed: The Manor and Liberty of Havering-atte-Bower 1500–1620*, Cambridge University Press, 2002; Winifred Brazier, *A Childhood in Havering-atte-Bower*, Ian Henry, 1981

Havering Park • *Havering*

An interwar development constituting the north-western part of the Collier Row district. The name is not in widespread use, although it is a bus destination and the council has recently designated it a ward. The royal hunting lodge at Havering possessed a wooded estate that encompassed all the land and buildings between present-day HAVERING-ATTE-BOWER and COLLIER ROW. The park was divided into farms in the 1650s, after monarchs had ceased to use the house. Late in the 18th century Havering Park Farm became one of the progressive farms for which the area was noted, pioneering advanced agricultural methods. The park was also the site of Hampden House, a mansion occupied by a succession of London businessmen and merchants during the 19th century. Following the creation of the Eastern Avenue (A12) in the mid 1920s, a variety of property developers piled into the area. The largest of these was T F Nash, who bought a large chunk of land north of Collier Row Road for a planned estate of 9,000 homes. Nash himself lived for a while at Hampden House and his firm laid on its own bus service for the estate's residents. By 1939, 2,000 houses had been completed. Building continued into the war, until work was suddenly halted. After the war green-belt legislation prevented the estate from spreading further into the countryside. Many of its more dreary properties have subsequently been disguised with a variety of cladding materials. In the Havering Park ward, 97 per cent of the residents are white and only a quarter of 1 per cent were born outside the EU – the lowest proportion in London. Only 8.4 per cent of those aged 16 to 74 are qualified to degree level or higher. More than a third of households contain dependent children.

Havering Country Park, which lies between the estate and the village of Havering-atte-Bower, has mature woodland, ponds, hay meadows and two grassland conservation areas.

✉ Romford RM5

👤 12,366

Havering Riverside • *Havering*

A new name for the Thames marshland of SOUTH HORNCHURCH, RAINHAM and WENNINGTON. The mudflats were used for grazing sheep from the Middle Ages and parts came under the plough as drainage was steadily improved. Vegetables were grown for the London market, especially with the coming of faster communications in the 19th century. The farms were noted for their asparagus, and for dairy cattle and pedigree Essex pigs. Gravel was extracted from other parts of the marshland and replaced by silt dredged from the Thames. Later in the 19th century industries were established along parts of the riverside, and many of these continue to operate, especially at remote COLDHARBOUR and on either side of Rainham Creek, while a large swathe of land east of the creek and stretching into Essex has been preserved by the Royal Society for the Protection of Birds as the RAINHAM MARSHES Nature Reserve. Brownfield sites are likely to be redeveloped over the next two decades as part of the borough's role in the THAMES GATEWAY regeneration scheme.

✉ Rainham RM13

Haverstock Hill • *Camden* (pronounced 'havvəstok')

A former artists' retreat, now a stretch of the A502 linking CHALK FARM with BELSIZE PARK. First recorded in Rocque's map of 1745, the name probably refers to a place where oats were grown and seems to have originally designated the whole slope rather than the road itself, which was then called Hampstead Road or London Road. Until the building of an orphanage, almshouses and a church in the mid 19th century, the hamlet of Haverstock Hill consisted of just the Load of Hay tavern (rebuilt in 1863) and a few cottages lying below the corner of England's Lane. An early resident was the writer Richard Steele, co-founder of both *Tatler* and *The Spectator*. Artists' studios replaced the cottages in 1872. The various estates bordering Haverstock Hill were sold off for development in the latter part of the 19th century, and a vestry hall built in 1878 was later extended to become HAMPSTEAD Town Hall. Belsize Park Tube station opened in 1907. Phases of infilling and rebuilding have since wrought significant changes, notably in the 1930s and 1970s. The amenities of the upper section of Haverstock

Hill are popular with the residents of Belsize Park, especially the Screen on the Hill cinema and the events and projects at the old town hall. In common with much of Camden, more than half the residents of the Haverstock ward are single, and almost 5 per cent are of white Irish descent.

George Clausen's *A Spring Morning, Haverstock Hill* (1881) is considered a definitive image of Victorian Britain. The painting hangs in Bury's municipal art gallery.

> ✉ NW3

> ♦ 11,224 (Haverstock ward)

> 🚇 Northern Line (Belsize Park, zone 2)

Hawley's Corner • *Bromley*

The southernmost distinct settlement in Greater London, situated at the junction of five roads, south of WESTERHAM HILL. A Christian mission was initiated in 1877 in a cottage at Hawley's Corner by Miss Thorneycroft, the daughter of a local farmer. After the Thorneycrofts moved away and the lease expired, a new chapel was established in nearby South Street. The former tearooms at the corner of Grays Road have been extended to become the Spinning Wheel pub and restaurant, while a tiny thatched cottage provides accommodation for the manager. The south-western quarter of Hawley's Corner, which includes Westerham Heights Nurseries, was transferred to the care of Sevenoaks district council in 1993.

> ✉ Westerham TN16

Haydons Road • *Merton*

The southernmost section of the A218, which runs from WANDSWORTH to MERTON, west of the River Wandle. The Haydon family had been living in Merton for over 200 years when George Haydon acquired Cowdrey's Farm in 1746. The site of the farmhouse is now marked by Cowdrey Road. The track that led to the farm from Merton High Street had been called Cowdrey Lane, but soon became known as Haydons Lane. In the 1840s Plough Lane branched eastwards off the northern end of Haydons Lane, in the direction of the Plough Inn, which lay across the Wandle. The arrival of the railway in the 1850s brought early suburban development as part of what was initially called New Wimbledon and later SOUTH WIMBLEDON. The Church of England established a mission in a small room off Haydons Lane in 1859. Around 1870 the lane was renamed Haydons Road. The sale of Cowdrey's Farm released 340 acres for building and a variety of investors descended on the site. The National Freehold Land Society laid out respectable streets of working-class housing but other projects were of inferior quality, and there were problems with overcrowding and poor sanitation. The locality was described as 'the poorest in the district' in the late 19th century. Just before World War I, Wimbledon Football Club built itself a new ground on a former refuse dump at the corner of Plough Lane. The club decamped to Crystal Palace in 1991 and then to Milton Keynes in 2003 (changing its name to Milton Keynes Dons) and the site is currently being developed with 570 flats, retail and business units and a surgery. Although the main streetscape of Haydons Road now presents a messy appearance, much of the housing in its hinterland is pleasant, including some new properties behind the station. The recent opening of an upmarket health club located off North Road is an indication of the area's changing profile.

Two women and a man who masterminded a million-pound prostitution ring in the area were jailed in 2003. The team brought unsuspecting Thai women to the UK and set up a brothel at 261A Haydons Road as a 'training centre' for them. The women were then sent to work in other brothels, or were 'sold on' to new 'owners'.

> ✉ SW19

> 🚆 Thameslink (zone 3)

Hayes • *Bromley*

An elongated suburb extending almost a mile-and-a-half southwards from BROMLEY. First mentioned in 1177, the name probably meant 'rough ground covered with brushwood'. Hayes Place was in existence by the 15th century and was rebuilt in the 1750s. By the time the railway arrived in 1882, Hayes was a flourishing village of around 600, but prospective commuters were deterred until the line was electrified in 1925, almost halving the journey time to CHARING CROSS. Ribbon development had already begun to creep along Hayes Road from Bromley when the banker Eric Hambro sold Hayes Place. Sheffield builder Henry Boot demolished the house in 1933 and laid out the Hayes Place estate. Several local firms put up more estates, including Hayes Hill, Pickhurst Manor, and Hayes Gardens. To cope with the increase in commuter traffic the station was rebuilt in 1935, and Station Approach became the main shopping area. After World War II, two major developments filled in the land between Bromley and Hayes. Bromley council laid out its own Hayes Place estate in the 1950s, with local shops on Chilham Way. Further north, the Building Design Partnership completed Hayesford Park in 1965, on the site of Hayes Food Farm. Influenced by the garden city movement, Hayesford Park mixes detached houses, bungalows, terraced houses and long blocks of flats, arranged round central shops that have since suffered from their proximity to Bromley. Hayes is blessed with two broad open spaces. On the south side, Hayes Common is one of the largest areas of unimproved acidic grassland in London, dotted with impressive older houses. To the north-east, Norman Park has extensive sporting facilities, including Bromley Football Club's ground and the home track of BLACKHEATH and Bromley Harriers Athletics Club. Like much of the borough, Hayes is comfortable, but not wealthy, suburbia. Almost 60 per cent of adult residents are married, 90 per cent are owner-occupiers and 96 per cent are white.

From 1754 until 1785, Hayes Place was a country seat of the Pitt family, leading figures of British imperial statesmanship. William Pitt the Younger, prime minister 1783–1801 and 1804–6, was born at the house in 1759. His father, William Pitt the Elder, the first Earl of Chatham and prime minister 1766–8, died here in 1778.

> ✉ Bromley BR2
>
> 👥 14,923 (Hayes and Coney Hall ward)
>
> 🚇 South Eastern Trains (zone 5)
>
> 📖 M Scott, *Bromley, Keston and Hayes*, Sutton, 1993; H P Thompson, *A History of Hayes in the County of Kent*, Jackdaw, 1978
>
> @ www.ideal-homes.org.uk/bromley/hayes.htm (London surburban history site)

Hayes • *Hillingdon*

A 20th-century agglomeration (and obliteration) of former medieval hamlets, centred two miles west of SOUTHALL, from which it is separated by the River Crane and the Paddington branch of the Grand Union Canal. The name has the same derivation as HAYES in Bromley and was first mentioned in the eighth century, when land here was granted to the archbishops of Canterbury. The archbishops subsequently extended their control of the area, and by the time of Domesday Book had become the sole landowner. The oldest building in the district is St Mary's Church, which may be of twelfth-century origin, but was rebuilt and extended during the next four centuries. Although lying close to the geographical centre of the ancient parish, the church does not seem to have been the focus of early settlement, which was instead spread loosely around the hamlets of WOOD END, BOTWELL, YEADING and HAYES END. HAYES TOWN (originally known as Cotman's Town) came later. Wood End was the largest of the hamlets by the late 16th century. The earliest recorded inn was the Adam and Eve, in 1665. When John Rocque mapped the area in 1754, a continuous ribbon of housing had evolved, running from the church through Wood End to Hayes End. The construction in 1796 of the Grand Junction (now Grand Union) Canal in the southwest of the parish altered the pattern of development. Brickfields, docks and cottages were established in the Botwell area and commercial activity increased after the coming of the railway in 1838, and especially after the opening of Hayes and HARLINGTON station in 1864. During the first half of the 20th century, Hayes became one of west London's prime industrial locations, and rows of terraced houses were built for the factory workers. Growth was especially rapid between the wars, when private and municipal estates filled most of the former farmland. Botwell became the main shopping area, but lost its identity within Hayes Town. Where it could find the space, the council added more housing after World War II, primarily in the vicinity of Yeading. Offices were built from the 1960s, including the headquarters of the now defunct Safeway supermarket group. The southern part of Wood End was the least spoilt, with public amenities taking the place of large private houses. Following a period of decline, future redevelopment is focused on mixed-use projects on the disused industrial sites in the south, and there are plans for the Heathrow Express to stop at Hayes and Harlington station. Demographic characteristics vary across the area, but in all wards except Charville (which borders HILLINGDON) most people are classified in the C2DE socio-economic groups. A significant minority of residents, particularly in the eastern half of the district, is of Indian origin.

The writer George Orwell, who lived and taught here in 1932 and 1933, described Hayes as 'one of the most godforsaken places I have ever struck'.

> ✉ Hayes UB3 and UB4

👥 59,561 (Barnhill, Botwell, Charville, Pinkwell and Townfield wards)

🚉 First Great Western Link; Heathrow Connect (Hayes and Harlington, zone 5)

📖 Catherine Kelter, *Hayes Past*, Historical Publications, 1996

@ hayes.middx.net (commercial community site)

Hayes End • *Hillingdon*

A residential and commercial corner of HAYES, located just over a mile west and slightly north of St Mary's Church. In the late Middle Ages, much of the parish of Hayes consisted of a string of cottages running towards HILLINGDON, and Hayes End was the cluster of homes at its outermost point. The hamlet was first mentioned by name in 1571 but is almost certain to have been in existence considerably earlier. By the end of the 16th century there were 22 dwellings in Hayes End, of which only seven were cottages, surrounded by more than 203 acres of enclosed land. Many 18th-century thatched tenements survived until the 1920s, after which the locality was extensively developed. A few older farm buildings remain, as do several 19th-century cottages and villas. Commercially, Hayes End is dominated by the Hayes Park office campus, constructed as the European headquarters for H J Heinz in the early 1960s. It has recently been radically redeveloped, although several of the original buildings have been retained. After a brief sojourn at STOCKLEY PARK, Heinz returned here in 2001.

✉ Hayes UB4

Hayes Town • *Hillingdon*

The name now given to the commercial core of the district – as opposed to Hayes Village, which is another name for the WOOD END locality. Hayes Town developed later than the outlying hamlets of the parish. There were twelve dwellings here in 1598, including St Mary's Vicarage, when the place was called Cotman's Town. Hayes Town was first mentioned in 1817, and the name of Cotman's Town slowly faded from use over the following 100 years. The streetscape of Hayes Town is very much a 20th-century creation, the result of the southward expansion of the parent district towards its railway station. This process has consumed the former hamlet of BOTWELL, which might have provided a more distinctive name for the area. The factories and offices of Hayes are close to the Grand Union Canal,

while the shopping centre is on Station Road and Coldharbour Lane, part of which was pedestrianized following the opening of the Hayes bypass (the Parkway) in 1992. The Hayes Town Partnership was established in 2002 to co-ordinate efforts to improve the lacklustre town centre and redevelop disused industrial sites. Recent developments have ranged from improvements in street furniture to the conversion of a postal sorting office into a health centre.

✉ Hayes UB3

👥 24,058 (Townfield and Botwell wards)

@ www.hayestowncentre.org.uk (Hayes Town Partnership site)

Hazelwood • *Bromley*

A northern satellite of CUDHAM, located halfway along the lane to GREEN STREET GREEN. The name is also spelt as two separate words. By London standards, this is a very isolated community, mainly consisting of bungalows built along a handful of private roads. The one-acre coppiced wood that gives the locality its name is situated just to the south-west. Although small, its chalk grassland is rich in ground flora, including toothwort and spurge-laurel. Amateur astronomers have begun to set up their telescopes at Hazelwood because it has one of the lowest levels of light pollution in the London area.

✉ Sevenoaks TN14

Headstone • *Harrow*

The northern part of HARROW, bordering PINNER to the west, graced by the only surviving example of a medieval aisled hall in outer London. The settlement was Hegeton in the early 14th century, probably 'the farmstead enclosed by a hedge'. A moated manor house was built in the 1310s and in 1397 this became the principal Middlesex residence of the archbishops of Canterbury. A great barn was built in 1506 for the manor farm. The estate was confiscated by the Crown in 1546, and sold on within a week. The house was remodelled in the 1630s, given an extra wing in the 1650s and further altered in 1762. However, it was subsequently used simply as a farmhouse and was allowed to deteriorate. Suburban development began to spread towards Headstone from WEALDSTONE in the 1880s, although a racecourse continued to operate until 1899, when it was suppressed after a riot started by Londoners. St George's Church, Headstone was consecrated in 1911 and Headstone Lane station opened in 1913. After World War I, private builders filled most of central Headstone's surviving gaps but the council (then Hendon rural district council) saved Headstone Manor and 63 acres of its grounds. Harrow council restored the great barn in 1973 and opened it as the borough's heritage museum, with an especially strong collection of ceramics and glass. After lying derelict for 20 years, the manor house is being restored. Since 2005 the house has been open to guided tours, while efforts are made to secure the funding needed to complete the restoration programme. Headstone is a relatively affluent place, particularly the Headstone North ward. The principal ethnic minority is of Indian descent, primarily of the Hindu religion.

> ✉ Harrow HA2
>
> ♦ 18,888 (Headstone North and Headstone South wards)
>
> 🚍 Silverlink Metro (Headstone Lane, zone 5)
>
> @ www.harrowarts.com/museum

Heart of London • *Westminster*
A business improvement district (BID) set up by the Piccadilly Circus Partnership to promote, prettify and protect the central WEST END. The zone is defined as 'circus to square' – that is, from PICCADILLY CIRCUS to LEICESTER SQUARE – and also includes the south-western end of SHAFTESBURY AVENUE and the northern part of Haymarket. Funded primarily by a levy on local businesses, the Heart of London Business Alliance aims to improve the area's streetscape and enhance its status as a 'world-class destination'. Among the project's initiatives are the appointment of 'guardians' to patrol the zone and the establishment of a police kiosk in Piccadilly Circus, which has proved popular as an information resource. A website features shopping, entertainment, dining and hotels. The BID was launched in February 2005 to run for two years, but the partnership is 'very confident' of obtaining support for a five-year extension from 2007. This is the most visible of five such schemes led by the London Development Agency and the Central London Partnership. The other four districts involved are BANKSIDE, HOLBORN, PADDINGTON and WATERLOO.

> ✉ W1; WC2; SW1
>
> @ www.heartoflondon.info

Heath Park • *Havering*
An Edwardian estate situated on the east side of ROMFORD, south of GIDEA PARK. Like nearby SQUIRREL'S HEATH, its name recalls the former heathland here. From the late Middle Ages this was the south-eastern corner of the manor of Stewards, which covered a swathe of land to the east of Romford. The Eastern Counties Railway cut the manor in half in the 1840s and the area nearest to Romford was sold and developed on both sides of the line during the second half of the 19th century. The Heath Park estate was laid out in the early years of the 20th century in a scheme that marked the expansion of Romford towards and beyond the railway line to UPMINSTER. Many of the properties were bay-fronted and generously proportioned, especially on Heath Park Road, and possessed fairly large gardens, although infilling has subsequently encroached on some of these. Heath Park School was established in 1906 and merged with Romford County High School in the early 1970s to form the Frances Bardsley School. In 2003 the lower school site, in Heath Park Road, was sold to developer Crest Nicholson for an upmarket housing development. The sale raised £7.5 million, which has been ploughed back into improvements and extensions to the upper school buildings on Brentwood Road.

This Heath Park should not be confused with Dagenham council's estate of the same name, built to the east of BECONTREE in the 1950s.

> ✉ Romford RM2 and RM1; Hornchurch RM11

Heathrow • *Hillingdon*
The world's busiest international airport, situated on the western edge of Greater London, south of the intersection of the M4 and M25 motorways. Although Heathrow made a relatively late appearance as a hamlet on the edge of HOUNSLOW HEATH – its presence was not recorded until 1453 – the area was rich in archaeological treasures, with evidence of Bronze Age farming and the only Iron Age temple colonnade in England. Aviation began here in 1930 and the government requisitioned the site as a bomber airfield shortly before the end of World War II. This seems to have been a ploy to sidestep public objections to Heathrow's intended commercial use when the war was over. Construction of the airport obliterated the hamlets of Heathrow, Perry Oaks and King's Arbour, together with the prehistoric sites. The first departure, in January 1946, was a British South American Airways flight for Buenos Aires. The terminal buildings at the centre of the airport site were

constructed between 1955 and 1968, when a 160-acre cargo site was added to the south, with a linking tunnel. The cargo area has often been the target of thieves and London's biggest ever robbery took place here in 1983, when £26 million worth of gold bullion and diamonds were stolen from the Brinks-Mat high security vault; most of the gold was never recovered. Terminal 4 was completed in 1986 and a fifth is under construction and due for completion in 2011. Controversial proposals to build a third runway were the subject of protracted consultation at the time of writing. Heathrow handles more than 67 million passengers and 1.3 million tonnes of freight every year. Within the airport perimeter, 68,000 people are employed and many firms in the surrounding localities depend on the airport for their existence. Recent transport improvements have included the Heathrow Express link to PADDINGTON, the Heathrow-FELTHAM Railair service and Heathrow Connect, a joint venture between BAA plc and First Great Western. Heathrow's central bus and coach station is the busiest in the UK. Based on Newall Road, the Heathrow airport visitor centre offers interactive exhibitions and views over the runway.

Heathrow has a held a long-running fascination for the author J G Ballard. Much of the action in his early shocker *Crash* (1973) took place on the highways and sliproads surrounding the airport, while 2003's *Millennium People* kicks off with a terrorist bomb attack here.

⊠ Hounslow TW6

ⵜ 10,217 (Heathrow Villages ward; includes Harlington, Harmondsworth, Longford and Sipson)

🚌 Heathrow Connect (Heathrow Central); Heathrow Express; Piccadilly Line (Terminals 1, 2 and 3; Terminal 4, zone 6)

📖 Philip Sherwood, *Around Heathrow: Past and Present*, Sutton, 2006

@ www.heathrowairport.com

Heaton Grange • *Havering*

A western extension of HAROLD HILL, located north of GALLOWS CORNER, and named after John Heaton. Born in 1740, Heaton was a City lawyer and auditor with offices in Old Burlington Street. In 1771 Heaton acquired the manor of Bedfords, near HAVERING-ATTE-BOWER, where he established his country seat. When Romford (Harold's Wood) Common was enclosed in 1814, Heaton paid £2,300 for five lots totalling 35 acres, but was awarded considerably more territory than he had actually paid for. He used the land to set up a model farm of 188 acres, which he called Heaton Grange. Heaton died at Bedfords four years later but contemporary accounts indicate that the farm was a success, and the ground was transformed into some of the most productive in the county. Romford council bought Heaton Grange in the 1950s and built an estate here. Its name is popular with local estate agents, who have been working to distinguish Heaton Grange from the rest of Harold Hill. Hilldene Primary School, on Grange Road, is a large and well-liked community school, but with a high level of pupil mobility.

⊠ Romford RM3

ⵜ 11,778 (Heaton ward, which includes part of Harold Hill)

Hendon • *Barnet*

A socially graduated residential district situated three miles north-west of HAMPSTEAD. Excavations in 1974 revealed Roman remains from c.AD 300 but Hendon's name (which means 'at the high down') was first recorded in 959, when it was a hamlet on the brow of Greyhound Hill. The ancient manor and parish of Hendon covered over 8,000 acres, mainly woodland that thrived on the heavy soil, with small settlements in the clearings. The manor belonged to Westminster Abbey from the 10th to the 16th century and, as the forest was cut down, haymaking became the chief activity. The farmhouse at Church Farm was built around 1660 and is now a borough museum. During the 18th century, Brent Street acquired several grand houses, along with the Bell Inn and a cluster of shops around the junction with Bell Lane. Hendon railway station was originally called WEST HENDON when it opened in 1868. Modern Hendon took form during the late 19th century as the hamlets around the station, Brent Street and Church End began to coalesce. A distinct social polarity emerged between the wealthy villas in the Parson Street and Sunny Gardens area and the working-class terraced houses further down the hill. By the 1890s Brent Street had become Hendon's main shopping centre. Hendon Central station opened when the underground extension to EDGWARE was completed in 1923. Shortly afterwards came the construction of the arterial roads that crisscross the district, bringing industry and new housing, especially along the North Circular

(A406). In 1931 Hendon was Britain's most populous urban district. The Hendon Technical Institute was established in 1939 and is now part of Middlesex University. During the late 1950s and early 1960s the council pulled down and rebuilt much of the housing stock, preserving the social gradient that begins in the disadvantaged lowlands of West Hendon and rises to the comfortable undulations of HOLDERS HILL. Thirty per cent of the residents of the Hendon ward are Jewish.

Hendon's greatest claims to fame are both located on the COLINDALE side of the M1: the Hendon Police College has been training London's cadets since 1935, while what remains of Hendon aerodrome now houses the RAF Museum.

✉ NW4

♦ 15,377 (ward)

🚆 Thameslink (Hendon, zones 3 and 4); Northern Line (Hendon Central, zones 3 and 4)

📖 Hugh Petrie, *Hendon and Golders Green Past*, Historical Publications, 2005

@ www.hadas.org.uk (Hendon and District Archaeological Society site)

Herne Hill • *Lambeth/Southwark*

Young professionals' territory, situated between BRIXTON and DULWICH. The area was part of the medieval manor of Milkwell, and one of its earliest buildings was the Half Moon Inn, which stood at the crossroads. The first mention of Herne Hill came in 1789; the name may derive from a prominent Dulwich family or it may mean 'hill by a nook of land'. Protective landowners restricted development here to a few homes for the wealthy and early in the late 18th century the hill was dotted with grand houses in a largely rural setting. Among the most impressive was Casino House, which had 15 acres of grounds landscaped by Humphry Repton. From the second half of the 19th century speculative developers moved into the area as leases on old properties came to an end. In an early scheme, the streets between Railton Road and Dulwich Road, now known as Poets' Corner, were laid out on the eastern half of Effra Farm by the Westminster Freehold Co. in 1855. Rapid change began with the opening in 1862 of Herne Hill station on the London, Chatham and Dover railway line, which also encouraged development in the vicinity of TULSE HILL. The line originally ran to ELEPHANT AND CASTLE and was extended to reach Holborn Viaduct in 1886. The Suburban Village and General Dwellings Co. put up terraced houses in Milkwood Road, Lowden Road and adjacent streets. By the early 20th century most of the large houses had been replaced by further terraces, with shopping parades along the main thoroughfares. The now-demolished Grand cinema opened opposite the station in 1914. After World War I, CAMBERWELL council bought the grounds of Casino House, which had been demolished earlier in the century, and laid out the Sunray estate of 'homes fit for heroes'. The estate was a model of building efficiency and architectural quality and is now designated an 'area of special character', with a remnant of Repton's landscaping forming Sunray Gardens. To the west, the Dorchester Court estate was built in 1936, in place of several Victorian villas. Following a period of decline, many of Herne Hill's houses have been restored and some subdivided properties have been reunified. The majority of residents in Lambeth's Herne Hill ward live in rented accommodation and the proportion of unmarried adults is almost twice the national average.

Herne Hill velodrome on Burbage Road has been dedicated to track cycling, with associated recreational uses, since 1891. There had recently been hopes of a major programme of upgrading but the necessary funds could not be raised and the velodrome closed in January 2005 after Southwark council pulled the plug on its funding. The track reopened in August 2005 when owners Dulwich College Estates agreed a three-year lease with British Cycling, but its long-term future remains uncertain.

✉ SE24

♦ 11,805 (Lambeth's Herne Hill ward)

🚆 Southern; Thameslink (zones 2 and 3)

📖 Patricia M Jenkyns, *The Book of Herne Hill*, Halsgrove, 2003; Don Bianco, *Herne Hill Heritage Trail*, Herne Hill Society, 2003

@ www.rich13.co.uk/hhs (Herne Hill Society site)

Heron Quays • *Tower Hamlets*

CANARY WHARF's little sister, originally an eight-acre quay but now extended by a further three acres to connect with Canary Wharf at its eastern end. Narrower than the other quays of the West India Docks, it formerly separated the Export and South Docks and was mostly occupied by offices and stores rather than warehouses. There was a *herring* shed on the quayside from around 1840, but never any trade in herons or with a place of that name. In an early chapter of Docklands redevelopment, Tarmac Properties drew up plans in 1981 for a mixed-use scheme that would cover the whole Heron Quays site, but only the first two phases were completed. These were high-tech cabins with monopitch aluminium-clad roofs and colourful enamel panelling. Although generally well-received, the buildings were not of the scale and grandeur of neighbouring developments. Despite proposals to build an apartment complex, the rest of the quay remained empty for more than a decade, mainly owing to uncertainty in the property market. In 2001 the Canary Wharf Group bought the site from Tarmac and began work on the HQ project, also known as Canary Wharf South. The scheme consists of five office blocks, of which the three tallest are around 500 feet high. Tenants include financial and legal companies, such as Morgan Stanley, Lehman Brothers and Clifford Chance. Heron Quays station has been rebuilt beneath the HQ2 podium, with a subway link to the Jubilee Line station via a new shopping centre called Jubilee Place.

To prove the viability of the proposed City Airport, Captain Harry Gee landed a Brymon Dash 7 on the quay in June 1982. Heron Quays roundabout has Pierre Vivant's *Traffic Light Tree*, a sculpture created from 75 working traffic signal heads.

✉ E14

🚊 Docklands Light Railway, Lewisham branch (zone 2)

Heston · *Hounslow*

A multicultural and multi-use district lying west of OSTERLEY Park and north of HOUNSLOW, between the M4 and the Great West Road (A4), and best-known for the motorway service station of the same name. Heston lies on what was once the heathland separating the great forest of north Middlesex and the marshes bordering the Thames. The name is probably of Saxon origin, meaning a settlement among the 'hese' or brushwood. It became a separate parish from ISLEWORTH in the 13th century and there followed a continuing rivalry between the two. Heston remained a small agricultural village for several centuries, renowned for the quality of its wheat. Although the enclosure of the heathland after 1813 brought some growth, rapid expansion did not occur until the inter-war years of the 20th century. On the western edge of the lo-cality, Heston Airport was operational from 1929 to 1946 and streets that have since been built here have names that commemorate famous aviators. It was at Heston in 1938 that prime minister Neville Chamberlain landed after signing the Munich Agreement with Adolf Hitler and gave his infamous 'peace in our time' speech. Commercial and light industrial development followed the creation of HEATHROW Airport in 1946. The airport provides employment for many of the district's inhabitants but also causes misery from aircraft noise and vortex strikes. Heston has proved a popular choice of residence with newly arrived immigrants from south Asia and many of its residents are of Indian origin. Sikhs, Muslims and Hindus are all well-represented.

Oliver Cromwell's daughter Elizabeth was a Heston resident. Jimmy Page, guitarist with the rock group Led Zeppelin, was born here in 1944.

✉ Hounslow TW5

👥 33,111 (Heston Central, Heston East and Heston West wards)

📖 Gillian M Morris and Andrea Cameron, *Hounslow As It Was: A Selection of Photographs with Captions of Hounslow, Cranford, Heston and Isleworth*, Hendon, 1977

Higham Hill · *Waltham Forest*

The disadvantaged north-western part of WALTHAMSTOW. Saxons made a clearing in the forest here and the manor of Higham is recorded in Domesday Book. The original Higham House was located here, near present-day Sutton Road. The house was subsequently rebuilt in the far east of the manor, facing WOODFORD GREEN. The manor went through several subdivisions and reunifications and this part was later called Higham Benstead. It was in the hands of the Heron family for many years but was at one point seized by the crown because of a marriage to the daughter of the 'traitorous' Sir Thomas More. The hill itself was common land with grazing rights permitted to local parishioners. A bridge across the River Lea was said to have been in existence in 1594, when a moderately large hamlet had evolved. The population then went into a decline until the enclosure of the common in 1850, which led to some tentative suburban development in the 1870s. By the end of the 19th century parts of Higham Hill had been densely built up, and some of the housing became overcrowded. Walthamstow council began the first of its many slum clearance and rebuilding projects here after World War I, in Millfield Avenue. Among the other schemes were the Higham Hill estate of 1920 and Priory Court, begun in 1946. Successive phases of redevelopment brought tower blocks in the 1960s and 1970s and large sums have been spent on neighbourhood renewal programmes in recent years. Unemployment levels are relatively high, while the largest proportion of men and women work in wholesale, retail and car repair activities. Around half of residents rent their homes, most from the council. Islam is the second most predominant faith after Christianity.

Higham Hill was the focus of an experiment in popular democracy in 2003 when the council set up electronic voting to decide spending plans for £200,000 worth of community funding, with results beamed onto a large video screen.

✉ E17

♁ 11,161

Highams Park • Waltham Forest

A residential district, public park and industrial estate situated south of CHINGFORD HATCH. The stuccoed manor house of Highams lies to the east, facing WOODFORD GREEN. Built in 1768 for Anthony Bacon MP, the house was next occupied by a former governor of Bombay. Highams' third owner, John Harman, called in Humphry Repton to landscape the grounds, and Harman's son Jeremiah sold the estate to Edward Warner in 1849. The Warners were a prominent family in the area and prime minister William Gladstone was among their guests here. When the station opened in 1873 (originally as Hale End) the family began to develop the grounds, making this one of the first parts of the wider district to be built up. The houses were generally more substantial than the family's projects further southwest in WALTHAMSTOW. The Corporation of London acquired 30 acres of Highams' grounds in 1891 to preserve them as part of Epping Forest. The station was rebuilt in 1900 and Highams Park continued to grow during the early decades of the 20th century, gaining factories, schools, churches and some Arts and Crafts amenity buildings. The Electric cinema was built in 1911 and was joined in 1935 by the Regal, which is now a snooker hall. Also in the 1930s, Essex county council built Highams Park Secondary School and Walthamstow council created the Highams Park, retaining Repton's landscaping in the vicinity of the six-acre lake, which has fishing

for carp, pike and tench. Considering that it not on a main through route and is close to Walthamstow, WOODFORD and CHINGFORD, Highams Park has a surprisingly large shopping centre around the station.

Extended boy band Blazin' Squad first came together at the end of the 1990s at Highams Park School.

✉ E4; Woodford Green IG8

♁ 10,075 (Hale End and Highams Park ward)

🚆 'one' Railway (zone 4)

High Barnet • Barnet

Modern maps usually treat High Barnet as the area north of Wood Street, and Chipping Barnet as the part to the south and south-east, but history does not recognize this distinction and nor does the local population. High Barnet made its first appearance as an alternative name for Chipping Barnet, or indeed for plain Barnet, in the late 16th century. Rising to 425 feet above sea level, Barnet does occupy an elevated position by London standards and it was popularly said to be the highest spot on the Great North Road (the former A1) between London and York. Another claim that there is no higher point along a direct line east to Russia's Ural mountains is not true. The High Barnet name failed to catch on until adopted by the Great Northern Railway Co. for the station it opened here in 1872. The company may have liked its superior sound or sought to imply that their service scaled Barnet's slopes further than it actually did. The name was retained when the station joined the underground network in 1940 and was consequently used to identify the newly suburbanized town, which some distinguished from the parish of Chipping Barnet. The council has been leading a revival of the older name but few residents bother with either prefix. See also CHIPPING BARNET.

✉ Barnet EN5

♁ 13,847

🚆 Northern Line, High Barnet branch terminus (zone 5)

Highbury • Islington

Famous as the former home of ARSENAL Football Club, Highbury is an elongated settlement in north ISLINGTON, between CANONBURY and FINSBURY PARK. In the 13th century the farms and woodland here came into the possession of the Knights Hospitallers, a military monastic order. The woods were mostly cleared during the 17th century, by which time the area had become known by its present name because of its relatively elevated position. In 1740 a tea and ale house opened at Highbury Barn; Oliver Goldsmith later wrote of the pleasant time he had spent here. In 1770, John Dawes, a stockbroker, began to acquire land, building a Highbury House for himself and granting building leases for the first suburban houses. Dawes died in 1788 and his son sold off most of the estate for further building. Before the century was out Highbury Fields were encircled by imposing terraces of houses. In the 1820s, Thomas Cubitt built Highbury Park, setting up his own brickfields nearby. Thirty years later Henry Rydon added Highbury New Park. Other developers constructed rows of villas in the 1860s and 1870s – again using the term 'park' to convey an impression of quasi-rural grandeur. This growth led to the opening of Highbury railway station in 1872, when it looked much more imposing than it does now. Highbury Fields were saved for the public in 1885. In the same year the present Highbury Barn opened, replacing the old tavern and pleasure gardens, which had become a scene of disreputable activities. The clock tower at Highbury Quadrant was erected in celebration of Queen Victoria's diamond jubilee in 1897. Arsenal Football Club took over the sports ground of St John's College of Divinity in 1913. Unlike most parts of suburban London, Highbury saw little change between the wars as the area was already fully built up, although a few of the grandest properties were supplanted by more affordable terraced houses and mansion blocks. Bombed sites were filled with new housing after World War II; the largest project was the London County Council's Quadrant estate, with 611 homes. The last of Highbury's handful of manufacturing firms moved out in the early 1960s. Like much of the borough, Highbury has an affluent minority and a less visible, less affluent majority. Young singles make up a high proportion of the adult residents. A number of early villas have survived, most of which have been subdivided.

The singer/songwriter Dido Armstrong comes from Highbury. An American EP issued to promote her first album was entitled *Highbury Fields*.

✉ N5

♦ 21,959 (Highbury East and Highbury West wards)

🚇 Silverlink Metro; WAGN Railway (zone 2); Victoria Line (Highbury and Islington, zone 2)

📖 Keith Sugden, *History of Highbury*, Islington Archaeology and History Society, 1984

Highbury Vale • *Islington*

Nowadays an estate agents' name for the area where Blackstock Road and Highbury Park meet, to the south of FINSBURY PARK. It has been suggested that this was the site of a Danish settlement, and possibly a battle, in the vicinity of the present Highbury Vale police station. Much of the locality was developed on the former grassland of Cream Hall Farm, which provided milk to north Londoners for around 100 years from the 1780s. Cream Hall itself was a 17th-century villa that stood where Riversdale Road is now. The street named Highbury Vale was laid out in about 1823 but was renumbered as part of Blackstock Road in the 1880s, when a grand shopping parade was built. St John's Church, Highbury Vale (later Highbury Park), was consecrated in 1881 and demolished in 1980. It had been named after the theological college that rented its ground to ARSENAL Football Club when it moved to HIGHBURY from WOOLWICH. St John's Highbury Vale School opened in 1936 and was praised by the educational standards agency Ofsted in 2000 for its high standards. Its pupils are mainly white with an increasing minority of African and Caribbean attendees.

✉ N5

High Elms • *Bromley*

Although the prominent signposting suggests a major settlement, High Elms is not a village but a collection of rural amenities set in almost a thousand acres of parks, woods and agricultural land, south of FARNBOROUGH. The Lubbock family acquired the estate in 1808 and progressively enlarged it, rearing sheep and cattle and growing cereal crops. A new mansion house was built in the 1840s, set in landscaped gardens. Sir John William Lubbock was a mathematician and astronomer who developed a method for calculating the orbits of comets and planets. His son, Sir John Lubbock, who was created the first Baron Avebury in 1900, was also a scientist – but perhaps his greatest claim to fame was to introduce the legislation establishing bank holidays when he was a member of Parliament; a bank holiday was once dubbed 'St Lubbock's Day'. Kent County Council bought High Elms in 1938 and the house was used as a nurses' training centre. High Elms mansion burned down in 1967, ironically on Bank Holiday Monday in August. Much of its estate is now a nature reserve open to the public and managed by Bromley council. Golf has replaced horse racing as the favoured sport and there is a nature centre, an old ice well and an Eton fives court. Although Dutch elm disease and the great storm of 1987 have taken their toll, the park is rich in a variety of trees planted by both the former owners and the Forestry Commission. Except for those living close by, High Elms is an undiscovered asset, ideal for walks and picnics and for encouraging children's appreciation of nature.

✉ Orpington BR6

Highgate • *Camden/Haringey*

A much-extended village standing on high ground north-east of HAMPSTEAD HEATH. Highgate took root around a village green peppered with ponds and elm trees, at the top of a 426-foot hill on the edge of the Bishop of London's estate. It was the bishop who erected a tollgate here sometime before 1354, when Highgate's name was first recorded. Later in the same century Dick Whittington is supposed to have sat upon a milestone on Highgate Hill and, inspired by the distant sound of Bow Bells, turned again to find fame and fortune in London. There are many holes in this story, one being that this is not the route to the Whittington family home in Gloucestershire. Nevertheless, a replica stone marks the alleged spot, surmounted by a 1964 statue of Whittington's cat. From the late 16th century a ribbon of houses began to form along Highgate Hill. The settlement was split down the middle between the parishes of ST PANCRAS and HORNSEY, as it now is between the boroughs of Camden and Haringey. The much-altered Lauderdale House was a home of Charles II's mistress Nell Gwynne. The Flask public house dates from 1663. From the late 17th century to the end of the 18th century Highgate filled with smart houses for City folk. Many of the properties survive, and so does the demographic profile. Highgate did not gain its own parish church until 1832, when St Michael's was built in place of a chapel of ease. Highgate Cemetery opened in 1839 and is now divided into the western (original) cemetery and the eastern (1854), separated by Swains Lane. With its memorials, mausoleums and catacombs, the cemetery is much loved by those of a gothic inclination. Sir Sydney Waterlow, like Dick Whittington a Lord Mayor of London, is commemorated with a statue in the park that he donated in 1889. The neo-Georgian mansion Witanhurst, on West Hill, is said to be the largest private house in London. Built in 1913 for a soap magnate, it recently achieved celebrity as the home for the BBC's *Fame Academy* students and was then put on the market for £32 million. Highgate's most important 20th-century buildings are Highpoint One and Two, designed in the 1930s by Berthold Lubetkin for Sigmund Gestetner, the copier king. Gestetner initiated the modernist project to provide housing for some of his TOTTENHAM HALE workers but, perhaps understandably, changed his mind and sold them privately. Lubetkin himself took a penthouse apartment in Highpoint Two. Highgate station opened in 1941, taking the name earlier used by what is now ARCHWAY station. This and other improvements in transport links contributed to the development of a new district to the north and east of the village that traded on the Highgate name.

The graves at Highgate Cemetery include those of William Foyle, founder of the bookshop bearing his name, Michael Faraday, Mary Ann Evans (George Eliot) and, most famous of all, Karl Marx. Funerals still take place and more recent interments include Sir Ralph Richardson, Sir Michael Redgrave, and Dr Y D Dadoo, first chairman of the African National Congress. A plaque on the wall of Waterlow Park marks the site of the poet Andrew Marvell's house. Another poet, A E Housman, lived on North Road and wrote *A Shropshire Lad* there. To have been 'sworn in at Highgate' was late 18th-century slang for being sharp or clever. 'Highgate resin' is another name for copalite, the ochre-coloured ancient fossil resin found in the London clay of Highgate Hill.

✉ N6

👥 20,802 (Camden and Haringey's Highgate wards)

🚇 Northern Line (zone 3)

📖 John Richardson, *Highgate Past*, Historical Publications, 1989

@ www.hamhigh.co.uk (*Ham & High* newspaper site)

Highlands Village • *Enfield*

A mid-market 'executive estate', mostly built by Barratt in the late 1990s, located between OAKWOOD and GRANGE PARK. Residents prefer to consider this the north-west corner of WINCHMORE HILL. In 1883 the Metropolitan

Asylum Board acquired 36 acres of the Chaseville estate and took advantage of the remote setting to erect a hospital for patients with contagious diseases. Originally called the Northern Hospital, but known locally as the pest-house, it was arranged in a street of pavilions winding around a central administration block. The neighbouring Enfield Isolation Hospital opened in 1900. In 1948, when the National Health Service was created, the Northern became a district general hospital and was renamed Highlands to avoid confusion with the Royal Northern Hospital, with which it had been grouped in the NHS organization; Enfield Isolation Hospital became South Lodge. Following the closure of the hospitals, the main Highlands block was demolished in 1997 and the surviving buildings, in red and yellow brick Queen Anne style, have been converted into apartment blocks as the centrepiece of a new 'village'. Around these lie a series of short cul-de-sacs of sympathetically styled houses. Pennington Drive, the development's main thoroughfare, is named after N G Pennington, the hospital's leading architect. Amenities include a community centre, nursery and surgery. A Sainsbury's superstore has replaced South Lodge. Blake Court is a 'very sheltered' private housing scheme for older people. At 41.3 years, the mean age of Highlands' residents is significantly older than the national and borough averages. Situated across WORLD'S END Lane from the village, Highlands School was the first new secondary school in the country to be built entirely through the private finance initiative. The school was opened in 2001 by the prime minister Tony Blair.

Highlands Hospital did important work with victims of encephalitis lethargica, a form of sleeping sickness portrayed in the 1990 movie *Awakenings*, which was based on a true story. Actor Robert de Niro visited the hospital as part of preparations for his much-praised role in the film.

✉ N21

👤 12,305 (Highlands ward)

High Street Kensington *see* KENSINGTON HIGH STREET

Highwood Hill • *Barnet*
The classy northern corner of MILL HILL, with a wealth of historic buildings, formerly known simply as Highwood. It was first identified separately from its parent manor of Hendon in the 14th century and was a fashionable country retreat during the 17th and 18th centuries. The diarist and traveller Celia Fiennes lived at Highwood Ash from 1713 to 1737. Highwood House was bought in 1825 by Sir Stamford Raffles, the founder of Singapore and the London Zoological Society. He lived here for only a year before he died but Lady Raffles stayed on until her own death in 1858. An older house on the estate had been the residence of Rachel, Lady Russell, whose husband was executed for conspiring to murder Charles II. The adjacent Hendon Park estate was the 140-acre property of William Wilberforce, the anti-slavery campaigner. To the south, Holcombe House was built for a City glove merchant in 1778. Herbert (later Cardinal) Vaughan bought the villa in 1866 and started a Catholic missionary college here. The school soon outgrew the premises so Vaughan built St Joseph's College, which lies to the south-west. Holcombe House then became home to a sisterhood of Franciscan nuns, who also soon moved to larger, purpose-built premises: the neighbouring St Mary's Abbey. When Holcombe House came back on the market in 1977 it was acquired for the Missionary Institute London, a collaborative undertaking that trains men and women for ministry and missionary work. The institute is due to close at the end of June 2007 owing to a lack of students. St Mary's Abbey has recently been converted into a luxury apartment complex called Highwoods, while the Franciscan sisters have moved into a new lodge next door. The more conventional but still very grand houses of Highwood Hill mostly date from various decades of the 20th century, especially the 1930s. The Rising Sun inn was converted from a 17th-century cottage to its present use in 1751.

Highwood Park House, on Nan Clark's Lane, doubled as a Mediterranean villa in various 1960s television series and featured in episodes of *Morse* and *Jonathan Creek* in the 1990s.

✉ NW7

Hill End • *Hillingdon*
A hamlet and its outlying farms, situated north of HAREFIELD, beyond the hospital. Although Hill End stands on relatively high ground, the name may derive from a former landowner rather than a topographical feature. There was a group of houses here by 1754 and in the latter half of the 19th century a number of cheap cottages were built for workers in the nearby chalk quarries and brickworks. Most of the present housing,

clustered around the rather neglected village green, was built after World War II. The hamlet is too quiet to have sustained its pub, so the Plough has been converted to a children's nursery. Farther up Springwell Lane, the narrowboats strung along the canal draw the eye from the ramshackle workshops and the disused landfill facility at the old quarry.

✉ Uxbridge UB9

Hillingdon • *Hillingdon*

A much-extended village, plentifully endowed with open spaces, situated midway between HAYES and UXBRIDGE. As befits a settlement that has given its name to the modern borough, Hillingdon has a long history. Once occupying a clearing in the dense woodland that covered the area, its name probably referred to 'the hill of a man called Hilda', although others have construed it as 'the fort on a hill' and cited dubious stories of a battle in which the Mercians defeated the West Saxons. The Church of St John the Baptist was in existence by 1100 and parts of the present structure date from the 13th century. The road to Oxford, which runs north-westwards through the middle of Hillingdon, divided the uncultivated north from the fertile south, where most of the early farms and dwellings were established. Several areas of common land had attracted settlement to their fringes by the late Middle Ages, including Hillingdon Heath, COLHAM GREEN, PIELD HEATH and GOULDS GREEN. The Red Lion has stood on the green west of the church since the 16th century and Charles I is said to have rested here in 1646. Numerous gentlemen's residences were built in the southern part of the parish and of the present-day survivors the most impressive are Cedar House and Hillingdon Court. Uxbridge gained economic and administrative ascendancy over Hillingdon and the village languished until the early 20th century, when tram services to London began. In the west, the government acquired the much-rebuilt Hillingdon House and its grounds in 1915 and established the airfield that became RAF Uxbridge. After World War I private developers began to expand the village into a commuter suburb, although many open spaces were retained as playing fields and recreation grounds. The council acquired Coney Green in 1926 and an ancient earthwork was later uncovered here. The conversion of the main road into a dual carriageway in the mid 1930s coincided with the fullest spate of growth to both the north and south, with the council supple-

menting the efforts of commercial builders. The new locality of NORTH HILLINGDON came into existence at this time. At Colham Green, post-war council estates greatly increased the population and Hillingdon Hospital was rebuilt in a high-rise design in 1962. The hospital is currently undergoing further redevelopment. The strength of Uxbridge as a commercial centre has prevented the old village from acting as a focus for the wider suburb, which has had the benefit of preserving some of its charm, despite the intrusion of the busy road. In the Hillingdon East ward, 80 per cent of the residents are white British but the socio-economic profile is more diverse; 75 per cent of householders own their homes.

Mary, Marchioness of Rockingham died at Hillingdon House in 1804. Her husband, whom she had married at the age of 16, served as prime minister in 1765–6 and again in 1782, when he died in office. The astrologer Russell Grant was born in Harvey Road in 1952.

✉ Uxbridge UB10 and UB8

♟ 11,878 (Hillingdon East ward; the remainder of Hillingdon falls in Brunel and Uxbridge North wards)

🚇 Metropolitan Line; Piccadilly Line (zone 6)

@ www.thisishillingdon.co.uk (online version of local newspaper)

Hither Green • *Lewisham*

A revitalized commuter suburb, situated south-west of LEE and east of CATFORD. In medieval times this was the location of the important hamlet of Romborough, but it seems likely that the whole population – and the place's very identity – was wiped out by the Black Death. The present name was coined in the 18th century to distinguish the new settlement – which was nearer to LEWISHAM parish church – from Further Green on Verdant Lane. After its woodland was cleared in the early 1600s this became an area of nursery gardens and, from the 1780s onwards, of prosperous merchants' villas, until the opening of the station and a fever hospital in the 1890s. The former stimulated the construction of housing for artisans and the middle classes and the latter scared away the rich. Nearly 3,000 homes were built from the turn of the century until the outbreak of World War I by Cameron Corbett, who also developed SEVEN KINGS and ELTHAM PARK. The dwellings varied in scale from modest terraced houses to superior detached properties. Although the estate was

243

short on amenities, Corbett's negotiation of cheap railway season tickets for the residents ensured its success. The Chiltonian biscuit factory operated near the station from 1913 until 1930, when the business moved to Lee. After World War II the council erected blocks of flats on estates like Hether Grove, but many of these have already been replaced, mainly because of their poor standards of construction. In 1960 a rail freight depot was opened south of St Mildreds Road, handling at its peak over two million tonnes of continental fruit and vegetables a year. In November 1967 a train derailment at Hither Green cost the lives of 49 people. Following the closure of Hither Green Hospital, the western part of the site was redeveloped for housing purposes in the late 1990s. A mixed-use development on the eastern half is nearing completion and will include housing, live-work units, a doctor's surgery, a nursery and some retail and commercial space. Meanwhile, the old biscuit factory is being converted to a mews layout with live-work spaces, triplex houses and residential lofts.

✉ SE6; SE13

🚆 South Eastern Trains (zone 3)

📖 Godfrey Smith, *Hither Green: The Forgotten Hamlet*, self-published, 1997

Hockenden • *Bromley*

A farming hamlet on the easternmost edge of the borough, skirted by the Swanley bypass (A20). Its Old English name was first recorded in 1240 as Hokindenne. David Mills, in his *Dictionary of London Place Names*, suggests that it means 'woodland pasture (for swine) associated with a man called Hōc'. The pasture probably consisted of rough scrub, fit only for a few pigs or geese turned out onto the common land with the permission of the lord of the manor. James Chapman of Paul's Cray Hill united the long-divided halves of Hockenden manor in 1791 when he added land bought from the heirs of William Wentworth, Earl of Strafford, to the land he had acquired from Sir John Dixon Dyke in 1767. The Chapman family were prominent local citizens from the 17th to the 19th centuries and there are memorials to them in the churchyards of ST MARY CRAY and ST PAUL'S CRAY. They are remembered by Chapman's Lane, a cross-country track where a colony of wild parakeets has now established itself. Hockenden House is a large farmhouse, part of which serves as a privately owned day nursery. Lower Hockenden Farm has two rows of red-brick, tin-roofed huts built for hop pickers and later used by fruit pickers. Hops have not been cultivated here for many years, but some still grow wild in the hedgerows.

Hockenden Wood lies to the south-west. The chestnut woodland conceals Brocken Hurst, the 50-acre home of the Naturist Foundation, which has extensive leisure facilities and space for tents and caravans.

✉ Swanley BR8

@ www.naturistfoundation.org

Hoe Street • *Waltham Forest*

An electoral ward and key thoroughfare in WALTHAMSTOW, linking High Road LEYTON with Chingford Road. Hoe Street station opened in 1872 at a time when the neighbourhood was still mainly dairy pasture. It is said that trains would wait at the station for would-be passengers seen running across the fields. The introduction of cheap workers' fares helped ensure speedy development of the surrounding area in the late 1870s and early 1880s. The Victoria Hall was built in 1887 and became the town's first cinema 20 years later. The rival Empress was built at the southern end of the street in 1913 by Good Bros, local builders and impresarios. The Victoria Hall was demolished in 1930 and replaced by the Granada cinema, later the EMD. Central Parade was completed in 1964, with flats, shops, a lecture hall and a clock tower. The station was renamed Walthamstow Central when the Victoria Line arrived in 1968. Hoe Street is nowadays almost entirely lined with shops, although it has declined in status since Selborne Walk shopping centre became the prime retail site in 1988. The EMD cinema closed in 2003 and was subsequently acquired by the Universal Church of the Kingdom of God but there are hopes that the building may yet reopen as a cinema. Hoe Street's population is ethnically diverse; the most significant minority is of Pakistani descent and Islam is the second religion after Christianity. The ward is not affluent. Of its 5,000 households, almost half have no access to a car.

Hell on Hoe Street (2002) is one of a series of Walthamstow-based crime novels by former probation officer Jeremy Cameron.

✉ E17

👤 11,579

🚆 'one' Railway; Victoria Line terminus (Walthamstow Central, zone 3)

Holborn • *Camden/City* (usually pronounced 'hoebən')

A former metropolitan borough and an office-dominated street running eastward from the north-east corner of COVENT GARDEN towards SMITHFIELD. An early settlement evolved on the edge of the City beside a 'hole bourne' or stream in a hollow. The stream became known as the River Fleet and was later covered by Farringdon Street and Farringdon Road. The depth at which that route runs beneath Holborn Viaduct gives an idea of quite how hollow the valley was. The road now called Holborn, which becomes High Holborn west of Gray's Inn Road, was in existence as Holeburnestreete by 1249. The Bishop of Ely built a town house at present-day Ely Place, where its 13th-century chapel, dedicated to St Etheldreda, survives today. The bishop's garden was noted for its strawberries and, in *Richard III*, Shakespeare has the Duke of Gloucester say, 'My lord of Ely, when I was last in Holborn / I saw good strawberries in your garden there / I do beseech you send for some of them.' Holborn developed as a medieval suburb of the City, with houses that steadily grew in impressiveness. Several lawyers' colleges were established, some later evolving into barristers' colonies, while others withered and died. Staple Inn was among the departed but its 16th-century timber-framed frontage remains. GRAY'S INN to the north of the street and LINCOLN'S INN to the south have prospered and expanded. From 1863, houses in the east of Holborn were demolished for the construction of Holborn Viaduct, which was opened by Queen Victoria in 1869. From that time until the present day Holborn has been progressively redeveloped with hefty office blocks. By far the most exquisite is the terracotta fortress of Holborn Bars, built for the Prudential Assurance Co. by Sir Alfred Waterhouse and his son Paul over the last quarter of the 19th century. The six-way junction at Holborn Circus became the site of the offices and printing works of the Mirror newspaper group, now replaced by Sainsbury's headquarters. Holborn was renowned for its medieval inns, all of which have either disappeared or been rebuilt. The deceptively narrow Cittie of Yorke pub dates from 1924 but parts of its barn-like interior are older. The 'MIDTOWN' label has recently been applied to a zone of redevelopment focused on the junction of High Holborn and Procter Street.

✉ WC1; WC2

👤 10,645 (Holborn and Covent Garden ward)

🚇 Central Line; Piccadilly Line (zone 1)

📖 John Lehman, *Holborn*, Macmillan, 1970; Brian Girling, *Holborn, Bloomsbury and Clerkenwell*, Tempus, 2000

Holders Hill • *Barnet*

The exclusive northernmost tip of HENDON, separated from FINCHLEY to its east by Dollis Brook. The track that is now Holders Hill Road was in existence by the 14th century and during the following century the land came into the possession of All Souls College, Oxford. The hill was called Oldershyll in 1584 and by its present name in 1750. The undulating and wooded landscape attracted some pretty villas, including Holders Hill House, a *cottage orné* which stood for most of the 19th century. The builder C F Hancock put up several properties in the Parson Street and Holders Hill area in the 1870s but other attempts to develop the area over the next two decades were largely unsuccessful because transport links were poor. The Abney Park Cemetery Co. converted the 42-acre Dollis Farm into Hendon Park (now Hendon) Cemetery in 1899 and soon afterwards Hendon Golf Club was founded on part of Holders Hill Farm. Demand for housing picked up with communications improvements that culminated in the arrival of the North Circular Road (A406) in the late 1920s. Strips of golf course and cemetery land were sold for housebuilding and Holders Hill Road was lined with expensive houses and blocks of private flats. The rebuilt Holders Hill House became Ravensfield College in 1931 and the Hasmonean School in 1947. A separate girls' school is located a mile to the west. The school caters primarily for Orthodox Jewish children and has been rated among the best comprehensive schools in London. The North Hendon Adath Yisroel Synagogue moved to its present purpose-built home in the boys' school's grounds in 1965. Holders Hill is extremely popular with wealthier members of the Jewish community and in recent years more luxury flats have been squeezed into every available space on and off the main road.

The political economist Jeremy Bentham did much of his writing at Dollis Farm on Holders Hill Road in the late 18th century. The farmhouse was demolished in 1930.

✉ NW4; NW7

Holland Park • *Kensington & Chelsea*

An attractive public park and highly fashionable residential quarter situated south of NOTTING HILL and north of KENSINGTON HIGH STREET. In 1607, Chancellor of the Exchequer Sir Walter Cope built the nucleus of Kensington House. On his death in 1614 the property passed to his son-in-law Henry Rich, first Earl of Holland, who greatly enlarged what became Holland House before his execution in 1649. Henry Fox, a wily character who later became Paymaster General, leased the house from 1726 and acquired the freehold around 1770, by which time he had become the first Baron Holland, though he was no relation of Henry Rich. The second finest home in the district was the 17th-century Campden House, now replaced by flats. This was the home of William Phillimore in the early 19th century, when he began to sell building plots. One of the first streets to be laid out was Bedford Gardens, begun in 1822 by William Hall when he was 20 years old. Hall built to a high standard but other speculators did not and the initial appearance of the district was decidedly mixed. By the 1850s Holland House had fallen into a state of disrepair and Fox's grandson was forced to follow Phillimore's example to raise funds for its renovation. Over a period of several decades a series of separate schemes encircled Holland House and its attenuated grounds. This phase of building was almost exclusively luxurious, and inferior properties from earlier in the century were progressively replaced. Sweeping stuccoed terraces constitute the most visible theme but some streets have mews cottages or red-brick mansions. Leighton House was built in 1879 to the extravagant taste of Frederic, Lord Leighton, classical painter and President of the Royal Academy from 1878 to 1896. Leighton was at the centre of a group of artists and architects who became known as the Holland Park Circle and his house survives as a palatial collection of Victorian art. Holland House took a direct hit by a bomb in 1941 and was reduced to a shell in the late 1950s. The grounds were opened to the public and an open-air theatre was set up at the rear of the ruined house. The variety of public and private splendour in the park and its surrounding streets makes this one of London's loveliest places to walk or to live. A new building for the Commonwealth Institute opened on the south side of the park in 1962 but this has since closed and its future is uncertain at the time of writing. In the Holland ward the proportion of adults qualified to degree level or higher is almost three times the national average.

The fictional 34 Claremont Avenue in Holland Park was Edina's home in Jennifer Saunders' television comedy series *Absolutely Fabulous*.

✉	W8; W11
👤	9,372 (Holland ward)
🚇	Central Line (zone 2)
📖	Caroline Dakers, *The Holland Park Circle*, Yale University Press, 2000
@	www.rbkc.gov.uk/leightonhousemuseum

Holloway • *Islington*

A linear residential settlement with a high proportion of council housing, bordering the road of the same name, stretching north-westwards away from Islington. From the 14th century the 'hollow way' began to lend its name to the scattered collection of dwellings along its length, dislodging the older manorial identity of TOLLINGTON. By the 16th century, three distinct hamlets comprised the district: UPPER HOLLOWAY, LOWER HOLLOWAY and Ring Cross, which had grown up around the junction with what is now Hornsey Road and was later absorbed by Lower Holloway. Dairy farms occupied most of the surrounding fields. Holloway was noted in the 18th century for the cheesecakes produced on the farms and sold at local taverns. By 1800 a few villas were appearing, together with some terraced housing in the south, but true suburban development did not begin until the 1840s. Freehold land societies intensified the housebuilding process from the 1850s. Holloway Prison opened in 1852 on a site that had previously been set aside for the burial of cholera victims; the prison became exclusively a women's jail around 1903. By this time the district was wholly built up, mostly with terraced houses – some of which were of substandard construction – but with a few streets of detached and semi-detached houses set well back from the commercial hubbub of HOLLOWAY ROAD itself in the NAG'S HEAD locality. From the early 20th century the borough and county councils knocked down houses and put up blocks of flats with increasing zeal until they were persuaded to desist in the 1970s. Over 45 per cent of homes in Holloway are rented from the council – one of the highest proportions in London.

Holloway provided a home for the fictional Charles Pooter in George and Weedon Grossmith's *The Diary of a Nobody*, which satirizes the pretensions of a lowly Victorian clerk; 1 Pemberton Gardens is said to represent the precise location of 'The Laurels, Brickfield Terrace'. In Nick Hornby's novel *High Fidelity*, the hard-to-find record shop is situated in a Holloway side street.

✉ N7; N19

🚶 11,214

Holloway Road • *Islington*

A major north London thoroughfare (A1), running north-westward from Highbury Corner to ARCHWAY. The road was in existence by the 11th century and was known as the 'hollow way' (the road in a hollow) by the early 14th century, when it had become the main route from the CITY OF LONDON to the north. In the 17th century, Holloway Road was notorious for its highwaymen but it became safer as houses began to connect the three hamlets along its length. The construction of Archway Road brought an end to the area's rural character in the 1820s. Holloway Road Tube station opened in 1906 where the hamlet of Ring Cross had stood. This section of underground line was constructed in tandem with the railway line running from KING'S CROSS to FINSBURY PARK – hence the station's location some distance from the more focal NAG'S HEAD locality. A prototype spiral escalator was installed at the station but never entered service. Supermarkets have changed the face of Holloway Road over the past few decades. Sainsbury's demolished a ravishing Victorian block of shops on its arrival in 1970. A Waitrose supermarket replaced Jones Brothers' department store in 1993. This and the opening of a Safeway (now Morrison's) supermarket at Nag's Head prompted Sainsbury's to sell out to Kwiksave (who subsequently retreated in favour of an Argos superstore). Generally, the road's mix of retailers is typical of inner (as opposed to central) London high streets, with the colourful exception of a cluster of fetish fashion shops near the junction with Liverpool Road. Second-hand shops are also in abundance. The London Metropolitan University gained an iconic landmark in 2004 with the opening of its graduate school, the capital's first building by the American architect Daniel Libeskind; it supplemented Rick Mather's curved white block of 2000, and a brutalist concrete tower from this campus's pre-1992 incarnation as the Polytechnic of North London.

Holloway Road was the first home of the Campaign for Nuclear Disarmament on its foundation in 1954, and of the National Youth Theatre – housed in the former People's Picture Palace – two years later. In the early 1960s, record producer Joe Meek created a string of hits at his home-cum-studio at 304 Holloway Road, including the Tornados' *Telstar*. Holloway Road was also the first of the capital's 'red routes'. Instituted in the 1990s to reduce traffic congestion, particularly stringent stopping and parking restrictions apply on London roads marked with double red lines.

✉ N7; N19

🚇 Piccadilly Line (zone 2)

Holwood • *Bromley*

A private estate in south KESTON, centred on the historic Holwood House. The name was first recorded in 1484 and means 'wood in a hollow'. Holwood House was built on a modest scale in the early 17th century and progressively extended. William Pitt the Younger acquired the house in 1784 and he employed the services of Sir John Soane to remodel and enlarge it further, while Humphry Repton improved the grounds. Holwood House became an important meeting place for political figures of the time and has been called 'the original Chequers', in a reference to the prime minister's official country retreat. The hollow trunk of the 'Wilberforce Oak' stands where William Wilberforce gave notice to Pitt that he had resolved to raise the question of the slave trade in the House of Commons. A commemorative stone bench is inscribed with a pertinent extract from Wilberforce's diary. On the other side of the house is an Iron Age hill fort called Caesar's Camp and the location of the source of the River Ravensbourne. Holwood House was rebuilt in 1826 by Decimus Burton after its predecessor had burned down. The house has recently been restored and 78 homes have been built on the site of a demolished 1970s outbuilding, but the rest of the parkland is protected from development.

✉ Keston BR2

Homerton • *Hackney* (pronounced 'hommə-tən')

A crowded part of east-central HACKNEY, dominated by council-built flats. Homerton was first recorded in 1343 and takes it name (which was often rendered as 'Humberton') from the farm of a woman called Hūnburh. In 1535 Sir Ralph Sadleir, principal secretary of state to Henry VIII, built a house on

Homerton High Street that was later owned by Thomas Sutton, reputedly the wealthiest commoner in England. By the early 17th century Homerton was the most populous part of Hackney and more than a dozen lords and knights had houses here, including the governors of Jersey and Guernsey. Some of these property owners were only occasional visitors to Homerton but Edward, Lord Zouche cultivated a physic garden here and extended it to other plots before his death in 1625. After the mid 18th century building began to spread well beyond the High Street. Berger's paint factory opened in 1780 and workers' cottages were built nearby. This was the start of a process of industrialization and urbanization that steadily drove the gentry away. By the mid 19th century, cramped terraces were spreading outwards to join Homerton with neighbouring localities. A connection formed especially readily between Homerton and Hackney since the two places had only been separated by a single field even in the Middle Ages. Homerton station opened in 1868 and the Eastern Hospital was built in 1871 to treat smallpox victims, clinching the exodus of wealthy residents. By the end of the 19th century Homerton was densely built up, mainly poor and even 'semi-criminal' in parts. Industry continued to expand, until factories filled half the available land by the 1920s, mostly in purpose-built premises rather than the converted houses that were common elsewhere in Hackney. After World War II, Hackney council put up dozens of blocks of flats as industry drifted away. The London County Council built the Wyke estate on the site of the Berger factory after it closed in 1960. Following extended periods of closure, Homerton station and the former Eastern Hospital reopened in the mid 1980s; Homerton Hospital achieved university status in 2002.

Now owned by the National Trust, Sutton House is a historical museum and contemporary art gallery, but with restricted opening times. Despite subsequent alterations and additions, this rare example of a Tudor red-brick house retains many early details, even in rooms of later periods, including original linenfold panelling and 17th-century wall paintings.

✉ E9

🚇 Silverlink Metro (zone 2)

📖 David Mander, *Hackney, Homerton and Dalston*, Sutton, 1996

@ www.nationaltrust.org.uk (for Sutton House)

Honor Oak • *Southwark/Lewisham*

A primarily working-class neighbourhood occupying high ground north of FOREST HILL. One Tree Hill has been claimed as the site of Boudicca's defeat by the Roman general Suetonius Paulinus, but this almost certainly occurred in the south Midlands. On May Day 1602 Elizabeth I is said to have picnicked beneath the hill's crowning tree. The story is of doubtful authenticity and it is even less likely that the queen got drunk and knighted the oak, as has been claimed. It is more probable that the tree marked the boundary of a group of manors known as the Honour of Lewisham. The present-day Honor Oak Road was the original 'Forest Hill', deforested in the 1780s and laid out with homes for prosperous Londoners. A decade later the East India Company set up a semaphore position on One Tree Hill to signal the arrival of its ships in the Thames. This was commandeered by the government during the time of the Napoleonic threat. Honour Oak station opened in 1865, stimulating housebuilding for the middle classes. St Augustine's Church was built in 1873 and the Honor oak was destroyed by a lightning strike around the same time. In 1896 a private golf club enclosed One Tree Hill, prompting an 'agitation' lasting several years, which was said to have drawn up to 100,000 demonstrators. CAMBERWELL council eventually bought the hill for £6,000 and opened it to the public in 1905, when a new oak tree was planted at the summit. The slopes of the hill are wildly wooded and the park is one the hidden gems of south London. Golfers now have to make do with the nine-hole Aquarius course, situated at the end of Marmora Road. Beneath the course lies Europe's largest underground reservoir, occupying 14 acres. Opened in 1909, the reservoir stores water pumped here from the treatment centre at HAMPTON. The Honor Oak estate was a major development of the late 1920s and early 1930s by the London County Council, with 27 brown-brick blocks of flats covering 25 acres. After Honor Oak station and its railway line were closed, the Greater London Council built more housing to the west in the mid 1970s. The recently enlarged Camberwell New Cemetery borders One Tree Hill. Southwark council came under fire in 2003 for covering hundreds of wobbly gravestones in yellow plastic bags because they were 'unsafe structures'. The council fares better with Honor Oak adventure playground, on Turnham

Road, which is one of the best of its kind.

✉ SE23; SE22; SE4

📖 John Nisbet, *The Story of the One Tree Hill Agitation, with a Short Sketch of the History of Honor Oak Hill*, Michael Counsell, 1997

@ www.honoroak.towntalk.co.uk (commercial local information site)

Honor Oak Park • *Lewisham*

The eastern part of HONOR OAK, situated between CROFTON PARK and FOREST HILL. Despite misconceptions to the contrary, Honor Oak Park was not the name of an open space; the designation was the invention of Victorian property developers. Although the railway was constructed through the district in 1839, no station was provided here until 1886, when those developers pitched in with a contribution of £1,000 towards its construction. Several sites in the area have been redeveloped in recent decades, most interestingly at Segal Close, to the south-east, and Walter's Way, to the west. These are both named after Walter Segal, who pioneered low-cost low-skill construction methods ideally suited to self-build projects. Lewisham council supported the schemes, which served as a model that has since been adopted by several other English councils. East of Brockley Rise, the former Guy's Hospital sports ground is now a King's College facility, currently undergoing a major upgrade funded with monies raised from the college's sale of a ground in Surrey to Chelsea Football Club. Underground railway services are planned to reach Honor Oak Park when the first phase of the East London line extension project is completed in 2010.

✉ SE23

🚆 Southern (zone 3)

Hook • *Kingston*

A suburb filling the area between CHESSINGTON and SURBITON. The name probably refers to a hook-shaped spur of land, although the 12th-century presence of John Hog, a mill owner later known as John del Hoc, has prompted some alternative etymological theories. The locality was earlier called Grappellingham, which mutated into Grapsome. The first cottages in Hook probably clustered near what is now the junction of Hook Road with Mansfield Road, when this was the southern edge of Surbiton Common and belonged to Merton Priory. The common was to remain sparsely populated until the coming of the railway, so Hook's smallholders and craftsmen

had to travel to Kingston to sell their wares. The hamlet's growth was constrained by the borders of neighbouring estates and it was many years before the population rose above a hundred, inhabiting about 20 dwellings. In the early 19th century, road improvements, enclosure and the sale of land by Kingston council led to a modest surge in Hook's growth as City merchants built villas here. St Paul's Church was consecrated in 1838. During the mid 19th century, building societies bought land here and broke it up for sale in smaller lots, often to help their shareholders qualify for the vote. Late in the century Hook became caught up in the rapid expansion of Surbiton as a railway suburb, a process that reached its apogee after the opening of the Kingston bypass in 1927. The largest project was the Hooklands estate of nearly 300 houses with attendant shops. Other roads were developed piecemeal by a variety of local builders. After World War II the last fields disappeared beneath blocks of council flats, except for some playing fields close to the bypass, while most of Hook's remaining older villas were replaced with more compact dwellings and additional rows of shops. Opened in 1960, the Hook underpass, which cut through the SOUTHBOROUGH locality, was one of the first such projects in the country. On the eastern edge of Hook an industrial and commercial zone has grown from a nucleus of wartime factories on Cox Lane. The council's new Hook Centre is due to open in November 2006 and replaces the former library and community buildings on Hook Parade. The centre is intended to act as a focus for regeneration efforts in the area.

The children's author Enid Blyton honed her craft while working as a nursery governess at Southernhay, 207 Hook Road. After the success of her first book she quit to take up writing full-time. The house has since been converted to flats and doctors' surgeries.

✉ Chessington KT9

🚶 8,721 (Chessington North and Hook ward)

📖 Mark Davison, *Hook Remembered*, Mark Davison, 1997; Marion Cicely Bone, *The Story of 'Hook in Kingston'*, The Parochial Church Council of St Paul, Hook, 1989

Hornchurch • *Havering*

A primarily interwar suburb situated to the south-east of ROMFORD. Evidence of occupation during Middle Palaeolithic times has been found near St Andrew's Church. Henry II founded a hospice here in 1159, which by

1222 had become known as the Monasterium Cornutum or Monastery of the Horns, possibly a reference to the local leather currying industry, which had either a bull's or a stag's head with horns as its guild sign. Hornchurch outgrew DAGENHAM in the late Middle Ages and became quite densely populated but in the 15th century Romford gained ascendancy as a centre of trade. A gently sloping bowl known as the Dell was a popular setting for wrestling matches and other sporting events, especially in the 18th century, and possessed one of the best-known cockpits in the London area. The Dell lay to the south-west of the church in the Mill Field, which was possibly the site of the monastery and is now a recreation ground. Leather remained at the heart of Hornchurch's commercial life until the 19th century, with shoemakers, tanners and dealers in animal skins. The medieval St Andrew's Church was partially rebuilt in 1802 and restored again in 1869. Subsequent renovations have included a stained-glass window featuring a red Ford Fiesta car. The railway came in 1885 and peripheral suburban development began ten years later with William Carter's creation of EMERSON PARK. During the 1920s and 1930s the whole of Hornchurch became a dormitory suburb, its population increasing threefold during this period. In the middle decades of the 20th century Hornchurch held urban district status, incorporating UPMINSTER, RAINHAM and HAROLD WOOD. The town centre was redeveloped in the late 1960s and early 1970s but some valuable older houses were preserved, including the 18th-century Langtons, now a register office. The Queen's Theatre moved from a converted cinema to purpose-built premises on Billet Lane in 1975, and has become one of outer London's most successful arts venues. Across the road is Fairkytes, a Georgian house that is now Hornchurch Arts Centre. Hornchurch Country Park occupies much of the former airfield of RAF Hornchurch, which was an important base for Spitfires during the Battle of Britain. To its west and south-west lie ELM PARK and SOUTH HORNCHURCH. Further south, brownfield sites on the Hornchurch Marshes are earmarked for development as part of HAVERING RIVERSIDE.

In 1795 'Gentleman' John Jackson defeated the 'WHITECHAPEL whirlwind' Daniel Mendoza in a famous fight at the Dell. Jackson's ungentlemanly technique included holding Mendoza by his hair while punching his head with his other hand. Boxers have rarely worn their hair long since.

✉ Hornchurch RM11 and RM12

♦ 37,652 (Hacton, Hylands and St Andrew's wards)

🚇 District Line (zone 6)

📖 Tony Benton, Upminster and Hornchurch, Tempus, 2004; Charles Thomas Perfect, Ye Olde Village of Hornchurch: Being an Illustrated Historical Handbook of the Village and Parish of Hornchurch, Ian Henry, 2005

@ www.queens-theatre.co.uk

Horn Park • Greenwich

A fruit farm turned council estate, situated between LEE and ELTHAM. The 12th-century manor formed a bulge in the boundary of Eltham parish, so 'horn' may have been used in its sense as a 'projecting corner'. The 345 acres of West Horne, as it was then known, were enclosed in the 15th century. The park keeper of 1481 had a moated lodge with a dairy, barn, stable, garden and orchard. By the end of the 17th century, the estate had been 'disparked' and converted to arable land, meadow and pasture. Around 1860 the silk merchant Thomas Blenkiron acquired Horn Park and used the farm for grazing racehorses. A new owner planted orchards at the beginning of the 19th century. The farmhouse stood near the present-day junction of Alnwick Road and Horncastle Road. The fruit farm's lease expired in 1930 and the first streets were laid out by private developers in the vicinity of Hornpark Lane. In 1936 Woolwich council cleared the orchards and began to build 198 homes as the first stage of the Horn Park estate, with early tenants coming from the more crowded parts of the borough. The estate was half-finished by the outbreak of World War II. Building resumed at a rapid pace when hostilities ceased, including some prefabricated bungalows that survived until the mid 1960s. The completed estate consisted of some 1,100 homes. Since 1964, Horn Park has been the home of Colfe's School. It was founded in Lewisham in 1652 by the Reverend Abraham Colfe with assistance from the Leathersellers' Company, though its origins go back as far as 1494. The school became independent in 1977. It has sections for children of all ages and has recently become co-educational.

✉ SE12

📖 David Kincaid, Kings and Commuters: Horn Park from the Saxons to World War One, self-published, 2000

Hornsey • *Haringey*

A late Victorian and Edwardian residential district situated between ALEXANDRA PARK and CROUCH END. The name was recorded as Haringeie in 1201 and had been corrupted to Harynsey two centuries later. Hornsey's heavily wooded hills belonged to the Bishop of London from at least 1321, when the village already had a church. St Mary's was subsequently rebuilt twice but only its late-15th-century tower now remains. By the 18th century Hornsey was a sizeable village where Londoners were building country retreats. Landowners began to lay out suburban streets from the 1810s but these were little exploited until after the opening of Hornsey station in 1850. Thereafter, progressively more compact dwellings filled the fields, and most of the available space had been exhausted by the time Hornsey became an urban district in 1895. Many of the estates were built by large developers like the British Land Co., the Birkbeck Freehold Land Co. and the National Freehold Land Society, which aimed to provide homes for clerks and skilled workers. With parks in most directions, the district had the country's lowest death rate in the early 20th century and was nicknamed 'healthy Hornsey'. The last gaps were plugged in the years before and shortly after World War I, partly by council housing. All building since the 1930s has replaced pre-existing structures, including the many properties that suffered irreparable bomb damage in World War II. With the subdivision of houses (sometimes into ten or twelve bedsits) and the construction of purpose-built flats Hornsey became increasingly working class in character from the 1950s. Thousands of English-born residents moved away, many of them to new towns in the Home Counties. Today, nearly three-quarters of residents are white, including a significant number of Turks. Almost all the usual main ethnic sub-groups are well represented; only the Pakistani community is smaller than the national average. Hornsey's extensive council housing has impeded the return of the middle classes but, in a recent surge upmarket, Thames Water's derelict site has been redeveloped as NEW RIVER VILLAGE. Payments made to the council by the village's developers have funded improvements to the High Street, including the restoration of St Mary's Tower and its clock in 2005.

In 1952 Colin Chapman founded the sports car manufacturing firm Lotus Engineering at 7 Tottenham Lane, in converted stables behind the Railway Arms. The impracticalities of producing cars in a residential neighbourhood forced the company to move to Cheshunt, Hertfordshire, in 1959 and later to Hethel in Norfolk. There has been talk of opening a small Lotus museum at the original site, where the first 100 Lotus Seven cars were built and the Elite was developed.

✉ N8

🚶 10,075

🚉 WAGN Railway (zone 3)

📖 Ken Gay, *From Forest to Suburb*, Hornsey Historical Society, 1996

@ www.hornseyhistorical.org.uk

Hornsey Rise • *Islington*

A mostly council-built street and locality situated in the far north of the borough, to the south of CROUCH END. The 'rise' is the steep slope up to the ridge known as the Northern Heights. From the mid 19th century various groups of properties were speculatively built here, with names such as Rose Cottages, Grove Villas and Victoria Terrace. The new community gained a church in 1861 with the consecration of St Mary's, on Ashley Road, which has since expanded its boundaries to incorporate the former parish of St Stephen's Church, Elthorne Road. Hornsey Rise in its current form dates from the late 1880s, when the vestry of St Mary's Church, Islington gave a unifying identity to the road's string of disparately named terraces, while Crouch End Crescent became Hornsey Rise Gardens. Hillrise Road was Upper Hornsey Rise from its creation in 1853 until it was renamed in 1936. Islington council instigated several housing projects in the area before and after World War II but a few Victorian villas survive here and there. The locality benefited from further municipal improvements in the mid 1980s, including the building of some pleasing flats and sheltered accommodation, the opening of the Hornsey Rise Health Centre, and the creation of the Philip Noel-Baker peace garden in Elthorne Park. In the Hillrise ward, the largest defined ethnic minority is of Irish descent, followed by black Caribbeans.

Britain's, a toy company that specialized in models, developed out of a business established at 28 Lambton Road by William Britain in the mid 19th century.

✉ N19

🚶 11,382 (Hillrise ward)

📖 Eric A Willats, *Streets with a Story: The Book*

251

of Islington, Islington Local History Trust, 1988

Hornsey Vale • *Haringey*

A family-friendly corner of HORNSEY, merging with CROUCH END to the west of Ferme Park Road. Until the late 1870s the ridge running across the district was known as the Hog's Back and its slopes consisted of farmland with just a few mansions, including Womersley House, the home of OXFORD STREET retailer Peter Robinson. Within the space of a few years the large houses were bought up and re-placed by a succession of developments, inclu-ding the Streatham and Imperial Estate Co.'s Ferme Park estate, which filled part of Farn-fields manor (also known as Harringay manor). Montague Road and neighbouring streets were laid out in the former grounds of a house called Abyssinia, which had faced Tot-tenham Lane. Further east, J C Hill developed the Rathcoole estate in the grounds of a house of that name and later put up shops on Totten-ham Lane. The Elder family's land west of Ferme Park Road was built up by the mid 1890s. Many of the early residents were Horn-sey tradesmen, industrial workers or lower middle-class commuters. The Stationers' Company moved its FLEET STREET-based school to Mayfield Road in 1895 and the Lon-don Diocesan Home Mission built an iron church on the same road three years later, which was replaced by the red-brick St Luke's in 1903. By the 1920s Hornsey Vale had some pockets of poverty but it has steadily risen in popularity since World War II, although a number of properties have been subdivided into flats. Hornsey School for Girls moved to its present site on Inderwick Road in 1971, and St Luke's Church, which had never been a success, was converted to flats later in the dec-ade. The Stationers' school closed in 1983 and its site was split into several parts, which are now occupied by the Abyssinia Court Close Care development, Weston Park Primary School and the Hornsey Vale Community Centre. Stationers Park is a small but highly regarded open space with a children's play area.

Although the film's credits call this Crouch End, location shooting for 2004 'rom-zom-com' *Shaun of the Dead* took place in Hornsey Vale. Our hero's home is on Nelson Road.

✉ N8

@ www.hornseyvale.org (community centre site)

Horns Green • *Bromley*

A small outpost of CUDHAM, which lies half a mile to the north, Horns Green is London's most south-easterly settlement. This was part of the extensive Kentish landholdings of the earls of Derby. The 17th earl sold the Cudham portion of the family's estates in 1909. Horns Green has a few 19th-century houses in Kent-ish flint and brick, but most of the properties are late 20th-century executive homes, set well back from the western side of the road.

✉ Sevenoaks TN14

Horsenden Hill • *Ealing*

Among the largest tracts of open space in north-west London, Horsenden Hill and its neighbouring golf courses separate the indus-try of PERIVALE and GREENFORD from the sub-urban streets of SUDBURY. Horsenden Hill was acquired by Ealing council in 1938 as part of its green-belt scheme and the park was exten-ded by the acquisition of neighbouring charity-owned land in 1942. The hill has been described as a 'miniature Hampstead Heath' and its summit offers one of the most panor-amic views in London. Paradise Fields wet-lands are a recent addition to the nature conservation areas surrounding the hill. Ac-cessed from the corner of Greenford Road and Rockware Avenue, the water features con-sist of two lagoons and two smaller ponds.

✉ Greenford UB6

📖 Eva Farley, *A Farm in Perivale*, self-published, 1985

Houndsditch • *City*

A poor relation among the City's commercial thoroughfares, extending south-eastward from BISHOPSGATE's junction with LIVERPOOL STREET to ALDGATE. The name was first recor-ded in 1275. Seemingly obvious explanations for the meaning of place names often turn out to be fallacious, but Houndsditch genu-inely seems to have been a trench where 'dead dogges were there laid or cast'; several canine skeletons were unearthed here in 1989, prob-ably dating from Roman times. During the Middle Ages, Houndsditch became the centre of the bellfounding industry. Then, as the use of artillery and small arms in warfare devel-oped during the 15th century, the metalwor-kers turned to the manufacture of guns and cannons. The ditch was filled in by the end of the 16th century, when second-hand clothes began to be sold here. For most of the 20th century the Jewish-owned Houndsditch Warehouse was a landmark local clothing business but it has since been replaced by one of the many austere office blocks that now line the street.

In December 1910 a group of Latvian anarchists killed three policemen and injured two others who interrupted them during a burglary attempt on a jeweller's shop in Houndsditch. On 2 January 1911, two of the gang were cornered and subsequently killed in the siege of Sidney Street, in STEPNEY.

✉ EC3

📖 Donald Rumbelow, *The Houndsditch Murders and the Siege of Sidney Street*, Penguin, 1990

Hounslow • *Hounslow*

A major commercial and strongly Asian residential district situated east of HEATHROW airport. Hounslow was first mentioned in Domesday Book and the name is a corruption of Old English words meaning 'hound's mound'. The mound may have been a burial tumulus but is not known whether the 'hound' element referred to the animal or a man of that name. A Trinitarian friary was established around 1200, in the vicinity of the present-day police station on Montague Road. At the time of the dissolution of the monasteries, the friary was the richest Trinitarian house in England. The friary's chapel subsequently evolved into Holy Trinity Church. By 1635 Hounslow had already acquired significance as a coaching halt, conveniently located just before the Bath and Staines roads diverged across HOUNSLOW HEATH. Although the village barely extended beyond the High Street, there were over a hundred residents and at least five inns, some of which had been in existence for more than a century. The separate village of LAMPTON lay to the north. In the 18th and early 19th centuries Hounslow was the first stop outside London for nearly all the westbound coaches; in 1833 over 200 coaches passed through every day. Hounslow station opened in 1850 on a loop of the Windsor, Staines and South Western Railway and within a decade new roads were being laid out for suburban housebuilding. Development was slow at first and accelerated only moderately after the arrival of the Metropolitan District Railway in the 1880s. In the early years of the 20th century the area around the High Street evolved into a proper town centre, and civic offices, a library and public baths were built on Treaty Road. Hounslow grew rapidly after World War I, absorbing Lampton and MASWELL PARK and creating the new district of HOUNSLOW WEST. After World War II, council housing erased the last remaining fields, notably at BEAVERS FARM. Holy Trinity Church was destroyed by arson and rebuilt in 1961. The High Street was progressively redeveloped from the 1960s onwards, with office blocks as well as shops. At this time large numbers of Asian immigrants began to settle in the area, at first because it was close to their point of arrival at Heathrow Airport, and then as a result of a snowball effect. In the mid 1980s the shops and new library of the Treaty Centre replaced the civic buildings of Treaty Road. In a continuing process of change, a major project in the town centre has recently added a supermarket and a multiplex cinema.

The heroine of the 2002 British movie *Bend It Like Beckham* plays football for the fictional Hounslow Harriers.

✉ Hounslow TW3 and TW4

👥 42,631 (Hounslow Central, Heath, South and West wards)

🚉 South West Trains (Hounslow, zone 5); Piccadilly Line (Hounslow Central; Hounslow East, zone 4)

📖 Andrea Cameron, *Hounslow Town Past and Present*, Sutton, 2005; Neil Chippendale (ed.), *Reminiscences from the Asian Community in Hounslow*, Heritage Publications and Hounslow Leisure Services, 1993

@ www.hounslow.info (council-sponsored local leisure and cultural activities site)

Hounslow Heath • *Hounslow*

A large park situated to the east of the River Crane in south-west HOUNSLOW, including a public golf course and nurseries. The removal of tree cover on the 'Warren of Staines' from the early 13th century created the bleakest terrain in Middlesex, eventually stretching from BRENTFORD to beyond the western boundary of modern London. Rudimentary agricultural usage developed after Henry VIII divided the land among 14 parishes in 1546. On several occasions great armies were mustered here, including those of Oliver Cromwell and James II. In the 17th century the heath covered 25 square miles and was peppered with gibbets, erected for the punishment of its notorious highwaymen. By the start of the 19th century it still encompassed 5,000 acres but a combination of enclosure and the exercise of squatters' rights rapidly diminished it. 'Hounslow Heath,' wrote William Cobbett in 1830, 'is a sample of all that is bad in soil and villainous in look. Yet this is now enclosed, and what they call "cultivated". Here is a fresh robbery of villages, hamlets and farm and labourers' buildings and abodes!' Sand and gravel mining began in the mid 19th century, wreaking further damage on the natural environment. In 1919, Hounslow Heath became the site of the first civil airport in the country. The earliest commercial flight was from Bristol to Hounslow and the inaugural scheduled air service was from Hounslow to Paris. On 12 November 1919 the first flight to Australia left Hounslow, arriving 28 days later. Commercial aviation moved to Croydon in 1920 and the airport closed. Its buildings were destroyed by fire in 1929 but a plaque in Staines Road marks the site. Gravel extraction continued until about 1976, with the resulting craters filled with domestic refuse. A regeneration programme has subsequently restored around 200 acres of heathland with gorse, broom and rushes. In 1991 most of the site was designated a statutory local nature reserve. A municipal golf course has been laid out on the heath's western edge and the unsightly tower blocks of the Hounslow Heath estate have claimed the south-eastern corner. Almost half the residents of the Hounslow Heath ward are Asian or Asian British, and the Christian, Hindu, Muslim and Sikh faiths are all well represented.

✉ Hounslow TW3 and TW4

♦ 11,115

📖 Gordon S Maxwell, *Highwayman's Heath: Story in Fact and Fiction of Hounslow Heath in Middlesex*, Heritage Publications/ Hounslow Leisure Services, 1994 (reprint of a 1935 publication)

Hounslow West • *Hounslow*

A utilitarian 20th-century extension of Hounslow, situated south-east of CRANFORD and separated from HATTON and NORTH FELTHAM by the River Crane. In almost every other instance in London, the use of a point of the compass after a place name is an indication of artificiality. There is no such place as Hounslow East, for example, just a station of that name. Where such a locality does take on a life of its own, residents tend to switch the order of the words; for example THAMESMEAD WEST is becoming West Thamesmead. But Hounslow West constituted an entirely new district, built on farmland that had formerly been part of HOUNSLOW HEATH. In the early 19th cen-

tury the only premises of note in the area were the Traveller's Friend public house on the Bath Road and Hounslow cavalry barracks to the south. Hounslow began to expand in this direction in the second half of that century, aided by the arrival of the Metropolitan District Railway at what was originally Hounslow Barracks station in 1884. Despite the electrification of the railway line in 1905, shortening journey times into London, the area west of the station remained in agricultural use until the late 1920s, when private developers began to lay out new streets of semi-detached houses. The station was renamed Hounslow West and rebuilt, to the design of Charles Holden, for the arrival of the Piccadilly Line in 1933. Shopping parades were built and the (now lost) Ambassador cinema opened in 1936. After World War II a large municipal housing estate covered the fields of Beavers Farm. The Church of the Good Shepherd was provided in 1957 for the newly created parish of Hounslow West. HEATHROW Airport trading estates operate on the western edge of the district. The rebuilt Traveller's Friend is now a McDonald's restaurant. The residential population is mainly Asian or Asian British, of whom most are of Indian origin. There is a moderate level of social and economic disadvantage across the ward as a whole, which is concentrated on the Beavers estate.

✉ Hounslow TW4

♦ 10,356

🚇 Piccadilly Line (zone 5)

@ www.good-shepherd.org.uk (church site)

Hoxton • *Hackney*

Formerly a working-class district in north-west SHOREDITCH, now fashionable with members of London's media and 'dotcom' industries. It is possible that hogs were once kept here but more likely that the farmer's name was Hōc. ST PAUL'S Cathedral owned the manor at the time of Domesday Book. There were attempts in the 1680s to make Hoxton a sort of 'North End' to rival the WEST END, but the creation of Hoxton Square and Charles Square failed to spark an inrush of wealthy homebuyers. Instead, Hoxton's open spaces retained their market gardens and gained hospitals, schools and public houses. A number of religious dissenters came to live here, most memorably the Ancient Deists of Hoxton, who believed that they conversed with the dead. In *The Birth of Modern London*, Elizabeth McKellar suggests that

Hoxton's unusual character encouraged 'an alternative building tradition even on the very edge of the commercial centre itself and ensured the continued survival of these buildings unmodernized throughout the 18th century'. This piecemeal development encompassed a wide range, from mean tenements to mansion houses. Among the professional men who settled here was James Parkinson of Hoxton Square. His *Essay on Shaking Palsy*, written in 1815, identified the disease that now bears his name. Hoxton Fields had disappeared beneath Hoxton New Town by 1850. Hoxton was home to the renowned Britannia Theatre, a music hall that Dickens compared with Milan's La Scala. Built in 1858, it became one of Victorian London's greatest palaces of entertainment. Converted to a cinema in 1923, then demolished after wartime bomb damage, its name lives on in the leisure centre at the corner of Shoreditch Park. Hoxton Hall, a saloon-style music hall built in 1863, survives and is used for community arts and education purposes. The White Cube, on Hoxton Square, is a contemporary art gallery consisting of a refurbished industrial building and a main gallery with a recent modular glazed extension. Despite the post-war replacement of slum terraces with slum tower blocks and the recent arrival of assorted creative types, Hoxton retains an identity and a spirit that has been lost in much of inner London.

The poet and playwright Ben Jonson killed fellow actor Gabriel Spencer in a duel on Hoxton Fields in 1598, evading a death sentence because he could read from the Latin Bible. The proto-feminist writer Mary Wollstonecraft was born in Hoxton, where her father was a silk weaver. In 2002, footballer David Beckham popularized a short haircut fronted with a narrow tuft that was nicknamed a 'Hoxton fin'.

✉ N1

👪 10,698

📖 Christopher Miele, *Hoxton Architecture and History Over Five Centuries*, Hackney Society, 1993; Bryan Magee, *Clouds of Glory: A Childhood in Hoxton*, Jonathan Cape, 2003

@ www.hoxtonhall.co.uk

Hurlingham • *Hammersmith & Fulham*

An exclusive residential locality and famous sporting club occupying the southern tip of the FULHAM peninsula east of PUTNEY BRIDGE station. First recorded in 1489 as Hurlyngholefeld, this was simply a field of very little consequence for several centuries, although the hamlet of Broomhouse evolved on its eastern side. In the late 17th century the field was divided into Little and Great Hurlinghams and early in the 18th century a plague pit was dug. Hurlingham House was built for Dr William Cadogan in 1760. The house was significantly enlarged in two subsequent stages but its original core remains. It later became home to the Duke of Wellington's elder brother and to several governors of the Bank of England. A pigeon shooting club was established at the house in 1869 and the club soon introduced the new sport of polo, becoming the headquarters of the British game. Polo ceased to be played at Hurlingham in 1939 and the Hurlingham Polo Association is now based in Oxfordshire. Nowadays, Hurlingham has facilities for tennis, croquet, cricket, bowls, squash, gymnastics and swimming. Streets to the north of Hurlingham Road were laid out from the early 1880s and to the south-west later in the decade. Schools and a business park lie east of the club's 42-acre grounds.

The athletics stadium at Hurlingham was used to film scenes in the Oscar-winning 1981 film *Chariots of Fire*.

✉ SW6

🚇 Putney Bridge (formerly Putney Bridge and Hurlingham; zone 2)

📖 H Taprell Dorling, *The Hurlingham Club, 1869–1953*, Hurlingham Club, 1953

@ www.hurlinghamclub.org.uk

The Hyde • *Barnet*

A stretch of the A5 running between WEST HENDON and COLINDALE, and its surrounding industry and housing. The name derives from 'hide', a measure of cultivatable land. First identified separately from its parent manor of HENDON in the 13th century, the Hyde had around a dozen dwellings in 1597. The village grew with the appearance of coaching inns during the 18th century, by which time it had become the principal settlement on the road between Cricklewood and Edgware. Hendon Brewery (as it was later called) was established at the Hyde in 1860 and remained active for almost a century. Suburban housing spread here during the early 20th century and the Hyde developed as an industrial centre during World War I, stimulated by the presence nearby of Hendon Aerodrome. In 1925 the Duple coachworks moved here from HORNSEY. At the end of the 1920s over 1,000 houses were built by Hendon council on sites vacated by wartime factories. Across Silk Stream, Schweppes put up Deerfield Cottages for workers at their bottling plant in West Hendon. Since 1970 the Duple site has been occupied by a variety of light industrial firms, while the Hyde House office block has replaced the former brewery. It is currently the headquarters of Barnet Health Authority.

The playwright Oliver Goldsmith lived at an earlier Hyde House, a farmhouse on KINGS-BURY Road, from 1771 to 1774. He wrote *She Stoops to Conquer* here and was visited by Dr Johnson, James Boswell and the painter Sir Joshua Reynolds.

✉ NW9

Hyde Park • *Westminster*

Central London's largest open space, situated west of MAYFAIR and north of KNIGHTS-BRIDGE. This was farmland known as the manor of Eia at the time of Domesday Book and was acquired by Henry VIII as one of his many hunting grounds. At that time the park was almost twice its current size and included present-day KENSINGTON GARDENS. In the early 1630s, Charles I opened the park to the public without any of the public pressure that usually presaged acts of royal generosity. After the king's execution the park was seized by the state but citizens continued to use it as a pleasure resort. At the Restoration, Charles II replenished the stock of deer in a newly created enclosure and surrounded the park with a high wall. Londoners camped out here during the Great Plague of 1665 in the hope of escaping infection. William III had his walk to Kensington Palace illuminated with 300 oil lamps, creating the first artificially lit highway. The walk was known as the *route de roi*, which later became corrupted to Rotten Row. Queen Caroline, wife of George II, commissioned a number of improvements to Hyde Park, as she did to several of London's royal parks. The most visible of her works is the Serpentine, a 28-acre lake that curves across the southern part of the park and twists north into Kensington Gardens. In 1828 iron railings replaced the park's brick wall. Hyde Park has a long tradition of hosting national celebrations, often on the occasion of royal birthdays or military victories. The most magnificent event of all was the Great Exhibition of 1851, in which a huge glass and iron structure known as the CRYSTAL PALACE was temporarily erected in the park. Political meetings have been permitted in Hyde Park since the late 1860s and the park is now London's usual

venue for protest rallies that are too large to fit into TRAFALGAR SQUARE. In 1930 George LANSBURY established an open-air lido, which is available for swimming throughout July and August. The Diana, Princess of Wales memorial fountain is an oval water chute, opened in 2004 but often closed since for maintenance or due to adverse weather conditions. The park is best known for its lake and its wide-open spaces but there are gardens and dells too, and plentiful sports facilities. Boating and rollerblading are among the most popular informal activities. The residential area encompassed by the Hyde Park ward is dominated by the private rental sector and a very high 15 per cent of all residents are students. To the north of the park, the classy Hyde Park estate was laid out from the late 1820s in a corner of BAYSWATER then known as Tyburnia.

During the 1860s Charles Dickens lived at several houses in the Hyde Park area, all now demolished. The bookseller and stationer W H Smith lived at 12 Hyde Park Street. Claude Monet's 1871 painting of Hyde Park hangs in the Museum of Art at the Rhode Island School of Design.

✉ W2 (main part); SW1; SW7 (southern edge); W1 (Park Lane edge)

♦ 10,330

@ www.royalparks.gov.uk

Hyde Park Corner • *Westminster*

A traffic roundabout said to be 'London's most vital junction' and its hotel-filled vicinity, located at the south-east corner of HYDE PARK. When the park first came into existence all the land here was part of it. Apsley House was built by Robert Adam in 1778 for the Lord Chancellor, Lord Apsley, and became the home of the Duke of Wellington in 1817. The duke made significant improvements to the house's grandeur and filled it with works of art that he had received as gifts. Apsley House was known as 'No.1 London' because it was the first dwelling on the London side of the former KNIGHTSBRIDGE tollgate. It is now a popular museum and gallery, largely unchanged since the time of the duke's residence. Hyde Park Corner Lodge and St George Hospital (now the Lanesborough Hotel) both date from the 1820s. This decade also saw the realization of a long-debated plan to create a grand feature at this important gateway to London. Decimus Burton's neo-classical Constitution Arch has been called 'England's answer to the Arc de Triomphe', although it is somewhat smaller than its Parisian counterpart. An oversized statue of the Iron Duke was later perched on the monument, which led to it becoming known as the Wellington Arch. When the arch was dismantled as part of a road-widening scheme and moved to its present position in 1882, Wellington's statue was removed and taken to Aldershot. Its position atop the arch was taken in 1912 by Captain Adrian Jones' bronze statue of *Peace Descending on the Quadriga of War*. London's smallest police station operated inside the Constitution Arch for a few years but closed in 1960, when the former crossroads at Hyde Park Corner became a roundabout, marooning the arch in its centre. A unit of cavalry parades through the arch each morning.

In 1952 the words 'Hyde Park Corner' were used as code within the royal household to communicate the death of George VI.

✉ W1; SW1

🚇 Piccadilly Line (zone 1)

Ickenham • *Hillingdon*

A genteel residential suburb situated between UXBRIDGE and RUISLIP. Excavations at Long Lane playing fields have produced evidence of a possible Iron Age settlement, superseded in the late first century AD by an extensive multi-phase field system, which was modified over the following three centuries. The estate was first recorded in Domesday Book as Ticheham, 'the farmstead of a man called Ticca'. St Giles' Church was in existence by the mid 13th century and the oldest part of the present building dates from the 1330s. Three substantial homes built from the 16th century onwards survive today: the modest manor house; Sir Edward Wright's ostentatious Swakeleys House, completed in 1638; and the mid 18th century Ickenham Hall, to which the Compass Theatre and Arts Centre is now attached. Charlotte Gell established almshouses, which were built in 1857 on land she had donated, and bequeathed funds for the construction of the canopied village pump, which was installed in 1866. The opening of a halt on the Metropolitan Railway in 1905 failed at first to alter the character of the village but the sale of most of the Swakeleys estate in 1922 hastened Ickenham's entry into METROLAND. The Drummond estate was laid out in the north, shops were built in Swakeleys Road, and Princess Victoria opened the village hall in 1927. Several more housing estates followed in the 1930s, including the Glebe, Swakeleys and Ivy House, while the so-called 'Ickenham garden city' took the place of Milton Farm. More private developments filled out the suburb in the 1950s and 1960s, after which vigilant protection of the green belt prevented further incursions. A proposal to build a national exhibition centre on Ickenham Marsh met with local opposition and the scheme went instead to Birmingham. Swakeleys House was restored and converted to offices in the early 1980s. Only the very centre of the old village remains well preserved, although on the outskirts there are three moated sites that are scheduled ancient monuments. Ickenham Marsh, managed by the London Wildlife Trust, has open oak woodland and scattered scrub, with damp meadows and marsh bordering Yeading Brook. There have been problems with unauthorized use of the marsh for motorbike scrambling. Ickenham Green has an area of unimproved acidic grassland. Sixty-three per cent of Ickenham's adult residents are married, a very high proportion. At 41.9 years, the average age is significantly higher than the national norm.

The diarist Samuel Pepys visited Sir Robert Vyner at Swakeleys House in 1665 and recorded in his diary being shown the preserved body of a black boy who had died of 'a consumption'. During the 1908 Olympic Games, the marathon passed through Ickenham, en route from Windsor Castle to WHITE CITY.

✉	Uxbridge UB10
👥	9,993
🚇	Metropolitan Line; Piccadilly Line (zone 6)
📖	Eileen M Bowlt, *Ickenham and Harefield Past*, Phillimore, 1996; James Skinner, *Ickenham*, Tempus, 2005
@	www.ickenham.co.uk (community site); www.ickenhamchurchnews.co.uk; www.compasstheatre.co.uk

Ilford • *Redbridge*

A strategic commercial centre, arguably the most important in outer east London, situated two miles north of BARKING. The name is a corruption of 'Hyleford', 'Hyle' being an old name for the River Roding, and meaning 'trickling brook'. In the first or second century BC an encampment or market existed to the south of the present town centre at a site called Uphall, which covered approximately 48 acres. Adeliza (or Adelicia), Abbess of Barking, founded a hospital around 1145, with a chapel that stands today on Ilford Hill. The original medieval settlement of Ilford may have been established on the opposite bank of the Roding, at what is now LITTLE ILFORD, but the eastern village soon grew larger, and was known as Ilford Magna by 1254, and later by the English form of Great Ilford. The mansion at VALENTINES PARK is an impressive but lonely survivor from the grand houses that were built in the 17th and 18th centuries, while brickworks brought employment for ordinary villagers. The station opened in 1839 but Ilford's onion and potato fields survived until the start of the 1880s, when the sale of the Clements estate sparked off a 30-year-long housing boom, led by Cameron Corbett south of the railway and at SEVEN KINGS and later by Peter Griggs in CRANBROOK. Two of the earliest industrial employers were Ilford Laundry at Ley Street, where the washing was hung out to dry in the surrounding fields, and Alfred Harman's Britannia Works, which made photographic materials and later changed its name to Ilford Ltd. Ilford Town Hall, now headquarters of the London Borough of Redbridge, was built in 1901 and the council was a pioneer of the municipal supply of electricity. The town expanded further northwards after World War I, especially with the construction of the Eastern Avenue (A12) in the mid 1920s, when GANTS HILL, NEWBURY PARK and BARKINGSIDE became part of the new Borough of Ilford. From the 1960s, Ilford town centre underwent radical reconstruction with office blocks replacing several historic buildings. In 1985 the Winston Way relief road diverted traffic from the centre, allowing the High Road to be pedestrianized. The Kenneth More Theatre was built in 1974 and is regarded as the borough's premier cultural venue. The Exchange, an art deco-style mall with over a hundred shops, opened in 1991. Plans for further improvements include a new focal point, Unity Square, which is due for completion around 2010 and will be followed by new roads that will free up space for high-rise towers to the west and medium-rise mixed-use schemes to the east.

⊠ Ilford IG1

♁ 36,514 (Clementswood, Loxford and Valentines wards)

🚌 'one' Railway (zone 4)

📖 Norman Gunby, *A Potted History of Ilford*, self-published, 1997; J E Tuffs, *Ilford: A Short History*, Troy Novant, 1995

@ www.ilford.org.uk (privately operated local information site)

Imperial Wharf • *Hammersmith & Fulham*
'London's premier riverside development', according to its creators, situated in the SANDS END district of FULHAM and separated by the railway line from CHELSEA HARBOUR. In 1824 the Imperial Gas Light and Coke Co. acquired the Sandford manor house estate and began producing gas here in 1829. Barges brought coal to the site, which expanded hugely over the following decades. By the middle of the 19th century, Imperial was London's leading gas company. A merger in 1876 created the even larger Gas Light and Coke Co., which continued to gobble up Sands End, causing distress to neighbouring market gardeners who were still trying to grow fruit and vegetables on the increasingly polluted soil. The company stopped up old rights of way, paying generous compensation to the council, and laid out its own Imperial Road and Imperial Square. Partly to thwart wage demands by local workers, large numbers of Germans were employed here until the outbreak of World War I. Further growth between the wars forced Macfarlane Lang's Imperial Biscuit Works to leave Townmead Road for a cleaner site. With the advent of North Sea gas in the 1970s the gasworks closed down and car breakers later occupied much of the site. At the turn of the 21st century, property developers St George began to build an extensive estate of luxury apartment blocks and town houses, with shops, cafés, restaurants and ten-acre park. The scheme also included provision for affordable housing.

⊠ SW6

@ www.imperialwharf.com (property developer's site)

Inns of Court The collective term for the Inner and Middle TEMPLE, GRAY'S INN and LINCOLN'S INN.

Island Gardens • *Tower Hamlets*
A station on the Docklands Light Railway and a small riverside park at the tip of the ISLE OF DOGS. After William Cubitt had built up the south-eastern quarter of the island (CUBITT TOWN), he leased land from the Admiralty to put a handful of grand villas along the waterfront to the south. To accompany these he commissioned a plantation, with dozens of varieties of trees and shrubs. The ground was planted but the villa scheme was a failure; only two were built and one of those lasted fewer than ten years. The other survived into the 20th century, eventually becoming a library. The plantation fell into neglect and by the 1880s it was derelict. In 1895 the London

County Council created a park with walks, a play area, bandstand and a 700-foot terrace offering a superb view across the Thames to Greenwich. The MILLWALL Extension Railway came here in 1872 and the station was named North Greenwich. The line carried some docks traffic as well as day-trippers who crossed to GREENWICH by ferry. The ferry service was discontinued after the opening of the foot tunnel in 1901. The inception of omnibus services and the departure of Millwall Football Club from the island in 1910 impaired the railway's viability and the station closed in 1926. It reopened in 1987 as Island Gardens, originally the southern terminus of the DLR. The station was relocated underground in Millwall Park when the line was extended to LEWISHAM in 1999.

Tower Hamlets council's improvements to the park in the 1980s included a refreshment house with a giant teapot and teacup. The subsequent painting of the brickwork detracts from its appearance.

⊠ E14

🚋 Docklands Light Railway, Lewisham branch (zone 2)

📖 Eve Hostetteler, *Isle of Dogs* (2 volumes), Island History Trust, 2000 and 2002

Isledon Village • *Islington*

A 1990s mixed-tenure project with 211 dwellings, situated in south-west FINSBURY PARK. 'Isledon' is an old form of ISLINGTON, although the estate is simply named after the road on which it is located. The seven-acre site formerly consisted of industrial buildings beside the railway. Shops and stalls on nearby Fonthill Road specialize in affordable designer clothes and there were proposals to build a national fashion centre here. However, these were abandoned after Finsbury Park residents pressed for the site to be put to a more locally oriented use. Several housing associations collaborated to build flats and maisonettes in 1994 and a second, smaller phase of modular town houses was completed in 1999. Community facilities include a doctor's surgery, a self-built nursery, workspaces and open space with a children's play area. A nursing home cares for elderly people and those with disabilities or mental health problems. The village drew praise for its integrated approach to urban design but critics disliked the heavy predominance of social housing and 'dead end' layout.

⊠ N7

Isle of Dogs • *Tower Hamlets*

An 800-acre tongue of land jutting into the Thames opposite DEPTFORD and GREENWICH, made into an island by the creation of the WEST INDIA Docks in 1802. The name, however, was in use by the early 16th century and its origin is not known. The most popular story is that Henry VIII kennelled his hunting dogs here, which is credible since Greenwich Palace was just across the river, but there is no proof of this. The first attempts at draining what was then called STEPNEY Marshes took place in the 12th century and the land was slowly converted to cornfields and pasture. However, several centuries elapsed before reliable protection from flooding allowed the development of riverside docks and industry. The opening of the West India Docks transformed the northern part of the peninsula and in 1815 two tollroads opened up the hinterland, though it was several decades before many brave (and poor) souls began to set up home here. William Cubitt built up the southeastern part of the peninsula in the 1850s, with industry along the waterfront and housing inland (CUBITT TOWN). Shortly afterwards, MILLWALL Docks opened and related industries and housing filled much of the eastern side. Large-scale municipal housebuilding projects brought many East Enders here after each of the world wars. Dock-related activity dominated the Isle of Dogs until the 1970s, when labour relations problems and the increasing size of cargo ships led to the growth of Tilbury and the coastal ports at the expense of London's docks. West India and Millwall Docks closed in 1980 and the following year their ownership passed from the Port of London Authority to the London Docklands Development Corporation. The LDDC's regeneration mission was a flagship project for Margaret Thatcher's Conservative government, which relaxed planning controls, granted tax incentives and invested in infrastructure, most visibly in the form of the Docklands Light Railway. The first phase of the DLR opened between Tower Gateway and ISLAND GARDENS in 1987. In the same year (after earlier, less ambitious plans had been discarded), construction work began at Canary Wharf, the centrepiece of the whole initiative. During the early 1990s a combination of recession, the ending of the Isle of Dogs' enterprise status and renewed competition from the CITY OF LONDON halted the commercial property boom. Land values tumbled, whole blocks lay empty and property developers went into liquidation. It was not until the beginning of the 21st century that construction projects regained their original momentum. The northern part of the Isle of Dogs has now become a shopping and leisure zone, in addition to its primary function as a hub of global capitalism, while the south has become an uneasy fusion of typical East End terraces and upmarket waterfront apartments.

In 1598 the dramatist Thomas Nashe wrote a seditious play called *The Isle of Dogs*, but the title may have been a sardonic reference to the whole island of Britain. Patricia Cornwell's lame detective story *Isle of Dogs* concerns a group of Americans whose ancestors came from here.

✉ E14

📖 Stephen Porter (editor), *Survey of London, vols 43 and 44: Poplar, Blackwall and the Isle of Dogs, the Parish of All Saints*, Athlone Press, 1994; Eve Hostetteler, *The Isle of Dogs* (2 vols), Island History Trust, 2000 and 2002

@ www.lddc-history.org.uk/iod/index.html

Isleworth • *Hounslow* (pronounced 'izəl-wəth')

A riverside town of ancient origin, situated east of HOUNSLOW. A copy of an Anglo-Saxon charter indicates that in 677 this was Gislheresuuyrth, 'the enclosed settlement of a man called Gīslehere'. The 'G' was not dropped from the name until the mid 13th century, by which time Isleworth had evolved into a village on a manorial estate. Following the dissolution of the monasteries, the increasing private ownership of land led to the development of Isleworth as a wealthy residential area. Among the titled residents, Lord Grey of Warke was living in a house on the south side of Swan Street in 1635. Rebuilding during the 18th century created the locality now known as OLD ISLEWORTH. The increase of horse-drawn traffic at the end of that century and the arrival of the South Western Railway's Hounslow loop line in 1849 prompted the richest residents to move farther out of London and encouraged the growth of market gardens in place of orchards. The earliest phase of suburban development took place in SPRING GROVE and WOODLANDS. The railway brought factories too, and Pears soap was made in Isleworth for a hundred years from 1862. The new residential quarter of ST MARGARETS filled the gap between Isleworth and TWICKENHAM at the end of the 19th century. The Great West Road (A4) came to the north of the district in the mid 1920s, bringing semi-

detached houses that joined Isleworth to Osterley. The construction of the MOGDEN waste water works in 1936 reduced the appeal of the south-western corner of Isleworth and locals have been protesting about the odours ever since. The council and private developers built numerous blocks of flats in the second half of the 20th century, further contributing to the inconsistent appearance of the area, but Old Isleworth has undergone something of a renaissance. Odeon Parade is a conversion of the old Isleworth Studios (formerly the Odeon cinema) into 36 apartments. Isleworth is the home of the massively redeveloped West Middlesex University Hospital and – on the Osterley border – of Sky TV. A third of all homes here are rented from the council.

Interior scenes for the 1968 film *Isadora*, starring Vanessa Redgrave as Isadora Duncan, were filmed at Isleworth Studios.

✉ Isleworth TW7

👥 10,745

🚂 South West Trains (zone 4)

📖 Christine Diwell (ed.), *Isleworth Remembered: Memories of Life in a Riverside London Village 1900–2003*, Isleworth Society, 2003

Isleworth Ait • *Hounslow*

An unspoilt island in the Thames, located off OLD ISLEWORTH at the mouth of the River Crane. In the 17th century there were four aits here but their dividing channels have since silted up and the island still floods regularly. It was formerly part of the Duke of Northumberland's SYON PARK estate. The duke permitted a swimming pool to be built here for the use of local children, but nothing of this remains. Isleworth Ait is now a nine-acre nature reserve managed by the London Wildlife Trust. The tall canopy of mixed woodland shelters treecreepers, kingfishers and herons; summer snowflakes and marsh marigolds; and two-lipped door snails and German hairy snails. In order to preserve the habitat, public access is discouraged.

✉ Isleworth TW7

@ www.wildlondon.org.uk (London Wildlife Trust site)

Islington • *Islington*

A gentrified inner London suburb, though still with a large working-class community, situated one and a half miles north of St Paul's Cathedral. In the year 1000, Islington was Gislandune, the 'hill of a man called Gīsla'. Until the dissolution of the monasteries, the village's lands were largely in the hands of religious institutions such as the canons of St Bartholomew, who gave their name to CANONBURY. Henry VIII hunted both animals and mistresses in what became MILDMAY PARK, remembered in street names such as King Henry's Walk. Islington was a staging post on the route north from London and the ANGEL takes its name from an inn on the turnpike road. The New River, built to supply London with water from Hertfordshire from 1609, passed through Islington on its way to the round pond at New River Head, south of the Angel. Its creator, Hugh Myddleton, is commemorated by a statue at ISLINGTON GREEN. By the late 18th century, tens of thousands of oxen and hundreds of thousands of sheep were passing along Islington High Street every year on their way to SMITHFIELD. By that time Islington was developing rapidly as a residential suburb, with elegant Georgian and Victorian squares proliferating in BARNSBURYand Canonbury, while UPPER STREET and Lower Street (now ESSEX ROAD) became busy shopping centres. The 64-acre Mildmay estate to the east was leased for the building of middle-class and working-class homes from the 1840s onwards. During this period, much of Islington became a 'walking suburb' – a dormitory for the thousands of clerks who walked to work in the CITY OF LONDON – while street traders came to CHAPEL MARKET. Islington's rural connection survived with the building of the Smithfield Club's Agricultural Hall in 1862. The hall was later used for almost every imaginable kind of event and was the original venue for Cruft's dog show. It is now a business design and exhibition centre. The opening of the palatial HIGHBURY and Islington station in 1872 symbolized Islington's role as the archetypal commuter suburb; appropriately Weedon Grossmith, co-creator of the archetypal suburbanite commuter Mr Pooter in *The Diary of a Nobody*, lived in Canonbury Place in the 1890s. Soon, however, the middle classes were choosing to move even further out of central London; large homes were subdivided and Islington became a working-class area. It was partly in grim appreciation of its down-at-heel grittiness that George Orwell chose to move into Canonbury Square in 1944. Islington suffered wartime bomb damage and post-war depopulation but from the late 1950s the process of gentrification began, bringing the middle classes back to restored and revived squares and terraces. Running in parallel was the

building of huge council estates such as the Marquess estate, off Essex Road, for a time reputedly the most crime-ridden in Europe and now the subject of a major regeneration scheme. The flourishing of the Camden Passage antiques market was another sign of changing times, as Upper Street in particular became a golden mile of smart shops and chic restaurants.

Walter Sickert painted *The Hanging Gardens of Islington* at his studio in Noel Street (now Noel Road) in 1925. The composer Benjamin Britten was an Islington resident for the last ten years of his life, although he died in Aldeburgh, Suffolk. The writer Joe Orton lived in Noel Road from 1959 until his murder in 1967 by his partner Kenneth Halliwell. The pair were imprisoned in 1962 for stealing and defacing Islington library books. Reproductions of the defaced and doctored book jackets are now part of the Joe Orton collection held by the borough's local history centre.

✉ N1

♦ 41,605 (Barnsbury, Canonbury, St Mary's and St Peter's wards)

🚇 WAGN; Victoria Line (Highbury and Islington, zone 2); Northern Line (Angel, zone 1)

📖 Mary Cosh, *A History of Islington*, Historical Publications, 2005

@ www.myislington.co.uk (commercial local information site); www.islingtongazette.co.uk (online local newspaper); www.geocities.com/redrken (informative privately operated local history site)

Islington Green • *Islington*

A small park located at the apex of UPPER STREET and ESSEX ROAD, generally identified as the centre of ISLINGTON. Upper Street and Lower Street (as it was) were Islington's principal thoroughfares from medieval times and the triangle of land at their junction formed an early focus. Archaeological excavations have revealed evidence of 15th-century tenements, demolished in the 17th century. By this time the triangle had become waste ground, especially popular for dumping dung. The Marquess of Northampton, lord of the manor of CANONBURY, granted the land to the vestry in 1777 and the green was cleared and enclosed with posts and rails. A watch house was built soon afterwards and trees were planted in 1808. Several public houses had long stood around the green, notably the Fox at the north-west corner. Sam Collins established the Lansdowne Arms in 1851 and subsequently converted it into a music hall that gained the popular nickname 'the chapel on the green'. Rebuilt in 1897 and later called the Islington Hippodrome, the music hall was irreparably damaged by fire in 1958. Funfairs are regularly set up on the green. The Screen on the Green is a well-established independent cinema, programming a mix of art-house and mainstream films.

William Gladstone, then Chancellor of the Exchequer, unveiled a statue of Sir Hugh Myddleton on the green in 1862, commemorating his entrepreneurial feat in bringing fresh water to London via the New River. Pupils from the fourth-form music class at Islington Green School sang the chorus to Pink Floyd's *Another Brick in the Wall* in 1979.

✉ N1

Ivybridge *see* MOGDEN

Jackson's Lane • *Haringey*

A Victorian road in north-east HIGHGATE, located just south-west of Highgate station. It acquired its name from Joseph B Jackson, an early 19th-century resident of a house called Hillside. Jackson's Lane previously crossed ARCHWAY Road and continued as a footpath, but this eastern part was renamed Shepherd's Hill when it was built up with some very pricey homes in the 1880s. The old lane, too, was developed around this time with detached houses and a mansion block, which closed in on some substantial Georgian properties. In 1893 a site on the corner of Archway Road was obtained for the construction of Highgate Wesleyan Methodist Church, which eventually opened in 1905 with an adjacent hall and Sunday school that had almost as great a capacity as the church. In the area between Southwood Lane and Jackson's Lane, Southwood House and its former grounds gave way in the late 1950s to a triangle of 30 terraced houses with a communal garden. Other large houses were demolished in the mid 1960s and replaced with flats or smaller houses. Many of the surviving Victorian properties have been subdivided into bedsits or small apartments. Highgate Methodist Church operated a counselling centre in the 1960s but closed in 1976. Since then the church has been converted into a theatre, while the adapted hall offers a wide range of arts classes, courses and activities.

✉ N6

@ www.jacksonslane.org.uk (arts centre site)

Jermyn Street • *Westminster*

A high-class thoroughfare situated south of PICCADILLY, particularly noted for gentlemen's tailoring. Originally, this was to have been the north part of a 'little town' planned around ST JAMES'S Square by Henry Jermyn, the Earl of St Albans, who leased the land from the Crown in the 1660s. Sir Isaac Newton lived here from 1697 until 1709, when he left for Chelsea. Newton stayed first at number 88, which was built soon after 1675 on land leased from the earl, and still survives. In 1700 he moved next door to number 87, which is no longer standing. William Blake was baptized at the Wren church of St James, on the corner of Church Place, once the most fashionable church in London. A Jermyn Street festival takes place in September.

The poet Thomas Gray and the author Sir Walter Scott both lodged in the street. In the early years of the 20th century Rosa Lewis, famed for her cooking and her open-minded hospitality, ran the Cavendish Hotel. Known as the Duchess of Jermyn Street, she is credited with saying, 'It doesn't matter what you do in the bedroom as long as you don't do it in the street and frighten the horses'. The 1970s television series *The Duchess of Duke Street* was loosely based on the story of her life.

✉ SW1

Joydens Wood • *Bexley*

A 320-acre woodland and the adjacent residential district east of NORTH CRAY. The western part of the wood falls within the London Borough of Bexley (with access from Vicarage Road, Old Bexley) but the rest, including all the housing, is in Kent. The name derives from the family of William Jordayne, a 16th-century resident of Dartford; the wood has also been known as Jordans in the past. The Forestry Commission acquired Joydens Wood in 1956 and later placed it under the management of the Woodland Trust, which opened it to the public in 1988. There are two nature trails through birch, Corsican pine, oak, pine and sycamore trees. A Saxon earthwork known as Faesten Dyke runs north–south through the wood.

✉ Bexley DA5

Julian Brimstone • *Bromley*

A hilltop hamlet three-quarters of a mile south-west of CHELSFIELD VILLAGE along Church Road towards PRATT'S BOTTOM. The London to Sevenoaks railway line passes through a tunnel beneath the hill. Chelsfield

Riding School is opposite the red-brick and tile house that gives the hamlet its name. It is unlikely that there was ever an individual called Julian Brimstone; complex theorizing about the derivation involves a corruption of the names of two former residents, a Mr Gillman and a Mr Brown. In 1961, Homesteads Ltd bought Brimstone Farm and laid out Brimstone Close as an extension of the Chelsfield Park estate. To the east is Chelsfield Lakes Golf Centre, a 'pay and play' operation created in 1993 and bought by American Golf (UK) in 2001.

In her autobiography *Time Remembered*, the novelist Miss Read recalls that as a child she walked to school in Chelsfield past violet and sage fields and Julian Brimstone's 'ivy-covered farmhouse', with its walnut trees and geese and ducks around the pond.

✉ Orpington BR6

📖 Miss Read, *Time Remembered*, Michael Joseph, 1986

Junction Road • *Islington*
A down-at-heel street connecting TUFNELL

PARK with UPPER HOLLOWAY. Junction Road was constructed as a feeder for the new ARCHWAY Road in 1813. Much of the area's original development was as cheap housing for working people who were displaced from ST PANCRAS and SOMERS TOWN by the railway building of the mid 19th century. Station Road marks the site of the former Junction Road railway station, which operated from 1872 to 1916, after which it was used solely by goods services until finally closed in 1960. Commuter groups continue to lobby for the station's reopening, so far without success. Only a quarter of the Junction ward's adult residents are married, an exceptionally low proportion. Most homes are rented from the council or a housing association. In 2004 Junction Road was branded 'the worst street in the borough' for its level of grime, graffiti and 'festering rubbish'. Archway Quasar, a 'combat arena' located at 13 Junction Road, is the locality's prime leisure venue.

✉ N19

👥 10,816 (Junction ward)

Kelsey Park • *Bromley*

A public park and its vicinity in south BECK-ENHAM. William Kelshulle owned land in Beckenham in 1408 and the estate was known as Kelsies by 1479. Edward Hasted suggests in his *History of Kent* that the family may have been here 'as early as the reign of King Henry III'. A mansion was built in the late 15th century by William Brograve and subsequently much enlarged. Its last residents, sometime after 1835, were the Hoare banking family. Much of the surrounding area was built up during the years before and after World War I, and Kelsey Park was opened to the public in 1913. The park now covers 32 landscaped acres, with the Beck opening out into two ribbon lakes. Kelsey Park School opened in 1968 at a new site on Manor Way, as a successor to Alexander Boys' School. The school now has specialist sports college status and takes pupils from a wide catchment area. Kelsey Park Mansion is an 'age exclusive' development of apartment homes for people over 55. Like most of Bromley, the Kelsey and EDEN PARK ward is overwhelmingly white and relatively affluent.

> ✉ Beckenham BR3

> ♀ 14,751 (Kelsey and Eden Park ward)

Kenley • *Croydon*

A wealthy residential suburb situated in the southernmost part of Greater London, half a mile east of COULSDON. Kenley did not make its first recorded appearance until 1255 but the name is of Old English origin, probably meaning 'the woodland clearing of a man called Cēna'. Kenley was part of the medieval manor and parish of Waddington (or Watendone or Wattenden) and was never a hamlet in its own right, but simply the name of a lane and a farm. Later it became part of the manor of Coulsdon. Waddington's church burned down in 1780, when it was being used as a barn. Around 1823 Kenley House was built on the site of Kenley Farm. When the Caterham Railway came through in 1856, Coulsdon

station was opened here but was soon renamed Kenley. From the mid 1860s, mansions and other superior houses began to dot the farmland and All Saints' Church was completed in 1872. Shops were built near the station, an old alehouse became the Pig and Whistle and the new village gained its own school in 1885. Gardner's pleasure resort drew daytrippers to nearby RIDDLESDOWN in the 1890s. By the early 20th century suburban building had replaced most of the farms, while a less affluent settlement began to take shape at LITTLE ROKE. Kenley airfield opened in 1917 and became an important fighter station during the Battle of Britain. The base closed in 1959 but the airfield continues to be used for gliding. From the 1950s many of the grandest Victorian and Edwardian properties were converted to flats or nursing homes or replaced by smaller houses and bungalows. Old Lodge Lane and Hayes Lane have some of the best surviving old buildings. Wattenden Primary School opened in 1968. Kenley House has been vacant since 2003 and plans for its restoration include the construction of around 30 homes in its grounds. Kenley Common, a 135-acre park managed by the Corporation of London, lies on the south-eastern side of the suburb. The typical Kenley resident is white, Christian, married, middle-aged, and a home and car owner.

Flying scenes for the films *Angels One Five* (1953) and *Reach for the Sky* (1956) were shot at Kenley airfield.

> ✉ Kenley CR8

> ♀ 13,525

> 🚉 Southern (zone 6)

> 📖 Grahame Brooks, *Kenley*, Bourne Society, 2000

> @ www.controltowers.co.uk/H-K/Kenley.htm (RAF Kenley site);
> www.southlondongliding.co.uk (gliding club site)

Kennington • *Lambeth/Southwark*

An area of terraced houses and tower blocks, east of VAUXHALL. First recorded in Domesday Book as Chenintune, the name probably meant 'the farm of a man called Cēna', although others have suggested 'place of the king'. In 1337 Kennington was given to Edward, the Black Prince, and a royal palace was built here. Though the palace has long gone, the manor has belonged to the eldest son of England's monarchs ever since as part of the Duchy of Cornwall. From 1622 the duchy started to grant leases to Kennington's residents, giving them an incentive to improve their properties. The construction of Westminster Bridge in 1750 brought accessibility and early popularity as a place of residence. Most of the modern layout of Kennington was set by 1799, although the south-western part, including Kennington OVAL, developed a little later. By 1818 the present street pattern was fully established and the village was becoming a semi-rural suburb with grand terraced houses of four or even five storeys. Kennington Common was a venue for fairs and executions; St Mark's Church stands on the site of the gallows. In 1848 a huge crowd assembled here intending to march on Parliament to present its Chartist petition. The march was banned and the crowd was persuaded by the Chartist leader Feargus O'Connor MP to disperse peacefully. In 1852 the common was converted to 'a pleasant place of recreation' and renamed Kennington Park. This was at a time of increasingly dense building all around, and with villas succumbing to multiple occupation. Karl Marx wrote in *Das Kapital* that Kennington was 'very seriously over-populated in 1859, when diphtheria appeared'. Kennington station opened on the Bank branch of the Northern Line (originally called the City of London and Southwark Subway) in 1890 and served the Charing Cross branch also from 1926. Tram and bus routes also converged here; Kennington was described in the 1920s as 'the Clapham Junction of the southern roads' and St Mark's became the tramwayman's church. Lambeth council built all kinds of municipal housing here from the early 1950s to the late 1970s, including several high-rise estates. East of Kennington Park, the London County Council's Brandon estate was its first such project to retain some existing terraces. Kennington's long decline is now being reversed as the advantages of its location prompt the reuniting of formerly subdivided properties.

Kennington was the birthplace in 1887 of Bernard Montgomery, later Field Marshal Viscount Montgomery of Alamein. The Brandon estate has Henry Moore's sculpture *Reclining Figure No.3*.

✉ SE11; SE17; SW8; SW9

👤 11,983 (Oval ward)

🚇 Northern Line (zone 2)

📖 Jill Dunman, *Lambeth, Kennington and Clapham*, Sutton, 1999; Edward Walford, *Walford's History of Stockwell and Kennington*, ed. John W Brown, Local History Reprints, 1996

@ www.vauxhallandkennington.org.uk (community site)

Kennington Oval *see* OVAL

Kensal Green • *Brent/Kensington & Chelsea/Hammersmith & Fulham*

A beautiful cemetery and increasingly fashionable residential quarter – more accurately, triangle – situated on the HARROW ROAD between WEST KILBURN and HARLESDEN. The 13th-century name 'Kingisholt', of which 'Kensal' is a corruption, meant 'king's wood', but the king in question remains unidentified. The green was first recorded in 1550, when it was surrounded by thick woodland. By the mid 18th century most of the trees had been cleared and farms had been established on land belonging to All Souls College, Oxford, followed later by brickworks. Over a million bricks were made here in 1825, soon after the enclosure of the green. The first suburban cottages and villas were built along Harrow Road and the village had half a dozen shops by 1829. Surprisingly, it was the opening of the cemetery in 1832 that made this a popular residential area. Laid out on 56 acres of land between Harrow Road and the Grand Union Canal, Kensal Green was the first of many suburban cemeteries created by joint-stock companies in response to the difficulties of finding burial space in central London churchyards. Father and son engineers Sir Mark and Isambard Brunel, the writers Thackeray and Trollope, and the French acrobat and tightrope walker Blondin are among those buried here. By the middle of the century the village was a sizeable and mixed community, inhabited by tradesmen, farm and cemetery workers and the Mancunian novelist William Harrison Ainsworth, who lived at Kensal Manor House and is also buried in the cemetery. Kensal Green gained a main-line station in 1860 and was densely built up in the last quarter of the century, mostly with compact dwellings. Kensal Manor House was demolished in 1939. From soon after World War II a West Indian community developed at Kensal Green, growing especially large in the 1960s and 1970s. In Brent's Kensal Green ward just over half the population is now white and the most significant minorities are of black Caribbean, Indian, white Irish and black African descent. The district has recently been undergoing a moderate level of gentrification as an overspill zone from unaffordable Notting Hill, in the process gaining a couple of trendy bars and some new town houses and live–work units.

G K Chesterton's poem *The Rolling English Road* makes reference to the cemetery in its famous couplet, 'For there is good news yet to hear and fine things to be seen / Before we go to Paradise by way of Kensal Green'.

✉ NW10; NW6

♦ 10,668 (Brent's Kensal Green ward)

🚉 Silverlink Metro; Bakerloo Line (zone 2)

📖 James Stevens Curl et al, *Kensal Green Cemetery*, Phillimore, 2002

@ www.kensalgreen.net (cemetery site)

Kensal Rise • *Brent*

As its name suggests, this late Victorian suburb occupies the slopes above KENSAL GREEN. A station opened on Chamberlayne Road in 1873, when houses were beginning to appear nearby. More farmland was released for building in the late 1880s and the first school opened. The most distinctive properties were on Clifford Gardens, where an old Hampstead man was employed to decorate the gables with what Brent council calls 'quaint and curious stucco scenes'. A national athletics ground was laid out in 1890 but never amounted to much and soon succumbed to the demand for building land. Kensal Rise gained one of the earliest free libraries in the area, opened in 1900 by Mark Twain. Shops and light industry appeared on Chamberlayne Road around this time but depressed market conditions brought housebuilding to a halt and unsold plots were used as sports grounds or allotments. Building resumed its ascent of the slopes after World War I, improving in quality as it approached BRONDESBURY PARK and WILLESDEN GREEN. By 1939 the district had fully merged with all its neighbours, although household sizes decreased between the wars and the population declined a little. By the 1960s parts of Kensal Rise were in a very dilapidated state,

and middle-class families moved away and big-name stores deserted Chamberlayne Road. The council replaced some of the inferior early houses with flats while supporting the renovation of other properties by housing associations. The locality has been recovering in recent years but it is losing its identity because estate agents treat it as part of QUEEN'S PARK. Gujarati, Arabic and Portuguese are the main minority languages spoken in the neighbourhood.

✉ NW10

🚉 Silverlink Metro (zone 2)

Kensal Town • *Kensington & Chelsea*

An infrequently used name for a heavily redeveloped part of north-east NORTH KENSINGTON, located between the Grand Union Canal and the main railway line into Paddington. Kensal New Town, as it was originally called, was laid out from the mid 19th century following KENSAL GREEN'S successful development. From the start, however, it was a poorer and less fashionable sister and deteriorated into a notorious slum. Until 1899 this was a detached part of the parish of St Luke's, Chelsea, covering about 140 acres, but was subsequently incorporated within the Royal Borough of Kensington, despite the latter's objections – the real reason for which seemed to be the abject condition of the inhabitants. In 1903 social reformer and statistician Charles Booth described it as 'an isolated district shaped like a shoe and just as full of children and poverty as was the old woman's dwelling in the nursery rhyme'. The main improvement before World War I was the Emslie Horniman Pleasance, a little park on Bosworth Road with features by the eminent architect C F A Voysey, now restored. From the 1930s the council began a programme of slum clearance and estate building that accelerated after World War II and erased much of the original street pattern. The process culminated on the east side with Ernö Goldfinger's Trellick Tower. This is a love-it-or-hate-it 30-storey concrete block with a distinctive separate lift and stair tower. Built to high standards and visible for miles, Trellick Tower is now Grade II-listed as a relic of a bygone age of monumental municipal building. Like much of North Kensington, Kensal Town is a very multicultural community, including Afro-Caribbeans, Portuguese and Moroccans.

✉ W10

📖 Jerome Borkwood, *From Kensal Village to*

Golborne Road: Tales of the Inner City, Kensington and Chelsea Community History Group, 2002

Kensington • *Kensington & Chelsea*

An eminently salubrious residential and institutional district situated north-west of CHELSEA. The name was first recorded in Domesday Book and probably derives from a Saxon farmer called Cynesige. Despite its exalted reputation, Kensington was a late developer. A few gentlemen's residences were built in the early 17th century, of which only two significant examples survive, in completely contrasting forms: Sir Walter Cope's mansion is now the bombed-out shell of Holland House, while Sir George Coppin's house has grown several times over to become Kensington Palace. In 1685 the developer Thomas Young began to lay out Kensington Square, but this long remained an isolated outpost of civilized London amid the fields and gravel pits that covered most of the parish. The joint monarchs William III and Mary II made Kensington Palace their home in 1689 and it was the favoured residence of their three successors. Queen Victoria was born and raised here but moved to Buckingham Palace on her accession to the throne in 1837. Coincidentally, it was only at this point that property developers began to seriously exploit Kensington's residential potential; in the 40 years from 1841 the population of the parish increased sixfold. The establishment of the museums and colleges of SOUTH KENSINGTON brought added prestige and in the second half of the 19th century the district filled with high-class stuccoed terraces and detached villas. Property developers made up the name 'WEST KENSINGTON' for what had formerly been Fulham's lowly NORTH END; by contrast, NORTH KENSINGTON was a genuine part of the medieval parish but has never been a prestigious locality. Grand exhibition halls were built at EARLS COURT and KENSINGTON OLYMPIA in the mid 1880s and KENSINGTON HIGH STREET became one of the most fashionable shopping centres in the capital. By the end of the century only three significant green spaces remained: KENSINGTON GARDENS, HOLLAND PARK and the cemetery at WEST BROMPTON. Some streets were even more superior than others: Kensington Palace Gardens and The Boltons are among the most expensive addresses in London, and indeed in the world. No fundamental changes affected Kensington's residential fabric during the 20th century but high commissions and embassies clustered around Kensington Gardens and hotels multiplied across the southern half of the district, ranging in scale from converted houses in Earls Court to a skyscraper on Cromwell Road. GLOUCESTER ROAD is the central thoroughfare of Kensington's hospitality industry.

Residents of Kensington Square have included the philosopher John Stuart Mill, the painter Sir Edward Burne-Jones and the actress Mrs Patrick Campbell. William Wilberforce held anti-slavery meetings at his home in Kensington Gore. Winston Churchill lived and died at 28 Hyde Park Gate. Muriel Spark's 1988 novel *A Far Cry from Kensington* observes life here through the eyes of a young widow of slender means. The board game *Kensington* enjoyed a flurry of popularity in the 1980s.

✉ W8 (Kensington); SW7 (South Kensington)

♰ 36,266 (Abingdon, Campden, Holland and Queen's Gate wards; excludes North and West Kensington)

📖 Barbara Denny and Carolyn Starren, *Kensington Past*, Historical Publications, 1998

@ www.mykensington.co.uk (commercial local information site)

Kensington Gardens • *Westminster/ Kensington & Chelsea*

A royal park adjoining the west side of HYDE PARK, of which it originally formed a part. Around 1605 Sir George Coppin, clerk of the Crown to James I, built a house here with 36 acres of grounds. Later known as Nottingham House it was acquired by the joint monarchs William III and Mary II in 1689 and remodelled as Kensington Palace. The palace was further extended by George I and has not significantly changed since. George II was the last reigning monarch to live here and his consort Queen Caroline employed Charles Bridgeman to lay out Kensington Gardens. Near the boundary with Hyde Park six pools formed by the River Westbourne were connected to form the Long Water and the Serpentine. The future Queen Victoria was born at Kensington Palace in 1819 and she chose Kensington Gardens as the site for the fabulously ostentatious Albert Memorial, erected in 1872 to commemorate her late husband's achievements. A tea pavilion built in 1934 was converted into the Serpentine art gallery in 1970 and has since staged a remarkable number of influential exhibitions for such a dinky space. A £4 million renovation programme was begun under the patronage of Diana, Princess of Wales, who lived at Kensington Palace, and completed in 1998. A prolonged restoration of the Albert Memorial took place around the same time. The streets surrounding Kensington Gardens are clustered with embassies, high commissions and the London residences of foreign potentates. Two former embassy buildings in Kensington Palace Gardens knocked together to form a single mansion were sold for £50 million in 2001, making this the only private residence in the world worth more than Bill Gates's Shangri-La in Seattle. Kensington Palace retains residential apartments and offices for several members of the royal family but visitors can tour the state apartments and view the royal ceremonial dress collection.

The gardens have inspired many artists and writers, including the poet Matthew Arnold and most famously J M Barrie, whose *Peter Pan in Kensington Gardens* introduced the little boy who refused to grow up. In 1912, Barrie commissioned the sculptor George Frampton to create a statue of Peter Pan, which stands by the Long Water. The gardens' status as 'the world capital of fairies, gnomes and elves' was buttressed by the addition in the late 1920s of the Elfin Oak, a tree stump carved with effigies of the 'little people'.

⊠ W2

📖 Edward Impey, *Kensington Palace: The Official Illustrated History*, Merrell, 2003

@ www.kensington-palace.org.uk

Kensington High Street • *Kensington & Chelsea*

A homogenized shopping street located one mile west of KNIGHTSBRIDGE and widely referred to as 'High Street Ken'. KENSINGTON'S medieval parish church of St Mary Abbots was rebuilt in the late 17th century, with a tower added in 1772. A ribbon village grew up haphazardly around it and by the mid 19th century the narrow street was jammed with traffic, its buildings were a hotch-potch and the backstreets had become a slum. Everything changed in the late 1860s. The Metropolitan Board of Works cleared the insanitary housing and widened the High Street. The church was rebuilt again and the underground station opened, providing easy access to VICTORIA and WESTMINSTER. Entrepreneurs opened shops that grew to become department stores. The most successful of these was Barkers, which absorbed its main rival Derry

and Toms in 1921. Barkers opened the present building at 99 Kensington High Street in 1932. In the last quarter of the 20th century the street went into a decline but this had the benefit of allowing quirkier boutiques and indoor markets to flourish, offering better bargains and more 'urban' styles than could be found in Knightsbridge, which seemed stuffy by comparison. Barkers switched to an arcade format, with floor space sublet to franchises, and sold its famous roof gardens to the Virgin Group. Over the past decade the street has staged a recovery that has forced out most of the independent retailers. Its distinctive, slightly bohemian air has evaporated and Kensington High Street now looks much like any other high street.

The political essayist and agriculturist William Cobbett owned and lived on a smallholding that stood on the south side of the High Street, roughly on the site of the station, in the early 19th century.

⊠ W8

🚇 Circle Line; District Line (zone 1)

Kensington Olympia • *Hammersmith & Fulham*

An exhibition centre located at the western end of HIGH STREET KENSINGTON. In the 18th century this was the site of a vineyard, which by all accounts produced a passable burgundy. Kensington station opened on a branch of the Metropolitan Railway in 1864 and was renamed Kensington (Addison Road) four years later. Following the success of the Agricultural Hall in ISLINGTON, which held military tournaments as well as every kind of animal show, the public demanded a larger arena where mock battles could be played out on a grand scale. In 1885 the National Agricultural Hall Co. bought 6 acres and 37 perches of nursery land just over Kensington's border in HAMMERSMITH. Olympia opened in 1886 and proceeded to stage a series of lavish entertainment spectaculars, although it struggled to turn a profit. Pleasure gardens were laid out in the grounds and some of the world's first motor shows were held in the hall in the early 20th century. The National Hall was added on the south-west side in 1922, which necessitated the demolition of some properties in WEST KENSINGTON Gardens. The remainder of this street was erased in 1929 during the construction of the Empire Hall, later known as Olympia 2. London's first multi-storey car park was built for Olympia in 1937. The station closed during World War II and reopened afterwards as Kensington Olympia, served by a District Line shuttle from EARLS COURT. Main-line passenger services via Willesden Junction and Clapham Junction resumed in 1994 and cross-country and suburban trains now call here.

The poet Samuel Taylor Coleridge lived opposite the site of the exhibition hall in 1811–12.

> ✉ W14

> 🚉 Silverlink Metro; Southern; District Line (zone 2)

> 📖 John Glanfield, *Earls Court and Olympia*, Sutton, 2003

> @ www.eco.co.uk (Olympia and Earls Court exhibition halls site)

Kent House • *Bromley*

Border territory between BECKENHAM and PENGE, taking its name from a house that used to be the first building in the county of Kent on the local road from London. The area was recorded in the twelfth century as a Norman-owned estate, half of which was leased to the Hospital of St Katherine by the Tower in 1240, by which time Kent House was in existence. The house was owned by a series of City merchants over the following centuries, including John Styles, who dealt in wool in London and Calais in the 15th century. Another merchant, Anthony Rawlins, died at Kent House in 1694 and bequeathed money to be used for almshouses. Rawlins' almshouses survive today in remodelled form, in a corner of St George's churchyard, Beckenham. The Russian banker and Lloyds insurer John Julius Angerstein acquired Kent House in 1784. It became a farmhouse from around 1806, and the 178-acre farm had grazing rights on Penge Common. Kent House station was built in 1884, off King's Hall Road. Its architecture differs from other stations on the line because of its later construction. Local builders immediately began to lay out the neighbouring streets for middle-class housing. Barnmead Road is named after Barn Meadow, one of the fields on Kent House Farm. Kent House became a nursing home and then a private hotel before being pulled down in 1957. Its site is now covered by Beckett Walk. Kent House station was damaged by an IRA bomb in 1993, after a train was stopped and evacuated there following warnings; there were no casualties. The local community is mainly white and English-speaking, with incomes that are a little below average.

William Makepeace Thackeray once stayed at Kent House and the author's notes for his unfinished novel *Denis Duval* suggest that it was intended to be the protagonist's home.

> ✉ Beckenham BR3

> 🚉 South Eastern Trains (zone 4)

Kentish Town • *Camden*

A tarnished but characterful district situated north of CAMDEN TOWN, primarily residential but with some commerce and industry. The name is of obscure Saxon or Celtic origin and is more likely related to a man called Kentish than to the county of Kent. The settlement evolved as a ribbon development on the road to HIGHGATE and there is some evidence that it moved northwards to its present location, having first begun near ST PANCRAS Church; indeed, it may be that St Pancras and Kentish Town were originally one and the same place. William Bruges lavishly entertained the Emperor Sigismund at his country house in Kentish Town in 1416. In the 17th and 18th centuries, highwaymen made the surrounding area notoriously dangerous. Their attacks became so frequent that a group of vigilantes was formed for the protection of travellers. The antiquarian Dr William Stukely was one of several men to seek out a rural retreat in Kentish Town in the mid 18th century. Later in the century the introduction of regular coach services, operating on improved roads, made Kentish Town increasingly convenient and it benefited from a pleasant setting beside the Highgate tributary of the River Fleet. Lord Nelson is supposed to have lived for a while at the Castle Inn, 'in order to keep an eye on the Fleet'. As late as 1840 this was still a half-rural village with a community of artists and engravers but it was almost entirely built over during the following 30 years. Its popularity was aided by a London doctor who praised the healthy air and clean water, calling Kentish Town 'the Montpelier of England', and came to live here himself. Mary Shelley, however, condemned the place as an 'odious swamp'. The last grazing land disappeared in the 1860s, when a station opened near the Bull and Gate coaching inn, forming a convenient transport interchange. Underground stations opened at South Kentish Town (now closed) and Kentish Town in 1907. During the first half of the 20th century parts of the district became run down and the council cleared the first set of dilapidated properties in the early 1930s. Plans for aggressive redevelopment were tabled after World War II but a milder version was implemented and by 1960 the middle classes were beginning to rediscover Kentish Town. Today the population is a typical inner-north London mix of blue-collar workers and young professionals, along with some better-off owners of refurbished Victorian properties. Community groups continue to press for improvements to Kentish Town Road, which television newsreader and long-time resident Jon Snow has described as 'one of the slummiest high streets in London'.

'Men begin in Kentish Town with £80 a year, and end in Park Lane with a hundred thousand. They want to drop Kentish Town; but they give themselves away every time they open their mouths.' So says Professor Higgins in Shaw's *Pygmalion*. Hip-hop singer Ms Dynamite (Niomi Daley) grew up in Kentish Town.

✉ NW5

👥 11,462

🚃 Thameslink; Northern Line (Kentish Town, zone 2); Silverlink Metro (Kentish Town West, zone 2)

📖 Gillian Tindall, *The Fields Beneath*, Phoenix, 2002 (reissue of a splendid 1977 study)

Kentish Town West *see* MAITLAND PARK

Kenton • *Harrow/Brent*

A flourishing multicultural community situated north-east of HARROW. Most of Kenton falls within Harrow borough, but the part south of Kenton Road lies in Brent. The name was first recorded in 1231, when it was already a well-established settlement. Late in the 19th century Kenton remained an agricultural village with only the most basic amenities. The 'gentlemen's seats' that peppered so many parts of outer London had not appeared here because of its relative inaccessibility. Kenton is one of several London suburbs whose centre was shifted by the siting of its railway station. The old village lay in the immediate vicinity of Kenton Grange, now in Woodcock Park. The opening of a station on the London and Birmingham (later London and North Western) Railway three-quarters of a mile to the west in 1912, and the expansion of Kingsbury's territory, pushed the village's midpoint towards WEALDSTONE. At first the railway brought more day-trippers than new inhabitants, but growth accelerated after 1925 with the popularity of the Harrow and WEMBLEY areas. St Thomas's Hospital and Christ Church College, Oxford sold their land in Kenton around

this time and estates were built with bucolic names like Woodcock Dell and Lyon Farm. In the ten years to 1931, when its development peaked, Kenton's population increased twenty-fold. A METROLAND brochure of the previous year pronounced that this once small hamlet, 'standing on a little-used country road, has now become a thriving colony and the country lane is a busy high road of traffic between Harrow, KINGSBURY GREEN and the main London Road to EDGWARE'. When the Travellers' Rest was rebuilt as the Rest Hotel in 1933, it became the largest public house in Middlesex. Harrow sewage farm was converted into Kenton recreation ground in 1936. St Mary's Church, built with money raised by the sale of its namesake in Charing Cross Road, was consecrated in the same year. Kenton is now popular with upwardly mobile members of the Asian community, particularly those of Indian descent, and has almost as many Hindus as Christians, as well as a significant Jewish minority in the south.

✉ Harrow HA3

👥 32,037 (Harrow's Kenton East and Kenton West wards, and Brent's Kenton ward)

🚃 Silverlink Metro (zone 4); Bakerloo Line (zone 4)

📖 M C Barrès-Baker, *Kenton*, Grange Museum of Community History and Brent Archive, 2001

Kenwood • *Camden*

A landscaped estate located to the north-east of HAMPSTEAD HEATH, south of Hampstead Lane. The park boasts a fine collection of trees and some of the most beautiful rhododendron gardens in London. Kenwood House, remodelled in the neoclassical style by Robert Adam in 1764, is an English Heritage property. Dr Johnson's thatched summerhouse used to stand in the grounds. The estate belonged to the earls of Mansfield until 1925, when the house and grounds were saved from developers in a campaign led by Sir Arthur Crosfield, whose achievement is marked by a plaque. Kenwood was bought by Edward Cecil Guinness, the first Earl of Iveagh, and on his death in 1927 he bequeathed the estate to the nation along with part of his collection of old master paintings; the Iveagh Bequest includes a Rembrandt self-portrait, one of only five Vermeers in Britain, Gainsborough's portrait of Countess Howe and works by Reynolds and Turner. Lakeside concerts, traditionally of classical music, are held at Kenwood in the summer. In recent years the programme has incorporated more accessible material, attracting larger audiences. This has aroused the ire of conservationist pressure groups and some nearby residents, including the actor Warren Mitchell.

Kenwood House has frequently served as a film location, including for scenes in *101 Dalmatians* and *Notting Hill*.

✉ NW3

📖 Julius Bryant, *Kenwood: Paintings in the Iveagh Bequest,* Yale University Press, 2003; John Carswell, *The Saving of Kenwood and the Northern Heights,* Aidan Ellis, 2001

Keston • *Bromley*

A semi-rural village situated two miles west of FARNBOROUGH. It is claimed that the name relates to Julius Caesar's presence in the area in 55 BC, although this is extremely improbable. However, it is likely that Romans settled here around AD 200 and relics of a Roman cemetery have been found. The old parish church, opposite the western end of Downe Road, was the centre of medieval Keston but, after the Black Death, development began anew a mile and a half to the north, in a clearing between HAYES Common and Keston Common. The latter was one of the first pieces of common land to be protected by Act of Parliament from further encroachment (in 1865) and now has perhaps the most diverse range of habitats of any common in London, with the greatest number of rare species. Most of the recent construction is hidden from the main road, allowing Keston to maintain the impression – by London standards – of an unspoilt rural community. The surrounding farmland is littered with evidence of Neolithic as well as Roman occupation, and there is a weatherboarded windmill dated 1716, and restored in 1913, but most of these sites are inaccessible to the public. Keston Ponds, near the private estate of HOLWOOD, are fed from the fancifully named Caesar's Well, the source of the River Ravensbourne.

✉ Keston BR2

👥 16,500 (Bromley Common and Keston ward)

📖 Muriel V Searle, *Hayes, West Wickham and Keston in Old Picture Postcards,* European Library, 1988

Keston Mark • *Bromley*

A largely 20th-century extension of KESTON, which lies half a mile to the south-west. This was once a hamlet on the northern perimeter of Keston parish; 'mark' means a boundary and was once common in place names, though few examples survive in the London area. A tree known as Mark's Oak used to stand in one of the fields of FARNBOROUGH Lodge. Keston Mark has now almost merged with BROMLEY COMMON to the north and LOCKS-BOTTOM to the east as a result of extensive private housebuilding. Many of the homes are expensive – particularly on the private Keston Park estate – but this is a characterless corner and there are car dealers and a garden centre where the village green should be. The Keston Mark public house used to be called the Red Cross but was renamed 'to avoid confusion with the international organization'; it is not clear what kind of confusion could have arisen.

✉ Keston BR2

Kevington • *Bromley*

Although situated just a mile to the south-east of ST MARY CRAY, this is a rural hamlet (also spelt Kevingtown), with farms, nurseries and old cottages. The name may come from Old English words meaning 'place on a small hill' or it may relate to a landowner named Cyfa. The Ordnance Survey map of 1876 shows Kevingtown and Kevington as two separate places, the former at the top of the hill, the latter on its western slope. However, this distinction no longer applies. The manor of Kevington was in the hands of the related Manning and Onslow families from the late Middle Ages to the mid 18th century, when Middleton Onslow sold it to Herman Behrens, a City merchant from Amsterdam who commissioned the construction of Kevington Hall, completed in 1769 by the architect Sir Robert Taylor. Behrens' descendants held the property until World War II, when the government requisitioned it to accommodate Canadian troops. Afterwards, Kent County Council used the hall as a primary school until the early 1980s. It is now privately owned, newly restored and available for conducted group tours by arrangement and for private functions. Next door, the former Shawcroft Special School, built in 1974 in a woodland setting on Crockenhill Road, has been renamed Oak View and is a commercially run, medium-security mental healthcare unit for adolescents. The hamlet lacks any amenities for residents and the former Kevington Arms is now Blueberry Farm. Once part of the Kevington manor estate, the 30-acre Warren is a woodland and meadow nature reserve managed by the London Wildlife Trust.

273

✉ Orpington BR5

@ www.kevingtonhall.co.uk

Kew • *Richmond*
An attractive village lying in a crook of the Thames, opposite CHISWICK and BRENTFORD. The name is probably derived from 'key-hough', the wood or 'hough' by the quay, and was first mentioned in 1327. When the Tudors made RICHMOND UPON THAMES a regular seat of their court, Kew benefited as a home for their courtiers. The Duke of Suffolk had a mansion here that was built and pulled down in the Tudor era. The house now called Kew Palace was built in the reign of James I by a Flemish merchant and hence became known as the Dutch House. The village had a chapel from the 16th century and St Anne's Church was built on Kew Green in 1714, when a public subscription raised the money and Queen Anne granted the plot of land. The village grew around the green and then southwards along the eastern edge of what is now KEW GARDENS. The green used to be a regular place for fairs until these became too riotous. Kew came to prominence as the resort of George II's family. The Hanoverians lavished money and attention on Kew House, or the Old Palace, and its grounds. The house was taken down in 1802 and a replacement was commenced but left unfinished by George III. To the east of Kew Bridge was the old Kew dock, which was once the centre of a thriving fishing industry until it was killed off by pollution in the Thames. The toll bridge was bought for free public use in 1873, by which time Kew Gardens station was bringing hundreds of thousands of visitors a year to the gardens and turning the village into a suburb. The massive archive repositories of the Public Record Office were built at the end of Ruskin Avenue in the mid 1970s, when the institution moved here from CHANCERY LANE. Further to the south-east, St James Homes have recently built 500 upmarket houses and apartments at Kew Riverside, on the site of a former sewage works. To the annoyance of some residents, a neighbouring recycling centre continues to operate and was refurbished in 2006. The residents of Kew tend to be white and well educated. Fewer than 10 per cent of homes are rented from the council or a housing association.

The landscape and portrait painter Thomas Gainsborough was buried in St Anne's churchyard in 1788.

✉ Richmond TW9

👥 9,445

⛴ Kew pier

📖 David Blomfield, *Kew Past*, Phillimore, 1994

@ www.pro.gov.uk (Public Record Office site)

Kew Bridge • *Hounslow*
A river crossing and station located where the Thames makes the first northward loop on its journey through London. The name is not much used for the station's hinterland, largely because KEW itself is on the opposite bank. Until 1759 a horse-ferry carried traffic across the river near here, owned for the last century of its existence by the Tunstall family, who also had a BRENTFORD limekiln business. The entrepreneurial Robert Tunstall commissioned the building of a wooden toll-bridge, which lasted 30 years before his son, also Robert, replaced it with a stone structure. The present bridge was designed by John Wolfe-Barry and opened in 1903 by Edward VII, in whose honour it was named, although its users continued to call it Kew Bridge. The construction of the bridge, in concrete and granite, was a joint project by the county councils of Surrey and Middlesex. Kew Bridge station, on the Hounslow loop line, opened in 1850. In 1869 the London and South Western Railway Co. built Kew railway bridge at STRAND ON THE GREEN to provide a shorter route for its line to RICHMOND. A gem among London's lesser-known collections, Kew Bridge Steam Museum is housed in a former water pumping station on Green Dragon Lane. The museum has a narrow gauge steam railway, an exhibition on the story of London's water supply and the world's largest collection of steam pumping engines, several of which can be seen in action at weekends.

A year after the first Kew Bridge opened Prince George was riding across it when a messenger reached him with news of his accession to the throne on the death of George II. The artist J M W Turner sketched and painted the second bridge several times in 1805.

✉ Brentford TW8

🚆 South West Trains (zone 3)

@ www.kbsm.org (Kew Bridge Steam Museum)

Kew Gardens • *Richmond*
The Royal Botanic Gardens occupy the northwestern part of the KEW peninsula, across the Thames from BRENTFORD. The gardens are a

convergence of three 17th-century projects: the Dutch House and the White House and their grounds, and the northward expansion of the royal gardens of RICHMOND UPON THAMES. Over the first three decades of the 18th century, and especially during the reign of George II, several properties in Kew were acquired or built for members of the royal household either as permanent residences or places of leisure. The Dutch House became Kew Palace, while the White House was rebuilt as the home of Frederick, Prince of Wales and his wife Princess Augusta. Queen Caroline appointed Charles Bridgeman and William Kent to embellish the landscape and add decorative buildings and most of their work was done in the early 1730s. The octagonal ten-storey pagoda was built in 1762 as a surprise for Princess Augusta, the Dowager Princess of Wales, and Capability Brown remodelled the gardens of Richmond (formerly Ormonde) Lodge for George III and Queen Charlotte in 1765, but the lodge itself was demolished in the following decade. Queen Charlotte is said to have designed the cottage that was built at the edge of the Old Deer Park in the early 1770s. At this time, Joseph Banks was made director of the gardens and set about importing, cultivating and then re-exporting consignments of exotic plants from Britain's colonies abroad. Banks set up satellite botanical gardens as far afield as St Vincent in the West Indies and Madras in India. The various gardens of Kew were united in 1802 and adopted as a national botanical garden in 1841. The Victorian directors enhanced Kew's role by introducing brokerage facilities for vital commodities like tea, coffee, rubber, quinine and cotton, while resisting attempts to turn the gardens from a scientific establishment into a pleasure park. Magnificent new buildings were erected for the cultivation of plants requiring different climatic conditions, including the Winter Garden (now the Temperate House) and the Palm House. Successive new buildings have subsequently entrenched Kew's status as world centre of botanical research, as well as a breathtaking spectacle. Kew Palace has recently reopened following extensive refurbishment and visitors are also being permitted occasional access to the pagoda. With nearly a million admissions a year, the gardens are a more popular attraction than London Zoo. In 2003 UNESCO declared Kew a world heritage site, in recognition of its 'unique cultural landscape'.

The 2004 BBC television series *A Year at Kew*, narrated by Alan Titchmarsh, was so popular with viewers that a second series was immediately commissioned.

⊠ Richmond TW9

🚇 Silverlink Metro; District Line (zones 3 and 4)

📖 Rupert Smith, *A Year at Kew*, BBC Books, 2004; Ray Desmond, *Kew: The History of the Royal Botanic Gardens*, Harvill, 1998

@ www.rbgkew.org.uk (Royal Botanic Gardens site); www.explore-kew-gardens.net

Kidbrooke • *Greenwich*

A socially mixed residential district situated south of CHARLTON and east of BLACKHEATH. A watercourse called Kid Brook runs to the south-west, but this may have been named after the settlement, as the derivation is probably 'marshy ground with kites'. Kidbrooke was an ancient manor, first documented in the twelfth-century records of the diocese of Rochester. The diocesan manuscript notes the presence of a chapel and this survived until around 1400. Its demise may have been the consequence of the depopulation of Kidbrooke by the Black Death in the mid 14th century. Woodland covered parts of the manor and Kidbrooke provided quality timber to London builders in the early 19th century. Most of the land was given over to pasture and arable use with a little market gardening until the 1860s, when housebuilding began to cut ribbons through the agricultural holdings and St James's Church was built. Kidbrooke station opened to the south in 1895 and a new road was laid to provide access from the village, where more villas clustered around the church. Kidbrooke station remained one of the quietest on the line until 1915, when a neighbouring military depot was built. Between 1925 and 1938, the Blackheath side of Kidbrooke disappeared under new roads and houses, notably in the form of the Kidbrooke Park estate. Rochester Way became a major traffic route in 1932. Upper and Lower Kidbrooke Farms survived until World War II but succumbed soon after. Kidbrooke School, which opened in 1954 near Brook Hospital in Lower Kidbrooke, was the first purpose-built comprehensive school in the UK. Greenwich council built the FERRIER estate in the 1970s and is now in the process of rebuilding it. Over half the homes in Kidbrooke are owner-occupied, while a third are rented from the council.

The comedian Jim Davidson grew up in Holburne Road. The actor Jude Law attended Kidbrooke School and has been quoted as saying, 'It was just a nightmare school. The vibe was really aggressive and racist, and all about gangs.' The school gained better publicity when it became the test bed for Jamie Oliver's popular and influential crusade to improve school catering standards in Channel 4's 2005 series *Jamie's School Dinners*.

✉ SE3

👤 12,098 (Kidbrooke with Hornfair ward)

🚆 South Eastern Trains (zone 3)

📖 Michael Egan, *Kidbrooke: 800 Years of a Farming Community*, Greenwich and Lewisham Antiquarian Society, 1983

Kilburn • *Brent/Camden*

The former heartland of London's Irish community, now more multicultural, located north-west of ST JOHN'S WOOD and MAIDA VALE. The name comes from a stream (which could have been 'cold bourne', 'cow's bourne' or 'King's bourne') that formerly constituted the upper part of the River Westbourne. Kilburn Priory was founded in the twelfth century on the site of a former hermitage and the Red Lion, which was said to date from 1444, may have begun life as the priory's guest house. The settlement grew as a minor halt on the London to St Albans road, with coaching inns built to serve the travellers along the stretch of Watling Street that is now Kilburn High Road (A5). A medicinal well was discovered near the Bell inn in the early 18th century and a pleasure garden was laid out in imitation of the one at Hampstead. After abortive attempts at estate building in the 1820s, the large houses and farms that had previously lined the main road were demolished to make way for terraces of houses, the first of which was built in 1850 after the opening of Kilburn station on the London to Birmingham line. At the same time, villas for the upper middle classes were built on the former estate of Kilburn Priory. Outlying areas like BRONDESBURY, Shoot Up Hill and WEST KILBURN were developed from the 1860s. A number of private schools opened, including one run by A A Milne's father, which the writer attended, as did H G Wells and the newspaper proprietor Alfred Harmsworth. The district became poorer later in the century, the schools closed, large houses were subdivided or took in lodgers, and a variety of immigrants began to move here, especially the Irish. Kilburn became a popular place for public entertainment and entrepreneurs established several variety theatres. When the Gaumont State opened here in 1937 it was Europe's largest cinema, with 4,000 seats. Much of the present housing in Kilburn is the result of slum clearance programmes in the 1930s and the replacement of bomb-damaged properties after World War II. Municipal authorities built several estates of flats into the 1970s and Irish settlers were joined by West Indians, Indians and Pakistanis. A few years ago, Kilburn High Road was named the 'Music Mile' by the London Tourist Board, with Irish and country music the main specialities, performed at pubs like Biddy Mulligan's. Nearly all these establishments have now gone and the Music Mile is no more, although several pubs still have an Irish flavour and/or clientele. The Tricycle Theatre is the district's leading cultural venue. Fewer than 10 per cent of Kilburn's residents are now Irish and many of these are of the older generation; the black African community is larger and − in the Brent half of the district − so is the black Caribbean community. Kilburn is shrinking as estate agents choose to market its fringes by other names; the writer Zadie Smith states her address as 'QUEEN'S PARK borders (Kilburn)'.

The band Kilburn and the High Roads gave punk singer/songwriter Ian Dury his first break in the early 1970s.

✉ NW6

👤 24,666 (Brent Kilburn ward and Camden's Kilburn ward)

🚆 Silverlink Metro (Kilburn High Road, zone 2); Jubilee Line (Kilburn, zone 2)

📖 Dick Weindling and Marianne Colloms, *Kilburn and Cricklewood*, Tempus, 2001

@ www.kilburn.towntalk.co.uk (commercial local information site); www.tricycle.co.uk

---

Kilburn Park • *Brent/Westminster*

The south-western part of KILBURN, between Kilburn High Road and WEST KILBURN. The area may have been part of Kilburn Priory's lands in the Middle Ages but the 'Park' element of the name was merely a builders' invention. In 1850 the Reverend Edward Stuart sold 47 acres here to a consortium of five developers, of whom the largest was James Bailey. They laid out roads and sewers and divided the site among themselves, subletting to smaller firms who built a few houses each. Several of the contractors aimed high with their early efforts but the isolated, muddy location failed to attract buyers and the estate remained incomplete for several decades. In the absence of middle-class residents, properties were soon subdivided, some containing as many as six households in the 1870s. At this time, the Reverend R C Kilpatrick commissioned an extraordinary church for Kilburn Park. St Augustine's is one of the most breathtaking Victorian churches in the whole of England, a fusion of French-inspired detailing and Anglo-Catholic tradition, with a soaring steeple. The body of the church was complete by 1877 but it was another 20 years before the spire reached its full height of 254 feet. Perhaps the church gave Kilburn Park the cachet it had previously lacked, for the remainder of the estate was built up in the late 1880s. The London Electric Railway came to Kilburn Park in 1915. Much of the area was damaged by World War II bombing and was afterwards subject to wholesale redevelopment and the addition of several council tower blocks. Many of Kilburn Park's residents are of black Caribbean and black African origin. Kilburn Park Primary School is a very highly regarded foundation school despite the social difficulties of its catchment area.

✉ NW6

🚇 Bakerloo Line (zone 2)

King George V • *Newham*

A Docklands Light Railway station located to the east of LONDON CITY AIRPORT. The King George V Dock was commissioned in 1910 as part of an improvement plan for the ROYAL DOCKS and opened for traffic in 1921. It was designed on the same lines as the ROYAL ALBERT Dock, except that its north side was flanked by two-storey, brick-built transit sheds, while a series of 'dolphin' jetties were positioned parallel to the south quay. The dock closed in the early 1980s and its western dry dock and all the buildings on its north quay were replaced by London City Airport. King George V station opened in 2005 and is designed to allow the further extension of the line under the Thames to WOOLWICH ARSENAL.

✉ E16

🚇 Docklands Light Railway, City Airport branch terminus (zone 3)

Kingsbury • *Brent*

A mixed METROLAND and municipally built suburb covering a large area north-east of WEMBLEY and west of HENDON. Known in ancient times as Tunworth, it was mentioned in Domesday Book as Chingesberie, which meant 'king's manor'. The unused 12th-

century church is an indication of Kingsbury's significance as a medieval settlement and an inscription at the police station records how local disputes were resolved by representatives from much of the modern borough. The growth of Kingsbury has seesawed between its southern and northern extremities. Kingsbury was first a village beside Black Pot Hill (now Blackbird Hill), and KINGSBURY GREEN was a hamlet one mile to its north. Kingsbury was severely affected by the Black Death. The old village was largely abandoned; a new one grew up around Kingsbury Green and by the late 19th century the original village was almost forgotten. Victorian development was substantial enough for Kingsbury to break away from Wembley in 1900 as an independent urban district. However, the separation lasted only 34 years and the district remained predominantly rural until well into the 20th century. In the 1920s NEASDEN and Kingsbury station (now Neasden) stimulated Metroland growth in the southern part of Kingsbury and the population increased eightfold in ten years. Immediately after this came the final construction stage of the Metropolitan Railway, from Wembley Park to Stanmore, and the opening of the underground station to the west of Kingsbury Green in 1932, whereupon the town's centre of gravity shifted once more. A further spate of private building included some notable follies and cottage-style houses by Ernest George Trobridge. Because Kingsbury is not a highly desirable area, most of Trobridge's delightful homes are not in the condition they deserve to be. After World War II, Wembley council built a large housing estate, destroying most of Kingsbury's historic buildings in the process.

There are two churches dedicated to St Andrew, sharing the same churchyard at the south end of Church Lane. This was the original location of the village of Kingsbury from Saxon times. St Andrew's Church on Old Church Lane is of medieval origin and is the only building in the borough with Grade I-listed status. The newer St Andrew's Church was erected as a result of the massive growth in the area's population following the opening of Neasden and Kingsbury station and the laying out of Kingsbury Garden Village. Formerly an Anglo-Catholic church located in Wells Street in the parish of St Marylebone, and conveniently already dedicated to St Andrew, it was transported to Kingsbury stone by stone in 1933.

✉ NW9

🚇 Jubilee Line (zone 4)

📖 M C Barrès-Baker, *Kingsbury,* Grange Museum of Community History and Brent Archive, 2001

Kingsbury Green • *Brent*

A small park and hilltop locality located at the junction of Kingsbury Road and Church Lane in north-east KINGSBURY. The early hamlet was almost wiped out by the Black Death in 1349 but growth resumed in the following century. By the late Middle Ages several roads converged on the green, which became the focus of the district's largest hamlet as new houses were built. The Plough inn was recorded in 1748. Some modest villas appeared here and at nearby ROE GREEN from the early 19th century but the area remained primarily agricultural until the 1920s. Thereafter, the whole of Kingsbury rapidly filled with suburban housing and the farm buildings and labourers' cottages were pulled down. The combination of encroaching interwar development and the straightening of Kingsbury Road in the 1970s reduced the green's area to a single acre, but there are much larger open spaces nearby. Kingsbury Green's name was used to identify all of north Kingsbury until relatively recently but because the station is called simply Kingsbury this usage has declined. At Kingsbury Green Primary School, pupils come mainly from Indian, Pakistani, white British, Bangladeshi, African, Caribbean and Chinese backgrounds.

✉ NW9

King's Cross • *Camden/Islington*

A run-down but rapidly changing inner-city district located one mile east of REGENT'S PARK, and formerly called Battle Bridge. The modern name comes from a statue of George IV that was erected at the junction of EUSTON Road, GRAY'S INN ROAD and PENTONVILLE Road in 1830. The statue was removed only 15 years later owing to its unpopularity with the local community. However, the name proved more resilient and was applied to the Great Northern Railway terminus when it opened in 1852, and subsequently to an expanding neighbourhood to the north and south, much of which was previously known as ST PANCRAS. King's Cross is one of central London's poorest districts and its shops, hotels and homes all reflect this. It has the highest concentration in western Europe of people living in short-term accommodation, and its streets are a gathering place for drug dealers and addicts, alcoholics, prostitutes and the homeless. Heavy policing and comprehensive use of closed-circuit television have reduced, but not eliminated, the more obvious manifestations of the area's problems. The King's Cross Partnership is overseeing a massive regeneration programme, which may not be completed until 2015. At the heart of the project is the redevelopment of 53 acres of railway land as a 'human city' named King's Cross Central. Behind King's Cross is Camley Street nature park. Created on the banks of the Regent Canal, it has a variety of wildlife habitats as well as a visitor centre and classroom.

In 1987, 31 people died in a fire at King's Cross station, which resulted in new safety measures that included a ban on smoking throughout the London Underground system. One victim of the conflagration was not identified until 2004. On 7 July 2005, Muslim extremists travelled into King's Cross Thameslink station from Luton, radiating out from the station to carry out suicide bombings on a bus and three Tube trains that killed 52 people.

King's Cross station hides two secrets: legend has it that Boudicca, queen of the Iceni, is buried beneath what is now platform 11, while Harry Potter and his schoolmates board the Hogwarts Express at platform $9\frac{3}{4}$.

✉ N1; WC1

🚶 11,413

🚇 Main-line: Great North Eastern Railway (Yorkshire, north-east England and Scotland); WAGN Railway (East Anglia and suburban services) Thameslink: Thameslink (Bedford to Brighton service) London Underground: Circle Line, Hammersmith & City Line, Metropolitan Line, Northern Line, Piccadilly Line; Victoria Line (zone 1)

📖 Michael Hunter and Robert Thorne (ed.), *Change at King's Cross*, Phillimore, 1990

@ www.kingsx.co.uk (community site); www.argentkingscross.co.uk (King's Cross Central)

Kingsland • *Hackney*

A historically poor and densely populated locality situated immediately west of DALSTON, of which it is nowadays considered a part. Its name derives from the former royal ownership of parts of Hackney. Samuel Pepys wrote in 1667 that he had boarded at Kingsland as a boy, 'and used to shoot with my bow and arrows in these fields. A very pretty place it is'. At that time the hamlet was slightly more populous than Dalston and it grew more rapidly in the 18th century, with inns strung out along what became Kingsland High Street and farmhouses behind. During the first quarter of the 19th century some terraces of very cramped houses were laid out, creating an increasingly sharp contrast with the early stages of respectable suburbanization in Dalston. Kingsland station opened in 1850 but closed when Dalston Junction opened in 1865. Without a station to its name Kingsland's identity faded; some late Victorian maps do not label it separately, already treating the area as part of Dalston's sprawl. In the 1880s Kingsland Green was built on, despite local protests. Throughout the second half of the 20th century, council intervention nibbled away at Kingsland's already meagre heritage, but more recent City Challenge funding has produced some improvements. Kingsland station reopened as Dalston Kingsland with the creation of the North London line (in its present form) in 1985. Kingsland High Street has a hotch-potch of inexpensive shops and other commercial premises, including the excellent Rio cinema (the third cinema on this site) and a former eel, pie and mash shop that is now a Chinese restaurant. Kingsland Waste, the stretch of Kingsland Road between Forest Road and Middleton Road, hosts a long-established Saturday market selling all kinds of goods.

✉ N1; E8

🚇 Silverlink Metro (Dalston Kingsland, zone 2)

King's Road • *Kensington & Chelsea*

'The longest catwalk in the world' runs southwestwards from SLOANE SQUARE to FULHAM, where it becomes New King's Road. It originated as a private highway from London to HAMPTON COURT, created by Charles II. In 1693 the Crown made a down payment on the construction of an intersecting processional route that would connect Chelsea's Royal Hospital with Kensington Palace, but only a short section south of King's Road was completed, which survives as Royal Avenue. The road's association with high fashion and style is not a recent phenomenon. Many of London's farms became nurseries in the 18th century and those bordering King's Road were regarded as the height of fashion. Would-be stars of market gardening who operated elsewhere had to open 'showrooms' here to promote their businesses. The royal highway became a public thoroughfare by degrees. In the mid-18th century passes were issued to 'proper' gentlemen but enterprising locals forged their own. King's Road opened formally to the hoi polloi in 1830, by which time houses and inns were scattered along most of its length. One of the oldest buildings was the WORLD'S END tavern, which gave its name to the neighbouring locality where the road runs closest to the river. Shops appeared later in the 19th century, especially towards the Sloane Square end, and James Whistler and friends founded the Chelsea Arts Club in 1891. The Duke of York's Headquarters, formerly an asylum for soldiers' children, became a base for the Territorial Army in the early years of the 20th century. A vestry hall was extended to a King's Road frontage in 1908 and survives as the Old Town Hall. Places of entertainment included the Palaseum and Gaumont cinemas, which still operate but under different names. Mary Quant opened the King's Road's first boutique in 1955 and by the mid 1960s the street had become a fashion centre that was rivalled only by CARNABY STREET. Gandalf's Garden and the Chelsea Drug Store were among the many hang-outs for hippies and curious onlookers. Punk clothing appeared at World's End in the early 1970s, a few years before its musical accompaniment. The street has become more straightforwardly commercial and less cutting-edge since those times, but remains immensely popular, as much for its bars and restaurants as its fashion retailers and galleries. The Duke of York's Headquarters was redeveloped with shops, cafés and an open paved area in 2003.

The actress Ellen Terry lived at 215 King's Road from 1904 to 1920. The fictional hero James Bond lived in Royal Avenue, as did the protagonists of Catherine Alliott's 2002 novel *A Married Man*.

✉ SW3; SW10

📖 Max Decharne, *King's Road: The Rise and Fall of the Hippest Street in the World*, Weidenfeld & Nicholson, 2005

Kingston Hill • *Kingston*

A tree-lined road running along the south-eastern edge of RICHMOND PARK. The name is only occasionally used to refer to the wider locality. Development, financed by the National Freehold Land Society and others, began in the mid 19th century, when a succession of villas was built along its length. St Paul's Church, Kingston Hill was built near the southern end of the road in 1878. Rebuilding and infilling over the course of the 20th century, especially in the 1930s, significantly increased the housing density. Gate lodges are often the only survival from the Victorian phase. In 1946 Kingston Technical College moved to its new home in Kingston Hill House, a mansion that had supposedly belonged to Lillie Langtry, mistress of the Prince of Wales (later Edward VII). The college also took over Kenry House, on the opposite side of the road, which had previously served as an Italian prisoner-of-war camp. The college became Kingston Polytechnic in 1970 and Kingston University in 1992. In 2004 the council designated Kingston Hill a conservation area; this includes the university campus and neighbouring housing and landscaping.

Just north of Richmond Park's Ladderstile Gate is Galsworthy House, formerly Parkfield, the birthplace of the novelist John Galsworthy in 1867.

✉ Kingston upon Thames KT2

@ www.kingston.ac.uk (Kingston University)

Kingston upon Thames • *Kingston*

The ancient capital of Surrey, and coronation place of Saxon kings, hence 'king's town'. There is considerable evidence of Roman occupation and it is claimed (though less credibly) that Julius Caesar crossed the Thames here. In 838 Kingston was chosen as the seat of the great council convened by King Egbert and presided over by Ceolnothus, the Archbishop of Canterbury. The town's long association with royalty continued in the tenth century with Edward the Elder, son of Alfred the Great, who was the first of seven Saxon kings to be crowned here. The Coronation Stone, probably the town's most notable possession, stands by the twelfth-century Clattern Bridge over the River Hogsmill, outside the more recent Guildhall. Kingston was an important royal manor by the time of Domesday Book, which declared that it had a church, five mills and three salmon fisheries; the borough's modern logo incorporates three salmon and a crown. Kingston's post-Norman significance owes much to its bridge, which was for nearly a thousand years the lowest Thames crossing except for LONDON BRIDGE. There has been a market in Kingston since at least the 13th century, and pottery, fishing, tanning and the wool trade were key industries throughout the Middle Ages. The grammar school was founded in 1561. Kingston was an important coaching town in the 18th cen-

tury but the Druid's Head is the only contemporary survivor from the inns of that period. The town's transport links were improved when a stone bridge replaced its wooden predecessor in 1828 but civic resistance blocked the arrival of the railway until 1863, although Kingston-on-Railway opened at SURBITON in 1838. Kingston's residential population leapt when private estates such as Richmond Park were added along Richmond Road in the 1930s. At the far end of that road, the pioneering Sopwith Aviation Co. was succeeded by Hawker Engineering, which manufactured cars and motorcycles as well as the aircraft for which it is best known. Kingston has become the prime retail location for south-west London, yet retains one of the best medieval street plans outside the City. Its flagship store, Bentall's, opened in 1867 and was reconstructed at the end of the 1980s, when it met with competition from John Lewis. At the same time a transformation began with the construction of a relief road, which permitted the pedestrianization of the town centre. A notable feature in the main shopping area is the domino set of telephone boxes, an installation by David Mach. In 2004 the town centre enterprises set up a pioneering business improvement district in a bid to retain Kingston's place among Britain's top 20 shopping destinations.

✉ Kingston upon Thames KT1 and KT2

👥 17,468 (Grove and Canbury wards)

🚌 South West Trains (zone 6)

📖 Francis Frith and Patrick Loobey, *Francis Frith's Kingston upon Thames*, Frith Book Co., 2004; Phil Andrews et al, *Charter Quay: The Spirit of Change – The Archaeology of Kingston's Riverside*, Trust for Wessex Archaeology, 2003; June Sampson, *Kingston Past*, Historical Publications, 1997

@ www.kingstononline.co.uk (commercial local information site)

Kingston Vale • *Kingston*

A suburbanized village, nestling between KINGSTON HILL and PUTNEY VALE, with RICHMOND PARK to the north-west and WIMBLEDON COMMON to the east. Formerly known as Kingston Bottom, the name was changed in deference to Victorian sensibilities. In its earliest days the hamlet was home to labourers who made their living in Richmond Park. The growing importance of HAMPTON COURT as a royal residence in the late 17th century brought inns to the vale, serving the needs of passing courtiers and messengers, as well as those travelling further in the direction of Portsmouth. Until the early 19th century a smithy, a handful of taverns and a group of cottages comprised the totality of Kingston Vale's housing stock. Grand villas began to appear thereafter, until these were almost as numerous as the cottages, which began to decline in number with the prevailing rural depopulation. In 1847 Kingston Vale acquired its own church, St John the Baptist, removing responsibility for the locality from the vicar of HAM. The original building was replaced by the present structure in 1861, erected on a site given by the Duke of Cambridge, who owned much of the land hereabouts. As in many parts of the borough, the construction of the Kingston bypass brought suburban development to Kingston Vale in the 1930s and the process continued after World War II. In the late 20th century, soaring property prices led to the closure of village amenities and their replacement by more housing.

Dorich House, now part of Kingston University, has works by the Russian sculptress Dora Gordine and a collection of Russian art and artefacts assembled by her husband. The house was built to the couple's design and is occasionally opened to the public.

Robin Hood's name features in many place-names in the locality but the legendary outlaw is not supposed to have visited these parts. From the 15th century, travelling troupes of players dressed up as the merry men, performed little plays and put on displays of archery. Henry VIII is said to have watched such entertainments in Richmond Park and their popularity was reflected in the naming of a nearby farm, an inn, a park gate and then other local places. A mid-19th-century church document referred to Kingston Vale as the 'Robin Hood district'.

✉ SW15

📖 Leonard W Cowie, *A History of the Parish and Church of St John the Baptist, Kingston Vale*, St John the Baptist Project 150 Committee, 1997; Clive Whichelow, *The Local Mystery of Robin Hood*, Enigma, 2000

@ www.kingston.ac.uk/dorich (Dorich House page of Kingston University site)

King Street • *Hammersmith & Fulham*
The principal shopping street of HAMMERSMITH, running from Hammersmith Broadway west to STAMFORD BROOK, where it meets

Chiswick High Road and GOLDHAWK ROAD. This was a turnpike road from 1717 and during the course of the 18th century it acquired houses, inns, stables and Cromwell's Brewery. Before it was covered over, Stamford Brook used to open out into a creek near the brewery. King Street gained its present name around 1794. Shops began to line the street towards the end of the 19th century. The street was widened in the 1930s, when Hammersmith Town Hall was built and many of the original shops were demolished. The construction of the A4 two decades later relieved the street of its role as part of the Great West Road. Nowadays, the big-name stores are clustered towards the eastern end, including those within the Ashcroft Square and Kings Mall precincts. The western part of King Street has a strong Polish presence, with retailers, services and a social centre serving the local community. The red brick and aubergine tiling of the Salutation Inn (1910) is one of the street's few architectural highlights.

The Lyric Theatre is a focal arts venue for west London. A new gilt and velvet auditorium has been rebuilt inside this 1970s concrete structure. The Latymer Arts Centre, at 237 King Street, is a new building with a four-storey atrium serving as a theatre foyer and art gallery.

✉ W6

Knightsbridge • *Westminster*
A prestigious locality and street situated south of HYDE PARK. The street is just under a mile long, running westward from HYDE PARK CORNER along the edge of the park to its north. The contemporary district of Knightsbridge stands a little to the west of the site of the original hamlet, occupying the area between Kensington Road, Cromwell Road and Brompton Road. There are at least four explanations of how the former bridge (over the River Westbourne) acquired its name, the quaintest and least likely being that two knights, on their way to seek the blessing of the Bishop of London, quarrelled and fought to their deaths here. In the 11th century the bridge gave its name to a village which performed functions that the City wished to exclude: livestock was slaughtered here and a leper hospital was built. As a western outpost of medieval London, its counterpart to the east was STRATFORD. The government established the first Knightsbridge (or HYDE PARK) Barracks after the Gordon riots of 1780, in case of further insurrection. With the growth

of KENSINGTON, CHELSEA and BELGRAVIA as high-class residential districts, retailers began to locate in Knightsbridge. Benjamin Harvey opened a linen shop in 1813 and passed the business on to his daughter on condition that she went into partnership with Colonel Nichols, adding luxury goods to the store's range. Charles Henry Harrod brought his tea-selling business from STEPNEY in 1849. Both Harvey Nichols and Harrods were rebuilt in the 1880s. Construction of the present Harrods store began in 1901, and Knightsbridge station opened in 1906. By this time, other stores lined Brompton Road, Knightsbridge and Sloane Street and were specializing in increasingly exclusive ranges. Dressmakers, furriers and milliners replaced shops that had catered to the more everyday needs of a local customer base. Food shops either moved out or, like Harrods, expanded into new lines. Over the course of the 20th century a more cosmopolitan mix of retailers and service outlets evolved but Knightsbridge retains a disproportionate number of stores catering to the very wealthy. Although best known for its shops, there are equally exclusive offices and residences – mostly large houses subdivided into flats. 'The Knightsbridge' is a complex of opulent apartments and mews houses opposite Knightsbridge Barracks, touted by its developers as 'the world's most desirable new address'.

Knightsbridge has been the scene of two six-day sieges. In 1975 three armed robbers took six Italians hostage in a Spaghetti House restaurant. Further west, on Princes Gate, SAS troops stormed the Iranian embassy on 5 May 1980, after gunmen had killed two hostages.

✉ SW1; SW7

🏃 8,949 (Knightsbridge and Belgravia ward)

🚇 Piccadilly Line (zone 1)

📖 John Greenacombe (ed.), *Survey of London, vol 45: Knightsbridge*, Athlone Press, 2000

@ www.harrods.com; www.harveynichols.com

Knight's Hill • *Lambeth*

A low-rent street that is part of the A215, rising from WEST NORWOOD to Norwood Heights, and named after a 16th-century family that owned a broad swathe of land in the area. The name Knight's Hill formerly applied to the entire ribbon development from BEULAH HILL to Brockwell Park but the road is now separated from the topographical feature called Knight's Hill, which lies east of Tulse Hill. Its summit is around 220 feet above sea level, distinctly lower than the highest point of the road. The grandest local resident was Lord Thurlow, Lord Chancellor from 1778 to 1783, who went to live at Knight's Hill Farm in the 1780s. It is said that he chose this modest dwelling to spite the architect who had overspent in building his nearby residence, Thurlow Park. To the south-east, NORWOOD NEW TOWN was built in the early 1850s on what used to be Knight's Hill Common. Of the several council estates in the locality, the Portobello is the largest. Completed in 1951, it fills 16 acres that were the site of a large house and its grounds. In 1964 a synagogue with meeting hall replaced a home for Jewish children. These were sold in the late 1970s. The Flemish-style building at 14–16 Knights Hill opened as a library in 1881, and has recently been refurbished as a youth and community centre. Knight's Hill playing field lies between Dassett Road and Furneaux Avenue. The ward of Knight's Hill has an ethnic profile similar to that of the borough as a whole, except for a relatively high percentage of mixed-race residents. Almost half the homes are owner-occupied, a significant proportion by Lambeth's standards.

✉ SE27

🏃 13,687

Knockholt • *Bromley/Sevenoaks, Kent*

The station lies just inside the London Borough of Bromley, but Knockholt itself is in Kent. The South Eastern Railway's route to Tonbridge ran through here from 1868 and the station opened eight years later. Originally called Halstead for Knockholt, its simpler but misleading identity dates from 1900. PRATTS BOTTOM or Badger's Mount would be more accurate (and colourful) names.

Edith Nesbit, author of *The Railway Children*, lived at Halstead Hall as a teenager. Despite the northern setting of the film of her novel, the story was probably based on her acquaintance with the stretch of line around here, with its cuttings and tunnels through the chalky North Downs. The family moved to Islington the year before the station opened; CHELSFIELD was the nearest halt until then.

✉ Sevenoaks TN14

🚉 South Eastern Trains (zone 6)

Ladbroke Grove • *Kensington & Chelsea*

A lively, racially mixed district centred on the street of that name, which runs between HOLLAND PARK and KENSAL GREEN. Sir Richard Ladbroke, a banker, MP and Lord Mayor of London in 1747, acquired four large parcels of land here in 1750. His heir planned an extravagant estate in 1823 with Ladbroke Grove as the central boulevard but financial difficulties forced the project into abeyance. John Whyte opened the Hippodrome racecourse on the still-undeveloped farmland in 1837 but it closed after four unprofitable years and work slowly resumed on the Ladbroke Grove estate. The resultant luxury housing is now generally referred to as 'NOTTING HILL', while Ladbroke Grove's name has become associated with the vicinity around the station. It opened on the Hammersmith and City Railway in 1864. The first buildings had only recently appeared on the road at that time. Of these, the most distinctive was the Elgin public house, although its sumptuously fitted interior dates from a makeover in the 1890s. The station's environs were smashed apart by the construction in the 1960s of the WESTWAY (A40), an urban motorway that now soars across the locality. However, a project that was at first disastrous for the community has been turned to good advantage and amenities of all kinds now flourish in its shadow. Like much of NORTH KENSINGTON, in the 1970s Ladbroke Grove became a hang-out for rock, punk and reggae artists, including Hawkwind, The Clash and Aswad, and retains a musical community today. The central section of the street is a focal part of the Notting Hill Carnival route and is further enlivened by links with PORTOBELLO ROAD, to its east.

In a train disaster sometimes called the 'Paddington' rail crash, 31 people were killed and more than 400 injured when a Thames Trains turbo hit a London-bound Great Western high-speed train near the Ladbroke Grove bridge on 5 October 1999.

✉ W10; W11

🚃 Hammersmith & City Line (zone 2)

Ladywell • *Lewisham*

The western side of LEWISHAM, separated from the High Street by the River Ravensbourne. As early as 1472 a spring was recorded on the site of what is now 148 Ladywell Road. It was called Our Lady's Well because of its supposed healing powers and was visited by pilgrims en route to Canterbury. In the 18th century the Ladywell area was sometimes called Bridge House, after a farmhouse that was the only significant structure. From the 1780s smallholders enclosed strips of waste bordering Ladywell Road, often applying to the manor court for squatters' rights and being granted 21-year leases. On the expiry of these leases the farmers became the direct tenants of the lord of the manor. In 1830 a brick bridge replaced the wooden footbridge that had formerly provided the sole connection with Lewisham. Ladywell station opened on the Mid-Kent Railway in 1857 and the Lady Well was covered over as terraced housing began to line Ladywell Road. To the west of the locality the Lewisham (now Ladywell) and DEPTFORD (now BROCKLEY) cemeteries opened in 1858. As has been pointed out, 'for much of its short history the dead population of Ladywell has outnumbered the living'. From the mid 1880s a cluster of municipal buildings provided various civic amenities, from a swimming bath to a coroner's court. In 1894 the five Thames-side parishes of the BERMONDSEY poor law union acquired Slagrave Farm and built the huge St Olave's workhouse, which opened amid scenes of extraordinary jubilation in 1900. Part of the workhouse survives as Ladywell Lodge; the rest has been replaced by Dressington Avenue. Council housing was built in Ladywell after each of the world wars, but some former meadows were left open because they were liable to regular inundation when the Ravensbourne overflowed. These now constitute Ladywell Fields, a 46-acre park divided by the railway lines into three separate sections. The creation of weirs and levées has eliminated the flooding problem and sections of the fields have been taken for an athletics arena and a major extension of Lewisham Hospital. Ladywell leisure centre opened in 1965, with a new swimming pool. Lewisham council has announced its intention to close the centre in 2007 and build a school that will open in 2010, when a replacement pool will be provided in Lewisham. The proposed three-year period without a pool has been the cause of widespread dismay. The residents of the Ladywell ward tend to be relatively young and well educated. Almost a quarter have no religious faith, one of the highest proportions in London.

Henry Williamson, the celebrated author of *Tarka the Otter* but less well regarded for his fascist connections, grew up in Eastern Road, on the border with Brockley. In 1984 the Henry Williamson Society and Lewisham council placed a commemorative plaque on the house where he spent the greater part of his childhood and youth, and which is the setting for the early volumes of *A Chronicle of Ancient Sunlight*.

> ⊠ SE13; SE4; SE6

> ♦ 12,430

> 🚇 South Eastern Trains (zone 3)

> 📖 Robert Smith, *The Well of Our Lady*, Ladywell Village Society, 1986

> @ www.saveladywellpool.com

Lambeth • *Lambeth*

An ancient south London district bordering the Thames opposite WESTMINSTER. The name probably meant that lambs were offloaded at a landing place here, although others suggest that it is a corruption of 'loamhithe', and thus refers to the muddy nature of the landing place. This was the spot from which archbishops of Canterbury took the ferry across to Westminster and thus made an ideal location for their London pied-à-terre. The archbishops were lords of the manor of Lambeth from 1197 and soon afterwards built a chapel and a residence on the riverside. The only surviving part is the undercroft of the chapel. The present Lambeth Palace contains elements from each succeeding century, all harmoniously integrated. The most recent phase of major work was a refurnishing and enlargement carried out for Archbishop Howley in the early 1830s by Edward Blore. By this time, a warren of streets surrounded the palace and

filled the former Lambeth Marsh, to its north. Residents worked at the wharves and boatyards on the waterfront, in small factories making whitewash or at Doulton's pottery. Although other bridges existed nearby, ferries continued to provide the most direct means of crossing the river until 1862, when a suspension bridge connected Lambeth Road with Westminster's Horseferry Road. Soon afterwards the construction of the Albert Embankment erased many of the riverside yards, while helping to protect the area from flooding. Lambeth Palace now found itself set well back from the river. St Thomas's Hospital moved from SOUTHWARK to a site north of the palace in 1871. Lambeth North station opened in 1906. The Bethlem Royal Hospital stood on Lambeth Road until 1930, when it moved to MONKS ORCHARD. The east and west wings of the hospital building were then demolished as part of the enlargement of Geraldine Mary Harmsworth Park, while the central portion became the new home of the Imperial War Museum. After a long period during which Lambeth Bridge was restricted to pedestrian use, it was rebuilt in 1932. Following the deterioration of the housing stock and severe bomb damage in World War II, the Greater London Council redeveloped the area south of Lambeth Road in the 1960s and its former character has been lost. Other streets made way for the expansion of St Thomas's Hospital. The Florence Nightingale Museum, on Lambeth Palace Road, is dedicated to the life and work of Britain's most celebrated nurse. The medieval parish church of St Mary-at-Lambeth was deconsecrated in 1972 and is now the Museum of Garden History. The former Lambeth Marsh is now thought of as the SOUTH BANK and WATERLOO areas.

The artist and poet William Blake lived for ten years in Hercules Road, just east of Lambeth Palace. Captain William Bligh lived round the corner in Lambeth Road and is buried in St Mary's churchyard. Somerset Maugham's first novel, published in 1897, was *Liza of Lambeth*. 'The Lambeth Walk' was a song from the musical *Me and My Girl* and was popularized by Lupino Lane, who first performed it at the Victoria Palace in 1937.

> ⊠ SE1; SE11

> ♦ 20,830 (Bishop's and Prince's wards)

> 🚇 Bakerloo Line (Lambeth North, zone 1)

> 📖 Sue McKenzie, *Lambeth: The Twentieth*

Century, Sutton, 1999 (covers the whole borough)

@ www.archbishopofcanterbury.org/palace;
www.museumgardenhistory.org;
www.florence-nightingale.co.uk;
london.iwm.org.uk

Lamorbey • *Bexley* (pronounced 'lammǝbee')

A former village, now absorbed into north SIDCUP, with a recent history dominated by facilities for young people. Lamorbey was originally spelt Lamienby, which became corrupted briefly to Lamb Abbey (hence the local Abbeyhill Park) before becoming fixed in its current form. The name derives from a local family, also known as Sparrow, which lived here from the late Middle Ages. On the death of Thomas Sparrow in 1513 the estate passed to James Goldwell, who built himself a house called Lamienby Goldwell. The house was rebuilt in 1744 and its grounds were laid out as a park. To its west lay the 16th-century Marrowbone Hall, which was demolished sometime before 1850. Owing to the proximity of Sidcup station, the village began to grow in the latter decades of the 19th century and the parish of Holy Trinity was created in 1878. Lamorbey's population almost doubled in 1902 when the Greenwich and Deptford Children's Homes (later known as The Hollies) opened on the site of Marrowbone Hall with accommodation for 587 children and over 60 staff. A school was built for the children on Burnt Oak Lane. After World War I the surrounding orchards, market gardens and nurseries began to disappear beneath streets of suburban housing and Lamorbey absorbed the neighbouring hamlet of Halfway Street. Some plots of land were sold to disabled ex-servicemen for £80 each. A new home for the Sidcup County School for Girls (now CHISLEHURST and Sidcup Grammar School) was built on the south side of Lamorbey Park in 1931. In 1950 Rose Bruford established her drama school at Lamorbey House, where she served as principal until 1967. The Hollies Children's Home closed in 1983 and the site was laid out with housing in the early 1990s. Some of the home's ancillary structures survive, notably Thomas Dinwiddy's clock-faced water tower. Holy Trinity Primary School is the largest voluntary-aided primary school in the diocese of Rochester. The campus of the college of speech and drama is currently undergoing extensive remodelling.

✉ Sidcup DA15

♦ 10,419 (Blackfen and Lamorbey ward)

▯ Jad Adams and Gerry Coll, *The Hollies: A Home for Children,* self-published, 2005

Lampton • *Hounslow*

The northern part of central Hounslow, lying immediately south of the Great West Road (A4). Its name comes from the Old English for a lamb farm. From the early 18th century, Lampton was the property of the Bulstrodes, lords of the manor of Hounslow, who devised an ambitious plan to develop the land on either side of Lampton Road in 1881. However, only a few grand houses were built, as economic conditions became unfavourable, and most of these have since been replaced. Until late in the 19th century Lampton remained a 'small village or hamlet in Heston parish … [with] few inhabitants, principally depending on agriculture and brickmaking'. The District Railway (now the Piccadilly Line) arrived here in 1884. Montague Road, Queen's Road and Balfour Road were laid out with terraced housing around the turn of the 20th century and the village began to merge into Hounslow. The Black Horse Inn (which had been in existence since at least 1759) was rebuilt in 1926. Opened in 1930, Lampton Park is situated to the west of the Lampton locality, with Hounslow Civic Centre and Lampton School.

✉ Hounslow TW3

Lancaster Gate • *Westminster*

A densely built-up but wealthy residential locality and hotel zone situated north-east of KENSINGTON GARDENS, halfway along BAYSWATER Road. It derives its identity from an entrance to the gardens, so-called in honour of Queen Victoria in her guise as Duchess of Lancaster. The area was laid out with prestigious terraced houses from the 1840s and Christ Church was built in 1855. The name 'Lancaster Gate' was at first applied only to a square around the church, then to the neighbouring street and then to the wider area, as this became one of the most prestigious addresses in London. By the 1870s almost every street in Lancaster Gate could boast a resident peer, MP or high-ranking military officer. In its heyday, Christ Church was nicknamed 'the thousand pound church' because of the large sums collected from the wealthy congregation every Sunday. Lancaster Gate station opened in 1900 on the eastern side of the locality, where it actually stands opposite Marlborough Gate. Hotels and private flats were built in the 1920s but these barely dented Lancaster

Gate's high-class reputation, and nor did the well-designed council flats that filled a handful of bomb sites after World War II. In the 1960s the station was rebuilt beneath the Court Royal Hotel, which was subsequently renamed the Royal Lancaster. Dry rot led to the demolition of the body of Christ Church in 1978 and the spire now finds itself attached to an ecclesiastical-looking block of flats. For over 70 years Lancaster Gate was the home of the Football Association, the governing body of English football. The FA relocated to SOHO Square in 2000, selling its old building to property developers for £7.25 million. The ward has a high proportion of young, well-educated, single residents living alone in privately rented accommodation. There are very few families with children or households with more than one pensioner.

Lytton Strachey, the eminent biographer, spent 25 years at 69 Lancaster Gate, while author J M Barrie lived around the corner at 100 Bayswater Road. Scenes in Woody Allen's 2006 light comedy *Scoop*, starring Scarlett Johansson, were shot in Lancaster Gate.

⊠ W2

♦ 12,003

🚇 Central Line (zone 1)

Langdon Park • *Tower Hamlets*
A planned Docklands Light Railway station in north POPLAR, situated at the bridge linking Carmen Street and Bright Street. Created as part of the 'sustainable communities initiative', the station will be centrally located in relation to the Teviot, Brownfield and LANSBURY estates. Local councillor Kevin Morton has called the £7 million project, 'a key step in breaking down the social Berlin Wall between Poplar and Docklands'. Better shopping facilities and new mixed tenure housing to the east of the railway are hoped to result. The station is due to open in mid 2007. Langdon Park is a small recreation ground to the north of the station site. Langdon Park School is a mixed community comprehensive school that draws its students from a relatively local catchment area. The national educational standards agency Ofsted describes the school as having 'rich cultural diversity'; two-fifths of pupils have a white British background, one-third are from Asian-Bangladeshi families, and most of the remainder are black or black British. The percentage of pupils living in overcrowded households is three times the national average, and almost three-quarters

are entitled to free school meals.

⊠ E14

🚇 Docklands Light Railway, Stratford branch (zone 2)

Lansbury • *Tower Hamlets*
A large council estate in the part of north POPLAR once known as Poplar New Town. Wartime bombing destroyed or damaged nearly a quarter of the buildings in this area, which was one of the first be redeveloped by the London County Council after 1945. In 1951 the barely finished Lansbury estate became the 'Live Architecture Exhibition' of the Festival of Britain. Critics were generally underwhelmed by the project, with one or two notable exceptions. Writing in *The New Yorker* in 1953 Lewis Mumford remarked, 'I shall be surprised if Lansbury is not one of the best bits of housing and urban planning anywhere'. Several more schemes filled out the area over the next three decades, including the large blocks of Lansbury West. Inevitably, much of the Lansbury estate has become run down. Tower Hamlets has transferred the estate to housing association ownership and it is presently undergoing regeneration. St Saviour's Church survives from 1864, and is now used by the Celestial Church of Christ, a Nigerian foundation. The church is encircled by the Arcadian scheme of self-built houses, dating from the late 1980s. The 15-acre Bartlett Park is Lansbury's largest open space. Chrisp Street has a daily market that meets a wide variety of local needs, with a special emphasis on exotic fruit and vegetables on Fridays and Saturdays. Opened in 2004, Chrisp Street Idea Store is a mix of library services, learning spaces, IT and a café housed in a glass building on the corner of East India Dock Road.

The estate is named after George Lansbury (1859–1940), a borough councillor and a local hero for his 'Poplarist' campaign demanding that London's richer boroughs should subsidize the poorer ones. He subsequently became Labour MP for Bromley and Bow and led the Labour Party in opposition from 1931 to 1935. The Poplar-born actress Angela Lansbury is his granddaughter.

⊠ E14

♦ 11,496 (East India and Lansbury ward)

📖 John Shepherd, *George Lansbury: At the Heart of Old Labour*, Oxford University Press, 2002

Latimer Road • *Kensington & Chelsea/ Hammersmith & Fulham*

A London Underground station and historically poor street lying on the western side of NOTTING DALE. The name originates from land endowed by Edward Latymer for the funding of Hammersmith's Latymer School in the early 17th century. The Metropolitan railway line to Hammersmith was built through the district in 1864 and a station opened four years later on Bramley Road, at the junction with a branch line running south to Addison Road. By this time cottage laundries and pigsties were replacing former brickfields and the station was nicknamed 'piggery junction'. Latimer Road's poverty drew municipal and philanthropic assistance. In 1880 the school board for London built the three-storey Latimer Road School, which now houses Kensington & Chelsea's pupil referral unit, and St Anne's Nursery School, which may be the oldest institution of its kind in London. Harrow School established a mission on the street in 1884 and a school in 1887. But deprivation continued well beyond the Victorian era as Horace Newte observed in *Sparrows: The Story of an Unprotected Girl* in 1915. 'Between Notting Hill and WORMWOOD SCRUBS lies a vast desert of human dwellings ... by scarcely perceptible degrees, there is a declension of so-called respectability, till at last the frankly working-class district of Latimer Road is reached.' The relationship between the street and the station was broken off by the construction in the 1960s of the WESTWAY (A40) and the West Cross Route (A3220) to SHEPHERD'S BUSH, when Latimer Road's southernmost section was renamed Freston Road. The Greater London Council planned to demolish much of Freston Road and replace it with industry and high-density flats but squatters occupied the houses and declared the Republic of Frestonia in 1977. The GLC backed down and granted the squatters temporary leave to stay, while the Bramley Housing Co-operative planned and built on a human scale. The first new homes were completed in 1985. The Freston/Latimer Road employment zone has several media-related businesses owing to the proximity of BBC Television Centre at WHITE CITY and the musical community of LADBROKE GROVE. Kensington & Chelsea council is trying to bring convenience retailers to the vicinity of the Tube station to counteract a deficiency in local shopping facilities.

In a classic chase scene in *The Lavender Hill Mob* (1951), all the police cars converge in a pile-up at the junction of Bramley Road and Freston (then Latimer) Road in front of the Bramley Arms, now part of the Chrysalis building. The pub also featured in the film *Sid and Nancy*.

✉ W10; W11

🚇 Hammersmith & City Line (zone 2)

Lawrie Park • *Bromley/Lewisham*

A Victorian estate located in the heights of UPPER SYDENHAM, on the north-eastern edge of Crystal Palace Park. The name is now primarily recalled only in the names of local streets, although estate agents have begun to speak of the 'Lawrie Park triangle'. The estate was enclosed by the 17th century and was acquired sometime before 1800 by John Lawrie. From the 1850s to the 1870s Lawrie Park became the exclusive end of SYDENHAM and was built up with some very handsome villas, many by George Wythes, the developer of BICKLEY. The Hall, former home of the Lawrie family, was sold to the Crystal Palace Co. and its grounds were built upon. The erection of the CRYSTAL PALACE and the consequent improvements in transport connections added considerably to the locality's fashionability. Some of the original houses remain but the inevitable infilling and replacements have diminished the original charm. Lawrie Park Road (formerly Lawrie Road) has Sydenham Lawn Tennis Club and St Christopher's Hospice.

Camille Pissarro's 1871 painting *The Avenue, Sydenham* depicts a view along Lawrie Park Avenue, looking towards St Bartholomew's Church. The National Gallery bought the work in 1984. W G Grace managed and led the short-lived London County Cricket Club in the early years of the 20th century while living at 7 Lawrie Park Road, a house demolished in the 1960s.

✉ SE26

Lea Bridge • *Waltham Forest/Hackney*

An industrial and working-class residential district straddling the River Lea east of CLAPTON. There has been water-related industry here since the time it was called Jeremy's Ferry. The first waterwheel was erected in 1707 and this was followed by mills grinding corn and even pins and needles, and a water pumping station. The mills presented an obstacle to navigation which was overcome by the opening of the Hackney Cut, from Lea Bridge to OLD FORD, in 1769. At around the same time, the Lea Bridge turnpike improved accessibility to the City and the district became fashionable for a while with merchants and bankers. On the eastern side of the river, Lea Bridge station (opened in 1840, but now closed) was the earliest railway connection in the LEYTON and WALTHAMSTOW area and soon brought the construction of workers' housing. During the latter part of the 19th century, filter-beds were constructed on both sides of the river and in the 1930s factories replaced agricultural smallholdings. Some of the old utilities and industries have since closed and the Middlesex Filter Beds have become a nature reserve within the Lee valley regional park. The western side of the district has remained primarily residential, and is sometimes known as MILLFIELDS. With European Union funding, Lea Bridge is now undergoing regeneration, providing infrastructure improvements to its industrial estates. The newly enhanced area has been given the name Lea Bridge (or Leyton) Gateway. Around half the population of Lea Bridge is white and a quarter is black or black British. The Asian community is predominantly of Indian descent on the Hackney side and of Pakistani descent in the Waltham Forest part.

Lee Valley Ice Centre hosts ice skating and ice hockey events, and has seating for 1,000 spectators. The neighbouring Lee Valley Stables have an indoor riding school and outdoor hacking facilities, as well as offering carriage driving and side-saddle tuition.

✉ E5; E10

♟ 22,197 (Leabridge, Hackney and Lea Bridge, Waltham Forest wards)

📖 Waltham Forest Oral History Workshop, *The Road to Jeremy's Ferry,* Waltham Forest Oral History Workshop, 2003

Leadenhall Market • *City*

A covered Victorian market situated just south of BISHOPSGATE, with access from Gracechurch Street. The area was built up during the latter part of the first century AD as Londinium spread northwards but reverted to farmland when the Romans withdrew. By 1309 a grand lead-roofed mansion called Leaden Hall had been built. Subsequently there was a granary here and a market for all kinds of food, cloth and ironmongery. Poultry was a speciality from 1321 and cheese from 1397. Richard Whittington, elected Lord Mayor of London in 1397 (twice), 1406 and 1419, was granted the leasehold on the manor of Leadenhall in 1408. The mansion burned down in

1484 and an open market was established on the site with the same variety of goods, but primarily fish, meat, poultry and corn. Samuel Pepys recorded that he bought a good leg of beef for sixpence in 1663, three years before much of the market burned down in the Great Fire. Leadenhall market continued to operate from a variety of buildings until the Corporation of London commissioned the present wrought-iron and glass-roofed buildings, which were completed in 1881. Architect Sir Horace Jones was also responsible for the Victorian market buildings at SMITHFIELD and BILLINGSGATE. The buildings were restored in 1991, bringing the luscious internal colour scheme back to life. Leadenhall market has now been colonized by fashion and accessory retailers, coffee shops and restaurants, although a butcher and a fishmonger valiantly hold out.

A gander that evaded slaughter at Leadenhall became a market favourite and was fed at local pubs. Nicknamed 'Old Tom', he allegedly survived to the age of 38. On his death in 1835 he lay in state at the market and was buried there.

✉ EC3

Leamouth • *Tower Hamlets* (pronounced 'leeməth')

An isolated pair of peninsulas, formed by the meanderings of the River Lea (here called Bow Creek) as it reaches the Thames. Although there are records of ships being unloaded here as early as 1297, there was little human activity apart from some farming and fishing until the late 16th century, when a house was built, with an orchard and a moat. A second incarnation of the house became a public house early in the 18th century. The creation of the EAST INDIA Dock in 1806 made road access to Leamouth even more difficult but encouraged industrial development and the building of homes for workers. The northern peninsula, known as Goodluck Hope, became a centre for glass-making and then for galvanized iron manufacture, which continued until the 1960s. The close-knit (and allegedly inbred) residential population was dispersed by a slum clearance programme in the 1930s. The Pura vegetable oil refinery now covers nearly all of Goodluck Hope. Leamouth's most enduring employer was the Corporation of Trinity House, which occupied the tip of the eastern peninsula from 1803 to 1988. The site is now used for arts and community projects while the restored chainstore and lighthouse host leisure and cultural events. Most of Leamouth is relatively unaffected by docklands regeneration but sooner or later it is likely to succumb to redevelopment in the form of office tower blocks or upmarket apartments.

> ✉ E14

> @ www.trinitybuoywharf.com

Leaves Green • *Bromley*
A hamlet surrounded by farms and common land, situated one mile north of BIGGIN HILL. The name is a corruption of Leigh's Green, which derived from a family who owned land here in the mid 15th century. The weatherboarded Kings Arms pub dates from the early 18th century and there are flint-faced cottages converted from the former CUDHAM workhouse, erected in 1731 but never much used. A cast iron coal post was erected on the green in 1861 to mark the point at which duty had to be paid on coal and wine being brought into the City of London. The post is now a Grade II-listed structure. Several original buildings survive in the village centre, although there has been some less attractive post-war development along Leaves Green Road, some of it highly priced. A 50-acre riding school dominates the western side of the village. Leaves Green Common, the village green, has been allowed to grow more wildly in recent years to let natural flora regenerate.

> ✉ Keston BR2

Lee • *Lewisham*
An aggregation of several formerly separate settlements situated south of BLACKHEATH and west of LEWISHAM. Lee was first mentioned in Domesday Book, with the same spelling as is used today, although there have been variants during the intervening period. The name means 'woodland clearing'. St Margaret's Church was built at the eastern end of Belmont Hill in the late Middle Ages and became the focus of the first hamlet in the parish. The next was in the Old Road area, where Pentland House was built in the mid 1680s. This is now a Goldsmiths College hall of residence. The Manor House was built nearby around 1771 and was sold in 1796 to Sir Francis Baring, co-founder of the Baring Brothers banking house. The house later became a military college and is now a public library, with 14 acres of gardens and a lake behind. LEE GREEN and the Tiger's Head public house lay to the east. Farms and labourers' cottages were the sole occupants of the recently deforested area further south. St Margaret's Church was rebuilt in 1814 as Lee became a popular retreat for City merchants because of its 'healthy and pleasant situation'. From 1825 Lee New Town covered the gardens of Lee Place, a moated mansion on the north side of Old Road that was demolished in 1824, growing up around Lee Church Street and Boone Street and giving shelter to those who provided services for the wealthy residents here and in BLACKHEATH PARK. In response to the very rapid growth of the district a new St Margaret's Church was built across the road from its predecessor in 1841. The ruins of the old church remain. Lee station opened in 1866, stimulating construction of housing for the middle classes to the south of the district. By the outbreak of World War I, the whole of Lee was crowded with suburban dwellings. The jerry-built slums of Lee New Town were demolished in stages from the 1930s to the 1960s, aided by wartime bombing, and much of that area is now occupied by council housing. Although its grandest houses have mostly gone, many Georgian and Victorian terraces survive and Lee has not been overly modernized except for the conversion of the larger houses into flats. Lee acquired a certain trendiness in the 1960s and a hint of this remains today.

Sir Edmond Halley, who gave his name to the comet, is buried in the churchyard of the old St Margaret's Church. The publisher Stanley Unwin, the best known of whose titles is *The Lord of the Rings*, lived in Handen Road. In the Sherlock Holmes story, *The Man with the Twisted Lip* lived in Lee.

> ✉ SE12; SE13

> 🚃 South Eastern Trains (zone 3)

Lee Green • *Lewisham*
Situated at the eastern end of Lee High Road, this was the original centre of LEE, which expanded north and west to meet BLACKHEATH and LEWISHAM, and then south to Lee station. The Tiger's Head public house was built in 1766 and became famous for its bowling green and notorious as a haunt of smugglers. In 1809 the first semi-detached houses were built near the green and piecemeal suburban development continued until 1825, when shops appeared and the bridge over the Quaggy River was enlarged. The latter allowed the river to flow more freely, reducing the risk of flooding, and over the following 40 years the village green vanished as the locality was intensely built up, mainly with small houses for labourers. Some of the 19th-century housing

was cleared before and after World War II in redevelopment projects, the largest of which was the mixed-use Leegate scheme. Lee Green has a wider choice of shops and restaurants than might be expected with Lewisham such a short distance away. More than three-quarters of the ward's residents are white – a higher proportion than in most of the borough – and 63 per cent of homes are owner-occupied.

✉ SE3; S12

🚶 12,057

Leicester Square • *Westminster* (pronounced 'lestə')

'The quintessence of the WEST END', according to Westminster council, linked to PICCADILLY CIRCUS by Coventry Street. Originally a square plot of Lammas land in the parish of St Martin's, the area acquired the name Leicester Fields when Robert Sidney, second Earl of Leicester, built a residence here in 1636. An early version of Leicester Square was laid out in 1665 and houses modelled on those in PALL MALL were built around it. From 1712 to 1760 Leicester House served as a palace for two princes of Wales and the square consequently became a fashionable promenade. In 1771 Sir Ashton Lever converted Leicester House to a 'museum of curiosities', which attracted smaller crowds than the street entertainers and gambling dens that were present by this time. Lever also established an archery club that practised in the house's grounds. He sold the house by lottery and it was demolished a few years later as part of a phase of rebuilding that brought traders and craftsmen to the square in place of private residences and created roughly its present layout. In 1782 Gedge's drapers became the first London store to boast a large glass shopfront. A cheap theatre was built on the site of Leicester House, and this was later converted into another drapers shop and then a hotel. The centre of the square was used for exhibitions and public lectures until gardens were laid out in 1874, with a central fountain and statue of Shakespeare and busts of notable former residents at each corner. Theatres, oyster rooms and Turkish baths were by then appearing and music halls included the Empire and the Alhambra. A few Georgian and Victorian buildings survive but most of the square now dates from the 1930s onwards and is especially renowned for its cinemas, which regularly host film premieres. On the south side of the square, the reduced price ticket kiosk for West End theatres has

become a minor institution. Capital Radio's headquarters is on the east side of Leicester Square. Nightclubs, bars and fast-food joints abound, and the square is a magnet for buskers, flyer distributors and itinerant preachers. The central gardens were relaid in 1990 following the construction of a subterranean electricity station that supplies much of the West End's power. Westminster council is planning to give the square another face-lift in time for the 2012 Olympics.

Former residents of Leicester Square include the 18th-century artists William Hogarth and Sir Joshua Reynolds. Betty Miller's 1934 novel *Farewell Leicester Square*, which controversially exposed British anti-Semitism, took its title from a line in the song *It's a Long Way to Tipperary*, as did Arthur La Bern's *Goodbye Piccadilly, Farewell Leicester Square*, filmed by Alfred Hitchcock as *Frenzy*.

✉ W1

🚇 Northern Line; Piccadilly Line (zone 1)

@ www.officiallondontheatre.co.uk/tkts

Leman Street • *Tower Hamlets* (pronounced 'leemən')

Together with Dock Street, Leman Street (A1202) connects WAPPING with WHITECHAPEL and the eastern part of the CITY OF LONDON. Although not the name of the locality, Leman Street is used as the main point of reference in a rather anonymous district, once the site of an extensive Roman cemetery and later known as Goodman's Fields. The original Goodman was a farmer here, but his son found it more lucrative to rent out the land for others to graze horses and grow vegetables. The fields adjoined the Abbey of the Sisters of St Clare until the dissolution of the monasteries in the 1530s. The nuns were called Minoresses, a name that survives in the street called Minories. Sir William Leman developed the area with substantial houses around 1710 and named several of the surrounding streets after his relatives. Some of the properties were occupied by Sephardic Jews. Leman Street has been little touched by changes in nearby Wapping. Architecturally, it is dominated by the old CWS building and the rather unsightly Leman Street police station, opened in 1891.

Leman Street was the first passenger station on the London and Blackwall line out of FENCHURCH STREET from 1840 until its closure in 1941, following bomb damage.

✉ E1

Lesnes Abbey • *Bexley* (pronounced 'less ness')

A new electoral ward encompassing the eastern side of ABBEY WOOD, plus WEST HEATH and part of the BOSTALL estate. The minimal remains of Lesnes Abbey, excavated in the 1950s and 1960s, lie at the foot of the gently sloping hill off Abbey Road. The abbey was founded in 1178 by Richard de Lucy as penance for his part in the events leading to the murder of Thomas Becket in Canterbury Cathedral in 1170. After Henry VIII's dissolution of the monasteries, the abbey fell into disuse and its walls crumbled. The ruins have been reconsecrated and services of worship are occasionally held on the site. The creation of the ward of Lesnes Abbey seems to be an administrative convenience rather than the union of a community, as its northern and southern parts have different characteristics. Overall, the ward's population is primarily white, Christian and home-owning, though slightly less so than the borough's population as a whole.

Lesnes Abbey Woods are 215 acres of ancient woodlands, with oak and sweet chestnut trees and 20 acres of wild daffodils in the spring. An exposed fossil bed contains the remains of shells, fish, reptiles and mammals. A memorial at the edge of the woods honours the designer William Morris, who used to pass the spot on his way from his home Red House to Abbey Wood station.

✉ SE2; Bexleyheath DA7; Belvedere DA17

♦ 10,947

Lessness Heath • *Bexley*

Although still shown on maps as an area on the south-east side of BELVEDERE, this is not a name in widespread use. Lessness was recorded in Domesday Book as Loisnes, when it possessed three fisheries. A century later it gave its name to Lesnes Abbey. Lessness was one of the medieval hundreds of Kent and meetings were held on the heath, which formerly covered a large tract of land west of ERITH. The heath was enclosed in 1812, when much of it was allocated to Christ's Hospital, which also owned Lesnes Abbey. Like many enclosures of the period, the rationale was that the land should be put to more intensive agricultural use during the Napoleonic Wars but little such improvement took place. The heath was later divided between the area's two great landowners, William Wheatley of Erith and Sir Culling Eardley of Belvedere, and they exploited the increase in its building value that followed the arrival of the North Kent Railway in 1849. Most of the heath was developed from the 1860s to the 1890s but fractions survived as parks and recreation grounds. Lessness Heath is now best known as the name of a large primary school on Erith Road. Most children at the school live in the immediate area, which has socio-economic characteristics that are slightly below average.

✉ Belvedere DA17; Erith DA8

Lewisham • *Lewisham* (pronounced 'luishəm' nowadays, formerly 'luiss(h)əm')

A large south-east London suburb and commercial centre, situated on the River Ravensbourne, one and a half miles south of GREENWICH. This was an ancient manor, granted by Elfrida, niece of King Alfred, to the Abbey of St Peter at Ghent. It was Lievesham at that time: probably the homestead of a man called Lēof or Lēofsa. Around half a dozen mills were operating on the river at the time of Domesday Book. These were later used for grinding steel as well as corn, and for weaving silk and tanning leather. St Mary's Church was begun at the end of the 15th century and the village progressively stretched out in an elm-lined ribbon along what is now the High Street. The length and prettiness of the settlement was said (with some credibility) to have so impressed James I that he declared, 'On my soul, I will be king of Lusen'. St Mary's vicarage dates from 1693 and the church was rebuilt in 1777, the base of the tower remaining from the medieval structure. In the 18th century the 'healthy air' encouraged a growing number of merchants to build residences here. However, like most south London districts except those on the bank of the Thames, its rapid growth did not begin until after the arrival of the railway in 1849. Until the 1870s developers built substantial houses for the upper middle classes, accompanied by a sprinkling of cheaper housing for those who provided their services. Thereafter, the wealthy began to leave and streets of more densely packed housing were laid out for clerks and artisans. Housing and civic amenities spilled across the Ravensbourne into neighbouring LADYWELL. Many of the earliest properties had already been demolished and replaced by the end of the 19th century. With its growth as a transport hub, served by two railway lines, trams and buses, Lewisham grew in importance as a shopping centre. The two largest businesses were both drapers' stores: Chiesman's and George Stroud. The town honoured Queen Victoria's diamond jubilee by erecting a clock tower, and a street market began in 1906. Much of the town centre had to be rebuilt following bomb damage in World War II, while municipal estates were laid out on the outskirts. The London County Council's Orchard estate, begun in 1963, was one of the largest. By that time Lewisham was becoming a multi-ethnic community, the largest minority being of black Caribbean origin. The Lewisham Centre, a shopping mall, opened in 1977. Chiesman's department store became an Army and Navy Store in 1983 and has recently been replaced by a police station. Stroud's was taken over by the Royal Arsenal Co-operative Society and its site is now a Yates's wine lodge. A ten-year programme of much-needed improvements to the town centre began in 2003, intended to brighten its appearance and reduce traffic congestion.

The musicians Ginger Baker, Maxi Priest, Matt and Luke Goss and Daniel and Natasha Bedingfield all grew up in Lewisham.

⊠ SE13

ⵌ 13,190 (Lewisham Central ward))

🚊 South Eastern Trains; Docklands Light Railway, Lewisham branch (zones 2 and 3)

📖 John Coulter, *Lewisham: History and Guide*, Sutton, 1994; Joan Anim-Addo, *Longest Journey: A History of Black Lewisham*, Deptford Forum, 1995

@ www.lewishamcentre.co.uk

Leyton • *Waltham Forest*

A Victorian suburb separated from HACKNEY by the River Lea, from which it takes its name. The village was also known as Low Leyton, from its setting on the river's flood plain; a patch of Leyton Marsh survives near LEA BRIDGE. Walnut Tree House, also known as Essex Hall, is probably the borough's oldest structure – though there is no record of precisely when it was built or for whom. Its timber-framed core dates from roughly 1500, with matching wings added later. St Mary's Church was built in 1658 but, like Walnut Tree House, it has since been much extended and altered. By the 18th century most of the marshes had been converted to fertile farmland, which was dotted with mansions, especially towards the area now known as BAKERS ARMS. There was little growth in the main village until the coming of the railway in the mid 19th century, which brought both industrial

development beside the Lea and the construction of a lower middle-class dormitory suburb. Thereafter, Leyton's population doubled every decade for the rest of the century. In particular, its growth in the 1880s was the fastest of any comparably sized town in England. The opening of Midland Road station in 1894 sealed the fate of the big houses in the north of the district. By the 1920s barely a scrap of land remained to be built upon. Heavy damage during the Blitz led to wholesale municipal reconstruction after the war, with the addition of tower blocks from 1961 onwards. Known until recently for the manufacture of neckties, Leyton has also been home to the factories of Aquascutum and Thermos, but manufacturing has declined in favour of service industries over the past few decades. In 1991 SPITALFIELDS market moved to Ruckholt Road in TEMPLE MILLS. The new Quadrant development within the grounds of Leyton Orient Football Club includes flats with a view of the pitch. White residents make up slightly less than half of Leyton's population. The other main ethnic minorities are of black Caribbean, black African and Pakistani descent. The average age of Leyton's residents is 31.7 years, which is relatively young. This is mainly the result of the large number of families with dependent children, including a high proportion of single-parent households.

CLAPTON Orient Football Club moved to Brisbane Road in 1937. The 'Orient' name had been the suggestion of a player who worked for the Orient Line shipping company, since it fitted the east London location. The club changed its name to Leyton Orient in 1946 and enjoyed its greatest period of success in the 1960s.

⊠ E10

ⵌ 12,522

🚊 Silverlink Metro (Leyton Midland Road, zone 3); Central Line (Leyton, zone 3)

📖 Keith Romig and Peter Lawrence, *Leyton and Leytonstone*, Tempus, 1995

@ leyton.info (privately operated local information site); www.leytonorient.com

Leytonstone • *Waltham Forest*

A cultural crucible situated between WANSTEAD and LEYTON, taking its name from an old milestone, which is now topped by a 19th-century Portland stone obelisk known as the 'high stone'. The stone stands at the junction of New Wanstead and Hollybush Hill – and finds itself in the borough of Redbridge, owing to boundary changes. The village evolved early as a roadside halt. A Rose inn was in existence in 1585 and Leytonstone High Road was more important than the High Road in Leyton by the end of the 16th century. A few large houses were built from the late 17th century – including the Pastures, now replaced by a youth centre – but Leytonstone did not gain as fashionable a reputation as its neighbour. Leytonstone House, built around 1800, is the oldest surviving mansion. It successively served as a brewer's residence, a school and a hospital and has now been converted to offices in the grounds of a Tesco superstore. William Cotton of nearby Wallwood House gave money for the building of the Church of St John the Baptist in the early 1830s and Leytonstone became a separate parish in 1845. It was still primarily a farming village when the first station opened in 1856 and remained quiet for a further two decades. The Cotton family gave the site for St Andrew's Church when their estate was developed with substantial suburban houses from the mid 1870s. Nearer STRATFORD, the district was rapidly built up with two-storey yellow-brick terraced houses in the 1880s, providing affordable accommodation (and season tickets) for city clerks. Change in recent decades has been almost entirely limited to the replacement of groups of Victorian houses with small blocks of flats. The latest developments include one- and two-bedroom apartments at the Zodiac, on the High Road. Despite the outward similarities of their convergent housing, Leytonstone and Leyton are demographically disparate. Leytonstone has fewer households with children, fewer black residents and a higher proportion of owner-occupied properties. The Leytonstone Festival has been held every July since 1995 and brings together a series of arts events at several venues.

Leytonstone's greatest son was the film director Alfred Hitchcock, who was born here in 1899. His parents ran a modest grocery store in the High Road, on a site subsequently occupied by a petrol station. Other local notables include the actor Sir Derek Jacobi, cricketer Graham Gooch, footballer David Beckham, broadcaster Jonathan Ross and musician Damon Albarn.

✉ E11

🚶 10,635

🚌 Silverlink Metro (Leytonstone High Road, zone 3); Central Line (Leytonstone, zones 3 and 4)

📖 Keith Romig and Peter Lawrence, *Leyton and Leytonstone*, Tempus, 1995

@ www.leytonstonefestival.org.uk

Limehouse • *Tower Hamlets*

Part gentrified, part solidly working-class, this EAST END district forms the north-western gateway to the ISLE OF DOGS. It takes its name from the limekilns that operated from the mid 14th century, converting Kentish chalk into quicklime for the capital's building industry. From the late 16th century ships were built at Limehouse and traders supplied provisions for voyages. Wealthy merchants erected fine houses on Narrow Street, especially in the early 18th century, and St Anne's Church was built in 1730 by Nicholas Hawksmoor. This is regarded as one of the architect's greatest achievements and has the highest church clock in London. In the 1740s a short-lived pottery produced England's first soft-paste porcelain, which was known as Limehouse ware. London's oldest canal, the Limehouse Cut, was constructed around 1770 to link the River Lea at BOW with the Thames here, thus saving a journey around the Isle of Dogs. With the growth of its docks, Limehouse acquired an immigrant population and became London's first CHINATOWN. The community was never very large but it gained a reputation for gambling and opium-smoking. Limehouse provided the backdrop for the *Dr Fu Manchu* films – indeed, their creator claimed that the character was modelled on a Chinese man of unusual appearance whom he had glimpsed on Limehouse Causeway one foggy night in 1911. Despite the 20th-century decline and closure of the London docks, the heart of old Limehouse survived the post-war municipal redevelopment that transformed so much of the EAST END. Narrow Street's houses were some of the first in London to undergo gentrification from the late 1950s and disused warehouses were converted to apartments in the 1970s and 1980s. Private developers have since added new units, some of which were erected with excessive haste to capitalize on the DOCKLANDS residential boom. Although there are still many Chinese restaurants, Bangladeshis now form the largest ethnic minority in Limehouse; the 2001 census recorded that only 2.7 per cent of residents were of Chinese descent.

The 1921 song *Limehouse Blues* was made famous by Gertrude Lawrence and has been recorded by Rosemary Clooney and Julie Andrews, as well as in instrumental form by Charlie Parker and others. According to the

Oxford English Dictionary, 'Limehouse' used to be a verb, meaning 'to make fiery political speeches such as Mr Lloyd George made at Limehouse in 1909'. The district gained another political connotation in 1981 when the short-lived Social Democratic Party was founded here, setting out its principles in the 'Limehouse declaration'.

> ⌧ E14
>
> ⫙ 12,484
>
> ⊞ c2c; Docklands Light Railway, all branches (zone 2)
>
> ▭ Daniel Farson, *Limehouse Days: A Personal Experience of the East End*, Michael Joseph, 1991

Lincoln's Inn • *Camden/Westminster*

A legal quarter and its neighbouring square, which is the largest in central London, situated south-east of HOLBORN station. The land belonged to Dominican priors who subsequently decamped to BLACKFRIARS, whereupon the Earl of Lincoln built a house here. The earl bequeathed his home to a college of lawyers, who moved in some time in the 14th century. The earliest buildings have not survived but the complex that evolved on the site has elements from every century since the 15th, including the Old Hall of 1492 and a chapel rebuilt in 1623. Property developer William Newton acquired the twelve acres of Lincoln's Inn Fields in two stages, in 1629 and 1638, and began to erect houses on each side except the east, which backed onto the buildings of the inn. It is said that Newton employed Inigo Jones as the scheme's architect but this is doubted by some. The only survivor from Newton's project is Lindsey House, home of the Earl of Lindsey in the early 18th century. Much of the square was inappropriately redeveloped in the 19th century but more recent neo-Georgian replacements have attempted to match the earlier scale. Sir John Soane bought 12 Lincoln's Inn Fields in 1792 and subsequently acquired numbers 13 and 14, and had rebuilt them all by 1824. Soane was the architect of the Bank of England, Dulwich Picture Gallery and three London churches, and he created an 'academy of architecture' within his home, which he left to the nation on his death. The resulting museum is a treasure house – or rather three interconnected houses – of art and artefacts, including Hogarth's *Rake's Progress*, preserved in an intimately domestic context. Of the square's other buildings the most notable is the headquarters of the Royal College of Surgeons, designed by Sir Charles Barry in 1835, which incorporates the Hunterian Museum. In nearby Portsmouth Street is the Old Curiosity Shop, erroneously claimed to have been the inspiration for Dickens' creation but looking very authentic all the same. Populated by strolling barristers during the day, Lincoln's Inn Fields until recently provided a dormitory for London's homeless after dark. Many have now been displaced to surrounding street doorways.

The actress and royal mistress Nell Gwynne lived in Lincoln's Inn Fields and her son, the Duke of St Albans, was born in her lodgings there. Anthony Trollope, who spent time in his father's chambers in Lincoln's Inn, wrote of it that 'we know of no place in London more conducive to suicide'. The inn was the first London home of Eric Gill, who has been called 'perhaps the finest English artist-craftsman of the 20th century'.

> ⌧ WC2
>
> ▭ William Holden Spilsbury, *Lincoln's Inn*, William S Hein, 1988
>
> @ www.lincolnsinn.org.uk (Honourable Society of Lincoln's Inn site); www.soane.org (Sir John Soane's Museum site); www.rcseng.ac.uk (Royal College of Surgeons of England site)

Lisson Green • *Westminster*

The old name for the locality now more commonly known as LISSON GROVE, situated in north-west Marylebone. This was once part of the medieval manor of Lilestone, which stretched north to HAMPSTEAD. Lisson Green was a 'little manor' that broke away as early as 1236, with its own manor house and one carue (c.100 acres) of land. The village's first attraction was the Yorkshire Stingo public house, probably visited by Samuel Pepys in 1666, on a flirtatious outing with a merry widow. In the mid 18th century the arrival of London's original bypass, the New Road, improved the area's accessibility and Lisson Green began to expand. The village faced EDGWARE ROAD, with the green itself behind; the two Edgware Road Tube stations are at opposite ends of the settlement's early extent. By the time of the construction of the Regent's Canal in 1810, the present street plan had been laid out and stuccoed houses were being built. Among those moving here for the country air were several artists and writers, who later decamped to ST JOHN'S WOOD. Sir Edward Baker (who gave his name to BAKER STREET) acquired the southern part of Lisson Green in 1821 and built large blocks of flats as an extension of MARYLEBONE, but further north the area began to decline as unscrupulous landlords put up shoddy houses and overfilled them with poor tenants, especially Irish labourers. Lisson Green became filthy, disease-ridden and, in parts, criminal. In 1885 the case of 13-year-old Eliza Armstrong, who was sold to a brothel keeper for £5, caused such an outcry that the law was changed and so was the name of the street where she lived (from Charles Street to Ranston Street), such was the dishonourable reputation it had gained. Philanthropists turned their attention to the locality and built artisans' cottages and airy tenements in place of the squalid slums. Municipal authorities took up the baton in the 20th century. Among their largest projects were the Lilestone estate, begun before and finished after World War II, and the Lisson Green estate, completed in 1974 and accommodating around 1,600 residents. The latter has recently been extensively revamped, correcting serious flaws in the original plan and its execution.

The Austrian composer Joseph Haydn sought the seclusion of a Lisson Green farmhouse for the summer of 1791, during his three-year stay in England.

✉ NW1

🕮 E McDonald and D J Smith, *Pineapples and Pantomimes: A History of Church Street and Lisson Green*, Westminster Libraries, 1992

Lisson Grove • *Westminster*

A cosmopolitan street running south-eastwards from ST JOHN'S WOOD towards MARYLEBONE, in parallel with EDGWARE ROAD. The neighbouring locality was known as LISSON GREEN until it became urbanized. One London street atlas still shows both place names, with Lisson Green lying to the east of Lisson Grove, but most now treat the whole area as Lisson Grove. The street was laid out in the late 18th century and was soon lined with stuccoed houses towards its southern end, while a white lead manufactory operated further north. For a while it was a smart address but within a few decades Lisson Grove had become very rough. The journalist George Augustus Sala remembered his childhood here in the 1830s, when 'the principal public buildings were pawnbrokers and "leaving shops", low public houses and beershops, and cheap undertakers'. From the 1850s, slum clearance projects slowly began to improve the quality of life in Lisson Grove, though it remained

poor. On the corner of Broadley Terrace the Artisans', Labourers' and General Dwellings Co. erected Portman Buildings in 1887; these have now been replaced by the luxury apartments of Portman Gate. In the late 1890s the construction of the railway line into Marylebone station separated Lisson Grove from REGENT'S PARK, bringing decline to its traders. The Portman market on CHURCH STREET closed in 1906 but trading continued at the roadside. After World War I, dining rooms at 35 Lisson Grove became a fish bar, which was called the Sea Shell from 1964. Now relocated to the corner of Shroton Street, the restaurant is one of London's best-known purveyors of fish and chips. Past customers have included Diana, Princess of Wales and Lord Lichfield.

The historical painter Benjamin Haydon described a Lisson Grove dinner party with William Wordsworth, John Keats and Charles Lamb at which Lamb got drunk and berated the 'rascally Lake poet' for calling Voltaire a dull fellow. In Shaw's play *Pygmalion* Eliza Doolittle comes from Lisson Grove, and the locality is also mentioned by the American writer Jack London.

✉ NW1

Little America *see* GROSVENOR SQUARE

Little Britain • *Hillingdon*

A lake and its vicinity located north-west of YIEWSLEY, bounded by the Grand Union Canal to the east and the River Colne (which also forms the border with Buckinghamshire) to the west; so-called because of its vaguely Britannic shape. There were houses at Little Britain by 1864 and in the late 19th century St Matthew's Church, Yiewsley, established a mission room here. Most of the Little Britain area is now a country park, a 15-acre chunk of the Colne Valley Park with access from Packet Boat Lane, Trout Lane or the canal towpath. There are wildlife walks and Little Britain Lake is noted for both its fishing and its waterfowl. Little Britain is designated a site of importance for nature conservation.

✉ Uxbridge UB8

Little Ealing • *Ealing*

The southernmost part of SOUTH EALING. The hamlet of Little Ealing was in existence by the mid 17th century, when its largest dwelling was Place House. The building now called Rochester House was probably built in the 1710s for John Pearce, a London distiller, and named after his son Zachary Pearce, Bishop of Rochester, who died here. Through his marriage in 1745, Sir Francis Dashwood – the founder of the notorious Hellfire Club – gained possession of Place House, but he sold or let it in the following year and the house was rebuilt later in the century. Fewer than 20 other homes stood in Little Ealing at that time. Place House was renamed Ealing Park in the early 19th century, when its grounds were landscaped by Humphry Repton. William Lawrence made further improvements after he acquired the property in 1838 and the young Queen Victoria is said to have stayed at the house. Ealing Park and 70 acres of grounds were sold for building in 1882 and the British Land Co. laid out roads to the south of the house, which became a convent. South Ealing station opened in 1883 and housing for the lower middle classes had spread to reach the old village by the early years of the 20th century. The opening of Northfield halt in 1908 both reflected and further stimulated the suburbanization of the area and the halt was rebuilt as NORTH-FIELDS and Little Ealing station in 1911. The remainder of the locality was built up between the world wars. In the late 1980s Place House (as it is once again called) became the girls' upper school of the King Fahad Academy. At the neighbouring Little Ealing Primary School, half the pupils are from ethnic minorities and a high proportion speak English as an additional language.

✉ W5

🚇 Piccadilly Line (Northfields, zone 3)

📖 Paul Fitzmaurice et al, *Little Ealing: A Walk through History*, Ealing Fields Residents' Association, 2002

@ www.littleealinghistory.org.uk

Little Heath • *Redbridge*

An area dominated by education and healthcare institutions at the north-western corner of CHADWELL HEATH. Little Heath was once a hamlet at the edge of Hainault Forest and may have been the site of the water source that gave Chadwell its name. It is home to a college and three schools. Redbridge College is a vocation-oriented establishment with an enrolment of over 7,000 students. Little Heath School is a special school for pupils with learning difficulties. Ethel Davis School is dedicated to children of all ages with physical disabilities. Grove Primary School is a community school for boys and girls aged from three to eleven years. There have been three hospitals in the vicinity of Little Heath. Good-

mayes was originally an asylum for the 'pauper lunatics of West Ham', while Chadwell Heath began life as an isolation hospital. The original Goodmayes and Chadwell Heath hospitals have been closed in recent years, but parts of both sites continue to be used for healthcare purposes. King George Hospital, a major NHS facility for the adjacent boroughs, opened in 1993. Little Heath was designated a conservation area in 1992. Hainault Road has the recent Little Heath development, by Bellway Homes.

Little Heath had its own church from 1862 until its demolition in 1933. St James's Church was built by Major Ibbetson as a chapel beside his residence at Heath House. Services continued until about 1930.

✉ Romford RM6

Little Ilford • *Newham*

The half-forgotten north-eastern corner of EAST HAM, situated on the opposite side of the River Roding (and the North Circular Road) from ILFORD itself. Domesday Book identifies this as the original location of Ilford and there was a wooden church here in Saxon times, which was rebuilt in stone in the early 12th century and then in brick in the 18th century. The parish of Little Ilford was the smallest in BECONTREE hundred, covering 768 acres in the 19th century. Very few people lived here until the hamlet began to grow slowly in the 1850s, gaining its first school in 1865. From the 1880s the creation of cemeteries in the area led to a rush on the remaining available building land. By this time, however, the wider district was being called MANOR PARK and the parish was absorbed into East Ham. Manor Farm was developed as the Manor House estate after 1895 and the manor house itself was demolished by 1901. The district was almost fully built up by 1910. Jerry-built housing that had degenerated into slums on Grantham Road, Alverstone Road and Walton Road was redeveloped by the council from the 1960s. Little Ilford is now an area with problems of social deprivation. At Little Ilford Community School, on Browning Road, more than half the pupils are eligible for free school meals. The Little Ilford ward is very ethnically mixed, with no single group predominating. The largest minorities are white, Bangladeshi, Indian and black African. A third of residents are Muslims, and nearly 30 per cent are under 16.

Little Ilford Park, formerly the grounds of Little Ilford manor house, is located at the eastern end of Church Road. It is said with some credibility to have inspired the Small Faces' song *Itchycoo Park*. Jack Cornwell Street commemorates a 16-year-old boy from Alverstone Road who was posthumously awarded the Victoria Cross for his gallantry at the Battle of Jutland in 1916.

✉ E12

✚ 13,329

Little India *see* SOUTHALL *and* WEST EUSTON

Little Italy • *Camden*
A nickname applied to the western side of CLERKENWELL because of its strong Italian connections, which go back at least two centuries. Also once known as Italian Hill, its boundaries are recognized as Clerkenwell Road, Farringdon Road and Rosebery Avenue. In addition to the Italian Church of St Peter, built in 1863, there are several local shops and services run by members of the Italian community, including a *scuola guida* (driving school), but the number of these is declining. The Italian population reached a peak here in the late 19th century. Until then, the Saffron Hill vicinity had been notorious for the pickpockets and fences portrayed in *Oliver Twist* and the authorities were glad to see these characters supplanted by the more respectable Italians. London's Italians are now spread more thinly throughout the capital, but Sunday worship at St Peter's still provides a focal point. The *Processione della Madonna del Carmine*, held on the Sunday after 16 July, is Little Italy's most important event. Except during wartime it has taken place every year since 1896.

Giuseppe Mazzini, the writer and political leader, lived in Laystall Street and founded an Italian language school in nearby HATTON GARDEN in 1841.

✉ EC1

📖 Sacheverell Sitwell, *Little Italy in London*, self-published, 1977

Little Paris *see* SOUTH KENSINGTON

Little Roke • *Croydon*
An affordable residential locality in north KENLEY, situated immediately west of RIDDLESDOWN, with a mix of owner-occupied and rented accommodation. The name means 'little place at the oak tree' and a Thomas atte Roke was recorded as living here in 1328. Roke Farm was in existence by 1762 and a substantial house called Little Roke later stood at the southern end of Roke Road. In the 1920s and 1930s Little Roke consisted of a small community of terraced and semi-detached cottages. The village had a primary school, a church hall and a surprising variety of shops, selling practically everything except clothing. Little Roke was almost entirely rebuilt during the second half of the 20th century, losing its amenities and its village character. Roke Primary School was rebuilt in 1994 and has a high percentage of pupils who speak English as an additional language. Two ancient oaks were measured in 2001, when they were threatened by a proposed development, and one was found to be almost 900 years old.

✉ South Croydon CR2

Little Stanmore • *Harrow*
A significant medieval parish lying west of EDGWARE and BURNT OAK, but now almost lost within neighbouring suburbs, notably CANONS PARK. St Lawrence's Church was built in white stone during the twelfth century, but the oldest surviving part of the present structure is its late-14th-century tower. The rest of the church was rebuilt in 1715, with a startlingly ornate interior that has woodcarvings attributed to Grinling Gibbons. The parish was also known as Whitchurch, from the original colour of St Lawrence's, and this name was applied to the hamlet that grew up around it, nothing of which has survived. Until the late 19th century the neighbouring Canons estate provided much of the hamlet's employment, and acted as a constraint on its growth. The first suburban avenues were laid out shortly before World War I but to the south there were open fields as far as KINGSBURY GREEN until METROLAND development created QUEENSBURY during the 1930s. The council built several groups of houses, including the Chandos estate, and opened the 27-acre Chandos recreation ground. Near Canons Park, properties were built to high specifications. At Little Stanmore Nursery, First and Middle School, 62 per cent of pupils speak a language other than English at home. The educational standards agency Ofsted rated the school's performance unsatisfactory in 2004 and applied a 'special measures' regime.

It is probable that Handel performed the first of his *Chandos Anthems* at St Lawrence's Church, although the story that he was inspired to compose *The Harmonious Blacksmith* while sheltering from the rain in a nearby forge is almost certainly apocryphal.

✉ Edgware HA8

@ www.little-stanmore.org (church's site)

Little Venice • *Westminster*

A canal intersection and its pretty, if flawed, vicinity on the border of PADDINGTON and MAIDA VALE. A pool was created here in the 1810s at the meeting point of the Regent's Canal and the Paddington arm of the Grand Junction (now Grand Union) Canal, and was originally known as Paddington Broadwater. A small island with willows and wildfowl makes a kind of roundabout at the junction, which was always intended as a spot for pleasure boats. The neighbouring area was built up in a piecemeal but harmonious fashion from the second quarter of the 19th century, especially with terraces and pairs of three-storey stuccoed houses. In her 1934 detective novel *Death of a Ghost*, Margery Allingham gave the name 'Little Venice' to a house overlooking the canal. The name caught on with estate agents after World War II and is still much used for the pricey properties in the locality. Any echo of Venice is very faint indeed, and the incongruous 1960s flats on Warwick Crescent mar its charm, but the jolly houseboats moored along the canalsides create a picturesque appearance. Artists' studios on the east side of the pool were demolished and replaced by a small park, named Rembrandt Gardens in 1975 to commemorate the 700th anniversary of the founding of the city of Amsterdam, the 'Venice of the North'. Public walkways were opened on both sides of the pool around this time. Most of Little Venice was part of the Maida Vale estate belonging to the Church Commissioners, who offered the freeholds for sale in the 1980s, when a number of houses were bought by property companies and converted into flats. More than half the adult residents of Little Venice are qualified to degree level or higher.

The poet Robert Browning, short-story writer Katherine Mansfield, playwright Christopher Fry, novelist Elizabeth Jane Howard and Icelandic chanteuse Björk are among those who have had homes in Little Venice.

✉ W2; W9

👥 8,100

📖 James Dowsing, *Little Venice*, Sunrise Press, 2001

Little Woodcote • *Sutton*

A rural hamlet situated two miles west of PUR-LEY, where Little Woodcote Lane meets Wood-mansterne Lane. When a gas pipeline was laid through Little Woodcote in 1968, flints of possibly Neolithic origin were uncovered. Other flints of varying ages have also been found here, indicating significant prehistoric occupation. However, there is little support for speculation that Little Woodcote was the site of a Roman town – perhaps the much sought-after Noviomagus. Evidence of the existence of an early medieval village is mixed but it seems that there was a settlement of some kind, which may have declined in population after the Black Death. To the west of Little Woodcote and the north of WOOD-MANSTERNE the future twelfth Earl of Derby created Oaks Farm and its walled garden as a 'model farmery' during the 1870s. The Oaks itself was a magnificent castle-like mansion, possibly based on a relocated tollhouse extended by Robert Adam. The house was demolished in the late 1950s. Surrey County Council provided smallholdings for ex-servicemen in Little Woodcote, retaining these until 1951. Located on what is now Sutton's south-eastern edge, much of the Oaks is now a park, sports centre and public golf course. The southern part has become a disused wilderness.

Lord Derby inaugurated two famous horse races at nearby Epsom, naming them after himself and his house.

✉ Carshalton SM5; Banstead SM7

📖 Margaret Cunningham, *The Story of Little Woodcote and Woodcote Hall*, Heritage in Sutton Leisure, 1989

Liverpool Street • *City*

A main-line railway station located at the corner of Liverpool Street and BISHOPSGATE, and the terminus for train services to the eastern and north-eastern suburbs, Stansted Airport and East Anglia. The street takes its name from Lord Liverpool, prime minister from 1812 to 1827. With so many other landmarks close by, only the immediate environs of the station are referred to as the Liverpool Street area. Although the London to East Anglia route first began to operate in the 1840s, it was not until 1874 that Liverpool Street station replaced Bishopsgate as the terminus. It is London's (and Britain's) fifth busiest station, measured by passenger 'footfall'. Improvements made in the early 1990s combined the restoration of many original features with sensible modernization, including a more spacious booking hall for London Underground services. In 2004 all main-line services operating out of Liverpool Street were consolidated within the 'one' Railway franchise, operated by the National Express Group.

Scenes in the films *Bridget Jones's Diary* and *Mission: Impossible* were shot in and around Liverpool Street station.

✉ EC2

🚃 Main-line: 'one' Railway (East Anglia and suburban services) London Underground: Central Line, Circle Line, Hammersmith & City Line, Metropolitan Line (zone 1)

📖 Nick Derbyshire, *Liverpool Street: A Station for the Twenty-First Century,* Granta, 1991

Lloyd Park • *Waltham Forest*
A public park located north of Forest Road in WALTHAMSTOW. In the Middle Ages the park formed the grounds of a moated house called Cricklewoods. The moat gave its name to Water House, which was built in the mid 18th century and was also known as Winns. In the mid 19th century this was the boyhood home of William Morris, the artist, craftsman and socialist. Later owners, the Lloyd family, gave the house to the people of Walthamstow in 1898, on condition that the council bought an adjoining 10 acres of its grounds. The remaining 86 acres of grounds were acquired by the Warner company, which laid out the Winns estate to the west. The housing bears the distinctive features of the company's extensive work in Walthamstow. Between 1911 and 1943, when Water House was known as Lloyd Park Mansion, it served as a clinic, providing free medical and dental care for the children of Walthamstow. Between the wars the council built houses at William Morris Close, enlarged the park and added a pavilion. The house became a museum of Morris's life and work in 1950; it also has a collection of paintings and sculpture donated by the artist Sir Frank Brangwyn, who was a pupil of Morris. The little Waltham Forest Theatre was built as part of the modernization of the pavilion in 1965. Slightly less than half the residents of William Morris ward are Christians – one of the lowest proportions in the borough.

✉ E17

👥 10,975 (William Morris ward)

Locksbottom • *Bromley*
The north-western corner of FARNBOROUGH, dominated by a new university hospital. The name (which is also spelt as two separate words) referred to the Lock family, who owned land in the valley in the 18th century.

A bridge was built over a brook here in 1725 at a cost of £2 1s 6d, plus 8s 7d for workmen's beer. Bromley board of guardians built a union workhouse at Locksbottom in 1845, a grey and ugly building surrounded by a high brick wall. In 1896 over 500 adults and children were living at the workhouse. From the early 20th century the addition of infirmary facilities marked the beginning of the institution's evolution into a hospital, a process that was complete by the late 1920s. This was a time when Locksbottom was losing its village character as suburban development began to spread here from ORPINGTON. Mock-Tudor shops were built in the 1930s but some have closed in recent years. To the west of the village, the Keston Park estate was laid out around Holwood Park Avenue. The luxury houses on this gated estate are regularly demolished and rebuilt to even higher specifications, with prices running well into the millions. Following an extensive programme of redevelopment, Farnborough Hospital reopened in 2003 as the Princess Royal University Hospital. Locksbottom's prime attractions are Ye Olde Whyte Lyon, a 17th-century coaching inn, and the Michelin-starred Chapter One, the AA Restaurant of the Year in 2004.

✉ Orpington BR6

London Airport see HEATHROW and LONDON CITY AIRPORT

London Bridge • *Southwark*
London's longest established Thames crossing and the name now applied to the historic environs of its southern side. The first bridge was built around AD 50 and, with its many successors, it was for nearly 1,700 years the city's only Thames bridge. Work on the construction of a stone bridge began in 1176 and St Thomas's Hospital was established in SOUTHWARK at around this time. The bridge of nursery rhyme fame stood for more than six centuries and was possibly the most painted of all the capital's scenes; it is represented in almost every gallery in London. Houses, shops and a chapel were built on the bridge, mills operated beneath several of its arches and until 1660 the heads of traitors were mounted on spikes by the southern gatehouse. Old London Bridge was replaced in 1831 and London Bridge station was built beside it in 1836, making this the oldest of the capital's present-day termini. The neighbouring area became increasingly congested, with the wharves at SHAD THAMES, the industry of BANKSIDE and the slums of the

BOROUGH. St Thomas's Hospital moved to LAMBETH in 1871 but a neighbouring hospital founded by Sir Thomas Guy has remained and progressively expanded, adding the world's tallest hospital tower in 1974. London Bridge was replaced again in the early 1970s and its predecessor was re-erected at Lake Havasu City, Arizona. The vicinity of London Bridge station is a significant commercial centre, notably in the form of LONDON BRIDGE CITY. Among the area's tourist attractions are the London Dungeon, on Tooley Street, and HMS *Belfast*, a floating museum of naval history.

Bedale Street played home to the heroine of the 2001 hit movie *Bridget Jones's Diary*.

✉ SE1

🚉 Southern; South Eastern Trains; Thameslink; Jubilee Line; Northern Line (zone 1)

📖 Patricia Pierce, *Old London Bridge*, Headline, 2001

@ hmsbelfast.iwm.org.uk; www.guysandstthomas.nhs.uk (Guy's and St Thomas's hospitals site); www.thedungeons.com (London Dungeon site)

London Bridge City • *Southwark*

A major commercial centre located on the south bank of the Thames between LONDON BRIDGE and TOWER Bridge; the westernmost of London's docklands rejuvenation schemes. Also called the London Bridge Quarter, it is built around the site of Hay's Wharf, which has been filled in and covered over with a glazed atrium to create Hay's Galleria, with shops, bars and restaurants for local office workers. The development includes a public park and a riverside walk between the two bridges. The proposed London Bridge Tower, already better known as the Shard of Glass, is due for completion by the end of 2010. If the project goes ahead as planned, this will be by far London's tallest building, at 1,016 feet, almost a third as high again as One Canada Square at CANARY WHARF.

✉ SE1

🚢 London Bridge City pier

@ shardlondonbridge.com; www.haysgalleria.co.uk

London City Airport • *Newham*

A short-take-off-and-landing airport located in eastern DOCKLANDS. The facility was proposed in 1981 by the London Docklands Development Corporation and Captain Harry Gee proved its viability by landing a Brymon Dash 7 at HERON QUAYS the following year. London City Airport opened in 1987 on the quays between the former KING GEORGE V and ROYAL ALBERT docks, with a terminal building of almost cosy proportions. The King George V Dock office buildings are used as a transit office. The runway was extended in 1990 to permit use by corporate jets, and a turning loop was provided in 2003, increasing the handling capacity. Only low-noise, mid-range airliners can use the airport, which offers flights to UK and European destinations. Nearly two million passengers now pass through City Airport each year, with a long-term target of five million. A Docklands Light Railway connection opened in 2005, supplementing the somewhat inconvenient shuttle bus services.

✉ E16

🚉 Docklands Light Railway, City Airport branch (zone 3)

@ www.londoncityairport.com

London Fields • *Hackney*

A 31-acre park located west of Mare Street in south-central HACKNEY and, by extension, the surrounding residential and commercial locality. The fields formerly lay just outside Hackney, on the London side, hence the name. A smattering of houses bordered the fields from the mid 17th century and the area was densely built up by the early 19th century, with better-off residents tending to live on the north side. Broadway Market developed around a row of two-storeyed shops in the 1820s. At this time the fields belonged to a handful of farmers, who were obliged to allow local people to graze animals here after the harvest had been gathered. Property developers almost got their hands on the fields in the early 1860s but the benefits of preserving such a useful space persuaded the Metropolitan Board of Works to acquire the land as a public park in 1872. London Fields station opened in the same year, on the Great Eastern Railway's new branch line from BETHNAL GREEN. Small-scale industries like bootmaking flourished in the streets to the south, which became increasingly poor and overcrowded. Council flats began to replace the slums from the early 1930s and London Fields Lido was opened. The Church of St Michael and All Angels was rebuilt after its predecessor was bombed in 1945 and has become very active in community work. Properties on Broadway Market were rehabilitated in the late 1970s and the street now has boutiques, art galleries and a Saturday market with farm produce, flowers, arts and crafts and clothing. Hackney council's sales of its properties on Broadway Market to the highest bidders have sparked a campaign against the 'social cleansing' of the locality. London Fields Lido closed in 1988 but pressure from the local community, which organized a clean-up of the neglected site, has recently prompted Hackney council to restore and reopen it as London's only 50-metre heated outdoor pool. Construction of a seasonal roof is planned to allow year-round opening. London Fields' Victorian properties have been undergoing gentrification over the past decade and developers have added private flats. In an indication of the area's changing image, an apartment block called Artisans has been built around a gated courtyard on Lansdowne Drive and sold with the slogan 'contemporary, cultural, connected'. At the same time, the industrial estate has been brought back to life by an influx of arts and media tenants. The park itself is not one of London's most beautiful: mature plane trees add a little greenery in season, but with tower blocks in all directions, London Fields presents a gloomy vista on a dull or wintry day. The ethnic communities of London Fields include those of Turkish, Caribbean, African and Bengali descent.

London Fields is the title of Martin Amis's sweeping examination of metropolitan mores in the late 20th century, but the story is set in and around Ladbroke Grove and Notting Hill.

✉ E8

🚇 'one' Railway (zone 2)

Lonesome • *Lambeth/Merton*

A railside residential locality situated on the STREATHAM/MITCHAM border, south-west of Streatham Vale Park. The name formerly applied to a much larger area but the rise of STREATHAM VALE has consigned it to obscurity. It is named after Lonesome (or Lonely) House, which was built around 1820. Established here because of the sparse population, the Lonesome chemical works produced naphtha to make waterproofed clothing and groundsheets for troops during the Crimean War. The company expanded its gas production facilities in the 1860s, demolishing Lonesome House in the process. The locality became more inaccessible when the railway divided it from Mitcham in 1868. Speculative

builders later started to lay out an estate here but the project was unsuccessful and Lonesome was described as a 'deserted village' early in the 20th century. However, expanding employment opportunities in Streatham soon brought new housebuilding, with residents fording the River Graveney on their walk to work. In the 1920s, before the building of Streatham Vale's Church of the Holy Redeemer, Lonesome's Mission of the Good Shepherd was based in a large wooden shed off Marian Road and conducted open-air evangelical work there. The chemical works closed in the 1930s and the site was divided between residential and non-noxious industrial uses. Industry did not finally disappear from Lonesome until the late 1960s. Lambeth council made a site available for a Gypsy encampment in the 1970s but this soon became overcrowded and was later closed. The recreation ground on Oakleigh Way has a children's play area and a nature reserve beside the railway. Lonesome First School on Grove Road takes pupils aged from three to eight years, and has higher than average numbers of pupils who speak a first language other than English, pupils eligible for free meals and pupils with special educational needs.

The ice hockey player Tony Whitehead was born in Lonesome in 1936 and played for Great Britain in 1962. His lengthy career included spells at two Streatham-based clubs, the Royals and the Redskins.

✉ SW16; Mitcham CR4

@ www.ideal-homes.org.uk/lambeth/ streatham/lonesome.htm (London surburban history site)

Longford • *Hillingdon*

A village located at the north-western corner of HEATHROW Airport, one mile south-west of HARMONDSWORTH. The name comes from an oblique crossing over the River Colne, for many years written – and pronounced – as two separate words. Longford grew up as a halt on the Bath Road and had 30 houses by 1337, but development was limited by the susceptibility to flooding of the low-lying land. Its waterside location made milling the dominant activity; from medieval times farmers brought corn, barley and wheat here. Paper mills came afterwards, and later still an associated printing works. The White Horse inn was in existence by the 17th century and survives today, together with a handful of houses and cottages from that period. Longford had a village shop by 1839. The opening of the Colnbrook bypass (A4) in 1929 and subsequent traffic exclusion measures and conservation area status have helped preserve Longford's remarkably villagey character, despite some intrusions from the late 20th century. To the east of the village there are several airport-related commercial premises. The Longford River is an artificial watercourse that Charles I had constructed to provide water for the lakes at Hampton Court and Bushy Park. The course of the river was changed in the 1940s as a result of the creation of London (now Heathrow) Airport and has been changed again with the construction of the new fifth terminal.

✉ West Drayton UB7

@ www.thisislongford.com (residents' association site)

Longfordmoor • *Hillingdon*

The westernmost place in Greater London, situated on the Bath Road (A4) between the River Colne and the Wraysbury River, beside the M25. Moor Bridge has provided the link to LONGFORD since the 15th century, and has also been known as High Bridge. SIPSON Farm seems to have been responsible for the bridge's maintenance for perhaps two centuries, until at least the 1820s. On its northern side are lakes formed from disused gravel workings. Mad Bridge crosses the Wraysbury River and leads to Poyle, now in the borough of Slough, where apple grower Richard Cox created the Orange Pippin around 1825. Longfordmoor finds itself more isolated than ever following the construction to the south of the access road connecting the M25 with HEATHROW'S new Terminal 5.

✉ West Drayton UB7

Longlands • *Bexley*

A comfortable and relatively aged community that, like most of the former hamlets hereabouts, is just 'part of SIDCUP' to most residents. It lies on the NEW ELTHAM side of that district. There was a settlement here from the 17th century and Longlands House stood from 1750 to 1886. For a long period it was home to George Russell, a mill owner and soap manufacturer with works at BLACKFRIARS and EAST GREENWICH. Longlands is a district of well-proportioned, pebble-dashed semi-detached houses, mostly built between the wars, with a few blocks of flats at the eastern end of Longlands Road. Some of the best properties were built by Cory and Cory in the late 1920s, with tile-hung bays, leaded windows and timber porches. Ninety-five per cent of Longlands' residents are white and 80 per cent are owner-occupiers. For this corner of London, the proportion of adults living alone is relatively high, partly owing to the significant number of widowed pensioners. The average age of Longlands residents is 42.6 years, much older than either the borough or the national norm. Longlands Primary School, on Woodside Road, takes an increasing number of children from single-parent families and rented accommodation, but relatively few from the private housing to the north of the school, according to a 2004 report by the educational standards agency Ofsted. The Longlands area is particularly well supplied with sports and recreation grounds.

✉ Sidcup DA15

👥 9,611

Lord's • *Westminster*

The cricket ground and international headquarters of the game, situated in south ST JOHN'S WOOD. By the late 18th century cricket had acquired a substantial following in north London and the game's upper-class followers wanted a more exclusive venue than the open meadow at White Conduit Fields. Accordingly, Thomas Lord – a Yorkshire-born bowler and a prosperous merchant – laid out a ground at Dorset Fields (now Dorset Square) and founded the MARYLEBONE Cricket Club. In 1814 he moved the operation to the site of a former duck pond in St John's Wood, and the success of the venture prompted him to build a pavilion and a tavern. Lord retired in 1825 and died seven years later, leaving behind a club that had become the country's leading cricket team and the game's recognized governing body. From 1838 lawn tennis was also played at Lord's and a sub-committee of the Marylebone club later formulated that game's first laws. In 1878 the MCC invited Middlesex County Cricket Club to make Lord's its home. Another three acres were added to the ground with the acquisition of Henderson's nursery – hence the 'nursery end'. An underground station was built at Lord's in 1868 (originally named St John's Wood Road), but closed with the opening of the present St John's Wood station in 1939. As well as the home games of the Marylebone and Middlesex clubs, the venue also hosts international test matches and the Eton v HARROW and Oxford v Cambridge fixtures. Cricket enthusiasts can take a tour of the ground on non-match days and visit the MCC Museum. The latest in a series of recent improvements at Lord's have been a major restoration of the pavilion and the construction of the futuristic media centre, which won the Stirling Prize in 1999. There are plans to use the venue for concerts and corporate events to help to pay for further upgrades to the facilities. At the 2012 Olympic Games, the archery competition will be held at Lord's.

✉ NW8

📖 Stephen Green, *Lord's: Cathedral of Cricket*, Tempus, 2003

@ www.lords.org

Loughborough Junction • *Lambeth*

A station and a knot of railway lines located halfway along Coldharbour Lane where BRIXTON meets CAMBERWELL. It derives its name from Henry Hastings, first Baron Loughborough. In 1660 Lord Loughborough acquired the old manor house of LAMBETH Wick, which came with 234 acres of farmland, extending into the area then known as Cold Harbour. The house later became a 'superior academy' for boys. The Lambeth Wick estate was sold off in three parts and built up from the 1820s onwards, with development progressing from north to south. The old manor house was demolished in 1854, when the Loughborough Park estate was laid out with 315 houses of varying degrees of grandeur. The Loughborough Hotel now occupies the site of the house. Loughborough Junction station opened in 1863, followed by another station to its west, originally called Loughborough Park, later East Brixton, which closed in 1976. At one point it was proposed to extend the Northern Line (as it now is) to Loughborough Junction, before the decision was taken to extend the line to CLAPHAM instead. By the end of the 19th century, many of the area's larger villas were being subdivided into flats. A number of these houses survive but much of the area's housing stock was lost in a post-war demolition programme around Coldharbour Lane to clear the way for an inner London ring road that never materialized. The council flats of the Loughborough estate subsequently filled the breach, notably the eleven-storey blocks around Barrington Road. Loughborough Park public gardens opened in 1972. Loughborough Primary School, on Minet Road, opened as a 'fresh start' school in 2002, serving the Loughborough estate. Around four-fifths of its pupils come from minority ethnic backgrounds and at least 28 different mother tongues are spoken.

Clockwork Studios on Southwell Road, which has workshops for artists and craftspeople, was the site of Fred Karno's Fun Factory before World War I.

✉ SW9; SE5; SE24

🚆 Thameslink (zone 2)

Lower Belvedere • *Bexley*

The northern and newer part of BELVEDERE, known from the 17th century as Picardy. Picardy may have been the name of a manor, but its origin is unknown and there is no evidence of any connection with the region of the same name in northern France. Lower Belvedere's oldest surviving building is the Ye Olde Leather Bottle public house on Heron Hill, opposite the junction with Upper Abbey Road. Said to date from 1643, when it was called simply The Bottle, the inn was rebuilt at the end of the 18th century. The North Kent Railway line was built through the district in 1849 and Belvedere station opened ten years later. Within a few years, rows of small houses began to be constructed for workers at the new Thames-side factories at ERITH and the CROSSNESS sewage works, opened in 1865. Picardy's grandest house, Heron Hill, was sold in 1884 and its grounds developed for housing. Trams and buses began to serve Lower Belvedere in the early years of the 20th century and the population grew large enough to justify the establishment of St Augustine's Church in 1915. Around the station the marshy ground hindered development and the land was occupied by a large community of travellers long after the rest of Belvedere had been built up.

✉ Belvedere DA17

🚆 South Eastern Trains (Belvedere, zone 5)

Lower Cheam • *Sutton*

The eastern part of CHEAM, centred around the southern end of Gander Green Lane and bordering WEST SUTTON. It was originally the manor of East Cheam and this name has regained some currency in recent years. The manor was in the possession of the archbishops of Canterbury from the time of Domesday Book until 1539, when Thomas Cranmer swapped the manor with Henry VIII; Cranmer gained Chislet Park in Kent, while the king was able to add more hunting land to nearby Nonsuch Park. At this time the hamlet consisted only of the manor house and a dozen cottages. The manor passed through various aristocratic hands after Henry's death, notably local grandees like the Lumley family. East Cheam manor house, which had been built by a tenant of Cranmer, was pulled down in 1800 by Philip Antrobus and replaced by Lower Cheam House. The Antrobus family were leading members of the Cheam gentry for over a century and their estate stretched north from Cheam Road up to what became Tate Road. The family gave land at the end of Gander Green Lane to Sutton Cricket Club in 1858. The club was forced to move its pitch westwards when the WIMBLEDON loop of what is now the Thameslink line was constructed in the late 1920s, using spoil from the railway cuttings to fill a disused chalk pit. Tennis and squash facilities have since been added. The Lower Cheam estate was sold and the house demolished in 1933, and Carlisle Road was laid out on its site. The area has seen additional housebuilding in recent years, especially Linden Homes' 122-unit Shearwater development by Cheam waterworks in 1999.

No. 23 Railway Cuttings, East Cheam was the home of Tony Hancock in his legendary radio and television comedy series *Hancock's Half Hour*. Co-writer Alan Simpson has said that he chose the locality because of its posh connotations and then 'killed it' with the (fictional) street name.

✉ Sutton SM1

Lower Clapton • *Hackney*

The part of CLAPTON that lies south of the Lea Bridge Road and north of HACKNEY, so called from the early 19th century. From the 17th century wealthy Londoners took advantage of the pleasant and accessible location to erect country seats here. Clapton House was built around 1680 on the east side of what is now Lower Clapton Road. Across the road a five-bay house was built in the late 1710s for a manufacturer of novelty chamber pots, and accordingly nicknamed Piss Pot Hall. Philanthropic institutions later converted some of the properties in the area and built new almshouses and care homes. Piss Pot Hall became the British Asylum for Deaf and Dumb Females. Clapton Square was laid out in 1816; it is now a conservation area. Opposite Clapton House, a landowning vicar, Thomas Baden Powell, endowed the site for St James's Church in 1840. From the 1860s developers began to build suburban terraces, at first close to the main arterial roads and then on new streets in the hinterland, aided in particular by the sale of the grounds of the London Orphan Asylum. Clapton House (latterly a school) was demolished in the 1880s and Thistlewaite Road, Newick Road and Mildenhall Road covered its grounds. By the outbreak of World War I, the southern end of Lower Clapton Road had merged with Hackney's Mare Street in a continuous line of shops. From the 1930s onwards municipal authorities built some council flats, and later replaced war-damaged properties, but with less intensity than in UPPER CLAPTON. The capacious and distinctive Round House, originally a Nonconformist chapel, was converted into a performing arts centre in 1996. Lower Clapton has a very diverse population, with ethnic minorities that include those of black Caribbean, black African, Indian, Bangladeshi and Turkish descent. Lower Clapton Road became known as 'murder mile' in the early 2000s after a spate of shootings.

The playwright Harold Pinter lived at 19 Thistlewaite Road as a boy, and went to school at HACKNEY DOWNS.

✉ E5

Lower Edmonton • *Enfield*

This is downtown EDMONTON, focused around EDMONTON GREEN, where Fore Street, Church Street and the Hertford Road meet. All Saints' Church was in existence by about 1140 and the present building dates from the 15th century, although it has been altered almost out of recognition since then. By the late 18th century Lower Edmonton was the administrative as well as the spiritual centre of the parish and a well-established settlement, although by no means large. There were 101 dwellings here in 1801. In the mid 19th century, ribbon development along Fore Street linked it with UPPER EDMONTON. In 1849 the Great Eastern Railway opened Church Street station (later Lower Edmonton) on a now-closed branch line to Enfield Town from Angel Road. Another branch line arrived in 1872 and Edmonton station was built, later called Lower Edmonton and now Edmonton Green. The second line was the more successful but even before the new station opened the railway had had an effect in Lower Edmonton; industry developed northward along the line, and the building of LIVERPOOL STREET station displaced thousands of City inhabitants, many of whom came to live here. Extensive shopping facilities and a street market at Edmonton Green drew visitors from miles around in the late 19th century. Much of Lower Edmonton was built up with housing by the outbreak of World War I and the process was completed in the two decades after hostilities ceased, closing the gap with neighbouring districts like BUSH HILL PARK. After World War II, Edmonton council and its Enfield successor comprehensively redeveloped what had become a run-down area, adding tower blocks in the 1960s. The 1990s saw a resurgence in private housebuilding, especially of small flats. Lower Edmonton is a multi-ethnic community; the main groups being white, black Caribbean and black African.

The Latymer School operates a selective admission policy and is rated one of the best state schools in the country. Founded in 1624 on Church Street, the school moved to Haselbury Road and went co-educational in 1910. Most of its pupils do not come from the immediate area and those that do are more likely to live in WINCHMORE HILL than Lower Edmonton. The educational standards agency Ofsted reported in 2005 that the school's excellent standards had risen 'even higher' than at the previous inspection. The entertainer Bruce Forsyth is among the school's alumni.

✉ N9

👥 12,686

🚉 'one' Railway (Edmonton Green, zone 4)

@ lower-edmonton.co.uk (privately operated local information site – if only every part of London had a website like this)

Lower Feltham • *Hounslow*

A 'non-existent place', according to FELTHAM'S leading historian, Kenneth Baldwin. 'Other than its mention on the Ordnance Survey maps of recent years, the writer, despite enquiry, knows of no authenticity for the misnomer "Lower" Feltham, having thus far found the expression first used in 1911,' wrote Baldwin. He speculated that the name gained currency when the northern and eastern parts of Feltham (which are on slightly higher ground) were built up before and after World War II, although he insisted that the new parts were never called Upper Feltham. Lower Feltham lies approximately 45 feet above sea level, while central Feltham is about 65 feet. Situated right on the London border, Lower Feltham is mostly surrounded by open country except where it connects with its parent to the north-east. Most of Lower Feltham's residents are white, although there are significant black and Asian minorities. The area suffers the problems of unemployment, social deprivation and crime.

West of the residential district is the Feltham Young Offenders' Institution, situated in a wasteland of nurseries and former gravel pits. It opened as Middlesex County Industrial School in 1859 and converted to its present use in 1919. In recent years Feltham has become Britain's most notorious youth prison. A prison inspectors' report in 2000 criticized it as 'rotten to the core', and suicides have been all too common. Channel 4's musical documentary *Feltham Sings* featured lyrics by Simon Armitage and performances by inmates. The programme won a BAFTA award in 2003.

✉ Feltham TW13

Lower Holloway • *Islington*

The southern part of HOLLOWAY, situated around the north end of CALEDONIAN ROAD. Lower (or Nether) Holloway was first recorded in 1553. From the late 17th century the area included COPENHAGEN House and its fields, which later became the site of a succession of amenities until the building of the present Caledonian Market estate. Very few people lived in Lower Holloway until the construction of Paradise Row in 1767. This terrace of 31 houses remained isolated until around 1800, when more small terraced houses and a few villas appeared in HOLLOWAY ROAD. The settlement soon absorbed the hamlet of Ring Cross, which had stood at the junction of Holloway and Hornsey Roads, prompting the establishment of a chapel of ease and, in 1815, parochial schools. Remoter parts of the district acquired some noxious industries, notably in the Belle Isle area, to the south-west. The cottages of Belle Isle and the farmland around were erased by cramped terraced housing in the 1860s and 1870s. Some of the most substandard housing was soon being replaced – by the Northern Polytechnic in 1896 and by London County Council flats from the early 1900s. Much larger housing schemes transformed the western part of Lower Holloway after World War II, and where larger houses survived they were often subdivided into flats. Lower Holloway retains some industrial and commercial premises to the present day but its character is primarily residential, with much of the housing stock built and then rebuilt by successive municipal authorities. A high proportion of residents are from ethnic minorities, especially of Nigerian and Ghanaian origin. The area is more often referred to as Holloway Road or Caledonian Road than Lower Holloway, mainly because of the nearby Tube stations, which both opened in 1906. There have even been attempts to reposition the area as 'Upper Islington'.

In September 1905, Hawley Harvey Crippen and his wife Cora moved in to 39 Hilldrop Crescent. Dr Crippen had practised as a dentist and a purveyor of patent medicines; Cora was a music hall singer. Cuckolded by the assertive, flirtatious Cora, Crippen turned to his young secretary, Ethel le Neve, and the two became lovers. Crippen poisoned his wife, cut up her body and buried her remains in the cellar. Finding himself under police suspicion, he boarded a steamer bound for Canada, accompanied by Ethel disguised as a boy. The ship's captain noticed that the pair behaved in an unusually affectionate manner and sent a wireless message to London. Chief Inspector Dew of Scotland Yard took a faster ship and intercepted them as they docked in Quebec. Both were tried for murder; Le Neve was acquitted but Crippen was found guilty, and hanged at PENTONVILLE prison on 23 November 1910.

✉ N7

📖 Richard Gordon, *The Private Life of Doctor Crippen*, House of Stratus, 2001

Lower Merton   *see* MERTON PARK

Lower Morden   •   *Merton*
Situated beside the Pyl Brook, south of RAYNES PARK, Lower Morden provides various facilities and amenities to a wide catchment area. In 1890, Battersea council bought 120 acres of Morden Common and laid out Battersea New Cemetery, now Morden Cemetery. The cemetery has Anglican and Nonconformist chapels and one of London's finest horse chestnut trees. In 1947, Merton, Morden and Carshalton councils created a joint cemetery, now Merton and Sutton Cemetery, on the other side of Green Lane. The North-East Surrey Crematorium opened in the northern section of Morden Cemetery in 1958. With cremation increasingly replacing burial, part of the cemetery was deemed surplus to requirements and Wandsworth council (Battersea's successor) laid out the attractive Four Acres estate at the southern end of Grand Drive from 1980. Garth Road (named after a former lord of the manor of Morden) has light industrial buildings and refuse destruction facilities. The scrapyard was in the news in 2002 when a 'mountain' of 3,000 refrigerators accumulated, awaiting environmentally sound disposal. Several of Lower Morden's employers specialize in services and supplies for the building and engineering sectors. The Lower

Morden ward takes in the affluent community of MORDEN PARK and thus exhibits high levels of employment and home and car ownership.

✉ Morden SM4; New Malden KT3

👥 8,561

📖 Peter Hopkins, *Lower Morden and West Barnes*, St Martin's Church, Morden, 1995

Lower Norwood   *see* WEST NORWOOD

Lower Place   •   *Brent*
A canalside corner of PARK ROYAL, bordering HARLESDEN, and now undergoing regeneration. The name is little-used except by a business centre on Steele Road, but the manor once embraced much of modern Park Royal, NORTH ACTON and WEST TWYFORD. A 15th-century house owned by Sir John Elrington is identified as having later become Lower Place Farm, which stood beside Barrett's Green. It may have been here that Sir John built a chapel in which Sir Thomas More's two daughters were married in 1525. The Paddington Canal, now part of the Grand Union Canal, and the London and Birmingham Railway sliced through the farm's land in 1801 and 1837 respectively. Acton council bought 13 acres of the farmland for the creation of North Acton Cemetery in 1893 and the Royal Agricultural Society acquired part of Goddard's, a neighbouring dairy farm at Lower Place, in 1901. The Central Middlesex Hospital opened in 1903 as a workhouse infirmary, but has since been much extended. McVitie's began making biscuits at Waxlow Road in 1906 and the factory is now the third largest biscuit producer in the world. The construction of the North Circular Road (A406) brought an end to farming at Lower Place as the remaining fields filled with factories, although some allotments remain from Lower Place's agricultural days. South of the canal the industry is mainly small-scale and the premises unremarkable, except for the glass-bricked Luxcrete head office on Disraeli Road. Steele Road provides access to the Grand Union Canal Walk. The Central Middlesex Hospital is currently undergoing a major programme of redevelopment to create an entirely new acute care hospital, an office building and more than 100 bed spaces for key workers.

The abandoned Acton Lane power station served as the atmosphere processing station in the film *Aliens* (1986) and as the interior of the Axis Chemicals plant in *Batman* (1989).

✉ NW10

Lower Sydenham • *Lewisham/Bromley*

The eastern end of SYDENHAM, flanking Sydenham Road (A212). The original village of Sydenham took shape here in the 17th century, but did not develop significantly until after the enclosure of Sydenham Common in 1810. Just off SOUTHEND Lane, Lower Sydenham station opened on the Mid-Kent Railway in 1857. New streets of an increasingly working-class character were laid out from the late 1860s, when St Michael and All Angels' Church was built. Sydenham recreation ground (now Mayow Park) was opened in 1878, before a crowd of 10,000. Many Germans made their home in Sydenham, some because of the entrepreneurial opportunities offered by Crystal Palace and some because of the musical associations of its pleasure gardens, and a German Evangelical church was founded in temporary accommodation in 1875 and replaced by a permanent structure in the early 1880s. At the same time, the Roman Catholic church of Our Lady and St Philip Neri was built at the corner of Watlington Grove and Sydenham Road. Over the last two decades of the 19th century Lower Sydenham was filled with housing, some on land that had belonged to St Olave's Church in Southwark. The poorest corner of the district was BELL GREEN, with its gasworks and jerry-built terraced houses. Home Park and Sydenham Library both opened in the early years of the 20th century and the station was rebuilt at its present site in the far south-east of the district in 1906. From the early 1930s industrial estates grew rapidly on Kangley Bridge Road and Worsley Bridge Road. By the outbreak of World War II there were 16 factories here and the best-known of these was Baird TV, founded by the British inventor of television John Logie Baird. After 1940 the company became Cinema-Television Ltd, which later switched its production to electronic instruments, including metal detectors. The Anglican, German and Roman Catholic churches were all destroyed by wartime bombing and rebuilt in the late 1950s. The German church was renamed in honour of Dietrich Bonhoeffer, its pastor in the 1930s, who was executed by the Nazis just before the end of World War II. St Michael's Church shares a site with the primary school of the same name. The largest ethnic minority groups at the school are of black Caribbean and black African descent.

The musicologist Sir George Grove, famed for the compendious *Dictionary of Music and Musicians* that bears his name, lived at 208 Sydenham Road.

✉ SE26

🚇 South Eastern Trains (zone 4)

Loxford • *Redbridge*

A densely built-up, multi-ethnic locality in south ILFORD. The name Loxford is rarely used by locals, who simply refer to the area as 'the BARKING end of Ilford Lane'. The medieval manor of Loxford was in the possession of Barking Abbey and in 1319 the Abbess of Barking was licensed to fell oaks in HAINAULT Forest to rebuild her house here after a fire. The present Loxford Hall dates from about 1830 and was enlarged around 1860. The terraced street plan of the Loxford Hall estate was laid out at the end of the 19th century as one of a cluster of developments that filled southern Ilford with relatively small and cheap houses. The first Loxford schools were opened in 1904. The council's Loxford Lane estate has a few variations of architectural detail on the basic low-rise theme but these are rendered ineffective by the poor materials and state of repair. Behind the estate is the sorry-looking Loxford Water, a tributary of the River Roding that forms the northern boundary to Barking Park. Loxford's main ethnic groups are white, Pakistani and Indian, and the South Asian community is served by a variety of specialist shops on Ilford Lane. Four-fifths of pupils at Woodlands Junior School speak a language other than English at home, and a quarter are from refugee families. Loxford School of Science and Technology is a community comprehensive school with specialist status as a third-phase technology college. The educational standards agency Ofsted rates the school highly despite the challenges posed by many pupils' disadvantaged backgrounds and rudimentary knowledge of English. Loxford Hall now serves as a child and family consultation centre for the North East London Mental Health Trust.

✉ Ilford IG1

👥 13,585

Luxted • *Bromley*

A hamlet in the very rural southern part of the borough, one mile south of DOWNE. The name dates back over 1,000 years, and was at one time recorded as Lukkestyle. To the east and north-east are the woods and chalk grassland of Twenty Acre Shaw, Hang Grove and Downe Bank, which have partial public access. These are sites of special scientific interest, rich in wildflowers, including eleven species of orchid. There is evidence that nearby farmland was ploughed from pre-Saxon times. Luxted Farm has an 18th-century house built using the knapped flint technique characteristic of the Kent countryside. The 20th century brought a variety of new construction to Luxted, beginning with the terraced Dunoon Cottages in 1905 and going downhill from there.

✉ Orpington BR6

Lyonsdown • *Barnet*

The south-western part of NEW BARNET, although for a while during the late 19th century the two names were virtually synonymous. It was first identified in an agreement dated 1553 referring to fields and grounds called 'the Lyon downs', and probably derives from a former resident of that name. Lyonsdown House was acquired in 1810 by Andrew Reid, of the brewing company that became Watney Combe Reid, who was later a high sheriff of Hertfordshire. Reid died here in 1841 and the house was demolished in 1862. Spurred by the proximity of New Barnet station, the British Land Co. then laid out the Lyonsdown es-tate. This was suburban development of the highest class: grand houses with games room and wine cellars, sweeping drives and separate side entrances for the servants. No shops were allowed on the estate. The imposing Church of the Holy Trinity was built in 1868, near the site of Lyonsdown House. Since those heady times many of the larger properties have been replaced or subdivided, and the spacious grounds of those that remain have been filled with smaller houses or tasteful blocks of flats. Some office blocks have gone up in Lyonsdown Road, also the location of the Society of African Missionaries and Lyonsdown Hall, which hosts meetings of clubs and societies.

The first public demonstration of motion picture projection in Britain was given by local photographer Birt Acres to the Lyonsdown Amateur Photographic Association on 10 January 1896. Four days later Acres repeated the show for the Royal Photographic Society and commercial performances began in PICCADILLY in March that year.

✉ Barnet EN5

Maida Hill • *Westminster*

A shifting and lesser-known locality situated somewhere to the south of MAIDA VALE. The fields here attracted little attention until the opening of the Paddington branch of the Grand Junction (now Union) Canal in 1801. Within a few years the first villas were built on Hill House fields, the highest part of PADDINGTON at 120 feet, together with a public house named the Hero of Maida. The hero was Major-General Sir John Stuart, who in 1806 led British troops to victory over a larger French force on the plain of Maida in southern Italy. By 1810 the locality was being marked as 'Maida' on maps. Shortly after this, construction work began on the Regent's Canal, which branched off from the Grand Junction Canal at what is now LITTLE VENICE. The Maida Hill tunnel, begun in 1812, was the first canal tunnel to be built in London and is the second longest, after Islington's. Its route had to be altered to avoid the Portman estate, which had refused passage through its property. The part of EDGWARE ROAD immediately north of the Regent's Canal was originally called Maida Hill, and later Maida Hill East, while modern Maida Avenue was formerly Maida Hill West. The joke about how God created Yorkshire – 'Maida Hill then Maida Vale' – indicates the order in which the district developed, as the first houses went up here and then spread northwards. These early properties were built in an Italianate style that was distinctively different from the later look of Maida Vale. In 1868 the whole stretch of the former Edgware Road north of the canal was united as Maida Vale and Maida Hill's name faded into obscurity for a while. It was later revived to identify the area to the south-west of Shirland Road, well to the west of its point of origin, which was called St Peter's Park when it was built up from the mid 1860s. This was a squatting hotspot in the 1970s and is now popular with young singles.

The author Wilkie Collins entered Maida Hill Academy in 1835. In Graham Greene's novel *Loser Takes All*, Bertram plans to get married at the fictional church of St Luke's, Maida Hill, but trouble ensues when the wedding is switched to Monte Carlo. Pre-punk rockers the 101ers, who mutated into The Clash, took their name from the house number of their squat in Walterton Road, now replaced by a low-rise block of flats. The band played a weekly residency at the nearby Chippenham public house.

✉ W9

Maida Vale • *Westminster*

Mansion block territory, located west of ST JOHN'S WOOD. The area belonged to the diocese of London in 1647, when it was covered by woodland and pasture. There were no structures apart from farm buildings until the end of the 18th century. Houses were built after 1807, to specifications laid down by the Church, which included the use of stock bricks and slate roofs. A short stretch of EDGWARE ROAD was called Maida Vale in 1828 although the name was not applied to the neighbouring locality until much later in the century. The main thoroughfare was lined with villas by the 1840s but several decades elapsed before the hinterland filled with houses, many built with red or multi-coloured bricks in a style advocated by John Ruskin. Maida Vale Hospital for nervous diseases opened in 1866 and staff here were later the first to identify and successfully operate on a brain tumour. In the 1880s Maida Vale gained a large Jewish community, perhaps constituting as much as a fifth of the area's residents. From around this time early villas began to be demolished and replaced by flats. The trend reached its peak in the early years of the 20th century when massive mansion blocks went up on the main road, with smaller blocks in the streets behind. Clarendon Court even boasted its own restaurant and booking office for theatres. Maida Vale station opened in 1915, one of the few built above ground on this section of the Bakerloo Line. Maida Vale recording studios were built on the site of a skating rink to house the BBC Symphony

Orchestra. The name 'Maida Vale' is now almost synonymous with 'live' studio music, courtesy of Radio 1's sessions, especially with the late John Peel. The Greater London Council built its Maida Vale estate in the early 1970s and the Church Commissioners sold the freeholds on its properties in the following decade. The Islamic Centre of England opened in 1998 at 140 Maida Vale. Randolph Avenue has the Iyengar Yoga Institute, the first purpose-built yoga centre in Europe. Maida Vale maintains a reputation as an address for wealthy dowagers, but in fact it has fewer pensioners living alone than most parts of the borough and most residents have never been married.

Maida Vale was the birthplace in 1855 of William Friese-Greene, the inventor of ciné film. The district was made famous by Alfred Hitchcock's *Dial M for Murder* in 1954, when a call to the Maida Vale telephone number MAI 3499 was the signal for a killing at the fictional 61A Charrington Gardens. The film was based on a 1952 West End play.

✉ W9

♦ 9,647

🚇 Bakerloo Line (zone 2)

📖 Kevin O'Sullivan, *Dial M for Maida Vale*, Westminster City Archives, 2000

Maitland Park • Camden

Victorian and post-war estates located on the western side of KENTISH TOWN, named after Ebenezer Maitland who was chairman of an orphanage that moved to HAVERSTOCK HILL in 1848. The orphanage was surrounded by open fields to its east at this time, when the Southampton family published a plan for building homes for the wealthier classes. What they actually produced was a more densely built-up estate for the less well-off. Some of the homes were built on plots bought by working people with the help of loans from co-operative building societies such as the Friends of Labour, which opened a branch in Maitland Park in 1866. Maitland Cricket Club was established in 1899 and played on PARLIA-MENT HILL and HAMPSTEAD HEATH until 1915. In the 1960s many of the original homes were demolished in a wave of council developments, of which the largest was the Maitland Park estate. Kentish Town City Farm was founded in 1972, when it was the first of its kind. It has subsequently served as a model in the development of the city farm movement as a whole. The farm is located on a four-and-a-half acre

site off Grafton Road, on the edge of GOSPEL OAK, where it uses some original buildings from the time the railway was built. Queen's Crescent is one of London's hidden cockney communities, with a street market held on Thursday and Saturday and plentiful independent shops. Nevertheless, it is an indication of the area's absence of amenities that the mayor of Camden cut a celebratory cake when she officially opened the street's first free cash machine in 2005.

The political philosopher Karl Marx lived at addresses in Grafton Terrace and Maitland Park Road from 1856 until his death in 1883. The grocers John James and Mary Ann Sainsbury opened their second shop at 159 Queen's Crescent in 1873 and lived upstairs here until 1886.

✉ NW3; NW5

🚇 Silverlink Metro (Kentish Town West, zone 2)

@ www.aapi.co.uk/cityfarm

Malden Green • Kingston/Sutton

A little-used name for the eastern end of OLD MALDEN, nowadays increasingly considered to be part of WORCESTER PARK. The green that gives the locality its name lies north-west of Worcester Park station and was also known as Lower Green. Like many village greens, this was common land that was progressively whittled away until a central fragment was saved in perpetuity. By the 19th century, the local authority was vigilantly guarding the green's integrity. William Baker, a CHEAM tea dealer, was found guilty of enclosing a quarter-acre in 1844 and told to remove his fence or pay a £20 fine. But in 1859 Worcester Park station was built on the common land and the railway line split the green in two. In 1908, Parliament passed an act authorizing the Metropolitan Commons (Malden Green) Scheme, which gave permanent protection to the five-acre common. Nevertheless, encroachment by various householders continued to cause problems and a local butcher had a hut forcibly removed from the green in 1925. The part of the green east of the railway line is now a sports ground, which was brought entirely under the authority of Sutton council in 1995. Malden Green Farm is a Grade II-listed farmhouse that juts into the green. The farm's remaining land recently disappeared beneath Barratt's Hollybrook development of 50 executive-style houses.

✉ Worcester Park KT4

Malden Manor • *Kingston*

An alternative name for part of OLD MALDEN. The present manor house was built in the 1620s and enlarged in the 18th century. The house stands near the Church of St John the Baptist at the western end of Church Road and is now a venue for meetings and functions, including weddings. It was the Southern Railway's naming of the station that prompted locals to start referring to its immediate vicinity as Malden Manor. The railway company was fond of mock-Tudor names at that time and had intended to call other stations on the line CHESSINGTON Court and Chessington Grange before settling for the more prosaic North and South labels. Built in 1938, Malden Manor station is a pleasing art deco structure that made innovative use of re-inforced concrete, but its appeal is now marred by the electricity pylon towering right outside. Malden Manor has very little council housing and a high number of retired people living in spacious homes, making it one of the most socially advantaged localities in south-west London. However, there is some deprivation across the tracks on the Sheephouse Way housing estate, an area that has suffered problems with graffiti and vandalism. The junction of Sheephouse Way and Manor Drive North has a shopping parade and the Manor public house. Malden Manor Primary School uses signage in Korean and Arabic to aid pupils who are at the early stages of acquiring English.

✉ Worcester Park KT4; New Malden KT3

🚆 South West Trains (zone 4)

@ home.cogeco.ca/~ford-ret/malden/malden.htm (station history site)

Malden Rushett • *Kingston*

A hamlet situated at crossroads south of CHESSINGTON World of Adventures, in the southernmost part of the 'tongue' of the borough that protrudes into the Surrey woodland. Eleventh-century Malden rambled across two manors, one of which has since become Malden Rushett, a reference to the rushes that grew here. The manor was heavily wooded at the time of Domesday Book and remained so for several hundred years. Sixty Acre Wood is a surviving part of the ancient woodland. Cultivation in the 17th century made use of a technique known as devonshiring, or denshiring – paring off old turf, burning it and spreading the ashes on the land. Malden Rushett, also known as Lower

Chessington or 'the Rushett', remained part of Malden parish until 1884 when it was transferred to Chessington. Before the transfer, residents of the hamlet's cottages had to go to (Old) Malden to be married, although they could be buried in Chessington. Some years later a temporary corrugated-iron mission house, of the sort known as an 'iron church', was erected with room for 60 cottagers, and 'improving' lectures were given. In the 1930s, the Southern Railway Co. planned to extend the Chessington branch line to Leatherhead, with ribbon development along the route and a sizeable town with its own station, probably at Malden Rushett. The plan was stymied by the outbreak of World War II and then by post-war designation of the area as green belt. A plan to locate an airport at Byhurst Farm also came to nothing, but Rushett Farm has a small landing strip. Silverglade business park has some technology company units. Telegraph Hill, at 240 feet, in the extreme south of the borough, is its highest point. Like other hills of the same name, it was a beacon point for the Royal Navy's semaphore system, relaying messages from London to Portsmouth.

✉ Chessington KT9

The Mall • *Westminster*

The ceremonial route leading from TRAFALGAR SQUARE's Admiralty Arch to Buckingham Palace, bordered by ST JAMES'S Park along most of its southern side. Charles II laid out the Mall in 1662 as a successor to the glorified croquet alley of PALL MALL. The boulevard grew in significance when St James's Palace became the monarch's principal home following the destruction by fire of the Palace of WHITEHALL in 1698. As the sport of pallemaille declined in popularity the Mall became a place of public promenade, later giving its name to the American cultural phenomenon the shopping mall, which was originally a store-lined street closed to vehicular traffic. With the accession of Victoria to the throne in 1837, Buckingham Palace became the new royal residence and the Mall's straight-line approach to the palace brought it even greater status. From the late 19th century the Mall served as the carriage drive for all royal processions and for the arrival of foreign dignitaries at Buckingham Palace. The construction of Admiralty Arch and the Victoria Memorial at opposite ends of the Mall in 1910 and 1911 brought greater formality to the ceremonial route. The Mall is usually lined with Union flags but during state visits these are inter-mixed with the appropriate national flags. The road is closed to vehicular traffic on Sundays, public holidays and state occasions. The Institute of Contemporary Arts and the Mall Galleries occupy the rear (Mall-facing) basements of the east wing of Carlton House Terrace.

Thomas Gainsborough painted *The Mall in St James's Park* around 1783, a scene described by Horace Walpole as 'all aflutter like a lady's fan'. New York's Frick Collection acquired the work in 1916.

✉ SW1

@ www.mallgalleries.org.uk; www.ica.org.uk

Manor House • *Hackney/Haringey*

A London Underground station, and by extension its immediate vicinity, located at the eastern corner of FINSBURY PARK. Before the creation of Seven Sisters Road, and thus of the crossroads, this was the site of a tollgate on GREEN LANES. The Manor Tavern (later Manor House) was built here in 1832. The public house had a licensed concert room from 1852 and boasted of a brief visit by Queen Victoria. For several years it was the meeting place for the Stoke Newington vestry. The arrival of the Piccadilly Line in 1932 prompted the widening of the crossroads and the old pub was demolished and rebuilt in its present form. The station's subsurface layout was by Charles Holden, who was responsible for much of the architecture on the extended Piccadilly Line. It is the only one of Holden's station that does not include structures at street level, though the large booking hall broke new ground in assisting passenger flow; Holden described it as 'an experiment in streamlined planning'. The station gave Hackney its first Tube connection, albeit at a remote corner, and this was a significant factor in the London County Council's decision to compulsorily purchase a great swathe of land here for the construction of the WOODBERRY DOWN estate. The outbreak of war halted development, which was not finally completed until 1962. The Manor House pub, which had been undergoing a steady decline, closed in the 1990s and a Costcutter supermarket now occupies the ground floor.

The Rolling Stones played weekly gigs at the Manor House in February and March 1963, when the pub hosted the Harringay Jazz Club. Shortly before its closure Bill Wyman commented that the Manor House was 'about the only old Stones venue that still exists' from the band's early days. The Who also performed there, in 1965.

✉ N4

🚇 Piccadilly Line (zones 2 and 3)

Manor Park • *Newham*

A network of Victorian terraces situated between FOREST GATE and ILFORD. Most of the area was part of the manor of LITTLE ILFORD until it gained a separate identity following the opening of its station. The new suburb took its name from the manor house built around 1810 for the lord of the manor of WEST HAM on his Hamfrith estate. The house still stands in Gladding Road but has been much altered and converted into flats. Manor Park station opened in 1872 and the Manor Park Cemetery Co. bought the eastern part of Hamfrith Farm in the same year. Streets of terraced housing were laid out on the neighbouring fields from the 1880s. In WOODGRANGE PARK, Cameron Corbett built to a higher standard than elsewhere in Manor Park, but kept costs down through efficiencies of scale. Little Ilford's Manor Farm was developed more cheaply as the Manor House estate after 1895. The street plan was determined by the railway lines that cut across the district and almost all the housing was low-priced and short on space but with adequate facilities. Most of the original properties survive intact. Romford Road (A118) is a busy thoroughfare, lined with a wide variety of shops, most of which are independent and cater to a very local catchment area. Towards the Ilford end, the road is noted for its many used-car dealers. Almost half the population of Manor Park is of Asian descent, with origins in most parts of the Indian subcontinent. Islam is the main religion.

The entertainer Stanley Holloway was born in Manor Park in 1890. The actress Greer Garson was born at 88 First Avenue in 1904.

✉ E12

👥 12,103

🚇 'one' Railway (zones 3 and 4)

Mansion House • *City*

The official residence of the Lord Mayor of London (who holds the office for only a year), situated at the western end of Lombard Street, opposite the BANK of England. The Church of St Mary Woolchurch Haw stood here until the Great Fire in 1666. The idea of commissioning a grand house for the mayor was first discussed after the fire but nothing came of it and the stocks market was built here instead.

Only when other large cities started to build such mansions did London decide it was not to be outdone. The site was chosen in 1736 and seven architects submitted proposals. The City's clerk of works, George Dance the Elder, won the competition with a Palladian design featuring a large Corinthian portico. Completed in 1752, the structure made innovative use of hidden iron chains running through the brick interior walls. Of the many receptions rooms, the grandest was the cavernous and sumptuous Egyptian Hall. Mansion House originally had an internal courtyard at first-floor level, but this was covered over when Dance the Younger made several improvements to the house's capacity and safety in 1795. Mansion House station opened in 1871, originally as the eastern terminus of the Metropolitan District Railway, which was extended to WHITECHAPEL in 1884. The station is located at the junction of Cannon Street and Queen Victoria Street but was given the name of the nearest landmark building. Mansion House was refurbished in the early 1990s at a cost of £11 million and the underground station was rebuilt at the same time. Mansion House is open by appointment only for visits by organized groups.

✉ EC4

🚇 Circle Line; District Line (zone 1)

📖 Sally Jeffery, *The Mansion House*, Phillimore, 1994

Mapesbury • *Brent*

A Victorian estate and conservation area located on the BRONDESBURY/CRICKLEWOOD border. Although it is not identified in street atlases, local residents proudly declare Mapesbury as their address. This area was part of the broad expanse of territory held by ST PAUL'S Cathedral from the end of the first millennium. Each of the cathedral's canons took responsibility for an individual manor, and Mapesbury derives its name from Walter Map, prebendary of the manor in the last quarter of the 12th century. The Ecclesiastical Commissioners succeeded St Paul's as the freeholder in 1840. The Mapesbury estate was mostly developed between 1895 and 1905 by at least twelve builders on the grounds of the 18th-century Mapes House. Other parts date from the late 1870s and the 1920s. The Ecclesiastical Commissioners sold the freeholds in the 1950s, mostly to private tenants, although the council bought a parcel of land at Shoot-up Hill. Many of the properties are of grand proportions, with four or five bedrooms. A number have been divided into flats, but the more recent trend is for conversion back into single dwellings. Over a third of the homes in Mapesbury are privately rented. Most residents are single and a high proportion are in their twenties. The largest separately identified ethnic minority is white Irish. The British Association of Psychotherapists and the Minster Centre, which trains psychotherapists and counsellors, are both based in Mapesbury Road. The BAP's headquarters was the home of the renowned clinician Oliver Sacks. In his memoir *Uncle Tungsten: Memories of a Chemical Boyhood*, Sacks recalled the night when a bomb fell in the garden – but later discovered that he had actually been away at boarding school at the time, and that his 'memory' was based on a dramatic letter written by his father.

In 2001, Keith Vaz MP, then Minister for Europe, was at the centre of a political scandal over payments made by the Hinduja brothers to Mapesbury Communications, a PR company registered in his wife's name and originally based at Vaz's home in Teignmouth Road. Paul Celan's short poem *Mapesbury Road*, written in German in 1971, is included in the collection *Poems: A Bilingual Edition*, with a translation by Michael Hamburger.

✉ NW2

🚶 13,242

Marble Arch • *Westminster*

A road junction and triple-arched monument at the north-eastern corner of HYDE PARK. This was the site of the medieval village of Tyburn, which became notorious as London's principal setting for public executions. Hangings took place here from the late 13th century and in 1571 a three-legged gallows was erected at the present corner of EDGWARE ROAD and BAYSWATER Road. Nicknamed the 'Tyburn tree', this new style of gallows had the advantage of permitting multiple hangings. This was replaced by a movable gallows in 1759, which was last used in 1783. John Nash designed the Marble Arch in 1828 as the main gateway to Buckingham Palace. Fashioned from white Carrara marble, the monument was inspired by the Arch of Constantine in Rome. When the palace was extended in 1851 the Marble Arch was moved to its present site, where it formed an entrance to Hyde Park. Like its counterpart at HYDE PARK CORNER, the arch has been left stranded on a traffic island as a result of traffic circulation improvements in the early 1960s. Proposals have recently been made to relocate the arch to Speakers' Corner, the area of Hyde Park where orators may declaim freely but will frequently be heckled by disrespectful audiences. The Odeon Marble Arch was built in 1967 in place of the former Regal cinema, as part of a shopping and office development on the corner of Edgware Road. The cinema had the largest screen in Europe but was broken up into a multiplex in 1996.

Noel Gay and Ralph Butler's 1932 composition *Round the Marble Arch* was a hit for Henry Hall and his orchestra.

> ✉ W1; W2

> 🚇 Central Line (zone 1)

> 📖 David Brandon and Alan Brooke, *Tyburn: London's Fatal Tree*, Sutton, 2004

Marble Hill • *Richmond*

'The 18th-century equivalent of Beverley Hills', according to Richmond council, bordering the Thames in east TWICKENHAM. George II had Marble Hill House built for his mistress Henrietta Howard in the 1720s and the elegantly simple Palladian villa became a playground for the celebrities of the day. The London County Council bought Marble Hill in 1902 and opened its parkland grounds to the public in the following year. The LCC's successor, the Greater London Council, restored the house beautifully in the mid 1960s. Open-air concerts are held in the grounds every summer and Marble Hill House is open to the public at weekends. Just along the riverside, Orleans House Gallery is an octagonal garden room and its service wings, which are the surviving parts of a house once occupied by Louis Philippe, Duc d'Orléans.

The artist J M W Turner lived at nearby Sandycombe Lodge, a house that he designed himself in 1812. Marble Hill House featured in the 1998 film *Shakespeare in Love*.

> ✉ Twickenham TW1

> 📖 Julius Bryant, *Marble Hill*, English Heritage, 2005

Marks Gate • *Barking & Dagenham*

A northern outpost of the borough, located a mile north of CHADWELL HEATH, and still surrounded by the fields of wheat, oats and barley that were once its *raison d'être*. Around 600BC a fortified hilltop village was established here, of which almost nothing remains but the hill itself. The medieval manor of Marks was one of BARKING'S oldest free tenements (an estate held for life or longer), with

its own manor court from the 14th century and special rights in HAINAULT Forest. Marks Hall, the 20-bedroom moated manor house, was built in the mid 15th century and demolished in 1808. The estate, which was much reduced over the centuries, was sold to the Crown in 1855. It is now part of Warren Farm, where a section of the moat survives, as does a 17th-century brick barn, which is still in use. Nearby were two other hamlets, now lost. Roselane Gate had its own entrance to the forest, at the northern end of Rose Lane near the Harrow public house. Padnall Corner was virtually wiped out when the Eastern Avenue was constructed. It was located at the bend in Padnall Road, and Padnall Hall stood to its west. Dagenham council built an estate at Marks Gate in the late 1950s. Much of Marks Gate's housing remains in municipal ownership and the area suffers from high levels of unemployment. City Limits is a popular local leisure facility, offering tenpin bowling, a fitness centre, bars and a restaurant.

In 1867, a 24-year-old Ilford labourer named James Bacon stabbed his wife to death in Marks Gate. What made this case unusual was that a chorus of public sympathy for the perpetrator led to his death sentence being commuted to ten years' imprisonment.

> ✉ Romford RM5 and RM6

> 📖 A E Baker, *A Miscellany of Marks Gate*, Barking and Dagenham Libraries, 1990

Marling Park • *Richmond*

The south-western corner of HAMPTON, bordered by playing fields that back onto the reservoirs of HANWORTH and Kempton Park. This was formerly Tangley Park, which was the site of a hotel built in 1869 that later became the Female Orphan Home when the institution moved here from WALTHAMSTOW. Major W B Marling purchased the estate and named it after himself in 1890. Development took place exceedingly slowly and most of the present properties date from the 1930s and 1950s, with semi-detached houses fronting tree-lined, grass-verged avenues. The varying finishes subsequently applied to the external walls aggravate the architectural disharmony. The name Marling Park is largely unrecognized by local residents, who think of this area as part of Hampton. Twickenham Rugby Football Club plays at the Parkfields ground on South Road.

> ✉ Hampton TW12

Marshalls Park • *Havering*

A popular corner of north ROMFORD, bounded by Main Road, North Street and the Eastern Avenue. Marshalls was a tenement on the east side of North Street, taking its name from a prominent family who lived in the vicinity from the 12th century. It was in the hands of the Thorowgood family throughout the 17th century, thereafter seeing a succession of owners, including the wonderfully named Onesiphorous Leigh of TOOTING. Marshalls was the only part of central Romford still undeveloped by the time of World War I. The estate was acquired and built up in 1924 by William Hunnable, vice-chairman of Romford urban district council and member for the Central ward. Hunnable died in 1928, at the age of 69. What is now Marshalls Park School was founded in the 1920s as the intermediate school for Romford. Marshalls House survived until 1959, when it was demolished to make way for an extension to the school. Following a recent period when it operated from two sites on opposite sides of the locality, the school was consolidated on the Pettits Lane site in 1999. The mock-Tudor semi-detached houses of Marshalls Park attract a relatively affluent population and the name is beloved of estate agents although it does not feature on most maps.

Marshalls Park school attracted media attention in 2003 by advertising for staff who 'must like chocolate'. The advertisement was said to have been highly successful.

✉ Romford RM1

Marsh Side • *Enfield*

A rarely used name for the eastern edge of LOWER EDMONTON, focused around the northern end of Montagu Road. The catchier 'PICKETT'S LOCK' (which lies just to the northeast) has become a more popular identity for this locality. Marsh Side was earlier known as Jeremy's Green or, more curiously, John a Marsh Green. The Marshes were a family of Norman origin who took a new surname from Edmonton Marsh, where they lived from the 13th century. John Marsh died around 1312 and divided his lands among four sons and two daughters in his will. It is therefore possible that Marsh Side gained its name because this was the Marsh family's side of EDMONTON, rather than on account of the undeniably boggy terrain. There were cottages and an inn here around 1600, surrounded by farmland. The inn was called the Cart Overthrown by 1752. In 1801 Marsh Side had 31 dwellings, including neighbouring farmhouses. Marsh Side at last showed signs of growth from the mid 19th century as Edmonton began to expand in all directions. Baptists established a chapel here around 1890 but the congregation must have proved unsatisfactory since it closed after barely five years. Industry and a sewage works filled most of the former farmland east of Montagu Road (which was earlier called Jeremy's Green Lane) during the first half of the 20th century, while housing was built to the west. The area was left heavily cratered by World War II bombing and never recovered its earlier vitality. Enfield council built the 22-storey Walbrook House at the eastern end of Bounces Road in the early 1970s. The construction alongside the railway line of Meridian Way in the early 1990s is helping to regenerate industrial and commercial life in the area. In 2002 Laing Homes laid out an estate to the east of Montagu Road, with properties ranging from one-bedroom flats to five-bedroom houses.

✉ N9

Maryland • *Newham*

A disadvantaged neighbourhood that is known only to most commuters as the last station before STRATFORD on the line into London, or for the gaudily panelled Henniker Point tower block. In 1638 the ILFORD-based merchant Richard Lee migrated to America, where he acquired an estate at Maryland Point on the Potomac River. After 20 years he returned to Ilford and bought land at Stratford, where he built a house that he called Maryland Point. The house was assessed for nine hearths in 1662, indicating that it was a building of substantial proportions. It was sold in 1678 and its subsequent fate is not known. Maryland Point first appeared as a place name on a map of 1696 and Daniel Defoe mentioned the existence of a 'new' settlement here in 1722. With the growth of Stratford in the mid 19th century the vicinity was built up as STRATFORD NEW TOWN and Maryland Point became a prosperous shopping thoroughfare. Maryland station opened in 1874. Following steady decline over the course of the following century the area now presents a low-rent aspect. The 23-storey Henniker Point was erected in 1969. Private apartment blocks have been built near the station in the past few years. The area has significant levels of social need and a high proportion of immigrants, both black and white. At Maryland Primary School around three-quarters of the pupils speak English as an additional language. Similar, but less marked, situations exist at St Francis' RC and Colegrave primary schools. Problems with anti-social behaviour recently led the council to designate a dispersal zone in the Maryland area.

On the death of Maryland's Richard Lee in 1664, his family returned to America, apparently in fulfilment of the conditions of his will. Lee's grandson Thomas established a plantation in Virginia in the late 1730s, which he named Stratford Hall, and this was the birthplace in 1807 of Thomas's grandson Robert E Lee, the most successful general of the Confederate forces during the American Civil War.

> ✉ E15

> 🚆 'one' Railway (zone 3)

Marylebone (or **St Marylebone**) • *Westminster* (various pronunciations, including 'marylǝbǝn' and 'marlybǝn')

A 'high status, non-family area', as demographers call it, situated south and west of REGENT'S PARK. Like neighbouring PADDINGTON, the borough of Marylebone once covered a much larger area than is generally associated with the name today, including almost the whole of the north side of OXFORD STREET, REGENT'S PARK (formerly Marylebone Park) and ST JOHN'S WOOD. The village that grew up by the path to PRIMROSE HILL was originally called Tyburn but after the construction of its church in 1400 it became known as St-Mary-a-le-bourne. An earlier church that had stood alone near present-day Oxford Street was abandoned after frequent vandalism and looting. St Mary's stood on the present Marylebone High Street, as did an older manor house, later known as Marylebone Place. LISSON GREEN evolved as the parish's principal outlying hamlet. Early in the 18th century high-class streets and squares began to spread north of Oxford Street. The grounds of the manor house became pleasure gardens in 1737, when the village remained sufficiently remote for its church to be 'much favoured for hasty or secret weddings.' In the 1750s an east–west highway was driven across the parish, north of the village; originally called the New Road, its stretch here is now the Marylebone Road. It took almost another century for the whole of Marylebone (except Regent's Park) to succumb to building. The pleasure gardens closed in 1778 and the manor house was demolished in 1791. Construction work began on the new parish church of St Mary

on Marylebone Road in 1814, while Thomas LORD'S Marylebone Cricket Club ground relocated from Dorset Square to St John's Wood Road. In 1861 Marylebone's population peaked at 161,680. The Great Central Railway Co. opened Marylebone station in 1897, causing disruption to neighbouring LISSON GROVE. This was the last of the London railway termini and the least commercially successful, but its underuse has precluded the need for subsequent expansion, leaving us with perhaps the capital's prettiest and most unspoilt main-line station building. Piecemeal redevelopment took place across Marylebone throughout the 20th century, with Marylebone Road seeing the most radical alteration, including mansion flats, curtain-walled office blocks, hotels and a new campus for what is now the University of Westminster. In addition to its style and design specialists, Marylebone High Street has central London's finest array of independent local shops, including bookshops, an ironmonger, and several specialist food stores. Its diversity and distinctiveness have made the street very popular with upmarket locals but the introduction of the congestion charge has reduced car-borne visits. The Marylebone High Street ward has fewer children than almost any other part of London. Most homes here are privately rented, one-person households.

In 1975 an IRA gang took a husband and wife hostage in Balcombe Street following a botched attack at a MAYFAIR restaurant and a police chase. The gang surrendered after a six-day siege.

> ✉ W1; NW1

> 🚆 Chiltern Railways terminus; Bakerloo Line (zone 1)

> 👥 8,860 (Marylebone High Street ward)

> 📖 Jack Whitehead, *The Growth of St Marylebone and Paddington*, Jack Whitehead, 2001; Mike Wood, *Discovering St Marylebone: Four Self-Guided Walks*, St Marylebone Society, 2001; Gordon Mackenzie, *Marylebone: Great City North of Oxford Street*, Macmillan, 1972

> @ www.marylebone.org (Marylebone Association site)

Maswell Park • *Hounslow*

A compact residential locality in south-east HOUNSLOW. The Maswell name was first recorded in the late 15th century and indicates the presence of a spring or stream belonging to a man called Mæssa. By the 19th century the name had become corrupted to 'Mazells'. 'Three roods, five perches' of Mazells were ISLEWORTH charity land, marked off from the surrounding fields by a boundary stone at each corner. The land was let to a BRENTFORD colonel, who sub-let it to a succession of farmers. The invention of the Maswell Park name dates from a late Victorian attempt to promote development here, but only a few short terraces of houses dotted the park by the outbreak of World War I. Most of Maswell Park was built up in the 1930s and a final gap was plugged in the late 1950s with the addition of Wolsey Close. Behind Maswell Park Health Centre a chunk of the original field survives as allotments. The Maswell Park hall on the corner of Inwood Road and Heath Road was registered as a non-denominational church in 1928. Now rechristened the Maswell Park Evangelical Church, it promotes social events such as jazz and soul gigs.

✉ Hounslow TW3

Mawney • *Havering*

A half-forgotten mini-suburb situated between ROMFORD and COLLIER ROW, and traversed by the River Rom. During the 14th century the manor of Romford came into the possession of the celebrated soldier Sir Walter de Mauny. Thereafter, the manor was called Mawneys, a form still used by local people and by the council. In the 19th century Mawney was known for its Gypsies, who worked in the fields and sold brushes and doormats to the cottages of the surrounding villages. The manor's 265 acres were sold for building in 1883 and Mawney's street pattern, like a letter 'A', was laid out in the 1890s in a development that marked the beginning of the outward expansion of Romford. Houses were built in small groups over a period of decades, gradually eroding the nurseries and smallholdings that had characterized the locality. Mawney Road School (located at the Romford end of Mawney Road, and now Mawney School) opened in 1896 to serve the new estate, and was enlarged in 1907. In 1925 the construction of Eastern Avenue (A12) divided most of Mawney from the town that had spawned it. Shortly afterwards came the estates of Collier Row, of which Mawney is now a satellite locality. Sixteen houses were demolished when one of the last flying bombs to fall in England hit Mawney Road, near the corner of Forest Road, on 26 March 1945. After the war, the creation of the green belt preserved farmland

to the south and west. Like much of the borough, Mawney is a homogenous community; the population is overwhelmingly white, Christian and home-owning, with relatively low levels of educational attainment.

When the Mawney Arms closed for refurbishment in 1999, its old fixtures and fittings were removed and reinstalled in a bar in Koh Samui, Thailand. The Thai establishment was renamed the Mawney Arms and displays the original pub sign.

✉ Romford RM7

♦ 12,556 (Mawneys ward)

Mayfair • *Westminster*

An elite residential and commercial quarter bounded by PARK LANE, OXFORD STREET, REGENT STREET and PICCADILLY. Like BELGRAVIA, its main rival as the most prestigious district in London, much of the land here became the property of Sir Thomas Grosvenor in 1677 on his marriage to EBURY heiress Mary Davies. In 1686 a two-week fair transferred from Haymarket to Great Brook Field, where Curzon Street and Shepherd Market now stand. In common with almost every London fair it became notorious for its 'loose, idle and disorderly' crowds and the event was exiled to BOW in 1764. By this time, the neighbouring fields had been laid out with high-class residential streets and squares, notably GROSVENOR SQUARE and BERKELEY SQUARE, while BOND STREET had filled with fashionable shops. Some of Mayfair's most charming streets are the ones that its developers reserved for tradesmen and which were later distinctively rebuilt; the 1890s terracotta frontages of Mount Street and Arts and Crafts houses in Mount Row provide the best examples. During World War II, wealthy residents evacuated themselves to the countryside and, when many chose not to return afterwards, Westminster council allowed the temporary conversion of some homes to offices, many of which were used by spies. As those permissions have expired, 'new money' has come into southern Mayfair and restored its reputation as a prime residential address. The most valuable property on the Monopoly® board, Mayfair is renowned for its exclusive boutiques, many of which hold a royal warrant. Bond Street seems almost downmarket compared with the rarefied retailers of South Audley Street and Curzon Street, which also has private gambling clubs, the offices of hedge funds and the Curzon Mayfair cinema. Auction houses cluster on Bond Street, art dealers around Cork Street and tailors in SAVILE ROW. The villagey Shepherd Market has emerged from a dubious past to gain bars and bistros. The less magnificent northern part of Mayfair is primarily taken up by offices and private colleges and clinics. Embassies and plush hotels are dotted all around.

Benjamin Disraeli, prime minister in 1868 and from 1874 to 1880, died at 19 Curzon Street in 1881. Other Mayfair residents have included the writers Richard Sheridan and Somerset Maugham and the musicians George Frideric Handel and Jimi Hendrix. Queen Elizabeth II was born at 21 Bruton Street in 1926. The romantic comedy film *Maytime in Mayfair* (1949), starring Michael Wilding and Anna Neagle, was set in the world of Mayfair haute couture.

✉ W1

📖 James Dowsing, *Mayfair: Simply London's Premier Address*, Sunrise Press, 2001; Carol Kennedy, *Mayfair: A Social History*, Hutchinson, 1986

Maypole • *Bromley*

A forgotten name for the south-eastern end of CHELSFIELD VILLAGE, close to the Kent countryside. This Maypole should not be confused with another village of the same name, north of JOYDENS WOOD, which lies just outside Greater London, in the borough of Dartford. Maypole's terraced cottages vary greatly in antiquity and loveliness. The former Maypole pub is now one of these cottages. On Hewitts Road, the Bo Peep (previously the White Hart) was once a base for wool smugglers. The building, in knapped flint with a tiled upper floor, dates from 1548.

✉ Orpington BR6

Maze Hill • *Greenwich*

A hillside road forming the eastern boundary of GREENWICH PARK since the enclosure of the common in the 15th century, and probably a cart track from the Thames to Blackheath for many years before that. Despite evidence that the road once led to a turf maze in BLACK-HEATH, the name appears to come from a 17th-century resident, Sir Algernon May. Gravel extraction dominated the east side of the hill until around 1650. After the workings had been exhausted the land was let to smallholders, who were gradually eased out to make way for the homes of gentlemen, scholars and naval officers. In the first half of the 20th century many of the houses were subdivided and some were destroyed in the Blitz.

The elaborate Maze Hill House was demolished in 1932 and replaced by an estate of smaller properties. At the junction of Maze Hill and Westcombe Park Road are the brooding towers of Vanbrugh Castle, built around 1720 by the playwright and architect Sir John Vanbrugh, who also designed Castle Howard and Blenheim Palace. Vanbrugh created a fortress-like complex of mock-medieval buildings, but only the centrepiece survived a spate of redevelopment in the 1890s and 1900s that followed the opening of Maze Hill station in 1876. The Blackheath Preservation Trust bought the site in 1976, restoring the castle and converting it into four dwellings. The northern part of the locality is now dominated by modern municipal housing, including 1960s tower blocks.

One of Greenwich's most renowned black residents, the former slave Olaudah Equiano, stayed for a while at 111 Maze Hill. A pioneering campaigner against the slave trade, Equiano published his autobiography in 1789.

✉ SE3; SE10

🚉 South Eastern Trains (zone 3)

📖 Neil Rhind, *Blackheath Village and Environs, 1790–1970*, vol II, Bookshop Blackheath, 1983

Merton • *Merton*

The compact remnant of a historic parish, situated midway between WIMBLEDON and MITCHAM, squeezed almost out of existence by newer suburbs with more marketable names. Gilbert le Norman, Sheriff of Surrey, founded the magnificent Merton Priory in 1115. In 1236 a group of leading barons held a Great Council here, forcing the Statutes of Merton onto the reluctant Henry III. Walter de Merton, Bishop of Rochester and Chancellor of England, was born at the priory. It was pulled down in 1538 and its stones were taken away to build Nonsuch Palace at CUDDINGTON. The site is now occupied by MERTON ABBEY MILLS. Merton remained a farming community, with textile-printing mills by the River Wandle, until the East India merchant Richard Hotham bought Moat House Farm in 1764 and enlarged the farmhouse, renaming it Merton Place. To the north-west, he built Hotham House, later Merton Grove. Admiral Horatio Nelson acquired Merton Place and its spacious grounds in 1802 and lived here in a ménage à trois with his mistress Emma and her husband Sir William Hamilton, whose death in 1803 removed the already thin veneer of respectability from their relationship. In September 1805 Nelson left from here for Trafalgar, where he died the following month. Emma Hamilton sold 'Paradise Merton', as she had called it, in 1808 and the house was demolished and the estate broken up in 1823. Subsequent development south of the High Street took a surprisingly urban form, with a dense little network of houses, small businesses, shops and alehouses. Trades included carpentry, saddlery and building. The southwestern part of Merton was developed from the 1870s as MERTON PARK, eventually surrounding the previously isolated medieval parish church of St Mary. The farmland north of the High Street was built over in the early 20th century and Merton Grove was demolished by 1913. In that year a bus garage was built in the High Street but the greatest stimulant to the wholesale suburbanization of the district (and the loss of Merton's identity) was the opening of COLLIERS WOOD and SOUTH WIMBLEDON stations in 1926. Much of Merton was rebuilt over the course of the 20th century, although a few older properties survive. The council redeveloped the run-down High Path area with terraced houses and low- and high-rise blocks of flats from 1951 to 1977, whereafter it began a more attractive project north of the High Street. The majority of southern Merton is given over to warehousing and light industry. A converted wine warehouse contains the offices, production suites and sets for *The Bill*, one of the longest-running drama series on British television.

The novelist Ford Madox Ford was born in Merton in 1873. Shaun Hutson's 1982 novel *Slugs* describes the invasion of Merton by gigantic and voracious gastropods.

✉ SW19

📖 Adam Spencer, *Merton: The Century in Old Photographs*, Sutton, 1999 (covers the borough)

Merton Abbey Mills • Merton

'The uncommon market', as it styles itself, situated on the bank of the River Wandle, south of Merantun Way (A24). Following the demolition in 1538 of MERTON Priory – an Augustinian house that was never an abbey – the land reverted to agricultural use, with a calico-printing mill operating on the riverbank by 1724. John Leach established a new mill in 1802, at which his son-in-law later produced colourful handkerchiefs. Towards the end of the 19th century that mill produced all the fabrics for Liberty's department store, which

subsequently took ownership of the operation; Liberty's printworks continued to operate until 1972. Merton Abbey station opened on the Tooting, Merton and Wimbledon Railway in 1868 but passenger services ceased after the arrival of the Northern Line at COLLIERS WOOD and SOUTH WIMBLEDON. One of the station's most regular commuters was the artist-craftsman William Morris, who leased a seven-acre site at Merton in 1881, refurbishing existing buildings and setting up a manufacturing base. For almost 60 years Morris & Co. produced a huge variety of decorative items here, including painted glass windows, tapestries, carpets and upholstery. The former railway line was replaced by Merantun Way in the early 1990s. The road's name refers to a doubtful link between Merton and the place where King Cynewulf of Wessex met his death. In *The Oxford Dictionary of London Place Names*, A D Mills calls this naming 'meretricious and deceptive'. Much of the site of Morris and Co.'s works is now occupied by the shops and market stalls of Merton Abbey Mills. The market is in full swing at weekends, with dozens of craft and food stalls, a heritage museum, a pottery and entertainment for children. An antique and bric-à-brac market operates on Thursday mornings. The remains of the priory's chapter house are open for group viewings by appointment. The Abbey Mills' working waterwheel is used as the symbol of the borough of Merton. After protracted planning delays, vacant parts of the Abbey Mills site have recently been redeveloped with a complex of apartment blocks by Countryside Properties. The scheme won a housing design award in 2005. Residents of the Abbey ward are twice as likely to be in their twenties as are those in the rest of the country.

✉ SW19

👥 9,526 (Abbey ward)

📖 Kevin Leyden, *A Historical Guide to Merton Abbey Mills*, Wandle Industrial Museum, 2000; David Saxby, *William Morris at Merton*, Museum of London Archaeology Service, 1995

@ www.mertonabbeymills.com

Merton Park • Merton

A leafy suburb situated on the south-western side of MERTON. John Innes was a successful City businessman who acquired Manor Farm in 1867 with the intention of profiting from the growth of WIMBLEDON by developing an estate here. He rebuilt the manor house (a former farmhouse) and made it his own home, while laying out broad avenues across the fields. The Merton Park estate was less successful than Innes had hoped, taking several decades to complete and evolving through different styles along the way. From plain beginnings, Innes moved on to a garden suburb approach, with extensive tree planting and picturesque houses. Much of the estate remained in agricultural use at this time and cottages were built for farm workers on Church Lane and Watery Lane. Lower Merton station opened in 1870 and its name was changed to Merton Park in 1887, after Innes had applied persistent pressure to the railway company. John Innes died in 1904 and was buried in the churchyard of St Mary the Virgin, the medieval parish church of Merton. A new phase of development then began, with Arts and Crafts houses by the architect J S Brocklesby, who lived at Long Lodge, on Kingston Road. The grounds of the manor house became John Innes Park in 1909, when a cricket pavilion and a wooden bandstand were added. The manor house itself became the core of Rutlish School in 1910. With the opening of stations at MORDEN and SOUTH MERTON, former allotments in the south were built up from the mid 1920s, with less imaginative designs than in the early phases. By this time, builders on adjoining plots were jumping on the Innes bandwagon and using the Merton Park name for their more affordable projects in areas such as Hillcross Avenue and Sandbourne Avenue. Merton Park Studios moved into Long Lodge and made 130 B-movies between 1934 and 1976, when the site was redeveloped with housing and offices. Merton Park station closed in 1997, when work began on converting the railway into a tram route, which opened in 2000. The Victorian and Edwardian heart of Merton Park is now a conservation area.

The artist Harry Bush painted many scenes in the immediate vicinity of his Queensland Avenue home (near South Wimbledon station) from the 1920s and was nicknamed 'the painter of the suburbs'. Former prime minister John Major was educated at Rutlish School. The novelist Edna O'Brien wrote her trilogy *The Country Girls* while living in Merton Park in the 1960s.

✉ SW19; SW20; Morden SM4

🏃 9,144

🚊 Croydon Tramlink, Route 1

📖 Geoffrey Wilson, *John Innes and the Birth of Merton Park 1865–1904*, John Innes Society, 1986; Geoffrey Wilson, *Merton Park: The Expanding Suburb 1914–31*, John Innes Society, 1986

@ www.stmarysmerton.org.uk

Metroland

The term 'Metroland' was coined by the Metropolitan Railway Co. in 1915 to describe its catchment area north-west of London, as part of a marketing campaign that lasted for two decades. In those days the Metropolitan Railway included the northern section of what is now the Jubilee Line and the arrival of the London Underground network transformed the appeal of dozens of previously remote villages like EASTCOTE, ICKENHAM, KENTON and KINGSBURY. The railway company had much to gain from the success of these new estates; as well as acquiring tens of thousands of fare-paying commuters, it was able to sell plots of land alongside the railway lines and around the stations.

John Betjeman made a BBC television documentary about Metroland and a book followed. The script is also available in various Betjeman collections. The scandalous Lady Margot Metroland was an invention of Evelyn Waugh, making appearances in *Decline and Fall* and other novels and stories. Julian Barnes' 1980 novel *Metroland* is the story of a young man's coming of age in the 1960s, set in north-west London and Paris. The 1999 film version starred Christian Bale and Emily Watson.

📖 John Betjeman, *Metroland*, BBC Publications, 1977; Liz Roberts, *Walks in Metroland*, Countryside Books, 1991

Midtown • *Camden*

A new name for HOLBORN and south-east BLOOMSBURY. Although 'Midtown' is the creation of property developers and letting agents, it is a useful designation for this resurgent area between the WEST END and the CITY OF LONDON, although some are overextending it to cover the entire southern part of the borough. The area's largest employers are government agencies and the professional services sector, including IT, telecoms, recruitment and smaller accountancy practices. The ten-storey Mid City Place on High Holborn is one of the most visible new developments. There is some concern that commercial floor space in Midtown is being eroded as terraced houses that had been subdivided into offices are being refurbished and returned to residential use. The striking Pearl Assurance building, opened in 1919, has recently been converted into a hotel.

✉ WC1

Mildmay Park • *Islington*

An increasingly cosmopolitan street and locality situated on the north-eastern edge of CANONBURY, north of Balls Pond Road. The estate was the property of the Halliday/Mildmay family from the early 17th century until the first half of the 19th century, when Lady St John Mildmay began to sell off land in lots for building. The main phase of activity did not come until a network of streets was laid out in the 1850s. The principal thoroughfares acquired substantial stuccoed properties while smaller streets were lined with two-storey terraced houses. The Mildmay Tavern was built in 1854 and St Jude's Church the following year. Balls Pond Road gained its name in 1865 from a pond near present-day Bingham Street; the pond derived its name from one John Ball, the owner in the mid 18th century of the lively tavern outside which the pond lay. Mildmay Park had a railway station and a synagogue from the 1880s until both closed in the mid 1930s, the latter because the exodus of middle-class Jews to more prosperous parts of London had caused the congregation to dwindle almost into non-existence. After World War II, several bomb-damaged zones were replaced with blocks of flats. Other sites were cleared and rebuilt in the 1960s. Mildmay is the easternmost electoral ward in Islington but exhibits the borough's typical mix of owners and renters, whites and non-whites, and young professionals and blue-collar workers. Most residents are single and do not own a car.

The town of Mildmay in Ontario probably took its name from the estate.

✉ N1

♦ 11,339 (Mildmay ward)

Mile End • *Tower Hamlets*

A contrasting district of 18th-century terraces and 1960s and 1970s tower blocks, situated west of BOW. The name derives from a hamlet, first recorded in 1288, that grew up one mile from ALDGATE. Mile End Road once formed the most imposing approach to London. Wat Tyler assembled his followers here during the Peasants' Revolt of 1381. The first Jewish burial ground on Mile End Road was established in 1657 by permission of Oliver Cromwell and

has been called one of the most hallowed spots for British Jewry. During the late 17th century STEPNEY expanded towards the southern side of Mile End Road, while the part of SPITALFIELDS that lay east of BRICK LANE evolved into a district known as Mile End New Town. Small groups of houses later appeared along Mile End Road itself, forming a hamlet called Mile End Old Town, although the name provided a more geographical than chronological distinction. Over the course of the 18th century the road was lined with a contrasting mixture of merchants' houses and industrial buildings, including a brewery and a distillery. A blue plaque at 88 Mile End Road marks the site of the house where Captain James Cook once lived. The road's hinterland remained primarily agricultural until the early 19th century, when two-storey terraced housing spread here from WHITECHAPEL and COMMERCIAL ROAD. Following an exodus of the mercantile population, the mostly poor Jewish community swelled. A large open space known as the Mile End Waste was used for political and religious meetings. In another of Mile End's contrasts, Dr Barnardo converted warehouses alongside the Regent's Canal into Copperfield Road Ragged School (now a museum) in 1876, while colleges were established on Mile End Road in the 1880s that became part of the University of London in 1915. Conditions in the district deteriorated during the first half of the 20th century and after World War II the London County Council and Stepney council cleared bomb sites and slums (including Captain Cook's house) and rebuilt intensively. Blocks of flats rose ever higher into the 1970s but housing associations have built less obtrusively in the past two decades. Opened in 2000, the Green Bridge across Mile End Road is clad in yellow plastic but is named after its linear park. Despite the drought-resistant plantings, the standard of maintenance is so poor that 'brown bridge' might be more appropriate. The road retains a selection of Georgian gems but these are overshadowed by the low-rent shops and takeaways that have replaced the grand emporiums of a century ago. A third of Mile End's residents are of Bangladeshi origin.

Pulp's song *Mile End* bewails life in a tower block squat off Burdett Road: 'The fifth floor landing smells of fish – not just on Friday, every single other day'. Platinum-selling rapper Dizzee Rascal comes from the district but his 2006 release *Waste Man* does not appear to refer to the Mile End Waste.

✉ E1; E3

♁ 22,940 (Mile End East and Mile End and Globe Town wards)

🚇 Central Line; District Line; Hammersmith & City Line (zone 2)

📖 John Gross, *A Double Thread: A Childhood Memoir in Mile End – And Beyond*, Chatto & Windus, 2001

@ www.raggedschoolmuseum.org.uk

Millbank • *Westminster*

A Thames-side street in south-east WESTMIN-STER, home mainly to institutions, and also a term used by estate agents to identify properties in the neighbouring locality. This was land belonging to Westminster Abbey when it was first recorded in 1546. The name referred to the presence of watermills on the embanked riverside. The last of these mills, which stood at the very northern end of Millbank, was pulled down early in the 18th century. Millbank Penitentiary opened in 1816, built in the shape of a six-pointed star and surrounded by an octagonal wall. This was the largest prison in the country and became infamous for its harsh regime, although its founding principles were relatively enlightened by the standards of the time. The penitentiary was demolished in 1892 and the Royal Army Medical College and the Tate Gallery were built on its site. The gallery's buildings were designed by Sidney J R Smith, the architect chosen by sugar magnate Sir Henry Tate, who had donated the paintings that formed the nucleus of the new collection and much of the necessary funding for the gallery's construction. The buildings have been progressively extended, most recently in 1987 with the opening of the Clore gallery, which houses works by J M W Turner. With the transfer of the post-1900 collection to Tate Modern on Bankside, the original buildings have been rebranded Tate Britain. In 1997 the Labour Party relocated its headquarters from working-class WALWORTH Road to the more glamorous 32-storey Millbank Tower, which stands just north of Tate Britain. To some, the move symbolized the ascendancy of Labour's modernizers, who were labelled the 'Millbank tendency'. In a cost-cutting exercise, Labour moved across Westminster to Old Queen Street in 2002. The former army medical college became home in 2005 to the Chelsea College of Art and Design, now part of University of the Arts London. Security service MI5 is headquartered at the forbidding-looking Thames House.

One of Turner's first experiments in oil, *Moonlight, a Study at Millbank* (c.1797), hangs in Tate Britain.

✉ SW1

🚢 Millbank Millennium pier

@ www.tate.org.uk

Millennium Quarter *see* SOUTH QUAY

Millennium Village • *Greenwich*

An urban village under development on the GREENWICH PENINSULA, south-east of the former Millennium Dome. Work began in 1999, when the scheme was hailed by the government as a 'blueprint for future sustainable developments', but the original architects resigned soon afterwards, accusing the developers of subverting the intentions of the project. The first 500 homes have been built, together with an ecological park and recreational areas. However, the continuing difficulties of the scheme were highlighted in January 2006, when Greenwich council granted outline planning permission for phases three, four and five but refused permission for the latter stages of phase one and the village square. Assuming the issues can be resolved the village should be completed soon after 2010. The Annandale School moved from EAST GREENWICH to John Harrison Way in 2001, when it became Millennium Primary School. Inspectors from the national educational standards agency Ofsted gave the school a good rating in 2006, quoting a pupil's remark that it is 'a great place to be and you really feel welcome'.

✉ SE10

@ www.gmvonline.com (residents' site)

Millfields • *Hackney*

The Borough of Hackney's side of the LEA BRIDGE area, usually considered to be an eastern part of CLAPTON. The great corn mills that gave the fields their name burned down in 1796. The excavation of brickfields in the 19th century revealed rhinoceros and elephant bones in North Millfields. In 1872 the Commons Preservation Society saved the 57 acres of North and South Millfields as public open spaces, and performed a similar service for nearby Clapton Common and Hackney Downs. Pond Lane was renamed Millfields Road in 1887, a time when terraced housing was beginning to extend here from Clapton. The district's mixed housing stock now includes both municipal and private properties, ranging from small flats to impressive villas. Among the council estates are Pond Farm, built in the 1950s, and the low-rise Millfields, which replaced Clapton stadium in 1980. At Millfields Primary School, on Hilsea Street, over half the pupils receive assistance in learning English as an additional language and ten per cent are from the families of asylum-seekers. A further three per cent are travellers' children. A 2001 inspection by the national agency Ofsted found a very high level of mobility; in one class over half the pupils had changed within the previous two years.

✉ E5

Mill Hill • Barnet
A rambling, multi-focal village-cum-suburb situated between EDGWARE and FINCHLEY, and possibly the London district most influenced by the Christian faith. Its self-explanatory name was first recorded in 1374. A tradition of religious nonconformity began with Quaker and Presbyterian communities in the 17th century. Quakers met at Rosebank, on the Ridgeway, from 1678 to 1719 and the weatherboarded building survives today. Across the road, in 1807 a group of Nonconformist ministers and city merchants founded a Protestant dissenters' grammar school, now Mill Hill School, in the former home of botanist Peter Collinson. New buildings were added in 1827 and have been supplemented by at least one additional structure in almost every decade since. Mill Hill did not acquire a separate Anglican church from HENDON until 1833 – and that was in the face of bitter opposition from the vicar of Hendon. Roman Catholics began the construction of St Joseph's College on Lawrence Street in 1869. This was the second stage of Cardinal Vaughan's project to create a training establishment for foreign missionaries, begun a few years earlier in nearby HIGHWOOD HILL. In 1887 the Sisters of Charity of St Vincent de Paul acquired Littleberries, a much-altered house of late 17th-century origin on the Ridgeway, and expanded it into a convent. The neighbouring St Vincent's Roman Catholic School opened in 1896. Methodists also built a school on the Ridgeway. By this time almost one-third of Mill Hill was covered by institutional buildings and their grounds – Mill Hill School alone covers 120 acres. This was an obstacle to the expansion of the village, as was its distance from the nearest stations on Bittacy Hill (MILL HILL EAST) and at what is now MILL HILL BROADWAY. As a result, most 20th-century de-

velopment took place in what was virtually a fresh suburb, in the vicinity of the Broadway, and churches were built there as the locality grew. Back on the Ridgeway, Jehovah's Witnesses moved to a new national headquarters at Watchtower House, built on the site of Bittacy House in 1959. The sect now operates here as the International Bible Students Association. Despite its history, Christians only make up half of Mill Hill's population. Jews account for another 17 per cent.

The University of London observatory is a familiar sight to drivers on the Watford Way (A1). Opened in 1929, the building now houses seven telescopes, a library and teaching space for University College London's department of physics and astronomy. The National Institute for Medical Research moved to its imposing purpose-built home on the Ridgeway in 1950. The institute doubled as Arkham asylum in the 2005 film *Batman Begins*.

✉ NW7

♦ 15,379

📖 Ralph Calder, *Mill Hill: A Thousand Years of History*, Angus Hudson, 1993

Mill Hill Broadway • Barnet
A main-line station and effectively MILL HILL'S town centre, although it is located well to the west of the settlement's old heart. The station – first called Bunn's Lane – opened in 1868 but the Midland Railway Co. neglected to promote suburban development in the vicinity. Shops did not appear in the locality until around 1910 and plans to build a garden suburb on 50 acres of land north-west of the station failed to get off the drawing board. Only a handful of residential streets had been laid out nearby by 1913. The Broadway, which had formerly been the lower end of Lawrence Street, gained its present name when the Watford Way (A1) cut through the area in the 1920s. Over the following decade the Broadway finally became a major shopping centre and most of the surrounding fields were converted to middle-class housing estates as Mill Hill's centre of gravity shifted away from the Ridgeway. However, even during this most intense phase of metropolitan expansion some open land remained near the station, owing to its distance from central London. The last few fields were covered by houses in the 1950s. Reflecting the piecemeal growth of the suburb, the fabric of St Michael and All Angels' Church was completed in 1956, 36 years after construction had begun. The Broadway

323

also has United Reformed and Roman Catholic churches, the latter rebuilt after subsidence problems. Since 1965 the elevated section of the M1 motorway has soared over the district, with the station on one side and the Broadway itself on the other. Mill Hill Broadway is one of the busiest stations in the borough and plans are in hand to increase the frequency of train services and improve bus access, but at the expense of parking spaces for the Broadway's shops.

✉ NW7

🚇 Thameslink (zone 4)

Mill Hill East • *Barnet*

An 'intensification' site for north London housing, situated midway between FINCHLEY and MILL HILL proper. The fields here belonged to All Souls College, Oxford from 1442. The medieval manor of Frith and Newhall lay to the north-east and was divided into Dollis, Frith, and Partingdale farms by the mid 18th century. The modern era came early to Bittacy Hill when the Great Northern Railway opened Mill Hill (later Mill Hill East) station and the North Middlesex Gas Co. built a gasworks in the 1860s. A pub and a few gasworkers' cottages appeared nearby but the railway service to London was slow and indirect so commuters were not interested and the surrounding area remained farmland. In 1909 the Middlesex Regiment moved into Inglis Barracks, which replaced Bittacy Farm. A council estate, including flats, was built at the foot of Bittacy Hill in the mid 1920s. South of the station, Mill Hill Homesteads bought Devonshire Farm in 1933 and laid out an estate. Further up the hill and over on the Frith manor lands, roads were laid out in the years before and after World War II. The barracks later became the base for the British Forces Post Office, which has recently moved to RAF NORTHOLT. There are plans to build 2,000 new homes by 2016 on the 94-acre site between Bittacy Hill and Frith Lane, but several controversies have impeded progress. These have included the discovery of low-level radioactive contamination, the excessive scale of some proposals, and objections from local residents that the 'concept of "social" housing does not match the character and profile of the whole of Frith Lane'. Meanwhile, Crest Nicholson has redeveloped the disused gasworks site with 250 homes, a supermarket and a health club.

Inglis Barracks were named in honour of Lieutenant-Colonel William Inglis of the 57th Foot (from 1882 the Middlesex Regiment), who was fatally injured at the Battle of Albuera in 1811. Inglis exhorted his troops to 'Die hard', and the 57th were afterwards nicknamed the 'Die-hards'. In 1988, 23-year-old soldier Michael Robbins was killed and nine others were injured by an IRA bomb at the barracks.

✉ NW7

🚇 Northern Line; Mill Hill East branch terminus (zone 4)

Mill Meads • *Newham*

A nature reserve and historic industrial district situated among the creeks and channels of the River Lea, south of STRATFORD. A 'mead' was a meadow and the mills were mainly of the tidal variety, taking advantage of the twice-daily swell of the river where it becomes Bow Creek. Products milled here from the 16th century included corn, gunpowder and, later, grain for distilling gin. To the south of the Channelsea River lay Sir William Congreve's rocket works, which made artillery that was used in the Napoleonic Wars and the Anglo-American War of 1812. The 'red glare' of these rockets at the Battle of Fort McHenry is referred to in the US national anthem. The northern part of Mill Meads is now primarily commercial, and the units operate increasingly in media-related fields such as design and display, and there are television studios at Three Mills. Other areas are still marshy wilderness, home to some rare aquatic flora and fauna. Among the architectural treasures of Mill Meads are the ABBEY MILLS pumping station and two surviving mills and a miller's house at Three Mills. Mill Meads are crossed by public footpaths that form a section of the Greenway route; some parts of this have recently been improved but others are in a disgraceful state.

✉ E15

Millwall • *Tower Hamlets*

Still a largely working-class residential district in the south-western part of the ISLE OF DOGS, though now intermingled with a dockside enterprise zone. Its name derives from the windmills that once lined the western embankment. Before the mills appeared this was Pomfret manor, the base for the earliest recorded Thames ferry east of the CITY OF LONDON, which plied between here and GREENWICH in the mid 15th century. Great Eastern pier was the site of the Scott Russell shipyard, where the steamship SS *Great Eastern* was built and launched in 1858, subsequently laying the first transatlantic telecommunications cable. In 1868, Millwall Docks opened to handle imports of timber and grain, and McDougall's flour works was established. The Millwall Extension Railway came in 1872, on the route now taken by the Docklands Light Railway. Millwall's industrial growth brought shipbuilding, engineering and chemicals, and an oil works owned by local resident Alexander Duckham. After World War I, 'homes for heroes' were erected on the Chapel House estate (named after a nearby medieval chapel) in a partnership between Poplar council and Millwall Lead Works. In the 1950s and 1960s, council blocks and maisonettes provided housing for local people whose homes had been destroyed in the Blitz. Along the riverside, more exclusive flats were constructed during the 1980s docklands boom, including Maconochies Wharf, the largest self-build development in Britain.

Workers from Morton's, a local confectionery firm, formed Millwall Football Club in the 1880s. The club played at several locations on the Isle of Dogs before establishing itself south of the Thames in 1910.

⊠ E14

♦ 12,892

🚇 Docklands Light Railway (Crossharbour, once Millwall Dock station, zone 2)

🚢 Masthouse Terrace (formerly Great Eastern) pier

Mitcham • *Merton*

A sprawling south London suburb with an ancient village at its heart, situated south of TOOTING. Medieval Mitcham consisted of four manors and two settlements, which were focused on the Upper and Lower Greens. Elizabeth I is said to have granted a charter for an annual fair after she had enjoyed watching the formerly unofficial festivities here. City gentlemen established country retreats here in the mid 17th century, attracted by the village's reputation for clean air at a time when London was frequently ravaged by epidemics, and Mitcham was nicknamed 'the Montpelier of England'. Robert Cranmer acquired the manor of Mitcham Canons in the 1650s and his family held the lordship for five generations. The Canons manor house was built in 1680 and is now a borough leisure centre, with an even older dovecote surviving in the grounds. Mitcham can make a strong claim to have the country's oldest cricket ground in

continual use, with good evidence that games were being played on the Cricket Green in 1685. From the mid 18th century large parts of Mitcham were given over to the cultivation of aromatic plants and shrubs, including camomile, poppies, liquorice and anise. The industry began when Ephraim Potter and William Moore took advantage of Mitcham's rich black loam to grow lavender, setting up a distillery at Tamworth Farm. Others soon followed, also producing oils of rose and peppermint. From its inception in 1801 the horse-drawn Surrey Iron Railway was used to transport Mitcham's horticultural produce to London. The iron railway went out of business in the 1840s, but its route was later used by steam trains and latterly the Croydon Tramlink. The opening of Mitcham Junction station attracted noxious industries rather than suburban homes, and helped bring large-scale lavender-growing to an end. Nevertheless, even after the physic gardens had been built over or converted to market gardens, the finest extracts were still described as 'Mitcham lavender oil'. It was not until much later in the century that private builders began to develop the village and outlying settlements such as PHIPPS BRIDGE and GORRINGE PARK, and the open spaces of MITCHAM COMMON were saved for public use in 1891. Shops were built around Fair Green, where the fair continued to be held until 1923, when it moved to Three King's Piece, on the common. Suburban and industrial development continued after World War I and the artificially quaint Mitcham Garden Village was completed in 1932. For over 60 years Locks Lane was the home of Renshaw's marzipan factory, built on a site that was originally a laundry. Municipal housing schemes were the dominant form of post-war construction, notably at POLLARDS HILL. There have been recent attempts to reintroduce some commercial cultivation of lavender to the district. Mitcham's limited rail connections have made it more affordable than districts at a comparable distance from central London, despite its wealth of green spaces. Around 60 per cent of the residents of the Cricket Green and Lavender Fields wards are white British, and the principal ethnic minorities are of black African and black Caribbean descent. The wards are socially very mixed.

Former Mitcham residents include the poet John Donne, who lived on the now untraceable Whitford Lane near Lower Green from 1605 to 1608 and, more prosaically, folk singer Ralph McTell, of *Streets of London* fame.

✉ Mitcham CR4

♦ 39,786 (Cricket Green, Figge's Marsh, Lavender Fields and Pollards Hill wards)

🚃 Southern; Thameslink City Metro (Mitcham Junction, zone 4); Tramstops Croydon Tramlink, Route 1 (Mitcham; Mitcham Junction)

📖 Nick Harris, *Mitcham*, Tempus, 1996

Mitcham Common • *Merton*

A 460-acre expanse of open terrain bisected by the Croydon Road (A236), south-east of the centre of MITCHAM. The common was cleared of its oak trees in Neolithic times and extensive grazing kept the acidic soil infertile. The parish workhouse was built at the northern end of Windmill Road in 1782. Gravel extraction in the 19th century created depressions and ponds, of which Seven Islands Pond is the largest. In 1891 the Mitcham Common Conservators took the land under their wing and ended destructive practices such as gravel extraction and turf removal, while permitting golfing in a limited area. As houses and factories surrounded the common in the early 20th century, commoners ceased collecting firewood and grazing sheep and cattle, and scrubby vegetation grew in an uncontrolled fashion. Land on each side of Cedars Avenue was ploughed and seeded during World War II. Post-war waste disposal created the common's low hills and destroyed some wetland habitats, but raised money for the conservators. From the 1980s the conservators have enhanced the acid grassland and heathland and the common's appearance is now much improved. The Windmill trading estate, which occupies the former workhouse site, has become very run-down and has recently been the subject of controversial proposals for its replacement with a mixed-use development.

In his metropolitan classic *Mother London*, Michael Moorcock writes of 'the endless and verdant Mitcham Common, with her ponds ... a soft green golf-course, copses, unthreatening marshes, stands of poplars, cedars and ... pedestrian bridges of wood and iron spanning a railway, sandy bunkers and depressions'.

✉ Mitcham CR4

@ www.mitchamcommon.org

Mogden • *Hounslow*

An old name for a part of south ISLEWORTH dominated by Thames Water's Mogden waste water works. Opened in 1936 on the site of Mogden farm, this is the second largest such plant in Europe, treating the sewage of a population of about 1.8 million from a 60-square mile catchment area of north and west London. Purified waste water from the plant is piped to ISLEWORTH AIT, where it is discharged into the Thames around high tide. Mogden has recently undergone a £40-million refit, but nearby residents still complain of unsavoury odours and raw overflows into the Thames after heavy rain. Electricity has always been generated from the waste methane to power the treatment works but in 1993 a combined heat and power plant was added. The 'Mogden formula' is a sewerage industry pricing structure that seeks to link charges to the volume and strength of trade effluent discharged. South Middlesex Hospital, which closed in 1982, was originally Mogden Isolation Hospital. The surrounding locality is rarely called Mogden now, perhaps because of the name's association with the waste water plant; Ivybridge is the preferred identity both for residential and commercial developments. The council's Ivybridge estate has some of the borough's highest levels of deprivation, although low-rise flats have recently been demolished, after lengthy delays. The main ethnic minorities are of Pakistani and black African descent; a number of refugee families have also been placed on the estate.

The Crane Walk runs through the middle of the Mogden works, beside the Duke of Northumberland's River, which was diverted as part of the construction programme.

✉ Isleworth TW7

@ www.mogden.org.uk (community site campaigning against odours from the Mogden works)

Monken Hadley • *Barnet*

Like neighbouring HIGH BARNET and CHIPPING BARNET, HADLEY and Monken Hadley are historically one and the same place but are now shown separately on maps. Monken Hadley, so-called because the manor once belonged to the Benedictine monks of Walden Abbey in Essex, tends to be identified as the part to the north. The origin of this distinction is that a 27-acre civil parish called Hadley was detached from the parish of Monken Hadley in 1894 and given to Barnet urban district council, while the remaining 668 acres became part of East Barnet Valley urban district. The two parts were reunited within the London Borough of Barnet in 1965, which created the conservation area of Monken Hadley in 1968. *See also* HADLEY.

✉ Barnet EN4 and EN5

Monks Orchard • *Croydon/Bromley*

An interwar middle-class housing development located on the borders of BECKENHAM and SHIRLEY, built in the grounds of a mental hospital. An ADDINGTON family called Monk owned a farm here sometime before the mid 17th century and Monksmead and Monks Orchard were the names given to their meadow and wood respectively. Lewis Lloyd acquired the estate in the early 1850s and named it after the wood. He built a mansion with 19 bedrooms, a billiard room, a library and a 36-foot dining room. An ornamental entrance lodge survives on Cheston Avenue. Monks Orchard was described in 1923 as 'typifying that which is best in the unspoiled English countryside' but within a year a large part of it had been acquired by the Corporation of London for the relocation of the Bethlem Royal Hospital from LAMBETH. Construction of the hospital began in 1928 and the mansion was demolished. The corporation did not require all the land it had bought so the remainder was sold off for housing and the present street plan was soon laid out. Most of the housing was built before the outbreak of World War II, with mock-Tudor the favoured style, although other properties have fewer pretensions to grandeur. Recent years have seen a spate of demolitions of existing houses and bungalows and their replacement by higher density schemes. The Monks Orchard Residents' Association has been fighting a rearguard action against what it perceives as overdevelopment.

The Bethlem Royal Hospital Museum was established at Monks Orchard in 1967. The museum holds the archives of the hospital and its sister institutions. The Bethlem Gallery was founded in 1998, housed in the creative workshops building of the hospital's occupational therapy department. In the following year patients and staff covered the façade with a ceramic relief, under the guidance of artist Timothy Clapcott. The gallery's collection of 'outsider art' has been called 'important and moving' in the *Fortean Times*, and four special exhibitions are held annually.

✉ Croydon CR0; Beckenham BR3

📖 Ian Muir and Pat Manning, *The Book of Monks Orchard and Eden Park*, Halsgrove, 2004

@ www.monks-orchard-web.org.uk (residents' association site);

www.bethlemheritage.org.uk (hospital archives and museum site)

Monument • *City*

A Portland stone column erected at the junction of Monument Street and Fish Street Hill, just north of LONDON BRIDGE. Built in 1677 by Sir Christopher Wren, the Monument commemorates the Great Fire that destroyed most of the City of London in 1666. It stands 202 feet high – its precise distance from the fire's source, a bakery in Pudding Lane – and is topped by a gilded flame. The pedestal originally carried an inscription blaming Roman Catholics for the fire. Referring to this, the poet Alexander Pope wrote, 'Where London's column pointing at the skies, / Like a tall bully, lifts its head and lies'. In 1831 the Corporation of London erased the offending words. Over 100,000 visitors a year climb the 311-step spiral staircase to the Monument's observation platform, now enclosed to prevent the suicides for which it was once notorious. The column was floodlit in 1994 and extensively restored the following year. Monument station opened in October 1884, on a section of track that completed what became the Circle Line. It was called Eastcheap for the first month of its existence.

✉ EC3

🚇 Circle Line; District Line (zone 1), with an escalator link to Bank station

📖 Adrian Tinniswood, *By Permission of Heaven: The True Story of the Great Fire of London*, Riverhead 2004; Neil Hanson, *The Dreadful Judgement: The True Story of the Great Fire of London*, Doubleday, 2001

Moorfields • *Islington/Hackney/City*

Moorfields was originally a large open space that stretched from the north side of the City wall towards HOXTON and ISLINGTON but the name is now principally used in the context of the Eye Hospital, which is located north of OLD STREET station. A back street named Moorfields survives nearer London Wall, by MOORGATE station. From 1415 the Moor Gate opened onto Moorfields, newly acquired by the Corporation of London. At that time the fields were marshland – the origin of the Walbrook watercourse and 'full of noisome waters' – although the Corporation soon set to work improving the drainage. The fields became too popular for the liking of locals, who planted hedges and dug ditches to keep out City ramblers. In 1514 a City posse tore down the hedges and filled in the ditches but many

327

were subsequently replaced. The wet fields frequently froze over in winter to form London's first skating rink, on which young men wearing 'shin-bone' ice skates played a game that involved tilting at their comrades with iron-tipped sticks. The fields were described in 1607 as 'a garden of this City and a pleasurable place of sweet ayres for citizens to walk in' and citizens took refuge here from the Great Fire in 1666. In 1675 the Bethlem Royal Hospital moved from BISHOPSGATE to Moorfields. Known as Bedlam, the asylum provided cheap entertainment for City dwellers who came to view the antics of the inmates. The hospital moved to Lambeth in 1815. Architect George Dance the Younger planned the redevelopment of Lower Moorfields in the late 18th century, creating Finsbury Square, Finsbury Circus and the surrounding streets. The scheme included the City of London's finest Roman Catholic church, St Mary Moorfields. This was demolished at the end of the 19th century, when the whole area was rebuilt, and replaced by the present, more recessive church on Eldon Street. Islington's Moorfields archaeological priority area covers almost all of the south-easternmost part of the borough.

In 1805 John Cunningham Saunders founded the world's first specialist eye hospital in Moorfields, prompted by an outbreak of trachoma among troops returning from the Napoleonic Wars in Egypt. The hospital moved to its present site on City Road in 1899.

✉ N1; EC1; EC2

📖 Peter K Leaver, *The History of Moorfields Eye Hospital*, Royal Society of Medicine Press, 2004

@ www.stmarymoorfields.net; www.moorfields.org.uk (Moorfields Eye Hospital)

Moorgate • *City*

A commercial street running from the north-west corner of the BANK of England northwards to the edge of the CITY OF LONDON. In 1415 'the Lord Mayor caused the wall of the City to be broken towards MOORFIELDS, and builded the postern called Moor Gate, for the ease of citizens to walk that way upon the causeways towards ISLINGTON and HOXTON'. The Moor Gate was demolished in 1761 and its stones were used to repair LONDON BRIDGE. Moorgate Street, as it was initially called, was constructed in the late 1830s as part of a new route to London Bridge. The part south of London Wall was flanked by a mix of offices

and residences in stuccoed terraces, only one of which survives today. The northern part of the street existed as a route across Moorfields towards the CITY ROAD before it was incorporated in the new approach road. The station, also originally named Moorgate Street, opened in 1865, at the expense of several little alleys and courts. The main station building that stands today dates from 1900, when what is now the Northern Line arrived. In the four decades before 1930 almost all of Moorgate was rebuilt with stone-faced office blocks, of which a handful of good examples remain. Much of the street has been rebuilt again over the past 20 years, with plentiful use of glass and steel. Shops, sandwich bars and other service providers line most of the street at ground level. Moorgate station's western ticket hall and the office block above it are being redeveloped in a scheme scheduled for completion in 2008.

The poet John Keats was born in a stable in Moorgate in 1795 and lived at No. 85 until he was nine years old. In the worst-ever crash on the London Underground, 44 people were killed in February 1975 when a train ran into the end wall at the terminus at 40 mph.

✉ EC2

🚊 WAGN Railway (secondary terminus); Circle Line; Hammersmith & City Line; Metropolitan Line; Northern Line (zone 1)

📖 Sally Holloway, *Moorgate: Anatomy of a Railway Disaster*, David & Charles, 1988

Morden • *Merton*

A sea of 1930s suburbia graced by two islands of parkland, located south-west of MERTON and MITCHAM. Early Morden developed around twin nuclei: St Lawrence Church (and later Morden Park House) in the south-west and Morden Hall in the north-east. Morden had been under the control of Westminster Abbey throughout the Middle Ages but it gained a resident lord of the manor in 1553. Richard Garth built Morden Hall and his descendants lived here for three centuries. St Lawrence Church was rebuilt in 1636, probably around the skeleton of a much older building. The Garths built Morden Park House for John Ewart around 1770. A snuff manufacturer and would-be country squire, Gilliat Hatfeild, bought Morden Hall in 1872 and protected the neighbourhood from early suburban development. In 1905, Morden still had 632 acres of grassland, 255 acres of arable land and 33 acres of woods. When the Northern Line (as it is now) was extended here from Clapham Common in 1926, the 17 miles from here to East Finchley made this the world's longest tunnel. A bus station opened the following year and extra services were soon laid on to try to divert passengers away from the already overloaded Tube station. Tube fares were set low with the deliberate intention of stimulating a housing boom in Morden and the plan worked. A whole new town grew up around the station, with shopping parades on either side of London Road. Semi-detached houses with sizeable gardens were the predominant property type, with mansion blocks on the main thoroughfares. In the late 1920s the London County Council commandeered 322 acres in the south-eastern corner of Morden for part of its ST HELIER estate. Gilliat Hatfeild died in 1941 and left Morden Hall Park to the National Trust; the hall itself is now a restaurant. The council bought MORDEN PARK in 1945, preserving 90 acres as open space and playing fields. In the early 1960s an office block was added to Charles Holden's station and the curved 14-storey slab of Crown House was completed, with an adjoining supermarket that has since been supplanted by Merton Civic Centre and a library. Morden cinema was demolished in the late 1970s and replaced by shops and flats. Other early amenities have since gone the same way.

✉ Morden SM4

🚇 Northern Line terminus (Morden, zone 4)

📖 Judith Goodman, *Merton and Morden: A Pictorial History,* Phillimore, 1995

Morden Park • *Merton*

A hilltop park and the comfortable residential district on its south-western edge, where the name has widely supplanted the less resonant LOWER MORDEN. There is evidence that a mound in Morden Park is a pagan burial site dating from early Roman times. This was monastic land belonging to Westminster Abbey before it was acquired as part of MORDEN manor by the Garth family in 1554. In 1768 Richard Garth, in partnership with the London merchant and distiller John Ewart, procured a private act of Parliament permitting the creation of the Morden Park estate. The double-fronted Morden Park House was built immediately afterwards as a retreat for the Ewart family. The estate passed through a succession of hands until it came into public ownership in 1936. At one time, the London County Council considered extending the ST

HELIER estate into the grounds, but the LCC leader Herbert Morrison was so impressed by the park's beauty that he declared it must be preserved. The LCC converted the northern half into playing fields, while the house became a headquarters for the borough's parks administration. Also in the 1930s, G T Crouch Ltd built the Morden Park Tudor estate on the site of a former pig farm in Lower Morden. Merton and Morden council added some houses in Tudor Drive in the 1950s. Fifteen acres on the east side of Morden Park were reserved for civic developments, where swimming baths were erected in 1967 and Merton Technical College was added five years later. The college has since become Merton College and Sixth Form Centre, and has been greatly expanded in recent years. Morden Park House has been restored and is used as the borough's register office.

✉ Morden SM4

@ www.merton.ac.uk (Merton College)

Morden South • *Merton*

A Thameslink station located half a mile south-west of MORDEN Tube station, but not a name used for the surrounding area. The railway line from WIMBLEDON to SUTTON opened in 1930. Like other stations on this line, Morden South is little more than a halt, with no booking hall or retail amenities. Traffic on the line never justified the expense of its construction, although the nearby Morden Tube station became one of the busiest commuter destinations on the network. London Underground's predecessors as operators of the Northern Line built a depot behind Morden South station and it might have been possible to create a Tube/rail interchange here but the two companies were antagonistic rather than co-operative. Express Dairies established a bottling plant on a former field between the two sets of rails, with its own siding and locomotive. After the dairy closed, London's Ahmadiyya Muslim community purchased the five-acre site for the construction of one of the largest mosques in Europe. Inaugurated in 2003, the imposing Baitul Futuh mosque cost £5.5 million, contributed by the community's members, and can accommodate up to 10,000 worshippers. Ancillary parts of the mosque are built around the fabric of the dairy and the old chimney was cleverly converted into a minaret, allowing a taller structure than would otherwise have been permitted.

✉ Morden SM4

🚆 Thameslink (zone 4)

@ www.alislam.org/mosques/index.html
(Baitul Futuh mosque site)

Mornington Crescent • *Camden*

A street and Tube station located at the junction of Hampstead Road and Camden High Street. The crescent was created in the 1820s and named after the Earl of Mornington. A decade later the Duke of Bedford's Figs Mead estate was laid out with stuccoed terraces of houses and was at first called Bedford New Town. Bombing raids on the nearby railway termini caused extensive damage to the area during World War II. St Pancras council replaced much of the 'new town' with the Ampthill estate in 1960 and the council's successor, Camden, reclad the three tower blocks in primary colours in the late 1980s. Greater London House is an imposing office block occupying the arc of the crescent and overlooking Harrington Square Gardens; it was formerly the Carreras 'Black Cat' cigarette factory. London Underground gained the opprobrium of commuters in the early 1990s when its refurbishment of Mornington Crescent Tube station was halted for several years owing to a shortage of funds. The station finally reopened in 1998, winning plaudits for its sympathetic restoration.

Except for CHEYNE WALK, few streets have rivalled Mornington Crescent as a creative hotbed. Among its former residents are the artists Spencer Gore, Clarkson Stanfield and Walter Sickert, who was living here when he founded the post-Impressionist Camden Town Group in 1911. The illustrator and political caricaturist George Cruikshank lived in Mornington Place. Mornington Crescent has given its name to a 'strategy' game played on the BBC Radio 4 show *I'm Sorry I Haven't a Clue*; successful play depends on sophisticated tactical proficiency as well as an encyclopaedic knowledge of London destinations.

✉ N1

🚆 Northern Line (zone 2)

📖 Tim Brooke-Taylor et al, *The Little Book of Mornington Crescent*, Orion, 2001

Mortlake • *Richmond*

A Thames-side settlement with a proud industrial past, lying opposite the tip of the CHISWICK peninsula. Domesday Book recorded the presence of a fishery and Mortlake's name probably derives from the Old English words 'mort', a young salmon, and 'lacu', a small stream (since lost). Although the manor of Mortlake was extensive, the village consisted of just a few riverside houses on a single street until 1619, when James I provided financial backing for the establishment of a tapestry works employing Flemish weavers. Charles I bought out the enterprise in 1636. The following year the king made himself less popular by compulsorily purchasing 732 acres of the parish as part of his vast new hunting ground at RICHMOND PARK. Later in the 17th century the village gained a sugar refinery and several maltings but the tapestry works closed in 1703. Around 1743 John Sanders founded his Mortlake pottery, becoming London's largest manufacturer of stoneware. Joseph Kishere, a former employee at Sanders' pottery, subsequently established his own pottery on the south side of the high street, making decorative pots known as Kishereware. During the latter part of the 18th century, when some fine houses were being erected by the river, James Weatherstone ran a successful brewery that he extended to the waterfront in 1807. The business went on to benefit from lucrative contracts to supply the British army in India with pale ale and was subsequently acquired by Watney's. Mortlake's entrepreneurial achievements continued when Richard Wesley Gale began bottling his prize honey here in 1919. A road-widening scheme spoilt the High Street in the 1960s but this failed to dent Mortlake's popularity with home-buyers (who tend to be middle aged and in secure jobs in the Mortlake and BARNES Common ward) and by the end of the 20th century many former amenities and commercial premises had been converted into, or replaced by, apartments. The Stag brewery is the only significant industrial enterprise still operating here, and now produces Budweiser lager for Anheuser-Busch.

The first varsity boat race was the result of a challenge issued to Oxford by Cambridge in 1829 and was rowed on the Thames at Henley. The second race was staged in 1836 between Westminster and Putney. Today the four-and-a-quarter mile course, which was first used in 1845, starts from the west side of PUTNEY BRIDGE and finishes by the Ship, a 16th-century inn situated just short of Chiswick Bridge. The race is held in March or early April, now usually on a Sunday. Around a quarter of a million people are estimated to watch the race from the riverbank.

⊠ SW14

♊ 9,925 (Mortlake and Barnes Common ward)

🚆 South West Trains (zone 3)

📖 Maisie Brown, *Barnes and Mortlake Past*, Historical Publications, 1997; Jack Howarth and Robin Hildyard, *Joseph Kishere and the Mortlake Potteries*, Antique Collector's Club, 2004

@ www.mortlake-online.co.uk (community site)

Mossford Green • *Redbridge*

A 'Barnardo-ville' in BARKINGSIDE, a third of a mile south-west of FULLWELL CROSS. Some early cartographers rendered the name as Mossfoot. There has been a hamlet here since the days when Barkingside was merely the name of the parish rather than a specific settlement. Edward Blore designed its Church of the Holy Trinity in 1840. Behind this lies Barkingside Cemetery. In 1873 Dr Barnardo established his village home for girls in the grounds of Mossford Lodge, which was leased to him rent-free as a wedding present. Six hundred girls were soon accommodated in 30 buildings; the Barnado's village became a mixed facility in 1939. Meanwhile, the hamlet of Barkingside was expanding – its first police station had formerly been the Mossford Arms – and the opening of Barkingside railway station in 1903 confirmed its local dominance. Mossford Green was soon swallowed up and its separate identity is now all but forgotten. One reminder is Mossford Green Primary School, on Fairlop Road. In 1975, Barnardo's opened the New Mossford Centre, on Civic Way, as a home for disabled children. Barnardo's village closed in 1986 and the New Mossford Centre closed in 1992 as part of Barnardo's plan to disengage itself from running children's homes. The surviving cottages of Barnardo's village have recently been restored and sold as private residences. Barnardo's headquarters is on Tanners Lane and the organization continues to support local charitable work. A Tesco supermarket now occupies part of the grounds of Mossford Lodge.

⊠ Ilford IG6

Motspur Park • *Kingston/Merton*

An interwar suburban locality situated on the south-eastern side of NEW MALDEN and best known for its sports grounds. Some locals treat part or all of neighbouring WEST BARNES as though it were in Motspur Park, a confu-sion abetted by the location of Motspur Park station. The Mot family lived in the area in the 14th century and gave their name to a farm that lay west of the present railway line. In 1627 the farm was called Motes Firs, a reference to the furze (gorse) that grew round about. It had become Motts Spur Farm by 1823, and was later Mosper Farm. The railway line was built through the district in 1859 but no halt was provided here and only a few villas had appeared by the early 20th century, when a station finally opened. Holy Cross Church was built on Douglas Avenue in 1908, and rebuilt 40 years later following wartime damage. In the mid 1920s the construction of the Kingston bypass (A3) and the electrification of the railway stimulated a construction boom, with numerous small builders putting up terraces of three-bedroom houses. New bus services were laid on and parades of shops and the Earl Beatty pub were built. Between 1927 and 1937 the number of season tickets sold at the station increased more than tenfold. The accessibility of Motspur Park also attracted London institutions, which created sports grounds that have since been protected from development. The BBC Sports Club based itself at the White House, while at the University of London's athletics ground, several world records were broken in the years before and after World War II. In 1999 the university sold its ground to Fulham Football Club, which set up a training complex covered with an air dome. In 2002 Kingston council refused an application from Bewley Homes to demolish the White House, on the grounds that it was 'a building of townscape merit', but in the following year the company went ahead anyway before the matter could be considered at a public inquiry, and subsequently won the right to redevelop the site with housing. In 2005 the Irish entrepreneur Ben Dunne acquired the neighbouring 21 acres of metropolitan open land from the BBC for £3 million. East of the railway line, the Sir Joseph Hood Memorial Playing Fields have public sports facilities and a nature conservation area.

Motspur Park provided the backdrop for *Brush Strokes*, a television comedy series about an amorous painter and decorator, which ran for five series between 1986 and 1991.

⊠ New Malden KT3

🚆 South West Trains (zone 4)

Mottingham • *Bromley/Greenwich*

A challenged residential district located east

of GROVE PARK (Lewisham) and dominated by an interwar council estate, which was built in the direction of CHISLEHURST. An Anglo-Saxon charter of 862 identified the boundary of land belonging to Mōda's people. The name Mōda suggests someone who was proud, bold and hard-working. This was farmland until the mid 19th century, with a handful of large houses on Mottingham Lane, including Mottingham House and Fairy Hall, which was rebuilt in 1856. In the absence of a significant settlement, Mottingham station was at first called ELTHAM when it opened in 1866. Cottages were built on what is now Mottingham Road, with the shops of the Terrace. The West Park estate was laid out with houses for the middle classes in the 1880s and St Andrew's Church was built in the fields between the station and the village. The Royal Naval School moved from NEW CROSS to Fairy Hall in 1889. The hall was acquired by the School for the Sons of Missionaries in 1912 to form Eltham College. In the same year the Ironmongers' Company, a City guild, built Sir Robert Geffrye's almshouses on Mottingham Road to replace homes in SHOREDITCH (which were then reconstructed at the Geffrye Museum in HAGGERSTON). Suburban development began after the Sidcup Arterial Road (A20) opened in 1923. The London County Council acquired Court Farm and began to lay out the Mottingham estate. Schools and shops were provided and the first of the estate's 2,000 homes were occupied in 1935. The King and Queen pub opened in 1937. Mottingham House was demolished in 1969 and replaced with the flats of Colview Court. The foundations of a Tudor mansion were uncovered during construction. The Greater London Council acquired the Geffrye almshouses in 1971, remodelled them and built new housing in the grounds. More housing replaced the King and Queen pub in 1992. The ward's population is overwhelmingly white, but in other respects Mottingham stands out from the rest of the borough of Bromley, literally and figuratively. It has fewer married couples, lower car and home ownership and lower levels of educational attainment than the borough as a whole. In her history of Mottingham, Winifred Parkinson lists 'poverty, poor health, disadvantaged families, unemployment [and] insufficient investment in youth' among the challenges facing the district in the 21st century.

The cricketer W G Grace lived at Fairmount on Mottingham Lane from 1909 until his death here in 1915. Punk rocker Siouxsie Sioux

attended Mottingham Secondary School.

✉ SE9

👥 10,114 (Mottingham and Chislehurst North ward)

🚆 South Eastern Trains (zone 4)

📖 Winifred H Parkinson, *Mottingham: From Hamlet to Urban Village*, Bromley Leisure and Community Services, 2005

@ www.eltham-college.org.uk

Mount Pleasant • *Camden/Islington*

A densely built-up street and locality in west CLERKENWELL, rising from Farringdon Road to GRAY'S INN ROAD, behind Rosebery Avenue. Coldbath Prison was built here in 1794, with accommodation for 1,800 inmates, making it the largest British jail of its time. The neighbouring fields were the site of a protest meeting in 1833 at which a policeman was stabbed to death, yet the inquest jury returned a verdict of justifiable homicide. In 1886 the Post Office took over the prison, converting it into a sorting office. From 1927 until 2003 the sorting office had its own subterranean rail link to Paddington and Whitechapel. A 405-room Holiday Inn has replaced the Mount Pleasant Hotel, which looked like a Victorian jail but was none the worse for that. Across the road, Exmouth Market now has few stalls but has become a popular place to eat and drink. At the southern end of Mount Pleasant, the narrow street is crowded with tenements and council flats.

The essayist Leigh Hunt and his brother John were detained at Coldbath Prison in 1812, awaiting trial for libelling the Prince Regent.

✉ EC1; WC1

Mount Pleasant • *Hillingdon*

A mixed-use locality, also known as HAREFIELD West, rivalling LONGFORDMOOR as the most westerly settlement in Greater London. Domesday Book recorded the presence here of mills on the River Colne. The construction of the Grand Junction (now Grand Union) Canal brought some quite noxious industries and their spoil heaps in the early 19th century, and it is likely that the name Mount Pleasant was applied ironically. Lime kilns, copper mills and iron works were followed later by factories making printing inks and rubber products. Uxbridge council built two phases of housing here, after each of the world wars, and private developers have taken advantage of the lake views, the canal and the Colne. Salamander Quay is a well-established commercial centre, specialising in high-tech industries. Royal Quay is a 1990s restoration of the old Coppermill Lock buildings, which have been designated a conservation area. Park Wood lies north of Mount Pleasant and the Old Park Wood nature reserve is managed by the Wildlife Trust, which calls it 'possibly the most varied piece of woodland in Middlesex', and praises its wealth of spring flowers, which include yellow archangel, lesser celandine, wood anemone and the uncommon coralroot bittercress, as well as a carpet of bluebells.

✉ Uxbridge UB9

Mudchute • *Tower Hamlets*

An urban farm and park on the Isle of Dogs, with a Docklands Light Railway station serving the residential community of south MILLWALL. Its undulations and its name derive from silted mud dredged from the Millwall docks in the 1880s and 1890s; before this, the site had been used for grazing and as a brickfield. Huge quantities of sludge were pumped here and spewed out of a giant pneumatic tube. Following complaints that the mud heap was a health hazard, 'mudchuting' ceased around 1910. Poplar council compulsorily purchased the site in 1918 and the land was used for allotments and piggeries until World War II, when gun emplacements were installed. The site was later considered for housing but in 1977 it became Mudchute Farm, a 32-acre public park consisting of a working farm, designated wildlife areas, riding stables, wooded areas and open parkland. The World War II pillboxes were adapted as pens for the livestock. Mudchute station and the adjacent formal garden occupy the site of Hawkins and Tipsons rope works, which stood here from 1881 to 1971. Creators of the famous 'Hercules' rope, they were also pioneers in the less glamorous field of nylon rope-making.

The action in Deborah Crombie's 1999 detective novel *Kissed a Sad Goodbye* starts with the discovery of a body in Mudchute Park.

✉ E14

🚉 Docklands Light Railway, Lewisham branch (zone 2)

Muswell Hill • *Haringey*

An 'exceptional example of a complete Edwardian suburb', as Haringey council rightly calls it, situated north-west of its original parent, HORNSEY. The topographic feature from which the district takes its name is now surmounted by the ALEXANDRA PALACE. Muswell is a corruption of 'mossy well' and there was a spring here that was reputed to have restored the health of Malcolm IV of Scotland. Sixty-four acres of the manor of Hornsey were given to the nunnery of St Mary, CLERKENWELL in 1152 for use as a dairy farm. The sisters also maintained a small chapel here and pilgrims visited the health-giving well. The vestry of Clerkenwell's St James's Church acquired the priory's farmland after the dissolution of the monasteries. Following the Hornsey enclosure award, which took effect in 1816, sedate villas began to appear and the growth of the village led to the building of St James's Church in 1842. However, the relative inaccessibility of Muswell Hill (which persists to this day) protected it from the first wave of suburban development that washed across north London in the mid 19th century. Neither the opening of Alexandra Palace nor a half-hearted railway connection significantly disturbed the semi-rural serenity, partly because some of the village remained under Clerkenwell's jurisdiction until the end of the century. The termination of this anomaly, combined with the sale of several grand houses and their spacious grounds, resulted in the comprehensive transformation of Muswell Hill in the 20 years from 1895, with just two building firms responsible for almost all the work, which resulted in a particularly harmonious effect. Some shops and street furniture were inappropriately modernized later in the 20th century and the council has been working with conservation groups to try to restore lost or damaged features. With its high property prices, Muswell Hill's inhabitants tend to be aged over 30 and qualified to degree level or higher.

Former residents of interest, if only for their names, include a 17th-century Master of the Rolls called Sir Julius Caesar and the 18th-century bon viveur Topham Beauclerk and his wife, the former Lady Diana Spencer. The Kinks released their *Muswell Hillbillies* album in 1971.

✉ N10

♀ 9,975

📖 Jack Whitehead, *The Growth of Muswell Hill*, Jack Whitehead, 1998; Ken Gay, *Muswell Hill History and Guide*, Tempus, 2002

@ www.muswell-hill.com (commercial local information site)

Nag's Head • *Islington*

A bustling commercial zone centred around the junction of SEVEN SISTERS Road and HOL-LOWAY ROAD, regarded by Islington council as one of the borough's two most important 'town centres'. The locality is named after a public house that has stood here for around 200 years. For much of the 19th century the Nag's Head marked the northernmost edge of ISLINGTON'S spread and was the terminus for its first tramway in 1871. The vicinity became a hub for retailers serving the expanding middle-class community of HOLLOWAY, and the pub was rebuilt in Italianate style. Despite the neighbourhood's demographic transformation during the 20th century, the Nag's Head remained the borough's largest shopping area until the 1990s, when it was overtaken by the ANGEL, which was more successful in attracting new investment and drawing visitors from outside its immediate hinterland. The small Nag's Head shopping mall opened in 1992, anchored by a Safeway (now Morrison's) supermarket. The Nag's Head street market on the south side of Seven Sisters Road is open every day. Although there is a wide range of goods on other days of the week, it sells only second-hand items on Wednesdays and has a flea market on Sunday mornings. The west side of Holloway Road has a hall of residence for London Metropolitan University students and a lavish art deco cinema, opened as the Gaumont in 1938 but now an Odeon. The Nag's Head itself spent its latter years as an Irish theme pub and has recently been converted to retail use. In the last few years, the streets around the Nag's Head have become a focus for the sale of contraband and counterfeit cigarettes. The police and the council launched a crackdown in 2006.

The poet and painter Edward Lear, best known for his nonsense verse, was born at Bowman's Lodge in 1812 and lived here until the age of 16. The lodge was named after an Elizabethan archery house and its site is now occupied by Bowman's Mews.

✉ N7

Nash • *Bromley*

A farming hamlet lying three-quarters of a mile south-west of KESTON. Its name means 'place at the ash tree'. A local patch of gravel deposits ensured dry foundations for the building of cottages. From the 15th century the Causton family of Bexley steadily increased its holdings in the area. The subdivision of land between family members and internecine squabbles in the 1610s and 1620s sparked off a decline in the Caustons' dominance, though they retained a presence here for a further century. For most of its existence, Nash has been wholly agricultural in character, inhabited by farmers and their labourers, and the occasional woodcutter. The hamlet still consists of only a handful of brick and flint cottages (most built before 1900), the 18th-century Nash House and a scattering of outlying farms. The Metropolitan Police dog training establishment moved to Layhams Road in 1953. Its 15-acre site has over 100 kennels and a unique, purpose-built facility performing artificial insemination using frozen genetic material that has been taken from working police dogs. The Nash circular walk is a four-mile trail through undulating countryside and woodland, taking in Keston as well as Nash. It begins at a car park off Heathfield Road on Keston Common, the highest point on the route.

✉ Keston BR2

Neasden • *Brent*

Once nicknamed 'the loneliest village in London', Neasden is now a characterless suburb sliced in two by the North Circular Road (A406) and separated from WEMBLEY by the River Brent. Its name may have meant 'nose hill', a reference to its location on a small promontory at the end of the Dollis Hill ridge. Before the Norman conquest Neasden may have been more important than WILLESDEN but it was no more than a 'retired hamlet' when enclosure was completed in 1823. At this time there were six cottages, four larger houses or farms, a public house and a smithy, grouped around the green. The dwellings included The Grove, which had been bought by a London solicitor named James Hall, and its former outbuilding, which Hall had converted into a house that became known as The Grange. In the 1870s, Neasden remained the most rural part of Willesden, although its housing stock had risen to around 50 and the Spotted Dog inn was attracting London daytrippers. Transport developments of various kinds shaped Neasden's subsequent evolution. Neasden station opened in 1880 (as KINGSBURY and Neasden) and a railway engineering works was established two years later, with workers' housing at Neasden Village, enlarged in the 1920s. Until the arrival of the motor car, Neasden's farms were largely given over to the rearing and stabling of horses. The North Circular Road was built in 1923, and over the next decade massive private housing estates swallowed up almost all the remaining farmland. A shopping centre was completed shortly afterwards and the Ritz cinema opened in 1935. All of Neasden's older houses were demolished during this period, except for The Grange; the Spotted Dog was rebuilt in mock-Tudor style. A number of houses were sacrificed to the enlargement of the North Circular in 1973, which blighted the shopping centre. Superstores and retail warehouses have since clustered around the road in the southern part of the district. In 1995 Neasden became the unlikely home of the biggest Hindu temple outside India: the Shri Swaminarayan Mandir. Until 2004 The Grange housed the borough's museum and archive, which has since moved to WILLESDEN GREEN. The Grange is to become a development unit supporting new business start-ups.

In the 1960s and 1970s *Private Eye* magazine seized on Neasden as a stereotypically bland address for 'nobodies' like Sid and Doris Bonkers. The model-turned-actress Twiggy came from Neasden. David Sutherland's children's novel *A Black Hole in Neasden* reveals a gateway to an alternate universe in a Neasden back garden.

✉ NW2; NW10

🚇 Jubilee Line (zone 3)

📖 Kenneth J Valentine, *Neasden: A Historical Study*, Skilton, 1990

@ www.mandir.org (Shri Swaminarayan Mandir site)

New Addington • *Croydon*

A new town, though never an officially designated 'New Town', in the far east of the borough, set on a steep hillside rising into the North Downs by nearly 200 feet along its north-south axis. New Addington's centre lies two-and-a-half miles south of the nearest railway station, at WEST WICKHAM. Domesday Book records that 'Albert the clerk holds of the king ADDINGTON. Osweard held it of King Edward. It was then assessed at eight hides; now at two. There is land for four ploughs ... woodland for 20 pigs'. This was the manor later known as Addington Temple, which covered roughly the area of modern New Addington. It remained farmland until well into the 20th century. In 1935 the First National Housing Trust acquired 569 acres of Fisher's Farm to lay out a garden village. Croydon council supported the plan as a way of reducing the over-crowding in its semi-slum urban areas, and over 1,000 homes had been built by the time that the outbreak of World War II halted construction. After the war the need for new housing was even more pressing, but there was also pressure to protect London's countryside. The borough took over the housing trust's unused land and acquired a further 400 acres, while the land west of Lodge Lane was designated as green belt. Construction to the original plan was completed by 1963, but continuing housing need prompted another extension to New Addington five years later. This latter part is known as the Fieldway estate and has become the most disadvantaged part of the district. As one of the largest estates in London without any nearby rail services, New Addington's inaccessibility was a major reason for the creation of Croydon Tramlink, which arrived here in 2000. Fieldway and New Addington are the borough's first and second most deprived wards and are the principal recipients of its regeneration funds. A 2001 planning document declared the council's aim to counter the perception that 'if you come to live in New Addington, you've failed'.

✉ Croydon CR0

👥 21,527 (Fieldway and New Addington wards)

🚇 Croydon Tramlink, Route 3 (King Henry's Drive; New Addington (terminus))

New Barnet • *Barnet*

A Victorian township that sprang up between CHIPPING BARNET and EAST BARNET following the opening of a station on the new Great

Northern Railway line in 1850. Station Road was built to provide access to Chipping Barnet. Houses went up on both sides of the railway tracks, with the pace of development accelerating towards the end of the 19th century. A clear distinction arose between the villas erected for the middle classes on the higher slopes to the west and the working-class housing and shops east of the tracks. Many of the latter homes provided domestic servants for the former. The grandest estate was LYONS-DOWN, to the south-west, laid out in the grounds of the former house of that name. Elsewhere, most of New Barnet had hitherto been meadowland. E Fergusson Taylor has been called 'the creator of New Barnet'. Taylor was an entrepreneurial estate agent and property developer who marketed his sites with a vigour that would make modern practitioners blush. He also encouraged the building of churches, a town hall, a temperance hall – and a coffee house that would divert would-be gin drinkers.

✉ Barnet EN4 and EN5

🚆 WAGN Railway (zone 5)

New Beckenham • *Bromley*

A Victorian creation in north-west BECKENHAM, increasingly succumbing to redevelopment. New Beckenham station opened on the Mid-Kent Railway in 1864 and very quickly gave its name to streets being laid out on COPERS COPE Farm, and soon afterwards to similar developments on neighbouring Foxgrove Farm. An iron Congregational church was built near the station and several private schools were established in the area, including at Minshall House, now replaced by the flats of Minshall Court. New Beckenham station was rebuilt in stages on a site to the north of its predecessor and completed in 1904, allowing trains from Beckenham Junction to stop. Remnants of the earlier station's platforms are still visible, together with a railwayman's cottage. During the first decade of the 20th century several large sports grounds were laid out in the north of the district, and these are now the home of the sports clubs of some leading financial institutions. The replacement of large Victorian houses with small blocks of apartments has been the dominant theme of building activity in the last few decades.

✉ Beckenham BR3

🚆 South Eastern Trains (zone 4)

Newbury Park • *Redbridge*

A nondescript area of mixed private and local authority housing in north-east ILFORD, straddling the Eastern Avenue (A12). The manor of Newbury was part of BARKING Abbey's extensive landholdings in the Ilford area until the dissolution of the monasteries, when Henry VIII granted it to Sir Richard Gresham. The land remained in wholly agricultural use until the late 19th century, when the first suburban houses were built, together with a primary school. In 1903 the Great Eastern Railway Co. opened the FAIRLOP loop, which linked WOODFORD with a junction on its main line between Ilford and SEVEN KINGS. This was a speculative project based on the assumption that Ilford's housing boom would bring continued northward expansion, and a substantial station was built at Newbury Park in anticipation of heavy traffic. A new school was provided and 142 house plots were offered for sale on the Newbury Park estate but investors failed to materialize. Only four plots were sold (on Hertford Road) at £42 each. It was not until the arrival of the Eastern Avenue in the mid 1920s that property developers filled the district with compact housing. To the south, the Plessey Co. began manufacturing electronic communications equipment on a new site at the junction of Ley Street and Vicarage Lane. In 1936 work began on a tunnel that would link the Central Line with the Fairlop loop at Newbury Park. Construction was halted by the outbreak of war and a Plessey production line was set up in the tunnel. At the end of 1947, underground trains finally replaced the old steam service and this was accompanied by the distinctive remodelling of the existing station, with an arched concrete canopy for buses, which won a Festival of Britain award for architectural merit. Newbury Park has a growing south Asian population, mainly of Indian and Tamil descent. At Newbury Park Primary School almost three-quarters of children speak English as an additional language.

✉ Ilford IG2

👥 13,074 (Newbury ward)

🚆 Central Line (zone 4)

New Charlton • *Greenwich*

A changing industrial area lying north of 'old' CHARLTON and east of the GREENWICH PENINSULA. The first factories were built around the time of the opening of the railway line to Angerstein Wharf in 1852. The wharf lies on the western side of New Charlton and the line was a private project for freight trains; it is still in use. Glass, rope and, later, cable manufacturing were the principal industries. Siemens opened its factory on the WOOLWICH border in 1863. William Cory built and operated barges that delivered coal and hay to London and took away refuse for disposal on the Kent and Essex marshes; more than a century later New Charlton is still a major base for the company, which now specializes in recycling and waste management. Charlton Athletic Football Club was founded by a group of teenagers on East Street (now Eastmoor Street) in 1905. New Charlton flourished between the wars but declined from the 1960s. The closure of the Siemens factory in 1967 caused an outpouring of dismay and anger that is hard to imagine now. Much of the heavy industry has since been replaced by trading estates or retail warehouses. Construction work began on the Thames Flood Barrier between New Charlton and SILVERTOWN in 1974 and it opened ten years later; this is the world's second largest movable flood barrier but it may need to be upgraded or replaced by 2030. The barrier control building is on the New Charlton side of the Thames and the nearby learning centre caters for school groups, while a smaller information unit and café are open to the general public. A riverside walk passes the barrier and the Anchor and Hope pub, to its west. Another Victorian pub, originally called the Lads of the Village and later the Thames Barrier Arms, is now an animal care clinic. As the last industries leave New Charlton, the valuable land is certain to be built up with housing, mainly in the form of apartment blocks with river views.

✉ SE7

🚢 Barrier Gardens pier

New Covent Garden *see* NINE ELMS

New Cross • *Lewisham*
A racially and socially diverse district located south-west of DEPTFORD. This was the site of a crossroads on the Kent/Surrey border and New Cross Heath was recorded in the 15th century, when the surrounding area was still heavily wooded. Two City guilds have had a defining influence on New Cross. The Worshipful Company of Haberdashers acquired much of the land in 1614 as an endowment for its charity. The company leased large houses to its members and other gentlemen in the 18th century and developed the land more intensively from the mid 19th century, after the coming of the railway. The Royal Naval School

opened in 1843 and the building was taken over by the Goldsmiths' Company's Technical and Recreative Institute in 1891. The institute evolved into Goldsmiths College and is now part of the University of London. Deptford Town Hall, completed in 1907, has maritime sculptures and carvings celebrating the old borough's heritage. Another New Cross landmark, the Super Kinema, opened in 1925 and is now the Venue nightclub. Much of the Victorian housing has been subdivided into flats, many of which are now occupied by Goldsmiths' students. Other houses were replaced in the 1970s by council estates and by the 15-acre Fordham Park. Over the second half of the 20th century many black people settled in New Cross, at first mainly from the Caribbean but later increasingly of African origin. The number of black or black British residents is now roughly equal to the number of white British residents. In 1981, 14 black youngsters died in a fire during a house party in New Cross Road. The police repeatedly rejected the possibility of a racist arson attack and 15,000 people marched through London to protest. The families held the 25th and final annual memorial service in 2006, having decided to focus on private remembrance and key anniversaries in the future. The Mayor of Lewisham has founded a commemorative bursary scheme in conjunction with Goldsmiths College.

Sir Barnes Wallis, who designed the bouncing bomb used in the 'Dambusters' raid in World War II, lived in New Cross for the first quarter of the 20th century. The actor Gary Oldman was born in New Cross in 1958. Carter USM's *The Only Living Boy in New Cross* was a top ten hit in 1992.

✉ SE14

👥 15,093

🚉 South Eastern Trains; East London Line branch terminus (zone 2)

@ www.goldsmiths.ac.uk; www.thevenuelondon.com

New Cross Gate • *Lewisham*
The western part of NEW CROSS, taking its name from a tollgate erected in 1718 at the top of what is now Clifton Rise. The gate was relocated in 1813 to the junction of New Cross Road and Peckham Lane (now QUEENS ROAD). This part of New Cross Road was built up from the 1820s with good-quality terraced housing. The station opened in 1839, originally as New Cross, and a prolonged period of

building began soon afterwards. Many early properties have since either been replaced or converted to new uses. Terraced houses on New Cross Road have had shops built over their front gardens, while houses elsewhere have been subdivided into flats. A Sainsbury's supermarket occupies the site of former locomotive sheds and workshops. The tram depot that was built in 1906 was replaced by a bus garage in the 1950s. The Electric Empire cinema that opened in 1909 is now a Clutch Clinic.

Charles Dickens kept a secret apartment here, a semi-rural retreat where he wrote *Bleak House* and later completed *Great Expectations*. The lodgings also provided him with convenient access to his mistress in NUN-HEAD.

✉ SE14

🚉 Southern; East London Line branch terminus (zone 2)

New Eltham • *Greenwich*

A predominantly white, working-class district situated south-east of ELTHAM proper and east of MOTTINGHAM. This was formerly the farming hamlet of Pope Street, which was centred on what is now Avery Hill Road. Pope Street was the original name of the station that opened here in 1878, primarily to serve first-class ticket holders who maintained rural retreats in the area. An early phase of building followed the arrival of the railway but the village retained a rural character to the end of the 19th century. Several of the old fields have survived, with their original boundaries, as sports grounds. The Beehive Inn was rebuilt in 1897 and used the adjacent field as a venue for trotting races and travelling circuses. New Eltham's remaining streets were laid out in the early 1930s and most of the present housing dates from that period. The community finally gained a library in 1931. A handful of light industrial enterprises opened, but most have since departed. One of the last to go was Dickerson's, a builders' merchant and plant hire contractor, which relocated to Norfolk in 1996 after 80 years in New Eltham. The company's Avery Hill Road site was soon built over with houses and flats. Infilling has added a number of newer properties, and there may be more building in future if further sports grounds are lost.

At present, the northern part of New Eltham is packed with sports facilities, among them the Sparrows Lane training ground of Charlton Athletic Football Club.

✉ SE9

👥 12,425 (Coldharbour and New Eltham ward)

🚉 South Eastern Trains (zone 4)

📖 John Kennett (ed.), *Memories of New Eltham*, Eltham Society, 1998

New End • *Camden*

The north-eastern corner of central HAMPSTEAD, east of Heath Street. With the development of Hampstead as a spa at the beginning of the 18th century, an ancillary quarter sprang up here with gambling dens and souvenir shops surrounded by new homes and lodging houses. The grandest surviving property was built in 1703 for the Sewells, a Quaker family, and later named Burgh House after its tenth owner, the wealthy clergyman Allatson Burgh. For a while New End was the poor corner of Hampstead, with its relatively humble cottages providing accommodation for artisans. The parish workhouse was founded here in 1800 and rebuilt in 1845, serving also as an infirmary and offices for the vestry, and later becoming New End hospital. As Hampstead's star rose, New End was enfolded in the embrace of its parent during the late 19th century. New End Primary School opened in 1906. Parts of New End were rebuilt in the 1930s, including the Old White Bear and the Duke of Hamilton public houses. The council added a few flats after World War II and most of the shops were gradually replaced by houses. After the closure of New End Hospital, the site was sold in 1986 to fund the redevelopment of the nearby Queen Mary's Maternity Home as a unit for the care of the elderly. Berkeley Homes converted the hospital buildings for residential use in 1996 and a year later New End School added a nursery in the grounds.

Since 1974, New End Theatre has occupied the former mortuary of New End Hospital, where Karl Marx was laid out before his burial in HIGHGATE Cemetery. Saved from conversion to offices in 1979, Burgh House is now home to the Hampstead Museum, which has a local history collection and watercolours from the Helen Allingham collection.

✉ NW3

@ www.burghhouse.org.uk; www.newendtheatre.co.uk

Newington • *Southwark*

The correct name for the southern part of SOUTHWARK, which is generally called ELE-

PHANT AND CASTLE to avoid confusion with STOKE NEWINGTON. It seems likely that Newington (which means 'new farmstead') grew up after about 1200, when the establishment of nearby Lambeth Palace brought increased traffic along the Kent road. Until the second half of the 18th century it remained a sparsely populated farming village with a little industry, notably the manufacture of clay tobacco pipes. Thereafter, new roads brought development opportunities and landowner Henry Penton (who created Pentonville) began to sell off some of his farmland. The 19th century saw increasingly dense housebuilding, mainly speculative but some philanthropic. Trinity Church was built in 1824 on land in the north of the parish that has belonged to the Corporation of Trinity House since 1661. The surrounding square was then laid out with smart terraced houses, many of which have since been converted laterally into flats across two or three house widths. With the magnificent exception of this estate, most of Newington was rebuilt in the course of the 20th century by a succession of municipal authorities. In 1975 Trinity Church became Henry Wood Hall, a rehearsal and recording venue for several orchestras, including the London Philharmonic. The population of Newington is multiethnic, with those of black African descent constituting the largest minority. Most residents rent from the council and do not own a car. Unemployment is high.

Newington Gardens is a small recreation ground beside the Inner London Sessions House, a Crown court. The park occupies the site of Horsemonger Lane Gaol, once the largest prison in Surrey, which stood here for nearly a century from 1791. That same year saw the birth in Newington Butts of Michael Faraday, the blacksmith's son who went on to become a pioneer in chemistry and electrophysics. Newington Butts is cockney rhyming slang for 'guts'.

✉ SE1

♦ 12,870

@ www.tnra.net (Trinity Newington Residents' Association site); www.hwh.co.uk (Henry Wood Hall site)

Newlands • *Barnet*

A handful of upmarket residential streets in north-west EDGWARE, squeezed between BROCKLEY HILL (A5) and Edgware Way (A41), with access from the former. Evidence of Roman cremation burials has been found at

Piper's Green Lane, formerly Green Lane. This was part of Edgware manor, which belonged to All Souls College, Oxford from 1443, as the neighbouring undeveloped land still does. The Newlands name may refer to former woodland newly brought into agricultural use, perhaps in the early 16th century. Piper's Green certainly had a farmhouse and outbuildings in 1597, when the college commissioned a map of its manor. Newlands underwent some tentative residential development from the early 19th century, including the building of Bromfield House and Newlands Grange, stucco houses demolished after World War II. Since that time a series of detached properties has been built along and off Piper's Green Lane. Some of the newer houses boast distinctive designs and substantial proportions, and occasional satisfying use of weatherboarding. The lane continues as a wooded footpath beside EDGWAREBURY golf course. The former common land at Piper's Green has been replaced by a sports ground.

✉ Edgware HA8

Newlands • *Southwark*

A residential enclave in south-east NUNHEAD, bounded by CAMBERWELL New Cemetery and by Nunhead Cemetery and waterworks. The original Newlands was a late-Victorian estate for the lower middle classes, built up in piecemeal fashion in the area north-west of Surrey Road. The estate was unsuccessful at first, not least because of the absence of mains drainage; properties here still had cesspools in 1883. The speculative builder Edward Yates laid out the much larger Waverley Park estate from 1884. The housing was followed successively by shops, a public house and a board school. In 1903, St Silas' Church was erected at the northern end of Athenlay Road. Beneath the Aquarius golf course is Europe's largest man-made underground reservoir, opened in 1909. Waverley School takes 11–16-year-old girls from six London boroughs and from a rich mix of ethnic groups and cultures.

✉ SE15; SE22

New Malden • *Kingston*

London's unlikely Korea Town, situated southeast of NORBITON. New Malden began to develop as a separate township from KINGSTON in the second half of the 19th century, boosted by the coming of the railway in 1846 and the opening of the Kingston loop line in the late 1860s, when Christ Church was built on Coombe Road. Until this time the area consisted mostly of farms and smallholdings, separated from Kingston by NORBITON COMMON. Some large villas were built on Kingston Road, and those that remain have almost all been converted to flats or offices. The first new roads to be laid out were the Groves named after trees, to the north-west of the station, which is now designated as a conservation area. New Malden became an urban district in 1894. Suburban development reached a peak in the 1930s, with modest terraced and semi-detached houses filling the area south of Kingston Road, and the town became a borough in 1936. New Malden has long had an industrial element and was subjected to bombing during the Blitz, which had the effect of clearing the way for more housing after the war. Motor vehicle repair is the dominant surviving form of light industry. Two 16-storey office blocks were built near the station in the mid 1960s, and more offices appeared later on Kingston Road. With around 10,000 Korean residents in the vicinity, New Malden has the largest and most concentrated Korean population in Europe. No one is quite sure how this came about. One explanation is that 1970s Korean expatriates followed the example of their ambassador and settled in WIMBLEDON, but when prices there rose excessively they decamped to nearby New Malden. The community is served by its own shops, restaurants and other enterprises, and several local churches hold services in the Korean language. New Malden also has a sizeable Tamil population, originating from Sri Lanka.

The sculptor Anthony Caro and the folk violinist Dave Swarbrick were both born in New Malden.

✉ New Malden KT3

🚊 South West Trains (zone 4)

📖 Stephen H Day, *Malden – Old and New,* Marine Day, 1990; Stephen H Day, *Malden – Old and New: Revisited,* Marine Day, 1991

New River Village • *Haringey*
A high-density, high-price housing estate in north-east HORNSEY, built on the 15-acre site of a former waterworks in the early years of the 21st century. This is one of several London projects undertaken by St James Homes, a joint venture between Thames Water and private developers the Berkeley Group that is capitalizing on the opportunities offered by disused utilities sites. Most of the housing units in the 'village' are studios and one- and two-bedroom flats but larger apartments,

maisonettes and houses are also included. The Victorian pump house has been converted into a restaurant, gym and art gallery, a linear park borders the New River, and almost all car parking has been pushed underground. New River Village won a housing design award in 2005 but critics have expressed fears that its brash appearance may not date well. More than 600 homes are planned for completion by 2008.

✉ N8

@ www.stjameshomes.co.uk

New Southgate • *Enfield*
An invented and then reinvented residential district situated to the south of ARNOS GROVE Tube station. It is not surprising that New Southgate should have had to borrow its name from its older neighbour because there was absolutely nothing here until the Great Northern Railway arrived, apart from two groups of farm buildings in Bowes Road. If this place was thought of at all, it was as an eastern extension of COLNEY HATCH – and this was the name originally given to the station when it opened in 1850. Betstyle Lodge appeared around this time and a gasworks was built to the south of the station in 1858. The wheel-shaped New Southgate Cemetery opened in 1861 as the Great Northern Cemetery and was set to become the site of the first crematorium in Britain until the Bishop of Rochester intervened and overruled the plan. The triangle bounded by High Road, Palmers Road and Bowes Road had filled with good quality housing by 1867, but went downmarket because the middle classes could not be persuaded to live so near to the lunatic asylum at Colney Hatch. The invention of the 'New Southgate' name was primarily a device designed to dissociate the settlement from the madness of Colney Hatch. St Paul's Church, New Southgate was consecrated in 1873. By 1897 New Southgate was fully built up and increasingly working class in character, but open country still separated it from WOOD GREEN to the south-east. The North Circular Road (A406) was completed by 1929, bringing more housebuilding to its hinterland. The area began to gain a Jewish population in the 1930s. After World War II, Southgate council looked at the bomb sites and the run-down housing, consulted with residents and in 1956 announced its intention to almost entirely rebuild New Southgate. The project began in 1959 with the erection of tower blocks in Highview Gardens that were completed in

1960. Enfield council took over the redevelopment programme in 1965 and completed it in the mid 1970s.

Jerome K Jerome, the prolific novelist, dramatist and essayist now chiefly remembered as the author of *Three Men in a Boat*, lived for part of his childhood at Springfield Road. The site of the house is now occupied by Garfield School. New Southgate Cemetery includes Caribbean, Greek Orthodox and Roman Catholic sections, and is the resting place of Shoghi Effendi, guardian of the Baha'i faith, who died while visiting London in 1957.

✉ N11

🚆 WAGN Railway (zone 4)

📖 David Pam, *Southgate and Winchmore Hill: A Short History*, Enfield, 1982

@ www.newsouthgate.com (cemetery site)

Newyears Green • *Hillingdon*

A scattered collection of small farms and civic amenities situated north of ICKENHAM and west of RUISLIP, and surrounded on all sides by green-belt farmland. The origin of the name, which is also spelt as three separate words, is uncertain. It is probably a corruption of a landowner's name but may refer to annual festivities – which would have been held on 'Lady Day', the feast of the Annunciation of the Blessed Virgin on 25 March, which was reckoned as the beginning of the year in England from the Middle Ages until 1752. Drawn in 1754, Rocque's map of Middlesex shows a small group of dwellings here. The dog-leg bend in Newyears Green Lane marks the point where the road used to fork off across HAREFIELD Lane (now Breakspear Road) to Ickenham but this route was closed after the enclosure of the fields in 1813. Despite its rural setting and idyllic name, much of Newyears Green is literally a dump. Newyears Green Lane has a recycling centre, waste transfer station and car breaker's yard. Not content with these facilities, flytippers deposit their loads in every available lay-by – usually right in front of the council's 'no tipping' signs. Dews Farm Sandpits, alongside Harvil Road, are managed by the London Wildlife Trust. There is woodland and scrub around varied grassland rich in flowers and insects.

✉ Uxbridge UB9

Nine Elms • *Wandsworth*

A predominantly commercial riverside area situated between BATTERSEA PARK and VAUXHALL. In the early 19th century market gardens filled most of the land here, growing asparagus and other vegetables for the London markets. In 1838 the London and Southampton Railway Co. opened its terminus at Nine Elms. The line was extended to Waterloo in 1848 and Nine Elms became the site of a goods yard and locomotive works. A gasworks was built and in 1865 this was the scene of the largest explosion in 19th-century London; a million cubic feet of gas ignited and eleven men were killed in the blast. The neighbouring housing was inevitably cramped and grimy and there was widespread poverty among the residents. In 1914 the pioneering Nine Elms Settlement, established by the Women's Freedom League in Everett Street (now demolished), served children with dinners of vegetarian soup and large slices of pudding, which they could either eat there or take home. From 1933 Battersea power station was built on the western side of Nine Elms. Sir Giles Gilbert Scott's structure has a steel girder frame and exterior brick cladding, and is said to be the largest brick building in Europe. It is actually two power stations, the second of which was not built until 1953, when the third and fourth chimneys were added. Following a progressive run-down, the power station closed in 1983 and has since been undergoing a protracted conversion into a major leisure destination. In 1974 Covent Garden's flower market and fruit and vegetable market moved to Nine Elms, taking over the site of the north and south railway goods depots. A large Royal Mail sorting office occupies the site of Everett Street. Other commercial premises now at Nine Elms include the Stationery Office and a Sainsbury's superstore. Waterside apartment complexes, such as Elm Quay, have added an upmarket residential aspect to the district.

✉ SW8

📖 Colin Allen, *Transplanting the Garden*, Covent Garden Market Authority, 1998

@ www.cgma.gov.uk (New Covent Garden Market site)

Noak Hill • *Havering*

A real village on a real hill, Noak Hill is perched amidst rolling farmland in the far north-eastern corner of Greater London. The name signified a place by an oak tree and was first recorded in 1490 but is certainly of considerably earlier origin. An area of Roman tiles '300 paces long' was discovered when the commons were enclosed. The late-17th-century Bear inn, on the edge of HAROLD HILL, was called the Goat House until 1715. Richard Neave acquired the Dagnam Park estate to the south in 1772 and bought his first property in Noak Hill in 1781. Neave was chairman of the West India Merchants, a director of the Hudson's Bay Company, governor of the Bank of England in the mid 1780s and later High Sheriff of Essex and was created baronet in 1795. Noak Hill Common and Havering Plain, which together covered almost 500 acres, were enclosed in 1814. Sir Thomas Neave continued to expand the family's property portfolio by purchasing the Angel and Bear public houses later in the decade and he converted the Angel into two cottages, which survive today. The attractive red-brick St Thomas's Church was built as a chapel of ease for Lady Frances Neave in 1842 and a school was added in 1848. Noak Hill remained a village of agricultural labourers and Neave family servants until after World War I, when another Sir Thomas Neave sold most of the family's property here at auction. The family retained their mansion, Dagnams, its park and Dagnam Park Farm until after World War II, and Dagnams was demolished in 1950. During the 1960s the Bear inn boasted a menagerie that was claimed to be the largest in the London area outside REGENT'S PARK. The little zoo was closed after the death of the pub's owner in the early 1970s. Although within audible distance of the M25 motorway and now inhabited by a commuting community, Noak Hill retains weatherboarded and thatched cottages, including the former gamekeeper's home. The old schoolhouse was converted into a restaurant in the late 20th century but has since reverted to private educational use.

✉ Romford RM4 and RM3

@ www.friendsofdagnampark.org.uk

Noel Park • Haringey

A multi-ethnic locality situated to the southeast of WOOD GREEN Tube station and sometimes called the Scotch estate. This had been 100 acres of farmland belonging to Dovecote House (also known as Ducketts) and was laid out by the Artisans', Labourers' and General Dwellings Co. between 1883 and 1907. The estate was named after the company's chairman, Ernest Noel MP. The project took advantage of the opening of a station on the Palace Gates branch line in 1878, which provided a convenient route to the docks and factories of east London, with early workmen's fares. Five types of houses were built, most of which were

offered at rents of less than £25 a year. St Mark's Church and Noel Park Board School opened in 1889, and the company demolished some mid-Victorian villas to build shops on Dovecote Avenue. Residents were entertained at the Empire Theatre from 1912 but no public houses were permitted on the estate. A later phase of housebuilding filling the gap between Moselle Avenue and Lordship Lane was completed by 1927, by which time the network of tightly packed terraces had over 2,000 houses. Noel Park and Wood Green station closed in 1963 and was demolished in the 1970s to make way for Wood Green Shopping City, while the old goods yard became the site of the Sandlings housing development. Noel Park's housing stock now consists mainly of multi-occupancy houses, rented accommodation and council housing. At Noel Park Primary School, 86 per cent of children are from ethnic minority backgrounds, mostly black African and black Caribbean.

After the closure of the Empire Theatre in 1955, Associated Television used it as a production studio for several years, and made the seminal hospital drama series *Emergency Ward 10* here.

✉ N22

♦ 11,472

Norbiton • Kingston

A downmarket eastern extension of KINGSTON UPON THAMES. The settlement was recorded in 1205 as Norberton, signifying a northern grange or an outlying farm, with its southern counterpart at SURBITON. In the mid 18th century Norbiton Hall was the residence of Sir John Phillips, whose Senegalese retainer Cesar Picton later became a respected coal merchant and gentleman of Kingston, in an early example of successful black entrepreneurship. Norbiton Hall and another grand house called Norbiton Place were swallowed by suburban London after the coming of the railways. The Kingston union workhouse moved to Coombe Road in the late 1830s, accommodating up to 320 inmates. The parish of Norbiton was created in 1842 and St Peter's Church was built by George Gilbert Scott. This was one of the great architect's first ecclesiastical efforts and he later unjustly dismissed it as 'ignoble'. An infirmary built alongside the Coombe Road workhouse became a separate institution in 1902, and is now Kingston Hospital. The borough's first council estate was begun on Cambridge Road in 1921 and subsequently extended in several phases. Like other parts of Kingston, Norbiton also had a manufacturing base. Celestion Ltd, best known for its loudspeakers, moved to a site opposite the church in 1929 and remained here until 1948. Norbiton Hall was rebuilt as a mansion block in the 1930s. Other purpose-built apartment blocks have begun to change the residential landscape in recent years. The former YMCA building on Coombe Road was reopened in 2003 as the Shiraz Mirza community hall and is intended to serve as a multi-cultural hub for the borough's residents and voluntary groups. Norbiton is the poorest ward in a rich borough, with more council housing and higher unemployment than most other parts of south-west London.

In a twist on the hackneyed use of Surbiton as the archetypal London suburb, writer David Nobbs set *The Fall and Rise of Reginald Perrin* in the Norbiton area. Starring Leonard Rossiter, this popular television comedy ran for three series in the late 1970s.

✉ Kingston upon Thames KT1 and KT2

♦ 8,844

🚉 South West Trains (zone 5)

@ www.shirazm.co.uk (Shiraz Mirza community hall site)

Norbiton Common • *Kingston*

A rarely used name for the southern part of NORBITON, and formerly a separate parish. Seven acres were marked out in 1697 to 'set the poor to work' cultivating flax. The whole 320-acre common was enclosed in 1808 and soon filled with farms and smallholdings. Norbiton Common Farm later became a branch of the KINGSTON workhouse. After the railway reached Norbiton in the 1850s much of the agricultural land was sold off for development. Around Kingston Road the original dwellings have almost all been replaced with council houses, which are now in a variety of states: some cared for, some not. Despite the council's specially targeted efforts, parts of Norbiton Common remain a blackspot for rubbish dumping and particularly for graffiti, which covers everything from garden fences to lamp-posts. The Mount Primary School, on Dickerage Lane, takes most of its pupils from the neighbouring council estates. In line with the area's ethnic profile, the school has a growing number of Korean children. Three of the school's dilapidated old buildings were demolished in 1993 and have been replaced by the executive homes of Archdale Place.

South of Kingston Road are the Kingsmeadow sports complex and the Searchlight youth and community centre. Kingsmeadow is home to Kingstonian Football Club and AFC Wimbledon – the breakaway club from Wimbledon Football Club, formed in 2002. Kingstonian moved here in 1989 and the ground was improved to Football League standard early in 2001.

✉ Kingston upon Thames KT1; New Malden KT3

@ www.kingstonian.net;
www.afcwimbledon.com

Norbury • *Croydon*

A multi-ethnic district consisting mainly of former council houses, situated between THORNTON HEATH and STREATHAM. The existence of a manor house was first noted in 1229 and it was known by 1359 as Northbury, the 'northern manor house' of Croydon. The manor extended across the London road and included the common that was later called Thornton Heath. It was in the possession of the Carews of BEDDINGTON for almost five centuries from 1385. Norbury Hall was built in 1802 and is said to have been designed by John Nash, although there is little evidence to support this claim. The grey-brick mansion is now a retirement home, with playing fields occupying its former grounds. From 1868 horse races were held on land to the west of the London road. Horses were brought here from STREATHAM COMMON station until a station was opened at Norbury in 1878 with long ramps leading down the embankment to the platforms. However, the increasingly unruly race meetings were halted soon afterwards. The railway connection failed to stimulate development and the open land attracted the attention of the London County Council in 1901. The LCC acquired 30 acres to the south-west of the station for one of its first 'out-county' estates, built beyond what was then the London boundary. Norbury station was rebuilt to handle the increase in traffic and an electric tram service ran along London Road. A first phase of nearly 500 terraced 'cottage homes' was mostly complete by 1910, accompanied within two years by a handful of shops – but no pubs were permitted. The manor house, which had become Norbury Farm, was demolished in 1914 and its site is marked by Manor Farm Road. After World War I, the LCC built a second phase of its cottage estate, influenced by the design of HAMPSTEAD GARDEN SUBURB. Croydon council added more municipal dwellings in the latter part of the 1920s and acquired the 18-hole North Surrey golf course in 1935, which it then laid out as Norbury Park. The park is traversed by an open section of the Norbury Brook, which is called the River Graveney to the west of Hermitage Bridge, said to be named after one or more hermits who once lived nearby. Since World War II the most visible change in Norbury has been the construction of office blocks on London Road (A23), mostly in the early 1960s. There are proposals to extend the Croydon Tramlink as far as Norbury, via Streatham. All the main ethnic minorities are well represented in Norbury and almost three-quarters of homes are owner-occupied.

Sherlock Holmes wanted Dr Watson to whisper 'Norbury' in his ear whenever he became over-confident, on account of his misinterpretation of the evidence in the case of *The Yellow Face*. The comedian Will Hay lived at 45 The Chase between 1927 and 1934. Hay was best known for playing a bombastic schoolmaster and appeared in 18 films during his Norbury residence; comedian and actor Roy Hudd unveiled a blue plaque on Hay's house in 2000. Norbury was also the home of Derek Bentley, controversially hanged for his part in the killing of a Croydon policeman in 1952.

✉ SW16

👥 13,812

🚆 Southern (zone 4)

📖 Raymond Wheeler, *Images of Norbury, Thornton Heath and Broad Green*, Tempus, 2002

North Acton • *Ealing*

A commercial zone divided from the rest of ACTON by the Western Avenue (A40) and generally considered part of the PARK ROYAL area, with a handful of residential streets in the far north-east that unexpectedly break the industrial monotony. From Elizabethan times the supposedly health-giving Acton Wells spa flourished on the eastern edge of the area, near OLD OAK COMMON. Wells House Road marks the site of the former assembly rooms, which later served as a school and then a farmhouse. Horse races were run at Acton Wells in the second half of the 18th century. Acton Cemetery opened in 1895 on Park Royal Road. A bridge across the railway line unites the cemetery's two halves, which have no remaining space for new graves although existing family plots continue to be used. The Central Line

Tube station opened in 1923, replacing an earlier Great Western railway service. In the 1930s, North Acton formed part of the industrial sprawl that made Acton the largest manufacturing town in south-east England between the wars. The John Compton Organ Works was among the best-known employers, building organs for churches, theatres and cinemas, including some magnificent Wurlitzer-style instruments. Bomb damage in the Blitz and post-war relocation caused progressive decline in the area from 1940. Today, much of North Acton's industry consists of small-scale operations, often in warehousing and distribution. A number of units have lain empty for some time. Some disused larger premises, such as the old Elizabeth Arden factory, have been converted to offices, workshops and studios for small businesses with the support of the Park Royal Partnership. The partnership hopes to encourage more redevelopment of this kind, creating a high-density, mixed-use zone that includes media-related enterprises and some residential units and local amenities.

✉ NW10

🚆 Central Line (zones 2 and 3)

North Beckton • *Newham*

The part of BECKTON bordering the northern end of Woolwich Manor Way (A117), mostly built up in the late 1980s. This is predominantly a network of short streets, even shorter cul-de-sacs and dinky homes, many built as part of social housing schemes. A handful of more imaginatively designed properties reveal that this was one of the later stages of Beckton's redevelopment, when the earlier insistence on uniformity was relaxed. North Beckton has high proportions of unemployed people and single-parent families. Many residents are from minority ethnic groups and a number of refugee families have been placed here. At the northern end of Woolwich Manor Way a former industrial waste tip was landscaped as 'the Beckton Alps' when the new town was built. Most of the waste was slag from Beckton gasworks but it also included debris from the basement of the new British Library, while a railway locomotive is said to be buried at the base. A dry ski slope was constructed on the hillside but this closed several years ago and longstanding plans to create an indoor winter sports complex have not come to fruition at the time of writing. Nearby, workmen digging deep flood drains for Thames Water have unearthed some of

London's oldest traces of organic life – the 6,000-year-old trunks of a yew and an oak, preserved in a peat bog.

✉ E6

North Cheam • Sutton

An interwar 'bus dependent' suburb situated east of WORCESTER PARK on London Road (A24). The absence of a station meant that North Cheam remained a primarily agricultural area into the 20th century. In 1901 much of Park Farm was acquired by 'Crystal Palace' Fireworks Ltd, owned by C J Brock and Co. The tin sheds in which the fireworks were made were widely dispersed across the fields and connected to a central building via a light railway. In 1904 the Daughters of the Cross converted the former Lord Nelson coaching inn into St Anthony's Convent and Hospital. The sisters subsequently opened a purpose-built hospital in 1914 and later added St Raphael's Hospice in the grounds; St Anthony's Hospital was rebuilt in 1975. The Sutton bypass skirted the eastern edge of North Cheam in 1926. It was around this time that the growth in London's bus services brought development opportunities to places beyond walking distance of a station. Developers made a selling point of North Cheam's open terrain, describing it as 'decidedly healthy, with invigorating and fresh breezes'. When C J Brock's moved to Hemel Hempstead in the early 1930s, builders immediately descended on its vacated site, erecting the first houses in a matter of weeks. Gleeson grabbed the lion's share of the land but other local firms were also involved. Cheam Park Farm Infants' School (now Junior School) and the Granada cinema opened in 1937. Some of North Cheam's more desirable properties later went up on roads in the south-east of the suburb, off Church Hill Road. Kimpton industrial estate has a reuse and recycling facility and a Tesco superstore on the site of a former sewage works. London Road has the offices of the *Surrey Comet*, a Sainsbury's superstore, and North Cheam Sports and Social Club, formerly a London Transport sports ground.

✉ Sutton SM3; Worcester Park KT4

📖 Tony Brett Young et al, *A Stroll Through North Cheam's Past*, North Cheam Liberal Democrats, 1991

North Chingford • Waltham Forest

The far north-eastern corner of CHINGFORD (and of the borough of Waltham Forest), not identified on most maps but well-signposted and known locally as 'the village'. Chingford station is here, inconveniently located for most of the district, but ideal for access to Epping Forest, although the closest part of the forest has more open space (and golf course) than woodland. The Great Eastern Railway's branch line originally terminated nearer CHINGFORD GREEN and its construction was beset by financial difficulties and wrangling between interested parties. It initially failed to bring significant suburban development but the railway company became convinced of its potential and extended the tracks 500 yards northwards, replacing the original station with the larger building that survives today. In the same year as the new station opened, the Epping Forest Act of 1878 put paid to the company's hopes of extending the line further and prevented extensive development to the north and east. However, the trains instead became popular with day-trippers, who thronged to visit the forest at weekends and especially on public holidays. Various amenities were provided for the visitors, of which the most impressive was the Royal Forest Hotel on Rangers Road. Opened in 1890, it was rebuilt in truncated form after a fire in 1912. The hotel is said to be haunted by a victim of the fire.

✉ E4

North Cray • Bexley

Half farming village, half council estate, flanking the A223 between BEXLEY and FOOTS CRAY. Changes seem to take place about every 200 years in North Cray. Edward Hasted records in his *History and Topographical Survey of the County of Kent* that it was owned by Sir John de Rokesle in the 12th century, the same period that the presence of a church is first mentioned. The estate changed hands in the 14th century through the marriage of Agnes de Rokesle to Thomas de Poynings. In 1557 Cardinal Pole, then Archbishop of Canterbury, united the parishes of Ruxley and North Cray, with the latter becoming the more dominant of the two. During the mid 18th century this part of the Cray Valley became a popular location for gentlemen's retreats, with grand houses and accompanying parkland created at North Cray Place and Vale Mascal. Capability Brown was probably responsible for the two landscaping projects, featuring a five-arch bridge over the River Cray and a Gothic bath house at Vale Mascal, both of which survive. Over the course of a decade from the late 1950s, the hitherto well-preserved village was irreparably altered by municipal projects.

North Cray Place was demolished and re-placed by the North Cray estate. The larger Be-densfield estate was built to its south: 485 homes in a mix of houses and flats laid out around short closes and communal greens. The village lane, its cottages and almshouses were obliterated by a dual carriageway. A me-dieval hall-house known as Woodbine Cot-tage was dismantled and re-erected at the Weald and Downland Open Air Museum in Singleton, Sussex. The remaining parkland of North Cray Place became part of Foots Cray Meadows, a public open space.

Built in 1760, Woollet Hall was the country seat of Viscount Castlereagh, the highly un-popular Foreign Secretary from 1812 to 1822. Believing he was being blackmailed for homo-sexuality, Castlereagh committed suicide here by cutting his throat with a penknife. Re-named Loring Hall, the house is now a private nursing home.

✉ Sidcup DA14

📖 Darrell Spurgeon, *Discover Bexley and Sidcup: Comprehensive Guide to Bexley, Bexleyheath, Welling, Sidcup, Footscray and North Cray,* Greenwich Guidebooks, 1993; Peter Tester, 'A Medieval Hall-House at North Cray', *Archaeologia Cantiana* 87, 1972

@ www.ideal-homes.org.uk/bexley/north-cray.html (London surburban history site); www.btinternet.com/~valemascal (Vale Mascal wedding venue site)

North Dulwich • *Southwark*
An attractive triangle of Edwardian housing that is as much a part of HERNE HILL as of DUL-WICH. Thomas Lett, a timber merchant, lived at Dulwich House in the early 19th century and the grounds covered most of the area bounded by Red Post Hill, Herne Hill and Half Moon Lane. The London Brighton and South Coast Railway Co. built North Dulwich station at the eastern corner of Lett's property in 1866. Charles Barry junior's original Ro-manesque station building survives today, al-though it has lost some of its lavish ornamentation. The trustees of the estate of Thomas Lett's widow offered leases to devel-opers at the end of the 19th century and house-building began in 1902. The trustees required that each property should be priced above £400, so design and construction standards were high. The houses lacked the external pre-tension of Victorian predecessors nearby but were elaborately appointed within. An Arts and Crafts hall was built on Red Post Hill in 1908 and later used as a church. The hall be-came a wing of St Faith's, the parish church of North Dulwich, on its completion in 1959. Es-tate agents now call the North Dulwich trian-gle 'highly sought after' and many of the houses have been subdivided into flats.

✉ SE24

🚉 Southern (zones 2 and 3)

North Ealing • *Ealing*
Despite the station name, the term 'North Eal-ing' is not widely used because of the range of alternative place names in the area. These in-clude HANGER HILL, BRENTHAM, PITSHANGER VILLAGE and CASTLEBAR. Early development here was confined to the rising ground of Cuckoo Hill and Castlebar Hill until the regu-lar flooding of the River Brent was brought under control in the early 20th century. North Ealing station is barely in Ealing at all, lying right on the border with WEST ACTON. Opened as part of the District Railway in 1903, its ser-vices transferred to the Piccadilly Line in 1932. On the other side of HANGER LANE, Ealing Village is a Grade II-listed art deco estate, cre-ated in the 1930s for people who worked at Ealing Studios, and is appreciated for its com-munal gardens, tennis courts, swimming pool and clubhouse. The homes were sold after the BBC bought the film studios in 1955. North Ealing Primary School is in the opposite cor-ner of the district, on Pitshanger Lane. Built in 1911 to serve the fast-growing population of Brentham, the school originally catered for girls and infants. It was extended in 1935. Standards here are very high and the school is oversubscribed. North Ealing is the most prosperous part of the borough.

✉ W5

🚉 Piccadilly Line (zone 3)

North End • *Bexley*
A disengaged working-class locality situated at the north end of CRAYFORD, and part of the borough's main regeneration zone. The name was first shown on a map drawn in the early 1760s. With the intensive development of neighbouring BEXLEYHEATH and ERITH in the latter part of the 19th century, quarries and brickworks were established here, together with a labourers' settlement. In 1919 Erith's Queen Street Baptist Church founded a mis-sion to serve this isolated community, with a hall on Arthur Street. After World War II, Crayford council built more than 170 semi-detached houses in and around Birling Road.

These were permanent, pre-fabricated units, built using the Easiform system, with concrete-panelled cavity walls. Although the houses were put up quickly and affordably, they were well-equipped with modern conveniences. The Arthur Street development of the early 1960s provided 265 dwellings in a mix of maisonettes and 13-storey blocks of flats. Construction-related businesses dominate the Northend trading estate, which is located on Northend Road (A206). Although just as white as the rest of Bexley, the North End ward (which includes SLADE GREEN) differs in several ways from the borough as a whole: unemployment is more endemic; educational attainment and home and car ownership are lower; 31 per cent of residents are aged under 20. In 2000 North End voters almost elected a British National Party activist to Bexley council, in what was perceived as an expression of desperation rather than extremism. The council has responded by taking steps to enhance community facilities.

✉ Erith DA8

👤 10,465

North End • *Camden*

A sparsely populated part of HAMPSTEAD HEATH, located at the apex of North End Way and Spaniards Road, and best known for its triangle of pubs. The Old Bull and Bush, a haunt of the artists Hogarth, Reynolds and Gainsborough, gave its name to a famous music hall song. The early-17th-century (but much altered) Spaniards Inn was formerly a toll-house and supposedly the residence of the Spanish ambassador to the court of James I. Alternatively, the name may simply derive from a former landlord whose nationality proved more pronounceable than his name. The tavern was the occasional rendezvous of the 'gentlemen of the road', as Alfred Noyes' poem *The Highwayman* recalls. Jack Straw's Castle celebrates the alleged hideout of Wat Tyler's lieutenant, but the present building dates only from the 1960s. Karl Marx and Friedrich Engels frequented its predecessor, as did Charles Dickens, who seems to have drunk almost everywhere. North End was the home of William Pitt (the Elder), Earl of Chatham in 1766–7. Wylde's Farm has played host to William Blake and the ubiquitous Dickens. Some of its lands were bought in 1905 to become the Heath Extension. From 1906 to 1940 the farmhouse belonged to Raymond Unwin, architect of HAMPSTEAD GARDEN SUBURB. In 1912 the dancer Anna Pavlova bought Ivy House, and

lived here until she died in 1931. North End was to have had the deepest Tube station in London, at the Bull and Bush, but residents' objections prevented it from ever opening. In the 1950s the partially built lower level was converted into an underground control centre for 'floodgates' on the deep Tube lines around central London. In case these gates ever need to be used in a war situation, the control room is allegedly 'blast-protected', even against sustained nuclear attack. Recent years have seen a growing number of futuristically styled properties inserted into North End, to the distress of some residents who want to preserve its rural charm.

The artist John Linnell took his family to live at Wylde's Farm (then known as Collins' Farm) in the 1820s to provide them with a refuge from the unhealthy air of London. His 1831 painting of the farm depicts a pastoral idyll reminiscent of a Constable landscape; the Museum of London acquired the work in 1963. The Victorian watercolourist Helen Allingham also painted the farm.

✉ NW3

North End • *Hammersmith & Fulham*

A former name for the settlement located at the north end of FULHAM. The fields here were part of the glebe lands belonging to Fulham rectory and were used for archery practice from the late Middle Ages. When the arrows ceased to fly early in the 17th century the land was gradually sold off for building and a handful of grand houses appeared. By 1745 a village had grown up on either side of North End Lane (now Road) between modern Lillie Road and Talgarth Road (A4). The village began to expand rapidly after 1814, when a chapel was built on Hammersmith Road that became St Mary's Church in 1835. By the mid 19th century North End had became one of the largest settlements in the manor of Fulham, with a mix of dwellings that included multi-storeyed houses with basement quarters for servants, shabby terraces and some old cottages. Market gardens still filled the neighbouring fields. North End station opened in 1874, prompting two Dorset builders – William Henry Gibbs and John P Flew – to select the village as the site for an ambitious scheme that they called the West Kensington estate. For the settlement's subsequent evolution, see WEST KENSINGTON.

The Florentine engraver Francisco Bartolozzi lived at Cambridge House for most of his long stay in London at the end of the 18th century. Samuel Richardson wrote his mould-breaking novel *Pamela* in 1740 while living at The Grange, a house owned from 1867 by the artist Edward Burne-Jones, who was visited here by John Ruskin and William Morris. The Grange was controversially demolished in 1958.

✉ W14; SW6

ℏ 10,904

🚇 District Line (West Kensington, zone 2)

North Feltham • *Hounslow*

A HEATHROW satellite district with industrial and trading estates north of the Duke of Northumberland's River, and housing to the south. In the days when this was an empty corner of HOUNSLOW HEATH, Bedfont gunpowder mills stood near Baber Bridge. The mills frequently blew up and had to be rebuilt. Swords were ground at another mill nearby. Stables dating from around 1800 survive from the former Feltham Lodge. A handful of mid-Victorian villas have survived north of Staines Road (A315) but the district has otherwise been entirely created since World War II. North Feltham was home to the National Maritime Institute until its submersion within British Maritime Technology, which is based at TEDDINGTON. The thriving North Feltham trading estate is dominated by logistics and support operations serving Heathrow Airport, and the aroma of international airline cuisine wafts from food preparation units. Hounslow Urban Farm was created in 1990 on the site of the borough parks nursery. It is London's largest community farm and its only approved rare breeds centre. The farm is located on Fagg's Road, just north of the ambulance and fire stations, and is open from Tuesday to Sunday and on bank holidays. North Feltham's other amenities include a Tesco supermarket, allotments and a waste tip.

✉ Feltham TW14

@ www.hounslow.info/urbanfarm

Northfields • *Ealing*

The south-western corner of EALING, with a history of fruit-growing and tightrope-walking – and street names that reflect this. From the 14th century this area was part of the manor of Coldhall, or WEST EALING. Great and Little Northfields were two large fields in the late Middle Ages, lying in the extreme west of Ealing parish. By the mid 17th century Northfield Lane (later Avenue) linked Little Ealing with the Uxbridge road and the manor

house of Coldhall probably stood near the southern end of the lane at that time. The Plough inn was in existence by 1722 but has since been rebuilt more than once. An orchard had been planted in Little Northfield by 1738 and in the 19th century the Steel family of market gardeners grew apples across the entire area on an almost industrial scale. In the 1870s the family built a fruit-packing warehouse, which still stands on the corner of Northcroft Road and Northfield Road. With the coming of electric trams to Uxbridge Road in 1901, the Steels turned property developers and began to grub up the fruit trees and lay out streets, initially between Uxbridge Road and Leighton Road. Julien Road, Wellington Road and Bramley Road, south of Northfields station, are named after cooking apples that the family cultivated. Northfield halt opened after the District Railway was electrified in 1908 and was rebuilt as Northfields and LITTLE EALING station in 1911. When Piccadilly Line services began the station was rebuilt again and given its present name, while a maintenance depot opened to the west. The Avenue cinema on Northfield Avenue was nicknamed the 'Spanish City' for its Moorish interior. Later an Odeon, the cinema was subsequently rescued from disuse by its conversion to a nightclub but it was demolished in 2005. Housebuilding later in the 20th century included closes behind the station that replaced former school premises in the 1970s. The Northfield ward is the most prosperous in the borough, with high levels of employment, educational attainment and home ownership. At Fielding Primary School on Wyndham Road, the most common languages spoken, after English, are Polish, Punjabi and Urdu.

The great French acrobat and tightrope walker Charles Blondin lived in Northfields from 1886 until his death in 1897 in a villa he called Niagara House, which stood opposite the Plough, probably on the site of Coldhall manor house. Blondin crossed Niagara Falls several times on a tightrope, once stopping midway to cook an omelette and once carrying his manager on his back. In 1861 he turned somersaults on stilts at the Crystal Palace, on a rope stretched 170 feet above the ground. Niagara House was demolished in the early 1930s and part of its grounds became Northfields recreation ground, now renamed Blondin Park. The adjacent Blondin nature area was created in 1997, with a community orchard, wildflower meadow and pond – but no waterfall.

✉ W5; W13

👤 12,477 (Northfield ward)

🚇 Piccadilly Line (zone 3)

📖 Richard Essen, *Ealing and Northfields*, Sutton, 1996

@ www.northfields.com (fitfully updated local information site)

North Finchley • *Barnet*

The primary commercial centre of Finchley, linked to CHURCH END by BALLARDS LANE. From the late 15th century this was an isolated spot called North End and there are no records of permanently inhabited dwellings here until the early 19th century, although the common land was occasionally used for troop encampments. The common was enclosed in 1816 and Ballards Lane was extended here to meet the Great North Road, now the High Road (A1000), in 1826. From around this time a London–Birmingham stagecoach called the Tally Ho stopped here to change horses, giving its name to the junction. By the late 1830s Tally Ho Corner had a cluster of dwellings, a chapel and the Torrington public house. A handful of artisans, including a female blacksmith, were based on Lodge Lane. A horse-drawn omnibus service ran from the Torrington to Charing Cross by 1851. Finchley and North End began to coalesce after the opening of stations at Finchley (now Finchley Central) in 1867 and Torrington Park (now WOODSIDE PARK) in 1872, whereafter the village came to be known as North Finchley. Christ Church and the Park Hotel were built in the late 1860s. North Finchley Board School (now Northside) opened in 1884 and new middle-class residential streets began to branch off the High Road. The introduction of trams in 1905 brought further growth and shops soon lined this section of the High Road in an unbroken continuum. By the outbreak of World War I, North Finchley offered leisure attractions too, including an ice rink and two cinemas. Between the wars the Tally Ho public house replaced the Park Hotel, several major retailers built imposing stores and an Odeon (later Gaumont) cinema opened in 1939. All this growth dragged the neighbourhood down a little and flats replaced some larger old houses. Some of the biggest retailers have since moved away but Barnet council still rates North Finchley as one of its three major town centres, along with CHIPPING BARNET (as it calls it) and EDGWARE. The Gaumont closed in 1979 and the Artsdepot has recently been built on its site. In addition to the arts centre, the development includes flats, a health and fitness centre, a bus interchange and more shops.

North Finchley has been home to a roll call of British comic talent: Spike Milligan lived in Holden Road, Eric Morecambe in Torrington Park and David Jason in Lodge Lane. Jason attended Northside School from the ages of five to 15, and opened the newly refurbished school in 2002.

✉ N12

North Greenwich • *Greenwich*

A modern name for the northern part of the GREENWICH PENINSULA, which lies east of the ISLE OF DOGS. Much of the peninsula was owned until recently by British Gas, which has progressively sold the site of its former gasworks. In 1996 North Greenwich was chosen as the site for the Millennium Dome, which became the largest single-roofed structure in the world on its completion almost four years later. North Greenwich station opened on the Jubilee Line extension to STRATFORD in 1999. It is said to be the largest underground station in the world, a feat permitted by the empty site that the developers were able to work with. A neighbouring part of North Greenwich is being developed as MILLENNIUM VILLAGE, but planning and funding issues have caused prolonged delays to the full exploitation of one of London's largest brownfield sites. Under a sponsorship deal with a mobile phone company, the Millennium Dome is set to reopen in 2007 as the O_2. This is touted as Europe's largest entertainment zone, with a Tutankhamun exhibition as the highlight of its inaugural year. Gymnastics and basketball events will be staged at the O_2 in the 2012 Olympic Games. By this time, a high-speed 'javelin' service from King's Cross is intended to reduce journey times to less than 20 minutes.

✉ SE10

🚇 Jubilee Line (zones 2 and 3)

📖 Iain Sinclair, *Sorry Meniscus: Excursions to the Millennium Dome*, Profile Books, 1999; S Perkins, *Dome: A Photographic Record of the Millennium Dome*, Booth-Clibborn, 2000

@ www.theo2.co.uk

North Harrow • *Harrow*

The north-western part of HARROW, centred on the station of that (misleading) name. Some residents consider HEADSTONE to lie within North Harrow. Just as SOUTH HARROW undermined the identity of ROXETH, developers' preference for the name of North Harrow snuffed out Hooking Green when suburban housebuilding began in the early 20th century. North Harrow station opened in 1915 and the district filled with affordable homes between the world wars. North Harrow Methodist Church opened in 1927 and Longfield School and St Alban's Church were built in the 1930s, the latter in a slightly Scandinavian style that drew high praise at the time. Following the closure in 2004 of a Safeway supermarket and the bowling alley above it, the site is being redeveloped with 112 flats and a new store, which is likely to open early in 2008. Just over half the pupils at Longfield School speak languages other than English, and Gujerati, Tamil, Urdu, Somali and Korean are the most common of these. The national educational standards agency Ofsted has commented that 'the social and economic background of pupils attending the school is favourable'.

> ✉ Harrow HA2 and HA1

> 🚇 Metropolitan Line (zone 5)

North Hillingdon • *Hillingdon*

An egg-shaped locality with its top cut off by the Western Avenue (A40). The north-south axis is Long Lane, which links HILLINGDON with ICKENHAM. From the Middle Ages, Rye Hill Field occupied much of the area, and belonged to the manor of Colham. The land remained largely unoccupied until the opening of Hillingdon station in 1923 and of the Western Avenue a decade later. Private builders put up houses in and around Sweetcroft Lane and the council built 220 homes on the Oak Farm Estate, which had formerly been Rye Fields Farm. A rash of 'executive-style' homes has spread within the last two decades. The locality is served by shops at Hillingdon Circus. Better known as the 'Master Brewer', the junction was a well-known bottleneck on the A40 but a short bypass, opened in 1994, has eliminated the problem. The Swedish home-furnishing retailer Ikea has proposed to make Hillingdon Circus the site for its first British 'high street' store, in a development that would include 240 flats. Planning permission was refused in November 2005 and the decision is under appeal at the time of writing. The educational standards agency Ofsted's most recent report on Ryefield Primary School found a culturally diverse intake, including Punjabi, Bengali, Urdu, Gujarati and Arabic

speakers. North Hillingdon Adult Education Centre is located on Long Lane.

> ✉ Uxbridge UB10

> 🚇 Metropolitan Line; Piccadilly Line (Hillingdon, zone 6)

North Hyde • *Hounslow*

A densely built-up residential and commercial locality tucked between the Grand Union Canal and the M4 motorway, south of SOUTHALL and west of NORWOOD GREEN. North Hyde was the northernmost part of the parish of HESTON – and indeed of the whole of the ISLEWORTH 'hundred', an ancient subdivision of the county consisting of 100 hides. A hide, often spelt hyde in place names, was the amount of land considered adequate for the support of one free family with its dependants, usually between 60 and 120 acres. The name dates from the 13th century, when Heston became a separate parish from Isleworth. At 100 feet above sea level it is one of the most elevated parts of a generally low-lying area. There is evidence of a farm here that belonged to the friars of Holy Trinity, and was thus excused from paying tithes to the local church. In the 18th century North Hyde was owned by the Bulstrode family, lords of the manor of Hounslow, who leased parcels of land to several farmers. Family documents record various disputes over their property here, including a court decision in 1731 that the tithes exemption remained in force. In 1794 the eminent botanist Sir Joseph Banks, who lived at nearby SPRING GROVE, noted that North Hyde had eight houses. The cutting of the canal across common land in 1801 prompted the establishment of a barracks and powder magazine with its own canal branch, now filled in. A small settlement grew up nearby, with cottages for labourers at the neighbouring brickworks. The barracks later became a Catholic boys' school, which survived until the 1930s. The council put up housing on North Hyde's fields before and after World War II and the surviving three acres of Barnes Farm are now given over to allotments.

> ✉ Southall UB2

North Kensington • *Kensington & Chelsea*

An ever-changing multicultural district sometimes considered to constitute the area lying west of LADBROKE GROVE and north of the WESTWAY (A40). A wider definition takes in neighbouring localities such as KENSAL TOWN, NOTTING DALE and beyond. Unlike 'WEST KENSINGTON', a name invented by property developers to improve the image of north Fulham, this area was genuinely part of the parish of KENSINGTON but was a poor district from the earliest days of its development. Until the mid 19th century the only buildings were at Notting Barns Farm but the neighbouring brickworks then gave way to mean dwellings and cottage industries and North Kensington was nicknamed 'Soapsuds Island' for its laundries. The island later floated off to ACTON as this part of London became more densely built up and polluted. Conditions barely improved through the first half of the 20th century and in the late 1950s the notorious landlord Peter Rachman let out a number of run-down properties here, after which the council stepped up its slum clearance programme. While the housing badly needed improvement, the scale of some of the rebuilding destroyed formerly tight-knit communities. The construction of the Westway was even more damaging and led to the foundation in 1971 of the North Kensington Amenity Trust (now the Westway Development Trust), to which the borough granted an 80-year sub-lease on 23 acres of land for the creation of social, educational and recreational facilities. North Kensington has one of London's largest multicultural communities. Caribbeans arrived in the first wave of post-war immigration, often disembarking from boat trains at KENSINGTON OLYMPIA and finding this to be the nearest affordable district within walking distance. Spanish and Portuguese migrants came here to work in the hotel and catering trade but some returned to their newly democratized homelands in the 1970s and 1980s. Moroccans and Filipinos settled next, also working in the hospitality industry, followed by East Africans more recently. As a result of this long tradition of resettlement, North Kensington has a high proportion of mixed-race residents. The district is renowned for its cutting-edge involvement in the music industry and has a number of recording studios. There are also problems with drugs and crime. In April 2003 the borough council made legal history by using civil law to obtain a court order banning five crack cocaine dealers from entering North Kensington, except to pick up their children or attend hospital appointments.

Between 1943 and 1953, John Christie strangled seven women and a child at 10 Rillington Place, since demolished in clearance for the construction of the Westway. Christie's victims included the wife and daughter of his neighbour Timothy Evans, who was hanged in 1950 for the murder of his child in a tragic mis-

carriage of justice. Bartle Road and Ruston Mews lie closest to the site of Rillington Place.

✉ W10

📖 Roger Mayne, *Photographs*, Jonathan Cape, 2001

@ www.historytalk.org (Kensington and Chelsea Community History Group site)

North Kingston • *Kingston*

Formerly the home of Kingston's most important industry and now a residential area with several educational institutions. In 1912 Thomas Sopwith established an aircraft factory on the site of a disused skating rink in Canbury Park Road. The company expanded massively during World War I, when a Sopwith Camel was said to have shot down the legendary Red Baron. In 1917 Sopwith acquired a 36-acre site at the northern end of Richmond Road, but this closed after three years as a result of the decline in demand for aircraft following the end of the war. Through the efforts of the test pilot Harry Hawker, the failing company was restructured as Hawker Engineering and production resumed at Canbury Park. The Leyland Motor Co. took over the Richmond Road site from 1928, while the former orchards and nurseries east of the road were replaced by the Richmond Park estate, which is now known as the Tudor estate because of its architectural style. The Tiffin Girls' School moved to its new Richmond Road buildings in 1937, and the council opened the Latchmere Road School to cope with North Kingston's growing population. Hawker returned to Richmond Road in 1948, while retaining technical facilities in Canbury Park until 1963. British Aerospace, the eventual parent company of what had become Hawker Siddely, closed the Richmond Road site in 1991, and the factory has since been replaced by housing.

The film actress Margaret Lockwood lived in Upper Park Road from 1960 until her death in 1990.

✉ Kingston KT2

North Lambeth • *Lambeth*

One of the most imprecisely defined districts in London. 'The history of this district was for many hundred years the history of Lambeth Palace', wrote S O Ambler in 1923, when things had already become less clear-cut. Some authorities now consider North Lambeth to consist of the VAUXHALL, WATERLOO and SOUTH BANK areas, but each of these has a distinct identity in its own right and the term 'North Lambeth' is only useful when it is necessary to consider the borough's riverside parts collectively. Lambeth council goes further and includes KENNINGTON, the OVAL and the northern tip of BRIXTON in its oddly-named 'North Lambeth town centre area'. Even the narrowest definition must include all of the borough north of Lambeth Road, which means Lambeth Palace (*see* LAMBETH) and the former Lambeth Marsh, now covered by Waterloo and the South Bank. (All possible parts of North Lambeth are discussed in their own entries.) SOUTH LAMBETH, on the other hand, is more widely recognized as a locality in its own right, although its borders too are indistinct.

✉ SE1, and possibly beyond

📖 J Dudman, *North Lambeth*, Sutton, 1996

🚇 Bakerloo Line (Lambeth North, zone 1)

North Ockendon • *Havering*

The only village in Greater London that is outside the M25, and the most remote from the city centre, North Ockendon lies two miles east of CORBETS TEY. It is a scattered farming community with labourers' cottages at its core on Church Lane. The flint-faced church of St Mary Magdalene dates from 1175 and retains elements from the 13th, 14th and 15th centuries. Among the monuments in the church are a number commemmorating members of the Poyntz family, the former lords of the manor. In 1593, John Morris married Katherine, daughter of Sir Gabriel Poyntz, and the couple jointly gained possession of the manor from Katherine's father. A descendant, another John Morris, was arraigned before the House of Lords in 1647 on charges of forging various evidences, including Acts of Parliament, to secure his title to North Ockendon and other manors. A timber-framed forge and bakehouse were built on Ockendon Road in the 17th century and survive today, as do cottages dating from around 1700. The village became part of HORNCHURCH Urban District in 1935, hence its present inclusion within Greater London. North Ockendon Hall was destroyed during World War II; its medieval moat is now part of Hall Farm. The farm is a flower nursery, while the moat is popular with anglers. After decades of decline, North Ockendon is growing again, with the construction of St Mary's Court accompanying the restoration of the church in 2003. Havering's outdoor pursuits centre Stubbers lies a mile to

the west, although the house that gave the estate its name was demolished in 1960. The much larger settlement of South Ockendon falls within the district of Thurrock, in Essex.

William Coys, who lived at Stubbers in the early 17th century, did pioneering work with plants and vegetables. He introduced hops as an ingredient in beer and cultivated exotic crops such as Jerusalem artichoke, ivy-leaved toadflax and the first yucca to flower in England.

✉ Upminster RM14

📖 Edward George Ballard, *Our Old Romford and District: Including Hornchurch, Upminster, Cranham, Corbets Tey, North Ockendon,* Swan, 1981

@ www.stubbers.co.uk (Stubbers Adventure Centre site)

Northolt • *Ealing/Hillingdon*

A large and unexciting set of housing estates, many of them council-built, situated northwest of GREENFORD. This was originally Northall, the northern counterpart to SOUTHALL. A settlement has existed at Northolt since the eighth century, originally on higher ground to the north-east of the church. The present St Mary's Church and a manor house were built in a shallow depression in the late 13th century and a village then began to take shape around the green. The manor house was thrice pulled down and twice rebuilt in the 14th century, and gained a moat, but was left in ruins after its last owner was hanged for treason. By 1500 there were four outlying hamlets in the parish, of which only WOOD END and WEST END retain vague identities today. From around 1700, when the village was first being called Northolt rather than Northall, the open arable fields were increasingly turned over to pasture and hay production for London's horses. The village remained quiet for another two centuries, mainly because of the poor state of the roads and the inadequate water supply. A railway halt opened at Northolt in 1907, but this at first had little effect on the village. To the west of the parish, Northolt aerodrome opened in 1915. Landowners gradually began to sell their farms for housing until the 1920s, when a second station opened at NORTHOLT PARK, and the coming of the Western Avenue (A40) and other arterial roads in the mid 1930s activated full-scale suburban growth. Northolt station was rebuilt for the arrival of the Central Line in 1948. Northolt became the main centre for Ealing council's post-war housebuilding programme, including experimental projects by the Ministry of Works, using mass-produced components like steel sheeting so that properties could be built rapidly. In the two decades after World War II, the council built almost 3,500 homes in the area, more than half its total for the whole borough. In 1958 Moat Farm was replaced by a privately built estate, and several infilling projects further increased the housing density later in the 20th century with a series of closes. Belvue Park and the old village centre retain some rural elements, and the moated site of the manor house is a scheduled ancient monument.

In the south-west of the district, at the intersection of Western Avenue and West End Road, is the Polish war memorial, nowadays better known as a traffic report landmark. Northolt airfield was the main base for the Polish Air Force during the early part of World War II. The monument, surmounted by an eagle, was unveiled in 1948 and is engraved with the names of the 14 squadrons of the PAF. Behind it is a wall with the names of all 1,241 members of PAF crews who died on operational flights.

✉ Northolt UB5

⋔ 26,308 (Northolt Mandeville and Northolt West End wards)

🚇 Central Line (zone 5)

@ www.fly.to/Northolt

Northolt Park • Ealing/Harrow

A post-war municipal housing estate occupying the northern part of NORTHOLT. This was a patch of open farmland until Northolt Park racecourse opened in 1929 as the national centre for the new sport of pony racing. The sport was cheaper to run than horseracing and the track's excellent facilities attracted large crowds over the next decade. The film and music hall star George Formby rode here in 1938 and returned the following year to make the Ealing Studios film *Come On, George*, performing all his own stunts. There was little racing after the outbreak of World War II and in 1940 the government requisitioned the site to intern Italian prisoners, later converting it to an army camp. Attempts to restart pony racing after the war were thwarted by Ealing council's determination to use the land to ease its housing shortage. The council compulsorily purchased the site for £250,000, although the start of building was delayed for

several years by the tardy withdrawal of the military. At the same time Harrow council laid claim to part of the site for its own council-house building programme. The first 64 houses were built in late 1951 in the north-west of the site and the grandstand was demolished in 1955. Ealing council eventually built around 1,200 homes on the Racecourse estate and Harrow council contributed another 200. Blocks of flats were added later on Newmarket Avenue. Apart from the street names, little evidence of the racetrack remains here. One of the stands was dismantled and moved to Brands Hatch motor-racing circuit, where it survives today.

The remaining green space of Northolt Park consists of little more than a recreation ground and some playing fields. Northolt High School is on Eastcote Lane and Northolt Park Infant School is on Newmarket Avenue.

✉ Northolt UB5

🚇 Chiltern Railways (zone 5)

@ ourworld.compuserve.com/homepages/ponyracing (Northolt Park Racecourse history site)

North Peckham • Southwark

A notorious council estate, situated north of Commercial Way in PECKHAM. Since the early 19th century this has been a densely populated district, becoming built up early owing to the convenience of access to the City, even on foot. All Saints Church, North Peckham, built in 1894, was the gift of the Gooch family in memory of Charles Cubitt Gooch. By the turn of the century the area had three dozen public houses. Built in the early 1970s, the North Peckham estate had 400 flats in five-storey blocks, linked by a second-floor pedestrian deck system over multi-storey parking. Originally considered enlightened for its avoidance of tall towers, it became hated and feared by all who lived or visited here. In November 2000 widespread public shock followed the murder of ten-year-old Damilola Taylor, who bled to death in a stairwell on the estate's Hordle Promenade after he was attacked by three other boys while on his way home from an after-school computer class at Peckham library. Major rehabilitation efforts are under way for North Peckham and its neighbouring housing projects, collectively known as the 'five estates'. The miserable flats are being demolished and replaced with 'village style' housing – indeed there have been attempts to reposition the area as Peckham

Village, but most locals have not taken this seriously.

✉ SE15

North Romford · Havering

An umbrella term for COLLIER ROW and its neighbouring localities, namely MAWNEY, HAVERING PARK, CHASE CROSS and RISE PARK. Some definitions of the area extend as far as NOAK HILL. Although the name still features as a bus destination, it is not favoured by residents. North Romford (later Forest Lodge) School opened on Lodge Lane in 1959, when it was the first comprehensive school in Essex. North Romford Community Centre is situated on Clockhouse Lane and hosts the meetings of several local clubs and societies. Bedfords Park, which the council describes as being in North Romford, lies to the east. Its 215 acres include a large lake, popular with anglers. A visitor centre opened in 2003 on the site of the former Bedfords House, reusing parts of the earlier building.

✉ Romford RM5

North Sheen · Richmond

The fading identity of what is increasingly marketed as the south-eastern corner of KEW. Unlike the genuinely ancient EAST SHEEN (and West Sheen, which was an earlier name for Richmond), North Sheen's name is little more than a century old and was the invention of speculative developers, who began building here in the 1880s. Until that time, this had been entirely agricultural land, except for the Beehive alehouse and Richmond gasworks, and the number of fruit trees was deemed 'unreckonable' by one observer. On gaining the area from MORTLAKE in the early 1890s, the new borough of Richmond built the workmen's dwellings of the Manor Grove estate around the gasworks and added more homes and Darell School in the early years of the 20th century. Fulham council laid out North Sheen Cemetery in 1926, and the inclusion of a Roman Catholic section subsequently brought the burials of many Poles. A Gothic chapel and the stone piers of the perimeter wall are the cemetery's most impressive features. St Philip and All Saints' Church, on Atwood Avenue, was consecrated in 1929. Although the church's exterior is merely pleasant, its remarkable interior consists of the timber frame of a 16th-century barn, removed from a farm in Oxted, Surrey. The whole exercise cost £5,000 and Southwark diocese suggests that it is probably the cheapest church

of its size ever built. North Sheen station opened in 1930, far later than any other stations on the line, and Lower Richmond Road (A316) was widened in 1933 as part of the creation of the Great Chertsey Road. The mock-Tudor Popham estate was laid out in 1936 and some particularly grand houses were built in Pensford Avenue, in the grounds of Reston House. Lower Richmond Road attracted apartment blocks and continues to do so whenever planning permission can be obtained. Darell Primary School has a diverse intake, and Bengali, Arabic, Cantonese and Japanese are among the home languages of its pupils.

✉ Richmond TW9

🚆 South West Trains (zone 3)

Northumberland Heath · Bexley

A family-friendly district standing on high ground in south-west ERITH, known locally as North Heath. The name Northumberland Heath has been in use since the 13th century and has no connection with the county; it means 'the heathland north of the watercourse'. This was 200 acres of common land that fell within Erith parish. In 1806 the lord of Erith manor, William Wheatley, allowed a workhouse to be built at Sussex Road. A workhouse offering temporary accommodation was called a 'spike' and the locality was nicknamed Spike Island. Wheatley gained ownership of most of the heath after its enclosure in 1815, and the pattern of fields that he created is reflected in the modern street plan. A windmill built in 1819 functioned until 1882, fortuitously serving as a beacon for vessels on the Thames. Its mill-house still stands. During the latter part of the 19th century a larger village began to take shape and the first school and church mission appeared. Mill Road and the southern ends of Brook Street and Bexley Road formed a triangle of terraced houses by the 1890s. St Paul's Church was consecrated in 1901, gaining its own parish four years later. By the 1930s the tram route between BEXLEYHEATH and Erith had led to a continuous ribbon development, new streets had been laid out south of Colyer's Lane and the land west of Lesney Farm had been developed. In 1955, Groom's bakery on Belmont Road merged with other independent bakers to form the massive British Bakeries conglomerate. Postwar changes have included the construction of eight-storey blocks of flats in the early 1960s and the recent creation of a clutch of cul-de-sacs, named after authors, on what was the northern part of Northumberland Heath recreation ground. Most residents of the ward are married, and over a third of households contain dependent children.

Among Northumberland Heath's early residents was the Meyer family, now remembered in Meyer Road. In 1929, Leo Meyer founded New Ideal Homesteads – in its day, southeast London's equivalent of Barratt and Wimpey rolled into one. NIH churned out suburban estates at great speed, giving little thought to landscaping. Rooms were small and prices rock-bottom, but the sales brochures employed flowery copy and colour illustrations to invoke visions of a bucolic paradise.

⌧ Erith DA8

♦ 10,482

@ www.ideal-homes.org.uk/bexley/northumberland-heath.html (London surburban history site)

Northumberland Park • *Haringey*

A multicultural, deprived satellite of TOTTENHAM, situated in the north-east corner of the borough. Marsh Lane (now Northumberland Park) station opened on the Northern and Eastern Railway in 1842, bringing development opportunities to the area's farms and market gardens. In an early municipal utilities scheme, the local board of health sank a 450-foot well near the station, which still supplies 180 thousand gallons a day to the London water system. A curving avenue was laid out in the late 1850s between Tottenham High Road and the station, on land behind the site of the Black House, a medieval mansion that had been owned by the dukes of Northumberland. The avenue was accordingly named Northumberland Park and was built up with villas for the upper middle classes. From 1885 until 1898 Northumberland Park was the home of Tottenham Hotspur Football Club, which played on former farmland beside the railway line. From the start of the 20th century factories were established in place of the surviving nursery gardens north of the station and the area remained an important industrial zone until after World War II. Over a 15-year period from the late 1950s a medieval farmhouse, disused industrial sites and most of Northumberland Park's villas were replaced by Tottenham council's expansive Northumberland estate of slab blocks and dull terraces. On the opening of the Victoria Line in 1968 an extensive depot was built beside the main-line railway tracks,

but plans to run a Victoria Line shuttle service to the station were later shelved. Northumberland Park School opened in 1972 in the former Tottenham County School's buildings and soon afterwards moved to its present purpose-built premises on Trulock Road. Employment levels in the locality are low and most residents rent their homes from the council or a housing association. The community's main ethnic groups are Turkish (including Kurdish refugees), white British, black Caribbean and black African. Northumberland Park has recently been the beneficiary of numerous co-ordinated projects aimed at improving residents' health and welfare, including more than 30 employment and training projects.

The secularist politician Charles Bradlaugh lived in Northumberland Park in the 1860s. As an MP from 1880, Bradlaugh was responsible for the introduction of the right of parliamentarians and court witnesses to affirm rather than take a religious oath, having been briefly imprisoned in the clock tower of the Palace of Westminster during his campaign. Mourners at his funeral in 1891 included Mahatma Gandhi.

⌧ N17

♦ 12,606

🚉 'one' Railway (zone 3)

North Wembley • *Brent*

A pleasant METROLAND suburb, bordering SOUTH KENTON and PRESTON. Although there was some early housebuilding in the 1890s, serious development did not begin until after the opening in 1912 of its station, which was also served by Bakerloo Line trains from 1917. A large industrial estate was laid out north-east of the station, and attracted a number of big-name tenants, including the British Oxygen Co., the Wrigley Co. and GEC. Imperial College bought land after World War I for an athletic ground but this was acquired by the council in 1936 and the college found a new site in HARLINGTON. After World War II the council added flats on the fringes of the area. The Church of St Cuthbert, North Wembley, was consecrated in 1959. Disused parts of the GEC industrial estate have recently been redeveloped with mixed-tenure houses and flats. The surviving commercial area is now called the East Lane business park. Vale Farm sports centre has extensive outdoor and indoor facilities, including swimming pools. Wembley High Technology College and Wembley

Manor Primary School both have diverse student rolls and no single ethnic group makes up a majority. In 2005 the primary school offered a £90,000 salary for the head teacher's post, a record for that sector, in a (successful) attempt to attract a suitable candidate. The school is an amalgamation of former infants' and junior schools and plans to move into new accommodation on the same site in 2008.

In a 2006 creative arts project, the City Mine(d) group set up a network of vacuum-suctioned tubes, connecting schools, pubs, shops and other meeting places in North Wembley. Locals were invited to draw their ideas on ping pong balls and feed them into the ends of the tubes, and the balls were later displayed at a fête held on the GEC playing fields. The project was subsequently repeated in Brussels, using the same set of materials.

> ✉ Wembley HA0 and HA9

> 🚇 Silverlink Metro; Bakerloo Line (zone 4)

> @ www.stcuths.org (possibly the most stylish church website in London)

Northwick Park • *Brent/Harrow*

A METROLAND suburb wedged between KENTON and HARROW. In 1905 Harrow School bought 192 acres of Sheepcote Farm to thwart plans for development near the school and the fields were converted into a golf course that opened two years later. The rest of the farm was laid out with streets by 1914 by the established owners of the land, the Churchill-Rushout family. Northwick Park was their estate in Worcestershire and several of the new roads were given the names of places in its vicinity. Housing was not built until after the opening of the station in 1923. Captain Spencer-Churchill's original intention was to create 'a unique specimen of town planning, the largest and best laid out estate near London' but the end result was more prosaic. In 1936 the council bought the remaining land for use as open space. Harrow Technical College, now part of the University of Westminster, was established here in 1959 and replaced most of Northwick Park golf course. The substantial Northwick Park Hospital was built from 1962 onwards on some of the public open space. The surviving 120-acre park has extensive sports facilities, including a new golf course and two Gaelic football pitches. The Northwick Park ward is the second least deprived in the borough and has the lowest crime level, according to measurements in 2004. Residents of white British and Indian origins each make up about

30 per cent of the population.

Sybil Fawlty receives treatment for an ingrowing toenail at Northwick Park Hospital in the classic 'Germans' episode of the television comedy *Fawlty Towers*, making a long journey from Torquay for a relatively minor procedure.

> ✉ Harrow HA1 and HA3

> 🚹 12,175

> 🚇 Metropolitan Line (zone 4)

Northwood • *Hillingdon*

A stockbroker-belt residential district located on the Greater London border, four miles north-west of HARROW. There was a manorial grange at Northwood in 1248, which may have been on the site of the present Grange on Rickmansworth Road. From at least the 14th century there was a hamlet here, separated from RUISLIP and EASTCOTE by Park Wood, Copse Wood and RUISLIP COMMON. A few cottages were recorded here in a survey of 1565 but the hamlet was slower to develop than Eastcote or Ruislip; after 200 years it consisted of only a few farms and dwellings, and by 1841 there were still only 41 occupied houses. Northwood retained its rural character until the late 19th century with many of the inhabitants engaged in supplying firewood to London as late as 1870. The main changes were the addition of Holy Trinity Church in 1854 and the extension of the Metropolitan Railway from PINNER to Rickmansworth in 1887, when a station opened at Northwood. F Murray Maxwell Hallowell Carew immediately bought up a large area around the station and sold off building plots along new roads named after himself. Further improvements to railway communications brought more residential development and the 1890s saw a number of large houses in their own grounds being built in the Green Lane area. Between Green Lane and Rickmansworth Road several streets were built up with smaller houses and continuous terraces. Northwood College came to Maxwell Road in 1893. After 1930 the pace of development in the wider area accelerated but much of this was south of Northwood, principally in NORTHWOOD HILLS and Ruislip. Many of Northwood's houses were ostentatiously grand and some have since been replaced by flats. Those that survive encompass a wide range of styles, including neo-Georgian, mock-Tudor, hacienda and neo-English baroque. The most luxurious properties tend to lie in the west of the district, which also has the London Bible College. Infilling and 'garden grabbing' continue wherever developers can find a vacant acre. Northwood has a high number of pensioners living alone, constituting more than a sixth of all households.

Although it was supposedly set in SURBITON, the 1970s television comedy *The Good Life* was filmed at 53 and 55 Kewferry Road in Northwood. This was native soil for actor Richard Briers, who grew up in nearby HATCH END and had served at RAF Northwood, also known as HMS *Warrior*, which is sited just across the London border in Hertfordshire's Three Rivers district. The base is now the permanent joint headquarters of joint and combined military operations by or involving the British armed forces.

✉ Northwood HA6

♦ 10,559

🚇 Metropolitan Line (zone 6)

📖 *Highways and Byways: 10 Walks Around Historic Ruislip, Northwood and Eastcote*, Ruislip, Northwood and Eastcote Local History Society, 1996

Northwood Hills • *Hillingdon*
The south-eastern end of NORTHWOOD, named to convey an impression of poshness. In the mid 18th century most of this area was part of RUISLIP COMMON and it remained wholly rural until Northwood's growth began to spill over in the early 20th century. On PINNER Road (A404), Northwood and Pinner Hospital began in 1919 as little more than a hut and gained a permanent structure in 1925. The Metropolitan Railway agreed to build Northwood Hills station on condition that the developer indemnified it against all losses for five years, but such was the project's success that the requirement was soon waived. The station opened in November 1933 and the construction of houses nearby began almost immediately afterwards and continued for two decades. Most of the properties were built on a more affordable scale than in Northwood itself, some in a flat-roofed modern style. Religious services were held from 1935 in a tent on the site of the present church of St Edmund the King, which was completed in 1964. Opened as the Northwood Hills Odeon, the Rex cinema was demolished in 1975 and replaced by a supermarket. The main ethnic minority in Northwood Hills is of Indian origin, and mostly Hindu. A relatively high 23 per cent of residents are aged over 60.

During the 1960s the young Elton John (born Reginald Dwight) lived at 30 Frome Court on Pinner Road with his mother and stepfather-to-be. At the age of 16, he began performing at the Northwood Hills Hotel every weekend, for £1 a night plus the proceeds of a whip-round.

✉ Northwood HA6; Pinner HA5

♦ 10,833

🚇 Metropolitan Line (zone 6)

📖 W A G Kemp, *The Story of Northwood and Northwood Hills*, self-published, 1955

@ www.saintedmundschurch.org.uk (church site includes parish history)

North Woolwich • *Newham*
An industrial settlement lying between the KING GEORGE V Dock and the Thames. There is speculation that this could have been the original WOOLWICH, later lending its name to the settlement south of the river. Wool from Essex sheep may have been landed or traded here by the Saxons. North Woolwich was mentioned in Domesday Book and for centuries was a detached portion of the county of Kent, and part of Woolwich parish. It consisted of virtually uninhabited marshland, used only as water meadows, until the arrival of the railway in 1847 and the introduction of a steam ferry service to the Royal Arsenal on the south bank of the river. Two years later its growth halted when Woolwich itself gained a railway connection, although the establishment of a pleasure park in 1853 generated some daytripper traffic. Created by the entrepreneur William Holland, the North Woolwich Gardens boasted the largest dance stage in London. East Ham council took the park into public ownership as the Royal Victoria Gardens in 1890. The building of the Royal Docks, culminating in the completion of the King George V Dock in 1921, brought factories and workers' housing to North Woolwich. As with other out-of-the-way places, there was a concentration of noxious industries. A new station opened in 1979 and the old building is now a railway museum.

✉ E16

Norton Folgate • *Tower Hamlets/City/Hackney*
Now just a short section of the A10 linking BISHOPSGATE with SHOREDITCH High Street, Norton Folgate was formerly a well-known mercantile neighbourhood. As Mr Burgess

says in Shaw's play *Candida*, 'I never met a man as didn't know Nortn Folgit before'. Until its merger with the parish of SPITALFIELDS in 1911, Norton Folgate was an extra-parochial liberty, which meant that it was outside the jurisdiction of any parish church. The playwright Christopher Marlowe was living here in 1589. A century later, Spital Square and its surrounding streets began to be built up with fine houses for silk merchants and master weavers, while artisans and journeymen occupied the diverging alleys and courts. Norton Folgate's residential population declined during the course of the 19th century as homes were converted into warehouses and business premises. When London's administrative boundaries were redrawn in 1900, a small part of Norton Folgate was included in the Metropolitan Borough of Shoreditch but the majority went to STEPNEY. Most of Norton Folgate is now occupied by modern offices, with more likely to appear in the near future as the City spreads northwards into Shoreditch.

The City of London Theatre, which specialized in 'domestic and temperance melodrama', opened on Norton Folgate in 1837 and closed in 1868. Puma Court, east of Spitalfields market, has almshouses 'for the poor inhabitants of the Liberty of Norton Folgate', built in 1860 to replace those of 1728.

The late Dennis Severs' house at 18 Folgate Street is an enchanting re-creation of a Huguenot silk weaver's family home. Its restricted public opening allows visitors to experience the sights, sounds and smells of domestic life in the 18th century (or thereabouts) in a way that no mass-access museum can achieve.

✉ E1

📖 Dennis Severs, *18 Folgate Street: The Life of a House in Spitalfields*, Chatto and Windus, 2001

Norwood • *Croydon/Lambeth*

A sprawling south London suburb that begins south of TULSE HILL and covers a broad south-easterly swathe almost as far as CROYDON. The Great North Wood of Surrey covered the whole of modern Norwood until the 17th century. The woods provided timber for building ships (including the *Golden Hinde*) and houses, a livelihood for charcoal burners and pig-keepers, and a home for Gypsies and squatters. A few early cottages survive on Arnulls Road, near the present Norwood Grove recreation ground. By the mid 18th century deforestation had created large areas of heathland.

From 1799 the enclosure commissioners sold or allocated plots of land of varying sizes and entirely new settlements arose. Where groups of small plots were sold, as in Lower and SOUTH NORWOOD, working-class housing frequently appeared. Where larger areas were acquired by individual landowners, for example on BEULAH HILL and in other parts of UPPER NORWOOD, substantial villas began to be built for City merchants, although the process did not accelerate until transport links improved. With the opening of Beulah spa in 1831, the Jolly Sailor station in 1839 and the relocation of the CRYSTAL PALACE to Sydenham Hill in 1854, Norwood rapidly filled with homes for the upper middle classes. Working-class enclaves like NORWOOD NEW TOWN provided reservoirs of tradesmen. Many of the properties were extravagantly grand and as early as the 1890s some succumbed to redevelopment, in the form of demolition or conversion to institutional use or into flats. After World War I, municipal projects altered the character of areas such as KNIGHTS HILL and GIPSY HILL. Council building continued to increase after World War II, peaking in the 1960s when many 19th-century homes were lost. Despite the ravages of the 20th century, much of Norwood retains a Victorian air. Because south London's major through routes skirt the edge of the district and it lacks a strategic shopping and leisure centre, it is less well-known than neighbours like STREATHAM.

James Thomson, who provided the lyrics of *Rule Britannia*, praised the rural seclusion of the Great North Wood in his *Hymn on Solitude*, published in 1729. 'Perhaps from Norwood's oak-clad hill, / When meditation has her fill, / I just may cast my careless eyes / Where London's spiry turrets rise, / Think of its crimes, its cares, its pain, / Then shield me in the woods again.'

✉ SE19

📖 Alan Warwick, *Phoenix Suburb*, Norwood Society, reissued 1991

@ www.virtualnorwood.com (community site); www.norwoodsociety.co.uk

Norwood Green • *Ealing*

The 'nice' part of SOUTHALL, according to some, situated to the north-west of OSTERLEY Park. Originally just called Norwood, it was first mentioned in a will of 832, which bequeathed the manor to the Archbishop of Canterbury. St Mary's Church is of Norman origin and was rebuilt in the mid 14th century, when the Plough Inn was established to serve labourers working on the project. Several handsome villas were built here in the late 18th and early 19th centuries, most of which have since been lost to suburban development, including Norwood Court and Bridge Hall. The finest survivor is Sir John Soane's Norwood Hall, which he designed for a friend in 1803 in a similar style to his own Pitshanger Manor. The house, which has original Soane drawings and a large walled garden, was modified and extended by the Unwin family in the late 19th century. Around this time the growing village absorbed its immediate western neighbour, Frogmore Green, and the church was given a new brick tower. Early in the 1920s the Unwins sold off much of Norwood Hall's land to the builders Warren and Wood. Their estate's streets are named after places in Dorset, Warren's home county. Norwood Hall itself and its remaining 19 acres of gardens were acquired by Middlesex County Council and converted into a horticultural college. Norwood House was demolished in 1927 and its land was sold off in small plots for building, while the General Housing Co. developed neighbouring sites. The elm trees that lined the ten-acre green were felled as part of a road-widening programme in 1928 and the pond was filled in soon afterwards, but the council compensated by creating Wolf Fields on the opposite side of Norwood Road. The formation of the borough of Southall-Norwood in 1935 echoed the physical convergence of the two settlements on the former brickfields between the railway line and the Grand Union Canal. A large part of Norwood Green was made a conservation area in 1969. Over a third of the ward's residents are of Indian origin, mostly Sikhs, and another third are white. Norwood Hall is now an Ealing tertiary college and its school of horticulture and floristry is managed by Capel Manor College at BULLS CROSS.

In his poignant autobiography *The Scent of Dried Roses*, Tim Lott depicts the suburban atmosphere of Norwood Green in the 1960s: 'The neat houses are decked out with a jumble of modest details of dreamed life – a caravan or boat in the front yard, a cartwheel on the wall, carriage lamps at the entrances.'

✉ Southall UB2

🏌 12,647

📖 Alan D Sabey (ed.), *Norwood Green in the Year 2000*, Norwood Green Residents' Association, 2000

Norwood Junction • *Croydon*

A commuter station serving SOUTH NORWOOD and north WOODSIDE, named after the diverging railway lines just to its south. The Jolly Sailor public house backed onto the CROYDON Canal in the early 19th century, and was popular with day-trippers who came to fish, take a summertime jaunt on a canal barge or ice skate in winter. When the canal closed in 1836, most of its bed was filled in and the London and Croydon Railway Co. appropriated the course for its line. With the opening of the line from West Croydon to London Bridge in 1839, a station was built here and named Jolly Sailor in honour of its neighbour. The route to East Croydon and on to Brighton opened two years later and the station was renamed Norwood Junction after the two lines' operating companies merged in 1846. High train fares initially deterred would-be commuters from settling so far out of London, but the building of the CRYSTAL PALACE at SYDENHAM invigorated the whole NORWOOD area. In 1854 a branch line to Crystal Palace opened, which was later extended to VICTORIA. South Norwood's growth prompted the rebuilding of the station in 1859, 80 yards to the south of its original site. London Underground has plans to extend the East London line to pass through Norwood Junction by 2010.

✉ SE25

🏌 South Eastern Trains; Southern; Thameslink (zone 4); also, from 2010, the East London Line

Norwood New Town • *Croydon*

'The world's first new town' (according to some), as we understand the term today, now demolished but still named on 21st-century maps. In the late 18th century Augustus Hervey, Earl of Bristol, bought a woodside cottage on KNIGHT'S HILL Common and acquired several acres of surrounding land from the Archbishop of Canterbury. Like many wealthy aristocrats he wanted to establish a London retreat to complement his City base and his country estate. Hervey greatly enlarged the cottage to create Norwood House, a mansion that is now the Virgo Fidelis Convent School. After his death, Hervey's mistress Mary Nesbitt lived on at Norwood House, playing a shadowy role in European political affairs as an agent of the British government. In the 1850s, following the decision to rebuild the CRYSTAL PALACE at nearby SYDENHAM, the exhibition's management company laid out a housing estate to the south-east of Norwood

House and rows of terraced cottages with tiny gardens were packed into a 9-acre area bordered by Rockmount Road and Oxford Road. Some of the properties were occupied by builders working on the Crystal Palace project. The new town was endowed with three public houses and enclosed by a high brick wall, which was mainly intended to prevent residents from disturbing the neighbouring community after payday carousing. Croydon council began to compulsorily purchase run-down properties from 1955 and by 1967 Norwood New Town had been entirely bulldozed. It was subsequently reconstructed with housing of less character and few amenities, on a landscape of softened gradients.

✉ SE19

📖 Beryl Cheeseman, *Treetops and Terraces*, Theban Publishing, 1994

Notting Dale • *Kensington & Chelsea*

A notoriously deprived enclave located to the west of the much better-known and better-off district of NOTTING HILL. In the mid 19th century this was a brickmaking area and Kensington Potteries was the largest employer. Gypsies lived here seasonally. From the 1860s Notting Dale was built up with cheap housing and the new residents scraped a living by taking in laundry or keeping pigs. Having started badly, conditions got worse and in 1893 the *Daily News* reckoned Notting Dale was the most 'hopelessly degraded' place in London. The social reformer and statistician Charles Booth charted terrible hardship just a few hundred yards from the wealth that radiated outwards from Lansdowne Crescent. Some of London's first housing associations began their work here and Octavia Hill took over the management of five run-down houses in St Katherine's Road. Do-gooders from KENSINGTON established churches, missions and Sunday schools but the underlying malaise persisted. Notting Dale's first Spanish immigrants were refugees from that country's civil war in the 1930s, while Caribbeans came soon after the *Empire Windrush* docked in 1948. Council flats replaced many of the slums from the 1950s onwards, notably in the form of the high-density Lancaster West estate of the late 1960s. Housing associations, including Octavia Housing and Care, now shoulder responsibility for the ongoing improvement of Notting Dale's dwellings.

The England footballer and 1996 player of the year Les Ferdinand grew up on the Lancaster West estate.

✉ W11; W10

📖 Shaaron Whetlor, *The Story of Notting Dale: From Potteries and Piggeries to Present Times*, Kensington and Chelsea Community History Group, 1998

@ www.octaviahousing.org.uk

Notting Hill • *Kensington & Chelsea*

Two contrasting districts in one, situated west of BAYSWATER. The name probably derives from a Saxon family called Cnottingas, sons of Cnotta, and was first recorded in 1356. The southern and largest part of Notting Hill was built up from the second quarter of the 19th century with the Norland and Pembridge estates in the south-west and south-east and the LADBROKE GROVE estate in the centre. Here, the grandest terraced houses rise to five storeys, with private communal gardens to the rear, yet the location made the properties affordable to the upper middle classes rather than the aristocracy of MAYFAIR and BELGRAVIA. Further north, Notting Hill blurs with what is now thought of as the Ladbroke Grove locality. By the late 19th century this borderland area had suffered a decline and extended families crowded into shared houses. The middle classes moved away and properties were subdivided into flats between the wars, while the central and southern parts of the district remained well-to-do. The arrival on Notting Hill's poorer fringes of West Indian migrants in the 1950s caused tensions that culminated in the Notting Hill riots of 1958. These were triggered by clashes in Nottingham the previous week, after which organized racists whipped up racial hatred among white youths in London. The riots brought the issue of 'race relations' to prominence in Parliament and the media, and partly in response to this a multiracial carnival was organized the following year at ST PANCRAS Town Hall. The carnival was held annually thereafter at a succession of halls before settling in Notting Hill from 1964. Notting Hill's contrasts extend west and east too, to the much poorer and lesser known district of NOTTING DALE and the frantically busy market on PORTOBELLO ROAD. London has many areas where rich and poor exist cheek by jowl but Notting Hill is perhaps the most remarkable, with rock stars and Hollywood actors living just a few streets from a crowded, multi-ethnic neighbourhood to the north and west.

G K Chesterton's comic novel *The Napoleon of Notting Hill* was published in 1904. The romantic comedy film *Notting Hill* (1999), starring Julia Roberts and Hugh Grant, featured locations in Elgin Gardens, Lansdowne Crescent, Portobello Road and NOTTING HILL GATE.

> ✉ W11
>
> 👥 33,803 (Colville, Norland, Notting Barns and Pembridge wards)
>
> 📖 Miranda Davies and Sarah Anderson, *Inside Notting Hill*, Pallas Athene, 2001
>
> @ www.mynottinghill.co.uk (commercial local information site)

Notting Hill Gate · *Kensington & Chelsea*

A visually dull but culturally interesting stretch of road situated at the meeting point of BAYSWATER Road, KENSINGTON Church Street, HOLLAND PARK Avenue and Pembridge Road. This was a lonely stretch on the 'way to Uxbridge' beside the Kensington gravel pits with a few cottages until a tollgate was set up in the mid 18th century. The gate stood at the junction with what was then Portobello Lane, now Pembridge Road, and was rebuilt twice over the following 100 years. As neighbouring streets were laid out, bars were placed across them to prevent traffic circumventing the tollgate. A higgledy-piggledy set of dwellings grew up along the roadway, some of which were demolished in the late 1860s when the railway first arrived. Coaches and omnibuses ran to several destinations in west Middlesex and numerous inns were built here, which were progressively replaced by shops. South of the main road, speculative developers crammed working-class families into back-street terraced houses, which are now highly sought-after and dubbed 'Hillgate Village'. In 1900, when the Central Line arrived, a local clergyman described conditions as 'worse than the East End' – but vicars were always saying that sort of thing about the worst parts of their parishes. In the late 1950s Notting Hill Gate was brutally redeveloped in a road-widening programme, creating a monotonous streetscape out of what had formerly been a characterful if messy thoroughfare and combining the two underground stations within a single concourse. The shopping facilities at Notting Hill Gate are unexciting compared with nearby PORTOBELLO ROAD but the locality has some chic eateries. The artist Damien Hirst ran the ultra-trendy Pharmacy restaurant here from 1997 to 2003, selling its fixtures and fittings for £11 million after its closure.

Notting Hill Gate has three venues that are popular with the cultural cognoscenti. The Coronet opened as a theatre in 1898 and became a cinema after World War I; Hugh Grant took Julia Roberts to see a film here in the romantic comedy *Notting Hill*. The Gate was converted from a coffee palace into a cinema in 1911, originally as the Electric. It took its present name in 1985. The Gate Theatre was established in 1979 in a room above the Prince Albert pub on Pembridge Road.

> ✉ W11
>
> 🚇 Central Line; Circle Line; District Line (zones 1 and 2)
>
> @ www.nhig.co.uk (Notting Hill Gate Improvements Group site)

Nower Hill · *Harrow* (pronounced to rhyme with 'slower')

A triangular area lying immediately east of PINNER, bounded by the Metropolitan railway line to the west and George V Avenue (A404) to the east. The road named Nower Hill, although barely 300 yards long, gained significance as part of the main route that connected HARROW with the village of Pinner. First recorded as 'atte Nore' in 1285, the name indicated a place at a flat-topped hill. Pinner is named after the same hill. By 1547 the area was known as Nower Field and by the mid 18th century it had become one of a cluster of scattered hamlets encircling Pinner, each containing little more than two or three tenements. In 1844 William Tooke bought 185 acres of land, now the site of Pinner golf course, and presented it to his son, who later built additions to his home in a somewhat grotesque manner, prompting its nickname of 'Tooke's folly'. The younger Tooke died in 1884 and a Gothic drinking fountain was erected in his memory on a small green at the junction of Nower Hill with Church Lane and Moss Lane. Nower Hill Cottage was considerably enlarged in 1895 for Ambrose Heal, and renamed Nower Hill House. The architects went on to design Heal's department store in TOTTENHAM COURT ROAD, which survives today – unlike Nower Hill House. Nower Hill remained largely undeveloped until the opening of the Metropolitan Railway station at Pinner in 1885, when development slowly began to spread in this attractive direction. Middlesex County Council opened Nower Hill High School in 1929 and the school has been progressively enlarged since World War II. Around 50 per cent of the pupils now come from ethnic minorities, and the largest of these groups is of Indian origin. Ofsted describes the school's catchment area as 'moderately prosperous ... with pockets of disadvantage'.

✉ Pinner HA5

@ www.nowerhill.org.uk (school site)

Nunhead • *Southwark*

A run-down district with a handful of highlights, situated east of PECKHAM RYE. The name was first mentioned in 1583, when Edgar Scot sold Thomas and William Patching certain estates 'lying at None-Head'. The name may relate to ownership of land here by the SHOREDITCH nunnery of St John the Baptist in the late 12th century. Others have suggested that it originates from a pub sign, but the sign itself could have derived from the same root. Nunhead was a market gardening hamlet when 58 acres were taken for All Saints' Cemetery in the late 1830s. The main entrance lodge was built on Linden Grove, where Charles Dickens later set up an apartment for his mistress. The cemetery is now an attractive wilderness, although parts have recently been restored. The Girdlers' Company and the Metropolitan Beer and Wine Trade Society built almshouses at Nunhead Green in the 1830s and 1850s respectively. Both groups of homes survive in good condition today, unlike the green. In 1854 the Southwark and Vauxhall Water Co. acquired a 14-acre site west of the cemetery and built four reservoirs, since replaced by two that are capable of delivering 43 million gallons a day. Brock's firework factory operated at Nunhead and in 1870 contracted to make two million cartridge tubes for the French army during the Franco-Prussian war. The company later moved to NORTH CHEAM. Nunhead station opened in 1871 and St Antholin's Church was built on Nunhead Lane in 1878. The district was built up in the 1870s and 1880s by a variety of speculative builders, mostly in a fairly haphazard fashion except for the more carefully planned Waver-

ley Park estate. This was the work of one of south London's pre-eminent speculative builders, Edward Yates, but it was not a great success; 310 of its 742 houses stood empty in 1907. The station was rebuilt on the opposite side of Gibbon Road from its predecessor when the line was electrified in 1925. The Gandolfi family moved their camera-making business to a former hatpin factory on Borland Road in 1928. The company's wooden cameras are said to be to the world of photography what Stradivarius violins are to music. Before and after World War II, the London County Council built numerous blocks of flats in the area, notably on the Nunhead estate in the 1950s, although some pockets of Victorian housing remain. Most homes in Nunhead are rented from the council or a housing association, and unemployment is high. Slightly more than one-third of residents are black or black British.

Charles Peace, the murderous Victorian burglar, made Evelina Road his London home. Nunhead-based Father Neil Horan hit the news in the early 2000s by disrupting the British Grand Prix in 2003 and the men's marathon at the 2004 Olympic Games; he was defrocked in 2005.

✉ SE15

👤 10,271

🚃 South Eastern Trains (zone 2)

📖 Ron Woollacott, *Nunhead Notables: A Guide to Some of the People Buried in Nunhead Cemetery*, Friends of Nunhead Cemetery, 2002; John D Beasley, *The Story of Peckham and Nunhead*, London Borough of Southwark, 1999

@ www.fonc.org.uk (Friends of Nunhead Cemetery site)

Nurserylands *see* HAMPTON NURSERYLANDS

Oakleigh Park • *Barnet*

A pricey residential locality situated east of WHETSTONE and south of EAST BARNET. Oakleigh Road is an old route, called Avernstreet in 1499 and by a number of other names in subsequent centuries, but its present identity dates from the Whetstone Freehold Estate Co.'s invention of the Oakleigh Park name after it acquired land here in 1869. Until then this had been Matthews Farm, the property of the Haughton Clarke family, who had made their money from the slave trade. When the station opened here in 1873 the estate company ensured that it too was named Oakleigh Park. The WFEC set out to build a high-class estate to capitalize on the quality of the wooded and undulating landscape and aimed to include a variety of morally and physically improving facilities at the showpiece Athenaeum Institute, which opened in 1881 with a grand concert. All Saints' Church was completed in 1883, with the sponsorship of FRIERN BARNET bigwig John Miles, who also laid out Myddleton Park. All Saints' is notable for its elaborate interior decoration, which took decades to complete. After an early flurry of interest the Oakleigh Park project soon ran out of steam. By the beginning of the 1890s Athenaeum Road and Oakleigh Park North and South had only 56 houses between them, while the institute was being used for industrial purposes. Other attempts to colonize the area were also slow to bear fruit. The former estate of the duke of Buckingham and Chandos was sold in 1892 but only Chandos Avenue had been partially developed by 1920. All Saints' Road, now Oakleigh Avenue, was still an empty track at this time. Oakleigh Park was eventually built up by the outbreak of World War II, partly by the council, which put up a 36-acre estate in the Russell Road area and in 1928 opened All Saints' School. New Ideal Homesteads, whose projects were mostly in south London, built more economical properties east of the railway line on 45 acres of Gallants Farm. The Oakleigh ward is distinguished by its relatively elderly population.

Oakleigh Park was a base for espionage and counterespionage during and after World War II. The Soviet Union's Tass news agency operated a radio monitoring station at The Lodge in Oakleigh Park North from 1941 to 1951. The Admiralty set up a base a few doors down at Tower House, allegedly so that they could keep an eye on the Russians and also for use as a safe house. Both buildings have since been pulled down and replaced by flats, and it is further alleged that the government overruled council objections to the demolition of Tower House so that its secrets might be buried forever.

✉ N20

♦ 14,740 (Oakleigh ward)

🚊 WAGN Railway (zone 4)

Oakwood • *Enfield*

A park and Tube station in the far north of SOUTHGATE that have given their name to the disparate private and municipal estates clustered around them. This was part of the woodland of ENFIELD CHASE, which in the 13th and 14th centuries belonged to the De Bohun family, whose name is still visible in these parts. In 1870 Samuel Sugden, a homeopathic chemist, bought land here, renovated a farmhouse and renamed it Oak Lodge and added a walled garden and an orchard. He also built an igloo-shaped ice house in the grounds, which survives today. Oak Lodge was demolished around 1920. Southgate council acquired the lodge's 64 acres of grounds and invented the name 'Oakwood' for the park it opened in 1927. The London Electric Co. extended the Piccadilly Line to COCKFOSTERS in 1933 and built a station here, which it at first called ENFIELD West. Oakwood School opened in the same year as the station but it was a couple of years before serious housebuilders ventured this far. John Laing and Co. then began to develop the South Lodge estate and by the outbreak of World War II most of modern Oakwood had taken shape. Some of the more luxurious homes are in the style known as 'stockbroker Tudor', with oversized eaves and chimneys. St Thomas's Church was built in 1941. More shops were added around the station in the 1950s and Enfield council now calls this 'Oakwood shopping centre', but that overstates the case. The council built a housing estate in the area around Green Road and Reservoir Road, to which it has recently made improvements. West Grove Community Primary School opened in 1998. The school has a large number of pupils of Mediterranean descent, including Greek, Greek and Turkish Cypriot and Italian, as well as a variety of non-European ethnic minorities. At De Bohun Primary School the main home languages spoken after English are Turkish, Somali and French. In 2004 more than a third of De Bohun's children came from refugee or asylum-seeking families and there was a correspondingly high level of pupil mobility.

Oakwood Park has an avenue of scarlet oak trees, which were planted annually by the mayor from 1945 until recently. Original field boundaries can still be seen from when the area was farmland.

✉ N14

🚇 Piccadilly Line (zone 5)

Old Bexley • Bexley

Also known as Bexley Village, this is the historic heart of BEXLEY, situated at the south-eastern corner of the modern suburb. The 'Old' prefix helped distinguish the village from Bexley New Town, as BEXLEYHEATH was called in the second half of the 19th century. A number of 18th-century buildings on the south side of the High Street were lost during redevelopment in 1966. The Old Mill burned down in the same year but it has since been rebuilt in replica form and is home to a restaurant and pub. The remainder of the village has been preserved following its designation as a conservation area in 1972. Among the surviving older properties are the King's Head public house, the former parish workhouse, Styleman's almshouses, High Street House and Cray House. St Mary's Church stands near the eastern end of the High Street, on Manor Road. Old Bexley cannot compete with Bexleyheath as a retail centre, so shops and other commercial premises have been converted to cafés, bars and restaurants in recent years. The late-Victorian Freemantle Hall serves as a community centre and hosts events such as record fairs.

✉ Bexley DA5

📖 Peter Tester, *Bexley Village*, Bexley Libraries, 1987

Old Brentford • Ealing

The south-eastern corner of BRENTFORD, located at the mouth of the River Brent, nowadays more commonly known as Brentford Dock. Medieval Brentford was divided between the parishes of HANWELL and EALING and the two halves were later distinguished as New and Old Brentford. New Brentford, which is no longer shown on maps, was associated with the manor of Bordeston, which came to be called BOSTON MANOR. The construction of the Grand Junction (now Grand Union) Canal began in 1793, enhancing Brentford's strategic significance and bringing increased industrial development to its riverside. With the coming of the railways, Brentford Dock was built under the direction of Isambard Brunel in the late 1850s to provide a road, rail and river freight link. From the 1950s the declining use of the canal and the subsequent growth of the motorway network rendered the dock redundant and it closed in 1964. The Greater London Council built a medium-rise housing estate on a large part of the railway and dock site in the 1970s and opened Brentford Dock marina in 1980.

✉ Brentford TW8

@ www.brentford-dock.net

Old Compton Street • Westminster

SOHO'S gay heartland, situated north of SHAFTESBURY AVENUE, running parallel with its middle section. The hunting fields here began to be built over during the last quarter of the 17th century and Old Compton Street soon became Soho's high street. It was named after landowner Spencer Compton, the Earl of Northampton, who died at the Battle of Hopton Heath in 1643. Compton's son Henry became Bishop of London and commissioned the building of St Anne's Church. New Compton Street, across CHARING CROSS ROAD, is named after him. By the end of the 18th century almost every house in Old Compton Street had a shop or tavern at ground level. Suppliers of kitchenwares were especially prevalent. Continental immigrants, notably French Huguenots, colonized the street from the start, and it has retained a cosmopolitan and bohemian character. From the early years of the 20th century, Old Compton Street was known for its delicatessens, one of which – King Bomba – was a focus for anti-fascist activities in the 1920s and 1930s, including a plot to kill

Mussolini. The Prince Edward Theatre was built at the eastern end of the street in 1930 and spent much of its life as a restaurant-cum-cinema. In the late 1950s the 2i's coffee bar at 59 Old Compton Street became the wellspring of British rock 'n' roll; Tommy Steele and Cliff Richard were among the young hopefuls discovered here. Over the past 15 years the street has developed a sufficiently distinctive character to mark it out from the other, 'straighter' parts of Soho. It is famed for its gay clubs and bars but also has specialist retail outlets for the gay community. The bombing of the Admiral Duncan pub by a right-wing fanatic in 1999 killed two people and injured more than 80.

The German composer Richard Wagner stayed in Old Compton Street early in his career, and composed his opera *The Flying Dutchman* here. The title track of the Vibratos' 2001 collection of Shadows-style guitar instrumentals, *The Ghost of Old Compton Street*, is a reference to the 2i's coffee bar.

✉ W1

📖 David Benedictus, *Streets of London: A Guide to the Five Streets Featured in the Thames Television Series*, Thames Methuen, 1985

Old Coulsdon • *Croydon*

An expanded village situated south-west of KENLEY. As its name suggests, this was the original COULSDON, which added the 'Old' when a new settlement grew up around Coulsdon South and SMITHAM stations. The Church of St John the Evangelist was in existence by the twelfth century, and has a 15th-century tower. The manor was held by the Abbey of St Peter, Chertsey from before the time of its appearance in Domesday Book until the dissolution of the monasteries. Thomas Byron acquired the extensive manorial estate in 1782 and the Byron family remained in residence here for 140 years, building Coulsdon Court in the 1850s. The progressive enclosure of Coulsdon Common led to litigation until its acquisition and preservation by the Corporation of London in the early 1880s. Until World War I the village consisted of a cluster of cottages and farm buildings around the green. Following the death of Edward Byron the Coulsdon Court estate was put up for sale in 1922 and the council bought the house and its parkland for a municipal golf course. In the years leading up to World War II, new roads were laid out centring on the village and lined with houses, including the Tudor village, to the south-

east. From 1967 Wates laid out the Coulsdon Woods estate on the hillside to the north of the village. Since 1968 a conservation area has protected the heart of Old Coulsdon, including Bradmore Green farmhouse and its 17th-century barn. However, on the outskirts, several small cul-de-sacs have filled former large gardens. Coulsdon Court was restored and extended in 1991 as the Coulsdon Manor Hotel. Coulsdon College, on Placehouse Lane, was formerly a boys' school and occupies the site of a medieval colliery. The village's most recent landmark is a millennium cairn and time capsule.

In 1776 Coulsdon Cricket Club played in the first-ever match to use three stumps. However, despite claims to the contrary, the game was staged at their opponents' ground in Chertsey, not on the green at Coulsdon.

✉ Coulsdon CR5

📖 Ian Scales, *Village Histories: Coulsdon*, Bourne Society, 2000; Roger Packham and Jean Tooke, *Coulsdon in Old Picture Postcards*, European Library, 1995

@ www.oldcoulsdon.co.uk (community site); www.theocra.org.uk (residents' association site)

Old Ford • *Tower Hamlets*

A waterside locality now dominated by post-1960s flats, situated in the far north of BOW. The name was first recorded in 1268, although a 'Robert of Aleford', mentioned in 1244, may have come from here. In the early Middle Ages this was an important crossing point of the River Lea on the main road from London into Essex; and there is archaeological evidence of active commercial traffic from the middle of the first century into the fourth century. However, the construction of a bridge at Bow supplanted the less reliable route through Old Ford. This was in part a consequence of the meadowland's vulnerability to flooding, a problem exacerbated by the prevalence of watermills along the River Lea, constricting its flow. The Hertford Union Canal was constructed on the northern edge of the locality in the late 1820s and its bank was lined with wharves, warehouses and sawmills. VICTORIA PARK opened to the north of the canal in 1845 and the London and Suburban Freehold Land and Building Society laid out the Victoria Park estate between ROMAN ROAD and the canal in the late 1850s. The southern half of the district was built up with compact terraced housing from the mid 1860s, following the opening of a station at Coborn Road (formerly Cut Throat Lane). Old Ford's waterworks were responsible for London's last cholera epidemic in 1866, although they were not shut down until 1891. Unlike neighbouring districts, no large-scale redevelopment took place here in the first half of the 20th century. The station closed in 1948 and some houses were demolished in 1959 to make way for the East Cross Route (A12), which cut off the area known as FISH ISLAND. In the early 1960s the London County Council lost patience with Poplar borough council's failure to redevelop the district and stepped in. The county council and its Greater London Council successor built a series of estates and were soon joined in the effort by Poplar's successor, Tower Hamlets council. As a result, most of Old Ford now consists of council houses and tower blocks in a mish-mash of designs and materials. On the site of the former wharves, new canalside apartment complexes are a more pleasing exception. The former Chisenhale veneer works has been converted into a gallery for young artists. At Old Ford Primary School children of Bangladeshi descent form the largest cultural group, and mostly speak Bengali or Sylheti. White British children are the second largest minority.

Sylvia Pankhurst ran the militant East London branch of the suffragette movement from rooms on Old Ford Road. On the same road she also opened a mother-and-baby clinic in a former pub (which she renamed the Mother's Arms) and a 'cost price restaurant'.

✉ E3

@ www.chisenhale.org.uk (Chisenhale Gallery)

Old Isleworth · Hounslow

The partial remnants of a riverside settlement that was overwhelmed by suburban development after the coming of the railways. The village was solidly established by the mid 17th century but nothing remains from this period. The 'very ancient' church of All Saints was rebuilt in 1707. The London Apprentice public house dates from 1731 and is said to have been named after the apprentice liverymen who rowed all the way here from the CITY OF LONDON on their days off. Despite the (all too common) claim that Henry VIII did some courting here, there is no evidence that a predecessor existed on the site. Church Street and Lower Square acquired some fine stuccoed terraced houses in the 18th and early 19th centuries, and several have survived. All Saints' Church was badly damaged by an arson attack during World War II, and the industrial wharves were devastated by enemy bombing. This destruction, combined with council clearances before and after the war, left large chunks of Old Isleworth desolate and it was several decades before the area was fully redeveloped. The church was rebuilt in 1970, with a modern extension tacked on. Other parts of the old town have since been subject to further modernization, especially in the late 1980s, with a complex of riverside terraces, offices and a pub. Recent gated blocks of loft-style apartments have further added to the disharmony, but Old Isleworth nevertheless retains enough heritage to justify its name. ISLEWORTH riverside is designated both a conservation area (which extends to include Syon Park) and a 'viewpoint in all directions', offering sights that include ISLEWORTH AIT, Richmond Old Deer Park and Kew Observatory.

✉ Isleworth TW7

@ www.oldisleworth.co.uk (community site)

Old Kent Road · Southwark

The property on the Monopoly board that nobody wants, the Old Kent Road (A2) runs from east NEWINGTON to NEW CROSS GATE. The road closely follows the line of the medieval route to Canterbury and formerly crossed the River Neckinger, which now runs underground. It was at that ford that the pilgrims watered their horses in Chaucer's *Canterbury Tales*. The road developed in an irregular fashion during the 19th century, with housing ranging from the elegant to the jerry-built, and factories that produced textiles and chemicals. From the 1840s the road's largest employer was the South Metropolitan Gasworks, which was run first by Thomas Livesey and then by his son George. The philanthropic George Livesey introduced a profit-sharing scheme for workers and donated a library on the Old Kent Road, which is now home to the Livesey children's museum; 7,000 people attended his funeral in 1908. Old Kent Road and HATCHAM station stood near the corner of Ilderton Road but it closed temporarily in 1917 and never reopened. The vitality of the road declined in the second half of the 20th century as its industries departed. Several commercial estates still operate but other sites lay derelict for more than a decade until they were taken over by retail warehouses. The Astoria cinema closed in 1968 and was demolished in 1984 and replaced by a DIY superstore. The Cantium retail park opened in 1992. Once known for eels, pie and mash, the Old Kent Road is increasingly popular for its clubs and other forms of nightlife. Marcia Road is a noteworthy recent project by Galliard Homes; its four-bedroom town houses replicate properties that stood here before but that had become too dilapidated for renovation.

Albert Chevalier's Victorian music hall song 'Knocked 'em in the Old Kent Road' was performed by Shirley Temple in the 1939 movie *The Little Princess*.

✉ SE1; SE15

@ www.liveseymuseum.org.uk

Old Malden • *Kingston*

A well-to-do suburb separated from TOLWORTH by the Hogsmill River and blurring with WORCESTER PARK to the south-east. The Church of St John the Baptist was in existence by the mid eleventh century and the manor was recorded in Domesday Book as Meldune, which meant 'the hill with a cross'. At 93 feet above sea level, the hill is not especially prominent. In 1264 Walter de Merton made Malden manor house the base for the educational foundation that subsequently became the University of Oxford's Merton College. This was perhaps the greatest advance in the development of higher education in London until the creation of the University of London. Despite the vehement opposition of Merton College, Elizabeth I took possession of the manor in the 1580s, in order to offer it to the Earl of Arundel in exchange for Nonsuch Palace. The college regained possession of the manor on appeal to the House of Lords in 1627. By this time, the manor house had been rebuilt, as had the church. The village remained primarily agricultural until the 19th century, focused around the twin hubs of the church and MALDEN GREEN, half a mile to its east. Industry took the form of a dozen gunpowder mills, strung out along the Hogsmill. Old Malden and Worcester Park station (later Worcester Park) opened in 1859 and the village began to grow slowly. The population rose from 320 in 1861 to around 700 by the end of the 19th century, including the parochial outpost of MALDEN RUSHETT. Meanwhile, a separate suburb took shape at NEW MALDEN, to the north. Old Malden today is very much a product of the 20th century, especially the period between the wars, when MALDEN MANOR station opened. The St John's and Plough Green conservation areas preserve a fine collection of older buildings and a fragment of the medieval landscape. Old Malden exhibits its afflu-

ence in various ways: more than 95 per cent of homes have central heating, unemployment is extremely low, and owner occupation and car ownership are high. Fifty-eight per cent of adult residents are married.

✉ Worcester Park KT4

👥 7,149

📖 Stephen H Day, *Malden – Old and New: Revisited*, Marine Day, 1991

Old Oak Common • *Hammersmith & Fulham*

A council estate and extensive railway sidings on the western side of WORMWOOD SCRUBS. The area was once covered by oak woodland, which also gave nearby ACTON its name. A spring was discovered on the western edge of the common in the late 17th century and a spa called Acton Wells flourished briefly. The common was enclosed in 1859. By this time the old wells had become the focus of a nascent settlement, supplemented in the 1870s by a *biergarten* run by London's German Club. At the end of the 19th century the village had a school and St Luke's Mission Church, which later became part of the parish of HARLESDEN. In 1905 the London County Council purchased almost 55 acres of Old Oak Common from the Ecclesiastical Commissioners for £30,000. Eight acres were later resold for the construction of what became the Central Line, recouping over a third of the initial outlay. Influenced by 'garden city' ideas, the first phase of the Old Oak estate was completed around 1911 and the streets were named in honour of former bishops of London. After World War I the LCC added another 736 houses, with the completed township accommodating around 4,600 residents. The Old Oak estate has undergone a major modernization programme since its transfer to housing association management in 1999. Regeneration funding is also helping to provide training initiatives and employment opportunities. The busy railway facilities at Old Oak Common service and refuel trains running out of Paddington station; a new heavy maintenance facility opened in 2002. To its south is North Pole International, a Eurostar rail depot.

✉ W12; NW10

👥 7,643 (College Park and Old Oak ward)

Old Southgate • *Enfield*

A designation used to distinguish the Southgate Green conservation area from NEW SOUTHGATE and from 1930s suburban SOUTH-

GATE. The council uses the Old Southgate name on some direction signs. The conservation area covers The Green, Cannon Hill and the southern half of the High Street and includes more than 500 buildings, of which around 20 are Grade II listed and five are Grade II* listed; Grovelands is Southgate's only Grade I-listed building. The Green itself is the highlight, with some fine cottages, terraces and Georgian houses.

✉ N14

⋔ 12,897 (Southgate Green ward)

@ www.southgategreen.org.uk (Southgate Green Association site)

Old Street • *Islington/Hackney*

An ancient route connecting CLERKENWELL with SHOREDITCH, bisected by the CITY ROAD. This was one of the earliest ribbon developments outside the City walls and was 'eald' (old) when its name was first recorded as Ealdestrate around 1200. Houses began to extend westward from Shoreditch High Street in the late Middle Ages and development intensified when HOXTON became a fashionable resort towards the end of the 17th century. Nearer the western end of the street, the growth of ST LUKE'S had a similar effect in the 18th century. In 1742, Samuel Whitbread invested in the Goat brewhouse, near the corner of Whitecross Street, where he produced porter. Soon outgrowing this small brewery, he moved to nearby Chiswell Street, where the business remained for over 250 years. In 1743 local jeweller William Kemp converted an existing pond on Old Street into the 50-metre Peerless Pool, which also served as a reservoir. Nicknamed the 'perilous pool', it was closed in 1850 and the site is now marked by Bath Street and Peerless Street. Old Street was heavily built up around this time but few of its early Victorian buildings remain, as a result of road widening in the 1870s and later slum clearance and bomb damage. Most commuters know Old Street for its station and the roundabout at the City Road junction, which is properly called St Agnes Well. The City and South London Railway (now the Northern Line) arrived here in 1901 and the Great Northern and City Railway (now WAGN Railway) followed just over two years later. Above ground, this is a cluttered corner, surrounded almost entirely by mundane modern structures and graced only by the terracotta grandeur of the former Leysian Mission, which moved here from Whitecross Street in 1904. The building was sold when the mission's work was merged with that of Wesley's Chapel in 1989 and has now been converted into flats. Old Street roundabout was given a facelift that included decorative arches in 1994 but the shopping precinct in the well remains slightly seedy.

✉ EC1

🚇 WAGN Railway; Northern Line (zone 1)

Old Town • *Croydon*

Now a dual carriageway section of the A236, north of the CROYDON flyover, and very rarely used as a name for the vicinity. In the mid 19th century Croydon's uncontrolled growth caused health and hygiene problems in what had become the fetid and insalubrious working-class quarter of Old Town. The Croydon improvement scheme of the early 1890s led to the widening of the High Street and swept away most of the Middle Row slum area.

✉ Croydon CR0

Oliver's Island • *Hounslow*

A small island in the Thames, lying off STRAND ON THE GREEN. Its name derives from a story that Oliver Cromwell once took refuge on the island but there is almost certainly no truth in this. The island was called Strand Ayt until a century after the Civil War, by which time the myth had arisen that Cromwell had used the Bull's Head in Strand on the Green as an intermittent headquarters. The story was further embellished with suggestions of a secret tunnel connecting the inn and the island, allegedly constructed to help Catholic priests escape Protestant persecutors. From the late 18th century Oliver's Island had a kind of tollbooth, a wooden structure styled like a small castle, which levied charges on passing craft to fund improvements to the river's navigability. The tolls were collected from a barge moored alongside the tollbooth. By 1865 there was a smithy, and barges were built and repaired on the island. In 1909 the Thames Conservancy assigned Oliver's Island to the Port of London Authority, which used it as a storage depot and as a wharf for derelict vessels. In 1958 the residents of Strand on the Green formed an amenity group for their locality that also took an interest in conservation on the island. The Strand on the Green Association was at the forefront of protests when the PLA tried to sell the island in 1971. The plan was dropped and Oliver's Island was instead leased to the London Natural History Society. The smithy was demolished in 1990.

▲ The Platform 9¾ sign at **King's Cross** station draws Harry Potter fans for a photo opportunity

▲ The architect EG Trobridge created a series of eccentrically picturesque houses in **Kingsbury** between the wars, including this one on Buck Lane

▲ *Out of Order* is an installation by David Mach, created in 1989 on Eden Street, **Kingston upon Thames**

▼ Harvey Nichols' flagship store opened in its present form on the corner of **Knightsbridge** and Sloane Street in the 1880s

▲ Leadenhall Market moved into its present wrought-iron and glass-roofed home in 1881

▲ This scene at **Lea Bridge** does not reflect the appearance of the wider area, much of which is given over to industry and utilities

▲ Former shipping containers have been converted to provide low-cost workspaces at **Leamouth**'s Container City

▲ Opened as the Regent's Canal Dock in 1820, **Limehouse** Basin became a marina in the 1980s and has since been surrounded by apartment blocks

◀ The Empire Theatre opened on **Leicester Square** in 1884; it was rebuilt as a cinema in 1928 and given a new interior in 1962

▲ The collegiate legal complex at **Lincoln's Inn** has a harmonious collection of buildings from every century since the 15th

▲ The 25 blocks of the **Lisson Green** estate were built on the site of Marylebone goods yard and were intended to house 5,000 people

▲ The Processione della Madonna del Carmine has been held annually in **Little Italy** for more than a century

▲ The canal intersection at **Little Venice** is lined with brightly painted houseboats, overlooked by houses from the second quarter of the 19th century

▲ To the west of **Little Woodcote**, the future twelfth Earl of Derby created Oaks Farm and as a 'model farmery' during the 1870s

◀ Norman Foster's City Hall was built to the east of **London Bridge City** in 2002 and will be overlooked by the 'Shard of Glass' if that project proceeds

▲ The 18th-century Ash Tree Cottage is by no means the oldest building on Bath Road in the well-preserved village of **Longford**

▲ **Lower Place** – Disraeli Road has the offices of Luxcrete, which markets the distinctive glass block walling used in the construction of Premier House

▲ Rushett Farm in **Malden Rushett,** a locality that has been saved from development by green belt protection

▲ Romford Road in **Manor Park** is noted for its used car dealerships

▲ The musicians George Friderich Handel and Jimi Hendrix lived in adjacent houses on Brook Street in **Mayfair**, but not at the same time

▲ **Maze Hill** – The architect and playwright Sir John Vanbrugh built this home for himself around 1720

▶ **Mill Hill** village is focused on the junction of the Ridgway and Milespit Hill, where Methodists built a red-brick chapel in 1893

▲ Now part of a conservation area, Thermopylae Gate in **Millwall** was named after a clipper on the Australian route

▲ Thames Water's **Mogden** waste water works opened in 1936 and is the second largest such plant in Europe

▲ The **Monument** to the Great Fire of London is 202 feet high, its distance from the fire's source in Pudding Lane

▲ **Morden** Hall Park is owned by the National Trust, which leases the house for use as a restaurant

▲ The former Black Cat cigarette factory at **Mornington Crescent** echoes the Egyptian temple to the cat-goddess at Bubastis

▲ The men's prayer hall in the Baitul Futuh mosque at **Morden South**

▲ A 1970s campaign against proposals to build a high-rise estate resulted in the creation of **Mudchute** Park and Farm

▲ Difficult retailing conditions confront many secondary suburban shopping parades, like this one in **New Eltham**

▲ **New Malden** is the main centre for London's Korean community

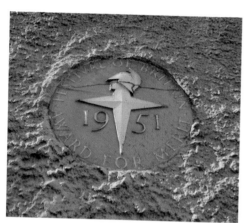

▲ Designed before World War II and built soon afterwards, **Newbury Park** bus station won an award for its distinctive use of concrete

▲ Old Keeper's Cottage on **Noak Hill** Road was the home of the Neave family's gamekeeper in the 19th century

▲ All kinds of vessels have become permanent homes at **Nine Elms** moorings

◀ Jack Straw's Castle, a former public house at the **North End** of Hampstead, has recently been converted to flats

▲ **North Feltham** – Hounslow Urban Farm is London's largest community farm

▲ Friars Lawn and the Grange are an attached pair of late 18th-century houses in **Norwood Green**

▲ The Muslim Cultural Heritage Centre opened in **North Kensington** in 1999

▲ **Notting Hill** – The fabulous terraces of Kensington Park Gardens were built in the early 1850s

▲ The distinctive peeling bark of a London plane, which stands by the pond and farmhouse on Bradmore Green in **Old Coulsdon**

▲ Church Street in **Old Isleworth**, with the tower of All Saints in the background

▲ **Oliver's Island** seen from the Surrey bank of the Thames, with Kew Railway Bridge behind

▶ **Osidge** was the home of the grocer and tea blender Thomas Lipton, who bequeathed his house as a hostel for nurses

▲ The peak-time ban on private cars results in the ascendancy of buses on **Oxford Street,** seen here from the roof of the John Lewis department store

▲ The Diageo drinks consortium has its headquarters at **Park Royal,** but has discontinued production at its nearby Guinness brewery

▲ Priscilla Sellon founded the Anglican Church's first sisterhood at 17 **Park Village** West

▲ **Perivale** – With its wonderful art deco detailing, the Hoover Factory on Western Avenue is widely considered to be London's finest (former) industrial building

◄ Opened in 1842, **Pentonville** is one of London's busiest 'local' prisons

▲ **Phipps Bridge** – When his terrace of workers' homes began to subside, the owner buttressed them with this castellated and 'ruinated' cottage

◄ This memorial sundial commemorates William Willett, who came up with the idea for daylight saving time as he rode through **Petts Wood**

▲ **Piccadilly Circus** was created by John Nash in 1819 and Alfred Gilbert's statue of Eros and the Trocadero (then a Lyons restaurant) were added in the 1890s

▶ Plans for new housing and small businesses on **Platt's Eyot** include the proposed construction of a new bridge to provide vehicular access

▲ D Silo at **Pontoon Dock** was restored by the London Docklands Development Corporation in 1994

▲ Although marred by unsympathetic 20th-century enlargement, **Pratts Bottom** retains some pretty groups of dwellings, like these weatherboarded cottages

▲ **Portobello Road** claims to become the world's largest antiques market on Saturdays and only Camden can rival the crowds it draws

▶ A crowd gathers at the summit of **Primrose Hill** to take in the superb view of the city at sunset

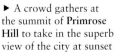

▲ The industrial wasteland around **Pudding Mill Lane** will be transformed for the 2012 Olympics

▲ The Artisans', Labourers' and General Dwellings Co. laid out the **Queen's Park** estate as a grid of terraces for the respectable working classes from 1873 onwards

▶ The Lodge is all that remains of the splendid set of buildings that made up **Reedham** orphanage

▲ Now a place of worship for Zoroastrians, this cinema in **Rayners Lane** features a representation of an elephant's trunk as the centrepiece of its art deco frontage

▶ A Parisian wine merchant opened the Café Royal on **Regent Street** in 1865, offering the then-rare prospect of French haute cuisine in the heart of London

◄ The riverside at **Richmond upon Thames** has a collection of fine buildings, open spaces and drinking establishments that can draw large crowds in the summer

◄ **Roehampton**'s Priory Hospital is internationally famous for the treatment of addictive disorders, often involving celebrities

▲ Queen Mary's Gardens were laid out in the 1930s, when the 17-acre Inner Circle of **Regent's Park** was first opened to the public

▲ The Corporation of London acquired **Riddlesdown** for public use in 1883

▲ **Royal Victoria** Dock is one of London's leading centres for sailing and windsurfing

▲ **Ruislip Common** has over 700 acres of glorious woodland and a sandy-beached lido that has no rival in Greater London

▲ The small and basic parish church of St Botolph was built in the early 14th century and survives as a barn at **Ruxley** Manor

▲ Much of the material that gave **Sandy Heath** its name was extracted for construction purposes in the 1860s and nowadays the terrain can often become boggy

▲ In 1970 the **Selsdon** Park Hotel was the scene of a meeting that changed the direction of British Conservatism

▲ The 2,500-acre **Richmond Park** (like others in London) began as a royal hunting ground and was opened to the public in 1904

▲ **Shadwell** – Former dock buildings converted to residential use at Free Trade Wharf

▲ **Shooters Hill** – Severndroog Castle commemorates the capture of the fortress of that name on India's Malabar coast

◀ When **Shoreditch** became fashionable in the 1990s, initially with the artistic community, former warehouses were converted for use as studios and galleries

▶ Tate & Lyle's sugar refinery at **Silvertown** is one of the few large-scale industrial plants remaining in London

◄ The Royal Court is widely regarded as England's foremost theatre for new playwrights and has staged works by Brecht, Ionesco, Beckett, Sartre, Wesker and Osborne

► The ruins and moat of the house called Howbury survive at **Slade Green**, together with a dilapidated Jacobean tithe barn

▲ **Smithfield** is the only remaining wholesale market in central London; its Victorian buildings have been refurbished to meet modern hygiene requirements

▲ Now a table dancing club, **Soho**'s Windmill Theatre famously claimed 'We never close' during the Blitz and was recently portrayed in the film *Mrs Henderson Presents*

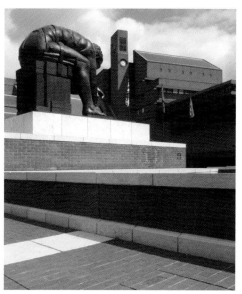

▲ **Somers Town** – Eduardo Paolozzi's sculpture of Isaac Newton is the dominant feature of the British Library's piazza

▲ **South Bank** – A second-hand book market operates under the arches of Waterloo Bridge, outside the National Film Theatre

▲ The opening of the National Theatre in 1976 marked the completion of the post-war creation of the **South Bank** arts complex

▶ Most of **South Bromley** has been rebuilt since World War II but Rutland Terrace survives on Oban Street from 1881

▲ **South Kensington** – The Victoria and Albert Museum has striven to compensate for its staid-sounding name by becoming the 'coolest' of London's great museums

▲ **Southall**'s Himalaya Palace cinema was restored in 2001 with the help of English Heritage and shows a mix of Hollywood and Bollywood films

▲ The medieval priory of St Mary Overie was rebuilt and enlarged during its centuries as a parish church and became **Southwark** Cathedral in 1905

▲ Saved from destruction by the **Spitalfields** Historic Buildings Trust, the houses of Fournier Street date were once leased to carpenters, merchants and silk weavers

▲ The run-down docks and warehouses of **St Katherine's** were transformed in the 1970s and 80s

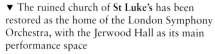

▲ The 385-feet Centre Point was London's only bona fide skyscraper when it was built in 1964 at **St Giles** Circus

▲ **St James's** Park is the oldest royal park in London and takes its name from a leper hospital founded by Queen Matilda around 1117

▼ The ruined church of **St Luke's** has been restored as the home of the London Symphony Orchestra, with the Jerwood Hall as its main performance space

◀ **St Margarets** – These houses in Ailsa Avenue played home to the Beatles in the film *Help*

▲ **Stanmore** – This stained-glass window at Bentley Priory commemorates the building's role as the Royal Air Force's Fighter Command Headquarters during World War II

▲ The pristine boulevards of **Stockley Park** are almost deserted even at lunchtime on a warm weekday

▲ A mural by Brian Barnes and **Stockwell** Park School pupils has made the entrance of this deep-level air-raid shelter into a war memorial

▲ **The Strand** – the Royal Courts of Justice are the home of the Court of Appeal and the High Court of Justice of England and Wales

▲ **Stoke Newington** – The tomb of William and Catherine Booth, the founder and mother of the Salvation Army, at Abney Park Cemetery

▲ This church on Marshgate Lane in **Stratford Marsh** is likely to succumb to the area's redevelopment for the 2012 Olympics

▲ Low Cross Wood Lane cuts through the ancient woodland of **Sydenham Hill,** which constitutes a surviving fragment of the Great North Wood

▲ Designed by Sir George Gilbert Scott, the **Strand** Chapel at King's College was beautifully restored in 2001

▲ Now the home of St Mary's College, **Strawberry Hill** was created by Horace Walpole in the 1750s and 60s and later extended by his relatives

▲ **Sundridge Park** – John Nash's imposing mansion is now a management centre and is not generally open to the public

▲ **Streatham Common** pumping station was built on Conyers Road in 1888, following the rapid growth in the area's population

▶ Hopes have been expressed that **Stroud Green** Road will become 'the next Upper Street', but with a more multicultural flavour

◀ **Surbiton** owed its early growth to the opening in 1838 of a station, which was stylishly rebuilt a century later

▼ The residents of **Taggs Island** live exclusively on houseboats; there are no permanent structures here

▲ When it was built in the 1820s, **Syon Park**'s Great Conservatory made pioneering use of glass and metal

▼ Camden council's flagship leisure centre opened at **Swiss Cottage** in 2006, partly funded by an associated apartment development

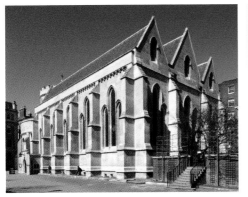

▲ **Temple** Church has become a major tourist attraction as a result of its appearance in the novel and film *The Da Vinci Code*

▲ **Three Mills** – Only two of the structures that gave this island its name have survived, of which the Clock Mill is the more picturesque

▲ The **Thames View** estate was built on reclaimed marshland in the 1950s

▲ **Tolworth** Tower was the work of Richard Seifert, who is said to have designed more London buildings than Christopher Wren

▲ Central London's **Theatreland** is focussed on Shaftesbury Avenue, where the Lyric was one of the first theatres to open, in 1888

▲ 100 yards long and 33 yards wide, the huge **Tooting Bec** lido was built in 1906

▲ The heavy-duty machinery that lifts the bascules of Tower Bridge is camouflaged by Gothic towers to harmonize with the neighbouring **Tower** of London

▲ The Granada Theatre on **Tooting Broadway**, now a bingo hall, is Britain's first Grade I-listed cinema building

▶ The grandest of **Tottenham Court Road**'s home furnishing stores, Heal's was extended southwards in 1937

◀ The Orange Tree in **Totteridge** became a public house in 1755, although the building has been much altered since then

▲ The National Gallery and the Church of St Martin-in-the-Fields form the backdrop to **Trafalgar Square**'s statues and fountains

▲ Lampooned in poetry by Wendy Cope and in a song by Carter USM, **Tulse Hill** is one of London's relatively 'unimproved' localities

▲ Built in 1803, **Upminster** windmill has been progressively restored in recent years

▶ Now an art gallery, this octagonal garden room and its service wings are all that survive of the **Twickenham** home of Louis Philippe, Duc d'Orleans

▲ Former residents of the **Vale of Health** include the writers DH Lawrence, Stella Gibbons, Compton Mackenzie and Edgar Wallace and the poet Rabindranath Tagore

▲ The creator of **Upper Woodcote** let gardens mature before building houses, resulting in lush scenes like this

▶ **Upney** – Built in the reign of Elizabeth I, Eastbury House is a National Trust property

▼ Solar panels on the 'ski ramp' roof extension of **Vauxhall** bus station provide power for most of its lighting

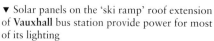

▲ The 15th-century Ancient House is one of several well-preserved old buildings in **Walthamstow Village**

▲ The layout of the original **Waterloo** station was so chaotic that it had to be rebuilt in the early 20th century but sections of earlier roofing were retained

▲ Cabmen's shelters were built all around London in the 1880s but this example in **Warwick Avenue** is one of just a few survivors today

◄ The 300 shops and 450 stalls of **Walthamstow** High Street and Selborne Walk are said to comprise Europe's longest daily street market

▲ Local youngsters pose in front of a Russian cannon that is displayed at **Welling** Corner in honour of the area's provision of homes for Woolwich Arsenal workers

▲ The **Westway** swings out over the Grand Union Canal and Trellick Tower looms in the distance

◀ Much used by rowers, sailors and canoeists, the **Welsh Harp** reservoir was created by damming the confluence of the River Brent and the Silk Stream

◀ **West Brompton** – The children's writer Beatrix Potter often walked in Brompton Cemetery and seems to have found names for her characters on the gravestones

▲ **Whipps Cross** – Waterlogged gravel pits have evolved into a popular beauty spot known as Hollow Ponds

▲ Even in an up and coming area like **Willesden Green**, the retail amenities can reflect a different reality

▶ As in nearby Harley Street, many of the properties on **Wimpole Street** are let by the Howard de Walden estate as doctors' or dentists' consulting rooms

▼ **Wimbledon Park** is dominated by the facilities of the All England Lawn Tennis and Croquet Club, which plans to install a retractable roof for Centre Court by 2009

▲ A major regeneration scheme is proposed for **Woodberry Down**'s 57 blocks of flats, built following World War II

▲ **Wood Green** is the primary leisure and shopping destination for a broad catchment area in north London

▲ Built in 1714, **Woodford Green**'s Hurst House is known as 'Naked Beauty' after a statue by the Italian sculptor Monti which used to stand in the garden

▼ The Board Room and Saloon of **Woolwich Arsenal** date from around 1717 and were probably the work of Sir John Vanbrugh

The island is now thickly wooded and a haven for cormorants, herons and Canada geese. Efforts are being made to control non-native tree and bird species.

✉ W4

Olympia *see* KENSINGTON OLYMPIA

Orpington • *Bromley*

An extensive dormitory town situated four miles south-east of BROMLEY. The place was first recorded in 1032 as Orpedingtun – the farmstead of a man called Orped, a name which meant 'active' or 'bold'. All Saints' Church is of Saxon origin and has a sundial inscribed in runes. The church was remodelled around 1200 and a priory was built nearby before 1270. The priory was enlarged and improved in the following two centuries and served both as a residence for the rector and chaplains and as an overnight stop for the priors of Canterbury Cathedral. Orpington and ST MARY CRAY rivalled each other for local ascendancy from the late Middle Ages but neither developed significantly until the 19th century. The opening of Orpington station in 1868 brought some early development to CROFTON and BROOM HILL and rebuilding on the High Street, while Orpington New Town was laid out on the edge of DERRY DOWNS. Until the end of the 19th century an annual fair was held on White Hart Meadow. At this fair William Cook, a poultry breeder who lived at Waldon Manor, developed and first presented 'Orpington Buff' chickens in 1894. They rapidly gained popularity as an excellent meat bird but lost out as the commercial roaster market developed, partly because of their excessively pale skin. With the provision of a larger station and improved rail services in 1904, developers began to buy up land east of the railway and true suburbanization was under way by the outbreak of World War I. During the war the Canadian province of Ontario funded the construction of a military hospital that later became Orpington Hospital. Housebuilding reached a crescendo in the late 1920s and 1930s, with winding tree-lined streets laid out in all directions. After World War II the suburb expanded to meet neighbouring villages and a large council estate was built on the edge of the green belt at RAMSDEN. A much larger All Saints' Church was consecrated in the late 1950s, with the medieval church becoming its ante-chapel, while the priory was attached to a new library. Many of the Victorian shops on the High Street were lost in the early 1970s during the building of the Walnuts shopping centre, which includes offices, a further education college and a police station. Behind the mall, the Walnuts Leisure Centre has swimming pools, sports courts and other facilities. At the southern end of the High Street the construction of a Tesco superstore and associated flats has caused controversy. Except on its far eastern side, Orpington is the epitome of comfortable suburbia, and its prime attraction is the museum and gardens of the priory.

In the days before tactical voting became commonplace, Orpington was the scene of a sensational by-election victory for the Liberals in 1962 when Eric Lubbock took the seat with a 27 per cent swing. The rock singer Billy Idol grew up in Orpington, as William Broad. Bugs Bunny's friend Miss Prissy is allegedly an Orpington Buff.

✉ Orpington BR6 and BR5

👥 15,078 (ward)

🚌 South Eastern Trains (zone 6)

📖 Dorothy Cox, *The Book of Orpington*, Barracuda, 1983

@ www.wsn.co.uk/orpington (local photograph archive)

Osidge • *Barnet* (pronounced to rhyme with 'sausage')

A comfortable 1930s suburban locality lying on a westerly slope beside the Pymmes Brook west of SOUTHGATE. Its name comes from Old English, meaning 'hedge belonging to a man named Osa'. Osidge was first recorded in 1176, in a charter from Henry II to the Abbot of St Albans referring to the abbot's woodland property here, where pigs were kept. The land was sold off after the dissolution of the monasteries in the mid 16th century and a substantial house was erected and parkland laid out. A condition of tenure was that the woods should supply faggots for the burning of heretics. In 1652 the house became the residence of the Hadley family. John Kingston of Oak Hill built a new Osidge in 1808, and promptly sold it. From 1893 this was the home of Thomas Lipton, who had been born into poverty in Glasgow and created a national chain of grocery stores. He is best remembered for his blends of tea, and for popularizing the beverage in the USA. After his death in 1931 most of the 60-acre estate was built up, but Lipton endowed his home as a hostel for nurses. The house still stands, in five acres of grounds, at 151 Chase Side, near the corner of Osidge Lane (originally called Blind Lane). Hugh Davies, the developer of the Osidge estate, advertised the proximity of Southgate station with a paraphrase of a popular song: 'Home, James, and don't spare the horses, it's a home on the Tube for me'. The properties are mostly semi-detached houses with generous gardens. To the west, the attractive but under-let Hampden Square has shops, restaurants and the Osidge Arms public house. Barnet's Conservative council came under fire in 2002 for proposing to install closed-circuit television cameras in the square, part of a ward newly won by the Conservatives, rather than in Labour-held areas with higher crime rates.

Whitehouse Way provided the backdrop to scenes in Mike Leigh's award-winning film *Secrets and Lies*. Jazz singer Amy Winehouse grew up on Osidge Lane.

> ✉ N14

> 📖 Alex Waugh, *The Lipton Story*, Cassell, 1951

Osterley • *Hounslow/Ealing*

The location of one of London's most magnificent stately homes, one-and-a-half miles west of BRENTFORD. Osterley was first recorded in 1274, and the name derives from Old English words meaning 'sheepfold clearing'. Sir Thomas Gresham, commercial agent and financial adviser to Elizabeth I, bought the manor of Osterley in 1562 and replaced the existing farmhouse with 'a faire and stateley brick house'. The banker Sir Francis Child acquired the house in 1713 and around 1760 his grandson commissioned Robert Adam (and probably others) to remodel the exterior and create lavishly furnished and decorated new rooms inside, while the grounds were landscaped and endowed with a chain of lakes. From the beginning of the 19th century Osterley Park House ceased to be a main place of residence. The neighbouring localities, formerly known as Thornbury Common and Scrattage, were occupied by farms, cottages and brickyards when Osterley and SPRING GROVE station opened on Thornbury Road in 1883. The common lay between Osterley Park and Spring Grove, while Scrattage was to its west. Little change took place until the construction of the Great West Road (A4), when suburban development began with luxury semi-detached houses on Wood Lane. Each had its own quarter-acre plot and was priced at a steep £2,500. The present station, a classic Charles Holden design, opened in 1934, and the old building is now a bookshop. In 1935, St Francis's Church was built on the Great

West Road. In 1939 the Earl of Jersey opened Osterley Park House to the public and ten years later gave it to the National Trust. The house is nowadays open to the public on most days in summer and at weekends in winter, and rooms can be hired for wedding ceremonies and receptions. In a ground-breaking move, the National Trust recently authorized its use for same-sex blessing ceremonies. Osterley Park, now split in two by the M4 motorway, includes woods, farms, sporting facilities and an ornamental lake. Brunel University's Osterley campus lies south of the Great West Road. North of the Grand Union Canal, which curves round the north of Osterley Park and along its eastern border, parts of the St Bernard's Hospital site have been redeveloped as Osterley View and Osterley Gardens.

Osterley Park has been a popular location for filming country house dramas, including the 1999 version of *Mansfield Park*. In recent BBC productions the house has played host to Leonardo da Vinci and Ludwig van Beethoven.

> ✉ Isleworth TW7

> 🚶 10,452 (Osterley and Spring Grove ward)

> 🚇 Piccadilly Line (zone 4)

> 📖 Eileen Harris, *Osterley Park, Middlesex*, National Trust, 1994

> @ www.osterleypark.org.uk (unofficial site)

Oval • *Lambeth*

The south-western corner of KENNINGTON, jutting into VAUXHALL, famed as the home of Surrey County Cricket Club. From the 17th century the land was used for growing fruit, flowers and vegetables; one tenant had to pay part of his rent in asparagus. The area takes its present name from a street layout devised in 1790, although the plan was never fully realized. In 1844 the Montpelier Cricket Club leased ten acres of the Oval's market gardens after it had been ejected from its ground at WALWORTH. Cabbage patches were buried under turf brought from Tooting Common. Shortly after the ground opened, a group of aficionados founded Surrey Cricket Club at a meeting in the neighbouring Horns Tavern; Surrey played its first county cricket match against Kent in 1846. An embankment was raised using soil excavated during the enclosure of the River Effra at Vauxhall Creek. As well as becoming the premier cricket ground south of the Thames, the Oval hosted the inaugural FA Cup final in 1872 and England's first rugby union matches against Scotland and Wales. Oval station, the Surrey Tavern and the members' pavilion were all built in the 1890s. The Duchy of Cornwall has been the ground's landlord from the start and in 1915 the future Edward VIII, then Prince of Wales and Duke of Cornwall, granted the club the right to use the Prince of Wales feathers as its insignia. The insurance company Brit became the Oval's sponsor in 2004, when redevelopment of the Vauxhall end began as part of a project to transform the ground into a broader sporting and entertainment venue.

England's wretched performance in a test match against Australia at the Oval in 1882 led the *Sporting Times* journalist Reginald Brooks to write a mock obituary in which he declared that the deceased body of English cricket would be 'cremated and the ashes taken to Australia'. Thus began the tradition of the two countries competing for the 'Ashes'. The Oval has given its name to cricket grounds in several former British colonies, including Sri Lanka and Barbados.

In the neighbouring Oval ward, more than two-thirds of residents are white – a high proportion for Lambeth – and the largest ethnic minority is of African descent. Archbishop Tenison's School was founded in 1685 and became a voluntary-aided church school in 1999. Around 80 per cent of pupils are from minority ethnic backgrounds and the school is heavily oversubscribed.

✉ SE11

⋔ 11,983

🚇 Northern Line (zone 2)

📖 Surrey County Cricket Club, *Darling Old Oval: A History of 150 Years of Surrey Cricket at the Oval, 1845–1995*, Cricket Lore, 1995

@ www.surreycricket.com

Oxford Circus • *Westminster*
The crossroads of OXFORD STREET and RE-GENT STREET. The junction was created in the early 1820s by the construction of Regent Street and was originally named Regent Circus North. Its southern counterpart – now called PICCADILLY CIRCUS – was a grander affair; there was never a circular arrangement to the buildings at the northern crossroads, just a rounding of corners. The Corinthian arcades of the circus itself were probably by John Nash, the architect of Regent Street, while the surroundings were developed by a local speculative builder, Samuel Baxter. By the

1890s the general public had started to refer to the junction as Oxford Circus, and it had become a notorious traffic blackspot, crowded with horse-drawn carriages from dawn until dusk. During this decade the linen draper Peter Robinson relocated here, operating premises at both the north-western and north-eastern corners, while Dickens and Jones took up residence at the south-eastern corner. A station on the Central London Railway opened on the east side of Argyll Street in 1900 and six years later the Waterloo and Baker Street Railway built a separate station on the opposite side of that street. Oxford Circus was rebuilt over an eleven-year period from 1912 as part of the reconstruction of Regent Street. Today the four corners are occupied by clothing and footwear stores. Curbs on the use of private cars in Oxford Street have helped reduce vehicular traffic, but pedestrians can cause congestion at Christmas time, when police officers are frequently needed to control the road crossings.

Christopher Ross's book *Tunnel Visions* collates the philosophical observations of a station assistant on the northbound Victoria Line platform of Oxford Circus Tube Station.

✉ W1

🚇 Bakerloo Line; Central Line; Victoria Line (zone 1)

📖 Christopher Ross, *Tunnel Visions*, Fourth Estate, 2001

Oxford Street • *Westminster*
Central London's 'jugular vein of consumerism' (as one anarchist group calls it), running east–west from ST GILES Circus to MARBLE ARCH. This was a medieval track, part of 'the way to UXBRIDGE', and was formerly known as Tyburn Road. The change to Oxford Street took place gradually between about 1718 and 1729 and the modern name probably derives from former landowners the earls of Oxford. The Lord Mayor of London had a banqueting house, a country seat used after hunting, which stood near the modern Stratford Place, opposite BOND STREET station. New Bond Street reached Oxford Street in the 1720s and the banqueting house was demolished in 1737 when houses, most of which still backed onto open fields, were beginning to line the street. The development of the neighbourhood culminated in the 1810s with the creation of RE-GENT STREET, which formed a crossroads at what is now OXFORD CIRCUS. Thereafter, small shops such as booksellers, shoemakers and

goldsmiths spread outwards from this focal point and the street became increasingly congested in the latter part of the century. John Lewis opened his first shop selling ribbons and haberdashery in 1864, progressively branching out into new lines. D H Evans followed soon afterwards. Grand emporiums made their appearance in the 1890s and the opening of four Central Line stations on the street in 1900 allowed customers to come from further afield. In 1902 the Bourne and Hollingsworth brothers-in-law moved their store to Oxford Street from WESTBOURNE GROVE, which had been a rival for shoppers' attentions. In 1909 Harry Gordon Selfridge opened Britain's first 'democratic' department store, where you could walk around as you pleased rather than being shown from counter to counter. Thereafter the street became single-mindedly devoted to retailing and the last private houses disappeared in 1930, to be replaced by a Gamage's department store. Marks and Spencer opened its Marble Arch store in 1930 and the Pantheon store in 1938. By this time, John Lewis's business had grown to fill a pair of department stores, but these were destroyed by fire after being hit by an oil bomb in 1940. The John Lewis store was rebuilt in its present form in the late 1950s. The first display of Christmas lights on Oxford Street was turned on in 1959 and the event is now a heavily publicized part of the promotional calendar, usually involving celebrities who appeal to an audience of parents and children. Some of the early department stores have left Oxford Street, to be replaced by small malls or the flagship stores of mass-market fashion groups or music retailers. Today the street shifts upmarket from east to west. The discount traders are mostly at the TOTTENHAM COURT ROAD end, while the big names cluster around Oxford Circus. Towards Marble Arch, stores increasingly cater for wealthy foreign tourists. Much of the south side is owned by Grosvenor Estates, which has recently collaborated with Westminster council in making environmental improvements.

Marks and Spencer's Pantheon store occupies the site of a pharmacy where in 1804 the writer Thomas de Quincey obtained his first supply of opium. In Geoff Nicholson's novel *Bleeding London*, the protagonist recalls that De Quincey called the street 'a stony-hearted stepmother who drinks the tears of children'.

✉ W1

@ www.oxfordstreet.co.uk (Oxford Street Association site)

Paddington • *Westminster*

Once a parish and metropolitan borough stretching as far as WEST KILBURN, but now a compact, densely built-up commercial locality surrounding the station that bears its name. A 'farmstead associated with a man called Padda' was first recorded in 998, but the settlement at PADDINGTON GREEN did not begin to grow until the 16th century, which was relatively late for a place so close to London. The landscape gained a predictable smattering of gentlemen's seats in the 18th century but was also much disfigured by gravel workings. From the start of the 19th century the village became the focus of a series of transportation initiatives that hastened its urban development. The Paddington branch of the Grand Junction (now Grand Union) Canal opened in 1801 and the canal company sponsored the construction of Grand Junction Street (now Sussex Gardens) and Praed Street, named after the company's chairman, William Praed. London's first horse-drawn bus service began operating from Paddington Green in 1829 and the Great Western Railway arrived in 1838, at first using a temporary terminus building that later became the site of a goods depot. Queen Victoria alighted here in 1842 after her first-ever train journey, which had begun in Slough, Berkshire. A permanent station opened in 1854, designed by the railway's chief engineer, Isambard Kingdom Brunel. In 1863 Paddington (Bishop's Road) station became the western terminus of the world's first underground railway line. By this time the village had become a crowded, semi-industrial suburb, and St Mary's Hospital had been built on Praed Street. The south-eastern part of the parish had meanwhile been built up as fashionable Tyburnia. Piecemeal rebuilding from the late 19th century to the present day has left central Paddington with a streetscape that ranges from fine Georgian terraced houses to some frankly seedy flats that are sometimes used for illicit purposes. The MARYLEBONE flyover and the elevated section of the WESTWAY (A40) were built in the second half of the 1960s, dividing the station and its environs from the settlement that had grown up around the green. A large-scale mixed-use development at PADDINGTON WATERSIDE is presently taking shape between the disunited halves, in the shadow of the Westway.

Alexander Fleming discovered penicillin in 1928 at St Mary's Hospital. The site of his original laboratory is now a museum devoted to his work. Former Paddington residents include the American polymath Benjamin Franklin and the German poet Heinrich Heine. Paddington is perhaps most famous for the children's book and television character Paddington Bear, who was found at the station and went to live in the suburban Brown household. In 2000 the books' author, Michael Bond, unveiled a 'life-size' bronze statue of Paddington in the station's new retail and eating area.

✉ W2

🚃 Main-line: First Great Western (south and south-west England, south Wales), First Great Western Link (southern England and suburban services), Heathrow Express (Heathrow Airport) London Underground: Bakerloo Line; Circle Line; District Line; Hammersmith & City Line (zone 1)

📖 Hans Norton, *Glimpses into the Past: Paddington, Little Venice and Maida Vale over the Years*, Paddington Waterways and Maida Vale Society Local History Group, 2005

@ www.newspad.co.uk (online local newspaper)

Paddington Green • *Westminster*

A rag-bag locality separated by HARROW ROAD and the end of the WESTWAY (A40) from the rest of PADDINGTON, but formerly the focus of the medieval village. From 1524 the White Lion pub stood on EDGWARE ROAD, opposite what is now the end of Bell Street. The parish church of St Mary was built in the 17th century and rebuilt in 1791, when the village had become popular as a rural retreat. During the

19th century Paddington Green lost its refined air as urbanization took hold. Edward Shillibeer operated London's first horse-drawn bus service from Paddington Green to the BANK in 1829, via the New Road. By the 1850s the surrounding area was densely built up, mostly with working-class terraced housing. The White Lion was rebuilt twice, becoming the Metropolitan Music Hall in the 1860s. Paddington Green Children's Hospital opened in 1883, financed by public donations. It has since been absorbed within St Mary's Hospital. Slum housing was cleared away from 1937 onwards, usually to be replaced by blocks of council flats. The Metropolitan Music Hall was demolished in 1962 as a consequence of construction work on the Marylebone flyover and was replaced by Paddington Green police station. This well-known landmark is the fortress to which suspected terrorists are usually taken for questioning in London. The IRA exploded a bomb outside the police station in 1992. St Mary's Church has a well-kept churchyard and the green itself might be pleasant were it not for 300 degree views of London at its most drab. Sarah Siddons surveys the southern aspect with an air of resignation; her white marble effigy is one of the few London statues to commemorate a member of the acting profession. The large amount of bed and breakfast accommodation in the area has led to the placement here of many refugees and asylum-seekers. At Paddington Green Primary School about a third of the pupils are from these families, and more than three-quarters have English as an additional language.

The Victorian music hall song *Pretty Polly Perkins of Paddington Green* became a big hit before World War I and was probably based on a real girl called Annette Perkins: 'She was as beautiful as a butterfly and proud as a queen / Was pretty little Polly Perkins of Paddington Green.' The green is the setting for scenes in the musical *Oliver!*. Paddington Green (and the surrounding four square miles) was the subject of a BBC television 'docu-soap' of that name which ran for six series from the end of 1998. The shows examined the lives of some of the area's colourful characters – including a transsexual prostitute and a safe-cracker.

✉ W2

Paddington Waterside • *Westminster*
A 21st-century mixed-use development situated in the vicinity of PADDINGTON station and the Paddington branch of the Grand Union Canal. This is one of the largest such schemes the capital has seen since the regeneration of DOCKLANDS. Most of the new building is taking place north of the station but the 80-acre Paddington Waterside 'footprint' takes in the station itself, new and old parts of St Mary's Hospital and existing buildings stretching from Eastbourne Terrace to the Hilton Metropole hotel on EDGWARE ROAD. Outline planning permission for the transformation of the former Paddington goods yard was granted in 1992 but its implementation was delayed by the downturn in the London property market. Construction began in 2000 but the ultimate form of the whole Waterside development is still under discussion and work may continue for up to ten more years. Westminster council rejected a plan for the 42-storey Grand Union Building, nicknamed the Paddington Eye, because it was inappropriately massive for the neighbourhood and the structure will now rise to 29 storeys. The first phase of the Sheldon Square office complex at Paddington Central was opened in 2002. Marks and Spencer moved its headquarters from BAKER STREET to Waterside House in 2004, and leisure and residential elements at Paddington Basin have recently been completed. Further extensions of Paddington Waterside are proposed for the longer term, including the relocation of North Westminster Community School and the redevelopment of its old site.

Algernon Newton's 1925 painting *Paddington Basin*, now in the art gallery at Brighton Pavilion, earned him the nickname 'the Regent's Canaletto'.

✉ W2

@ www.paddingtonwaterside.co.uk (regeneration partners' site); www.paddingtonbasin.co.uk (developers' site); www.paddingtoncentral.co.uk (property sales site)

Pall Mall • *Westminster*
A prestigious thoroughfare in ST JAMES'S, connecting the southern end of St James's Street with TRAFALGAR SQUARE. The name is now usually pronounced as in 'pallet' and 'mallet' but was earlier delivered as 'pell mell', as indicated in John Gay's poem *Fair Pall Mall* (1716), 'O bear to me the paths of fair Pall Mall / Safe are thy pavements, grateful is thy smell!' This pronunciation was later used by the manufacturers of the upmarket American cigarette brand Pall Mall, which took its name from the street. Pall Mall and then the MALL devel-

oped in the mid 17th century as boulevards where the well-to-do of Westminster played the imported sport of pallemaille, a cross between croquet and polo, but without the horses. Pall Mall later became a fashionable meeting place, famed for its coffee- and chocolate-houses. Members of the nobility built houses on the south side of Pall Mall, with gardens backing onto St James's Park. In the 19th century numerous gentlemen's clubs were established on Pall Mall; several remain here today, including the Athenaeum, the Reform Club and the Travellers' Club. In the second half of the 19th century Pall Mall's name became synonymous with the War Office, which stood here until 1906. In addition to its clubs, Pall Mall is now home to serviced offices, the Institute of Directors and the Royal British Legion.

Thomas Gainsborough lived at Schomberg House in Pall Mall between 1774 and 1788, and painted the *Blue Boy* here. The *Pall Mall Gazette* was an evening newspaper founded in 1865, which aimed to add human interest to its political coverage.

✉ SW1

📖 J M Scott, *The Book of Pall Mall*, Heinemann, 1965

Palmers Green • *Enfield*

'A poor man's MUSWELL HILL', as Pevsner called it, consisting of an Edwardian core surrounded by interwar estates on the borders of SOUTHGATE, WINCHMORE HILL and BOWES PARK. There was a Palmers Field here in 1204 and a road called Palmers Green in 1324 but there is no record of a settlement until the late 16th century, when there were four houses. The Broomfield Park estate belonged to the City of London alderman Sir John Spencer in 1599. Two centuries later Sir William Curtis, another alderman, acquired nearby Cullands Grove. It is Curtis who is remembered in the name of Alderman's Hill – and who is credited with originating the term the 'three R's' for reading, writing and arithmetic; some sources suggest that he meant this in all seriousness. After Curtis's death, Cullands Grove was acquired by John Taylor of Grovelands, who demolished the house and incorporated the grounds into his estate. By 1801 Palmers Green had 54 dwellings, including two inns and two farms. Despite the opening of the station on Aldermans Hill in 1871, little development occurred at first, mainly because wealthy landowners like the Taylor family had no need to sell. One estate was offered in lots in 1879 but few houses had been built on it by the end of the 19th century. The sale of several more estates after the death of their owners and a rush of interest from builders resulted in the development of almost all the land near the railway between 1900 and 1918. Large semi-detached houses went up on the Taylors' lands between Aldermans Hill and Fox Lane. The 54-acre Broomfield Park opened to the public in 1903. In the 1920s and 1930s semi-detached and terraced houses appeared south of Broomfield Lane and in the east of the district, south of Hedge Lane. After World War II, building was mainly confined to the replacement of bomb-damaged properties. Recent new builds have primarily consisted of flats, while a number of larger houses have been subdivided. Consequently a large number of Palmers Green's residents live in private rented accommodation. The ward also has the borough's highest proportion of 'other white' residents, which mostly means those of Greek or Turkish descent.

Palmers Green is best known to the highbrow as home to the poet Stevie Smith and to the lowbrow for its mention in Jona Lewie's 1980 novelty hit *You'll Always Find Me in the Kitchen at Parties*. Stevie Smith was born in Hull in 1902 but her family moved to Palmers Green less than five years later. They settled at 1 Avondale Road, which was to remain her home until she died in 1971. Smith's writings contain many thinly disguised allusions to Palmers Green and its residents, including an unpleasant caricature of her bank manager. Paul Scott, author of the *Raj Quartet*, grew up in Palmers Green.

✉ N13

🚶 13,197

🚌 WAGN Railway (zone 4)

📖 Alan Dumayne, *Once Upon a Time in Palmers Green*, self-published, 1993

Park Hill Village • *Croydon*

An estate agents' name for the 120-acre estate straddling Park Hill Road in south-east central CROYDON. Originally built for the keeper of the deer park of the archbishops of Canterbury, Park Hill House stood near to where Stanhope Road now lies. Reconstructed several times, it was demolished in 1949. The mid-Victorian Park Hill estate, laid out by the Ecclesiastical Commissioners, was mostly replaced with some fine Wates-built houses in the late 1960s and early 1970s. The 'village' has tree-lined roads, landscaped areas and a mix of town houses, detached houses and small apartment blocks. Many of the houses are split-level to accommodate the sloping terrain. Park Hill Junior School opened in 1968 and an infant school followed soon afterwards. St Matthew's Church, on the corner of Chichester Road, relocated here in 1971 in response to declining attendances at its predecessor in George Street. Opened in 1888, Park Hill recreation ground is a 15-acre park beside the railway line, in which a disused water tower, 125 feet tall, is a local landmark. On the opposite side of the locality, the Croydon Tramlink now runs through the short Park Hill tunnels that were cut in the 1880s for the WOODSIDE and SOUTH CROYDON Railway. Fossils of prehistoric mammals and a giant flightless bird were unearthed when the tunnels were dug.

✉ Croydon CR0

Park Lane • *Westminster*

The second most valuable property on the British Monopoly® board came into existence on the eastern border of HYDE PARK after Henry VIII enclosed the park in the early 16th century. It remained a rough track called Tyburn Lane until the 18th century. As MAYFAIR grew, titled gentlemen erected mansions on the east side of the road. Dorchester House was built in 1751 but did not gain that name until after its acquisition by Joseph Damer, who was made first Earl of Dorchester in 1792. The Grosvenor family, later the dukes of Westminster, lived on Park Lane from 1806. From the 1820s the road was intensively built up with very fine houses. In 1869 Dorchester House was rebuilt for Robert Stayner Holford in the style of a Renaissance palace. The German financier Alfred Beit commissioned Aldford House in 1897. With such fine views across the park, even the high values of its 18th- and 19th-century mansions did not deter property speculators from redeveloping the road between the wars, mostly with luxury hotels. When the art deco Park Lane Hotel (now the Sheraton Park Lane) opened in 1927 it was the first British hotel with a bathroom for every bedroom. The Grosvenor House Hotel opened in 1929 and in the same year Dorchester House was dismantled and re-erected in Scotland. The floors and ceilings of the highly specified hotel that replaced Dorchester House were lined with compressed seaweed for improved soundproofing. In 1962 part of Hyde Park was taken to allow Park Lane to be made into a dual carriageway and the road was diverted at the south end to enter HYDE PARK CORNER by the side of Apsley House. A cavernous underground car park was built beneath Hyde Park, with single-storey space for 1,100 cars and innovative automatic entry barriers. The 28-storey Hilton became a new London landmark on its completion in 1963. The noisiness of Park Lane has prompted proposals to put most of the street into a tunnel, but this dream is unlikely to be realized. In 2004 the Princess Royal unveiled a stylish memorial to animals that have died in war at Brook Gate, on the edge of Hyde Park. In addition to its hotels, Park Lane also has prestige offices and showrooms for exclusive car marques. Only near its northern end is there any semblance of conventional retailing at street level.

Park Lane residences signify high social status for Frederick Augustus Bullock in Thackeray's *Vanity Fair* and for the Honourable Ronald Adair in Conan Doyle's *Adventure of the Empty House*. The National Trust was founded at a meeting in Grosvenor House in 1895. Herbert Wilcox directed the romantic comedy film *Spring in Park Lane* (1948), which starred Michael Wilding and Anna Neagle, who had lived at Aldford House.

✉ W1

Park Langley • *Bromley*

A select estate in south BECKENHAM, still undergoing development. It is likely but not certain that the 'langan leage' recorded in a charter of 862 can be identified with this place, although the next mention of Langley does not come until the 13th century, when the Langley (or de Langele) family were in possession of the estate, and had probably taken their name from it. The Langley estate passed through a succession of eminent hands until it was acquired in the 1820s by Emmanuel Goodhart, whose family retained it into the 20th century. In 1908 the Lewisham building firm H & G Taylor bought 700 acres of the estate, intending to create a garden suburb of the highest quality, with a golf course, substantial detached and semi-detached houses, curving avenues and a circular amenity building, with shops and a church. One of the houses was built as the centrepiece of the 1910 Ideal Home Exhibition at KENSINGTON OLYMPIA and reassembled here following the exhibition. Henry Wellcome bought Langley Court and 105 acres of land in 1918 to set up research laboratories for his pharmaceutical company. At the same time, Taylor's resumed work on its 'garden city'. Although the company considered the golf course to be the 'jewel in the crown' of Park Langley, its architectural highlight was the petrol station built at Looking Glass Corner in 1929. Designed in what Pevsner calls 'a rampant *Road to Mandalay* style', it later became known as the Chinese garage. Parts of Park Langley were not fully developed until after World War II, while the amenity centre failed to materialize and its site was used for Langley Park Schools. Wellcome ended research at Langley Court in 1995 and its grounds have seen extensive housebuilding in the early 21st century, including the Langley Park and Langley Waterside estates.

✉ Beckenham BR3; West Wickham BR4

@ www.plra.org.uk (Park Langley Residents' Association site); www.chinesegarage.co.uk

Park Royal • *Brent/Ealing*

An extensive industrial and commercial estate in the far north of ACTON, between the Western Avenue (A40) and the Grand Union Canal. Formerly the village of Twyford, the present name derives from the Royal Agricultural Society exhibitions held here from 1903 to 1905. Munitions factories were built on the site during World War I, and it developed as an important industrial estate after hostilities ended. There were stadiums for greyhound racing and football. Employers included H J Heinz and the Waterlows printing company. Drinks conglomerate Diageo has its headquarters here. Built by Sir Giles Gilbert Scott in 1934, the neighbouring Guinness brewery closed in 2005, owing to Diageo's excess production capacity. Following the closure of several of Park Royal's factories in the 1970s and 1980s, parts of the area became derelict. The Park Royal Partnership plans to address the decline with a massive increase in the size of the Park Royal estate, bringing 25,000 new jobs by 2012, and a related improvement in the quality of the built and landscaped environment. Contrary to the general trend towards exclusively high-tech business parks, manufacturing industry will continue to play a part. A new Central Line stop is proposed, making Park Royal an interchange station on the London Underground. Park Royal is also known to the public for its Asda superstore and the Royale leisure park, which includes a nine-screen multiplex cinema and a 36-lane bowling alley. The complex lies on the opposite side of Western Avenue from the main estate.

✉ NW10

🚇 Piccadilly Line (zone 3)

📖 M C Barrès-Baker, *Twyford and Park Royal*, Grange Museum of Community History and Brent Archive, 2001

@ www.parkroyal.org (Park Royal Partnership site)

Park Village • *Camden*

A delightful pair of streets situated on the south-western edge of CAMDEN TOWN, created in the 1820s by John Nash as part of his master plan for REGENT'S PARK. Park Village West, which survives intact, is a crescent located just north of Regent's Park barracks, off Albany Street. Park Village East meanders gently south as an extension of Prince Albert Road. Nash and his protégé James Pennethorne combined stuccoed villas and terraced houses of sharply differing proportions and styles, including Gothic, Italianate and Tudor, on either side of an arm of the Regent's Canal that was later filled in. The village was a model for subsequent Victorian estates and has even been identified as *the* first modern suburb, albeit in miniature – but there are many other contenders for the title, which is so hard to define, from CLAPHAM to Cambridge, Massachusetts. Among the early residents was Dr James Johnson, physician to William IV. Johnson lived at 12 Park Village West, possibly the most impressive villa in the whole development. A few doors away at No. 17, Priscilla Sellon founded the Anglican Church's first sisterhood in 1845, which was soon followed by others in England and North America. Just a generation after its completion, half of Park Village East was torn down to make way for the London and Birmingham Railway. Units of the University of Westminster are located at 100 Park Village East, including the Policy Studies Institute and the Centre for the Study of Democracy.

✉ NW1

Parliament Hill • *Camden*

A 319-feet hill and 267 acres of fields now constituting the south-east corner of HAMPSTEAD HEATH. A mound to the north-west of the hill may be a Bronze Age round barrow. Parliament Hill's name was not recorded until around 1875, and despite its recentness is of uncertain origin. The obvious explanation is that the hill provides superb views of Westminster and central London in general. A more specific and legendary reason is that

Guy Fawkes and his co-conspirators intended to watch the blowing up of the Houses of Parliament from here and this story is echoed in an earlier name, Traitors' Hill. The Hampstead Heath Enlargement Act formally joined the hill and fields to the heath in 1889, ensuring their permanent preservation. Had they been protected earlier, South Hill Park would not have been built. At the time of the extension Lord Mansfield was planning further development in the area of the present athletics track but he was instead restricted to creating Tanza Road, which joined up two pre-existing streets. The flats of Parliament Court were built on the South End Farm estate next to the railway in 1937. There are extensive and varied sports facilities in the GOSPEL OAK crook of the fields surrounding Parliament Hill and William Ellis schools. Parliament Hill Lido dates from the late 1930s and is open all year round, but unheated. This Grade II-listed amenity is run by the London Borough of Camden and owned by the Corporation of London. The recently refurbished athletics track is the base for HIGHGATE Harriers and London Heathside athletics clubs. Parliament Hill Fields is regarded as north London's premier kite-flying spot.

The poet John Betjeman was born in the 'red-brick gloom' of Parliament Hill Mansions in Lissenden Gardens in 1906.

⊠ N6; NW3; NW5

@ www.highgateharriers.org.uk;
www.londonheathside.org.uk

Parsons Green • Hammersmith & Fulham

A highly gentrified locality in central FULHAM, arranged around a triangular green and the larger Eel Brook Common, which lies to its north-east. Evidence of an Iron Age settlement has been discovered at Lady Margaret School. The green's name derives from the presence of Fulham rectory, which stood on the site of St Dionis' Church from the 14th century. A clump of trees on the west side of the green was known as Parson's Grove by 1424. Parsons Green had only 16 ratepayers in 1625 and the village remained sparsely populated for the next two centuries. The White Horse coaching inn was a meeting place for Fulham Albion Cricket Club, one of the first in England. It is said that the parson played bowls on the green in the early 18th century, when the old rectory was demolished and replaced by two brick-built houses. Wealthy Londoners were able to build country retreats here with spacious grounds because the land was not progressively subdivided into small tenements, as it was at nearby WALHAM GREEN. From the 1840s suburban dwellings began to replace Parsons Green's grandest houses, although some survived as schools. The Midland District Railway opened a station in 1880 and within a decade an irregular grid of terraced houses had filled the entire vicinity. St Dionis' Church and the White Horse were rebuilt and the village pond, known as Colepitts, was drained. Twentieth-century change has mostly been limited to infilling, and the replacement of St Mark's School, a Co-op dairy depot and some former light industrial premises by housing, shops and offices. Following its enlargement in 2002 a conservation area now takes in the whole of Parsons Green between New Kings Road and the railway line.

Maria Fitzherbert, the clandestine 'wife' of George, Prince of Wales (subsequently the Prince Regent, and then George IV), lived at East End House in the early 19th century. Media queen Janet Street-Porter grew up in a ground-floor flat on Elmstone Road in the years immediately following World War II, when Fulham was a working-class district.

⊠ SW6

👫 10,280 (Parsons Green and Walham ward)

🚇 District Line (zone 2)

Parson's Pightle • Croydon (pronounced 'pyetal')

A corner of the extensive swathe of green belt that lies south-west of OLD COULSDON. Parson's Pightle was an 18th-century house that served as the rectory for Coulsdon's Church of St John the Evangelist. A 'pightle' was a small enclosure or croft. The parsonage was rebuilt in stone as a private residence in 1841. Some of the grounds have been preserved as part of Happy Valley Park but the house was demolished in the 1960s during the construction of a housing estate. The estate's main thoroughfare is named after the most illustrious occupant of Parson's Pightle, Admiral Sir William Goodenough, who commanded the Royal Navy's second light cruiser squadron during World War I. The sports ground at Parson's Pightle is home to Purley John Fisher Rugby Football Club.

⊠ Coulsdon CR5

Peckham • Southwark

A steadily recovering but still deprived district situated east of CAMBERWELL. Peckham appears in Domesday Book as Pecheham, meaning a 'homestead by a hill' – probably a reference to what is now called TELEGRAPH HILL. At the time it was an insignificant place of 240 acres. Henry I gave it to his illegitimate son Robert, Earl of Gloucester, and it served as a royal hunting ground. King John favoured Peckham with the grant of an annual fair which survived into the 19th century. It remained a rural area until the Industrial Revolution, growing crops for the London market. The Grand Surrey Canal linked Peckham to the Surrey Docks (now SURREY QUAYS) in 1826 and Thomas Tilling's horse-drawn buses operated from 1851, helping open up the area to Londoners moving out of the city. New estates such as Peckham Park, also known as Peckham New Town, were built from the early 19th century onwards and NORTH PECKHAM became a desirable middle-class suburb. Its respectability was confirmed by the opening of the Jones and Higgins department store on Rye Lane. However with the OLD KENT ROAD acquiring industry such as a gasworks, and south Peckham being developed with the lower middle class in mind, its upmarket reputation was always vulnerable. It flourished just as ably as a working-class suburb, with jobs provided by employers such as Samuel Jones, which made the Butterfly brand of gummed papers. Peckham suffered in the Blitz and after the war bombsites in the north were merged into the new Burgess Park. By the time of ten-year-old Damilola Taylor's death on the North Peckham estate in 2000, the area had become a byword for inner city crime and decline. Change was already in hand, however, with the Peckham Partnership's regeneration of its grimmest estates and the opening of Will Alsop's landmark library in 2000 on Peckham Square, created by the infilling of the Grand Surrey Canal. Improvements in the BELLENDEN renewal area include street furniture by sculptor Anthony Gormley and painter Tom Phillips. Peckham is the only ward in London where black and black British people make up a majority of the population. Over a third of all residents are of black African descent, by far the highest proportion in London.

The poet Robert Browning was educated at Peckham in the 1820s, and the actor Jeremy Irons was briefly a social worker here. One of the most famous addresses in British television comedy was Peckham's fictional Nelson Mandela House, the home of the Trotter family in *Only Fools and Horses*. The neighbourhood also featured in Channel 4's 'ethnic sitcom' *Desmond's*, which ran from 1989 to 1995. The footballers Rio and Anton Ferdinand were born and raised in Peckham.

✉ SE15; SE5

👥 56,943 (Livesey, Nunhead, Peckham, Peckham Rye and the Lane wards)

📖 John D Beasley, *Peckham and Nunhead Memories*, Tempus, 2000

@ www.peckhamsociety.org.uk

Peckham Rye • *Southwark*

A triangular common and its adjoining public park, located on the south side of PECKHAM. Legend has it that Boudicca died of poisoning here. Peckham Rye was first mentioned by name in the early 16th century. 'Rye' is a corruption of 'rīth', Old English for a small stream. The medieval common was surrounded by market gardens in the second half of the 18th century and local people resisted encroachments in 1766 and 1789. Peckham Rye station opened in 1866, some way to the north but close enough to stimulate suburban development. In 1868 CAMBERWELL vestry bought out the lord of the manor's rights to the common, permanently preserving it as public open space. The London County Council acquired the neighbouring 51 acres of Homestall Farm in 1892 and laid it out as Peckham Rye Park. The LCC began the Rye Hill estate on the NUNHEAD side of the common in 1939 but did not complete it until 1964. Austin's, one of the largest antiques and second-hand dealers in Europe, operated near the northern tip of the common until 1994. The site is now occupied by Austins Court. More than half the homes in the Peckham Rye ward are owner-occupied, a high proportion by the borough's standards. Peckham Rye Park reopened in 2005 after a year-long closure for the restoration of its delightful Victorian features. The replanted gardens were quickly vandalized and night-time guard-dog patrols were introduced.

William Blake had his first 'vision of angels' as a young boy on Peckham Rye. Muriel Spark wrote *The Ballad of Peckham Rye* in 1960. Peckham Rye Lido, which closed in 1987, and Camberwell Old Cemetery, which lies to the south, both featured in the 1969 film *Entertaining Mr Sloane*, based on a play by Joe Orton. Peckham or Peckham Rye is cockney rhyming slang for a tie.

✉ SE15; SE22

👥 11,248

379

🚆 South Eastern Trains; Southern (zone 2)

📖 John D Beasley, *Peckham Rye Park Centenary,* South Riding Press, 1995

@ www.foprp.org.uk (Friends of Peckham Rye Park site)

Penge • *Bromley* (pronounced 'penj')

A less favoured corner of the borough, lying on the south-eastern side of CRYSTAL PALACE Park. The name derives from Celtic words meaning 'head of the wood'; Pencoed in Wales has exactly the same origin. This is one of the few Celtic place names in London and suggests the survival of a native British contingent after Anglo-Saxon colonization. In 957 King Eadwig (or Edwy All-Fair) granted the manor of BATTERSEA to 'Lyfing, his faithful minister', together with swine pasture at Penge, which remained a detached portion of Battersea parish for more than a thousand years. Gypsies continued to make camp in the woods here until the early 19th century, when the construction of the Croydon Canal brought daytrippers to Penge and ANERLEY, and later the first residents after the enclosure of the common in 1827. The canal was replaced by a railway in 1839 and Penge (now Penge West) station opened but soon closed again, owing to the lack of passengers. The Church of St John the Evangelist was built in 1850, when the population of the village had risen to over a thousand, including the residents of two groups of almshouses. Soon afterwards, the relocation of the Crystal Palace to SYDENHAM brought explosive growth to the area. The station reopened in 1863 and the London, Chatham and Dover Railway opened another station in the same year, which lay within BECKENHAM and is now called Penge East. In 1866 the Duke of Westminster sold Porcupine Field on favourable terms to the Metropolitan Association for Improving the Dwellings of the Industrious Classes and the charity laid out its only country estate here, which it named after Alexandra, Princess of Wales. Because Penge lay on the lower slopes of Sydenham Hill, speculative developers generally built smaller houses than in the heights of UPPER NORWOOD or UPPER SYDENHAM and this contributed to the high density of population, which had risen to over 13,000 by 1871. Penge became an urban district in 1900 and was transferred from Surrey to Kent. The area was very badly damaged by bombing during World War II and of the several consequent reconstruction projects the largest was the council's Groves estate, now run by the Broomleigh Housing Association. Several of the estate's tower blocks have been demolished as part of a recent regeneration scheme. Only 78 per cent of the residents of the Penge and Cator ward are white, a very low proportion in comparison with the rest of the borough of Bromley. The principal minorities are of black African and black Caribbean descent. More than a quarter of homes are rented from a housing association. Unemployment is almost twice the borough average.

John Mortimer's irascible barrister Horace Rumpole often referred to the 'Penge bungalow murders' case as his greatest triumph; the full story was finally revealed in the 2004 novel of that name.

✉ SE20

👥 16,687 (Penge and Cator ward)

🚆 South Eastern Trains (Penge East, zone 4); Southern (Penge West, zone 4)

📖 David R Johnson, *Around Crystal Palace and Penge,* Sutton, 2004; Peter Abbott and the Anerley Writers Circle, *The Book of Penge, Anerley and Crystal Palace,* Halsgrove, 2002

@ www.virtualpenge.com (community site)

Pentonville • *Islington*

An underprivileged inner-city district situated between KING'S CROSS and the ANGEL, ISLINGTON. In 1730 pleasure gardens and tearooms opened at White Conduit House, and survived for almost a century. The composer James Hook was organist at the gardens and a cricket pitch was tended by Thomas Lord, who went on to establish a ground of his own in MARYLEBONE. Britain's earliest bypass, the New Road, brought access to the land west of Islington in 1756. The development opportunity was seized by Captain Henry Penton, MP for Winchester, who began to lay out what has been called London's first planned suburb during the latter years of the 18th century. The Palladian St James' Church was erected in 1787 (and rebuilt in facsimile in 1990 as flats and offices) and the estate was completed around 1820. A few of the original houses survive in CHAPEL MARKET, which, as Chapel Street, marked the Penton estate's eastern boundary. Almost a mile to the north, Pentonville Prison was built in 1842 to a radical radial plan. Its designers, Joshua Jebb and Sir Charles Barry, created what was literally a model institution, since it has been called 'the most copied prison in the world'. By 1850 London had reached out to merge with the new suburb and most of the buildings that now line Pentonville Road (as this section of the New Road was renamed) date from that period onwards. By the late 19th century parts of Pentonville had degenerated into slums, which were cleared in stages from the 1930s. The district is now dominated by post-war council housing; the Priory Green estate of 1951 was among the first. Some blocks have already been rebuilt with a more humane design, while others have had elaborate security measures installed, largely to prevent usage of common areas by the drug addicts of King's Cross. Pentonville Road is steadily shifting upmarket, especially near the Angel, where the Crafts Council has its headquarters and gallery.

It has been said that Pentonville's high ground is a sacred site, associated with Merlin and pagan worship. In *London: The Biography*, Peter Ackroyd speculates on alternative meanings of 'pen' and 'ton' that relate to holy waters. Ackroyd knows all about Henry Penton but suggests that a parallel derivation might exist, asking, 'Can one place assume different identities, existing in different times and in different visions of reality?' On a more rational note, the philosopher John Stuart Mill was born in Pentonville in 1806.

✉ N1

📖 Robert Stephen Duncan, *Peerless Priceless Pentonville: 160 Years of History of Pentonville*, self-published, 2000

@ www.craftscouncil.org.uk

Perivale · *Ealing*

An industrial and residential area in east GREENFORD, bounded by the River Brent and the Paddington branch of the Grand Union Canal. Perivale was originally Greenford Parva, or Little Greenford, and the name may be a corruption of Parva. Alternatively it may derive from 'pure vale' or 'pear vale'. Stories have been told of a sequence of mysterious deaths at the medieval Perivale Mill, but there is little documentary evidence even for the mill's existence. The manor of Perivale evolved in the late Middle Ages, with links to the Mercers' Company of the City of London. The manor house was demolished by 1850, when the village started to show the first shoots of growth and the church was refurbished by the little-known Ealing architect R Willey. Perivale remained very quiet into the early years of the 20th century. The station opened in 1904 but the village still had fewer than 100 inhabitants

by the time of the 1911 census. The availability of open land and the coming of the Western Avenue (A40) brought industry after 1930, including Sanderson's wallpaper factory. Residential estates followed, notably Perivale Park, built to the west of the station by Cliffords Estates, which boasted of its 20 different styles of elevation. Developments to the north of the industrial area included local shops on Bilton Road. By 1951 Perivale's population had risen to almost 10,000. Today, just over half the residents of Perivale are white and the largest minority is of Indian descent. In most respects, Perivale's socio-economic profile is representative of the borough as a whole, though a little more affluent. Perivale Wood is an ancient woodland formerly known as Braddish Wood, and privately owned by the Selborne Society. This is the second oldest nature reserve in the country but is not generally open to the public.

Perivale's architectural highpoint is undoubtedly the Hoover Building, on the Western Avenue. 'One of these days the Hoover factory's gonna be all the rage / In those fashionable pages,' prophesied Elvis Costello in 1978. This art deco masterpiece by New York architects Wallis Gilbert and Partners was completed in 1933. It closed in 1982 and reopened ten years later, magnificently restored, with the rear of the building converted into a Tesco superstore.

✉ Greenford UB6

👥 13,441

🚇 Central Line (zone 4)

📖 Frances Hounsell, *Greenford, Northolt and Perivale Past*, Historical Publications, 1999

Perry Hill · *Lewisham*

A section of the A212 running northwards from BELL GREEN to Catford Hill, taking its name from the Middle English word for a pear tree. Saxon or Jutish farmers may have settled in a forest clearing here as early as the sixth century. The name 'Perrystrete' was recorded in 1473, gradually mutating into Perry Street Hill and then Perry Hill. Place House, the manor house of SYDENHAM, stood until 1810 near to where Perry Hill now becomes Catford Hill. Tradition has it that Elizabeth I had the house built for the Earl of Essex and frequently visited him there, but there is no evidence for this. From around 1870 the area was built up as far south as Castlands Road. Beyond this was Perry Hill Farm, which belonged to the Leathersellers' Company. Its farmhouse was once known as Clowders, now remembered in a street name, as is one of its meadows, Priestfield. The farm succumbed to suburban housebuilding early in the 20th century. The locality now has interwar blocks of council flats, some low-rent shops and light industry, and run-down properties.

Oddly, a plaque at 37 Woolstone Road honours John Linnell and William Blake. But, as Lewisham council is quick to point out, 'This plaque is a copy of one on a house in North End Road, HAMPSTEAD. Neither Linnell nor Blake had any connection with the Perry Hill area and this house was not built until after their deaths.'

✉ SE6

Perry Vale • Lewisham

A new ward in south-east FOREST HILL, covering an area originally known as Perry Slough. In contrast to the older settlement of Perry Hill, from which it borrowed its name, settlers did not colonize the marshy ground here until the 18th century. Rocque's map of 1745 shows Perry Slough on the western edge of cultivated land, beyond which was still thick forest, with barely a dwelling in sight. Following the opening of Forest Hill station (originally Dartmouth Arms) in 1839, the area was built up with homes for wealthy city commuters. Among the new residents was a community of Germans who had their own church in Dacres Road. Perry Vale's demographic profile is now similar to that of the borough as a whole, with just a few indications of slightly superior affluence. No. 11 Shaw's Cottages, in Perry Rise, is an 'ecological self-build private house' with a grass roof supported by tree trunks.

The Irish poet Thomas Dermody died in Perry Vale in 1802, at the age of 27. He was buried at St Mary the Virgin Church, Lewisham.

✉ SE23

♦ 14,513

Petersham • Richmond

A prosperous village almost surrounded by green spaces, situated south of RICHMOND UPON THAMES. The land belonged to St Peter's Abbey in Chertsey from the seventh century, although its name refers to the homestead of a man called Peohtrīc or Patrick rather than the saint. In the Middle Ages it was a place of sanctuary where no one could be arrested. When the abbey handed Petersham to the Crown in the 15th century, the village fell under the same jurisdiction as its close neigh-

bour HAM. The present St Peter's Church was built in 1266 and was almost totally rebuilt in 1505, with subsequent additions that include a 17th-century tower and distinctive Georgian box pews. Petersham's role as a refuge for the London rich has left it with a legacy of fine Stuart and Georgian houses and it has been called the most elegant village in England. The Dysart family, who lived at Ham House from the 17th century, are remembered in the name of one of Petersham's pubs, the Dysart. Lord John Russell (later the first Earl Russell) founded a village school in 1851 and the present primary school is named in his honour. The red-brick All Saints' Church was begun in 1901 and has since found its vocation as a recording studio. Gordon House, home to the eccentric Duchess of Queensberry in the 18th century, was converted into London's German School in 1971, with new buildings added over the following decade. Petersham Park, Common and Meadows are extensions of Richmond Park. The meadows form the tranquil foreground of the famous vista of south-west London from Richmond Hill. The riverside path from Richmond is popular for weekend outings and walkers may take advantage of the ferry that still crosses the Thames to TWICKENHAM close to Ham House.

The explorer George Vancouver retired to Petersham and wrote A Voyage of Discovery here. He died in 1798 and is buried in St Peter's churchyard. Charles Dickens wrote most of Nicholas Nickleby while staying at Elm Lodge in the 1830s.

✉ Richmond TW10

♦ 9,678 (Ham, Petersham and Richmond Riverside ward)

▭ John Plant, Ham and Petersham at 2000, Richmond Local History Society, 2000

@ www.russell.richmond.sch.uk

Petticoat Lane • Tower Hamlets/City

A historic market street located north of ALDGATE. In 1373 this was the muddy Berwardes Lane. In 1500 it had become an elm-lined avenue called Hog Lane. By 1603 it was known as Petticoat Lane, probably because dealers in old clothes operated here. The word 'petticoat' formerly embraced a wider variety of skirts than it does now. An outbreak of plague in 1625 drove away the local nobility and the area was colonized by Dutch and French immigrants, who began selling their wares. British traders followed and a major market had developed by the mid 18th century. In 1830 the lane's name was prudishly changed to Middlesex Street but this has never entered popular usage. At the end of the 19th century the road was widened and lined with shops. Most retailers dealt in clothes but others offered takeaway foods such as hokey-pokey and wallywallies. When more and more street traders set up stalls here the authorities tried at first to expel them, sometimes finding excuses to drive buses or fire engines through the crowds. The Corporation of London relented in 1927 and introduced a regulation scheme for stallholders' pitches. Sunday trading was legalized in 1936, in response to the wishes of the EAST END'S large Jewish community. Nowadays, Wentworth Street has a weekday market and this spreads into Middlesex Street and its offshoots on Sundays, when over 1,000 stalls operate. Clothing and textiles are still the main speciality but bargains of all kinds are on offer. The market attracts millions of visitors every year but many younger customers have migrated to nearby Brick Lane or SPITALFIELDS, or forsaken the East End for CAMDEN TOWN.

Vidal Sassoon, 'the man who invented modern hairdressing', lived in a Petticoat Lane tenement and was apprenticed to a hairdresser nicknamed 'the professor'. In the face of the blackshirted anti-Semitism troubling the East End at that time, Sassoon became active in a Jewish paramilitary group and left the country in 1948 to fight for Israeli independence.

✉ E1

📖 Jo Adam Joseph, *Souvenir Guide to Petticoat Lane*, Petticoat Lane Preservation Co., 1975

Petts Wood • *Bromley*

The acme of Kentish suburbia, situated midway between CHISLEHURST and ORPINGTON, and previously divided between those two parishes. The wood is believed to have been planted in the last quarter of the 16th century by the Pett family, who were leading shipwrights for 200 years and are mentioned in Pepys' diaries. Not until 1872 was the first house said to have been built here, and named Ladywood. William Willett came up with his idea for daylight saving time while riding through Petts Wood just after dawn one morning in the early 1900s. Basil Scruby, an entrepreneur from Harlow in Essex, had already built more affordably at NEWBURY PARK and elsewhere when he turned his attention to Petts Wood in 1927, securing an option on 400 acres of woodland and strawberry fields and proceeding to buy it in sections. In the same

year, the National Trust acquired the remainder of the wood and erected a granite sundial in William Willett's honour. Scruby appointed the architect Leonard Culliford to lay out roads that emphasized the natural curves of the landscape, rather than simply cutting across it. He also paid the Southern Railway Co. £6,000 to open a station in 1928, and provided the site for the passenger building and a goods yard. Shops, the Daylight Inn hotel and the Embassy cinema were built in the vicinity of the station from the early 1930s. Scruby leased groups of plots to numerous builders, including his Harlow friends Walter Reed and George Hoad. The various subcontractors soon built up the eastern side of Petts Wood in a variety of grandiose styles, with mock-Tudor predominating. St Francis's Church was built on Willett Way in 1935. From around this time, Scruby began to sell off the land west of the railway line but as a result of his financial difficulties he was unable to exert control over the quality of building. Much of this area was developed by Morrell's and New Ideal Homesteads, both major players in the suburbanization of rural south London. On the edge of Scruby's land, other developers added some modernist houses and chalets, a few in the voguish 'suntrap' style. Congregational (later United Reformed), Methodist and Roman Catholic churches were built in the 1950s and 1960s. The Embassy cinema closed in 1973 and was replaced by a Safeway supermarket in 1982, whereupon five local shops closed within months, but generic factors have also played their part in the subsequent decline of the centre's village character. With only 7.9 per cent of its population in the 20–29 age group, the Petts Wood and Knoll ward has fewer young adults than almost any other part of London. Over 95 per cent of residents are white, and almost two-thirds of adults are married.

In 1940 General Charles de Gaulle and his wife rented 41 Birchwood Road after the fall of France but they judged Petts Wood to be at risk of bombing, so the family moved to rural Shropshire while the general stayed in a Mayfair hotel. The dour entertainer Jack Dee was born in Petts Wood in 1964.

✉ Orpington BR5; Chislehurst BR7

🚶 13,627 (Petts Wood and Knoll ward)

🚆 South Eastern Trains (zone 5)

📖 Peter Waymark, *A History of Petts Wood*, Petts Wood and District Residents

@ www.pettswood.org.uk (residents' association site)

Phipps Bridge • *Merton*

An improved but still less than popular housing estate in north-west MITCHAM, separated from MERTON'S industrial zone by the River Wandle. Its 16th-century name probably derives from a local family called Pipp but could come from 'pipe', which used to mean 'the channel of a small stream'. Twelve Roman graves have been found here and the bridge may have carried a main road until MORDEN Hall's grounds became parkland in the 16th century. A reference in a document of 1572 to 'the stone walls of the bridge known as Puppes Bridge' indicates the presence of a substantial structure that was subsequently demolished. After 1700 the riverside here became part of an extensive textile industry, led by Huguenot entrepreneurs. The technique of using copper plates to print cloth was pioneered at Phipps Bridge in the mid 18th century. The owner of Wandle Villa built a row of riverside cottages for his workers in the 1820s. When subsidence began to affect them, he added as a buttress a castellated and 'ruinated' cottage that is now owned by the National Trust. The first significant housebuilding came in the late 19th century with the laying out of streets between Church Road and the southern part of Phipps Bridge Road. In the 1960s, Phipps Bridge was zoned for high-rise council housing, which subsequently became very run down. From the mid 1990s the tower blocks were demolished and replaced with low-rise units. Over 1,000 homes were built in the space of four years, and existing properties were improved in one of London's largest estate action schemes of recent times. The new properties are managed by housing associations. The regeneration charity Groundwork Merton set up projects with young people to improve their aspirations and help them realize their potential, and worked with the community to create a new park on a patch of derelict land, with a multi-sports and skateboard arena.

✉ SW19; Mitcham CR4

🚊 Croydon Tramlink, Route 1

📖 E N Montague, *Phipps Bridge, Phipps Mill and Bunce's Meadow*, Merton Historical Society, 1999

@ www.groundworklondon.org.uk/trusts/ merton (Merton pages of Groundwork site)

Piccadilly • *Westminster*

The road that now runs from HYDE PARK CORNER to PICCADILLY CIRCUS was part of an ancient route known as 'the way to Colnbrook' or 'the way to Reading'. The western and eastern halves were later called Hyde Park Road and Portugal Street, the latter in honour of Catherine of Braganza, queen consort of Charles II. It is said that in the late 16th or early 17th century, a house was built here by Robert Baker, a tailor who had got rich by selling a kind of starched collar called a piccadil. (There is some dispute as to whether Mr Baker's trade was actually in 'piccadil' collars or 'pickadilla' cakes.) The house was playfully nicknamed 'Piccadilly Hall' and although other residences soon followed, the locality acquired the name of the first. Most of the area belonged, as it still does, to the Crown but in 1661 royal trustees granted long leases to Henry Jermyn, who began to develop the area to the south. The 17th-century Burlington House was modified in seminal Palladian style in the early 18th century, when a string of taverns and shops began to line the road. These included bookstores run by John Hatchard and John Debrett, and by William Pickering, founder of the Aldine Press. William Fortnum and Hugh Mason opened a shop in 1707 that evolved into a department store now particularly renowned for its food hall. Robert Jackson began blending tea at his warehouse in Piccadilly early in the 19th century. The delightful Burlington Arcade was built to the west of Burlington House in 1818 and the house itself was purchased by the government in 1854. It became home to a clutch of learned societies and the Royal Academy of Arts, now best known for its annual summer exhibition of new British art. By the end of the 19th century Piccadilly had become fashionable as both a shopping and a residential area for the rich and famous. London's first steel-framed building, the Ritz Hotel, opened in 1904. From 1905 to 1910 many of the earliest buildings were swept away in a road-widening project. The most impressive store built thereafter was the six-storey Simpsons of Piccadilly in 1936, now the flagship store of the Waterstone's bookselling chain. The British Academy of Film and Television Arts is based at 195 Piccadilly, originally the home of the Royal Institute of Painters in Watercolours. Among the street's other institutions are the Hard Rock Café and the offices of several national airlines. GREEN PARK lies to the south-west.

'Piccadilly polari' (or 'palare') was a slang language used by the gay community in the late 1950s and 1960s and popularized by the characters Julian and Sandy on the BBC radio show *Round the Horne*. Actor and scriptwriter Jeremy Lloyd drew on his experiences working as an assistant at Simpson's when he co-created the television sitcom *Are You Being Served?* in the early 1970s.

✉ SW1

📖 Francis Sheppard, *Robert Baker of Piccadilly Hall and His Heirs*, London Topographical Society, 1982

Piccadilly Circus • *Westminster*

Once the 'hub of the British Empire' and now the focal point of the WEST END, located at the point where MAYFAIR, SOHO and ST JAMES'S meet. Regent Circus South, as it was first named, was created by John Nash in 1819 as a crossroads on REGENT STREET. PICCADILLY led south-westwards towards HYDE PARK CORNER and Coventry Street provided a short connection with LEICESTER SQUARE. There was no roundabout but the buildings at the corners were given curved frontages. The Criterion Theatre opened in 1874. The layout was disrupted in the late 1880s by the addition of SHAFTESBURY AVENUE on the north-east side, which forced the rebuilding of the London Pavilion Music Hall, now a shopping mall. Sir Alfred Gilbert's statue of Eros, officially the Angel of Christian Charity, was erected in 1893 to commemorate the good deeds of Lord Shaftesbury. It was the first public monument in the world to be made of aluminium. J Lyons and Co. established the Trocadero restaurant, now a leisure centre, in 1896. Piccadilly Circus station opened on the Bakerloo Line in March 1906 and on the Piccadilly Line in December. The station was rebuilt in 1928 to provide increased capacity. As the result of continual road alterations the circus has now become triangular in shape and Eros has been relocated. Piccadilly Circus has been home to a succession of famous stores, including Swan & Edgar and Lillywhites, but is even better known for its illuminated billboards, especially the 99-feet wide Coca-Cola sign. The Tube station, pavements and road junction are among the busiest in London; there can be a traffic jam here at three in the morning.

Almost throughout its history Piccadilly Circus has served as a meeting place for various subcultures, including prostitutes and their clients, gay men – especially before the legalization of homosexuality – and 'dropouts' and drug dealers in the 1960s and 1970s. The recently created HEART OF LONDON project aims to ensure that its attractions are now more family-oriented.

✉ W1

🚇 Bakerloo Line; Piccadilly Line (zone 1)

📖 David Oxford, *Piccadilly Circus*, Tempus, 1994

Pickett's Lock • *Enfield*

A 125-acre leisure zone situated in north-east Edmonton, named after a lock on the River Lee Navigation, rebuilt in 1855. Gravel deposits were worked here from the late 19th century to the 1950s, after which the site was used as a landfill site. Pickett's Lock Centre opened in 1973 on the bank of the William Girling reservoir. The centre includes a 12-screen multiplex cinema, multi-purpose sports centre, 18-hole golf course with driving range, and a camping and caravan site. However, the majority of the site is green-belt open space devoted to informal leisure use. In 2000, Pickett's Lock was selected as the new home for British athletics, the proposed site for the 2005 world athletics championships and the focus of a planned Olympic bid. However, the Millennium Dome fiasco and difficulties in funding the rebuilding of Wembley stadium prompted the government to reconsider its involvement in the project and the scheme was abandoned. Plans to add a station at Pickett's Lock Lane have also come to nothing. However, the sports centre is now deemed to be close to the end of its usable life and the council proposes to demolish it and replace it with a regional (rather than national) athletics centre. The area around the western end of Pickett's Lock Lane was the site of new housing developments at the start of the 21st century. Land to the south of Deephams sewage works has been identified as an area of opportunity by the council, possibly involving 'unneighbourly industrial uses' because of its relative isolation from residential areas.

✉ N9

Pield Heath • *Hillingdon*

A partially developed locality lying south of Brunel University and north-west of HILLINGDON Hospital, either side of the River Pinn. Its 16th-century name is pronounced 'peeled', which is what it means: a piece of heathland stripped bare of vegetation. A horticultural nursery was established here in 1895 and it had been joined by five others within two decades, covering a total of 65 acres. Only a small part of Pield Heath has since been built upon, with the construction of a school, a convent and a few cul-de-sacs of uninspiring semi-detached houses. In 1963, Brunel University bought the parcel of land south of Pield Heath Road from Middlesex County Council for use as playing fields, at a cost of £10,000. The riverside footpath through the fields has recently been improved by Hillingdon council as part of the Celandine route linking PINNER with the Grand Union Canal at COWLEY. The enhancements include resurfacing and the addition of new seats and trees. The rest of Pield Heath was occupied by nurseries until they closed in 1984. Part of that land is now Hillingdon Garden Centre, but the remainder lies in a state of semi-dereliction because the green-belt designation prevents housebuilding and no other suitable use has been found. Pield Heath House School caters for children with special needs. It is run by the Sisters of the Sacred Hearts of Jesus and Mary and takes pupils from all over north-west London. In an exceptional commendation, the educational standards agency Ofsted described this award-winning school as 'wonderful'.

✉ Uxbridge UB8

Pimlico • *Bromley*
Unrecalled by all except the oldest residents, this was a hamlet that grew up to the south of APERFIELD during the latter part of the 19th century. The name is still shown on some maps and although its origin is not known it is probably the same as that of the better-known Pimlico in central London. Pimlico mill operated at the corner of Main Road and Edward Road until 1879 and was dismantled around the turn of the century. Its site is now occupied by Mill House. The hamlet has been consumed by BIGGIN HILL, although Pimlico Wood remains.

✉ Westerham TN16

Pimlico • *Westminster*
A stuccoed residential enclave situated southeast of VICTORIA station. It probably took its name from a well-known public house in HOXTON, owned by one Ben Pimlico, who also brewed Pimlico ale in the early 17th century. The earliest incarnation of Pimlico here was a group of taverns and coffee-houses clustered south of Buckingham House. These were squeezed out when the mansion became Buckingham Palace in 1825 and the name drifted further south to a new residential area under development by Thomas Cubitt, which had at first been called South BELGRAVIA. Cubitt used soil excavated during the construction of ST KATHERINE'S docks to level the marshes, while covering the open sewers that had formerly traversed them. He built factories for making the building materials on an 11-acre site now covered by Dolphin Square and laid out Pimlico with a more populist eye than his project in Belgravia, with a pub on almost every corner – though these were as much for the builders as future residents. Cubitt died in 1855 and is commemorated by a statue on Denbigh Street. Pimlico became popular with artists and writers and a literary institute was founded in 1861, next door to the busy Monster tavern. The south-western part of Pimlico gained a reputation as a red-light district in the latter part of the 19th century, allegedly aided by its proximity to the Houses of Parliament. Pimlico was very badly damaged by bombing in World War II, arguably suffering the worst destruction outside the EAST END, and large parts were rebuilt with municipal housing after hostilities ended. The biggest projects were the Churchill Gardens estate, which was completed in 1962 and has been called 'almost a small town', and the later Lillington Gardens estate. The flats of Sherborne House replaced the ruined Monster tavern. The rest of Pimlico had slipped from genteel to shabby by this time, partly as a result of laws on leasehold and rent capping, which deterred property owners from making improvements, but it staged an impressive recovery in the last quarter of the 20th century. Many of Pimlico's terraced houses have been converted into reasonably priced hotels or subdivided into flats for the upwardly mobile but the more recent trend is towards their reunification as private houses.

In the 1948 Ealing comedy film *Passport to Pimlico*, residents declare their independence from the United Kingdom. A N Wilson's first novel, *The Sweets of Pimlico*, won the John Llewellyn Rhys Prize in 1978. The writers George Eliot and Joseph Conrad both lodged in Pimlico, and artist Aubrey Beardsley and composer Sir Arthur Sullivan had homes here.

✉ SW1

🚇 Victoria Line (zone 1)

📖 Adam Stout, *Pimlico: Deep Well of Glee*, Westminster City Archives, 1997; Isobel Watson, *Westminster and Pimlico Past*, Historical Publications, 1993

Pinner • *Harrow*
Sprawling to the north-west of HARROW, Pinner is a 20th-century nutshell encasing a much

older kernel. The name is probably of Saxon origin, meaning 'place by a peg-shaped ridge'. From the 1230s this ridge had a church and a street of houses leading down to a brook that was later called the River Pinn. To the north lay woodland and a large common, while smallholders cultivated plots in the south. PINNER GREEN and NOWER HILL were among the outlying farming hamlets. Pinner Park was a 250-acre deer reserve for the lord of the manor of Harrow, protected by a high bank and two ditches. The Church of St John the Baptist was rebuilt in 1321 and the saint's feast day was celebrated at a midsummer fair from 1336. The fair is still held every June. By the 16th century the village had a butcher, a baker, a candlestick-maker and several other cottage tradesmen. Wealthy outsiders began to take an interest in the area, including the Bacon family, who acquired Pinner Park, and Sir Christopher Clitherow, Lord Mayor of London in 1635, who bought Pinner Hill and Pinner Wood. During the early 19th century, in the first significant shift in Pinner's character since medieval times, large farms supplanted Pinner's many smallholdings, making it a place of fewer farmers and more agricultural labourers, whose numbers then declined as dairy farming began to replace crop-growing. The opening of Pinner (later HATCH END) station in 1842 brought remarkably early suburban growth in the form of the isolated WOODRIDINGS estate by the mid 1850s. At this time, around 40 per cent of the population of Pinner was engaged in agriculture or related occupations, but this dropped to about 15 per cent by 1881, when twice that proportion were working as domestic servants. The arrival of the Metropolitan Railway in 1885 brought more suburban growth, mostly of a superior form. In the early years of the 20th century the suburb expanded eastwards, meeting the even faster-growing Harrow at HEADSTONE and NORTH HARROW. Large projects between the wars included estates at RAYNERS LANE in the south-east and PINNERWOOD PARK in the north. Townhouses and blocks of flats completed the picture in the 1960s and 1970s. Despite the intrusion of a supermarket near the station, the old village is relatively well-preserved, with a profusion of timber-framed buildings. As appearances suggest, the residents of Pinner live in comfortable circumstances and four in five householders own their homes. More than two-thirds of the population is white British; the largest minority (eleven per cent) is of Indian descent.

Among Pinner's many notable residents have been the illustrator W Heath Robinson, the Nazi diplomat Joachim von Ribbentrop, the astronomer Patrick Moore, the actor Ronnie Barker and the singer Simon Le Bon. In the late 1930s the novelist Howard Spring contributed to *The Villager*, the journal of the Pinner Association. In the early 1990s the young actress Jane March earned the tabloid nickname 'the sinner from Pinner' for her steamy performances in a succession of soft-core porn movies.

✉ Pinner HA5

♦ 19,156 (Pinner and Pinner South wards)

🚍 Metropolitan Line (zone 5)

📖 Alan W Ball, *The Countryside Lies Sleeping*, Riverhill Press, 1981

@ www.pinnerlhs.freeserve.co.uk (local history society site); pinnerassociation.co.uk

Pinner Green • *Harrow*

A quiet northern corner of PINNER. The affix 'Green' often refers to the original centre of a district, but Pinner Green was a separate hamlet from its namesake as early as the Middle Ages. A windmill stood on the green in 1565. Several cottages were built in the 18th century and the Bell inn was licensed in 1751. A toll-bar was erected at Pinner Green in 1809, to raise funds for the improvement of the road to Rickmansworth. Pinner Cricket Club began playing on the green in 1892. When the area was being developed with housing in the mid 1930s the land was put up for sale and the club could not afford the asking price, but Hendon district council stepped in to preserve it as the Montesole playing fields, named after the club's president of the time. The fields also have football pitches and tennis courts. With the interwar expansion of the locality and the creation of the PINNERWOOD PARK estate, shops and a pub were built along the short stretch of road called Pinner Green. More recently a Tesco supermarket has opened on Ash Hill Drive. New homes continue to be built in the locality, the latest of which are the 22 apartments of the Viewpoint, arranged in a set of linked blocks. Pinner Green Social Club is based at the Greenwood Hall on Rickmansworth Road.

'I was born in a council house at 55 Pinner Hill Road. It was quite rural – there was a farm opposite,' recalled Elton John, who was christened Reginald Dwight in 1947. The family later lived in Potter Street, until Elton's parents divorced in 1962.

✉ Pinner HA5

@ www.pinnercc.co.uk (Pinner Cricket Club)

Pinnerwood Park • *Harrow*

A pair of hillside housing estates built on former farmland north of PINNER GREEN. In 1547 Pinner Wood covered 127 acres but was cut back progressively to its present five acres. Pinnerwood House was built around 1600 and although much altered and reduced in size it survives today, with 17th-century panelling in its entrance hall. Nearby Pinnerwood Cottage was built in 1867 and Pinnerwood Farm has a farmhouse dating from the later 19th century. The farm is set in 120 acres of land devoted to grazing and haymaking, and also breeds horses. In the 1930s the Artisans', Labourers' and General Dwellings Co. laid out the Pinnerwood Park estate with over 400 houses. The company had hitherto built for the skilled working classes, as its name suggests, but this was a middle-class garden suburb, aimed at those who could afford the train fare to the City. Pinner Wood School opened in 1939. Harrow council added an estate of its own in the 1960s. Close to Pinner Hill golf course there are several pockets of more luxurious accommodation where back garden swimming pools are not uncommon. Pinner Wood itself occupies the central part of the golf course and was formerly linked to Oxhey Wood, which lies to the north. Pinner Wood First and Middle Schools are on Latimer Gardens. Both schools draw pupils from a relatively wide catchment area and have high proportions of children from ethnic minorities.

Edward Bulwer-Lytton (later the first Baron Lytton) wrote his long-winded crime novel *Eugene Aram* at Pinnerwood House in 1832.

✉ Pinner HA5

Pitshanger Village • *Ealing*

An estate agents' label for one of the most advantaged parts of NORTH EALING, centred on Pitshanger Lane and sometimes taken to include the garden suburb of BRENTHAM. The name was first recorded in 1493, and may refer to a wooded slope frequented by hawks or kites. Pitshanger manor once covered an area stretching from HANGER HILL to Mattock Lane. Pitshanger Farm (for a while called Pitch Hanger Farm) lay in the north of the manor in the 18th and 19th centuries, latterly keeping dairy cattle. Pitshanger Lane (originally Pitshanger Road) followed its present route by 1894. Between the start of the 20th century and the outbreak of World War I the area was transformed, first by the creation of Brentham to the north, and then by the building of houses, shops, churches and a school along Pitshanger Lane. The farmhouse at Pitshanger Farm was demolished in 1908, but some of its land was preserved as Pitshanger Park, now part of Brent River Park. The Pitshanger Community Association organizes a Pitshanger party in the park each summer and 'Light up the Lane', held in Pitshanger Lane to mark the start of the Christmas festivities. Sir John Soane's Pitshanger Manor is located well to the south of the 'village', in Walpole Park, off Mattock Lane.

✉ W5

@ www.pitshanger.org.uk (residents' association site)

Plaistow • *Bromley* (usually pronounced 'playstow')

An area of mixed socio-economic character, situated at the northern end of BROMLEY. The name was first recorded in 1278 and indicated a place where people gathered to play games. The exceptionally wealthy Swiss banker Peter Thellusson bought the Plaistow estate in 1777 and built Plaistow Lodge. Thellusson died in 1797 after writing the most complex will in English history, which forced an immediate change in testamentary law and provided inspiration for Dickens' novel *Bleak House*. The area was still wholly rural when an iron church was built beside the lodge in 1875 but three years later Plaistow station opened on the new line to Bromley North. The arrival of the railway prompted the People's Freehold Land Society to finance the development of an estate for tradesmen and the lower middle classes. The four-acre Plaistow Cemetery opened on Burnt Ash Lane in 1893 and is notable for its grand entrance lodge. The cemetery has 4,000 graves and few spaces now remain. Plaistow station was rebuilt in 1896 and renamed SUNDRIDGE PARK to avoid confusion with Plaistow in east London. By this time, Plaistow was creeping towards fusion with Bromley as suburban housebuilding expanded. In 1926 a private developer erected a seven-foot high wall across Valeswood Road, at its junction with Alexandra Crescent, in response to residents' complaints that 'vulgar' people from the DOWNHAM estate were taking a short cut through Plaistow to Bromley town centre. Bromley council refused to remove the wall and it survived for more than a decade. St Andrew's Church, which Pevsner calls 'really very poor', replaced St Mary's Mission Church in 1929. Plaistow Lodge became Quernmore Secondary School and is now Parish Church of England Primary School. The exterior of the building survived the conversion almost intact but nearly all the original internal features have been lost.

In the mid 1950s David Bowie attended Burnt Ash Junior School, while living in Plaistow Grove.

✉ Bromley BR1

♠ 14,374 (Plaistow and Sundridge ward)

🚇 South Eastern Trains (Sundridge Park, zone 4)

📖 Muriel V Searle, *Bickley, Widmore and Plaistow*, European Library, 1990; Patrick Polden, *Peter Thellusson's Will of 1797 and its Consequences on Chancery Law*, Edwin Mellen Press, 2002

Plaistow • *Newham*

A traditionally working-class district situated on the south-east side of WEST HAM. Although it has now acquired the cockney pronunciation 'plarstow', the name probably derives from 'play-stow', a place of recreation, although a link has been suggested with a former lord of the manor, Hugh de Plaiz. In the 18th century, Plaistow was a popular retreat for 'sedate merchants and citizens of credit and renown', including George III's brother, the then Duke of Cumberland, who bought a mansion with extensive grounds where he stabled his racehorses. Like many villages at this distance from the capital, the intrusion of the railway drove the gentry away during the 19th century, as it brought an influx of more ordinary inhabitants. And as in other parts of east London, noxious industries decamped here from across the River Lea, deterring the middle classes. An extra factor pushing Plaistow downmarket was the laying of the long barrow of the Northern Outfall Sewer in 1864, bringing working people first as constructors and then as residents. The old mansions were demolished and their grounds were replaced with constricted streets of shabby tenements and, despite the proximity of the outfall system, unsanitary conditions. Perhaps it was more than coincidence that John Jeyes began to make his patented germicidal fluid in Plaistow in 1885. John Curwen founded the Tonic Sol-Fa Press at Plaistow's Congregational Chapel, helping the masses to read and play music more easily by means of his simplified notation. The construction of the Royal Docks brought another wave of industrial incomers. Extensive municipal rebuilding after World War II replaced bomb-sites. Plaistow remains one of the most disadvantaged parts of London. At Lister Community School, on St Mary's Road, an exceptionally high proportion of pupils (80 per cent) are eligible for free school meals. Plaistow's ethnic profile alters from north to south. The West Ham side has a stronger Asian presence, while the part nearer CANNING TOWN has more white people. Black and black British residents are relatively evenly spread across the district.

The Irish statesman and philosopher Edmund Burke lived at Brunstock Cottage in Balaam Street from 1759 to 1761. Will Thorne, the pioneer trade unionist who founded the precursor of the modern GMB union, was MP for Plaistow from 1918 until 1945. Ian Dury's *Plaistow Patricia*, from the album *New Boots and Panties*, was a bitterly angry rant about the effect of inner-city turpitude on one woman's life. The actress Honor Blackman and the rock singer David Essex were born in Plaistow.

✉ E13

♠ 25,068 (Plaistow North and South wards)

🚇 District Line; Hammersmith & City Line (zone 3)

📖 George Taylor, *Around Plaistow*, Chalford, 1996

@ www.lalamy.demon.co.uk/plaistow.htm (local history pages on personal site)

Plashet • *Newham*

Largely forgotten other than as the name of its school and zoo, Plashet lies just north-east of UPTON PARK. Its name means 'a clearing in the wood'. The grand Plashet House was the home of the prison reformer Elizabeth Fry from 1809 to 1829, while her daughter Katherine (who gave her name to Katherine Road) moved into nearby Plashet Cottage. Both properties were demolished in the 1880s when the estate was covered with terraced housing. A similar fate befell Potato Hall on Romford Road. In 1891 Plashet Park became EAST HAM'S first public park. The tree-lined Plashet Grove once had its own little shopping centre, rather than the rudimentary convenience stores that remain today. However, it does now have an award-winning bridge linking two school sites, described as 'a cross between a Miro sculpture and a Chinese lantern'. The former Trebor sweet factory on Katherine Road was refurbished and extended as residential accommodation in 2004. Plashet's ethnic composition is unusual, not because it is overwhelmingly Asian, but because it mixes people of Indian, Pakistani and Bangladeshi descent. Plashet Girls' Secondary School is popular and oversubscribed, partly because many local families prefer single-sex schooling; 87 per cent of the pupils are from Asian backgrounds.

The locally based poet Benjamin Zephaniah has versified upon his habit of jogging in Plashet Park. Opened on Rutland Road in 1964, Plashet Zoo has a collection of child-friendly animals and a butterfly house.

✉ E6; E7

Platt's Eyot • *Richmond*

The westernmost and one of the largest of London's Thames islets, now also called Port Hampton Business Island by its private owners. The words 'eyot' and 'ait' are used interchangeably to denote the small islands of the Thames and the two are pronounced identically. Platt's Eyot is linked by a narrow bridge to the Lower Sunbury Road. Until the 1880s osiers were grown here, a species of willow used for basket-making. The islet owes its hilly topography to the dumping of soil excavated during the creation of additional filter beds at Hampton waterworks at the end of the 19th century. Platt's Eyot was home to the Thorneycroft boatyard, which built torpedo boats in both world wars. The islet was also formerly a base for the river police. Although its features are on a small scale, Platt's Eyot has an unexpected amount of both woodland and light industry, together with amenities like a café and public conveniences for workers and sailors. Many of the islet's workshops and studio units currently lie empty, but its moorings are almost fully occupied. It seems likely that a group of upmarket houses and flats will be built on the islet within the next few years.

✉ Hampton TW12

Plumstead • *Greenwich*

A Victorian outgrowth of WOOLWICH, which lies to its west. This place where the plum trees grew was first recorded around 970 as Plumstede. It is possible that the Romans planted orchards here on an agricultural scale. The present St Nicholas' Church was built in the 12th century and given an incongruous tower in the early 1660s. The village was of little consequence at this time and remained so until the early 19th century, with scattered farms

and minor country houses and a high street that stretched towards Woolwich. The largest landowner was the Pattison family of Burrage House, which lay on the western slope of Plumstead Common. The Pattisons sold a sandpit as the site for WOOLWICH ARSENAL station, which opened in 1849 and brought the first growth to west Plumstead. Keen to profit further from their property, the family sold Burrage House too, which was demolished so that the railway could be extended onwards into Kent. To the south of the railway, Burrage Road was laid out and the first terraces of Burrage Town were built on Sandy Hill Road for workers at Woolwich Arsenal. Superior houses meanwhile began to appear on Plumstead Common Road. The enlargement of the arsenal as a result of the Crimean War and the opening of Plumstead station in 1859 sparked an explosion of growth across the district. The Herbert estate was laid out north of SHOOTERS HILL but Queen's College, Oxford was stymied in its attempt to cover Plumstead Common with a high-class development. Almost all the rest of the district was covered with housing and attendant amenities before the end of the 19th century. Former chalk mines west of Wickham Lane were built over in the early 20th century, but some properties later collapsed and the London County Council had to fill the mines with fly ash to prevent further subsidence. The downsizing of Woolwich Arsenal after World War I brought decline to Plumstead and its population fell by almost 10,000 in the 1920s. Many of the departing residents did not move far; this was a period of massive growth in neighbouring districts like WELLING and ELTHAM. After World War II, council projects transformed the western side of Plumstead. The largest of these was the Glyndon estate, with almost 2,000 dwellings, which was begun in 1959 and not completed until 1981 and has recently been undergoing regeneration. Woolwich Mosque was built on Plumstead Road in 1996; seven per cent of Plumstead's residents are Muslims. Slightly less than two-thirds of the population is white, with other ethnic groups well-represented.

✉ SE18

🚶 14,112 (27,991 including the Glyndon ward)

🚆 South Eastern Trains (zone 4)

📖 Edward Hasted, *Hasted's History of Plumstead*, ed. John W Brown, Local History Reprints, 1997

Plumstead Common • *Greenwich*

A wiggling chain of open spaces covering an undulating plateau in south PLUMSTEAD, linking to Winn's Common in the east. The parish workhouse stood at Winn's Common in the 18th century and a windmill was built on Plumstead Common in 1764. Villas and terraces of houses began to appear on Plumstead Common Road in the 1840s. This was a time when parishioners made the most of their grazing rights on the common and there were objections when the landowners, Queen's College, Oxford, began to enclose some of the land. The situation worsened in 1871 when the college granted the army permission to use the common as a training ground and the right of public access was withdrawn. When the leader of a protest march was imprisoned, commoners rioted to secure his release. An Act of 1877 authorized the Metropolitan Board of Works to purchase the common. This was a period of heightened (and high-class) suburban development in the neighbourhood, when new streets such as Wrottesley Road were laid out. The Slade (now Greenslade Primary) School opened in 1884. Two years later, WOOLWICH ARSENAL workers founded Dial Square Football Club at a meeting in the Prince of Wales public house on Plumstead Common Road. The name was soon changed to Royal Arsenal and the club played its early home games on Plumstead Common. By the outbreak of World War I the vicinity of the common had filled with housing, accompanied by shops and churches. The modernist architect Berthold Lubetkin added a unique terrace of four houses on Genesta Road in 1935. Plumstead Common has some of the most varied terrain of London's open spaces, including wooded ravines, ponds, puddingstone boulders, and an ancient burial mound on Winn's Common.

✉ SE18

📖 Alex and Julia Cowdell et al, *Our Common Story: A Celebration of Plumstead Common*, Plumstead Common Environment Group, 2004

@ www.pceg.org.uk (Plumstead Common Environment Group site)

Poets' Corner

An estate agents' term for any collection of vaguely attractive streets named after poets. These include parts of ACTON, HANWELL and HERNE HILL. Some local authorities have also joined in the name game, particularly with regard to designations for conservation areas. The term is inspired by the section of Westminster Abbey devoted to poets' memorials.

Pollards Hill • *Croydon/Merton*

Although not shown on some maps, this is a distinct district lying on the eastern edge of MITCHAM, south-west of NORBURY. Pollards are trees that have been cut back to promote the growth of new, short branches. Most of the woodland was cleared in the Middle Ages, becoming the meadows and dairy pasture of New Barns Farm, also known as Galpins. The 'physic gardener' James Arthur grew aromatic herbs here in the mid 19th century. TOOTING BEC Golf Club bought the farmhouse and around 100 acres of land in 1905 and cleared what remained of the woodland on Pollards Hill. The golf club was unsuccessful and so was a successor, the Pollards Hill golf club. The site is now occupied by Tamworth Manor High School and neighbouring housing. Outward development from Mitcham was slow until the council identified the area as a suitable site for 'homes for heroes' after World War I. Even then, development plans were uncompleted by the outbreak of World War II. When these hostilities ended, Mitcham council quickly grabbed the remaining land for the erection of prefabricated dwellings to ease the borough's housing shortage. The first homes were ready in January 1946. The council added six-storey maisonette blocks in the early 1950s. During the following decade the prefabs were replaced by a pioneering 'perimeter planning' scheme of low-rise flats and houses, set around a series of squares, bounded by Recreation Way. The project was completed in 1971. Seven hundred of these properties have recently been refurbished and a further 190 units constructed in a five-year phased programme. Two-thirds of the residents in Merton's Pollards Hill ward are white and the principal ethnic minorities are black African, black Caribbean, Indian and mixed race. Just over 70 per cent of homes are owner-occupied, but there are high levels of unemployment.

The author Christopher Street has suggested that a set of triangular ley lines connects Pollards Hill with the churches of St Mary's in ADDISCOMBE and BEDDINGTON. These lines are ancient routes across the countryside that follow alignments linking sacred sites; there is evidence of prehistoric earthworks at Pollards Hill. Some people claim that mystic forces are associated with ley lines.

SW16; Mitcham CR4

9,914 (Merton's Pollards Hill ward)

Ponders End · *Enfield*

An industrial and multiracial working-class residential district on the eastern edge of EN-FIELD. The name was first recorded in the late 16th century and probably derives from one John Ponder, who was living here in 1373. In 1664 the hamlet had 58 dwellings, one of which was a mansion that had reputedly been a residence of the earl of Lincoln. The ancient manor house of Durants Arbour stood to the east of the High Street until it was destroyed by fire in the late 18th century. A flour mill built around this time survives today as the borough's oldest industrial structure, part of Wright's bakeries. When Grout and Baylis established their crape (black gauze) mill in 1809, Ponders End was an L-shaped hamlet strung loosely along the High Street and South Street with a separate group of houses at Scotland Green. The lack of restrictions on building, together with the presence of the River Lea and the early arrival of the railway in 1840, brought more factories and workers' cottages from the mid 19th century. Terraced housing began to spread in the 1860s, while industry monopolized the area east of the railway line, as it still does. Housebuilding accelerated in the 1890s following improvements in transport links and the opening of the Ediswan factory on Duck Lees Lane, in a former jute mill. The factory was responsible for a remarkable variety of scientific inventions, including tungsten filament lamps, the radio valve and rayon. Ponders End continued to expand during the early years of the 20th century but market gardens still divided it from ENFIELD HIGHWAY at the outbreak of World War I. By the mid 1930s it had fully coalesced with eastern Enfield. After World War II the council redeveloped some of the most run-down housing and later erected several tower blocks near the junction of South Street with Alma Road. Ponders End has the highest proportion of young adults of any ward in the borough. It has high levels of social housing and skilled manual workers. All the main ethnic minorities are present in Ponders End, and there is a notable concentration of Bangladeshi families.

'I had thought in a green old age (oh green thought!) to have retired to Ponders End (emblematic name, how beautiful!)', wrote Charles Lamb to Wordsworth. 'The University of Ponders End' was a popular student nickname for Middlesex Polytechnic, which now really is a university.

Enfield EN3

12,978

'one' Railway (zone 5)

Pontoon Dock · *Newham*

A Docklands Light Railway station located in WEST SILVERTOWN. This was the site of a repair facility originally called the Victoria Graving Dock, built in the late 1850s on the south side of the ROYAL VICTORIA Dock, as it was later called. Using an innovative system of hydraulic jacks, vessels were raised out of the water on pontoons, which were then drained of their ballast water and shunted into a finger dock for repair or overhaul. There were four of these splayed fingers at each end of the dock but most have now been filled with concrete. By the end of the 19th century ships had become too big for the equipment to lift and the dock switched to handling grain imports. Massive silos were built on the quayside, into which grain was pumped by suction. Several of the granaries and flour mills were damaged in the SILVERTOWN explosion of 1917 and replaced in the years before World War II, notably by Spillers Millennium Mills and the CWS Mills. Most of the dockside buildings were demolished in the early 1990s during preparation for the creation of Silvertown Quays, a shopping, office, housing and leisure development.

E16

Docklands Light Railway, City Airport branch (zone 3)

Pool of London · *City/Tower Hamlets/ Southwark*

The *Oxford English Dictionary* explains that a pool is a deep and still place in a river and that London's pool is 'the part of the Thames between LONDON BRIDGE and Cuckold's Point', which is located at the north-eastern tip of the ROTHERHITHE peninsula. However, this definition includes the Lower Pool, which is the stretch between WAPPING and LIMEHOUSE. The London Development Agency and other bodies have made the Pool of London the focus of a regeneration and tourism programme for the shoreline between London Bridge and just beyond TOWER BRIDGE, embracing attractions from BOROUGH market (Southwark) in the west to ST KATHERINE'S docks (Tower Hamlets) in the east. Despite a publicity campaign, the term has yet to re-enter common parlance. 'It has not caught on as well as I had hoped,' admitted Usha Mistry of the Pool of London Partnership in 2003. Government funding for the ten-year scheme ceases in 2007.

In the days of London's docks, 'pool-price' was the wholesale price of coal at the Pool of London.

@ www.poologflondon.co.uk (includes forthcoming events)

Poplar • Tower Hamlets

An EAST END district situated immediately north of the ISLE OF DOGS and taking its name from the native trees (*Populus canescens* and *Populus nigra*) that once thrived on the moist alluvial soil beside the marshes. From the 17th century Poplar provided homes for workers at the docks that lined the river front from LIMEHOUSE around the Isle of Dogs to BLACKWALL. It became one of London's first multi-ethnic districts, with inhabitants of Indian, Chinese and 'Nubian' origin. The opening of the WEST INDIA Docks in 1802 stimulated a rapid growth in housing development, mainly mean terraces of rented cottages. Poplar Fields, the area north of East India Dock Road, was built up as Poplar New Town from the 1830s to the mid 1850s. By the late 19th century, poverty and overcrowding were rife. The borough of Poplar, created in 1900, soon gained a reputation for political radicalism, especially for the Labour council's demand that London's wealth should be distributed more evenly among its constituent parts. The borough's determination to relieve adequately the suffering of its poor was nicknamed 'Poplarism' by the *Glasgow Herald* in 1922 and the term became generic for allegedly spendthrift Labour councils. The district now consists almost entirely of council flats and houses dating from the 1950s to 1970s, notably on the LANSBURY estate. In 1981, public housing accounted for 97.6 per cent of Poplar's dwellings. Docklands regeneration has since brought some private residential and commercial properties. Only a few structures, mainly churches, pubs and public buildings, pre-date World War II.

Joseph Stalin, leader of the Soviet Union from 1924 to 1953, lived in Poplar in the early 1900s as a political refugee.

✉ E14

🚊 Docklands Light Railway, all branches (zone 2)

📖 John Hector, *Poplar Memories*, Sutton, 2003

@ www.poplarharca.co.uk (social housing

landlord's site)

Portobello Road • Kensington & Chelsea

A characterful market street winding in a north-north-westerly direction from NOTTING HILL GATE, where it branches off Pembridge Road. Vice-Admiral Edward Vernon defeated a Spanish fleet at Porto Bello (now Portobelo in Panama) in 1739 and the farm that stood here was renamed in honour of the victory. The country track that traversed its fields was later called Portobello Lane. In 1801 the Grand Junction (now Grand Union) Canal cut across the northern part of the lane, which has since been further truncated by the railway and the redevelopment of KENSAL TOWN. From the mid 19th century the LADBROKE GROVE estate progressively filled the territory to the south-west and the owners of Portobello Farm began to sell off their land for housing. Traders set up shop along the lane to provide goods and services for their wealthy neighbours. As development slowly moved northwards (and socially downwards) over the remainder of the century, terraces of working-class housing lined the rest of the road. In 1864 Portobello farmhouse was sold to the Little Sisters of the Poor, who built St Joseph's Convent on the site of its orchard. The delightful Electric cinema opened in 1910 and now rivals EAST FINCHLEY'S Phoenix as the capital's oldest working cinema. Over the second half of the 20th century the shops and stalls of Portobello Road increasingly specialized in antiques and bric-à-brac, creating one of the most distinctive street markets in London. The area's character was further enhanced by the music scene that evolved here from 1969, when Island Records moved to nearby Basing Street. Live music venues and specialist record shops appeared on Portobello Road in the 1970s and punk, reggae and later rap and hip-hop artists performed and recorded here and often rented (or squatted) homes in the vicinity. Portobello Road has stalls every weekday and is especially big on Saturdays, when it claims to become the world's largest antiques market. The street is also good for fashion and food. Its popularity may prove to be its downfall; traders have recently sought the council's help in preventing generic outlets like coffee bars from squeezing out the traditional shops that have made Portobello what it is. A plaque on the wall of 115 Portobello Road commemorates June Aylward, who established the street's first antiques shop.

✉ W11; W10

📖 Shaaron Whetlor and Liz Bartlett, *Portobello: Its People, Its Past, Its Present*, Kensington and Chelsea Community History Group, 1996

@ www.portowebbo.co.uk (commercial local information site); www.portobelloroad.co.uk (Portobello Antique Dealers Association site)

Pot Kilns • *Havering*

One of the smallest hamlets in London, and unnamed on most maps, Pot Kilns lies north of CRANHAM on Bird Lane, just off the Southend Arterial Road (A127). From 1708 this was the centre of the UPMINSTER brickfields, one of the largest employers in the district. The first brick kiln was built in 1774. Tiles were also produced, and a variety of pots – hence the locality's name. These were mainly chimney pots but also flower pots and kale pots, which were used for making broth or pottage. Pot Kiln Farm was shown on a map of 1825. The kilns were operated by members of the Branfill family until the late 1850s and later by the Upminster Brick Co. and its successors. The main kiln, known locally as 'the dome', was 45 feet in diameter and 70 feet high. Another was nicknamed 'the shaft'. Brickmaking continued here until 1933, when the Essex Brick and Tile Co. went into voluntary liquidation. Pot Kilns now consists of just two short terraces of houses built in the 1880s for the local workers, set among pasture, spinneys and hedgerows. Pantile Cottages run alongside the lane while Plain Tile Cottages jut southwards. Several of the properties have been 'improved' but some of their original character and detailing survive. Pot Kiln Wood is a 17-acre Woodland Trust property. To the north are farms and nurseries along Hall Lane and Tomkyns Lane, with farmhouses and cottages. Great Tomkyns has a 14th-century barn with Grade II*-listed status but it is in a poor state of repair.

✉ Upminster RM14

📖 Pat Ryan, *Brick in Essex: The Clayworking Craftsmen and Gazetteer of Clayworking Sites*, self-published, 1999

Poverest • *Bromley*

The western side of ST MARY CRAY. The remains of Romano-British villas and a bathhouse have been uncovered on Poverest Road. The bathhouse was in use from around AD 270 to AD 400 and probably served a small farmstead that extended southwards. The foundations are on show inside a public viewing building. A Saxon burial ground to the north and east of the bathhouse was in use between the mid fifth and sixth centuries. Margaret de Pouery owned a manorial estate here in 1327 and the locality's name is a corruption of hers, via the form 'Poverish' in the 19th century, when the vicinity remained wholly agricultural. Terraced cottages were built to house workers of the paper mills beside the River Cray and micro-localities gained colourful nicknames like Sloper's Island and Dipper's Slip. The Fordcroft estate was laid out from 1882, with plots for 217 homes and a tavern, although most of the homes were never built and the tavern opened as a grocer's instead. In 1892 ORPINGTON Baptist church opened the Fordcroft Mission Hall, which is now in community ownership as Poverest Coronation Hall. The first council houses were built immediately after World War I and a flurry of residential development followed the construction of the Orpington bypass (Cray Avenue, A224) in the mid 1920s. New roads were given names inspired by the presence of a spinney called Robin Hood Shaw and shops were built on Marion Crescent. Commercial enterprises tended to consist of businesses such as scrapyards, coal merchants, hauliers and demolition specialists. In the late 1950s, Orpington council compulsorily purchased most of the houses on the Fordcroft estate and rehoused the residents in RAMSDEN. Unusually, much of the area that was cleared was left as open space, but this may have been a consequence of inertia rather than a considered decision not to redevelop the sites. One former raspberry field became Poverest recreation ground (also known as Poverest Park) and Bromley council acquired the neighbouring Covet Wood in 1991. Local shops have faced the usual difficulties as a result of competition from nearby superstores and Poverest Road post office closed in 2004. According to a 2004 report by the national educational standards agency Ofsted, most pupils enter Poverest Primary School with levels of knowledge and understanding that are well below average.

✉ Orpington BR5

@ www.poverest.org.uk (community site)

Pratts Bottom • *Bromley*

An expanded village situated on the London/Kent border, a mile south of CHELSFIELD. The 14th-century name derives from the family of Stephen Prat and the low-lying location of the settlement, nestling in a valley at the foot of Rushmore Hill. Chelsfield Grange, now known locally as The Grange, may have been built in the late 15th century but has since been remodelled and enlarged. The Bull's Head public house was in existence by the early 17th century, when poorhouses for the parish of Chelsfield were built on the common land. A toll gate was erected on the London to Rye road in 1748. The Porcupine inn stood at the top of Rushmore Hill by 1791, when its sale particulars referred to the village as 'Spratts Bottom'. The armed hold-up of a mail coach at Pratts Bottom in 1798 prompted the offer of a £240 reward but the highwayman was never caught. In the early 19th century the village gained a reputation as fertile territory for recruitment to the Mormon faith as a result of its remoteness from the parish church at Chelsfield. The quaint, simple little All Saints' Church was built in response to the rapid growth of Pratts Bottom later in the century, when The Grange served as a grammar school. The turnpike cottages were demolished when the road was widened in the late 1920s. Grange Drive and Orchard Road were laid out in the 1930s and 1950s on the former grounds of The Grange. With its terraces of weather-boarded and flint cottages and its ancient inn, Pratts Bottom has been called 'almost the archetype of English villages' but unsympathetic late-20th-century housebuilding has undermined its charm. Residents of the Chelsfield and Pratts Bottom ward tend to be white, middle-aged, married homeowners with at least one car. Pratts Bottom Primary School had 52 pupils at the time of its 2005 inspection by the national educational standards agency Ofsted, and the roll is growing as a result of the school's improving reputation.

- ⊠ Orpington BR6
- ♀ 14,068 (Chelsfield and Pratts Bottom ward)
- ⬚ Judith Hook, *Pratts Bottom: An English Village*, Norman-Stahli Publishing, 1972
- @ www.prattsbottom.co.uk (community site)

Preston · *Brent*
A comfortable, multi-ethnic corner of NORTH WEMBLEY, south-east of KENTON. The name, which meant 'priest's farmstead', is not widely used locally. Domesday Book recorded the presence of a landowning priest in the district. A settlement was in existence by the mid 13th century, when the hamlet of Uxendon had also appeared, just to the east. The Babington plot to assassinate Elizabeth I was hatched and foiled at Uxendon, with the resul-

tant execution of 14 conspirators. John Lyon, the yeoman who founded HARROW School, lived at Preston in the 16th century and bequeathed his farm to provide funds for the upkeep of the school. The Horseshoe inn gained a licence in 1751, when houses had begun to cluster around the green. Preston House was built early in the 19th century and its subsequent tenants included a surgeon, a cigar importer and a solicitor. Encroachments reduced the size of the green, while the vicinity remained agricultural, with farms shifting increasingly to the production of hay for London's horses. George Timms acquired Preston House in 1880 and turned the grounds into a tea garden, which survived into the 20th century. A proposal to build a station on the Metropolitan Railway was vetoed in 1896 because the locality remained so sparsely populated. A wooden halt opened to serve the shooting events of the 1908 Olympic Games, which were held at Uxendon Farm. In the 1920s and early 1930s Harrow School and Oxford's Christ Church college sold their Preston estates, while Wembley council upgraded the country lanes. Shops and the Preston Park Hotel were built in the late 1920s, with many more shops following in the 1930s, together with a primary and secondary school. A proper station was built at Preston Road in 1931 in response to the rapid spread of housing across the district. A Liberal synagogue opened in 1947 to serve the substantial Jewish community and the Church of the Ascension was consecrated a decade later. A council estate replaced Lyon's Farm in the early 1960s, when Preston House was also demolished. No single ethnic group is in a majority in Preston, although the white and Indian groups together make up two-thirds of the total population. The vast majority of the Indian population is Hindu. At Preston Park Primary School, 44 languages are spoken, the most common being Gujarati, Urdu, Japanese, Tamil, Somali and Arabic.

- ⊠ Wembley HA9; Harrow HA3
- ♀ 12,832
- 🚇 Metropolitan Line (Preston Road, zone 4)
- ⬚ M C Barrès-Baker, *Preston and Uxendon*, Grange Museum of Community History and Brent Archive, 2001

Primrose Hill · *Camden*
A delightful vantage point and its outrageously expensive residential surroundings, situated immediately north of REGENT'S PARK.

The woodland here was granted to Eton College by Henry VI at a time when the name Primrose Hill was first coming into use. The hill was cleared of trees in the mid 17th century and remained as farmland until the arrival of the railway, when both the college and the neighbouring landowner, Lord Southampton, seized the opportunity to sell building plots. St Mark's Church was begun in 1851, and a station opened in the same year, under the name Hampstead Road. Shortly afterwards Chalcot Square was laid out with stuccoed Italianate villas, while its central garden was planted with acacia trees. The Crown acquired the summit of the hill for public use, granting the college some land near Windsor in exchange. Primrose Hill Road was built in the 1870s to improve access to the college estate. By 1900 the present built environment was almost complete. Primrose Hill has long had a small manufacturing presence. Chalcot Road's Utopia Village has been home to piano-making, electrical engineering and a record company, from which it takes its present name. Primrose Hill in the 1960s has been described as 'the very last word in London bohemia', but now it is simply posh. However, neighbouring council estates exhibit considerable levels of deprivation and there are refugee families from Kosovo and Somalia. The sightlines from Primrose Hill towards St Paul's Cathedral and the Palace of Westminster are among a handful of officially designated strategic views that are safeguarded from inappropriate development. Regent's Park Road has a cluster of agreeable shops, cafés and restaurants. Primrose Hill station closed in 1992.

Sylvia Plath wrote her autobiographical novel *The Bell Jar* while living in Chalcot Square between January 1960 and the summer of 1961. The poet W B Yeats and writers Alan Bennett, Kingsley Amis and Martin Amis are among other literati who have lived locally. *Primrose Hill* is the title of a 1982 track by local band Madness and a 1999 debut novel by Helen Falconer. So many film scenes have been shot in Primrose Hill lately that residents have begun to complain about the frequent disruption.

✉ NW1; NW3; NW8

👥 11,574 (Camden Town with Primrose Hill ward)

📖 Simon Jenkins, Alan Bennett et al, *Primrose Hill Remembered*, Friends of Chalk Farm Library, 2001

@ www.primrosehill.com (commercial local information site)

Prince Regent • *Newham*

A Docklands Light Railway station located on the east side of CUSTOM HOUSE. Unlike the other royally associated stations in the area, Prince Regent is not named after a dock but after the road that runs northward from here to PLAISTOW. The route was in existence from the late Middle Ages and was formerly known as Trinity Marsh Lane, then as Prince Regent's Lane in the 19th and early 20th centuries and is now Prince Regent Lane. The station's design anticipated intensive development of the neighbouring land, so staircases and platforms are wider here than elsewhere on the BECKTON part of the line.

✉ E16

🚈 Docklands Light Railway, Beckton branch (zone 3)

Priory Park • *Haringey*

Some residents and traders use this name for the locality situated between MUSWELL HILL and HORNSEY. The Warner family rebuilt their house as the Priory in 1823, with a Gothic exterior and some fittings from Wanstead House in WANSTEAD PARK, which had recently been demolished. The house gave its name to Priory Road, which lay to the south and is lined by some distinctive plane trees. In 1842 Henry Warner endowed land for the building of St James's Church, Muswell Hill. The last occupant of the Priory was the wine merchant Herbert Reader Williams, who chaired the Hornsey school board, founded Hornsey Liberal Party and launched campaigns to save Highgate Woods and the southern side of ALEXANDRA PARK (which bordered his property) from housing development. CROUCH END'S clock tower was erected in his honour. In the face of Hornsey's rapid urbanization, the council bought land to the south of Priory Road in 1887 and opened a park here seven years later. Williams died in 1897 and a clutch of local developers, notably John Farrer, began to lay out the Priory estate soon afterwards. Pevsner praises the estate's 'relaxed terraces of gabled houses with decorative pargeting and timberwork'. The Priory itself survived until 1902, when it was replaced by more roads of terraced housing spreading towards Alexandra Park. The park was enlarged in 1926.

✉ N8

Pudding Mill Lane • *Newham*

Barely 500 yards in length, Pudding Mill Lane short-circuits Marshgate Lane in south-west STRATFORD. Pudding Mill River, one of the BOW back rivers, is a very minor tributary of the River Lea. The mill that gave its name to the river and the lane was wind-driven, unlike its many water-powered neighbours. The history of the mills in this area is somewhat uncertain but the Pudding Mill was probably named because of its shape and was demolished during the first half of the 19th century. The later Nobshill (or Knobs Hill) Mill survived until the early 1890s. Until 1998 there was just a passing loop at this point on the Stratford branch of the Docklands Light Railway, which here runs alongside the main line into LIVERPOOL STREET, and above the Central Line. The station was built for the convenience of workers at the utilities and industrial estates that pocked STRATFORD MARSH over the course of the 20th century. This is one of London's most obscure destinations – indeed one 21st-century street atlas seems unaware of its existence – but it has assumed greater significance since the neighbourhood became the site for the 2012 Olympic Park. The station will become a transport interchange for the games, but will have to be closed during the construction phase. The lane itself will be replaced by peripheral Olympics facilities. The little Pudding Mill River is likely to disappear under the main stadium. Pudding Mill Lane should not be confused with Pudding Lane, the source of the Great Fire of London.

> ✉ E15

> 🚉 Docklands Light Railway, Stratford branch (zones 2 and 3)

Purley • *Croydon*

A moneyed 20th-century suburb located on the southern outskirts of CROYDON. In 1200 this was Pirlee, which most authorities suggest was 'the woodland clearing where the pear trees grow'. However, it has been credibly argued that the name may have been brought by an immigrant from Purley Magna, near Reading, who owned an estate in SANDERSTEAD. Until the 19th century this remained an inconsequential settlement consisting of Purley House (later Purley Bury) and a scattering of farmsteads. In 1801 the population density was less than one person per acre. Godstone Road station was opened in 1840 for the use of residents of Godstone, which lay eight miles away. The station closed in 1847 owing to lack of passengers but reopened in 1856 as Caterham

Junction, prompting the construction of the first villas in an area then known as Foxley Hatch. The station was renamed Purley in 1888. Christ Church was completed on the Brighton road in 1878 and gained its own parish two years later. A waterworks was built on Brighton Road in 1901, when suburban growth was beginning in the hinterland of the railway lines. Villas on Brighton Road were demolished and replaced by shops, which also lined the High Street, and a cottage hospital opened in 1909. The population density had reached nine persons per acre by 1911. Purley expanded rapidly between the world wars, especially after the construction of Croydon's bypass, Purley Way (A23), in 1928. The Astoria cinema opened in 1934 and Purley's shops reached a peak in 1939 but their numbers progressively declined after World War II. From the 1960s, office blocks were built on the arterial routes. A 2002 report rated Purley as having the highest average household income in the country but this affluence is not visible in the kebab takeaways and charity shops in the vicinity of Purley Cross, where independent retailers have been adversely affected by supermarket developments, such as the Tesco that replaced the waterworks.

The politician John Horne Tooke established his reputation with *The Diversions of Purley*, his medley of etymology, grammar and politics, in 1782; Peter Ackroyd later gave the same title to a book of poems. Former residents of Purley include the actor Peter Cushing, the cellist Jacqueline du Pré and the supermodel Kate Moss. A mention in Monty Python's famous *Nudge Nudge* sketch – 'Say no more! Purley!' – made the suburb the butt of metropolitan humour in the late 1960s. The stereotype was reinforced by the setting here of *Terry and June*, a television comedy that ran from 1979 to 1987.

> ✉ Purley CR8

> 👤 12,998

> 🚉 Southern (zone 6)

> 📖 A Higham (ed.), *Purley*, Bourne Society, 1996

Purley Oaks • *Croydon*

A popular residential locality straddling the Brighton Road (A235) between Sanderstead and Purley. Until the late 19th century horses and cattle grazed at Purley Oaks Farm, which retained an ancient barn and several of the trees that had given the estate its name. Brighton Road School was built in 1873 at a time when the area was still undeveloped. Purley Oaks station opened on the line to Brighton in 1899 and the farm was offered for sale at auction in 1903. The conditions of sale ensured that houses were built for the professional classes and the first properties were occupied within two years. Servants and live-in maids were the norm but the need for garages was not recognized at that time. Much of the surrounding land remained open and in 1916 James Relf established a market garden near the station. After World War I the area was almost entirely built up with suburban housing. Brighton Road School was renamed Purley Oaks in 1922 and rebuilt in 1940. The present Purley Oaks Primary School takes pupils from a large catchment area and from a wide range of socio-economic backgrounds. Twenty-two per cent have English as an additional language, although few are at the early stages of learning English. The former Purley Oaks dump on the Brighton Road reopened as a reuse and recycling centre in 2005.

✉ Purley CR8

🚉 Southern (zone 6)

Putney • *Wandsworth*

FULHAM's counterpart on the south side of the Thames, lying west of WANDSWORTH. Putney – the landing place of either the hawk or a man called Putta – was Putelei in Domesday Book but this was probably a transcription error and it is recorded as Puttenhuthe in 1279. The present St Mary's Church dates from the 15th century and was the setting for the Putney debates of 1647, when members of the New Model Army argued with the Levellers over the future form of the Commonwealth. Its position on the Thames was the making of Putney as an early place of recreation and some commerce, with a busy ferry trade until the construction of a wooden bridge in 1729. PUTNEY HEATH was used for duelling from the 18th century and gentlemen's residences spilled onto the heath from fashionable ROEHAMPTON in the early 19th century. St Mary's Church was extensively rebuilt in 1837 and the railway arrived in 1844. From this time, large estates began to be sold for building and market gardens and orchards were erased as Gothic and Italianate villas spread out from the High Street and up Putney Hill. PUTNEY BRIDGE was rebuilt in stone in 1886 and the accompanying embankment enhanced the town's growing reputation as a riverside pleasure resort. At the same time the High Street was widened and most of its old buildings were lost. Public houses, banks and large shops steadily filled the street in the en-

suing decades. The manufacture of spark plugs brought unexpected industrial growth to PUTNEY VALE from 1912. Between the world wars, middle-class suburban expansion filled the remaining gaps between Putney and its neighbours, especially to the west. Among those who laboured on the building sites was the young Laurie Lee, who lived in digs on Lower Richmond Road and on Werter Road in the 1930s, during his early years as a writer. Nearer to Putney Heath, a number of grand houses survived until after World War II, when many were replaced by council estates. Office blocks came to the High Street and East Putney from the 1960s. The surprisingly ordinary High Street has been slowly improving but its shops are outdone by Wandsworth's, while its restaurants and bars struggle to compete with those of BARNES and Fulham. Putney's riverside does not have the industrial history of downstream districts, so there has been less opportunity for the construction of modern apartment blocks. Developers have instead turned their attentions inland, where the most imaginative recent development has been a small complex on Dryburgh Road that includes four near-circular flats. On the same road, the award-winning Putney leisure centre has a very wide variety of facilities.

The Antarctic explorer Captain Lawrence Oates, best known for his last words, spent his boyhood at 309 Upper Richmond Road, now marked by a blue plaque.

✉ SW15

👥 38,228 (East Putney, West Putney and Thamesfield wards)

🚉 South West Trains (zones 2 and 3)

📖 Brian Evans, *Putney*, Sutton, 1997

@ www.putneysw15.com (community site)

Putney Bridge • *Hammersmith & Fulham/ Wandsworth*

A busy river crossing linking PUTNEY and FULHAM, and the name of the station on its north side. The Earl of Essex erected a temporary bridge here in 1642 to facilitate troop movements. In 1729 local master-carpenter Thomas Phillips completed the first permanent structure, to the design of Sir Jacob Ackworth. The bridge originally had 26 arches (later reduced to 23), ranging in width from 14 to 32 feet. It provided the only dry crossing of the Thames between the City and Kingston and soon generated toll revenues of £1,500 a year. Sir Joseph Bazalgette was responsible for the bridge's replacement in 1886. Constructed from Cornish granite, the new bridge also served as an aqueduct, carrying water mains under the footway. Bazalgette's bridge was widened in the 1930s. Putney Bridge station (originally Putney Bridge and Fulham) opened in 1880 as the terminus of the Metropolitan District Railway's newly extended WEST BROMPTON branch. In 1889 a rail bridge was constructed downstream of the road bridge, allowing a connection with the London and South Western Railway at EAST PUTNEY. Putney Bridge has been the starting point for the University Boat Race since 1845, and it was the finishing point for the five preceding races, which began at Westminster. The competition takes place on a Saturday or Sunday near Easter between teams from Oxford and Cambridge universities. It is the best-known event in the rowing calendar, and was in many ways the inspiration for the modern sport. The four-and-a-quarter-mile slog to Mortlake is usually over in less than 20 minutes.

The writer Mary Wollstonecraft tried to drown herself by leaping from Putney Bridge one night in October 1795. Watermen pulled her unconscious from the river.

✉ SW6; SW15

🚇 District Line (zone 2)

Putney Heath • Wandsworth

The northern continuation of WIMBLEDON COMMON and, as a residential area, the southernmost part of PUTNEY. It is said that when the Swedish botanist Linnaeus saw the golden bloom of the furze on Putney Heath, he fell on his knees thanking God for its beauty. Bowling Green Close marks the site of a series of greens created from the late 17th century by Wimbledon's lords of the manor, the earls Spencer. The scientist David Hartley built himself a house called Wildcroft in 1776, employing experimental techniques he had devised to prevent the spread of fire. His work is commemorated by an obelisk on the heath, designed by George Dance. Jerry's Hill commemorates Jerry Abershaw, who was set upon a gallows here in 1795 after being hanged on Kennington Common for shooting a Bow Street runner. Several duels were fought on Putney Heath in the 18th and 19th centuries, including between eminent politicians: William Pitt, the Younger, a local resident and the prime minister of the day, duelled on the heath with a fellow MP in 1798; and in 1809 the Foreign Secretary, George Canning, was injured in the thigh in a duel with the Secretary of

War, Viscount Castlereagh, following a disagreement over the deployment of troops in a failed military campaign earlier that year. From the early 19th century, Putney Heath began to attract country seats of the sort that had been filling neighbouring ROEHAMPTON, although not on the same scale. The fifth Earl Spencer allowed the heath to become (literally) a tip in the 1860s, as part of a deliberate strategy to obtain the right to enclose it and then sell building plots. However, after a long legal battle the common was saved for public use and cleaned up by an appointed body of conservators, funded by a rates levy on local residents. The heath has woods, wilderness, grassland and five ponds. During the course of the 20th century most of Putney Heath's little palaces were demolished, often to be replaced by small blocks of luxury flats, such as those at Wildcroft Manor.

The actress Sarah Siddons lived in a 'little nutshell' on Putney Heath in the late 18th century, possibly a cottage next to Bowling Green House, where William Pitt the Younger died in 1806. A more obscure former prime minister, Frederick Robinson, Viscount Goderich, died at his home in Putney Heath in 1859.

✉ SW15; SW19

📖 Tony Drakeford and Una Sutcliffe (ed.), *Wimbledon Common and Putney Heath*, Wimbledon and Putney Common Conservators, 2000; Clive Whichelow, *Secrets of Wimbledon Common and Putney Heath*, Enigma, 2000

Putney Vale • Wandsworth

A micro-locality with a place in motor-racing history, separating WIMBLEDON COMMON from RICHMOND PARK. Newlands Farm was a medieval enclosure that fell into disuse and became overgrown. The farm was revived in 1630. The first significant structure in Putney Vale was the Halfway House, later the Bald Faced Stag, a public house established around 1650. The notorious highwayman Jerry Abershaw made the tavern the base for his operations from 1790 until 1795, when he was hanged at the age of 23. The 47-acre Putney Vale Cemetery was established in 1891, a crematorium and garden of remembrance being added later. Shortly before World War I, 175 acres were added to Wimbledon Common, including much of Newlands Farm. The extension incorporated playing fields at Putney Vale, now noted for rugby, which were named in honour of the scheme's sponsor, Richardson Evans. In 1912, working in the cellar of the disused Bald Faced Stag, racing car driver Kenelm Lee Guinness developed a spark plug that could withstand very high engine temperatures. Its applicability to fast cars, motor cycles and aeroplanes made the invention an immediate success and KLG became the largest employer in the area, with over 1,400 workers in 1918. Smith's Industries bought the company in 1927 and built a new factory just in time for the outbreak of World War II. Smith's main factory was demolished in 1989 and replaced by an Asda supermarket, a McDonald's burger bar and a petrol station. In the mid 1950s Wandsworth council built the Putney Vale estate of 370 dwellings on land that had been earmarked for a possible extension of the cemetery.

As well as making spark plugs and special engines, Kenelm Guinness built two world record-breaking cars at his Robin Hood engineering works in Putney Vale. Malcolm Campbell reached 175 mph driving *Bluebird* on Pendine Sands in 1927. Two years later Henry Segrave achieved 231 mph with *Golden Arrow* in Daytona, Florida.

✉ SW15

Pymmes Park · *Enfield*

A lovely 53-acre park and neighbouring residential locality situated north-west of SILVER STREET station. Pymmes House was built by William Pymme in 1327. During the late 16th century the property was in the possession of William Cecil, first Baron Burghley, who also built the magnificent Burghley House in Stamford, Lincolnshire. William was succeeded by his son Robert (later the first Earl of Salisbury) as the chief minister of Elizabeth I. Robert Cecil is said to have spent his honeymoon at Pymmes. The house remained in the hands of the family until 1801. The Nawab Nazim of Bengal lived here in 1868. At the end of the 19th century the council obtained part of the estate from the Ray family and opened it to the public, enlarging it in 1906. Most of the surrounding terraced housing was built around this time. Pymmes House was destroyed by fire in 1940, although a Tudor walled garden survived and has been restored. Parts of the park were lost during the expansion of the North Circular Road (A406) but the council recently obtained a heritage lottery grant for restoration of the Victorian parkland. Pymmes Brook flows from HADLEY via SOUTHGATE to join the River Lea at PICKETT'S LOCK; its course from Pymmes Park onwards is almost all underground now.

✉ N18

Queensbury · *Harrow/Brent*

An interwar suburban creation situated south of LITTLE STANMORE, and popular with Indian families. In 1920 Geoffrey de Havilland leased the former London and Provincial Flying School site and established his aircraft company at Stag Lane, in what was then defined as EDGWARE. De Havilland manufactured numerous famous aeroplanes here, including several varieties of 'Moth'. In 1934 the company moved to Hatfield in Hertfordshire and much of present-day Queensbury was laid out on the site of the disused airfield. To the west, Honeypot Lane – a narrow track named for its stickiness when wet – was transformed into a residential and industrial artery. Although the Metropolitan Railway had begun its service to STANMORE at the end of 1932, it was two years before a station was added here, not just to encourage housebuilding but because so much growth had already taken place. The railway company ran a newspaper competition to devise a name for the station, and the winning entry played on the new town's association with KINGSBURY. Queensbury Park opened in 1936. Shops were built in the vicinity of the station, one of which served as a Methodist Sunday school and place of worship until a brick church was opened on Beverley Drive in 1938. Anglicans worshipped in a wooden hut on Waltham Drive until All Saints Church was consecrated in 1954, by which time Queensbury was the most densely populated ward in Wembley borough. The Essoldo cinema became a bingo hall in the 1960s and has since been replaced by the housing of Essoldo Way, while superstores have appeared on Honeypot Lane. Asians and Asian British residents – mostly of Indian descent – now make up half of Queensbury's population, with whites adding another third. Hinduism and Christianity are the main religious faiths. Around four-fifths of homes are owner-occupied.

The aviatrix Amy Johnson learnt to fly at Stag Lane. In 1930 she became the first woman to fly from England to Australia, piloting a de Havilland Gipsy Moth from CROYDON to Darwin. The aircraft is now on display at the Science Museum.

> ✉ Stanmore HA7; Edgware HA8
>
> 🚶 23,230 (Brent's Queensbury ward and Harrow's Queensbury ward)
>
> 🚇 Jubilee Line (zone 4)

Queen's Park · *Brent/Westminster*

Two conservation areas of the same name, located either side of the Bakerloo/Silverlink railway line south-west of KILBURN. The northern area (now in the London Borough of Brent) tends to be spelt without an apostrophe. To the south, the Queen's Park estate was laid out from 1873 by the Artisans', Labourers' and General Dwellings Co. on land acquired from All Souls College, Oxford. The company ran into some financial difficulties but successfully completed its grid of 2,200 terraced cottages for the respectable working classes in just over a decade. Avenues were numbered from first to sixth, and streets were named in alphabetical order from A to P. Meanwhile, the United Land Co. laid out tightly packed terraces of housing on a neighbouring site in WEST KILBURN. North of the railway line, Queen Victoria opened the International Exhibition of the Royal Agricultural Society in 1879. The open space that survives north of Harvist Road was a section of the showground and was opened to the public as Queens Park in 1887. The park's immediate vicinity was built up over the following 25 years, much of it with generously proportioned detached and semi-detached houses. At that time, the streets to the south-west of the park were considered to be in KENSAL RISE and the streets to the northeast in Kilburn. However, this pricey little locality now asserts its own identity as Queens Park. Many of United Land's terraces were demolished and replaced by the Mozart estate, which won a design award in 1973 but subsequently became a particularly unpopular place to live. Other council building replaced some of the Queen's Park houses south of

Droop Street. In Brent's Queens Park ward the majority of homes are owner-occupied but in Westminster's Queen's Park ward most are rented from the council or a housing association.

Queen's Park Rangers Football Club was formed in 1882 by the old boys of Droop Street Board School. Originally called St Jude's, the club took its present name after a merger with Christchurch Rangers in 1886. QPR has played outside the Queen's Park neighbourhood for the majority of its existence, mostly at its present ground in Loftus Road. The team was in and out of top-flight football from the late 1960s to the mid 1990s, but has struggled in recent years, both on the pitch and off it, with persistent financial problems.

✉ W10; NW6

♦ 21,579 (Brent's Queens Park ward and Westminster's Queen's Park ward)

🚇 Silverlink Metro; Bakerloo Line (zone 2)

📖 Erica McDonald and David J Smith, *Artizans and Avenues: A History of the Queen's Park Estate*, City of Westminster Libraries, 1990

Queens Road, Peckham • *Southwark*

A section of the A202 joining PECKHAM High Street with NEW CROSS Road (A2). Most of the road falls within Peckham but the eastern end is in New Cross and it was formerly known as DEPTFORD Lane or Peckham Lane. The surrounding neighbourhood consisted of market gardens until about 1840 when a network of terraces called New Peckham began to be laid out. Its station (originally Peckham) opened on a new section of line between East Brixton and London Bridge in 1866. In the same year the road was renamed in honour of Queen Victoria and the station soon followed suit. From 1893, the street's principal business was Evans Cook, which began as a second-hand furniture store and subsequently diversified into removals. Doctors George Scott Williamson and Innes Pearse of the Royal Free Hospital opened the Pioneer Health Centre at 142 Queens Road in 1926. The doctors chose the area because it contained a cross-section of society. They provided regular medical checks and gave advice on healthy living, and found much more sickness than they had expected. In 1935 the centre moved around the corner to St Mary's Road, into purpose-built premises that still look modern today. Another significant doctor who practised in Queens Road in the 1930s was Dr Harold Moody. A Jamaican immigrant who studied medicine at King's College, Moody was the founder of the League of Coloured Peoples and the father of several talented and high-achieving black Britons. A blue plaque marks his former surgery at 164 Queens Road. Modern housing developments in the Queens Road area include Peckham's Acorn estate and the Somerville estate in New Cross. Quay House, on Kings Grove (formerly Kings Road), is a 2001 conversion of a 1930s dairy depot into an architect's office, sculpture studio and home with a new-build development of three flats above.

✉ SE14; SE15

🚇 Southern (zone 2)

Queens Road, Walthamstow *see* WALTHAMSTOW QUEENS ROAD

Queenstown Road • *Wandsworth*

BATTERSEA's Queenstown (formerly Queen's) Road runs from CHELSEA Bridge along the eastern edge of BATTERSEA PARK, snakes under a complex of railway viaducts and then heads south towards CLAPHAM. The area has been dubbed the Battersea Tangle because of the network of railway lines here. To the east of the Clapham end of the road is the Park Town estate, built in the 1860s for middle-class families. The rapid emergence of a heavy railway presence reduced the desirability of the properties, which were soon subdivided for occupation by manual workers. Queen's Road station was opened by the London and South Western Railway in 1877, with a second platform and a new booking office added in 1909. It was renamed Queenstown Road Battersea in 1980 and given Grade II-listed status in 2001. Today, the street exhibits some of the sharpest polarities in inner London, with cheap takeaways and pricey restaurants; run-down or closed-down general stores and specialist fashion boutiques; dilapidated, subdivided terraced houses and swanky new apartment blocks. At an average of four rooms per household, properties in the area are significantly smaller than the national average. Most are rented. Despite Battersea's fashionability, Berkeley Homes has preferred to use the name 'Chelsea Bridge Wharf' for its major new development at the northern end of Queenstown Road.

The Victorian Gothic church of St Philip the Apostle, Queenstown Road, was built to serve the community of Park Town. Post-war renovations included a stained-glass window depicting Battersea power station. St Philip's stands within the Catholic tradition of the

Church of England and has adapted to the area's changing profile by introducing a weekly Ethiopian liturgy.

✉ SW8

♦ 12,505 (Queenstown ward)

🚃 South West Trains (zone 2)

📖 Priscilla Metcalf, *The Park Town Estate and the Battersea Tangle*, London Topographical Society, 1978; J E Connor, *The Railway Stations of Battersea and Wandsworth*, Connor & Butler, 1998

Queensway • *Westminster*

A central north-south axis of the Bayswater district, consisting mostly of 20th-century apartment blocks with shops and restaurants at street level. This was formerly Black Lion Lane, which ran from KENSINGTON to WESTBOURNE GREEN. Black Lion Gate survives at the north-western corner of Kensington Gardens. The lane was a favourite ride of the young Princess Victoria and after her coronation it was renamed Queen's Road. This was changed to Queensway a century later to distinguish it from the many other Queen's Roads. The vicinity was late to develop because it was on lower ground than nearby PADDINGTON and Westbourne Green, but from the mid 19th century the proximity of the West End began to attract upper middle-class professionals who appreciated its rural setting. By the 1890s a cosmopolitan variety of shops had lined the street and Whiteley's department store moved here from WESTBOURNE GROVE in 1911. The Porchester baths, with the most elegant swimming pool in London, opened in 1925. Queens Ice and Bowl, as it is now called, opened in 1930 and has been central London's only permanent ice rink ever since. Queensway remained a prestigious shopping centre until the mid 20th century, when the residential neighbourhood began to decline in status. Large houses were subdivided for multiple occupation or converted into budget hotels, while others were demolished to make way for council blocks. Students, immigrants and tourists became the area's principal denizens. The shops went downmarket and Whiteley's closed in 1981. From the mid 1980s an influx of wealthy Arabs to Bayswater brought an upturn in Queensway's fortunes and a change in its character. With its Palestinian grocers, Egyptian newsagents, Persian cafés and Lebanese restaurants, modern Queensway has been called 'an oasis for London's Arab diaspora'. Whiteley's reopened in 1989 as a shopping mall with a food court and cinema. Confusingly, Queensway station is at the corner of Bayswater Road, while Bayswater station is on Queensway.

✉ W2

🚃 Central Line (Queensway, zone 1); Circle Line; District Line (Bayswater, zone 1)

📖 Clare Melhuish, 'Queensway Mix: A case-study in architectural anthropology', www.iniva.org/celluloid/melhuish.html, 1995

Rainham • *Havering*

An industrial and residential district located three miles south of HORNCHURCH. Because of its situation beside the Ingrebourne River, with access to the Thames via Rainham Creek, there appears to have been human occupation of the area virtually since the ice retreated. Prehistoric implements have been found in the marshes and there is evidence of a Saxon burial ground. The name is probably a corruption of 'Reoginga-ham', Saxon for 'settlement of the ruling people'. The squat, flint-faced Church of St Helen and St Giles was built around 1178 and survives virtually unaltered. Rainham subsequently evolved as a dual-purpose agricultural and trading settlement. As London grew, market gardens were established here and their produce was taken up the Thames on barges, which returned laden with coal and manure. The medieval wharf was improved in the late 1710s by its owner, Captain John Harle, who went on to build Rainham Hall a decade later. This compact, elegant house is now a National Trust property but its opening hours are extremely limited. Rainham station opened in 1854 and the village began to expand, following the typical pattern that begins with larger villas for the well-off and then gives way to cheaper accommodation for the masses as advancements in transport provide improved accessibility. From around 1880 the village crept eastwards, and after World War I the sale of smallholdings brought growth to the New Road area. A war memorial clock tower was erected in the centre of the village in 1920 and a large Jewish cemetery was established on Upminster Road North in 1938. Private and council housebuilding continued after World War II, especially in the north. South of the railway line, industrial premises line Ferry Lane but the former rifle ranges on RAINHAM MARSHES have been saved from development by the creation of a nature reserve. The council is supporting plans to build a casino on Ferry Lane, which could act as a catalyst for the significant transformation of its immediate vicinity. There are sufficient remaining elements of old Rainham to suggest what a charming marshland village this once was, but these have been engulfed by unsightly additions from the second half of the 20th century. Rainham Hall and St Helen's and St Giles' Church, for example, gaze across the road at a library and social services offices that are truly offensive.

The popular crime writer Martina Cole spent part of her childhood in Rainham and uses local settings in some of her books. Rainham Steel's advertising hoardings are a familiar sight at major football matches. The steel stockholder and distributor was formed in 1973 and is based on Manor Way.

> ✉ Rainham RM13

> ♟ 12,114 (Rainham and Wennington ward)

> 🚌 c2c (zone 6)

> 📖 S Curtis, *Dagenham and Rainham Past*, Phillimore, 2000

Rainham Marshes • *Havering*

A desolate landscape of marshland and silt lagoons situated east of RAINHAM Creek, and part of the ecological and development zone now called HAVERING RIVERSIDE. In the Middle Ages the monks of Lesnes Abbey grazed their sheep on the pasture here, and around 400 acres were in arable use in 1309. The first incarnation of the Three Crowns inn may have been built beside Rainham Creek as early as 1550, serving passengers for the Rainham ferry, which carried Canterbury-bound pilgrims across the Thames. The agricultural land was extended by 185 acres through reclamation in the 17th century. The Three Crowns was rebuilt in the early 19th century and wharves and industrial premises appeared on the riverfront from the 1880s and later filled much of Ferry Lane. In 1906 the War Office bought a swathe of the mudflats for use as rifle ranges, but these became relatively inactive after World War II. The Three Crowns was mostly demolished in the early 1970s, and more recently the rerouted A13 and the Channel Tunnel rail link have been constructed across the marshes. In 2000 the Royal Society for the Protection of Birds acquired 850 acres of Rainham, Wennington and Aveley Marshes from the Ministry of Defence for the creation of the society's only nature reserve in Greater London. Not surprisingly, the reserve is of particular note for its diverse bird interest, especially its wading birds, wintering wildfowl, finches and birds of prey. The reserve also supports some scarce wetland plants and insects and has one of the highest densities of water voles in the country. An environment and education centre has been built across the London border in Purfleet, Essex.

In December 2005 nearly 2,000 people visited the RSPB's Rainham Marshes reserve to see a rare sociable plover, only the second recorded appearance of the species in London.

✉ Rainham RM13

@ www.rspb.org.uk/reserves/guide/r/rainhammarshes

Ramsden • *Bromley*

A council estate situated on the far eastern edge of Orpington, with views over open country from the tower blocks. Little is known of the origin of the name, but it may have meant 'woodland pasture for rams'. The Ramsden estate, a mix of terraced housing and high- and low-rise blocks, was constructed in the late 1950s and 1960s. Although Ramsden is regarded as grotty and crime-ridden by many Orpingtonians, this is by comparison with most other parts of the district, rather than with deprived estates elsewhere. Broomleigh, the housing association now responsible for much of Ramsden, is in the process of regenerating the estate, in a programme touted as 'Ramsden's Revival'. The six-phase project will ultimately involve demolishing and replacing most of the existing housing and creating a more traditional street pattern. New buildings will rise to no more than four storeys. The housing density was intended to be similar to that of the original estate but has since been revised downwards. The project began in 2003 and will provide a roughly even split of homes for sale and for rent, with improved play areas, more parking spaces and several homes specifically tailored for disabled people. Phase two was completed in 2006.

A scheme in which young residents worked with street artists to create graffiti-style paintings ran into problems in 2005. Posters were painted in the community centre and then mounted on hoardings around the Ramsden estate but police cautioned one great-grandfather when he tore down several boards just before the press arrived for their unveiling.

✉ Orpington BR5

Ratcliff • *Tower Hamlets*

Although the name is still shown on some maps, sometimes spelt 'Ratcliffe', this historic locality has become lost in LIMEHOUSE. Ratcliff was situated at the point where, today, Docklands-bound traffic disappears below ground into the Limehouse Link Tunnel. The hamlet first developed around the junction of two Roman roads as they converged on *Londinium*. Ratcliff had a dock as early as the 14th century and there are records of timber deliveries from Surrey and the conscription of craftsmen from East Anglia to build ships for the king in the 1350s. Sir Hugh Willoughby sailed from Ratcliff in 1553 on an expedition that opened the trade route to Moscow. In 1576 Martin Frobisher departed on the first of his voyages in search of the north-west passage to Asia. Ratcliff Highway, which led to the City, was a notorious haunt for London's low life in the 18th and 19th centuries. In the Ratcliff Highway murders of 1811, two entire households were brutally slain. The prime suspect hanged himself while awaiting trial.

Ratcliffe Highway is a much-recorded shanty-style folk song.

✉ E1; E14

📖 P D James and T A Critchley, *The Maul and the Pear Tree: The Ratcliffe Highway Murders, 1811*, Thorndike, 1988

Raven's Ait • *Kingston*

A small island in the Thames lying between Hampton Court Park and south-west Kingston. The Kingston Rowing Club, established in 1858, was based here and held annual regattas. In the 20th century Hart's boatyard operated an on-demand ferry service to the islet and the Navy League trained sea cadets here. Raven's Ait continues to be used as a base for water sports, especially sailing and rowing. Kingston council acquired the islet in 1996 and leases it to a conference and banqueting business, which promotes its use for weddings and as a film location, the former successfully, the latter less so. A private launch carries visitors across from the Kingston shore.

✉ Surbiton KT6

@ www.ravensait.co.uk (business marketing site)

Ravensbourne • *Bromley*

A station in east BECKENHAM, named after the river that rises near KESTON Ponds and flows north to join the Thames near GREENWICH. Legend has it that Julius Caesar encamped his troops at Keston and observed a raven frequently alighting nearby. He guessed that the bird might be quenching its thirst and ordered that its landing spot be examined, whereupon a little spring was found, which was then used to supply water for the legion. However, in the 14th century the river was called Rendesburne, which is probably derived from Old English words meaning 'boundary stream'. The present version of the name is probably an example of folk etymology. The River Ravensbourne forms the boundary between several sets of parishes along its course, and near the station it separates Beckenham from BROMLEY. One of the last of Beckenham's many stations, Ravensbourne opened in 1892 on the CATFORD loop line and new roads were soon laid out nearby. However, Victorian development ceased when it reached the ends of Foxgrove Road and the Avenue, possibly because less hilly sites elsewhere offered richer pickings. Crab Hill was an unmade road in 1900, when Ravensbourne Road (later Avenue) had only six houses. Two-thirds of the properties on the road were built between the world wars. The London County Council built flats near Ravensbourne station in the late 1950s, when the station still had 'the air of a sleepy rural halt', according to the local paper.

> ✉ Beckenham BR3; Bromley BR1

> 🚇 South Eastern Trains (zone 4)

Ravenscourt Park • *Hammersmith & Fulham*

A public park and its neighbouring residential locality, situated at the western end of HAMMERSMITH. From at least the 14th century this was the manor of Pallingswick or Paddenswick. In 1746 Secretary to the Admiralty Thomas Corbett bought the estate and rebuilt the manor house, naming it Ravenscourt after the bird on his family's coat of arms. Parts of the 80-acre estate were leased to tenant farmers after Corbett's death. George Scott, who lived at Ravenscourt from 1812 to 1859, progressively sold off chunks of his land for housebuilding and insisted on high standards of architecture and construction. He also improved the parkland and added flower gardens. Some of the new houses were soon demolished during the building of the railway that cut across the southern end of the estate. The station opened in 1877, and was called Shaftesbury Road for the first eleven years of its existence. In 1887 Scott's heirs sold Ravenscourt and 32 acres of grounds to the Metropolitan Board of Works, which converted the gardens into a park. 'To my mind this indeed is the most beautiful park in London', wrote W H Hudson in *Birds in London* in 1898. Queen Charlotte's Hospital opened in a large Victorian house on the west side of the park in 1929. Two years later the Royal Masonic (now Ravenscourt Park) Hospital replaced some neighbouring houses. Ravenscourt served as a public library in its later years but was destroyed in an air raid in 1941. Ravenscourt Park was designated a conservation area in 1974 and plans to demolish old houses in Paddenswick Road were abandoned. Queen Charlotte's Hospital has recently relocated next to Hammersmith Hospital at WORMWOOD SCRUBS and its former site is being redeveloped with housing, a community centre, doctors' surgery and shops. Half of Ravenscourt Park's residents are single and a similar number are university educated. Among the area's many ethnic minorities the Polish community is the most visible, with a cultural centre on KING STREET and specialist shops nearby.

> ✉ W6

> 🚶 10,791

> 🚇 District Line (zone 2)

> 📖 Rosamund Vercoe, *Ravenscourt*, Fulham and Hammersmith Historical Society, 1991

Rayners Lane • *Harrow*

A suburban conglomeration to the west of HARROW, taking its identity from the Tube station, which was itself named after the long and winding road that runs through here on its way from SOUTH HARROW to PINNER. From medieval times, smallholders used the lane when carting their grain to the mill on Pinner Green. It was originally called Bourne Lane, because it crossed several streams, including YEADING Brook. The Rayner family, who lived here in the first half of the 19th century, were not property owners but working tenants of the farmer who had acquired the neighbouring land. The countryside around the wooden rail halt at Rayners Lane was completely transformed in the decade before World War II, mainly by T F Nash, Harrow's biggest interwar housebuilder. Nash constructed narrow gauge railway sidings at High Worple to bring in materials for the project and created the shopping parade on Alexandra Avenue. The locality now has a large Asian and British Asian population, most of whom are of Indian descent. Hinduism is the main religion after Christianity. The typical resident is a married homeowner, probably with children and one or two cars.

The Grosvenor (later Odeon) cinema, designed by F E Bromige, is one of London's finest suburban cinema buildings. Opened in 1935, its art deco frontage features an abstract representation of an elephant's trunk. The building is now a centre of worship for members of the Zoroastrian faith, and was used as the location for *Eyes Down*, a recent BBC television comedy set in a bingo hall.

> ✉ Harrow HA2; Pinner HA5

> 👥 10,038

> 🚇 Central Line; Piccadilly Line (zone 5)

Raynes Park • *Merton*

To some an enduring community, to others an 'underwhelming commuter suburb', situated one-and-a-half miles south-west of WIMBLEDON. Edward Rayne owned and managed Park House Farm from 1822, dividing the land into three 'parks': for pasturing sheep and cows, for growing peas, turnips and swedes, and for producing hay for local horses. After his sudden death in 1847, Rayne's widow retained the farm until her son's financial mismanagement forced her to sell to the lord of the manor of Morden, Richard Garth, in 1867. Garth laid out Grand Drive and in 1871 funded the opening of a station, named after the farm's former owner. Poor market conditions restricted property sales, so Garth leased some of the land as playing fields and a golf course. A few shops and houses were built in the 1880s, but it was not until the extension of Wimbledon's Worple Road to Raynes Park in 1891 that growth began to pick up and two shopping parades were built opposite the station. Nevertheless, it was several decades before the area was fully built up, despite the arrival of tram services in 1907. With plenty of space still available for non-residential purposes, Carter's Tested Seeds Ltd purchased 19 acres west of WEST BARNES Lane in 1909 and built a large complex of offices, laboratories and workshops. The largest of the area's speculative developers was George Blay, who bought the CANNON HILL estate in 1924 and obtained a government subsidy to build freehold houses. Firstway was the first road he laid out, followed by an extensive series of other 'ways'.

The former golf course, which lay west of Grand Drive, is remembered in the names Greenway, Fairway and Linkway. Raynes Park County School for Boys opened in 1935 and has since become Raynes Park High School, a mixed comprehensive. Carter's left Raynes Park in 1966 and the council acquired its site for housing, laying out streets with names ending in 'Gardens'. Raynes Park Library was rebuilt in 2005, as part of a development that includes 29 sheltered flats.

Raymond Briggs, creator of *The Snowman* and *Fungus the Bogeyman*, was educated at Raynes Park County School for Boys. Jeff Beck's 1971 album *Rough and Ready* includes the instrumental track *Raynes Park Blues*, alternatively titled *Max's Tune*, in a reference to keyboard player Max Middleton, who wrote the piece while he was living in the area.

> ✉ SW20; New Malden KT3

> 👥 9,395

> 🚇 South West Trains (zone 4)

> 📖 Evelyn M Jowett, *Raynes Park with West Barnes and Cannon Hill: A Social History*, Merton Historical Society, 1987

> @ www.rpwbresidents.org.uk (residents' association site); www.raynespark.merton.sch.uk (High School site)

Rectory Road • *Hackney*

A very mixed commercial and residential thoroughfare in south-east STOKE NEWINGTON. In the early centuries of its life the road was the northern part of SHACKLEWELL Lane, which looped from DALSTON to Stoke Newington Common. St James's Church, West Hackney, was built by Sir Robert Smirke in 1824 and its rectory lay down the lane that is now Manse Road. In 1864 the Great Eastern Railway Co. won permission to construct a branch line running to the east of Shacklewell Lane. Builders quickly grabbed the opportunity to replace market gardens with houses along this section of the lane, which was renamed Rectory Road. The railway line and Rectory Road station opened in 1872. Soon afterwards, development around Garnham Street cut off Rectory Road's north tip, diverting travellers onto Northwold Road. As housing filled the neighbourhood ever more densely, the street's character slipped downmarket. The Tyssen estate, the landowner, was given permission to convert some of the larger houses to industrial use in 1933 after warning the council that the alternative was multiple occupation. Rectory Road station was rebuilt in the 1970s. For most of its length, Rectory Road is part of the Stoke Newington one-way system, deflecting City-bound traffic on the A10 away from Stoke Newington High Street. Three early-19th-century houses survive at the southern end of the road, and have Grade II-listed status. The Rectory ward was abolished at the last boundary reorganization and Rectory Road now divides the wards of HACKNEY DOWNS and Stoke Newington Central. A Labour-held ward before its eradication, the Rectory ward ranked in the top 10 per cent of the nation's most deprived wards, but that represented only a middling score within this borough.

✉ N16

🚊 'one' Railway (zone 2)

Redbridge • *Redbridge*

A well-connected suburban locality in north Ilford, situated at the junction of the Eastern Avenue (A12), the North Circular Road (A406) and the southern end of the M11 motorway. There have been at least four bridges across the River Roding here. The earliest, known as Hockley's Bridge after a medieval landowner, was standing in the 16th century. A red-brick bridge was built in 1642 and survived for two centuries, after which an iron bridge was erected in its place. The Red House was an inn that stood on the Ilford side of the river. Red-brick terraced houses, now mostly pebble-dashed, were built here at the beginning of the 20th century using materials from the Ilford brickfields. Another spate of house-building followed the arrival of the Eastern Avenue in the mid 1920s, when the iron bridge was replaced by the present crossing. Redbridge station opened in 1947 on a new section of the Central Line, with platforms just 26 feet below road level. The arrival of the Tube could have prompted further building beside the river but the land was protected from development. In 1965 the newly created London Borough of Redbridge united the borough of Wanstead and Woodford with the borough of Ilford. The two had formerly been separated by the River Roding and the new borough's name was chosen because the bridge symbolized their linkage. Redbridge has been nicknamed 'diesel alley' because so many cab drivers choose to live here. The Redbridge roundabout has been rated London's worst accident blackspot.

✉ Ilford IG4

🚊 Central Line (zone 4)

Reedham • *Croydon*

A suburb fathered by an orphanage, situated south-west of PURLEY. After training as a watchmaker and clock repairer, Andrew Reed chose instead to become a Congregationalist minister. He founded a children's home that soon outgrew its lodgings in RICHMOND and STAMFORD HILL and raised funds to buy a new site in the Surrey hills. The Asylum for Fatherless Children opened in 1858 with a capacity of 300. Reed died four years later, aged 75, and the asylum's name was changed to Reedham in his honour. When the station opened in 1911 it also took the name Reedham, as did the village that grew up nearby. Declining numbers and increasing debts forced the governors to close the home in 1980 and the site was sold to pay off debts and set up the Reedham Trust. Based at the Lodge, the only remaining building, the trust sponsors boarding school education for children with difficult home circumstances.

✉ Purley CR8

🚊 Southern (zone 6)

📖 H E Rolph, *The Home on the Hill: The Story of Reedham*, Reedham Old Scholars Association, 1981

@ www.reedham-trust.org.uk

Regent's Park • *Westminster/Camden*

A royal park and the neighbouring residential area lying north of MARYLEBONE Road. Formerly known as Marylebone Park, this was a royal hunting ground leased to the dukes of Portland. When the Portland lease expired in 1811 the Prince Regent (later George IV) commissioned architect John Nash to devise a masterplan for a large part of London's WEST END, with Regent's Park as its crowning glory in the north. Nash originally envisaged a palace for the prince, surrounded by a private royal park, which would in turn be encircled by fine houses. The park was landscaped but only the grand stuccoed terraced houses on the perimeter and a handful of villas were built and George IV later chose to live at Buckingham Palace. The Zoological Society of London established a scientific zoo in the north of Regent's Park in 1828 and both the zoo and the park's gardens were opened to the public in the mid 1840s. Queen Mary's Gardens were laid out in the 1930s. Cecil Sharp House, at 2 Regent's Park Road, was built in 1930 as a centre for traditional folk music. It is home to the Vaughan Williams Memorial Library, a national archive dedicated to the preservation of English folk music and dance. After inheriting $40 million from her grandfather Frank Winfield Woolworth, Barbara Hutton built Winfield House in 1937 and donated it as a home for the American ambassador after World War II; visiting US presidents often stay here. With the support of the British government, George VI gave land on the west side of the park for the creation of an Islamic centre, in memory of Muslim soldiers who had died fighting for the British Empire. The London Central Mosque (also known as Regent's Park Mosque) opened on the same site in 1977. London Zoo has been voted the capital's favourite visitor attraction and large parts of it are being redeveloped at present to remove cages and bars and create more natural forms of enclosure. The park has some of London's most extensive sporting grounds, with tennis courts, football, cricket, softball and rugby pitches and capacious changing facilities. An open-air theatre operates in the summer months and concerts are staged on the bandstands. The Regent's Park locality takes in radically contrasting housing stock, ranging from fine Georgian villas to Camden council's deprived Regent's Park estate. St John's Lodge, on the Inner Circle, achieved the record price for a London home when it sold for nearly £50 million in 1994.

In 1823 a pioneering exhibition of revolving architectural displays opened at the Diorama, in Park Square East. One of London's worst calamities happened on Regent's Park lake in winter 1867 when ice gave way beneath hundreds of skaters and 40 young men died.

✉ NW1

♟ 23,013 (Westminster's Regent's Park ward and Camden's Regent's Park ward)

🚇 Bakerloo Line (zone 1)

📖 Ann Saunders, *Regent's Park*, Bedford College, 1981

@ www.royalparks.gov.uk/parks/regents_park; www.zsl.org/london-zoo

Regent Street • *Westminster*

A prestigious WEST END shopping street, curving south and then east from Portland Place to PICCADILLY CIRCUS (which was originally called Regent Circus South). Lower Regent Street continues south to Waterloo Place. In 1811 the architect John Nash planned the street for the Prince Regent (later George IV) as the central thoroughfare of a scheme linking his home at Carlton House with the proposed site of a palace in REGENT'S PARK. Regent Street was completed in 1825 to widespread acclaim. The Polytechnic (Britain's first such institution) was founded at the northern end of the street in 1838, later becoming the Regent Street Polytechnic and ultimately forming the nucleus of the University of Westminster. Meanwhile, flaws were becoming apparent in Regent Street's commercial practicality. Colonnades had to be removed because streetwalkers had taken to lurking in their shadows and by the end of the century the intimate scale of the shops had become inappropriate to retailers' needs. A protracted rebuilding programme began in 1902, resulting in the present streetscape. Only All Souls' Church survives from the original project, at the street's far northern end. Regent Street remains the property of the Crown Estate, which oversees a continuous programme of investment designed to keep it at the forefront of the West End shopping experience. The street was repaved in 1992 using 2,000 tons of Pennine stone, in a £3 million scheme replacing concrete that had proved unequal to the task. Regent Street has three large hotels, and new stores have recently been opening at the rate of about a dozen a year, mostly flagship outlets for international fashion brands at the upper end of the mass market. Of the longer-established stores, Jaeger and Aquascutum are among the latest to have undertaken major refurbishments. Heddon Street, made famous on the cover of David Bowie's *Ziggy Stardust* album, has become a 'food quarter'. Hamley's claims to be the world's oldest, largest and best-stocked toyshop, with over 50,000 different items on sale.

Parisian wine merchant Daniel Nicolas Thévenon opened the Café Royal in 1865, offering the then-rare prospect of French haute cuisine in the heart of London. Oscar Wilde dined here in 1892 with the Marquess of Queensberry and his son Lord Alfred Douglas.

✉ W1; SW1

📖 Hermione Hobhouse, *A History of Regent Street*, Phillimore, 2003

@ www.regentstreetonline.com

Richmond Hill • *Richmond*

A superior road and its vicinity, located south of RICHMOND UPON THAMES town centre. Charles I used to ride up the hill to hunt in RICHMOND PARK and the view from the summit has attracted artists and poets since the 17th century. Grand houses lined the hill at well-spaced intervals during the late 18th century, including Downe House, Ancaster House, The Wick, and Wick House, which was built for Sir Joshua Reynolds. The Star and Garter inn was rebuilt as a chateau-like hotel in 1864 and in its early days played host to exiled crowned heads of Europe. The Richmond Hill Hotel of 1865 is now the PETER-SHAM Hotel. The grounds of Buccleuch House and Lansdowne House were laid out as the Terrace Gardens in 1887 and have become a favourite spot for couples posing for wedding pictures. The view from the hill was protected by Act of Parliament in 1902 after developers had proposed to build on Petersham Meadows and MARBLE HILL. The Star and Garter inn was replaced in 1924 by a sumptuous home for disabled sailors, soldiers and airmen, the future use of which is now the subject of debate. Richmond University is the home of the American International University in London. The campus is set in a six-acre site, centred on an impressive neo-Gothic structure that was originally the Wesleyan Theological Institution. At the nearby Vineyard Primary School on Friars Stile Road, one is not surprised to learn that the proportion of children receiving free school meals is well below the national average.

The view from Richmond Hill has inspired the composer Henry Purcell, the poets James Thomson and William Wordsworth, the art critic John Ruskin and countless artists, notably J M W Turner and Philip Wilson Steer. Downe House has been home to the dramatist Richard Sheridan, the actor John Mills and the rock star Mick Jagger.

✉ Richmond TW10

@ www.richmond.ac.uk

Richmond Park • *Richmond*

London's greatest royal park, extending over 2,500 acres south-east of RICHMOND UPON THAMES town centre. Charles I created the park in 1637, ordering its brick-walled enclosure so that he might hunt deer. The enclosure was highly unpopular with local people, even though the king allowed them to walk and to gather firewood here – a right that still exists. When Charles was beheaded, Parliament granted the park to the City of London, which prudently returned it to Charles II on his restoration. In 1751 Princess Amelia took up residence in the White Lodge (built as a retreat for her father, George II) and excluded the public

from the park until the courts overturned the ban seven years later. In his role as Deputy Ranger, Viscount Sidmouth introduced a series of plantations from 1819 onwards, principally of oak trees, but also Spanish chestnut, beech, hornbeam, sycamore and larch. There are now more than a dozen woods, the most beautiful of which is the 42-acre Isabella Plantation. As a result of public pressure, Edward VII disbanded the Royal Hunt and opened the park to the public in 1904. George V granted permission for the park's eastern section to be turned into a golf course, on the understanding that it was for 'artisans' who could not afford membership of a private club. The course opened in 1923 and was followed by another two years later. The Isabella Plantation was extensively replanted with ericaceous shrubs in the 1950s and 1960s. Sidmouth Wood has become a bird sanctuary; over a hundred different species have been recorded throughout the park, and pheasant and partridge are raised. Richmond Park has several hundred fallow and red deer, and a wide variety of woodland wildlife, including badgers and foxes, although the official mole-catcher has been made redundant. Sheep ceased to be grazed in 1980. At the centre of the park are the Pen Ponds, where coarse fishing is allowed by permit. The White Lodge, which had been occupied by a succession of princes and princesses, became the home of the Royal Ballet School's Lower School in the mid 1950s.

Pembroke Lodge was the home of Lord John Russell, prime minister in 1846–52 and 1865–6, and of his grandson, the philosopher Bertrand Russell. Princess Alexandra lives at Thatched House Lodge, which in its present form is largely the work of Sir John Soane. In 1997 Jenny Tonge won the newly created constituency of Richmond Park for the Liberal Democrats, making her Richmond's first non-Conservative MP for 130 years.

✉ Richmond TW10; SW14; SW15

🏃 107,194 (parliamentary constituency)

📖 Joanna Jackson, *A Year in the Life of Richmond Park*, Frances Lincoln, 2003

@ www.royalparks.org.uk/parks/
richmond.park

Richmond upon Thames • *Richmond*

A delightful Thames-side town, situated nine miles south-west of central London. This was Sheen (or Shene or West Sheen) in the Middle Ages. Royal courts were held at the manor house from the end of the 13th century and

Edward III died in 1377 at what had become Sheen Palace. Henry VII rebuilt the palace after a fire in 1497 and named it Richmond after his earldom in Yorkshire. Richmond Palace was the birthplace of Henry VIII, and Elizabeth I spent many summers here, maintaining a wardrobe of 2,000 dresses in a purpose-built storehouse. After her death in 1603 the Stuarts allowed this stately collection of buildings to fall into decay and the palace was demolished in 1650. All that now remains are the Wardrobe and the gateway, beside Maids of Honour Row. The presence of the palace had stimulated the growth of the village, which was at this time concentrated on Hill Street, George Street, the Quadrant and KEW Road. Richmond had also become a place to which rich Londoners fled by boat to escape epidemics. The discovery of a medicinal spring in the 1670s brought demand for accommodation for visitors and soon afterwards wealthy Londoners started renting properties and buying land on which to establish small estates, although the creation of the Old Deer Park and RICHMOND PARK constrained the town's ability to spread. The Richmond wells fell out of favour and closed in 1763 but the town saw more growth in the latter part of the 18th century, when Richmond Bridge was built, cottages filled the lanes and large villas lined the riverside and RICHMOND HILL. The finest of the homes by the river was Asgill House, on Old Palace Lane, one of the first major projects of the architect Sir Robert Taylor. The Thames remained a popular method of travelling to Richmond and a steamer route opened in 1816. A horse-drawn omnibus connected London and Richmond from 1830 but this was overtaken by the arrival of the railway in 1846. By the end of the 19th century suburban development had left little land available for building and only a few surviving mansions with grounds. Of those that remain, two have become hotels. Richmond Theatre was built on the Green in 1899. Over the course of the 20th century parades of shops replaced many of the Georgian dwellings but the town centre nevertheless retains more character than most of its outer London rivals. From the late 1950s a growing demand for office space was satisfied both by the conversion of existing buildings and the construction of purpose-built blocks. The riverside between the bridge and Water Lane was redeveloped, incorporating and restoring some of the existing buildings, in the late 1980s. With its beautiful green, mall-free shopping streets and plenitude of places to eat and drink, Rich-

mond draws numerous visitors and can become crowded in summer. Among its many sports teams, the town is home to the London Welsh and Richmond rugby football clubs.

The Chilean revolutionary leader Bernardo O'Higgins lived at Clarence House in the Vineyard at the start of the 19th century. In the late 1850s the novelist George Eliot and her husband lodged at 8 Parkshot, now the site of the magistrates' court. Leonard and Virginia Woolf lived at Hogarth House on Paradise Road, where they founded the Hogarth Press in 1917.

✉ Richmond TW9

♦ 20,045 (North Richmond and South Richmond wards)

🚇 Silverlink Metro terminus; South West Trains; District Line (zone 4)

⛴ Richmond pier

📖 John Cloake, *Richmond: Past and Present*, Sutton, 1999

@ www.richmond-online.co.uk (community site); www.guidetorichmond.co.uk

Riddlesdown • *Croydon*

Chalk downland in north KENLEY, and its neighbouring residential locality. Part of Riddlesdown is a scheduled ancient monument containing Neolithic remains. Saxon graves have been discovered on Riddlesdown Road and their alignment suggests that the route was in use in the seventh century. Riddlesdown was first mentioned by name in 1277 and derives from Old English and Middle English words meaning 'cleared woodland on a hill'. The woodland is believed to have consisted of beech trees, which flourish on chalky soil. A lime quarry was in existence by the late 18th century and continued to operate for nearly 200 years. The Corporation of London acquired the majority of Riddlesdown in 1883, preserving it as open space. The acquisition resolved a dispute between the owner of nearby LITTLE ROKE House and the lord of the manor, who had been attempting to encroach on the common land. Riddlesdown National School catered for children from PURLEY and Kenley in the years when the hamlets were first evolving into suburbs. Gardner's Pleasure Resort was established in 1892 at the foot of Riddlesdown, drawing day-trippers in their thousands. Riddlesdown station opened in 1927 and a tunnel carries the railway line southwards beneath the down. The neighbouring area soon filled with some pleasing houses and small parades of shops were built near the station, although only one was occupied ten years later. Developers nevertheless persisted and built another parade in 1939, which proved equally difficult to let. In 1962 Riddlesdown Residents' Association successfully defeated an attempt to build six three-storey blocks of flats near the station but the sites were eventually developed in the 1980s. Riddlesdown High School is a voluntary-aided mixed comprehensive and has been accredited as a specialist science college since 2004. Few pupils come from homes experiencing economic hardship, and nearly 80 per cent are from white British backgrounds.

✉ Purley CR8

🚆 Southern (zone 6)

@ www.riddlesdownresidents.org.uk

Rippleside · *Barking & Dagenham*
A commercial locality in south-east BARKING, north of the marshland of Ripple Level. In Old English a 'ripple' was a strip of land and Ripple Street was in existence here by the 16th century, later becoming Ripple Side before taking its modern form, Ripple Road. A newly created local burial board laid out Rippleside Cemetery in 1894. Across the dual carriageway from CASTLE GREEN, the area is dominated by commercial estates and the rail sidings and depots of Ripple Lane Freightliner terminal, but plans have been abandoned for Rippleside to have a station on the new line to the Channel Tunnel. South of the railway lie the new residential developments of BARKING REACH and an 'urban common' called the Ripple. A range of habitats has developed on this former industrial site now run by the London Wildlife Trust, with orchids, grass snakes and harvest mice.

✉ Barking IG11; Dagenham RM9

@ www.wildlondon.org.uk (London Wildlife Trust site)

Rise Park · *Havering*
The south-eastern part of COLLIER ROW. Much of the farmland here was acquired during World War I by Tommy England, a local trader and property speculator. Housebuilding started in the 1920s and accelerated in the 1930s. England donated the land for the 23-acre public park, which opened in 1937. In the same year the Rise Park estate went on the market, through local agents Hilbery Chaplin. Their literature proclaimed that with its rural atmosphere and various different types of houses

this was 'undoubtedly one of the most attractive estates in Romford … For the housewife who requires less work and does not wish to climb stairs there are bungalows, detached or semi-detached.' Prices started at £610 freehold. The area suffered bombing during the Blitz and saw further building after World War II. The very popular Rise Park Junior School was built in 1957. A 1999 report by the educational standards agency Ofsted revealed that there were no pupils with English as an additional language and under two per cent from ethnic minority backgrounds, extremely low figures compared with London as a whole.

✉ Romford RM1

Roe Green · *Brent*
A 'garden village' and its neighbourhood in north KINGSBURY, south-west of COLINDALE. Earlier called Row Green, its name derives from the Middle English 'wro', meaning 'a nook or corner; a retired or sheltered spot'. Derived from the Old Norse 'wrá', this represents a rare appearance in the London area of a word brought by the Vikings. A large house stood here from as early as the 14th century and was joined by another around 1730. A hamlet of moderate size grew up around the green over the course of the 18th and 19th centuries. In 1835 the four Sidebottom brothers of Roe Green were drowned while bathing in the Welsh Harp reservoir. Kingsbury Manor, now in Roe Green Park, was built in 1899 for the Duchess of Sutherland. During World War I a housing estate was begun at Roe Green for aircraft workers at the HYDE. Built on garden suburb principles, the estate contained 250 homes, an inn, six shops and a doctor's house. It was designed by Sir Francis Baines, who had earlier created the WELL HALL estate for the workers of WOOLWICH ARSENAL. Prisoners of war assisted in the construction work. The surrounding area was built up during the late 1920s and the early 1930s. Later in the decade the council bought land for the creation of the 42-acre Roe Green Park, which has a well-maintained walled garden. The village was made a conservation area in 1968 and, unlike Kingsbury Green, retains a genuinely villagey aspect. At Roe Green Junior School, on Princes Avenue, the largest ethnic group is of Indian heritage.

In 1928 John Logie Baird received the first television pictures from the continent in a laboratory he had set up in the coach house of Kingsbury Manor.

✉ NW9

Roehampton • *Wandsworth*

'The last village in London', according to its historian, now augmented by assorted institutions and a pioneering council estate, lying on the western side of PUTNEY. The settlement gained an identity in the 14th century, at first as East Hampton and then Rokehampton. The 'roke' element may have referred to the presence of rooks, rocks or oaks. By 1498 the village had an inn and 20 houses, but the first dwelling of significance was Roehampton House, which was rebuilt from a hunting lodge around 1630. For the third quarter of the 17th century this was the home of Christiana, Countess of Devonshire. Among her guests here were the political philosopher Thomas Hobbes and most of the leading figures of the Restoration court. In 1777 the house was demolished and replaced by Roehampton Grove, eliminating confusion with another Roehampton House that later became part of Queen Mary's Hospital. Medfield Street and Roehampton High Street constituted the nucleus of the village in the 18th century, while handsome villas peppered the surrounding hills and vales, occupied by a succession of eminent figures. By the late 19th century, high-class suburban homes were increasingly in evidence and the aristocracy began to move away. Institutions and colleges took over some of the mansions but most were demolished during the 20th century. Private and council estates filled their former grounds, notably the Alton estate, built in the 1950s. Roehampton Priory claims to be London's oldest private psychiatric hospital and has treated many celebrities for problems such as exhaustion, depression and alcoholism. The former Roehampton Institute is now Roehampton University. Seven per cent of Roehampton's residents live in communal establishments – an exceptionally high proportion.

The 19th-century prime minister Benjamin Disraeli, also a writer, created an Earl and Countess of Roehampton in his autobiographical novel *Endymion*. The poet Gerard Manley Hopkins studied at the Jesuit seminary at Manresa House. In sharp contrast, the risqué writer Frank Harris twice lived in Roehampton with his extremely young wife-to-be, Nellie O'Hara; Harris said that Roehampton and the French Riviera were his favourite places in the world.

✉ SW15

♀ 13,011

📖 Jacqueline Loose, *Roehampton: 'The Last Village in London'*, London Borough of Wandsworth Libraries and Arts, 1979

@ www.roehampton.ac.uk (Roehampton University site)

Roman Road • *Tower Hamlets*

An EAST END market street running between north BOW and east BETHNAL GREEN. Evidence of Roman transit has been discovered here but the road is thought unlikely to have been in significant use at that time. It was called Green Street from about 1790 and a section was earlier known as Driftway. The development of GLOBE TOWN from the late 18th century brought commerce to the road and a market began to operate here in 1843. The invention of the road's present name seems to have been a kind of mid-19th-century marketing ploy, inspired by the discovery of Roman remains at OLD FORD. Roman Road assumed greater importance after the opening of VICTORIA PARK and it was widened in the mid 1870s. The surrounding area was widely rebuilt in the mid 20th century and in 1959 the council provided an off-road market area as part of one of its flat-building schemes. As is often the case in such situations, traders proved reluctant to leave the street, which remained crowded with barrows and stalls. The street market nowadays operates at the eastern end of the road on Tuesdays, Thursdays and Saturdays, when its cheap fashion stalls are especially busy. The neighbouring premises keep conventional hours and most serve the local community but a few are of the 'traditional East End' variety while others specialize in aspects of interior design. Tower Hamlets council opened its first 'idea store' multi-purpose community facility on Gladstone Place in 2002. Although the vicinity has a variety of ethnic minorities, the proportion is relatively low in comparison with many other parts of the borough.

In 1994 Rachel Whiteread's award-winning *House*, a concrete sculpture cast from the interior of a demolished home on Grove Road, was itself demolished at the philistine insistence of Bow neighbourhood council.

✉ E2; E3

Romford • *Havering*

The 'capital' of Havering since the Middle Ages, situated five miles east of ILFORD. The name was first recorded in the mid 12th century and probably referred to a broad (or 'roomy') ford across the Beam River, which was later called the River Rom locally. The settlement initially evolved to the south-west of the modern centre, around a chapel dedicated to St Andrew that was in existence by 1177. Henry III granted Romford the right to hold a market in 1247 and added permission for a Whitsun fair three years later. The focus of the village shifted to the new marketplace, whereupon it is said that the chapel was swallowed up by an earthquake although its bells could still be heard on St Andrew's Day. By the 15th century the market was well-known for the sale of leather goods made in nearby HORNCHURCH, and by the 17th century it had become a very large agricultural market, selling farm tools, livestock, fruit and vegetables. As a coaching halt on the London to Colchester road the town gained a plethora of inns and hotels. In 1799 Edward Ind bought a small brewery and later joined forces with Octavius and George Coope to form a partnership that became one of the largest brewers in the country. The town was still small and its environs almost entirely agricultural when the Eastern Counties Railway arrived in 1839, boosting both the market and the brewing industry. Landowners began to sell off their estates for suburban development in a protracted process that began with a now-vanished New Romford and Laurie Town and continued well into the 20th century with schemes such as MARSHALLS PARK. Romford gained its role as a strategic shopping centre as early as the 1920s, profiting from a popular combination of new branches of national retailers and long-established local firms centred on the so-called 'Golden Mile' of South Street and North Street. Here and in the High Street, cottages and slum terraced houses were demolished to make way for wider thoroughfares and modern commercial premises. At the same time, light industrial premises appeared on the outskirts, especially along the Eastern Avenue (A12), north of which a new township mushroomed around COLLIER ROW. While the residential district expanded in every direction, enlightened councillors and developers ensured that a string of green spaces garlanded the growing borough, a status it attained in 1937. The town centre was redeveloped after the construction of the ring road in the late 1960s. The former Ind Coope brewery lay unoccupied for over a decade before its recent reconstruction as apartments, with additional houses and a retail and leisure development. In the Romford Town ward, 7.2 per cent of the residents are non-white, a high proportion by Havering's standards.

The old Essex proverb 'go to Romford to be new-bottomed' referred to the market's reputation for well-made leather breeches. In the late 1660s the colourful adventurer 'Captain' Thomas Blood lived at an apothecary's shop in Romford under an assumed name. In 1671 he almost succeeded in stealing the crown jewels. The snooker player Steve Davis has been nicknamed 'Romford Slim' or, less kindly, 'the Romford Robot'.

> ✉ Romford RM1 and RM7
>
> 🏃 13,200 (Romford Town ward)
>
> 🚃 'one' Railway (zone 6)
>
> 📖 Brian Evans, *Remembering Romford*, Sutton, 2005
>
> @ www.romford.org (privately operated local history site)

Rosehill · *Sutton*

The southern tip of ST HELIER, although its early developers marketed it as part of CARSHALTON. There is much confusion over whether to spell the name as one or two words; this gazetteer uses 'Rosehill' for the locality and 'Rose Hill' for the road that connects Rosehill with Angel Hill and Sutton High Street. There is no documentary support for the assumption that this was a hill where wild roses grew; the locality simply takes its name from Rosehill Farm (later Rosehill House), which stood here from at least the mid 18th century. At that time the notoriously marshy road to London was improved with the introduction of a turnpike and a toll-house was built at Rosehill, which marked the boundary point between the bailiwicks of the Croydon and Reigate Turnpike Trust and the Surrey and Sussex Trust. Around 1866, after the abolition of the turnpike, the toll-house was taken down and moved to WRYTHE Green, where it was rebuilt, enlarged and named Woodcote House. Following the London County Council's creation of the St Helier estate and the opening of the station at Sutton Common in 1930, developers turned their attention to this area, building semi-detached houses and the apartment block and shops of Rosehill Court, with an adjoining Gaumont cinema that provided the main leisure amenity for St Helier. A hundred acres of former farmland became Rosehill Park, which is split into east and west parts by Rose Hill. The Gaumont became a Mecca bingo hall in 1961 and is a listed building. The Rose public house has been replaced by a supermarket. Bellway Homes' new complex at Rose Hill Triangle has 175 apartments, with retail units and affordable housing at the apex. Rosehill Park has a synthetic, floodlit football/hockey pitch and the recently expanded Sutton junior tennis centre, which is claimed to be one of the best equipped in the country with 22 indoor, outdoor and clay courts.

The comedy scriptwriter Ray Galton was living in Rosehill when he co-created East Cheam as Tony Hancock's address in the classic radio (and later television) series *Hancock's Half Hour.*

⊠ Sutton SM1

@ www.geocities.com/raycrawley/ gaumont.html (personal site with memories of Rosehill)

Rotherhithe • *Southwark*

A broad Thames peninsula formerly dominated by its docks, situated between BERMONDSEY and DEPTFORD. Rotherhithe, known as Redriffe to Samuel Pepys, is variously translated as 'mariner's haven' or 'landing place for cattle'. Both explanations point to its role as a river landing, the importance of which increased as London gradually expanded eastwards. Bermondsey Abbey exerted a strong influence, with the monks helping to build and maintain the area's defences against flooding. Rotherhithe's moated manor house was originally owned by the Clare family but passed into Edward III's ownership in the mid 14th century. Henry IV visited in 1412 for a rest cure for leprosy. The site of the house lies opposite one of Rotherhithe's two most famous pubs, the Angel, from where Judge Jeffreys reputedly watched executions on the far bank at WAPPING. The other, the Mayflower, dates from the 16th century but acquired its name when the Pilgrim Fathers' ship stopped there in 1620 before setting off for the New World. The ship's captain, Christopher Jones, is buried in St Mary's Church, which may have Saxon origins. Pepys' service with the Navy Board brought him regularly to Rotherhithe, where a typical diary entry from February 1665 shows he 'did drink some strong waters and eat some bread and cheese'. Another attraction of the Stuart era was Rotherhithe's Cherry Gardens, recalled by today's Cherry Garden Pier. Rotherhithe both built and broke up ships, notably the Trafalgar veteran *Temeraire*, immortalized by Turner on its last voyage. Rotherhithe built some of the first steamships and the first iron ship, the *Aaron Manby.* The growth of the Surrey Docks

(now SURREY QUAYS) brought seamen from all over the world, a fact vividly illustrated by its three Scandinavian seamen's missions. The massive GREENLAND DOCK dates from the late 17th century and was London's major whaling base until the 19th century. Marc Brunel and his son Isambard completed the first tunnel under the Thames in 1843, commemorated by a small museum near the Mayflower. Rotherhithe's population grew from just over 10,000 in 1801 to almost 38,500 in 1901. A century later it is attracting a new population of riverside dwellers in upmarket flats along Rotherhithe Street, one of London's longest roads. Seventy-five per cent of Rotherhithe's residents are white, while the largest minority is of black African origin. Forty-four per cent of homes are rented from the council and a further 25 per cent from private landlords or housing associations. Nearly six per cent of properties have been bought through a shared ownership scheme, the highest proportion in London.

The entertainer Max Bygraves was born in Rotherhithe in 1922. Michael Caine was born in the charity wing of the now demolished St Olave's Hospital in 1933, the son of a Billingsgate porter; 70 years later the actor unveiled a council plaque at the hospital's surviving gatehouse, on Ann Moss Way, off Lower Road.

⊠ SE16

♁ 11,395

🚇 East London Line (zone 2)

📖 Stephen Humphrey, *The Story of Rotherhithe,* London Borough of Southwark, 1997

@ www.brunelenginehouse.org.uk

Roundshaw • *Sutton*

The Roundshaw estate was built in the late 1960s on land that was part of CROYDON Airport until it closed in 1959. It was named after Roundshaw Park, which now acts as a kind of village green and in turn took its name from a round grove of trees. The estate's street and building names commemorate aviation companies, aircraft and individual pioneers. Roundshaw's first tenants came from within the borough but the Greater London Council later took responsibility for part of the estate, rehousing East Enders here. Although unpopular with its neighbours, Roundshaw was at first perceived as a 'luxury estate', with spacious accommodation and centrally supplied heating and hot water. Rents were relatively high. But within a decade deficiencies in construction quality had become increasingly obvious, and antisocial behaviour led to (exaggerated) talk of a 'no go zone' in the 1980s. The Apeldoorn estate to the south was built privately on council land in the 1980s but the house prices put property there out of the reach of most Roundshaw tenants. The council eventually addressed the root problems of the original estate with a comprehensive re-generation programme involving private builders and social housing groups. Over 1,000 high-rise pre-cast concrete units have been demolished and replaced with a similar number of low-rise houses and flats built in traditional street patterns, allowing all the current residents to remain on the estate if they wish. A new community building, the Phoenix Centre, opened in 2004. The late de-cision to include Shaw Way in the project means that final completion of all work is un-likely to be achieved before 2008.

Roundshaw Downs is a local nature reserve covering about 94 acres of chalk grassland, most of which was once part of the airfield. The downs are showing increasing biodiver-sity in both flora and fauna, especially birdlife. In summer, tracks are cut in the grass to aid access.

✉ Wallington SM6

Roupell Park • *Lambeth*

First a showy private estate and then a council estate of high-rise flats, situated east of STREATHAM HILL on the BRIXTON/STREAT-HAM border. Between 1810 and 1819, metal dealer John Roupell and his son Richard Palmer Roupell spent £10,000 buying up parts of Lord Thurlow's extensive estate. Richard Roupell and the eldest of his four illegitimate children, William, began to plan a prestigious development from the late 1830s, centred on Christchurch Road and Palace Road. When Richard Roupell died in 1856, William des-troyed his father's will and forged a new one in order to gain control of his property here and in Southwark. In the following year Wil-liam Roupell was elected MP for Lambeth after a notoriously corrupt campaign. By the 1860s, Roupell Park had been mostly comple-ted, though spasmodic progress continued in an easterly direction. Very little of the original housing has survived. William Roupell en-joyed a lavish lifestyle and had spent almost all the family's wealth and lost most of its land by 1862. Fearing the exposure of his forgery, he fled to Spain, but soon returned voluntarily

to face trial. He was given a life sentence and spent the next 14 years in prison, after which he returned to the family home at Aspen House. The house became an open-air school for delicate children in the 1920s. The area to the west of Roupell Park was a virtual slum in the first half of the 20th century, with narrow roads crowded with rundown cottages, old farm buildings and light industrial units. The Blitz and a flying bomb inflicted destruction in World War II. After hostilities ended, Wandsworth council (which was responsible for the locality at that time) cleared the whole site and built the Roupell Park estate. The council also began to reclaim part of the wasteland of Rush Common for use as a public open space. The Greater London Council added the Palace Road estate in the 1970s.

✉ SW2

📖 Judy Harris, *Streatham Heritage Trail: Roupell Park and Leigham Court*, Streatham Society, 2002; Judy Harris, *The Roupells of Lambeth*, Streatham Society, 2001

Rowley Green • *Barnet*

A farming hamlet in north-west ARKLEY, right on the border with the Hertfordshire borough of Hertsmere. The first element of its name dates from the late 13th century, when it meant a 'rough woodland clearing'; the later second element indicated the presence of a village green, now lost to trees and shrubs since cattle grazing stopped after World War II. Adjacent to Arkley golf course (in fact almost enveloped by it), the twelve-acre Rowley Green Common is a remnant of the meadowland with two large ponds and a bog formed from old gravel diggings, surrounded by mature oaks and bir-ches. The common was made a local nature re-serve in 1991 and thus accorded statutory protection. It is jointly managed by the Lon-don Wildlife Trust and the Hertfordshire and Middlesex Wildlife Trust.

✉ Barnet EN5

Roxeth • *Harrow*

Still a separate locality, situated north-east of SOUTH HARROW, but the strength of its iden-tity has been sapped by developers' and railway companies' preferences for the Harrow name. Happily, the council has recently resurrected the ward of Roxeth. First recorded in 845, the name may mean 'rooks' place' or may be related to a farmer called Hrōc. A family called Rox-eth owned the freehold here in the 12th and 13th centuries, but they took their name from their landholding, which had become a manor by 1514. A moated manor house called Roxeth Place stood opposite the present junction of Roxeth Hill and Northolt Road. Further north, the weatherboarded Roxeth farmhouse was built on Bessborough Road around 1700, and survives today. In the 1840s Roxeth became one of the first parts of the borough to experience some suburban development, although this was almost entirely on the HARROW ON THE HILL side. The village had around 150 houses by the end of that decade, of which ten were farmhouses. In 1855 a gasworks was built on Roxeth Marsh, which pushed the area downmarket for a while. Two schools and Christ Church were built, and shops and pubs clustered along Middle Row (now Road). When the Metropolitan District Railway station opened in 1903 it was with the convoluted designation 'South Harrow for Roxeth and NORTHOLT'. The railway line crossed Roxeth Marsh on a viaduct. Until this time, parts of Roxeth had remained resolutely rural but farmers soon sold up and the once-extensive common land was progressively eroded. Harrow council built some houses in the 1920s and private developers filled the rest of the area by the outbreak of World War II. The council added system-built flats in the 1960s. Just over half of Roxeth's residents are white; the largest minority is of Indian descent, and mainly Hindu. Three-quarters of homes here are owner-occupied.

R M Ballantyne, the Scottish writer of children's adventure books, lived for eight years in Mount Park Road until his death in 1894.

✉ Harrow HA1 and HA2

👤 10,538

🚇 Piccadilly Line (South Harrow, zone 5)

📖 T L Bartlett, *The Story of Roxeth*, Harrow Libraries, 1992

Royal Albert • *Newham*

A Docklands Light Railway station for the Royal Albert Dock, which lies to the south. The dock was constructed from 1875 in response to the ever-increasing size of ships, which had become too big even for the neighbouring Victoria Dock. It was opened in 1880 by the Duke of Connaught on behalf of Queen Victoria. The quayside was lined with single-storey transit sheds rather than old-style warehouses and this was the first dock in London to be lit by electricity. As trade evolved, the dock began to specialize in chilled meats, bananas and tobacco. The Lower Gallions entrance was constructed in 1886 to compete

with the threat posed by new docks being built by the East and West India Docks Co. at Tilbury. The Royal Albert Dock Seamen's Hospital was established in 1890 as a branch of the Dreadnought Seamen's Hospital, GREENWICH. The London School of Tropical Medicine was founded at the hospital in 1899 and remained there until its relocation to Bloomsbury in 1920. The Royal Albert Dock was damaged in World War II and did not fully reopen until 1956. With its closure in the early 1980s, almost all the buildings were demolished. LONDON CITY AIRPORT was laid out on the south quay, office blocks replaced the former cold stores at the north-west corner and University of East London premises have been built at CYPRUS. The dock itself is now used for rowing and regattas. To the east, the Albert Basin is presently the focus of a regeneration scheme that ultimately aims to provide up to 3,000 homes and live/work units, together with commercial and light industrial units that will create a similar number of jobs.

✉ E16

🚇 Docklands Light Railway, Beckton branch (zone 3)

Royal Arsenal *see* WOOLWICH ARSENAL

Royal Botanic Gardens *see* KEW GARDENS

Royal Docks • *Newham*

The collective name for the ROYAL VICTORIA, ROYAL ALBERT and KING GEORGE V docks, located between BECKTON and CANNING TOWN and the riverside districts of SILVERTOWN and NORTH WOOLWICH. The three docks opened in 1855, 1880 and 1921 respectively, each designed to handle the ever-increasing size of ocean-going vessels. The docks progressively adapted to changes in the nature of trade, with lineal quays replacing jetties and transit sheds replacing warehouses. An improvement plan of 1929 resulted in better approach roads and the clearance of slums in Silvertown; 3,600 residents were displaced, most of whom were found new homes in WEST HAM. The Royal Docks suffered devastating bomb damage in World War II. They were subsequently repaired and reopened but soon began to decline as a result of the increasing use of containers and the consequent rise of the docks downstream at Tilbury in Essex. The Royal Docks were closed in the early 1980s and are now used for sailing and rowing, while their quays have been redeveloped primarily for commercial purposes, the largest of which is the new Royals business park. LONDON CITY AIRPORT was laid out between the Royal Albert and King George V docks. Plans to create a highly imaginative £2 billion 'water city of the 21st century' around the docks were shelved after the recession of the early 1990s. The recently created ward of Royal Docks is at present the borough's smallest by far, but this will change within a few decades as more housing is constructed as part of the THAMES GATEWAY plan.

✉ E16

👥 6,186

📖 Stephen Pewsey, *Stratford, West Ham and the Royal Docks*, Sutton, 1999

Royal Oak • *Westminster*

An 'improving area' (according to estate agents) situated on the eastern side of WESTBOURNE GREEN. The Royal Oak public house stood here from at least the 18th century. In the late 1830s the Great Western Railway line split the Paddington district into northern and southern halves, reinforcing an existing distinction between the wealth of BAYSWATER to the south and the relative deprivation of the canalside streets to the north. The land here was owned at that time by one William Penney, who made a high compensation claim for his loss. A little-served halt at Royal Oak brought some more industry and poor housing to the vicinity. There were pleasure gardens at the Royal Oak in the 1840s and most of the neighbouring area was built up around this time, with very few gaps remaining by 1855. The Hammersmith & City Railway came through here in 1864 and its Royal Oak station was built on the site of William Penney's house seven years later, whereupon Great Western Railway services were withdrawn. In the 1930s the construction of the hall, library and baths at what is now Porchester Leisure Centre raised the tone of the area and provided what is still a much-appreciated amenity. The elevated section of the WESTWAY (A40) compounded the north–south division in the mid 1960s. The rebuilt Royal Oak public house stands at 88 Bishop's Bridge Road, on the corner of Porchester Road. Modernized in recent years, it no longer has quite the rough reputation it once had. To the north of the railway line, much of the area between Royal Oak and Paddington stations has been filled by the PADDINGTON WATERSIDE development.

✉ W2

🚇 Hammersmith & City Line (zone 2)

The Royals *see* ROYAL DOCKS

Royal Victoria • *Newham*

A Docklands Light Railway station in southeast CANNING TOWN, named after the Royal Victoria Dock, which lies to its south. The dock was promoted by railway contractors and constructed on a flood plain that was purchased for little more than its agricultural value. Opened in 1855, the Victoria Dock could take the largest steamships and had the latest hydraulic engines to open its gates. It was taken over in 1864 by the London and St Katherine's Dock Co., which needed larger facilities and it became the Royal Victoria Dock when the company added the Royal Albert Dock in 1880. The accompanying rail sidings of the Royal Victoria Exchange were the largest of their kind in the country. The dock handled frozen meats, fruit, butter and tobacco, as well as general goods. Ships were initially unloaded at jetties but a system of 'simple lineal quayage' later proved more suitable for the increasingly large vessels. The dock continued to adapt to changing circumstances and in the 1930s and early 1940s grain silos were erected at PONTOON DOCK and a new north quay was built. At the same time, the western entrance was closed, allowing the construction of SILVERTOWN Way. Very long transit sheds were rented by shipping lines specializing in trade with specific countries, such as Argentina, Canada, the USA, Australia and New Zealand. The Royal Victoria Dock closed in the early 1980s and most of its buildings were soon demolished. Surviving warehouses have been converted to flats. The ExCeL exhibition and conference centre dominates much of the north quay, while chain hotels have been built to its east. A high-level pedestrian bridge was constructed across the dock in 1999 to provide access to the DLR stations for residents of the new housing developments of WEST SILVERTOWN.

✉ E16

🚇 Docklands Light Railway, Beckton branch (zone 3)

Ruislip • *Hillingdon* (pronounced 'ricelip')

An archetypal interwar Middlesex suburb, strung along the outer edge of built-up London north of RAF NORTHOLT aerodrome. The first element of its name refers to the rushes that grew on the marshy banks of the River Pinn; the second element may be a corruption from 'slæp', a wet slippery place, or 'hylpe', a leap. At the time of Domesday Book, when Ruislip's name was first recorded, the land here was mostly woodland, of which 600 acres survive, in Park Wood, Copse Wood and Mad Bess Wood. The medieval manor of Ruislip covered all of what became Ruislip (originally Westcote), NORTHWOOD and EASTCOTE. From the 15th century the manor was in the hands of King's College, Cambridge. The college leased the land for farming until the arrival of the railway brought the prospect of development at the start of the 20th century. For a while Ruislip flourished as a resort for day-trippers, with tea gardens and assorted diversions. King's College sold the first portion of its land for building in 1905, around what is now Kingsend. This was followed by a plan to create an estate of over 7,500 homes, filling much of central and north Ruislip and socially graded from luxury properties in the north to less expensive houses in the south. In contrast to the garden suburbs that characterized other parts of outer London, there was little provision for the retention of existing natural features. Nevertheless, the low-density housing, spacious gardens and landscaped streets made Ruislip an appealing prospect for city dwellers who hankered after a life in the country. Other developers extended the new suburb with estates of varying quality in the 1920s and 1930s and Ruislip–Northwood urban district council built some municipal dwellings before and after World War II. SOUTH RUISLIP attracted some industrial development. During the 1960s a handful of office blocks were built in the vicinity of the area's stations, notably at Ruislip itself. In common with many suburban districts, the shopping parades have seen several retail outlets replaced by fast-food takeaways. Ruislip also has a number of sit-down restaurants, mostly Indian and Chinese.

In 1961 the bungalow at 45 Cranley Drive was discovered to have been the communications centre of the 'naval secrets' spy ring, which passed information from Portland research station to the Russians. The tenants, Helen and Peter Kroger, were jailed, and later exchanged in a spy swap. Middle-class life in London's country suburbs was colourfully satirized by Leslie Thomas in his 1974 novel *Tropic of Ruislip* (subsequently unsuccessfully televised as *Tropic*). The model Jordan bought a bungalow in Courtfield Gardens in 2000, but stayed there for only a year.

✉ Ruislip HA4

▲ 43,338 (Eastcote and East Ruislip, Manor, South Ruislip and West Ruislip wards)

🚇 Metropolitan Line; Piccadilly Line service in peak hours (zone 6)

📖 Eileen M Bowlt, *Ruislip Past*, Historical Publications, 1994

@ www.ruislip.co.uk (community site)

Ruislip Common · Hillingdon

An amenity area at the northern end of the district, bordered on most sides by Ruislip Woods. Evidence of late Bronze Age occupation has been found here. Poor's Field was first recorded as common wasteland in 1295. Ruislip Common once had a hamlet called Park Hearne, with a number of half-timbered cottages that were lost when the valley was flooded by the Regent's Canal Co. to create Ruislip Reservoir in 1811. The reservoir was designed as a feeder for the Grand Junction Canal, but was never particularly successful at performing this task. The canal company developed the reservoir as a lido in the mid 1930s and Ruislip–Northwood urban district council took it over in 1951. The main lido building was demolished in 1994, after a fire the previous year. With its woodland setting, sandy beach, pub and miniature railway, Ruislip Lido justifiably attracts thousands of local people each summer. Early plans for the development of the Ruislip Manor estate proposed the building of houses almost up to the water's edge, but negotiations with King's College, Cambridge, the landowner, saved most of Park Wood for the public in 1932. Four years later, Copse Wood and Mad Bess Wood were also acquired. Ruislip's first council houses were built shortly afterwards on Reservoir Road. In 1997 English Nature designated Ruislip Woods a national nature reserve, the first in a metropolitan district. Breakspear Crematorium, on the west side of the common, is the second largest in London and is run jointly by the boroughs of Harrow and Hillingdon. The Breakspear name is common hereabouts and this has given rise to unconfirmed speculation that Nicholas Breakspear, the only English pope, once lived nearby.

The *Titanic* sank at Ruislip Lido in the 1958 film *A Night to Remember*, and scenes for the 1961 musical *The Young Ones*, starring Cliff Richard, were filmed on the beach, with local teenagers appearing as extras.

✉ Ruislip HA4; Northwood HA6

@ www.ruisliplidorailway.org (Ruislip Lido Railway site)

Ruislip Gardens • *Hillingdon*

The smallest of Ruislip's localities, separated from RAF NORTHOLT aerodrome by the YEADING Brook. The manorial landowner, King's College, Cambridge, created New Pond Farm on West End Road in 1872, and built a farmhouse of the same name. The fields were spared in the original development plan for RUISLIP, but succumbed after the opening of the station on the Great Western Railway's Birmingham line in 1934, when the Ruislip Gardens estate was laid out, accompanied by the Bell public house and the shops of New Pond Parade. The estate was known to residents as 'the Gardens'. Ruislip Gardens School opened in 1939. It was closed after the outbreak of war because of its proximity to RAF Northolt but reopened in 1941. The Central Line was extended to WEST RUISLIP in 1948, on tracks parallel with the main line, and a new station was built at Ruislip Gardens. Main-line services continued to run for another ten years. Around 10 per cent of pupils at Ruislip Gardens Primary School come from homes where English is not the first language. Parents based at RAF Northolt often send their children here, which results in a relatively high pupil turnover. South of the station, new flats have just been built on a former Ministry of Defence site in Carmichael Close, including affordable homes for key workers.

John Betjeman's 1954 poem *Middlesex* opens thus: 'Gaily into Ruislip Gardens / Runs the red electric train, / With a thousand Ta's and Pardon's / Daintily alights Elaine.'

⊠ Ruislip HA4

🚇 Central Line (zone 5)

Ruislip Manor • *Hillingdon*

The south-eastern part of RUISLIP, bordering EASTCOTE. A wooden rail halt opened at Ruislip Manor in 1912, when this area was still open countryside. The station was completely rebuilt in its present form in 1938, to a design by Charles Holden. Virtually all of Ruislip Manor was laid out as a single private housing estate by George Ball from 1933 to 1939, and called Manor Homes. The estate should not be confused with the original plan for the development of central Ruislip (initially called Ruislip Manor) or with the Ruislip Manor cottage estate north of the railway line. Ball acquired the land from King's College, Cambridge, which had previously entertained

the notion of creating here a garden suburb similar to the one at Hampstead. The 2,238 houses were all built to one of two basic types, mostly in terraces of four or six, although a few were semi-detached. They were priced within the reach of working people, starting at £450, and many were sold to men from the north who had come to London to find work during the Great Depression. Other buyers came from industrialized parts of west London, such as ACTON, in search of an affordable rural residence. Nowadays, most adults in Ruislip Manor have some educational qualifications, but not a degree. Ninety per cent of the residents are white, and almost as many are homeowners.

The music hall stars Elsie and Doris Waters opened Ruislip's first British Restaurant on Victoria Road in 1941. British Restaurants were wartime canteens, intended to feed the masses economically.

⊠ Ruislip HA4

👥 10,902 (Manor ward)

🚇 Metropolitan Line; Piccadilly Line service at peak hours (zone 6)

@ www.ruislip.co.uk/manorhomes (Manor Homes page on community site)

Rushey Green • *Lewisham*

Part of downtown CATFORD, an electoral ward and a section of the A21. The name, which is self-explanatory, took various forms, including Rushet Green and Rush Green, before becoming fixed in its present form in the 17th century. The hamlet had a medieval moated house, probably the precursor of the grand Rushey Green Place, which became the property of the 'beautiful and imperious' Mary Fitz of Lewisham, of whom it is said that she 'outwitted and outlived four husbands'. The common land at Rushey Green was enclosed in 1810, but the south-western corner was allocated to the parish in compensation. Cottages and shops soon began to appear, all of which have since been replaced at least once. Priory Farm, which stood from the late 17th century, was demolished in 1877. Ringstead Road and the western end of Brownhill Road now occupy its site. Today, Catford has a significant shopping centre at Rushey Green, including the Catford Island retail and leisure park. Lewisham Town Hall stands at the corner of Catford Road and Rushey Green. The 850-seat Broadway Theatre is a 1930s structure, refurbished in 2002. A little over half of Rushey Green's residents are white, and nearly a third are black or black British.

✉ SE6

👥 13,215

Rush Green • *Barking & Dagenham/Havering*

A predominantly white working-class neighbourhood, situated south-west of ROMFORD. The hamlet, with its green where the rushes grew, was first recorded in 1651 and retained a concentration of small farms until the late 19th century. In 1871 the Romford Burial Board opened a cemetery on Crow Lane to replace the former parochial graveyard. The first residential development was the Birkbeck estate of 1885, consisting of West Road, Wolseley Road, Grosvenor Road and Birkbeck Road. Rush Green Hospital opened in 1900 as an isolation unit for Romford, DAGENHAM and HORNCHURCH and was enlarged to become a general hospital after the creation of the BECONTREE estate. Romford council built some of its earliest houses in Rush Green in the 1920s. A mission hall was provided at Rush Green in 1946 and the brown-brick St Augustine's Church was built on Birkbeck Road in 1958, later gaining its own parish made up of corners of Romford, Dagenham and Hornchurch. That the Church of England set up these institutions so recently is an indication of how slowly the hamlet evolved into a suburb. Rush Green College was established in 1961 and has since expanded to become the vocationally oriented Barking College. The area has seen significant housing association building in the past ten years, and there has been a small increase in the size of its ethnic minority population. Rush Green Hospital closed in 1995 and its site has now been covered by houses arranged in a series of cul-de-sacs with flowery names. Despite the open spaces that flank it on most sides, Rush Green feels like an untidy part of east London's peripheral sprawl; its unfocused form may in part be due to its position on the border of two boroughs.

The entertainer Max Bygraves lived on Thornton's Farm Avenue after World War II and performed in local pubs.

✉ Romford RM7

@ www.barking-coll.ac.uk (Barking College site)

Russell Hill • *Croydon*

An educational locality in north-west PURLEY, where the ground rises to over 360 feet above sea level. The area was referred to as Beggar's Thorn in a 10th-century charter of King Edgar and was later known as Beggar's Bush. The Warehousemen, Clerks and Drapers School was opened by the Prince of Wales (subsequently Edward VII) in 1886. The site was named Russell Hill in honour of the school's president, the former prime minister John Russell, the first Earl Russell, whose family seat lay at Kingston Russell in Dorset. The school bought the 100-acre Ballards estate in COOMBE (Croydon) in 1923 to provide additional accommodation for its growing roll. It vacated Russell Hill in 1961 to consolidate all teaching at the Ballards campus and is now the Royal Russell, an independent, fee-paying school with a separate trust funding the education of foundation students. Since 1962 the Russell Hill site has been occupied by the Margaret Roper and Thomas More schools, which are voluntary-aided Roman Catholic primary and secondary schools.

✉ Purley CR8

Russell Square • *Camden*

Central London's second largest square, located to the north-east of the British Museum in BLOOMSBURY. The Russell family, earls of Bedford from 1550, gained possession of Bloomsbury by marriage into the Southampton family in 1669. The area remained mostly open fields until the mid 18th century. The square was laid out in 1801 by Humphry Repton on land called first Southampton Fields and subsequently Long Fields. James Burton was the designer of the original buildings that surrounded the square, only a few of which now remain. Built at the turn of the 20th century, the Russell Hotel is a chateau-style terracotta extravagance, regarded as the finest work of the architect Charles Fitzroy Doll. The hotel has recently completed a somewhat overdue refurbishment. Russell Square Gardens were relaid in 2002, returning them to something like their appearance in the early 1800s by reproducing the original twisting paths and planting a new lime walk. Low branches have been removed from some older trees and the park is now better lit and once again railed and gated. Some of the changes were designed to deter gay men from using the gardens as a cruising area.

Russell Square is the main setting for the events of William Thackeray's 'novel without a hero', *Vanity Fair*. The poet T S Eliot worked for nearly 40 years for the publishers Faber & Faber at 24 Russell Square, a building now occupied by the School of Oriental and African Studies.

✉ WC1

🚌 Piccadilly Line (zone 1)

Ruxley • *Bexley/Bromley*

A predominantly rural area with some light industry beside the main roads, situated immediately east of FOOTS CRAY. The terrain rises further east to around 100 feet above sea level at Upper Ruxley, on the Kent border. This was Rochelei in Domesday Book, and the name may have indicated a place frequented by rooks. In the Middle Ages, Ruxley gave its name to the local hundred, or administrative district, of which it was the central meeting place. The small and basic parish church of St Botolph was built in the early 14th century and survives (barely) as a barn at Ruxley Manor, which is now home to a garden centre. The parish was combined with that of St James, NORTH CRAY, in 1557. The hamlet of Ruxley is said to have been abandoned at that time, possibly as a result of bubonic plague. Ruxley gravel pits were dug from 1929 to 1951 and now constitute one of London's few areas of relatively undisturbed water south of the Thames. The River Cray flows through three of the pits and a fourth is fed by springs. The surrounding swamp and fen vegetation supports a remarkable diversity of birds, butterflies, dragonflies and beetles. Access is only possible by prior arrangement with the warden. To the east of the lakes lie Ruxley Wood, Ruxley Park golf course and Bromley Ski Centre.

✉ Sidcup DA14; Orpington BR5

Saffron Hill *see* FARRINGDON and LITTLE ITALY

St George in the East • *Tower Hamlets*

This quaint parish name for the northern part of WAPPING has dropped out of use although it is still shown on some 21st-century maps. The parish was created in 1729, the year of the church's completion on Cannon Street Road. St George in the East was one of three EAST END churches designed by Nicholas Hawksmoor, the others being at SPITALFIELDS and LIMEHOUSE. There was never a recognizable settlement called St George in the East, but the parish name provided a useful identity for the formerly anonymous area north of the docks. The central thoroughfare was Cable Street, so called for its ropeyards. Two squares and a handful of streets were laid out but market gardens occupied much of the parish until the end of the 18th century. With the construction of COMMERCIAL ROAD and the coming of railways and heavy industry to the East End, St George in the East became a solidly urban and extremely poor parish over the course of the 19th century. The Prince of Denmark pub was enlarged in the 1850s to become Wilton's Music Hall, which survives today as a rare example of its kind, though in need of restoration. Jewish immigration changed the character of the area from the end of the century, creating a garment district in the north of the parish. SHADWELL station was called Shadwell and St George in the East during the early part of the 20th century. After World War I the municipal authorities began to build blocks of flats and to provide public health amenities. In the 1930s Sir Oswald Mosley's British Union of Fascists attempted to divide Christians and Jews in the East End. Mosley organized a march of 3,000 of his blackshirted followers in October 1936, which was blocked by protesters' barricades at the junction of Cable Street and LEMAN STREET, in the so-called 'battle of Cable Street'. Following devastating bomb damage in World War II, St George in the East was redeveloped as an almost entirely residential area, including high-rise flats in the 1970s. Subsequently, Docklands regeneration has impinged on the parish, without transforming it.

The Men They Couldn't Hang's rock-folk song *Ghosts of Cable Street* recalls the events of 1936. A 1982 mural painted on the side of the former St George's vestry hall depicts the 'battle' in heroic fashion. Ensign Street and Grace's Alley were used as locations for the 1994 film *Interview with the Vampire*, starring Tom Cruise and Brad Pitt.

✉ E1

🚊 East London Line; Docklands Light Railway, all branches (Shadwell, zone 2)

St George's Fields • *Westminster*

A green and gated estate identified as a locality by only one street atlas, which calls it St George's Field. It is situated to the north of BAYSWATER Road, a quarter of a mile west of MARBLE ARCH. This was a burial ground from 1763, later used for archery, games and as allotments. The land was owned by St George's Church in Hanover Square, which sold it to developers in 1967. Completed in the early 1970s, the estate has 300 apartments – studios and one- and two-bedroom flats – in five-storey balconied blocks with garage parking beneath. The blocks are set in a couple of acres of lush little gardens with some mature trees. A few tombstones remain, arranged three deep along the north wall. This is one of the capital's loveliest post-war estates – a BARBICAN or BRUNSWICK centre on a more human scale. Estate agents use the word 'oasis' for St George's Fields with some justification.

These St George's Fields should not be confused with their former namesake in SOUTHWARK, a popular gathering place and scene of the Wilkite Riots in 1768, when eleven agitators were shot by troops.

✉ W2

@ www.st-georges-fields.co.uk (estate property site)

423

St Giles • *Camden*

The area just to the south-east of TOTTEN-HAM COURT ROAD station is properly known as St Giles, but the term is rarely used, perhaps because this was once London's most notorious neighbourhood. It came into existence in the year 1101, when Henry I's wife Matilda founded a hospital for lepers here. There have been three churches of St Giles-in-the-Fields; the present one dates from 1734. Until the mid 19th century the St Giles district was a 'rookery' – a home for every kind of villain and misfit – conveniently close to the rich pickings offered by the gentry up west. Its slums provided refuge from the officers of the law, who would seldom venture into the warren in pursuit of a fleeing criminal. The turning point came in 1840, when the police defeated a gang of counterfeiters after a battle lasting several hours. Within a year the authorities were planning to force New Oxford Street through the district in a deliberate act of decontamination by demolition. The creation of SHAFTESBURY AVENUE and CHARING CROSS ROAD in the late 1870s and 1880s continued the process and by 1891 the population of the parish of St Giles in the Fields was less than half what it had been in 1821. During the course of the 20th century almost all the surviving early housing was replaced by a mix of offices, light industrial premises, shops and council flats. The much-signposted but little-known St Giles Circus is overlooked by the 385-feet Centre Point tower block, which was London's only bona fide skyscraper when it was built in 1964. Developer Harry Hyams came in for heavy criticism because he left the building empty for many years, content to benefit from the escalation in its capital value while he paid no rates. A hundred squatters occupied it in 1974. Now a Grade II-listed building, Centre Point's tenants include the Confederation of British Industry and the Vespa Lounge, a popular lesbian bar. Recently, as intensive policing has driven drug vendors and users from Charing Cross and King's Cross, parts of St Giles have once again acquired a reputation for illegal activities. To the south, Denmark Street is nicknamed Tin Pan Alley for its historic recording studios and music shops. There are big budget plans for a new office and leisure complex here.

William Hogarth's shocking drawing *Gin Lane*, published in 1751, depicts the evils wrought on St Giles by the unfettered activities of London's distillers.

✉ WC2

📖 F Peter Woodford (ed.), *Streets of St Giles*, Camden History Society, 2000

St Helier • *Merton/Sutton*

An extensive overspill estate, separated from Mitcham by the River Wandle, built between the wars by the London County Council to rehouse people from inner London slums. This had been farmland, best known for growing lavender, which was processed locally. In 1926 the LCC chose this 825-acre site for its second largest development in London after BECON-TREE. The estate was completed in 1936 and named in honour of Lady St Helier, a prominent philanthropist and council alderman who had died while the development was under construction. The other St Helier, chief town of Jersey, objected to the choice of name and vainly advocated 'Jeuneville', as Lady St Helier was known as Lady Jeune before her husband was given a peerage. In keeping with the ideals of the time, St Helier was laid out as a 'garden city', with cottage-style terraced houses, an eighth of the site devoted to open spaces and the maximum possible retention of natural features. As at Becontree, a dedicated light railway brought construction materials to the site. Too large to be a single community, St Helier was divided into sectors, each with its own amenities. In all, 9,000 homes were built to house 40,000 people, with 18 schools and seven churches. Many of the roads were given the names of religious centres, marking the former ecclesiastical ownership of lands hereabouts, notably by Merton Abbey. To help newcomers orient themselves, street names were arranged alphabetically, from Abbotsbury Road in the north-west to Winchcombe Road in the south-east. St Helier Hospital opened on the site of a former pig farm in 1938; John Major, prime minister from 1990 to 1997, was born here in 1943. Some additional houses were built in the 1950s. Most homes in St Helier are now owner-occupied and it has become a good place to buy a relatively inexpensive property.

The former CARSHALTON sports arena reopened as the Sutton Arena Leisure Centre on Middleton Road in 2003. Among its facilities the complex has a fitness centre, multipurpose sports hall, outdoor track and athletics facilities.

✉ Morden SM4

👥 19,953 (Sutton's St Helier ward, and Merton's St Helier ward)

🚆 Thameslink (zone 4)

⬚ Paul Harper, *St Helier Estate*, Merton Leisure Services, 1998

St James's • *Westminster*

Originally a swamp but subsequently one of the WEST END's most prestigious quarters, St James's lies south of PICCADILLY and west of WHITEHALL. Queen Matilda, the consort of Henry I, founded the original St James's as a hospital for 'leprous maidens' around 1117. With the progressive eradication of leprosy in Britain, the house had been turned into a convent by the mid 15th century. When Whitehall Palace burned down in 1512, Henry VIII drained and enclosed the surrounding marshland and in 1531 built another palace in place of the former hospital. The new park was used for the royal hunt and for troop mustering and manoeuvres. St James's Palace served as a military prison during the Civil War. At the Restoration, Charles II landscaped the park in the style of Versailles and divided the neighbouring bailiwick between his mistress the Duchess of Cleveland and his friend Henry Jermyn, who created St James's Square in the late 1660s. In 1685, St James's was made a separate parish (from St Martin-in-the-Fields) and Christopher Wren built St James's Church, with interior carvings by Grinling Gibbons. The church contains the grave of John Christie, the auctioneer. When Whitehall Palace burned down again in 1691, St James's Palace succeeded it as the royal seat, and the district, by now fully built up, became the royal precinct. White's opened as a coffeehouse in 1693, later developing into a gentlemen's club. Similar institutions followed, including Boodle's, Brooks's and the Athenaeum, making St James's the heart of London's clubland. In the late 1820s John Nash created the park as it exists today, as well as Carlton House Terrace. Around this time St James's also became notorious for its brothels and gambling dens. Poor construction necessitated extensive rebuilding from the mid 1850s, and the residential character of St James's shifted from the aristocratic to the merely upper middle class, while art galleries, restaurants and gentlemen's outfitters gradually replaced the less reputable establishments. Very recently St James's has become a major European centre for specialist investment houses known as 'hedge funds'. In April 2003 the St James's-based *Economist* magazine estimated that nearly 100 institutions controlled assets of around $300 billion, 'which would mean that more money is managed in St James's than in Frankfurt'.

St James's Palace remains the official residence of the sovereign, although since the accession of Queen Victoria in 1837 the monarch has lived at Buckingham Palace. Today it is the London residence of the Princess Royal and Princess Alexandra, and houses the offices of several departments of The Queen's household. Neighbouring Clarence House, formerly the home of Queen Elizabeth the Queen Mother, is the London residence of the Prince of Wales and the Duchess of Cornwall. At No. 4 St James's Square a blue plaque identifies the former home of Nancy Astor, the first woman to sit in Parliament, while No. 10 was the home of three prime ministers, including Gladstone.

✉ SW1

🚶 8,658 (the St James's ward stretches all the way to Aldwych)

🚇 Circle Line; District Line (St James's Park, zone 1)

⬚ E J Burford, *Royal St James's*, Robert Hale, 1988

St James Street • *Waltham Forest*

A local amenity zone and shopping street in west WALTHAMSTOW, forming a dog-leg bend link between BLACKHORSE ROAD and Markhouse Road. St James Street was formerly Marsh Street, but at least part took its present name soon after the building of its church in 1842. St James Street station opened on the Liverpool Street to Chingford line in 1873. Much of the surrounding area was developed by a local builder, Sir Courtenay Warner, during the 1890s. The Clock House estate took its name from the Warner family home, part of which is still standing at the corner of Mission Grove and Pretoria Avenue and has recently been restored. Warner's houses were built to a high standard with distinctive external features, including a letter 'W' on many of the properties. A replacement St James's Church was built in 1902 and demolished 60 years later and the site is now occupied by a health clinic. The council acquired some of the Clock House estate in the 1960s and has designated Leucha Road a conservation area. The St James Sure Start programme aims to tackle problems associated with child poverty and social exclusion in the neighbourhood.

St James's Park and Low Hall sports ground lie to the south-west of the station. The latter contains the Pump House steam and transport museum, a Grade II-listed Victorian enginehouse remodelled in 1897 to take a pair of

Marshall steam engines, which are still in working order.

✉ E17

🚉 'one' Railway (zone 3)

St Johns • Lewisham

The southernmost part of DEPTFORD, spilling into north-west LEWISHAM. In 1773 Stone House became the area's first significant building. It was designed by the architect George Gibson for his own use, in a floridly church-like style that prompted its nickname of 'Comical House'; the house has recently been restored. At the end of the 18th century much of the land north of Lewisham Way was owned by Jonathan Lucas, who was mostly in South Carolina running a large rice-milling business. Shipbuilding was flourishing in Deptford at that time as a result of the war with France and accommodation for workmen and their families was in short supply, so in 1795 Lucas began to build houses on what is now Albyn Road. From 1805 he laid out a series of new streets in the northern part of his estate, which was soon known as Deptford New Town. Following the second Treaty of Paris in 1815 the value of Lucas's land declined but growth resumed after the London and Greenwich Railway came to Deptford in 1836. Better-quality houses were built after 1840, although on a smaller scale than in BROCKLEY, its neighbour to the south-west. In 1855 St John's Church and vicarage were built on the site of the former Lucas family home and its garden. The suburb was almost complete by the time it gained its own station in 1873 and it remains relatively intact today. Despite high unemployment in the area, a 2001 survey put St Johns in the top 1 per cent of 'areas to buy property' because prevailing values did not fully reflect the economic and social potential of the locality. This potential has yet to be fully realized, as the very mixed condition of the housing and shops indicates. St Stephen's Church of England Primary School on Albyn Road has almost equal numbers of pupils of white, Caribbean and African ethnicity. Nearly three-quarters come from homes where English is an additional language.

Britain's third-worst rail disaster occurred at St John's in December 1957 when a rear-end collision in fog caused a bridge to collapse onto the wreckage, killing 90 people.

✉ SE8

🚉 South Eastern Trains (zone 2)

St John's Wood • Westminster

A plush 19th-century suburb with interwar augmentation, situated on the north-west side of REGENT'S PARK. The name was recorded in Latin form at the end of the 13th century, when the land came into the possession of the Order of the Hospital of St John of Jerusalem. The English name was first mentioned in 1524. Henry Samuel Eyre, a London wine merchant, purchased the estate from the Earl of Chesterfield in 1732. St John's Wood did not evolve in the same way as many other smart parts of London. Its low-lying situation, poorly served by roads, did not attract gentlemen's seats and yet the Eyre family were keen to profit from its development, unlike more protective and resistant landowners elsewhere. In 1794 they commissioned a plan that would have seen St John's Wood laid out in the same style as the spa town of Bath, but this was stymied by recession during the Napoleonic Wars. To the south of the Eyre estate, the area around St John's Wood High Street was built up as Portland Town in the early 19th century, with housing for the working classes. Thomas LORD'S cricket ground moved from Dorset Square to St John's Wood Road in 1814. The Eyre family laid roads across their estate in the 1820s and agreed building contracts with a number of small firms, who did most of their work in the 1840s. Standards were kept high and the new inhabitants were bankers, merchants and gentlemen of independent means. Most residents were wealthy enough to keep their own carriage and mews were built to accommodate the horses and staff. Later phases of building, especially towards the west, were less exclusive. St John's Wood was well-served by omnibuses from the late 1850s, with stabling for horses becoming plentiful as a consequence, and Marlborough Road station opened in 1868. Portland Town was redeveloped from the 1890s, with a mix of institutional buildings and mansion blocks, together with shopping parades on the High Street. Elsewhere, blocks of private flats replaced many of the early Victorian houses during the 1930s. A new station was built in 1939 and opened as St John's Wood, whereupon Marlborough Road station closed. After World War II the municipal authorities rebuilt so extensively in the north and west that some parts of the former Eyre estate are no longer thought of as being in St John's Wood. However, the surviving Victorian properties and the classiest of the flats and mansion blocks form a charming and prestigious enclave, which reaches its acme on Avenue Road.

The Hungarian film producer Alexander Korda lived on Avenue Road from 1933 to 1939 and the composer Benjamin Britten lived on St John's Wood High Street in the mid 1940s.

✉ NW8

🚇 Jubilee Line (zone 2)

📖 Richard Tames, *St John's Wood and Maida Vale Past*, Historical Publications, 1998

St Katherine's • *Tower Hamlets*
A revitalized part of the former London docks, located between WAPPING and the TOWER. In 1147 Queen Matilda established a church-cum-hospital, which adapted and survived here until the coming of the docks. During the Middle Ages the boggy land was frequently inundated when the Thames wall was breached, but in the early 16th century the marshes were drained by Cornelius Vanderdelft, allowing waterfront development to begin. The busy settlement that grew up here was torn apart after Parliament passed the St Katherine Docks Act in 1825. Over 11,000 people were displaced by the works, which swept away slums like Dark Entry, Cat's Hole and Pillory Lane. Construction was led by the great railway builder Thomas Telford, in his only major project in London. Some 2,500 men were employed to move rubble and soil (including the remains from the churchyard) into barges that were then taken upriver by the contractor Thomas Cubitt and used as foundation material for properties in BELGRAVIA and PIMLICO. Telford created the docks around two connected basins, giving an exceptionally long quayside for such a small area of enclosed water. Warehouses were erected on the dockside, with roadways running directly behind – another innovation, which reduced handling and pilferage. St Katherine Docks opened in October 1828 and the last of the warehouses was completed the following year. Additional warehousing was constructed in the 1850s. With its tight security, St Katherine's specialized in high-value exotic goods such as ivory, indigo powder, shells and feathers, as well as handling staples like tea and wool. The docks were wrecked by wartime bombs but limped on until their final closure in the late 1960s. In the 1970s and 1980s St Katherine's was redeveloped in a pioneering mixed-use project that created private and public housing, offices and leisure facilities. The Dickens Inn was fabricated in antique style around the innards of a relocated warehouse, and a retracting foot-bridge was added at the entrance to the centre basin in 1994. With its yachts, cobbled causeways, cafés and shops St Katherine's is a tourist attraction by day, while the bars and restaurants draw City workers at night. Like many other DOCKLANDS quarters, the neighbouring housing exhibits a great disparity in wealth between its newcomers and the more established inhabitants. The area's ranking on the 'deprivation index' is falling, but some residents remain in disadvantaged circumstances.

✉ E1

👤 11,245 (St Katherine's and Wapping ward)

🚤 St Katherine's pier

@ www.skdocks.co.uk

St Leonard's Hamlet • *Havering*
A late 20th-century estate of 250 homes between RUSH GREEN and HORNCHURCH. In 1889 the Poor Law guardians of the parish of St Leonard's, SHOREDITCH, bought Harrow Lodge Farm and built the Hornchurch Cottage Homes. The guardians' intention was to give orphans and poor children their own little community, in contrast to the institutionalized world of the workhouse. The settlement, which became known as St Leonard's, consisted of a group of cottages set around a village hall where children were taught vocational skills. Boys also had military band training and many of them subsequently entered the armed forces. In the settlement's early days as many as 500 children were here at a time but the roll ultimately dwindled to around 100. For the last two decades of its existence St Leonard's was run by Tower Hamlets council, which closed it and sold the 86-acre site and its buildings in 1984. Evidence later emerged of systematic child abuse during the period of Tower Hamlets' stewardship, which led to Operation Mapperton, a police investigation that resulted in the jailing of the former superintendent and another care worker in 2001. The estate that has replaced the cottage homes has passable townhouses on one side, and on the other, executive homes in cul-de-sacs branching off St Leonard's Way. At first the developer failed to live up to a promise to restore the main building and serious deterioration occurred. Eventually it was converted into residential units. Hornchurch Sports Centre and Harrow Lodge Park now occupy the remainder of the former farmland.

William Pett Ridge's realist novel *A Son of the State* (1899) tells the story of a Hoxton orphan who is sent to live in the cottage homes.

✉ Hornchurch RM11

St Luke's • *Islington*

A little-used name for the area surrounding the western half of OLD STREET. After its marshes were drained in the 16th century, a hospital was built for plague victims which stood until 1736. From medieval times until the slum clearance programme of the 1870s, its position on the edge of the CITY OF LONDON made St Luke's a haven for all kinds of prohibited activities, from astrology and wizardry to bear-baiting and prostitution. Thieves and pickpockets could make regular forays into the City and then lose any pursuer in the maze of courts and alleyways around Whitecross Street, which nowadays has a more respectable weekday market. The reputation of St Luke's as a 'rookery' – a zone of criminality – reached a peak in the first half of the 19th century. 'Flash houses' – drinking dens and lodging houses where criminal plans were laid and stolen goods fenced – were more numerous here than anywhere else in London. By 1900, southern St Luke's had become a district of workshops and warehouses, with new tenement blocks providing homes for law-abiding citizens. However, many of the worst elements simply decamped to the other side of Old Street and this part remained disreputable until the 1930s. St Luke's School was founded in 1698. It is a justifiably popular and oversubscribed primary school.

St Luke's Church was completed in 1733 and is attributed to Nicholas Hawksmoor and John James. The church tower is a fluted obelisk topped by a golden dragon that cockneys to this day insist is really a plague flea. Problems caused by settlement led to the church's closure in 1959, and the removal of its roof. It lay derelict until 2003, when an education centre and rehearsal hall for the London Symphony Orchestra were built in its shell. The Grade I-listed exterior has been faithfully restored and a new extension added.

✉ EC1

@ www.lso.co.uk (London Symphony Orchestra site)

St Margarets • *Richmond*

A gentrified part of north-east TWICKENHAM, separated from ISLEWORTH by the River Crane. From the 16th century this area was the northern part of Twickenham Park, with a house on the boundary of Isleworth and Twickenham parishes. The house was demol-

ished by 1805 and the estate was broken up. Around 1830 the Marquis of Ailsa built a house called St Margarets on the site of a 17th-century property that had once been home to the dramatist Richard Sheridan. The marquis died in 1846 and the St Margarets estate was put up for sale in the 1850s. Ailsa's house was demolished and replaced by one built for, but never occupied by, the second Earl of Kilmorey; in 1856 this house became home to the Royal Naval Female School. In 1867 the earl also rebuilt the neighbouring Gordon House, which also subsequently became part of the naval school. By this time, new roads had been laid out on the St Margarets estate, but little building had taken place. The station opened in 1876, well to the south of the house from which it took its name and effectively redefining the extent and focus of the St Margarets area. Despite the railway connection, growth remained sluggish and developers resorted to building terraced cottages instead of detached villas. By the end of the 19th century St Margarets was fully built up. The construction of Twickenham Bridge and the Chertsey Road (A316) in the early 1930s necessitated the demolition of some properties here but others were built further west. Kilmorey House (formerly St Margarets) was hit by a bomb in 1940, after which the Royal Naval Female School moved away and the buildings later became a teacher training college. The college went through a series of identity changes before it closed in 2005, with the remaining staff and students moving to Brunel University's Uxbridge campus. The St Margarets area was considered merely ordinary for much of the 20th century, but it has now become very popular with the professional classes. The St Margarets and North Twickenham ward has one of the highest employment levels in London. Most residents are white, university-educated homeowners.

Charles Dickens lived at Ailsa Park Villas in 1838 and is said to have written *Oliver Twist* there. The Turk's Head pub featured in the Beatles' film *A Hard Day's Night*, while the Fab Four lived in Ailsa Avenue in *Help*. The films' interiors were shot at nearby Twickenham Studios.

✉ Twickenham TW1

♟ 9,946 (St Margarets and North Twickenham ward)

🚃 South West Trains (zone 4)

📖 A C B Urwin, *Twickenham Parke: An Outline of*

the History of Twickenham Park and the St Margarets Estate, self-published, 1965

St Mary Cray • Bromley

An industrial and low-cost residential district situated to the north-east of ORPINGTON. In a confusion with neighbouring ST PAUL'S CRAY, the district is often erroneously referred to as 'St Mary's Cray', sometimes even by those who live in the vicinity. Once known as South Cray, it was first recorded in 1032 when King Canute granted land here and at Orpington to the priors of Christ Church, Canterbury. St Mary's Church was built in the early 13th century and soon gave South Cray its present name. During the Middle Ages the market at St Mary Cray was second only in importance to BROMLEY's in this part of Kent and several mills operated beside the River Cray. In his late-18th-century *History of Kent*, Edward Hasted described the place as a 'populous, handsome village'. A paper mill, later part of Wiggins Teape, operated from around 1806 and banknotes and stamps were printed here from 1860, the year in which the station opened. In the latter part of the 19th century a series of restorations to the church masked its medieval origins. On the Orpington side of the district, a small estate was laid out in the POVEREST area. The construction of the Orpington by-pass (A224) in 1926 marked the start of the area's modern industrial growth. The St Mary Cray section of the bypass, which was named Cray Avenue, obliterated Manor Farm. In 1936 the farm's former oast house became the first home of electrical manufacturer Morphy Richards. The 1950s and 1960s brought the heaviest phase of both industrial development and council housebuilding, erasing nearly all evidence of the original village, although a very few early-18th-century houses survive, together with some Victorian terraces on the High Street. Most of the industry is sited between Cray Avenue and the River Cray, with housing spreading up the slopes on either side. St Mary Cray's characterless appearance has been attributed to the austerity of the post-war period, but more recent commercial development has failed to bring any improvement. However, regeneration schemes are making beneficial changes to the housing estates. The Cray Valley East ward is 95 per cent white and a relatively high proportion of adults are divorced, separated or widowed. Levels of educational attainment are low.

The actor Leslie Grantham, best known for his appearances and disappearances in *East-*

Enders, grew up on a council estate in St Mary Cray.

✉ Orpington BR5

👤 14,663 (Cray Valley East ward)

🚆 South Eastern Trains (zone 6)

📖 John Blundell, *An Illustrated Guide to St Mary Cray and the Upper Cray Valley*, St Mary Cray Action Group, 1999; Edward Hasted, *Hasted's History of St Mary Cray*, ed. John W Brown, Local History Reprints, 1997

St Marylebone see MARYLEBONE

St Mary's • Tower Hamlets

St Mary Matfelon was built among the cornfields west of STEPNEY between 1250 and 1286 as a chapel of ease to St Dunstan's Church, and its white stone fabric gave Whitechapel its name. The chapel became a church in 1338. It was rebuilt after a great storm in 1362 and again in 1673, through the generosity of one William Meggs, who also endowed almshouses on a neighbouring site. The church was rebuilt yet again in 1880 after a disastrous fire, while the almshouses were replaced by St Mary's Tube station in 1884, later renamed St Mary's (Whitechapel Road). This closed in 1938 when ALDGATE EAST station was relocated eastwards, reducing the distance between the two. The station building was destroyed by bombing in 1940 and so was the church, which this time was not rebuilt. The neighbouring district has long been renowned for its poverty and still scores highly on indices of deprivation.

✉ E1

St Mary's Village • Hackney

Britain's first 'demand-led pepper-potted mixed tenure development', which means that residents are offered the choice of where they want to live and with what form of tenure, without being segregated into social and private housing zones. Situated off Eastway in HACKNEY WICK, the village takes its name from the nearby parish church of St Mary of Eton and replaces the run-down tower blocks of the Trowbridge estate, built in the 1960s. It is the product of co-operation between Hackney council, local residents, housing associations and private sector builders. The 220 homes range from one-bedroom apartments to four-bedroom family houses, including a variety of special needs accommodation and several live−work units. The properties have been offered for shared ownership, low-cost home ownership or market sale. Income generated from the outright sale of homes is being reinvested in the area to provide benefits such as a community centre, play area, doctor's surgery, local shop and environmental improvements.

> ✉ E9

St Pancras • *Camden*
Nowadays the identity of the district situated to the north-east of BLOOMSBURY and formerly a metropolitan borough extending as far north as HIGHGATE. The saint's name is an anglicization of the Latin St Pancratius, a 3rd-century martyr who was beheaded at the age of 14. Usage of the misnomer 'St Pancreas' is a sure sign of a newcomer to London or an overzealous spellchecker. The old church that was dedicated to St Pancras may be of 7th-century origin and was probably rebuilt in the 12th century. However, its parishioners migrated northwards to Kentish Town and the church was left isolated in the fields. St Pancras Old Church survives on Pancras Road but a neo-Grecian church of the same name was built in 1822 on the corner of present-day Euston Road and Upper Woburn Place to serve the streets that were spilling out of Bloomsbury at this time. This was never an area of the highest class and it deteriorated with the arrival of the railway termini, the first of which was EUSTON in 1837. North of the Euston Road conditions became particularly bad in the parts of SOMERS TOWN that were not taken for station buildings or goods yards. St Pancras station and the Midland Grand Hotel were built from 1865 to 1874 by Sir George Gilbert Scott for the Midland Railway Co. Scott was a builder of churches and a restorer of great cathedrals and this experience shows in his work here. The hotel's interior is, if anything, even more opulent than its façade but it was converted to office use after 1935 and renamed St Pancras Chambers. The offices too were closed in the mid 1980s when the building failed to pass fire regulations. British Rail tried in vain to gain permission to demolish the hotel building and it has long remained empty, while the platforms behind have been underused. Finally, a new use has been found for the station and from 2007 it will become the primary London terminus for Channel Tunnel rail services, and the hotel will be returned to its original purpose.

The Museum of London has a wonderful evocation of the station's cathedral-like qualities in John O'Connor's sunset view from Pentonville Road, painted in 1884. The dramatist George Bernard Shaw was a St Pancras vestryman and councillor from 1897 to 1903, during which time he worked to establish the first free ladies' public lavatory in the borough.

> ✉ WC1; NW1

> ♁ 12,490 (St Pancras and Somers Town ward)

> ⊞ Main-line: Midland Mainline (Leicester, Nottingham, Derby, Sheffield). London Underground: services shared with King's Cross (zone 1)

> ▯ Jack Simmons, *St Pancras Station*, Phillimore, 2003

> @ www.ctrl.co.uk (Channel Tunnel rail link)

St Paul's • *City*
The cathedral of the diocese of London and Britain's best-loved building, crowning Ludgate Hill. The first St Paul's Cathedral was built in 604 and rebuilt in 962 following Viking raids. In 1087 Old St Paul's was begun in grand Norman style; its completion took over 200 years. Throughout the Middle Ages and beyond, the cathedral's costs were met by tithes levied on tenants of its extensive landholdings. The ways in which the cathedral's prebendaries managed the estate, resisting or encouraging development, influenced the growth of several of modern London's suburbs. In 1512 Dean Colet established St Paul's School in the churchyard. Old St Paul's burned down in the Great Fire of 1666, after which Sir Christopher Wren was commissioned to produce a design for a new cathedral, which was completed in 1710. The cathedral is built of Portland stone and surmounted by a dome inspired by St Peter's Basilica in Rome, with an acoustically conductive Whispering Gallery that runs around its interior circumference. The capacious crypt contains more than 200 memorials. St Paul's famously survived bombing raids during the Blitz, thanks to good fortune and the valiant efforts of firefighters, and it became a symbol of London's wartime resistance. The state funeral of Sir Winston Churchill took place here in 1965. A £40 million restoration programme is on schedule for completion in time for St Paul's 300th anniversary. The cathedral is toured by nearly a million visitors every year, while many more simply jump off their sightseeing coaches, pose for a photograph and move on. The neighbouring Paternoster Square development of offices and shops was a 1960s blight

on the cathedral's beauty, but in 1993 plans were approved for a replacement project of classically designed buildings, which gained the endorsement of the Prince of Wales. The recession in the property market delayed implementation but work was completed in 2003. The following year the London Stock Exchange relocated to new headquarters at 10 Paternoster Square, and Temple Bar was re-erected near the cathedral's north-west tower. This Portland stone arch had served as a gateway to the City of London for two centuries but was removed to a Hertfordshire park when its narrowness began to cause traffic congestion at its original location at the meeting point of Fleet Street and the Strand.

Modern Freemasonry began on 24 June 1717, when four London fellowships met at the Goose and Gridiron alehouse in the churchyard of St Paul's Cathedral and founded the world's first Grand Lodge.

✉ EC4

🚇 Central Line (zone 1)

📖 D Keene et al (eds), *St Paul's: The Cathedral Church of London 604–2004,* Yale University Press, 2004; Ann Saunders, *St Paul's: The Story of the Cathedral,* Collins and Brown, 2001

@ www.stpauls.co.uk

St Paul's Cray • *Bromley*

Primarily a municipally built residential area, beginning a mile south-east of CHISLEHURST and stretching eastwards to the edge of the green belt. Evidence of a Bronze Age enclosure with timber huts has been uncovered here, together with various artefacts of the period. St Paulinus was buried at Rochester in 644 and the original village church dedicated to him may date from shortly after that time. The village was simply called Craie in Domesday Book and became Craye Paulin after the church was rebuilt around 1200. Meanwhile, South Cray became ST MARY CRAY and grew larger than its parent over the course of the Middle Ages. Gray's Farm covered much of the present residential area from the 18th century. Riverside mills made use of the valley's many trees to manufacture paper. Away from the river and the heart of the old village, most of St Paul's Cray remained in agricultural use until well into the 20th century. The London County Council began to lay out the St Paul's Cray estate immediately after World War II and the first residents moved in during 1949. Council building continued into the 1960s.

Private developers added homes on the western side of the district, including some large detached properties near St Paul's Cray Common. The stylish copper-roofed St Barnabas's Church was built in 1964 and the old church was declared redundant in 1977. St Paulinus's Church served as a day centre for the elderly for several years and has recently been converted to offices. Most of the former council houses have been bought by their occupants and many of these have since been resold, but numerous residents continue to live in deprived circumstances, especially in the south-eastern quadrant. In the Cray Valley West ward, 95 per cent of the population is white and levels of educational attainment are very low. Almost two-thirds of homes are owner-occupied and over a quarter are rented from a housing association. Light industry and retail parks cluster beside the River Cray.

✉ Orpington BR5

🚶 16,121 (Cray Valley West ward)

📖 Edward Hasted, *Hasted's History of St Paul's Cray,* ed. John W Brown, Local History Reprints, 1997

Sanderstead • *Croydon*

A long ribbon of 20th-century suburban housing, stretching more than two miles south-eastwards from its station on the edge of PURLEY to Hamsey Green, which lies just outside the Greater London border. Sondestede was recorded in an Anglo-Saxon charter of around 880, when the manor was presented to the Bishop of Winchester. The name referred to a homestead built on sandy ground. The present All Saints' Church dates from 1230, with an unusually shaped tower of 1310. The church has memorials to the Atwood family, Sanderstead's principal landowners until the late 17th century. Sanderstead Court was built in 1676 and altered and modified in the 18th century. In the 19th century the Wigsell family of Sanderstead Court owned 85 per cent of the parish: 1,839 acres. Sanderstead was an 'estate village', with tradesmen serving the Wigsells and their farms but the family forbade the building of a public house. Sanderstead station opened in 1884 but failed to stimulate growth owing to its distance from the village. From the early 20th century Sanderstead began to expand and between the world wars suburban development spread from north to south. Sanderstead Court became the SELSDON Court Hotel in 1928. The shops of Cranleigh Parade were built on the east side of Limpsfield Road between 1932 and 1938. Estates begun before World War II were completed in the 1950s, when most of the bomb-damaged Sanderstead Court was demolished. A surviving corner became the clubhouse for Selsdon Park golf club and the rest of the site was built up with two-storey terraced houses. The timber-framed White House, on Limpsfield Road, is the most impressive survivor from the old village. Sanderstead at last gained a pub, the Good Companion on Tithepit Shaw Lane, as the result of a 1995 boundary change. A double murder in the pub's car park shocked the community in 2002. The over-sixties outnumber twenty-somethings by more than three to one in Sanderstead, one of the highest ratios in London.

✉	South Croydon CR2
♦	12,165
🚆	Southern (zone 6)
📖	Joy Gadsby (ed.), *Sanderstead*, Bourne Society, 1998
@	www.sanderstead.com (community site); www.sanderstead-parish.org.uk

Sands End • *Hammersmith & Fulham*

FULHAM's former industrial district, now the site of high-profile riverside developments. In the Middle Ages the western part of Sands End was occupied by Fulham town meadows, where villagers grazed their cattle on the marshes, while Sandford manor lay to the north-east. The manor came into the possession of Westminster Abbey during the reign of Henry VII. Its Elizabethan manor house became a saltpetre factory in 1762 and various other kinds of factory later, including a pottery and a bleach and die works. As drainage was improved, orchards and market gardens appeared but these were gradually erased by riverside industries, starting with the Imperial gasworks in the 1820s. The Kensington Canal was cut across the district but proved unprofitable and was later replaced by a railway line. Rows of terraced housing were laid out inland from 1870. Fulham council built a power station in 1901 and a larger distribution centre in 1936. On Townmead Road, Macfarlane Lang baked biscuits and Van den Bergh's made margarine until the mid 1930s. From the end of World War II the warehouses, works and wharves progressively closed down, leaving a wasteland by the 1980s. Many of the larger Victorian terraced houses were converted to flats.

The council designated Sands End's river frontage a conservation area in 1991 to protect it from unsympathetic development, following some early excrescences. A Sainsbury's superstore has filled the site of the power station, CHELSEA HARBOUR has been created in place of a former coalyard and the gasworks is now the huge IMPERIAL WHARF development. Other projects have included the Harbour Club Sports Centre, the Carnwath Road industrial estate and apartments at Regent on the River. Sandford manor house, which now stands on Rewell Street, has been restored and converted to offices.

It is said that Nell Gwyn lived at Sandford manor house for a while, where Charles II visited her, but Nell was the sort of character who inspired many stories. The essayist and politician Joseph Addison certainly lived at Sands End in the early 18th century, quite probably at the manor house.

✉	SW6
♦	9,723

Sandy Heath • *Camden*

The part of HAMPSTEAD HEATH that lies in the apex of NORTH END Road and Spaniards Road, between East Heath and WEST HEATH. Its name reflects its earlier character, before large quantities of sand and gravel were excavated in the 1860s for making bricks and laying railways. Sandy Heath is now low-lying, with ponds, bogs and woodland. The raised path known as Rotten Row runs across the heath, linking North End to Spaniards End. Despite some steep climbs, Sandy Heath was popular with both walkers and cyclists, but Camden council has banned the latter category, causing a minor furore. Volunteers from Heath Hands help with gorse management, so that paths remain passable.

✉	NW3

Savile Row • *Westminster*

A street known for high-class tailoring that runs parallel with REGENT STREET, south of Conduit Street. In order to alleviate his financial difficulties, the third Earl of Burlington offered developers the five or six acres of land behind Burlington House in 1717. Savile Row was laid out in the early 1730s and named after Burlington's wife, Lady Dorothy Savile. Noblemen and high-ranking military officers were among the early tenants. For a while Savile Row attracted some physicians' and surgeons' practices and was something of a precursor of HARLEY STREET. Tailors began to set up shop in the streets of the Burlington estate in the late 18th century, making a first appearance on Savile Row by 1806. Beau Brummell was an early patron of this fashionable new quarter. By 1838 the street was teeming with tailors, and when Henry Poole inherited his father's Old Burlington Street business in 1846 he enlarged the premises and created a new entrance on Savile Row. Poole became Savile Row's foremost tailor, fitting out monarchs and, later, Hollywood stars. Hawkes & Co, later to become Gieves & Hawkes, moved to Savile Row in 1912. Successful apprentices of the leading firms have often started their own businesses on the street, as have several cloth merchants. Recent arrivals have included some of the leading names in contemporary male couture. The street has become an international byword for gentlemen's tailoring; the Japanese word for a suit, *sebiro*, is a direct transliteration of 'Savile Row'.

The headquarters of the Beatles' Apple Corporation were at 3 Savile Row, previously the home of the Albany club and of Lord Nelson and Lady Hamilton. The band's famous rooftop concert, its final performance, took place here in January 1969.

> ✉ W1

> 📖 Stephen Howarth, *Henry Poole, Founders of Savile Row*, Bene Factum, 2003 Richard Walker, *The Savile Row: An Illustrated History*, Thomson, 1989

> @ Several Savile Row tailors have websites; two of the best are: www.8savilerow.com (Kilgour site); www.henrypoole.com (Henry Poole & Co. site)

Scott's Lodge • *Bromley*

Known only to the cartographers at Philips, this is apparently the name for a tiny settlement in the far south-eastern corner of London, where Grays Road meets CUDHAM Lane South. The lodge itself lies just outside the borough in the parish of KNOCKHOLT. Originally called White Lodge, in reference to its finish, this is an undistinguished double-roofed property standing in mature gardens, much altered around 1900. An unsubstantiated story has it that the house was renamed in honour of a 14th-century predecessor on the site, built by Ralph Scot.

> ✉ Sevenoaks TN14; Westerham TN16

Seething Wells • *Kingston*

A wonderfully named watering hole in west

SURBITON, on the bank of the Thames. It takes its name from a spring which was said to 'bubble up' from the ground beside the Portsmouth Road (A307). Noted in the 18th century as 'cold in summer and warm in winter', the spring was thought to cure complaints of the eye – though this was a claim made for many others too. By the early 19th century the riverside had a wharf and osier beds, while the fields inland were divided into many smallholdings. Following several outbreaks of cholera in London, the Metropolis Water Act of 1852 legislated that drinking water should not be extracted from the Thames below TEDDINGTON. This immediately prompted the Lambeth Water Co. to relocate its reservoir and works to Seething Wells. Shortly afterwards, the Chelsea Water Co. established its works next door. Around 200 residents were evicted to make way for the schemes. The two waterworks eventually descended into the hands of Thames Water, which closed most of the operations in the early 1990s and sold the land for housing. A Victorian pump house has been converted into a health and leisure club. Kingston University has built halls of residence here, which are well-regarded for the quality of accommodation but not for their remote location. The waterworks' former filterbeds have been designated as metropolitan open land and are rich in wildlife.

The ranting punk poet and journalist Steven Wells adopted the pseudonym Seething Wells in the late 1970s.

> ✉ Surbiton KT6

Selhurst • *Croydon*

A socially deprived part of north CROYDON. Selhurst was first recorded in 1225 and its name may mean either 'dwelling where the sallow willows grow' or 'dwelling in a wood'. A bag of Saxon coins was dug up during the construction of the railway. Selhurst (later Heaver's) Farm was in existence by the early 19th century, when the Croydon Canal skirted its southern and eastern edges. The construction of the canal brought growth to the village and a chapel was built for navvies and bargees. Following the closure of the canal in 1836 a railway track was laid along its route. A settlement of 50 or more dwellings had grown up by the mid 19th century, with the White Horse public house at its centre and a handful of larger houses on its fringes, of which Dagnalls was the most substantial. Croydon races were held at Heaver's Farm from 1858 until the mid 1860s. Selhurst station opened in 1865, followed by churches and schools as the village evolved into a suburb of Croydon. Girls' and boys' schools jointly known as the Selhurst Schools opened in 1904 and saw both good times and bad before both institutions closed in 1988. The boys' school has since reopened as Selhurst High School, while the girls' school has become the Brit School, a city technology college specializing in performing arts and technology. Over half of Selhurst's residents are white and a quarter are black or black British. Levels of car and home ownership are low compared with the rest of the borough and unemployment is higher. The proportion of single-parent households is twice the national average. The Selhurst rail depot occupies much of the eastern side of the locality, and was formerly the site of Crystal Palace Football Club's ground, the Nest. Before its abolition, Railtrack introduced a new population of newts and toads onto the railway land as part of a project to create a small wildlife sanctuary around two new ponds and over 600 newly planted trees.

✉ SE25

🏃 14,591

🚆 Southern (zone 4)

📖 John Gent and Isabel MacLeod (eds), *The Selhurst Schools 1904–2004*, Old Croydonians' Association, 2004

@ www.selhurstcommunity.org.uk (Selhurst High School site)

Selhurst Park • *Croydon*
Once the largest estate in SOUTH NORWOOD, situated on the north side of SELHURST, and now best known as the home of Crystal Palace Football Club. Selhurst Park was a gated estate of high-class housing, tentatively begun in the late 1850s between Upper Grove and Oliver Grove. The gate pillars from Oliver Grove were later re-erected at the entrance to South Norwood recreation ground. The project soon foundered and the land went through several changes of hands and at least one bankruptcy. One of the most distinctive houses was Selhurst Lodge, built around 1860 in the style of an Indian bungalow for a retired army officer who had served in the subcontinent. The house was demolished within 30 years and its site is now occupied by Bungalow Road. Most of the other large houses have also since been replaced by more affordable properties. Parts of Selhurst Park remained undeveloped at the end of World War I, when Crystal Palace Foot-

ball Club leased a ground known as the Nest near Selhurst station. The Nest held 25,000 spectators but views were poor, especially when smoke from shunting engines drifted across the pitch, so the club acquired a disused brickworks in Selhurst Park in 1922. The team played its first game at the new ground in 1924, when there was just one stand, with open terraces on the other three sides. The stadium was completely modernized in the 1990s, a period when it was also home to Wimbledon Football Club, and now has seating for 26,300 – little more than the terraces held when the ground first opened. Sainsbury's operates a superstore within its grounds.

✉ SE25

📖 Nigel Sands, *Crystal Palace Football Club, 1905–1997*, Sporting and Leisure Press, 1997

@ www.cpfc.co.uk (Crystal Palace Football Club site)

Selsdon • *Croydon*
A prosperous southerly outpost of CROYDON situated in an elevated position to the northeast of SANDERSTEAD. Its name could have meant 'dwelling on a hill'; Selsdon is on very high ground by London standards, some of it above 500 feet. Most of Selsdon used to be a single farm, covering more than one square mile, and owned for a long time by the Church. Its woodland was used for pheasant shooting in the 19th century, with clearings and rides that can still be seen. In 1923 the farm was sold off and split up. The early 19th-century farmhouse-cum-mansion became Selsdon Park Hotel and was much extended, and its parkland was laid out as a golf course in 1929. Subsidized by the local council, the Surrey Garden Village Trust bought 300 acres of the farm with the aim of dividing it into parcels where war veterans could settle and make a living off the land. Unlike most garden villages, Selsdon was not connected to an existing suburb and new residents had to travel to Sanderstead or Croydon to do their shopping. The plots of land turned out to be too small for their intended purpose but made wonderful back gardens. When developers started to clear more of the wood in 1925, campaigners launched an appeal to preserve 16 acres. An unexpected degree of success permitted the acquisition of nearly 200 acres, which were presented to the National Trust, with the local authority taking responsibility for their maintenance. North of Addington Road, Littleheath Wood was similarly saved in 1932.

Selsdon station, which closed in 1983 (when it was still lit by gas lamps), was nowhere near Selsdon itself. Opened in 1885 as Selsdon Road, it was on the unsuccessful WOODSIDE and SOUTH CROYDON Railway.

In February 1970 the Conservative leader Edward Heath convened his key advisors at Selsdon Park Hotel to draw up a new manifesto with an emphasis on tax cuts and free market economics. Labour prime minister Harold Wilson saw this as the thinking of a political Neanderthal, whom he branded 'Selsdon Man', but Heath won the general election four months later.

✉ South Croydon CR2; Croydon CR0

👭 11,879 (Selsdon and Ballards ward)

📖 Ralph Rimmer, *South Croydon and Selsdon*, Nonsuch, 2005; Brian J Salter (ed.), *Selsdon and Croham*, Living History, 1983

Seven Kings • *Redbridge*

A 'people's suburb', as its developer described it, in eastern ILFORD. Legend has it that in Saxon times seven royal huntsmen met here by a stream at a clearing in the Hainault Forest, pausing while their horses drank. Sadly, a less romantic explanation has a greater ring of truth: that the name is a corruption of *Seofecingas*, which meant 'settlement of Seofeca's people'. Seven Kings, or at least the part with the street plan that looks like an egg slicer, has been called 'the town built in a year'. This was 1898–9, when local developer Cameron Corbett laid out an estate of good quality houses that clerks and lower grade civil servants could afford. It was nicknamed Klondike by its first residents, because of its rapid growth and relative inaccessibility, but a station was quickly opened and Seven Kings soon had 10,000 inhabitants, with Corbett adding the Mayfield estate to the south and Downshall to the north. The attractive Seven Kings bungalow estate of the 1920s and 1930s is now a conservation area. Like neighbouring parts of Ilford, Seven Kings has become popular with Asian families, especially those of Indian origin. Three-quarters of homes here are owner-occupied. In 1991, Redbridge council tried to convert Seven Kings Park into a new cemetery, but was dissuaded by a 10,000-signature petition.

At the Tate Britain gallery the artist Michael Landy created a full-size replica of his parents' house at 62 Kingswood Road, on the Seven Kings/GOODMAYES border. The installation, entitled *Semi-detached*, was demolished after the six-month show in 2004.

✉ Ilford IG3

👭 11,910

🚇 'one' Railway (zone 4)

📖 Peter Foley, *Seven Kings and Goodmayes: Origins and Early Development*, Heptarchy [note the pun], 1993

Seven Sisters • *Haringey*

A poor, multi-ethnic neighbourhood encircling the junction of Seven Sisters Road and the High Road in SOUTH TOTTENHAM. It is said that some time around 1350 seven elm trees were planted in a ring around a walnut tree by the roadside at Page Green by seven sisters when they were about to go their separate ways. A Protestant martyr was later supposed to have been burnt here, after which the walnut tree flourished without growing bigger. Although parts of the story are almost certainly mythical, the trees certainly existed in the 17th and 18th centuries. The walnut had died by 1790 but the elms lasted long enough to give their name to a turnpike road built in 1833 to provide improved access from Tottenham to Westminster. Seven Sisters Road became a ribbon development of large villas, some with gardens backing onto the New River. The elms were removed around 1840, although the seven daughters of a Tottenham butcher later planted a new set, which has not survived. Seven Sisters station opened on the Great Eastern Railway in 1872, rapidly bringing two-storey terraced houses to newly built streets in place of an earlier scattering of middle-class villas. Many of the properties were allowed to deteriorate during the first half of the 20th century and some were cleared after World War II. Seven Sisters station became a Victoria Line interchange in 1968 and over the following decade Haringey council built several small estates of low-rise flats. The low-rent shops in the vicinity of the station bear witness to the deprivation of this corner of the borough, although the presence of the Tube station has pushed up house prices. Thirty-six per cent of the residents are white British and just over a quarter are black or black British. At 31.7 years, the average age of residents is very low. The most common languages spoken at Seven Sisters Primary School are English, Turkish, Somali, Bengali and Kurdish.

✉ N15

👭 13,179

🚇 'one' Railway; Victoria Line (zone 3)

Sewardstone • *Epping Forest, Essex*

Sewardstone, SEWARDSTONEBURY and GILWELL PARK lie outside Greater London but within the E4 London postal district. The discovery of a dug-out oak canoe indicates the possibility of an Iron Age settlement in Sewardstone and the name probably identifies a Saxon farmer. The manor of Sewardstone occupied the southern part of the parish of Waltham Holy Cross and it was first recorded in 1177, when Henry II made a grant of land here to the canons of Waltham Abbey. The manor held its own courts from the 13th century. The hamlet lay on the old route to the abbey from CHAPEL END in WALTHAMSTOW. One of the earliest recorded dwellings in Sewardstone was the Pentensary, which was the home of the abbey's pittancer. A pittancer's job was to distribute pittances, which were originally pious bequests made to religious houses. Other properties standing here in the late 17th century included the Netherhouse in Sewardstone Road and Carrolls at Sewardstone Green. In 1674 the manor was purchased by James Sotheby, a noted antiquarian and book collector, although not apparently connected with the auctioneers of the same name. His son William Sotheby was a translator of the classics and a poet. The manor remained in the hands of the Sotheby family for over 200 years. There was a silk factory here in 1806, to which poor boys and girls were sent from Enfield's CHASE SIDE workhouse. By 1813 CHINGFORD post office was delivering mail to Sewardstone, which was the reason for its later inclusion in the E4 postal district. Waltham School Board built a primary school here in 1874 but this closed in 1939, after which children had to travel to a new school in YARDLEY LANE. In addition to some desirable residential properties, Sewardstone has a string of nurseries and garden centres, which are more concentrated here than anywhere else in the London area except CREWS HILL. The Sewardstone Marsh nature reserve is part of the Lee Valley Regional Park, and the park authority also runs a campsite nearby. The marsh is popular with birdwatchers and is accessed from Godwin Close, off Sewardstone Road.

✉ E4

@ www.leevalleypark.org.uk (for park and campsite information)

Sewardstonebury • *Epping Forest, Essex*

A wealthy (in parts, fabulously wealthy) village nestling in a quiet corner of Epping Forest north of CHINGFORD. In the 19th century this was a remote hamlet with a lonely road that became impassable in bad weather. Barbara Ray, in her history of Chingford, relates that a pupil-teacher who lived at Sewardstonebury arrived at Chingford infants' school so wet and muddy that there was no alternative but to send her home again. Now there are luxury houses strung along the length of Bury Road, the main thoroughfare, and in the private estate to the west. Hornbeam Lane is, by local standards, positively modest. Every second property in Sewardstonebury seems to have builders at work – remodelling or extending the house or landscaping the grounds. Whole new palaces regularly replace insufficiently grand mansions. Sewardstonebury has no shops, church or pub but there are golf courses to the north and south. The West Essex course, created by James Braid in 1900, was designed to make full use of Epping Forest's natural attributes. With undulating fairways and small, sloping, quick greens, it is reckoned a challenging par 71.

✉ E4

@ www.westessexgolfclub.co.uk

Shacklewell • *Hackney*

A multiracial neighbourhood with some light industry, almost squeezed out of existence by HACKNEY and STOKE NEWINGTON, which lie on either side. The name may refer to a well-spring in a sunken place or where animals could be shackled (tethered), but was not recorded until 1490 despite its probable Old English origin. In the early 16th century Sir John Heron, reputedly the richest man in Hackney, owned a large estate centred on a manor house here; its site is now covered by shops. Several villas for gentlemen were built during the course of the 18th century, interspersed with lesser properties for tradesmen, two pubs and a dairy on the south side of the village green. Side roads subsequently proliferated, many lined with cramped terraced houses, but Shacklewell remained an isolated settlement until Hackney expanded outwards to meet it in the mid 19th century. Perch Street, Seal Street and April Street were laid out in the early 1880s with good quality terraced houses for working people, and Shacklewell Green was taken into public ownership. By the early 20th century Shacklewell had gained a synagogue and some industrial premises, while a number of larger houses were being knocked down and replaced by more terraces. Parts became a slum and several streets were cleared in the 1930s to make way for municipal and philanthropic housing projects. More flats followed after World War II. The conversion of the synagogue to a mosque is an indication of the shift in Shacklewell's ethnic mix in recent decades. KINGSLAND Secondary School (opened as DALSTON County School in 1937) has a significant proportion of pupils from Turkish and Kurdish backgrounds, some of whom speak little English and have minimal experience of formal education. At Shacklewell Primary School (opened in 1951), over 80 per cent of children are from black, Indian, Pakistani, Bangladeshi, Turkish or Chinese backgrounds.

✉ N16; E8

Shad Thames • *Southwark*

A riverside street, and by extension the surrounding area, located on the south bank of the Thames, east of TOWER Bridge. The name is a corruption of 'St John at Thames', a reference to the Knights of St John, the former landowners. The parish church of Horselydown was dedicated to St John when it was built in 1728. Horselydown was the medieval name for this area but has now faded from use. This stretch of the shoreline became the core of BERMONDSEY and SOUTHWARK's 'larder of London', dominated by the tea, coffee, spice and dried fruit warehouses of Butler's Wharf, which were completed in 1873. A century later the last warehouses closed and the area was redeveloped from the mid 1980s, with offices, shops, cafés, bars and restaurants. Shad Thames is still criss-crossed by the overhead goods gantries that linked the warehouses, many of which retain interior fitments too. The Design Museum, brainchild of Sir Terence Conran, occupies the main building of the former Butler's Wharf complex. Founded in 1989, it is dedicated to explaining how everyday objects work and why they look the way they do. On Maguire Street, the Bramah Tea and Coffee Museum is a collection of artefacts connected with these beverages and tells the story of their trading impact on the port of London.

Before its makeover Shad Thames featured as a location in *Dr Who* and the movies *Oliver*, *The French Lieutenant's Woman* and *The Elephant Man*.

✉ SE1

@ www.designmuseum.org;
www.bramahmuseum.co.uk

Shadwell • *Tower Hamlets*

Now the north-eastern part of WAPPING, but once a separate TOWER hamlet. Shadwell's Old English name means 'shallow well'. Archaeological excavations have revealed evidence of a Roman quarry here, subsequently used as a cemetery, with a mausoleum tower. By the 3rd century the area had been divided into plots, where domestic residences were built. A leather bikini has been discovered in a timber-lined tank dating from the 4th century. After this period the site was abandoned to agricultural use. A succession of Norman landowners amassed an estate here that Bishop de Fauconberg bequeathed to the dean and chapter of ST PAUL'S on his death in 1228. Further augmentation brought the property to nearly 100 acres by the end of that century. The picturesque Prospect of Whitby (as the pub is now called) may date from around 1520, although it has been much altered and 're-antiqued' since. Maritime industries brought growth to Shadwell from the 1630s and a chapel was built in 1656. Shadwell became a parish in 1669, when its 8,000 residents included many seafarers. St Paul's Church, which recalls the identity of the former landowners, was built in 1820, by which time conditions in the parish had become insanitary. Philanthropists converted a building in Glasshouse Fields to one of London's earliest public wash houses in the 1840s. In *London: A Pilgrimage* (1872), Blanchard Jerrold wrote of 'the densely-packed haunts of poverty and crime – in the hideous tenements stacked far and wide, round such institutions as the Bluegate Fields ragged schools in Shadwell' and Gustave Doré provided an appropriate illustration of the scene. Some of the slums disappeared in the construction of the docks in the 1850s and more were cleared in the 1860s but the character of the district did not fundamentally alter until after World War II, when council blocks sprouted in all corners. The architecture has changed, but according to calculations by the Low Pay Unit, Shadwell still has some of the worst deprivation of all London's wards. Most homes are rented from the council or a housing association and employment levels are very low. Half the population is of Bangladeshi origin and Islam is the principal religion. The average age of residents is an exceptionally low 30.2 years.

✉ E1

👥 12,078

🚇 East London Line; Docklands Light Railway, all

branches (zone 2)

📖 David Lakin et al, *The Roman Tower at Shadwell*, Museum of London Archaeology Service, 2002

Shaftesbury Avenue • *Westminster/Camden*

The central thoroughfare of London's THEA-TRELAND, connecting PICCADILLY CIRCUS with the eastern end of New Oxford Street. The road-building project was planned from 1877 by the Metropolitan Board of Works' architect George Vulliamy and the celebrated engineer Sir Joseph Bazalgette. Construction entailed the unification and widening of the existing Richmond, King and Dudley Streets and the creation of a wholly new section between Rupert Street and Piccadilly Circus. This disrupted the layout of Piccadilly Circus and necessitated the demolition and rebuilding of the London Pavilion. East of CHARING CROSS ROAD, also newly created, slum housing was cleared in the ST GILES district. The avenue opened in 1886 and was named after Anthony Ashley Cooper, the seventh Earl of Shaftesbury, a campaigner for the eradication of the slums who had died in the previous year. Heavy terraces lined much of the road, with shops at street level and flats above, many of which were used as consulting rooms, offices or chambers. The first theatres to open were the Shaftesbury and the Lyric in 1888. The Lyric survives but the original Shaftesbury was destroyed during World War II. The Royal English Opera House opened in 1891, flopped, and became the Palace Theatre the following year. The avenue's architecture came in for some early criticism but progressive rebuilding on the north side improved its status, especially with the construction of a string of theatres in the first decade of the 20th century, namely the Apollo, Hicks (renamed Globe, now Gielgud), Queen's and Prince's (now Shaftesbury). The last theatres to open on the avenue were the Prince Edward in 1930 and the Savile in 1931. The latter has spent most of its life as a cinema, currently named the Odeon COVENT GARDEN. The Curzon cinema opened in 1959 as the Columbia, in the basement of an office development. In addition to its theatres and cinemas, a mixture of tourist-oriented shops and restaurants occupies much of the western part of the avenue. East of Cambridge Circus the tenants are more idiosyncratic, including fancy dress and science fiction stores. Work is currently under way at the adjacent Queen's and Gielgud theatres to provide a communal foyer and build the 500-seat Sondheim Theatre above the Queen's, creating the first new theatre in Shaftesbury Avenue since 1931.

✉ W1; WC2

@ www.thisistheatre.com

Shepherd's Bush • *Hammersmith & Fulham*

A lively and sometimes edgy residential district and minor cultural zone, situated north of HAMMERSMITH. Shepherd's Bush derives its name from shepherds who used to rest their flocks on the triangular green on their way to market in London. In 1657 Miles Syndercombe hired a cottage that stood on the site of the present Bush Hotel and planned to use a primitive form of machine-gun to assassinate Oliver Cromwell on his way to HAMPTON COURT, but was betrayed by his accomplices. Shepherd's Bush remained entirely rural until the late 18th century, when ribbons of housing appeared along the main roads, followed by terraces to the north. By 1830 semi-detached houses were going up on the west side of the green but fields lay to the south for several more decades. Stations have opened and closed at Shepherd's Bush since 1844 but the first really useful halt was built on the Hammersmith & City Railway in 1864. Shepherd's Bush was almost wholly built up by the time the Central Railway's 'tuppenny tube' reached here in 1900. The Empire Theatre, nicknamed the 'Coliseum of west London', opened in 1903 and Lime Grove Studios followed in 1910. Both were subsequently taken over by the BBC and used as television studios. By the 1930s much of Shepherd's Bush had become very run down and the council cleared slums and built flats during the third quarter of the 20th century. South-east of the green, an ugly car park and shopping precinct replaced old shops. The Bush Theatre opened in the upstairs dining hall of the Bush Hotel in 1972. The Shepherd's Bush Empire was converted into a rock venue in 1994. Construction work is underway on a massive retail and leisure centre on the WHITE CITY side of the district, while the council is working to make the area around the green more pedestrian-friendly. Large parts of the area remain socially disadvantaged but Shepherd's Bush has become popular with young graduates. 'It's all happening in Shepherd's Bush. We're the new bushgeoisie!' says Gerald the Suffocator in Candace Bushnell's 2000 novel *Four Blondes*.

No. 24 Oil Drum Lane, Shepherd's Bush

West, was the home of Steptoe and Son in the television comedy series of that name. Post-grunge rock band Bush take its name from the district, although the word's other connotations played a part in the choice.

> ✉ W12
>
> ♦ 10,249 (Shepherd's Bush Green ward)
>
> 🚇 Silverlink Metro; Central Line; Hammersmith & City Line (zone 2)
>
> 📖 *Around The Bush: A History of Shepherd's Bush*, Shepherd's Bush Local History Society, 2000
>
> @ www.shepherds-bush-empire.co.uk

Shirley • *Croydon*

A relatively (in parts very) affluent neighbourhood situated between ADDISCOMBE and ADDINGTON. The name was first recorded in 1314 and could have meant 'shire clearing', in reference to its location near the border between Surrey and Kent, or 'bright clearing'. In the 17th century Shirley was a hamlet beside a common on the old road from Croydon to West Wickham. Shirley House was built in 1721 and was later acquired by Colonel John Maberley, who made his fortune as a contractor to the army. Maberley went bankrupt in 1834, primarily as a result of a failed banking venture but partly because of the huge amounts he had spent on improvements to the house. By this time the quaint village of Shirley was beginning to grow and a chapel was built in 1835. The chapel was replaced in 1856 by St John's Church, built to the design of George Gilbert Scott. Shirley House was converted into the Shirley Park Hotel in 1912. Much of present-day Shirley was built up in the 1930s with semi-detached houses, though a few Victorian buildings survive. Later developments to the south in UPPER SHIRLEY and in the north at SHIRLEY OAKS are of contrasting characters. The Whitgift Foundation acquired Shirley Park Hotel in 1965 and Trinity School (formerly the Whitgift Middle School) moved to a new building on its site. More than a quarter of Shirley's residents are in the higher and intermediate managerial, administrative and professional socio-economic groups.

Walking down a local lane in 1880, the Reverend William Wilks found a lone poppy with a white border to its red petals. He carefully marked the flower and returned in the autumn to collect its seed. Next spring he planted out several hundred seedlings in his garden at the vicarage in Shirley Church Road and bred progressively paler plants, including an all-white variety. Still known as the Shirley poppy (*Papaver rhoeas Shirley*), the distinctive feature of Wilks's flower is the absence of a black blotch at the base of each petal. Wilks later became secretary of the Royal Horticultural Society and was responsible for the beginnings of the society's annual flower show.

> ✉ Croydon CR0
>
> ♦ 13,978
>
> 📖 Raymond Wheeler, *Shirley and Addington*, Tempus, 2003

Shirley Oaks • *Croydon*

The northern and more affordable part of SHIRLEY, bordering MONKS ORCHARD. Land here was in the hands of the archbishops of Canterbury from the Middle Ages and was leased to Colonel Maberley of Shirley Park in the early 19th century. Oaks Farm was in existence by 1800. In 1903 the Bermondsey board of guardians built the cottage homes of the Shirley schools, later called the Shirley Oaks Children's Home, on the neighbouring Shirley Lodge Farm. Around 400 children lived in 38 large cottages, and other amenities included a sick bay, swimming bath, laundry and workshops, with a school at the north of the site. In 1930 the home passed to the London County Council and in 1965 to the London Borough of Lambeth. Following the closure of the home in 1982, Heron Homes acquired the 72-acre site and built Shirley Park Village. Except for the conversion of a handful of cottages and the entrance lodge, the buildings were all demolished but the new housing was generally well-received. The 50-bed Shirley Oaks Hospital was built on the site of the school in 1986 and is part of BMI Healthcare. In 2000 Shirley Oaks residents funded and installed their own close-circuit television cameras at either end of Blackthorne Avenue in a successful bid to reduce graffiti and car dumping.

> ✉ Croydon CR0
>
> 📖 Jad Adams and Gerry Coll, *The History of Shirley Oaks Children's Home*, Deptford Forum Publishing, 2000

Shooters Hill • *Greenwich*

The ancient woodland of Shooters Hill and its accompanying residential locality lie between PLUMSTEAD and ELTHAM. The road of the same name was part of Watling Street, the Roman road to Dover, and now forms a section of the A207. At 432 feet the summit is one of the highest points in Greater London. The name was first recorded in 1226 and probably derives from the use of the slopes for archery practice, although other sources suggest a link with highwaymen. Henry IV ordered the clearance of trees bordering the road in an unsuccessful bid to protect travellers from 'violent practices'. In the 18th century several aristocrats and knights cleared parcels of woodland to erect grand houses with landscaped gardens, now all lost. In Castle Wood, Lady James commissioned the Gothic folly Severndroog Castle in 1784 to commemorate her late husband's capture of the fortress of that name on India's Malabar coast. From the mid 19th century a village began to develop on the hillside, soon gaining a police station, church and school. Early 20th-century amenities included an ornate octagonal water tower, a fire station that has recently been converted into flats – one of which retains the firemen's pole – and in 1927 the Memorial Hospital. George Wimpey laid out the Shooters Hill estate in the 1930s but most of the higher parts of the hill were saved from further development by the London County Council, which made a series of acquisitions between the wars to create a public open space that is now designated a site of special scientific interest. Oxleas Wood and Woodlands Farm were threatened by plans to construct a link road to a proposed east London river crossing, but these were abandoned in 1993 following a long-running battle by conservationists that ended with victory in the European Court. The demographic profile of the Shooters Hill ward is closer to that of the country as a whole than the rest of the borough, except that its non-white minorities make up a fifth of the population, compared with less than a tenth for England generally.

Byron's *Don Juan* (1823) has the short poem *London from Shooters Hill*. 'Don Juan had got out on Shooters' Hill / Sunset the time, the place the same declivity / Which looks along that vale of good and ill / Where London streets ferment in full activity.' Charles Dickens' novel *A Tale of Two Cities* opens on Shooters Hill.

✉ SE18

🚶 12,854

📖 Tony and Douglas Johnson (eds), *Aspects of Shooters Hill*, Shooters Hill Local History Group, 1989

@ www.ideal-homes.org.uk/greenwich/main/ shooters-hill.htm (London surburban history site)

Shoreditch • *Hackney/Tower Hamlets*

A high-density employment area situated north of LIVERPOOL STREET station. The former parish and borough of Shoreditch embraced HOXTON and HAGGERSTON; the vicinity of the medieval village is now sometimes called SOUTH SHOREDITCH. The name is of Old English origin and refers to a dyke by a steep bank but the more romantic explanation, espoused in Thomas Percy's *Reliques*, is that Jane Shore, mistress of Edward IV, died in a ditch here in 1527. Augustinian nuns founded a priory in Shoreditch in the 12th century but significant development did not begin in the area until the 16th century, when building extended northward from BISHOPSGATE. Houses lined the High Street and a few more ran westwards on OLD STREET. The Theatre and the Curtain were the first London theatres when they were built west of the High Street in the fourth quarter of the 16th century. Shoreditch was one of the first 'outer London' districts to fuse with the City and the parish had around 10,000 inhabitants by 1750, together with 15 almshouses and St Leonard's Church. Within 100 years the population had increased tenfold, with many residents working in local industries, especially the furniture, upholstery and timber trades. Philanthropists and the borough and county councils replaced slum housing with blocks of flats but the area remained overcrowded until after World War II. Central Shoreditch is still crammed with Victorian warehouses and industrial buildings, contrasting grimly with the marble and glass of the neighbouring CITY OF LONDON. Printing, engineering, furniture and clothing industries maintain a presence here but new technology is the rising star. The southernmost tip of the district, beyond Worship Street, has the greatest concentration of office blocks, merging geographically and architecturally with the City. In the early 1990s Shoreditch became popular with a wide spectrum of the arts and media communities, ranging from sculptors to website designers. The trend stuttered as a result of rising rents, and perhaps an excess of hype, but the phenomenon is far from dead; Soho House recently opened a hotel, brasserie and art-house cinema on Ebor Street, while Shoreditch Town Hall has been restored as a cultural and leisure venue.

In Britain's biggest cash robbery, £6 million, weighing five tons, was taken from a Security Express warehouse in Curtain Road on Easter

Monday in 1983. *Shoreditch Tw*t* was a 2002 Channel 4 television production based on the content of a long-running fanzine (which did not use an asterisk) that lampooned the lifestyle of local media trendies. Malcolm Needs' unsuccessful 2003 film *Shoreditch* unravelled the mystery of a corpse found in the cellar of a derelict jazz club. Stewart Home's 2004 novel *Down and Out in Shoreditch and Hoxton* is set simultaneously in the present day and the Jack the Ripper era.

> ✉ EC2; E1; N1

> 🚌 East London Line (limited service: weekdays and for the Sunday markets at Brick Lane and Columbia Road, zone 2)

> @ www.shoreditchtownhall.org.uk; www.myshoreditch.co.uk (commercial local information site)

Shortlands · *Bromley*

A prosperous south-western corner of BROMLEY, previously called Clay Hill. Evidence of an Iron Age hill-fort was discovered at Toots Wood in 1889, together with fragments of Roman pottery, indicating the presence of a moderately significant settlement. The medieval field pattern here consisted of sets of long and short fields, called Longelonds and Shortelonds, and the latter gave their name to a house built at the beginning of the 18th century. The house and its extensive farmland were acquired in 1848 by railway magnate William Wilkinson, who built several cottages for his agricultural labourers. In 1858 the West End and Crystal Palace Railway Co. opened Shortlands station, prompting Wilkinson to sell his farm's 163 acres for development. The oak and birch trees of Kingswood were cleared as the Shortlands estate took shape. Wilkinson died in 1865, leaving an endowment for the construction of St Mary's Church. In a second phase of development around 1880 the Westmoreland Road area was built up with a group of handsome villas known as the South Hill Park estate. Shortlands House served as a hotel for the first half of the 20th century and then became a school, now called Bishop Challoner's School. A number of maisonette blocks were built in the 1960s and 1970s. Shortlands residents are overwhelmingly white home-owners and tend to be relatively well-educated. The houses are comparatively large, although a third have only one occupant. At 41.7 years, the average age of residents is significantly higher than in most parts of the capital.

George Grote, born at Shortlands House in 1794, wrote an authoritative history of Greece in twelve volumes, without ever visiting the country, and served as MP for the City of London, president of University College, London and vice-chancellor of the University of London. In 1869 he refused the offer of a peerage. Grote died two years later and was interred in Westminster Abbey's Poets' Corner.

> ✉ Bromley BR2

> ⚥ 9,303

> 🚆 South Eastern Trains (zone 4)

> 📖 Muriel V Searle, *Shortlands*, European Library, 1992; Len Hevey, *Shortlands*, self-published, 1991

Shrublands · *Croydon*

A post-war council estate situated in the south-eastern corner of SPRING PARK. When the woods and farmland of Spring Park were suburbanized in the 1920s, the part between Links View Road and SHIRLEY Church Road escaped the process by being converted into a 137-acre golf course. But after World War II, Croydon council responded to its acute housing shortage by compulsorily purchasing the course and filling the northern part of the site with prefabricated homes. The southern part was retained as public open space. The council built a permanent estate in the late 1950s and early 1960s with a mix of short terraces of houses and three-point blocks of flats. The houses had back gardens and the blocks all offered close access to communal greensward and children's play areas. Shops, a community hall and a doctor's surgery were among the amenities. The estate now has 260 houses, most of which have been sold to private owners, and 770 flats. Since 1995, £5 million-worth of improvements have been carried out, including measures to improve security and reduce the fear of crime. In 2001 the council launched an action plan to improve further Shrublands' housing, health and environment. To the south of the estate is the 68-acre Shirley Heath, once known as Jackson's Common, which has a mix of woodland, open heath, football pitches and play areas.

> ✉ Croydon CR0

> @ www.shrublands.net (community site)

Sidcup · *Bexley*

A primarily 1930s suburb situated between CHISLEHURST and BEXLEY. The name was first recorded in 1254 and is derived from Old

English words meaning either a 'fold in a hill' or a 'flat hilltop'. This was essentially a field name and there is no record of a hamlet existing here until 1675. One nearby house called Frognal, which had pre-dated the hamlet, was rebuilt on several occasions between the 15th and the early 18th centuries. The village gained an inn, a forge and a scattering of country seats, including Sidcup House, which was built in 1717. Sidcup Place, as it is now called, was said to have been built in 1743 by an officer in the army engineers as a star-shaped fort. If this is true, the house was soon remodelled on more conventional lines and has since been much extended. The Church of St John the Evangelist held its first services in 1844 and the village soon acquired its first terraced housing in Church Place. Sidcup station opened in 1866 on the Dartford loop line and second-class (rather than third-class) season ticket-holders almost immediately began to settle here. It was the siting and naming of the station that determined Sidcup's subsequent pre-eminence over neighbouring villages like FOOTS CRAY and the now-absorbed Halfway Street, which until then had been of equal or greater significance. In the 40 years after 1871, Sidcup's population rose from 390 to 8,493. The new residents were housed in small estates built by individual developers and the properties were substantial detached or semi-detached villas, with gardens as large as a quarter of an acre. Almost all the early building took place in the hinterland of Station Road; north of the tracks the hamlet of LAMORBEY remained largely undisturbed until the establishment of the Greenwich and Deptford Children's Homes in 1902. In 1917 the grounds of Frognal became the site of a hospital, which specialized in the treatment of soldiers and sailors with facial and jaw injuries. It has since evolved into Queen Mary's Hospital. After World War I, and especially in the ten years from 1929, a building boom carried Sidcup across the railway line and south to the new by-pass (A20) to fill roughly its present sprawling extent, while a denser network of streets encircled the old village. Apart from the construction of council estates soon after World War II, the main changes in the second half of the 20th century were the widespread extension of private homes, with features such as garages and granny flats, and the building of offices in central Sidcup. Privately built apartment blocks continue to be squeezed in wherever planning permission allows. The Sidcup ward has very low unemployment, high home ownership and a relatively high number of pensioners living alone.

Its ethnic profile is overwhelmingly white.

In Harold Pinter's influential 1960 play *The Caretaker*, the tramp Davies (played originally and in the film version by Donald Pleasence) insists repeatedly but implausibly that everything will be all right if he can only get down to Sidcup.

✉ Sidcup DA14 and DA15

♦ 10,432

🚉 South Eastern Trains (zone 5)

📖 John Mercer, *The Sidcup Story*, Bexley Libraries and Museums Department, 1988

@ website.lineone.net/~shadlow/sidcup.html (privately operated local information site)

Silver Street • *Enfield*

A street and residential locality in south-west EDMONTON, and the home of Enfield's civic centre. The nucleus of what became UPPER EDMONTON stood at Silver Street's original eastern end, at the junction with Fore Street, while further west was the isolated hamlet of Tanners End. Despite its suburban setting, Silver Street retains several historic buildings. The White Lodge, now a medical practice, is a 16th-century clapboard building with a 19th-century exterior and a walled garden with an ice house. Joseph Whitaker, the founder of *Whitaker's Almanack*, lived and died there. Millfield House, built in 1792, has become an arts centre that houses a library and the Millfield Theatre. The Edmonton board of guardians built a workhouse in 1842 that eventually evolved into the North Middlesex Hospital; some of the original buildings survive. Silver Street station opened in 1872 on the new line to Enfield. Most of the housing was built around the end of the 19th century, following the opening of PYMMES PARK to the public. Silver Street's length and significance as a thoroughfare were diminished by the creation of the Sterling Way section of the North Circular Road (A406). This involved the demolition of residential and hospital buildings, and Silver Street station found itself detached from its namesake.

Michael Menson, whose band Double Trouble had chart success in the 1980s, died in hospital two weeks after he was found in Silver Street in January 1997, having been set alight. Controversially, the police initially treated the incident as suspected suicide, but later conceded that it had probably been a racially motivated attack. Three men were jailed for their parts in the killing.

✉ N18

🚇 'one' Railway (zone 4)

Silvertown • *Newham*

A steadily regenerating dockland district situated between the Thames and the ROYAL DOCKS. Industry and accompanying housing grew up on the marshes after the construction of the railway line to NORTH WOOLWICH in 1847. The town takes its name from one of the first manufacturers, Samuel Winkworth Silver's India-rubber, Gutta-percha, and Telegraph Co., which opened in 1852 and grew to occupy 15 acres and employ 3,000 workers. The district had become known as Silvertown by the late 1850s and Silvertown station opened in 1863. Henry Tate set up his sugar-cube factory in Silvertown in 1877 and four years later Abram Lyle began to produce golden syrup at nearby Plaistow Wharf, formerly an oil storage facility. The presence of these works, together with treacle refineries and jam-makers, gave rise to the nickname 'the sugar mile'. During the late 19th century the strip of land north of Albert Road was built up with workers' terraced houses. London's largest-ever explosion occurred in 1917 at the Brunner Mond munitions factory; 73 people were killed and most of the town was destroyed, only to be rebuilt after World War I along the same lines as before. During World War II, Silvertown was a prime target for German bombing. On one occasion a ring of fire forced the Woolwich ferries to mount a Dunkirk-style evacuation of the inhabitants. Tate and Lyle's sugar refinery was rebuilt from the 1950s and is the district's leading present-day employer. Silver's rubber works was demolished in the 1960s and many other industries have also moved away, leaving sites for new housing, especially at WEST SILVERTOWN. Silvertown station was closed permanently in 2006, as a side-effect of a project to build a new Docklands Light Railway extension.

The effect of wartime bombing in Silvertown is shown in Graham Sutherland's *Devastation: An East End Street* (1941, Tate Britain). Mark Knopfler's *Silvertown Blues*, from his album *Sailing to Philadelphia*, tells of the changes taking place here at the end of the 20th century.

✉ E16

📖 Melanie McGrath, *Silvertown: An East End Family Memoir*, Fourth Estate, 2002

Single Street • *Bromley*

A rural hamlet clustered around the lane of the same name, situated south-east of LUXTED. The manor of Berterye (which was spelt in all sorts of ways) was in existence by 1145 and gave its name to nearby BERRY'S GREEN. According to John Phillipot's *Visitation of Kent*, written around 1619, the crusader Simon Manning was 'lord of the castle and town of Bettrede'. The site of the 'castle' – the manor house – is now lost but the 'town' is assumed to have been the hamlet later known as Single Street. The Manning family retained an important role in parts of the modern borough of Bromley for several centuries and they were also lords of the manor of KEVINGTON. Single Street's present name was first documented as late as 1871, in an Ordnance Survey map, but it may be of Old English origin; a 'sengel' was a burnt clearing. In the latter part of the 20th century the hamlet expanded as far as green-belt restrictions would permit but it retains some older properties, including Bell Cottage, which is said to be of 16th-century origin. Single Street lies at the southern tip of the proposed world heritage site covering the area around Charles Darwin's former home at DOWNE, but its later housing is excluded.

✉ Westerham TN16

Sipson • *Hounslow*

A linear village stretching three-quarters of a mile along Sipson Road, most of which lies just west of the M4 HEATHROW spur road. Gravel excavations have revealed Neanderthal hand-axes and Bronze Age loom-weights, the latter providing the earliest known evidence of weaving in the London area. A small cremation cemetery from the middle Bronze Age has also been discovered. Sipson was first mentioned by name in 1214, as Sibwineston, and there were 14 houses here by 1337. Wheat and rye were grown by the 16th century and an oast house was built for malting and brewing. Following enclosure of most of the common land, the village grew slowly from the late 18th century, when Sipson House was built. However, it remained of minor importance in 1836, when Pigot & Co.'s Directory commented that, 'The dwellings in this place are but few and those of rather mean appearance'. A workhouse stood at Sipson Green until around 1860 and an infants' school was built soon after this. In the late 1890s an old farm was converted into a jam factory, which survived until about 1920. The buildings were taken over by a furniture manufacturer, which switched to making caravans in 1947. Over the second half of the 20th century the character of the village was greatly affected by the growth of Heathrow. Sipson House has been converted to office use by the British Airports Authority and renamed Sipson Court, with only its original façade surviving. Sipson is now hemmed in to the south and north by Heathrow hotels, and many local residents work at these establishments or at the airport.

Charles Dickens may have come up with the name for the protagonist of *A Christmas Carol* while on a visit to Sipson House. However, opinions are divided as to whether the inspiration came from nearby Scroogeall Cottages or from a local shepherd who assured Dickens that his sheep would be able to 'scrooge' through a narrow gate.

✉ West Drayton UB7

Slade Green · *Bexley*

The easternmost settlement in London south of the Thames, situated north of BARNES CRAY, and not held in high regard by most Bexleyites. This was formerly the manor of Howbury, recorded simply as Hov in Domesday Book, from the Old English 'hōh', a heel of land. Slade Green was first mentioned in the 16th century, but the name is probably of earlier origin. A 'slade' was 'a little dell or valley; or a flat piece of low, moist ground' and it was certainly the latter meaning that applied here. The ruins and moat of the house called Howbury constitute a scheduled ancient monument and a Jacobean tithe barn survives, but in deteriorating condition. Howbury's surroundings were fields on the edge of CRAYFORD Marshes until industrial development began here in the late 19th century, mainly in the form of brickmaking and barge-building. The station opened in 1900, followed by locomotive sheds and carriage sidings. The South East and Chatham Railway Co. built a small estate of railway workers' homes and a matching public house on Oak Road. The cottages are arranged in groups of four and designed to look at first glance as though each set is a single dwelling. Prolonged railway ownership kept the Oak Road estate relatively unspoilt and it is now a conservation area. The bulky Church of St Augustine opened in 1911. The council built flats, bungalows, semi-detached houses and shops in the late 1950s. The system-built flats were demolished around 1990 and replaced by much more pleasant housing. Bellway Homes received permission to build homes off Slade Green Road in the mid 1990s in return for providing the Ray Lamb Way relief road. Barratts built the Watermead Park estate on reclaimed marshland later in the decade. The railway depot is still Slade Green's major employer. The former Slade Green Secondary School now houses council offices. Slade Green junior and infant schools share neighbouring sites on Slade Green Road. The latest reports by the national educational standards agency Ofsted speak of an 'area of substantial material hardship' and state that Czech and Turkish are the most commonly spoken languages after English. By the end of the 20th century the locality was suffering from neglect but the council has recently invested in environmental improvements.

✉ Erith DA8

🚆 South Eastern Trains (zone 6)

📖 Edward Thomas, *Slade Green and the Crayford Marshes*, Bexley Local Studies and Archive Centre, 2001

@ www.sladegreen.org (community site); www.sladegreen.com (commercial local information site)

Sloane Square · *Kensington & Chelsea*

Now seen as the 'gateway to the KING'S ROAD', Sloane Square was laid out in the late 1780s as part of the HANS TOWN development. Both the town and the square were named after landowner Hans Sloane. The square functioned as a service provider for the new district, with stables, sheds, workshops, bakehouses and some accommodation for staff. In 1868 the Metropolitan District Railway Co. opened Sloane Square station and in 1877 Peter Jones took over a drapery establishment at this end of the King's Road that quickly grew to occupy a series of disconnected buildings. The store was unified into a single grand emporium during the redevelopment of Hans Town in the late 1880s, which also saw the construction of the Royal Court Theatre on the site of the former Court Theatre. These changes to the square's perimeter resulted in roughly the current layout, except that the roads then met at a central crossroads. In the early years of the 20th century many of the surviving houses from the first phase of the square's existence were demolished and replaced, including a philanthropic dispensary that had stood on the south side, now the site of a branch of Boots. A circulatory traffic system was introduced in 1929, and the centre of the square was paved over. The present Peter Jones store opened in 1937 to widespread architectural acclaim for its pioneering use of curtain-walling; it has recently been extensively modernized. Sloane Square station was rebuilt in 1940, only to be destroyed in an air raid within a year. In 1948 the Royal Academy endowed the square with a fountain in recognition of the contribution of CHELSEA to London's artistic life. Council proposals to restore the square's original crossroads layout were withdrawn in 2007, following negative public reaction.

The Royal Court Theatre is regarded as England's foremost home for new playwrights. It has staged works by Bertolt Brecht, Eugène Ionesco, Samuel Beckett, Jean-Paul Sartre, Arnold Wesker and, perhaps most influentially of all, John Osborne's *Look Back in Anger* in 1956. The term 'Sloane Ranger' was coined in the 1980s to denote rich young women who affect a country look in the metropolis.

> ⊠ SW1; SW3

> 🚊 Circle Line; District Line (zone 1)

> @ www.royalcourttheatre.com

Smitham • *Croydon* (pronounced as in 'with 'em')

A station in COULSDON. The name was first recorded in 1331 as Smetheden, and derives from words meaning 'smooth valley'. The floor of the valley was known as Smitham Bottom and was a desolate area in the 18th century, a haunt of highwaymen and a place of encampment for Gypsies. The Red Lion inn was in existence by 1735 and cricket matches and prize fights were later held on Lion Green. To the south-west Portnalls Farm was acquired in 1878 as the site for the New Surrey Lunatic Asylum, subsequently known as Cane Hill, and a few houses were built at Smitham soon afterwards. When a station opens in a thinly populated place it usually bestows its name on the settlement that grows up around it. If not, the station's name is changed to match its new catchment area. But when the railway arrived here in 1904 the ensuing township borrowed the identity of the established village of Coulsdon, which now calls itself OLD COULSDON and yet the station's name has remained unchanged. However, Croydon council has recently proposed that the station should be renamed Coulsdon to 'reinforce the identity' of the district. Apart from the station, Smitham's name is used only by the well-regarded Smitham Primary School.

> ⊠ Coulsdon CR5

> 🚊 Southern (zone 6)

Smithfield • *City*

Properly known as West Smithfield, this is the home of London's main wholesale meat market and of Bart's Hospital, located just west of the BARBICAN. The Romans used this 'smooth field' as a cemetery in the 3rd and 4th centuries and it was later the site of public executions, including the burning of witches and martyrs. The priory church of St Bartholomew the Great and an adjoining hospital were established in 1123 by Rahere, who is sometimes described as a court jester but was 'more of a priest than a fool', as Rudyard Kipling put it. Both institutions survive today, though nothing remains of the hospital's original building and only a little of the church's. Bartholomew's Fair was held annually from 1133. The event, which began on St Bartholomew's day (24 August) and lasted for several days, was the national market for the sale of cloth. Oxen were sold here from 1305 and the Corporation of London gained the right to collect market tolls from 1400, although it was not until 1638 that a formal charter was granted. Cattle were driven here from as far away as the Isle of Skye in Scotland. Geese waddled from Norfolk wearing little cloth shoes on their feet. The agricultural revolution of the 18th century brought extraordinary developments in animal fattening techniques. In 1795 the average carcass sold at Smithfield weighed twice what it had done in 1710. The scale of operations at the livestock market created an increasingly hazardous public nuisance but self-interested parties long resisted relocation to a more suitable site. Finally, the Smithfield Market Removal Act of 1852 moved the trade in live animals to COPENHAGEN Fields. Had the law not intervened market forces would have, because the growth of the railways was making it increasingly viable to bring in farm-killed meat. Bartholomew's Fair was suppressed in 1855 and Smithfield's street pattern was reconfigured, focused on new central buildings for the market. These have since been refurbished to bring them up to European Union hygiene standards – all very different from the picture of 'filth and mire' conjured up by Dickens in *Oliver Twist*. Smithfield is the only significant wholesale market that has not relocated outside the City and meat is delivered by refrigerated trucks that are barely able to negotiate the narrow streets. In 1994 the Court of Appeal ruled that the

Corporation owns Smithfield whether or not it is used as a market, and thus the possibility remains that the butchers will be displaced so that more profitable use can be made of the site.

The Scottish nationalist William Wallace was executed at Smithfield in 1305, and Wat Tyler, who led the Peasants' Revolt, was stabbed to death here by the Lord Mayor of London in 1381. The artist William Hogarth was christened at St Bartholomew's Church in 1697. Ben Jonson's most famous work, *Bartholomew Fair*, was written about the rogues he met at Smithfield. The poet John Betjeman had a home in Cloth Fair from 1955. He moved out in 1977, when he had finally had enough of the din of Smithfield's juggernauts.

✉ EC1

📖 Alec Forshaw, *Smithfield Past and Present*, Robert Hale, 1990

Snaresbrook • *Redbridge*

An elegant and well-preserved residential locality in north-west WANSTEAD, seven miles from central London. The name was first recorded in its present form in 1599; its first part is of uncertain origin, although it could be connected with the use of snares for trapping animals or birds in Epping Forest. The stream that gave the village its name is no longer visible above ground. Snaresbrook evolved as a coaching halt on the road to Epping in the late 17th century, when horses were changed at the Spread Eagle. The present Eagle Hotel is of early-18th-century origin and is the oldest inn in Wanstead. A detached portion of Epping Forest survives near Eagle Pond, formerly Snares Pond. Most of Snaresbrook's Georgian houses were built along the east side of Hollybush Hill, which still has its hollies. In 1843 Leopold I, King of the Belgians, opened the infant orphan asylum, which subsequently became the Royal Wanstead School and is now Snaresbrook Crown Court. Snaresbrook station opened in 1856 on the Loughton branch of the Eastern Counties Railway. The Merchant Seamen's Orphan Asylum was built in 1862 and later served as a convent and then a hospital. The New Wanstead estate was laid out south of the station and the remainder of the area filled out during the rest of the century, culminating with the Drive estate, which was begun in 1896. The railway line was electrified in 1947, when it became part of the Central Line. A conservation area stretches all the way along Hollybush Hill and Woodford Road into SOUTH WOODFORD. Snar-

esbrook has relatively few young families. Pensioner households outnumber those with dependent children, a reversal of the national norm.

✉ E11

🚶 10,854

🚇 Central Line (zone 4)

Soho • *Westminster*

Arguably London's most vibrant place, and long-time centre of 'alternative' mores, this compact commercial quarter is bounded on the west, north and east by REGENT STREET, OXFORD STREET and CHARING CROSS ROAD. In the south, CHINATOWN forms a less well-defined border. Soho now encompasses the entire area once known as Kempsfield, of which it was originally just a part. Its name is said to derive from a cry similar to 'tally-ho', for this was a hunting ground in the 16th century. Built up after 1679 by the speculative builder Richard Frith, Soho at first attracted aristocrats but soon provided a haven for Greek Christians and Huguenots fleeing religious persecution. The House of St Barnabas was established on Greek Street in 1846 as a refuge for homeless women. German, Italian and Hungarian radicals came to Soho after the failed revolutions of 1848. Some of these migrants opened restaurants specializing in their national cuisine, attracting London's bohemian community from the early part of the 20th century and especially in the 1930s and 1940s. After World War II, Soho became notorious as the WEST END'S red-light district. Legislative changes have pushed prostitution off the street corners and into dingy upstairs flats, but various sex-related enterprises persist at street level. In 1959 the tenor saxophonist Ronnie Scott founded a jazz club on Gerrard Street, which moved to its present site at 47 Frith Street in 1965. On Soho's western side, CARNABY STREET gained worldwide fame in the 1960s as the heart of 'swinging' London. Since the late 1980s, gay Soho has been focused on OLD COMPTON STREET. Soho is home to advertising, media and film distribution companies (especially on Wardour Street) and is famed for its pubs and clubs, a declining proportion of which are colourfully seedy. As well as the sex shops, there are boutiques specializing in fashion accessories, while Berwick Street has a traditional outdoor market. A small but active residential community struggles to prevent Soho's transformation into a zone of continuous commotion. The council's attempt to pedestrianize much of Soho in 1999 was abandoned after just six months and its streets have returned to their normal traffic-clogged state. Golden Square and Soho Square have the only green spaces, the latter graced by a 17th-century statue of Charles II and a charming gardeners' shed of Victorian origin that pretends to be even older. The perimeter of Soho Square has a French Protestant church, St Patrick's Roman Catholic Church and the headquarters of the Football Association, while Soho Street has a Radha Krishna temple and Govinda's restaurant. The Soho Jazz Festival, held annually at the beginning of October, is probably the biggest event of its kind in the country.

Some London districts are lucky to have played home to a single obscure 'celebrity', whose fame often needs elucidation. Soho's truly legendary residents are so numerous that there is space here only to mention the names of Canaletto, Casanova, Hogarth, Blake, Mozart, Constable and Marx. John Logie Baird constructed and demonstrated his 'televisor' at 22 Frith Street. Colin MacInnes's novel *Absolute Beginners* is arguably *the* great Soho story, although the same cannot be said of the film.

✉ W1

📖 Judith Summers, *Soho*, Bloomsbury, 1991; Murray Goldstein, *Naked Jungle: Soho Stripped Bare*, Reynolds and Hearn, 2005

@ www.thesohosociety.org.uk; www.ronniescotts.co.uk

Somers Town • *Camden* (pronounced 'summers town')

Sandwiched between EUSTON and ST PANCRAS stations, Somers Town has been transformed several times in its 200-year existence. At the end of the 17th century Sir John Somers, appointed Lord Chancellor and created Baron Somers of Evesham in 1697, acquired the local freehold. The arrival of the New Road (now Euston Road) improved access to the area and in 1793 a Frenchman, Jacob Leroux, leased land from the Somers family for building. His scheme was not as profitable as he had hoped because war and recession forced down the value of property, and the neighbourhood soon acquired a 'shabby genteel' status. Refugees from the French Revolution bought some of the houses. No. 29 Johnson Street, now Cranleigh Street, was the home of the young Charles Dickens when it was newly built in 1824. The construction of the great railway

termini in the mid 19th century brought in thousands of labourers, while many residents were displaced by the clearance of four acres for St Pancras station and the subsequent establishment of a goods depot in 1875. Some were resettled in homes built for them by the Midland Railway. The depot's site is now occupied by the British Library. This massive red brick building, designed by Colin St John Wilson, opened in 1998 after years of controversy and delays, allowing the Library to move its headquarters and core collection into a separate home from the British Museum. Inside, it is more inspiring than one might guess from the rather brutal exterior. In front of the library is a large piazza, with a bronze statue of Isaac Newton and an amphitheatre that is occasionally used for outdoor events. Most of the streets behind the library are now filled with late 20th-century council housing. The residential mix is multi-ethnic, with an especially strong Bangladeshi presence.

In 1830, Somers Town saw the first-ever Metropolitan Police fatality when PC Joseph Grantham was kicked to death while trying to break up a street fight. In 2004, Somers Town became London's first 'good behaviour zone' in a scheme introduced by Camden council using powers under the newly introduced Anti-Social Behaviour Act.

✉ NW1

👥 12,490 (St Pancras and Somers Town ward)

📖 Malcolm J Holmes, *Somers Town: A Record of Change*, London Borough of Camden, 1985; Steven Denford and F Peter Woodford (ed.), *Streets of St Pancras: Somers Town and the Railway Lands*, Camden History Society, 2002

@ www.bl.uk (the British Library)

South Acton • *Ealing*

The most deprived part of the ACTON sprawl, dominated by the post-war South Acton estate. South Acton was farmland until the 1859 enclosure award but thereafter began one of the most intensive phases of development seen in the London area at that time. The British Land Co. acquired several fields and laid out a network of terraced streets. Thousands of new Londoners arrived from all over the British Isles in search of a job and an affordable home. Many men were employed as labourers in nearby brickfields while their wives worked in Acton's burgeoning laundry industry, either for one of the larger concerns of 'Soapsuds Island' or taking in washing at home. South Acton gained a railway station in 1880 on what is now the North London line, and a Tube station in 1905, on a short spur line from AC-TON TOWN. By this time the settlement had a population of 15,000, many of whom were living in increasingly overcrowded surroundings. Conditions barely improved throughout the first half of the 20th century. It was not until after World War II that the municipal authorities acted to clear the slums. The council compulsorily purchased all the properties on streets that lay immediately north of South Acton station and began to replace these with blocks of flats, the first of which were completed by 1954. South Acton Tube station closed in 1959. More blocks of flats went up in the early 1960s, including two of 22 storeys. These subsequently exhibited many of the problems typical of such projects, and some have since been demolished as part of a major regeneration programme involving several housing associations. Two-thirds of South Acton's residents are white and the main ethnic minority is of black African (especially Somali) descent. Most homes are rented, primarily from the council or privately.

Until 1988, Harlech Tower, in Park Road East, doubled as Peckham's Nelson Mandela House in the classic television comedy series *Only Fools and Horses*.

⊠ W3

♁ 13,318

🚋 Silverlink Metro (zone 3)

Southall • *Ealing* (pronounced 'south-all')

A primarily Asian residential and commercial district, separated from HAYES to the west by the Grand Union Canal and from HANWELL to the east by the River Brent. Southall was first mentioned in 1198 and the early hamlet seems to have grown up around SOUTHALL GREEN. This remained a rural part of the manor of Norwood even after the cutting in 1796 of the Grand Junction (now Grand Union) Canal and the opening of Southall station in 1839. In the second half of the 19th century the main change to the landscape was the appearance of brickfields, with cottages for their labourers. Widespread development did not begin until the 1890s, with factories flanking the railway line. As in other parts of the borough, it was the arrival of affordable and convenient electric trams in the early years of the 20th century that brought a surge in suburban housebuilding. By 1944 overcrowding was said to have reached 'acute' proportions but recommendations that industrial development should cease were not followed. From the late 1950s onwards, Asian immigrants began to settle in Southall. Its proximity to HEATHROW and the availability of work in local factories were both influential factors, but the subsequent escalation has been a snowball phenomenon that could have happened almost anywhere. Punjabis are the main ethnic sub-group and the principal religion is Sikhism, but there are also many Hindus and Muslims, from East Africa, Pakistan and Bangladesh. Around the vibrant central shopping areas of the Broadway and South Road over three-quarters of the residents are now of Asian origin. Southall gained a reputation as the Asian community's equivalent of BRIXTON with the racist murder of Gurdip Singh Chaggar in 1976, the death of the protester Blair Peach following a National Front meeting in 1979 and the Southall riots of 1981. Comparative calm subsequently descended, although there has been internecine political violence, including the murder of a Sikh newspaper editor in 1994. As wealthy Indians move out to leafier suburbs, new ethnic groups are taking their place, including Somalis and, most recently, Afghan Sikhs. The Sri Guru Singh Sabha Gurdwara, on Havelock Road, is the largest Sikh temple outside India. Havelock Road is named after Sir Henry Havelock, a British general who distinguished himself in the Afghan and Sikh Wars in the 1830s and 1840s and played a leading role in suppressing the Indian Uprising in 1857–8, and some campaigners have suggested that the road should be renamed. On Glade Lane, in the midst of Southall's industrial district, is London's only independent steam railway centre, run by volunteers from the Great Western Railway Preservation Group.

The unsuccessful 2003 gangster movie *Triads, Yardies and Onion Bhajees*, subtitled *Once Upon A Time In Southall*, updated the 'legend' of 1980s Asian gang the Holy Smokes.

⊠ Southall UB1 and UB2

♁ 64,470 (Dormers Wells, Lady Margaret, Norwood Green, Southall Broadway and Southall Green wards)

🚋 First Great Western Link; Heathrow Connect (zone 4)

📖 Jonathan Oates, *Southall and Hanwell*, Tempus, 2002

@ www.southall.co.uk (business and community site); www.southallbid.co.uk (Southall business improvement district site); www.gwrpg.co.uk (GWR Preservation Group site)

Southall Green • *Ealing*

The core of the early village of SOUTHALL, flanking the road now called King Street to the south and the Green to the north. The manor house was built (or rebuilt) in 1587 and although it has since been altered and restored, it remains the most authentic survival of its kind in London. The village at Southall Green had grown to significant proportions by the end of the 18th century, when 33 houses were in existence. The appearance of the area was altered when the railway cut across to the north in the late 1830s but factories and houses did not begin to crowd in until much later in the century. By the mid 1890s Southall Green was the most densely populated area in the district and its early cottages were soon rebuilt as the pressure for factory workers' accommodation mounted. The council acquired the manor house in 1913, eventually restoring the building and using it as offices. A feasibility study in 2005 recommended against opening a centre for culture, diversity and heritage in the manor house and its future use has yet to be decided. The manor house grounds are open to the public in daylight hours and have yew trees and a mulberry tree said to have been planted by Henry VIII. The vicinity of the green is sometimes now referred to as Old Southall. Two-thirds of the residents of the Southall Green ward are Asian or Asian British, of whom the great majority are of Indian descent.

✉ Southall UB2

👥 12,895

South Bank • *Lambeth*

A Thames-side cultural quarter situated opposite the Victoria EMBANKMENT, attracting over six million visitors every year. After the marshes were drained at the beginning of the 18th century, the area successively became home to a pleasure garden, LAMBETH waterworks and the Lion brewery. Work on the construction of County Hall, the home of the London County Council (LCC) and its successor the Greater London Council, began in 1912 and it was opened in 1922, with extensions added later. Since the abolition of the GLC, County Hall has been converted to provide hotel accommodation, and is also home to the London Aquarium and an art gallery specializing in the work of Salvador Dali. At the opposite end of the South Bank, the Oxo Tower was built in 1930 in art deco style, with the word 'Oxo' spelt out in the shape of its windows to dodge restrictions on riverside advertising. The tower now boasts an expensive restaurant. Between these two landmarks lay a derelict industrial wasteland that the LCC proposed to develop on a monumental scale. The Royal Festival Hall was built for the 1951 Festival of Britain, together with an array of attractions like the Dome of Discovery and the Skylon. The temporary structures were replaced by the Shell Buildings and a series of arts venues in the 1950s and 1960s. The National Theatre contains three auditoria: the Olivier, Lyttelton and Cottesloe theatres. The National Film Theatre hosts a repertory programme aimed mainly at serious cineastes. The Queen Elizabeth Hall is a concert venue, grouped with the Purcell Room and Hayward Gallery, completed by the Greater London Council in 1968. Areas below this complex are a prime destination for skateboarders and roller-bladers. South-west of the arts complex the Jubilee Gardens were laid out in 1977 and now possess the capital's most successful recent tourist attraction, the London Eye. This 443-foot-high observation wheel was intended as a temporary attraction when it opened at the end of 1999, but was so successful that a 25-year extension to its lease was granted in 2006. Behind ITV's London Studios, the Coin Street project is a complex of housing association homes, small shops, community offices, bars and cafés. Gabriel's Wharf has designer-maker workshops, restaurants and temporary exhibitions. The aesthetic overhaul of the South Bank's main cultural venues has been the subject of prolonged debate, but despite the intermittent unveiling of grand designs it is unlikely that money will be found to make radical changes in the near future.

Feliks Topolski's mural of 20th-century events is painted on panels mounted in three railway arches under the approach to Hungerford Bridge. The Banners project lined the streets of the South Bank with 66 banners, each 20 feet high, which are illuminated at night.

✉ SE1

🚢 Festival pier

@ www.london-se1.co.uk (community site); www.southbanklondon.com (arts events site)

South Barnet • *Barnet*

An infrequently used name for the far south-

449

eastern corner of Barnet, bordering South-gate's OSIDGE. It was formerly also known as Sans or Sarnes Barnet – that is, 'without (meaning 'outside') Barnet'. A delightful alternative version was Sarnets Barnet. During the 12th century the Bishop of London gave South Barnet to the Order of the Hospital of St John of Jerusalem, as part of its holdings at FRIERN BARNET. The endowment was confirmed by King John in a charter of 1199. When suburban development began in the early 20th century South Barnet gained its own church, St Michael's, on the BRUNSWICK PARK estate. In 1972 the parish was broken up and incorporated into the four neighbouring parishes. The church was demolished and in 1977 the Church Commissioners cleared the site and sold the land for housing. Thus ended the independent history of South Barnet; most locals now consider their home to be in EAST BARNET or Brunswick Park. The area is relatively prosperous and a high proportion of households has access to a car or two. When Parkside Gardens and Brookside South were made part of the new No. 382 bus route in 2003, more than 200 residents signed a petition opposing the service.

✉ Barnet EN4

South Beddington • *Sutton*

Despite its (little-used) name, this is generally considered to be WALLINGTON's south-eastern quadrant. The evolution of the Church of England's places of worship here illustrate the fits and starts by which South Beddington developed after the railway arrived in Wallington. When the first church was erected on Sandy Lane in 1872 it was not said to be in South Beddington but in BANDON HILL, such was the infancy of the new locality. St Michael and All Angels was a high Anglican daughter church of St Mary's Church, BEDDINGTON. The decision early in the 20th century to pull down the wooden church and replace it with a brick-built structure smacks almost of hubris, for it was an elegant and capacious edifice – a far cry from the tin shacks that had been erected in some other new suburbs. Indeed, the old church was sold to a parish in Nottingham (for a sixth of its initial cost), where it was reassembled and stood for another 60 years. Bandon Hill Infants' (later Primary) School took over the Sandy Lane site. The new St Michael's Church was built on Milton Road and now claimed the growing South Beddington as its parish. Construction began in 1906 and the church opened the following year, al-

though it was unfinished; money had run out and the architect's intentions could not be fully realized. The church was finally completed in the 1920s by the same architect, but to a design that still fell short of his original plan. South Beddington was transformed by the creation of the ROUNDSHAW council estate in the 1970s. St Paul's Church is an ecumenical daughter church of St Michael's, recently rebuilt as part of the estate's regeneration programme.

✉ Wallington SM6

♟ 10,423 (Beddington South ward)

@ www.st-michaels-beddington.org

South Bermondsey • *Southwark/Lewisham*

The south-eastern corner of BERMONDSEY, scarred by railway lines and trackside industry. South Bermondsey (originally Rotherhithe) station opened in 1866 on Rotherhithe New Road. The streets to the south-east were laid out from the end of the 1870s. The station was relocated to its present site between Ilderton Road and Bolina Road in 1928. Much of the area was redeveloped with council estates, industrial estates and trading estates during the mid 20th century. Lewisham council cleared the housing to the east of Bolina Road in the 1960s and created an open space called Senegal Fields, which was named after the longest of the lost roads. In 1993 this became the site of MILLWALL Football Club's stadium, the New Den, which has a capacity of 20,146. The club had previously played a quarter of a mile away at Cold Blow Lane. Southwark's South Bermondsey ward is relatively poor, with a low level of owner occupation and high numbers of single-parent and one-person households. Most residents do not have access to a car. The main ethnic minority is of Black African descent.

✉ SE16

♟ 11,631

🚆 Southern (zone 2)

@ www.millwallfc.co.uk

Southborough • *Bromley*

The south-eastern corner of the BROMLEY district, bordered to the east by PETTS WOOD. A house called South Barrow stood here from as early as the 17th century. By the mid 19th century the settlement had acquired a few more large houses and around 16 cottages. BICKLEY station was originally called Southborough when it opened in 1858, but confusion frequently arose with another Kentish village of the same name near Tunbridge Wells; present-day residents say that the Royal Mail makes the same mistake. South Barrow was altered and enlarged on several occasions in the second half of the 19th century and became Belmont School in 1901, catering for the 'daughters of gentlemen'. After the school's closure in 1922 the building became The Cloisters, an old people's home, and later served as an office of the War Damage Commission. It was demolished in 1954 and replaced by Birdham Close. Southborough Primary School is one of the few amenities to use the place name. This is a relatively large school and around 10 per cent of pupils are from ethnic minority backgrounds. Jubilee Country Park lies to the north-east of Southborough. During World War II the land was requisitioned from the West Kent Golf Club (which moved to HIGH ELMS) for use as gun emplacements and subsequently was let for grazing. In 1977 Bromley council decided to commemorate the Queen's silver jubilee by acquiring the 63-acre site for use as a park and opened it to the public four years later. As well as ancient London clay meadows, the park includes the oak woodlands of Thornet Wood and Blackbrook Wood.

✉ Bromley BR2 and BR1

Southborough • *Kingston*

HOOK's half-forgotten little sister, situated to the west of TOLWORTH. The name comes from Southborough Lodge, which took its name from the same 'barrow' that gave its name to BERRYLANDS. Thomas Langley built the house in 1808 on a bare part of SURBITON Common, when it was said that the only structure visible from it was Hampton Court. Soon afterwards the track that is now the A243 became a turnpike road and Southborough Gate was installed at the junction of the lane from Long Ditton to Ewell. Improved roads and the sale of some building plots brought Southborough's first population surge in the 1860s, with the construction of several grand villas. Among these was The Rhodrons, owned by law publisher Robert Norton Stephens, who funded a temperance meeting place for local working men. In the 1880s the tollgate was removed and the Southborough estate was broken up, with modern Tolworth taking shape on some of this land. In 1927 the Kingston bypass crossed Hook Road and a roundabout was constructed. This became the site for

Southborough's most prominent landmark, the Ace of Spades roadhouse, which incorporated a garage, a mock-Tudor restaurant built with timbers from the barn at Haycroft Farm, and a swimming pool that was demolished when the Hook underpass was constructed. The Ace of Spades was popular with visiting Americans, while locals preferred the Southborough Arms, which moved to larger premises in 1934 and is now the Cap in Hand. In the years before World War II, Southborough was fully suburbanized and most of its villas were demolished in the process. The shops of Ace Parade and Arcade Parade were constructed on the site of Haycroft House and on land that had belonged to The Rhodrons. Southborough Boys' School opened in 1963.

The newspaper magnate Lord Beaverbrook was an early customer of the Ace of Spades' repair shop in 1928 after his car collided with a lorry at the roundabout. The former world heavyweight boxing champion Max Baer set up his training camp at the Ace of Spades in preparation for two fights at HARRINGAY Arena in 1937.

✉ Surbiton KT6

South Bromley • *Tower Hamlets*

A little-used name (although still recognized by older residents) for the south-eastern part of BROMLEY-BY-BOW, which has been sliced and diced by communications improvements over three centuries. The small but elaborately ornamented Bromley Hall was built in the late 15th century as the manor house of Lower Bromley, perhaps for a courtier at Greenwich Palace, and radically remodelled soon after 1700. The house has since served as a calico printing works, gentleman's seat, charity home, carpet warehouse and most recently as offices. The construction in 1770 of a short canal called the Limehouse Cut separated South Bromley from its parent and the locality thereafter evolved as an extension of POPLAR. From the mid 19th century, factories were established beside Bow Creek with workers' housing further inland, focused on St Michael and All Angels' Church, which has since been converted to flats. Between 1864 and 1885 David McIntosh laid out compact but sturdy terraces to the east of St Leonard's Road, some of which survive today. McIntosh's Scottish origins show in the street names. Poplar gasworks and neighbouring Abbott Street date from the 1870s. John Abbott was a former chemist who also built at OLD FORD. Following extensive wartime damage, Poplar council began work on its Abbott estate in 1947 and from the 1950s to the 1970s the London County Council and its Greater London successor showered South Bromley with more flats. Many of the early estates have since been rebuilt on a less impersonal scale, although some were highly regarded in their time. The Northern Approach Road (A12) leading to the Blackwall Tunnel split South Bromley down the middle in the 1960s and its eastern half was further isolated by the construction of office blocks on the other side of the East India Dock Road in the 1990s.

The most notable of South Bromley's many blocks of flats is Ernö Goldfinger's 26-storey Balfron Tower of 1967. This was the first public housing project by the architect, whom Ian Fleming so disliked that he gave his name to a Bond villain.

> ✉ E14

Southbury • *Enfield*

An electoral ward and station in east ENFIELD, on the western fringes of PONDERS END. Southbury field was recorded in 1572 as covering 237 acres. The field was traversed by a footpath that was made into a public road in 1803, at first known as Nags Head Road but renamed Southbury Road later in the century when an eastward extension towards the River Lea was named Nags Head Road. In 1891 the Great Eastern Railway opened a new line to Cheshunt with a station at Southbury Road. With the arrival of electric trams on Hertford Road in 1909, passenger train services ceased. The following year Southbury Road itself was widened to take trams. After the construction of the Great Cambridge Road (A10) in 1924, factories were built in the vicinity of the station, including electrical equipment manufacturers. Housing began to fill out the area at around the same time, as Enfield and Ponders End expanded to meet each other here. The railway line was electrified in 1961, when the station was reopened as Southbury. In recent decades, superstores and a multiplex cinema have replaced several former industrial units. Nearly two-thirds of homes in the Southbury ward are owner-occupied and a third are one-person households. Educational attainment among the adult population is relatively low. At Southbury Primary School, 43 per cent of pupils speak English as an additional language, according to a 2001 report by the educational standards agency Ofsted; and pupil mobility is very high, which means that relatively few children start and finish their educa-

tion at the school. The proportion of children from disadvantaged backgrounds is much higher than average. Turkish, Kurdish and Bengali are the most common of the 20 first languages spoken.

> ✉ Enfield EN1 and EN3
> 🚶 12,466
> 🚉 'one' Railway (zone 5)

South Chingford • *Waltham Forest*

The area west of HIGHAMS PARK, stretching across to the River Lea and including, by some definitions, CHINGFORD MOUNT. It was by the river here that CHINGFORD probably began, with a group of Saxon huts supported on poles above the marshes. Excavation of a reservoir nearby revealed a primitive canoe, which is preserved in the British Museum. A Chingford Hall has stood in the vicinity for over 1,000 years; the present building dates from around 1840 and was converted to office use after World War II. In the mid 19th century, South Chingford consisted of just the hall, Chingford Mill, the Ferry House and three farms. There was a gradual build-up of housing in the area from the late 19th century, beginning at SUFFIELD HATCH, but significant construction of terraced housing did not take place until the 1930s, when South Chingford ceased to be a rural farming community. This was followed by industrial growth along the Walthamstow Avenue section of the North Circular Road (A406) and construction of the Chingford Hall council estate south of Maple Avenue. The estate suffered from a high crime rate in the 1980s but several of its high-rise blocks have since been demolished and a wide-ranging (and well-funded) social action programme has helped improve the residents' sense of security. It is now owned by a subsidiary of the Peabody Trust. South Chingford's best-known employer was the Durex condom factory, which closed in 1994.

> ✉ E4
> 🚶 10,680 (Valley ward)

South Croydon • *Croydon*

A relatively expensive residential part of CROYDON with ill-defined borders. The medieval manor of Haling Park covered 400 acres of the western side of the district. Elizabeth I granted the manor to Lord Howard of Effingham in 1592. Blunt House was built in 1759 to the east of South End, in a parkland setting. Nearby, a tollgate was set up on the Brighton road, at its junction with SELSDON Road. The turnpike road was heavily used by farmers bringing livestock to London, and Croydon cattle market was established in Drovers Road in 1848. The Haling Park estate was sold for building in 1850 and its northern part was laid out with winding avenues lined at discreet intervals with Italianate villas. The great majority of these have been replaced, often by flats, but those that survive comprise the Waldrons conservation area. St Peter's Church was built in 1851, to the design of Sir George Gilbert Scott, whose brother was to be the last resident of Blunt House. The church burned down while a spire was being added in 1864 and was rebuilt the following year, when South Croydon station opened. The subsequent growth of the district brought the destruction of most of its older buildings, and the Swan and Sugarloaf and Red Deer public houses were rebuilt on a grander scale. St Augustine's Church was consecrated in 1884. The WOODSIDE and South Croydon Railway opened in 1885 but was never a success, although it remained in existence for almost a century. Blunt House was demolished in 1889 and replaced by Aberdeen Road and Ledbury Road. In response to the southward expansion of the district, the council opened the Brighton Road (now South Croydon) recreation ground in 1895. Horse-drawn trams had terminated at the site of the old tollgate but from 1901 electric trams ran as far as the Royal Oak in PURLEY. South Croydon bus garage opened in 1915. The Whitgift School moved to Haling Park in 1931 and has since been progressively extended. Away from the school grounds, terraced and semi-detached houses filled the surviving open spaces or replaced Victorian mansions. The livestock market closed in 1935 and the market buildings were replaced by flats. In October 1947 a train crash at South Croydon killed 31 people. Since World War II, change in the area has mostly been limited to the subdivision of large houses into flats and the extension of smaller properties. At the Howard Primary School, on Dering Place, the majority of pupils come from ethnic minorities but this does not reflect the demographic profile of South Croydon as a whole.

The journalist and moralist Malcolm Muggeridge grew up in Birdhurst Gardens, the son of a Croydon Labour councillor. The actress Dame Peggy Ashcroft, known especially for her Shakespearean roles, was born at Tirlemont Road in 1907. She won an Oscar for her performance in the 1984 film *A Passage to India*, directed by Sir David Lean, born three months after her, just around the corner at 38

Blenheim Crescent. Lean's other film credits include *Brief Encounter* (1946), *The Bridge on the River Kwai* (1957), *Lawrence of Arabia* (1962), *Doctor Zhivago* (1965) and *Ryan's Daughter* (1970).

✉ South Croydon CR2 and CR0

🚃 Southern (zone 5)

📖 Ralph Rimmer, *South Croydon and Selsdon*, Tempus, 1994

@ www.whitgift.co.uk (Whitgift School site)

South Dagenham • Barking & Dagenham

A designation for the 'opportunity site' in the vicinity of DAGENHAM DOCK. Most of South Dagenham's 200 acres consist of land vacated by the Ford Motor Co. following the radical downsizing of its operations here. Four firms of consultant architects drafted proposals for the site in 2002, and one spoke of the potential for 'heroic change', recommending a very mixed development with zones of low- and high-density housing, retailing, offices and industry. It now seems likely that that the eastern and western halves of South Dagenham will be designed by separate firms but in the light of the scale of the opportunity and the need to co-ordinate with the evolving planning framework for the THAMES GATEWAY, the final form of the development remained undecided at the time of writing.

✉ Dagenham RM9

South Ealing • Ealing

A distinct community from EALING proper, South Ealing is centred on the twin hubs, one ancient and one modern, of its church and Tube station. In the Middle Ages, St Mary's Church was at the heart of Ealing itself and this area was known as 'the town', as opposed to 'the village' of LITTLE EALING, which lay further south. Around 1698 the old rectory at St Mary's became home to Great Ealing School, which evolved into one of London's finest educational institutions and survived for two centuries. St Mary's Church was rebuilt in 1740 after its medieval predecessor had fallen into a ruinous state. Described as 'a monument of Georgian ugliness', it was rebuilt again in 1860. By this time the Great Western Railway had arrived at Haven Green and Ealing's centre of gravity was shifting northward to the Uxbridge Road. South Ealing gained its own station in 1880 and the first homes for the lower middle classes began to appear. By 1894 the locality had electricity for homes and street lighting but it is an indication of its marginal position that the municipal authorities built an isolation hospital here after the outbreak of smallpox in 1902. The borough's first council houses were built in South Ealing in the following year – an attractive pair of terraces called Municipal Cottages. In 1907 the electrification of what became the Piccadilly Line gave builders the opportunity to begin the full-scale suburbanization of South Ealing. Today, local shops line both sides of South Ealing Road all the way down to the cemetery and the border with BRENTFORD, where there is some new housing. Although Little Ealing is still shown on maps, it has become lost within South Ealing as far as many residents are concerned.

Pupils at Great Ealing School included Cardinal Newman, the writers William Thackeray, Captain Marryat and T H Huxley, and the librettist W S Gilbert. During his years of exile in the early 19th century, Louis Philippe, king of the French from 1830 to 1848, taught geography and mathematics at the school.

✉ W5

🚊 Piccadilly Line (zone 3)

South End • *Camden*

A hamlet from Elizabethan times, South End now constitutes the south-eastern corner of HAMPSTEAD, in the vicinity of HAMPSTEAD HEATH station. South End (or Hoylands) Farm remained unaffected by the growth of Hampstead until 1854, when the farm was split in two by the Hampstead Junction Railway. The landowners, the dean and chapter of ST PAUL'S Cathedral, sold eight acres to the railway company for £7,000, leaving the hapless tenant farmer with two 16-acre remnants on either side of the line. The Ecclesiastical Commissioners took control of the farm in 1868 and the estate management company Cluttons began to exploit its building potential on their behalf. Starting in the south, plots were progressively sold off, although it was the northern part that was the first to be developed, mainly on account of its superior elevation. The local authority acquired the manorial waste at South End Green in 1874 and a local philanthropist donated the ornate drinking fountain here seven years later. Parliament Hill and Nassington Road were laid out in 1878, with properties that were relatively affordable by middle-class standards. Almost all of South End was built up by the close of the 19th century. Horse-drawn bus services for Hampstead used to terminate at South End Green, as did omnibuses until well into the 20th century. In

its first municipal housing project, Hampstead council built the flats of South End Close shortly after World War I, issuing bonds to help raise the £200,000 needed. The Royal Free Hospital relocated to Pond Street in 1974, but it was another four years before it was officially opened by The Queen. The hospital's performance is rated highly but the main building is a monstrosity. A £50-million makeover is currently under way to extend its working life by another 60 years.

The writer George Orwell lived in South End from 1934 to 1936 and worked at Booklovers' Corner, later a chess players' cafe, now a pizza takeaway. South End Green features in both John Wyndham's *Day of the Triffids* and John le Carré's *Smiley's People*.

✉ NW3

🚇 Silverlink Metro (Hampstead Heath, zone 3)

@ www.royalfree.nhs.uk

Southend • *Lewisham*

The last part of the borough to be built up, Southend's 16th-century name refers to its position in relation to LEWISHAM, which lies two-and-a-half miles to the north. In the 18th century Ephraim and John How used the water power of the Lower Mill on the River Ravensbourne to manufacture cutlery that was said to be the best in England, examples of which are held by the Victoria & Albert Museum. For most of its existence the Upper Mill ground corn for local farmers but it was also used for cutting wood and, by the late 19th century, for generating electricity. The village straddled a main route from Kent into London and mail coaches and farmers' wagons used to stop at the Green Man or Tiger's Head inns. Southend was home to some of Lewisham's most wealthy inhabitants, including the Forster family of Southend Hall, which stood just south of the junction of Whitefoot Lane and Bromley Road (A21). Henry Forster was a popular local figure in the early 20th century and, after 26 years' service as MP for Sevenoaks, he became the first MP for the borough of Bromley from 1918 until he was ennobled in 1919. Both his sons were killed in World War I and after the war Lord Forster gave part of his estate for the creation of a park in their memory. With the approach of Lewisham's suburban spread, the rich left for the more distant Kentish countryside and their large houses were converted to other uses. One became a hotel and another a mental hospital, while the Britannia Film Co.

bought Southend Hall for use as a studio. The extension of the tram network to Southend brought day-trippers from Lewisham, and the village was a resort for residents of the huge council estates built at DOWNHAM and BELLINGHAM in the 1920s. Lower Mill's pond was turned into a boating lake called Peter Pan's Pool. Private developers soon moved in on the village itself and its large houses gave way to much smaller ones. Many of the institutional buildings that had been provided for the old village and the interwar suburb were demolished in the 1980s and replaced by shops. Most of the recognizable fascias today tend to be those of 'limited range discounters'. The old millpond is now known as the 'Homebase pond', after the neighbouring DIY store.

Jack Cade, the leader of the Kentish rebellion of 1450, allegedly hid for a while on the island in the centre of the village pond, which may have been somewhat larger at that time.

⊠ SE6; Bromley BR1

Southfields • *Wandsworth*

This was the south field of WANDSWORTH's Lammas land, divided from its northern counterpart by the track that became WEST HILL. When the name was first recorded in 1247, the field occupied only the north-eastern quarter of the present settlement. The remaining area was shared between three manors, of which Wimbledon was much the largest. East and west Southfields developed at different speeds. In the west, Earl Spencer sold some building plots in 1836, allegedly to pay off gambling debts. Various styles of houses began to appear, mostly detached and with generous gardens. The success of WIMBLEDON PARK subsequently added impetus. As demand shifted towards more affordable properties, these villas were replaced within a century by terraced and semi-detached houses. In the east there was no preliminary villa stage. The opening of the station in 1889 prompted dense suburban housebuilding on former farmland, notably in the form of the Southfields grid. The process reached a peak in the early years of the 20th century, boosted by the electrification of the railway. At the consecration of the capacious St Barnabas Church in 1908 the Bishop of Southwark commented that Southfields had developed 'almost with mushroom growth'. This was the outer edge of the metropolitan conurbation at that time, and families moved here in search of a quasi-rural lifestyle. According to the *Daily Chronicle* in 1912, Southfields had the closest haystacks to central London. The last of the hayfields disappeared between the wars and light industrial units were set up near King George's Park. After World War II, private and council estates replaced most of the remaining villas. On the western edge of Southfields, the London County Council's Ackroydon estate of the early 1950s was Britain's first high- and low-rise mixed complex in a greenfield setting. It paved the way for the much larger ALTON estate at ROEHAMPTON, begun soon afterwards. Southfields has become increasingly popular with young professionals in recent years, a transformation manifested in trendier bars and specialist food shops.

Southfields station offers convenient access to the All England Lawn Tennis and Croquet Club, and shuttle bus services between the station and the grounds are laid on each summer during the fortnight of the Wimbledon tennis championships.

⊠ SW18; SW19

♀ 14,063

🚇 District Line (zone 3)

📖 Neil Robson, *Roomy Villas: The Story of Southfields Grid and its Surroundings*, self-published, 2000; Simon Catling, *The Changing Face of Southfields*, self-published, 1991

Southgate • *Enfield*

A 1930s dormitory suburb located two miles south-west of ENFIELD. The hamlet that grew up by the southern entrance to ENFIELD CHASE was first mentioned in 1370. The gate stood near the present site of the Tube station. Another settlement grew up along South Street, in the vicinity of Southgate Green. Much of the surrounding area was woodland at this time, providing a resource for the poor – and for the king, who owned the chase. Here on the edge of the chase several estates came into existence from the late Middle Ages, often with large houses at their hearts, and after the chase was enclosed in 1777 a similar process took place when this land was divided up among already wealthy knights and gentlemen. Southgate thus became known for its elegant mansions and the wealthy London merchants who owned them. This state of affairs persisted well into the 19th century, because of the absence of main roads, the hilly terrain that kept away the early railway builders and the disinclination of several of the larger estates' owners to sell their land. A few new streets were laid out after 1853 but speculative builders found few takers for the large houses they had started to erect and they soon desisted. By the outbreak of World War I Southgate was still essentially rural. After the war improvements in bus services brought some ripples of interest from potential commuters but it was the arrival of the Piccadilly Line in 1933 that really turned the tide. In the space of six years the area was almost entirely built up with houses and shopping parades, except for chunks of parkland that the enlightened council had acquired earlier. The few remaining gaps were rapidly plugged in the 1950s. Since then some larger houses have been replaced by flats. A relatively high proportion of properties in Southgate are privately rented. The northern ward of Southgate has significant Jewish and Chinese minorities while the southern ward of Southgate Green has large communities of Indian and Irish origin.

From the 15th century Grovelands was one of Southgate's grandest private estates. Its mansion was built in 1797 by John Nash for a Tottenham brewer and brandy merchant, with grounds landscaped by Humphry Repton. The estate ultimately became part of the Walker family's huge Southgate landholding, which also included ARNOS GROVE. Southgate council acquired part of the grounds as a public park just before World War I and the rest of the land was sold for building. The mansion became a military hospital and since 1985 has been the Grovelands Priory private clinic. The former Chilean dictator Augusto Pinochet controversially convalesced here in 1998.

✉ N14

👤 25,000 (Southgate and Southgate Green wards)

🚆 Piccadilly Line (zone 4)

📖 Alan Dumayne, *The Old Borough of Southgate*, Sutton, 1998

South Greenford · *Ealing*

More the name of a station than that of a true locality, and situated more to the east than the south of Greenford proper, on the northern edge of Perivale Park. South Greenford halt opened in 1926, much later than the other stations on the Greenford to Ealing line. The halt was conveniently situated for access to the Western Avenue (A40), which was then under construction. The council completed one of Greenford's earliest municipal estates on Cow Lane in 1935. The lane was renamed Cowgate Road a year later and Perivale Mater-

nity Hospital was built next door to the station in 1937. The hospital was demolished in the 1990s and the site is now occupied by the houses of Haymill Close. The sports ground to the south of Stockdove Way was formerly the site of Ealing Isolation Hospital.

✉ Greenford UB6

🚆 First Great Western Link (zone 4)

South Hackney · *Hackney*

A product of benign landowners and a by-product of VICTORIA PARK, which lies to its south and east. Until late in the 18th century South Hackney consisted of a cluster of houses and cottages surrounded by meadows, orchards, a brick-field and market gardens producing vegetables, flowers and seeds. The fields belonged to more than 60 different landowners, of whom the most dominant were the Cass and Norris families, followed by St Thomas's Hospital and the heirs of William Thompson of STAMFORD HILL. Leases at that time tended to be for 61 years and many came up for renewal in the 1780s, when the landlords began to lay out some streets for house-building. Construction quality varied considerably, descending at worst to the near shanty conditions of Hackney Bay, which may have been nicknamed in reference to the criminality of the Botany Bay penal colony, founded in Australia in 1788. Hackney Bay occupied the eastern part of the present Cassland Road. The leases next expired just as Victoria Park was being created and plots were auctioned subject to conditions intended to raise South Hackney's social profile. Speculative builders were slow to take advantage of the opportunity but the area was finally built up by the 1870s, except for the Lammas land at Well Street Common. Houses in the south and west were generally of higher quality than those in the north and east. During the 20th century some larger properties not protected by restrictive covenants were subdivided for multiple occupation or even converted into factories. Others were replaced from the 1930s onwards, often by municipal estates. The Kingshold estate became the largest – and most miserable – of these when it was extended after World War II (and prefixed 'New'). Most of this latter phase was demolished and rebuilt at the end of the 1990s. South Hackney is an ethnically mixed community that includes a well-established black minority of both Caribbean and African descent.

Jack Cohen, the Whitechapel-born founder of the Tesco supermarket empire, made his first sales from a hired barrow in Well Street market in 1919. The market still operates, with around 90 pitches specializing in clothing and food.

✉ E9

📖 Isobel Watson, *Gentleman in the Building Line: The Development of South Hackney,* Padfield, 1989

South Hampstead • *Camden*

Although street maps show South Hampstead as the area west of SWISS COTTAGE, the term is not widely used and might have faded from use altogether were it not for the presence of its station and the will of local estate agents. Some prefer to consider it part of WEST HAMPSTEAD. South Hampstead was built up in the late 19th century, to the west on land that had belonged to Kilburn Priory and to the east on the estate of the Maryon Wilsons, lords of the manor of Hampstead. The houses were often terraced or closely spaced but gardens were long and the streets wide and leafy. Among the architects was Banister Fletcher, who later created Brentford's Gillette factory. The London and North Western Railway opened Loudon Road station in 1879, and closed it in 1917. The original station building, which has not survived, was a picturesque wooden lodge with a pair of tall triple chimney stacks. Five years later the station reopened as South Hampstead, no longer served by mainline trains but by the electric trains of the New Line, which ran from EUSTON to QUEEN'S PARK. Many of South Hampstead's substantial properties have since been subdivided into flats. Several purpose-built blocks of flats and maisonettes were added in the 1960s, some by the council. South Hampstead Girls' School is located across the Finchley Road in Maresfield Gardens.

✉ NW6

🚌 Silverlink Metro (zone 2)

South Harefield • *Hillingdon*

A modern name for the part of HAREFIELD that lies south of St Mary's Church. By 1333 the Knights Hospitallers had established a cell at Moorhall, in what is now South Harefield. Harefield manor house was said to have stood south of the church, and to have been visited by Elizabeth I and John Milton before being burned down in 1660. A house called the Place (later Harefield Place) was built on the site around 1750 and was demolished in the 1810s. Far to the south, a station opened on the line

between WEST RUISLIP and Denham in 1928 but a proposed housing estate did not materialize owing to the landowner's financial difficulties and the station closed three years later. Greenbelt designation has restricted post-war development to the canal side of the main road, mostly north of Moorhall Road. Widewater Place is a courtyard-style office development built in 1991, with an impressive central water feature. Harefield Place nature reserve consists of two parcels of woodland that include parts of lake edges and two ponds. Park Lodge Farm is an educational centre and working farm run by Hillingdon council. Harefield Moor, with its dozen lakes, lies between Harvil Road and the River Colne, and is home to Hillingdon Outdoor Activities Centre.

✉ Uxbridge UB9 and UB10

South Harrow • *Harrow*

An amorphous district filling most of the southern tip of the borough. The opening of South Harrow station in 1903, together with other communications improvements, drew suburban housing into the area hitherto known as ROXETH and much of the land near HARROW and along Northolt Road was built up by the outbreak of World War I. Welldon Park School opened in response to the area's growth in population. Further west, Oxford's Christ Church college sold its farmland for building in 1931 and the prominent suburban housebuilder T F Nash built a substantial estate that spread from here to Rayners Lane. In an indication of the cachet of the Harrow name, SUDBURY Hill station was called South Harrow when it first opened and NORTHOLT PARK was called South Harrow and Roxeth. The South Harrow Piccadilly Line station was rebuilt at its present location in 1935. The parish of St Paul, South Harrow was created in 1937, with a strikingly modernist grey-brick church on Corbins Lane. The Roman Catholic parish of St Gabriel's, South Harrow was based in a temporary church that has never been replaced. After World War II, Harrow council built over 250 houses, flats and maisonettes, and added more homes in the 1960s. Although its borders are hard to define, South Harrow has a clear centre in the shops on Northolt Road, with a little market under the railway arches and a Waitrose supermarket that draws custom from a wide catchment area. The 21-acre Alexandra Park is the area's largest open space. South Harrow became increasingly ethnically diverse in the latter decades of the 20th century. At Welldon Park

Middle School pupils speak a total of 26 non-English languages.

Screaming Lord Sutch, leader of the Official Monster Raving Loony Party, was found dead at his South Harrow home in 1999. A post-mortem later confirmed that he had hanged himself after a long battle with depression.

> ✉ Harrow HA2

> 🚇 Piccadilly Line (zone 5)

South Hornchurch • *Havering*

A 20th-century working-class settlement situated to the north-west of RAINHAM, between the River Beam and the River Ingrebourne. From around the 13th century the district was dominated by the manors of Mardyke, Whybridge and Dovers. The latter took its name from a family that had been granted the town of Dover by William I, the Conqueror. In the early 17th century, Mardyke became the seat of Sir Sebastian Harvey, a lord mayor of London. Farmland and orchards ringed the manor houses, and cherries were among the local produce. A cherry fair was held annually until around 1800. The Cherry Tree public house was in existence by 1773, and Cherry Tree Lane formed part of the route to Rainham until it was bypassed by new roads following the opening of the docks in east London. The settlement began to expand in the late 19th century, with the first school opening in 1899, but it was not until the 1920s that a wave of housebuilding transformed the agricultural landscape. Plans to build 1,215 homes on 103 acres of Mardyke Farm were approved in 1925 and the same year saw a smaller development begin at Whybridge. The latter was a messy affair, with some of the construction failing to meet acceptable standards and Hornchurch council stepped in to take control. The Rainham builders Smith and Black bought and developed Dovers Farm in 1937. Just before its absorption within Havering, Hornchurch council built its first high-rise estate, at Mardyke, including six 12-storey blocks. Like much of the borough, South Hornchurch has a high proportion of white residents – nearly 95 per cent. Educational attainment is poor; 40 per cent have no qualifications, while only 7 per cent are qualified to degree level or above, about a third of the national average. South Hornchurch has a very high concentration of skilled manual workers. Brittons is a popular comprehensive school, drawing an increasing number of pupils from a growing area, including the neighbouring borough of Barking and Dagenham.

At the northern end of Rainham Road, Bretons is an 18th-century manor house built by a gentleman farmer on the ruins of a Tudor house and restored in 1975. In the grounds are a brick barn and walled garden.

> ✉ Rainham RM13

> 👥 12,592

> 📖 Frank Lewis, *A History of Rainham, with Wennington and South Hornchurch*, P R Davies, 1966

South Kensington • *Kensington & Chelsea*

South-west London's museum and academic quarter. The efforts of government minister Sir Henry Cole and the influence of Prince Albert drove the creation here of the Victorian age's finest expression of intellectual achievement. Using proceeds from the 1851 Great Exhibition, an 88-acre site was acquired on the edge of BROMPTON, streets were laid out and Sir William Cubitt began erecting the first art galleries, which were nicknamed 'the Brompton boilers' for their utilitarian appearance. These were taken down in the 1860s and parts were rebuilt in BETHNAL GREEN, where they now accommodate the Museum of Childhood. Prince Albert died in 1861 and the Albert Hall was built in his memory, opposite KENSINGTON GARDENS. The hall's neighbours on Kensington Gore include scientific institutions and arts and music colleges. The Natural History Museum brought the British Museum's rocks, fossils and skeletons to Cromwell Road in 1881. The Victoria and Albert Museum – originally a museum of manufacturing – was opened in its present form by Edward VII in 1909. The Science Museum followed in 1928. The Royal College of Science, the Royal School of Mines and the City and Guilds College became the Imperial College of Science and Technology in 1953. A 20-year expansion programme then produced most of the college's present buildings. The residential streets of South Kensington are lined with four- and five-storey stucco houses, many of which have been converted to flats, but remain unaffordable to most. Most of the properties are part of the Wellcome Trust and Thurloe estates, which stamp down hard on rogue leaseholders who paint their front doors pink. Each of the South Kensington museums is visited by between one and two million people annually. The Science Museum has Charles Babbage's calculating machine, Stephenson's *Rocket* and the Apollo 10 command module that made the first manned flight around the moon. The museum perhaps tries too hard for the 'wow' factor, while failing to make the most of its interactive technology. The Natural History Museum, by contrast, maximizes information and packs in far more exhibits. A £100-million Darwin Centre opened at the Natural History Museum in 2002. The magnificent Victorian and Edwardian buildings of the Victoria and Albert Museum contain the National Art Library and some of Britain's best collections of artefacts, including works in silver and glass as well as more mainstream materials. The V&A has striven to compensate for its staid-sounding name by becoming perhaps the 'coolest' of London's great museums. A 'FuturePlan' is presently under way, aiming to reintegrate the museum's disparate galleries.

Amid its other claims to fame South Kensington is also London's 'Little Paris', with francophone bookshops, doctors, dentists and other specialist services, as well as several French restaurants. The Institut Français, in Queensberry Place, hosts cultural events and presents (mainly) French films at the Ciné Lumière. The French Consulate is on Cromwell Road but the embassy is in Knightsbridge. *Ici Londres*, the magazine for London's French community, carries a cartoon strip entitled *South Ken' Boulevard*.

✉ SW7

🚇 Circle Line; District Line; Piccadilly Line (zone 1)

📖 Abigail Willis, *Museums and Galleries of London*, Metro Publications, 2005; *Blue Guide: Museums and Galleries of London*, Blue Guides, 2005

@ www.nhm.ac.uk (Natural History Museum); www.sciencemuseum.org.uk; www.vam.ac.uk (Victoria and Albert Museum)

South Kenton • *Brent*

A METROLAND station and its immediate vicinity in NORTH WEMBLEY. The locality is distinct from KENTON itself but merges imprecisely with PRESTON to its east. The South Kenton and Preston Park estate was laid out from 1927 and was completed soon after the opening of South Kenton station in 1933. Several firms of builders were involved in the project, including Fred and Charles Costin, who were responsible for most of the houses in Windermere Avenue. The estate was provided with its own park, school, shopping parades and pub. The Church of the An-

nunciation, South Kenton, was completed in 1938. Until the creation of the London Borough of Brent in 1965, South Kenton was part of the borough of Wembley, while the rest of Kenton lay within Harrow urban district. The church hall accommodates several local groups, including the South Kenton and Preston Park Residents' Association and the Windermere Nursery, which opened in 1987.

✉ Wembley HA9

🚇 Silverlink Metro; Bakerloo Line (zone 4)

@ www.skppra.co.uk (residents' association site)

South Lambeth • *Lambeth*

A densely built up locality, separated from its parent district by KENNINGTON, but increasingly overshadowed by VAUXHALL and STOCKWELL. South Lambeth was an extensive manor in the Middle Ages, stretching almost as far as MITCHAM. The manor was probably in the possession of the Crown for much of its existence, until it was absorbed within Vauxhall at the end of the 13th century. In the early 17th century the botanist John Tradescant acquired a three-acre plot and set up home here. Together with his son, Tradescant amassed an unrivalled collection of trees, shrubs and flowers, with an emphasis on species from the Americas. When the younger Tradescant died in 1662, the collection passed to the astrologer and alchemist Elias Ashmole. Ashmole built up a large estate in South Lambeth and later leased Tradescant's house, but he moved the botanical rarities to Oxford, where they formed the nucleus of the Ashmolean Museum. Several grand houses were built in South Lambeth during the 18th century, but only a few fragments of their walls remain today. One of the earliest industrial enterprises was the Beaufoy vinegar distillery, which moved here in 1810. The parts that survive are rated one of the best examples of early industrial building in the borough. Two developments in transportation stimulated the growth of South Lambeth as a residential district in the first half of the 19th century. The building of Vauxhall Bridge in 1816 linked South Lambeth Road with WESTMINSTER. Two decades later the Southampton Railway established its London terminus at NINE ELMS, and that area's subsequent industrialization stimulated a requirement for workers' housing nearby. Interwar and post-war municipal estates have since replaced many of the early dwellings, and most of the surviving 19th-century terraced houses are now in conservation areas.

✉ SW8

📖 Prudence Leith-Ross, *The John Tradescants: Gardeners to the Rose and Lily Queen*, Peter Owen, 1998

South Merton · *Merton*

A station in the southern part of MERTON PARK, not a distinct locality in its own right. This end of John Innes's landholdings remained almost entirely undeveloped until the opening of MORDEN station in 1926, when housing began to spread south of Martin Way. South Merton station opened in 1929 on the new line from WIMBLEDON, which was extended to SUTTON in the following year. Only a tiny ticket office was provided but a large concrete base was laid for the future construction of a proper station building, which has never been constructed. The vicinity was wholly built up by the mid 1930s, except for Mostyn Gardens, east of the station. This ten-acre park has a play area and an ornamental garden. A multi-sports court opened on the site of former tennis courts in 2004, after five years of planning and fundraising led by the youth pastor of Morden Baptist Church. The facility is linked to the neighbouring Poplar Primary School and is available for public use outside school hours.

✉ SW19; SW20; Morden SM4

🚇 Thameslink (zone 4)

South Norwood · *Croydon*

A densely built-up part of NORWOOD that evolved after the opening of a station at NORWOOD JUNCTION. The first references to this part of Croydon Common came in the mid 15th century, with an account of the rent for a coppice called Cholmerden, later the site of Goat House and nowadays of Sunny Bank. By 1678 Goat House stood in 19 acres of grounds. South Norwood lake was created at the beginning of the 19th century as a reservoir to feed the Croydon Canal. On the conversion of the canal to a railway line in the late 1830s, bridges were constructed at Goat House and Portland Road (A215). In 1848 just two wooden cottages stood in the High Street (A213) but development began soon afterwards in Portland Road and St Mark's Church was built on Albert Road in 1852. Construction began on the over-ambitious SELHURST PARK estate and large Italianate houses were built in the vicinity of St Mark's, of which a few survive, mostly conver-

ted to flats. The High Street was lined with shops in the early 1860s. From 1867, William Ford Stanley ran a factory in Belgrave Road, where he manufactured the mathematical, scientific and surveying instruments that he had invented. Stanley lived locally and in 1902 he endowed and designed the Stanley Halls and an adjacent technical trade school. In 1907 the people of South Norwood erected a clock tower in Station Road in honour of Stanley's golden wedding anniversary. Edwardian and half-timbered 1930s semi-detached houses and low-rise council houses filled out South Norwood over the course of the 20th century. South Norwood Country Park covers 120 acres to the south-east of the district and has wildflower meadows and wetland areas. Recent social issues have included shopkeepers' allegations that South Norwood is unduly affected by aggressive begging and residents petitioning to save a local petrol station from being replaced with flats on the grounds that it was the nearest thing they had to a community centre – a suggestion that reflected unjustly on the continuing role of the Stanley Halls. Over a fifth of South Norwood's residents are black or black British, most of Caribbean descent.

From 1891 to 1894 Sir Arthur Conan Doyle lived at 12 Tennison Road, where he wrote 21 Sherlock Holmes stories after he had given up medical practice to pursue his writing career. Punk rocker Captain Sensible went to Stanley Tech on South Norwood Hill, according to his song *Croydon*, a track from the album *Women and Captains First*.

✉ SE25

👥 14,590

🚇 Southern; South Eastern Trains; Thameslink (Norwood Junction, zone 4); East London Line from 2010

South Quay · *Tower Hamlets*

An ever-expanding Docklands development located on the southern side of the former West India Docks, with road access from Marsh Wall. Until regeneration began in the 1980s the quayside was occupied by warehouses storing produce from the Far East. The first phase of Richard Seifert's South Quay Plaza was completed in 1987 and, as Peterborough Court, was home to the *Daily Telegraph* until it moved to CANARY WHARF in 1992. Despite favourable early indications that encouraged developers' ambitions, South Quay has had a chequered history. Receivers were called in during an earlier phase of development after lack of interest from potential tenants, and floor space was offered at less than a quarter of CITY OF LONDON prices but uptake was still slow. In February 1996 the IRA broke its 18-month ceasefire with a massive truck bomb at Marsh Wall, causing two deaths and up to a £100 million-worth of damage to property. Much of the bomb site lay dormant until work began in 2001 on the Millennium Quarter, a 50-acre mixed development co-ordinated by the London Borough of Tower Hamlets, which will include a rebuilt station, commercial premises, thousands of residential units – of which more than a quarter will be 'affordable' – a hotel, shops, restaurants, and new leisure and community facilities. The Quarter will not be completed until around 2016 and aspects of its final form have yet to be determined.

✉ E14

🚆 Docklands Light Railway, Lewisham branch (zone 2)

South Ruislip · *Hillingdon*

A sprawling residential and industrial area situated more to the south of EASTCOTE than of RUISLIP, but considered an integral part of the latter by most residents. Ralph Deane created Bourne Farm here sometime in the 1810s. A century later the farm was almost chosen as the site for an airfield, but an alternative location to the south-west was chosen and NORTHOLT aerodrome was born. South Ruislip remained almost entirely farmland until the opening of the station (at first called Northolt Junction) in 1908. Ralph Hawtrey Deane sold two of his fields to British Freehold in 1910, and more land the following year. The first shops were built around 1912 on Station Approach. Some of the earliest homes in South Ruislip were poorly constructed, prompting the council to adopt a plan that sought to regulate building quality. Thereafter, a succession of land development companies acquired additional plots from the Deane family and began a sequence of housebuilding that was to proceed continuously for over 50 years, interrupted only by the two world wars. This was supplemented by industrial growth in the 1950s. From 1951 to 1966 a United States Air Force base oversaw tactical air operations and provided logistical support to the Seventh Air Division. The site of the base is now occupied by the Victoria retail park, near the Queensmead Sports Centre. South Ruislip is becoming increasingly multi-ethnic, and is proving especially popular with families of Indian descent. The local residents' association is one of the strongest in London, with around 4,500 members.

✉ Ruislip HA4

👤 10,823

🚆 Chiltern Railways (limited service); Central Line (zone 5)

@ www.srra.org.uk (residents' association site)

South Shoreditch · *Hackney*

More of an administrative term than a recognized locality, South Shoreditch represents roughly the part of the borough of Hackney that lies south of OLD STREET. This has been a bustling area since Elizabethan times, when it was the site of nurseries and leisure destinations such as beer gardens and theatres. Charitable religious foundations set up institutions and almshouses here. London started to expand across the surviving fields of South Shoreditch from around 1720, attracting support industries for the City. In the 19th century, large-scale and noxious factories moved away to more rural sites, leaving craftsmen who specialized in furniture and printing. South Shoreditch is now home to contemporary business sectors that include hospitality and catering, multimedia, fashion and product design. For the most part, the old warehouses and workshops have proved remarkably adaptable to changes of use dictated by the evolving needs of City customers. However, a number of these premises were demolished and replaced by office blocks late in the 20th century, some time after such strategies had been discredited in residential situations. Accusations were levelled at Hackney council that its motive in allowing this 'clean sweep' solution was simply to gain an increase in rateable value per square foot. The Hackney Society argued for special measures of the kind that had fostered the rejuvenation of Birmingham's jewellery quarter. The council made South Shoreditch a conservation area in 1991 and published a supplementary planning document in 2006 that seeks to maintain the area's special character while promoting its economic vibrancy.

✉ EC2

📖 Michael Hunter et al, *South Shoreditch: A Survey of Historic, Industrial and Commercial Buildings with a Strategy for the Area*, Hackney Society, 1986

South Street • *Bromley*

Although it still appears on maps, South Street is really a lost hamlet, renamed WESTERHAM HILL in the early 1920s. The original name dated from the 18th century and referred to its position south of BIGGIN HILL on the road to Westerham. The name fell out of favour because it was overly generic. Like other villages hereabouts, South Street's principal crop was strawberries, grown on a dozen farms and sold at COVENT GARDEN. The other crops were grown for feeding to horses; South Street staged an annual horse show and its stud farm bred bloodstock. Changes in land use caused a decline in the demand for agricultural labour and consequent rural depopulation. The village post office and shops have gone but the Fox and Hounds public house remains, catering to a wide catchment area. South Street Baptist Chapel was founded in 1887, but succumbed to 'Westerhamization' and changed its name after World War II. The chapel's history provides some indication of the ups and downs of the community. It had to be rebuilt in 1911 to accommodate a growing congregation, and the old building was converted into a schoolroom. It became a church in 1932 and a church hall was added in 1960. Thereafter, attendance began a steady decline.

✉ Westerham TN16

South Teddington • *Richmond*

The part of TEDDINGTON bordering BUSHY PARK, and merging with HAMPTON WICK to its south. There were no buildings here at all until the opening of Hampton Court gasworks on Sandy Lane in 1851. Soon afterwards, John Langdon-Down founded Normansfield Hospital on the Kingston Road. Langdon-Down carried out groundbreaking work on the diagnosis and treatment of learning disabilities and described the physical and mental features associated with a condition that became called mongolism, and which is now known as Down's syndrome. After the railway reached Teddington in 1863 this area developed so rapidly that it was given the name New Found Out. Sadly, the more prosaic present name soon replaced it. Anglican and Roman Catholic church schools were founded in 1865 and 1884 respectively. At the latter, the ground floor served as the school and the upper floor as a chapel until the Church of the Sacred Heart of Jesus was built in Kingston Road in 1893. By the end of the century housing had spread south of Bushy Park Road, with scat-

tered dwellings reaching north along the Kingston Road. The present St Mark's Church replaced a Victorian mission hall in 1939, gaining its own parish. Collis Primary School, named after its Victorian founder, moved to Fairfax Road in 1972 and into its present building a decade later. Normansfield Hospital survived until 1997, when the site became the subject of a protracted wrangle over redevelopment plans and the proposed restoration of its Grade II*-listed theatre (for stage plays, not surgery). Also on the border of Hampton Wick, the former gasworks is now the site of a major mixed-use development scheme, including 200 apartments.

✉ Teddington TW11

📖 O Conor Ward, *John Langdon-Down: A Caring Pioneer,* Royal Society of Medicine, 1998

@ www.collis.richmond.sch.uk; www.sacredheart.richmond.sch.uk

South Tottenham • *Haringey*

A shabby south-eastern corner of the borough, located north of STAMFORD HILL and UPPER CLAPTON. Despite the growth of central TOTTENHAM, most of the land here remained undeveloped in the mid 19th century and the local board of health chose a site on Markfield Road near the River Lea to build its sewage works. A disastrous decline in the efficiency of the works in the 1860s was alleged to have been responsible for the deaths of 4,000 people, when untreated sewage was discharged into the Lea. A beam engine was eventually installed and this operated until the works' closure, after which it was restored as part of a museum that nowadays opens on the second Sunday of each month. Further west, developers built some substantial villas for the middle classes and St Ann's Church opened in 1861. However, the character of the district changed rapidly with the provision in the 1870s of improved transport connections, which included South Tottenham and SEVEN SISTERS stations and an omnibus service to the ANGEL, ISLINGTON. New streets of two-storey terraced houses were laid out across the area and occupied by working-class or lower middle-class commuters. The North-Eastern Fever Hospital (now St Ann's) opened in 1892. A group of German bakers settled in South Tottenham and built a Lutheran church in Antill Road in 1901. Increasing poverty in the district led to the opening of a soup kitchen on St Ann's Road before World War I. In the second half of the 20th century South Tottenham became a prime place of settlement for immigrants from the West Indies, spearheading the establishment of Tottenham's present sizeable black community. Many of South Tottenham's Victorian streets have survived, but some were replaced in the 1970s by a variety of council-built low-rise projects. At Gladesmore Community School on Crowland Road, two-fifths of pupils are of black Caribbean or black African descent and a tenth are white British. However, these figures do not necessarily mirror the local demographics since a large proportion of pupils travel long distances to this increasingly popular school.

✉ N15

🚊 Silverlink Metro (zone 3)

@ freespace.virgin.net/lec.orm (Markfield Beam Engine and Museum site)

South Twickenham • *Richmond*
A quiet corner of the extensive suburb of TWICKENHAM, situated south-east of TWICKENHAM GREEN. The poet Alexander Pope moved to a riverside villa in South Twickenham in 1719. He laid out gardens on the other side of the road called Cross Deep (named after the neighbouring stretch of the Thames), which were connected with the house via a tunnel. Pope expounded his seminal thinking on the 'Genius of the Place' – the need for harmony with nature in landscape design – while writing in this garden. When Baroness Howe bought the property in 1807, she commissioned Ryan House next door and demolished the villa. The tea merchant Thomas Young put up a new villa on the site in 1842. By this time, the enclosure of the nearby common land had brought some early development to South Twickenham, but the main phase of suburban building came from the 1880s onwards. St Catherine's Convent School moved to Pope's Villa in 1919. It is now St James Senior School for Boys. Cross Deep had other imposing houses, including Radnor House and Cross Deep Hall, but these were destroyed by bombing in World War II. Radnor Gardens occupies the site of these houses and several of their neighbours. The South Twickenham ward is notable for the high number of residents in the 16–29 age group. The proportion of ethnic minority residents is very low.

✉ Twickenham TW1

👤 9,027

South Wandle • *Croydon/Sutton*
A commercial and industrial regeneration area, located to the east of SUTTON and the west of CROYDON town centres, and forming part of the wider Wandle Valley industrial area. The main existing commercial zones are at Beddington Lane and Purley Way. A 2003 regeneration plan describes South Wandle as a regionally important manufacturing zone, an affordable location for small and medium-sized enterprises and a major logistics and retail location for south London and south-east England. The project aims to turn South Wandle into a major business area by 2008. There are obstacles to overcome, especially in terms of the unpleasant environment that the area is perceived to have.

✉ Wallington SM6; Croydon CR0

👤 38,200 (Sutton's Beddington North ward, and Croydon's Broad Green and Waddon wards)

Southwark • *Southwark*
South London's most ancient town, situated directly across the Thames from the CITY OF LONDON. Its Old English name of Sudwerca means 'southern defensive work or fort'. Southwark can lay claim to the longest history of any part of London, since it was here that the Romans chose to build the first bridge across the Thames following the invasion of AD43. The settlement was an integral part of Roman Londinium, with public, industrial and domestic buildings on islands and reclaimed marshland. Its fortunes were always tied to those of the City on the opposite bank as it benefited from the flow of trade and transport across the river and also acted as a place of refuge and retreat. A church was built on the site of the present-day Southwark Cathedral in around 607 and dedicated to Mary Overie, a local saint whose father was as a Thames ferryman. It came under the jurisdiction of the bishops of Winchester, who built their palace on a site to the west. The church was rebuilt in the twelfth century and again in 1207 following a fire. Its resident Augustinian friary was dissolved in 1540 and it was rededicated to St Saviour, the nave being rebuilt in the late Victorian era after a period of decline and disrepair. Famous members of the congregation include John Harvard, founder of Harvard University, who was born in Southwark in 1607. The bishops' palace was destroyed by fire in 1814 and today little remains except for its rose window, although its prison – the Clink – lives on as a street name and a

universal term. The first Southwark Bridge was privately built in 1815, and subsequently bought by the Corporation of London using rent money from the tenants of LONDON BRIDGE. The present bridge was completed in 1921. Southwark's marshy terrain constrained its expansion for centuries but as river commerce grew it became a trading and industrial centre, focused on the area known as the BOROUGH.

✉ SE1

⚕ 26,173 (Cathedrals and Chaucer wards)

🚇 Jubilee Line (zone 1)

📖 Richard Tames, *Southwark Past*, Historical Publications, 2001; John D Beasley, *Southwark Remembered*, Tempus, 2001

South Wimbledon • *Merton*

The part of WIMBLEDON that lies on the 'other side' of the railway tracks – the eastern, as much as the southern, part of the district. Very little development took place here until the 1850s, when Wimbledon became a junction, rail services improved and commuter traffic began to increase. The first phase of building took place nearer MERTON because water supplies and drainage were more reliable on the higher ground. The Liberal National Freehold Land Society, politically aligned with the Liberal Party, was the first to buy land south of the Broadway. The society laid out streets named after Liberal prime ministers and lent small-scale developers the capital to construct a few houses at a time. Many of the newcomers to these streets were working class, employed on the railway or in construction or as servants to the gentry of Wimbledon. Further east, speculative builders with less idealistic motives built homes for the middle classes. In 1867 a local heiress, Keziah Peache, endowed Bertram Cottages, 16 'model' homes that were let out at subsidized rents. At this time the area was known as New Wimbledon but the name South Wimbledon soon began to take hold. The population increased eightfold in the two decades to 1881. South Wimbledon became a distinctly deprived locality in the late 19th century and the death rate here was twice as high as that in Wimbledon proper. The last remaining fields were sold for building by 1900 and South Wimbledon began a slow climb towards respectability, aided by the arrival of the London Underground network in 1926. This is still the more affordable part of Wimbledon but very popular with young professionals.

Nigel Williams's 1992 comic novel *They Came from SW19* revolves around events at the fictional First Church of Christ the Spiritualist, South Wimbledon. Williams chose an apt setting; the locality at one time had more Nonconformist adherents than Anglicans.

✉ SW19

🚇 Northern Line (zones 3 and 4)

South Woodford • *Redbridge*

A separate community rather than just the southern part of WOODFORD, situated north of SNARESBROOK. The northern part of this locality evolved much earlier than the rest, with cottages clustering around St Mary's Church in the late 18th century. A row of grander houses to the east included Elmhurst, Holmleigh and West Lodge. Following the opening of the station (originally as George Lane) in 1856, a network of streets was laid out on both sides of the railway and Hermon Hill was lined with houses as far as Snaresbrook. An iron church was brought from Camden Town and re-erected on Hermon Hill in 1882. Local benefactors the Misses Nutter provided the permanent Holy Trinity Church later in the decade and its parish was taken partly from Woodford and partly from WANSTEAD. From the early 20th century developers began to build houses for clerical commuters on the sites of older villas and the process accelerated between the wars, when South Woodford also became the entertainment centre of the wider district. Most of the remaining old buildings were demolished in the 1960s and replaced by council housing. In 1969 three tower blocks were erected in the grounds of Elmhurst as halls of residence for Queen Mary College. The halls were sold for development in 2003 and the site is presently being redeveloped with around 400 private homes, most of which will be flats. Elmhurst will be refurbished as part of the scheme, which is due for completion around 2010. South Woodford's aspirational character is reflected in the specialist shops on George Lane, which include a notable sausage-maker. A conservation area protects the area around the northern part of the High Road. The majority of residents are of white British origin, and a range of other ethnic groups make up the remainder.

The crime writer Ruth Rendell was born in South Woodford, where her parents both worked as teachers.

✉ E18

🚇 Central Line (zone 4)

Spencer Park • *Wandsworth*

A conservation area at the extreme northern end of WANDSWORTH COMMON. The Spencer family, wealthy Warwickshire landowners, acquired Wandsworth Common in the early 18th century and this was the north-eastern corner of their estate. From 1829 William Wilson, the co-founder of Price's candle factory at VAUXHALL, rented a mansion here from the Spencers. The fifth Earl Spencer (great-great-uncle of Diana, Princess of Wales) sold the mansion's lease in 1866 and substantial villas soon began to go up on the newly created street named Spencer Park and on the present-day Wandsworth Common North Side. The earl transferred the remainder of the common to a preservation group. Council flats replaced a few of the properties in the 1960s, but many Victorian Gothic originals survive. One house has a roof based on that at HAMPTON COURT Palace; others made pioneering use of concrete. The remnants of a mid-19th-century wind-pump at the southern end of Windmill Road have Grade II-listed status. The pump used to extract rainwater from the railway cutting and deposit it in a picturesque lake with islands, nicknamed the Black Sea. The lake was drained in the 1870s and a park was laid out with formal walks and greenery for the benefit of the area's new residents. Spencer Park (later John Archer) School used the Royal Victoria Patriotic Building from 1957 until 1974, when purpose-built classrooms were erected on the site. These were demolished in 1994 after the school had been declared redundant.

The railway cutting at Spencer Park was the location of the Clapham rail crash in December 1988, in which 35 people died after three trains collided.

✉ SW18

Spitalfields • *Tower Hamlets*

A 'deprived, dangerous and exotic' district, successively known as Petty France, Little Jerusalem and Banglatown, situated between SHOREDITCH and ALDGATE. Walter and Rose Brown founded the hospital and priory known as St Mary Spital in 1197. The hospital was closed in 1538 and its buildings were adapted as homes and workshops in the first of a series of changes of use that came to characterize the district. Suburban expansion began after the Great Fire of London in 1666 and Spitalfields market was established in the 1680s. Over the following decades refugees from French religious persecution settled in Spitalfields in their thousands. These Huguenot exiles were attracted by an existing silk-weaving industry, which they expanded greatly. They built numerous chapels, and fine houses that served as both homes and workshops, with large attic windows providing good light for weavers to work by. Nicholas Hawksmoor's Christ Church was consecrated in 1729 and its 225-foot spire remains the area's landmark. By the early 19th century the silk-weaving industry was declining in the face of cheap foreign imports and the increasingly anglicized Huguenots dispersed around London. They were replaced by poor Jews from Amsterdam, whose specialist trade was the manufacture of cigars and cigarettes. After 1845, Spitalfields' cheap accommodation attracted Irish immigrants fleeing their country's potato famine, many of whom helped to build London's docks. Philanthropic organizations began to replace slum housing with model dwellings from the 1860s. Jewish refugees from the pogroms in Russia formed the next wave of newcomers after the 1880s, bringing skills in tailoring and cabinet-making, and strengthening Spitalfields' role as a trading district. New buildings for the fruit, vegetable and flower market were erected in 1893 and extended in 1928. By the mid 20th century Spitalfields' Jews were moving away to suburbs in north and east London. A Bengali community established itself in the 1960s – although Muslims from the Sylhet district of Assam had been settling here since the late 19th century. The area around BRICK LANE has accordingly been dubbed Banglatown. Spitalfields wholesale market moved to a purpose-built site in Leyton in 1991 and its buildings have since become home to the only retail market in London that can even vaguely rival CAMDEN TOWN for its youth appeal. However, the value of the site leaves its future in almost continuous doubt. Christ Church was restored and fully reopened in 2004 after almost 50 years of closure. In recent years surviving weavers' houses have been renovated and warehouses have been converted to apartment blocks with galleries and cafés at street level, but behind these conspicuous developments this is still a district of run-down tenements, where overcrowding is high and incomes are low. By most measures of deprivation, no other London ward comes close to Spitalfields.

What became Europe's largest chain of opticians began here in 1750 when John Dollond opened a shop selling spectacles. The music hall performer Bud Flanagan was born in Hanbury Street in 1896, as Chaim Reuven Weintrop. The artists Gilbert and George moved to Spitalfields so long ago that at first they heard only Yiddish accents here.

E1

8,383 (Spitalfields and Banglatown ward)

Anne J Kershen, *Strangers, Aliens and Asians: Huguenots, Jews and Bangladeshis in Spitalfields, 1660–2000*, Routledge, 2005; C Thomas, *Life and Death in London's East End: 2000 Years at Spitalfields*, Museum of London Archaeology Service, 2004; William Taylor, *This Bright Field*, Methuen, 2001

@ www.spitalfieldssociety.org (amenity society); www.spitalfields.org.uk (council information site); www.visitspitalfields.com (commercial local information site)

Springfield Park • *Hackney/Waltham Forest*

A 33-acre public park and neighbouring council ward situated beside the River Lea in UPPER CLAPTON. Spring Hill took its name from a line of springs that runs along the valley side. Roman remains, including a stone coffin, were discovered in the 1820s; a Roman villa may have stood here. From at least 1664, much of the land belonged to the Webbe family, including Spring Hill Farm. Thomas Webbe later developed a small industrial zone around a riverside creek, with cottages for workers. The five-bay-windowed Springfield House, also known as the White Lodge because of its stucco finish, was built in the 1820s. When the house and a neighbouring property, The Cedars, went on the market in 1902, the county and borough councils stepped in and bought them with help from public donations. Thomas Garland then sold Spring Hill House so that its grounds could be added and Springfield Park opened in 1905. The White Lodge was retained as a refreshment house and many mature trees were preserved but other houses, outbuildings and cottages were demolished. Spring Lane was rerouted along the edge of the park. The Springfield housing estate, completed in 1940, consists of five-storey blocks of flats arranged around a large courtyard. The Keir Hardie and Webb estates followed in the 1950s. The Springfield estate was remodelled in 1982 following consultation with residents about how best to overcome the many problems that had developed here. The old creek was re-excavated as Springfield marina in 1969. The Springfield ward borders STAMFORD HILL and nearly a quarter of its residents are of the Jewish faith. The main ethnic minorities are of black African and black Caribbean descent. A very high proportion of households contains dependent children. The ward has London's highest percentage of people working in education.

E5

10,859 (Hackney's Springfield ward)

Spring Grove • *Hounslow*

A well-preserved, and in parts grand, suburb situated south-east of OSTERLEY, known until the late 19th century as Smallbury Green. The settlement grew up on common land that once lay between ISLEWORTH and HESTON and takes its modern name from a house built during the Civil War for Sir John Offley. Within the grounds was a spring, providing water that was piped to the house. Another mansion replaced the original Spring Grove just over a century later. Sir Joseph Banks, the botanist and pioneering developer of KEW GARDENS, lived at this house for 40 years and laid out the gardens with a lake and springs and a magnificent variety of plants. He died here in 1820. The London and South Western Railway branch line arrived in 1849, with a station at Isleworth originally called Spring Grove. A year later the builder Henry Davies bought the Spring Grove estate and constructed a number of merchants' villas of classical design with stone facings. Davies himself lived at Thornbury House, now Campion House, in Thornbury Road. The recession of the 1870s and unwise speculation by many residents brought depression to the locality and prosperity did not return for nearly 20 years. In 1886, Spring Grove House was sold to Andrew Pears, great-grandson of the creator of the famous translucent soap. Pears rebuilt Banks's house as the mansion that is now home to West Thames College. In the early 20th century, terraced houses began to appear, followed by semi-detached houses after World War I, at which time there was also some industrial development alongside the Great Western Railway line. Finally, in the 1960s and 1970s, blocks of flats replaced many of the original Davies houses. Spring Grove was designated a conservation area in 2002.

The young Robert Louis Stevenson stayed in the area briefly, and somewhat unhappily, with his uncle. He went to school at Burlington House, which stood in Witham Road. In 1992 the guitar pop band the Bluetones came together in Spring Grove, originally calling themselves the Bottlegarden.

✉ Isleworth TW7

♦ 10,452 (Osterley and Spring Grove ward)

🚋 South West Trains (Isleworth, zone 4); Piccadilly Line (Osterley, zone 4)

@ www.geocities.com/davidjorr/springgrove/ springgrove.htm (Spring Grove Conservation Area Group site)

Spring Park • Croydon/Bromley

A largely interwar settlement bordered by MONKS ORCHARD to the north, WEST WICKHAM to the east, ADDINGTON to the south and SHIRLEY to the west. This was a patch of inferior farmland until it was enhanced in the first half of the 19th century by the addition of new roads and an accompanying change of identity from Cold Harbour to Spring Park (an existing local name) as part of a plan to encourage the building of mansions in the area. A wealthy MP, Sir John Temple Leader (who later started a sizeable British colony near Florence in Italy), bought Spring Park in the mid 1830s and engaged the innovative Hewitt Davis as tenant farmer. By improving the soil and drainage, Davis transformed the land from rough heathland into a model farm. Agricultural associations organized trips here to learn from his achievements. Spring Park House stood on the present-day Farm Drive, at first in isolation but gradually encroached upon by lesser properties. Suburban development started in the 1920s and accelerated in the 1930s, absorbing the hamlet of Starve Acre on the Addington Palace estate. After World War II, council housing filled the remaining gaps, with only the municipal open spaces escaping development. All Saints Church, on Bridle Road, is a distinctively modern redbrick building, built in 1956 by the architectural partnership Curtis Green, Son and Lloyd. It is a Grade II-listed building. The Corporation of London cares for the heathland and coppiced woods of Spring Park, which fall within the borough of Bromley. Smaller clumps of the woodland also survive around Miller's Pond and north of Links View Road, which was named for a former golf course laid out in 1922 on land now covered by the Shrublands estate.

Shirley and West Wickham telephone numbers used to be prefixed with 777 because this was the numeric equivalent of the first three letters of Spring Park.

✉ Croydon CR0; West Wickham BR4

Squirrel's Heath • Havering

An unexceptional residential locality situated immediately east of GIDEA PARK station. The name probably derives from 13th-century landowners rather than the local wildlife. The heath was enclosed in the early 19th century but it was the coming of the railway in 1839 that brought growth. Wagon works and a tarpaulin factory were sited here soon afterwards, long terraces of industrial cottages were erected to house the workers and local services flourished as a consequence. In 1858 two houses in Factory Road (now Elvet Avenue) were converted into a school, which was enlarged in 1895. It was not until 1911 that a station, originally called Squirrels Heath and Gidea Park, was built to serve the new suburb to the west. Soon, its grander neighbour absorbed Squirrel's Heath. By 1939 the area was completely built up, mostly with good quality houses and generous gardens. Tower blocks of flats were added in the 1960s and 1970s, replacing some of the 19th-century terraces. Squirrel's Heath Junior School opened in the same year as the station, replacing the Factory Road school, and the building has changed little since then. It shares its Salisbury Road site with an infants' school. The Squirrel's Heath ward takes in ARDLEIGH GREEN and extends north to GALLOWS CORNER. It has a high proportion of white, married, Christian residents living in owner-occupied homes.

✉ Romford RM2; Hornchurch RM11

♦ 11,780

Stamford Bridge • Hammersmith & Fulham

Now the home of Chelsea Football Club, Stamford Bridge stadium opened in 1877. It is named after a 15th-century crossing at Counters Creek, which formed the boundary between FULHAM and CHELSEA. The bridge was at a 'sandy ford', which became corrupted to 'Stamford'. In its early years the stadium was used primarily by the London Athletic Club and also hosted greyhound racing and baseball. In 1904 the ground was bought by the building contractor Gus Mears, who had already acquired a neighbouring market garden. Resisting a tempting offer for the site from the Great Western Railway, Mears and his brother set out to create London's premier footballing venue, commissioning the east stand from the great stadium builder Archibald Leitch. The remainder was terraced with spoil from construction work on the underground railway network. Mears considered the names 'KENSINGTON' and 'London' for the new club, before settling on 'Chelsea', which started the 1906–7 season in division two of the Football League. The erection of a tin roof over the south terrace in 1930 gave rise to the nickname 'the Shed' and this end of the ground became the home of the team's most zealous supporters. The club was a founding member of the Premier League in 1992. From 1994 to 2001 the stadium was completely redeveloped, with associated leisure and hotel facilities. The Russian businessman Roman Abramovich bought the club in 2003, and immediately spent almost £100 million on new players; Chelsea has since become one of the most formidable football clubs in Europe.

✉ SW6

📖 Brian Mears and Ian Macleay, *Chelsea: A 100-year History*, Mainstream Sport, 2004

@ www.chelseafc.com

Stamford Brook • *Hounslow/Hammersmith & Fulham*

A compact and comfortable locality squeezed between HAMMERSMITH and CHISWICK and centred on Stamford Brook Common (also known as the Green). It is named after a stream that ran through the area, which in turn took its name from a 'stony ford' at the Great West Road (A4). A hamlet of 'seven cottages or tenements' was recorded in 1699, amidst strips of arable farmland and pasture. A century later, when there were 168 dwellings in TURNHAM GREEN, Stamford Brook had only four houses. One of these was The Brook, which was bought in 1878 by Thomas Hussey, a builder who had leased 50 acres of meadowland at Stamford Brook for brickmaking. Hussey supplied tens of millions of bricks for Jonathan Carr's development at nearby BEDFORD PARK and soon began to put up his own houses on what became Stamford Brook Avenue. In 1902 he leased The Brook to the artist-craftsman Lucien Pissarro and his wife Esther, who spent the rest of their days here. The early years of the 20th century saw the last of Stamford Brook's market gardens and orchards disappear as the village became a suburb. Mansion blocks were erected on the south side of the common, although disappointing sales forced developers to return to more conventional housebuilding. Stamford Brook station opened in 1912, much later than the other stations on the line, and the council

provided some sports facilities on the common in the same year. Houses were built on the site of the tennis courts in 1934. Stamford Brook lost two landmarks in the 1980s with the unsympathetic conversion of St Mary's Church into flats and the demolition of the former Commodore cinema, which had spent its latter years as a bingo hall. Parts of the old tram depot (later a bus garage) have also been converted to flats.

Camille Pissarro stayed with his son when he was living on Bath Road in 1897 and painted several views of Stamford Brook, although some are incorrectly catalogued as portrayals of Bedford Park. Lucien and Esther Pissarro designed a typeface called Brook for their woodcutting venture, the Eragny Press.

✉ W6

🚇 District Line (zone 2)

📖 Reginald Coleman and Shirley Seaton, *Stamford Brook: An Affectionate Portrait*, Stamford Brook Publications, 1997

Stamford Hill • *Hackney/Haringey*

Located north of STOKE NEWINGTON, Stamford Hill is one of London's most distinctive quarters, with a highly independent community of about 15,000 Hasidic Jews. In the 13th century this was 'Sandford' Hill, where a sandy ford crossed a tributary of the River Lea. In the late 18th and early 19th centuries its elevated situation attracted wealthy merchants, notably Moses Vita Montefiore, an Italian Jew who died here in 1789. The arrival of trams and trains in 1872 set off a 20-year building programme that established the present layout of Stamford Hill, including shops on Dunsmure Road by 1884. From this time onwards, and particularly after the 1920s, upwardly mobile Jews moved here from the EAST END, as they did to DALSTON and Stoke Newington. Several synagogues were relocated or founded here. Some larger old houses were converted for use as Jewish schools or other institutions, while their grounds were split into lots and sold off for further housebuilding. The London County Council and the Guinness Trust built estates in the 1930s. The LCC added more blocks after World War II, as did the Samuel Lewis Trust. This was a period of Hasidic Jewish immigration from eastern Europe, creating a 'square mile of piety' at Stamford Hill. The Hasidim have their own schools, conventicles and kosher food shops. They wear 18th-century frock coats and black hats and are the sole British Jewish group still to speak Yiddish; outside Israel, only New York has a larger community of Hasidic Jews. Stamford Hill also has residents of black African, black Caribbean, Turkish and Kurdish descent.

Because of Stamford Hill's special character, it has been the subject of television documentaries and the setting for television drama. Programmes include a Channel 4 documentary, *Volvo City*, and the 1993 BBC play *Wall of Silence*. The latter caused controversy with its portrayal of a psychopathic Hasidic murderer, played by Warren Mitchell. The 'Volvo City' nickname derives from the (receding) popularity of this car marque with the community. Stamford Hill was the fictional home of Marcus, the young prodigy in *Madam Sousatzka*, Bernice Rubens' 1962 novel.

✉ N16

🚇 'one' Railway (zone 3)

Stanmore · *Harrow*

An expansive and expensive suburb running into open countryside west of BROCKLEY HILL and east of HARROW WEALD. The name was first recorded in Domesday Book as Stanmere, a stony pool. It was later known as Great Stanmore, to distinguish it from the separate settlement of LITTLE STANMORE, which lay to the south-east. In the Middle Ages the village is thought to have clustered around the manor house and church, which stood near the present-day junction of Wolverton Road with Old Church Lane. An Augustinian priory was founded a mile and a half to the north-west, probably in the early 13th century. Elsewhere, the surroundings were mostly empty heathland, later known as Stanmore Common. Perhaps because of the Black Death, the old village was abandoned and a new settlement grew up to the north, on the Uxbridge road, where the Church of St John the Evangelist was consecrated in 1632 by Archbishop Laud. Beginning with STANMORE PARK in the 1720s, several very grand houses were either newly built or greatly enlarged from existing properties. Bentley Priory was built in 1766 on the site of the Augustinian priory, and remodelled in the 1790s by Sir John Soane for the eccentric James Hamilton, later the Marquess of Abercorn. Public houses were licensed in various locations across the parish, including the Abercorn Arms in 1803. The village itself remained little changed until the 1820s, when substantial villas began to cluster around the church and manor house. Meanwhile, the rebuilding of mansions continued, notably

Stanmore Hall in the late 1840s, when a new St John's Church was also built, in the same churchyard as its namesake. In the 1880s Frederick Gordon converted Bentley Priory into a grand but not very successful hotel, and established a railway company that built a line to Stanmore. More villas followed and Stanmore Golf Club was founded in 1893. In 1925 the Air Ministry bought Bentley Priory and it became the Royal Air Force's Fighter Command Headquarters during World War II. Modern suburban development began after the construction of the Metropolitan Railway (later the Bakerloo and now the Jubilee Line) in 1932, when St Bartholomew's Hospital sold its land in the south of the parish and a network of new roads was laid out west of Honeypot Lane and extending to BELMONT. Some open spaces were preserved in this area by the creation of sports grounds for City companies. The RAF acquired Stanmore Park in 1938 and demolished the mansion. Stanmore's main-line station closed in 1952 and the building has been converted to a house. Many other properties also remain from the late-Victorian and Edwardian phase of Stanmore's growth, but their large gardens have been lost to infilling. Stanmore College (as it is now called) opened in 1969 as the country's first purpose-built sixth-form college. RAF Stanmore Park closed in 1997 and has been replaced by housing, and the future of the RAF station at Bentley Priory is under review. The 120-acre Stanmore Common has more rare plant species than any other open space in London except KESTON Common and HAMPSTEAD HEATH, and some scarce moths, flies and beetles.

The Prince Regent (later George IV) met with the exiled Louis XVIII of France at the Abercorn Arms in 1814. Queen Adelaide, widow of William IV, died at Bentley Priory in 1849.

✉ Stanmore HA7

🚇 Jubilee Line northern terminus (zone 5)

📖 Eileen M Bowlt, *Stanmore Past*, Historical Publications, 1998

@ www.stanmore.ac.uk (Stanmore College)

Stanmore Park · *Harrow*

An electoral ward and a major new housing estate situated west of central STANMORE. Stanmore Park was a mansion built in the 1720s, probably on the site of an older moated house. The Marquess of Abercorn acquired the estate in 1839 but, since he had his own seat not far away at Bentley Priory, he sold the mansion to the banker George Carr Glyn in 1848. In the 1880s Stanmore Park became a boys' preparatory school, and it continued in this role until its sale in 1938. The mansion was then demolished and RAF Stanmore Park air base was laid out in its 56 acres of grounds. The base became the headquarters of Balloon Command and was later part of the Strike Command group. RAF Stanmore Park closed in 1997 and in 2001 a judicial review upheld the council's decision to allow Laing Homes to build 411 homes on the site – the largest housing development ever submitted for approval in the modern borough. Construction has recently been completed and the results are relatively pleasing. The Stanmore Park ward has a high number of older residents and a significant Jewish population. The principal ethnic minority is of Indian descent.

✉ Stanmore HA7

👥 9,339

📖 John F Hamlin, *History of Royal Air Force Bentley Priory and Stanmore Park*, London Borough of Harrow, Library Service, 1997

Staples Corner • *Barnet/Brent*

A road intersection located between CRICKLEWOOD and WEST HENDON, formed when the North Circular Road (A406) cut across the Edgware Road (A5) in the mid 1920s. The junction is named after the Staples and Co. mattress factory, which was located on the south-west corner, and not the stationery superstore that has now cleverly sited itself here. Staples and Co. was the first of more than 50 factories built here between the wars, erasing the hamlet of Oxgate, although the 16th-century wattle-and-daub Oxgate Farmhouse survives on Coles Green Road. In the early 1970s the junction's character was effaced by the building of the Edgware Road flyover and the termination of the M1 motorway just to the east. Shortly after the 1992 general election an IRA bomb caused massive damage, particularly to a DIY superstore, and the flyover was closed for several months. At 100 lb the bomb was one of the largest ever planted on the British mainland. The following year another, much smaller, device was also detonated in the vicinity. The former industries of Staples Corner have been replaced by car dealers, retail warehouses and a multiplex cinema, and south-east of the junction a brownfield site has been redeveloped with housing. A landmark tower has been proposed for Staples Corner to mark this gateway to London, and it is likely that the recent extension of BRENT CROSS in this direction will be accompanied by new apartment blocks. Writing in the *New Statesman* in 1998, Paul Barker suggested that, 'Hell must be something like Staples Corner. Piranesian flyovers, demonic roundabouts, traffic swirling about like the legions of the damned'.

✉ NW2

Starch Green • *Hammersmith & Fulham*

An old name for the locality north of RAVENSCOURT PARK, now used only (if at all) for the immediate vicinity of Seven Stars Corner, at the junction of GOLDHAWK ROAD and Askew Road. It was also called Gagglegoose Green. The green had a pond, which was filled in from 1926 and is now an open space. Starch Green acquired its name from the laundries that operated here in the 18th and 19th centuries. Another speciality of the district was rabbit-breeding for the City meat markets.

✉ W12

Stepney • *Tower Hamlets*

Once the capital of the EAST END, Stepney is now reduced in extent and significance to a collection of flats and terraces wedged between COMMERCIAL ROAD and MILE END Road. The name is a corruption of Stibenhede – Stibba's haven. It was first recorded in the early 11th century and this was the only east London district to be entered in Domesday Book, when the principal landowner was the Bishop of London. By the 16th century the episcopal manor of Stepney covered almost all of what became known as the East End. Following the growth of the Tudor navy and the mercantile marine, Stepney became a popular place of residence for seamen and retired naval officers. From the late 17th century, and especially in the early 18th, speculative developers built small groups of houses here, which included some short rows of terraced houses, a groundbreaking innovation at that time. Over the course of the 19th century Stepney's character was transformed as London expanded to absorb it. Commercial Road lived up to its name by filling with shops and other businesses. Towards the end of the century Jewish immigrants poured into Stepney and numerous small synagogues opened, together with dedicated institutions for the new community, such as schools and a hospital. Slum clearance began in the 1930s and this was combined with the rebuilding of bomb sites after World War II. Old neighbourhoods were erased as the borough and county councils erected some of the East End's most colourless and ungainly estates. Those who could afford to move out did so, including most of the Jewish population, leaving behind them a community of the dispossessed. During the 1950s and 1960s Stepney's criminal minority acquired a reputation as small-time conmen, poor relations of the more notorious gangs in neighbouring WHITECHAPEL and BETHNAL GREEN. In the early 1970s council building reached a nadir, as cheap blocks were crammed into the last few available sites. By the end of the decade conservationists were fighting to save the terraced houses that survived from the late 17th to early 19th centuries and these have since been rehabilitated. From the 1980s immigrants, from the New Commonwealth became the dominant ethnic groups, especially those from the Sylhet district of Bangladesh. Council signage in Stepney is generally written in both English and Bengali script.

During the siege of Sidney Street (also known as 'the battle of Stepney') in 1911, two Latvian anarchists, wanted for the murders of three policemen in HOUNDSDITCH, died in a house fire during an armed assault commanded by Winston Churchill. The actor Terence Stamp and the playwright Arnold Wesker were both born in Stepney in the 1930s.

✉ E1

📖 Tim Baker (ed.), *History of the County of Middlesex: Stepney, Bethnal Green,* Victoria History of the Counties of England, 1999; Fermin Rocker, *The East End Years: A Stepney Childhood,* Freedom Press, 1998

Stepney Green • *Tower Hamlets*

A station, road and park located in north-central STEPNEY. Although Stepney is one of east London's most ancient settlements, Stepney Green is a 19th-century invention. Both the road and its neighbouring common land were formerly called MILE END Green. There are earlier mentions of a green at Stepney but these do not necessarily identify the present locality. The green was flanked by fine houses in the 17th and 18th centuries and some of these survive today. For half its length the road is divided in two by Stepney Green Gardens, created in 1872 from a remaining strip of the old Mile End Green. From the late 19th century, when this had become a strongly Jewish area, self-help companies built tenement blocks, of which the most distinctive is Stepney Green Court. Stepney Green station opened on Mile End Road in June 1902. Like

the rest of Stepney, the vicinity of the green was heavily redeveloped with municipal housing from the 1930s to the 1970s. Stepney Green Park was formed at the end of this period in order to provide some much-needed open space, but sadly at the expense of good early-19th-century houses. The St Dunstan's and Stepney Green ward is estimated to have London's highest proportion of people in social grade E. At Stepney Green Secondary School, four-fifths of pupils are eligible for free school meals and 98 per cent are from the Sylheti-speaking Bangladeshi community.

In 1905 the ringleader of the mutiny aboard the Russian battleship *Potemkin,* torpedo quartermaster Afanasy Matushenko, sought refuge at an anarchist and socialist meeting place in Dunstan House on Stepney Green. Matushenko soon returned to Russia, where he was caught and hanged in 1907. Bernard Kops, an East Ender of Dutch-Jewish parentage, achieved recognition in 1959 with his first play, *The Hamlet of Stepney Green,* an optimistic reworking of Shakespeare's *Hamlet.*

✉ E1

🚶 12,679 (St Dunstan's and Stepney Green ward)

🚇 District Line; Hammersmith & City Line (zone 2)

Stockley Park • *Hillingdon*

A business park with surrounding leisure facilities, situated north of the Grand Union Canal one and a half miles east of WEST DRAYTON. A 350-acre site, previously derelict, was transformed in the late 1980s into a commercial science park, now regarded as the foremost development on the 'West London Corridor'. It provides one of the largest public parks and open spaces to be created in London in the 20th century, and is touted as an example of what can be achieved by public–private partnerships and at no cost to the local community. Architectural critics were divided over Stockley Park's aesthetics, and some industry commentators have called it 'grim' and 'dreary', hardly what its creators intended, but the site changed hands several times after the project began. Nevertheless, the list of early occupiers reads like a who's who of high-tech, although some companies have since moved away. The business area is set in a landscaped country park with an 18-hole public golf course. Plans for a rail link and a station, HEATHROW North, to be based just outside Stockley Park have not come to fruition but the park's tenants have had some success in reducing vehicle usage through cycle-to-work and car-sharing schemes.

Following a spate of late-night car cruising in 2002, security barriers were erected to prevent use of the park as a through route, so the tree-lined boulevards are almost empty of traffic except for under-used buses and kids racing their bikes. And even at lunchtimes only a handful of workers take a stroll or make use of the green spaces.

✉ West Drayton UB11

@ www.stockleypark.co.uk

Stockwell · Lambeth

An ethnically and socially mixed neighbourhood, often regarded as the northernmost part of BRIXTON. The name, which referred to a wellspring by a tree trunk or stump, was first recorded in 1197. A century later Stockwell achieved manorial status but it remained under the sway of VAUXHALL long afterwards. Henry VIII's chief minister Thomas Cromwell may have stayed at the manor house, which was surrounded by a wide moat and four acres of gardens. After its release by the Crown in 1598, the manor was held by the viscounts Montagu in the 17th century, the Chute family in the 18th and the Thornycrofts in the 19th. All these owners chipped away at its extent by selling off land here and there. Stockwell Green formed the nucleus of the settlement, with the manor house on its north side and a public well in the south-west corner. The Swan, the Plough and the Old Queen's Head were the earliest public houses. The manor house was demolished around 1755 and a new mansion was built which survived for less than a century – a period in which Stockwell changed from a collection of nurseries with the usual scattering of grand houses into a nascent 'villa land'. William Cox of Kennington began to develop Stockwell Park as a high-class estate after 1838, whereupon several other builders pitched in with variations on his theme. Many of the villas were terraced or otherwise tightly packed, which has helped ensure their survival to the present day. Several public and philanthropic institutions were established in the 1860s, including an orphanage and a college. Commodious churches replaced cramped chapels. Stockwell Green was built over in the 1870s despite attempted resistance via the courts. Stockwell became the southern terminus of London's first deep Tube line in 1890 but it was not until after World War II that the landscape was again trans-

formed, this time by the construction of several large municipal estates, notably the London County Council's Stockwell Gardens (on the site of Stockwell College), the Greater London Council's Springfield estate and Lambeth council's Stockwell Park. A third of Stockwell's residents are black or black British and nearly 15 per cent are non-British white, including a thriving Portuguese community.

In 1873–4 the artist Vincent van Gogh lived at 87 Hackford Road, on the eastern edge of the district. The same street also contains the Type Museum, which claims to have the most extensive typographic collection in the world. Founded here in 1995, the museum is housed in a former veterinary hospital.

✉ SW9

♦ 13,416

🚇 Northern Line; Victoria Line (zone 2)

📖 Ken Dixon, Alan Piper et al, *Brixton Heritage Trails: Six Walks Around Brixton and Stockwell*, Brixton Society, 2001; Edward Walford, *Walford's History of Stockwell and Kennington*, ed. John W Brown, Local History Reprints, 1996

@ www.typemuseum.org

Stoke Newington · Hackney

A traditionally nonconformist community, in every sense, situated north-west of HACKNEY. The medieval village grew up around the twin nuclei of Newington Green and the junction of Church Street with what is now Stoke Newington High Street. Outsiders of all kinds were recorded here from the 15th century – for example: two Flanders men were residents in 1436, a clergyman was jailed for repeating gossip about the queen in 1562, and a shot was fired at the king from a Stoke Newington house in 1675. In 1709 the parish built four houses to accommodate Protestant refugees from the Rhine Palatinate. Among the wealthy Quakers living in the town houses on Church Street was John Wilmer, who in 1764 was buried in a vault in his garden with a bell attached to his wrist in case he was not dead. From the 1820s, developers began to turn their attention to Stoke Newington. One of the most prolific builders was Thomas Widdows of Church Street, allegedly 'a most lascivious old fellow', whose projects included the MANOR HOUSE public house at the far north-western corner of the parish. The beautiful Abney Park Cemetery was laid out in 1840 on unconsecrated ground, which made it popular with

Nonconformists. Stoke Newington station opened in 1872, prompting a renewed flurry of development that included the rebuilding of many of the High Street's busy commercial premises. Quaker resident Joseph Beck helped establish CLISSOLD PARK in 1889. Terraced streets and some more classy avenues filled the rest of the district by the end of the 19th century, when poor Jewish immigrants from Russia, Poland and Germany were arriving in the south of Stoke Newington. In the 1930s wealthier Jews came to the northern part of the borough and they were subsequently supplemented by Hasidic Jews from eastern Europe, especially in the STAMFORD HILL area. Before and, especially, after World War II, council flats replaced rows of houses in the more overcrowded parts of the district and the massive WOODBERRY DOWN estate was built in the north-west. From the 1960s, West Indians, Greek Cypriots and Turks further enhanced the diversity of the community. During the 1980s, Stoke Newington became something of a 'new Islington', a working-class district increasingly colonized by the young middle classes, many of them politically radical and working in arts-related professions. A host of shops and wine bars sprang up to serve these 'Stokeys', whose lifestyle was satirized by comedians such as Alexei Sayle. The area also became known for the free availability of drugs and in 1994, after the biggest inquiry of its kind for 20 years, the Police Complaints Authority reported that this had been due partly to widespread corruption among officers at Stoke Newington police station. In the 21st century Stoke Newington is less of a radical hotbed but remains eminently cool.

The writer and religious Nonconformist Daniel Defoe married a girl from Newington Green in 1684 and tried to raise civet cats here to make perfume. John Wesley, the founder of Methodism, occasionally retreated to Stoke Newington in the early 1780s. The philosopher John Stuart Mill and the author (and Quaker) Anna Sewell lived here in the 1810s and 1820s respectively, when they were both young children. Other residents have included the writers Joseph Conrad and Edgar Allen Poe and the glam rock star Marc Bolan, who spent his childhood at 25 Stoke Newington Common.

✉ N16

♦ 10,133 (Stoke Newington Central ward)

🚆 'one' Railway (zone 2)

📖 Isobel Watson, *Hackney and Stoke Newington Past*, Historical Publications, 1998; David Mander, *Look Back, Look Forward! An Illustrated History of Stoke Newington*, Sutton/London Borough of Hackney, 1997

@ www.n16mag.com (online local magazine); www.abney-park.org.uk

Stonebridge · *Brent*

A troubled but improving council-built estate and its vicinity, situated north-west of HARLESDEN. The name derives from the stone bridge of 1745 that carried the HARROW ROAD (A404) over the River Brent. Until very late in the 19th century this was the site of Stonebridge Farm and of WILLESDEN's first sewage works but it was then rapidly built over, although some earlier large houses survived for a while. After World War I, Willesden council built houses west of Brentfield Road as part of its response to Lloyd George's call for 'homes for heroes'. During the 1950s the council planned a massive redevelopment covering almost 100 acres of Stonebridge. More than 2,000 units were built, mostly in high-rise blocks, the first of which opened in 1967. Many existing streets were erased, together with the shops on Hillside. Despite the council's good intentions, the Stonebridge estate soon proved flawed in its design and execution, and residents felt that little interest was shown in their welfare. The body of elderly tenant John Sheppard was discovered in 1993 after he had lain dead in his flat for three years. The Stonebridge Housing Action Trust took over management of the estate in 1994 and has done its best to make improvements, replacing some of the blocks with less austere terraced housing as part of a multi-million pound effort to enhance the quality of life here, and extensive further regeneration is planned. The Fawood Children's Centre, opened officially in 2005, was built in 2004 on a tiny budget but with huge imagination, to the design of architect Will Alsop; some critics have rated it the best London building since the Gherkin. Nevertheless, the Stonebridge estate continues to suffer from high levels of drug-related crime, burglary, violence and unemployment, although criminal incidents have been falling lately. A contract killing of two sisters and their mother's partner in Clark Court brought the estate back into the media spotlight in 2005. A number of refugee families have been placed on the estate, many from sub-Saharan Africa. Stonebridge has the second highest proportion of black residents of any ward in London, after PECKHAM.

In 1998 Stonebridge provided the setting for the Channel 4-backed film *Babymother*, a largely affirmative black musical by Julian Henriques with a cast of local people. The boxer Audley Harrison grew up on the Stonebridge estate.

> ✉ NW10

> ♦ 15,943

> 📖 M C Barrès-Baker, *Stonebridge*, Grange Museum of Community History and Brent Archive, 2001

> @ www.stonebridgehat.org.uk (Stonebridge Housing Action Trust)

Stonebridge Park • *Brent*

Formerly a high-class estate located on the eastern side of STONEBRIDGE, just north-west of HARLESDEN. Following the opening of WILLESDEN JUNCTION station in 1866 developers planned a flamboyant estate (although the finished result was a little less grand) that was originally known as Harlesden Park, and later as Stonebridge Park. The Midland Railway Co. opened Harrow Road station (later Stonebridge Park) in 1875 and within a year more than 60 detached and semi-detached villas had been built, together with the Stonebridge Park Hotel on the section of the HARROW ROAD called Hillside, where a significant shopping centre soon evolved. Terraced houses were built for tradespeople in streets to the west of Stonebridge Park. The Church of St Michael and All Angels was built in 1891 and gained its own parish a year later. Some of the estate's larger houses were subdivided in the early years of the 20th century but there was little new building from this time onwards. The original Stonebridge Park station closed in 1902 but a new one opened a decade later on the London and North Western Railway. The station was served by electric trains on the forerunner of the Bakerloo Line from 1917. No. 14 Stonebridge Park was used as a military hospital during World War I and subsequently became the Edgar Lee Home for boys with rheumatic hearts. The estate retained its popularity into the 1930s, when numerous members of the local board and council lived here. Most of the villas succumbed to the council's redevelopment of the wider area after World War II, and only two of the original properties now remain. Stonebridge Park no longer has an identity distinct from the rest of Stonebridge.

> ✉ NW10

> 🚆 Silverlink Metro; Bakerloo Line (zone 3)

Stonegrove • *Barnet/Harrow*

A heterogeneous residential locality straddling both the A5 and the EDGWARE/STANMORE border. In the 15th century the area became part of the extensive landholdings of All Souls College, Oxford. The Stonegrove name did not make its first appearance until the early 19th century and probably referred to woodland lying near a milestone on Watling Street. Several buildings soon made use of the new name (which was then spelt as two words), including Stone Grove House, Lodge, Court and Cottage. In 1829 Edgware entrepreneur Charles Day built a symmetrical group of eight almshouses beside Watling Street, this section of which is now called Stonegrove. Until well into the 20th century Stonegrove's handful of villas remained entirely surrounded by open land. Between the wars, middle-class suburban housing covered much of the locality, as it did elsewhere in Edgware. Most of the early houses were lost at this time, but Day's almshouses have survived. Stonegrove Park was created in 1934 and its facilities now include a playground and tennis courts, but it has suffered from vandalism in recent years. In 1957 Hendon council erected the tower blocks of the Spur Road estate in spite of local residents' resistance. Harrow council built some innovative terraced housing for the elderly and disabled around a village green in 1968, while on its side of the border Barnet council (the successor to Hendon) laid out the Stonegrove estate. In a major regeneration scheme, ownership of the Spur Road and Stonegrove estates is being transferred to the Family Housing Association while the council will offer neighbouring land for private sale. The project is the subject of a staged approach, with some elements depending on the outcome of pending negotiations.

Founded in 1935, the Edgware and District Reform Synagogue moved in 1951 to Sidbury Lodge, at 118 Stonegrove. A new main building with a high-capacity synagogue hall and a function hall opened in 2001. The EDRS claims to be the largest synagogue in Europe, with around 2,000 family members.

> ✉ Edgware HA8

> @ www.edrs.org.uk (Edgware and District Reform Synagogue site)

The Strand • *Westminster*

A commercial and institutional thoroughfare running eastward from CHARING CROSS and meeting FLEET STREET just west of the junction with CHANCERY LANE. The name was first recorded in 1185 and derives from the Old English word meaning 'bank' or 'shore'. The road formerly ran close to the Thames but now finds itself lying inland as a result of the construction of the Victoria EMBANKMENT. Many maps still give the Strand as the name of the district that everyone else knows as Covent Garden. Forming part of the connection between the early twin centres of WESTMINSTER and the CITY OF LONDON, the Strand has been a place of settlement for centuries. John of Gaunt's Savoy Palace was destroyed in the Peasants' Revolt of 1381 and is now the site of a sumptuous hotel. Edward Seymour, Duke of Somerset, built a riverside mansion on the Strand in 1547, which later served as a royal residence. Somerset House was rebuilt after 1775 and has been put to several purposes by the government, most famously as the central record office for births, marriages and deaths. The buildings are now used by the Inland Revenue and the art galleries of the Courtauld Institute. In the late 1820s King's College was founded on a site next to Somerset House, and Simpson's-in-the-Strand opened as a 'cigar divan'. In 1867, Karl Marx described the Strand as 'a main thoroughfare which gives strangers an imposing idea of the wealth of London', but he went on to point out that behind its grand institutions lay streets teeming with the city's underclass. The temple-like buildings of the Royal Courts of Justice were erected east of the ALDWYCH in the 1870s. Much of the Strand was lined with offices over the course of the 20th century, of which the most imposing is the Shell-Mex building of 1931.

Charles Dickens frequented the Roman bath on Strand Lane – as did his character David Copperfield. Founded in 1890 and published monthly until 1950, the *Strand* magazine was a mixture of factual articles, short stories and serials. Its early success was driven by the appearance of Arthur Conan Doyle's 'Sherlock Holmes' stories, which appeared in almost every issue until 1927. Other famous contributors included Kipling, Chesterton, Tolstoy and Simenon. The short-lived Strand cigarette brand was launched at the end of the 1950s, promoted with the line 'You're never alone with a Strand'.

✉ WC2

Strand on the Green • *Hounslow*

A quaint riverside village and pub-crawl paradise, situated just east of KEW BRIDGE. It was simply 'Strand' from the 13th century to the 17th century, from the Old English word for a bank or shore. This was a fishing community with a ferry service to KEW, and one of the medieval settlements that comprised CHISWICK. In its early days there was no path along the riverbank, just a series of interconnecting wharves. During the 18th century the village attracted wealthy residents who built some grand homes here; and the Ship, Bull's Head, Bell and Crown, and City Barge public houses all came into existence. The opening of the first Kew Bridge in 1759 improved accessibility, increased land values and drew some of George III's courtiers when the king was living at Kew Palace. By 1800 a continuous footpath ran along the bank, although it was liable to flooding at high tide. Orchards and market gardens lay behind the waterfront properties but by the end of the 19th century these were succumbing to building development, and fishing was dying out as the prime livelihood of local families. An increasing number of alleyways provided links to the waterfront. Chiswick council erected the borough's first municipal housing in Strand on the Green in 1903 and the whole locality was built up by the 1930s. Some bomb-damaged properties were replaced after World War II and older cottages were renovated. Until the 1970s, Strand on the Green retained some industrial premises, which were replaced by residential accommodation as they successively closed.

The German-born painter Johann Zoffany lived at 65 Strand on the Green from 1790 until his death in 1810. Zoffany sometimes used local fishermen as his models, for example as Christ's disciples. The author Margaret Kennedy lived for a while at Strand Green House and made it the setting for her 1924 bestseller *The Constant Nymph*. Other village residents have included press baron Hugh Cudlipp, poet Dylan Thomas, writer Nancy Mitford and actor Donald Pleasance.

✉ W4

📖 Jennifer Buckle, *Victorian Legacy: Strand-on-the-Green As It Was*, Portia, 1992

Stratford • *Newham*

An important commercial and industrial centre situated north-west of WEST HAM, of which it was once a part. Excavations for the Jubilee Line extension uncovered the remains of horses that may have been killed as part of religious rituals around 300BC. Cistercian monks founded Langthorne Abbey in the marshes near the River Lea in 1135 and it grew to become one of the richest religious houses in England. The village was originally known as Stratford Langthorne – 'street ford near Langthorne Abbey' – to distinguish it from Stratford atte BOW, on the other side of the river. The construction of Bow Bridge attracted early agricultural industry east of the Lea. The village was a centre for the slaughter of livestock brought from East Anglia and for baking bread, using corn ground at the riverside mills on STRATFORD MARSH. In 1844 (the year that the poet Gerard Manley Hopkins was born here), Stratford began to be transformed as a result of the Metropolitan Building Act. This forced noxious industries to move outside London, and Stratford was the first place across the border in Essex, with good road and water connections into the city. The well-established mills, distilleries and breweries were joined by engineering works, printers, ink and dye works and every kind of processor of coal, oil, manure and animal bones. In 1847, George Hudson established the Eastern Counties Railway's locomotive works here and railway workers' housing was built at what became known as STRATFORD NEW TOWN. The town centre was built up with shops, public houses, places of entertainment and municipal institutions in the late 19th and early 20th centuries. The best surviving examples from this period are on the south side of the Broadway. In 1965 Stratford became the seat of government for the newly created borough of Newham, and the council soon set about demolishing much of the old town and building a lacklustre shopping centre and municipal tower blocks. More sympathetic regeneration around the turn of the 21st century has brought an almost metropolitan style to the town centre, especially around the small cultural quarter, which has the Theatre Royal Stratford East and the Stratford Picturehouse. Stratford's property values saw some of the biggest increases in London in the early 2000s. The town's appeal can only grow with the arrival of the Channel Tunnel rail link in 2007, the construction of STRATFORD CITY and its focal role in the staging of the Olympic Games in 2012.

The former Greater London Council chairman Tony Banks took the title Baron Stratford in 2005 after standing down as MP for West Ham.

✉ E15

476

♦ 12,278 (Stratford and New Town ward)

🚆 'one' Railway; Silverlink Metro; Central Line; Jubilee Line; Docklands Light Railway terminus (zone 3)

📖 Stephen Pewsey, *Stratford: A Pictorial History*, Phillimore, 1993

@ www.stratfordeast.com (Theatre Royal Stratford East)

Stratford City • Newham

A 'major metropolitan centre' soon to be built on former railway lands north and west of STRATFORD town centre. The 180-acre development will sit next to the site of the 2012 Olympic Park, and is planned to include more than 4,500 homes, 2,000 hotel rooms, a secondary school, a primary health care centre and several million square feet of offices, shops and leisure facilities. Landmark buildings are promised for the £4 billion scheme. The flood plain will be raised using material excavated in the building of the Channel Tunnel rail link. Outline planning permission for the scheme was granted early in 2005 but the subsequent takeover of the main promoter, Chelsfield plc, caused uncertainty regarding much-needed collaboration in the construction of the Olympic village. After the London Development Agency threatened to compulsorily purchase the site the issue was resolved amicably. Building is likely to begin at Stratford City in 2007 and the 'city centre' should be fully operational by 2010. Peripheral phases may not be completed for a further ten years.

✉ E15

@ www.futurestratford.com

Stratford Marsh • Newham

An industrial zone located west of STRATFORD town centre, soon to be transformed into a focal part of London's 2012 Olympic Park. In the Middle Ages watermills and windmills stood here, such as the one that gave its name to PUDDING MILL LANE. From the 18th century efforts were made to unite some of the channels of the River Lea that criss-crossed the marsh, notably via the creation of the River Lea Navigation. This reduced the number of crossing points required by Stratford Causeway, now the south-western end of the High Street (A118). The ecclesiastical parish of Stratford Marsh was established in 1852 and survived for just over a century. From 1867 the Carpenters' Company began to develop the land it held around present-day Carpenters

Road with a mix of factories and housing. Over the course of the 20th century a mish-mash of utilities, warehouses, yards and scrap-heaps filled most of the area, while diverse natural habitats flourished by the waters' edges. In 1966 Marshgate Lane became the site of the first nuclear reactor to be built for a UK university. It was commissioned for the department of nuclear engineering at Queen Mary College and was deactivated in 1982. The marsh is traversed by the inappropriately named Greenway, a pedestrian and cycling path that forms part of the Capital Ring, a 75-mile orbital route. One observer has summed up Marshgate Lane thus: 'Imagine the worst car-breaker, Rottweiler-ridden, broken glass, pit-bull terrier, burn anything, change-the-plates street, and it's here.' For all its roughness, Stratford Marsh has nurtured industries that Londoners do not want near their own homes and has provided urban photographers with endless opportunities for incongruous juxtapositions. All this is about to change as construction work begins on London's Olympic Park, which will be centred on Stratford Marsh. As plans stand at the time of writing, the main stadium will replace the Marshgate trading estate, just south of the City Mill River's divergence from the Lea. The aquatic centre will be located beside the Waterworks River. The area south of the Olympic Park and the new STRATFORD CITY will be redeveloped as the Carpenters' District, with the usual mix of facilities and amenities for such projects, and tall and medium-height towers that are intended to contain five million square feet of office space.

✉ E15

Stratford New Town · *Newham*

A seldom-heard name nowadays for the area midway between STRATFORD and LEYTON Central Line stations, but once the home of rail workshops to rival Swindon or York. In one of London's earliest railway developments, the Eastern Counties Railway line reached here in 1839 on its way to Romford. Eight years later the company made Stratford the site of its main works. Streets of workers' housing branched off Leyton Road in a development initially called Hudson Town after 'Railway King' George Hudson, the ECR chairman, who had joined the company in 1845. Within four years Hudson had fallen from grace in a fraud scandal, and the settlement's name was subsequently changed to Stratford New Town. The Great Eastern Railway succeeded the insolvent ECR in 1862. Stratford's sidings still accommodate freight and container terminals and will play a part in the Channel Tunnel rail link.

✉ E15

♁ 12,278 (Stratford and New Town ward)

Strawberry Hill · *Richmond*

A riverside locality situated between TWICKENHAM and TEDDINGTON, centred on one of London's most sumptuous mansions. In 1698 the Earl of Bradford's retired coachman built or bought a house here, which was acquired in 1747 by the politician and man of letters Horace Walpole. He renamed the house Strawberry Hill, after a field in the grounds. Strawberries are known to have been grown in the area before this time and commercial fruit gardens were later established nearby. Like HAMPTON HILL and MARBLE HILL, there is no real hill here, merely a slight elevation of the terrain. Walpole spent much of his life adding extra rooms and features to the 'little cottage', creating a Gothic fantasy set in a nine-acre landscaped garden that became famous throughout Europe. After Walpole's death in 1797 the property passed to his relatives, the Waldegrave family. Frances, widow of the seventh Earl of Waldegrave, added a new wing of her own design in 1862. In the following year the railway passed to the west of the house but it was ten years before a station opened in Strawberry Hill. Some have suggested that the station was built at the behest of the countess, for the convenience of her house guests, but it is more probable that property speculators pressurized the railway company into providing the facility. One of these developers was Chichester Fortescue, Frances's fourth husband, who laid out streets of villas on the edge of the family estate. Housebuilding continued to fill the area into the early 20th century. St Mary's College moved from BROOK GREEN to Strawberry Hill in 1925, and the mansion was further extended. The college is now part of the University of Surrey, with an emphasis on teacher training.

✉ Twickenham TW1 and TW2

🚃 South West Trains (zone 5)

📖 Anna Chalcraft, *A Paper House: Horace Walpole at Strawberry Hill*, Highgate, 1998; Anthony Beckles Willson, *Strawberry Hill: A History of the Neighbourhood*, Strawberry Hill Residents' Association, 1995

@ www.smuc.ac.uk (St Mary's College)

Streatham • *Lambeth* (pronounced 'strettəm')

An extensive south London suburb, stretching southwards from BRIXTON to NORBURY. Streatham was first recorded in Domesday Book as Estreham, but this is likely to have been a transcription error, since the name simply means 'street ham', a reference to a small settlement beside the Roman road. St Leonard's Church gained its own parish in 1291 and was rebuilt in the 14th century; it has since been almost totally rebuilt again. The estate of Streatham was part of the manor of TOOTING BEC in the Middle Ages, when more hamlets grew up at separate points along the road. After the Reformation and as the woodland was cleared the district was broken up into several farms and some of the landowners began to sell these off in the 18th century. Given Streatham's remoteness from London, most of the houses built at this time served as country retreats and the most important of these was the Thrale family's home at STREATHAM PARK. The first suburban dwellings appeared at the northern edge of the district in the 1830s, on STREATHAM HILL, and soon afterwards in ROUPELL PARK. Full suburbanization began after the opening of railway stations in the mid 19th century and the process reached a peak between 1880 and 1914, when the parish's cottages, mansions and fields were erased by a series of estates. The High Road and Streatham Hill (both sections of the A23) became a major shopping centre and, after World War I, an entertainment destination too. Streatham baths and ice rink both opened in 1934. The muddy south-west corner known originally as Lower Streatham was the last part of the district to be built up, whereupon it was renamed STREATHAM VALE. By the mid 1930s Wandsworth council had built blocks of flats at several locations across the district and municipal building accelerated after World War II. In the latter decades of the 20th century Streatham gained a multi-ethnic population; a slight majority of residents are now of white British descent. The largest minorities are of Caribbean and African origin. The amenities of Streatham Hill and High Road have struggled to recover from the depression of the 1980s, after which the John Lewis Partnership closed its department store here, and in a 2002 poll BBC radio listeners voted the High Road 'Britain's worst street … with its increasingly high level of violent crime'.

In 1959 Thomas Llewellan Jones wrote 'The Man Who Really Was Tarzan' for the *Man's Adventure Magazine*, in which he told the story of William Mildin, the 14th Earl of Streatham, who was shipwrecked in 1868 and then spent 15 years living in the African jungle. However, Jones's tale was as fictional as those of Edgar Rice Burroughs. Cynthia Payne, whose true story was filmed as *Personal Services*, ran a high-class brothel at her home in Ambleside Avenue, next door to the home of composer/conductor Carl Davis. The Mayor of London, Ken Livingstone, was born in Shrubbery Road, while Streatham's best-known contemporary daughter is the supermodel Naomi Campbell.

✉ SW16

♦ 51,769 (St Leonard's, Streatham Hill, Streatham South and Streatham Wells wards)

🚆 Southern; Thameslink (zone 3)

📖 Patrick Loobey, *Streatham in Old Photographs*, Sutton, 2003; John W Brown, *Streatham*, Tempus, 1999

@ www.streathamsociety.org.uk

Streatham Common • *Lambeth*

A butterfly-shaped open space and its surrounding housing, situated at the south-eastern corner of STREATHAM'S sprawl. Streatham wells were discovered in 1659 and were exploited as a tourist attraction. Well House was built in 1783 and later renamed The Rookery. After the water became contaminated in the early 1790s a new well was dug on Valley Road. Around 1820 David Wilson set up a silk mill opposite the west end of the common in an unsuccessful attempt to bring mass production to this cottage industry. P B Cow's India Rubber Works took over the site within two decades, making the famous Cow adhesive gum. Streatham Common station opened in 1862, originally as Greyhound Lane. The Metropolitan Board of Works acquired Streatham Common from the Ecclesiastical Commissioners in 1884, preserving it as a public open space. The vicinity was laid out with streets of pleasing villas, notably on the Coventry Park Estate, briefly making Streatham a fashionable address for the middle classes, while the very wealthy moved away. Streatham Common pumping station was built in 1888 to a delightful Moorish design and survives today on Conyers Road. Streatham's well water, which was said to have three times the mineral content of Epsom's, was bottled and delivered locally in the early years of the 20th century. The London County Council acquired The Rookery estate in 1912 and demolished the dilapidated house, opening its formal gardens to the public. A 200-year-old cedar in the gardens is one of the oldest in the country. Just over the borough border is NORWOOD Grove, another fine municipal garden, but this time with its house surviving; the hall was formerly the home of Arthur Anderson, one of the founders of the P&O shipping line. A Sainsbury's supermarket replaced Cow's works in the late 1980s, when the surviving textile mill was converted to a service block. The surviving Victorian and Edwardian houses in the neighbourhood have been recolonized by the middle classes in recent years and two-thirds of householders in the Streatham Wells ward are classified in the ABC1 socio-economic categories.

⊠ SW16

♦ 12,746 (Streatham Wells ward)

🚉 Southern (zone 3)

📖 *Sexby's History of Streatham Common*, Local History Publications, 1989

Streatham Hill • Lambeth

Not quite 'the REGENT STREET of south London' that its creator intended but a significant leisure zone on the STREATHAM/BRIXTON border. The eastern half of the area was part of the huge grounds of Leigham Court, a mansion that stood from around 1820 near to what is now the southern end of Mount Nod Road. The Royal Asylum of St Anne, a philanthropic boarding school for boys from poor families, moved to Streatham Hill from Aldersgate in 1825. Large villas began to line the main road, each with around an acre of garden, but the early arrival of the railway brought a switch to more compact suburban building. Streatham Hill was the district's first station when it opened in 1856 on the Crystal Palace branch line of the London, Brighton and South Coast Railway. The Artisans', Labourers' and General Dwellings Co. acquired Leigham Court in 1894 and built more than 1,000 homes, demolishing the original mansion in 1908. When leases on villas south of Telford Avenue began to expire in the 1920s, they were progressively acquired by Hugh Sewell Kingdon, whose project to create an entertainment centre involved a restaurant, dance hall, theatre, cinema and shops. The road was widened and the entire hinterland was soon built up. A higher proportion of flats and mansion blocks than elsewhere in the outer suburbs reflects the area's commercial vitality in the 1930s.

Pullman Court occupies the site of the Royal Asylum. This is a striking group of Grade II*-listed modernist blocks by Sir Frederick Gibberd, who went on to design Liverpool's Roman Catholic cathedral. In 1962, Streatham Hill theatre was converted into a bingo hall and the Gaumont Palace cinema became the largest bowling alley in Europe. The Locarno has remained a dance venue, under a variety of names including the Cat's Whiskers and Caesars.

The brothers and future show business impresarios Lew Grade, Bernard Delfont and Leslie Grade bought a flat for themselves and their mother in Pullman Court soon after it was built in 1935. The Clash's Mick Jones grew up at his grandmother's flat in Christchurch Road. Jones later sang of weekend dances in Streatham in the song *Stay Free*.

⊠ SW2; SW16

🚉 Southern (zone 3)

📖 *A Walk around Streatham Hill*, Streatham Society, 1982

@ www.pullmancourt.org.uk (residents' association and architectural history site)

Streatham Park • Wandsworth/Lambeth

A SOUTHWARK brewer, Ralph Thrale, built the substantial but not palatial Streatham Park in the 1730s on the foundations of a medieval house. Thrale had obtained a lease on 100 acres of TOOTING Common from the Duke of Bedford, allegedly in return for a constant supply of ale and porter at the duke's principal seat, Woburn Abbey. In 1767, Hester Salusbury married Ralph's son Henry at St Anne's Church in Soho and went to live with him at Streatham Park, taking her mother along too. Henry Thrale was MP for Southwark in the 1770s and his vivacious wife was a socialite who kept a revealing diary of her early years here. Dr Johnson was a close friend of the family and such a regular guest that he had his own apartment at Streatham Park. When Henry Thrale died in 1781, he left the house to Hester, who remarried and moved away. She later returned to Streatham Park for a while, but in such reduced circumstances that she had to auction its entire contents. When Hester died in 1821, her four daughters inherited the property and soon sold it. A succession of subsequent owners allowed Streatham Park to fall into an increasingly ruinous state and the house was demolished in 1863. From the 1870s the estate was developed for high-class suburban housing, a process that took 60 years to complete. Dixcote, at 8 North Drive, built in 1897, is the largest house in London by the renowned architect C F A Voysey. Most of the late Victorian villas have been replaced by council housing, principally the Greater London Council's Fayland estate of the 1960s. Those villas that remain now constitute a conservation area with some very mature landscaping, including an avenue of trees from the Thrale estate that now lines West Drive.

When Streatham Park was pulled down, *Punch* magazine commented that its timbers should be cut up and made into snuff boxes as 'relics of the immortal Sam' [Johnson].

✉ SW16

📖 Mary Hyde, *The Thrales of Streatham Park*, Harvard University Press, 1977

@ www.thrale.com (Thrale genealogy site)

Streatham Vale • *Lambeth*

The south-westernmost part of STREATHAM, formerly known as Lower or South Streatham, but once a corner of MITCHAM. For several centuries there was little here but fields, the River Graveney and a track connecting Mitcham with NORWOOD. The route was often used by Gypsies, who had camps in both villages. The Greyhound Inn, established around 1730, became a popular resting place for these travellers. The opening of Greyhound Lane station in 1862 barely stirred this remote spot and the lane remained a muddy track for several decades more. In 1875 the station was renamed Streatham Common and half of Greyhound Lane became Streatham Vale. The first houses appeared, mainly on Eardley Road, and a handful of industries were established, bringing local employment opportunities. Suburban development got under way abruptly from 1922 as the Streatham Vale estate took shape. Two private building firms shared most of the work, R H Miller laying out Abercairn Road and its offshoots, while Wates of Norbury built eastwards from Streatham Vale to the railway line. In the three years from 1929 a profusion of amenities were provided and improvements made. Schools opened on either side of Streatham Vale; the Greyhound Inn was rebuilt; the Graveney was channelled into culverts to prevent flooding; Streatham Vale Park was laid out on the site of an abandoned brickworks; and the new parish church of the Holy Redeemer was consecrated. Streatham Park Cemetery opened in 1920 on Rowan Road, so far south of Streatham Park itself that it lies in the London borough of Merton. The comic actor Will Hay was buried in the cemetery in 1949. The cemetery has a variety artists' section dedicated to lesser-known performers from the music hall era. An adjoining Jewish burial ground opened in 1932.

✉ SW16

📖 I C A Isaac, *Vale Vistas: The Story of Streatham Vale and its Parish Church*, Victoria, 1982

Stroud Green • *Haringey/Islington*

'An interesting, not very well known, Victorian urban landscape', according to local historian Ken Gay, situated north of FINSBURY PARK station and south of HORNSEY VALE. The name is of 15th-century origin and indicates a marshy place overgrown with brushwood. The first large building here was Stapleton Hall, which was built in 1609 for Sir Thomas Stapleton, possibly on the site of an earlier house. The hall became a public house in the 18th century and had an 80-acre farm in the mid 19th century. Housebuilding began around 1870 and spread from Stroud Green Road (originally Tollington Lane) north-eastward into HORNSEY parish, with the grandeur of the terraced streets increasing as the new district thrived; three-storeyed houses became the norm. Most of the streets have names with royal associations; Cornwall Road, for example, honours the duchy rather the county. Stroud Green gained its own station in 1881, on the Edgware, Highgate and London line, with shops and coal delivery offices around it. Such was the density of building that relatively new houses had to be demolished to make way for Stroud Green School in 1897. Stroud Green station closed in 1954 and the railway track has now become the Parkland Walk. Stapleton Hall was converted to apartments and new wings were added in 1989. Many houses have been subdivided and the locality is favoured by young graduates. In 2002 the Finsbury Park Business Forum's coordinator optimistically declared, 'We can really see Stroud Green Road becoming the next UPPER STREET … but [we will] make sure it retains its multicultural flavour'. Although mainly white, Stroud Green's population has significant black Caribbean and African minorities. At Stroud Green Primary School the main languages, other than English, are Turkish, Yoruba, French and Twi-Fante, which is spoken primarily in southern Ghana. More than half of 16- to 74-year-olds in Stroud Green are qualified to degree level or higher, 60 per cent of the adults are single and almost a third have no religion – exceptionally high figures compared to national averages.

The actor Bob Hoskins lived at 46 Upper Tollington Park from the age of three, and was educated at Stroud Green School.

> ✉ N4

> 👥 10,324 (Haringey's Stroud Green ward)

> 📖 Ken Gay, *Stroud Green and Finsbury Park: A Walk*, Hornsey Historical Society, 1997

> @ www.stroudgreen.net (community site)

Sudbury • *Brent*

A peaceful residential backwater situated west of WEMBLEY. The name was first recorded in the late 13th century as Suthbery – the southern manor house. Its northern counterpart may have been the manor house of HARROW. Sudbury Court was the principal Middlesex residence of the archbishops of Canterbury until the end of the 14th century, after which Sudbury manor was divided and leased out. Sudbury Common at this time stretched from Wembley to the foot of Harrow Hill. From 1630 the manor was in the hands of the family that became the Churchill-Rushouts, who much later developed NORTHWICK PARK. Squatters erected cottages on the common in the 17th century. Gradual improvements to the Harrow Road (A4005) brought the first houses and inns, including the Swan, the Black Horse and the Mitre, and the village consisted of 70 properties in 1759. Several substantial houses were built following the enclosure of the common in 1817. This was the first part of the Wembley area to undergo suburban development and when present-day Wembley Central station opened in 1842, it was initially called Sudbury. Shops were established around the Swan and schools opened in 1846 and 1880. Sir George Barham, the founder of the Express Country Milk Supply Co. (now Express Dairies plc), came to live in Sudbury in 1895 and the grounds of his mansion now form Barham Park. By the end of the 19th century the population had reached almost 1,000. In the first decade of the 20th century Sudbury gained two electric train services as well as electric trams. Day-trippers visited the Swan's tea garden and a racecourse operated for a while, on the site of the present Methodist church. Many of the Victorian villas were quickly demolished and their grounds were developed with housing. Outlying farms suffered the same fate after World War I, and development was further stimulated in the mid 1920s when the British Empire Exhibition was staged at Wembley. By the outbreak of World War II the suburb had four churches, a cinema and Charles Holden-designed stations at Sudbury Hill and Sudbury Town. Wembley council built the Sudbury Farm estate after the war and the Churchill-Rushouts laid out the Sudbury Court estate. Most of the old buildings of Sudbury were demolished during the 1950s, including Barham House. Construction continued in the 1960s and 1970s, mostly in the form of privately-built blocks of flats. Sudbury Cottages constitutes the smallest of Brent's conservation areas, preserving all that remains of the historic core of the early settlement that grew up at Sudbury Court. Like neighbouring Wembley, Sudbury is very popular with families of Indian descent, who make up more than a quarter of the population.

> ✉ Wembley HA0; Greenford UB6; Harrow HA1

> 👥 12,307

> 🚉 Chiltern Railways (Sudbury Hill Harrow; Sudbury and Harrow Road (limited service), zone 4); Piccadilly Line (Sudbury Town; Sudbury Hill, zone 4)

> 📖 M C Barrès-Baker, *Sudbury*, Grange Museum of Community History and Brent Archive, 2001

Suffield Hatch • *Waltham Forest*

A residential locality situated just west of CHINGFORD HATCH. First recorded in the 13th century, Suffield is a corruption of South Field, the name of a farm that in 1758 occupied 82 acres of land south of present-day New Road, which was formerly Southfield Road. A hatch was a gate that would have prevented cattle straying onto the roads from the forest waste. The farm's field pattern indicates that the land here was probably enclosed relatively late. The Suffield Hatch estate was auctioned in 1880 as 'eligible building land suitable for cottage property' but substantial construction did not occur until the 1930s, and development in the grounds of CHINGFORD Hospital has greatly expanded the population since then. The 50-acre Larkswood Park is the largest in Chingford and some of the trees in Larkswood were part of the ancient Epping Forest. A late 16th-century farmhouse has been preserved, though much altered. The former Larkswood swimming pool became a leisure centre in 2001. The area's main ethnic minorities are of Turkish and Greek origin.

> ✉ E4

Summerstown • *Wandsworth*

A light industrial enclave located beside the River Wandle, where TOOTING meets WIMBLEDON. The street named Summerstown links Plough Lane with Garratt Lane (A217). From the late Middle Ages there were mills beside the river, which frequently flooded the area. 'Dutchmen' are recorded as manufacturing brass plates for kettles and frying pans around 1631 and there is also evidence of Huguenot silk-weaving and wig-making here. In the 18th and early 19th centuries the hamlet provided labour for the Wandle's mills. Summerstown's Romanesque parish church of St Mary replaced an earlier chapel in 1904 and is now Grade-II listed. Wimbledon, Lambeth and Streatham cemeteries lie to the west, south and east respectively. The writer and poet Edward Thomas cycled through Summerstown just before the outbreak of World War I and described the scene in his evocative travelogue *In Pursuit of Spring*. Observing a damp meadow, factories and dirty houses, he concluded that a 'mixture of the sordid and the delicate in the whole was unmistakable'. Summerstown has recently been the focus of extensive housebuilding but developers claim the new properties are in desirable EARLSFIELD, despite the SW17 address.

Marc Feld, later to become the rock star Marc Bolan, moved with his family to one of the new Sun Cottages in Summerstown in 1962. This was a comedown from the street cred he had enjoyed when living in STOKE NEWINGTON and he spent as much time as possible in the clubs of SOHO.

✉ SW17

Sundridge • *Bromley*

The north-eastern part of BROMLEY, spread around the golf courses of SUNDRIDGE PARK. First mentioned in a charter dated 987, Sundridge (or Sundresse, as it was originally known) was in the hands of the Le Blund family for several centuries from around 1220. From the 17th century a succession of wealthy Londoners lived here and a three-storey brick house was built on the southern slope of the Quaggy River valley early in the 18th century. Sir Claude Scott purchased that house in 1795 and demolished it on the advice of Humphry Repton, building the present mansion on the opposite slope and creating the park. To the south, on Sundridge Avenue, Robert Whyte junior built a grand house for his family in 1899. After his death, Whyte's widow and daughters saw through his plan to create a

music room capable of holding up to 80 guests. Family concerts featured performances by Sir Adrian Boult, Paul Tortelier and many others. In 1968 the house became an arts centre that now attracts nearly 20,000 visitors a year; Julian Lloyd Webber, Cliff Richard, James Galway and David Bowie have performed there. Several architecturally impressive houses from the mid 20th century are clustered around Sundridge Park station, on Plaistow Lane, Edward Road and Lodge Road. Two of the most highly regarded are Godfrey Samuel's By the Links (1935) and Ivor Berresford's cedar-clad Brooklyn (1958).

The Russian anarchist Peter Kropotkin lived for several years at 61 Crescent Road. David Bowie spent his childhood from 1955 to 1965 at 4 Plaistow Grove.

✉ Bromley BR1

🚶 14,374 (Plaistow and Sundridge ward)

@ www.bromleyarts.com/rac/rac.html (Ripley Arts Centre site)

Sundridge Park • *Bromley*

Although some maps identify SUNDRIDGE and Sundridge Park as discrete places, the latter is simply an evolution of the former − a later name for the estate of Sundridge, its mansion and parkland, now a management centre and a golf club. The two names are used interchangeably for the neighbouring residential area. Sundridge Park was created in the late 1790s for Sir Claude Scott. The stuccoed mansion was designed by John Nash and the work was completed under the direction of Samuel Wyatt. The surrounding farmland was transformed into parkland to a plan by Humphry Repton. When the railway line to BROMLEY NORTH opened in 1878, the Scott family had a station built for their private use. Towards the end of the 19th century Sir Edward Scott began to sell off the estate and a rebuilt station opened to the public as Sundridge Park in 1896. The park became a golf course, with a new clubhouse opened in 1903 by the prime minister, A J Balfour. What began as a nine-hole course has since grown into a pair of what Pevsner called 'unusually umbrageous' 18-hole courses. The mansion functioned as a luxury hotel until after World War II and became a management centre in 1956. A new block of residential accommodation was completed in 1970.

Sir Edward Scott won fame for breeding pheasants, and his namesake the Prince of Wales (the future Edward VII) was equally well-known for his love of killing them. Understandably, the two men became friends and the future king often visited Sundridge Park for game-shooting weekends.

> ✉ Bromley BR1

> 🚆 South Eastern Trains (zone 4)

> 📖 Ken Wilson, *Sundridge Park*, Sundridge Park Management Centre, c.1991

> @ www.spgc.co.uk (Sundridge Park Golf Club site)

Surbiton • *Kingston*
The embodiment of London suburbia, partly because it sounds like a contraction of 'suburban town', Surbiton originated in the twelfth century as a farm located south of KINGSTON UPON THAMES – and 'southern homestead' is the real meaning of the name. In 1648, Royalist and Parliamentarian forces clashed in a skirmish on Surbiton Hill in which the 19-year-old Lord Francis Villiers was killed, possibly on the site of the present-day Villiers Path. Surbiton Place was built in the mid 18th century for William Roffee, a distiller who kept a fleet of pleasure boats on the Thames and held parties that were attended by royalty. The house was later acquired and enlarged by the Earl of Uxbridge. In the early 19th century the hamlet consisted of around 40 dwellings and the Waggon and Horses public house but because Kingston brushed the railway aside, Surbiton acquired a station very early. This opened as Kingston-on-Railway in 1838, and over the following half-century high-class housing spread across the new suburb, which was also known as Kingston New Town or New Kingston. Thomas Pooley began an ambitious estate but overreached himself, and in 1844 control of the project passed to his bankers, who donated sites for the district's first church and school. Alexander Raphael of Surbiton Place built St Raphael's Roman Catholic Church in 1847 but died not long after its completion. William Woods bought the Surbiton Place estate and retained the mansion, while putting up villas in the vicinity of Surbiton Road and Portsmouth Road. From the early 1850s, waterworks were constructed beside the Thames at SEETHING WELLS. Surbiton laid claim to Ealing's title of 'queen of the suburbs' but by the end of the 19th century its fashionability had begun to decline, although growth continued in more modest form. The opening of the Kingston bypass (A3) in 1927 helped stimulate a building boom that filled the former farmland of TOLWORTH, SOUTHBOROUGH and

BERRYLANDS. Compact blocks of flats replaced some Victorian villas nearer the town centre and later on the Surbiton Place estate. In 1931 Surbiton Place was demolished and its site was built over. Surbiton station was rebuilt in a modernist style in 1938. Office blocks appeared in the town centre from the late 1950s and a small number of Victorian properties were compulsorily purchased and replaced by council housing in the Alpha Road area. Surbiton station, now a Grade II-listed building, was voted Britain's 'most improved station' after its £3 million refurbishment in 1998. Surbiton's image is not a suburban myth; the overwhelming majority of residents are white, middle-class homeowners.

The town's reputation was fostered in the early 1900s by literary works such as Barry Pain's *Eliza*, which poked fun at the home life of a clerk, and Keble Howard's *The Smiths of Surbiton*. The Avenue, Surbiton, was the setting for the BBC television comedy series *The Good Life*, in which a suburban couple adopted a self-sufficient lifestyle, but the exterior scenes were actually filmed in NORTHWOOD. Real-life Surbiton residents have included Alfred Bestall, the creator of Rupert Bear, Helen Sharman, the first Briton in space, and campaigning anti-apartheid exile Donald Woods.

> ✉ Surbiton KT6 and KT5

> 🚶 29,113 (St Mark's, Berrylands and Surbiton Hill wards)

> 🚆 South West Trains (zone 6)

> 📖 Robert Statham, *Surbiton Past*, Phillimore, 1996

Surrey Quays • *Southwark*
The redeveloped site of the former Surrey Docks, which includes GREENLAND DOCK and CANADA WATER. In 1695 Wriothesley Russell (later second Duke of Bedford) married Elizabeth Howland and the Russell family thus gained control of the potentially valuable Rotherhithe peninsula. He was 14 at the time and she was 11. Excavation of the Howland Great Wet Dock (later Greenland Dock) began the following year and work was completed by 1700. In the 1790s theft and congestion caused chaos in the POOL OF LONDON, creating an intense demand for additional inland facilities, and over the following century several rival companies filled 372 acres of the peninsula with a series of new docks. Ruinous competition between the companies prompted their merger in 1865 as the Surrey Commercial Docks Co. The East London Railway traversed

the docks in 1869 and Deptford Road (later Surrey Docks) station opened in 1884. The Port of London Authority assumed control of the docks after its establishment in 1908. World War II brought the devastation of the built environment and displacement of the local population. Many evacuees never returned and those that did were in desperate need of rehousing. Bermondsey council built blocks of flats, while the PLA partially rebuilt the docks. However, with the decline of the whole of the London DOCKLANDS, the Surrey Docks were progressively shut down in the 1960s and closed completely in 1970. The whole estate was acquired by the Greater London Council and some grandiose schemes were mooted, including a Channel Tunnel rail terminal, an Olympic park and a vertical take-off and landing (VTOL) airport. However, a recession in the commercial property market meant that most of the site was redeveloped with mixed-tenure housing after the London Docklands Development Corporation took over in 1981. Most of the docks were filled in, unlike those across the river. Shopping and leisure facilities filled most of the Canada Dock site. A small part of Lavender Dock became a pond and ecological study area for schoolchildren. The renaming of Surrey Docks station as Surrey Quays in 1989 caused some resentment at the time but has since established the area's reinvented identity. Private housebuilding has continued into the 21st century, with developers referring to projects in parts of DEPTFORD as 'near Surrey Quays'. Almost a third of the residents of the Surrey Docks ward are in their twenties and there are relatively few children or old people. More than four-fifths of the population is white, a very high proportion by the borough's standards.

Local band Squeeze sang about the Surrey Docks on 'It's Not Cricket', a track from the album *Cool for Cats*.

✉ SE16

♦ 11,346 (Surrey Docks ward)

🚇 East London line (zone 2)

📖 Stuart Rankin, *A Short History of the Surrey Commercial Docks*, Rotherhithe Local History Society, 1999

@ www.btinternet.com/~se16 (privately operated local information site)

Sutton • *Sutton*

A busy town since the Victorian era, situated four miles west of CROYDON. Domesday Book provided the first reliable mention of the estate, as Sudtone. The name means 'south farmstead' and may have referred to its position in relation to MORDEN or MITCHAM. Little is known of medieval Sutton, which may not even have existed as a focused settlement until much later. By the mid 18th century the village consisted of a loose ribbon of houses along the High Street. At the first census in 1801, Sutton had fewer inhabitants than CHEAM or WALLINGTON, and far fewer than CARSHALTON, but the increase in coaching traffic on the Brighton road and the subsequent arrival of the railway in 1847 brought early growth. The medieval parish church of St Nicholas was demolished and replaced by the present church in 1864. Soon after this, more railway connections were added and lord of the manor Thomas Alcock developed a prestigious estate that formed the new parish of BENHILTON, and endowed All Saints' Church. Alcock also laid out the streets of Newtown, east of the High Street, but left it to an assortment of builders to put up cramped terraced housing for the working classes. Shops and several pubs lined Lind Road, but few of the original properties have survived. By 1881 Sutton had grown larger than its three rivals combined. Some very grand homes were built in south Sutton towards the end of the century but these too have mostly been replaced by flats or smaller houses. One stately survivor on Worcester Road, The Russettings, has been preserved as the borough's register office. The town continued to expand, especially after trams came from Croydon in 1906, but having already grown so much it lacked the space for the kind of Edwardian or interwar development that transformed its neighbours. In 1914 the council created Manor Park from the grounds of three large houses, none of which had ever been a manor house. The WEST SUTTON and SUTTON COMMON localities filled with compact housing in the 1930s, following the construction of the Sutton bypass (A217) and the railway loop line to WIMBLEDON. After World War II, and especially in the 1960s, much of the old town centre was redeveloped with shops and offices, although not on the scale witnessed in Croydon. Initiatives since the mid 1970s have included the pedestrianization of the High Street and the opening of the multi-use civic centre, the Secombe Theatre and the Times Square and St Nicholas shopping centres. Away from the town centre, developers continue to seek planning permission to demolish Victorian properties and replace them with small apartment blocks. More than four-fifths of residents are of white British origin and a clear majority are categorized within the ABC1 social groups – overwhelmingly so in the Sutton South and Sutton West wards.

Sutton inspired the BBC radio serial *Mrs Dale's Diary*, the daily account of a doctor's wife and her family, which ran from 1948 to 1969. The raconteur and pioneer of open effeminacy Quentin Crisp was born in Sutton in 1908. His life was portrayed by John Hurt in *The Naked Civil Servant*, filmed for television in 1975.

> ✉ Sutton SM1 and SM2
>
> ♦ 38,498 (Sutton Central, Sutton North, Sutton South and Sutton West wards)
>
> 🚆 Southern; Thameslink (zone 5)
>
> 📖 Sara Goodwins, *Sutton Past and Present*, Sutton, 2004
>
> @ www.suttonguardian.co.uk (online local newspaper); www.suttontheatres.co.uk

Sutton Common • *Sutton*

A station in north SUTTON on the WIMBLEDON loop of the Thameslink line, but the name is rarely used to identify the neighbourhood. Sutton Common was a club-shaped swathe of farmland stretching northwards from the old village. Sutton Green stood at its northern end and was left as open space when the common was enclosed and divided into pasture and arable land in 1809. Later in the 19th century some large villas were erected here with spacious gardens. Between the wars these properties were replaced with cheaper, more densely built-up terraced and semi-detached houses, a process that accelerated with the opening of the station in 1930. The Southern Railway Co. had gained permission to build a line to Wimbledon in 1910 but had not proceeded until it faced the threat of competition from a potential extension of the Northern Line from MORDEN to Sutton. Some of Sutton Common's roads, such as Fairlands Avenue and Hurstcourt Road, are named after houses that once stood there but have been demolished. Sutton Common recreation ground, which is designated as Metropolitan Open Land, has a children's playground, tennis courts, a basketball court and a pavilion that has been restored following a fire in 1999. Glenthorne High School, on Sutton Common Road, is a mixed comprehensive school that has arts college status. Only four per cent of its pupils are from ethnic minorities, reflect-

ing the absence of racial diversity in the area. The ward of Sutton Common was merged with NORTH CHEAM in 2002 to create Stonecot.

> ✉ Sutton SM1 and SM3
>
> 🚆 Thameslink (zone 4)

Swiss Cottage • *Camden*

A well-endowed amenity centre serving a wide catchment area north of ST JOHN'S WOOD, but with pockets of deprivation in its immediate vicinity. FINCHLEY ROAD and Avenue Road converged here in the 1820s and Adelaide Road cut across Eton College's land in 1830. By 1841 the Swiss Cottage tavern stood on the island formed at the junction of the three roads. It has since been rebuilt and enlarged while retaining its chalet style. A steady programme of housebuilding on the Eton estate accelerated after the opening of Swiss Cottage station in 1868. This was the terminus of a line that was intended to be extended later to HAMPSTEAD but instead went to WILLESDEN GREEN in 1879. Shops progressed northwards along Finchley Road in the 1880s. In the late 1930s a bulky Odeon cinema and the flats of Regency Lodge filled out the tavern's island site. Bombs aimed at the railway line did extensive damage during World War II and 35 acres of the Eton estate were afterwards redeveloped with high- and low-rise blocks of flats. A library and swimming pool and a new home for Hampstead Theatre opened in the early 1960s. As these and other local facilities have become in need of renewal, Camden council has been investing in Swiss Cottage on a scale not seen since the days of Victorian municipal largesse. An £85 million project includes a leisure centre, community centre, social and private housing and a park. The council has provided new stalls with credit card payment facilities for Eton Avenue market and the food traders are becoming more Gordon Ramsey than gorblimey.

Based on a childhood experience, Wilkie Collins made the Swiss Cottage turnpike the setting for a scene in his 1862 novel *The Woman in White*. The 'Swiss Cottage slickster' was a greased-back hairstyle that flourished briefly in the early 2000s.

> ✉ NW3; NW6
>
> ♦ 11,663
>
> 🚆 Jubilee Line (zone 2)
>
> 📖 Carola Zentner and Elaine Hallgarten, *Insider's Guide to Hampstead and Swiss Cottage*, Searchlight, 1994

Sydenham • *Lewisham/Bromley*

A formerly grand Victorian suburb situated south of DULWICH and FOREST HILL. This was Chipeham in 1206, probably the farmstead of a man called Cippa, and the name evolved in stages over several centuries. The last change, when the 'p' became a 'd', did not occur until the late 17th century. By this time two distinct settlements had evolved: one around BELL GREEN in present-day LOWER SYDENHAM and the other in what is now Sydenham Wells Park, where the presence of springs with alleged medicinal qualities was drawing visitors. These two halves of Sydenham were divided by the Croydon Canal, which was constructed from 1801, and by Westwood Common, which was enclosed in the 1810s. When the canal company went bankrupt, a railway line was laid along the course of the filled-in canal and Sydenham station opened in 1839, after which houses for wealthy Londoners began to appear on the former common. In 1854 the CRYSTAL PALACE was brought from HYDE PARK and rebuilt on the southern ridge of SYDENHAM HILL in the south-west corner of the district. This event transmuted the fortunes of the extended village. Improvements in communications made Sydenham the best connected place south of the Thames. Hotels and every kind of amenity catered to the needs of the tens of thousands of tourists. Grand houses were built for the new residents, including Crystal Palace managers and directors, in UPPER SYDENHAM and LAWRIE PARK, with attendant accommodation for those who provided their services or laboured less lucratively at the palace. A huge gasworks was built at Bell Green, which became one of the most densely built-up parts of outer London. Sydenham's population doubled every ten years in the three decades to 1871 and doubled again over the remainder of the 19th century, reaching around 40,000. The appeal of the Crystal Palace declined in the 20th century but its destruction by fire in 1936 was still a tremendous blow. Many of Sydenham's grandest houses were replaced by homes for the new breed of commuter, while municipal estates were built in several corners, for example at Sheenewood in Lawrie Park, High Level Drive in Upper Sydenham, the Dacres estate in Lower Sydenham, in the Kirkdale area north of Sydenham station, and at Bell Green. On Dartmouth Road, Sydenham School was greatly enlarged to become a comprehensive in 1957. Despite the changes, the hilly terrain and surviving vestiges of its Victorian heyday continue to endow Sydenham with a distinctive character, although the town centre is in need of regeneration.

The Antarctic explorer Sir Ernest Shackleton lived at 12 Westwood Hill.

✉ SE26

♦ 15,353

🚇 Southern (zone 3)

📖 Joan P Alcock, *Sydenham and Forest Hill: History and Guide*, Tempus, 2005

@ www.virtualsydenham.com (community site); www.sydenham.org.uk (community site); www.sydenhamsociety.com (civic amenity site)

Sydenham Hill • *Southwark/Lewisham*

A station and road lying on the western edge of UPPER SYDENHAM. This part of London is filled with place names that begin with 'Upper' or end with 'Hill', but Sydenham Hill rises higher than most, topping 350 feet at the southern end of the road that shares its name. For this reason, it was chosen as the site for the CRYSTAL PALACE, which was rebuilt here in 1854. The northern end of the locality is as much a part of DULWICH as of Upper Sydenham, and if SYDENHAM had not had a strong reputation of its own the station would probably have been called South Dulwich when it opened in 1863. With the attraction of the palace and the benefit of the railway, numerous villas were built on the hill, especially in the third quarter of the 19th century, some of which were themselves pretentiously palatial. South of the station, Kingswood House was remodelled in the 1890s as a stone-faced baronial castle for the founder of the Bovril company. The grounds were sold for development after World War II and the house is now a community centre. Most of the other large houses in the locality were demolished over the course of the 20th century and replaced with housing that varies widely in grandeur and aesthetic quality. The most architecturally significant is the Tecton partnership's Six Pillars, on Crescent Wood Road, which was built for a school headmaster in 1935. Six Pillars was refurbished in 2003 and is occasionally opened to the public. Sydenham Hill Wood constitutes a surviving fragment of the Great North Wood that once stretched from Croydon to Camberwell. It possesses a rich mosaic of ancient and recent woodland and is home to woodpeckers and warblers, bamboo and bluebells. Dulwich and Sydenham Hill golf course lies to the north.

The television pioneer John Logie Baird lived at 3 Crescent Wood Road.

✉ SE26

🚃 South Eastern Trains (zone 3)

@ www.sydenham.org.uk/six_pillars.html

Syon Lane • *Hounslow*

Classified as a 'London distributor road', it connects SYON PARK and OSTERLEY Park, which are the grounds of west London's finest stately homes. The lane formerly had other grand villas, including Wyke House, which became a private lunatic asylum in the 19th century, and the Duke of Marlborough's Syon Hill. Syon Lane station opened on the HOUNSLOW loop line in 1849. Just to the north, the former Gillette factory was designed in 1937 by the relatively undistinguished Sir Banister Fletcher, when he was 71. Pevsner speaks of its 'incongruous, timidly modernistic grandeur', but it outshines most industrial buildings. Syon Lane is bisected by the Great West Road (A4) at Gillette Corner and BRENTFORD'S main business district lies east of this junction, where there is a Tesco superstore and a small shopping parade. Sports grounds and their clubhouses now dominate the northern part of the lane, with football clubs on the west side and rugby clubs on the east. Beyond these are the compact Wyke Green and the much larger Wyke Green golf course, on the edge of Osterley Park. The Syon ward covers an area between the railway line and the river. This is a diverse ward where residents are equally likely to be buying their home or renting it; to be single or married; and to have a degree or no qualifications at all.

✉ Isleworth TW7

👤 9,717 (Syon ward)

🚃 South West Trains (zone 4)

Syon Park • *Hounslow*

Syon Park occupies a long stretch of the riverside between BRENTFORD and ISLEWORTH and Syon House is the London seat of the dukes of Northumberland. The north-eastern part of the park was the scene of the battles of Brentford in 1016 and 1642. In 1431 the English followers of the teachings of St Bridget of Sweden moved their headquarters here from TWICKENHAM and built Syon Abbey, which took its name from the biblical Mount Zion. There are few remnants of the abbey but archaeological surveys have located the sites of some former outbuildings and determined that the main structure may have been almost as large as Salisbury Cathedral. When Henry VIII dissolved the monastic establishments in the 1530s, he gave the estate to Edward Seymour, the uncle of his son, the future Edward VI. During the first part of Edward's brief reign, Seymour was created first Duke of Somerset and 'Protector of England', acting as regent – and sovereign in all but name – for the child monarch. An admirer of Italian Renaissance architecture, he built Syon House in that style over the foundations of the west end of the abbey church between 1547 and his death by execution in 1552. The house retains the abbey's vaulted undercroft below the Great Hall. Two centuries later Sir Hugh Smithson, later the first Duke of Northumberland, acquired the estate through his marriage to Elizabeth Seymour. The couple employed Robert Adam to remodel the interior of the house and Capability Brown to landscape the grounds, creating a showpiece that is now open to the public.

Syon House is also available for private hire and as film location. It featured in *The Madness of King George*, the 1994 film of the play *The Madness of George III*, and more recently in *Gosford Park* and *The Golden Bowl*. In an effort to address west London's 'lack of profile' compared with the EAST END, a recent tourism initiative has highlighted attractions such as Syon Park. Syon is the only known area of tall grass washland along the Thames in London. Tide Meadow has reed grasses and rye grass, with marshland plants including the very poisonous hemlock water dropwort. Herons and flocks of overwintering birds use the tidal muds.

✉ Brentford TW8

📖 *Syon*, Heritage House Group, 2003

@ www.syonpark.co.uk

Taggs Island • *Richmond*

A populous Thames atoll formerly called Walnut Tree Island or Garrick's Upper Eyot, located between HAMPTON and HAMPTON COURT. Willows grew here and their branches were used for basket-making. From the 1850s the convenient nearby presence of Hampton Court station drew day-trippers to the island's shabby pub and skittle alley, the Angler's Retreat. Thomas Tagg set up both a home and a boat-building business here in 1868 and soon took over the lease of the Angler's Retreat and rebuilt it as a hotel, where guests included the French actress Sarah Bernhardt. Grand houseboats were moored around the island, one of which was rented in 1887 by the author J M Barrie. George Tagg took over his father's business but poor summers and unfavourable economic conditions forced him to sell up in 1903. Tagg remained manager of the hotel until 1912, when it was acquired by the impresario Fred Karno, who built an opulent hotel that he called the Karsino and an equally luxurious houseboat for himself, the *Astoria*. Charlie Chaplin is said to have stayed on the boat. Custom was initially brisk at the hotel but the outbreak of World War I caused a decline in trade from which it did not recover, despite relaunches as the Thames Riviera and later the Palm Beach. During World War II, munitions were produced on the island and a bridge was built to carry them to the shore. Karno's hotel was demolished in 1971, when Taggs Island had become derelict. The centre of the island was excavated in 1983 to create a lagoon that increased the capacity for houseboats and a bridge capable of carrying cars was built. The island's community is entirely based on houseboats; there are no permanent structures here.

The musician David Gilmour bought the *Astoria* in 1986 and converted it into a floating studio. Pink Floyd's albums *A Momentary Lapse of Reason* and *The Division Bell* were recorded on the boat.

✉ Hampton TW12

@ www.taggs-island.com (superb community site)

Teddington • *Richmond*

A very large and very comfortable Victorian suburb, located south of TWICKENHAM. It was first documented in the 11th century, although it is not mentioned in Domesday Book, and its name probably derives from words meaning 'farmstead of a man called Tuda'. In the Middle Ages the village grew near the river, around St Mary's Church and the manor house. The oldest main road ran along the route of the Twickenham Road and Kingston Road and connected the London–HOUNSLOW road with the bridge from HAMPTON WICK to KINGSTON in 1219. There was a fishing weir on the Thames at Teddington between 1345 and about 1535. A road, now Waldegrave Road through to Park Road, probably came into existence to cater for traffic to HAMPTON COURT, a royal palace from about 1525. Some large houses were built as a result of the increasing popularity of nearby RICHMOND in the 17th and 18th centuries, the first probably in 1672. One of the few remaining is Elmfield House, which is now used by Richmond council. By the 18th century a few houses existed along the High Street, with another settlement in Park Road. The common land, which was part of HOUNSLOW HEATH, and the open fields to the north and south of the village were enclosed in 1800. Teddington Lock was constructed in 1811 and marks the end of the tidal reach of the Thames. It was rebuilt with an additional side-lock in 1857. The sale of the manorial estate and the opening of Teddington station in 1863 led to a deluge of middle-class housing being built, including at SOUTH TEDDINGTON. Small terraces went up between Stanley Road and Waldegrave Road, and Broad Street became a street of shops. Manor Road had been laid out in 1861 but the rest of that end of the high street, although it grew rapidly, was not so densely filled. By 1871 the parish of Teddington had four times as many houses as a decade earlier. Among the major buildings opened in the 1870s and 1880s were St Peter's Church, a cottage hospital, a town hall and St Alban's Church. Of these, only the churches survive, the latter as the Landmark Arts Centre. A footbridge over the lock replaced the ferry from 1889. The National Physical Laboratory opened in 1902 (see BUSHY PARK). The coming of tram services in 1903 stimulated building around the Kingston Road area and by the outbreak of World War I most of the existing streets and housing were in place. More commercial premises opened after World War II, primarily in the form of offices and workshops, and a council estate was built at Udney Park. Teddington business park opened in 1984 on the site of an old coal yard in Station Road. In recent years blocks of upmarket flats have been built wherever planning permission can be obtained. Teddington's population is predominantly white, middle-aged and well-educated.

After receiving a legacy in 1857, R D Blackmore bought Gomer House, now demolished. He established a peach orchard here and wrote numerous novels, including the romantic adventure story *Lorna Doone*. No. 131 Waldegrave Road was the birthplace and childhood home of Noel Coward. There has been filmmaking at Teddington Studios since 1912 but it boomed after Warner Bros leased and then bought the studio in the 1930s, when it was said to have produced 10 per cent of British films. It was substantially rebuilt after being bombed during World War II and became a television studio in 1958. Recent productions here include *The Office* and *Pop Idol*.

✉ Teddington TW11

👥 9,615

🚃 South West Trains (zone 6)

📖 K Howe, *Teddington Past and Present*, Hendon Publishing, 1994

@ www.teddington-online.co.uk (community site)

Telegraph Hill · *Lewisham*

An electoral ward and a two-part park, situated between NEW CROSS and NUNHEAD. The hill rises to around 150 feet and is so called for a semaphore signalling station that was established here in 1795. Until then, this had been Plow'd Garlic Hill. The signalling station was one of the points from which news of Wellington's victory at Waterloo was flashed to London. It was removed in 1823. The area

was part of the Worshipful Company of Haberdashers' extensive landholdings in the manor of HATCHAM. The company had already built terraced housing on its land nearer New Cross Road when it commissioned a study of the development potential of Telegraph Hill in 1859. The surveyor recommended 'the erection of dwelling houses of a high standard' on wide tree-lined streets. The company added Haberdashers' Aske's School for boys and girls (named after one of its members Robert Aske, and now Hatcham College) in 1875, a separate Haberdashers' Aske's girls' school in 1891 and St Catherine's Church in 1894. In the following year the London County Council opened Telegraph Hill Park to the public. The Victorian housing of Telegraph Hill now constitutes a distinctive enclave, with a relatively diverse middle-class population that includes a significant number of welfare professionals. The strong community spirit is demonstrated by the Telegraph Hill Society's well-maintained website.

In the 1840s the poet Robert Browning lived near New Cross Road at Telegraph Cottage.

✉ SE14

👥 14,426

📖 Raymond Thatcher, *Hatcham and Telegraph Hill: An Historical Sketch*, Lewisham Historical Society, 1982

@ www.thehill.org.uk

Temple · *City*

A pair of autonomous enclaves of the CITY OF LONDON, forming two of the four Inns of Court, situated south of the western half of FLEET STREET. The Military Order of the Knights Templar, a monastic order founded during the Crusades, established a church and residential quarters by the river around 1160. Temple Church was built in two phases and completed in 1240. The order's clergy occupied a consecrated precinct on the east side of the church and the knights, squires and various lay brothers lived to the south and west. The Order was suppressed in 1312 and Parliament voted its buildings to the Order of the Hospital of St John of Jerusalem, which leased them to students of law. There is some debate about when, why and even *if* the college divided itself into two separate Inns of Court. (They were called 'inns' because their members lived communally.) The usual explanation is that at some time in the late 14th or early 15th centuries the lawyers agreed on the split for administrative purposes. Another theory holds that there were always two societies, which later came to be called the 'Inner Temple' and 'Middle Temple' because the former lay nearer the City while the latter occupied the buildings in the middle of the complex. Most of the medieval buildings were destroyed in the Great Fire and in three subsequent fires in the second half of the 17th century and the Temple was rebuilt to a more collegiate plan. The grounds were extended southwards with the construction of the Victoria EMBANKMENT in 1870, when Temple station opened. The Temple and its church were badly bomb-damaged during World War II but sensitive restoration has preserved the other-worldly intimacy of this enclave, where the courtyards are still illuminated by gas lamps. Law is no longer taught here and barristers' chambers occupy most of the buildings.

The American Senator at Temple Bar is one of Anthony Trollope's lesser-known works. Television companies have made frequent use of the Temple, in productions as diverse as the BBC's *David Copperfield* and ITV's *The Bill*.

⊠ EC4 (Temple station is in WC2)

🚌 Circle Line; District Line (zone 1)

@ www.innertemple.org.uk;
www.middletemple.org.uk

Temple Fortune • *Barnet*

An overlap locality separated from HENDON by the River Brent and the North Circular Road (A406), and sharing characteristics with its neighbours to the south and east. This was part of the manor of Blechenham in Saxon times. The first part of its present name refers to ownership of the land hereabouts by the Knights Templar from 1243. The second part of the name may be a corruption of 'fore-ton', a farmstead that lay before somewhere – probably Hendon as one travelled from London. John Rocque's map of 1754 was the first to identify Temple Fortune, when a single farmhouse stood here by a small green. Temple Fortune remained isolated until the arrival of the FINCHLEY ROAD in the late 1820s. The Royal Oak was established as a coaching inn and terraces of cottages began to appear; two on Hendon Park Row are the only survivors. By 1880 most of the open land had been enclosed and in 1903 Eton College's holdings north of HAMPSTEAD were divided into three farms, one of which was named Temple Fortune Farm. Within a few years the eastern side of Temple Fortune was developed as part of the 'artisans' quarter' of HAMPSTEAD GARDEN SUBURB and shopping parades with flats above were built as part of the suburb's quirky philosophy of banishing commercial enterprise to the fringes of the estate. The style of the parades was inspired by the walls of medieval towns like Rothenburg in Bavaria. Meanwhile, GOLDERS GREEN expanded into the south of the locality following the opening of its station in 1907. Decoy Farm, which had occupied the north and west of Temple Fortune, was built over from the mid 1920s. On Cranbourne Gardens, St Barnabas's Church replaced an earlier chapel in 1934. Like its neighbouring localities, Temple Fortune is now popular with members of the Jewish community but its property prices have sailed out of the reach of artisans of any faith.

Aida Foster founded a school of drama in Temple Fortune in 1927 and ran it until the 1970s. She later claimed that Elizabeth Taylor had been a pupil but Ms Taylor has not confirmed this. *EastEnders* and *Carry On* star Barbara Windsor certainly attended the school, taking four buses to get here from STOKE NEWINGTON and feeling a little out of place among the well-heeled local girls.

⊠ NW11

Temple Mills • *Waltham Forest*

An industrial, commercial and railway area beside the River Lea in west LEYTON. A crossing point on the river brought early human activity and evidence has been found of a Roman camp nearby. In 1185 William of Hastings, steward to Henry II, granted land here to the Knights Templar, who later built wooden watermills. After the dissolution of the order in the 14th century its property passed through a variety of hands (including the Crown's) and milling and related agricultural industries continued to grow. A White Hart tavern stood at Temple Mills from the early 18th century. In the latter part of the 19th century the mills were demolished and the Great Eastern wagon works were moved northwards from STRATFORD, with marshalling yards spreading inexorably. The works were modernized in 1958 as part of a programme that made them the largest in Britain. British Rail later added a Freightliner terminal. In 1991 the Corporation of London relocated SPITALFIELDS market to a site north of Ruckholt Road and the A12 was extended across Temple Mills later in that decade. The area's other principal occupant is the Lee Valley Sports Centre. Elsewhere there is derelict wasteland, recolonized by grasses, bracken, bramble, thistle and flea-bane. Temple Mills will be transformed for the 2012 Olympic Games. The velopark will be built north of the A12, with the hockey centre to the south. The Olympic village will be laid out on the former railway lands further to the south-east. In addition to the sports facilities, Temple Mills may gain its own station as a permanent legacy of the games.

✉ E10

Thames Gateway • *Newham/Barking & Dagenham/Havering/Bexley*

A planners' designation for a corridor extending either side of the Thames in outer east London and beyond. Thames Gateway is the proposed site for a raft of projects that will create mixed residential communities by attracting people on a range of incomes, as well as providing employment areas and shopping and leisure facilities. Most of the building in Greater London will take place on former industrial land, some of which is at risk from flooding. In 2004 the London Mayor, Ken Livingstone, suggested that a second Chinatown could be among the future attractions in London's part of the Thames Gateway but the developments presently taking place are less imaginative than this. A 2006 report from the Institute for Public Policy Research found that east Londoners considering moving to the Thames Gateway found the new homes 'monotonous and characterless'. The report also noted concerns that the neighbourhoods could lack adequate public services and transport infrastructures, while people from black and minority ethnic communities were worried about the availability of culturally specific goods and services. Up to 120,000 new homes may be built by 2016.

📖 Jim Bennett and James Morris, *Gateway People: The Aspirations and Attitudes of Prospective and Existing Residents of the Thames Gateway*, Institute for Public Policy Research, 2006; A Power et al, *A Framework for Housing in the London Thames Gateway*, London School of Economics, 2004

@ www.london-riverside.co.uk (development company site)

Thamesmead • *Greenwich/Bexley*

Once dubbed the 'town of the 21st century', Thamesmead is a vast agglomeration of municipal and private housing estates, with some peripheral industry, situated on former marshland between WOOLWICH and ERITH. The Thames here makes its most northerly ex-

cursion within Greater London, so Thamesmead is on the same latitude as Westminster. Its name was the winning entry in a newspaper competition. Because of its size, the town plan was subdivided into localities by points of the compass. After the land was vacated by the military, the Greater London Council developed Thamesmead spasmodically from the mid 1960s until the early 1980s. The first buildings used pre-cast concrete but this was subsequently abandoned in favour of less grim materials. The topography is dominated by a series of lakes and canals that drain surface water as well as providing good fishing and relieving the starkness of the built environment. Following the abolition of the GLC, the estate's ownership transferred to Thamesmead Town Trust, now Trust Thamesmead. The company was later split into three parts: a housing association, a land developer, and a charitable trust responsible for regeneration. The founders' vision of a futuristic community has largely been discarded in favour of traditional British suburban housebuilding. Large sums of money from local government, national government and European Union sources continue to be ploughed into improvement and expansion. The focus of this investment will be on THAMESMEAD SOUTH, which has acquired a poor reputation compared with the newer parts of the town. Because of the switch from tower blocks to conventional houses, forecasts of Thamesmead's final population have halved from the original target of 100,000.

The *Thamesmead Gazette* was a community newspaper that switched to online publication in 1995, becoming probably the best website of its kind in London. The site was forced to close in 2004 as the result of an injunction taken out against it following the publication of a story about mail-order brides.

✉ SE28; SE2; Erith DA18

🚶 22,456 (Bexley's Thamesmead East ward and Greenwich's Thamesmead Moorings ward)

📖 Foreman and Bossert, *Thamesmead Rediscovered*, Alan Conisbee and Associates, 1998; Valerie Wigfall, *Thamesmead: Back to the Future*, Greenwich Community College Press, 1997

@ www.trust-thamesmead.co.uk

Thamesmead Central • *Greenwich*

The town's riverside amenity area, with housing to the immediate south and east. Construction began here in 1971 and included the

491

pumping station at Thamesmere, which was required to regulate the drainage canals and lakes that are essential to keep the town from flooding. As its name suggests, Thamesmead Central offers the majority of the town's retail facilities – but these are woefully inadequate for a settlement of such proportions.

✉ SE28

Thamesmead East • *Bexley*

Originally the industrial and commercial part of THAMESMEAD, begun in 1979. The Modern Art Glass factory received architectural praise when it was first erected on Hailey Road. Even today, it is suggested that its apparent ordinariness demonstrates its influence on subsequent design trends. Following the abolition of the Greater London Council in 1986 and the establishment of the Thamesmead Town Trust, a previously unplanned phase of house-building began here, around the eastern part of Yarnton Way. The Business Academy was established in 2002 and moved fully into its present buildings a year later. It is one of very few state schools to offer education for pupils from 4 to 19 years. After an inspection in 2005, the national educational standards agency Ofsted rated the school inadequate, but said that pupils believed it was improving. The Thamesmead East ward is the borough's priority area for business development, with its highest available level of grants. Plans include a technology park with 80 units for production based on the use of information technology. The scale of the proposals has caused some consternation among environmentalists, who fear the destruction of grazing marshland.

✉ Erith DA18

👥 10,701

@ www.thebusinessacademy.org

Thamesmead North • *Greenwich/Bexley*

The last of the exclusively residential zones of THAMESMEAD, as originally planned, and the part that estate agents are calling 'sought after'. Work began on this northern sector in 1977. The locality would have been given a more individual identity had it been called CROSSNESS, which is the name for the tip of the shoreline here. However, that is also the name of the neighbouring sewage works. Planners adopted a more flexible and traditional approach to the layout and architecture of Thamesmead North. Existing trees were retained and the houses were built in brick

with pitched, tiled roofs. As in Thamesmead Central, drainage canals act as water features. A golf course was laid out to the east. Several private firms built roads of housing in Thamesmead North in the late 1990s, often marketing the properties as starter homes. Developers subsequently switched their attention to THAMESMEAD WEST.

✉ SE28

Thamesmead South • *Bexley*

The most populous but not the most popular of Thamesmead's zones, meeting ABBEY WOOD to its south. The Lakeside locality, built around Southmere Lake, was where THAMESMEAD started in 1967 and architecturally it mixes good intentions with bad mistakes. The main non-residential features are the health centre, the Lakeside leisure centre, Thamesmead Baptist Church, and the shops and community facilities at Tavy Bridge. Thamesmead South is the only part of the new town to have been completed as originally planned, but is already undergoing 'renewal', which will involve some demolition, much refurbishment and the construction of new flats, shops, offices and community facilities.

Stanley Kubrick used Thamesmead South for location scenes in his 1971 masterpiece *A Clockwork Orange*. Southmere Lake doubles as the Flat Block Marina, an old tramp is attacked under a walkway by the shopping centre and Alex dumps his fellow droogs into the water beside Binsey Walk. The area was depicted again in *Beautiful Thing*, Jonathan Harvey's 1996 portrayal of life in the vicinity of Tavy Bridge.

✉ SE2; Erith DA18

Thamesmead South West • *Greenwich*

The least significant of THAMESMEAD's sectors, known solely for Belmarsh Prison. Access is from Western Way (A2016), the main route across the Plumstead marshes. Planned from 1982 and built on 77 acres of the disused WOOLWICH ARSENAL site, the prison opened in 1991. It holds around 900 inmates and acts as both a local jail for south-east Londoners and a remand centre for high-risk prisoners, who are held in a separate mini-prison with its own perimeter and enhanced surveillance. To improve security and reduce the amount of staff time spent escorting prisoners to court, a magistrates' court and a Crown court were constructed between the prison and Western Way, and are linked to the prison via a tunnel. Despite its modernity, Belmarsh has suffered from overcrowding and staff shortages. In recent years the detention of terrorist suspects without trial has led civil rights campaigners to brand the prison 'Britain's own Guantanamo Bay'.

The notorious convict Charles Bronson held three other prisoners hostage at Belmarsh in 1996, fruitlessly demanding a helicopter to Cuba, an axe, submachine guns, a cheese sandwich and an ice cream. Other high profile inmates have included the train robber Ronnie Biggs and former Conservative ministers Jeffrey Archer and Jonathan Aitken. In 1999, Aitken penned *A Ballad from Belmarsh Gaol*, published in *The Spectator* magazine.

✉ SE28

Thamesmead West • *Greenwich*

The newest of the residential zones of THAMESMEAD, situated north of PLUMSTEAD. Unlike the rest of the new town, Thamesmead West stands on land that had previously been built upon. This was the site of many of the workshops and storehouses of WOOLWICH ARSENAL. Thamesmead West has been progressively extended towards the north-east in recent years. Developers and estate agents are calling the area West Thamesmead, partly because it sounds less inelegant but perhaps also to emphasize that this is the most detached of all the town's zones. It includes GALLIONS REACH URBAN VILLAGE. West Thamesmead Business Park lies in the area shown on maps as THAMESMEAD SOUTH WEST. It is the borough's largest industrial estate.

✉ SE28

Thames View • *Barking & Dagenham*

A dismal council estate trapped between CREEKMOUTH and the A13. This was marshland until the mid 1950s, when the council began to build over 2,000 homes, using piles and rafts to secure the foundations. Bastable Avenue is the main thoroughfare. Hemmed in by industrial sites and with soulless architecture and a pervading air of dilapidation, this is east London at its most depressing. There is no Thames view from ground level. The estate's ethnic mix includes residents of white, black African and black Caribbean descent, but relatively few of Asian origin. In recent years the council has placed here a number of refugee and asylum-seeking families, mainly from Eastern Europe. Thames View has been the subject of a Sure Start initiative to promote the physical, intellectual and social development of babies and young children. Its organi-

zers commented, 'The estate itself is isolated, the community fragmented, with little access to communal facilities. Services are basic, educational attainment poor, life chances limited.' To the east of Thames View is the new BARKING REACH development, which has begun with the Great Fleete estate. Although merely acceptable in terms of its design and build quality, it looks dazzling in comparison with Thames View.

Newlands Park, the only open play area on the estate, was refurbished in 2001 as part of the National Lottery-funded A13 Artscape project. The improvements include a leaf-shaped layout, landscaping, skateboarding facilities and new play areas.

✉ Barking IG11

Theatreland • *Westminster/Camden*

A media and tourist industry term for the quarter in which most of the WEST END's playhouses are to be found, centred on Cambridge Circus and SHAFTESBURY AVENUE. The word has been in use for about a century and the theatres are mostly of Victorian construction. The City of Westminster captions selected street signs with a Theatreland logo, although most guidebooks cast their net more widely than the council, embracing around 40 establishments in roads such as Haymarket, Coventry Street, CHARING CROSS ROAD, St Martin's Lane, the STRAND, ALDWYCH and Covent Garden's DRURY LANE and Earlham Street. Among the greatest London theatres are the Duke of York's, which premiered *Peter Pan*, the Haymarket, which dates from 1821, and the Palace, which opened in 1891 as the Royal English Opera House but soon became the Palace Theatre of Varieties. Other illustrious theatres include the Adelphi, Cambridge, Garrick, Her Majesty's and Wyndhams. On the fringes are the WHITEHALL theatre, the Dominion in TOTTENHAM COURT ROAD and the London Palladium in Argyll Street.

✉ W1; WC2

📖 Ronald Bergan et al, *The Great Theatres of London*, Andre Deutsch, 2004; Zoë Wanamaker et al, *London's Theatres*, New Holland, 2002; Edwin Heathcote, *Theatre London: An Architectural Guide*, Batsford, 2001

@ www.londontheatre.co.uk; www.officiallondontheatre.co.uk

Thornton Heath • *Croydon*

A sprawling south London suburb extending

from the edge of SELHURST PARK in the east to POLLARDS HILL in the west. The heath was originally common land covering 36 acres and stretching northwards towards NORBURY, with a pond used for watering horses and cattle. Charcoal burners carried water from the pond along what is now Colliers Water Lane. A gallows was set up near the pond and six men were hanged here simultaneously in 1722. The Wheatsheaf coaching inn was built on London Road later in the century. After its enclosure in 1799, most of the heath was used for farming but parts near the pond were sold for development and some substantial houses were built on the east side of London Road. With the opening of the station on the Croydon to Balham line in 1862 a settlement known briefly as New Thornton Heath began to evolve in its vicinity. The Croydon workhouse relocated to the north of BROAD GREEN in 1866 and its infirmary was built nearby in 1881. The buildings subsequently became Queen's Hospital and Mayday Hospital; Queen's Hospital closed in 1987 and housing has now filled its site, while the Mayday has grown to become one of south London's largest university hospitals, with 740 beds. By the end of the 19th century Thornton Heath was almost fully built up and shops lined the High Street, with St Alban's Church and a civic clock tower at opposite ends. The station was rebuilt in 1897 to handle the growing population of commuters. In 1953 the village pond was filled in and replaced by a small ornamental lake, which survived for two decades. St Andrew's Roman Catholic Church was built on Brook Road in 1970. Despite progressive rebuilding throughout the 20th century, much of late Victorian Thornton Heath survives, although the area has not succumbed to gentrification. Just over half of Thornton Heath's residents are white and the principal ethnic minorities are of black Caribbean and black African descent.

Thornton Heath hit the headlines in November 1999, when a naked man wielding a samurai sword ran amok in St Andrew's Church, leaving a dozen worshippers injured.

✉ Thornton Heath CR7

👥 14,784

🚉 Southern (zone 4)

📖 Raymond Wheeler, *Images of Norbury, Thornton Heath and Broad Green*, Tempus, 2002

Threadneedle Street *see* BANK

Three Mills • *Newham*

An industrial island formed by the dividing and recombining tributaries and channels of the River Lea, situated in MILL MEADS between BROMLEY-BY-BOW and WEST HAM. This has been a trading site for over 900 years, although little is known about the tidal mills that operated here in the Middle Ages. Three Mills' name was in use from the 16th century but none of the structures survives from that period and only two mills have stood here for much of the time since then. Ian Nairn wrote of the two remaining mills that they 'form a focus like a village green and tie a knot in the Lea valley'. House Mill, which dates from 1776, is the largest watermill in Britain and its milled grain was a source of much of London's flour – and gin. World War II bombing brought its active life to an end but it has now been restored as a showpiece, though its opening hours are presently very restricted. The more picturesque Clock Mill was rebuilt in 1817 from an earlier mill. Other buildings on the island were destroyed by fires and bombs in the first half of the 20th century. The River Lea Tidal Mill Trust has been working to improve public access to and usage of House Mill. Most of the island is now occupied by film and television studios owned by the London Development Agency. Alongside the studios, Copthorn Homes have converted the gin distillery's former storehouse into an apartment block.

Productions at Three Mills Studios have included the television series *Footballers' Wives* and *Bad Girls* and the feature films *28 Days Later*, *Lock, Stock and Two Smoking Barrels* and *Tim Burton's Corpse Bride*. This was also the site of the *Big Brother* house, used for the first two series of the Channel 4 reality show before its relocation to Elstree in Hertfordshire.

✉ E3; E15

@ www.housemill.org.uk (River Lea Tidal Mill Trust site); www.3mills.co.uk (Three Mills Studios site)

Tokyngton • *Brent* (pronounced 'toke-ing-tən')

Primarily an interwar garden suburb, situated in south-east WEMBLEY. Although it was sometimes called Oakington, the name does not derive from its tree cover but from 'the farm of the sons of Toca' and was first mentioned in 1171. The manor rivalled Wembley for economic significance in the Middle Ages and had a chapel that survived into the 18th century. After a brief spell as Oakington Park in the mid 19th century, the last decades of the manor's rural existence were as Sherrin's Farm. The Great Central Railway line ran across the north of the farm in 1906 and the lord of Tokyngton manor, Sir Audley Neeld, entered into an agreement with Wembley council to develop a 'garden city' estate of semi-detached houses in 1913. Work began the following year, paused during World War I and resumed afterwards. The estate was the borough's first exercise in town planning and is now a conservation area. Neeld extended the estate in 1932 and later conveyed 21 acres, together with the dilapidated Tokyngton manor house, to the council for use as open space. A proposal to convert the manor house into a library was rejected and in 1939 it was blown up in an exercise designed to test the readiness of air raid precautions. After World War II the council built low-rise blocks of flats, partly in place of bomb-damaged houses. The construction of the Bakerloo Line depot at STONEBRIDGE PARK in the far south of the locality proved an unpopular development in the 1970s. Most homes in the Tokyngton ward are owner-occupied and the largest ethnic group is of Asian descent, primarily Indian. Christianity, Hinduism and Islam are the main religions. At Oakington Manor Primary School, 80 per cent of pupils come from ethnic minorities and most speak English as an additional language.

✉ Wembley HA9

👥 11,836

📖 M C Barrès-Baker, *Wembley and Tokyngton*, Grange Museum of Community History and Brent Archive, 2001

Tollington • *Islington*
One of the original constituent parts of ISLINGTON, first mentioned in a charter of around 1000 in which the Saxon bishop of London was recorded as being the overlord of 'Gislandune and Tollandune'. The manor merited its own entry in Domesday Book and covered almost half the parish of Islington in the Middle Ages, but by the 14th century HOLLOWAY was supplanting Tollington as the identity of the settlement that lay north of the village of Islington. Tollington's manor house, also known as the Lower Place, stood beside the road to Hornsey on a site later occupied by a pub called the Devil's House and now filled by Kinloch Street. Devil's Lane was a nickname for Tollington Lane and derived from

the highwayman Claude Duval, who frequented this vicinity until his execution in 1669. The pub functioned until at least 1811, latterly under a more wholesome name. The Tollington Park estate was laid out in fits and starts from the 1840s in a variety of classical styles, but much of the area has since succumbed to redevelopment. In the 1960s and 1970s, Islington council built four housing estates in west FINSBURY PARK, collectively known as the Tollington estates. Among the streets erased for these developments was Campbell Road, which had earlier gained a reputation as 'the worst street in north London'. The larger two estates, Andover and Six Acres, have suffered serious structural and social problems but in a 2003 ballot residents rejected a move to housing association management that would have provided £140 million in regeneration investment. The council has since attempted to address the estates' difficulties in collaboration with the London Housing Board, community groups and the police. The Tollington ward has a wide cross-section of ethnic groups, including a relatively large minority of Bangladeshi descent.

✉ N4; N7

👥 12,462

📖 Jerry White, *Campbell Bunk: The Worst Street in London between the Wars*, Pimlico, 2003

Tolmers Village • *Camden*
An urban community in WEST EUSTON, with Tolmers Square in its south-west corner. The square was laid out with housing from 1861 to 1864 on land belonging to the New River Co., and named after a Hertfordshire hamlet near the river's source. The properties were built to a standard that was designed to attract the middle classes, but they were deterred by its close proximity to EUSTON station, and the houses in this irredeemably poor quarter were soon subdivided for multiple occupation. By 1871, 5,000 people were crammed into a twelve-acre area, which continued to evolve in a piecemeal fashion with many properties undergoing several changes of use. The square's Congregational church became a cinema in 1923. Greeks and Cypriots settled here after World War II, followed a few years later by the first Asians, who began to open restaurants on Drummond Street. From the late 1950s the neighbourhood attracted the interest of property developers who saw the potential for the replacement of houses with offices,

and residents began a long campaign of resistance. In the early 1970s the struggle to save Tolmers Village, as it was dubbed, became a cause célèbre with the Left, and students from nearby University College joined with squatters and trade unionists in resisting evictions. The activists failed to prevent the destruction of much of the original housing, but succeeded in persuading Camden council to compulsorily purchase the site from the property company Stock Conversion. Plans to construct half a million square feet of office space were abandoned and Tolmers Square was rebuilt with council flats and a Young's pub.

The Museum of London has Christopher Hall's 1954 painting of the square.

⊠ NW1

📖 Nick Wates, *The Battle for Tolmers Square*, Routledge & Kegan Paul, 1976

Tolworth • *Kingston*

The 'scrag end of the borough', as the *Evening Standard* once controversially described it, straddling the Kingston bypass south-east of SURBITON. Tolworth was recorded as 'Taleorde' in Domesday Book (after a man called Tala) and mutated through 'Talworth' before the present version of the name became fixed in the late 19th century. The manor was given to Henry, Earl of Westmoreland by Elizabeth I, and was bought by Nathaniel Polhill, MP for SOUTHWARK, in 1781. For most of the 19th century the earls of Egmont were Tolworth's principal landowners. St Matthew's Church was built on the border with Surbiton in 1875. The largely unexplained generosity of a Coutts banker resulted in a church that was much larger than the locality needed, but which was appreciated by the inhabitants of the villas springing up along Ewell Road at the time. In the 1880s, brickfields in Red Lion Lane (now Road) and William Hipwell's 550-acre dairy farm were the major employers. Tolworth Isolation Hospital was built in 1889 in the face of vigorous local objections. On the death in 1897 of Charles George Percival, the seventh Earl of Egmont, the farmland was sold for development, although progress was slow at first, partly because of poor drainage. The manor house burned down in 1911. With the opening of the Kingston bypass in 1927, a massive programme of expansion began, with houses and amenities replacing farms such as Tolworth Lodge. Ewell Road was recut and Tolworth Broadway appeared. Tolworth central school was built on the site of Fullers Farm. This became Tolworth Girls' School, a

secondary modern now rated 'exceptionally effective' by the educational standards agency Ofsted and heavily oversubscribed. Tolworth station opened in 1938. The Tolworth Tower, designed by Richard Seifert and built in 1964 on the site of the former Odeon cinema, is the tallest building in outer London. Its 22 storeys reach 265 feet and the supermarket at ground level was the largest in southern England when it opened. In the late 1960s the creation of an underpass helped relieve congestion at Tolworth Junction. Like other parts of the borough, Tolworth has a sizeable Korean community. A high proportion of homes is owner-occupied and contains dependent children.

⊠ Surbiton KT6

🏃 9,531 (Tolworth and Hook Rise ward)

🚌 South West Trains (zone 5)

📖 Mark Davison and Paul Adams, *Tolworth Remembered*, Mark Davison, 2000; Patricia J Ward, *From Talworth Hamlet to Tolworth Tower*, self-published, 1975

@ www.thecornerhouse.org (community arts centre)

Tooting • *Wandsworth*

A densely populated multiracial district situated west of STREATHAM. The name is of uncertain Anglo-Saxon origin and may have referred to 'the people of the lookout place'. The manors of Tooting (subsequently TOOTING GRAVENEY) and TOOTING BEC were in existence by the time of Domesday Book and each became the centre of a farming village over the course of the Middle Ages, in the valleys of the Wandle and Graveney rivers. In the 18th century, country homes began to appear, including Hill House at Tooting Graveney and FURZEDOWN House in the locality that later took its name. Houses also lined the High Street and a few of these early buildings have survived. The area attracted some villas and institutions from the mid 19th century, when Charles Dickens' essay *The Paradise at Tooting* exposed the wrongdoings at an asylum for pauper children on TOOTING BROADWAY. Tooting Junction station opened in 1868 on the Tooting, Merton and Wimbledon Railway. This did not immediately stimulate suburban growth but later in the 19th century the area between the station and Tooting Broadway became the first part of Tooting Graveney to be filled with suburban housing. Meanwhile, development spread towards Tooting Bec from Balham, although Tooting Common was preserved as open space. The main-line station was relocated to its present position in 1894 and renamed Tooting. The London County Council built a cottage estate at Totterdown Fields in the early years of the 20th century, and the huge Tooting Bec lido opened in 1906. The arrival of the Underground in 1926 brought the completion of Tooting's transformation from a pair of villages into a London suburb; the medieval parish church was replaced and the fabulous Granada cinema was built on the Broadway. Later residential development has mostly involved the replacement of former institutional buildings, including hospitals – although St George's remains and is one of the biggest hospitals in the country. Tooting has been called 'Little South India' for the size of its Asian, notably Tamil, population and for its variety of affordable South Indian restaurants. The main streets have shops specializing in saris and Asian sweets, jewellery and videos. Tooting also has a mosque and an Islamic bank. A 2002 study of 18- to 34-year-olds showed that Tooting has the highest proportion of young 'singletons' in London and the growing number of bars reflects their desire to meet each other.

Perhaps because it has a silly sounding name, Tooting has been the setting for several television comedies, including *Hugh and I* and *Citizen Smith*, which used the Castle public house for location scenes. Planetary expert Pete Mouginis-Mark named a Martian meteorite crater after his Tooting birthplace in 2005. Tooting is cockney rhyming slang for a light kiss, from Tooting Bec – a peck.

✉ SW17

🏃 13,261

🚌 Thameslink (zone 3)

📖 Patrick Loobey, *Balham and Tooting*, Tempus, 2001; Frank Staff, *Tooting Rambles*, self-published, 1985

@ pages.britishlibrary.net/tooting; www.tootinglife.com (town centre partnership site)

Tooting Bec • Wandsworth

The names Tooting Bec and Upper Tooting are interchangeable. Most maps show the area as Upper Tooting but residents usually call it Tooting Bec because of the name of the station. At the time of Domesday Book there were two TOOTING manors. The more northerly of the pair was given by William I, the Conqueror, to Richard of Tonbridge, who in turn endowed it to the abbey of Notre Dame du Bec in Normandy. There is speculation that the monks of Bec may have established a priory here around which a settlement coalesced in the 12th century, but if this is the case, its site has not been located. By the 16th century Tooting Bec was the largest village in the parish of STREATHAM. The manor passed through various monastic and secular hands before and after the Reformation, ending up as part of the Duke of Bedford's extensive holdings in the area. The Metropolitan Board of Works acquired 218 acres of Tooting Bec Common in 1875. Poor drainage delayed suburban development in Tooting Bec until the problem was overcome in the late 19th century. At that time the grandest villa was Park Holme, which may have occupied the site of the medieval manor house. Tooting Bec Asylum was built in 1903 on the site of another building referred to as a manor house but lacking historical justification for the name. Tooting Bec lido opened in 1906 and the South London Swimming Club was formed there the same year. The pool is the widest in Europe and one of south London's most delightful leisure amenities. Park Holme was demolished in 1924 and replaced by the Bell estate, named after the house's last owner, Eliza Bell. Tooting Bec station opened in 1926, originally as Trinity Road. Tooting Bec Asylum closed in 1995 and the site was redeveloped by Fairview Homes as Heritage Park, which has nearly 1,000 homes and limited community facilities.

✉ SW17

🚌 Northern Line (zone 3)

@ www.rix.dial.pipex.com/tooting (privately operated site about Tooting Bec Common)

Tooting Broadway • Wandsworth

A station and shopping parade located at the crossroads of the A24 and A217, which was known in the past as Tooting Corner. This was part of the manor of TOOTING GRAVENEY and the manor house stood near here. Peter Drouet's asylum for pauper children at Surrey Hall faced the Broadway in the mid 19th century. Set in seven acres of grounds, it was a sizeable and profitable operation for Drouet until disgraceful sanitary conditions contributed to an outbreak of cholera in 1848 in which more than 100 children died. Drouet was put on trial for felonious killing but found not guilty. He sold up soon afterwards and the tragic episode prompted major municipal improvements to the area's drainage. At the end of the 19th century there were still a few private houses interspersed among the shops on the Broadway. Trams began to serve Tooting Corner in 1903, frequently derailing on the sharp turn. A statue of Edward VII attired as commander-in-chief of the army was erected on the corner in 1911. That year marked the completion of London County Council's Totterdown estate and the influx of new residents stimulated a transformation in the scale of the shopping facilities. Tooting Broadway station opened in 1926. The Granada cinema of 1931 (now a bingo hall) has the most magnificent interior of its kind in London, a cathedral-like design modelled on the lavish American picture palaces of the era. It was the first British cinema to be given Grade I-listed status. The independent shops and stalls of Broadway market and the nearby streets reflect the neighbourhood's wide ethnic diversity. Tamil, Konkani, Ibo, Tagalog and Creole French are among the most common languages spoken at St Boniface Primary School on Undine Street.

The nearby Salvador estate is named after a wealthy Tooting family who played a leading role in the establishment of the first Jewish settlement in America.

✉ SW17

🚇 Northern Line (zone 3)

📖 Janet Weeks, *The Paradise at Tooting: An Account of the Tragedy at Drouet's Infant Pauper Asylum*, Local History Publications, 2000

Tooting Graveney • *Wandsworth/Merton*

The more southerly of the two manors into which TOOTING was divided at the time of Domesday Book. The manor was owned by Chertsey Abbey and was leased in the twelfth and thirteenth centuries to the Graveney (or Gravenel) family, who may have taken their name from the village of Graveney in north Kent. Tooting Common was also split into two parts, along the boundary between the parishes of STREATHAM and Tooting Graveney; an avenue of trees was later planted to mark the boundary. In 1803 Benjamin Oakley built Tooting Lodge, which he soon sold to Rees Goring Thomas. When Thomas acquired the lordship of the manor of Tooting Graveney in 1811, he renamed the lodge the Manor House. The medieval parish church of St Nicholas, which was distinguished by a circular tower, was demolished in the 1830s and replaced by the present structure with a 'vast

barn' of a nave, which has since been subdivided into more manageable parts. By the 1860s several villas had been built among the market gardens and the new lord of the manor applied to enclose Tooting Graveney Common. Following a court victory by commoners, the common remained free of speculative building and was transferred to public ownership in the mid 1870s under the terms of the Metropolitan Commons Act. In his *Handbook to the Environs of London*, published in the following year, James Thorne described Tooting Graveney as 'very pleasant and apart from the common, very commonplace'. Until this time, the villages of Tooting Bec and Tooting Graveney (also known as Upper and Lower Tooting) had remained separate, but they were linked by suburban housing over the latter years of the 19th century. West of the common, the London County Council acquired Totterdown Fields and in 1901 began to lay out its first cottage estate here. By 1911 the estate had 1,229 houses but only four shops. All Saints' Church was built as the centrepiece of the new estate, in imposing Gothic style. The auctioneers Greasbys have been in Longley Road since 1919, and nowadays hold fortnightly sales of unclaimed lost property from London Transport, including countless mobile phones, as well as contraband seized by customs. Tooting Graveney has a multiracial community and Merton's Graveney ward (which straddles the railway line east of Tooting station) is the most ethnically diverse in the borough. At Graveney School, in the FURZEDOWN locality, the main secondary languages spoken by pupils are Urdu, Gujarati, Tamil and Punjabi.

✉ SW17

👥 22,597 (Wandsworth's Graveney ward and Merton's Graveney ward)

@ www.greasbys.co.uk

Tottenham • *Haringey*

A densely built-up, multiracial district situated six miles north of the Tower of London. 'Toteham' (the farmstead of a man called Totta) was first recorded in Domesday Book, as was a weir at present-day TOTTENHAM HALE. From the 12th century Tottenham's accessibility to London attracted wealthy merchants and religious institutions to its wooded slopes, although the main village consisted only of a cluster of dwellings at Tottenham Green. Six inns were recorded on the High Road in the mid 15th century and a jousting competition called the Tournament of Tottenham was said to draw visitors from Islington, Hackney and Highgate. Tottenham manor house (now Bruce Castle) lay almost a mile to the north of the green. Henry VIII made a payment to the hermit of Tottenham when he visited the house in 1517. Over the course of the next two centuries mansions, private schools, groups of almshouses and other charitable institutions were built near the High Road, while extensive woodland survived to the west and the marshy meadows lay undisturbed to the east. Only in the late 18th century did development begin to branch away from the High Road along old tracks like WHITE HART LANE and new roads like BRUCE GROVE. Tottenham remained suburban rather than urban until the coming of the railways to the east side of the parish in the 1840s and the west side in the 1850s. WOOD GREEN, formerly an outlying hamlet, grew especially rapidly and had established itself as a separate middle-class district by the early 1870s. At this time a railway at last cut through central Tottenham, west of the High Road. Speculative developers had already built numerous houses in anticipation of this event and they stepped up their efforts over the following two decades, until Tottenham had spread to meet its neighbours in all directions. In the early 20th century, places of entertainment were built on the High Road, Tottenham Hotspur Football Club won early trophies and industry came to the marshes. The last pockets of farmland disappeared in the 1920s, when municipal housebuilding began in earnest. After World War II, council flats dominated the construction programme, with massive projects in the 1960s – notably at NORTHUMBERLAND PARK and BROADWATER FARM – and smaller, low-rise estates in the 1970s, for example at SEVEN SISTERS. This was a period of significant change in Tottenham's residential profile, with the arrival of immigrants first from the Caribbean, especially in SOUTH TOTTENHAM, and later from Turkey and Africa.

The expression 'Tottenham shall turn French' was a late medieval equivalent of 'pigs might fly'. In the Tottenham Outrage of 1909, PC William Frederick Tyler was shot in the head by armed robber Paul Hefeld, whom he was pursuing (*see also* HALE END).

✉ N17

🚶 61,282 (Bruce Grove, Northumberland Park, Tottenham Green, Tottenham Hale and White Hart Lane wards)

🚆 'one' Railway (Bruce Grove; White Hart Lane, zone 3)

📖 Chris Protz and Deborah Hedgecock, *Tottenham and Wood Green: Past and Present*, Sutton, 2003

Tottenham Court Road • *Camden*

A commercial thoroughfare running along the western edge of BLOOMSBURY, noted for its furniture and electronics retailers. This was the route from ST GILES to the manor house of Tottenhall, a name that had become corrupted to Tottenham by the time of the house's demolition in the early 18th century. The change was influenced by public familiarity with the north London district of TOTTENHAM, although the manor had no connection with that place. The manor house stood on the site of the present 250 Euston Road, and excavations there have uncovered early Saxon pottery, a series of 13th- to 14th-century yard surfaces and the remains of medieval and Tudor walls. From the late 18th century and especially in the 19th century, Tottenham Court Road was known for the manufacture of furniture, especially cabinets. Some of the workshops later turned to piano-making. Furniture retailing grew in tandem with the manufacturing industry and several grand stores opened in the 1910s and 1920s. The finest of these was Heal's, which is now paired with a branch of Habitat. The Dominion Theatre was built at the southern end of the Tottenham Court Road in the late 1920s. Beneath the street lies the bunker from which General Eisenhower directed the Allied forces' liberation of Western Europe; it is now used for the secure storage of documents and data. To the present day, the street's main specialism north of GOODGE STREET is furniture retailing, accompanied by a wide variety of other businesses, including the UK flagship branch of the Spearmint Rhino chain of lapdancing clubs. Further south, Tottenham Court Road is famed as a centre for electronics retailers, especially hi-fi and video equipment and, increasingly, computers. Many of the businesses are now Asian-owned and compete vigorously on price. Making a diagonal link with Oxford Street at the southwestern end of Tottenham Court Road is the hidden-away Hanway Street, which has some recherché shops and bars, including several with Spanish connections.

In George Bernard Shaw's play *Pygmalion*, Eliza Doolittle sells flowers on the corner of Tottenham Court Road. In Lerner and Loewe's musical adaptation, *My Fair Lady*, Eliza lives in a Tottenham Court Road tenement, although she goes home to Drury Lane in the original play. Tottenham Court Road station was the scene of David's attack on a lone commuter in John Landis's spoof horror film *An American Werewolf in London*.

> ✉ W1 (boundary with WC1 runs along eastern side)

> 🚇 Central Line; Northern Line (zone 1)

Tottenham Hale • *Haringey*

A collection of commercial and council estates on the east side of TOTTENHAM. There is evidence of pre-Norman economic activity and residents of 'the Hale' were recorded from the late 13th century, although the first mention of *Tottenham* Hale did not come until 1754. By this time the settlement was Tottenham's largest satellite, with an inn and several dozen dwellings. The village had more than 600 inhabitants in 1840, when the Northern and Eastern Railway arrived and Tottenham (now Tottenham Hale) station was built. From the early 1860s suburban development began to connect Tottenham Hale with its parent district and its separate existence had been wholly lost by the 1890s. Over the first half of the 20th century factories were built, primarily between the railway line and the River Lea, and Tottenham Hale became one of the borough's primary industrial zones. The best-known employer was the Gestetner factory on Broad Lane, which employed 6,000 staff at the peak of its production of stencil-duplicating equipment. From the late 1950s, much of Tottenham Hale was redeveloped with municipal housing, which was generally of a higher architectural standard than other estates in the area, for example at NORTHUMBERLAND PARK. The Greater London Council's Ferry Lane estate of the late 1970s was accompanied by the opening of a new primary school. Disused factories were subsequently replaced by shed-style warehousing and the Ferry Island and Tottenham Hale retail parks. Although a relatively little-known destination, Tottenham Hale is one of outer London's busier stations – on a par with Hampstead – because it is an interchange for the line to Stansted Airport. Buildings by the architect Will Alsop, murals by the artist Bruce McLean and decorative features that include a 'tower of time', 'bridge of signs' and 'path of the people' attempt to enliven the environment, but they have not been well cared for so the effect is spoiled. Just under half the residents of the Tottenham Hale

ward are white. The other significant ethnic minorities are of black Caribbean and black African descent, and numerous refugees from Turkey, Iraq and Somalia have been placed on local council estates. There is a high level of unemployment and of households with children, including single-parent households. Most residents live in rented accommodation but waterside apartments on Ferry Lane have recently attracted private homebuyers.

> ✉ N17; N15

> 👥 12,728

> 🚇 'one' Railway; Victoria Line (zone 3)

Totteridge • *Barnet*

An unaffordably lovely ribbon village strung along the road from WHETSTONE to HIGHWOOD HILL and set amidst farmland, parks and golf courses. Opinions differ on the derivation of the first part of its name, which was first recorded as Taderege in the 12th century. Most experts now propose an association with a man called Tāta, but others have suggested that 'tot' meant either a height or a place of worship. The 'ridge' part is undisputed: Totteridge sits on a crest that rises well above 400 feet. The land here was part of the Bishop of Ely's medieval estate at Hatfield in Hertfordshire. The Church of St Etheldreda was mentioned in a document of 1250. It is said that Edward I visited in 1305 and the bishop had a house and chapel here by 1357, on the site of the present Totteridge Park. The church was rebuilt in 1790, by which time it had become St Andrew's, and its churchyard has a yew tree that is over 1,000 years old. Several structures survive from the late 17th and early 18th centuries, mostly farm outbuildings. The oldest mansion is Totteridge Park, built in 1750 but remodelled in the early 20th century. The renowned architect R Norman Shaw was responsible for Ellern Mede in 1877. Shaw's plans for the house's interior are now with the Royal Academy. Totteridge's other mansions are mostly recent creations, as the village has become a haven for business and media moguls who wish to retreat behind high walls and security gates. Since the early 1990s more than a dozen seven-figure properties have been built, and there would have been more had it not been for green-belt restrictions. Totteridge Village has all the rural essentials: shops, primary school, cricket club, village hall and the Orange Tree public house. Totteridge Fields are ancient hay meadows managed by the London Wildlife Trust. The

Totteridge ward has a large Jewish community, and residents tend to be married, middle-aged homeowners, often with dependent children.

✉ N20

♁ 14,449

🚇 Northern Line (Totteridge and Whetstone, zone 4)

📖 Pamela Taylor and Joanna Corden, *Barnet, Edgware, Hadley and Totteridge: A Pictorial History*, Phillimore, 1994

@ www.totteridgeresidents.org

Tower • *Tower Hamlets/City/Southwark*

The Tower of London and Tower Bridge are the capital's most famous landmarks east of the CITY OF LONDON. The immediate vicinity was formerly an autonomous district called the Liberty of the Tower and is now part of the borough of Tower Hamlets. William the Conqueror began construction of the White Tower on the site of Roman fortifications in the late 1070s. An encircling wall was built in 1097. Twenty more towers were eventually added and the site was progressively extended in several stages, primarily in the 13th and 14th centuries. The Tower has served as a fortress, a royal palace, a prison, storehouses and an arsenal. Yeoman Warders, commonly known as Beefeaters, have guarded the Tower since the reign of Henry VII. Charles II introduced the public display of the Crown jewels and is said to have decreed that at least six ravens should always be kept at the Tower. Despite the high price of admission, the Tower of London is visited by more than two million people every year. Tower subway was constructed in 1870. It served first as a tramcar tunnel and was then converted to pedestrian use; it now carries water mains. Tower of London station (now Tower Hill) opened in 1882. Tower Bridge was built from 1886 under the direction of the engineer Sir John Wolfe Barry and the architect Sir Horace Jones. As the furthest bridge downstream at that time it was necessary to construct the roadway in the form of two counterbalanced see-saws, or bascules, which could be tipped using hydraulic engines. The advanced engineering was clothed in Gothic towers to harmonize with the neighbouring fortress. The bridge was opened (literally) by the Prince of Wales in 1894. The bascule-raising machinery was converted to electric power in 1976, allowing many internal areas to be opened up to visitors. Tower Gate-

way station opened in 1987 as the original western terminus of the DOCKLANDS Light Railway system. City Hall was built across the Thames from the Tower in 2002, and is the base of the Greater London Authority and the Mayor of London.

Several monarchs, especially Henry VIII and Elizabeth I, made use of the Tower as a prison and place of execution for those who had fallen out of favour with them. Among their victims were Sir Thomas More, who was executed on Tower Hill, and Anne Boleyn, Catherine Howard and the Earl of Essex, who were all beheaded at the Tower.

✉ EC3 (Tower of London); E1 and SE1 (Tower Bridge)

♁ 161 (City of London's Tower ward)

🚇 Circle Line; District Line (Tower Hill, zone 1); Docklands Light Railway terminus (Tower Gateway, zone 1)

🚢 Tower Millennium pier

📖 Derek Wilson, *The Tower of London*, Allison & Busby, 1998; Honor Godfrey, *Tower Bridge*, John Murray, 1988

@ www.tower-of-london.org.uk; www.towerbridge.org.uk

Trafalgar Square • *Westminster*

London's best-known square, located immediately north-west of CHARING CROSS. Excavations here have produced significant findings of elephant and hippopotamus remains, dating from around 120,000BC. The Church of St-Martin-in-the-Fields has stood to the north-east of the square since the 13th century and has been twice rebuilt. From the 14th to the 19th centuries the present Trafalgar Square was the site of the royal mews, where Geoffrey Chaucer once toiled as a clerk of works. The square was laid out in 1830 and named after the battle at which Admiral Horatio Nelson died. Seven years later William Wilkins' National Gallery was erected on the north side. This was followed in 1843 by Edward Baily's statue of Nelson, erected in celebration of his naval victories at Cape St Vincent, the Nile, Copenhagen and Trafalgar and mounted on a granite column 184 feet high. In the same year an equestrian statue of George IV was placed on a plinth in the north-east corner of the square, with statues of imperial generals Charles James Napier and Henry Havelock later added in the south-west and south-east corners. It is said that the vacant plinth in the north-west corner has been earmarked for a statue of Elizabeth II after her death. It was not until 1867 that Nelson's memorial was finally completed by the installation of Sir Edwin Landseer's four bronze lions. Admiralty Arch, which separates the MALL from Trafalgar Square, was designed by Sir Aston Webb in memory of Queen Victoria. Its central arch gate is only opened on ceremonial occasions. Canada House and South Africa House, the high commissions of their respective countries, overlook the east and west sides of the square. From the Chartists of 1848 to the poll tax rioters of 1990, Trafalgar Square has been a focal destination for protest marches and demonstrations against the government. Developments at Trafalgar Square since 1991 have included the addition of the Sainsbury wing to the National Gallery, the inauguration of the 'fourth plinth project' to temporarily showcase new (and often controversial) works of art, the pedestrianization of the area between the square and the National Gallery and the virtual eradication of the infamous pigeon population. Every Christmas the city of Oslo donates a Norwegian spruce for the square, in recognition of Britain's assistance to Norway during World War II.

C W Murphy's 1902 composition *I Live in Trafalgar Square* has been recorded by Stanley Holloway, Georgia Brown and Warren Mitchell.

✉ WC2

📖 Roger Hargreaves, *Trafalgar Square through the Camera*, National Portrait Gallery, 2005; Jean Hood, *Trafalgar Square: A Visual History of London's Landmark through Time*, B T Batsford, 2005; Rodney Mace, *Trafalgar Square: Emblem of Empire*, Lawrence & Wishart, 1987

@ www.nationalgallery.org.uk; www.stmartin-in-the-fields.org

Tubbenden • *Bromley*

Although not shown on most maps, Tubbenden is a recognized designation for the part of ORPINGTON that lies between CROFTON and FARNBOROUGH. Like other local places with names ending in 'den', this would have been a patch of woodland pasture, probably associated here with a man named Tubba. The name was first recorded in 1240. Orpington chickens were once bred in Tubbenden by William Henry Cook, whose father had created the breed. The site of the farm is now covered by Maxwell Gardens, named after another prominent local family, whose home was called Tuppendence (Tubbendens). In 1804 Eliza Maxwell married Thomas Young, a distinguished physicist, physician and Egyptologist known as 'Phenomenon Young', who did ground-breaking work on deciphering the Rosetta Stone and on the wave theory of light and the interference phenomenon. On his death in 1829 he was buried at Farnborough, in the family vault of the Maxwells. The baronetcy Evans of Tubbenden was created for Sir Francis Henry Evans, a lieutenant of the City of London who came originally from Lancashire, and conferred on him by Edward VII in 1902; the baronetcy became extinct in 1970. Tubbenden was considered an outlying part of Farnborough before Orpington's expansion, and its fields were covered with orchards until the early years of the 20th century. The housing stock is a mixture of ages and qualities. Tubbenden Infants' School was awarded Beacon status in 1999 and the junior school is also well-regarded.

✉ Bromley BR6

Tufnell Park • *Islington*

A distinctive 19th-century residential scheme, characterized by wide, tree-lined streets and individually styled housing, situated northeast of KENTISH TOWN. From early times this was part of the manor of BARNSBURY, which in the 15th century possessed a moated farmhouse at what is now the eastern end of Tufnell Park Road. William Tufnell inherited the manor in 1754 and soon afterwards changed his surname to Jolliffe. The estate later passed to his brother and down through his family, thus regaining the Tufnell connection. The area was known for its dairy farms until the early 19th century but in 1822 the family sought permission to grant building leases and created Tufnell Park Road two years later. Other roads were named after branches of the extended family. Most of the terraced houses were built in the 1850s and 1860s, often with separate gabled roofs to make them look like semi-detached houses. Only two architects were employed throughout the project but they built adventurously, differentiating each street and sometimes every villa within a street. Façades were often plain but imaginatively ornamented, especially around the windows. The Byzantine-style church of St George was included as part of the project, endowed for the Free Church of England in 1868. Tufnell Park station opened in 1907. Like much of Victorian north London, the 20th century brought the subdivision of many of the houses and municipal replacement of others, so that most of Tufnell Park's residents now live in flats, rented privately or from the council or housing associations. More recently, some houses have been reunited as the middle classes recolonize the locality, especially on the western side. Tufnell Park's main ethnic minorities are of Turkish, Bangladeshi and Somali origin.

The musician and campaigner Bob Geldof lived in a squat on Tufnell Park Road in 1977. Channel 4's comedy series *Spaced* was set at the fictional 23 Meteor Street (actually Carleton Road), Tufnell Park. The show's acutely accurate portrayal of twenty-something flat-sharing life made it a cult hit.

> ✉ N7; N19

> 🚇 Northern Line (zone 2)

Tulse Hill • *Lambeth*

A socially disadvantaged locality situated on the south-eastern edge of BRIXTON. Three estates, Bodley, Upgrove and Scarlettes were united in 1352 under the ownership of the Hospital of St Thomas the Martyr, an Augustinian priory then located in SOUTHWARK. Henry VIII seized the property at the dissolution of the monasteries and by 1563 a house called Brockalle was in existence, near the present junction of Norwood Road and Rosendale Roads. In 1656 the estate was in the hands of the Tulse family. Sir Henry Tulse was Lord Mayor of London in 1683–4 and made a fortune from the west African slave trade. In 1807 the estate was divided in two. John Blades, a City glass manufacturer, acquired the eastern part, and he demolished the old house and built Brockwell Hall on the hilltop in 1813. Dr Thomas Edgar, a legal writer, later gained possession of the western part of the estate through his marriage to Mary Cressingham. He acquired an additional strip of land giving access to BRIXTON HILL, created the curving sweep of Upper Tulse Hill and began to build a high-class estate here. In 1855 Jonah Cressingham gave land for the construction of Holy Trinity Church, which was built in the face of objections from nearby vicars who feared a lightening of their collection plates. The opening of HERNE HILL station in 1862 prompted John Blades' grandson to build some large detached houses on the perimeter of the Brockwell Hall estate. Brailsford Road and Arlingford Road were laid out with terraces of houses and shops in the late 1880s. Lambeth council and the London County Council acquired Brockwell Hall and its grounds in 1891 and opened Brockwell Park in the following year. The park was later enlarged and is now one of south London's best-known amenities and a popular venue for summer events. Brixton Skating Palace opened at the far northern end of Tulse Hill in 1901, on a site occupied earlier by a large villa and later by a carpet superstore. In 1939 the LCC began construction of the large Tulse Hill estate, where the Mayor of London, Ken Livingstone, grew up. Throughout the post-war decades Lambeth council added smaller estates, continuing into the early 1980s with the completion of Cressingham Gardens, which has 306 dwellings. A large number of Tulse Hill's residents still rent their homes from the council, although private gated estates have recently been built in the area. St Martin in the Fields Girls' High School is very highly regarded. The majority of pupils are of black Caribbean or African descent and the school bucks the national tendency for these ethnic groups to underperform at GCSE level, despite pupils' below-average socio-economic background.

It is hard to imagine Tulse Hill as the birthplace of astrophysics, but in 1856 the astronomer Sir William Huggins built a private observatory here, where he conducted pioneering research into the spectra of stars, nebulae and comets. Huggins continued his work in Tulse Hill until 1908, dying here two years later. The locality has frequently been the subject of jokey references. Carter USM's 1991 album *101 Damnations* includes a track called *24 minutes from Tulse Hill*. Wendy Cope created a Tulse Hill-based character called Jason Strugnell, whose verses parodied the work of well-known poets: 'If men deride and sneer, I shall defy them / And soar above Tulse Hill on poet's wings — / A brother to the thrush in Brockwell Park'.

> ✉ SW2 (the station is in SE27)

> 🚶 13,119

> 🚇 Southern; Thameslink (zone 3)

> 📖 Margaret Siddall, *From Schoole to School*, Devonshire House, 1999 (a history of St Martin in the Fields School)

> @ www.brockwellpark.com

Turkey Street • *Enfield*

The road linking BULLS CROSS with ENFIELD WASH, and a small conservation area. It seems likely that the street took its name from a former resident named something like Tuckey, and that the 19th-century corruption to 'Turkey' was the result of what linguists call 'folk etymology'. The street's existence was first recorded in 1427 and was the location of a hamlet of ten houses in 1572. The watercourse that intertwines with the eastern section of the street was earlier called the Maiden's Brook but is now usually called Turkey Brook. By the mid 18th century the first Plough inn was in existence, as was a bridge across the brook, which used to be navigable to this point. Further west, another bridge carried the street across the New River. Enfield's first almshouses were built in Turkey Street by Ann Crowe. In her will of 1763 she left money to repair them and to buy coal for the inmates. The original almshouses were replaced by the present group in the early 1890s. A station opened in 1891 but disappointing residential growth and a poor service that involved changing trains at WHITE HART LANE made the line unprofitable and passenger services were withdrawn after electric trams began to run along Hertford Road in 1909. After World War II the council built large estates to the north but a few early-19th-century houses and cottages have survived on Turkey Street itself. With the introduction of an electrified service to LIVERPOOL STREET in 1961 the station was reopened. The Turkey Street ward occupies a long strip between the Great Cambridge Road (A10) and Hertford Road (A1010). More than a fifth of homes in the ward are rented from the council, a high figure by Enfield standards. Eighty-five per cent of residents are white. The ward has the borough's highest proportions of skilled manual workers and of those with a long-term illness.

Enfield Crematorium opened in 1938 and is now run by the London Borough of Haringey. It is located to the south-west of Turkey Street station. Covering an area of nearly 50 acres, it is one of London's largest crematoria.

> ✉ Enfield EN1 and EN3

> ♦ 12,744

> 🚆 'one' Railway (zone 6)

reaching London; nearly 1,000 men died in the ensuing Battle of Turnham Green. In an infamous incident in 1680, the Earl of Pembroke killed an innocent bystander with a thrust of his rapier while in a drunken rage; Pembroke was temporarily held in the Cock and Half Moon tavern, but his high status effected his release and he escaped punishment. Sir George Barclay and 40 conspirators plotted in vain to assassinate William III upon the green in 1696. The common was rife with highwaymen and in 1776 a lone gunman robbed the Lord Mayor of London and his retinue. None of this lawlessness deterred several noble families from establishing country retreats here in the 18th century, while the village grew in significance as a coaching halt on the road to Bath. In 1821 the Horticultural Society of London began to lay out a garden that extended from the south of the green towards Chiswick. The society organized an annual fête that was the forerunner of the modern Chelsea Flower Show. Turnham Green gained its church in 1843 and a station in 1877. By the end of the 19th century the substantial villas that had lined Chiswick High Road at discrete intervals were being replaced by a ribbon of terraces with shops at street level, while the hinterland filled with a mix of properties, generally getting smaller the later they were built. Turnham Green is now very popular with young professionals, many of whom rent their homes privately. One-person households are common and statistics show relatively few families with children, although a stroll down Chiswick High Road can give a different impression. Over 70 per cent of all 16- to 74-year-olds were employed at the time of the 2001 census, an exceptionally high figure.

John Heath-Stubbs' 1968 poem *Turnham Green* commemorates the Italian poet Ugo Foscolo, who died here in 1827. The novelist E M Forster lived in Arlington Park Mansions.

> ✉ W4

> ♦ 10,184

> 🚆 District Line; limited Piccadilly Line service (zones 2 and 3)

Turnham Green · *Hounslow*

The commercial centre of CHISWICK since the mid 19th century, straddling Chiswick High Road. By 1630 a hamlet separate from the riverside settlement at Chiswick was firmly established around the green, with 60 ratepayers. In 1642 an army of 24,000 Roundheads assembled to prevent Charles I from

Turnpike Lane · *Haringey*

The southern tip of WOOD GREEN, where the High Road meets Harringay's GREEN LANES. Turnpike Lane itself runs west to HORNSEY and was formerly called Tottenham Lane, as it still is to the south-west. In the early 18th century the road through Wood Green became increasingly busy as travellers sought a route that avoided the WHETSTONE turnpike on the Great North Road. An act of 1710 authorized the introduction of a turnpike at Hornsey, although tolls were not levied until 1739. The Stamford Hill and Green Lanes Turnpike Trust finally erected a gate here in 1765. For the next 27 years this was the only tollgate on Green Lanes, which at that time extended much further north. The highwayman Dick Turpin allegedly leapt the spike-topped gate on his horse Black Bess on one occasion, when pursued by a posse led by the chief constable of Westminster. The turnpike system was abolished in 1872 and the gate was dismantled. By this time, the Wellington public house was standing at the corner of Turnpike Lane and the High Road, now the site of a Burger King restaurant. Turnpike Lane station opened in 1932 on the newly extended section of the Piccadilly Line from Finsbury Park to Arnos Grove. The art deco Turnpike Parade was built beside the station entrance, with a cinema that survived until the enlargement of the neighbouring bus station in 1999. Together with Westbury Avenue, which runs north-east towards Tottenham, Turnpike Lane has become a low-rent overspill from the retail agglomeration of Wood Green. Much of the lane is now lined with shops, takeaways and hairdressers serving the diverse local community, which includes recent immigrants from the eastern Mediterranean as well as longer-established residents originating from the Caribbean and the South Asian subcontinent, especially Bangladesh.

During the 1980s the singer Sade lived near Turnpike Lane station before her breakthrough.

✉ N8, bordering N15 and N22

🚇 Piccadilly Line (zone 3)

Twickenham • *Richmond*

A pleasing, if slightly twee, riverside residential district, situated south-west of RICHMOND UPON THAMES. Pottery and flints found in Church Street date from 3000 BC and some evidence of Roman occupation has also been found. There is mention made of a settlement at Twickenham, on the ground by EEL PIE ISLAND, in AD 704. It is thought that a church stood on the site of St Mary's at the end of the 11th century. The village grew during the Middle Ages along Church Street and King Street and in alleys from them to the river, and was surrounded by stretches of open field and meadows. By the 17th century a hamlet called Heath Row was linked with the main village by buildings along Heath Road. The present street pattern of central Twickenham was all but established by 1635. In the early 16th century Richmond and HAMPTON COURT had both become royal palaces. Twickenham lay between them and members of the royal households began to build homes in the area. A small number of the best houses, including Orleans House, MARBLE HILL House and York House, occupied the riverside and in the 18th century the village's grassy riverfront contributed to the famous view from RICHMOND HILL. The terraces of Montpelier Row and Sion Row were built in the early 1720s. Traffic to the area increased with the building of a bridge to replace the ferry to Richmond in 1777. A good deal of building took place to the west of the green after the enclosure of 1818. Further population growth followed the coming of the railway to Twickenham in 1848. The original station was located at the northern end of Grosvenor Road and Queen's Road, across London Road from its present site. Most of the neighbouring area was developed between 1880 and 1895, as was ST MARGARETS. York Street was created in 1899 to bypass Church Street, which was too narrow to cope with the Richmond traffic. The increased traffic and the easier access by railway made Twickenham less of a riverside retreat than it had been and in the latter part of the 19th century the large estates started to be broken up and sold off for plots for smaller houses. In 1909 Twickenham became the first permanent home of the Rugby Football Union. The site now covers 30 acres beside the Duke of Northumberland's River and the stadium seats 75,000. There is a museum beneath the east stand with interactive displays, period set pieces and items from the famous Langton collection. The Harlequins rugby team plays nearby at the Stoop Memorial Ground, named after their legendary player and statesman of the game A D Stoop. In 1920 Twickenham was largely built up and developers shifted their attention outwards to localities such as WHITTON. By the 1950s most of the large houses that had characterized the district had submitted to the spread of more affordable housing. Despite the desirability of its housing and the visitor numbers generated by the presence of the stadium, the shops and restaurants of Twickenham lack the pulling power of those in Richmond.

Twickenham's residents have included philosopher and statesman Sir Francis Bacon and the novelist Henry Fielding; while the writers John Gay, Jonathan Swift and Alexander Pope were nicknamed 'the three Yahoos of Twickenham' by Henry Bolingbroke. Pope was perhaps Twickenham's most devoted champion, calling his retreat 'my Tusculum' after Cicero's villa outside Rome.

✉ Twickenham TW1 and TW2

38,335 (St Margarets and North Twickenham, South Twickenham, Twickenham Riverside and West Twickenham wards)

South West Trains (zone 5)

J M Lee, *The Making of Modern Twickenham*, Historical Publications, 2005

@ www.twickenham-museum.org.uk; www.rfu.com (Rugby Football Union site)

Twickenham Green • *Richmond*

A surviving fragment of TWICKENHAM Common and by extension its vicinity, situated on the south-western side of the town centre. This was formerly the south-eastern tip of HOUNSLOW HEATH and a workhouse was built here in 1725. In the early 19th century, Workhouse Road, now First Cross Road, joined the older routes to HANWORTH and HAMPTON to create the green's present triangular shape. The workhouse, its almshouses and its grounds occupied around half the area of the present-day green after the enclosure of Twickenham Common in 1818. The remainder was allocated to 'the Twickenham poor' as part of compensation for their loss of rights to gather firewood from the common. Holy Trinity Church was built in Gothic revival style in 1841. The workhouse was demolished around 1845 and, apart from a few cottages on First Cross Road, the vicinity of the green was not built up until later in the 19th century. From the late 1950s the architect Eric Lyons designed several little groups of houses and flats in the vicinity of Twickenham Green for the innovative private housebuilder Span Developments. The green today is surrounded mainly by Victorian properties, several of which have become restaurants. Prince Edward, Earl of Wessex opened a new cricket pavilion on the green in 2005.

✉ Twickenham TW1

James Strike, *The Spirit of Span Housing*, self-published, 2005

Underhill • *Barnet*

A mixed area of rented and privately owned housing lying 'under' BARNET Hill. The settlement grew up at a confluence of several old lanes, where Silver Crispin rebuilt a cottage alehouse as the Red Lion in the mid 18th century. Poor children were cared for at Underhill Cottages at the start of the 19th century; the one nearest Mays Lane was formerly a tollhouse on the turnpike road. When Barnet Fair was at its height it took over streets right across the town but the main fairground filled the fields of Underhill. The Edgware, Highgate and London Railway Co. planned a line to Barnet in 1866 and its proposal to build the terminus at Underhill was approved but the company was bought out by the Great Northern Railway, which changed the route and pushed on to HIGH BARNET. Underhill still had only a few dwellings when construction of CHIPPING BARNET sewage farm began here in 1874, and dairy cattle continued to graze on Sharpe's Farm into the 20th century, while common lodging houses stood nearby. The Three Horseshoes and Queen's Arms were closed in 1928 as part of the council's drive to reduce the number of pubs in the area, a policy known as 'the Barnet comb-out'. In the early 1930s the Grasvenor estate was laid out beside the railway line and the Old Red Lion was rebuilt. The London Borough of Barnet built the Dollis Valley housing estate on the site of the former sewage farm in the late 1960s, and more than a fifth of homes in the Underhill ward are still rented from the council.

Barnet Football Club moved to the Underhill stadium on Barnet Lane in 1907. (Underhill also hosts home games for ARSENAL reserves.) The Bees have long wanted to move to a new home but every proposed site has been dogged by controversy and their eventual future may lie outside the borough.

✉ Barnet EN5

♁ 15,721

Upminster • *Havering*

A predominantly white, home-owning dormitory suburb situated east of HORNCHURCH, enriched by a handful of important old buildings. Celtic farmers who lived here from about 500 BC created the distinctive rectilinear field pattern in the southern part of the area. Upminster's name derives not from some great cathedral, but from the parish church, said to have been founded in the seventh century by St Cedd, bishop of the East Saxons. The present church, dedicated to St Laurence, was built facing the village green in the early 13th century and its original tower survives intact. A thatched barn was built near Hall Lane in the mid 15th century and now accommodates an agricultural and folk museum, which is usually open on weekend afternoons once a month in summer. The village had a population of 370 in 1695 – still small but almost a tenfold increase from the time of Domesday Book. During the late 18th century Sir James Esdaile rebuilt Gaynes manor house for himself as a Palladian villa and added other substantial houses in the area, several of which were occupied by members of his family. James Nokes erected a windmill on his farm on the western side of the village in 1803. Recent conservation work has returned this attractive smock mill to working order. In 1885 the Great Eastern Railway brought Upminster within half an hour of London but this still represented an unacceptable journey for most potential commuters. In addition, major landowners were not yet ready to sell their estates. The first major phase of housebuilding came when the ILFORD developer Peter Griggs set his sights on Upminster in 1906. He proposed to create a 'new town on an American plan', covering 700 acres of the Upminster Hall estate. The hall itself has survived as a clubhouse for Upminster golf course. The best houses were planned for the area north of the railway, with gardens up to half an acre in size. Shops and smaller homes would be built to the south, while community facilities would include a high-class preparatory school and a doctor's house. New streets were laid out, most of which were named after former manorial families. The scheme progressed at a varying rate, according to prevailing economic conditions, with some building continuing throughout World War I. Smaller estates were added by other developers after the war and central Upminster was fully built up by 1938. A last phase of building in the 1950s and 1960s extended the suburb further north and east, with properties of a similar appearance to the better homes built between the wars. Upminster has recently been showing the first signs of evolving into a modern multicultural community but it has a long way to go yet.

William Derham was rector of St Laurence's from 1689 until his death in 1735. Dr Derham lived at High House, where he wrote his two great works, *Physico-Theology*, and *Astro-Theology*. He also made notes on sunspots, the moons of Jupiter and the migrations of birds, as well as compiling meteorological tables, making most of his observations from the church tower. His Royal Society papers describe how he measured the speed of sound from the tower, with the help of paired pocket watches, a telescope and friends who would fire a distant gun at a precise moment. More recently, the rock singer Ian Dury grew up in the suburb, and entitled his 1981 album *Lord Upminster*.

✉ Upminster RM14

🚶 12,674

🚆 c2c; 'one' Railway shuttle service to Romford; District Line terminus (zone 6)

📖 Tony Benton, *Upminster and Hornchurch*, Tempus, 2004; Tony Benton with Albert Parish, *Upminster: The Story of a Garden Suburb*, Britton Wallant, 1996

@ www.upminster.com (community site); www.upminsterwindmill.co.uk (preservation trust site)

Upminster Bridge · *Havering*

The penultimate eastbound station on the District Line, situated between UPMINSTER and HORNCHURCH. The name refers to the road bridge over the River Ingrebourne at the foot of Upminster Hill, the meeting point of Upminster Road and St Mary's Lane. In 1782 the vestry board proposed a stone-built replacement for the old wooden bridge, but the plan was rejected. This proved a false economy because subsequent timber repairs cost as much as building a bridge of stone. Construction of a sturdier crossing had to wait until 1891, following heavy rain and disastrous floods three years earlier in which the Bridge House Inn had been badly damaged. The new bridge was twice the width of its predecessor and had a time capsule of local documents and publications sealed into the foundations, seven feet below the road surface. As it appears today, the bridge is possibly the dullest such structure in London. Nearby, speculative housebuilding began before World War I and the area was fully developed by around 1930, with the station opening in 1934. Replacements, 'improvements' and continuous infilling have resulted in the messy appearance of the area's domestic architecture. The local shops, also a mixed bunch, are mainly of the low-rent variety.

Hornchurch Stadium, on Bridge Avenue, was built in 1952. The stadium has athletics facilities and is home to AFC Hornchurch, known until the collapse of its sponsor as the 'Chelsea of non-league football'.

✉ Hornchurch RM11; Upminster RM14

🚆 District Line (zone 6)

Upney · *Barking & Dagenham*

A former village, now absorbed within eastern BARKING. Upney is something of a rarity in the geography of London: a place that has lost its identity despite having a station that bears its name – which means 'higher island', implying that it was once surrounded by marshes. Most of Upney's housing was built between the wars as part of the council's slum clearance programme. The dominant feature of the locality is Barking (originally Upney) Hospital. Shortly before World War I, local people raised the money to found the hospital, and new blocks were added in the 1930s and 1960s. Most of the site was sold for residential development in 1999, although some specialist acute facilities have survived. The former maternity wing, opened in 1987, is now the Upney Lane Centre, an outpatients and minor injuries unit, with a local branch of Moorfields Eye Hospital. Wilcon Homes has built houses and maisonettes, while Hanover Housing Association has added flats for the elderly, with associated care facilities. The Wilcon housing, centred on Goodey Road, is of reasonably high quality and has introduced the phenomenon of Jaguars and Mercedes (albeit often 'previously owned') parked in residents' drives. The junction of Upney Lane and the Drive has the essential amenities: a post office, fish and chip shop and tanning centre. A significant minority of residents are of Indian or Pakistani origin and, after English, Punjabi and Urdu are the most widely spoken languages.

Across Ripple Road (A123) is Eastbury Manor House, a National Trust property managed by the borough council as an arts, heritage and community resource. This Grade I-listed mansion was built for an Essex merchant during the reign of Elizabeth I. In the early 17th century the house attracted wealthy Catholic families who could practise their religion there in relative safety from persecution, and some Gunpowder Plot mythology has therefore become attached to it. The National Trust has recently completed the renovation of the west wing. A Roman coffin was discovered in a nearby back garden in 1932.

✉ Barking IG11

🚆 District Line (zone 4)

Upper Belvedere • *Bexley*

Street atlases do not distinguish between Upper and LOWER BELVEDERE, but most of the local signage refers specifically to the former, which is the southern part of the district. The settlement was developed from 1856 by landowner Sir Culling Eardley, who lived at Belvedere House. He intended this to be a high-class residential area and, apart from a few rows of cottages, most of the properties were substantial villas with generous gardens. All Saints' Church was consecrated in 1861. Because the residents were expected to have servants and carriages, the introduction of public transport was resisted into the 20th century, preserving the village's appearance. A surge of building in the 1930s began to transform Upper Belvedere into a more conventional suburb and from the mid 1960s the replacement of older properties, including shops on Nuxley Road, advanced the process. As local historian John Pritchard comments, 'the village so largely created by the Eardley family was rapidly losing its original character by 1965'.

✉ Belvedere DA17

Upper Clapton • *Hackney*

Manorial courts began to divide Clapton into upper and lower halves around 1800 and the terminology soon entered popular parlance. Upper Clapton Road was formerly Hackney Lane and Clapton Common was Broad Common. From the late 18th century, labourers' cottages began to cluster along the southern

end of Upper Clapton Road and on Kate's Lane (now Northwold Road). Grander properties were erected in the direction of STAMFORD HILL, mostly detached but with a few high-class terraces. In the latter half of the 19th century, construction spread beyond the main thoroughfares into a network of newly created streets that joined up with STOKE NEWINGTON and SHACKLEWELL to the west. Towards the River Lea, the grounds of three large houses were saved by the creation of Springfield Park in 1905. By this time Upper Clapton had its own shops, schools, pubs and places of worship. A few houses were converted for use as clothing workshops after World War I. From the early 1930s, metropolitan and local authorities seized on Upper Clapton as a suitable location for large-scale housing projects. Some of the schemes utilized surviving open ground and some replaced slum housing but others were built at the expense of sound Georgian villas and terraced houses. Hackney council added system-built tower blocks in the 1960s and 1970s before switching to low-rise blocks in its last phase of municipal construction. There has been relatively little new building since; the largest recent project has been the redevelopment of the former LEA BRIDGE tram depot as a mixed-use site, with 105 residential units in six blocks. With its concentrated stock of social housing, Upper Clapton is a deprived area and the transient population includes a number of refugee families. The largest ethnic minority is of black Caribbean descent. Upper Clapton Road has gained a reputation as a hotbed of crime in recent years, with offences ranging from muggings to drive-by shootings.

Upper Clapton Football Club is one of England's oldest rugby teams – but it no longer plays anywhere near here. Founded in 1879, the club moved to Epping in 1933.

✉ E5

Upper Edmonton • *Enfield*

The densely populated southern part of EDMONTON, focused on SILVER STREET, ANGEL ROAD (A406) and Fore Street (A1010), which form the arms of the crossroads at the ANGEL, EDMONTON. From the late Middle Ages ribbon development along the coaching road to Hertford created a hamlet at Fore Street, with several well-known inns. The Bell became so famous that more than one establishment laid claim to the name and at one time there was an Old Bell and an Oldest Bell. Like all places on the eastern side of the modern borough, industry developed beside the River Lea in the 19th century, with nearby terraced housing for workers. Grander properties were built on and around Silver Street. Between these asymmetric halves the spine of Fore Street experienced aggressive expansion in the 1880s and 1890s. Large old houses in its hinterland were pulled down and replaced by cramped terraces, often built so poorly that Edmonton council prosecuted some jerry-builders, forcing a few to demolish properties. At the beginning of the 20th century the council bought PYMMES House and preserved its grounds as a much-needed public park. With this exception, almost the entire remainder of Upper Edmonton was soon built up. Few of the structures possessed any architectural merit except the Gothic St John's Church on Dyson's Road. Municipal housing projects transformed large parts of the area after World War II. The Sterling Way section of the North Circular Road disfigures Upper Edmonton but traffic congestion has been reduced by the construction of the Fore Street underpass at the end of the 1990s. The Upper Edmonton ward forms a long east–west band along the border with Haringey and bears more socio-economic resemblance to neighbouring TOTTENHAM than to most parts of its parent borough of Enfield. The typical resident is a young manual worker living in social housing. Unemployment and crime levels are high, and incomes and car ownership low.

✉ N18

🚶 14,843

Upper Elmers End • *Bromley*

Districts in this area merge together even more than in most other parts of London, and Upper Elmers End is essentially a lost hamlet that used to lie near the bend in the middle of Upper Elmers End Road (A214), centred on the Rising Sun public house. Much of the surrounding area was part of Park Farm in the 19th century. In 1882 Upper Elmers End was divided from EDEN PARK and the rest of ELMERS END by the Mid-Kent Railway line. The West Kent brewery dominated the hamlet, which had fewer than 20 houses at the start of the 20th century. The brewery later became Kempton's bakery, which specialized in meat pies from the 1930s. This was a time when the council was developing the area with small semi-detached houses. Some of the Victorian houses and cottages in Upper Elmers End were very pleasing but the survivors were replaced by council flats in the 1950s. Holly Crescent and Lodge Gardens are named for Holly Lodge, a former bailiff's house that was let to a series of middle-class occupants from the late 19th century. The primary commercial enterprise in the locality is the Masters Renault dealership, which occupies the site of several former small businesses.

✉ Beckenham BR3

Upper Holloway • *Islington*

The part of HOLLOWAY that lies between Camden Road and ARCHWAY, extending – by some definitions – just beyond Hornsey Road to the east and JUNCTION ROAD to the west. Most of the early structures in Upper Holloway stood in the area now known as Archway. During the 17th century several inns appeared along the northern section of HOLLOWAY ROAD, the first of which was the Mother Red Cap, which was said to be a haunt of prostitutes in the 1630s. Little residential development took place until the 1840s. The first investors built substantial villas with generous grounds but within a decade land societies began to lay out streets of terraced houses for leaseholders who would thus qualify for the vote. However, many of these developments were not completed until the 1870s and plenty of space remained between each of the new estates. Over the next two decades smaller houses filled these gaps and clerks and artisans filled these houses. By the end of the century, detached villas that had been built 50 years earlier were being knocked down and replaced by more terraces. From as early as 1901, municipal authorities set about demolishing some of the more inferior properties and constructing progressively larger blocks of flats. By 1967 Islington council and the Greater London Council had nearly 50 sizeable estates in the area either completed or in progress. Many local people felt that the process had gone too far and that the councils were now needlessly destroying good quality houses. The Holloway Tenant Co-operative, which may have been the first of its kind in England, was one of a series of groups that successfully persuaded the authorities to switch from rebuilding to rehabilitation, and to rehousing existing tenants in the same neighbourhood. The most desirable parts of Upper Holloway remain in the area where settlement first began, which some estate agents now like to call 'HIGHGATE borders'.

Marie Stopes opened Britain's first birth control clinic at 61 Marlborough Road in 1922. The Mother's Clinic for Constructive Birth Control occupied a converted house, with a confectioner and a grocer as neighbours. It aimed to be homely and welcoming 'to mothers or fathers'. By 1925 the clinic had become so popular that it moved to its present location in Whitfield Street, FITZROVIA.

✉ N7; N19

🚋 Silverlink Metro (zone 2)

Upper Norwood • Croydon

The central part of the huge Victorian suburb of NORWOOD, situated south-west of CRYSTAL PALACE. The two identities overlap and some residents of the east side of Upper Norwood refer to the area as Crystal Palace. During the first half of the 19th century grand houses with large grounds filled much of Upper Norwood. Only in the Woodland Road area and the triangle formed by Westow Hill, Church Road and Westow Street was housing built for the working classes. By 1845 Upper Norwood had a population of over 3,000. The reconstruction of the Crystal Palace on SYDENHAM Hill in 1854 catapulted Upper Norwood to the height of fashion as a place of residence. Varied amenities were built to serve the tourists, including the Queen's Hotel. Successively more imposing mansions were built, often with ostentatious ornamentation, especially on BEULAH HILL. A variety of facilities met the needs of the more diverse population in the north-east of the district. Westow Street market grew up in the 1880s and operated for around 70 years. Upper Norwood recreation ground was opened to popular acclaim in 1890. Upper Norwood Library opened in 1900 and is now jointly owned by Croydon and Lambeth councils but operates independently of both – a unique arrangement for a British public library today. As the popularity of Crystal Palace waned, so did Upper Norwood's appeal to the wealthy, and private developers and Croydon council began to buy up some of the largest houses. Most of the properties were still in good condition but changing socio-economic conditions had left fewer people able to afford them. Some were converted into flats but builders generally found it more cost-effective to build a whole new street in place of the house and its former grounds. Despite a century of rebuilding, many of the original villas of Upper Norwood have survived and are protected by a large conservation area. The Norwood Heights retail complex was built on the site of Barker's piano store and factory and a Salvation Army citadel. The Upper Norwood ward has a broad spread of ethnic minorities, of which the lar-

gest are of black Caribbean and Indian descent. Almost two-thirds of homes are owner-occupied.

The French novelist Emile Zola lived at the Queen's Hotel at the end of the 19th century. His photographs of the local area have been collected into a book (see below). Camille Pissarro's depiction of a snowscape at *Fox Hill, Upper Norwood* hangs in the National Gallery. It is said that Madame Tussaud came to live in exile at Effingham Lodge, and set out from here with her touring waxworks exhibition. In *The Sign of Four*, Sherlock Holmes solves the mystery behind the murder of Bartholomew Sholto of Pondicherry Lodge, Upper Norwood.

✉ SE19

👥 14,190

📖 Jean-Claude Le Blond-Zola et al, *Emile Zola: Photographer in Norwood, South London 1898–1899*, Norwood Society, 1997

Upper Ruxley see RUXLEY

Upper Shirley • Croydon

The southern part of SHIRLEY, nestling between the ADDINGTON Hills and the Addington and Shirley Park golf courses. The enclave of Badger's Hole evolved on squatted land in the mid 18th century and a hamlet of weatherboarded cottages followed in the 19th century, centred around the junction of Oaks Road and Upper Shirley Road. A post mill was built in 1810 and was replaced after a fire by the present tower mill in 1854. Its boat-shaped, weatherboarded cap is of a distinctly Kentish design. The village had a brewery for most of the second half of the 19th century and in 1868 two cottages were converted into the Surprise inn, while temperance tea gardens offered an abstemious alternative. The Coloma Convent School was founded on the eastern side of Upper Shirley Road in 1869. In 1954 John Ruskin Grammar School moved from Croydon to a new site on Upper Shirley Road, with Shirley windmill in its grounds. The school was demolished in 1991 to make way for housing development. Shirley windmill was restored to working order and opened to the public in 1995. Coloma was rated one of the 123 best secondary schools in England in an 'honours list' produced by the educational standards agency Ofsted in 2005. To the south lies the exclusive enclave of Shirley Hills, which has been called 'Croydon's BISHOPS AVENUE', and its main residential road is coincidentally named Bishops Walk. Houses backing onto one of the two golf courses fetch prices in the millions.

✉ Croydon CRO

@ www.coloma.croydon.sch.uk (school site)

Upper Street • *Islington*

The central thoroughfare of ISLINGTON, and part of the A1, stretching for one mile between HIGHBURY Corner and the junction with Liverpool Road at its southern end. There used to be a Lower Street too, but this is now ESSEX ROAD. Honorius, Archbishop of Canterbury, established Islington's parish of St Mary here in 628, under the aegis of ST PAUL'S Cathedral. St Mary's Church was originally called Our Lady of Islington. Upper Street was part of the cattle-droving route to SMITHFIELD and a King's Head tavern is supposed to have existed from about 1543. By the early 17th century the street had a sprinkling of gentlemen's houses and tradesmen's cottages. But before the century was out the gentry had begun to depart and several of their houses were converted to inns. Sir John Miller's house, which stood near Theberton Street, had become the Pied Bull by 1725. An unsubstantiated story persists that this had earlier been the residence of Sir Walter Raleigh. A variety of developers put up short rows of houses for the middle classes and by 1735 Upper Street was almost entirely built up, although much of the hinterland remained open. Islington became a popular place for Londoners to spend a day out and the number of public houses multiplied. Dr William Pitcairn established a four-acre botanical garden opposite Cross Street. During the 19th century the rows of houses were rebuilt as commercial premises, at first catering for the growing local population and later attracting customers from further afield. The street's non-stop commerce prompted the vicar of St Mary's Church to campaign against Sunday opening, resulting in the founding the Lord's Day Observance Society in 1831. Despite Islington's ever-diminishing status as a residential district, Upper Street's outfitters and drapers grew in prestige, and their trousseaux and underclothes were especially highly prized. A section of the street was rebuilt in widened form and lined with substantial terraces of shops, while smart new frontages were added to the surviving older premises. In the mid 1920s the Church Missionary Society College was replaced by Sutton's model dwellings, a pleasing estate with Arts and Crafts details, and Islington Town Hall was built. Meanwhile, the big stores lost the battle with their rivals 'up west' and Upper Street went into a slow decline that lasted until Islington's increasingly young and well-educated population presented new opportunities after the 1960s. Sisterwrite was Britain's first feminist bookshop when it opened on Upper Street in 1978, the King's Head began to stage theatrical performances and the Hope and Anchor became London's leading pub venue for the burgeoning punk rock scene. Upper Street's variety of restaurants is now almost unrivalled outside the WEST END and there are all kinds of specialist shops, notably the antiques traders of Camden Passage.

Charles Wesley wrote *Hark the Herald Angels Sing* while serving as assistant curate at St Mary's Church in 1738. The illustrator Kate Greenaway came to Upper Street with her family in 1852. In 1994 Tony Blair and Gordon Brown dined at Upper Street restaurant Granita (now closed), where they allegedly thrashed out the deal that led to Blair becoming prime minister and Brown chancellor.

✉ N1

📖 Jim Connell, *Illustrated History of Upper Street, Islington*, Stowlangtoft, 1991

Upper Sydenham • *Lewisham*

The faded western half of SYDENHAM, now dominated by blocks of council housing. In Elizabethan times, forestry was an important industry here, providing charcoal and wood for shipbuilding. By the end of the 18th century the forest had been almost completely cleared and dairy farming had become the dominant occupation. The erection of the CRYSTAL PALACE in the 1850s and the opening of Upper Sydenham railway station (now closed) prompted the complete building over of Sydenham Common with some very grand suburban housing. But its success proved short-lived and the area fell out of fashion within a decade. Its real beginnings as a dormitory suburb were in the 1880s when the 'new middle classes' began to arrive. In the 1960s and 1970s a large group of council blocks were erected. Wells Park is all that remains of the 500-acre common. It takes its name from the nearby springs that were discovered around 1640 at the top of what was then Pig Hill (now Peak Hill).

✉ SE26

Upper Tooting *see* TOOTING BEC

Upper Walthamstow • *Waltham Forest*

More commonly known as 'the WOOD STREET

area', this is the eastern part of WALTHAM-STOW, north of WHIPPS CROSS. It lies on the upper part of the slope that rises from the River Lea towards the ridge of London clay. This was muddy dairy pasture until the Walthamstow Enclosure Act of 1848, after which developers began to transform it. Writing in 1861, local historian Ebenezer Clarke commented, 'Mud Island and Hog Corner have been converted into Salter's Buildings and Paradise Row, stagnant ponds and offensive ditches have been filled in or covered over … and if we continue to improve we shall be approaching an earthly paradise.' Much of the heavenly housing was replaced in the 1930s by estates such as The Risings but a number of Victorian properties remain. The mid-18th-century Walthamstow House, on Shernhall Street, was once the home of Sir Robert Wigram, whose family also owned two surviving mansions on Forest Road. The parkland to the east of Upper Walthamstow is part of Epping Forest.

✉ E17

Upper Woodcote · *Croydon*

A garden village in west PURLEY and a paradise for tree lovers and horticulturalists – if they can afford it. In 1859 James Watney bought 800 acres of the Carew family's BEDDINGTON estate and his grandson sold about a third of the land to chartered surveyor William Webb in 1888. Webb planted trees, flowers and hedgerows that were allowed to mature before homes were built and offered for sale. The coming of the tram to Purley in 1901 spurred him to make a start on construction and the first dwelling to be completed was Upper Woodcote House, which Webb himself moved into. Cottages were then studded around a village green in the south-west corner, originally for Webb's workmen but soon snapped up by commuters. The outer roads of the estate were mostly built up with semi-detached properties, and these have been the worst affected by traffic and by alterations and infilling. Most of the inner roads were laid out from 1907 and the plots developed between 1912 and 1920. Webb planted Rose Walk with 6,000 rose bushes, the South Border with herbaceous plants and Silver Lane with a double row of silver birch and a host of bulbs and wild flowers. The Promenade de Verdun came last, lined with an avenue of Lombardy poplars with their roots in soil brought from Armentières and sifted to remove shrapnel. At the end of the avenue is a granite obelisk dedicated to the memory of French soldiers who died in World War I. The estate was virtually complete by 1925 and contains around 230 houses, which themselves are of varying architectural merit, but in an incomparable setting. Webb expounded his landscaping theories in a short but well-illustrated publication that is still available from antiquarian booksellers. The council conferred conservation area status on Upper Woodcote Village in 1973, extending this to cover the rest of the estate a decade later. There is a blanket tree preservation order and no subdivision of plots is allowed.

✉ Purley CR8

📖 Vanda Bouri, *A Century of Garden First: Introducing the Webb Estate Conservation Area*, The Webb Estate Society, 1994

Upton · *Bexley*

The south-western part of BEXLEYHEATH, lying east of DANSON PARK. Indications of Bronze Age habitation have been discovered here. A 17th-century farm building, once known as Wye Lodge, survives in much-altered form on Lion Road. Upton was an isolated heathland hamlet with a handful of pretty cottages and a couple of public houses when Philip Webb and William Morris came here to build the idealistic Red House. The pair had conceived the notion while rowing down the River Seine in the summer of 1858. With its informal, asymmetric design, the house represents one of the earliest expressions of Arts and Crafts principles. The German scholar Herman Muthesius later described it as 'the first private house of the new artistic culture, the first house to be conceived as a whole inside and out, the very first example in the history of the modern house'. Morris lived here from 1860 to 1865. BEXLEY Cottage Hospital (now Upton Day Hospital) opened at 14 Upton Road in 1884. Towards the end of the 19th century, Bexleyheath began to spread towards Upton with the building of the Oaklands estate south of the Broadway. Ribbon development along Upton Road in the late 1920s and early 1930s marked the absorption of the hamlet into the suburbs.

The architect Edward Hollamby bought Red House in 1952 and restored it, living there until his death in 1999. The National Trust subsequently acquired the property for around £2 million. To protect Red House and some nearby cottages, much of Upton is designated a conservation area and the house itself has Grade I-listed status.

✉ Bexleyheath DA6

📖 Jan Marsh, *William Morris's Red House: A Collaboration Between Architect and Owner*, Pavilion, 2005

Upton • *Newham*

'The pretty rural hamlet of Upton is a little more than a mile north-east of WEST HAM church,' wrote James Thorne in 1876. No longer rural and no longer much heard of, Upton gained its name from a position on higher ground. It was the home of a community of Quakers from the late 18th century onwards. The Spotted Dog on Upton Lane is Newham's oldest building, albeit much transformed from its 16th-century origins. It is said to have been the site of Henry VIII's dog kennels, and had a popular tea garden and cricket ground before 1900. No sooner had Thorne's words appeared than the hamlet began to be built over with housing for the factory workers of West Ham. Because of the station and the football ground, UPTON PARK is now much better known than its parent.

Joseph Lister, who pioneered antiseptic surgery, was born in Upton Lane in 1827.

✉ E7

Upton Park • *Newham*

A densely built-up district situated between WEST HAM and EAST HAM, and best known as the home of West Ham United Football Club. The station opened on the London, Tilbury and Southend Railway in 1877 and the Upton Park estate was built following the sale of PLASHET House and its grounds in 1883. The surrounding area was developed from the 1890s, while GREEN STREET filled with shops and a market was established on Queens Road. The housing consisted almost entirely of uniform, compact terraces for clerks and the skilled working classes. Construction standards were mostly satisfactory but one or two estates were rushed up with less care. District Railway trains began serving the station in 1902 and the old hamlets of Plashet, UPTON and Green Street gradually dissolved within the new district of Upton Park. Council blocks, not one of which matches another, were wedged into every available gap in the Victorian terraces in the 1960s and 1970s. During the first half of the 20th century Upton Park possessed a large Jewish community, which has now been replaced by an even larger south Asian population. At Upton Cross Primary School, all the children are from ethnic minorities and 97 per cent come from homes where English is not the first language.

West Ham United moved to Green Street's Boleyn ground in 1904, nine years after their formation as Thames Ironworks Football Club and four years after they had changed their name to attract broader support.

✉ E6; E13

🚇 District Line; Hammersmith & City Line (zone 3)

📖 Micky Smith, *For the Claret and Blue*, Blake, 2004 (West Ham's answer to Nick Hornby's *Fever Pitch*)

Uxbridge • *Hillingdon*

The administrative and commercial centre of the borough, situated on the western edge of Greater London, south of the Western Avenue (A40). The name almost certainly derives from the Wixan tribe who settled various parts of Middlesex in the seventh century. Their bridge would have crossed the River Colne. However, no document recorded the existence of the village until the mid twelfth century, when it was called Wixebrug. St Margaret's Church began life as a chapel of ease to HILLINGDON church in the early 13th century. A market house was built by 1513 and soon afterwards a ribbon of timber-framed houses lined the Oxford road from the Colne to what is now Vine Street. The Bennet family owned a mansion called The Place, where Royalist and Parliamentary representatives drew up an abortive treaty to end the Civil War in 1645. The mansion was later reduced in size and renamed the Treaty House and is now a pub called the Crown and Treaty. During the 18th century Uxbridge flourished as a coaching halt, with shops and inns on the High Street, and the present market building was built in 1788. The construction of the Grand Junction (now Grand Union) Canal in the 1790s brought industry to UXBRIDGE MOOR and by 1801 passenger barges were running daily to PADDINGTON. The transport links helped confirm Uxbridge's supremacy over Hillingdon as a market town, particularly for corn. Coach traffic continued to increase and the town had 54 licensed premises in 1853. Three years later the first railway station opened and road travel began to wane, with many inns and their stables converting to private dwellings. From the late 19th century, private housebuilding began to spread towards COWLEY and Hillingdon, and subsequently to the north, encouraged by the construction in 1904 of the Metropolitan Railway terminus in

Belmont Road. The council built outlying estates after World War I and in the 1930s demolished slum properties in the crowded centre. Uxbridge Lido opened in 1935, and is soon to be the centre of a new leisure complex. The Underground station was rebuilt at its present location in 1938. From the late 1960s the council embarked on the wholesale redevelopment of the town centre, paving the way for the present appearance of the shopping and leisure area. Two shopping centres now dominate the High Street: the Pavilions, which holds a weekly craft market, and the Chimes, which includes a nine-screen cinema. Listed buildings in the Old Uxbridge conservation area have been refurbished. Brunel University moved to Uxbridge in 1967 and has since greatly expanded its campus. To the southeast of the town centre stands Hillingdon civic centre, built in the mid 1970s in an original and influential style that avoided the grandly monumental approach taken by most town halls. Swish apartment blocks have recently added a new dimension to the residential profile.

✉ Uxbridge UB8

⚥ 33,740 (Brunel and Uxbridge North and South wards)

🚇 Metropolitan Line terminus; Piccadilly Line terminus (zone 6)

📖 James Skinner, *Around Uxbridge*, Tempus, 2004; K R Pearce, *Uxbridge*

People, Sutton, 1999

@ www.brunel.ac.uk;
www.pavilionsuxbridge.co.uk;
www.thechimes.uk.com

Uxbridge Moor · *Hillingdon*

A canalside industrial area of south-west UX-BRIDGE. The Grand Junction (now Grand Union) Canal was dug through the moor in 1794, connecting Uxbridge with the Thames at BRENTFORD. By 1800 the link to Birmingham was complete. Wharves and warehouses were constructed along the canal and coal for the surrounding district was offloaded here, while corn was taken aboard. Oil and mustard mills, glass and gas works prompted the building of workers' homes, followed by the Church of St John's on the Moor in 1838 and a ragged school eight years later, both on Waterloo Road. Uxbridge Moor is still a commercial zone, but this now takes the form of a network of industrial estates and business parks. The London Wildlife Trust manages a stretch of the bank that has willow woodland and meadows, at the north end of Riverside Way industrial estate, where a branch of the River Colne flows into the canal.

Cricket was played on the moor from at least 1735. Uxbridge cricket club was founded here in 1789, and England played Kent at the ground in the same year. The club moved to Uxbridge Common in the 1820s.

✉ Uxbridge UB8

V

Valence • *Barking*

An electoral ward in north BECONTREE. Agnes de Valence, whose name derived from the French abbey of Valence, retired to DAGENHAM following the death of her third husband in 1291. On Agnes's demise in 1309 her brother Aylmer, later Earl of Pembroke, took possession of the estate and held it until his death in 1342, when he was buried in Westminster Abbey. Valence House may have been built in the 14th century but was subsequently enlarged, then reduced and then enlarged again, as well as being remodelled on other occasions. At its heart, the present house is of late-17th-century origin. The Valence estate was broken up in 1806 but little building took place here until the creation of the Becontree estate. The London County Council bought Valence House in 1901 and sold it to Dagenham council in 1926. It subsequently served as council offices and a library and is now partly a museum that is popular for local school visits. The council is proud of Valence House, but this is primarily a reflection of the borough's dearth of quality historic buildings. Valence moat, despite its modest proportions, is popular with young anglers. Valence Park, between Becontree Avenue and Valence Wood Road, has tennis courts but not much else. Like the rest of Becontree, the Valence ward has a predominantly white population. The most significant ethnic minority is of black African heritage. A majority of homes here are now owner-occupied but most of the remainder are still rented from the council. Valence Junior School is on Bonham Road. Among the small number of pupils whose first language is not English, Turkish, Punjabi, Portuguese and Yoruba are the most widely spoken tongues.

Football pundit and former England manager Terry Venables was born in Valence Avenue in 1943. He lived in Bonham Road and attended Valence School.

✉ Dagenham RM8

8,775

@ www.barking-dagenham.gov.uk/4-valence/valence-menu.html (Valence House Museum site)

Valentines Park • *Redbridge*

A public park and neighbouring Edwardian estate situated on the north side of central ILFORD. The name probably derives from a 16th-century landowner. A house was built here in the late 1690s, probably for Elizabeth Tillotson, widow of an archbishop of Canterbury, but successive enlargements and improvements have erased almost every trace of this building. The mansion that stands today dates primarily from phases of work in 1769 and 1811. The council acquired most of the grounds and opened them in 1899, originally as Central Park. Following the death of the mansion's owner in 1902, Ilford council bought the remainder of the grounds and extended the park. Begun in 1909, the Valentines Park estate was one of the last of the Victorian and Edwardian schemes that entirely transformed Ilford from farmland to suburb within the space of two decades. The council acquired Valentines mansion itself in 1912 and it served as a home for Belgian refugees during World War I and later as offices for the local public health authority. With the formation of the London Borough of Redbridge in 1965, Valentines became home to the council's housing service, which vacated the building in 1993. It lay empty and increasingly shabby until its exterior was restored in 2002. Over £3 million of council and lottery money has been secured for the renovation of the interior, and it is hoped to open the building to the public from 2009. Valentines Park is one of east London's loveliest spots, with formal gardens, lakes and landscaped parkland, as well as 26 tennis courts. The Valentines ward is ethnically diverse; the main groups are of white, Indian or Pakistani origin. A high proportion of homes are privately rented.

✉ Ilford IG1

11,643 (Valentines ward)

⬜ Len Dowling, *Valentines Park, Ilford: A Century of History*, Redbridge Libraries, 1999

@ www.2-sixteen.org.uk/vm (Valentines Mansion page of council site)

Vale of Health • *Camden*

A mini-village in north HAMPSTEAD, with more to it than most maps suggest. This part of HAMPSTEAD HEATH was originally known as Gangmoor, and later as Hatches (or Hatchett's) Bottom, after an early-18th-century cottager. The Hampstead Water Co. created a pond here in 1777, which drained enough of the formerly malarial marsh to allow houses to be built. For much of its early existence, Hatches Bottom was not regarded as a picturesque village but as an intrusive presence on the heath. The essayist Leigh Hunt lived here from 1816 to 1818 and regularly hosted meetings of writers and poets, who included Shelley, Keats and Byron. In 1851 the village had 57 adults and 30 children crammed into 18 houses. With the opening of the Hampstead Junction Railway in 1860, day-trippers began to swarm here in summertime and the Hampstead Heath Hotel and Vale of Health tavern were built, neither of which has survived. In 1877 the Athenaeum Club opened in a chapel-like building, later becoming an Anglo-German society with over 1,000 members. By 1890 the village had 53 houses. Those who wished to attract visitors invented and propagated the 'Vale of Health' name, although this did not fully supplant the older identity until the mid 20th century. The village now consists mainly of attractive villas and cottages, often separated by narrow passageways, together with two small blocks of private flats. Residents formed the Vale of Health Society in 1973 to resist inappropriate development and marked its 25th anniversary by founding Heath Hands, the first volunteer corps dedicated to Hampstead Heath.

Former residents include the artist Stanley Spencer, the writers D H Lawrence, Stella Gibbons, Compton Mackenzie and Edgar Wallace, and the Nobel prize-winning Indian poet Rabindranath Tagore.

✉ NW3

⬜ Helen Bentwich, *The Vale of Health on Hampstead Heath, 1777–1977*, High Hill Press, 1977

Vauxhall • *Lambeth/Wandsworth* (pronounced 'voxhall' or 'voxall')

A recently improved Thames-side locality and transport interchange in south-west LAMBETH, and formerly the site of London's most fashionable pleasure gardens. The Gascon mercenary Falkes de Bréauté gained possession of the manor in 1233 through his marriage to wealthy widow Margaret de Redvers and built Falkes' Hall, later called Fox Hall. Jane Vaux, possibly a descendant of Falkes de Bréauté, owned a house here in 1615 with eleven acres of grounds called the Spring Gardens, which were opened as a pleasure park in 1660. Samuel Pepys recorded later in the decade that he went 'by water to Fox-hall, and there walked in Spring Garden'. The park reopened in 1732 with greatly enhanced attractions and the construction of WESTMINSTER Bridge in 1750 improved its accessibility. Such was the prestige of Vauxhall Gardens, as they were formally called from 1785, that similar parks were laid out in several cities, including the Tivoli Gardens in Copenhagen. Many borrowed the Vauxhall name. In Russia, the station pavilion at the Pavlovsk pleasure gardens outside St Petersburg was named *Vokzal*; Pavlovsk was the destination of the first Russian railway line, which arrived there from the city in 1837, and the word *vokzal* is still an old-fashioned word for 'station' in Russian. Vauxhall Gardens closed in 1859 after two decades of financial difficulties but a small remnant, Spring Gardens, survives opposite the northern end of South Lambeth Road. A little to the south, Vauxhall Park opened in 1890. Industry and commerce flourished along Vauxhall's riverside for more than three centuries, and still does at NINE ELMS. The Vauxhall Ironworks Co. built its first car in 1903, badged with Falkes de Bréauté's heraldic griffin; a plaque at Sainsbury's petrol station on Wandsworth Road marks the site of the factory. The company relocated to Luton in 1905 and became Vauxhall Motors two years later. The present Vauxhall Bridge opened in May 1906, replacing the 19th-century Regent Bridge. Much of Vauxhall was rebuilt with blocks of low-rise flats in the 1930s and parts had become very run-down by the early 1990s, since when the area has been transformed in a variety of ways. The Secret Intelligence Service (MI6) moved to a purpose-built headquarters at Vauxhall Cross in 1993 and other parts of the riverside have since filled with luxury apartment blocks that have proved popular with senior politicians. Inland, surviving Georgian and Victorian terraced houses have been gentrified, while huge sums have been spent on the regeneration of council housing. Vauxhall's Portuguese community has opened cafés and restaurants, while a 'village' of gay bars and nightclubs has also evolved. Transport for London completed London's most distinctive bus station at Vauxhall Cross in 2004, with 'ski-ramp' solar panels that power most of the station's lighting.

The pleasure gardens feature prominently in Thackeray's *Vanity Fair*, although Captain Dobbin finds 'the Vauxhall amusements not particularly lively'. Thomas Hood's *At Shining Vauxhall* is one of several poems inspired by the gardens. The Victoria & Albert Museum has Thomas Rowlandson's watercolour *Vauxhall Gardens* (1784). Singer/songwriter Morrissey lived in the area for a while and released the album *Vauxhall and I* in 1994.

✉ SW8; SE11

♦ 110,431 (parliamentary constituency)

🚉 South West Trains; Victoria Line (zones 1 and 2)

@ www.vauxhallsociety.org.uk; www.vauxhallpark.org.uk

Victoria • *Westminster*

A main-line railway terminus and its neighbourhood, located half a mile south of Buckingham Palace. The first use of the queen's name in this area came one year after her accession in 1837 with the creation of Victoria Square, just south of the Royal Mews. Victoria Street cut through WESTMINSTER'S worst slum district in 1845, displacing 5,000 poor, most of whom decamped south of the Thames. In 1860, Grosvenor (or Victoria) railway bridge began to carry trains across the river to a new station under construction on a site vacated by the Chelsea Water Co. following its relocation to SEETHING WELLS. Until then services had terminated south of the river at NINE ELMS. The line north of the Thames followed part of the route of the former Grosvenor Canal. To appease the Duke of Westminster, the local landowner, goods trains were banned, shrubs were planted, long, glass train sheds were built and the tracks were even lined with rubber beds. The station formally opened in 1862, with services to Kent running from its eastern 'Chatham' side, while the larger 'Brighton' half mainly served destinations in Sussex. In 1868 the Midland District Railway opened its station at Victoria as part of the 'inner circle' line. The two halves of the main-line station were rebuilt and given their present facades between 1906 and 1909. The presence of the station brought warehouses and furniture repositories to its hinterland, while offices on

Victoria Street displaced earlier industries like printing, brewing and milling. The Royal Standard Music Hall was demolished and replaced by the Victoria Palace Theatre in 1910. The art deco New Victoria (now Apollo Victoria) opened in 1930 as a cine-variety theatre. Victoria Coach Station was built on Buckingham Palace Road in 1932, also in art deco style. From 1959 onwards, small hotels and blocks of flats and chambers on Victoria Street were progressively demolished and replaced with large office buildings, often with shops at street level. The Victoria Line arrived in 1968, and the Victoria Place and Colonnades shopping malls were constructed over the tracks of the Brighton side in the 1990s. The modern Victoria area has amenities that adequately meet the needs of local office workers and those in transit but little to make it a destination in itself except for its two theatres, which have cultivated a reputation for musicals. The council is seeking a 'renaissance of Victoria' via staged improvements to the main-line and London Underground stations and their environs, but would like the coach station to move elsewhere.

✉ SW1

🚉 Main-line: South Eastern Trains; Southern (Kent, Sussex and suburban services) London Underground: Circle Line; District Line; Victoria Line (zone 1)

@ www.transportforlondon.gov.uk/vcs (Victoria Coach Station)

Victoria Dock A commonly used short form of ROYAL VICTORIA Dock and the former name for CUSTOM HOUSE station.

Victoria Embankment *see* EMBANKMENT

Victoria Park • *Tower Hamlets/Hackney*

A 213-acre park with lakes and many amenities situated between SOUTH HACKNEY and Bow's OLD FORD locality. The park was created to beautify the EAST END, provide recreational space and improve public health. Two possible sites were considered: at BOW COMMON and in south-east HACKNEY. The consultant planner Sir James Pennethorne recommended Bow Common, which he felt was less flat and dull. However, the Hackney option was preferred, primarily because the land was cheaper, although landscaping proved unexpectedly expensive. There were nurseries and orchards here before, but the fruit trees were cut down for fear that they would provide an incentive to thieving and disorder. Disorderly gatherings had been a feature of the neighbouring Bonner's Fields, most of which subsequently disappeared beneath access roads and housing. Victoria Park opened unofficially in 1845, while landscaping was still in progress and before the lakes had been created. Numerous ornamental structures were added in subsequent decades but most have been lost as a result of war-time bombing or neglect. The creation of the park stimulated housebuilding in its vicinity. New streets were laid out and substantial terraced houses and detached villas filled the area over the following three decades. Victoria Park had a station on the North London line from 1856 to 1943, with access from the north side of Wick Road. Some housing was replaced after the 1960s by private and council flats but a conservation area now protects most of the Victorian properties, which have been described as 'forever up-and-coming but never quite making it into the Islington league'. Estate agents refer to the area as 'Victoria Park village'. The park became the sole responsibility of the London Borough of Tower Hamlets in 1994.

Victoria Park has hosted political gatherings throughout its history, including Chartist rallies soon after it opened, striking dockworkers' meetings in the late 19th century and a Rock against Racism carnival in 1978 that was attended by more than 80,000 people.

✉ E9, E3; E2

👥 12,066 (Hackney's Victoria ward)

📖 Philip Mernick and Doreen Kendall, *A Pictorial History of Victoria Park*, East London History Society, 1996

Waddon • *Croydon*

The western side of CROYDON, noted for its business and retail parks. The name was first recorded in the twelfth century and derives from Old English words meaning 'woad hill'. Traces of Bronze Age and Iron Age habitation have been found here, including caves. The Waddon Court estate covered most of the area from the Middle Ages, when mills operated along the River Wandle. The river was later used to irrigate watercress beds and to feed the extensive lakes of Waddon Court. Industrialization began in 1867 with the construction of Croydon gasworks on Waddon Marsh. Free-thinking Christians established Brotherhood House on Stafford Road in 1896, and it later became a socialist home called Morris House. Adjacent aerodromes were opened at BEDDINGTON and Waddon during World War I and in 1920 these were amalgamated to form Croydon Airport. Its classically inspired terminal and the Aerodrome Hotel opened on Purley Way in 1928, in time for aviator Amy Johnson's pioneering solo flight from Croydon to Darwin, Australia, in 1930. The creation of Purley Way (A23) to bypass Croydon brought dozens more factories to the area, while Croydon corporation built the Mitcham Road and Waddon housing estates. The corporation acquired 150 acres of land opposite the airport for use as sports fields. Industry also covered the former watercress beds of Waddon Marsh and the remainder of the Waddon Court estate was sold for housing, together with the grounds of neighbouring Waddon Lodge. Here too, the corporation stepped in and preserved surviving parts of Waddon Ponds for public use. During World War II, Croydon Airport was converted to military use and it closed permanently in 1959. The Imperial Way industrial estate filled much of the eastern side of the site, while Sutton council built the ROUNDSHAW estate on its part. Airport House now has serviced offices, a restaurant and an infrequently open museum. There are plans to create a supercasino here. Industry began to withdraw from Waddon in the 1970s and the sites of former factories have since been filled by warehouses and superstores, especially along Purley Way, where hotels and leisure venues have also flourished. The largest of the developments is Valley Park, where an Ikea store opened in 1997. The residential part of Waddon has a typical demographic profile for the borough, except that it is a little less affluent and has slightly more inhabitants who are single and live in council housing.

✉	Croydon CR0
👥	13,393
🚌	Southern (zone 5)
🚌	Croydon Tramlink, Route 1 (Waddon Marsh)

Walford • *Walford*

A stereotypical east London district, situated in the fictional borough of the same name. Little of Walford's history is known prior to 1985. Its name may be connected with the 19th-century London historian Edward Walford or perhaps indicates early settlement of the area by Celts, as is also likely in the cases of WALWORTH and WALLINGTON, (the Old English word 'wala' has the same root as 'Wales'). The ford could have crossed one of the tributaries of the River Lea, but Walford's precise location is difficult to pin down. The architecture of the surprisingly busy Albert Square appears to date from around the 1880s and bears a close resemblance to part of Fassett Square, on the HACKNEY/DALSTON border. However, aerial views have centred on POPLAR, while Walford East Tube station seems to lie to the east of BOW ROAD. Unlike many east London quarters, the population is still primarily white working-class, although various ethnic minorities have a token presence. Living standards seem to be relatively acceptable, although there are characteristics that would normally be indicators of deprivation. All the businesses and shops are privately owned and run. There are no local branches of high street chains, no Tesco Metro, nor even a Budgen's, and no bank or building society. At least there is still a post office.

✉ E20

🚇 District Line; Hammersmith & City Line (Walford East, zones 2 and 3)

📖 Rupert Smith , *'EastEnders': 20 Years in Albert Square*, BBC Books, 2005

@ www.bbc.co.uk/eastenders

Walham Green • *Hammersmith & Fulham*

A largely disused name for the area now called FULHAM BROADWAY and its surroundings, which are simply considered to be central FULHAM. The village was first mentioned in 1383 as Wandongrene, when Fulham itself was a hamlet beside the Thames. The triangular green was surrounded by elm trees and occupied the area now filled by Vanston Place and Jerdan Place. By the mid 17th century it possessed all the essentials of a traditional English village green: a pond, stocks, a whipping post and a pub. Meanwhile, the neighbouring estates were progressively divided and subdivided, creating a network of smallholdings for market gardeners, artisans and tradesmen. This form of development discouraged the creation of extensive rural retreats and instead sowed the seeds of Walham Green's evolution into the future commercial centre of Fulham. During the 18th century, groups of cottages gave way to rows of houses, which were in turn replaced by terraced streets over the course of the 19th century. St John's Church was built on the site of the pond in 1828. Walham Green station opened in 1880 and shops and places of entertainment soon lined the Broadway. Fulham Town Hall was built in 1890, following the earlier gravitation here of petty sessions and manorial courts. By the end of the century the green had been erased and the whole neighbourhood was densely built up with working-class housing, of a respectable character at the centre but less so in the backstreets. Within a couple of decades much of the area had become very run-down and the council began a programme of slum clearance and rebuilding in the early 1930s. The station was renamed Fulham Broadway in 1952 because none of the borough's stations mentioned Fulham and local traders thought the old name sounded too rustic.

✉ SW6

🚶 10,280 (Parsons Green and Walham ward)

🚇 District Line (Fulham Broadway, zone 2)

Wall End • *Newham*

A ward situated between BARKING and EAST HAM, and the locality centred on the Duke's Head public house. The name is also spelt as one word but neither form is widely used. From the Middle Ages, Wall End was an isolated hamlet on the road to Barking. It was the 'end', or outlying part, of East Ham where an embankment prevented the River Roding from flooding. From 1804 to 1827 a pair of cottages in Wall End constituted East Ham's workhouse, afterwards becoming private homes again. In the mid 19th century there were only about 20 houses here but most of the area was built up between 1880 and 1910. The riverside part of Wall End consists of light industry, much of which is not flourishing. Regeneration efforts have included the construction of a pedestrian footbridge across the river. In 2001 a national survey put Wall End in the top 1 per cent of localities for potential growth in house prices, a comparable ranking with the more obvious HOXTON. This was because its property values did not fully reflect the economic and social potential of the district. Most of Wall End's residents are Asian or Asian British, with Indian, Pakistani, Bangladeshi and 'other Asian' origins all well represented. The area is especially popular with young families.

✉ E6

🚶 12,932

Wallington • *Sutton*

An extensive commuter suburb, situated east of SUTTON. The name derives from the same root as 'Wales' and almost certainly denoted an early Celtic settlement. Wallington's status as a hundred – an extensive administrative area – indicates its medieval importance, as did the size of its Norman manor, but the village had become BEDDINGTON's inferior by the late Middle Ages. It was part of Beddington parish but had a chapel that was outside the jurisdiction of the parish priest in the 16th century, with its own graveyard. A paper mill was in existence in 1771, later grinding flour and ultimately making chocolate. The millpond survives as the Grange boating lake. Early in the 19th century the hamlet consisted of just a few cottages and an inn, grouped around the village green, together with a handful of outlying houses. The construction of the Croydon to Epsom railway in 1847 triggered lasting changes. The owner of the Carshalton Park estate forbade the building of a station on his land, so CARSHALTON station (now Wallington) was sited here, to the south of the village. Nathaniel Bridges, lord of Wallington manor, began to lay out an estate of Gothic villas to the east of Manor Road in the early 1860s. Bridges sponsored the construction of Holy Trinity Church and Wallington became a separate parish from Beddington in 1867. Development was not rapid but by the 1910s the growing town was expanding across the former lavender fields and a new centre had taken shape along Woodcote Road to the south of the station. Wallington was the larger partner in its 1915 pairing with Beddington as an urban district, and it subsequently absorbed BANDON HILL and SOUTH BEDDINGTON. Between the world wars many of the largest early-Victorian properties were replaced by smaller properties and a town hall (now a Crown Court) and library were built on Woodcote Road. Other houses on the Bridges estate were replaced by flats after World War II. Since the construction of Wallington Square in the early 1960s the area around the station has become the borough's second commercial centre after Sutton itself, with several office blocks. Eighty-five per cent of Wallington's residents are of white British origin and over 70 per cent of homes are owner-occupied.

The writer and artist Mervyn Peake lived at 55 Woodcote Road as a young man in the 1920s and again in the 1950s, after his father died and left him the house. The rock guitarist Jeff Beck was born in Wallington in 1944. The Beatles, The Who and the Rolling Stones were among artists who performed at Wallington Public Hall in the early 1960s. Wallington resident Craig Shergold achieved the world record in get-well cards, with over a hundred million. Despite a successful brain tumour operation in 1991, Internet appeals for cards continued to circulate for many years afterwards, to the increasing desperation of Craig's family.

> ✉ Wallington SM6

> ⚥ 19,576 (Wallington North and South wards)

> 🚉 Southern (zone 5)

> 📖 John Phillips et al, *Carshalton, Wallington and Beddington*, Tempus, 1995

Walthamstow • *Waltham Forest* (pronounced 'wallthəmsto')

The commercial and administrative centre of the borough, situated to the east of the River Lea between LEYTON and CHINGFORD. Its name is a corruption of three words: 'weald' (forest), 'ham' (a plot of land) and 'stow' (a

place). The superfluous final syllable was added later to distinguish it from Waltham Cross. Walthamstow began to develop relatively early for a village this far from the CITY OF LONDON. In the 18th century it was a collection of hamlets providing a popular country retreat for the wealthy, but enclosure in 1850 started the spread of terraced housing northwards across the parish and the bankers and merchants soon retreated still further. Gas was laid on in 1854 and the railway arrived in 1872. Most of the district was built up by the end of the 19th century, although new estates continued to be squeezed into the remaining gaps until the 1930s. Walthamstow greyhound stadium opened in 1931. The stadium is located north of the Crooked Billet roundabout, in Chingford, and is by far London's most successful venue of its kind, although its future is uncertain. On the western side, factories appeared beside the Lea; Andrex toilet paper was named after St Andrew's Mill, where it was first made in 1936. The borough council acquired the former Lammas lands of WALTHAMSTOW MARSHES for public use. They are now part of the Lee Valley Regional Park and have been designated a site of special scientific interest. In 1968 the Victoria Line arrived at HOE STREET station, which was renamed Walthamstow Central. A shiny new bus station opened in 2004, putting the scruffy railway building to shame. Modern Walthamstow has a comprehensive shopping centre around Hoe Street and the Selborne Walk mall, opened in 1988. From Monday to Saturday, the High Street hosts what has been touted as 'Europe's longest street market'.

The pop band East 17, teen idols of the early 1990s, called their first album *Walthamstow*.

> ✉ E17

> ⚥ 67,001 (Chapel End, High Street, Hoe Street, Markhouse, William Morris and Wood Street wards)

> 🚉 'one' Railway (zone 3); Victoria Line terminus (Walthamstow Central, zone 3)

> 📖 David Mander, *Walthamstow Past*, Historical Publications, 2001

> @ www.walthamstowmemories.net, www.wsgreyhound.co.uk (Walthamstow Stadium)

Walthamstow Marshes • *Waltham Forest*

An area of semi-natural wetland lying in the south-western corner of WALTHAMSTOW, across the River Lea from UPPER CLAPTON. In the Middle Ages the marshland covered a larger area than it does today and was more perilous to cross. Walthamstow Marshes came under the jurisdiction of the Havering and Dagenham commissioners of sewers in the 16th century, which very slowly improved their drainage. Like many of London's surviving open spaces, these were Lammas lands, where local people had the right to graze their livestock at certain times of the year. From the mid 19th century railway and water companies bought out some of these rights, notably for the waterworks at COPPERMILLS. The Lammas rights were not fully extinguished until Walthamstow council acquired the land in 1930. A series of reservoirs filled the northern part of the marshes, while the council undertook to preserve 100 acres in the south as public open space. Flood relief measures were approved in 1938 but these were not fully implemented until 1960. The Lee Valley Regional Park Authority acquired the marshes in 1971 and is now responsible for their care and preservation. Much of the surviving marshland is designated a nature reserve and a site of special scientific interest. Rare breeds of cattle have been reintroduced here in recent years. A pressure group called the New Lammas Lands Defence Committee strives to resist incursions into Hackney, Walthamstow and Leyton marshes, which are proposed surprisingly frequently, and inappropriate developments on their edges.

Alliott Verdon Roe assembled his Avro No. 1 triplane under a railway arch on Walthamstow Marshes and made the first all-British powered flight from here in 1909. Centenary events are planned to celebrate his achievement. Film director Joe Wright, whose recent credits include *Pride and Prejudice* (2005), made his first short film, *Whatever Happened to Walthamstow Marshes*, in 1991.

✉ E17

📖 G A Blakeley, *Walthamstow Marshes and Lammas Rights*, Walthamstow Antiquarian Society, 1951

Walthamstow Queens Road • *Waltham Forest*

A station and street in central WALTHAMSTOW, named after Queen Victoria. Walthamstow Burial Board opened its non-denominational cemetery in 1872 and Queens Road was created to provide a route to Hoe Street. Another link ran westward from the cemetery but only later was this stretch also named Queens

Road. In 1894 the Midland Railway Co. built the Tottenham and Forest Gate Railway, assisted by a small contribution from the London, Tilbury and Southend Railway Co., and Queens Road station opened with the line. Despite its name, the station is not on Queens Road but at the northern end of Edinburgh Road. The arrival of the railway accelerated the rate of housebuilding in the area, and this part of Walthamstow soon lost its remaining fields. At the south-western end of Queens Road the Kelmscott Leisure Centre has indoor facilities for fitness training, martial arts, badminton and squash and an outdoor sports arena.

✉ E17

🚇 Silverlink Metro (zone 3)

Walthamstow Village • *Waltham Forest*

A delightful conservation area and recent 'best London village', situated in UPPER WALTHAMSTOW, and also known as Church End. There was a clearing in the forest here at the time of Domesday Book and the first church was built in 1145. The present St Mary's seems to have evolved somewhat haphazardly from that structure. The timber-framed Ancient House (formerly the White House) dates from the 15th century, with a west wing rebuilt in the 16th. Sir George Monoux founded almshouses on Vinegar Alley in 1527, together with a school that later relocated to CHAPEL END. A Nag's Head pub stood in the village by 1675. The Vestry House, which began life in 1730 as the parish workhouse, is now a local history museum and borough archive. Squire's almshouses were built in 1795, while Orford House and The Chestnuts date from the early 19th century. Most of the village was built up in the 20 years following the enclosure of Church Common in 1850, including a new Nag's Head on Orford Road in 1859. The village was saved from subsequent disfigurement by the opening of the station at HOE STREET, which drew commercial development away to the west. The Ancient House was lovingly restored in 1934. The council made a number of environmental improvements to Walthamstow Village in 1980 and the Ancient House was repaired again in 2002.

✉ E17

📖 *Walthamstow Village*, Walthamstow Historic Local Books, 1996

@ www.walthamstowvillage.net (residents' association site)

Walworth • *Southwark*

A crowded and socially disadvantaged district situated east of NEWINGTON. Formerly noted for its robust working-class community, Walworth (like Newington) is losing its identity as newcomers regard it simply as part of 'the ELEPHANT AND CASTLE area'. The remains of a mammoth have been found under the streets of Walworth and there is evidence of human occupation since the Stone Age, 4,500 years ago. Walworth – 'the enclosed settlement of the Britons' – grew up between Kennington Park Road (A3) and the OLD KENT ROAD (A2), which developed along the lines of two of the ancient roads fanning out from LONDON BRIDGE to the south coast. Canterbury Cathedral was a large landowner from the late Saxon era onwards. Walworth was long a rural area producing fruit and vegetables in abundance; one local nurseryman had a list of 320 varieties of gooseberries. In the mid 17th century there were only a few houses along what is today Walworth Road (A215) but growing numbers of tradesmen set up shop here as traffic from London increased. Walworth Common was one of London's most popular cricket grounds in the early 18th century. One of the grandest surviving examples of Walworth's early development is Surrey Square, built in the 1790s by the architect Michael Searles. St Peter's Church in Liverpool Grove was built to a design by Sir John Soane in 1825 to serve the rapidly growing community; over the course of the 19th century, Walworth's population increased eightfold, reaching 122,200 in 1901. Great areas of Walworth were rebuilt after World War II, notably in the form of the massive Heygate and Aylesbury estates, which were planned in the 1960s and completed in the 1970s. The Labour Party's headquarters were in Walworth from 1981 to 1997, when it moved to MILLBANK. Its Walworth Road building was renamed John Smith House, after the party's former leader. Tony Blair visited the Aylesbury estate soon after Labour's 1997 election victory but a vote by residents brought a halt to its regeneration; now fears over its safety have hastened redevelopment plans. The Heygate estate will be replaced as part of the Elephant and Castle redevelopment scheme. The Cuming Museum, located in the Town Hall building at 151 Walworth Road, was founded on the personal collection of Richard Cuming and his son Henry, and has been supplemented by relics unearthed during excavations in the Southwark area. On permanent display is the Lovat collection of London superstitions, mostly charms and cures for rheumatism. East Street has a very traditional London street market. The largest ethnic groups in the area are of white British and black African origin.

The mathematician and astronomer Charles Babbage – inventor of a forerunner of the computer – was born in Crosby Row (now Larcom Street) in 1791. Charlie Chaplin was born in East Street in 1889, the son of music hall entertainers. *Pride of Walworth* (1995) is one of a series of south London romances by Mary Jane Staples.

> ✉ SE17

> 👥 24,697 (East Walworth and Faraday wards)

> 📖 Mary Boast, *The Story of Walworth*, London Borough of Southwark, 1993

> @ www.visitsouthwark.com/the-cuming-museum

Wandsworth • *Wandsworth*

A prominent riverside commercial centre, flanked by PUTNEY to its west and BATTERSEA and CLAPHAM to the east. There is evidence that a Saxon named Wendel had established a fishing settlement here by 693. All Saints' Church was in existence by 1234. Farming and market gardening constituted the principal inland occupations until the late Middle Ages. By the 16th century the first breweries were operating in Wandsworth and the landlord of the Ram inn was brewing his own beer by 1581. Like many villages close to London, Wandsworth attracted wealthy City gentlemen seeking a spot to build a country villa. The king's embroiderer, William Brodrick, had a house near the present Putney Bridge Road by 1605. At Sword House (now the site of Wandsworth police station) Sir Everard Fawkener played host to Voltaire during his two years' exile from France in the late 1720s. The arrival of Huguenot refugees enhanced the town's commercial vigour and cloth weaving, dyeing, bleaching and printing all flourished beside the River Wandle. Dutch metal workers established an iron smelting works, specializing in cookware. Transport improvements in the 19th century made Wandsworth a viable place of residence for City workers and during Victoria's reign the district filled with housing, together with new public buildings and parks. During the mid 19th century the Young family took control of the Ram brewery, where brewing continued until 2006. Satellite localities evolved at EARLSFIELD from the 1880s and at SOUTHFIELDS in the early years of the 20th century.

Interwar slum clearance brought municipal housing projects. Bomb damage in the early 1940s was the spur to an extensive programme of post-war redevelopment, including more council estates, while many residents chose to move south to outer suburbs like CROYDON or the new town of Crawley. Wandsworth gasworks closed in 1971 and development began along the riverside. In the same year the famously dowdy Arndale shopping centre was built on the site of amenities that had included a greyhound stadium and swimming baths. It has since been rebuilt as Southside, with 110 retail units, a fitness centre and a 14-screen multiplex cinema, while surrounding tower blocks are being radically remodelled. Apartment complexes are replacing disused industrial premises in the town centre and by the Thames, notably at the Riverside Quarter on the Wandle delta. The Courthouse, on Garratt Lane, is home to the Wandsworth museum.

Half the characters in the 2003 blockbuster movie *Love Actually* seem to come from Wandsworth, including Martine McCutcheon's Natalie, who lives at the 'dodgy end' of the district. The film's climax is set at a nativity play in Wandsworth – actually shot at Putney's Elliott School.

✉ SW18

🚶 52,555 (Earlsfield, Fairfield, Southfield and Wandsworth Common wards)

🚋 South West Trains (Wandsworth Town, zone 2)

📖 Dorian Gerhold, *Wandsworth Past*, Historical Publications, 1998

@ www.wandsworthtown.com (community site); www.southsidewandsworth.com

Wandsworth Common • *Wandsworth*

A wide strip of open land stretching from east Wandsworth to the edges of TOOTING and BALHAM. There has been a common here since the time of Domesday Book, and its two halves became known as BATTERSEA West Heath and WANDSWORTH East Heath. By the mid 18th century the whole was known as Wandsworth Common and it occupied roughly twice its present area. More than 50 piecemeal enclosures nibbled away at the common from 1794, including for railway building from the mid 1830s. One of the largest chunks was taken for the Royal Victoria Patriotic Asylum in the late 1850s. Also in that decade, the Reverend John Craig set up the largest (but

not best) telescope in the world and its site is remembered in an area called the Scope, now a nature reserve. Following a campaign to preserve the open space, Earl Spencer, the lord of the manor, agreed to transfer the common to public ownership, except for the area that was subsequently developed as SPENCER PARK. The elected group of conservators failed to prevent the common's deterioration into a large mud patch and the Metropolitan Board of Works took over in 1887. The so-called 'toast-rack' of streets between Baskerville Road and Trinity Road was laid out from the 1880s. The largest remaining assemblage of stonework from the medieval London Bridge survives in the ground floor façade of 49 Heathfield Road and in the garden walls in front of numbers 49 to 73 – except for one property where the wall has been tastelessly replaced. These structures were built using rubble from Stone House, a residence demolished around 1909. The London County Council extended Wandsworth Common by 20 acres in 1912 and it now covers 175 acres. The Royal Victoria Patriotic Asylum became an orphanage and in World War II a detention centre, holding the Nazi defector Rudolph Hess, among others. It is now a sought-after apartment complex. Built in its former grounds in 1955, and retaining pre-existing trees and views, the Fitzhugh estate consists of five eleven-storey council blocks. The Wandsworth Common ward has relatively little ethnic variety; the largest minority is of black Caribbean descent, and accounts for only 3.4 per cent of the population.

✉ SW11; SW12; SW18

🚶 13,555

🚋 Southern (zone 3)

📖 Lt.-Col. J J Sexby, *Sexby's History of Wandsworth Common*, ed. John W Brown, Local History Reprints, 1996

Wandsworth Road • *Lambeth*

A motley commercial and residential thoroughfare running from VAUXHALL towards CLAPHAM JUNCTION. A section of an ancient route out of London, Wandsworth Road marked the northern edge of the parish of CLAPHAM. This was farmland with some market gardens until the late 18th century and the first structure of note was the Nag's Head public house, at the junction with North Street. The Plough brewery was built nearby in 1820, while some handsome villas began to line the north-eastern part of the road; very few of these have survived. At this time the

Whidbourne family acquired the Union Grove area and developed a high-class estate. On Wandsworth Road, shops and artisans' terraced houses and cottages advanced progressively south-westward. From the late 1850s to the early 1870s the area underwent a spate of development that included almshouses, commercial parades, Christ Church on Union Grove, Wandsworth Road station on the London, Chatham and Dover Railway line and the rebuilding of the Plough. Most of Union Grove's villas were replaced by the Larkhall estate in 1930, which was built with a cursory nod in the direction of 'garden city' principles. This was a private development that quickly ran into financial difficulties and had to be completed by the London County Council. The LCC purchased more of the Whidbourne land in 1935 and added the Springfield estate. The presence of an ammunition works on Stewart's Road made the area a target of bombing in World War II and the resulting damage led to extensive post-war redevelopment. The process was not completed until the end of the 20th century and included three petrol stations and the Greater London Council's Carey Gardens and Westbury estates.

The musicologist Sir George Grove, who compiled the compendious *Dictionary of Music and Musicians* that now bears his name, was born in 1820 in Thurlow Terrace, which was demolished during the building of Wandsworth Road station.

✉ SW8

🚆 Southern (zone 2)

📖 Alyson Wilson (ed.), *The Buildings of Clapham*, Clapham Society, 2000

Wanstead · *Redbridge*

An increasingly popular suburban village, situated at the apex of the A11 and A12, north-east of LEYTONSTONE. In prehistoric times this was a coastal area and archaeological investigation has revealed evidence of Palaeolithic as well as (much later) Roman habitation. The name of Wanstead, which may mean 'white house' or 'house on the wen-shaped hill' or 'place where wagons are kept', was first recorded in 824 and there was a woodland hamlet here by 1100. Early settlement was confined to the vicinity of the manor house at what became WANSTEAD PARK, with its nearby Church of St Mary. Neighbouring farms progressively turned to market gardening as access to London improved. The village began to attract wealthy

residents from the mid 18th century, considerably later than places such as WOODFORD. When the church was rebuilt in its present form in 1790 there were just 120 houses here, four-fifths of which were gentry-owned. High-class suburban development began to the north around 1860, after the opening of a station at SNARESBROOK. More affordable estates were laid out in the south of the parish at CANN HALL and ALDERSBROOK around the turn of the century but in Wanstead itself builders continued to erect substantial houses until the outbreak of World War I. Smaller properties appeared after the war as developers sought to make the most of the few remaining plots. The construction of the Eastern Avenue (A12) in the mid 1920s and the sale of Nightingale Farm in the late 1930s brought housing to the east and far north respectively. After World War II and the opening of Wanstead station in 1947, construction was limited to the replacement of several hundred bomb-damaged houses, followed by later in-filling and the construction of small blocks of flats in place of some of the largest old houses. The High Street was redeveloped from the early 1970s, when many of its older buildings were demolished. Despite the plain appearance of the newer premises, the street retains a villagey air, aided by the presence of a large green on the west side. The rerouting of the A12 to provide a better link to the M11 necessitated some demolition and tree-felling in the mid 1990s, in the face of active resistance by conservationists. A 'best London village' award in 2002 reflected the wealth of green space on Wanstead's doorstep, its well-preserved Victorian residences and – at the time – its value for money, although this has since become less evident. Most residents are white, middle-aged homeowners, but younger professionals are choosing to move here if they can afford it.

Former residents include the dramatist R B Sheridan, the politician George Canning and the poet Thomas Hood – who all lived at a variety of addresses in the London area – and William Penn, the founder of Pennsylvania.

✉ E11

👥 11,506

🚆 Central Line (zone 4)

📖 Ian Dowling and Nick Harris, *Wanstead and Woodford*, Tempus, 1995

Wanstead Flats · *Redbridge*

Not a housing estate but one of the largest expanses of common land in east London, although it does not compare with HAMPSTEAD HEATH or WIMBLEDON COMMON because it is so featureless. The flats constitute the southernmost part of Epping Forest but most of the trees were cleared several centuries ago. The area was formerly known as the Lower Forest or Wanstead Heath and commoners had 'rights of turbary' here, which meant that they could dig peat for fuel. In the late 18th century an annual market for cattle from Wales, Scotland, and the north of England took place from the end of February to the beginning of May. Commoners consistently resisted attempted encroachments by neighbouring landowners and fought legal battles with Lord Mornington, Earl Cowley and others from the 1850s until the flats were preserved under the Epping Forest Act of 1878. From later in the century until the outbreak of World War I, an Easter pleasure fair was held here. The terrain is now mainly acidic grassland with some playing fields, and is popular with horse riders.

✉ E7; E11; E12

Wanstead Park • *Redbridge*

A public park and a name used by estate agents for the neighbouring residential locality, situated to the south-east of WANSTEAD Tube station. Wanstead manor house stood on the north side of the present-day golf course, near the parish church of St Mary. The house was originally a small building called Wanstead Hall but was enlarged in 1499 so that it could serve as a royal hunting lodge. The park was formed by enclosing part of Epping Forest in the mid 16th century. Wanstead House (as it became known) was rebuilt in 1722 on a magnificent scale but was demolished in 1834 after its contents had been sold to pay off the debts of the spendthrift William Pole-Wellesley, nephew of the Duke of Wellington. The Corporation of London acquired the grounds in 1880 and opened them to the public two years later. Wanstead golf course was laid out on and around the site of the mansion in 1893. The park's landscaped grounds were allowed to grow wild but some more formal elements have recently been reintroduced. The many ponds and islands, fed by the River Roding, are a haven for birds. Wanstead Park and a select few houses on its doorstep are designated a conservation area.

In 1717 the Astronomer Royal James Bradley and his uncle James Pound set up one of the world's largest telescopes in Wanstead Park, mounted on a maypole brought from the Strand.

✉ E11

🚇 Central Line (Wanstead or Redbridge, zone 3)

📖 O S Dawson, *The Story of Wanstead Park*, Thomas Hood Memorial Press, 1995 (reprint of 1894 publication); William Addison, *Wanstead Park*, Corporation of London, 1973

Wapping • *Tower Hamlets*

A recolonized waterfront neighbourhood conveniently located between the CITY OF LONDON and DOCKLANDS. Wapping is an Old English place name meaning 'the settlement of Wæppa's people'. The modern heart of Wapping lies on the strip of alluvial plain once known as Wapping Marsh, but the original settlement stood on a higher gravel terrace, around what became the Highway. Construction of a wharf in 1395 sowed the seeds of a 15th-century riverside hamlet called Wapping-on-the-Woze (mud). Full-scale waterfront development with storehouses and tenements followed the draining of Wapping Marsh around 1540 and the newer village outgrew its predecessor, ultimately appropriating its name. Convicted mutineers and pirates were brought from Marshalsea Prison in SOUTHWARK to Wapping's Execution Dock, where they were hanged. Their bodies were then left in cages while three tides washed over them. Captain William Kidd was dispatched in this fashion in 1701 and a modern riverside pub is named after him. London Dock was constructed at Wapping in 1805 and specialized in rice, tobacco, wine and brandy. The neighbourhood inevitably became overcrowded and was allowed to deteriorate until the London County Council implemented a comprehensive slum clearance scheme in 1926. The docks closed in the late 1960s, and were mostly filled in, although some stretches of decorative waterway have been retained. When Rupert Murdoch's News International established its printing works here in 1986, the 'Wapping dispute' grabbed the headlines as sacked workers and their supporters picketed the plant for a year. Housebuilders squeezed the maximum possible number of flats, town houses and warehouse conversions into Wapping's winding streets during the last two decades of the 20th century, targeting most of these at young professionals, although some units were initially reserved for local people. Many properties have been bought to let rather than for owner occupation, sometimes resulting in reduced standards of upkeep. Wapping Lane and Wapping High Street now have fashionable restaurants and bars (and estate agents) that reflect the area's changed character. The long and narrow Town of Ramsgate public house stands beside the slippery Wapping Old Stairs, which lead down to the river. The former Wapping hydraulic power station has been converted into a visual arts, music and dance venue. Away from the riverside, Wapping is also home to a significant proportion of the East End's Bangladeshi community.

The maritime explorer Captain James Cook lodged near Wapping Lane in the 1750s. Cook was the mate of a Whitby merchantman that was lying off Wapping when he joined the Royal Navy as a seaman on the *Eagle*. He returned to Wapping in 1762 to marry a local girl.

✉ E1

♦ 11,245 (St Katherine's and Wapping ward)

🚇 East London Line (zone 2)

📖 Madge Darby, *Waeppa's People: History of Wapping*, Conner & Butler, 1988

Warren Street • *Camden*

A 400-yard Georgian street running westwards off the northern end of TOTTENHAM COURT ROAD. In the latter part of the 18th century this was an access road for the newly built properties on what is now Euston Road. Warren Street was laid out with three-storey terraced houses in 1799 by Charles Fitzroy, first Baron Southampton. Variations in architectural detail have led to suggestions that several speculative builders may have been involved in the project. Fitzroy named the street after his wife, Anne Warren. Anne was the daughter of Admiral Sir Peter Warren, who founded New York's Greenwich Village and gave his name to more than one Warren Street in America. The new street soon became a popular place of residence for artists, especially engravers. During the 19th century Warren Street was in the news when the radical MP Sir Charles Dilke was accused of conducting an adulterous affair here, and when a gunman murdered a resident and a pursuing policeman. The Northern Line station opened in 1907, originally as Euston Road, but this was changed to Warren Street within a year. The station's 1930s stone façade is by Charles Holden. The street deteriorated in the second half of the 20th century, when used-car dealers operated premises at street level while leaving the upper floors empty. Other properties were neglected by absentee landlords. In 1967, Warren Street became the Victoria Line's southern terminus for the first three months of the line's existence. The street now possesses a diverse mixture of retailers and providers of professional services. Among the specialist shops are a couple of noteworthy booksellers.

The mosaic featured on the walls of the Victoria Line platforms is a visual pun on the station's name. The artist created a maze that would be difficult to unravel in less than the typical three minutes' interval between trains.

✉ W1

🚇 Northern Line; Victoria Line (zone 1)

Warwick Avenue • *Westminster*

A broad, stuccoed street in southern MAIDA VALE, running north-westwards from the HARROW ROAD at LITTLE VENICE to Sutherland Avenue. This was originally a track called Green Lane and was named Warwick Road (later changed to Avenue) on the street plan produced in 1827 by George Gutch, surveyor to the Bishop of London. Gutch named the road after Jane Warwick, of Warwick Hall near Carlisle, who had married into a landowning family here in 1778. The first houses, some of which were very large, were erected in the 1840s by the Warwick Avenue bridge over the Paddington arm of the Grand Junction (now Grand Union) Canal. The neighbourhood was largely built up within two decades and most of the properties survive today. St Saviour's Church on Warwick Avenue was consecrated in 1856 and its section of the road was widened to create a grand approach, making this perhaps the broadest avenue in London. The church, however, was never wealthy, partly because the area acquired such a large Jewish community. With all this development, nearby Welford's dairy, dairymen to Queen Victoria, had to send its cattle to fields in WILLESDEN and HARLESDEN and the dairy building relocated to new premises at the corner of Shirland Road and Elgin Avenue in 1882. One of London's few surviving cabmen's shelters was built on the avenue around this time. Warwick Avenue station opened in 1915 as an intermediate stop on the Bakerloo Line's new extension from PADDINGTON to QUEEN'S PARK. The station was originally to have been called Warrington Crescent and it is perhaps surprising that it has not since been renamed Little Venice. St Saviour's Church was rebuilt in 1976 in a project that incorporated the new flats of Manor House Court. There are shops on Formosa Street, which crosses the northern part of the avenue.

David Ben-Gurion, the first prime minister of Israel, lived at 75 Warrington Crescent in

1920. Early punk musician Matt Dangerfield converted his basement flat on Warrington Crescent into a recording studio in the mid 1970s. The Damned, The Clash, Generation X and the Sex Pistols are said to have made their first recordings here.

✉ W9; W2

🚇 Bakerloo Line (zone 2)

Waterloo • *Lambeth*
A railway terminus and its immediate environs, situated in the far north of LAMBETH, close to the SOUTH BANK arts complex. Residential settlement and the provision of amenities increased on Lambeth Marsh following the opening in 1817 of the first Waterloo Bridge, which was named in honour of the British victory at the Battle of Waterloo two years earlier. The Royal Coburg Theatre opened in 1818, becoming the Royal Victoria in 1833. St John's Church, on Waterloo Road, was the first of a series known as the 'Waterloo churches', after this one, that were built with the aid of a parliamentary grant. The London and South Western Railway Co. opened Waterloo station in 1848. Six years later the London Necropolis Co. added a separate station to carry coffins and mourners on a dedicated line to Brookwood Cemetery. Waterloo Junction (now Waterloo East) station opened on the South Eastern Railway in 1869. Goods yards and other railway facilities replaced several streets, while many of the surviving properties were converted to cheap lodging houses for railway workers. The main station was ill-equipped to deal with the growth in passenger numbers over the course of the 19th century and was entirely rebuilt over an extended period from 1900. Opened by Queen Mary in 1922, Waterloo is now Britain's largest and busiest railway station, handling 75,000 arriving passengers in the morning peak hours alone. Waterloo International station is at present the London terminus for the Channel Tunnel rail services and has one of the most complex and impressive steel and glass roofs ever built. As a result of subsidence, Waterloo Bridge was controversially demolished in 1936. The present bridge opened in 1942, after construction work had continued throughout the Blitz. Many of the streets behind Waterloo station were torn down in the 1960s and replaced with council flats. Lower Marsh gives the best indication of the area's former character, and retains a busy street market. After serving as a music hall, temperance hall and opera house in the 19th century, in the inter-

war years the Old Vic Theatre, as the Royal Victoria was now known, became under Lilian Baylis's management the home of opera, dance and theatre companies that were the nascent national companies of the postwar period. The Old Vic is now a leading repertory theatre that has flourished recently under the artistic directorship of the American actor Kevin Spacey. Adjacent to the South Bank complex, the BFI London IMAX Cinema has a screen ten storeys high, housed inside a spectacular £20 million glass structure.

The Kinks' *Waterloo Sunset* (1967) is widely regarded as the most evocative of London's popular anthems. In 1999 lead singer Ray Davies made the well-received feature film *Return to Waterloo*, in association with Channel 4.

✉ SE1

🚇 Main-line: South West Trains (Southampton, Portsmouth, south-west England) Waterloo East: Southern; South Eastern Trains (southern counties and suburban services, zone 1) London Underground: Bakerloo Line; Jubilee Line; Northern Line; Waterloo & City Line (zone 1)

🚤 Waterloo Millennium pier

@ www.lower-marsh.co.uk (commercial local information site); www.oldvictheatre.com

Watling • *Barnet*
The London County Council's largest 'outcounty' estate north of the Thames after BECONTREE and situated on the north side of BURNT OAK, which itself lies in southern EDGWARE. In 1321 John the Goldbeater is recorded as owning a farm here, which survived for a further five centuries and belonged at one time to James Marshall, co-founder of Oxford Street's Marshall and Snelgrove department store. When Burnt Oak station opened in 1924 the LCC bought a well-wooded 500-acre site by Silk Stream and began to lay out a 'cottage estate' on garden city principles, with wide main roads and retaining mature trees wherever possible. The project was named after Watling Street, the Roman road from London to St Albans which ran close by. The farm buildings were demolished in 1927 and the first homes were ready for occupation in the same year. By the spring of 1930 more than 4,000 houses and a few flats had been completed in a variety of architectural styles, some influenced by HAMPSTEAD GARDEN SUBURB. Only half the properties were built of bricks and mortar; the remainder mostly used

rough-cast concrete or tarred weatherboarding, partly because of a shortage of skilled bricklayers; 250 houses were assembled from steel panels made on rejigged production lines at aircraft factories. St Alphage's Church was built in 1927 on Montrose Avenue. Its pulpit came from the recently demolished St Mark's Church, which had stood in the LEMAN STREET area of WHITECHAPEL. Only one school had opened by 1928 but the vicinity had seven more within a decade. Many of the early residents came from Islington and St Pancras and for a while a quasi-cockney community spirit prevailed. The shops and market on Watling Avenue had the flavour of CHAPEL MARKET and the campaigning *Watling Resident* newspaper sold 3,000 copies at its peak in August 1929. Middle-class neighbours did not like what they saw and nicknamed Watling 'Little Moscow', although communist candidates gained only 80 votes in local elections. By the mid 1930s, assimilation and a broader variety of incomers combined to dilute Watling's early character. The estate has been designated a conservation area, but too late to prevent widespread pebble-dashing. Watling market operates on Saturdays at the rear of Burnt Oak station, which was formerly called Burnt Oak (Watling).

✉ Edgware HA8

🚇 Northern Line (Burnt Oak, zone 4)

Wealdstone • *Harrow*

A north-eastern extension of HARROW, taking its name from a stone, first recorded in the 16th century, marking the division between Harrow and Harrow Weald. The station, on the London–Birmingham railway, opened in 1837 and was originally called Harrow but its name was changed to Harrow and Wealdstone in 1897. The area around the station was among the first in outer London to undergo railway-stimulated suburban development. Terraced housing spread in all directions, with many new streets named after contemporary politicians. Several major factories were established in the late 19th century, most notably that of Kodak Ltd, which had its own artesian wells. Kodak is still the borough's largest private employer. In October 1952, Wealdstone station was the scene of Britain's second-worst rail disaster, when a collision between three trains resulted in 112 deaths. The Grade II-listed station building, which dates from the early part of the 20th century, was fully refurbished in 2003, gaining a heritage award for improving accessibility while preserving his-

toric features. Like many parts of the borough, Wealdstone is now popular with members of the Asian community, especially those of Indian origin. The council has recently targeted the area for regeneration efforts.

In 2002, Wealdstone became the butt of a long-running series of jibes by broadcaster Terry Wogan on his BBC Radio 2 breakfast show, prompted by a light-hearted dispute with a colleague. In an interview with the *Harrow Observer*, Wogan asked, 'Why should he claim to live in Harrow when we know he lives on the more unmarketable side of the hill, which is Wealdstone?'.

✉ Harrow HA3

👥 8,963

🚌 Silverlink Metro (zone 5); Bakerloo Line terminus (Harrow and Wealdstone, zone 5)

📖 Ron Brown, *The Book of Wealdstone*, Barracuda, 1989

Well Hall • *Greenwich*

A wartime housing estate in north ELTHAM, containing the grounds of the former Tudor building of that name. Well Hall was recorded as early as the 13th century and its great house was built for the landowner Sir William Roper and his wife Margaret, daughter of Sir Thomas More, after their marriage in 1521. Sir Gregory Page bought the property in the 1730s and demolished the house but its inner moat and barn have survived, the latter as a pub. In 1905 WOOLWICH council created Well Hall Road (now the A205) from the country track that had been Woolwich Lane, and it became a tram route in 1910. Following the outbreak of World War I, the government acquired 96 acres of farmland on either side of Well Hall Road to build an estate for munitions workers at Woolwich. Construction workers were drafted in from all parts of London to build 1,300 homes on 'garden city' lines and the project was completed by December 1915. Despite the urgency, the Ministry of Works team, led by Francis Baines, achieved high architectural standards, especially in terms of stylistic variation. Many of the three miles of roads curved with the contours of the land and field boundary trees were retained where possible. The streets were named after men with historical associations with Woolwich, mostly in munitions production. In 1925 the government sold the Well Hall estate to the Royal Arsenal Co-operative Society, which renamed it the Progress estate. The house that Sir Gregory Page built to replace Well Hall (which was later given the same name) was pulled down in 1931 and the gardens of Well Hall Pleasaunce were laid out in its place. A swathe of land across the estate had been left empty for the planned construction of Rochester Way (A2), which came through in the early 1930s, leading to the creation of the Well Hall roundabout. At the same time Sir Gilbert Scott's Church of St Barnabas was relocated here from WOOLWICH DOCKYARD. Its church hall is named in honour of the comedian Frankie Howerd, who grew up in Arbroath Road. The estate gained conservation area status in 1975 and the Co-operative Society sold its interest in the estate to the Hyde Housing Association in 1980. The Well Hall Odeon, which later became the Coronet, closed in 1999 and has since lain derelict and vandalized. A development of shops and flats is proposed for the site, with the exterior of the cinema remaining unchanged.

Lovelace Green is named after the poet Richard Lovelace, who was born at Woolwich in 1618. He is best known for the lines 'Stone walls do not a prison make / Nor iron bars a cage', from his poem 'To Althea, From Prison'. The writer Edith Nesbit lived at Well Hall from 1899 to 1922, the politician Herbert Morrison lived with his family in Well Hall Road from 1923 to 1929, and the actress Sylvia Syms grew up in Maudsley Road in the 1930s.

> ✉ SE9
>
> 📖 R G Rigden, *Well Hall*, London Borough of Greenwich, 1960

Welling • *Bexley*

A 'major district centre', second only within the borough to BEXLEYHEATH, which lies to its east. Welling was first mentioned in 1362 as 'Wellyngs' and its name may have indicated the presence of a well or spring, or may derive from Ralph Willing, who held land in Bexley earlier in the century, but it is rarely clear in such cases whether the place name or the personal name came first. Welling evolved as a coaching halt on the route to Dover. Inns like the Nag's Head and Guy, Earl of Warwick were later joined by a ribbon development of premises belonging to craftsmen and tradesmen, behind which lay farms and market gardens. From 1849 the North Kent Railway enabled farmers to deliver perishable produce quickly to the London markets. However, this was too early for the presence of a station to stimulate suburban housebuilding and Welling remained predominantly rural until the 1920s,

with the exception of some high-class housing on the Belle Grove estate. Between the wars a welter of large and small developers descended on Welling and its outlying farms, building low-cost houses for the lower middle classes and skilled working classes, notably at FALCONWOOD. Welling station was rebuilt in enlarged form in 1931. Welling's shopping centre stretches for almost a mile along Bellegrove Road (A207) and includes around 300 outlets. A Russian cannon is on display at Welling Corner, in recollection of the accommodation formerly provided for WOOLWICH ARSENAL workers at EAST WICKHAM, which Welling has now absorbed. Since 1988 the Conference football club Welling United has played at Park View Road (A207) on the edge of DANSON PARK. Welling achieved notoriety in the early 1990s as the home of the British National Party, which was blamed for an increase in racialist violence in this overwhelmingly white area.

> ✉ Welling DA16
>
> ♦ 10,535 (Falconwood and Welling ward)
>
> 🚉 South Eastern Trains (zone 4)
>
> 📖 Peter Tester, *East Wickham and Welling*, Bexley Local Studies and Archive Centre, 1991
>
> @ homepage.ntlworld.com/welling.website (privately operated local information site); www.wellingunited.com

Welsh Harp • *Brent/Barnet*

A 340-acre nature reserve centred on the 125-acre Brent reservoir, situated between KINGSBURY and WEST HENDON. The Harp and Horn inn stood on the Edgware Road near Brent Bridge from the mid 18th century and had been renamed the Welsh Harp by 1803. It came to be known as the Old Welsh Harp after another inn named the Upper Welsh Harp was built further north. In the mid 1830s the confluence of the River Brent and the Silk Stream was dammed to create the Brent (or Kingsbury) reservoir, in order to supply the Paddington branch of what is now the Grand Union Canal. The Welsh Harp reservoir, as it became known, was enlarged in the early 1850s and the Old Welsh Harp gained enormous popularity as a destination for daytrippers. Sporting events of all kinds were held here, especially boxing matches, with ice skating in winter. A music hall song called *The Jolliest Place That's Out* praised the Welsh Harp's attractions. So great was the appeal of the pub and the reservoir that the Midland Railway opened Welsh Harp station in 1870 to cater for excursion traffic. The station closed in 1903 and the reservoir's appeal declined with the urbanization of the surrounding area, especially after the creation of the North Circular Road (A406), which had the benefit of allowing wildlife habitats to form. The Old Welsh Harp was rebuilt in 1937 but was later demolished to make way for the STAPLES CORNER flyover. In the 1948 Olympic Games, rowing competitions were held on the reservoir, which remains much used by rowers, sailors and canoeists. A conservation group and environmental education centre were established in the 1970s. Welsh Harp Village is a recently built estate in east Kingsbury, jutting into West Hendon playing fields. Brent's Welsh Harp ward covers the area to the west of the reservoir and includes north NEASDEN. The ward is ethnically diverse, with no single group constituting a majority.

> ✉ NW9; NW2; NW10

> 👥 12,405

> @ www.brentres.com (Welsh Harp Conservation Group site)

Wembley • *Brent*

A 20th-century commercial and residential creation with a significant Indian community, situated nine miles north-west of central London. It was recorded as Wembalea – 'Wemba's clearing' – in a charter of 825. Although Wembley was called a 'township' in 1212, the medieval settlement seems never to have grown very large. The hamlet was assessed as one of the wealthiest in HARROW in the mid 16th century but this was probably because its chief landowners, particularly the Page family, also owned property elsewhere. Much of Wembley was common land, which the Pages led the way in enclosing from the early 17th century. In 1805 the village had one inn, two mansions, three farmhouses and around 20 other houses. Wembley station opened in 1845 but six years later the population of Wembley and TOKYNGTON was still only 203. Although a few large houses were built in subsequent decades, it was not until the end of the century that a sudden rush of activity erased the old village and created a residential and industrial suburb. The Wembley Hill estate was laid out from 1899 and Wembley Hill (now Wembley Stadium) station opened in 1906, stimulating housebuilding to its south. The Wembley House and Wembley Dairy Farm estates fol-

lowed soon afterwards and by 1920 a continuum of built-up streets linked the district with ALPERTON, to the south. The arrival of the Bakerloo Line was meanwhile attracting factories and housing to NORTH WEMBLEY, while a garden suburb was laid out at Tokyngton. In the mid 1920s, the British Empire Exhibition was held at WEMBLEY PARK, endowing the borough with its most famous asset: Wembley Stadium. The council built estates before and after World War II and, on the largest scale of all, at CHALKHILL in the late 1960s. This was also a time of office construction along several main roads and the building of new shops in central Wembley. The arrival of Asian immigrants from India and east Africa began to transform the district at this time and Ealing Road is now one of London's four leading shopping areas for Asian goods, along with SOUTHALL, TOOTING and Upton Park's GREEN STREET. The Wembley Central ward has London's highest percentage of people born outside the European Union, at 54.5 per cent. White and black minorities each constitute about a fifth of the population and Hinduism is the most common religion. There are relatively few pensioners and people living alone, and a high number of households with dependent children.

A satirical version of the successful, well-educated Indian families who characterize METROLAND Wembley appears in the hit BBC television series *The Kumars at Number 42*.

> ✉ Wembley HA9 and HA0

> 👥 22,838 (Wembley Central and Tokyngton wards)

> 🚆 Chiltern Railways (Wembley Stadium, limited service, zone 4); Silverlink Metro; Bakerloo Line (Wembley Central, zone 4)

> 📖 Geoffrey Hewlett, *Wembley*, Tempus, 2002

Wembley Park • *Brent*

The north-eastern quadrant of WEMBLEY and the home of its newly rebuilt stadium. From the early 19th century, Wembley Park was a country estate with a mansion at its centre and grounds laid out by Humphry Repton. The estate was sold in 1881 and part was acquired by the Metropolitan Railway Co. Wembley Park station opened in 1894, followed two years later by adjacent pleasure gardens. The gardens were the brainchild of the railway company's chairman, Sir Edward Watkin, who aimed to create London's greatest leisure attraction, including a tower that would be taller than the Eiffel Tower. The project was a failure in every respect. The gardens failed to draw sufficient visitors, and the property was taken over by the Wembley Park Estate Co. The tower reached a height of 200 feet when problems of finance and subsidence caused its abandonment. Watkin's Folly, as the tower was dubbed, was pulled down in 1907. The pleasure grounds continued to be used for events of various kinds and were chosen as the site for the British Empire Exhibition, which was held in 1924–5. This was a mammoth affair, which involved the construction of new roads over a wide area, and the widening of existing ones, and the introduction of mains drainage to the district. The improvements enabled the suburban development of the surrounding area at the same time. The greatest of the exhibition buildings was Empire (later Wembley) Stadium, which was completed a year before the show, when it staged the FA Cup final between WEST HAM United and Bolton Wanderers. The spectators vastly exceeded the stadium's 127,000 capacity and, after spilling onto the pitch, were cleared with the aid of a policeman mounted on a white horse. Greyhound racing began at Wembley in 1927, a year after the craze had been initiated at Belle Vue in Manchester. Many of the exhibition buildings were afterwards leased for light industrial use but the stadium was retained as the home of English football. The Empire Pool and Arena was built next to the stadium in 1934. Wembley Town Hall, later used by the London Borough of Brent, was built in 1939 on Forty Lane. By this time the remainder of Wembley Park had been fully developed as a mixed residential and industrial area and most of the wealthy inhabitants had left. The council built the disastrous CHALK-HILL estate south of Forty Lane in the late 1960s, and this has recently been fully redeveloped. In the latter part of the 20th century, parts of the exhibition site were converted to retail use, including warehouses and a Sunday market, and a conference centre opened in 1977. Wembley Stadium closed in 2000 and was rebuilt on a different axis over a protracted period, with a retractable roof and a landmark lattice arch. The stadium forms the centrepiece of a redevelopment project covering most of the old exhibition site. Football matches in the 2012 Olympic Games will be played at Wembley Stadium.

In addition to its sporting role, the old Wembley Stadium hosted many live music events, most famously the Live Aid concert of 1985. Wembley Arena continues to serve as a major concert venue. Among the artists who have released 'live at Wembley' albums are Queen, Hawkwind, Beyoncé, Placido Domingo and Pearl Jam.

✉ Wembley HA9

🚇 Jubilee Line; Metropolitan Line (zone 4)

📖 Glen Isherwood, *Wembley: The Complete Record 1923–2000*, Sports Books, 2006

@ www.wembleystadium.com
www.whatsonwembley.com (Arena and exhibition and conference centre events site)

Wennington • *Havering*

A remote and dispersed village situated two miles south-east of RAINHAM, on the outer edge of east London. First recorded in the tenth century as Winintuna, it was probably the home of a Saxon chief named Wynna. Westminster Abbey held the manor of Wennington from 1066, and possibly from considerably earlier. A manor house was in existence by 1198 and the Church of St Mary and St Peter was built around this time. Much of the fabric of the present church dates from the 14th century. The manor house was called Wennington Hall by 1345 and was probably plundered in the Peasants' Revolt of 1381. The principal manor became known as Wennington Westminster to distinguish it from neighbouring Wennington Enveyse and was briefly seized by the Crown in the 14th century when its tenant landlord was imprisoned as a rebel. The area of the manor varied greatly over the centuries but reached a peak in 1664, when it covered 563 acres, which consisted mostly of marshland that had progressively been reclaimed over several centuries. Noke (or Noak) House was built in the 17th century and in 1808 it became the joint workhouse for Rainham, Aveley and West Thurrock. It served this purpose until 1836 and was later converted into five cottages. Wennington Hall, which had become a farmhouse, was rebuilt in the early 1850s and was later modified and refaced with red brick. Arguably, Wennington's heyday came during the 60 years following 1868 when the training ship *Cornwall* was moored at nearby Purfleet and terraced cottages were built here for some of the staff, with a neighbouring laundry. A few council and private houses were built near the square village green in the 1920s, when the population reached a peak of 432. In 1956, SEVEN KINGS Housing Association built 20 semi-detached houses on the site of Wennington House. Several of the village's older buildings were demolished in the second half of the 20th century, but survivors include three groups of cottages and Wennington Hall Farm, which stands at the junction of Wennington Road and New Road (A1306). The village has around 300 inhabitants, most of whom live in houses scattered along the south side of Wennington Road. To the south lie the barren Wennington Marshes, much of which now form part of the RSPB's RAINHAM MARSHES nature reserve.

✉ Rainham RM13

👤 12,114 (Rainham and Wennington ward)

📖 Frank Lewis, *A History of Rainham, with Wennington and South Hornchurch*, P R Davies, 1966

@ www.wenningtonvillage.org (community site)

West Acton • *Ealing*

Possibly the most desirable part of this sprawling suburb and the last to be built up, West Acton remained rural at a time when SOUTH ACTON was already becoming a slum. John Cary's 1786 map of Middlesex reveals no indication of habitation between Tile Kiln House on Hanger Lane and Fryes Place, east of Horn Lane. Ten years later West Lodge was built on the south side of Uxbridge Road. To its north, an 1805 map shows a set of fields belonging to Sir Harry Featherstonehaugh. In 1876, James Thorne observed that much of ACTON had already succumbed to bricks and mortar but 'on the west are some pretty lanes'. Suburban housebuilding here began on the eastern edge of EALING, when semi-detached houses went up on the West Lodge estate in the first decade of the 20th century. The lodge itself is still standing but has been converted to office use. The 1920s brought the improvements in communications that would transform the area. West Acton station opened on the newly extended Central Line in 1923 and later that decade the Western Avenue (A40) made London easily accessible by road. Noel Road was one of the first new streets to be completed, with semi-detached properties priced at around £800 to appeal to the middle market. In 1924 a subsidiary of the Great Western Railway Co. laid out an estate of appealing little houses and some shops near the main railway line. Reserved for railwaymen, the homes were designed by GWR architect T Alwyn Lloyd, a protégé of Raymond Unwin. West Acton School opened on Noel Road in 1937. By the outbreak of World War II, today's West Acton

had largely taken shape. As well as the usual smattering of young professionals and antipodean flat-sharers, West Acton now has Japanese families who want to be near the excellent Japanese school in Creffield Road.

The television sitcom *Rings on Their Fingers*, starring Diane Keen and Martin Jarvis, which ran for three series from 1978 to 1980, was set in West Acton.

✉ W3

🚇 Central Line (zone 3)

West Barnes • *Merton*

A family-oriented locality situated east of NEW MALDEN. The history and the identity of West Barnes are entangled with that of RAYNES PARK, for the latter was built almost entirely on the site of the former. In the 14th and 15th centuries Merton Priory owned two sets of barns where the produce of its estates was stored. West Barns Farm stretched from Merton Common to the Beverley Brook. The farm was sold after the dissolution of the monasteries and in the early 17th century the land was divided between two brothers, creating Park House Farm and Moat Farm. Richard Garth, lord of the manor of Morden, acquired Park House Farm in 1867 and slowly developed it as Raynes Park. Moat Farm survived until the 1920s when it broken up by the construction of the Kingston bypass and Bushey Road. Sydney Edward Parkes' company, Modern Homes and Estates, bought land between West Barnes Lane and the railway line, building mock-Tudor homes with a government subsidy. Phyllis Avenue and Arthur Road are named after Parkes' children. Another builder, William Palmer, named Estella Avenue after his daughter. As well as blurring with Raynes Park to the north, West Barnes has an indistinct border with MOTSPUR PARK in the vicinity of its station. The West Barnes ward has a high level of owner occupation and relatively few one-person households.

✉ New Malden KT3

👤 9,559

📖 Evelyn M Jowett, *Raynes Park with West Barnes and Cannon Hill: A Social History*, Merton Historical Society, 1987

@ www.rpwbresidents.org.uk (residents' association site)

West Beckton *see* CUSTOM HOUSE

Westbourne Green • *Westminster*

Definitions vary, but Westbourne Green is now generally considered to constitute the very mixed locality midway between BAYSWATER and MAIDA VALE, north of the WESTWAY (A40). There is much overlap and confusion between Westbourne Green, Grove and Park, but Westbourne Green was the original settlement and the other two places did not acquire their identities until 19th-century developers gave their names to roads. In the 13th century this was the 'place west of the stream (or bourne)' and it gave its name to the River Westbourne, which later provided water for the Serpentine in HYDE PARK. The whole of the western half of PADDINGTON parish was known as Westbourne Green by the 17th century, when the area had just a few mansions and the green was a popular beauty spot. In the following century houses and inns were built around the green but concentrated development did not come until the arrival of the Grand Junction (now Grand Union) Canal in 1801. The canal enhanced the scenery and drew speculative builders from the 1820s. The coming of the railway during the following decade encouraged further housebuilding until the district had expanded to meet its neighbours on all sides by the 1880s. On its fringes the newly enlarged district mostly abutted well-to-do places like Bayswater, NOTTING HILL and Maida Vale and the quality of building here was suitably high. But more compact dwellings were built along the HARROW ROAD and this central part of Westbourne Green soon went into a decline from which it has never properly recovered. The county and borough councils replaced the most run-down housing with blocks of flats from the 1950s onwards, while the Westway disfigured the area in the mid 1960s. The Westbourne Green Sports Complex opened in the mid 1970s and it has been the focus of Westminster council's recent efforts to make wider improvements to the area's inadequate amenities, which include the creation of an 'academy' secondary school. In the Westbourne ward the principal ethnic minorities are of black Caribbean, black African, Bangladeshi and white Irish descent. Islam is the main religion after Christianity. The majority of homes have relatively few rooms and are rented from the council or a housing association.

From 1805 until 1817 the actress Sarah Siddons had a country retreat at Westbourne Farm, later named Desborough House after a nearby meadow. Her brother Charles Kemble lived next door at Desborough Lodge.

✉ W2; W9

♦ 10,075 (Westbourne ward)

Westbourne Grove • *Westminster*

A recently revived commercial thoroughfare running westward from QUEENSWAY towards NOTTING HILL. This is the smallest of the Westbourne localities, consisting of a single street and its offshoots, but it was the commercial heart of BAYSWATER in the latter half of the 19th century. The road was created in the late 1830s and soon extended. Cottages and villas lined both sides and most of these had front gardens. From the mid 1850s shops began to replace the houses. Many of these ventures failed and the road was nicknamed 'bankruptcy row' when William Whiteley opened his first little shop here in 1863. Whiteley proved to be a very astute merchant and by 1876 he had acquired 15 adjacent shops, creating London's first 'great emporium'. This did not please smaller local traders and there was an outcry each time the store branched into a new line of business, much as there is today when supermarket chains widen their range. Whiteley's buildings were always mysteriously catching fire but were soon rebuilt. William Whiteley was shot dead in his office in 1907 by a man claiming to be his illegitimate son and his legitimate sons moved the store to Queensway in 1911, after which Westbourne Grove went into a decline. In recent years antique dealers and upmarket boutiques have recolonized the street, which also has a growing number of restaurants with an exotic variety of cuisines. It is possible that Westbourne Grove will again become 'the BOND STREET of the West' that it was once dubbed.

✉ W2; W11

Westbourne Park • *Westminster/Kensington & Chelsea*

A fashionable residential locality occupying a crescent of land made by the elevated section of the WESTWAY (A40), north-east of NOTTING HILL. A mansion called Westbourne Place stood north of here in the 1640s, with grounds stretching in this direction. The property was later renamed Westbourne Park. After the Great Western Railway came through the district in the late 1830s, a station was opened here, originally called Green Bridge. In the mid 1850s the house was demolished and its grounds were covered by the generously proportioned semi-detached villas of Westbourne Park Road and Westbourne Park Villas, where the writer Thomas Hardy lived in the 1860s. For a while the new settlement was known as 'Westbournia'. In response to the influx of Roman Catholics to neighbouring North Kensington, the Poor Clare order established a monastery on Westbourne Park Road, with separate chapels for nuns and visitors. Westbourne Park was served by the Hammersmith & City Railway from 1866 and the station brought some commerce to the area, but vibrations caused the collapse of four tradesmen's houses in Westbourne Park Passage (now lost) in 1869. The station was rebuilt on its present site in 1871. Later in the century Westbourne Park Road was extended westwards by the simple device of renaming Cornwall Road. Like much of the surrounding area, Westbourne Park had declined by the middle of the 20th century and many houses had been subdivided. The notorious slum landlord Peter Rachman bought his first property on St Stephen's Gardens in the early 1950s, targeting newly arrived West Indian immigrants, whose difficulties in finding accommodation made them easier to exploit. Westminster council later acquired groups of run-down homes, rehabilitating some and replacing others with flats. Westbourne Park was popular with hippies in the 1960s and has since attracted more respectable (and wealthy) figures from the worlds of fashion and music, with chic eateries and organic grocers that draw celebrity customers. The area's population has declined as houses formerly occupied by several families have been reunited into single households.

The blue door that featured prominently in the film *Notting Hill* belonged to a converted chapel in Westbourne Park Road, once owned by the film's scriptwriter and co-producer Richard Curtis. The door was sold for £5,750 to a PORTOBELLO ROAD antiques dealer in 1999.

✉ W11; W2

🚇 Hammersmith & City Line (zone 2)

📖 H E Bonsall and E H Robertson, *Dream of an Ideal City: Westbourne Park, 1877–1977*, Westbourne Park Baptist Church, 1978 (despite its promising title, very much about the church rather than the locality)

West Brompton • *Kensington & Chelsea*

Squeezed almost out of existence by FULHAM, CHELSEA and EARLS COURT, between which it lies, West Brompton was an area of fields and market gardens until the late 18th century. Much of the land was acquired from 1801 by the Gunter family, confectioners of BERKELEY

SQUARE. Over the course of the 19th century the Gunters and their lessees built thousands of houses on newly created streets, named after a variety of family associations. Edith Grove, for example, honours Captain Robert Gunter's daughter, who died of scarlet fever at the age of eight. Finborough Road is named after the country seat of the Pettiward family, another local landowner. Brompton Cemetery was founded in 1837 as the West of London and Westminster Cemetery. It has a formal layout, with a central chapel based on St Peter's Basilica in Rome. Previously the land had been fields and market gardens, mainly owned by Lord Kensington. An additional four-and-a-half acres was obtained in 1844 from the Equitable Gas Co., giving access to FULHAM ROAD. The cemetery was compulsorily purchased from the private owners in 1852 by the General Board of Health, becoming the first and only London cemetery under government control. Around 200,000 people have been buried here, including eleven holders of the Victoria Cross, 3,000 Chelsea Pensioners, the suffragette leader Emmeline Pankhurst, and Richard Tauber, the singer and operetta composer. In 1997 the Sioux Indian chief Long Wolf was reburied in South Dakota, having been interred at Brompton in 1892. The children's writer Beatrix Potter often walked in the cemetery and seems to have found the names for many of her characters on the gravestones here.

Dylan Thomas's first London home was 5 Redcliffe Street, where he was surrounded by 'poems, butter, eggs and mashed potato'. The Finborough public house has a highly regarded upstairs theatre, opened in 1980.

✉ SW10

🧍 8,625 (Redcliffe ward)

🚇 Silverlink Metro service (limited); District Line (zone 2)

@ www.royalparks.gov.uk/parks/ brompton.cemetery/(Brompton Cemetery pages on Royal Parks site); finboroughtheatre.itgo.com (Finborough theatre site, including local history section)

Westcombe Park • *Greenwich*

Situated west of CHARLTON and north of KIDBROOKE, Westcombe Park is, in character, an extension of BLACKHEATH and GREENWICH. The manor of Combe (Old English for a valley or hollow) lay in the Charlton area, and West Combe had its own identity before the Norman Conquest, separated from the rest of the manor by what is now West-combe Hill. The land came into Crown possession before being granted to Richard II's butler, Gregory Ballard, in an arrangement witnessed by Geoffrey Chaucer. Westcombe remained farmland throughout the Middle Ages, but its subsequent history is dominated by two 18th-century properties. Westcombe Park was created in the 1720s as a 50-acre garden for the new Westcombe House, a mansion that stood for around 130 years and whose tenants included the general and colonial administrator Robert Clive ('Clive of India') and the banker Alexander Baring. Nearby, in 1774, the wealthy and well-connected merchant John Julius Angerstein built a villa called Woodlands. Angerstein was the first chairman of Lloyd's of London; he devised a ground-breaking scheme for a national lottery and acquired paintings that formed the nucleus of the National Gallery collection after his death in 1823. Woodlands later became home to the Yarrow shipbuilding family and then to the Little Sisters of the Assumption. During the 1850s and 1860s, land to the south of Westcombe Park Road was laid out as the Vanbrugh Park estate. The success of this project, and the opening of the station in 1876, prompted the sale of Westcombe Park for the building of middle-class housing. However, despite grand aspirations and an architectural competition, several decades elapsed before all the plots were taken up. After World War II, rising property values encouraged infilling by private housebuilders, while the municipal authorities demolished several properties to make way for council flats. Subsequent pressure from preservation societies has prevented further debasement of the area.

✉ SE3

🚈 South Eastern Trains (zone 3)

📖 Neil Rhind, *Blackheath Village and Environs, vol. II*, Bookshop Blackheath, 1983

West Croydon • *Croydon*

A transport hub in north-central CROYDON and a name sometimes applied to the BROAD GREEN and north WADDON areas. The Croydon Canal opened in 1809 and joined the Grand Surrey Canal near NEW CROSS GATE. The canal closed owing to lack of traffic in 1836 and the London and Croydon Railway took over much of its route from 1839, when West Croydon station opened on the site of the canal basin. An atmospheric propulsion system was ex-perimentally introduced on the line in 1845 but withdrawn within a year, owing to technical difficulties. Trains served WIMBLEDON from 1855 until 1997, when this line was closed and replaced by Route 1 of the Croydon Tramlink system. West Croydon is to become the southern terminus of the greatly extended East London Line in 2010.

✉ Croydon CR0

🚈 Southern (zone 5)

🚈 Croydon Tramlink, Routes 1, 2 and 3

West Drayton • *Hillingdon*

An airport satellite district situated north-west of HEATHROW. West Drayton is generally considered to be separated from YIEWSLEY by the railway line, although the parish and ward boundaries differ. The name is a corruption of Drægton – a place where small boats could be dragged across the marshes from the River Colne. St Martin's Church is of 12th-century origin. The manor was known as West Drayton by the 15th century, distinguishing it from DRAYTON GREEN in Ealing. Henry VIII gave the manor to Sir William Paget in 1547 and his family held it until the 18th century, when the substantial manor house was pulled down. Its brick wall and gatehouse have survived, in reduced form. The subsequent lords of the manor, the de Burgh family, lived at Drayton Hall, which is now an office building. West Drayton remained a small village in an agricultural parish until the opening of its station in 1838. The railway brought a little horticulture and a lot of brickmaking to the fields and West Drayton was described in 1887 as having 'the sordid air of an industrial village', with rows of inferior cottages for la-bourers. Over the following half-century the village filled with housing for artisans, City clerks and railway workers. Housebuilding was especially intense between the world wars and included the creation of West Drayton Garden City, 'a grand retreat for jaded city workers', which was built on the site of a for-mer golf course and racetrack. With the station located so close to Yiewsley, the two settle-ments merged, both on the ground and in the form of an urban district, which was estab-lished in 1930. The council cleared some slum areas and began building large estates at Bell Farm and Wise Lane, which were completed after World War II. The outer fringes of the district have been preserved as green-belt land. West Drayton was home to the UK's air traffic control centre until the operation moved to Swanwick, Hampshire in 2002, although some computer control systems remain here. West Drayton Green is a conservation area, with 18th-century properties that include Southlands, now an arts centre. The ward has a predominantly white population, most of whom own their own homes, although a significant minority rent from the council.

✉ West Drayton UB7

👤 11,589

🚃 First Great Western Link (zone 6)

📖 James Skinner, *West Drayton and Yiewsley*, Tempus, 2003; Philip Sherwood, *Around Hayes and West Drayton: A Third Selection*, Sutton, 2002

West Dulwich • *Lambeth/Southwark*

A Victorian and Edwardian railway suburb bordering DULWICH, TULSE HILL and WEST NORWOOD. 'West Dilwysh' was first recorded in 1344. Hesitant growth began here after the opening of Dulwich station in 1863 (it did not become West Dulwich until 1926). The railway company laid out Thurlow Park Road, Rosendale Road and Turney Road to provide access to the station, although these were at first unsurfaced. Building frontages were advertised but take-up was slow. Rosendale Road's eventual width and grandeur is supposedly the consequence of a plan to make it part of a grand processional route to the CRYSTAL PALACE. A speculator attempted to profit from this by laying out Tritton Road in its path, hoping to be bought out, but his bluff was called and the scheme was abandoned. All Saints Church was built in 1891. A spectacular structure for such a modest suburb, it deservedly has Grade I listed status. The first houses in West Dulwich were very select, but properties became progressively more affordable as development spread westward. The main phase of construction came in the years before World War I, although gaps were still being filled in the 1930s. The area suffered badly in World War II. West Dulwich Congregational Church, which stood on Chancellor Road (now Chancellor Grove), was wiped out by a direct bomb strike in 1940. All Saints Church was damaged but subsequently restored. Five V1 rockets fell on West Dulwich in 1944, prompting a postwar reconstruction programme that included the creation of the Rosendale Road estate. The unlucky All Saints Church was gutted by a fire in 1999 and has had to be restored yet again. Turney Special School and Rosendale Primary

School occupy neighbouring sites at the northern end of the locality. At Rosendale School almost a third of the pupils speak English as a second language and there is a high level of pupil mobility. It was rated as a 'good school with some outstanding features' in a 2005 report by the educational standards agency Ofsted.

The Japanese artist Yoshio Markino lodged in Martell Road in 1901 while working for a tombstone maker at West Norwood Cemetery. Pop funsters the Bonzo Dog Doo Dah Band first came together at 164A Rosendale Road, in 1962.

✉ SE21

🚃 South Eastern Trains (zone 3)

West Ealing • *Ealing*

A Victorian and Edwardian residential area situated between HANWELL and EALING. In the 18th century this was Ealing Dean (or Dene), one of three settlements in the area, the others being Great Ealing and LITTLE EALING. A dean was a wooded vale. Ealing Dean consisted of arable farmland, a few orchards, a small settlement on Mattock Lane and two coaching inns on Uxbridge Road. The Green Man inn boasted stabling for 100 horses. The railway line was built through the district in 1838 but a station did not open here until 1871. The latter half of the 19th century saw villas erected on the north side of Uxbridge Road, with a few semi-detached properties on the opposite side. To the south were the parish allotments, on land once known as Jackass Common. By the end of the 19th century most of the land between Uxbridge Road and the railway line had been built up with terraced housing and a few semi-detached houses, some of which were of very poor quality. There was a little industry, mostly small businesses, and local shops began to line Uxbridge Road. In 1903 the first brick-built church was consecrated and West Ealing library opened. The three-acre Dean Gardens replaced some of the allotments in 1910. The park now hosts an annual fair. Other than the replacement of some properties damaged in World War II, West Ealing saw little change until the early 1980s, when redevelopment south of the Broadway brought a Sainsbury's and a new library. West Ealing's retailers are handicapped by the proximity of bustling Ealing Broadway, which has prompted some of the larger stores to move out in recent years. Its homes are more affordable than other parts of Ealing, but many have been stripped of their original features. New blocks of upmarket apartments have been added recently.

Perhaps the greatest excitement ever seen in West Ealing was in 1964, when a train carrying the Beatles stopped at West Ealing station to avoid fans waiting at Paddington. The band were taken into the booking office, where they signed autographs, and left by car within a few minutes. Parts of the gangster film *Snatch* were shot on location in West Ealing, and much of the Dick Francis novel *Twice Shy* is set in the fictional West Ealing School.

> ✉ W5

> 🚌 First Great Western Link; Heathrow Connect; Heathrow Express (zone 3)

> 📖 Ealing library's *West Ealing fact sheet* is one of a series on the borough's localities

West End · *Ealing*

The south-western part of NORTHOLT, which was built up immediately before and after World War II. This was one of four outlying hamlets in the parish of Northolt, with its own green, measuring roughly three acres, a pond and a watering place for livestock. West End was virtually self-contained, with a few dwellings, a public house, two shops and two smithies, but residents had to travel to Northolt to attend church or school. A brickfield operated to the south-east from 1835 and a few cottages were built for its workers, after which almost no development took place for nearly a century. Most of the hamlet was owned by a succession of lords of the manor of Down (later Down Barns) until the estate was sold off in 1920, following the death of Lord HILLINGDON. West End Farm was acquired for development in 1936 although the farmhouse survived until the 1970s, with a milk distribution depot operating from its rear. In 1948 Ealing council bought much of the former Medlar Farm, part of which it preserved as Rectory Park. The rest was built up with houses (including some prefabs at first), shops and a school. On the other side of Church Road (A312) the council took a similar approach with Lime Tree Farm in the 1950s, naming the roads of its new estate after actors. To the west, Down Barns Farm has survived as part of the green belt. The brickfield became home to the construction company Taylor Woodrow and is now the site of GRAND UNION VILLAGE. The Northolt West End ward has some pockets of significant social disadvantage.

> ✉ Northolt UB5

> 👥 13,420 (Northolt West End ward)

> 📖 C H Keene, 'A Short History of the Hamlet of West End, Northolt, Middlesex', Ealing Library, 1985

West End · *Hillingdon*

A forgotten name for a former farming hamlet located on the south-western edge of HARLINGTON. Elder Farmhouse was in existence by the 17th century and its present brick front was added in 1752, by which time a small settlement had grown up nearby. The Pheasant public house was built on West End Lane around 1800 and now has a striking restaurant extension. The Pheasant Nursery, which takes its name from the pub, occupies the fields behind. Most of the present housing dates from the 1890s onwards. By the 1980s, the expansion of Harlington as an airport satellite had erased the separate identity of West End.

> ✉ Hayes UB3

West End · *Westminster*

The UK's leading leisure destination, this is *the* West End. The term has been in use since the early 19th century but there is no agreement on its ambit. The West End undoubtedly takes in the entertainment area around LEICESTER SQUARE, PICCADILLY CIRCUS and SHAFTESBURY AVENUE, and the shopping district of OXFORD STREET, REGENT STREET and BOND STREET. SOHO and MAYFAIR are certainly constituent parts, but many authorities go further afield. P H Ditchfield's 1925 book *London's West End* takes in CHELSEA and NOTTING HILL but popular understanding has changed since then. Although nowadays seen as the HEART OF LONDON, the West End is a comparative newcomer to the capital's social scene. When the CITY OF LONDON first took shape, its prime entertainment zone was located across the Thames at SOUTHWARK. With the shift of government and ecclesiastical influence to WESTMINSTER, development spread along the riverbank but did not at first reach this far inland. By the early 17th century numerous fine houses dotted the fields, while the London masses remained concentrated in the City. Noxious industries were pushed downriver (and downwind) and the EAST END took shape. Entrepreneurial landowners began to lay out high-class streets and squares north of Westminster from the late 17th century but many of these were soon colonized by artisans, craftsmen and refugees, driving the upper classes to ever more distant new suburbs. Early in the 19th century shops in the West End began to cater for the many rather than the privileged few, and music halls and other places of entertainment were built. In the 1810s, John Nash enhanced the new district's prestige with the creation of Regent Street and what are now OXFORD CIRCUS and Piccadilly Circus. Offices, hotels and colleges moved here from the City, driving away more residents. In the mid 19th century the building of the great railway termini in a ring around the West End cemented its focal status. The 20th century brought cinemas and dance halls and further intensification of the existing service industries. Collective improvements in personal wealth from the late 1950s encouraged more day-trippers and short-stay visitors from around the United Kingdom and an ever-growing number of foreign tourists. In some cases, rising rents and rates forced niche providers to find more affordable places to do business. In recent years the West End has suffered a slight decline in the face of competition from out-of-town shopping malls and leisure parks. Vehicle congestion charging and terrorism have deterred some. Nevertheless, around one million people continue to visit the West End every day. Shops and other businesses combined to form the New West End Co. in 2005, which aims to develop a 'revitalization' strategy, and the Mayor of London and relevant local councils, notably Westminster, are working to similar ends.

Surprisingly few artistic or literary titles, or even guide books, have devoted themselves to the West End by name. The Pet Shops Boys' 1986 hit *West End Girls* does not ostensibly concern London's West End but the Dire Straits song *Wild West End* does.

> ✉ W1

> 🚶 7,463

> 📖 Will Adams and Tricia Adams, *Central London: Westminster and the West End*, Past & Present, 2003; Erika Diane Rappaport, *Shopping for Pleasure: Women in the Making of London's West End*, Princeton University Press, 2001

> @ www.mywestend.co.uk (commercial local information site)

Westerham Hill • *Bromley*
The modern name for the locality formerly known as SOUTH STREET, but additionally taking in HAWLEY'S CORNER. Westerham Hill is also the identity of the stretch of the A233 running southwards from the Fox and Hounds public house. The ribbon development with

its small Baptist church is surrounded by farmland that was formerly noted for its strawberries and the rearing of racehorses. Some high-class housing has been built in recent decades, endowed with extensive grounds. One property with an indoor swimming pool complex went on the market for £1.8 million in 2006. Main Road has a variety of rural small businesses, including boarding kennels, pest control, and the Saddlery and Gun Room, a country pursuits supplier.

> ✉ Westerham TN16

> @ www.westerham.hill.btinternet.co.uk (Westerham Hill Baptist Church site)

West Euston • *Camden*
A 'renewal priority area' extending westward from EUSTON station to Albany Street and covering the REGENT'S PARK estate and Crown estate housing and the commercial area of Regent's Place with Euston Tower and Abbey House. West Euston takes in Drummond Street, which is one of several parts of London nicknamed 'Little India', in this case because of its restaurants rather than the ethnicity of residents, who are more likely to be of Bangladeshi origin. West Euston has high levels of multiple deprivation, which means that local people suffer disproportionately from crime and disorder problems, high levels of unemployment, low incomes, low levels of educational attainment, greater health problems and lower quality of housing. West Euston Partnership was established in 1992 to help tackle these issues and receives funding from a variety of public resources and from local businesses. Its projects have included a 'one-stop shop' community resource and advice centre on Hampstead Road and the 'h-pod' on Cumberland Market, a centre intended to improve community health which opened in 2006.

> ✉ NW1

> @ www.westeustonpartnership.co.uk

Westferry • *Tower Hamlets*
A Docklands Light Railway station located on the eastern edge of LIMEHOUSE. West Ferry Road (as it was called until the 1920s) was created, together with its eastern counterpart, when local landowners and businessmen established the POPLAR and Greenwich Ferry Roads Co. to make turnpikes to the Greenwich ferry in 1812. This marked the opening-up of the inland part of the Isle of Dogs although it was several decades before the

peninsula was fully colonized. The company abandoned its horse-ferry service in 1844 but continued to levy tolls until the Metropolitan Board of Works bought out the owners and removed the tollgates in 1885. Westferry Road has been progressively diverted and extended, finally meeting West India Dock Road when the London County Council demolished the Rosher estate in 1960. This junction is the site of Westferry station, opened in 1987 as one of the original 15 stops on the Docklands Light Railway. The immediate vicinity remains largely unregenerated, with just a handful of unexceptional commercial premises. Before World War II the neighbourhood was the centre of the Chinese East End. Westferry Road is the site of the recent Canary South residential development, which has included the conversion of a fire station to flats and the building of a new fire station further along the road.

A blue plaque in Westferry Road celebrates the building in 1858 of Brunel's SS *Great Eastern*, the largest steamship of the 19th century. The gardens at Westferry Circus have railings and gates by Giuseppe Lund symbolizing the seasons.

✉ E14

🚇 Docklands Light Railway, all branches (zone 2)

@ www.tfl.gov.uk/dlr/stations/
westferry.shtml

West Finchley • *Barnet*

A less distinct or historic settlement than its northern and eastern counterparts, West Finchley is focused on its Tube station, which is located midway along Nether Street. The street wiggles between CHURCH END and NORTH FINCHLEY while BALLARDS LANE takes the direct route. There were brick houses and weatherboarded cottages on Nether Street from the Middle Ages but the land to its west remained well-wooded into the 18th century, when the elm trees were cut down and it was turned over to haymaking. A path called Lovers (or Love) Walk traversed the locality in 1800, and still does. Jersey Farm Dairies was established between Nether Street and Dollis Brook around 1887 and kept a herd of 100 cows. Some of the farm buildings survived until the early 1920s, when developers were beginning to turn their attention to this unexploited edge of the now-popular FINCHLEY district. West Finchley station did not open until 1933, 60 years after the construction of the Great Northern Railway's branch line to

High Barnet, which became part of the underground network in 1940. Stations usually stimulated development (indeed that was often their main purpose) but West Finchley opened in response to a flurry of building that was already well under way, creating a new little suburb. Housing density has increased since World War II with the insertion of some flats but the banks of the brook remain verdant. Two-thirds of West Finchley's residents are white and the largest ethnic minority is of Indian origin. Young people in their twenties make up a relatively high proportion of the population, often renting their homes privately, and comparatively few households have dependent children.

The skull and flesh of a crocodile were found in Dollis Brook in 1996 by an RSPCA inspector walking his dog.

✉ N3

🚶 14,264

🚇 Northern Line (zone 4)

West Green • *Haringey*

A culturally diverse locality situated northeast of HARRINGAY. This was formerly one of the chain of greens linked by GREEN LANES. To its east lay Downhills, later called Mount Pleasant House, which was built some time before 1728. This house was replaced in 1789 by a three-storey brick mansion set in several hundred acres, with ornamental gardens and a grove of trees sweeping down to the Moselle River. Possibly because of the arrival of the railway at TOTTENHAM HALE in 1840, West Green began to develop relatively early, with local builder Edward Clarke and others laying out the first streets in the 1850s. West Green gained its own station in 1878, on the Palace Gates branch line. At the end of the 19th century the British Land Co. bought the Downhills estate, selling it to the local authority in 1902. The council demolished the mansion and built on the fields but the ornamental gardens were kept as a park. West Green suffered a decline in the years after World War II as middle-class families moved out to the new suburbs and houses were divided into flats. The Essoldo cinema closed in 1958 and West Green station and its line were axed as part of the Beeching cuts in the 1960s. West Green has recently been the subject of a neighbourhood renewal project that has sought to tackle the poor state of many of the multiple-occupancy properties in the area, with the aim of generating spin-off benefits such as a reduction in 'feelings of hostility and fear of crime'. The West Green Learning Resource Centre opened in 2002. This is a landmark building, created to provide a catalyst for change in a part of the borough where there have been problems of under-achievement. West Green's residents originate from a variety of countries, including Turkey, Greece, Somalia and Bangladesh.

✉ N15; N17

♟ 11,884

📖 Peter Curtis, *In Times Past*, Hornsey Historical Society, 1991

West Ham • *Newham*

Formerly an important industrial district situated south-east of STRATFORD. Ham, which means a settlement or homestead, was recorded in the 10th century as a village situated between the great Forest and the marshes of the Thames and the Lea. The first separate mention of West Ham came two centuries later. West Ham belonged to the Abbey of Stratford from 1135 to 1538 and suffered economically after the dissolution of the monasteries. It recovered in the 17th century with the growth of the leather and weaving industries. Then came an influx of City businessmen seeking a rural retreat. In 1762 the King's surveyor recorded 455 mansions and 245 cottages in West Ham. The mansions may not all have matched the modern understanding of the word, but this was certainly a settlement of well-to-do merchants. However, its location to the east of the River Lea gave West Ham a strategic 'gateway' position in relation to the capital and also allowed the siting of noxious industries that were not permitted nearer the City. From the 1840s, chemical works, textile factories and distilleries all located here, and cheap workers' housing replaced the mansions. The greatest growth came during the latter half of the 19th century, when West Ham gained the sobriquet 'the factory centre of the south of England' and became its largest and fastest-growing borough. Following the death of the philanthropist Samuel Gurney, his home, Ham House, was demolished and in 1874 its grounds were opened as West Ham Park in an effort to provide, literally, a breathing space for the residents of the overcrowded district. West Ham was ravaged during the Blitz and its fortunes waned after World War II as the industries departed, the docks closed and many east Londoners sought homes in Essex or in the new towns of the Home Counties.

Modern West Ham is a truly multiracial community, with significant numbers from all the main ethnic groups.

East London's pre-eminent football team, West Ham United, plays at nearby UPTON PARK. The club was founded as Thames Ironworks Football Club in 1895 and gained promotion to the first division of the Southern League in 1899, turning professional in the same year.

✉ E7; E13; E15

♟ 12,637

🚇 c2c (zone 3); District Line; Hammersmith & City Line; Jubilee Line; (zone 3)

📖 Stephen Pewsey, *Stratford, West Ham and the Royal Docks*, Sutton, 1999

@ www.lalamy.demon.co.uk/timeline.htm (local history pages on personal site)

West Hampstead • *Camden*

A stepping-stone residential area for upwardly mobile young professionals, situated to the south-west of its HAMPSTEAD parent between the FINCHLEY ROAD and KILBURN High Road. Lacking its own supply of spring water and situated away from the main roads, medieval West End barely qualified as a hamlet until a few country houses were built here from the 17th century onwards. The tendency for West End Lane to become impassably muddy after heavy rain further enhanced the hamlet's isolation. In 1815 West End remained exceptionally quiet – so much so that its inhabitants claimed to have heard the cannon fire at Waterloo. The construction of the Finchley Road brought few additions to a population that consisted of a handful of squires and some farm labourers, gardeners and craftsmen. By 1851 West End had one inn and two beershops. Railways were the prime stimulus of growth in many country corners of modern London, but few places were transformed as wholly as West End. With the arrival of the Hampstead Junction Railway in 1857, the Midland Railway in 1868 and the Metropolitan and St John's Wood Railway in 1879, the new suburb of West Hampstead spread in all directions. Some of the new estates were the work of big developers like the United Land Co., whose inclination was to build fairly densely, and during the latter decades of the 19th century parts of West Hampstead became increasingly working-class in character, with policeman, travelling salesmen and railwaymen mixing with clerks and artisans.

Engineering workshops operated near the railway lines. Twentieth-century building was limited mainly to interwar blocks of flats in the north of the district, often in place of Victorian houses that had already become rundown. From the 1940s many Czechs settled here, though almost all have since moved further out to the north-western suburbs. The West Hampstead ward now has relatively few families and a great number of young single people. A large proportion of homes are privately rented and fewer than a quarter of adults are married, compared with more than half for the country as a whole. This socio-economic profile is evident in the upmarket cafes that have lined West End Lane in recent years.

Former residents include the singers Olivia Newton John and Jimmy Somerville, the author Doris Lessing, the actress Emma Thompson and the playwright Joe Orton, who lived on West End Lane with his lover Kenneth Halliwell from 1951 to 1959.

> ✉ NW6

> ♦ 10,053

> 🚇 Silverlink Metro; Thameslink; Jubilee Line (zone 2)

> 📖 Christopher Wade (ed.), *The Streets of West Hampstead*, Camden History Society, 1975; Dick Weindling and Marianne Collom, *Kilburn and West Hampstead Past*, Historical Publications, 1999

> @ www.cityneighbours.com (NW3 and NW6 community site)

West Harrow • *Harrow*

An early 20th-century extension of HARROW, with some later council housing and retirement flats. Housing began to spread across the open fields after the electrification of the Metropolitan Line in 1905, running first along Pinner Road and then branching off into new streets. In less than a decade the area around the newly extended railway line to Uxbridge had been built up. Vaughan School accepted its first pupils in 1910 and West Harrow station was opened at the request of residents late in 1913. In the same year, St Peter's Church was completed on Sumner Road, although an intended tower was never built. The church has since been converted to a 'Christian centre'. West Harrow Cricket Club was founded in 1918 by a group of ex-colonials. Nowadays, the club's membership is primarily of Indian ethnic origin. The 26-acre West Har-

row recreation ground is the locality's principal amenity, with facilities for football, cricket, tennis and basketball, and it is the base for West Harrow Bowling Club. West Harrow Cricket Club, however, moved to HEADSTONE Manor recreation ground in 1999. The residents of West Harrow are predominantly white, but one-fifth is of Indian origin and Hinduism is the second most common religion, after Christianity. The 2006 inspection of Vaughan School by the national educational standards agency Ofsted reported that almost half the pupils are bilingual, but only a few are at the early stages of learning English.

> ✉ Harrow HA1 and HA2

> ♦ 9,690

> 🚇 Metropolitan Line (zone 5)

West Heath • *Bexley*

A part-Victorian, part-interwar locality that many residents consider to be part of BOSTALL HEATH. West Heath House was built in the early 19th century for Sir Samuel Hulse, who was aide-de-camp to the Prince Regent, later George IV. Hulse grabbed some common land to enlarge the grounds of his house, which has resulted in the dog-legged line of Bedonwell Road. The king visited West Heath House after Hulse had risen to become a field marshal and treasurer of the royal household. Lessness Park was an Italianate mansion built in the mid 19th century, with grounds that extended north to Woolwich Road and included a cricket pitch. The pitch was used by West Heath Cricket Club and W G Grace once played there. West Heath House was rebuilt in 1878 but no tenant could be found, so part of the grounds was sold off and several large villas were built, some of which have survived. Burcharbro Road was laid out in the 1890s and gains its curious name from its builders, Burrowes, Charlesworth and Brodie, who also developed neighbouring Pinewood Road. West Heath House was occupied until 1921 by Sir Tom Callender, who owned a cable manufacturing company in ERITH. The house was afterwards converted into flats and the remainder of the grounds was developed at the same time. Edward Blackwell built houses on West Heath Road in 1930 and added more properties to the south in the following year. Blackwell had worked in Australia, hence the name of Canberra Road. Lessness Park was demolished in the mid 1930s and its site was developed with housing, mainly bungalows.

A line of trees fronting Woolwich Road (A206) was preserved and a small plot was saved as West Heath recreation ground, which opened in 1937. This was temporarily commandeered for prefabricated housing after World War II to accommodate families made homeless by bombing. One of the largest Victorian houses on Woolwich Road became St Joseph's Convent School and later a campus of Bexley College, which in 2005 gained planning permission to convert the building to flats and to add more housing in its grounds. The high density of the proposed scheme has drawn complaints from local residents.

✉ SE2; Bexleyheath DA7

West Heath • *Camden*

An extension of HAMPSTEAD HEATH with an increasingly separate identity, lying west of North End Way and south of Golders Hill Park. West Heath was the site of an important Stone Age encampment, dating from the era when man first began to abandon a nomadic lifestyle and establish settlements. Excavations have uncovered over 100,000 flints. Horse races were held on West Heath from the 1730s. On the heath's west side the Leg of Mutton Pond is so called because of its shape. Like Sandy Road, it was probably created in the early 19th century as part of a poor relief scheme. Sandy Road was sometimes known as Hankins's folly, after Thomas Hankins, surveyor of the highways. The Metropolitan Board of Works added West Heath to its Hampstead Heath protectorate in 1872. Inverforth House (originally The Hill) was built around 1895 on the site of an earlier house on North End Way and in 1904 it became the first London home of the soap magnate W H Lever, later Viscount Leverhulme. Lever spent considerable time and money beautifying the house, which became a hospital after his death and has since been converted to private flats. However, most of the grounds have been added to the heath. The grounds of some other large houses south of West Heath were taken for gated developments in the 1980s and 1990s. The weatherboarded Jack Straw's Castle on West Heath Road is named after a ringleader of the Peasants' Revolt who is said to have addressed crowds from a haywagon here. A coaching inn stood on the site from 1721 but was wrecked by a World War II bomb and rebuilt in the early 1960s. Regrettably, the pub has also recently been converted to private flats. West Heath has acquired a reputation as one of London's prime cruising grounds for gay men, especially after dark; some estimates put the total number of participants in the thousands. There have been attacks on people cruising and indecency prosecutions.

Hampstead-educated poet Thom Gunn published a collection of verse entitled *Jack Straw's Castle* in 1976.

✉ NW3

📖 Desmond Collins et al, *Excavations at the Mesolithic Site on West Heath, Hampstead, 1976–1981*, Hendon and District Archaeological Society, 1991

West Hendon • *Barnet*

One of the borough's poorer quarters, West Hendon is now separated from HENDON proper by the M1 motorway. The land was once part of Tunworth (now KINGSBURY) but, by passing into the ownership of Westminster Abbey, became part of the parish and manor of Hendon in the late tenth century. Although the locality attracted visitors following the creation of the WELSH HARP reservoir in the 1830s, no settlement existed here until the opening of Hendon main-line station in 1868. Over the latter part of the 19th century West Hendon evolved as a new suburb, consisting almost entirely of terraced housing. A Baptist mission hall was built in 1885 and Nonconformists joined Anglicans in contributing to St John's School, built in 1889, after seeing shoeless children walking to CHURCH END in WILLESDEN. The Church of St John the Evangelist held services in temporary buildings until its permanent home was consecrated in 1896. In the same year the opening of the Schweppes bottling plant brought further growth to the locality. West Hendon Broadway was fully built up by the outbreak of World War I, although open fields still stretched south to CRICKLEWOOD railway sidings at this time. The North Circular Road (A406) cut across these fields in the 1920s. In February 1941 a V2 rocket killed 80 West Hendon residents and made 1,500 homeless. Much of the surviving housing stock was demolished and rebuilt between the 1940s and the late 1960s. The closure of the Schweppes plant in 1980 contributed to the area's economic decline and West Hendon is now the focus of a major regeneration scheme. This will entail the demolition of the post-war estate and its replacement with more than 2,000 new homes, together with community facilities, a civic square, and environmental and road improvements. Slightly more than half of West Hendon's residents are white, while a fifth are of Indian origin.

✉ NW9

👤 14,587

🚆 Thameslink (Hendon, zone 3)

📖 Reginald Somes, *Encompassing History of St John the Evangelist, West Hendon and Its Environs*, R H Somes, 1995

West Hill • *Wandsworth*

WANDSWORTH's western slope, rising from the valley of the River Wandle towards PUTNEY HEATH. West Hill underwent the two-stage development process common to many localities that began to grow in the mid 19th century. Spacious villas with large gardens lined the south side of the main road, spreading into the southern hinterland and then to the north. This stage was largely complete before the end of the century. In the years before and after World War II most of these properties were replaced with streets of terraced and semi-detached houses and with council estates. Several of the area's street names commemorate the houses that stood there before. On West Hill itself private flats and townhouses were a feature of the second wave of building. The West Hill ward was at the centre of allegations of gerrymandering in 1994, when the Labour Party claimed that council tenants were moved out of two tower blocks so that the flats could be sold to private buyers. Nevertheless, nearly a quarter of homes in the ward remain in council ownership. The De Morgan Centre opened in 2002 at 38 West Hill, a former reference library. The centre is devoted to the study of 19th century art and society, and houses the permanent collection of work by William De Morgan, a ceramic artist, and his wife Evelyn, a painter.

✉ SW18

👤 14,356

@ www.demorgan.org.uk

West India Quay • *Tower Hamlets*

A DOCKLANDS Light Railway station and its immediate vicinity, located in the northwestern corner of the ISLE OF DOGS and named after the docks that occupied the site for most of the previous two centuries. During the course of the 18th century the number of vessels discharging their cargoes at London's riverside docks almost trebled and with this growth came overcrowding and increased pilferage. Liverpool had shown that wet docks provided a solution and a group of merchants, together with the West India Company and the

Corporation of London, chose the Isle of Dogs as their preferred site, since other investors already had plans for WAPPING and the peninsula's distance from London was perceived to provide added security from theft. The West India Docks opened in 1802, divided into separate import and export docks – setting a precedent in dock construction. South of the export dock the City Canal traversed the Isle of Dogs. The canal proved a commercial failure and was subsequently enlarged to become the South Dock. Sugar, rum, teak, mahogany and coffee made up the docks' principal imports. The following century saw successive phases of enlargement, increased competition, financial difficulty and mergers with other London docks. Perhaps the most significant event, with hindsight, was the company's decision in 1881 to build a new dock at Tilbury, rather than further enlarging the West India Docks. Additional expansion did eventually come, especially after the creation of the Port of London Authority in 1908, but the docks' long-term fate had by then been sealed. Most of the West India Docks were wrecked during World War II, after which the facility slowly declined until its closure in 1980. The quays have since been redeveloped Manhattan-style as CANARY WHARF, HERON QUAYS and SOUTH QUAY. The surviving warehouses of the North Quay have been rebranded 'West India Quay', and provide amenities for local workers and residents, with bars and restaurants, a multiplex cinema and the obligatory health club. West India Quay also has new apartment blocks and the Museum in Docklands, based in the former No. 1 Warehouse.

✉ E14

🚆 Docklands Light Railway, Lewisham branch (zone 2)

@ www.museumindocklands.org.uk

West Kensington • *Hammersmith & Fulham*

'A modern district within the parish of FULHAM', as it was called in 1890, when it had recently become the new name for NORTH END. In 1876 speculative builders William Gibbs and John Flew began to lay out their West Kensington estate on land that had belonged to the confectioner James Gunter. Their architecture was repetitive but each house was given distinctive leafy plasterwork above the door and windows. Gibbs bought and enlarged Mornington Lodge as his own home. The two entrepreneurs persuaded the railway company to change the name of the station to West Kensington and built over 1,200 homes here but depressed market conditions in the 1880s brought the process to a halt, leaving vacant lots and unoccupied properties. The absence of access routes across the two railway lines was another drawback and the West Kensington Estate Co. went under in 1885. From the early years of the 20th century, interest in West Kensington revived. The district became popular with artists and writers and such was the demand that developers squeezed in more buyers by building mansion blocks, sometimes in place of existing rows of houses. Fulham council put up flats in the 1920s, demolishing Mornington Lodge, and with the opening of the West Cromwell Road (A4) in 1942 access was at last improved, although at the expense of some Gibbs and Flew houses. The council built extensively but not prettily in the southern part of the district in the decades after World War II, culminating in the West Kensington estate of the early 1970s. West Kensington's slightly seedy post-war reputation has receded in recent times with the arrival of a stream of young professionals. Sixty-three per cent of the residents of the North End ward are single and more than half the adults of working age have a degree. The definition of the West Kensington area has contracted over the last century as the names of BARONS COURT and EARLS COURT have gained currency, but some residents of the North End Road are still keen on the KENSINGTON cachet.

Scottish residents of West Kensington have included *Whisky Galore* author Compton Mackenzie, who lived on Avonmore Road as a child, and Renton and Sickboy, who stayed in a Talgarth Road flat in the 1996 film *Trainspotting*.

✉ W14

🚇 District Line (zone 2)

📖 Pamela Daphne Edwards, *West Kensington and Shepherd's Bush*, European Library, 1995

West Kilburn • *Westminster*
A fuzzily defined area, lying north of the HARROW ROAD and west of MAIDA VALE. The far eastern side of the locality was developed as St Peter's Park from the mid 1860s. Named in honour of former landowners Westminster Abbey, St Peter's Park included Bravington Road and the streets to its east, but its identity has been lost and the area is now sometimes

called MAIDA HILL. Across to the west, the Artisans', Labourers' and General Dwellings Co. built the charming terraced cottages of the QUEEN'S PARK estate after 1873. In the centre of West Kilburn, the United Land Co. completed Beethoven and Mozart Streets by 1886 and added Herries and Lancefield Streets within the following decade. Large parts of West Kilburn were rebuilt with council flats after World War II, while housing associations have been active here since the mid 1960s, in some cases co-operating with former squatters to rehabilitate rundown properties.

The comic actor Norman Wisdom was born in 1915 at 91 Fernhead Road, an address that he considers to be in PADDINGTON.

✉ W9; W10

Westminster • *Westminster*
The seat of Britain's government and home of some of its most important religious institutions. It lies on the west bank of the Thames opposite LAMBETH, from where it was once possible to cross the river at low tide to a marshy island of thorn trees, Thorney Island. There was a place of worship here from the 2nd century, and perhaps even earlier. From 785 it was the site of a monastic foundation which Edward the Confessor re-endowed and to which he added a large, stone abbey church, consecrated in 1065; this was referred to as the 'west minster' to distinguish it from the 'east minister', ST PAUL'S Cathedral in the City of London. In the mid 13th century Henry III instigated the reconstruction of the church in the Gothic style, and the building grew to its present form over the following three centuries, with two western towers added later by Hawksmoor. Westminster Abbey has been the setting for coronations since 1066 and is the burial place of 18 monarchs, including Elizabeth I. Its nave is the tallest in the country and at its west end lies the grave of the Unknown Warrior. Geoffrey Chaucer's tomb began the tradition of Poets' Corner, where memorials have since been erected to great British writers from Shakespeare to Dylan Thomas. The abbey attracts over three million visitors a year. Behind the abbey is the Royal College of St Peter at Westminster, which was founded in 1179. It is better known as Westminster School.

Westminster Palace was a residence of English kings from the mid 11th century. Parliament emerged in the late 13th century as an extension of the king's council. The Lords sat at Westminster Palace from the end of the 14th century but the Commons did not gain a permanent foothold there until 1547. The palace was destroyed by a devastating fire in 1834, London's biggest conflagration since the Great Fire in 1666. Westminster Hall, the crypt of St Stephen's Chapel and the Jewel Tower survived and a new, purpose-built structure was erected around these by Charles Barry and Augustus Pugin and brought into service in 1867. The chamber of the House of Commons was destroyed in a 1941 air raid. It was sensitively rebuilt by Sir Giles Gilbert Scott and reopened in 1950. The Palace of Westminster is also known as the Houses of Parliament. To the north of the palace, WHITEHALL is the prime location for government departments, but many others are situated in the streets to the south and west. The prestigious but plain Queen Elizabeth II Conference Centre is a government building used mainly for private-sector and professional events.

Methodist Central Hall stands opposite the Palace of Westminster. Opened in 1912, the hall hosted the first meeting of the United Nations in 1946. On the far western side of Westminster, just off Francis Street, is Westminster Cathedral, the cathedral church of the Roman Catholic archdiocese of Westminster. Built at the end of the 19th century on the site of a former prison, it is dedicated to the Most Precious Blood of Our Lord Jesus Christ.

William Wordsworth's sonnet *Composed upon Westminster Bridge* has been called the best-known poetic tribute to a city in the English language. It was written after the poet and his sister Dorothy crossed the bridge at dawn on 3 September 1802.

📧 SW1

🚇 Circle Line; District Line; Jubilee Line (zone 1)

🚢 Westminster Millennium pier

📖 Simon Bradley and Nikolaus Pevsner, *London: Westminster* (Buildings of England series), Yale University Press, 2003

West Norwood • *Lambeth*

Despite its name, this is the northern part of NORWOOD, and is poorer but more characterful than much of this sprawling district. Lower Norwood, as it was earlier called, began to grow early in the 19th century as small parcels of former common land were sold off for building. A later scheme at Royal Circus was of a much more ambitious nature, aiming to fill the space between Canterbury Grove and Leigham Vale with curving terraces of houses, but wealthy buyers preferred detached

or semi-detached villas and the project was a failure. The Norwood House of Industry, a workhouse school, was built in 1810 on Elder Road. Most of the buildings have been demolished but the lodge and the front block of the old school survive and have been converted to residential use. St Luke's Church was built at the apex of KNIGHTS HILL and Norwood Road in 1825. Opened in 1837, West Norwood Cemetery was an early example of a non-denominational, landscaped public cemetery. An area was reserved for London's Greek community. Among those buried here are Sir Henry Tate, who founded the sugar company and art gallery that bear his name, the household management writer Mrs Beeton and the potter Sir Henry Doulton. A residential home for 220 Jewish orphans opened in 1866, later becoming the Norwood Orphanage. As Lower Norwood filled with middle-class housing the name 'West Norwood' was adopted in 1885 in response to residents' sensitivities. Since that time the district has declined in prestige and gained a multi-ethnic community, especially of African and Caribbean origin. Despite the perception that West Norwood is essentially a residential area, it has the largest concentration of industrial land in the borough, focused on the triangle south of the station. Businesses have complained at the lack of room for expansion, and the same problem has deterred major retailers, although this may have benefited the many independent shops. Lambeth council has been investigating the possibility of bringing additional open-air retailing to West Norwood, probably at Lansdowne Hill, where a Thursday market already operates. The Norwood Action Group is campaigning for the social, environmental and economic regeneration of West Norwood and the surrounding area.

A 'big modern villa of staring brick, standing back in its own grounds' in Lower Norwood provides the setting for the Sherlock Holmes story *The Adventure of the Norwood Builder*. Camille Pissarro's painting *Lower Norwood, Londres, Effet de Neige* hangs in the National Gallery.

📧 SE27

🚇 Southern (zone 3)

@ www.fownc.org (Friends of West Norwood Cemetery site); www.norwoodaction.org.uk (Norwood Action Group site)

West Ruislip • *Hillingdon*

The south-western corner of Ruislip, bordering Ickenham. The station opened in 1906 as Ruislip and Ickenham. At this time King's End Farm occupied much of the area and its entrepreneurial owner George Weedon created Poplars sports fields here after the coming of the railway. The fields complemented the tea garden Weedon had opened near the junction with the High Street, and offered all the fun of the fair. The farmhouse served as a clubhouse for Ruislip golf course from 1939. The Central Line arrived at West Ruislip in 1948. It had been intended to extend the service to Denham, but plans were abandoned when the introduction of green-belt regulations prevented further development here. Green-belt protection also constrained the expansion of West Ruislip, although the old farmhouse was demolished in 1951 and houses were built on the site. A new golf clubhouse was erected near the station. Just south of the station, RAF West Ruislip was formerly a United States Air Force base and is currently used by the US Navy. The base also owns accommodation in Blenheim Crescent. Housing has been built on a redundant part of the airbase.

The locality's most notable mention in a creative work is a reference in the barber's prelude to Monty Python's 'Lumberjack Song' to the 'flatulent elm of West Ruislip'.

> ✉ Ruislip HA4; Uxbridge UB10 (south of the railway line)

> 🚉 Chiltern Railways (limited service); Central Line terminus (zone 6)

West Silvertown • *Newham*

A set of new urban developments with mixed-tenure housing and some innovative amenities, situated south of ROYAL VICTORIA Dock. From the mid 19th century until the early 1980s, riverside factories and quayside warehousing occupied the former marshes. Since the closure of most of the industrial premises West Silvertown has been undergoing extensive regeneration. In the 1990s the London Docklands Development Corporation sponsored the creation of Britannia Village, a self-supporting community with housing of modest architectural standards. Britannia Village Primary School opened on Westwood Road in 1999 and its building is described by Ofsted as 'delightful … an excellent working environment'. Around half the pupils come from ethnic minorities and 40 per cent speak English as an additional language. Thames Barrier Park was completed in 2000 and boasts the most distinctive public gardens created in London in recent decades. The park is

flanked by apartment blocks built by Barratt at the same time: Barrier Point and Tradewinds. West Silvertown station opened in 2005. Construction is under way of a major mixed-use scheme at PONTOON DOCK called Silvertown Quays, a 59-acre development that will have 5,000 residential units and a conservation-oriented aquarium, to be operated by the Zoological Society of London and scheduled to open in 2008. The final phases of the Silvertown Quays project will include community facilities such as a primary school, health facilities, more public spaces and a community hall, and are due for completion before 2020.

> ✉ E16

> 🚉 Docklands Light Railway, City Airport branch (zone 3)

> @ www.silvertownquays-london.com (developers' site);
> www.westsilvertownfoundation.co.uk

West Smithfield *see* SMITHFIELD

West Sutton • *Sutton*

The western side of SUTTON gained its first low-cost suburban housing as early as the 1860s, later followed by an extensive gasworks, but the hinterland of the present station remained largely rural until well into the 20th century. Gander Green Lane was still a country road in the 1920s. At the end of that decade the Southern Railway Co. constructed the loop line from Sutton to WIMBLEDON, electrifying it from the start to increase commuter appeal. The opening of West Sutton station in 1930 brought a dense network of terraced and semi-detached houses to neighbouring streets. In a recent development at Sydney Road, the Lavender Housing Partnership has replaced outmoded sheltered accommodation with a mix of houses, flats and studios for social rent and sale. The Sutton West Centre, on Robin Hood Lane, provides various educational and welfare services for the local community.

Non-league Sutton United Football Club plays at the borough sports ground on Gander Green Lane, adjacent to West Sutton station. The club was formed in 1898 and moved to its present ground in 1919.

> ✉ Sutton SM1

> 🚉 Thameslink (zone 5)

> @ www.suttonunited.net

West Thamesmead *see* THAMESMEAD WEST

West Thornton · *Croydon*

London street atlases give no name to the territory between southern THORNTON HEATH and MITCHAM COMMON, but West Thornton's name is sometimes used locally and constitutes an electoral ward. There was a small settlement here by the 18th century, from which some of the cottages survived until relatively recently. With the expansion of Croydon in this direction, WADDON MARSH Lane was renamed Thornton Road. The road was widened as part of a bypass scheme for the town and to provide access to Croydon aerodrome in the 1920s. At this time, the southern part of the area began to fill with offices and factory estates, several of which remain today, while others have been replaced by housing. The ward is culturally diverse with no single ethnic group constituting a majority. There are many families with children, including single-parent households. Most homes are owner-occupied, but unemployment is relatively high. Those that are employed tend to be semi-skilled and unskilled manual workers. At West Thornton Primary School just over half the pupils speak English as an additional language.

✉ Thornton Heath CR7

♦ 16,498

West Twyford · *Ealing/Brent*

An old name, still shown on some street signage, for what is now the westernmost part of PARK ROYAL. The locality is also sometimes called Twyford Abbey, after its oldest building. Twyford was mentioned in Domesday Book and the name derives from the Old English 'twī-fyrde', a reference to two fords that crossed the River Brent. The village consisted of ten dwellings and a chapel in the 13th century, but seems to have become depopulated soon afterwards. By 1593 the manor house was the only inhabited property and this situation was unchanged in 1808, when the house was rebuilt in 'Tudor-gothick' style. A dozen or so other homes were built over the next hundred years and mushroom farms were established. Following the opening of the Royal Agricultural Society's showground, Park Royal and Twyford Abbey station was built in 1903, and survived until 1931. By this time West Twyford was becoming part of the industrial sprawl of ACTON, and the Guinness brewery and others built housing for workers. West Twyford's population rose from 311 in 1931 to 2,995 in 1951. The area has since declined as the result of the progressive closure of factor-

ies in Park Royal. The manor house was used as a nursing home by the Roman Catholic Alexian Brotherhood for most of its rebuilt life, and consequently became known as Twyford Abbey. It has lain empty since 1991 and a proposal for its refurbishment as housing was rejected by the Mayor of London in 2005, primarily because the plan also involved building on neighbouring open land. Next door to the 'abbey', West Twyford Primary School draws children from a catchment area that the national educational standards agency Ofsted describes as 'not especially prosperous, nor seriously deprived'. About 40 per cent of pupils do not speak English as their first language; Arabic is the most commonly spoken language after English.

✉ NW10

📖 M C Barrès-Baker, *Twyford and Park Royal*, Grange Museum of Community History and Brent Archive, 2001

Westway · *Westminster/Kensington & Chelsea/Hammersmith & Fulham*

The part of the A40 dual carriageway stretching from EAST ACTON to PADDINGTON. The term is generally used to refer to the two-and-a-half mile elevated section that connects WHITE CITY with Marylebone Road. Begun in 1964, the Westway was conceived as a solution to congestion caused by the absence of a link between central London and the interwar Western Avenue. The Greater London Council forced this state-of-the-art highway through the NORTH KENSINGTON area amidst allegations of Soviet-style disregard for the effects on the local population. Angry protests greeted Michael Heseltine, then Parliamentary Under-Secretary for Transport, when he opened the Westway in July 1970, and the GLC was forced to rehouse some residents living adjacent to the road. Beneath its elevated section the Westway Project added artistic embellishments and the North Kensington Amenity Trust (later the Westway Development Trust) helped to establish leisure and cultural amenities.

The Westway's bleak underbelly has frequently featured as a film and pop video location, and punk rockers The Clash and The Jam employed Westway imagery. *Westway* was the title of a long-running radio soap opera broadcast on the BBC World Service and BBC7. The story focused on a health centre in the fictional Westgrove Park, a locality evidently associated with WESTBOURNE GROVE and WESTBOURNE PARK. The Westway provides the setting for J G Ballard's novel *Concrete Island*. Ballard has compared the Westway with Cambodia's temple city Angkor Wat, calling it 'a stone dream that will never awake'.

West Wickham • *Bromley*

A relatively uniform interwar suburb situated west of HAYES, on the border with the London Borough of Croydon. The name is of early Anglo-Saxon origin and denoted a homestead that was associated with an even earlier Romano-British settlement. The 'West' prefix was added in the 13th century, to distinguish it from EAST WICKHAM, which lies some ten miles to the north-east, on the north side of WELLING. In 1469 the manor was sold to the Norfolk lawyer Henry Heydon, who rebuilt the Church of St John the Baptist and the manor house, Wickham Court. Heydon married Anne Bullen, great-aunt to Henry VIII's queen Anne Boleyn. Samuel Lennard acquired Wickham Court in the late 16th century and his family remained lords of the manor of West Wickham for almost four centuries. Early settlement in the village was scattered, probably beginning around the church and only later spreading up Corkscrew Hill to the present High Street. Tax returns from 1779 indicate that this was one of the three wealthiest villages in the present borough. Both the church and Wickham Court were remodelled in the 19th century; the latter's castle-like appearance was augmented by the addition of battlements and other modifications. At the eastern end of the High Street, R Norman Shaw extended West Wickham House in 1871, making influential use of his favoured Queen Anne style. The railway came here from EL-MERS END in 1882 but there was little scope for development until 50 acres of West Wickham Common were enclosed by Sir John Lennard and sold for building. The remaining 25 acres were preserved in 1892 with the aid of the Corporation of London. From the mid 1920s the electrification of the railway and the death of the protective Sir John Lennard brought a surge in housebuilding and the creation of the CONEY HALL estate from 1933. After World War II, West Wickham gained office blocks and an enhanced role as a shopping centre. Wickham Court served as a teacher training college until the arrival of the Schiller International University in 1978. After the university moved the higher education facility

to its WATERLOO campus, the mansion became a combined nursery and primary school in 2002 and added a senior department in 2005. West Wickham has a relatively elderly population, with a large number of pensioners and very few twenty-somethings. Nearly 95 per cent of the population is white, and 90 per cent of homes are owner-occupied. Less than 5 per cent of the housing stock dates from before 1918.

In 2000, Channel 4 Television returned 17 Braemar Gardens to its probable appearance in the 1940s and a family from West Yorkshire lived there for nine weeks as they would have done during World War II. To complete the illusion, West Wickham shopkeeper Nigel Lovegrove transformed his delicatessen into a 1940s-style grocer's, where the family did all their shopping. The house was also recreated at the Imperial War Museum.

West Wimbledon • *Merton*

An increasingly popular term describing the area immediately south of WIMBLEDON COMMON, taking in CROOKED BILLET, COPSE HILL, COTTENHAM PARK and some or all of RAYNES PARK. Many commentators consider 'West Wimbledon' to be an artifice, trading on the cachet of the WIMBLEDON name in an attempt to elevate the image of Raynes Park. Such techniques have been widely used by property developers and estate agents in areas close to many of London's more prestigious suburbs, such as Hampstead, Harrow and Dulwich, and more recently Clapham and Greenwich. And it is not a new phenomenon here; in 1937 the Southern Railway vetoed a proposal to rename Raynes Park station West Wimbledon. Christ Church, Copse Hill, became the mother church of the newly created parish of West Wimbledon in 1961. Merton council uses the term 'West Wimbledon' for the local conservation area, but this covers a relatively limited part of the district.

✉ SW20

@ www.christchurch-westwimbledon.org

Whetstone • *Barnet*

A stylish extended village situated on high ground between BARNET and NORTH FINCHLEY. It was first recorded as 'Weston' in the late 14th century, disproving the myth that the name derives from a large whetstone used to sharpen blades before the Battle of Barnet, and referring instead to the settlement's location west of FRIERN BARNET, its parochial parent. Whetstone grew up as a ribbon village on the Great North Road, which was flanked by houses and inns here by 1677. Most of its inhabitants were employed in woodland-related industries like charcoal burning or provided services to passing travellers, who had to pay a toll to use the road from 1825 until 1862. TOTTERIDGE and Whetstone station opened on the Great Northern Railway's branch line to HIGH BARNET in 1872. A few smart villas were built on the outskirts in the mid 19th century but the village itself had a reputation for drunkenness and brawling – and for outbreaks of typhoid – and remained solidly working-class until the 1920s. From this time semi-detached houses were built for the lower middle classes in the hinterland of the High Road, while more exclusive properties went up on land overlooking Dollis Brook. Around 1930 the first office blocks were built on the High Road, which also gained an impressive array of shops. Underground trains served the station from 1940. The eleven-storey, L-shaped office block now accommodating Barnet council offices was opened in 1966 as Ever Ready House, headquarters of the battery company. The modern High Road reflects the increasingly affluent nature of its catchment area, with smart cafés and restaurants, a Waitrose supermarket and a Friday farmers' market.

Claims that comic actor Stan Laurel lived in Whetstone some time before World War I have not been substantiated.

✉ N20

🚇 Northern Line (Totteridge and Whetstone, zone 4)

📖 John Heathfield, *Around Whetstone*, Sutton, 1994

Whipps Cross • *Waltham Forest*

A road junction and its vicinity, separating the eastern edge of WALTHAMSTOW from the northern tip of LEYTONSTONE. It is said that persons found stealing sheep or deer from adjacent parts of Epping Forest were whipped all the way from here to Walthamstow, but a more likely explanation of the name is that it is a corruption of Phippe's Cross, after late-14th-century resident John Phippe. Forest House was built in 1683 for a Huguenot banker and survived for almost three centuries. Several Georgian properties, built around 1767, survive along Whipps Cross Road (A114), which is now a conservation area. Residential development began in earnest during the 1850s after the enclosure of common land to the west. A terrace of four large Victorian houses has been converted into the Sir Alfred Hitchcock Hotel. The stately Whipps Cross Hospital was built in the grounds of Forest House in 1903. Four years later, the Whipps Cross Lido was dug without mechanical assistance as a winter unemployment relief scheme. In common with neighbouring parts of Walthamstow, Whipps Cross had a film studio in the early 20th century: the Precision Film Co. operated here from 1910 to 1915. Whipps Cross Lido was closed and filled in by the Corporation of London in the early 1980s but a nearby series of waterlogged gravel pits survive as the Hollow Ponds – or Hollow Pond, since they all join into one. The pond is designated a site of special scientific interest and serves as a boating lake in summer. Whipps Cross Hospital is presently undergoing a phased programme of redevelopment that will result in the creation of a totally new hospital by 2012.

The footballer David Beckham was born at Whipps Cross Hospital maternity unit in 1975.

✉ E11; E17

📖 Alwin Dormer, *Whipps Cross University Hospital: A View of its History*, Forest Medical Society, 2002

@ www.whippsx.nhs.uk (Whipps Cross University Hospital site)

Whitechapel • *Tower Hamlets*

A historic EAST END melting-pot situated east of ALDGATE. Some time in the 13th century the Church of St Mary Matfelon was founded and became known as *alba capella* or the white chapel. Around 1350, St Mary's became a parish church – although it survived only a few decades more before being rebuilt – and Whitechapel was the name given to the parish. The process of industrialization began locally in the late 15th century with the establishment of construction trades: brick- and tile-making, lime-burning and woodworking, accompanied by what John Stow later called the 'building of filthy cottages'. Jewish immigrants from Spain and Portugal settled here in the late 17th century, forming the nucleus of a community that would become known as 'the Jewish East End'. They were later joined by Germans, who established a Lutheran chapel and a Roman Catholic church. New industries included clothing, sugar refining, brewing and engineering. Whitechapel Bell Foundry moved to its present site from HOUNDSDITCH in 1738. It was here that the hour bell of the Great Clock of Westminster (known as Big Ben) and Philadelphia's Liberty Bell were cast. Construction of the London (now Royal London) Hospital began on the site of Red Lyon Farm in the 1790s, and it later gained fame for treating the 'elephant man' Joseph Merrick. A modest suburb evolved in the neighbouring streets, but many of the houses have since been replaced by ancillary hospital buildings. Over the course of the 19th century, Whitechapel's industries lost out to foreign competition while its housing became more overcrowded, especially after an influx of Ashkenazi Jews. One street of 176 houses had 2,516 inhabitants in 1881. Increasing hardship bred crime and prostitution, and the latter brought the district its enduring notoriety with Jack the Ripper's murders in 1888. Stories of white slavery may sound like urban myths, but there is well-documented evidence that this trade took place here around the end of the 19th century with local girls being tricked or threatened into working in the brothels of Buenos Aires, Cairo and Constantinople. Philanthropists worked hard to alleviate conditions, establishing every kind of life-improving institution, from soup kitchens to the Whitechapel Art Gallery, which is still a major cultural resource for the East End. Although it has its share of post-1960s monstrosities, Whitechapel was spared the wholesale redevelopment that took place further east after World War II, and thus retains enough dark alleys and cramped courts to attract 100,000 participants in Jack the Ripper walking tours every year. As Whitechapel's Jews moved to outer north and east London, their place was taken by south Asian immigrants, especially from the 1970s, and the majority of the population is now of Bangladeshi origin; 15,000 worshippers attended the inauguration of the London Muslim Centre in 2004. Half the housing is rented from the council or a housing association, a quarter is rented privately and a quarter is owner-occupied.

In the late 18th century Whitechapel produced one of Britain's most illustrious boxers, Daniel Mendoza, whose fame was so great that he became the first Jew to be permitted to address George III. Whitechapel has been the subject of dozens of books, mostly devoted to Jack the Ripper, but Iain Sinclair explored its dark side in a different way in *White Chapell, Scarlet Tracings* (1987).

⊠ E1

♦ 12,046

🚇 District Line; East London Line; Hammersmith & City Line (zone 2)

📖 Paul Begg, *Jack the Ripper*, Robson, 2004

@ www.whitechapelbellfoundry.co.uk; www.whitechapel.org (Whitechapel Art Gallery site)

White City • *Hammersmith & Fulham*

The northern part of SHEPHERD'S BUSH, now dominated by graceless corporate and residential monoliths. The original White City was a 200-acre complex built on both sides of Wood Lane with 25 palaces and halls, most covered in white stucco, a network of Venetian-style canals and a 150,000-capacity stadium. The Jewish-Hungarian émigré Imre Kiralfy was the driving force behind the project and appropriated its name from the White City at the Chicago Columbian exhibition, which he had visited in 1893. Opened in 1908, the venue hosted the Franco-British Exhibition and the Olympic Games in its inaugural year. Its last show, the Anglo-American Exposition, came just six years later and was closed prematurely because of the outbreak of World War I. By the early 1930s the exhibition halls had fallen into dereliction but the stadium was used by QUEEN'S PARK Rangers Football Club for two seasons. Finding this unprofitable, the club returned to its earlier home in Loftus Road. The London County Council demolished the beautiful but crumbling palaces and began to erect the 52-acre White City estate, which was completed after the war. Much of the rest of the exhibition site became home to BBC Television in the late 1950s. The BBC has progressively expanded the complex, building its corporate headquarters on the site of the old stadium in 1990. Across Wood Lane, a 37-acre shopping and leisure scheme is under construction, with associated affordable housing and new transport links.

White City's most famous resident was The

Who's guitarist Pete Townshend. His 1985 solo album was entitled *White City*, which he describes as 'a joke of a name' in the track *White City Fighting*. Tim Lott's novel *White City Blue* explores a number of male friendships forged in W12.

> ✉ W12
>
> ♦ 11,997 (Wormholt and White City ward)
>
> 🚌 Central Line (zone 2)
>
> 📖 Edward Platt, *Leadville: A Biography of the A40*, Picador, 2001

Whitehall • *Westminster*
The symbolic home of the executive branch of British government and the Civil Service, located south of TRAFALGAR SQUARE. The street becomes Parliament Street south of the Cenotaph. Evidence of prehistoric, Roman and Saxon activity has been found and the area has been continuously occupied since the 9th century. Walter de Grey, Archbishop of York, bought a property in the area soon after 1240 and called it York Place. Henry VIII rebuilt and extended the house to create the Palace of Whitehall, with amenities that included tennis courts, a bowling alley, a cockpit, formal gardens and orchards. During subsequent reigns, Whitehall became more a place of accommodation than recreation. In 1649, Charles I was executed outside the Banqueting House, which is the only part of the palace that now survives, the rest having been destroyed by fire in 1698. Whitehall was progressively rebuilt with offices of state. In 1735, Prime Minister Sir Robert Walpole moved into 10 Downing Street, a terraced house built on the cheap some 50 years earlier by the soldier and diplomat Sir George Downing, after it had been joined with a much grander property at the rear. The Treasury was completed in 1736 and by the end of the 18th century most of the key government offices were based in Whitehall. During the 19th century Whitehall became the administrative centre of the British Empire, and further building work by John Soane and Charles Barry brought architectural cohesion to the assortment of buildings. The Cenotaph is the United Kingdom's primary national war memorial. It was constructed from Portland stone in 1920 to the design of Sir Edwin Lutyens. The Cabinet War Rooms were adapted from an existing storage area beneath the Office of Works on King Charles Street and Winston Churchill began directing the British war effort from here in October 1939. The rooms were opened to the public in 1984 by the Imperial War Museum, which added a Churchill Museum in 2005.

In the mid 18th century, Whitehall provided the setting for a plethora of works by the Venetian artist Canaletto, most of which are now in private collections. The Whitehall farces were a series of plays performed at the Whitehall Theatre in the 1950s and 1960s, usually starring Brian Rix.

> ✉ SW1
>
> 📖 Peter Hennessy, *Whitehall*, Pimlico, 2001 (a history of the civil service)
>
> @ www.number-10.gov.uk; cwr.iwm.org.uk (Cabinet War Rooms)

White Hart Lane • *Haringey*
A long and winding thoroughfare connecting the High Roads of TOTTENHAM and WOOD GREEN, best known as the name (although not the actual address) of Tottenham Hotspur Football Club's stadium. The road was in existence by 1619, when its western part was called Apeland Street. The White Hart inn stood on the east side of the High Road in Tottenham and was used for court sessions in the 1650s. Some very grand country retreats were built along the lane in the 17th and 18th centuries but settlement remained sparse until around 1810, when suburban villas gradually began to spread westward from Tottenham's High Road. White Hart Lane station opened on the Great Eastern Railway in 1872 and its vicinity soon took on a more urban character. In 1901 the London County Council bought land between White Hart Lane and Lordship Lane for one of its first out-of-town cottage estates. The White Hart Lane estate was built in several stages and completed in the late 1920s. At the last census, 44 per cent of homes in the ward were rented from the council, a very high proportion, and 12 per cent did not have central heating; only 44 per cent of 16- to 74-year-olds were employed. At White Hart Lane Comprehensive School, Turkish is the most widely spoken mother tongue, followed by Kurdish, Somali, English, Bengali and Albanian. Tottenham's end of White Hart Lane has some of the borough's most affordable properties.

Tottenham Hotspur Football Club was formed (originally as Hotspur FC) from an older cricket club in 1882. 'Hotspur' was a nickname for Sir Henry Percy, eldest son of the first Earl of Northumberland, whose family subsequently became major landowners in Tottenham. Most of the club's founders were old boys of St John's Presbyterian School and Tottenham Grammar School. The newly professional club moved from NORTHUMBERLAND PARK in 1899 to a site behind the White Hart inn and soon became one of the most successful teams in southern England. Spurs' greatest achievements of recent times came in the 1960s (including the League and FA Cup double in 1961) but they were subsequently overshadowed by their long-time north London rival ARSENAL. Spurs is noted for its loyal fan base among north London's Jewish community.

✉ N17; N22

♁ 11,985

🚉 'one' Railway (zone 3)

📖 Alison Ratcliffe, *Tottenham Hotspur*, Rough Guides, 2005

@ www.spurs.co.uk

Whitewebbs • *Enfield*

A country park and golf course situated two miles north of ENFIELD TOWN on the east side of CREWS HILL. A mansion called Whitewebbs (also spelt as White Webbs) stood here from the mid 16th century and in 1570 it was granted to Robert Huicke, physician to Henry VIII and Elizabeth I. A small group of cottages coalesced around the mansion over a period of decades. The Gunpowder Plot was said to have been hatched at Whitewebbs in 1605, though this claim is also made for Eastbury Manor House in UPNEY, Barking. Land to the north of Whitewebbs Road became part of Theobalds Park on its enclosure in 1611 and was later turned over to farming. Following the much later enclosure of ENFIELD CHASE Dr Abraham Wilkinson established the 134-acre Whitewebbs Farm, which he subsequently enlarged, demolishing the old house and building a new one in 1791. This Whitewebbs was revamped in the style of a French chateau in 1881 and has since become an old people's home. A pumping station was built in 1898 to feed a loop of the New River and is now home to Whitewebbs Museum of Transport, which also hosts antiques fairs, model railway exhibitions and other events. Enfield council purchased the Whitewebbs estate from Sir Duncan Orr-Lewis in 1931 and divided it into a municipal golf course and a public park. The park consists of a mixture of open space and ancient woodland in which there are streams and small lakes.

✉ Enfield EN2

@ www.whitewebbsmuseum.co.uk

Whitton • *Richmond/Hounslow*

A residential suburb situated on the southeastern edge of HOUNSLOW and separated from TWICKENHAM by the Duke of Northumberland's River and the River Crane. Its name means 'white farm'. A heathside hamlet since the 11th century, Whitton's first spur to growth was the building of two great houses, Kneller Hall and Whitton Place. The German artist Sir Godfrey Kneller was the leading portrait painter of his day and founded the English Academy of Painting in 1711, the same year that he moved into his new house here. In 1725 the Earl of Islay, later third Duke of Argyll, built Whitton Place, a property so grand that one of its outbuildings later became a separate mansion. The first Kneller Hall was demolished in 1847 and replaced by the present building, where the Duke of Cambridge founded the Royal Military School of Music in 1857. Whitton did not acquire a separate church from Twickenham until 1862 and was still largely rural in character, with several strawberry gardens, until suburbanization began in earnest at the beginning of the 20th century. Developers knocked down Whitton Park's fine old buildings in 1911 and laid out a housing estate. The Chertsey Road (A316) sliced off the district's south-east corner in the early 1930s. Later that same decade Whitton acquired a High Street, with around 100 shops, on what had previously been a peaceful stretch of Percy Road. By 1950, bungalows and semi-detached houses had covered most of Whitton's former gardens and parkland. Because of the proximity of desirable Twickenham, house prices have risen relatively rapidly, especially in what estate agents call the Kneller Hall area, which has seen additional housebuilding recently. More than four-fifths of homes are owner-occupied, a very high proportion. During the summer months the Royal Military School of Music stages a series of outdoor concerts at Kneller Hall.

The rock singer and songwriter Elvis Costello grew up in Whitton, where his father had developed his own musical talents at the Royal Military School of Music.

✉ Twickenham TW2

♁ 9,149

🚉 South West Trains (zone 5)

@ www.army.mod.uk/schoolarmymusic (Corps of Army Music site)

Widmore • *Bromley*

A suburbanized hamlet located on the east side of BROMLEY, but in danger of being squeezed out of existence by estate agents' fondness for desirable BICKLEY. The name was first recorded as Withmere in 1226, and probably derives from Old English words meaning 'the pool where the willows grow'. Roman cinerary urns have been discovered here but no other evidence to support the suggested presence of a significant Roman settlement. Muriel Searle quotes an old story that Widmore would have been the site of Bromley's medieval church but for divine intervention: 'Bromley old church was attempted to be built at Wigmore [sic] but what was built by the men by day was carried away by night, and the stones placed where it now stands, so that the architect was at length obliged to acquiesce, and then the building regularly proceeded.' Instead of becoming the town centre, Widmore remained a quiet hamlet until well into the 19th century, disturbed only by the presence of a brickworks. After 1845, landowner John Wells began selling fields north of Widmore Road and the first substantial houses appeared in the district that was for a while known as New Bromley. By the late 1850s Widmore's 40 'pleasant residences' outnumbered its working-class cottages. Also north of Widmore Road lay the mansion of Freelands, whose occupants had included an ex-governor of the Bank of England and the widow of an archbishop of Canterbury. The estate was sold in 1888 and became the nucleus of Holy Trinity Convent, now a college. Much of present-day Widmore, south of Widmore Road, was formerly parkland belonging to the Bishop of Rochester's Bromley Palace. The land was developed as the Palace estate in the 1920s and 1930s. Bromley Adult Education College is headquartered at the Widmore Centre on Nightingale Lane.

✉ Bromley BR1

📖 Muriel V Searle, *Bickley, Widmore and Plaistow*, European Library, 1990

@ www.bromleyadulteducation.ac.uk (Widmore Centre site)

Widmore Green • *Bromley*

The old heart of the village of Widmore, separately identified on some maps to distinguish it from the later suburban sprawl to the south. The village green had a pond that was fed by water running off the slopes of Sundridge and Bromley. Villagers treated the green as common land for centuries but legal documents record a dispute over the ownership of the pond and its surroundings in 1637. A Methodist chapel was erected on Chislehurst Road in 1776, and it is possible that John Wesley visited here. Just over a century later the chapel was replaced by a larger building in Tylney Road, which survived until 1975. The historic focus of Widmore Green is the Oak public house, with some adjacent older properties and two parades of shops.

✉ Bromley BR1

Willesden • *Brent*

A densely developed district separated from WEMBLEY to its west by the River Brent. The name referred to a hill by a spring or stream and its first confirmed appearance was in Domesday Book in 1086, when the manor was owned by the dean and chapter of ST PAUL'S Cathedral. The shape of Willesden's parish remained largely unchanged for almost a thousand years and stretched as far as the present-day districts of BRONDESBURY, CRICKLEWOOD and PARK ROYAL. At the centre of the parish, settlements formed around St Mary's Church and the manor house at CHURCH END and to the east at WILLESDEN GREEN. An intermediate hamlet grew up at CHAPEL END after 1820. From the middle of the 19th century substantial houses were built for City merchants and professionals but Willesden's character began to change after the coming of the railways. WILLESDEN JUNCTION station opened in 1866, prompting the growth of HARLESDEN as a separate district. The Metropolitan Railway had a more direct effect on the growth of Willesden itself, with a station opening at Willesden Green in 1879 and at NEASDEN the following year. The rapid spread of working-class housing made Willesden the fastest-growing district in the London area during the 1890s. With the arrival of bus and tram services, shopping centres and industry flourished from the beginning of the 20th century, while northward residential development covered the farmland of DUDDEN HILL and DOLLIS HILL. Willesden became a municipal borough in 1933 and the incoming Labour council immediately set about building estates in the outlying areas not yet covered by housing. So keen was the council to reduce overcrowding that it left few open spaces, with the notable exception of Gladstone Park, in the far north of the then borough's area. Willesden's importance as an industrial area declined markedly after World War II and factories were steadily replaced by warehouses or residential schemes. During the 1960s and 1970s many of the late-Victorian terraces in Church End – and Willesden's town hall – were pulled down and replaced by blocks of council flats and the area is currently undergoing regeneration. Migrants from the Caribbean, the Indian subcontinent, West Africa and most recently the Antipodes have created one of London's most diverse communities.

Willesden formed the backdrop for ITV's long-running series *Minder*, but its greatest modern claim to fame is as the setting for Zadie Smith's 2000 story of interracial relationships, *White Teeth*. 'Zadie Smith is to Willesden what Shakespeare is to Stratford-upon-Avon,' said *The Times*.

> ✉ NW10
>
> 📖 A Spencer, *Willesden*, Sutton, 1996; Len Snow, *Willesden Past*, Phillimore, 1994

Willesden Green • *Brent*

The east end of WILLESDEN, now seen as more desirable than other parts of the district because it escaped wholesale redevelopment with high-rise council estates after World War II. This was the geographical centre of Willesden parish from the late Anglo-Saxon period, when a hamlet grew up in a forest clearing beside a tributary of the River Brent. St Mary's Church and Willesden manor house formed the nucleus of the separate settlement of CHURCH END, to the west. Cottages and farmhouses clustered around the spacious green during the Middle Ages and eleven people were assessed for rates here in 1687. The Spotted Dog inn was in existence by the mid 18th century, when orchards had been planted. Several villas were built after enclosure in 1823, together with tradesmen's premises and more cottages. Villas were built for the upper middle classes from the 1860s but the arrival of the Metropolitan Railway in 1879 marked the end of this phase. Willesden Green had been dominated by one large farm, Bramley's, and one mansion, Gowan House, and both were bought by the United Land Co., which sold on plots to builders of cramped terraced houses. In 1887 St Andrew's parish church was built on the High Road and by 1901 the ward had 18,948 inhabitants, whom the vicar described as mostly poor, irreligious and accustomed to spending Sundays in bed. After World War II the council planned to clear and rebuild the entire area except for the immediate vicinity of the station but implemented only a fraction of its proposals. With

its low property values, Willesden Green became a popular place for immigrants to settle from the late 1950s, including many from Ireland and the Caribbean. From the 1980s, regeneration funding brought improvements to the High Road (A407), including the opening in 1989 of a new library. More recently, the area has attracted young adults on a tight budget and the ward now has a large number of residents in their twenties – more than twice the national average. Most people rent their homes and do not have access to a car. Unlike most of the borough, whites and Christians are in a slight majority.

Willesden Green is the title of a mock-country song by the Kinks, recorded for the 1971 film *Percy*.

> ✉ NW2; NW10
>
> 👥 12,714
>
> 🚌 Jubilee Line (zones 2 and 3)
>
> 📖 M C Barrès-Baker, *Willesden Green*, Grange Museum of Community History and Brent Archive, 2001

Willesden Junction • *Brent/Hammersmith & Fulham*

A rail interchange and neighbouring 'area of intensification' situated north of OLD OAK COMMON. Despite its name the station is very much in HARLESDEN – indeed its opening in 1866 was primarily responsible for Harlesden's transformation from a rural to an urban character. Most main-line services stopped here in the early days and the railway company ran buses to STONEBRIDGE PARK and CHURCH END. The station was unexpectedly successful, drawing trade and workmen to the immediate vicinity. Marshalling yards and engine sheds were added from 1873. Colonel R J Nightingale Tubbs developed an estate of terraced housing primarily for railway workers and the London and North Western Railway built Harley Terrace for its employees in the 1890s. Underground services reached Willesden Junction in 1915. During the 20th century the land between the railway lines and the Grand Union Canal filled with industrial estates, some of which are now in a neglected state but are the subject of Hammersmith and Fulham council's renewal efforts. Hythe Road is dominated by 'London's largest car supermarket', a multi-site operation with thousands of second-hand cars. Willesden Junction bus depot opened in 2003 on Station Approach. Silverlink Metro has been running an increasing number of services out of Willesden Junction in recent years and the station is targeted for further development as a connective hub.

The UK's first fully realistic bus simulator came into use at Willesden Junction bus depot in 2005. Trainee bus drivers have to navigate the fictional London district of Firsdon, which is named after the project's co-sponsors, bus operator First and Transport for London. People involved in the project have given their names to Firsdon's buildings and streets, which include Livingstone Drive.

> ✉ NW10

> 🚌 Silverlink Metro; Bakerloo Line (zone 3)

Wimbledon • *Merton*

The home of tennis and a Victorian and Edwardian suburb, situated two miles south of PUTNEY. The name derives from Old English words meaning 'the hill of a man called Wynnman (or Wymbald)'. A battle is believed to have been fought here by the kings of Wessex and Kent in 598. The parish church of St Mary is of Saxon origin but has been rebuilt three times since the Middle Ages. Around the 13th century, a collection of cottages and farmsteads were established on the heights of WIMBLEDON COMMON, which functioned as a grazing and hunting ground and a source of wood and water, but a settlement did not begin to coalesce around the present-day High Street for another 400 years. The village was long part of the manor of MORTLAKE, held by the archbishops of Canterbury. After the Reformation the powerful Cecil family took a lease on the rectory and then built the first of a succession of manor houses in what is now WIMBLEDON PARK. The first station opened in 1838, augmented by a link with CROYDON in 1855. From then onwards the parkland started to be sold off for redevelopment and Wimbledon grew rapidly as a desirable suburb, especially in the COPSE HILL and COTTENHAM PARK areas of WEST WIMBLEDON. To the south 'New Wimbledon' (later SOUTH WIMBLEDON) was mushrooming between the railway line and MERTON, accounting for half the population of 16,000 in 1881. The arrival of the District Railway in 1889 enhanced the prestige of villas in Wimbledon Park but many of the early properties here were replaced with more affordable homes from the 1920s, when the All England Lawn Tennis and Croquet Club took up residence in Church Road. Change after World War II was mostly limited to the subdivision of large houses and the construction of relatively unobtrusive blocks of municipal and private flats. With the disappearance of the

great houses, the Wat Buddhapadipa, a Thai Buddhist temple on Calonne Road, can claim to be Wimbledon's grandest building today. The Broadway, with its Centre Court shopping centre, offers a comparatively gritty contrast to the upmarket village on the hill, which has appealing boutiques, bars and restaurants. Other amenities on the Broadway include the Polka Theatre, which specializes in productions for young audiences, and the New Wimbledon Theatre. The last decade has witnessed a remarkable influx of white South African immigrants, who tend to work in finance, health, education or social services and speak English rather than Afrikaans.

The poet and novelist Robert Graves was born in Wimbledon in 1895. *The Wimbledon Poisoner* (1990) was the first in Nigel Williams's series of comic novels set in the area. In Graham Swift's *The Light of Day* (2003), George Webb's detective agency operates out of an office above a tanning studio on the Broadway.

> ✉ SW19

> 👥 92,622 (parliamentary constituency)

> 🚌 South West Trains; District Line terminus; Croydon Tramlink interchange (zone 3)

> 📖 Richard Milward, *Wimbledon Past*, Historical Publications, 1998

> @ www.wimbledonvisitor.com (tourist information site);
> www.newwimbledontheatre.co.uk;
> www.polkatheatre.com

Wimbledon Chase • *Merton*

A station, open space and small conservation area situated on the western edge of Merton. Wimbledon Chase was a group of fields on the southern side of WIMBLEDON where stag hunts were organized during the 19th century. Rail services began to operate from the station in 1929, when the first section of the Wimbledon to SUTTON line opened as far as SOUTH MERTON. The line ran through the council's Whatley estate at CANNON HILL and the railway company was obliged to build a mile and a half of embankment to minimize the loss of estate land. An eight-acre conservation area lies to the north-east of the station and takes in Chatsworth Avenue, Richmond Avenue and Quintin Avenue, which were built in the early years of the 20th century on the site of Merton Hall Farm. The terraced and semi-detached houses are varied in style but complementary in character, with good use of moulded bricks, terracotta panels and decorative glazing. Nearer the station, most properties date from the 1920s and 1930s, with some later infilling and recent compact blocks of flats. Housing on the south side of Kingston Road occupies the site of Bakers End farmhouse, later called Broadwater House. To the north, the narrow strip that remains of the Chase itself has been preserved as a public footpath and an open space with some mature trees. The well-regarded Wimbledon Chase Primary School is situated on Merton Hall Road. It began life in 1924 as Wimbledon County School for Girls. Wimbledon Chase Middle School took over the buildings in 1969 and became a primary school in 2001.

John Howard Martin was an early pioneer in film production, specializing in short films and comic features, often involving trick photography. In 1913 he set up his own studio at 2/4 Quintin Road and went on to establish MERTON PARK studios in the 1920s.

⊠ SW20

🚊 Thameslink (zone 3)

Wimbledon Common · *Merton*

A plateau of bogs and heathland stretching from RICHMOND PARK to WIMBLEDON town. This is London's largest common, covering 1,200 acres including PUTNEY HEATH. Its most ancient feature is Bensbury Camp, popularly though misleadingly known as Caesar's Camp, a hill-fort that probably dates from around the seventh century BC. The common was for centuries part of the manor of MORTLAKE, owned by the archbishops of Canterbury, with rights of hunting and grazing granted to local tenants. It acquired a reputation as a duelling ground: the politicians Pitt the Younger, Castlereagh and Canning were among those who fought here. Earl Spencer gained legal authority to enclose the common in 1803, but backed down in the face of local protests. The best-known landmark on Wimbledon Common is the windmill, built in 1817 to grind corn and now a museum devoted to windmills and woodworking. The common has been in public ownership since 1871, but only when the National Rifle Association left for Bisley in 1889 did full freedom of movement become possible. Golf was played informally on the common from the early 19th century, and the London Scottish Golf Club (later the Royal Wimbledon Golf Club) was founded there in 1864. Players are required to wear a red sweater or jacket (originally a red coat) on the golf course. In 1948 the

council opened Cannizaro Park at the common's south-eastern corner. This had been the gardens of Warren House, once owned by the Duke of Cannizaro, whose exotic name stuck to the estate even after the house burned down in 1900. The gardens are particularly admired for their rhododendrons and azaleas.

In a cottage beside the windmill, Robert Baden-Powell began to write *Scouting for Boys* in 1907. Elizabeth Beresford created the *Wombles of Wimbledon Common* in 1968 and the environmentally conscious creatures gained their own television series in 1973.

⊠ SW19; SW20

@ www.wpcc.org.uk (Wimbledon and Putney Commons Conservators site)

📖 Tony Drakeford and Una Sutcliffe (eds), *Wimbledon Common and Putney Heath*, Wimbledon and Putney Commons Conservators, 2000

Wimbledon Park · *Merton/Wandsworth*

A Victorian and interwar conservation area in north WIMBLEDON, and the home of British tennis. In 1588, Sir Thomas Cecil built the first of Wimbledon's four manor houses, a two-storey brick mansion with a deer park and 20 acres of gardens, near the rectory that his father had acquired some 40 years earlier. The estate was sold to the Spencer family in the early 18th century and inherited by 11-year-old John Spencer in 1748, whereupon his trustees doubled the size of its grounds to more than 1,200 acres. In 1765, the year in which he was created an earl, Spencer commissioned Capability Brown to landscape the park and create a 30-acre lake where there had once been a bog. After the death of the third earl in 1845, the Spencers sold all their property here to insurance magnate John Augustus Beaumont. He soon began releasing large chunks of the northern half of the park to wealthy individuals who commissioned architects and landscape gardeners to create prestigious homes. The park was mooted as a possible site for the CRYSTAL PALACE but the price of land was too high and its management company chose Sydenham instead. Beaumont sold Wimbledon Park House in 1872 and began to lay out the roads surrounding it, although many plots stayed on the market until the arrival of the District Railway in 1889. In that year Beaumont's daughter, Lady Lane, leased part of the park to cricket, tennis and golf clubs, while land near the railway line was built up with terraced housing of smaller proportions than the neighbourhood had seen before. In 1914, Lady Lane sold the remainder of the park to the council for public use. During the 1920s and 1930s, developers filled the grounds of the earliest and grandest properties with detached houses of a more modest size but still of high quality and with large gardens. The All England Lawn Tennis and Croquet Club moved from Worple Road to Church Road in 1922. The club hosts the Wimbledon tennis championships every June–July, and over half a million spectators attend over a two-week period.

Mary Anne Evans, better known by her pen name George Eliot, lived at Holly Lodge, 31 Wimbledon Park Road, where she completed *The Mill on the Floss*. The children's storyteller and illustrator Raymond Briggs was born in Wimbledon Park in 1934.

✉ SW19

🚌 District Line (zone 3)

📖 Bernard Rondeau, *Wimbledon Park: From Private Park to Residential Suburb*, self-published, 1995

@ www.wimbledon.org (Wimbledon tennis championships site)

Wimpole Street • *Westminster*

A 'long unlovely street', according to Tennyson, which runs north–south through central MA-RYLEBONE and is now best known for dentistry. Wimpole Hall is a palatial house in Cambridgeshire that belonged to the Harley family, developers of the Cavendish estate. Begun around 1724, Wimpole Street had just seven houses by the end of the decade. The Irish statesman and philosopher Edmund Burke was living here in 1759, at a time when the street was beginning to fill with substantial, if uninspiring, terraced houses. Upper Wimpole Street was created after the closure of Marylebone Gardens in 1778. Like Harley Street and the rest of the immediate area, Wimpole Street soon attracted the cream of London's fashionable society, before being colonized by doctors, mainly from the 1820s. Later still, the street gained popularity with opticians and dentists; Arthur Conan Doyle opened his ophthalmic practice in Upper Wimpole Street in 1891. The Royal Society of Medicine came to 1 Wimpole Street in 1912. The British Dental Association and the General Dental Council are both based in the street and private dental consultants still abound here.

A different kind of suffering has guaranteed the street's place in history. Elizabeth Barrett was kept a virtual prisoner at 50 Wimpole Street by her tyrannical father before eloping to Italy with fellow poet Robert Browning in 1846. The story of *The Barretts of Wimpole Street* became the subject of a play and a 1934 film, remade in 1957 with John Gielgud as the patriarch. In Jane Austen's *Mansfield Park* (1814), Mr Rushworth takes a house in Wimpole Street after his marriage. Professor Henry Higgins lives at 27A Wimpole Street in George Bernard Shaw's play *Pygmalion*. Paul McCartney stayed at 57 Wimpole Street, the home of his girlfriend's parents, from 1963 to 1966. He wrote *I Wanna Hold Your Hand* and *Yesterday* here.

✉ W1

@ www.bda-dentistry.org.uk (British Dental Association site)

Winchmore Hill • *Enfield*

A superior Edwardian and interwar suburb focused on an agreeable village green, separated since the 15th century from SOUTHGATE to its west by the Grovelands estate. The origin of the name is uncertain but it is probably a corruption of a personal name (Wynsige) plus 'mere', which could have meant a boundary or a pond. When the hamlet was first recorded in 1319 its inhabitants subsisted by coppicing oak trees or cultivating assarted fields (fields cut out of woodland). A Quaker community existed here in 1688. By 1801 a thriving settlement had grown up around Winchmore Hill Green and on several of the roads that led to it, mixing elegant houses and weatherboarded cottages. A spa flourished briefly in the early 19th century after well-water was found to contain Epsom salts. St Paul's Church was built in 1827 and refurbished after a fire in 1844. A station opened in 1871 on the Great Northern Railway's new branch line to ENFIELD TOWN. Winchmore Hill had around 500 houses by 1882 but most of the landed gentry whose estates abutted the village could not be tempted to sell to the builders so there was little further development for the next two decades. This hiatus was similar to the situation that prevailed in Southgate and PALMERS GREEN, largely because they shared the same clique of landowners. But Southgate had no station at that time and Palmers Green lacked a picturesque core, so it was Winchmore Hill that grew faster and better when the great estates finally came onto the market in the early years of the 20th century. In 1909 ambitious plans were announced to create a 'woodland city' at

559

Winchmore Hill Wood but these came to nothing. When they ran out of greenfield sites builders bought up some early villas with spacious gardens and replaced them with groups of smaller properties and by 1935 Winchmore Hill was almost entirely built up. Property specifications ranged from adequate to deluxe, reaching their apogee in Broad Walk. A conservation area covers much of the old village centre west of the railway line. The typical Winchmore Hill resident is a home-owning, high-level manager in good health.

The poet Thomas Hood came to live in Rose Cottage on Vicars Moor Lane in 1829 and his wife bore their third child here. Although the Hoods were not wealthy, their home was a grander affair than its quaint name suggests. The family moved to WANSTEAD in 1832.

> ✉ N21
>
> ♟ 12,225
>
> 🚉 WAGN Railway (zone 4)
>
> 📖 Stuart Delvin, *A History of Winchmore Hill*, Regency Press, 1989

Winsor Park • *Newham*

A rarely used name for the part of EAST BECKTON centred on Winsor Terrace, which was built in the 1870s to house employees of Beckton's new gasworks. Frederic Winsor was the anglicized name of Friedrich Albrecht Winzler, the Bavarian founder of the Gas, Light and Coke Co.. Now one of the oldest surviving parts of this greatly regenerated district, its generously proportioned end-of-terrace houses were reserved for the company foremen, while the underlings had to be content with two-up, two-down dwellings. Winsor Primary School, at the southern end of East Ham Manor Way, serves a multinational catchment area. The educational standards agency Ofsted has reported that almost half the pupils speak English as an additional language and that they come from 35 different countries. Not surprisingly, performance in English at key stage 2 is among the worst in London, but the school's performance is rated as effective.

> ✉ E6

Woodberry Down • *Hackney*

A very large housing estate situated just east of MANOR HOUSE, comprising the area within a loop of the New River. This was dairy farmland until the 1820s, when it was opened up by new roads and the conversion of disused clay pits into reservoirs alleviated the threat of flooding. By the early 20th century it had become 'the posh end of STOKE NEWINGTON', home to several wealthy Jewish families and to Albert Chevalier, the music hall artiste. In 1934, despite powerful opposition, the London County Council compulsorily purchased all of Woodberry Down and the construction of an 'estate of the future' began after World War II. By the time the project was completed in 1962, 57 blocks of flats had been erected on 64 acres of land. The 2,500 homes have a mix of deck access and lobby access, with the majority being two- or three-bedroom flats. Woodberry Down School, now closed, became one of Britain's first purpose-built comprehensive schools in 1955. Like some other utopian schemes, Woodberry Down is today a flawed place in which to live, with an array of characteristic inner-city issues and flats that have structural problems, water penetration and few amenities. A regeneration plan is under way to provide new and refurbished housing and improve residents' 'life chances'. Proposals under discussion at the time of writing envisage the replacement of all existing social rented housing and the provision of 1,226 new dwellings, possibly including tower blocks (euphemistically referred to as 'tall buildings'), with improvements to community retail and service provision as well as public open space.

> ✉ N4
>
> 📖 Woodberry Down Memories Group, *Woodberry Down Memories: The History of an LCC Housing Estate*, ILEA Education Resource Unit for Older People, 1989 (a model of participative local history); Harriett Reynolds Chetwynd, *Comprehensive School: The Story of Woodberry Down*, Routledge & Kegan Paul, 1960

Woodcote • *Croydon/Sutton*

Originally an extensive estate stretching from present-day CLOCK HOUSE in the south to WALLINGTON in the north. Most street atlases now identify Woodcote as the locality on the western side of PURLEY, which is treated in this gazetteer as UPPER WOODCOTE. The name was first recorded in 1200 and means 'the cottage in or by a wood'. Woodcote was the grounds and farmland of a mansion known at various points in its existence as Woodcote, Woodcote Lodge and Woodcote Hall. The first lodge stood from at least the early 16th century, surrounded by sheep pasture and rabbit warrens, and it was home to a succession of wealthy owners and leaseholders. The earliest parts of the present Woodcote Hall date from before 1820. Parts of the Woodcote estate were sold off for housebuilding from the latter half of the 19th century. The earliest large-scale development was the creation in the 1860s of CARSHALTON ON THE HILL on the western edge of the estate. In 1901 William Webb built Upper Woodcote House as the centrepiece of a pioneering garden estate. With the accessibility brought by the railway, the north-eastern part of Woodcote was absorbed within Wallington between the wars. Well-proportioned Victorian villas were knocked down and replaced with suburban houses, while flats and shops lined Woodcote Road. At the south-western end of the former estate, LITTLE WOODCOTE has remained largely unspoilt to the present day. Woodcote Hall was extensively restored in 1963 and is now entirely surrounded by modern Wallington. It stands on Woodcote Avenue, at the corner of Park Hill Road.

✉ Purley CR8; Wallington SM6; Carshalton SM5

Woodcote Green • *Sutton*

A semi-rural locality situated on the far southern edge of WALLINGTON. The green itself is a small triangle at the junction of Sandy Lane South and Woodcote Road (A237). Surrey County Council built some houses at Woodcote Green in 1912 and much pricier properties have since filled the former fields east of Woodcote Road. A garden centre and nursery, established in 1959, occupies 26 acres of Woodcote Green. Wallington High School for Girls moved to a purpose-built complex west of the green in 1965 and acquired specialist status in engineering in 1994. A third of the students at this high-performing selective school are non-white, mostly of Asian descent.

There are other Woodcote Greens in England, including one not far away in Epsom.

✉ Wallington SM6

@ www.woodcotegreennurseries.co.uk;
www.wallingtongirls.sutton.sch.uk

Wood End • *Ealing*

The north-eastern part of NORTHOLT, but widely considered to represent the northern tip of GREENFORD. The settlement originated from a 13th-century grant of land to the Hospital of St Thomas of Acon, a City monastery. The manorial estate of around a hundred acres was originally known as Le Freres or Freres Place and the hamlet of Wood End grew up around the capital messuage – the estate's

principal group of dwellings. Wood End lived up to its name by retaining substantial woodland well into the 18th century. By the late 19th century the estate was in the hands of William Perkin, the pioneering chemist of GREENFORD GREEN. Perkin's land was sold in 1907 and the estate was broken up after 1920. The Royal Air Force erected a radio mast on Wood End Lane in 1926, briefly delaying the incursion of suburban housebuilding, which began in earnest in the 1930s. In response to Wood End's growth, a school was built in 1931 and progressively enlarged over the next few years. The council's Wood End estate suffers from a relatively high level of deprivation, with a number of overcrowded households. The majority of pupils at Wood End infant and junior schools come from the estate. After English, the schools' most widely spoken languages are Gujarati, Punjabi, Farsi and Cantonese.

The rock keyboard player Rick Wakeman grew up here and went to Wood End infant and junior schools.

✉ Northolt UB5

Wood End • *Hillingdon*

Now the north-central part of HAYES, with community facilities. While its name is broadly self-explanatory, John Field suggests in *Place Names of Greater London* that it may allude to the 'part of the woodland for 400 swine referred to in the Domesday Book description of the manor of Hayes'. Although there is evidence of Anglo-Saxon settlement in nearby Hayes, YEADING and BOTWELL, no mention was made of Wood End until the early 16th century. However, it was probably occupied earlier, since by the 1590s it consisted of 25 dwellings, 16 of them cottages, surrounded by enclosed land. Wood End House was built in the 17th century. By 1754 Wood End, HAYES END and Hayes formed a continuous area of houses, the majority on the south-western side of the main road to UXBRIDGE. The area was agricultural and largely remained so until the latter part of the 19th century. Between 1901 and 1903 the London United Tramways Co. extended its line from SOUTHALL to Uxbridge along the main road and some building took place in Wood End before World War I. The northern ends of Tudor Road, Cromwell Road and North Road were developed and some houses were built around Hemmen Lane and Church Road. Most of the residential property in the area surrounding Wood End was built between the wars, mostly as a result of industrial development in other parts of Hayes. Barra Hall, formerly known as Grove Lodge, was purchased by the council in 1923 and afterwards used as the town hall. Wood End House continued to accommodate council departments until its demolition in 1960. Its site is now occupied by the gardens of the Beck Theatre, which was built in the mid 1970s. Barra Hall was renovated and opened as a Sure Start children's centre in 2005. The hall's grounds are an attractive public park with an open-air theatre. Wood End Park Primary School is a very large community school located at the south-western edge of the locality. Just over a third of pupils speak English as an additional language, and Punjabi, Urdu, Gujarati and Somali are the most prevalent minority languages.

✉ Hayes UB3

Woodford • *Redbridge*

'The geographical and social high point of east London', situated to the north-east of WALTHAMSTOW, from which it is separated by a sliver of Epping Forest. Woodford takes its name from a ford across the River Roding at present-day WOODFORD BRIDGE. Like CHINGFORD to the west, the district was for centuries a collection of separate hamlets in forest clearings. Even before the Restoration, wealthy Londoners had begun to build grand houses here, and others later rented rooms for the summer. In the mid 18th century these rooms were said to be more expensive than in the capital itself. By the time Woodford was deforested in the early 19th century there were so many mansions with large gardens that there was hardly any room for agriculture. Before the opening of the station in 1856, 'Woodford' was another name for the vicinity of St Mary's Church, also known as Church End, but the name now encompasses the whole district. The coming of the railway brought suburban development, but not of the densely terraced kind so common elsewhere, because the railway company did not offer cheap fares for workmen. The council also conspired to keep out the lower classes by refusing entry to trams. The British Land Co. bought the Woodford Hall estate in 1869 and laid out new roads west of the church. A series of similar developments in the grounds of old houses followed over the next 60 years and almost the whole of modern Woodford was built up by the outbreak of World War II. The privately developed estates were often of the highest quality, especially in the west. More affordable properties

were built in SOUTH WOODFORD and east of the railway line, together with some post-war council estates, the largest of which is Broadmead, completed in 1968. This central part of Woodford has two main shopping streets: Snakes Lane, which is split in two by the railway, and Broadmead Road. The Broadway, with its curved terraces of attractively detailed three-storey shops nuzzling up to the station, is now one of Woodford's many conservation areas. Further east, Ray Park was formerly the grounds of the 17th-century Ray House. Ironically, negotiations for its purchase by Bryant and May were abruptly halted when the house was devastated by fire. The company used the grounds as a sports facility in the middle decades of the 20th century. Ray Park's nurseries now produce a quarter of a million bedding plants for the borough every year.

Winston Churchill was MP for Woodford for 40 years from 1924. Former Labour prime minister Clement Attlee lived at 17 Monkhams Avenue. Other past residents have included the artist, craftsman and socialist William Morris and the suffragette Sylvia Pankhurst.

✉ Woodford Green IG8

🏃 41,844 (Bridge, Church End, Monkhams and Roding wards)

🚇 Central Line (zone 4)

📖 Peter Lawrence and Georgina Green, *Woodford: A Pictorial History*, Phillimore, 1995; Reginald L Fowkes, *Woodford Then and Now*, After the Battle, 1990

@ www.wansteadandwoodfordguardian.co.uk (online version of local newspaper)

Woodford Bridge • *Redbridge*

A pleasant residential enclave divided from the rest of WOODFORD by the M11 motorway and spreading over the Essex border into the Epping Forest district. Before the first bridge was built in the 13th century, there was a woodland ford across the River Roding on the road to Abridge. The medieval village that grew up by the river was the first settlement in the area and the origin of the name 'Woodford'. Complaints were made about the state of the horse bridge in 1404 but it was not until 1573 that it was replaced by a wooden cart bridge. A stone bridge replaced the wooden crossing in 1768 but this was destroyed by floods only three years later. Understandably, a more resilient structure was then erected, which remained here for almost two centuries. St Paul's Church was built on the upper green in 1854 and restored after a fire later in the century. Woodford Bridge had 1,188 inhabitants in 1871, when suburban expansion was just beginning. Several attractive properties survive from the latter decades of the 19th century as part of a conservation area, as do rows of Edwardian shops. The fastest period of growth came in the 1930s and most of the present housing dates from this period. The Ashton playing fields were opened in 1937 to celebrate the incorporation of the Borough of Wanstead and Woodford. Woodford Bridge was the last of Woodford's hamlets to connect with what had by then become the main body of the district. The ward is socially and economically mixed, and 80 per cent of residents are of white British origin. Fewer than 10 per cent of pupils at Roding Primary School are at an early stage of learning English.

✉ Woodford Green IG8

👤 11,211 (Bridge ward)

Woodford Green • *Redbridge*

The west-central part of WOODFORD, and for centuries its most fashionable hamlet. The wide village green stretches along the eastern side of the High Road (A104) for almost a mile and is claimed to have the oldest village cricket field still in use. There was a windmill on the green in the 17th century that formed the nucleus of a hamlet called Woodford Row. By the time the mill was demolished in 1757 a cluster of mansions had begun to appear. One of the grandest of these, Hurst House, was built in 1714 for a prominent brewer and is still a private home. The house was known as 'the Naked Beauty', after a statue by the Italian sculptor Francesco Monti that stood in its garden. Woodford County High School for Girls is based at Highams, a mansion built to the west of the green in 1768, with gardens that were later landscaped by Humphry Repton. Its huge grounds stretched a considerable way into WALTHAMSTOW and were afterwards developed as the HIGHAMS PARK. Woodford New Road (A104) provided a stimulus to further development when it was cut through the forest in 1829, allegedly to expedite the king's journeys to Newmarket. After the mid 19th century the High Road became a prestigious shopping centre for the wider district. Epping Forest continued to cover much of the area until the 1880s, when high-class suburban estates began to be developed. In the early 20th century the locality absorbed the hamlet of Church End to its south, forming a continuum with SOUTH WOODFORD. By the outbreak of

World War II it had also fully merged with WOODFORD WELLS to the north. A statue of Winston Churchill, the local MP for 40 years, was erected on the green in 1959. A village sign near the corner of the High Road and Broadmead Road depicts forest cattle, All Saints' spire, a cricket wicket and the Churchill statue.

The author James Hilton wrote the novels *Goodbye Mr Chips* and *Lost Horizon* at his home in Oak Hill Gardens. Both stories were turned into successful films.

✉ Woodford Green IG8

@ www.woodford.redbridge.sch.uk (Woodford County High School for Girls)

Woodford Wells • *Redbridge*

The northernmost of the ribbon of hamlets that has coalesced to form the modern district of WOODFORD. The presence of a spring was recorded in 1285, although its precise location is unknown. Despite claims for the medicinal properties of its waters, an 18th-century spa was never a commercial success but the name has stuck. Because of its remoteness, there was little residential development here until the mid 19th century, when some detached and semi-detached villas were built in the village, together with some outlying mansions. All Saints' Church was built at the northern end of WOODFORD GREEN in 1874 on a site given by Henry Ford Barclay of Monkhams, one of Woodford's grandest homes. In 1889 Bancroft's School moved from MILE END to palatial red-brick premises on the west side of the High Road (A104). Roman Catholic and United Free churches were constructed around the turn of the 20th century. The grounds of several former mansions were built up before and after World War I. The Knighton estate was developed from 1931, although 47 acres of its wood survive, and the northern part of the Monkhams estate was laid out as a garden suburb in the 1930s, with infilling continuing long after the war. Woodford Wells' conservation area is effectively an extension of Woodford Green's, covering the immediate vicinity of the High Road almost to the borough border. Woodford Wells' distance from the heart of the main shopping area has made it harder for shops to flourish here, despite the relative affluence of most residents. The typical household in the Monkhams ward has 6.1 rooms, significantly higher than in most parts of London, and the average resident is five years older than in the borough as a whole. At Wells Primary School, few pupils are entitled to free school meals and 17 different ethnic heritages were represented in 2005, although by far the largest consisted of those from a white British background.

The Devil in Woodford Wells is a semi-autobiographical novel by the drama critic Harold Hobson, with plentiful local detail and history.

> ✉ Woodford Green IG8

> 📖 Harold Hobson, *The Devil in Woodford Wells*, Longmans, 1946

Woodgrange Park • *Newham*

An attractive Victorian estate with recent additions, located on the border of FOREST GATE and MANOR PARK. The name is applied only to the immediate vicinity of the station. Woodgrange, which means 'a farm in a forest clearing', was first recorded in 1198, when it was in the possession of Stratford Abbey. The manor remained in agricultural use until it was sold to Thomas Corbett in the 1850s. Corbett and his son Cameron sold part of the farm for use as a cemetery and developed the remainder over a 15-year period from 1877, with building progressing from east to west. This was Cameron Corbett's first such project and he went on to become one of London's greatest suburban housebuilders. The Woodgrange estate was a well-planned development of 700 homes with architectural detailing that echoed Victorian railway stations. The first burials took place at Woodgrange Park Cemetery in 1889 and Woodgrange Park station opened on a spur of the Tottenham and Forest Gate Railway in 1894. The Woodgrange estate was designated a conservation area in 1976, but not before many original features had been lost. Woodgrange Park Village is a small housing association estate built in the 1990s to the east of the station. Controversy arose in 2000 when developers Bellway Urban Renewal exhumed more than 12,000 bodies from a disused part of Woodgrange Park Cemetery in preparation for building 120 new apartments. The bodies, many of them Blitz victims, were reinterred elsewhere in the cemetery but local residents expressed disapproval of the way in which the remains were handled. Besides English, the languages of Woodgrange Park include Bengali, Punjabi, Urdu and Gujarati.

> ✉ E7; E12

> 🚇 Silverlink Metro (zones 3 and 4)

Wood Green • *Haringey*

A strategic shopping centre situated two miles west of TOTTENHAM. Wood Green was first recorded in 1502 as a clearing on the edge of Tottenham Wood. Until the mid 19th century it remained an outlying hamlet in Tottenham parish, of much less significance than neighbouring HORNSEY. St Michael's Church was built in 1844 and the village began to grow in anticipation of the coming of the railway. Wood Green's first station and school both opened in 1859, new roads were laid out north of the church and were lined with villas for the middle classes, while several charitable organizations built almshouses here. A pleasure ground opened in ALEXANDRA PARK, followed by an entertainment palace in 1873. In 1883 the Artisans', Labourers' and General Dwellings Co. began work on the NOEL PARK estate, one of the largest projects of its kind in Victorian London. Wood Green gained municipal independence from Tottenham in 1894 and has had a local government headquarters ever since, now in the form of Haringey's Civic Centre. In the early decades of the 20th century almost all the remaining gaps were filled by middle-class houses in the north, working-class terraces in the south and factories near the railway lines. The London County Council built the WHITE HART LANE estate on the surviving farmland between Wood Green and Tottenham. After World War II the retailers on the High Road began to outperform all their nearby rivals and by the mid 1960s Wood Green had become north London's most important shopping destination. In the mid 1970s the defunct Palace Gates station and many neighbouring buildings were demolished to make way for Wood Green Shopping City, a mall straddling the High Road, which elsewhere is flanked by a very mixed range of outlets. Cinemas and affordable restaurants have since broadened Wood Green's leisure appeal. For a century Wood Green was home to Barratts, the confectioners, but it moved out in 1980 as part of a general trend for offices and shops to replace manufacturing as the district's principal employers. The company's former factory on Clarendon Road has now become the focus of the Wood Green 'cultural quarter', an arts- and media-based regeneration scheme. Several of the projects based here function as production facilities for the creative industry, rather than attractions for the general public, and this has resulted in widespread misunderstanding of the cultural quarter's purpose and derision of its well-signposted and unduly pretentious name. Among the area's many ethnic communities, the largest groups are Turkish, black African (especially Somali) and black Caribbean.

✉ N22

🚇 Piccadilly Line (zone 3)

📖 Chris Protz and Deborah Hedgecock, *Tottenham and Wood Green: Past and Present*, Sutton, 2003; Albert Pinching, *Wood Green Past*, Historical Publications, 2000

Woodlands • *Hounslow*

A triangular-shaped group of tree-lined streets in west ISLEWORTH, bounded by the Duke of Northumberland's river to the east, the railway to the west and Worton Road and Bridge Road to the south. The name was first recorded in 1485 and refers to arable strips of land beside a wood. Until the early 19th century the only structures on what was then known as HOUNSLOW Field were some farm buildings and a moated house, both near the southern extremity of the modern locality. The land was enclosed in 1818 and most of it went to the Duke of Northumberland. Enclosure came relatively late here, probably because the soil was already being worked efficiently and intensively by the many market gardens. The arrival of the Hounslow loop railway in 1850 brought the first suburban villas to the northern tip of the triangle. Building plots were divided by substantial yellow brick walls, many of which still survive to show the former pattern of field division. St John's Church and the Woodlands public house served the spiritual and temporal needs of the new community. Stimulated by the development of the Great West Road (A4), the southerly expansion of Woodlands accelerated after 1925 with the construction of the Warren estate, named after developer R T Warren, a local builder. Houses and bungalows were built, first along existing thoroughfares and then on newly laid out streets, with a park at the centre. The council facilitated mortgages for would-be residents in an early encouragement of owner occupation. The last phase of Woodlands' development came after World War II, with the building up of Bridge Road and Worton Road, the creation of Gibson Close and the opening of Oaklands School on Woodlands Road (earlier called Hounslow Field Road). Oaklands is now a special school catering for 11- to 19-year-olds with severe, profound and multiple learning difficulties. It is highly regarded for the progress its pupils achieve.

✉ Isleworth TW7

📖 Stuart Bagnall, 'The Woodlands, Isleworth:

Continuity and Change in One Suburban District', (University of Liverpool, unpublished thesis, 1998)

Woodmansterne • *Croydon*

Woodmansterne station and the housing in its immediate vicinity are in Greater London, on the western edge of COULSDON, but the village proper is in Surrey. The station was one of the more recent main-line stations to open anywhere in London, in 1932.

✉ Coulsdon CR5

🚇 Southern (zone 6)

Woodridings • *Harrow*

An early commuter estate situated between the River Pinn and Uxbridge Road in southwest HATCH END, and no longer identified on most maps. Following the arrival of the railway, the first 50 houses were laid out on former farmland in 1855. Borrowing an Italianate design lately used in SWISS COTTAGE and ST JOHN'S WOOD, the properties were intended to attract families who wanted a grand residence but could not afford a more exclusive address. The large red-brick semi-detached houses with their ostentatious façades and gentrified names were set well back from the road. Most homes had two or three servants, often drawn from nearby PINNER. Milk was delivered from Woodridings Farm, on the other side of Uxbridge Road, until the land was developed in the mid 1920s.

Horatia Nelson-Ward, the daughter of Admiral Lord Nelson and Lady Hamilton, lived on the Woodridings estate towards the end of her life. Chandos Villas was the first marital home of Isabella Beeton, who in the late 1850s wrote here the articles that became *Beeton's Book of Household Management*. The house was destroyed by a direct hit in the Blitz and a shopping parade now stands in its place.

✉ Pinner HA5

Woodside • *Croydon*

A much-modernized Victorian village, situated on the north-eastern edge of CROYDON. Woodside was first mentioned in 1332 and its name refers to its location on what was formerly the edge of the Great North Wood. The farmland was mainly used for grazing because the heavy soil was difficult to plough. The only permanent structure recorded at Woodside in the 17th century was the Black Horse inn. William Marshall owned a 300-acre farm stretching across Woodside and ADDISCOMBE in the 1780s and published details of the soil conditions of his fields for the benefit of other farmers, and his records proved most useful to brickmakers in identifying sites for clay pits. Ashburton Park, later Stroud Green House, was built in 1788 and a hamlet had grown up around the green by the early 19th century. Two weatherboarded cottages survive from this period. In the 1850s, the brickmakers were at work across much of the neighbourhood, especially on the dominant Heath Lodge estate, owned by John Morland. Croydon races were run at Stroud Green Farm from 1866 and Woodside station was opened in 1871, delivering racegoers and horses to the course. The railway brought growth to the village too, in the form of both detached villas and workers' terraced houses. In the 1880s St Luke's Church was built and Stroud Green House was rebuilt as a school, later becoming a home for alcoholics and then an orphanage. Horse racing ceased in 1890, by which time the village was becoming a suburb. Board schools were built on Morland Road. Croydon council acquired the Ashburton Park estate in 1927, converting Woodside orphanage into a library and the grounds into a public park. Woodside's piecemeal evolution over the course of the 20th century has had some messy effects but several pleasing Victorian villas have survived, especially in the vicinity of the green. The station was replaced by a tramstop in 2000, with an additional stop to the south-west at Blackhorse Lane. Woodside has a relatively large black and black British community, most of whom are of Caribbean descent. Few residents are aged over 60.

✉ SE25; Croydon, CR0

♦ 15,715

🚋 Croydon Tramlink, Routes 1 and 2

📖 Lilian Thornhill, *Woodside*, North Downs Press, 1986

Woodside Park • *Barnet*

A garden suburb and its late Victorian precursors, situated on the western side of NORTH FINCHLEY at the confluence of Folly and Dollis brooks. During the 16th century the Peacock family of Redbourn in Hertfordshire acquired land here as part of an extensive estate. The family's descendants sold the land to Sir John Lade, whose son and namesake built Frith manor house in 1790 but had to sell off a neighbouring farm to pay gambling debts. Woodside was sparsely populated at this time owing to its remoteness and poor soil, which was mainly used for haymaking. Around 1840

Joseph Baxendale built Woodside House in WHETSTONE, with grounds that extended well to the south-west. Woodside Park station opened in 1872, originally as Torrington Park, and Joseph Baxendale died in the same year, bequeathing Woodside House as a ladies' retirement home. The charity that was entrusted to run the home sold off much of its grounds to developers, the most significant of whom was Henry Holden, who began to lay out new roads near the railway line on what he called the Woodside Park estate. Holden built Woodside Hall as a community asset in 1885 but progress was limited, on Holden's estate and elsewhere, and by the end of the century only dairy cattle populated the 200 acres of Frith Manor Farm. In the late 1920s a new developer began buying up land on the western side of Dollis Brook. Fred Ingram set about creating a 100-acre garden suburb with three-bedroom semi-detached houses in a variety of complementary styles. He named the new roads after the haunts of his Sussex boyhood. The project was a success and Ingram slowly expanded the suburb until war intervened. Post-war expansion was limited by green-belt restrictions and new building was mainly confined to the Southover area. Like much of Finchley, Woodside Park has attracted Jewish residents and Woodside Hall became a synagogue in 1950. More recently the suburb has also become popular with Japanese families.

✉ N12

🚇 Northern Line (zone 4)

Wood Street • *Waltham Forest*

A commercial thoroughfare in UPPER WALTHAMSTOW, north of WHIPPS CROSS. A small linear settlement was established here by the 7th century, one of the four that later formed the parish of WALTHAMSTOW. At the time of Domesday Book, Wood Street's farms were arable but they later converted to dairy production and market gardening for the London market. From the 17th century several large houses were built on the outskirts of the hamlet. The Clock House, completed in 1706, was the home of Sir Jacob Jacobson, a prosperous Dutch merchant. Wood Street remained rural and a separate settlement until the mid 19th century, after which speculative builders began to lay out a series of two-storey terraced houses that soon joined it with Walthamstow. The process received a boost from the opening of the railway station in 1873, which offered early workmen's fares on the line into LIVERPOOL STREET. Many residents lived in reduced circumstances and the Wood Street Philanthropic Society distributed free soup during the winters of the early 20th century. Wood Street had two film production studios: one operated from 1914 until 1932, at first making silent movies and then talkies, some with big budgets and well-known actors. Much of the locality was rebuilt in the 1930s and several factories were established in the vicinity, one of which replaced the film studio. Hawker Siddeley manufactured transformers at its Fulbourne Road site from the early 1930s until 2003. At one time Wood Street station was intended to be the terminus of the Victoria Line, but at a late stage this was switched to Hoe Street, now Walthamstow Central. The demographics of the Wood Street ward are very similar to those of the borough as a whole: almost two-thirds of its inhabitants are white and there is a broad spread of other ethnic groups. Council tenants make up a relatively large percentage of the population.

The Wood Street Walk was an annual eight-mile run sponsored by the owner of a local café from 1920. It was open to anyone living within a mile-and-a-half of Wood Street and the first prize was a Christmas dinner with all the trimmings. There have been occasional attempts to revive the event since the 1950s but, as the authors of Wood Street's history point out, the London Marathon now seems to have greater appeal.

> ✉ E17
>
> 👥 11,331
>
> 🚊 'one' Railway (zone 4)
>
> 📖 J W Howes and A D Law, *'Right up Your Street':*
>   *A Short History of Wood Street,*
>   Walthamstow Historical Society, 1994

Woolwich • *Greenwich* (pronounced 'woolidge')

A historic naval town, now much altered, situated three miles east of GREENWICH. A community has existed by the river at Woolwich since at least the Iron Age, and the Romans built a fort here. The Old English place name probably means 'trading place for wool', but no evidence has been found of a wool market. Henry VIII initiated shipbuilding here and the town's military facilities subsequently expanded to fill the entire waterfront, while pottery, glass, bricks and tiles were produced inshore. In 1695 the Royal Laboratory was established next to Tower Place. The laboratory manufactured explosive armaments and was the pre-

cursor of the Royal Arsenal. A burst of activity from 1716 to 1720 saw the construction of a brass foundry, the barracks, a new mansion house and the 'great pile' of buildings at Dial Square, which was probably the work of Nicholas Hawksmoor. The town was soon entirely built up, except for the common, which was used for artillery practice. Shops lined the main streets and Woolwich became north Kent's principal commercial centre. Such was the pressure of expansion that growth began to spill over into PLUMSTEAD in the 19th century and later into Eltham. But the dockyard closed in 1869 and the Royal Military Academy relocated to Sandhurst in 1947. The arsenal ceased manufacturing in 1967 and closed altogether in 1994. These events brought a period of decline to Woolwich from which it is only now recovering. At present, the proportion of council tenants in Woolwich is very high while owner-occupation is very low. The town also has an exceptionally large number of single-parent households. Woolwich is touted by some property consultants as south London's 'next big thing' because of its improving transport links, the developments on the Royal Arsenal site and its selection of well-built Georgian terraces.

In an IRA bombing in November 1974, two died and many more were injured when a device was hurled through a window of the King's Arms, opposite the Royal Artillery Barracks. In 1975 Woolwich acquired the UK's first McDonald's hamburger restaurant, which took the place of a branch of Burton's, the tailors. The Woolwich Building Society, founded in 1847, moved its headquarters to Bexleyheath in 1989.

> ✉ SE18
>
> 👥 27,734 (Woolwich Common and Woolwich Riverside wards)
>
> 🚊 South Eastern Trains (Woolwich Dockyard, zone 3; Woolwich Arsenal, zone 4)
>
> 📖 John Peters, *Woolwich Remembered*, John Manning Peters, 2002
>
> @ www.greenwich.gov.uk/Greenwich/ LeisureCulture/Walks/ HistoricWoolwich.htm (borough council site)

Woolwich Arsenal • *Greenwich*

A railway station and former armaments factory and barracks, located on the eastern side of WOOLWICH. The arsenal began life in 1695 as the Royal Laboratory, manufacturing explosives, fuses and shot. It was established on a site known as Woolwich Warren – remembered now in Warren Lane – which was known for its large rabbit population. In 1716 the Royal Regiment of Artillery was formed here, followed in 1741 by the Royal Military Academy. Both moved to WOOLWICH COMMON early in the 19th century. In 1805 the Royal Arsenal was officially established and no expense was spared in making this the world's foremost munitions works. Woolwich Arsenal station opened in 1849 on the London to Dartford line. Erected on the site of a former sandpit, the station has since been rebuilt twice. By the early 20th century the Royal Arsenal covered 1,285 acres. Including its testing ranges, the site measured three miles long by one mile wide, and had three separate internal railway systems. At the outbreak of World War I the Royal Arsenal employed over 70,000 workers. After World War II, declining demand for armaments prompted diversification into manufacturing for civilian purposes, from railway trucks to automated equipment for the silk-weaving industry. The Royal Ordnance factory closed in 1967, although many of the buildings continued to be used for testing and storage. Much of the new town of THAMESMEAD covers the arsenal's eastern testing ranges. The final military withdrawal came in 1994 and the buildings were taken over by English Partnerships for the development of housing, light industry and leisure facilities. Royal Arsenal West has become Firepower – The Royal Artillery Museum. A new Greenwich Heritage Centre opened at Building 41 in 2003.

Workers from the Royal Arsenal set up a buyers' co-operative in 1868, operating at first from members' houses in Plumstead and then from 147 Powis Street as the Royal Arsenal Co-operative Society. In 1886 another group of workers established a football club, known initially as Dial Square, and then Royal Arsenal. On moving to Highbury in 1913 the club shortened its name to Arsenal.

> ✉ SE18

> 🚌 South Eastern Trains (zone 4)

> 📖 Beverley Burford and Julian Watson (ed.), *Aspects of the Arsenal: Royal Arsenal, Woolwich*, London Borough of Greenwich Library Support Services, 1997

> @ www.firepower.org.uk (Royal Artillery Museum site)

Woolwich Common • *Greenwich*

An elongated open space at the southern ex-

tremity of WOOLWICH, and its neighbouring residential area. The common formerly covered a much wider area, extending into CHARLTON, but was gradually encroached upon for the construction of army quarters. At the height of Britain's empire building in the 18th century and the first half of the 19th century, much of the British Army camped on Woolwich Common until called forward to the Royal Arsenal to collect stores and ammunition before embarking on ships moored in the Thames. Between 1776 and 1802, new barracks were built here for the Royal Regiment of Artillery. In 1808 the Royal Military Academy moved to the east side of the common. The academy taught every branch of military science, as well as French and Latin, writing, fencing and drawing. Among the magnificent military buildings on the common is the Rotunda, designed by John Nash for an exhibition in St James's Park in 1814 and moved here six years later, when it became the first military museum. In 1848 a circular reservoir was dug on top of the common by convicts. The common continued to be used as an artillery firing range until 1860. The Royal Military Academy closed at the outbreak of World War II and afterwards became part of the Royal Military Academy at Sandhurst. Woolwich Common is still home to 16 Regiment Royal Artillery. The Woolwich Common housing estate was built in four phases between 1968 and 1981 on the site of the Barrack Tavern and an area of Regency terraced housing; the latter included 1 Kemp Terrace, which was the birthplace and home of General Gordon. The council has introduced one of Britain's most comprehensive closed-circuit television monitoring systems on the estate. The Woolwich Common ward has relatively large minorities of black African and Indian origin.

Charlton Athletic Football Club played on Woolwich Common between 1907 and 1909.

> ✉ SE18

> 🚹 14,967

> 📖 Darrell Spurgeon, *Discover Woolwich and Its Environs: A Comprehensive Guide to Woolwich, The Royal Arsenal, Woolwich Common, Plumstead, Shooters Hill and Abbey Wood*, Greenwich Guidebooks, 1996

Woolwich Dockyard • *Greenwich*

A station in west WOOLWICH, formerly serving the town's extensive naval facilities. In 1513 Henry VIII founded a dockyard at Woolwich to build the royal ship *Henri Grace à Dieu*, popularly known as the 'Great Harry'. Subsequent expansion brought a rope yard, ordnance storage and a gun battery to the waterfront, which at that time may have lain as much as 200 feet south of the present shoreline. Elizabeth I came to Woolwich in 1559 to mark the launch of her ship *Elizabeth Jonas*. During the 17th and 18th centuries the docks were progressively extended westwards. Behind the docks the town grew too, with housing, shops and industry. From 1776, redundant naval vessels were moored offshore to house prisoners who would otherwise have been sent to the American colonies, then in rebellion against the Crown. Convict labour was used to build new wharves and to dredge silt from the river. The yard was extended in 1833 and again in the 1840s, when modern docks were built. Woolwich Dockyard station opened in 1849 on the South Eastern Railway's new line from London Bridge to Dartford, Gravesend and Strood. The prison hulks were abolished in 1858 and the yard closed in 1869, when the site was handed over to the War Department for use as an annexe of the Royal Arsenal.

The Thames may be crossed at Woolwich by the ferry (which has been free since 1889) or through a foot tunnel, opened in 1912. Woolwich Reach is also traversed by the Thames flood barrier.

> ✉ SE18

> ⋔ 12,767 (Woolwich Riverside ward)

> 🚍 South Eastern Trains (zone 3)

Worcester Park · *Sutton/Epsom & Ewell, Surrey*

One of few districts that blithely straddle the London border as though it were not there, Worcester Park falls partly in the Surrey district of Epsom and Ewell, and merges with OLD MALDEN, to its north-west. The suburb takes its name from Worcester House, built by the fourth Earl of Worcester, who in 1606 was appointed the keeper of Nonsuch Great Park. The house stood on high ground near the southern end of present-day Royal Avenue. The station opened in 1859 on the edge of MALDEN GREEN, but high-class suburban development did not begin until the 1890s, when the novelist H G Wells lived for a while at 41 The Avenue. Wells satirized the social arrangements of Victorian Worcester Park (under the alias of 'Morningside Park') in his 1913 novel *Anne Veronica* and called it 'a suburb that had not altogether, as people say, come off'. Wor-

cester Park spread north towards MOTSPUR PARK between the wars. More recently, former sewage works have been replaced by a luxury development of 'New England style housing' called the Hamptons. In Sutton's Worcester Park ward over 70 per cent of 16- to 74-year-olds are employed, 87 per cent of homes are owner-occupied and 83 per cent of households have access to a car, all indicators of affluence. However, the number of people qualified to degree level or above is fractionally below the national average.

In 1851 the pre-Raphaelite artists Sir John Millais and William Holman Hunt spent the summer at Worcester Park Farm. Millais probably painted the landscape background for his celebrated work *Ophelia* (1852), now in the Tate Britain gallery, from a meadow beside the Hogsmill River, although the precise spot is still the subject of debate. The crime writer Simon Brett was born in Worcester Park in 1945.

> ✉ Worcester Park KT4

> ⋔ 9,874

> 🚍 South West Trains (zone 4)

> 📖 David Robert Rymill, *Worcester Park and Cuddington: A Walk Through the Centuries*, Buckwheat, 2000; Barbara C L Webb, *Millais and the Hogsmill River*, self-published, 1998

World's End · *Enfield*

A little-used name for a semi-rural locality separated from the western side of ENFIELD by Salmon's Brook. World's Ends were once dotted all around the outer edges of London as this was a popular name for a remote house or farm, often located at a parish boundary. This World's End straddled the border between the parishes of Enfield and Edmonton when it was established as a 19-acre farm after the enclosure of ENFIELD CHASE in 1777. Boundary changes in each of the following two centuries brought World's End entirely within Enfield's bailiwick. The enclosure act also stipulated that new roads be constructed across the former chase and World's End Lane (as it was later called) was one of these. In 1889 an outbreak of infectious diseases prompted the Enfield local board to buy World's End Farm for £2,000 to build an isolation hospital. A temporary set of iron buildings was erected in 1891 adjoining the newly built Northern (later HIGHLANDS) Hospital and replaced by a permanent structure at the end of the decade. Across World's End Lane, Enfield Golf Club was founded in 1895 on the former Swannell's Farm, which had been part of the Old Park estate. To the north, houses were built along and off Slades Hill in the 1930s. The construction of Merryhills Primary School had almost finished when war broke out in 1939 and special permission was granted for the work to be completed, since there was no other school within a mile and the area had greatly increased in population over the previous decade. A few more streets were laid out after World War II but most of the surrounding countryside has been preserved as part of the green belt.

✉ N21; Enfield EN2

World's End • Kensington & Chelsea

The cheaper but still trendy part of CHELSEA, located towards the western end of KING'S ROAD, where it dog-legs from the SW3 into the SW10 postal district. A 17th-century tavern and tea gardens bestowed their name on the hamlet that stood in this once-remote spot. As central Chelsea grew ever more fashionable in the 19th century, its working population was forced to move west and many settled here, in jerry-built and overcrowded tenements. Larger houses were soon subdivided for multiple occupation. In 1901 a parish priest commented that 'the all-pervading odour about the World's End is of fried fish; and ... there are dull streets of houses, many of which bear every sign of poverty with its too often attendant squalor'. The council earmarked World's End Passage for demolition but nothing was done for nearly three decades, until philanthropic trusts funded rebuilding. In 1969, despite opposition from preservationists, the council demolished eleven acres of two-storey houses and put up the tower blocks of the World's End estate. The punk movement of the late 1970s can take some credit for the renaissance of this stretch of King's Road. Boutiques at World's End pioneered early punk fashion and their successors still confer a distinctive personality on the quarter.

In 1970, Vivienne Westwood and Malcolm McLaren opened Let It Rock at 430 King's Road, selling 1950s clothes and memorabilia. Four years later the shop became Sex, and then Seditionaries, playing a seminal role in the genesis of both punk and new romantic styles. In 1981 Westwood renamed the shop again, this time as World's End.

✉ SW10

📖 Donald James Wheal, *World's End: A Memoir of a Blitz Childhood*, Century, 2005

Wormwood Scrubs • Hammersmith & Fulham

An open space and neighbouring institutional facilities, located to the north-east of EAST ACTON. First recorded in 1189 as Wormholt Scrubs, this was wasteland created by the felling of trees, with poor soil that was suitable only for grazing. The scrubs formerly stretched north as far as the HARROW ROAD. In 1801 the Paddington branch of the Grand Junction (now Grand Union) Canal cut off the northern section, which by that time had been mostly enclosed. From the late 1830s railway lines detached other parts of the common, which were later built on except for an area to the east, known as the Little Scrubs. After 1859 volunteer forces conducted rifle shooting exercises on the scrubs. Wormwood Scrubs Prison was built using convict labour to the designs of penal reformer Sir Edmund du Cane. The prison replaced MILLBANK Penitentiary and opened in stages from 1874. A model institution at the time of its creation, it subsequently gained a reputation for low standards of sanitation and poor prisoner–staff relations, exacerbated by problems of overcrowding. Hammersmith Hospital was built next to the prison in 1905 and has since been joined on the site by Queen Charlotte's Hospital. South of the WESTWAY, Hammersmith council laid out the Wormholt estate on garden city principles in the early 1920s. At the corner of Wood Lane and Du Cane Road stands the present Burlington Danes Church of England School a co-educational comprehensive that evolved out of two schools that came to Wormwood Scrubs between the wars. The West London stadium opened in 1967 at the end of Artillery Lane. It was renamed in 1993 after the most famous member of host club Thames Valley Harriers, Linford Christie, and refurbished in 2005. The stadium is also home to the London Blitz American Football Club and the London Nigerian Rugby Union Football Club.

In October 1966 the British spy and Soviet double-agent George Blake escaped over the wall of Wormwood Scrubs Prison and fled to Moscow. He had served just over five years of a 42-year sentence for passing on secrets to the Russians – the longest jail term ever imposed by a British court.

✉ W12

📖 Jocelyn Lukins et al, *The Scrubs*, Shepherd's Bush Local History Society, 1998

@ www.thamesvalleyharriers.com

The Wrythe • *Sutton*

A combination of council estate and conservation area situated at CARSHALTON's northern cusp. The name was first recorded as 'Rithe' in 1229, and later misspelt as 'Rye'. It did not gain an initial 'W' until the 19th century. A rithe was a small stream, usually one occasioned by heavy rain. Gravel was extracted here from late medieval times. The area was subject to frequent flooding from an overflowing pond on the west side of Green Wrythe Lane and this may explain why there was so little habitation here for so long. A cottage appeared and disappeared during the 17th century but the first enduring structure was a workhouse, built in 1792. Later named Leicester House, it went on to serve as a convalescent asylum and then as a succession of private schools. Beyond its grounds the Wrythe was common waste that stretched considerably further north than the green does today. Improvements in drainage in the early 19th century brought the beginnings of a hamlet at Wrythe Green, which had two dozen dwellings by around 1850. A handful of houses survive from this era and now form the nucleus of the Wrythe Green conservation area. The disused ROSEHILL tollhouse was re-built here around 1866 and given an extra floor and distinctive herringbone weatherboarding. It was renamed Bedford Cottage, later changed to Woodcote House. A herb farm operated nearby until after World War I. Leicester House was vacated in the 1930s and pulled down after World War II owing to its neglected condition. The Durand Close council estate was popular with young families when it was built in the 1960s but suffered a decline and has recently been the subject of a major regeneration programme. Woodcote House was saved from demolition and restored in 1977. The Wrythe's population is relatively poor by the borough's standards, and over 90 per cent are white. Green Wrythe is an oversubscribed primary school, on Green Wrythe Lane.

The Salvation Army has a hall on Green Wrythe Lane but in the 1880s it held noisy open-air prayer and hymn meetings on the green until locals bombarded members with soot, flour and abuse.

✉ Carshalton SM5

🏃 10,384

Yardley Lane • *Waltham Forest*

Best-known as a bus destination, Yardley Lane and its council estate are situated in the extreme north-western corner of Chingford, off Sewardstone Road (A112). The lane probably takes its name from William Yerdele, a resident of SEWARDSTONE in 1400. The former Yardley House was the country residence of Sir John and Lady Harriet Silvester of BLOOMSBURY. Sir John was Recorder of the City of London in 1803 and commandant of the Chingford Volunteers. Richard Hodgson built Hawkwood House nearby in the late 1840s, when he was lord of the manor of Chingford St Pauls. The house was demolished following bomb damage but its lodge survives. The Yardley Lane estate was built in the 1930s and Yardley Lane Primary School opened in 1939. The sailing facilities of King George's Reservoir lie to the west. Just across the Essex border to the north-east is Yardley Hill, which has gentle slopes ascending to 220 feet, making it popular with walkers and cross-country runners. The hill falls within the bounds of Epping Forest and the forest's conservators have recently reintroduced cattle to the heathland here.

✉ E4

Yeading • *Hillingdon* (pronounced 'yedding')

A fast-growing residential district situated north-east of HAYES, of which it was formerly a sub-manor. Yeading Brook, which separates the district from Hayes, rises in HARROW and joins the Grand Union Canal just to the south-west of Yeading. In 757 Aethelbald, King of Mercia, made a grant of land that mentioned Geddinges, as Yeading was then known. A survey of Hayes conducted in the late 16th century did not mention Yeading and a century later it was the smallest hamlet in the manor, with just 13 householders. Brickfields and brickmakers' cottages and the Union inn were in existence by the late 1820s. In his *Handbook to the Environs of London*, published in 1876, James Thorne commented that Yeading's few inhabitants were 'always found civil'. A temporary smallpox hospital was built at this isolated spot in 1903 and the village had only 20 dwellings in 1938. After World War II housing estates, first municipal and then private, spread across to the canal. Roman Catholic and Anglican churches were built in 1961. Housebuilding has continued into the 21st century wherever space permits and Yeading has also been earmarked by the borough council as a location for future commercial development. The residents come from a variety of social and cultural backgrounds. Sixty per cent are white and the main ethnic minority is of Indian origin. Sikhs constitute the largest religious minority and Springfield Road has the country's first state-funded Sikh primary and secondary schools, the Guru Nanak. At Yeading Junior School over 70 per cent of pupils speak English as an additional language.

Yeading Football Club was formerly based at the Warren on Beaconsfield Road, a ground that featured prominently in the 2002 film *Bend It Like Beckham*. The club merged with close neighbours Hayes in 2007 and the combined outfit now plays at the latter's Church Road ground, retaining the Warren for social activities, as a training base and the home ground for reserve and youth team games.

✉ Hayes UB4

♟ 11,923

@ www.yeadingfc.co.uk

Yiewsley • *Hillingdon*

The northern half of the 'composite suburb' of Yiewsley and WEST DRAYTON, which local MP John Randall has referred to as 'Siamese twins'. It was first recorded in 1235 as Wiuesleg, probably 'the woodland clearing of a man name Wifel'. Gravel excavation has revealed hundreds of prehistoric hand-axes and the remains of a Bronze Age cemetery but it was not until the 16th century that a hamlet had taken shape here. Yiewsley Grange was built around this time but has since been almost entirely altered and now serves as offices. Unlike West Drayton, the hamlet remained inconsequential until the early 19th century, when industry grew up alongside the canal, together with mean cottages for workers. The opening of West Drayton station in 1838 accelerated the industrial and residential growth, while houses for the middle classes lined the High Street. St Matthew's Church was built in the late 1850s and enlarged in 1898, when suburban housebuilding was beginning to cover the fields. The houses in the High Street were converted to commercial use, with shop units filling their front gardens. Yiewsley's earliest links were with UXBRIDGE but by the 1910s these had been lost as the fusion with West Drayton took hold. Land was acquired from St Thomas's Hospital in 1926 'to be used in perpetuity for the recreation of the people of Yiewsley', and now consists of grassy areas, two bowling greens, tennis courts and play parks, with a swimming pool and library. After the formation of Yiewsley and West Drayton Urban District in 1930, much of the Victorian housing was cleared to make way for municipal estates. Yiewsley remains the more commercial half of the district, with industrial estates fringing the canal, while a high-tech business park has been laid out to the east, at STOCKLEY PARK. Eighty-five per cent of Yiewsley's residents are white and 21 per cent of residents rent their homes from the council, relatively high figures for the borough.

The rock guitarist Ron Wood grew up in a council house in Yiewsley and formed The Birds here in 1964. He went on to play with the Jeff Beck Group, The Faces and the Rolling Stones.

✉ West Drayton UB7

♦ 11,056

🚌 First Great Western Link (West Drayton, zone 6)

📖 James Skinner, *West Drayton and Yiewsley*, Tempus, 2003